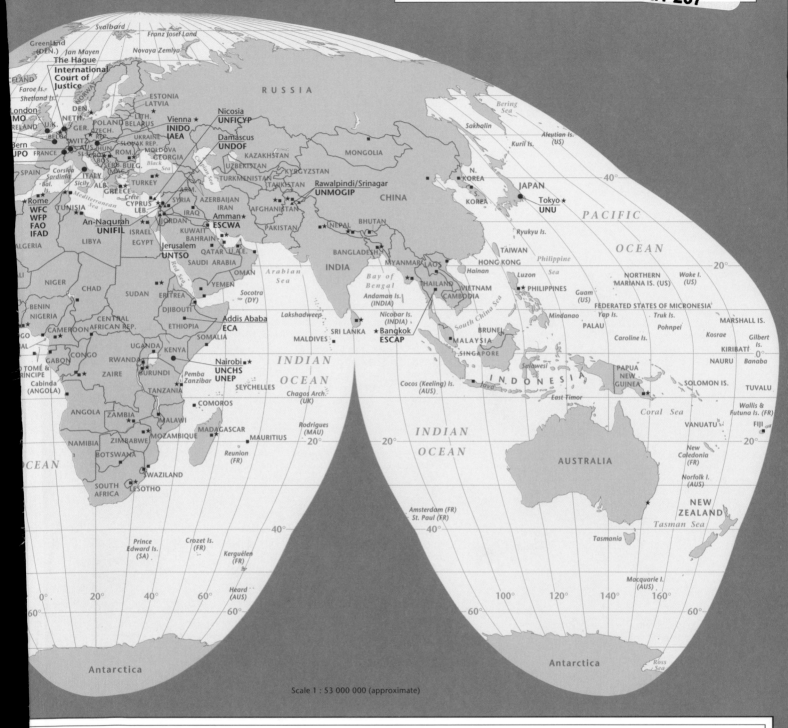

Scale 1 : 53 000 000 (approximate)

SPECIALIZED AGENCIES AND OTHER AUTONOMOUS ORGANIZATIONS WITHIN THE SYSTEM

Berne:
UPU -Universal Postal Union
Geneva:
GATT -General Agreement on Tariffs and Trade
ILO -International Labour Organization
ITU -International Telecommunication Union
WHO -World Health Organization
WIPO -World Intellectual Property Organization
WMO -World Meteorological Organization
London:
IMO -International Maritime Organization
Montreal:
ICAO -International Civil Aviation Organization
Paris:
UNESCO -United Nations Educational, Scientific and Cultural Organization

Rome:
FAO -Food and Agricultural Organization of the United Nations
IFAD -International Fund for Agricultural Development
Vienna:
IAEA -International Atomic Energy Agency
UNIDO -United Nations Industrial Development Organization
Washington:
IFC -International Finance Corporation
IMF -International Monetary Fund
The World Bank { -International Development Association (IDA) -International Bank for Reconstruction and Development (IBRD)

REGIONAL COMMISSIONS

Addis Ababa:
ECA -Economic Commission for Africa
Bangkok:
ESCAP -Economic and Social Commission for Asia and the Pacific
Geneva:
ECE -Economic Commission for Europe
Santiago:
ECLAC -Economic Commission for Latin America and the Caribbean

WORLDMARK ENCYCLOPEDIA OF THE NATIONS

Volume 1

ISSN 1531-1635

WORLDMARK
ENCYCLOPEDIA OF THE NATIONS

UNITED NATIONS

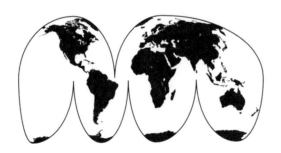

Formerly published by Worldmark Press, Ltd.

GALE GROUP

Detroit
New York
San Francisco
London
Boston
Woodbridge, CT

Gale Group Staff

Shelly Dickey, Project Editor
William H. Harmer, Contributing Editor
David Riddle, Jennifer M. York, Assistant Editors
Rita Runchock, Managing Editor

Mary Beth Trimper, Composition and Electronic Prepress Manager
Evi Seoud, Assistant Composition and Electronic Prepress Manager
NeKita McKee, Buyer

Kenn Zorn, Production Design Manager
Michael Logusz, Graphic Artist

ISBN 0-7876-0511-5 (set)
ISBN 0-7876-0512-3 (volume 1)
ISBN 0-7876-0513-1 (volume 2)
ISBN 0-7876-0514-X (volume 3)
ISBN 0-7876-0515-8 (volume 4)
ISBN 0-7876-0516-6 (volume 5)
ISBN 0-7876-4809-4 (volume 6)
ISSN 1531-1635

Printed in the United States of America

CONTENTS

Editorial Staff

Editor in Chief: Timothy L. Gall

Senior Editors: Jill Coppola and Mary Sugar

Associate Editors: Alana Andrews, Chandra P. Balasubramani, Glennon K. Brady, Lynne Brakeman, Nelia Dunbar, Rebecca N. Ferguson, Susan Bevan Gall, David M.Goodrich, Nese B. Guendelsberger, Robert Halasz, James Henry, Jeneen M. Hobby, Kim Humiston, Roman Jakubowycz, Daniel M. Lucas, Elizabeth Park, Caroline Sahley, Ann P. Standley, Susan Stern, George Sutcliffe, James Scott Volpe, Craig B. Waff, Jennifer Wallace, Rosalie Wieder, Douglas Wu, Michael Zannoni

Cartographers: Maryland Cartographics, Inc.; Scott B. Edmonds, President: Stephanie K. Clark, Deborah G. Freer, Tracy R. Morrill, Justin E. Morrill, Judith G. Nielsen, John P. Radziszewski

Copy Editors: Deborah Baron, Janet Fenn, Mary Ann Klasen

Typesetting: Bridgette Nadzam, Brian Rajewski, Deborah Rutti

Data Input: Judith Raday Arth, Dawn Babos, Lee Ann DeWolf, Janis K. Long, Maggie Lyall, Cheryl Montagna, Deborah Ridgway, Tajana G. Roehl, Karen Seyboldt, Kira Silverbird, Karen J. Sippola

Proofreaders: Deborah Baron, Jan Davis, Janet Fenn, Ruta Marino, Jennifer Wallace

Editorial Assistants: Katie Baron, Jennifer A. Spencer, Daniel K. Updegraft

Contributors

Shown below are contributors to the present and previous editions, in most cases followed by their affiliation or status at the time the contribution was made.

AHMED, BASHIR. Researcher/Writer.

ALBA, VICTOR. Author, *Transition in Spain: From Franco to Democracy.*

ALISKY, MARVIN. Director of Center for Latin American Studies and Professor of Political Science, Arizona State University.

ANTHONY, JOHN. Assistant Professor of Middle East Studies, School of Advanced International Studies, Johns Hopkins University.

ARNADE, CHARLES W. Chairman, The American Idea, and Professor of History, University of South Florida.

ASHFORD, DOUGLAS E. Department of Political Science, Cornell University.

AUMANN, MOSHE. Counselor, Embassy of Israel, Washington, D.C.

AYTAR, VOLKAN. Binghamton University.

BARBER, WILLIAM J. Associate Professor of Economics, Wesleyan University.

BARRON, MURIEL T.

BASS, ELIZABETH M. Economist-Editor, Research Project on National Income in East Central Europe, New York.

BENITEZ, ALBERTO. Department of Economics, Florida International University.

BENNETT, NORMAN. Professor of History, Boston University.

BERG, ELLIOT J. Professor of Economics, University of Michigan.

BERG, NANCY GUINLOCK.

BERNELL, DAVID. Johns Hopkins University.

BERNSTEIN, MARVIN. Professor of History, State University of New York at Buffalo.

BIRNS, LAURENCE R. Director, Council on Hemispheric Affairs.

BONGIORNO, JOSEPH A. St. John's University.

BOSTON UNIVERSITY, AFRICAN STUDIES CENTER. John Harris, Professor of Economics and Director of African Studies Center; James C. Armstrong, Head, African Studies Library, Editors; Norman Bennett, Professor of History, Boston University; Valerie Plave

Bennett, Energy Resources Co.; Heinz A. Bertsch; Edouard Bustin, Professor of Political Science, Boston University; Sid A. Chabawe; Tobias Chizengeni; William D. Coale; Leon Cort; Bernardo P. Ferraz, Fellow, Massachusetts Institute of Technology; Kathleen Langley, Associate Professor of Economics, Boston University; Jay I. Mann; Sandra Mann; Marcos G. Namashulua, Instructor, Political Science, Brandeis University; Jeanne Penvenne; Stella Silverstein; Henry Steady; Dominique Western.

BOUCHAER, TOUFIC. Second Secretary, Embassy of Syria, Washington, D.C.

BOXILL, IAN and BOXILL, RACHAEL. University of the West Indies.

BRADBURY, R. W. Professor of Economics, College of Business Administration, University of Florida.

BRAVEBOY-WAGNER, JACQUELINE ANNE. City University of New York.

BROCK, LIZA. Researcher/Writer.

BRODY, ALAN J. Department of Political Science, Cleveland State University.

BUTWELL, RICHARD. Dean for Arts and Science, State University of New York at Fredonia.

CARPADIS, CHRISTINA. Researcher/Writer, Cleveland, Ohio.

CARTER, GWENDOLEN M. Director, Program of African Studies, Northwestern University.

CASTAGNO, ALPHONSO A. Director, African Research and Studies Program, Boston University.

CASTAGNO, MARGARET. Author, *Historical Dictionary of Somalia.*

CELIK, AYSE BETUL. Binghamton University.

CHANG, A. S. Hong Kong Correspondent, Institute of Foreign Studies, Tokyo; formerly Professor of Economics, National Chi-nan University, Shanghai.

CHEN, NANCY. Population Division, United Nations Department of Economic and Social Information.

COLEMAN, JAMES S. Director, African Studies Program, and Professor of Political Science, University of California, Los Angeles.

COLLINS, ROBERT O. Professor of History, University of California, Santa Barbara.

COMPTON, ROBERT W., JR. Western Kentucky University.

CORBIN, PETER B. Interregional Adviser, UN Department of Technical Cooperation and Development.

CORDERAS, DESCÁRREGA, JOSÉ. Royal Geographical Society, Valverde (Spain).

COUFOUDAKIS, VAN. Indiana Univeristy-Purdue University.

COWAN, L. GRAY. Dean, School of International Affairs, State University of New York, Albany.

CUMINGS, BRUCE G. Professor of Political Science, Swarthmore College.

CZIRJAK, LASZLO. Associate, Columbia University.

DALL, CHRISTOPHER. College of William and Mary.

DE GALE, SIR LEO. G.C.M.G., C.B.E., Governor-General, Government of Grenada.

DOCKING, TIMOTHY W. Boston University.

DUNBAR, CHARLES F. President, Cleveland Council on World Affairs.

DUNKLE, JOHN R. Associate Professor of Geography and Physical Science, University of Florida.

EINHORN, ERIC. University of Massachusetts at Amherst.

ENGEL, DAVID. New York University.

EVANS, LAURENCE. Professor of History, Harpur College.

EYEK, F. GUNTHER. Professorial Lecturer in History and International Relations, American University.

EZRA, MARKOS. Population Studies and Training Center, Brown University.

FALL, BERNARD B. Professor of Government, Howard University.

FERETTI, EVELYN. Department of Agricultural Economics, Cornell University.

FINLAND, GOVERNMENT OF. Statistical Office, Helsinki.

FLETCHER, N.E.W. Personal Assistant to the Governor-General, Government of Grenada.

FLETCHER, WILLARD ALLEN. Professor and Chairman, Department of History, College of Arts & Sciences, University of Delaware.

FONER, PHILIP S. Professor of History, Lincoln University.

FRY, GERALD W. University of Oregon.

FULLER, BENNET, Jr. Researcher/Writer.

GALLIS, PAUL E. Congressional Research Service, Library of Congress.

GAGNON, V. P., JR. Ithaca College.

GANJI, MOHAMMAD H. Chancellor, Amir Showkatul-Mulk University, Birjand, Iran.

GILBERT, ERIK O. Arkansas State University.

GITTELMAN, ELIZABETH. Researcher/Writer.

GOBLE, PAUL A. Carnegie Endowment for International Peace.

GOUTTIERRE, THOMAS E. Dean, International Studies and Programs; Director, Center for Afghanistan, University of Nebraska at Omaha.

GOVEA, RODGER M. Associate Professor, Department of Political Science, Cleveland State University.

GRAYBEAL, N. LYNN. Researcher/Writer.

GREEN, KATHRYN L. California State University, San Bernardino.

GREENHOUSE, RALPH. US Information Agency.

GROELSEMA, ROBERT. Civil Society Analyst, Africa Bureau, US Agency for International Development, US Department of Agriculture

GRUNDY, KENNETH W. Marcus A. Hanna Professor of Political Science, Case Western Reserve University.

GUENDELSBERGER, JOHN W. Professor of Law, The Claude W. Pettit College of Law, Ohio Northern University.

GUENDELSBERGER, NESE. Attorney at Law, Ada, Ohio.

HAGERTY, HERBERT G. Foreign Service Officer (ret.), US Department of State.

HALE, PATRICIA. Researcher/Writer, West Hartford, Connecticut.

HEANEY, JAMES J. Managing Editor, *Webster's New World Dictionary*.

HEILMAN, BRUCE. University of Dar es Salaam, Tanzania.

HEINTZEN, HARRY. African Department, Voice of America.

HIDALGO-NUNEZ, Claudio. Researcher/Writer.

HISPANIC AMERICAN REPORT. Ronald Hilton, Editor; Donald W. Bray, Ronald H. Chilcote, James Cockcroft, Timothy F. Harding, Sir Harold Mitchell, Assistant Editors; Ann Hartfiel, Andrew I. Rematore, Editorial Assistants; Eugene R. Braun, Marjorie Woodford Bray, Lee Ann Campbell, Jorge Caprista, Manuel Carlos, Frances Chilcote, Nancy Clark, Richard L. Cummings, Carlos Darquen, Anthony Dauphinot, Nicholas H. Davis, Joan E. Dowdell, Jerome Durlak, Pan Eimon, Peter L. Eisenberg, Richard Eisman, Claire E. Flaherty, Charles Gauld, Hugh Hamilton, Timothy Harding, Paul Helms, Raymond D. Higgins, Saul Landau, Wendy Lang, Joyce Lobree, Thomas Marks, Marilyn Morrison, Frank Odd, Molly Older, D. Wingeate Pike, Gabriel Pinheiro, Luis Ponce de León, Kenneth Posey, James Purks, Lawrence L. Smith, Maud Maria Straub, Linda Striem, David F. Thompson, Pamela Throop, Alice Wexler, Ann Wyckoff, Allen Young, Michael J. Zimmerman, Contributors.

HOFFMAN, GEORGE W. Professor of Geography, University of Texas at Austin.

HUNSBERGER, WARREN S. Professor of Economics, American University (with the assistance of Alan D. Smith, Information Officer, Consulate-General of Japan, New York).

HVIZDOS, SCOTT. Researcher/Writer.

HWANG, S. MARTIN. Binghamton University.

INDOCHINA RESOURCE CENTER. Washington, D.C., D. Gareth Porter, Director.

INGHAM, KENNETH. Director of Studies, Royal Military Academy, Sandhurst.

INGRAMS, HAROLD. Adviser on Overseas Information, Colonial Office, London.

INTERNATIONAL INSTITUTE FOR AERIAL SURVEY AND EARTH SCIENCES. F. J. Ormeling, Head of Cartography Department; C. A. de Bruijn, P. Hofstee, A. B. M. Hijl, Department of Urban Surveys.

ITZKOWITZ, NORMAN. Associate Professor of Oriental Studies, Princeton University.

JUDD, KAREN. Researcher/Writer, New York, New York.

JUNION-METZ, GAIL. President, Information Age Consultants.

KALIPENI, EZEKIEL. Department of Geography, University of Illinois at Urbana-Champaign.

KANTOR, HARRY. Professor of Political Science, Marquette University.

KAPLAN, FREDRIC M.

KARCH, JOHN J. Professorial Lecturer, Institute for Sino-Soviet Studies, George Washington University.

KATZ, MARK N. Associate Professor of Government and Politics, George Mason University.

KATZMAN, KENNETH.

KIM, JULIE. Congressional Research Service, Library of Congress.

KING, MAE C. Harvard University.

KINGSBURY, ROBERT C. Assistant Professor of Geography, Indiana University.

KIRLI, CENGIZ. Binghamton University.

KIROS, TEODROS. Boston University.

KISH, GEORGE. Professor of Geography, University of Michigan.

KITIGWA, MIRAJI. University of Dar es Salaam, Tanzania.

KOLEHMAINEN, JOHN I. Chairman, Department of Political Science, Heidelberg College.

KOLINSKI, CHARLES J. Professor of History, Florida Atlantic University.

KOPECKY, DEAN. Researcher/Writer.

KOSTANICK, HUEY LOUIS. Professor of Geography, University of Southern California.

KRANZ, WALTER. Press and Information Officer, Principality of Liechtenstein.

KURZER, PAULETTE. Department of Political Science, University of Arizona.

KYLE, DAVID. Texas A&M University.

LAATIKAINEN, KATIE VERLIN. Wilkes University.

LAYACHI, AZZEDINE. St. John's University.

LAZERSON, JOSHUA. Researcher/Writer.

LEE, ROBERT H.G. Assistant Professor of History, State University of New York at Stony Brook.

LEMARCHAND, RENE. Director, African Studies Center, University of Florida.

LENGYEL, EMIL. Professor of History, Fairleigh Dickinson University (in collaboration with Catherine Logan Camhy).

LEWIS, H. A. G.O.B.E., Fellow, Royal Geographical Society (United Kingdom).

LEWIS, STEVE. Researcher/Writer.

LEWIS, WILLIAM H. Department of Anthropology and Sociology, American University.

LICHTENSTADTER, ILSE. Center for Middle Eastern Studies, Harvard University.

LINDO, WILLIAM. Government Information Services, Government of Belize.

LOBBAN, RICHARD A., JR. Department of Anthropology, Rhode Island College.

LOBOS, IGNACIO A. Journalist, Honolulu, Hawaii.

LODRICK, DERYCK O. Visiting Scholar, Center for South Asian Studies, University of California, Berkeley.

LONGMAN, TIMOTHY. Vassar College.

LUX, WILLIAM R. Assistant Professor of History, University of Alabama.

LYNCH, CATHERINE. Assistant Professor, Department of History, Case Western Reserve University.

MA, JUNLING. Researcher/Writer.

MARCUS, LAWRENCE. Washington University.

MARKS, HENRY S. Professor of History, Northeast Alabama State Junior College.

MATHEWS, THOMAS G. Secretary-General, Association of Caribbean Universities and Research Institutes, Puerto Rico.

McCANN, JAMES C. Boston University.

McDONALD, JAMES L. Senior International Policy Analyst, Bread for the World.

McGUIRE, CARL. Professor of Economics, University of Colorado.

McHALE, VINCENT. Chairman, Department of Political Science, Case Western Reserve University.

McINTIRE, ROBERT C. Associate Professor and Chairman, Department of Political Science, Millikin University.

McLELLAN, ROBERT S. US Information Agency.

MacLEOD, MURDO. University of Florida.

McLOUGHLIN, GLENN. Specialist in Science and Technology Policy, Congressional Research Service, Library of Congress.

MENDELL, MARCIA EIGEN.

METZ, RAYMOND E. Interim Director, University Libraries, Case Western Reserve University.

MILLER, NATHAN. Associate Professor of History, University of Wisconsin, Milwaukee.

MILLETT, ALLAN R. Mason Professor of Military History, The Mershon Center, The Ohio State University

MILNE, R. S. Professor of Political Science, University of British Columbia.

MIRANTE, EDITH. Project Maje, Portland, Oregon.

MONCARZ, RAUL. Professor, Department of Economics, Florida International University.

MORTIMER, MOLLY. Former Commonwealth Correspondent, *The Spectator*, London.

MOSELEY, EDWARD. Assistant Professor of History, University of Alabama.

MUNRO, ALLISON DOHERTY.

NAVIA, PATRICIO. Department of Politics and Center for Latin American Studies, New York University.

NETOS, ELEFTHERIOS. Candidate, Kent State University.

NEW YORK UNIVERSITY, DEPARTMENT OF POLITICS. I. William Zartman, Editor; John Entelis, Oladipo Coles, Jeffrey Knorr, Marie-Daniele Harmel, Contributors.

NICHOL, JAMES. Congressional Research Service, Library of Congress.

NICHOLSON, NORMAN L. Professor of Geography, University of Western Ontario.

NOROOZI, TOURAJ. University of Utah.

O'DELL, ANDREW C. Professor of Geography, University of Aberdeen.

OH, JOHN K. C. Professor of Political Science, Marquette University.

OLCOTT, MARTHA BRILL. Professor, Department of Political Science, Colgate University.

OLIVER, ROBERT T. Head, Department of Speech, Pennsylvania State University.

PANORAMA DDR. Berlin.

PAPP, TIBOR. Columbia University.

PATAI, RAPHAEL. Editor, The Herzl Press.

PAYNE, WALTER A. Professor of History, University of the Pacific.

PENIKIS, ANDREJS. Columbia University.

PETROV, VICTOR P. Professor of Geography, California State College.

POLAND, EMBASSY OF. Washington, D.C.

POLK, WILLIAM R. Director, Adlai E. Stevenson Institute, University of Chicago.

PRAGOPRESS. Prague.

PRECHT, HENRY. Adjunct Associate Professor, Department of Political Science, Case Western Reserve University.

PRICE, GEORGE. Premier, Belize.

RANAHAN, JOHN. Lake Ridge Academy.

RASHID, TAUFIQ. Indiana University.

RASHIDUZZAMAN, M. Professor of Political Science, Glassboro State College.

REINES, BERNARD. Researcher/Writer.

REYNOLDS, JONATHAN T. Livingstone College.

RIEDINGER, JEFFREY M. Michigan State University.

RITTERBUSH, DEACON. Researcher/Writer.

ROBINSON, KENNETH E. Director, Institute of Commonwealth Studies, and Professor of Commonwealth Affairs, University of London.

ROBINSON, RICHARD D. Lecturer on Middle Eastern Studies, Center for Middle Eastern Studies, Harvard University.

ROSBERG, CARL G., JR. Associate Professor of Political Science, University of California.

ROSEWATER, GAIL. Researcher/Writer, Cleveland, Ohio.

ROTBERG, ROBERT I. Professor of Political Science and History, MIT.

RUPEN, ROBERT A. Associate Professor of Political Science, University of North Carolina.

RUS, VLADIMIR. Department of Slavic Literature (ret.), Case Western Reserve University.

SANDS, WILLIAM. Editor, *The Middle East Journal*.

SANTOS, MARIA J. Senior Evaluator, United States General Accounting Office.

SCHULTZ, CRAIG. Researcher/Writer.

SEBUHARARA, R. CHARLES. Binghamton University.

SHABAD, THEODORE. Correspondent, *New York Times*.

SHAMBAYATI, HOOTAN. Middle East Center, University of Utah.

SHEIKHZADEH, AHMAD. Columbia University.

SHEPHERD, GEORGE. Professor of Political Science, University of Denver.

SIRACUSA, CHRISTINA. Researcher/Writer.

SMITH, ALAN HEPBURN. Associate Professor of Finance, Marquette University; formerly Permanent Secretary, Ministry of Finance, Ghana.

SORICH, RICHARD. East Asian Institute, Columbia University.

SOVIET ENCYCLOPEDIA PUBLISHING HOUSE.

STEVENS, RICHARD P. Director, African Language and Area Center, Lincoln University.

STOLL, JOSEPH W. Supervisor, Cartography Laboratory, University of Akron.

STUMPF, JEANNE MARIE. Department of Sociology, John Carroll University; Department of Anthropology, Kent State University–Geauga Campus.

SYRACUSE UNIVERSITY, FOREIGN AND COMPARATIVE STUDIES PROGRAM. Peter Dalleo; Thomas C. N. Evans; Robert G. Gregory, Professor of History; Elisabeth Hunt; Roderick J. Macdonald, Professor of History; Thomas F. Taylor.

SYRACUSE UNIVERSITY, PROGRAM OF EAST AFRICAN STUDIES. Fred G. Burke, Director; John R. Nellis, Administrative Assistant; and Gary Gappert, Nikos Georgulas, Richard Kornbluth.

URDANETA, CARMEN. Researcher/Writer, Boston, Massachusetts.

UTHUP, THOMAS. Binghamton University.

VANDENBOSCH, AMRY. Director Emeritus, Patterson School of Diplomacy and International Commerce, University of Kentucky.

VIVIANI, NANCY. Department of Economics, Australian National University.

WAGNER, EDWARD W. Associate Professor of Korean Studies, Harvard University.

WALKER, WENDY. Researcher/Writer.

WALLACE, JENNIFER. Researcher/Writer.

WARFEL, DOUGLAS. Researcher/Writer.

WEBB, RAYMOND P. Milton Academy.

WENNER, MANFRED W. Associate Professor of Political Science, University of Northern Illinois.

WERNSTEDT, FREDERICK L. Associate Professor of Geography, Pennsylvania State University.

WESTNEAT, ARTHUR S. School for Public and Environmental Affairs, African Studies Program, Indiana University.

WIEDNER, DONALD L. Chairman, Department of History, Temple University.

WILBER, DONALD N. Author, *Iran Past and Present.*

WILMINGTON, MARTIN W. Professor of Economics, Pace College.

WINDER, R. BAYLY. Chairman, Department of Near Eastern Languages and Literatures, New York University.

WISE, RENATE. Center for Middle Eastern Studies, The University of Texas at Austin.

WOEHREL, STEVEN. Specialist in European Affairs.

WOLFE, GREGORY D. Portland State University.

WRIGHT, WINTHROP R. Professor of History, University of Maryland.

YUGOSLAV FEDERAL COMMITTEE FOR INFORMATION.

ZULU, LEO. Department of Geography, University of Illinois at Urbana-Champaign.

ACKNOWLEDGMENTS

A basic part of the editorial preparation of the *Worldmark Encyclopedia of the Nations* consists of keeping continuously abreast of the work of governments. The editors wish to express their gratitude to the many government officials the world over who so kindly gave their cooperation. Grateful acknowledgment is made for the invaluable material, used throughout the encyclopedia, drawn from the mass of documents issued by the United Nations and its specialized agencies. Gratitude is expressed for the assistance given by numerous officials of the UN, the specialized agencies, and the intergovernmental and nongovernmental organizations.

The editors would like to specifically thank the staffs of the United Nations Public Inquiry Unit (headed by Ms. M. Hosali) and the Dag Hammarskjöld Library (headed by Ms. Rima Bordcosh) for the many hours they spent tracking down answers to particularly obscure questions. Special thanks is extended to the following individuals and units for substantive contributions on the work of their organizations: Jackie Aidenbaum and Mary Lou Murphy, DHA; Marie Paul Aristy, Chief Information, Communication and Documentation Unit, INSTRAW; Vera Azar and Lina Arafat, ESCWA, United Nations; Nassrine Azimi, UNITAR; Max Bond, UN University; Sabine Bauer and Sylvie Bryant, UNDCP; Borjana Bulajic, Social Affairs Officer, INSTRAW; Michael Cassandra, Centre for Disarmament Affairs, United Nations; Mary Covington, ILO; Padraig Czajkowski, Centre for Human Rights, United Nations; Jacqueline Dauchy, Director, Codification Division, Secretariat of the Commission on International Law, United Nations; Shalini Dewan, Chief, Editorial and Publications Section, Division of Communications, UNICEF; Allen Dorsey, ICRC Delegation to the UN; Fred Eckhard, Rolando Gomez, and Jane Gaffney, Office of Spokesman for the Secretary-General; Lynn Failing, Deputy Chief, Public Information Office, UNRWA; Donald E. Fitzpatrick, Special Assistant to the Under Secretary General for Administration and Management, United Nations; Hirut Gebre-Egziabher, Project Officer, Division of Information, UNICEF; Christine Graves, FAO; Marilla B. Guptil, United Nations Archives; H. J. Frick, Chief, Official Relations Branch, ILO; Nandasiri Jasentuliyana, Director, Office for Outer Space Affairs, United Nations; Maurice Jorgens, DOALOS; Mary Lynn Hanley, Chief, Editorial and Audio Visual Branch, Division of Public Affairs, UNDP; James T. Hill, Senior Economist, and Marva Coates, FAO; Margaret A. Kelly, Secretary, ECOSOC, United Nations; George Kell and Nina Weckstrom, UNCTAD; Julie A. Kimbrough, Media and NGO Liaison Officer, IFAD; Roger Kohn, Head of Information Office, IMO; Pamela Maponga, Secretariat of the Special Committee on Apartheid, United Nations; Luciana Marulli-Koenig, Chief Information Support Unit, Dept. of Policy Coordination and Sustainable Development, United Nations; William Lee, UNRWA; Ian McDonald, Chief Editor, IMF; Mehri Madarshahi, Department of Administration and Management, UN; Isabelle Marsalles, Electoral Assistance Division; Alex Marshall and Stirling Scruggs, UNFPA; Allegra Morelli, Director, Information Division, IFAD; Ozdinch Mustafa, Senior Political Affairs Officer, Trusteeship Council, United Nations; Marie Okabe, Senior Liaison Officer, UNHCR; Lisa Pachter, International Relations Officer, Office of the Vice President, United Nations Affairs, World Bank Group; Sarah Parkes, ITU; Carrie Power, UNIFEM; Andrew Radolf, UNESCO; Aurora Rodriguez, UNIDO; Ann Rogers, Senior Economist, Department of Policy Coordination and Sustainable Development, United Nations (for information on the World Food Council); Simeon Sahaydachny, Legal Officer, International Trade Law Branch, Office of Legal Affairs, UNCITRAL; Sunil Saigal, Acting Chief, Division of Resources Mobilization, Bureau for Resources and External Affairs, UNDP; Samir Sanbar, Under Secretary General, Department of Public Information, United Nations; Wesley Scholz, United States Department of State (for information on the Law of the Sea Convention); Jim Snissen, UNEP; Maria-Sabina Yeterian-Parisi, Economic Affairs Officer, Policy Coordination and External Relations Service, UNCTAD; Dorothy Thibodeau, Public Affairs Division, IMF; Celinda Verano, WHO Office at the UN; D. Williams, WMO; David J. Woods, Director, Information Division, GATT; External Relations Division, UNIDO; Communications and External Relations Section, UNIFEM; Division of External Relations, UNHCR; Adrienne Cruz, Publications, Dissemination and Reference Centre, UNRISD; Department of Public Information, UPU; Department of Public Relations and Information, WIPO; and the Secretariat of the World Meteorological Organization.

This encyclopedia greatly benefited from statistics and information requested of the governments of the nations profiled in these volumes. The following persons, personally or through the auspices of their offices, graciously responded to our request for information: Mr. Arben Tashko, Embassy of the Republic of Albania; Mr. Hamid Belhadj, Embassy of the Democratic and Popular Republic of Algeria; Ms. Debbie O. Profper, Embassy of Antigua and Barbuda; Mr. Garnik Ashotovich Nanagulian, Embassy of the Republic of Armenia; Mr. Christopher Sweeney, Embassy of Australia; Mr. Martin G. Eichtinger, Embassy of Austria; Mr. Djeikhoun Nazim Molla Zade, Embassy of the Republic of Azerbaijan; Mrs. Diane A. Dean, Embassy of the Commonwealth of the Bahamas; Mr. Othman Abdulla Mohammed Rashed, Embassy of the State of Bahrain; Mr. K. M. Ejazul Huq, Embassy of the People's Republic of Bangladesh; Mr. Charles Chesterfield Burnett, Embassy of Barbados; Mrs. Gisele Louise Eggermont, Embassy of Belgium; Mrs. Yvonne Sharman Hyde, Embassy of Belize; Mr. Augustine Moipolai Pone, Embassy of the Republic of Botswana; Mr. Eduardo Botelho Barbosa, Brazilian Embassy; Mr. Ahmad Hajijukin, Embassy of the State of Brunei Darussalam; Ms. Djeneba Yasmine Traore, Embassy of Burkina Faso; Mr. Pierre Ndzengue, Embassy of the Republic of Cameroon; Mr. L. Ian MacDonald, Embassy of Canada; Mrs. Maria I. M. Correa Reynolds, Embassy of Chile; Mr. Antonia F. Copello, Embassy of Colombia; Mr. Kresimir Cosic, Embassy of the Republic of Croatia; Mr. Miltos Miltiadou, Embassy of the Republic of Cyprus; Mr. Joergen Grunnet, Royal Danish Embassy; Mr. Issa Daher Bopuraleh, Embassy of the Republic of Djibouti; Dr. Dario Suro, Embassy of the Dominican Republic; Mr. Kamel Abdel Hamid Mohamed Ahmed, Embassy of the Arab Republic of Egypt; Mr. Eerik Niiles Kross, Embassy of Estonia; Mr. Demissie Segu Segu, Embassy of Ethiopia; His Excellency Pita Kewa Nacuva, Embassy of the Republic of Fiji; Mrs. Pirkko Liisa O'Rourke, Embassy of Finland; Mr. Jean Mendelson, Embassy of France; Mr. Gottfried Haas, Embassy of the Federal Republic of Germany; Miss Mara Marinaki, Embassy of Greece; His Excellency Kenneth Modeste, Embassy of Grenada; His Excellency The Most Reverend Agostino Cacciavillan, Apostolic Nunciature; Mr. Rosny Montoya Flores, Embassy of Honduras; Miss Klara Breuer, Embassy of the Republic of Hungary; Mr. Jon Egill Egilsson, Embassy of Iceland; Mr. Sanjay Bhatnagar, Embassy of India; Mr. Subekti Dhirdjosaputro, Embassy of the Republic of Indonesia; Mr. Nimrod Barkan, Embassy of Israel; Mr. Alessandro Vaciago, Embassy of Italy; Mr. Seiichi Kondo, Embassy of Japan; Mr. Marwan J. Muasher, Embassy of the Hashemite Kingdom of Jordan; Mr. Byong Suh Lee, Embassy of Korea; Dr. Ali Ahmad Al Tarrah, Embassy of the State of Kuwait; Mr. Ints Upmacis, Embassy of Latvia; Mr. Tsepiso Jeffrey Malefane, Embassy of the Kingdom of Lesotho; Dr. Alfonse Eidintas, Embassy of the Republic of Lithuania; Miss Colette Kinnen, Embassy of Luxembourg; Mr. Robert B. Mbaya, Embassy of Malawi; Mr. Alfred M. Falzon, Embassy of Malta; Mr. Banny DeBrum, Embassy of the Republic of the Marshall Islands; Mr. Amadou Diaw, Embassy of the Islamic Republic of Mauritania; Mr. Joaquin Gonzalez Casanova, Embassy of Mexico; Mr. Kodaro M. Gallen, Embassy of the Federated States of Micronesia; Mr. Nadmidyn Bavuu, Embassy of Mongolia; Mr. Antonio Paulo Elias Matonse Jr., Embassy of the Republic of Mozambique; Mr. Japhet Isaack, Embassy of the Republic of Namibia; Mr. Frans L.E. Hulsman, Embassy of the Netherlands; Mr. Robert Carey Moore Jones, Embassy of New Zealand; Mr. Enrique Vanegas, Embassy of Nicaragua; Mr. Adamou Abdou, Embassy of the Republic of Niger; Mr. Tore

Tanum, Royal Norwegian Embassy; Mr. Salim Al Mahrooqy, Embassy of the Sultanate of Oman; Mr. Malik Zahoor Ahmad, Embassy of Pakistan; Miss Lerna L. Llerena, Embassy of the Republic of Panama; Mr. Christopher Mero, Embassy of Papua New Guinea; Mr. Jose M. Boza, Embassy of Peru; Mr. Boguslaw M. Majewski, Embassy of the Republic of Poland; Professor Maria Graca S. Almeida Rodrigues, Embassy of Portugal; Mrs. Natal'ya P. Semenikhina, Embassy of the Russian Federation; Mr. John P. Irish, Embassy of St. Kitts and Nevis; Ms. Undine George, Embassy of Saint Lucia; Ms. Cecily A. Norris, Embassy of Saint Vincent and the Grenadines; Dr. Hamad Ibrahim Al Salloom, Embassy of Saudi Arabia; Mr. Marc R. Marengo, Embassy of the the the Republic of Seychelles; Miss Siong Fun Lim, Embassy of the Republic of Singapore; Mr. Jaroslav Smiesny, Embassy of the Slovak Republic; Mr. Gregor S. Zore, Embassy of the Republic of Slovenia; Mr. Atukoralalage A. Wijetunga, Embassy of the Democratic Socialist Republic of Sri Lanka; Mr. Abdalla Khidir Bashir, Embassy of the Republic of the Sudan; Mrs. Lindiwe Audrey Nhlabatsi, Embassy of the Kingdom of Swaziland; Mr. Ingmar J. Bjorksten, Embassy of Sweden; Mr. Francois Barras, Embassy of Switzerland; Ms. Souad Mourazen Al Ayoubi, Embassy of the Syrain Arab Republic; Mr. Ally O. Mjenga, Embassy of the United Republic of Tanzania; Mr. Oussama Romdhani, Embassy of Tunisia; Mr. Ahmet Mahfi Egilmez, Embassy of the Republic of Turkey; Mr. Dmitro Y. Markov, Embassy of Ukraine; Mr. Atiq Mubarak Marzoog Khamis, Embassy of the United Arab Emirates; Mr. Nicholas W. Browne, British Embassy; Mr. Carlos Maria Irigaray, Embassy of Uruguay; Mr. Ramon Hernandez, Embassy of the Republic of Venezuela; Mr. Lazarous Kapambwe, Embassy of the Republic of Zambia; Mr. Mark Grey Marongwe, Embassy of the Republic of Zimbabwe. Special acknowledgment goes to Margaret Hunter, Embassy of Turkmenistan and Veronica Rentmeesters, Embassy of Eritrea for their help in providing current information on their respective countries.

The following individuals and agencies deserve special acknowledgment for their generous assistance: Ernest Carter, USDA, Foreign Agricultural Service; Orlando D. Martino, Chief, Branch of Latin America and Canada, US Department of the Interior, Bureau of Mines, Division of International Minerals; Bernadette Michalski, Energy Analyst, US Department of the Interior, Bureau of Mines, Division of International Minerals; Hendrik G. van Oss, Economic Geologist, US Department of the Interior, Bureau of Mines, Division of International Minerals; Lowell Feld, Energy Information Administration, Energy Markets and Contingency Information Division; Matthew E. Brosius, Deputy Head of Center, Organization for Economic Co-operation and Development; Rosario Benevides, Salomon Brothers; Sarah Baker, BP America, Reference Center.

FOREWORD

Although the United Nations is often in the news, its basic nature, its possibilities and its limitations are not widely understood. In its first fifty years the organization has enormously expanded, both in membership and in the scope of its work. During that period, both governments and the public have made it responsible for a variety of dangerous and complex problems, usually without providing adequate means to tackle them. This has meant that the United Nations is mostly better known for its shortcomings than for its achievements.

At its foundation the main functions of the UN were the maintenance of international peace and security, disarmament, and various forms of post-war reconstruction. The founders, however, recalling that the part which economic and social disorder had played in creating the conditions for the second world war, provided, in the Charter, a resounding mandate for the promotion of "the economic and social advancement of all peoples" as well as of human rights and fundamental freedoms. The shortcomings of this side of the UN's work, by far the largest part in terms of staff and programs, is perhaps the most serious disappointment of the organization's first fifty years.

The UN itself is only the instrument of its member governments. Apart from the leadership, and the limited powers of initiative, of the Secretary General, the organization depends for its effectiveness and for its development on the support and the political will of the governments. Peacekeeping operations and the intermediary role of the Secretary General have spasmodically enjoyed such support, although there is now a serious controversy as to how much the UN ought to become involved in human disasters which are not threats to international peace. On the economic and social side there has been a far greater reluctance to give the UN a leading role.

The UN is now going through the most important transition of its history. Virtually all of its recent peace and humanitarian operations are concerned with violent situations within the boundaries of a single state, rather than with conflicts between states as in the past. The media and the public seem increasingly to see the organization as the police and rescue organization of a world community that does not yet exist. However reluctant governments may be to authorize and to provide the necessary resources for such a role, there can be little doubt that if the UN fails to carry it out, along with a far more effective lead in economic and social matters, the organization will become increasingly irrelevant to the great global problems which will determine the future of the human race. We already have many problems of "one world." If the UN does not begin to deal with them effectively, it will cease to be useful, and the future will be correspondingly more hazardous.

The so-called UN system covers, in theory at any rate, virtually the entire range of human activity. After fifty years it needs reorganization, reform and renewal. However, its Charter and its fundamental institutions are sound. If the world organization is to be strengthened to meet the enormous challenges of coming years, it is essential that the public understand it, so that it can be both intelligently criticized and strongly supported. This Encyclopedia provides a comprehensive and accessible basis for such understanding.

BRIAN URQUHART
Scholar-in-Residence, The Ford Foundation
August 1994

PREFACE

TO THE SEVENTH EDITION

Carved in stone, opposite the home of the United Nations, is an inscription taken from Isaiah: ". . . and they shall beat their swords into plowshares, and their spears into pruning hooks: nation shall not lift up sword against nation, neither shall they learn war any more." The Prophets' sense of moral justice, which was the foundation of their vision of peace as expressed in this inscription, has not yet been accepted as a basis for political behavior. Indeed, developments in recent years have cast a dark shadow over the United Nations. The passage of resolutions and the toleration of practices inconsistent with the spirit of the Charter have not only instilled doubt about the effectiveness of the organization as a political instrument but have also undermined the spirit of fairness and cooperation that once characterized the work of the specialized agencies. In the 1930s, the world witnessed the loss of moral force and then the political decline of the League of Nations. No friend of peace could wish its successor a similar fate. It is the fervent hope of the editors of this encyclopedia that political influences will not further undermine the substantive achievements of the United Nations.

The problems of peace preoccupy the minds of people everywhere. The ever-intensifying complexities of our times, while serving to increase the responsibility of a larger number of persons, often also augment the individual's feeling of helplessness. Yet, knowledge of other lands and ability to see their people as fellow human beings can enable the individual to overcome this feeling of helplessness and to act for himself and others. In this spirit this work was conceived and is offered, with the hope that it may not only find many specific uses, but may bring into focus a broader world view for the reader, and thus contribute to international understanding.

MOSHE Y. SACHS
Editor and Publisher, First through Seventh Editions

FOREWORD

TO THE FIRST EDITION

This encyclopedia is different from all others produced in recent years. It is not simply a collection of miscellaneous facts for ready reference. It resembles more the pioneer work of those encyclopedists who ushered in the era of enlightenment in 18th-century France, in that it mirrors the life of men and nations at a great turning point in history, when the national state system of absolute sovereignties has to find new adjustments under the sovereignty of science. The old safeguards for security—mountains and oceans—no longer hold against the impact of an atomic age. The United Nations is the mirror of this new world in which international life becomes more and more interdependent. The political framework is therefore filled in by a comprehensive survey of the major interests of people everywhere. Such an encyclopedia should prove a valuable guide to the understanding not only of the United Nations but of our time.

JAMES T. SHOTWELL
6 August 1874–17 July 1965
Chairman, Editorial Advisory Board First Edition

The swift course of domestic and world events, part of a hastened process of change, requires an enormous increase of basic understanding by peoples of the multiple factors influencing the tempo and direction of national developments. The pattern of intercultural penetration and cross-fertilizing exchanges of scientific and technological knowledge rests upon a concept of fundamental unity of diverse approaches to the central objective of all human endeavors: the creation of a better world, with general equality of opportunity to all individuals, everywhere.

Within a planet shrunk into community bounds by the progress of communications there are no substantial sectors of mankind still completely isolated from the main currents of 20th-century thought and action. A growing sense of identification among men is fostered by the adoption of certain basic standards of human rights and the slow growth of supranational law rooted in the fundamental principles that are common to all juridical systems.

No period in history has witnessed such accelerated search for adequate answers to the riddles that have so long beset humanity. Metaphysical explanations of the universe and of the individual's place within it vie with each other in the vast and only superficially explored realm of emotions; rationalized conceptions of economic and social philosophies contend in the marketplace of personal loyalties with a violence that frequently threatens to rend asunder the fabric of overall unity; and the march forward of freedoms and improvements in the status of people throughout our earth is largely clouded by the supercharged treatment of political affairs in the media of mass communication.

At a time when people everywhere are truly eager for accurate, comprehensive, and timely information about themselves and their neighbors in the closely related various geographic areas, the vastness and multiplicity of the field to be covered promotes reporting that serves little the needs of the average person: it is either too detailed in breadth and depth, so that only specialists can profit from its availability, or sketchy and fragmentary, to the point where it contributes more to confusion than enlightenment of the users.

A specific reason has made necessary a new approach to analytical and basic data on each country, as a separate political unit, and as a member of the vast family of nations all constitute together: the universality of their interest in the maintenance of international peace and security through the joint exercise of agreed-upon powers to restrain violence; to police disturbed areas where peaceful relations are endangered; to promote the application of legal procedures to the adjudication of their differences; and to strike at the very sources of controversy, which are rooted in the deep chasms among their economic and social standards and their consequent basic inequalities of status.

So-called realists may continue to voice their belief that conflict among nations is an outgrowth of their dynamic development, and that only practical arrangements which create "balances" of power can establish an equilibrium within the diverse segments of the world; and theorists of the biological inevitability of war still proclaim the materialistic concept that only a concentration of authority in the hands of some overwhelmingly strong state can eliminate actual armed conflict and bring to subjected peoples the "benefits" of a freedomless "pax romana." But mankind has made great strides since the days of empires, the conquest of colonial dependencies, the plagues and misery that fixed the general expectation of human life under thirty years, and the spiritual darkness of illiteracy and isolation from the mainstreams of culture of variegated philosophical, religious, and scientific concepts.

Under principles of ethics the peoples and the nations emerged as possessors of rights and bearers of responsibilities, and morality took its place in the councils of power. The advancement toward a universal rule of law has been too slow for the idealists and yet most encouraging to those who believe that peaceful evolutionary progress achieves more durable results than violent revolutionary change. The steady process of codification of generally recognized juridical principles and the formulation of new ones through general consensus constitute one of the most hopeful signs of this restless era of change. International compacts such as the Covenant of the League of Nations and the Charter of the United Nations incorporate moral concepts side by side with legal standards. They recognize that there are both ethical and juridical duties and rights that must be observed by states in their reciprocal relations and in respect of their inhabitants, subjects, and citizens.

So far-reaching are the changes already wrought within the world community, particularly for its less developed segments, that the normal processes of history have lost considerable significance in the face of new realities recently created.

Feeling that none of the encyclopedias and specialized sources of information do sufficient justice to these accomplishments in political freedom, economic development, social progress, and the practice of international cooperation, Worldmark Press, Inc., decided to publish a basically new encyclopedia devoted to the nations.

After identifying the outward symbols of each state: the capital, a map, the flag, the national anthem, the monetary unit, the system of weights and measures, holidays, and time, each article proceeds to cover, as thoroughly as available data permit, 50 individual phases of the country's life, so as to furnish an overall picture of its present as rooted in the past evolution of its institutions, customs, and traditions. A precise definition of location, size, and extent of the individual territory is given, so that the reader can visualize, as a living reality, that which the map depicts graphically. Topography, climate, and flora and fauna supplement the other natural physical features of the respective nation.

More than by any other factor, countries are what they are because of man's exertions to create his own environment, so population, ethnic groups, and language are the next items covered. Together with the section devoted to religion, they give a basic understanding of the demographic phenomena that determine the basic institutions, political, economic, and social, of each sovereign unit.

Transportation and communications follow in the description of the positive factors working for the consolidation of each country's internal unity and of the reconstruction of the wider oneness of mankind.

Next there is a historical survey, in most cases kept brief because of the availability of comprehensive ones in other sources of general information.

As a result of the individual national experience various types of governmental authority have been either adopted from the similar experience of other peoples or created to meet different requirements. In the operation of governments, there are diverse types of machinery which correspond to particular political philosophies and which the citizens control through political parties.

Local governmental structures supplement the system of deliberative and executive authorities in charge of public interests.

Knowledge of the organizational pattern of the judiciary acquires considerable importance for all kinds of individual and corporate activities within a particular nation, so information is furnished thereon.

The internal stability of a country and its international security are made clear by adequate data on the organization and potential of the armed forces.

Because the pattern of migrations has undergone great changes, information on their effect upon demographic developments in each state is of deep significance for any evaluation of manpower prospects and consumer potentials.

No nation is an isolated unit itself. The extent to which each government engages in international cooperation is a useful indicator of its concern with the peaceful handling of potential sources of tensions and conflicts.

One of the phases of internal development with an international impact relates to the wide range of the economy. This encyclopedia deals comprehensively with income, labor, agriculture, animal husbandry, fishing, forestry, mining, energy and power, industry, domestic trade, foreign trade, balance of payments, banking, insurance, securities, public finance, taxation, customs and duties, foreign investment, and economic policy.

It also gives information on health, social welfare, and housing, important in the economically less developed nations as a mainspring of economic activity and financial investment for what is called the infrastructure, vital as a prerequisite of other actions to promote production, employment, higher standards of living and, in general, a broader enjoyment of basic human rights and fundamental freedoms.

The domestic activities mentioned in the two previous paragraphs aim to help in the struggle against illiteracy which, even in more advanced countries, reduces the number of citizens actively engaged in political life and is instrumental in the growth and maintenance of discriminatory practices and arbitrary stereotypes within each nation and between many nations. It is of the utmost importance to know the educational facilities available for supplying trained political leaders, administrators, economists, social workers, medical personnel, and technicians. And to data on teaching establishments is added information on libraries and museums and on the organizations set up by the people of each country to promote their collective interests and welfare.

The press and other media of information and enlightenment constitute an important index of the cultural standing of the people; the degree of their freedom is the best evidence of the intellectual maturity of government and governed, and a significant indicator of the degree to which essential human rights in the field of opinion are truly respected.

Perhaps the most effective way to advance reciprocal understanding is by contacts among peoples of different countries and with each other's natural environment. The conditions which must be met for the purposes of tourism are fully explained.

Dependencies for which each individual state assumes international responsibilities are described in detail. Finally a brief roll of famous persons is a biographical listing of national figures. An up-to-date bibliography closes each nation's description.

But in our day and era nations are not islands unto themselves, busy solely with internal problems of varying magnitude. The field of exclusively domestic concern is shrinking under the tremendous impact of easy communications among nations.

While the United Nations and regional organizations of states, directly or through their subsidiary or associated organs, may and do deal with practically every field of human interest, other organizations restrict their jurisdiction to the more specific areas of economic or social matters. They handle issues at the universal and at the close neighborhood levels and, large or small, they each play a part in the process of international cooperation to improve and give constructive meaning to the relations among peoples. Even military pacts have gradually broadened the scope of their concern as a result of the finding that merely negative aims do not afford by themselves the stability and coherence for which they were brought into being. The Secretary-General of the United Nations, Mr. Dag Hammarskjöld, has repeatedly stated his views that any collective action conducted outside the United Nations, but consonant with the spirit of its charter, can be considered as cooperation toward the fundamental objectives of the world organization.

Because we live under the impact of global issues that affect every individual, for good or for ill, and because also of the advance of democratic processes domestically and internationally, more and more people are now actively concerned with the course of world affairs. The best channels to voice their hopes are the governments democratically elected and responsible to the wishes of the citizenry. When the people disagree with their authorities, whose judgment must necessarily take into account factors not always of public knowledge, the people then can use their nongovernmental bodies to express their prevailing views.

The *Worldmark Encyclopedia of the Nations* is a pioneer effort. It is our earnest hope that this first edition may prove a truly useful tool to everyone.

BENJAMIN A. COHEN
18 March 1896–12 March 1960
Editor in Chief, First Edition

NOTES

GENERAL NOTE: The Tenth Edition of *Worldmark Encyclopedia of the Nations* (WEN) includes a sixth volume, "World Leaders." The 193 entries in "World Leaders" provide biographical profiles of the person who is the head of the nation's government and who bears primary responsibility for the country's policy. The profiles are arranged alphabetically by country, and begin with the leader's name (with guide to pronunciation) and title, accompanied by a recent photo. The introductory sections provide a brief summary of the nation's status, including location, geography, and characteristics of society. (Researchers seeking more detailed information on any aspect of the country and its people may refer to the full country entry in the appropriate volume of WEN.) Sections profile the leader's personal background, rise to power, leadership, and outline his or her domestic and foreign policy positions. Finally, the leader's official mailing address is provided, along with a list of sources used in preparing the profile. The profiles were researched and written by knowledgeable experts, whose names and institutional affiliations appear at the end of each entry.

Reflecting the ever-changing status of the world geopolitical situation, the Tenth Edition includes entries for 194 countries, and for 6 describing dependencies. One new country profile, East Timor, was added following the 1999 referendum on independence in that former Indonesian province. Alternatively, the entry for Portuguese Asian Dependency (Macau) has been eliminated, with the information being incorporated into the China entry; as of December 1999 Macau came under Chinese authority. Similarly, the entry for United Kingdom Asian Dependency (Hong Kong) was eliminated with the Ninth Edition; as of 1997 Hong Kong came under Chinese authority. The Tenth Edition is the first to record changes in the world's economy following the creation of the euro zone by the nations of the European Union. The Eighth Edition of this encyclopedia (1995) reported on the dramatic changes in the world in the early 1990s, including the dissolution of the USSR, Czechoslovakia, and Yugoslavia; the unification of Germany; the unification of Yemen; and the independence of Eritrea. These changes resulted in twenty-five new country articles. Whereas the First Edition of the *Worldmark Encyclopedia of the Nations,* in one volume, contained 119 articles, the present Tenth Edition, in six volumes, now contains 200.

In compiling data for incorporation into the Tenth Edition of the *Worldmark Encyclopedia of the Nations,* substantial efforts were made to enlist the assistance of the government of every nation in the world, as well as of all pertinent UN agencies, who cooperated by supplying data and by revising and updating materials relevant to their sphere of interest. Material received from official sources was reviewed and critically assessed by the editors as part of the process of incorporation. Materials and publications of the UN family and of intergovernmental and nongovernmental organizations throughout the world provided a major fund of geographic, demographic, economic, and social data.

In compiling historical, economic, and political data, primary materials generated by governments and international agencies were supplemented by data gathered from numerous other sources including newspapers (most notably *The European,* the *Financial Times,* the *New York Times,* and the *Wall Street Journal*); periodicals (most notably *Current History, Elections Today, The Economist,* the *Far Eastern Economic Review,* and *World Press Review*); and over 150 World Wide Web sites hosted by government agencies and embassies.

The reader's attention is directed to the Glossary of Special Terms for explanations of key terms and concepts essential to a fuller understanding of the text.

COUNTRY NAMES: Country names are reported (as appropriate) in three forms: the short-form name, as commonly used in the text; the English version of the official name; and the official name in the national language(s). When necessary, textual usages of some short-form names have been rectified, usually through the substitution of an acronym for the official name, in order to strike a better balance between official usages and universal terminology. Thus the following short-form names have been adopted throughout (except in historical context to preserve accuracy): DROC (Democratic Republic of the Congo—known as Zaire prior to the Ninth Edition); ROC (Republic of the Congo); FRG (Federal Republic of Germany); North Korea: DPRK (Democratic People's Republic of Korea); and South Korea: ROK (Republic of Korea). In addition, Vietnam has replaced Viet Nam to reflect common usage.

MAPS: Spellings on the individual country maps reflect national usages and recognized transliteration practice. To clarify national boundaries and landforms, dark shading has been applied to waters, and lighter shading to lands not within that nation's jurisdiction. Cross-hatching has been used to designate certain disputed areas. Rivers that run dry during certain times of the year are indicated by dashed instead of solid lines.

FLAGS AND NATIONAL EMBLEMS: All depictions of flags, flag designations, and national emblems have been reviewed and, where necessary, corrected or changed to reflect their official usage as of 2000. In almost all cases the flags and emblems were drawn in an electronic format by One Mile Up, Inc. and are used with their permission. In general, the term "national flag" denotes the civil flag of the nation.

CURRENCY: In most cases, currency conversion factors cited in the Tenth Edition are as of March 2000. New with this edition, currency conversions for the euro are provided to reflect the initiation of foreign exchange in the euro as of 1 January 1999.

WEIGHTS AND MEASURES: The general world trend toward adoption of the metric system is acknowledged through the use of metric units and their nonmetric (customary or imperial) equivalents throughout the text. The two exceptions to this practice involve territorial sea limits, which are reported in nautical miles, and various production data, for which (unless otherwise stated) units of measure reflect the system in use by the country in question. All tons are metric tons (again, unless otherwise indicated), reflecting the practice of the UN in its statistical reporting. For a complete listing of conversion factors and an explanation of symbols used in the text, see p. 342 of this volume.

HOLIDAYS: Except where noted, all holidays listed are official public holidays, on which government offices are closed that would normally be open. Transliterations of names of Muslim holidays have been standardized. For a fuller discussion on these points, and for a description of religious holidays and their origins and meanings, see the Glossary of Religious Holidays in this volume.

INCOME: Statistics on national income were obtained from sources published by the World Bank and the US Central Intelligence Agency. World Bank figures are for gross national product (GNP), defined as the value of all goods and services produced within a nation in a given year, plus income earned abroad, minus income earned by foreigners from domestic production. CIA figures are for gross domestic product (GDP), defined as the value of all final goods and services produced within a nation in a given year. In most cases, CIA figures are given in purchasing power parity terms.

BALANCE OF PAYMENTS: Balance of payments tables were computed from the International Monetary Fund's *Balance of Payments Yearbook*. In some cases, totals are provided even though not all components of those totals have been reported by the government of the country. Accordingly, in some instances numbers in the columns may not add to the total.

FAMOUS PERSONS: Entries are based on information available through July 2000. Where a person noted in one country is known to have been born in another, the country (or, in some cases, city) of birth follows the personal name, in parentheses.

BIBLIOGRAPHY: Bibliographical listings at the end of country articles are provided as a guide to further reading on the country in question and are not intended as a comprehensive listing of references used in research for the article. Effort was made to provide a broad sampling of works on major subjects and topics as covered by the article; the bibliographies provide, wherever possible, introductory and general works for use by students and general readers, as well as classical studies, recent contributions, and other works regarded as seminal by area specialists. The country article bibliographies were supplemented with information obtained from a search conducted between June and August of 2000. An extensive bibliography listing the key references used for this edition appears on page 351 of this volume. However, it is not a complete listing since many fact sheets, brochures, World Wide Web sites, and other informational materials were not included due to space limitations.

THE UNITED NATIONS SYSTEM

THE UNITED NATIONS FAMILY OF ORGANIZATIONS

| **INTERNATIONAL COURT OF JUSTICE (IJC)** | **GENERAL ASSEMBLY** | **ECONOMIC AND SOCIAL COUNCIL (ECOSOC)** | **SECURITY COUNCIL** | **SECRETARIAT** | **TRUSTEESHIP COUNCIL (suspended)** |

Main and other
  sessional committees
Standing committees and ad
  hoc bodies
Other subsidiary organs and related
  bodies

UNRWA
United Nations Relief and
  Works Agency for Palestine
  Refugees in the Near East

IAEA
International Atomic Energy
  Agency (autonomous)

Select Offices, Programs and Funds

INSTRAW
International Research and Training
  Institute for the Advancement of
  Women

UNCHS (Habitat)
UN Centre for Human Settlements

UNCTAD
UN Conference on Trade and
  Development

UNDP
UN Development Programme

UNEP
UN Environment Programme

UNFPA
UN Population Fund

UNHCR
Office of the UN High
  Commissioner for Refugees

UNICEF
UN Children's Fund

UNIFEM
UN Development Fund
  for Women

UNITAR
UN Institute for Training and
  Research

UNU
United Nations University

UNDCP
UN International Drug Control
  Programme

WFP
World Food Programme
  (UN/FAO)

ITC
International Trade Centre
  (UNCTAD/WTO)

UNHCHR
UN High Commissioner for Human
  Rights

UNIFEM
UN Development Fund for Women

UNRISD
UN Research Institute for Social
  Development

INIA
International Institute on Aging

ICSC
International Civil Service
  Commission

Functional Commissions
Commission for Social
  Development
Commission on Human Rights
Commission on Narcotic Drugs
Commission on the Status of
  Women
Commission on Population and
  Development
Commission on Sustainable
  Development
Commission on Science and
  Technology for Development
Commission on Crime Prevention
  and Criminal Justice
Statistical Commission

Regional Commissions
Economic Commission for Africa
  (ECA)
Economic Commission for Europe
  (ECE)
Economic Commission for Latin
  America and the Caribbean
  (ECLAC)
Economic and Social Commission
  for Asia and the Pacific (ESCAP)
Economic and Social Commission
  for Western Asia (ESCWA)
Sessional and standing committees
Expert committees
Ad hoc committees
Related bodies

Specialized Agencies
ILO
International Labor Organization
FAO
Food and Agriculture Organization
  of the United Nations
UNESCO
United Nations Educational,
  Scientific and Cultural
  Organization
WHO
World Health Organization

World Bank Group
(Bretton Woods Institutions)
IBRD (World Bank)
International Bank for
  Reconstruction and Development
IDA
International Development
  Association
IFC
International Finance Corporation
MIGA
Multilateral Investment Guarantee
  Agency
ICSID
International Centre for Settlement
  of Investment Disputes

Technical Agencies
IMF
International Monetary Fund
ICAO
International Civil Aviation
  Organization
UPU
Universal Postal Union
ITU
International Telecommunication
  Union
WMO
World Meteorological Organization
IMO
International Maritime
  Organization
WIPO
World Intellectual Property
  Organization
IFAD
International Fund for Agricultural
  Development
UNIDO
United Nations Industrial
  Development Organization
WTO
World Trade Organization
  (formerly GATT)

Military Staff Comittee
Standing committees
Ad hoc bodies

International Criminal Tribunal
  for the Former Yugoslavia
International Criminal Tribunal for
  the Territory of Rwanda

Peacekeeping operations
(as of January 2000)
MONUC
United Nations Organization
  Mission in the Democratic
  Republic of the Congo
UNAMSIL
United Nations Mission in Sierra
  Leone
MINURSO
United Nations Mission for the
  Referendum in Western Sahara
UNTAET
United Nations Transitional
  Administration in East Timor
UNMOGIP
United Nations Military Observer
  Group in India and Pakistan
UNMOT
United Nations Mission of
  Observers in Tajikistan
UNMIBH
United Nations Mission in Bosnia
  and Herzegovina
UNMOP
United Nations Mission of
  Observers in Prevlaka
UNFICYP
United Nations Peacekeeping Force
  in Cyprus
UNOMIG
United Nations Observer Mission in
  Georgia
UNMIK
United Nations Interim
  Administration Mission in
  Kosovo
UNDOF
United Nations Disengagement
  Observer Force
UNIKOM
United Nations Iraq-Kuwait
  Observation Mission
UNIFIL
United Nations Interim Force in
  Lebanon
UNTSO
United Nations Truce Supervision
  Organization

STRUCTURE OF THE UNITED NATIONS SYSTEM

The UN system is often referred to as a "family" of organizations. The charter of the UN, signed in San Francisco on 26 June 1945, defined six main organs of the new world body, each with specific tasks and functions. However, because it was impossible to foresee all the demands that might be made on the organization, provision was made for extending its capacities as the need arose. Thus, three of the main organs are specifically empowered to establish "such subsidiary organs" as may be considered necessary for the performance of their functions. In addition, Article 57 of the charter provides that the various specialized agencies established by intergovernmental agreement and having international responsibilities in economic, social, cultural, educational, health, and related fields "shall be brought into relationship" with the UN. Since the signing of the charter, the UN has established numerous subsidiary organs and has entered into relationship with various independent organizations. Reproduced opposite is a chart showing the various organs and bodies within the UN system.

For assistance in interpreting the chart, a brief survey of the UN's main organs, the different categories of subsidiary organs, and the related agencies is given below. A detailed description of the functioning of each of the main organs and an account of the work of selected subsidiary organs are contained in later chapters of the first section of this volume. The structure and work of the UN specialized and technical agencies are described in the second section.

MAIN ORGANS OF THE UN

1. *The General Assembly,* composed of representatives of all member states, is the UN's central deliberative body, empowered to discuss and make recommendations on any subject falling within the scope of the charter itself. It also approves the UN's budget and determines—alone or with the Security Council—part of the composition of the other main organs, including the Security Council.
2. *The Security Council,* a 15-member body, has primary responsibility for maintaining international peace and security. In times of crisis, it is empowered to act on behalf of all member states and to decide on a course of collective action that is mandatory for the entire membership. The charter names five states as permanent members of the Security Council: China, France, the United Kingdom, Russian Federation, and the United States (those that were chiefly responsible for the defeat of the Axis powers in 1945). The remaining Security Council members are elected by the General Assembly for two-year terms.
3. *The Economic and Social Council (ECOSOC)* is assigned the task of organizing the UN's work on economic and social matters and the promotion of human rights. It consists of 54 members elected for three-year terms by the General Assembly.
4. *The Trusteeship Council* operated the UN trusteeship system established under the charter. It was originally composed of member nations administering trust territories, the permanent members of the Security Council, and a sufficient number of other members, elected by the General Assembly for three-year terms, to ensure an equal division of administering and non-

administering powers. After 1975, it was composed of the five permanent members of the Security Council—the United States, the sole remaining administering power, and the four permanent nonadministering powers. The last trust territory, the Pacific island of Palau, voted for affiliation with the United States in late 1993. The Trusteeship Council voted in 1994 to suspend operation, convening only at the request of its President, a majority of its member states, the General Assembly, or the Security Council.
5. *The International Court of Justice* is the principal judicial organ of the UN. It consists of 15 judges elected to nine-year terms by the General Assembly and the Security Council voting independently. It may not include more than one judge of any nationality. The Members of the Court do not represent their governments but are independent magistrates.
6. *The Secretariat* is the administrative arm of the organization. It is headed by a Secretary-General appointed by the General Assembly upon the recommendation of the Security Council for a five-year, renewable term.

SUBSIDIARY ORGANS OF THE UN

The UN Charter specifically confers the right to create subsidiary organs upon the General Assembly, the Security Council, and the Economic and Social Council. The subsidiary bodies fluctuate in number from year to year, according to the changing requirements of the main organ concerned. Both the General Assembly and the Economic and Social Council, for instance, often create subsidiary bodies to assist them in new fields of concern and dissolve others that have completed their work. Some of the subsidiary organs in turn set up their own subsidiary units—working groups, subcommittees, and the like.

Subsidiary Organs of the General Assembly

The General Assembly's subsidiary organs range in complexity and status from temporary committees to semiautonomous institutions that maintain their own secretariats or administrative departments. The names of the institutions or programs in existence in 2000, most of which were set up under the joint aegis of the General Assembly and the Economic and Social Council and operate through ECOSOC, appear in the lower left-hand column of the UN Family of Organizations chart. The remaining subsidiary organs are too numerous to list; the chart merely indicates their principal types: main and other sessional committees, standing committees and ad hoc bodies, and other subsidiary organs and related bodies.

The main and sessional committees comprise representatives of all member states and are formally reconstituted at each regular General Assembly session to discuss the various items on the agenda for that year. Two sessional committees are not committees of the whole—the 28-member General Committee, which reviews the General Assembly's agenda prior to its adoption at each session, and the nine-member Credentials Committee, which examines the credentials of delegations sent to each General Assembly session.

There are many standing committees, ad hoc bodies, and other subsidiary organs and related bodies. Some of the more important of these are:

- the Advisory Committee on Administrative and Budgetary Questions (ACABQ), a 16-member expert committee which reviews the budgets submitted by the Secretary-General;
- the Committee for Programme and Coordination, a 34-member committee, that reviews the programmatic aspects of the Secretary-General's budget;
- the 18-member Committee on Contributions, which recommends the scale of assessments that nations are required to pay as their share of the United Nations budget;
- the Administrative Committee on Coordination (ACC), established by ECOSOC in 1946. It is composed of the Secretary-General and the executive heads of the specialized agencies and the International Atomic Energy Agency. Its purpose is to supervise implementation of agreements between the UN and the specialized agencies, as well as to ensure the full coordination of activities of these bodies.

The ACC carries out its work through three main committees: the Consultative Committee on Administrative Questions; the Consultative Committee on Programme and Operational Questions; and the Interagency Committee on Sustainable Development. These committees oversee interagency cooperation on topics such as sustainable development, new and renewable sources of energy, international drug abuse control, outer space activities, demographic estimates and projections, women, disabled persons, prevention of crime, youth, water resources, nutrition, statistical activities, long-term development objectives, rural development, and science and technology for development.

An important ACC subcommittee is the Advisory Committee for the Coordination of Information Systems (ACCIS), based in Geneva, which was established in 1983 to facilitate access by member states to United Nations information and to improve the information infrastructure within the UN system. ACCIS advises UN organizations that wish to update or replace their information systems, and promotes the use of common standards to facilitate the electronic exchange of information. ACCIS publishes guides and directories of UN information sources and databases. It also maintains three important databases: Database of United Nations Databases and Information Services (DUNDIS), available both online and as a diskette; Database of United Nations Serial Publications (UNSER), available as a diskette; and the Register of Development Activities of the United Nations System (RDA), available as a diskette.

Substantive committees have been set up by General Assembly resolutions to study specific subjects of interest—for example, the peaceful uses of outer space, South Africa's former system of apartheid, and independence for colonial territories. Such committees, whose members are elected by the General Assembly or appointed by its president, usually meet several times a year. At each regular session, they report on their deliberations. They continue as long as is considered necessary. Even when their mandate seems completed, they are not necessarily formally disbanded but may be adjourned indefinitely and reactivated when the need arises. It is through these committees that the General Assembly accomplishes most of its work outside the spheres of responsibility that are specifically entrusted to the Economic and Social Council, the Trusteeship Council, or the various semiautonomous bodies referred to above.

Subsidiary Organs of the Security Council

The Military Staff Committee was established by the charter to advise the Security Council on the military aspects of maintaining international peace. However, the Military Staff Committee secretariat, though it holds regular formal meetings, has never been consulted on any of the UN's peacekeeping operations. The other subsidiary bodies shown on the chart in the lower right-hand column were set up, as their names suggest, to conduct the council's peacekeeping operations in the areas specified. Between June 1948 and March 2000, there were 53 peacekeeping operations, of which 38 were complete. (For further information on the work of these bodies, see the chapter on International Peace and Security.)

The Security Council, as of early 2000, maintained two standing committees, each including representatives of all Security Council member states: Committee of Experts on Rules of Procedure (studies and advises on rules of procedure and other technical matters); and Committee on Admission of New Members. Additionally, there are various ad hoc committees, established as needed; these comprise all council members and meet in closed session. In early 2000, the following ad hoc committees had been formed: Security Council Committee on Council meeting away from Headquarters and Governing Council of the United Nations Compensation Commission established by Security Council resolution 692 (1991).

The Security Council, acting under Chapter VII of the charter, which deals with "action with respect to threats to the peace, breaches of the peace, and acts of aggression," may set up committees to monitor noncompliance by member states with its resolutions. As of May 2000, the following committees had been set up: in 1966, when it imposed mandatory economic sanctions against the illegal regime in Southern Rhodesia; in 1977, when it imposed a mandatory arms embargo against South Africa; in 1991, after Iraq's unsuccessful invasion of Kuwait, to supervise the elimination of Iraq's weapons of mass destruction; in 1992, concerning the situations in the Libyan Arab Jamahiriya and Somalia; in 1993, concerning Angola; in 1994, concerning the volatile situation created by Hutu rebels in Rwanda; in 1995, concerning Liberia; in 1997, in the wake of years of civil war in Sierra Leone; and in 1999, concerning Afghanistan.

Subsidiary Organs of the Economic and Social Council

As indicated on the chart, there are four types of subsidiary organs of the Economic and Social Council:

1. the semiautonomous bodies (organizations, programs, and funds);
2. regional commissions;
3. functional commissions; and
4. sessional, standing, and ad hoc committees.

UN SPECIALIZED AND TECHNICAL AGENCIES

The specialized and technical agencies are separate autonomous organizations with their own policy-making and executive organs, secretariats, and budgets. The precise nature of their relationship with the UN is defined by the terms of special agreements that were established with the Economic and Social Council and subsequently approved by the General Assembly, as provided for in Article 63 of the charter. Since Article 63 also empowers the Economic and Social Council to coordinate the activities of the specialized agencies through consultation and recommendations, they are required to report annually to it.

Mention should be made here of the special status of the General Agreement on Tariffs and Trade (GATT), which was succeeded by the World Trade Organization. At its inception in 1948, GATT was a treaty establishing a code of conduct in international trade and providing machinery for reducing and stabilizing tariffs. The treaty was concluded pending the creation of a specialized agency to be known as the International Trade Organization, whose draft charter was completed in 1948 but was never ratified by the important trading powers. With the successful conclusion of the Uruguay Round of GATT, a new body, the World Trade Organization, supplanted it in 1995.

(For further details, see the chapter on the World Trade Organization.)

The International Atomic Energy Agency (IAEA) is distinguished from the other agencies in that it was specifically established under the aegis of the UN and is therefore considered in a category by itself. The IAEA reports annually to the General Assembly and only "as appropriate" to the Economic and Social Council. Because of the nature of its work, the IAEA also reports to the Security Council, again only "as appropriate."

THE BRETTON WOODS INSTITUTIONS

These institutions were created before the United Nations itself, at a conference at Bretton Woods, New Hampshire, in the United States in 1944. In the UN Charter, however, they were considered to be an integral part of the system of UN agencies. However, their agreements with the UN bind them only loosely to the rest of the system. The nature of these organizations is very different from the one country, one vote basis of the UN and the other specialized agencies (see World Bank and International Monetary Fund [IMF] in the second part of this volume). Membership in the Bretton Woods institutions is subject to financial subscription, and voting is weighted according to members' shares, effectively giving wealthy countries more control than poorer countries. When the World Bank became affiliated with the United Nations, it maintained its complete independence as far as coordination, refused to provide regular information to the UN, limited UN attendance at its meetings, and insisted on a clause eliminating any UN involvement in its budgets. While there is growing cooperation between the World Bank and some UN technical cooperation funds, like the United Nations Development Programme (UNDP), a 1993 study by the Joint Inspection Unit found that there was not much operational cooperation between the UN system organizations and the World Bank organizations.

THE SIZE AND COST OF THE UN SYSTEM

Since the early 1980s, the United Nations has been criticized for being a "vast, sprawling bureaucracy," and politicians have not hesitated to call it "bloated" or "swollen." This perception led to a drive for reform in the mid-1980s during which major contributing countries initiated a 13 percent staff cut. Another round of "rationalization" of the system and its secretariats was initiated in 1991. Tightening the budget remained a focus throughout the 1990s. The UN budget for the 2000–01 biennium was expected to amount to US$2,535 million. Joseph Connor, the Under Secretary-General for Management, said this budget, which was virtually at the same level as that of the 1998–99 biennium, "showed remarkable financial discipline." The virtual no-growth budget had been made possible by reduction of administrative costs and a reallocation of resources to the prime activities of the United Nations, including the maintenance of international peace and security, the promotion of sustained economic growth and sustainable development, and the development of Africa. Further, the UN's cash balance at the end of 2000 was forecasted to be about US$110 million, marking the first time in about six years that the organization had ended up with a plus balance. Part of this had been made possible by the level of contributions made by the United States, which was among the nations that had been in arrears. Mr. Connor hastened to add to the list of the UN's prime activities human rights promotion, the effective coordination of humanitarian assistance efforts, the promotion of justice and international law, disarmament, drug control, and the fight against crime prevention and international terrorism.

COMPARISON WITH THE LEAGUE OF NATIONS

The League of Nations grew out of the catastrophe of World War I (1914–18). Though the idea of the establishment of a body in which the nations of the world could settle their disagreements had been put forth periodically since antiquity, the League, created at the 1919 Paris Peace Conference, was the first organization of sovereign states designed to be universal and devoted to the settlement of disputes and the prevention of war. The League's failure to prevent the outbreak of World War II in 1939 did not destroy the belief in the need for a universal organization. On the contrary, it bred a determination to learn from the mistakes of the past and to build a new world body more adequately equipped to maintain international peace in the future.

The differences between the League of Nations and the UN begin with the circumstances of their creation. First, whereas the Covenant of the League was formulated after hostilities were ended, the main features of the UN were devised while war was still in progress. The more comprehensive powers assigned to the UN for the preservation of peace may owe something to the urgent conditions in which it was conceived. Second, the Covenant was drawn up in an atmosphere of divided attention at the Paris Peace Conference and was incorporated as part of the peace treaty with Germany. Although countries were permitted to ratify the Covenant and the treaty separately, the link between them was not good psychology and contributed, for example, to the unwillingness of the US Senate to ratify the Covenant. In contrast, the UN Charter was drafted as an independent legal instrument at a conference especially convened for the purpose. Third, the Covenant was hammered out behind closed doors, first by the five major powers of the era—France, Italy, Japan, the UK, and the US—and eventually in conjunction with nine other allied nations. The final text of the UN Charter, on the other hand, was the product of combined efforts of 50 nations represented at the 1945 San Francisco Conference and therefore took into account the views of the smaller nations, especially their concern to give the new organization far-reaching responsibilities in promoting economic and social cooperation and the independence of colonial peoples.

VOTING

Under the Covenant, decisions of the League could be made only by unanimous vote. This rule applied both to the League's Council, which had special responsibilities for maintaining peace (the equivalent of the UN's Security Council), and to the all-member Assembly (the equivalent of the UN's General Assembly). In effect, each member state of the League had the power of the veto, and, except for procedural matters and a few specified topics, a single "nay" killed any resolution. Learning from this mistake, the founders of the UN decided that all its organs and subsidiary bodies should make decisions by some type of majority vote (though, on occasion, committees dealing with a particularly controversial issue have been known to proceed by consensus). The rule of unanimity applies only to five major powers—France, China, the UK, the US, and the Russian Federation—and then only when they are acting in their capacity as permanent members of the Security Council. The Security Council also proceeds by majority vote, but on substantive (though not on procedural) matters, it must include the concurring votes of all the permanent

members. (See the section on Voting in the chapter on the Security Council.)

CONSTITUTIONAL POWERS TO PREVENT WAR AND END AGGRESSION

The Charter was designed to remedy certain constitutional defects and omissions in the Covenant that the founders of the UN believed had been partly responsible for the League's inability to halt the drift toward a second world war in the 1930s. These defects and omissions included the absence of any provision imposing a total ban on war, the provision of an overly rigid procedure for negotiating disputes between states, and the failure to vest the League's Council with sufficient powers to prevent the outbreak of hostilities or to terminate hostilities that had already begun.

The Covenant forbade military aggression but did not reject the limited right of a state to start a war, provided that it had first submitted the dispute to arbitration, judicial decision, or the Council of the League. If one party accepted the findings of the negotiating body and the second did not, the first might then resort to war legally after a "cooling-off" period.

The Charter recognizes no circumstances under which a nation may legally start a war. Article 51 does guarantee the right to individual or collective self-defense, which is a right to respond to an illegal armed attack but not to initiate one. If the Security Council decides that a "threat to the peace" exists, it has the power to order collective enforcement measures. These are mandatory for all member states and may include economic sanctions or military measures, but the power rarely has been invoked. (See the chapter on International Peace and Security.)

MEMBERSHIP

The League never became the universal organization that had been envisaged. Moreover, it failed to secure or retain the membership of certain major powers whose participation and cooperation were essential to make it an effective instrument for preserving the peace. Despite President Wilson's advocacy, the US did not join, and the USSR joined only in 1934, when the League had already shown itself unable to contain the aggressive policies of Germany, Italy, and Japan. The three aggressor states themselves withdrew their membership during the 1930s to pursue their expansionist aims. The UN, on the other hand, is approaching the goal of universality, with only a few smaller countries still unrepresented. By May 2000, its membership had reached 188.

PROMOTION OF HUMAN WELFARE

The UN Charter not only lays down specific injunctions for international economic and social cooperation, based on respect for the principle of equal rights and self-determination of peoples, but also has established a special organ—the Economic and Social Council—to conduct the organization's activities in this sphere. Throughout its existence, the UN, together with its specialized agencies, has gradually assumed primary responsibility for assisting the economic and social development of nonindustrialized member nations, most of them former colonial territories that joined the world body long after it was founded. The UN's many projects have become the cornerstone of the development policies adopted by almost all these countries. Since the Covenant of the League contained no provisions for a coordinated program of economic and social cooperation, there can be no comparison between the respective achievements of the two organizations in this respect. Nevertheless, the League performed valuable work in several fields: notably, working to eliminate the illegal sale of women and children, the "white slave" trade; providing assistance for refugees; reducing traffic in opium and other dangerous narcotics; and getting nations to lessen trade restrictions.

ADMINISTRATION OF COLONIAL TERRITORIES

Instead of sharing the colonial possessions of their defeated enemies as the traditional spoils of victory, the founding members of the League, with admirable foresight and restraint, regarded these territories as international mandates, and certain member states were designated to administer them on behalf of the world organization. This mandate system in a modified form was continued in the trusteeship system evolved by the founders of the UN. However, unlike the Covenant, the Charter expressly stipulates that the administering countries have an obligation to promote the progressive development of the territories placed in their charge toward self-government or independence.

BALANCE SHEET OF THE LEAGUE OF NATIONS

The League failed in its supreme test. It failed to contain the aggressive action of the Axis powers—Japan, Germany, and Italy—and thus failed to halt the drift toward a new world war. Beginning in 1931, Japan, a permanent member of the League's Council, waged a war of aggression against China, in defiance of both the Council and the Assembly. Although the League did impose economic sanctions against Italy, another permanent member of the Council, when it wantonly invaded Ethiopia in 1935, support was halfhearted and the action unsuccessful. The League was unable to do anything against the illegal reoccupation of the Rhineland in 1936 by Germany, still another permanent member of the Council; nor could it offer more than verbal protests against German and Italian intervention in the Spanish Civil War or the forcible incorporation of Austria into Germany in March 1938 and of Czechoslovakia into Germany the following year. The cumulative effect of these failures strengthened Hitler's belief in the impotence not only of the League itself but also of its principal remaining members. During the summer of 1939, when the world moved ever closer toward war, and even when Hitler's armies marched into Poland on 1 September 1939, not a single member called for a meeting of the League's Council or Assembly.

The League's balance sheet in political matters was not wholly negative, however. It was able, for example, to settle the dispute between Finland and Sweden over the Aland Islands, strategically located in the Gulf of Bothnia; the frontier controversy between Albania, Greece, and Yugoslavia; the potentially explosive border situation between Greece and Bulgaria; and the dangerous conflicts between Poland and Germany over Upper Silesia and between Germany, Poland, and Lithuania over Memel. Through the League's Permanent Court of International Justice, a border controversy between Czechoslovakia and Poland was settled, as were the disputes between Great Britain and Turkey over the Mosul area and between France and Great Britain over the nationality of Maltese residents in the French protectorates of Morocco and Tunisia. The League also stopped the incipient war between Peru and Colombia over territorial claims in the upper Amazon basin.

In addition to these successful peacekeeping activities, the League financially assisted the reconstruction of certain states, notably Austria, and was responsible for administering the Free City of Danzig and the Saar Territory. (The latter was transferred to Germany following a plebiscite in 1935.) It also carried out important humanitarian work. Some of its nonpolitical activities continued throughout World War II, and its secretariat did valuable preparatory work for the emerging UN. The League of Nations was not officially dissolved until April 1946, five months after the new world body came into being.

THE UN'S GREATER SCOPE

The field of activity and the responsibilities of the UN are considerably more extensive than those of the League. Of the specialized agencies in the UN system, only three—the ILO, the ITU, and the UPU—antedate the UN. The League, furthermore, never sponsored any such enterprises as those undertaken by, for example, the UN Development Program, the UN Environment Program, or the World Food Program. Membership in the League did not oblige a nation to join the Permanent Court of Justice, whereas all members of the UN are automatically parties to the Statute of the International Court of Justice, which is an integral part of the Charter.

Like the League, the UN has recorded several important successes in halting local armed conflicts and the spread of disputes: for example, in the Congo, Kashmir, and, over long periods, Cyprus. However, it has often proved unable to take effective action in any situation where the interests of either the US or the former USSR are closely involved or where the two giant powers seem committed to opposite sides of disputes involving smaller nations. Thus, it was unable to check the Soviet invasion of Hungary in 1956 and of Czechoslovakia in 1968; it was unable to take any action to halt the fighting that raged in Indochina during most of its existence; and, though progress has been made, it has not succeeded in finding a permanent solution to the prolonged crisis that has periodically erupted in Arab-Israeli wars in the Middle East.

The UN's ineffectuality in such situations caused a loss of confidence in its relevance in international political relations. Nor was it a source of consolation that there was no discernible drift toward a world war, for in most cases where the US and the former USSR found themselves almost at the point of actual confrontation, as in the 1962 Cuban missile crisis, they tended to resolve their differences bilaterally, not under the aegis of the UN.

On the other hand, if the two great powers did not always find it convenient to allow the UN to play too decisive a role in political matters, they found it equally impractical to bypass the world organization altogether.

Unlike the League, the UN is the center of a network of organizations whose activities reach into many aspects of the national life of every member state. As such, it has come to be regarded as an indispensable part of the machinery for conducting multi-level international relations. In a world transformed by the collapse of the former Soviet bloc, the UN is coming of age and may begin to fulfill the dreams of its founders. While its authority continues to be challenged by countries that remain on the fringe of the world community, the United Nations may be seen as an embryonic world government.

THE MAKING OF THE UNITED NATIONS

The creation of the UN at the San Francisco Conference in June 1945 was the culmination of four years of concentrated preparation. During these years, the idea of a world organization to replace the League of Nations was first debated and then fleshed out. Many of the important principles of the UN adopted at San Francisco were derived from earlier conferences.

DEVELOPMENTS LEADING TO THE SAN FRANCISCO CONFERENCE

1. *The Inter-Allied Declaration (London Declaration) of 12 June 1941.* In a dark hour of World War II, representatives of the UK, Australia, Canada, New Zealand, and the Union of South Africa and of the governments-in-exile of Belgium, Czechoslovakia, France, Greece, Luxembourg, the Netherlands, Norway, Poland, and Yugoslavia assembled at St. James's Palace in London. It was there that each pledged not to sign a separate peace and declared: "The only true basis of enduring peace is the willing cooperation of free peoples in a world in which, relieved of the menace of aggression, all may enjoy economic and social security. . . . " Ten days later, Hitler launched his attack against the Soviet Union.

2. *The Atlantic Charter of 14 August 1941.* British Prime Minister Winston S. Churchill and US President Franklin D. Roosevelt met aboard the cruiser USS *Atlanta* off the coast of Newfoundland and signed a declaration giving the first indication that the two powers would strive for the creation of a new world organization once peace was restored. In it, they announced "certain common principles . . . of their respective countries . . . for a better future for the world: the need for a secure peace; the abandonment by all nations of the use of force; the disarmament of aggressors; and the establishment of a wider and permanent system of general security."

3. *The Declaration by United Nations of 1 January 1942.* With the Japanese attack on Pearl Harbor on 7 December 1941 and the entry of the US into the war, the conflict assumed even wider dimensions. Japan's initial successes were staggering, and it was clear that the coalition against the Axis powers (Germany, Italy, Japan, and their allies) would need to be strengthened.

   On New Year's Day 1942 in Washington, DC, representatives of 26 states signed a declaration whose preamble called for subscription "to a common program of purposes and principles embodied in the . . . Atlantic Charter" and explicitly referred to the need for promoting respect for human rights on an international basis. In that declaration, the phrase "united nations" was first used. It had been coined by President Roosevelt to express the unity of the signatory nations in their determination to withstand the onslaught of the Axis powers. The declaration was subsequently signed by the governments of 21 additional states.

4. *The Moscow Declaration of 30 October 1943.* This declaration laid the foundation for the establishment of a new world body to replace the League of Nations. Meeting at a time when victory seemed in sight, the US, British, and Soviet foreign ministers and an ambassador from China drew up the Declaration of Four Nations on General Security, which recognized "the necessity of establishing at the earliest practicable date a general international organization based on the principle of sovereign equality of all peace-loving States, and open to membership by all such States, large and small, for the maintenance of international peace and security."

5. *Dumbarton Oaks Conference, Washington, 21 August–7 October 1944.* The Dumbarton Oaks conference was the first big-power meeting convoked specifically to discuss the establishment of a new world organization. At the beginning of the conference, the delegations offered widely differing proposals. On some of these divergent views they eventually reached agreement. For example, the British and Soviet delegations accepted an American position that favored a strong role for the General Assembly, in which all member states would be represented and which, therefore, would be the most "democratic" of the UN organs. There was agreement that a small Security Council should be "primarily responsible for the maintenance of international peace and security" and that the big powers should have the right of veto in that body. However, a deadlock developed over a Soviet proposal that a big power might exercise this right in disputes in which it was itself involved. This the US and the British refused to accept.

6. *Yalta Conference, February 1945.* The resultant deadlock was resolved at a meeting in Yalta attended by Prime Minister Churchill, President Roosevelt, and Marshal Stalin. The "Yalta formula," actually a compromise proposed by the US and rejected by the USSR at Dumbarton Oaks, provided that if any of the Big Five powers was involved in a dispute, it would not have the right to veto Security Council recommendations for peaceful settlement of the issue but would be able to veto a Security Council decision to invoke sanctions against it. After some initial objections from Churchill, the three leaders at Yalta also managed to agree on the basic principles of a trusteeship system for the administration of certain dependent territories under the aegis of the projected world body.

   On 11 February 1945, the three leaders announced that a conference would be convened in San Francisco on 25 April 1945 for the "earliest possible establishment of a general international organization" along the lines proposed at Dumbarton Oaks.

THE SAN FRANCISCO CONFERENCE, 25 APRIL–26 JUNE 1945

Despite the sudden death of President Roosevelt in early April, the United Nations Conference on International Organization convened as scheduled. President Roosevelt had been working on his speech to the conference before he died. That never-delivered address contains the often-quoted words: "The work, my friends, is peace; more than an end of this war—an end to the beginning of all wars; . . . as we go forward toward the greatest contribution that any generation of human beings can make in this world—the contribution of lasting peace—I ask you to keep up your faith. . . ."

China, the USSR, the UK, and the US acted as the sponsoring powers, and 46 other states participated, comprising all those that had signed the Declaration by United Nations of 1 January 1942 or had declared war on the Axis powers by March 1945.

The huge conference was attended by 282 delegates and 1,444 other officially accredited persons from those 50 countries and by representatives of scores of private organizations interested in world affairs (50 from the US alone). The daily output of documents averaged half a million pages.

Major Modifications in the Dumbarton Oaks Draft for the UN Charter

After much debate, the smaller and medium-sized nations succeeded in restricting the Big Five's use of the veto in the Security Council. Herbert V. Evatt, then deputy prime minister of Australia, who was in the forefront of that fight, declared: "In the end our persistence had some good effect. The Great Powers came to realize that the smaller powers would not accept a Charter unless certain minimum demands for restriction of the veto were accepted, viz., that there should be no veto upon the placing of items on the [Security Council] agenda and no veto on discussion [in the Security Council] . . . . If this vital concession had not been won, it is likely that discussion of matters in the open forum of the Security Council would have been rendered impossible: If so, the United Nations might well have broken up."

Another major change resulted from the desire of the smaller nations to give the world organization more responsibilities in social and economic matters and in colonial problems. Accordingly, the Economic and Social Council and the Trusteeship Council were given wider authority than was provided for in the Dumbarton Oaks draft, and they were made principal organs of the UN.

Creation of a New World Court

The San Francisco Conference also unanimously adopted a constitution—called the Statute—for an International Court of Justice to be incorporated as a main organ of the UN and to succeed the Permanent Court of International Justice established by the League of Nations. The Statute, which had originally been drafted by jurists from 44 nations meeting in Washington in April 1945, became part of the Charter of the UN.

Unanimous Acceptance of the Charter

The UN Charter touches on so many delicate and complex matters that its unanimous acceptance has often been ascribed to the particularly auspicious circumstances prevailing in the spring of 1945. In spite of some dissonance, the San Francisco Conference was imbued with a spirit of high mission. The Charter was worked out within two months. It was signed by 50 nations in all its official languages in an impressive ceremony on 26 June 1945. The five official languages at that time were Chinese, English, French, Russian, and Spanish. The sixth official UN language, Arabic, was not adopted until 1973.

ESTABLISHMENT OF THE UN, 24 OCTOBER 1945

The new world body officially came into being on 24 October 1945, when the Charter had been duly ratified by all permanent members of the Security Council and a majority of the other original signatory powers. This date is universally celebrated as United Nations Day.

SUBSEQUENT CHARTER AMENDMENT

Like other political constitutions, the UN Charter contains provisions for its own amendment. Amendments to the Charter come into force when they have been adopted by a vote of two-thirds of the members of the General Assembly and ratified by two-thirds of the UN member states, including all the permanent members of the Security Council.

The amendments that have been adopted are essentially adjustments made to take account of the huge increase in UN membership, which has more than tripled since 1945. As originally constituted, the 11-member Security Council and the 18-member Economic and Social Council were considered adequate to reflect the different interests of the various geographical groupings of states within the organization. However, the admission to the UN during the late 1950s and early 1960s of large numbers of newly independent African, Asian, and Caribbean countries created additional groupings. To accommodate their interests without jeopardizing those of the older groups, the General Assembly, in 1963, adopted amendments to Articles 23, 27, and 61 of the Charter. The first amendment enlarged the membership of the Security Council to 15; the second required that decisions of the Security Council be made by an affirmative vote of nine members (formerly seven); the third enlarged the membership of the Economic and Social Council to 27. All three amendments officially came into force on 31 August 1965.

The Economic and Social Council was enlarged to 54 by an amendment to Article 61 of the Charter, which was adopted by the General Assembly in 1971 and became operative on 24 September 1973.

Charter Review. Under the Charter, a general conference of UN members "for the purpose of reviewing the Charter may be held at a date and place to be fixed by a two-thirds vote of the members of the General Assembly and a vote of any seven members [amended to nine, as of 1965] of the Security Council." In addition, the Charter provided that if such a conference was not held by the tenth regular assembly session (in 1955), the proposal to call such a conference should be placed on the agenda. Accordingly, the 1955 General Assembly considered the matter and decided that a general review conference should be held at an "appropriate" but unspecified date in the future. A committee consisting of the full UN membership was established to consider the time and place at which the conference should be held. The Security Council concurred in the General Assembly's decision by a vote of 9 to 1, with 1 abstention. The committee met every two years until September 1967 without recommending a conference. It then became inactive, recommending that any member state might request it to meet.

At its 1974 session, the General Assembly established a 42-member Ad Hoc Committee on the Charter to consider specific proposals from governments for "enhancing the ability of the United Nations to achieve its purposes." The committee reported to the 1975 Assembly session that there was a fundamental divergence of opinion on the necessity for carrying out a review of the Charter and made no recommendations for action. The General Assembly decided, however, to continue the committee as a Special Committee on the Charter of the UN and on the Strengthening of the Role of the Organization and increased its membership to 47. In pursuit of its mandate, the committee has met every year since 1975 and has reported to each session of the General Assembly.

For example, in 1988 the Special Committee recommended, and the General Assembly adopted, a "Body of Principles for the Protection of All Persons under Any Form of Detention or Imprisonment"; in 1990 it proposed the rationalization of existing UN procedures, which were adopted by the General Assembly; and in 1991, the Special Committee considered the final text of the *Handbook on the Peaceful Settlement of Disputes between States.* That same year the General Assembly requested that the Secretary-General publish and disseminate the handbook.

The Special Committee also considers proposals concerning cooperation between the United Nations and regional organizations in the maintenance of international peace and security, conciliation rules of the United Nations, and assistance to other states affected by the imposition of sanctions by the decision of the Security Council, pursuant to Article 50 of the Charter.

PURPOSES AND PRINCIPLES

The main aims of the UN are set forth in the Preamble to the Charter, in which "the peoples of the United Nations," assembled in San Francisco in June 1945, expressed their determination

"to save succeeding generations from the scourge of war, which twice in our lifetime has brought untold sorrow to mankind, . . .

"to reaffirm faith in fundamental human rights, in the dignity and worth of the human person, in the equal rights of men and women and of nations large and small, . . .

"to establish conditions under which justice and respect for the obligations arising from treaties and other sources of international law can be maintained, and

"to promote social progress and better standards of life in larger freedom. . . ."

To accomplish these goals, they agreed

"to practice tolerance and live together in peace with one another as good neighbors, . . .

"to unite their strength to maintain international peace and security, . . .

"to ensure by the acceptance of principles and the institution of methods, that armed force shall not be used, save in the common interest, and

"to employ international machinery for the promotion of the economic and social advancement of all peoples . . . ."

PURPOSES
The aims of the UN are embodied in a set of purposes and principles contained in Articles 1 and 2 of the Charter, summarized as follows:

1. to maintain international peace and security and, to that end, to take effective collective measures for the prevention and removal of threats to the peace and for the suppression of acts of aggression or other breaches of the peace, and to bring about by peaceful means, and in conformity with the principles of justice and international law, adjustment or settlement of international disputes or situations that might lead to a breach of the peace;
2. to develop friendly relations among nations based on respect for the principle of equal rights and self-determination of peoples, and to take other appropriate measures to strengthen universal peace;
3. to achieve international cooperation in solving international economic, social, cultural, or humanitarian problems and in promoting and encouraging respect for human rights and for fundamental freedoms for all without distinction as to race, sex, language, or religion; and
4. to be a center for harmonizing the actions of nations in attaining these common ends.

PRINCIPLES
In pursuit of these purposes, the Charter stipulates that the UN and its members are to act in accordance with the following principles:

1. that the organization is based on the sovereign equality of all its members;
2. that all members are to fulfill in good faith their Charter obligations;
3. that they are to settle their international disputes by peaceful means and without endangering peace, security, and justice;
4. that they are to refrain in their international relations from the threat or use of force against other states;
5. that they are to give the UN every assistance in any action that it takes in accordance with the Charter and shall not assist states against which the UN is taking preventive or enforcement action;
6. that the UN shall also ensure that states that are not members act in accordance with these principles insofar as is necessary to maintain international peace and security; and
7. that nothing in the Charter is to authorize the UN to intervene in matters that are essentially within the domestic jurisdiction of any state, though this principle is not to prejudice the application of enforcement measures made necessary in the event of a threat to or breach of the peace.

MEMBERSHIP

As of May 2000, the UN had 188 member states, including 51 charter members (the 50 countries that sent representatives to the San Francisco conference, plus Poland, which ratified the charter shortly afterward) and 137 states that have joined the organization since 1945, the great majority of them former colonial territories that have achieved independence. The table in this chapter shows the growth of UN membership, the roster lists the members of the UN in alphabetical order and gives the dates of their admission to the UN. The roster does not take account of the several federations or unions of states that were created or dissolved during membership.

Thus, Syria, an original member, ceased independent membership on joining with Egypt to form the United Arab Republic in 1958. On resuming its separate status in 1961, Syria also resumed separate membership, which is still officially dated from the country's original day of entry. Tanganyika and Zanzibar joined the UN as separate states in 1961 and 1963, respectively, but in 1964 merged to form the United Republic of Tanzania, with a single membership officially dated from Tanganyika's day of entry.

Similarly, The Federation of Malaya joined the United Nations on 17 September 1957. On 16 September 1963, its name was changed to Malaysia, following the admission to the new federation of Singapore, Sabah (North Borneo), and Sarawak. Singapore became an independent state on 9 August 1965 and a member of the United Nations on 21 September 1965.

The Federal Republic of Germany and the German Democratic Republic were admitted to membership in the United Nations on 18 September 1973. Through accession of the German Democratic Republic to the Federal Republic of Germany, effective from 3 October 1990, the two German states have united to form one sovereign state.

The unification of the two Germanys began a process of realignment of nations that intensified as communist governments collapsed throughout Eastern Europe. In only two years 15 separate states from the former USSR were admitted to membership. As a result of this sweeping change, the former Union of Soviet Socialist Republics (an original member of the United Nations) became the Russian Federation. In a letter dated 24 December 1991, Boris Yeltsin, then president of the Russian Federation, informed the Secretary-General that the membership of the Soviet Union in the Security Council and all other United Nations organs was being continued by the Russian Federation with the support of the 11 member countries of the Commonwealth of Independent States.

Czechoslovakia also was an original member of the United Nations. On 10 December 1992, its Permanent Representative informed the Secretary-General that the Czech and Slovak Federal Republic would cease to exist on 31 December 1992 and that the Czech Republic and the Slovak Republic, as successor states, would apply for membership in the United Nations. Following the receipt of their applications, the Security Council, on 8 January 1993, recommended to the General Assembly that both the Czech Republic and the Slovak Republic be admitted to United Nations membership. Both were admitted on 19 January 1993.

In 1993, the proposed admission of a part of the former Yugoslavia, which had been known as the Republic of Macedonia, formed the subject of protest from the government of Greece, which considers the name "Macedonia" to pertain to one of its internal states. Now bearing the unwieldy name of "The Former Yugoslav Republic of Macedonia," the new country became a member on 8 April 1993.

ADMISSION OF MEMBERS

In the words of Article 4 of the Charter, membership in the UN is open to all "peace-loving states which accept the obligations contained in the present Charter and, in the judgment of the Organization, are able and willing to carry out these obligations." The original members are the states that participated in the San Francisco Conference, or that had previously signed the Declaration by United Nations, of 1 January 1942, and subsequently signed and ratified the Charter.

The procedure of admission is as follows. A state wishing to join submits an application to the Secretary-General, in which it formally states its acceptance of the Charter obligations. The application is forwarded to the Security Council. If the Security Council, by a vote of at least nine members (formerly seven), including all the permanent members, recommends the application, membership becomes effective on the day that it is approved by a two-thirds majority of the General Assembly. In other words, if any one of the Security Council's permanent members vetoes it, or if it fails to obtain a sufficient majority in the Security Council, the application does not reach the General Assembly at all.

Up to 1955 there were bitter controversies and years of stalemate in the Security Council over the applications of some countries. Usually one or more of the Big Five was on bad terms with the applying state, or it would choose to withhold consent as a bargaining point against the other big powers. Finally, on 14 December 1955, by a compromise, 16 countries were admitted together. Since then, new applications have only exceptionally caused controversy. Most of the applicants have been newly independent states that applied for membership immediately after attaining their independence. In almost all cases they have been admitted without delay and by unanimous vote.

The outstanding exceptions were the applications of the Republic of Korea (ROK), which applied in January 1949; the Democratic People's Republic of Korea (DPRK), which applied in February 1949; South Vietnam, which applied in December 1951; and North Vietnam, which applied in December 1951. The two Vietnams and the ROK sought action on their applications in 1975. The Security Council, by a narrow vote, decided not to take up the ROK's application, and the US subsequently vetoed membership for the Vietnams, citing as a reason the Security Council's earlier refusal to consider the membership application of the ROK. In response to a General Assembly recommendation, however, the Security Council in 1977 recommended the admission of the newly established Socialist Republic of Vietnam, and that country became a member in September 1977. The DPRK and the ROK maintained observer status at the General Assembly until September 1991, when both were admitted to membership simultaneously.

WITHDRAWAL FROM MEMBERSHIP

While the Covenant of the League of Nations contained provisions for the legal withdrawal of members, the UN Charter deliberately omits all reference to the subject. The majority feeling at the San Francisco Conference was that provisions for withdrawal would be contrary to the principle of universality and might provide a loophole for members seeking to evade their obligations under the Charter.

Thus, when the first—and so far the only—case of withdrawal arose, the procedure had to be improvised. On 1 January 1965, Indonesia, which then was pursuing a policy of confrontation against the newly formed Federation of Malaysia, announced that it would withdraw from the UN and its related agencies if Malaysia were to take its elected seat on the Security Council. Three weeks later, Indonesia's foreign minister officially confirmed withdrawal in a letter to the Secretary-General, who, after consultations with the Indonesian mission to the UN, merely noted the decision and expressed hope that Indonesia would in due time "resume full cooperation" with the world body. Following a coup later in 1965, Indonesia sent a telegram to the Secretary-General, just before the opening of the 1966 General Assembly session, announcing its decision to "resume full cooperation with the UN and to resume participation in its activities."

Arrangements were made to ensure that Indonesia's reentry would take place with minimum formality. Hence, it was decided that Indonesia need not make a formal reapplication via the Security Council but that the matter could be handled directly by the General Assembly. Citing the telegram as evidence that Indonesia regarded its absence from the UN as a "cessation of cooperation" rather than an actual withdrawal, the General Assembly's president recommended that the administrative procedure for reinstating Indonesia could be taken. No objections were raised, and Indonesia was immediately invited to resume its seat in the General Assembly. In short, the problems raised by the first case of withdrawal from the UN were solved by treating it as if it had not been a matter of withdrawal at all.

Although South Africa withdrew from three of the UN's related agencies—UNESCO, FAO, and the ILO—because of the antiapartheid sentiments of their members, it did not withdraw from the UN itself, despite numerous General Assembly resolutions condemning apartheid and recommending stringent sanctions. South Africa rejoined UNESCO and the ILO in the late 1990s.

SUSPENSION AND EXPULSION

The Charter provides that a member against which the Security Council has taken preventive or enforcement action may be suspended from the exercise of the rights and privileges of membership by the General Assembly upon the recommendation of the Security Council. However, only the Security Council, not the General Assembly, has the power to restore these rights. Any member that "has persistently violated the Principles" of the Charter may be expelled from the UN by the same procedure. Up to the end of 1999, no cases of suspension of rights or expulsion had been recommended by the Security Council.

Many states called for the expulsion of South Africa because of its apartheid policies, but no formal proposal to this effect was made. In 1974, the General Assembly called upon the Security Council to review the relationship between the UN and South Africa in the light of the constant violation by South Africa of the principles of the Charter and the Universal Declaration of Human Rights. The Security Council considered a draft resolution submitted by Cameroon, Iraq, Kenya, and Mauritania that would have recommended to the General Assembly the immediate expulsion of South Africa under Article 6 of the Charter. Owing to the negative votes of three permanent members (France, UK, US), the draft resolution was not adopted. After the council had reported back to the General Assembly on its failure to adopt a resolution, the president of the General Assembly, Abdelaziz Bouteflika of Algeria, ruled that the delegation of South Africa should be refused participation in the work of the General Assembly. His ruling was upheld by 91 votes to 22, with 19 abstentions. Although remaining a member of the UN, South Africa was not represented at subsequent sessions of the General Assembly. Following South Africa's successful democratic elections of May 1994, after 24 years of refusing to accept the credentials of the South African delegation, the General Assembly unanimously welcomed South Africa back to full participation in the United Nations on 23 June 1994. It also deleted its agenda item on "the elimination of apartheid and the establishment of a united, democratic and non-racial South Africa."

REPRESENTATION OF NATIONS IN THE UN

The members of the UN are nations, not governments. Whereas the UN may concern itself with the character of a government at the time that a nation applies for admission and may occasionally defer admission on these grounds (Spain under the Franco government, for example, applied for membership in 1945–46 but was not admitted until 1955), once a nation becomes a member, any governmental changes thereafter do not affect continuance of membership—provided, of course, that the nation continues to fulfill its Charter obligations. Nor, under the Charter, is the admission of a new nation dependent upon whether other nations individually recognize and have diplomatic relations with the government concerned. Though the relations of individual members with a nation applying for membership will affect the voting in the Security Council and the General Assembly, strictly speaking, the only consideration enjoined by the Charter is the judgment by the members that the applying nation as represented by its government is "willing and able" to carry out its UN obligations. As a result, there are several nations in the UN that do not recognize or have diplomatic relations with each other.

Nations have to be represented at UN proceedings by delegations that are specifically authorized by their governments to speak on their behalf. Thus, when a new ambassador appears, or when a new session of a UN organ convenes, it is necessary to examine the credentials of persons claiming to represent member states. The nine-member Credentials Committee, appointed by the General Assembly at the beginning of each session, must be satisfied that the person was duly appointed by his or her government and that that government is the official government of the respective member nation. The matter can become controversial at the UN if, for example, two rival governments both claim to be the only legitimate government of a member state and each demands that its own representative be seated.

A case in point was China. The long unresolved issue of its representation in the UN had been one of the most important and controversial items on the General Assembly's agenda. In 1971, however, the General Assembly decided "to restore all its rights to the People's Republic of China and to recognize the representatives of its government as the only legitimate representatives of China to the United Nations, and to expel forthwith the representatives of Chiang Kai-shek from the place which they unlawfully occupy at the United Nations and in all the organizations related to it."

United Nations Member States
(as of 1 May 2000)

MEMBER STATE	DATE OF ADMISSION	MEMBER STATE	DATE OF ADMISSION
Afghanistan	19 November 1946	Haiti	24 October 1945
Albania	14 December 1955	Honduras	17 December 1945
Algeria	8 October 1962	Hungary	14 December 1955
Andorra	28 July 1993	Iceland	19 November 1946
Angola	1 December 1976	India	30 October 1945
Antigua and Barbuda	11 November 1981	Indonesia	28 September 1950
Argentina	24 October 1945	Iran	24 October 1945
Armenia	2 March 1992	Iraq	21 December 1945
Australia	1 November 1945	Ireland	14 December 1955
Austria	14 December 1955	Israel	11 May 1949
Azerbaijan	2 March 1992	Italy	14 December 1955
Bahamas	18 September 1973	Jamaica	18 September 1962
Bahrain	21 September 1971	Japan	18 December 1956
Bangladesh	17 September 1974	Jordan	14 December 1955
Barbados	9 December 1966	Kazakhstan	2 March 1992
Belarus	24 October 1945	Kenya	16 December 1963
Belgium	27 December 1945	Kiribati	14 September 1999
Belize	25 September 1981	Korea, Democratic People's Republic of	17 September 1991
Benin	20 September 1960	Korea, Republic of	17 September 1991
Bhutan	21 September 1971	Kuwait	14 May 1963
Bolivia	14 November 1945	Kyrgyzstan	2 March 1992
Bosnia and Herzegovina	22 May 1992	Lao People's Democratic Republic	14 December 1955
Botswana	17 October 1966	Latvia	17 September 1991
Brazil	24 October 1945	Lebanon	24 October 1945
Brunei Darussalam	21 September 1984	Lesotho	17 October 1966
Bulgaria	14 December 1955	Liberia	2 November 1945
Burkina Faso	20 September 1960	Libyan Arab Jamahiriya	14 December 1955
Burundi	18 September 1962	Liechtenstein	18 September 1990
Cambodia	14 December 1955	Lithuania	17 September 1991
Cameroon	20 September 1960	Luxembourg	24 October 1945
Canada	9 November 1945	Madagascar	20 September 1960
Cape Verde	16 September 1975	Malawi	1 December 1964
Central African Republic	20 September 1960	Malaysia	17 September 1957
Chad	20 September 1960	Maldives	21 September 1965
Chile	24 October 1945	Mali	28 September 1960
China	24 October 1945	Malta	1 December 1964
Colombia	5 November 1945	Marshall Islands	17 September 1991
Comoros	12 November 1975	Mauritania	27 October 1961
Congo	20 September 1960	Mauritius	24 April 1968
Congo, Democratic Republic of the	20 September 1960	Mexico	7 November 1945
Costa Rica	2 November 1945	Micronesia (Federated States of)	17 September 1991
Côte d'Ivoire	20 September 1960	Republic of Moldova	2 March 1992
Croatia	22 May 1992	Monaco	28 May 1993
Cuba	24 October 1945	Mongolia	27 October 1961
Cyprus	20 September 1960	Morocco	12 November 1956
Czech Republic	19 January 1993	Mozambique	16 September 1975
Denmark	24 October 1945	Myanmar	19 April 1948
Djibouti	20 September 1977	Namibia	23 April 1990
Dominica	18 December 1978	Nauru	14 September 1999
Dominican Republic	24 October 1945	Nepal	14 December 1955
Ecuador	21 December 1945	Netherlands	10 December 1945
Egypt	24 October 1945	New Zealand	24 October 1945
El Salvador	24 October 1945	Nicaragua	24 October 1945
Equatorial Guinea	12 November 1968	Niger	20 September 1960
Eritrea	28 May 1993	Nigeria	7 October 1960
Estonia	17 September 1991	Norway	27 November 1945
Ethiopia	13 November 1945	Oman	7 October 1971
Fiji	13 October 1970	Pakistan	30 September 1947
Finland	14 December 1955	Palau	15 December 1994
France	24 October 1945	Panama	13 November 1945
Gabon	20 September 1960	Papua New Guinea	10 October 1975
Gambia	21 September 1965	Paraguay	24 October 1945
Georgia	31 July 1992	Peru	31 October 1945
Germany	18 September 1973	Philippines	24 October 1945
Ghana	8 March 1957	Poland	24 October 1945
Greece	25 October 1945	Portugal	14 December 1955
Grenada	17 September 1974	Qatar	21 September 1971
Guatemala	21 November 1945	Romania	14 December 1955
Guinea	12 December 1958	Russian Federation	24 October 1945
Guinea-Bissau	17 September 1974	Rwanda	18 September 1962
Guyana	20 September 1966	St. Kitts and Nevis	23 September 1983

United Nations Member States
(as of 1 May 2000)

MEMBER STATE	DATE OF ADMISSION	MEMBER STATE	DATE OF ADMISSION
St. Lucia	18 September 1979	Thailand	16 December 1946
St. Vincent and the Grenadines	16 September 1980	The Former Yugoslav Republic of Macedonia	8 April 1993
Samoa	15 December 1976	Togo	20 September 1960
San Marino	2 March 1992	Tonga	14 September 1999
Sâo Tomé and Principe	16 September 1975	Trinidad and Tobago	18 September 1962
Saudi Arabia	24 October 1945	Tunisia	12 November 1956
Senegal	28 September 1960	Turkey	24 October 1945
Seychelles	21 September 1976	Turkmenistan	2 March 1992
Sierra Leone	27 September 1961	Uganda	25 October 1962
Singapore	21 September 1965	Ukraine	24 October 1945
Slovakia	19 January 1993	United Arab Emirates	9 December 1971
Slovenia	22 May 1992	United Kingdom	24 October 1945
Solomon Islands	19 September 1978	United Republic of Tanzania	14 December 1961
Somalia	20 September 1960	United States of America	24 October 1945
South Africa	7 November 1945	Uruguay	18 December 1945
Spain	14 December 1955	Uzbekistan	2 March 1992
Sri Lanka	14 December 1955	Vanuatu	15 September 1981
Sudan	12 November 1956	Venezuela	15 November 1945
Suriname	4 December 1975	Vietnam	20 September 1977
Swaziland	24 September 1968	Yemen	30 September 1947
Sweden	19 November 1946	Yugoslavia	24 October 1945
Syrian Arab Republic	24 October 1945	Zambia	1 December 1964
Tajikistan	2 March 1992	Zimbabwe	25 August 1980

Growth of United Nations Membership

YEAR OF ADMISSION	MEMBERS	YEAR OF ADMISSION	MEMBERS
1945	Argentina, Australia, Belgium, Bolivia, Brazil, Belarus (formerly Byelorussia), Canada, Chile, China, Colombia, Costa Rica, Cuba, Czechoslovakia (readmitted in 1993 as two separate states, the Czech and Slovak Republics), Denmark, Dominican Republic, Ecuador, Egypt, El Salvador, Ethiopia, France, Greece, Guatemala, Haiti, Honduras, India, Iran, Iraq, Lebanon, Liberia, Luxembourg, Mexico, Netherlands, New Zealand, Nicaragua, Norway, Panama, Paraguay, Peru, Philippines, Poland, the Russian Federation (formerly the USSR), Saudi Arabia, South Africa, Syria, Turkey, Ukraine, United Kingdom, United States of America, Uruguay, Venezuela, Yugoslavia	1963	Kenya, Kuwait
		1964	Malawi, Malta, Zambia
		1965	Gambia, Maldives, Singapore
		1966	Barbados, Botswana, Guyana, Lesotho
		1967	People's Democratic Republic of Yemen (since 1990, merged with Yemen)
		1968	Equatorial Guinea, Mauritius, Swaziland
		1970	Fiji
		1971	Bahrain, Bhutan, Oman, Qatar, United Arab Emirates
		1973	Bahamas, Germany (formerly the German Democratic Republic and the Federal Republic of Germany)
		1974	Bangladesh, Grenada, Guinea-Bissau
		1975	Cape Verde, Comoros, Mozambique, Papua New Guinea, Sao Tomé and Principe, Suriname
1946	Afghanistan, Iceland, Sweden, Thailand		
1947	Pakistan, Yemen (formerly Yemen Arab Republic)		
1948	Myanmar (formerly Burma)		
1949	Israel		
1950	Indonesia	1976	Angola, Samoa, Seychelles
1955	Albania, Austria, Bulgaria, Cambodia (formerly Kampuchea), Finland, Hungary, Ireland, Italy, Jordan, Lao People's Democratic Republic (formerly Laos), Libya, Nepal, Portugal, Romania, Spain, Sri Lanka	1977	Djibouti, Vietnam
		1978	Dominica, Solomon Islands
		1979	St. Lucia
		1980	St. Vincent and the Grenadines, Zimbabwe
		1981	Antigua and Barbuda, Belize, Vanuatu
1956	Japan, Morocco, Sudan, Tunisia	1983	St. Kitts and Nevis
1957	Ghana, Malaysia	1984	Brunei Darussalam
1958	Guinea	1990	Liechtenstein, Namibia,
1960	Benin, Burkina Faso, Cameroon, Central African Republic, Chad, Congo, Côte d'Ivoire, Cyprus, Gabon, Madagascar, Mali, Niger, Nigeria, Senegal, Somalia, Togo, Zaire	1991	Democratic People's Republic of Korea, Estonia, Federated States of Micronesia, Latvia, Lithuania, Marshall Islands, Republic of Korea
		1992	Armenia, Azerbaijan, Bosnia and Herzegovina, Croatia, Georgia, Kazakhstan, Krgyz Republic, Republic of Moldova, San Marino, Slovenia,
1961	Mauritania, Mongolia, Sierra Leone, Tanzania	1993	Andorra, Czech Republic, Eritrea, Monaco, Slovak Republic, the Former Yugoslav Republic of Macedonia
1962	Algeria, Burundi, Jamaica, Rwanda, Trinidad and Tobago, Uganda	1994	Palau
		1999	Kiribati, Nauru, Tonga

UNITED NATIONS HEADQUARTERS

THE HEADQUARTERS BUILDINGS

When the UN came into being on 24 October 1945, it had no home. On 11 December 1945, the US Congress unanimously invited the UN to make its headquarters in the US. In February 1946, the General Assembly, meeting for its first session in London, voted for the general vicinity of Fairfield and Westchester counties, near New York City, but sites near Philadelphia, Boston, and San Francisco also were considered during 1946. Then came the dramatic offer by John D. Rockefeller, Jr., to donate $8.5 million toward the purchase of properties along the East River in midtown Manhattan. The City of New York rounded out the zone and granted rights along the river frontage. By November 1947, the General Assembly approved the architectural plans, and nine months later, the UN concluded a $65 million interest-free loan agreement with the US government. The director of planning for UN headquarters was Wallace K. Harrison of the US. The international board of design consultants included G. A. Soilleux, Australia; Gaston Brunfaut, Belgium; Oscar Niemeyer, Brazil; Ernest Cormier, Canada; Ssu-ch'eng Liang, China; Charles le Corbusier, Switzerland; Sven Markelius, Sweden; Nikolai D. Bassow, USSR; Howard Robertson, United Kingdom; and Julio Vilamajo, Uruguay.

The first structure to be completed, in the spring of 1951, was the 39-story marble and glass Secretariat building. In 1952, the conference building (with the three council halls and a number of conference rooms) and the General Assembly building were ready.

Thus, it was five or six years before the UN was permanently housed. In the interim, the Secretariat was established provisionally at Hunter College in the Bronx, New York, and in August 1946, the UN moved to the Sperry Gyroscope plant at Lake Success, Long Island. Several General Assembly sessions took place in the New York City Building at Flushing Meadow, and in 1948 and 1951, the body met at the Palais de Chaillot in Paris.

A library building at the headquarters site, erected and equipped through a $6.6 million donation by the Ford Foundation, was dedicated in 1961 to the memory of former Secretary-General Dag Hammarskjöld.

Various furnishings and works of art for the conference and General Assembly buildings and the library have been donated by member governments. Adjoining the public lobby in the General Assembly building is the Meditation Room, dedicated to those who have given their lives in service to the UN. It includes a stained glass window by Marc Chagall on the theme of "Peace and Man." The public gardens north of the General Assembly building contain sculpture and plantings donated by governments and individuals.

The United Nations headquarters was designed to serve four major groups: delegations, who now represent 188 member states and who send more than 3,000 persons to New York each year for the annual sessions of the General Assembly; the Secretariat, numbering 14,166 throughout the world; visitors, who average 1,500 a day; and journalists, of whom more than 450 are permanently accredited while twice that number are present during major meetings.

For a small fee, visitors may join one of the Secretariat's tours of the headquarters buildings, conducted daily in 20 languages by 47 guides from 28 countries.

Capacity

Because of the increase in the number of member states, the seating capacity of the conference rooms and the General Assembly Hall has been enlarged. A major expansion of office and meeting facilities at UN headquarters was undertaken in the 1980s.

About 30,000 men and women from some 150 countries work for the UN and its related organs and agencies—about one-third of them at UN headquarters and the other two-thirds at offices and centers around the globe. (See also the chapter on the Secretariat.)

Conference Services

UN headquarters, together with the organization's offices in Geneva and Vienna, provide the interpreters, translators, writers, editors, and conference personnel required for the many UN meetings throughout the world, as well as for other meetings held under UN auspices.

Telecommunications System

The UN has its own telecommunications system. UN headquarters is linked by radio with the offices in Geneva and Vienna, which, in turn, provide liaison with UN organs and offices in different parts of the world.

Computer System

As part of the fundamental modernization and reorganization of the United Nations, the organization's bank of IBM mainframes was replaced in stages by an Integrated Management Information System (IMIS). The first phase of the replacement, completed in early 1994, implemented a personnel system covering recruiting, hiring, promotions, and moving. Four hundred users at the headquarters were connected to Unix servers with personal computers using Windows software. Eventually all administrative applications were transferred to four Unix systems organized in client-server architecture. The phased installation of this multi-million-dollar system at various UN offices and agencies around the world continued in 2000. Other users, such as the United Nations Development Program (UNDP), the United Nations Children's Fund (UNICEF), and the International Labor Organization (ILO), had progressively adapted the software to their special requirements. In late 1998, a report of independent experts, initiated at the General Assembly's request, favorably evaluated IMIS from both the technical and cost perspectives. Their recommendations, as well as those of the General Assembly and the Board of Auditors, were subsequently addressed.

UN Postal Administration

UN stamps are issued under separate agreements with the postal authorities of the US, Switzerland, and Austria and are valid for postage only on mail deposited at UN headquarters in New York and at the UN offices in Geneva and Vienna. UN stamps may be obtained by mail, over the counter, or automatically through the Customer Deposit Service in New York, Geneva, or Vienna. Only revenue from the sale of stamps for philatelic purposes is retained by the UN. In addition to producing revenue, UN stamp designs publicize the work of the organization and its related agencies.

RECORDS AND DOCUMENTS

Library

The Dag Hammarskjöld Library contains approximately 400,000 books, 14,500 maps, over 80,000 periodicals and newspapers, and several hundred thousand documents and microfiches. The collection includes not only UN materials but also League of Nations records in its Woodrow Wilson Reading Room, as well as a general reference library on subjects related to the work of the UN. The library is for use by delegations, permanent missions, and the Secretariat and by scholars engaged in advanced research.

Archives

The United Nations Archives, located at 345 Park Avenue South in New York, dates from the establishment of the United Nations. Its 35 linear feet of holdings include both inactive administrative records created by Secretariat offices, as well as archival records that constitute the organization's institutional memory. Each year, approximately 50 researchers cull its archives for information about the UN's predecessors, the Secretary-General's "good offices" role, and the organization's mediating and peacekeeping activities.

The earliest records emanate from predecessor organizations, including the International Penal and Penitentiary Commission (1893–1951); United Nations Relief and Rehabilitation Administration (1943–48), which assisted liberated areas devastated by World War II; United Nations War Crimes Commission (1943–49) whose 17 Allied members together developed procedures for apprehending and punishing war criminals; and the United Nations Conference on International Organization (1945), at which the United Nations was chartered.

From its very beginning, a number of regional conflicts required that the new organization assume the role of peacekeeper. Consequently, the UN Archives maintains records associated with a wide variety of peacekeeping missions, ranging from the UN Special Committee on Palestine (1947), to the organization's electoral mission in Cambodia. Issues arising from colonialism also required early UN involvement. Archival holdings document the establishment of trusteeships for supervising elections and the transition to independence. The organization's technical assistance function in international social and economic development is, likewise, reflected among the archives' records.

Records are generally open for research at the end of 20 years. Strictly confidential records, or those with special restrictions (such as the War Crimes Commission records), require express authorization for access. Those wishing to research UN Archives records should request an appointment by writing to Chief, Archives Unit, United Nations Archives, PK-1200, United Nations, New York, NY 10017.

Documents Services

UN headquarters houses one of the world's largest photocopying and printing plants. Most UN documents are produced in photocopy form for the use of members and the Secretariat. Some documents, as well as many reports and studies, are issued as UN publications for sale to the public. They are available in the bookshop at UN headquarters and from distributors worldwide.

In the United States and Canada, Bernan Associates (formerly UNIPUB) distributes UN publications and publishes scholarly books by the United Nations University Press. It also distributes the publications of the Food and Agricultural Organization (FAO), International Atomic Energy Agency (IAEA), World Trade Organization (WTO), and the United Nations Educational, Scientific and Cultural Organization (UNESCO). Bernan is located in Lanham, Maryland, and can be reached from the United States at (800) 274-4888 or via email at query@bernan.com. The Bernan Associates web site can also be accessed at www.bernan.com. Other UN publications are available from the United Nations Publications Sales Section at UN Headquarters, (212) 963-8302 or (800) 253-9646 (for North America, Latin America, Asia, and the Pacific); and from the Geneva Sales Office and Bookshop, (41 22) 734 1473 (for Europe, Africa, and the Middle East). The UN Publications office also has a web site at http://www.un.org/Pubs/sales.htm, where the searchable catalog (available in English, French, and Spanish) of UN publications may be accessed and orders placed.

PUBLIC INFORMATION SERVICES

At its first session, in 1946, the General Assembly decided to create a special Department of Public Information (DPI) in the Secretariat. Recognizing that the UN's aims cannot be achieved unless the world is fully informed of its objectives and activities, the General Assembly directed that DPI should work to promote the fullest possible informed understanding of UN affairs. Accordingly, the UN provides a steady stream of information on its activities, covering virtually all media—press, publications, radio, television, films, photographs, and exhibits.

Press, Publications, and Photographic Services

DPI provides information to news correspondents and facilitates their access to meetings, documents, and other news sources. In any given year, several thousand press releases are issued at UN headquarters, including accounts of meetings, texts of speeches, announcements of special programs, and background or reference papers. DPI holds daily briefings and helps to arrange press conferences for members of delegations and senior members of the Secretariat and the specialized agencies.

Booklets, pamphlets, and leaflets covering the work of the UN are published in many languages. The *UN Chronicle*, issued quarterly in English, French, Spanish, and Arabic, reports on UN activities. The *Chronicle* now has its own web site at www.un.org/Pubs/chronicle, which includes information on the contents of individual issues as well as links to selected articles and cover images from the magazine. DPI also issues a *Yearbook of the United Nations*.

To illustrate UN activities in the field, photo missions are periodically undertaken throughout the world. The photographs obtained, together with extensive coverage of events at UN headquarters and other principal conference centers, are widely used by newspapers, periodicals, book publishers, and government information agencies. Posters and photo display sets are prepared for exhibition at UN headquarters and for worldwide distribution.

DPI press releases, background information releases, and other public information documents are available on the Internet by accessing http://www.un.org/news/. United Nations documents (major reports, and resolutions of the General Assembly, Security Council, and ECOSOC) can be accessed by Internet users. In the United States, many large libraries provide a free window onto the Internet, allowing access to some of the UN documents.

Radio, TV, and Film Services

A major responsibility of DPI is to assist the accredited correspondents of national and commercial broadcasting organizations in their coverage of the UN's work. In radio, correspondents may use studios and recording equipment at UN headquarters, and New York is linked with distant capitals by shortwave or radiotelephone. Film and television correspondents may receive visual coverage of principal meetings of the Security Council and the General Assembly, as well as of press conferences and briefings. Satellite transmissions carry this material around the world.

DPI broadcasts meetings of principal UN organs by shortwave and produces its own radio programs in the six official UN languages (Arabic, Chinese, English, French, Russian, and Spanish), reaching listeners in more than 100 countries. UN films and programs are produced not only for television but also for groups in schools, universities, and nongovernmental organizations.

Public Inquiries Unit

The Public Inquiries Unit handles individual inquiries from researchers and the general public seeking specific information about the United Nations and its subsidiary organizations. The unit can refer callers to the appropriate UN department or organization, and send by mail UN documents such as reports by the Secretary-General to the General Assembly or Security Council.

UN Information Centers

The network of United Nations Information Centers (UNICs), Services (UNISs) and Offices (UNOs) links Headquarters with the people of the world. Located in 78 countries, these branch offices of the United Nations Department of Public Information help local communities obtain up-to-date information on the United Nations and its activities. As of May 2000, 30 UNICs had created their own web sites, in local languages: UNICs in Antananarivo, Athens, Bonn, Brussels, Buenos Aires, Copenhagen, Harare, Islamabad, Lisbon, London, Madrid, Mexico City, Moscow, New Delhi, Panama City, Paris, Prague, Rabat, Rome, Tokyo, Tunis, Vienna, and Washington, DC; UNIC/UNIS Beirut, UNISs Bangkok and Geneva; and UNOs Armenia, Belarus, Ukraine, and Uzbekistan. These sites post calendars of events sponsored by the Centers along with information on major UN activities, such as the General Assembly Special Session on the World Drug Problem and the establishment of the International Criminal Court. The centers maintain up-to-date reference libraries of UN publications and documentation and answer public inquiries. DPI material is translated into local languages by the centers, which work closely with local media, information agencies, educational authorities, and nongovernmental organizations in their area. The centers also inform UN headquarters about local UN activities, which, in turn, are publicized by DPI. In 1996, the UN began integrating the functions of its information centers into the office of the UN representative/resident coordinator in the respective host country.

PRIVILEGES AND IMMUNITIES

The charter provides that in all territory of its member states, the UN shall hold whatever legal capacity, privileges, and immunities are necessary for the fulfillment of its purposes and that representatives of member states and officials of the UN shall have a status allowing them independent exercise of their functions. On 13 February 1946, the General Assembly adopted the Convention on the Privileges and Immunities of the United Nations. As of May 2000, 188 countries, including the US, had acceded to this convention. UN staff on official business can travel on a *laissez-passer* issued by the UN.

Countries that have acceded to the convention exempt the salaries of UN officials from taxation, except for the US and several other countries, where special reservations apply. These salaries,

however, are subject to a "staff assessment," an internal UN taxation. The UN itself is exempt from all direct taxes, customs duties, and export and import restrictions on articles for official use.

Virtually all member states have established permanent missions to the UN in New York. Their personnel enjoy privileges and immunities similar to those of diplomatic missions.

HEADQUARTERS AGREEMENT BETWEEN THE UN AND THE US

A special headquarters agreement, signed by Secretary-General Trygve Lie and US secretary of state George C. Marshall at Lake Success on 26 June 1947, has been in force since 21 November 1947. It defines the 18 acres of land in New York City located between 42nd and 48th Streets and First Avenue and the Franklin D. Roosevelt Drive as the Headquarters District of the United Nations. Subsequently, by supplemental agreements between the UN and the US, additional office space located in buildings in the vicinity has been included in the Headquarters District. The Headquarters District is "under the control and authority of the United Nations as provided in this agreement." It is the seat of the UN, and the agreement stipulates that the district "shall be inviolable." Federal, state, and local personnel on official duty may enter it only with the consent of the Secretary-General. The UN may make regulations for the area. US federal, state, and local law, insofar as it is inconsistent with UN regulations, does not apply here; otherwise, the US courts would have jurisdiction over actions and transactions taking place in the Headquarters District. The UN may expel persons from the district for violations of regulations. In such cases, and generally for the preservation of law and order, US authorities have to provide a sufficient number of police if requested by the Secretary-General. "No form of racial or religious discrimination shall be permitted within the Headquarters District." Other detailed provisions in the agreement between the UN and the US deal with the important matter of the accessibility of the seat of the UN to non-US citizens.

EMBLEM AND FLAG OF THE UN

The General Assembly adopted an official seal and emblem for the organization. The UN emblem depicts in silver against a light blue background a map of the earth, projected from the North Pole, and encircled by two symmetrical olive branches. It is a slight modification of a design selected by the US Office of Strategic Services for buttons used at the San Francisco Conference in 1945. The particular shade of blue is now officially called United Nations blue. The emblem is used only for UN publications and conferences and other officially approved purposes.

The first UN flag was used in Greece in 1947 in a region where there was fighting. The flag has the UN emblem in white against a background of United Nations blue.

The flag may be displayed not only by the UN and the specialized agencies and by governments but also by "organizations and individuals to demonstrate support of the United Nations and to further its principles and purposes." It is considered "especially appropriate" to display the UN flag on national and official holidays; on UN Day, 24 October; and at official events in honor of the UN or related to the UN.

THE UNITED NATIONS BUDGET

Under the Charter, it is the task of the General Assembly to "consider and approve the budget of the Organization" and to apportion the expenses of the UN among the member nations. From an administrative standpoint, the expenditures of the UN may be said to fall into two categories: expenditures that are included in what is termed the "regular budget," to which all members are obliged to contribute; and expenditures for certain high-cost items or programs, for which are established separate, or "extrabudgetary," accounts or funds financed by special arrangements that do not necessarily involve obligatory payments by UN members.

Included in the regular budget are the costs of services and programs carried out at UN headquarters and all overseas UN offices; the expenses of the International Court of Justice; and debt services charges, which are also listed as "special expenses."

Outside the regular budget, member states also are assessed, in accordance with a modified version of the basic scale, for the costs of peacekeeping operations. The number and cost of these operations has been aggravated in recent years, in large part due to political instability in Eastern Europe, Western Asia, and Africa. In the period 1992–93, the Secretary-General estimated the cost for these operations increased sixfold. In a report to the Economic and Social Council, he stated, "It would be mistaken to try to attach an order of importance or priority between peace and security on the one hand, and economic and social development on the other. The two are so closely interlinked as to be indivisible." This underlying philosophy provides the rationale for the growth in the number of peacekeeping operations and the expansion of their mandates beyond the previously traditional observer status, to activities such as disarming and demobilization of forces, humanitarian assistance, human rights monitoring, electoral verification, and civilian police support. Each peacekeeping operation is approved and budgeted separately.

Following is a list of 15 UN observation or peacekeeping operations under way as of May 2000, along with the original starting date: United Nations Truce Supervision Organization (UNTSO), June 1948; United Nations Military Observer Group in India and Pakistan (UNMOGIP), January 1949; United Nations Peacekeeping Force in Cyprus (UNFICYP), March 1964; United Nations Disengagement Observer Force (UNDOF) in Golan Heights, June 1974; United Nations Interim Force in Lebanon (UNIFIL), March 1978; United Nations Mission for the Referendum in Western Sahara (MINURSO), April 1991; United Nations Iraq-Kuwait Observation Mission (UNIKOM), April 1991; United Nations Observer Mission in Georgia (UNOMIG), August 1993; United Nations Mission of Observers in Tajikistan (UNMOT), December 1994 (mission was being liquidated as of May 2000); United Nations Mission in Bosnia and Herzegovina (UNMIBH), December 1995; United Nations Mission of Observers in Prevlaka (UNMOP) in Croatia, January 1996; United Nations Interim Administration Mission in Kosovo (UNMIK), June 1999; United Nations Transitional Administration in East Timor (UNTAET), October 1999; United Nations Mission in Sierra Leone (UNAMSIL), October 1999; and United Nations Organization Mission in the Democratic Republic of the Congo (MONUC), November 1999.

As of 31 May 1999, unpaid contributions for the peacekeeping operations with separate assessed budgets amounted to US$1.5 billion. Shortfalls in the receipt of assessed contributions

were met by delaying reimbursements to states that contributed troops, thus placing an unfair burden on them.

United Nations activities that are financed mainly by voluntary contributions outside the regular budget include: the United Nations Development Programme (UNDP), the World Food Program (WFP), the Office of the United Nations High Commissioner for Refugees (UNHCR), the United Nations Children's Fund (UNICEF), the United Nations Relief and Works Agency for Palestine Refugees in the Near East (UNRWA), and the United Nations Population Fund (UNFPA).

The member states of the specialized agencies decide on each agency's budget and scale of assessments separately from the United Nations itself.

COMMITTEES ASSISTING THE GENERAL ASSEMBLY IN FINANCIAL MATTERS
In 1946, the General Assembly established two permanent subsidiary organs concerned with administrative and budgetary affairs. The Advisory Committee on Administrative and Budgetary Questions is responsible for expert examination of the UN budget and the administrative budgets of the specialized agencies. The committee's 16 members, elected by the General Assembly for staggered three-year terms, serve as individuals, not as government representatives. The Committee on Contributions advises the General Assembly on the apportionment of the expenses of the UN among the member nations. Its 18 members are elected for three-year terms and also serve as individuals.

PROCEDURE FOR DETERMINING THE REGULAR BUDGET
Every other year, the Secretary-General presents detailed budget and appropriations estimates for the following biennium. (Until 1974 there were annual budgets.) These estimates are reviewed and sometimes revised by the Advisory Committee. The programmatic aspects are reviewed by the 34-member Committee for Program and Coordination.

Appropriations (Gross) 1946–1999 (in US$)

YEAR	APPROPRIATION	YEAR	APPROPRIATION
1946	$19,390,000	1967	133,084,000
1947	28,616,568	1968	141,787,750
1948	39,285,736	1969	156,967,300
1949	43,204,080	1970	168,956,950
1950	44,520,773	1971	194,627,800
1951	48,925,500	1972	208,650,200
1952	50,547,660	1973	233,820,374
1953	49,869,450	1974–75	606,033,000
1954	48,528,980	1976–77	745,813,800
1955	50,228,000	1978–79	996,372,900
1956	50,683,350	1980–81	1,339,151,200
1957	53,174,700	1982–83	1,472,961,700
1958	61,121,900	1984–85	1,611,551,200
1959	61,657,100	1986–87	1,711,801,200
1960	65,734,900	1988–89	1,748,681,800
1961	71,649,300	1990–91	2,134,072,100
1962	85,818,220	1992–93	2,362,977,700
1963	92,876,550	1994–95	2,580,200,200
1964	101,327,600	1996–97	2,608,274,000
1965	108,472,800	1998–99	2,488,302,000
1966	121,080,530	2000–01	2,535,689,200

BUDGET FOR THE 2000–01 BIENNIUM

AREA OF EXPENDITURE

PURPOSE OF EXPENDITURE	AMOUNT (US$)
OVERALL POLICY-MAKING, DIRECTION AND COORDINATION	
Overall policy-making, direction and coordination	47,675,100
General Assembly affairs and conference services	425,970,200
TOTAL	473,645,300
POLITICAL AFFAIRS	
Political affairs	137,756,000
Disarmament	14,067,900
Peacekeeping operations	76,094,700
Peaceful uses of outer space	3,667,700
TOTAL	231,586,300
INTERNATIONAL JUSTICE AND LAW	
International Court of Justice	20,864,500
Legal affairs	34,522,300
TOTAL	55,386,800
INTERNATIONAL COOPERATION FOR DEVELOPMENT	
Economic and social affairs	113,112,600
Africa: New Agenda for Development	5,883,400
Trade and development	87,685,500
International Trade Centre UNCTAD/WTO	19,248,700
Environment	8,743,400
Human settlements	13,757,400
Crime prevention and criminal justice	5,299,100
International drug control	15,037,800
TOTAL	268,767,900
REGIONAL COOPERATION FOR DEVELOPMENT	
Economic and social development in Africa	78,455,200
Economic and social development in Asia and the Pacific	57,031,600
Economic development in Europe	40,554,600
Economic and social development in Latin America and the Caribbean	78,857,500
Economic and social development in Western Asia	50,336,200
Regular programme of technical cooperation	41,995,300
TOTAL	347,230,400
HUMAN RIGHTS AND HUMANITARIAN AFFAIRS	
Human rights	41,163,400
Protection of and assistance to refugees	41,940,000
Palestine refugees	21,667,900
Humanitarian assistance	18,841,800
TOTAL	123,613,100
PUBLIC INFORMATION	
Public information	143,605,500
TOTAL	143,605,500
COMMON SUPPORT SERVICES	
Management and central support services	441,857,400
TOTAL	441,857,400
INTERNAL OVERSIGHT	
Internal oversight	19,220,600
TOTAL	19,220,600
JOINTLY FINANCED ACTIVITIES AND SPECIAL EXPENSES	
Jointly financed administrative activities	7,844,300
Special expenses	53,001,200
TOTAL	60,845,500
CAPITAL EXPENDITURES	
Construction, alteration, improvement and major maintenance	42,617,400
TOTAL	42,617,400
STAFF ASSESSMENT	
Staff assessment	314,248,000
TOTAL	314,248,000
DEVELOPMENT ACCOUNT	
Development Account	13,065,000
TOTAL	13,065,000
TOTAL EXPENDITURES	2,535,689,200

Aside from the regular budget, the General Assembly also allots a certain amount of money for unforeseen and extraordinary expenses and determines the level of the UN's Working Capital Fund, to which member nations advance sums in proportion to their assessed contributions to the regular budget. The fund is used to finance appropriations pending receipt of contributions and may also be drawn upon by the Secretary-General for other purposes determined by the General Assembly.

Since the expenses of the organization can never be precisely predicted, the Secretary-General reviews actual expenditures for the current year at each regular session of the General Assembly and proposes adjustments in the original appropriations. Usually, a supplemental budget is voted, but occasionally the General Assembly votes reductions.

Income Estimates

It was estimated that expenditures for 2000–01 would be offset in the amount of US$361,298,000, to be derived as follows:

1. *income from staff assessment*: US$318,911,500;
2. *general income*: US$37,178,000
3. *services to public*: US$5,209,400.

Under UN regulations, a percentage of the earnings of the entire UN staff is deducted in lieu of taxes and credited to "income." In order to avoid double taxation of staff members of US nationality, they are reimbursed by the UN for the taxes (federal, state, and city) levied on their UN earnings. The withholdings from the salaries of UN personnel of all other nationalities are credited to the member states' accounts against their assessed contributions. After taking into account staff assessments and other items of income, the net estimated amount remaining to be raised through assessed contributions from member states for the biennium 2000–01 totaled US$1,201,274,400.

ASSESSED CONTRIBUTIONS OF MEMBER STATES TO THE REGULAR BUDGET

The scale of contributions of member states is established by the General Assembly on the recommendation of its Committee on Contributions. The basic original criterion for the apportionment of UN expenses was the ability to pay, with comparative estimates of national income taken as the fairest guide. Other factors, such as the comparative income per capita, the ability of contributors to obtain foreign exchange, and, until 1974, the dislocation of national economies arising out of World War II, also were taken into account. In this way, the US share was at first 39.89 percent, gradually declining to 31.52 percent for 1971–73.

In 1972, the General Assembly established a ceiling on the rate of assessment of the highest contributor, set at 25 percent. At the same time, it lowered the minimum rate of assessment to 0.02 percent (later lowered to 0.01 percent and in 1997 lowered again, to 0.001 percent) and requested the Committee on Contributions to give attention to the special economic and financial problems of developing countries.

In an effort to introduce what it termed greater fairness and equity in the scale of assessments, the General Assembly, in 1981, requested the Committee on Contributions to prepare a set of guidelines for the collection of more uniform and comparable data and statistics from member states and to study alternative methods of assessing "the real capacity of member states to pay."

Based on 1998 figures, the top ten contributors for 2000 would be assessed at the following rates (percentages):

United States	25.0%
Japan	20.6%
Germany	9.9%
France	6.5%
United Kingdom	5.1%
Italy	5.4%
Russian Federation	1.1%
Canada	2.7%
Spain	2.6%
Netherlands	1.6%

Contributions by Nonmember States

States that are not members of the UN but participate in certain of its activities (principally the International Court of Justice, the regional commissions, the UN Conference on Trade and Development, and the control of narcotic drugs) contribute toward expenses of such activities according to a scale of assessments established by the General Assembly. Following are the assessment rates established for the nonmember states in 1999:

COUNTRY	ASSESSMENT
Holy See (Vatican)	0.001
Kiribati	0.001
Nauru	0.001
Switzerland	1.215
Tonga	0.001
Tuvalu	0.001

PROPOSALS TO EASE THE UN'S FINANCIAL DIFFICULTIES

By and large, the regular budget has never created major disputes among the member states, and most governments have usually paid their dues relatively punctually. However, beginning in 1963, the USSR refused as a matter of principle to contribute to certain items in the regular budget, such as the UN Commission for the Unification and Rehabilitation of Korea until its dissolution by a consensus vote of the 1973 Assembly, or to those parts of the regular budget devoted to the redemption of UN bonds (a method of raising funds for certain UN peacekeeping operations). France has taken a similar stand in connection with the redemption of the bonds. In addition, a number of countries have refused to contribute to the special accounts for peacekeeping operations. It was chiefly these controversial expenditures which precipitated the UN's financial emergency in the mid-1960s.

In July 1962, the International Court of Justice, at the request of the General Assembly, issued an advisory opinion in which it declared that the expenses of the first UN Emergency Force in the Middle East and the UN Force in the Congo constituted expenses of the organization within the meaning of Article 17, paragraph 2, of the Charter and should thus be borne by member states as apportioned by the General Assembly. The Assembly accepted the court's opinion in December 1962, but debate over peacekeeping operations and the financial difficulties continued. A number of other factors, moreover, contributed to the precariousness of the financial position of the organization, notably the lateness of many member states in paying their assessed contributions, the currency fluctuations of the 1970s (marked by two devaluations of the US dollar, on which the UN budget is based), and inflation.

A Group of High-Level Intergovernmental Experts to Review the Efficiency of the Administrative and Financial Functioning of the UN, appointed by the General Assembly in 1985, submitted to the General Assembly in the following year its recommendations for enhancing the efficiency and reducing the expenditures of the organization. Implementation of the group's recommendations was the condition which a number of states, including the US, placed on further payment of their assessments.

Among the solutions proposed in 1985 were an increase in the Working Capital Fund to US$200 million, the issue of certificates

of indebtedness in the amount of the arrears—in effect, borrowing from member states—and borrowing on the open market.

In 1992, Secretary-General Boutros Boutros-Ghali requested that the Ford Foundation assemble an independent advisory group to recommend ways to create a secure, long-term financial base for the organization. The group, co-chaired by Shijuro Ogata, former Deputy Governer of the Japan Development Bank, and Paul Volcker, former Board of Governors' Chairman of the United States Federal Reserve Bank, issued its report in February 1993. Entitled "Financing an Effective United Nations," it suggested the following measures:

- Dividing UN expenditures into three categories: a regular budget financed by assessed contributions; peacekeeping financed by a separate assessment; and humanitarian and development activities financed largely by voluntary contributions.
- Requiring UN member states to pay dues in four quarterly installments, instead of a single lump sum at the beginning of the year; and granting the organization authority to charge interest on late payments.
- Appropriation by some nations of their UN contribution earlier in the year.
- Acceptance by member states of significantly increased peacekeeping costs over the next few years, and financing future cost from national defense budgets.
- Creation by the UN of a $400 million revolving reserve fund for peacekeeping; and consideration of a unified peacekeeping budget, financed by a single annual assessment. The report concluded that proposals for additional, nongovernmental sources of financing the UN were "neither practical nor desirable."

Also in 1993, the Joint Inspection Unit (JIU) of the Secretariat issued a report declaring: "The old financial malaise is emerging with renewed evidence. What was a chronic illness is becoming a critical one." Among JIU proposals:

- Governments should adjust their national legislations to avoid obstacles to paying their UN contributions in full and on time.
- Replenishment of the proposed UN Peace Endowment Fund could take advantage of initiatives, such as the issuance of special stamps by member states, with revenues turned over to the organization.
- Countries could turn over to peacekeeping operations funds earmarked for aid to developing countries in which the existing critical situation is an impediment to using those funds.
- In parallel with financing, cost saving is indispensable to solving the financial crisis. Fighting waste and reducing expenses must take place in all areas of the organization.

The fundamental requirement for the essential financial stability of the UN, however, remained the full and timely payment by all member states of their assessments, in accordance with Article 17, paragraph 2, of the Charter, which states that: "The expenses of the Organization shall be borne by the Members as apportioned by the General Assembly."

In 1994, the UN General Assembly created the Office of Internal Oversight Service (OIOS) as a department within the Secretariat to independently monitor reports of waste, fraud, and mismanagement within the UN. OIOS focuses on high-risk activities, such as peace-keeping operations, humanitarian activities, and procurement while simultaneously providing oversight to all activities of the UN. OIOS provides oversight through internal auditing, management consulting, investigations, monitoring, inspection, and evaluation.

In 1996, efforts at managerial reform targeted five areas of management: cost structure, human resources, information, tech-

Scale of Assessments
(as of December 1997 for calendar year 2000)

MEMBER STATE	PERCENT	MEMBER STATE	PERCENT	MEMBER STATE	PERCENT	MEMBER STATE	PERCENT
Afghanistan	0.003	Denmark	0.692	Libyan Arab Jamahiriya	0.124	San Marino	0.002
Albania	0.003	Djibouti	0.001	Liechtenstein	0.006	São Tomé and Principe	0.001
Algeria	0.086	Dominica	0.001	Lithuania	0.015	Saudi Arabia	0.562
Andorra	0.004	Dominican Republic	0.015	Luxembourg	0.068	Senegal	0.006
Angola	0.010	Ecuador	0.020	Madagascar	0.003	Seychelles	0.002
Antigua and Barbuda	0.002	Egypt	0.065	Malawi	0.002	Sierra Leone	0.001
Argentina	1.103	El Salvador	0.012	Malaysia	0.183	Singapore	0.179
Armenia	0.006	Equatorial Guinea	0.001	Maldives	0.001	Slovakia	0.035
Australia	1.483	Eritrea	0.001	Mali	0.002	Slovenia	0.061
Austria	0.942	Estonia	0.012	Malta	0.014	Solomon Islands	0.001
Azerbaijan	0.011	Ethiopia	0.006	Marshall Islands	0.001	Somalia	0.001
Bahamas	0.015	Fiji	0.004	Mauritania	0.001	South Africa	0.366
Bahrain	0.017	Finland	0.543	Mauritius	0.009	Spain	2.591
Bangladesh	0.010	France	6.545	Mexico	0.995	Sri Lanka	0.012
Barbados	0.008	Gabon	0.015	Micronesia	0.001	Sudan	0.007
Belarus	0.057	Gambia	0.001	Monaco	0.004	Suriname	0.004
Belgium	1.104	Georgia	0.007	Mongolia	0.002	Swaziland	0.002
Belize	0.001	Germany	9.857	Morocco	0.041	Sweden	1.079
Benin	0.002	Ghana	0.007	Mozambique	0.001	Syrian Arab Republic	0.064
Bhutan	0.001	Greece	0.351	Myanmar	0.008	Tajikistan	0.004
Bolivia	0.007	Grenada	0.001	Namibia	0.007	Thailand	0.170
Bosnia and Herzegovina	0.005	Guatemala	0.018	Nepal	0.004	The former Yugoslav Republic of Macedonia	0.004
Botswana	0.010	Guinea	0.003	Netherlands	1.632	Togo	0.001
Brazil	1.471	Guinea-Bissau	0.001	New Zealand	0.221	Trinidad and Tobago	0.016
Brunei Darussalam	0.020	Guyana	0.001	Nicaragua	0.001	Tunisia	0.028
Bulgaria	0.011	Haiti	0.002	Niger	0.002	Turkey	0.440
Burkina Faso	0.002	Honduras	0.003	Nigeria	0.032	Turkmenistan	0.006
Burundi	0.001	Hungary	0.120	Norway	0.610	Uganda	0.004
Cambodia	0.001	Iceland	0.032	Oman	0.051	Ukraine	0.190
Cameroon	0.013	India	0.299	Pakistan	0.059	United Arab Emirates	0.178
Canada	2.732	Indonesia	0.188	Palau	0.001	United Kingdom of Great Britain and Northern Ireland	5.092
Cape Verde	0.002	Iran (Islamic Republic of)	0.161	Panama	0.013	United Republic of Tanzania	0.003
Central African Republic	0.001	Iraq	0.032	Papua New Guinea	0.007	United States of America	25.000
Chad	0.001	Ireland	0.224	Paraguay	0.014	Uruguay	0.048
Chile	0.136	Israel	0.350	Peru	0.099	Uzbekistan	0.025
China	0.995	Italy	5.437	Philippines	0.081	Vanuatu	0.001
Colombia	0.109	Jamaica	0.006	Poland	0.196	Venezuela	0.160
Comoros	0.001	Japan	20.573	Portugal	0.431	Vietnam	0.007
Congo	0.003	Jordan	0.006	Qatar	0.033	Yemen	0.010
Costa Rica	0.016	Kazakhstan	0.048	Republic of Korea	1.006	Yugoslavia	0.026
Côte d'Ivoire	0.009	Kenya	0.007	Republic of Moldova	0.010	Zambia	0.002
Croatia	0.030	Kuwait	0.128	Romania	0.056	Zimbabwe	0.009
Cuba	0.024	Kyrgyzstan	0.006	Russian Federation	1.077	Total	100.000
Cyprus	0.034	Lao People's Democratic Republic	0.001	Rwanda	0.001		
Czech Republic	0.107	Latvia	0.017	Saint Kitts and Nevis	0.001		
Democratic People's Republic of Korea	0.015	Lebanon	0.016	Saint Lucia	0.001		
Democratic Republic of the Congo	0.007	Lesotho	0.002	Saint Vincent and the Grenadines	0.001		
		Liberia	0.002	Samoa	0.001		

nology, and work programs. This approach has required reductions and redeployment of staff. Between 1984–95 and 1996–97, the UN eliminated 2,046 positions, and about 1,000 of the budgeted posts that exist now are kept vacant. Travel was reduced by 26% in 1996, and printing costs were reduced by 27% in early 1996, as more than 270,000 UN documents have become available electronically.

On 23 March 2000, Under-Secretary-General for Management Joseph E. Connor told the General Assembly's Fifth Committee (Administrative and Budgetary) that in 1999 the United Nations "took a step back from the financial brink." While regular budget and tribunals assessments were as expected, there was an increase in peacekeeping assessments in 1999, he added. Even with that increase, the obligatory cost to member states for all UN activities in 1999 was the lowest in six years: the actual assessment for 1999 came to just over US$2 billion. The UN had more cash than the previous year largely because of payments made by the United States to avoid losing its vote in the General Assembly. Total available cash at the end of 1999 jumped to some US$1.093 billion, from US$736 million in 1998. Amounts owed to the United Nations were also lower, at US$1.758 billion, down from US$2.031 billion a year earlier. And the level of the United Nations debt to its member states—some US$800 million—was also significantly lower than the previous three years.

THE GENERAL ASSEMBLY

The first of the UN organs established by the charter, the General Assembly is the pivot of the organization. All member states are represented. Each country, large or small, has one vote, and each country chooses its own representatives.

FUNCTIONS AND POWERS

The central position of the General Assembly is firmly established in a series of charter provisions encompassing a wide range of functions and powers. First are the provisions setting forth its powers as the major deliberative body of the UN. With two exceptions (described below), the General Assembly has the right to discuss and make recommendations on any subject that falls within the scope of the charter itself, including the functions and powers of the other organs. Hence, it is in the General Assembly that all of the UN's important projects (except for the Security Council's peacekeeping operations) originate—those dealing with political questions, disarmament, economic and social development, human rights, decolonization of dependent territories, and development of international law.

The second group of charter provisions defining the pivotal position of the General Assembly concerns the financing of the UN. The General Assembly is empowered to "consider and approve" the budget of the organization (which includes that of the International Court of Justice at The Hague), and it also has the right to determine how the expenses shall be apportioned among the member nations.

Lastly, the General Assembly's position is secured by provisions that give it specific powers in relation to the other organs. Thus, both the Economic and Social Council and the Trusteeship Council are constituted under the direct authority of the General Assembly to carry out designated tasks in their respective spheres. The administrative arm of the UN, the Secretariat, is also at the disposition of the General Assembly. The General Assembly's powers, however, are much more limited where the Security Council and the International Court of Justice are concerned. Designed in some respects to be more powerful than the General Assembly, the Security Council is in no way answerable to the body for its activities—although it is required to make an annual report and, when necessary, special reports. Also, whereas the General Assembly is empowered to make recommendations to the council concerning the maintenance of international peace, it cannot give the council instructions. In the case of the International Court of Justice, any attempt to render its activities answerable to the General Assembly would have prejudiced the independent status that is normally accorded to judiciary bodies throughout the world. Nevertheless, inasmuch as the General Assembly not only has budgetary power but also elects the non-permanent members of the Security Council and, concurrently with the Security Council, all the judges of the International Court, it can be said to exercise an appreciable degree of indirect control over both these bodies.

Thus, the one UN organ on which all member states have the constitutional right to be represented is able to make its will felt throughout the organization, and indeed the entire UN system. Because its powers closely resemble those of a national parliament, the General Assembly has been described as a "world parliament." Parliamentary powers are not to be confused, though, with governmental powers. Except insofar as the Economic and Social Council, the Trusteeship Council, and the Secretariat are bound to carry out its requests, the General Assembly has no power to legislate and cannot enforce its decisions upon individual member nations. The only sanctions that the General Assembly can wield against an uncooperative member are the suspension of the rights and privileges of membership and expulsion from the organization, but even these sanctions can be invoked only on the recommendation of the Security Council. In effect, then, all General Assembly decisions are purely recommendations that reflect world public opinion; they have moral, though not legal, force. At the end of this chapter, an attempt is made to assess their effectiveness on this score.

Charter Restrictions on the Assembly's Power to Discuss and Recommend

The charter imposes two major restrictions on the General Assembly's powers to discuss and make recommendations. The first is embodied in the principle set out in Article 2, paragraph 7 of the charter, which states: "Nothing contained in the present Charter shall authorize the United Nations to intervene in matters which are essentially within the domestic jurisdiction of any state or shall require the Members to submit such matters to settlement. . . ." This principle is not so restrictive as it might seem, for whether a given issue is or is not of a domestic character is decided by the General Assembly itself. It can and often does override by majority vote the attempt of a member nation to bar a particular topic from debate by invoking Article 2, paragraph 7 of the charter. The most notable case in point was the General Assembly's annual discussion of South Africa's apartheid policy (before it was abolished) despite South Africa's contention that the matter was within its domestic jurisdiction. (See section on "Apartheid in South Africa" in the chapter on Human Rights.)

The second restriction is to be found in Article 12 of the charter, which states that while the Security Council is exercising its functions in respect to any international dispute or situation, "the General Assembly shall not make any recommendation with regard to that dispute or situation unless the Security Council so requests." This stipulation, then, clearly establishes the absolute primacy of the Security Council over the General Assembly in times of crisis. Here, the main object of the founders of the UN was to ensure against the possibility of the smaller nations forming a majority bloc to interfere with any decisions that might be made by the Big Five acting in concert as permanent members of the Security Council, where each possesses the right of veto. (For a discussion of the veto right, see the chapter on the Security Council.)

Extension of the Assembly's Power to Discuss and Recommend through the Uniting for Peace Resolution

Designed to secure maximum unity of action in moments of acute danger, Article 12, in fact, proved to be the chief obstacle to action of any kind during successive crises in the years just after World War II. The effectiveness of the entire system presupposed a spirit of unanimity among the great powers in their determination to end a particular dispute that appeared to threaten international peace and security. However, on each postwar occasion when the great powers might have been expected to display unanimity, the USSR and the four other permanent members of the Security Council took opposite sides in the dispute. As a result, precisely because each of them possessed the veto, all council action was deadlocked. Meanwhile, the General Assembly, prevented from taking action of its own accord because of Article 12, was forced to stand by helplessly.

It was the seriousness of the Korean crisis that finally impelled the General Assembly to take steps to break through its constitutional straitjacket. Following a deadlock in the council in 1950, when the USSR vetoed a United States-sponsored resolution in connection with the entry of the People's Republic of China into the Korean conflict on the side of North Korea, the General Assembly adopted a resolution that enabled it to circumvent the restrictions imposed by Article 12. This act, which came to be known as the "Uniting for Peace Resolution," provides that if the Security Council, because of lack of unanimity among its permanent members, fails to exercise its primary responsibility in the maintenance of peace, in a case where there appears to be a threat to the peace, breach of the peace, or act of aggression, the General Assembly shall consider the matter immediately with a view to making recommendations to members for collective measures, including if necessary the use of armed force. Although the Uniting for Peace Resolution thus considerably extends the General Assembly's powers with respect to maintenance of international peace and security, it in no way represents an attempt to usurp the Security Council's prerogatives. Nor does it attempt to arrogate to the General Assembly the enforcement powers that the charter accorded to the Security Council alone. Even under the Uniting for Peace Resolution, the General Assembly can only recommend that members undertake collective peacekeeping measures; it cannot oblige them to do so. Nor can it impose peacekeeping action against the will of the parties to a dispute. It must obtain their explicit consent to the presence of UN personnel—observer commissions, mediators, troops—in their territories.

The Uniting for Peace Resolution has been invoked in several major crises: the Middle East (1958, 1967), Hungary (1956), Suez (1956), the Congo (1960), Afghanistan (1980), Palestine (1980, 1982), Namibia (1981), the occupied Arab territories (1982) and illegal Israeli actions in occupied East Jerusalem and the rest of the occupied Palestinian Territory (1997, 1998, 1999). In all cases, the emergency special sessions addressed situations in which the Security Council found itself deadlocked. (See the discussion of peacekeeping operations in the chapter on International Peace and Security.)

ORGANIZATION

Sessions

The General Assembly meets once a year in regular sessions that begin on the third Tuesday in September. Usually these sessions last about three months, ending before Christmas, but there is no fixed time limit, and many times the General Assembly has adjourned, continuing the session after the holidays. Special sessions on a particular topic may be held at the request of the Security Council, or of a majority of UN members, or of one member if the majority of members concur. An emergency special session may be called within 24 hours by the Security Council on the vote of any nine members, or by a majority of UN members, or by one member if the majority concur.

Through 1999, the Assembly convened 22 special sessions on issues that demanded attention over the years, including problems of Palestine, UN finances, Namibia, disarmament, international economic cooperation, apartheid, drugs, the environment, population, and sustainable development of small island developing states.

Sessional Committees

Most of the substantive work during regular session is conducted through seven "Main Committees," which are reconstituted at every session. Each is composed of representatives of all member nations.

- The *First Committee* deals with disarmament and related international security matters.
- The *Second Committee* deals with economic and financial matters.
- The *Third Committee* is concerned with social, humanitarian, and cultural matters and human rights.
- The *Fourth Committee* handles special political questions and questions concerning the granting of independence to colonial territories.
- The *Fifth Committee* deals with the administrative and budgetary matters of the organization.
- The *Sixth Committee* debates legal questions, including the general development and codification of international law.
- The *Special Political Committee,* was created in 1948 as an ad hoc committee of the whole to discuss the Palestine question. Never disbanded, it was subsequently absorbed by the Fourth Committee.

The General Assembly maintains two other sessional committees, both of which deal with General Assembly procedure. However, neither is a committee of the whole. The 29-member *General Committee,* composed of the General Assembly president, the 21 vice presidents, and the chairmen of the seven main committees (see Election of Officers, below), examines the provisional agenda of each session and makes recommendations on the inclusion or exclusion of items and on their assignment to the appropriate main committee. The *Credentials Committee* is a nine-member body appointed by the General Assembly at the beginning of the session to examine the credentials of representatives and to work out any problems that might arise in this connection.

Plenary Meetings

Since all the main committees are committees of the whole, the distinction between the General Assembly meeting in committee and meeting in plenum is largely one of protocol. Always conducted by the president or a vice president, plenary meetings are much more formal affairs. Normally, no one below the rank of head of delegation may actively participate in the proceedings, and no one is allowed to speak from his or her chair but must go to the speaker's rostrum. (None of the conference rooms in which the committees meet is provided with a speaker's rostrum.) The Assembly Hall itself is reserved for plenary meetings and is rarely used by the committees.

It is in plenary meetings that all formal or ceremonial functions occur: opening and closing of the General Assembly session, election of officers and members of other organs, adoption of resolutions and decisions on all agenda items, and addresses by heads of state or government or by other high national officials who visit the UN while the General Assembly is in session. Plenary meetings also constitute the forum for the statements of general policy that the head of each member delegation is entitled to make as part of what is known as the "general debate," which takes place during the first three weeks or so of the regular session. Because of the great number of questions which the General Assembly is called upon to consider (over 170 agenda items at the 1999–2000 session) it allocates most questions to its seven main committees.

Voting Procedure

Each member of the General Assembly and its committees has one vote. Article 18 of the charter decrees that decisions on "important" questions shall be made by a two-thirds majority of the members present and voting. Among the important questions specified are recommendations with regard to maintenance of peace and security; election of the nonpermanent members of the Security Council and of the members of the Economic and Social Council and the Trusteeship Council; admission of new UN members, suspension of rights and privileges of membership, and expulsion of members; questions relating to the operation of the trusteeship system; and budgetary questions. Decisions on other questions, including the determination of additional categories of important questions requiring a two-thirds majority vote, are made by a simple majority of the members present and voting. The phrase "members present and voting" means members casting either affirmative or negative votes; members who abstain are considered as not voting. Thus, although the number of abstentions is usually listed for information purposes, it does not count in the final tally as to whether a resolution has received the requisite majority—provided that the rules of quorum have been observed. A quorum is constituted when a majority of the members are present; no decision may be taken without one. The president of the General Assembly, however, may declare a meeting open and permit the debate to proceed when at least one-third of the members are present. The chairman of a main committee may open a meeting when one-quarter of the members are present.

Voting may be by a show of hands, by roll call, or, in certain instances such as elections, by secret ballot. The normal method was intended to be by a show of hands, but any member can request a roll call. There has been an increasing tendency to do so, especially on the more contentious issues. Before a roll-call vote is taken, a lot is drawn to determine the country that is to vote first. Starting with that country, voting proceeds according to the alphabetical order of the official names of states in English. Mechanical voting equipment was installed in the Assembly Hall and first used at the 1965 session. Similar equipment is used in some conference rooms.

Seating Arrangements

The charter allows each member state a maximum of five representatives in the General Assembly. Most members, in addition to their five representatives, send five alternative representatives and a number of advisers to each session. Six seats are assigned to every delegation in the Assembly Hall. Both in the hall and in conference rooms, delegations are seated in alphabetical order according to the official names of the countries in English. The seating is rearranged before each session by drawing lots to select the country with which the alphabetical seating will start.

Election of Officers

At each regular session, the General Assembly constitutes itself anew. During the opening meetings, the main officers are elected, who serve until the end of the session. If a special or emergency session is called, it is normally presided over by officers elected in the previous September.

The first officer to be elected is the president. Delegates vote by secret ballot, and a simple majority suffices. In choosing the president, regard has to be paid to the equitable geographical rotation of the office among the following groups of states: African, Asian, Eastern European, Latin American, and Western European and other states. By tacit agreement, no representative of a permanent member of the Security Council ever is elected president of the General Assembly or chairman of a committee.

General Assembly Presidents

1.	1946	Paul-Henri Spaak	Belgium
2.	1947	Oswaldo Aranha	Brazil
3.	1948	Herbert V. Evatt	Australia
4.	1949	Carlos P. Romulo	Philippines
5.	1950	Nasrollah Entezam	Iran
6.	1951	Luís Padilla Nervo	Mexico
7.	1952	Lester B. Pearson	Canada
8.	1953	Vijaya Lakshmi Pandit	India
9.	1954	Eelco N. van Kleffens	Netherlands
10.	1955	José Maza	Chile
11.	1956	Prince Wan Waithayakon	Thailand
12.	1957	Sir Leslie Munro	New Zealand
13.	1958	Charles Malik	Lebanon
14.	1959	Víctor Andrés Belaúnde	Peru
15.	1960	Frederick H. Boland	Ireland
16.	1961	Mongi Slim	Tunisia
17.	1962	Sir Muhammad Zafrulla Khan	Pakistan
18.	1963	Carlos Sosa Rodríguez	Venezuela
19.	1964	Alex Quaison-Sackey	Ghana
20	1965	Amintore Fanfani	Italy
21.	1966	Abdul Rahman Pazhwak	Afghanistan
22.	1967	Corneliu Manescu	Romania
23.	1968	Emilio Arenales Catalán	Guatemala
24.	1969	Angie E. Brooks	Liberia
25.	1970	Edvard Hambro	Norway
26.	1971	Adam Malik	Indonesia
27.	1972	Stanislaw Trepczynski	Poland
28.	1973	Leopoldo Benites	Ecuador
29.	1974	Abdelaziz Bouteflika	Algeria
30.	1975	Gaston Thorn	Luxembourg
31.	1976	Hamilton S. Amerasinghe	Sri Lanka
32.	1977	Lazar Mojsov	Yugoslavia
33.	1978	Indalecio Liévano	Colombia
34.	1979	Salim A. Salim	Tanzania
35.	1980	Rüdiger von Wechmar	Federal Republic of Germany
36.	1981	Ismat T. Kittani	Iraq
37.	1982	Imre Hollai	Hungary
38.	1983	Jorge E. Illueca	Panama
39.	1984	Paul J. F. Lusaka	Zambia
40.	1985	Jaime de Piniés	Spain
41.	1986	Humayun Rasheed Choudhury	Bangladesh
42.	1987	Peter Florin	German Democratic Republic
43.	1988	Dante M. Caputa	Argentina
44.	1989	Joseph Nanven Garba	Nigeria
45.	1990	Guido de Marco	Malta
46.	1991	Samir S. Shihabi	Saudi Arabia
47.	1992	Stoyan Ganev	Bulgaria
48.	1993	Samuel R. Insanally	Guyana
49.	1994	Amara Essy	Côte d'Ivoire
50.	1995	Diogo Freitas do Amaral	Portugal
51.	1996	Razali Ismail	Malaysia
52.	1997	Hennadiy Udovenko	Ukraine
53.	1998	Didier Opertti	Uruguay
54.	1999	Theo-Ben Gurirab	Namibia

Note: General Assembly presidents normally preside over special and emergency special sessions of the world body during their tenure. The exceptions were: José Arce of Argentina, who presided over the second special session in 1948, and Rudecindo Ortega of Chile, who presided over the first and second emergency special sessions held in 1956.

Following the election of the president, the main committees are officially constituted and retire to elect their own officers. Here again the matter of equitable geographical representation arises, and it is precisely regulated by a resolution adopted by the General Assembly in 1963. Of the seven committee chairmen, two must be chosen from African states and one each from Asian, Eastern European, Latin American, and Western European or other states. The seventh chairmanship rotates in alternate years between representatives from Asian and Western European or other states.

The final officers to be elected are the 21 vice presidents. Of these, 16 are elected in accordance with a geographical pattern: six from African states, five from Asian states, three from Latin American states, two from Western European and other states, and one from an Eastern European state. (The election of the president of the General Assembly has the effect, however, of reducing by one the number of vice presidencies allocated to the region from which the president is elected.) The remaining five vice presidents represent the permanent members of the Security Council: China, France, the Russian Federation, the United Kingdom, and the United States.

AGENDA OF THE ASSEMBLY

Under the General Assembly's rules of procedure, the provisional agenda for a regular session must be issued no later than 60 days before the opening. However, up to 30 days before the opening, the Secretary-General, any of the other principal organs of the UN, or any member of the UN may request the inclusion of supplementary items. Additional items may also be included at any time if a majority of the General Assembly agrees.

Normally, the agenda includes well over 100 items. The great majority of substantive (that is to say, nonprocedural) items arise out of decisions made by previous sessions, and their inclusion in the agenda is automatic. Thus, the General Assembly frequently requests the Secretary-General, a special committee, or another UN organ to submit a special report on a given topic. The report, at the time that it is due, automatically becomes part of the agenda item on the topic. There also are several items that the General Assembly is obliged to consider at each session under the Charter—for example, the annual report of the Secretary-General on the work of the UN and the reports of the three councils.

Adoption of the Agenda

The adoption of the agenda is not a mere formality. The General Assembly has to approve the entire agenda and may amend or delete any item by majority vote. A decision to reject a particular member's request to have an item placed on the agenda could have considerable political significance. It is the function of the General Committee (which could be described as the steering committee) to make recommendations to the General Assembly on the inclusion of requested items in the agenda. Most of the pros and cons of including a controversial item in the agenda are thrashed out in this committee rather than in plenary, and the committee's proceedings sometimes afford a preview of the positions that countries will take on certain questions when they come up for substantive debate. Another important function of the General Committee is to recommend the assignment of agenda items to the various main committees for debate. It may also recommend that an important item be debated in plenary without being referred to a committee.

EFFECTIVENESS OF THE ASSEMBLY

Depending on the nature of the question and on the views of the majority, General Assembly debates may lead to one or a combination of the following: recommendations, phrased in varying degrees of urgency, to individual countries or to all countries; initiation of studies and reports; creation of new UN organs, committees of inquiry, and permanent special bodies that are assigned specific tasks; and adoption of international covenants, treaties, and agreements.

Significance of the Enlarged Membership and Changing Voting Patterns

Since 1960, when the impact of the number of newly independent African and Asian nations first began to make itself felt in the UN, the General Assembly's voting patterns have undergone a marked alteration. Until then, the majority of controversial resolutions had tended essentially to reflect a simple East-West division of opinion. In the resulting lineup of votes, the Western view, marshaled under the leadership of the United States, easily attained comfortable majorities on most issues, since it was supported not only by the countries of Western Europe but by the

Latin American states as well. The formation of what has come to be known as the "Afro-Asian group," coupled with the general detente in East-West relations, introduced a new element into the voting equation.

Interested in wielding influence within the world body and preoccupied with the problems of development and decolonization rather than with cold war issues as such, African and Asian countries sought to unite themselves into an independent or "nonaligned" voting bloc. On occasion, the unity of the group is split by divided interests. This division occurs most frequently in major political issues of special importance to the big powers, when some small countries may find it expedient to associate themselves with the big power on which they are dependent for financial aid. At other times, notably on items connected with economic development, African and Asian nations may join the developing countries of the Latin American group in order to create a formidable voting bloc that can force through requests to which the highly developed nations, from East and West alike, may be reluctant to accede.

Then again, the emergence of what is in effect a floating third voting force in the General Assembly has resulted in the creation of special alliances as occasion demands. For example, the former Soviet bloc and the nonaligned groups often combined to defeat or harry the West on colonial issues. This development also opened up possibilities for striking voting bargains on individual draft resolutions. Accordingly, one group might support an initiative taken by a second group in exchange for the latter's support on a different item.

The indiscriminate wielding of voting strength by small nations is subject to the law of diminishing returns. Indeed, many small nations have shown indications of growing restraint, realizing that there is little point in pushing through resolutions requiring, for example, increased expenditure on economic development if the big powers, which make the largest financial contributions, are not prepared to implement them. Similarly, these nations have recognized that there is little to be gained from trying to compel the big powers to go beyond their own pace in agreeing upon measures for disarmament or for resolving their differences on peacekeeping issues.

One important outcome of the growing recognition by the small nations of the practical limitations of their voting strength, coupled with the realization by the Western powers that they no longer can be certain of majority support, even on items of particular importance to them, has been a general recourse wherever possible to compromise resolutions that command unanimous or nearly unanimous support. However, notwithstanding this partial solution to the problems created by the emergence of a floating third voting force in the General Assembly, the big powers, especially those from the West, have become increasingly dissatisfied with this situation, and some of their leaders have come to question the principle of "one country, one vote."

While the decisions of the General Assembly have no legally binding force for governments, they carry the weight of world opinion on major international issues, as well as the moral authority of the world community. Even so, the fact that a resolution receives an overwhelming majority vote does not guarantee its effectiveness. Nor does the fact that a resolution was adopted by a slender margin necessarily mean that it will serve no purpose. In general, it may be said that a resolution will be effective insofar as its adoption is not regarded by any country as inimical to its national interests. The most effective resolutions, then, are those that concern matters on which all members are prepared to accept a degree of compromise (though this acceptance may not necessarily be reflected in the actual voting) and that establish goals all members are eager to achieve or to which they have no objection. Like the UN itself, resolutions can be only as effective as the membership wants them to be.

THE SECURITY COUNCIL

Under the charter, the members of the UN vest in the Security Council primary responsibility for maintaining international peace and security. To facilitate its work and to ensure quick and effective action when required, the council has certain powers and attributes not accorded the other organs of the UN. Thus, the council is empowered by the charter to enforce its decisions and prescribe them as a course of action legally binding upon all UN members. However, these prerogatives can be invoked only in times of gravest crisis and under explicit conditions laid down in the charter. Otherwise, the Security Council, like the General Assembly, can only recommend and advise.

Another distinctive feature of the council is the membership and voting privileges accorded to the five countries that were chiefly responsible for the defeat of the Axis nations in World War II and, at the time of the San Francisco Conference, were regarded as militarily the most powerful countries in the world. By the terms of these privileges, China, France, the USSR, the United Kingdom, and the United States were each accorded permanent membership on the Security Council and the right to veto any substantive decision adopted by the majority of the other members. The underlying consideration here was the desire to preserve the unanimity of the Big Five—that is, to ensure that no peacekeeping action would be taken against the will of a country considered sufficiently powerful to oppose the council's decision with military force and so open up the possibility of a third major international war.

Since all five countries were actually specified by name in the relevant charter provisions, an amendment or revision of the charter would be required to name different nations as permanent Security Council members. In turn, a charter amendment requires ratification by all five permanent members of the Security Council before it can come into force. In 1971, a major change was brought about without altering the names of permanent members. The General Assembly voted that the right to represent China belonged to a delegation that the People's Republic of China would name and expelled the delegation from the Republic of China (Taiwan). On 24 December 1991, Boris Yeltsin, president of the new Russian Federation, sent a letter to the Secretary-General informing him that the Russian Federation, as the "continuing state" of the former USSR, would occupy the seat of the former USSR on the Security Council. The letter stated that the Russian Federation had the support of the 11 member countries of the Commonwealth of Independent States, most of whom subsequently became members of the United Nations. The precedent for this switch was cited as the 1947 accession of the newly independent India to the UN membership held by the former British India.

MEMBERSHIP

To expedite decision and action, the membership of the Security Council was deliberately restricted to a small number. Originally an 11-member body, it was subsequently enlarged to 15 members by a charter amendment that came into effect on 31 August 1965.

With five seats permanently assigned, the remaining 10 are filled by other UN members elected by secret ballot in the General Assembly for two-year terms. Five seats on the Security Council become vacant each year. Nonpermanent members of the council are ineligible for immediate reelection upon retirement. In electing the nonpermanent members of the Security Council, the General Assembly is required to pay due regard to the past and potential contribution of nations to the maintenance of international peace and security, as well as to equitable geographical distribution. In view of the power of the council, nations attach great importance to the choice of the nonpermanent members.

The problem of ensuring equitable geographical distribution of members elected to the Security Council has not been easy to resolve. Prior to the council's enlargement, there had been a long-standing difference of views on a "gentlemen's agreement" reached in the early days of the UN that was intended to guarantee that the six nonpermanent seats would be so distributed that one of the seats would always be held by a Soviet bloc country. However, until 1960, only Poland and the Ukraine were elected, and each served for only one two-year term. In the 1959 election, Poland and Turkey competed for the nonpermanent council seat for the two-year term 1960–61. After 52 ballots, the General Assembly gave the seat to Poland on the basis of the following compromise: though elected for two years, Poland would resign its seat at the end of the first year and Turkey would be the sole candidate to fill the unexpired term. Under a similar arrangement, Romania held a seat for 1962, resigning it for 1963 to the Philippines. To avoid the recurrence of such situations after the enlargement of the council, the General Assembly established a fixed pattern for the geographical distribution of the 10 nonpermanent seats: five from African and Asian nations, one from East European nations, two from Latin American nations, and two from West European and other nations.

The accession of the Russian Federation, a vastly less powerful state than the former USSR, to a permanent seat on the Security Council set off a discussion among the UN membership about the need to make changes to the structure of the Security Council to better reflect the radical changes in the world and the organization's overall membership. The 48th General Assembly established an Open-Ended Working Group on the Question of Equitable Representation on and Increase in the Membership of the Security Council, which held its first meeting in New York on 19 January 1994. The Working Group submitted an informal report to the Secretary-General summarizing the results of its survey of the membership. It found that virtually all member states of the UN favored an increase in the membership of the Security Council. There was little unanimity, however, on the criteria for revising the council's composition. Responses received by the Working Group proposed increasing membership by as few as four (to 19) or more than doubling its size (to 31). Some members suggested the number of permanent members be increased at least by one (to six), or perhaps as much as seven (to 12). Most states responding to the survey agreed that an increase in membership should not diminish the council's efficiency. While most members favored continuing the categories of permanent and nonpermanent memberships, new categories were suggested: permanent seats without power of veto; rotating permanent seats, with or without power of veto; and semipermanent seats or extended membership. Some of the possible criteria put forward for new Security Council permanent membership included size of peacekeeping and financial contributions, the size of population and territory, economic potential, regional importance, geopolitical situation, and military capability.

In 2000, the Security Council consisted of the five permanent members: China, France, the Russian Federation, the United Kingdom, and the United States; the 10 nonpermanent members, elected for a two-year period, were Argentina, Bangladesh, Canada, Jamaica, Malaysia, Mali, Namibia, Netherlands, Tunisia, and Ukraine.

ORGANIZATION OF THE COUNCIL

The Security Council is organized to function continuously and to meet as often as necessary. Hence, a representative from each member state must always be available so that in an emergency the council can convene at once. Chairmanship rotates among the council's member states according to their English alphabetical order, a new president (as the chairman is called) presiding every month. It is up to the president to decide whether to preside during the discussion of a question that directly concerns his own country.

Council members normally are represented by the heads of their permanent missions to the UN, who have the rank of ambassador. Any state that is not currently a council member but is a party to a dispute under consideration by the council must be invited to send representatives to participate in the proceedings, though without the right to vote. (In these circumstances, the disputing states concerned usually send a high government official, very often the foreign minister.) When the council is discussing a matter other than an actual dispute, the decision to invite the participation of any UN member states whose interests are directly affected is left to its discretion. The council has usually acceded to requests for such invitations. It has also granted representatives of national liberation organizations the opportunity to speak at a number of meetings.

The Security Council has held sessions away from its New York headquarters on two occasions, in Addis Ababa, Ethiopia, in 1972, to consider questions relating to Africa, and in Panama City, Panama, in 1973, to consider questions relating to Latin America.

VOTING

Each member of the Security Council has one vote. On questions of procedure, a motion is carried if it obtains an affirmative vote of any nine members. On substantive matters, a resolution requires the affirmative votes of nine members, including the concurring votes of the permanent members. However, any member, whether permanent or nonpermanent, must abstain from voting in any decision concerning the peaceful settlement of a dispute to which it is a party.

The Veto

The veto power and its exercise by permanent members remains a central characteristic of the mechanism of the Security Council, although, since the end of the cold war, a new climate of collegiality has made its use rare. Though the word "veto" does not occur in the charter, it is the common-usage term for the power of any of the five permanent members to defeat a resolution by voting "nay."

Negative votes cast in the council by its permanent members constitute an exercise of their veto power only on substantive questions, not on procedural matters. Moreover, by long-standing practice, the charter provision stipulating that all substantive resolutions must obtain the concurring votes of the permanent members has been interpreted to mean that, provided a permanent member does not actually vote "nay," a resolution may still be carried.

The veto power, then, is the constitutional instrument for giving expression to the requirement—discussed at the opening of this chapter—that before the Security Council invokes its authority in peacekeeping action, the big powers should first resolve their differences on how a particular crisis should be handled. However, although the principle of ensuring unanimity among the big powers was the major consideration underlying the institution of the veto, it was not the only one. A complementary consideration was the need of the major powers to ensure that their decisions would not be overridden by a majority vote of the smaller nations. In effect, conferring the right of veto upon a few powerful countries was tacit acknowledgment of the natural conflict that exists between their interests and those of the less powerful nations. It was a recognition of the fact that, despite differing social systems and power rivalry, the large countries often share more interests with each other than they do with smaller nations having social systems and tenets similar to their own. And it was for exactly this reason that the smaller countries represented at the San Francisco Conference made strenuous but unsuccessful efforts to prevent the institution of the veto power in the charter.

FUNCTIONS AND POWERS

The functions and powers assigned to the Security Council under the charter are the following:

- to maintain international peace and security in accordance with the principles and purposes of the UN;
- to investigate any dispute or situation that might lead to international friction and to recommend methods of adjusting such disputes or the terms of settlement;
- to determine the existence of a threat to the peace or an act of aggression and to recommend what action should be taken;
- to call on members to apply economic sanctions and other measures not involving the use of force in order to prevent or stop aggression;
- to take military action against an aggressor; and
- to formulate plans for the establishment of a system to regulate armaments.

The Security council also is empowered to exercise the trusteeship functions of the UN in areas designated as "strategic" (only the Trust Territory of the Pacific Islands was so designated).

Finally, the Council recommends to the General Assembly the admission of new members and the appointment of the Secretary-General and, together with the General Assembly, elects the judges of the International Court of Justice.

MAINTAINING INTERNATIONAL PEACE AND SECURITY

By the very act of joining the UN, all members "confer on the Security Council primary responsibility for the maintenance of international peace and security and agree that in carrying out its duties under this responsibility the Security Council *acts on their behalf*" (italics added). They also consent "to accept and carry out" the decisions of the council on any peacekeeping action that may be required. Under Article 39 of the charter, the Security Council's powers to take such enforceable decisions come into effect only when a definite "threat to the peace," an actual "breach of the peace," or a particular "act of aggression" has occurred. Only if the council decides that one of these circumstances prevails may it invoke its power to take a course of enforcement action that constitutes a legally binding commitment on all UN members. With regard to disputes between states that, in the opinion of the council, have not yet led to a definite threat to the peace or do not constitute an actual breach of the peace or an act of aggression, it may simply recommend measures for a peaceful settlement.

The extreme caution with which the founders of the UN

assigned governmental prerogatives to the Security Council is reflected in the fact that its peacekeeping powers are set out in two quite separate chapters of the charter. Chapter VI establishes the council's advisory functions in assisting the peaceful settlement of disputes. Chapter VII defines the kind of action that it may take in the event of threats to the peace, breaches of the peace, and acts of aggression.

Peaceful Settlement of Disputes

Under Chapter VI of the charter, the parties to any dispute "the continuance of which is likely to endanger the maintenance of international peace and security" are enjoined to seek a settlement of their own accord by peaceful means, including "negotiation, enquiry, mediation, conciliation, arbitration, judicial settlement, or resort to regional agencies or arrangements. . . ." When can the Security Council itself intervene? On this point, the charter is as unrestrictive as possible. By no means does every "situation" of conflicting interests lead to an actual dispute. Yet the council need not wait until a situation has given rise to friction before taking action. It may take the initiative of investigating any dispute, or any situation that might lead to international friction or give rise to a dispute, in order to determine whether the continuance of the dispute or situation is likely to endanger the maintenance of international peace and security. Moreover, any nation, whether a member of the UN or not, has the right to bring any dispute or threatening situation before the Security Council (or before the General Assembly). Should the parties to a dispute fail to settle their differences by peaceful means of their own choice, they are bound under the terms of the charter to refer the problem to the council.

Once the council has decided to intervene in a dispute, it can take several courses of action. It may recommend one of the methods of settlement listed in the charter; it may itself determine and recommend other "procedures or methods of adjustment" that it deems appropriate; or, if it considers that the continuance of the dispute is likely to endanger international peace and security, it can decide to recommend substantive terms of settlement.

Threats to the Peace, Breaches of the Peace, and Acts of Aggression

If, in its opinion, there is a threat to the peace, the Security Council has the duty to maintain peace and security by preventing the outbreak of actual hostilities. If there has been a breach of the peace or an act of aggression, its duty is to restore international peace and security.

The Security Council is empowered by the charter to call upon the parties to comply with any provisional measures that it deems necessary or desirable. Such immediate instructions to the quarreling states are intended, without prejudice to the rights of the parties, to prevent an aggravation of the conflict. For example, the council may demand the immediate cessation of hostilities and withdrawal of the forces from the invaded territory. If either or both parties do not comply with these demands, the council "shall duly take account" of the failure to comply. In this event, the farthest-reaching prerogative of the Security Council can come into play—namely, its right to institute sanctions against the recalcitrant state or states.

Here again, the discretion of the Security Council is very wide. When the council finds that a threat to the peace, breach of the peace, or act of aggression exists, it is authorized, though not compelled, by the charter to invoke sanctions. Even if its first provisional demands are not heeded, it may continue to press for peaceful settlement or take various other actions, such as the dispatch of a commission of inquiry, short of sanctions. On the other hand, the Security Council is free to invoke whatever enforcement measures it may consider necessary under the circumstances. It need not begin with the mildest but may, as in the

Korean conflict, immediately start with the severest type of sanction—namely, the use of military force—if it considers that less drastic measures would be inadequate.

Types of Sanctions. The charter does not provide an exhaustive list of sanctions that the Security Council may invoke, but it mentions two types: sanctions not involving the use of armed forces, and military sanctions.

Sanctions not involving the use of armed forces may be of two kinds. One is the severance of diplomatic relations with one or more of the belligerent states. The other is economic sanctions, including partial or complete interruption of economic relations and communications, such as rail, sea, and air traffic, postal and telegraphic services, and radio. The purpose is to isolate the country or countries against which they are directed, physically, economically, and morally. For example, a would-be aggressor that is denied certain strategic materials may be compelled to cease hostilities. If successful, such measures have great advantages over military sanctions. They impose fewer burdens on the participating countries and fewer hardships on the population of the areas of conflict. They also avoid the danger that once military action on behalf of the UN has been taken, war may spread.

Military sanctions, the charter stipulates, may include demonstrations by air, sea, or land forces; blockade; or "other operations by air, sea, and land forces," the latter including actual military action against the offending country or countries.

Once the Security Council has decided on specific sanctions, all members of the UN are under legal obligation to carry them out. The council may, however, at its discretion, decide that only certain member states shall take an active part, or it may demand that even nonmember states participate in economic sanctions to make them effective. The charter also stipulates that before any member state not represented on the Security Council is called upon to provide armed forces, that country must, upon its request, be invited to participate in the council's deliberations, with a right to vote on the employment of its own contingents.

The Security Council has invoked its powers to impose sanctions judiciously.

In December 1966, the council imposed mandatory economic sanctions against the illegal Smith regime in Southern Rhodesia (now Zimbabwe).

The council instituted a voluntary arms embargo against South Africa in 1963 on the grounds that arms supplied to that country were being used to enforce its policy of apartheid. In November 1977, it imposed a mandatory arms embargo against South Africa. Although the General Assembly requested the Security Council to consider mandatory economic sanctions (in 1977) and a mandatory embargo on oil and oil products (in 1979), the council did not act. (The General Assembly passed a resolution calling for a mandatory oil embargo and economic sanctions against South Africa at its 44th session in 1989.)

On 6 August 1990, in response to Iraq's invasion of Kuwait, the Security Council, in its Resolution 661, imposed tight sanctions: a full trade embargo barring all imports from and exports to Iraq, excepting only medical supplies and humanitarian food aid. The Security Council further indicated its resolve by passing Resolution 665 on 25 August 1990, authorizing member states to use force to block shipments of goods to Iraq. Finally, on 25 September, it passed Resolution 670 mandating a complete air transport blockade of Iraq.

In 1991, at the request of the foreign minister of Yugoslavia, the Security Council imposed its first mandatory arms embargo in Europe in an effort to quell the rising tide of insurrection between ethnic groups in that country. By 30 May 1992, Yugoslavia had dissolved into four states: Slovenia, Croatia, Bosnia-Herzegovina, and the Federal Republic of Yugoslavia (Serbia and Montenegro). At that time, Slovenia, Croatia, and Bosnia-Herzegovina were admitted to UN membership. The Security Council, in Resolution

757, imposed mandatory trade sanctions against the Federal Republic of Yugoslavia, excepting only shipments of food and medicine for humanitarian purposes.

On 31 March 1992, the Security Council adopted an arms and air traffic embargo on Libya (Resolution 748) in response to requests by France, the United Kingdom, and the United States. Those countries sought to force Libya to extradite two Libyan nationals indicted in those countries for the 21 December 1988 bombing of Pan Am Flight 103 over Lockerbie, Scotland, in which 270 persons died, and the bombing of UTA Flight 772 on 19 September 1989 in Niger, in which 171 persons died. On 11 November 1993, the Security Council voted to widen those sanctions (Resolution 883) to include freezing Libyan bank accounts, closing the offices of Libyan Arab Airlines, and prohibiting the supply of materials for construction and maintenance of airports. The sanctions also banned the supply of pumps, turbines, and motors used at export terminals and oil refineries.

On 16 June 1993, the Security Council adopted wide-ranging economic and trade sanctions (Resolution 841) against the military regime in Haiti which had unseated Haitian president Jean-Bertrand Aristide in 1991. President Aristide had been elected to office in a UN-supervised election. The council acted in conjunction with similar sanctions imposed by the Organization of American States. In brief, the Security Council directed members not to sell oil, weapons, ammunition, military vehicles, military equipment, and spare parts to Haiti. In addition, it authorized members to blockade the country to prevent those items from being delivered to Haiti. It also authorized member countries to freeze Haitian funds. The sanctions were briefly lifted when negotiations produced the Governors Island agreement of 3 July 1993, in which the military regime agreed to restore President Aristide with the assistance of a UN peacekeeping mission (called the UN Mission in Haiti or UNMIH). On 11 October 1993 the first deployment of UNMIH was prevented from landing at Port au Prince and the sanctions were reinstated three days later. On 6 May 1994, the Security Council adopted an expansion of sanctions (Resolution 917) against Haiti. Multinational forces were peacefully deployed in Haiti on 19 September 1994, and President Aristide returned shortly thereafter. On 29 September 1994, the Security Council suspended the sanctions (Resolution 944).

On 30 May 1993, in its Resolution 918, the Security Council imposed an arms embargo on Rwanda. It imposed the embargo in an effort to protect its UN Assistance Mission for Rwanda (UNAMIR) and other international humanitarian relief workers, as well as the civilian population, from the rampant lawlessness and violence that had broken out in connection with the resumption of that country's civil war between ethnic Hutu and Tutsi factions. In May 1994, violence broke out between the factions, and killings were widespread. In July 1994, the Security Council established a commission of experts to investigate violations of international humanitarian law (Resolution 935), and an International Tribunal was established on 8 November 1994 (Resolution 955) to prosecute persons responsible for the genocide.

The Security Council's previous reluctance to invoke its ultimate prerogatives is attributable to two main factors. There is a very strong argument that in most cases punitive measures are ineffective and may even harm chances for a peaceful settlement. The provisions on the UN security system make it clear that peace is to be preserved whenever possible without recourse to force. The second major factor is that, before the end of the cold war, one or two of the permanent members would take different positions from the other three or four, so that in most cases the council's sympathies were divided between the opposing parties. Not only did division between the permanent members preclude punitive measures against one side, but it also seriously inhibited definitive action of any kind. For example, the initial action of sending a UN command into Korea was made possible only by

the absence of the USSR from the council at the time (in protest against the council's decision on Chinese representation). Had the Soviet Union been there, it would presumably have vetoed the necessary resolutions. An example of the reverse situation is the issue of South Africa's apartheid policies. Beginning in 1960, the African nations appealed regularly to the Security Council to institute mandatory economic sanctions against South Africa in the hope of forcing it to terminate the apartheid system. The former USSR frequently expressed itself in favor of such a move, but the Western permanent members—in particular, South Africa's major trading partners, the United Kingdom and the United States—were reluctant to impose economic sanctions.

In the post-cold war era of collegiality in the Security Council, the Russian Federation and the United States rarely found themselves on opposite poles of an argument, and imposing sanctions as a method to force other member states to comply with Security Council directives was much easier to accomplish.

Armed Forces for the UN

Although the charter contains provisions to equip the Security Council with armed forces in case of need (the Covenant of the League of Nations contained no such provisions), these requirements have not been implemented. Under the charter, all UN members "undertake to make available to the Security Council, on its call and in accordance with a special agreement or agreements, armed forces, assistance, and facilities, including rights of passage, necessary for the purpose of maintaining international peace and security." These agreements were to determine the number and types of military forces to be provided by the nations, their degree of readiness, their location, and so on, and they were to come into effect only after ratification by the countries concerned according to their respective constitutional requirements. (With this provision in mind, the United States Congress in December 1945 passed the "UN Participation Act," authorizing the president of the United States to negotiate a special agreement with the Security Council on the detailed provision of United States forces; the agreement would then require approval by legislative enactment or joint resolution of the United States Congress.) The troops and weapons would remain part of each country's national military establishment. They would not become international forces, but they would be pledged to the UN and, at the request of the Security Council, would be placed at its disposal.

However, the plan to place armed forces at the disposition of the Security Council required wide international agreement on a number of steps before it could be put into operation. The charter provides for the establishment of a Military Staff Committee composed of the chiefs of staff (or their representatives) of the five permanent members to advise and assist the council on all questions relating to its military requirements. The first task that the council assigned the Military Staff Committee was to recommend the military arrangements to be negotiated with member states. The committee was never able to reach agreed positions that could serve as the basis for negotiation and at an early date took on the characteristics of a vestigial organ.

Peacekeeping

Peacekeeping operations are not mentioned in the charter, yet they, as opposed to enforcement measures, are the means that the Security Council has most frequently used to maintain the peace. It has dispatched observer missions and troops in several crises. (The council's major peacekeeping operations and those undertaken by the General Assembly are described in the chapter on International Peace and Security.) Although the arrangements for the provision of armed forces foreseen in the charter have not been realized, the UN has nevertheless been able to establish peacekeeping forces on the basis of voluntary contributions of troops by member states.

Until the end of the cold war, the formula had always been that the disputants themselves must expressly invite the council to take peacekeeping measures (the special situation of Korea being the only exception—see the chapter on International Peace and Security.) With the eruption of ethnic and nationalistic conflicts in Eastern Europe and Africa after the end of the cold war, the Security Council recognized that the increasing number and complexity of peacekeeping operations warranted review. In May 1993, it requested the Secretary-General to submit a report containing specific new proposals to improve the capacity of the UN in peacekeeping. The Secretary-General submitted his report on "Improving the capacity of the United Nations for peacekeeping" in March 1994. In response to this analysis, on 3 May 1994, the Security Council issued a statement setting forth factors to be considered in establishing UN peacekeeping operations. The factors to be considered in the establishment of new peacekeeping operations included:

- whether a situation exists that presents a threat to international peace and security;
- whether regional or subregional organizations already exist and can assist in resolving the situation;
- whether a cease-fire exists and whether the parties have committed themselves to a peace process intended to reach a political settlement;
- whether a clear political goal exists and whether it can be reflected in the mandate;
- whether a precise mandate for a United Nations operation can be formulated; and
- whether the safety and security of UN personnel can be reasonably insured; in particular, whether the parties to a dispute offer reasonable guarantees of safety to UN personnel.

The council also required an estimate of projected costs for the initial 90 days of a new peacekeeping operation, and for its first six months, and an estimate of the total annual cost, before authorizing any new missions. In the case of mission extensions, it also required estimates of the financial implications.

In both "An Agenda for Peace" (1992) and his March 1994 report, the Secretary-General proposed that a new mechanism had to be developed to enable a quick response to international crises. Under normal circumstances, the process of designing a mission, obtaining commitments for troops and equipment, establishing a budget, and obtaining approval for new peacekeeping missions could take as long as three months. The Security Council welcomed the Secretary-General's proposal to devise stand-by arrangements under which member states would maintain an agreed number of troops and equipment ready for quick deployment. A Stand-by Arrangements Management Unit was established to keep track of units and resources available for this purpose.

SUBSIDIARY ORGANS
Besides supervising peacekeeping operations (listed in the chapter on International Peace and Security), the Security Council also has established various standing committees and ad hoc bodies.

United Nations Special Commission (UNSCOM)
After the UN-sanctioned multinational force repulsed Iraq from Kuwait in April 1991, the Security Council passed Resolution 687 setting forth the terms for an official cease-fire. This resolution led the UN into previously uncharted waters. It required Iraq to "unconditionally accept the destruction, removal or rendering harmless of . . . all chemical and biological weapons and stocks of agents and all ballistic missiles with a range greater than 150 kilometers...." Iraq also was forced to agree to place all its nuclear

weapons materials under the custody of the International Atomic Energy Agency (IAEA). The resolution gave Iraq 15 days to submit a complete inventory of all its weapons of mass destruction.

To verify and implement this condition, the Security Council created the United Nations Special Commission (UNSCOM). Its mandate is to carry out immediate on-site inspections of Iraq's biological, chemical, and missile capabilities; to take possession for destruction, removal, or rendering harmless of all chemical and biological weapons and all materials for research, development, support, and manufacture of such weapons; to supervise the destruction by Iraq of all its ballistic missiles with a range greater than 150km, including major parts, repair, and production facilities; and to monitor and verify Iraq's compliance with its undertaking not to use, develop, construct, or acquire any of the items specified above. UNSCOM also works with inspectors of the IAEA, who are charged with similar tasks in the area of nuclear armaments.

In October 1991, UNSCOM reported to the Security Council that Iraq at first adopted an attitude of noncooperation, concealment, and outright falsification. The Security Council responded with Resolution 707 (1991) condemning Iraq's violation of Resolution 687 and making nine specific demands. In March 1992, Iraq declared that it was no longer in possession of any of the weapons described in Resolution 687, but the Security Council did not accept this. In June 1992, Iraq again supplied what it said were "full, final and complete reports," on the weapons programs covered by Resolution 687. These reports also were considered to be suspect. Using aggressive surprise inspection techniques, UNSCOM and IAEA were able to compile significant information on Iraq's weapons capabilities.

UNSCOM's investigations revealed that Iraq had acquired a massive stockpile of weapons of mass destruction and ballistic missiles. The international community was horrified to learn that Iraq had established a military research program to develop biological weapons that had long been banned by international disarmament agreements (to which Iraq was ostensibly a party). UNSCOM discovered that the microorganisms involved in this research program included anthrax, botulin toxin, and gas gangere. Although no facilities for the production of these biological weapons were found, UNSCOM did discover huge stockpiles of deadly chemical weapons, including warheads, aerial bombs, and artillery shells meant to deliver a variety of nerve gas agents, tear gas, and mustard gas.

IAEA/UNSCOM inspections also revealed three clandestine uranium enrichment programs and found conclusive evidence of a nuclear weapons development program aimed at an implosion-type weapon. The secret development of these materials, bypassing regular inspections by the IAEA, put Iraq in violation of its undertakings as a member of IAEA. The IAEA also found that Iraq had violated its obligations under the Nuclear Non-Proliferation Treaty. By mid-1992 the IAEA had removed and destroyed most of the materials and facilities and forced Iraq to destroy its nuclear complex at al-Athir, where most of the nuclear weapons research had taken place. The IAEA transported Iraq's nuclear fuel to Russia, where it was diluted from weapons grade to civilian reactor quality.

In December 1999, the phase-out of UNSCOM was announced: The Security Council adopted Resolution 1284, establishing the new United Nations Monitoring, Verification and Inspection Commission (UNMOVIC) to assume the responsibilities of monitoring the elimination of weapons of mass destruction in Iraq. UNMOVIC took over UNSCOM's assets, liabilities, and archives and was mandated to "establish and operate a reinforced, ongoing monitoring and verification system, address unresolved disarmament issues, and identify additional sites to be covered by the new monitoring system." At the time, the Council also expressed its intention to suspend and eventually lift sanctions against Iraq once certain conditions were met, including Iraq's demonstration of full cooperation for a period of 120 days. UNMOVIC was still being organized in spring of 2000.

War Crimes

International Criminal Tribunal for the former Yugoslavia (ICTY). Reports of widespread violations of international humanitarian law in the bloody conflict among the states of the former Yugoslavia led the Security Council to establish a Commission of Experts in October 1992. The commission was established to investigate the reports and submit its findings to the Security Council. In January 1993 the commission sent a first report describing the discovery of a mass grave in Croatia, and thousands of allegations of grave breaches of the Geneva Conventions and international humanitarian law. In February 1993, the Security Council adopted Resolution 808, establishing an international tribunal for the prosecution of persons responsible for the crimes discovered by the Commission, the first such tribunal since the war crimes trials conducted after World War II. By May 1993, the Secretary-General had submitted a detailed report to the Security Council setting forth the tribunal's legal basis, method of proceeding, and its statute. It was established as a subsidiary organ of the Security Council under Chapter VII of the charter. Its headquarters would be at The Hague, Netherlands.

On 25 May 1993, the Security Council passed Resolution 827, approving the report and establishing the tribunal "for the sole purpose of prosecuting persons responsible for the serious violations of international humanitarian law committed in the territory of the former Yugoslavia between 1 January 1991 and a date to be determined by the Security Council upon restoration of peace...." The General Assembly elected 11 judges to the tribunal in September 1993. However, it was not until 7 July 1994 that South African judge Richard Goldstone was chosen to lead the prosecution team and he served until 30 September 1996, after which Louise Arbour of Canada became chief prosecutor. As of March 2000, the ICTY president was Claude Jorda (France) and the vice-president was Florence Ndepele Mwachande Mumba (Zambia); presiding judges were David Anthony Hunt (Australia), Richard George May (United Kingdom), and Almiro Simoes Rodrigues (Portugal); and judges were Lal Chand Vohrah (Malaysia), Fouad Abdel-Moneim Riad (Egypt), Mohamed Shahabuddeen (Guyana), Rafael Nieto-Navia (Colombia), Mohamed Bennouna (Morocco), Patrick Lipton Robinson (Jamaica), Patricia Wald (United States of America), Fausto Pocar (Italy), and Liu Daqun (China).

As of April 2000, 39 of the accused were in custody; one, Zejnil Delalic, was released, pending an appeal; state arrest warrants had been issued against all accused and were outstanding on 28 people, including Yugoslav President Slobodan Milosevic; and there were outstanding international arrest warrants for seven of the accused. Proceedings had been completed for four men, all of whom were sentenced to prison terms ranging from several years to 45 years. The heaviest sentence to date had been handed to Tihomir Blaskic, who was found guilty "by virtue of his individual and superior responsibility" on three counts of crimes against humanity, six counts of grave breaches of the Geneva Conventions, and ten counts of violations of the laws or customs of war. Five other cases, involving a dozen of the accused, were in appeals before the chamber; another four cases were ongoing; and ten were in the pre-trial stage. Updates on the proceedings were being posted regularly on the UN's web site at http://www.un.org/icty/index.html.

International Criminal Tribunal for Rwanda (ICTR). On 1 July 1994, the Security Council requested the Secretary-General establish a three-member Commission of Experts to investigate allegations of mass killings of civilians and genocide in Rwanda, during the re-eruption of civil war in that country in April 1994. It had been reported that as many as 250,000 civilians may have died in ethnic violence. On 8 August 1994, the new government of Rwanda, led by members of the Tutsi ethnic group, notified the Secretary-General that it would cooperate with an international war crimes tribunal. The new government hoped that the promise of an international tribunal under the auspices of the UN would allay the fears of hundreds of thousands of ethnic Hutu citizens who were refusing to return to Rwanda from refugee camps in neighboring countries due to fear of reprisals and prosecution by the new government.

On 8 November 1994 the Security Council passed Resolution 955, establishing the tribunal and empowering it to prosecute persons responsible for serious violations of international humanitarian law in Rwanda and Rwandan citizens responsible for such violations committed in neighboring states during 1994.

Following the election of the first judges, the tribunal began its work in November 1995. Progress was initially slow and the tribunal was criticized for incompetence. In 1998 Judge Lennart Aspegren (of Sweden) announced his resignation, protesting bad management and inadequate working conditions. Meanwhile, Rwanda had begun to hold trials of its own. In a press conference held 5 March 1999, Louise Arbour, then chief prosecutor of the UN tribunals for the former Yugoslavia and for Rwanda, told correspondents that the contrast was becoming increasingly dramatic between the remarkable willingness to endorse and support the work of the tribunals on the African continent and the tolerated non-compliance in the case of the states of the former Yugoslavia: Of the 36 accused by the Rwanda Tribunal, 34 had been apprehended, arrested, and transferred by African states to a detention unit at Arusha, Tanzania. This was in dramatic contrast to the lack of cooperation that the tribunal for the former Yugoslavia was experiencing, in which numerous arrest warrants remained outstanding.

As the Rwandan death toll mounted (approaching one million dead), the tribunal pressed on with its work. In 1999 the Security Council appointed Carla Del Ponte (Switzerland) as the tribunal's chief prosecutor; she began work 11 August of that year. In spring 2000, the judges were Navanethem Pillay (Republic of South Africa; president of the ICTR), Erik Møse (Norway), Asoka de Zoysa Gunawardana (Sri Lanka), Laïty Kama (Senegal), William Hussein Sekule (United Republic of Tanzania), Mehmet Güney (Turkey), Lloyd G. Williams (Jamaica and St. Kitts and Nevis), Yakov Arkadievich Ostrovsky (Russian Federation), Pavel Dolenc (Slovenia), Claude Jorda (France), Mohamed Shahabuddeen (Guyana), Lal Chand Vohrah (Malaysia), Rafael Nieto-Navia (Colombia), and Fausto Pocar (Italy).

As of April 2000, 29 indictments had been issued against 50 individuals; a total of 44 individuals were detained under the authority of the tribunal. The tribunal had handed down several judgements, including that of Jean Kambanda, the former prime minister of Rwanda, who pleaded guilty to crimes of genocide, and Jean Paul Akayesu, Georges Anderson Ndrubumwe Rutaganda, Clement Kayishema, and Alfred Musema, who were sentenced to life imprisonment. The Akayesu judgement and the Kambanda sentencing were the first ever by an international court for the crime of genocide. Tribunal updates were being posted on the ICTR's web site at http://www.ictr.org/.

THE ECONOMIC AND SOCIAL COUNCIL

Many of the most outstanding accomplishments of the UN to date are in the economic and social fields. Under Article 55 of the charter, the organization is committed to promote the following goals:

"(a) higher standards of living, full employment, and conditions of economic and social progress and development;

"(b) solutions of international economic, social, health, and related problems; and international cultural and educational cooperation; and

"(c) universal respect for, and observance of, human rights and fundamental freedoms for all without distinction as to race, sex, language, or religion."

The responsibility for UN activities aimed at the achievement of these goals is vested in the General Assembly and, under its authority, the Economic and Social Council.

FIELDS OF ACTIVITY

The activities of the Economic and Social Council, carried out through its subsidiary bodies in cooperation with the specialized agencies, have touched on all aspects of human well-being and affected the lives of people everywhere. A list of the major spheres of activity supervised by the council is given below; the chapters on Economic and Social Development, Technical Cooperation Programs, Social and Humanitarian Assistance, and Human Rights contain further information on matters directly under its purview.

Economic Development. Although this field encompasses both developed and developing nations, emphasis is on the problems of the latter group. The activities of the council include evaluating long-term projections for the world economy; fostering international trade, particularly in commodities, between industrialized and nonindustrialized countries; improving the international flow of private and public capital; promoting industrialization and the development of natural resources; resolving related political and legal issues, such as permanent sovereignty over natural resources and land reform; developing programs of technical cooperation for developing nations; and applying the latest innovations of science and technology to improve the industrialization of developing countries.

Social Progress. Among the social problems handled under the aegis of the council are housing, population, international traffic in narcotic drugs, the welfare of children in the developing countries, and the status of the world's refugees, the aging, and the disabled. Particular attention is paid to the role of women in development.

Human Rights. The council and its subsidiary organs have elaborated a series of important principles for the promotion of fundamental freedoms. Measures include the Universal Declaration of Human Rights and a number of declarations and recommendations on specific rights—for example, the rights of women, freedom of information and the press, and racial equality. The most recent declaration was adopted in Vienna in June 1993, namely, the "Vienna Declaration and Programme of Action."

Related Special Problems. An example of a special problem of interest to the council is the improvement of statistical techniques, since efficient statistics are essential to economic and social development. Work in this field includes techniques to improve world statistics in specific economic branches, such as industry and finance; standards of national statistical services; and methods of comparing statistics from different countries.

Problems Dealt with by the UN Related Agencies. The specialized agencies, the World Trade Organization (WTO), and the International Atomic Energy Agency (IAEA) undertake a wide range of activities in the economic and social fields. It is a function of the council to coordinate these activities. Accounts of each of the related agencies are given in the separate chapters devoted to them.

FUNCTIONS AND POWERS

Under the charter, the council is authorized to make or initiate studies, reports, and recommendations on economic, social, cultural, educational, health, and related matters; to make recommendations to promote respect for, and observance of, human rights; to prepare draft conventions for submission to the General Assembly on matters within its competence; to call international conferences on matters within its competence and in accordance with rules prescribed by the UN; to enter into agreements, subject to the approval of the General Assembly, with specialized agencies; to coordinate the activities of the specialized agencies and obtain regular reports from them; to perform, with the approval of the General Assembly, services at the request of member nations or the specialized agencies; to consult with nongovernmental agencies whose work is related to matters dealt with by the council; to set up subsidiary organs to assist its work; and to perform any other functions that may be assigned to it by the General Assembly.

COMPOSITION

Originally, the Economic and Social Council consisted of 18 members, but the amendments to the charter that came into force on 31 August 1965 raised the number to 27. Another amendment that came into force on 24 September 1973 increased the membership to 54.

When the council was constituted in January 1946, the General Assembly elected the council's first 18 members for staggered terms: 6 members each for one, two, and three years, respectively. Subsequently, all terms were changed to three years, so that each year one-third of the membership is elected by the General Assembly.

The General Assembly resolutions adopting the amendments to the charter that increased the membership of the council also laid down an equitable pattern for the geographical distribution of the additional seats. The 54 members are elected with respect to geographic representation (i.e., to include members from African states, Asian states, Latin American states, Middle Eastern States, and European and other states). Elections are by a two-thirds majority vote on a secret ballot in the General Assembly, and immediate reelection of members is permissible. Although the permanent members of the Security Council have no privileged position on the Economic and Social Council and the charter does not guarantee them membership in the council, it has been the custom to reelect them continuously. In general, the General Assembly has less difficulty in agreeing on its Economic and Social Council selections than in filling Security Council vacancies. Moreover, if, in the opinion of the council, a matter on its agenda is of particular concern to a UN member not represented on the council, it may invite that state to participate in its discussions but without a vote.

In 2000, ECOSOC had the following members: Algeria, Angola, Austria, Bahrain, Belarus, Belgium, Benin, Bolivia, Brazil, Bulgaria, Burkina Faso, Cameroon, Canada, China, Colombia, Comoros, Costa Rica, Croatia, Cuba, Czech Republic, Democratic Republic of the Congo, Denmark, Fiji, France, Germany, Greece, Guinea-Bissau, Honduras, India, Indonesia, Italy, Japan, Lesotho, Mauritius, Mexico, Morocco, New Zealand, Norway, Oman, Pakistan, Poland, Portugal, Russian Federation, Rwanda, Saint Lucia, Saudi Arabia, Sierra Leone, Sudan, Suriname, Syria, United Kingdom, United States, Venezuela, and Vietnam.

PROCEDURE

In 1993, the Economic and Social Council undertook a major restructuring. Whereas it used to hold two sessions each year, one at UN headquarters in the spring and one in Geneva in the summer, it now holds only one substantive (5- to 6-week long) meeting per year in summer, rotating each year between Geneva and New York. A president and four vice-presidents are elected by the council for each year. The council also holds an organizational session in January to plan its program of work for the year.

Each of the 54 members of the council has one vote. The big powers possess no veto or other special voting privilege. A proposal or motion before the council may be adopted without a vote unless a member requests one. When a vote is taken, decisions are carried by a simple majority of the members present.

SUBSIDIARY ORGANS

The council accomplishes its substantive work through numerous subsidiary organs in the form of commissions, committees, and ad hoc and special bodies. In Article 68, the charter specifically states that the council "shall set up commissions in economic and social fields and for the promotion of human rights. . . ." Several types of commissions and other organs have been set up within this provision, including the regional commissions, to deal with economic and social problems in the different geographical areas of the world, and the functional commissions, to handle social, human rights, and environmental questions.

Regional Commissions

There are five regional commissions: the Economic Commission for Europe (ECE); the Economic and Social Commission for Asia and the Pacific (ESCAP); the Economic Commission for Latin America and the Caribbean (ECLAC); the Economic Commission for Africa (ECA); and the Economic and Social Commission for Western Asia (ESCWA). Each has its own staff members, who are considered part of the regular staff of the UN. Regional commission expenditures come out of the regular UN budget. The regional commissions are discussed in the chapter on Economic and Social Development.

Functional Commissions

Since 1946, the council established functional commissions and subcommissions to advise and assist it in its work.

The *Statistical Commission,* with 24 members, assists in developing international statistical services, promoting the development of national statistics and improving their comparability, coordinating the statistical work of the specialized agencies and the central statistical services of the UN Secretariat, and advising the UN organs on general questions relating to the collection, analysis, and dissemination of statistical information.

The *Commission on Population and Development,* with 27 members, studies population changes, including migration, and their effect on economic and social conditions and advises on policies to influence the size and structure of populations and on any other demographic questions on which the UN or its specialized agencies may seek advice.

The *Commission for Social Development,* with 46 members, advises the council on social policies in general and on all matters in the social field not covered by the specialized agencies; it gives priority to the establishment of objectives and programs and to social research in areas affecting social and economic development.

The *Commission on Human Rights,* with 53 members, makes recommendations and prepares reports to the council on human rights questions, including the status of women, the protection of minorities, the prevention of all forms of discrimination, and the implementation of international conventions on human rights. Its various working groups are composed of experts nominated by members to explore problems such as arbitrary detention, involuntary disappearances, and the rights of indigenous peoples.

The Commission on Human Rights has also established working groups on specific human rights questions, including slavery, indigenous populations, minorities, enforced or involuntary disappearances, and mental health detainees. It also encompasses a Subcommission on Prevention of Discrimination and Protection of Minorities.

The *Commission on the Status of Women,* with 45 members, prepares reports on matters concerning the promotion of women's rights in the political, economic, social, and educational fields and makes recommendations to the council on matters requiring immediate attention in the field of women's rights. The commission has established a working group on communications concerning the status of women.

The *Commission on Narcotic Drugs,* with 53 members, advises the council and prepares draft international agreements on all matters relating to the control of narcotic drugs. Over the years, the commission has established five subsidiary bodies. The Subcommission on Illicit Drug Traffic and Related Matters in the Near and Middle East and the Meeting of Heads of National Drug Law Enforcement Agencies (HONLEA), Asia and the Pacific, were the first subsidiary bodies to be established; both were convened for the first time in 1974. The need for similar coordination in other regions of the world led to a global network of HONLEA meetings: the Meeting of HONLEA, Africa, was established in 1985; the Meeting of HONLEA, Latin America and the Caribbean, in 1987; and the Meeting of HONLEA, Europe, in 1990.

The *Commission on Science and Technology for Development.* The United Nations has been concerned with the effects of advances in science and technology to world peace and social development since its inception in 1945 at the dawn of the nuclear era. In 1963 the first United Nations Conference on the Application of Science and Technology for the Benefit of the Less Developed Countries met in Geneva and began to form an agenda for international action. This was followed in 1979 by the United Nations Conference on Science and Technology for Development, held in Vienna, which produced the Vienna Programme of Action. In affirmation of the conference's program, the General Assembly established an Intergovernmental Committee on Science and Technology for Development, open to all states, to draw up policy guidelines, monitor activities within the United Nations system, promote implementation of the Vienna Programme, identify priorities, and mobilize resources. In 1989, on the tenth anniversary of the 1979 Conference, the General Assembly expressed its disappointment with the implementation of the Vienna Programme of Action and eventually decided to transform the Intergovernmental Committee and its subsidiary body, the Advisory Committee on Science and Technology for Development, into a functional commission of ECOSOC (General Assembly Resolution 46/235).

The Commission on Science and Technology for Development met for the first time in May 1993. It has 53 members elected by ECOSOC for a term of four years on the principle of equitable geographic distribution. At its first session, the commission recommended to ECOSOC that it be charged with the following tasks:

(a) assisting the council in providing science and technology policy guidelines and recommendations to member states, in particular developing countries;

(b) providing innovative approaches to improving the quality of coordination and cooperation in the area of science and technology within the United Nations system, with a view to ensuring optimum mobilization of resources;

(c) providing expert advice to other parts of the United Nations systems.

The *Commission on Crime Prevention and Criminal Justice* was established in December 1991 by General Assembly Resolution 46/152. An existing ECOSOC Committee on Crime Prevention and Control was dissolved, and its funds were made available to the new commission, which met for the first time in April 1992. The new commission is charged with developing, managing, monitoring, and reviewing implementation of the Crime Prevention and Criminal Justice Programme created at a Ministerial Meeting held in Versailles, France, in 1991. In addition, it will consult member states on the drafting of a convention on crime prevention and criminal justice. Priority areas of the commission include: national and transnational crime; organized crime; economic crime, including money laundering; the role of criminal law in the protection of the environment; crime prevention in urban areas; and juvenile and violent criminality. The main difference between the former committee and the new commission is that the decisions of the commission will be decisions of the governments, rather than of independent experts. Decisions at this level were considered essential to tackle the problems of drug trafficking, illegal arms sales, terrorism, dumping of industrial waste, and criminal negligence resulting in environmental degradation, corruption, and financial offences.

The *Commission on Sustainable Development.* As a result of the UN Conference on Environment and Development (UNCED) held in Rio de Janeiro in 1992, the council established a new functional commission in February 1993: the Commission on Sustainable Development. The new, 53-member commission began its work of monitoring the implementation of UNCED's Agenda 21 action plan with its first session in New York in June 1993. The commission's mandate includes: monitoring progress towards the UN target of providing 0.7 percent of gross national product of industrialized countries for official development assistance; considering information on the implementation of environmental conventions; and recommending action to the General Assembly. The commission will interact with other UN intergovernmental bodies, regional commissions, and development and financial institutions. A high-level Advisory Board, consisting of eminent persons from all regions of the world, will provide input to the commission and the council through the Secretary-General.

Other Subsidiary Organs

Article 68 of the charter provides that, in addition to the commissions specifically mentioned in the charter, the council should establish "such other commissions as may be required for its functions." With three exceptions, however, the other subsidiary organs created have not been given the name

"commission." Instead, they are called "standing committees" or "expert bodies."

In 2000, ECOSOC had the following standing committees and expert bodies: Committee for Programme and Coordination; Committee for Development Planning; Committee on Non-governmental Organizations; Committee on Natural Resources; Committee on Economic, Social and Cultural Rights; Committee on New and Renewable Sources of Energy and on Energy for Development; United Nations Group of Experts on Geographical Names; Commission on Human Settlements; Meeting of Experts on the United Nations Programme in Public Administration and Finance; Ad Hoc Group of Experts on International Cooperation in Tax Matters; and Committee of Experts on the Transport of Dangerous Goods.

Semiautonomous bodies, which generally report both to the council and to the General Assembly, include the following: International Research and Training Institute for the Advancement of Women (INSTRAW), UN Conference on Trade and Development (UNCTAD), UN Development Program (UNDP), UN Environment Program (UNEP), UN Population Fund (UNFPA), Office of the UN High Commissioner for Refugees (UNHCR), UN Children's Fund (UNICEF), UN Institute for Training and Research (UNITAR), and UN University (UNU). The Joint UN/FAO World Food Program (WFP), however, reports to the council only.

RELATIONS WITH NONGOVERNMENTAL ORGANIZATIONS

The charter empowers ECOSOC to make arrangements to consult with international organizations of private citizens, known as nongovernmental organizations (NGOs) and distinguished from intergovernmental organizations. Consultations with NGOs bring informed opinion other than that of governments and their officials before the council and provide it with a source of special experience and technical knowledge. NGOs granted consultative status are divided into two categories. Those in Category I are organizations with a general interest in the work of the council, and their activities are particularly germane to it and to the UN as a whole. Those in Category II are organizations with an interest in some particular aspect of the work of the council. In May 1987, 35 NGOs were listed in Category I and 299 in Category II. Another 490 were listed on the NGO roster for consultation as the occasion arises. By the late 1990s, more than 100 NGOs were listed in Category I, more than 600 in Category II, and more than 800 were listed on the roster for occasional consultation, for a total of more than 1,500 NGOs in consultative status. All such officially recognized organizations may send observers to the public meetings of the council and its commissions and may submit memoranda for circulation. Representatives of Category I organizations are entitled to participate in council debates and propose items for the agenda. Representatives of Category II organizations may, with the permission of the chair, make oral statements at council meetings.

Consultative status in Category II has been granted to nearly all important international business associations, cooperative societies, farmers' organizations, trade unions, and veterans' organizations; to leading professional groups, such as associations of architects, engineers, lawyers, newspaper publishers and editors, social welfare workers, tax experts, and many others; and to various women's and youth associations. Many associations formed along denominational lines—Greek Orthodox, Jewish, Muslim, Protestant, and Roman Catholic—also have consultative status. Most organizations that enjoy such official UN standing are international, in that they have members in more than one country. An organization whose membership is restricted to one particular country may obtain consultative status in the council only with the consent of the country's government.

The participation of NGOs in the work of the council took a

historic turn during preparations for the Conference on Environment and Development (UNCED) held in 1992 in Rio de Janeiro. More than 1,400 NGOs participated in UNCED, and their contributions to the historic conference were acknowledged to be invaluable. In view of this remarkable participation, the Secretary-General recommended that relevant and competent NGOs be accorded unusual participation in and access to ECOSOC's new functional commission, the Commission on Sustainable Development, which will monitor the progress of implementation of UNCED's Agenda 21 action plan.

Since many delegations expressed the need to transform the United Nations into a forum that was more accessible to NGOs, ECOSOC established a Working Group on the Review of Arrangements for Consultations with Non-Governmental Organizations in 1993. The Working Group held its first session in June 1994 with a mandate to review the arrangements for consultation with nongovernmental organizations, arrangements which had not been revised since they were first adopted by the council in 1968.

In his 1994 *Agenda for Development* Secretary-General Boutros Boutros-Gali noted that NGOs undertake development projects valued at more than US$7 billion annually. He stated: "The time has arrived to bring NGO and United Nations activities into an increasingly productive relationship of consultation and cooperation." In 1996 ECOSOC adopted a resolution regarding consultation with NGOs that recognized the growth of national and regional NGOs, the broadening role of the Committee on Non-Governmental Organizations, and the adoption of standard rules for the participation of NGOs in UN international conferences. ECOSOC recommended that the General Assembly examine the question of participation of NGOs in all areas of work in the UN.

ORGANIZATION OF INTERNATIONAL CONFERENCES

In accordance with a charter provision, the council from time to time calls for international conferences on special world problems falling within its sphere of competence. Thus, in the 1990s, the UN held conferences on such subjects as the environment, population, food, housing, and the status of women. These conferences led to the establishment of the UN Environment Program, the World Food Council, the Center for Human Settlements (Habitat), and other programs and to the adoption of world plans of action for the environment, clean water, population, the aging, the disabled, and other subjects of international concern.

PROPOSED RESTRUCTURING

In his 1992 *Agenda for Peace,* Secretary-General Boutros Boutros-Ghali issued a wide-ranging strategy for the future of the United Nations system, including proposals for changes in ECOSOC. It was suggested that those would reflect changes in the very definition of economic and social progress that had naturally resulted from the dissolution of the former USSR. In addition, a wealth of information now existed on successful and unsuccessful efforts at development, information that in itself called for a fundamental change in the structure of the United Nations so that it could respond more effectively to its members' needs in the area of economic and social development.

In his *Agenda,* the Secretary-General proposed that ECOSOC report to the Security Council on economic and social developments that might pose threats to international peace and security. He also urged the creation of a high-level, intersessional mechanism to enable ECOSOC to react in a timely way to new developments. He also called for lines of communication between the General Assembly and ECOSOC to be clarified and streamlined. In addition, the Secretary-General urged that the relationship between ECOSOC and its subsidiary bodies be redefined. For example, he reported to the General Assembly in 1992 (A/47/434) that members of ECOSOC were frustrated by discussing the same issues four times in the same calendar year: in the council's subsidiary body, in the committee session, in the council plenary, and in the General Assembly.

Intense negotiations occurred during a resumed session of the 47th session of the General Assembly in June 1993. A draft package of reforms was proposed that had as its main aim eliminating duplication of work in the General Assembly and ECOSOC and providing guidelines for a division of labor. For example, it was suggested that the governing bodies of the UN Development Programme (UNDP), UN Population Fund (UNFPA), and the UN Children's Fund (UNICEF) be transformed into smaller executive boards under the overall authority of ECOSOC. Other proposals would have affected the procedures of ECOSOC and would have subsumed the council's two subcommittees (on economic and social issues) into the plenary body.

Although there was clearly a consensus on the need for reform and rationalization, the developing countries (in particular those countries that make up the Group of 77) blocked passage of the package because of concerns over the numerical and regional composition of governing bodies of the different funds and programs of the United Nations. The smallest countries felt that the drastic reduction in representation would exclude them from participation in the decision-making processes of these bodies. In March 1996 Secretary-General Boutros Boutros-Gali emphasized ministerial participation and increasing involvement of the new global leaders for the revitalization of ECOSOC. In July 1996 he noted that ongoing reform efforts produced significant improvements but that ECOSOC's capacity to monitor and coordinate the work of the UN system needed to increase.

THE TRUSTEESHIP COUNCIL

Unlike the other main organs of the UN, the Trusteeship Council was established for the purpose of executing a closely defined system of operations. This is the trusteeship system, which was devised to adapt the League of Nations mandate system to meet the requirements of a new era.

The 1990s witnessed the graduation of the last of the Trusteeship Territories to independence or free association status. This historic achievement represents the official end of colonization as an official political system. In only 50 years the Trusteeship Council presided over the orderly, democratic transfer of power from developed nations to their former colonies.

The Trusteeship Council voted in 1994 to convene only at the request of its President, a majority of its member states, the General Assembly or the Security Council.

THE MANDATE SYSTEM OF THE LEAGUE OF NATIONS

In its political aspect, the history of the world could be read as the history of the creation and disintegration of successive empires, a chain of vicious cause and effect that has brought much bloodshed and wretchedness. After World War I, however, a concerted effort was made for the first time, in a limited way, to break the chain. Recognizing that colonies are a source of friction and jealousy among wealthy nations, the victorious Allies decided not to appropriate for themselves the colonies of their defeated enemies. Instead, those territories belonging to imperial Germany and the Ottoman Empire that were considered unable to function as independent states were placed under international administration supervised by the League of Nations.

The founders of the League created three types of mandates for the administration of these territories by nations acting as "Mandatories of the League of Nations." Class A mandates covered territories that were considered to be ready to receive independence within a relatively short period of time. These territories were all in the Middle East: Iraq, Palestine, and Transjordan, administered by the UK; and Lebanon and Syria, administered by France. Class B mandates covered territories for which the granting of independence was a distant prospect. These territories were all in Africa: the Cameroons and Togoland, each of which was divided between British and French administration; Tanganyika, under British administration; and Ruanda-Urundi, under Belgian administration. To the territories classified under Class C mandates virtually no prospect of self-government, let alone independence, was held out. These territories included South West Africa, administered by the Union of South Africa; New Guinea, administered by Australia; Western Samoa, administered by New Zealand; Nauru, administered by Australia under mandate of the British Empire; and certain Pacific islands, administered by Japan.

The terms of the mandate system implied an acknowledgment of the right of the peoples of the colonial territories belonging to states defeated in war to be granted independence if they were thought to have reached a sufficiently advanced stage of development. However, no provision was made in the League Covenant specifying that the countries designated to administer the mandated territories should take steps to prepare these peoples for eventual self-determination.

THE UN TRUSTEESHIP SYSTEM

Although the Covenant of the League forbade wars of aggression—that is, wars of conquest—the League's founding members did not see the need to underwrite this provision in a positive assertion of the principle of equal rights and self-determination of peoples. The UN Charter embodies an implicit recognition of the belief that denial of equal rights and the right of peoples to self-determination is a potential cause of war.

Thus, Article 1 of the Charter sets forth as a basic purpose of the UN "to develop friendly relations among nations based on respect for the principle of equal rights and self-determination of peoples, and to *take other appropriate measures to strengthen universal peace*" (italics added). Article 76, which sets out the main objectives of the international trusteeship system that was to replace the mandate system of the League, leaves no doubt of the value attached to its role as a means of helping the UN, in the words of the Preamble to the Charter, "to save succeeding generations from the scourge of war." The article reads as follows:

"The basic objectives of the trusteeship system, in accordance with the Purposes of the United Nations laid down in Article 1 of the present Charter, shall be:

"(a) to further international peace and security;

"(b) to promote the political, economic, social, and educational advancement of the inhabitants of the trust territories, and their progressive development towards self-government or independence as may be appropriate to the particular circumstances of each territory and its peoples and the freely expressed wishes of the peoples concerned, and as may be provided by the terms of each trusteeship agreement;

"(c) to encourage respect for human rights and for fundamental freedoms for all without distinction as to race, sex, language, or religion, and to encourage recognition of the interdependence of the peoples of the world; and

"(d) to ensure equal treatment in social, economic, and commercial matters for all Members of the United Nations and their nationals, and also equal treatment for the latter in the administration of justice. . . . "

Thus, in addition to emphasizing the importance of the trusteeship system as an instrument for peace, Article 76 defines the framework for the elaboration of obligations that the countries designated to administer the territories placed under UN trusteeship must undertake toward the peoples concerned. In essence, these obligations amount to a pledge on the part of the administering authorities to work toward the liquidation of the trusteeship system itself by preparing the peoples in trust territories for independence, or at least self-government.

The Trust Territories and Their Administering Authorities

The Charter does not specify the actual territories to be placed under UN trusteeship. Article 77 merely states that the system shall apply to three categories: (1) territories still under mandate, (2) territories "detached from enemy states as a result of the Second World War," and (3) territories voluntarily placed under the system by states responsible for their administration.

On the question of designating the administrators of trust territories, the Charter is equally nonspecific. It states simply that the individual trusteeship agreements shall designate the authority in each case, which may be "one or more states or the Organization itself." The provision that the UN itself may serve as an administering authority is a compromise solution that was adopted when it was decided at the San Francisco Conference to abandon an ambitious plan, originally proposed by China and initially supported by the US, to make the UN directly responsible for the administration of all trust territories.

It was decided that the powers that had administered mandates on behalf of the League of Nations were to conclude agreements with the new world organization and administer the same territories that were still dependent. There was one exception. The Pacific islands, which after World War I had been given to Japan as Class C mandates, were, by a special arrangement embodied in the Charter, classified as a strategic area to be administered by the US under a modified trusteeship.

As a result of agreements worked out by the General Assembly, 11 trust territories were placed under UN trusteeship, and seven countries were designated as administering authorities. These figures exclude the former German colony of South West Africa, which after World War I had been mandated to the Union of South Africa, because South Africa refused to place the territory under UN trusteeship. The distribution of the territories and their respective administering authorities was as follows:

in East Africa: Ruanda-Urundi administered by Belgium, Somaliland by Italy, and Tanganyika by the UK;

in West Africa: Cameroons administered by the UK, Cameroons by France, Togoland by the UK, and Togoland by France;

in the Pacific: Nauru, administered by Australia and on behalf of New Zealand and the UK, New Guinea by Australia, Western Samoa by New Zealand, and the Pacific islands of the Marianas, Marshalls, and Carolines by the US.

In September 1975, when New Guinea acceded to independence, the Trust Territory of the Pacific Islands became the only Territory on the agenda of the Trusteeship Council.

By virtue of a Trusteeship Agreement approved by the Security Council in 1947, the Territory was placed under United States administration as a strategic area under the terms of Article 83 of the Charter. In compliance with the provisions of that Article, the Trusteeship Council reported to the Security Council on all matters concerning the Territory, which was comprised of four entities (Northern Mariana Islands, the Federated States of Micronesia, the Marshall Islands and Palau).

Negotiations on the future political status of the Trust Territory of the Pacific Islands began in 1969. In 1975, the Northern Mariana Islands, in a referendum observed by the Trusteeship Council, chose to become a Commonwealth of the United States. In a series of referendums held in 1983 and duly observed by the Trusteeship Council's Visiting Missions, the Federated States of Micronesia and the Marshall Islands opted for a status of Free Association with the United States, while in Palau, the 75% majority required under its Constitution for the approval of the compact of Free Association with the United States could not be obtained in that and six later referendums.

In 1986, the Trusteeship Council, noting that the "peoples of the Federated States of Micronesia, the Marshall Islands, the Northern Mariana Islands and Palau have established constitutions and democratic political institutions providing the instruments of self governments," recommended an early termination of the Trusteeship Agreement.

In December 1990, the Security Council considered the status of the Trust Territory of the Pacific Islands and adopted, by 14 votes to 1, resolution 683 (1990). By that resolution, the Council determined the objectives of the Trusteeship Agreement had been fully attained with respect to those three entities and that therefore the applicability of the Trusteeship Agreement to them had been terminated. Palau, therefore, remained the only entity under

the 1947 Trusteeship Agreement. The Trusteeship Council at its annual regular sessions continued to review the situation in Palau.

In November, 1993, the Pacific island of Palau, the last of the islands remaining under the Trusteeship Agreement, succeeded in passing a referendum for the approval of the compact of Free Association with the United States. In January 1994, the Council requested the United States and Palau to agree on a date on or about 1 October 1994 for the full entry into force of the Compact of Free Association, and expressed the hope that, in the near future, the Trusteeship Agreement would be terminated by the Security Council (see chapter on Independence of Colonial Peoples).

THE TRUSTEESHIP COUNCIL

The fact that the Trusteeship Council was made a main organ of the UN is evidence of the importance attached to the role of the trusteeship system. The Council's functions, however, are decidedly more limited than those of the other main organs, for it acts, as the case may be, under the direct responsibility of the General Assembly in respect to trusteeships not involving areas designated as strategic or of the Security Council in respect to trusteeships relating to areas designated as strategic. The Charter provisions make it clear that the Trusteeship Council only "assists" the General Assembly and the Security Council in implementing the trusteeship system. It had a purely executive capacity in supervising the day-to-day operations of the system.

Composition

The Charter provides that the Council is to be composed of three groups of members: the countries administering trust territories, permanent members of the Security Council that do not administer trust territories, and a number of other UN members elected for three-year terms by the General Assembly to ensure an equal division between administering and nonadministering countries in the Council.

Until 1960, the Council consisted of 14 members: 7 administering members; 2 permanent nonadministering members; and 5 other nonadministering countries elected for three-year terms by the Assembly. As the various trust territories gained independence, the size and composition of the Council changed. The Assembly decided that after 1968, the Council would be composed only of administering powers and the nonadministering permanent members of the Security Council. On 16 September 1975, when Papua New Guinea, which includes the former trust territory of New Guinea, achieved independence, Australia ceased to be a member of the Council. This change left a membership of five: one administering power, the US, and four nonadministering permanent members of the Security Council—China, France, the USSR (today, the Russian Federation), and the UK.

Procedure

Each member of the Trusteeship Council has one vote. Decisions are made by a simple majority vote. The permanent members of the Security Council have no veto or other special voting privileges. Before 1968, the Council held two regular sessions a year, and afterwards, one. Special sessions may be called on the decision of the majority of the members or at the request of the Security Council or the General Assembly. The president and vice-president are elected at the beginning of each regular session and serve for one year.

Powers

In carrying out its supervisory and administrative functions, the Council was specifically authorized under the Charter to consider reports submitted by the administering authority; to accept petitions and examine thin consultation with the administering authority; to provide for periodic visits to the trust territories at times agreeable to the respective administering authorities; and to formulate a questionnaire on the political, economic, social, and educational progress in each trust territory, which the administering authorities were required to answer.

OPERATION OF THE TRUSTEESHIP SYSTEM

Trusteeship and Strategic Area Agreements

Since trusteeship territories were merely entrusted to the administering authorities, the precise terms of the agreement had to be carefully prescribed for each territory and approved by a two-thirds vote of the General Assembly, or by the Security Council in the case of a strategic area.

Article 82 of the Charter provided that there may be designated in any trusteeship agreement a strategic area or areas, which may include part or all of the trust territory concerned. In such cases, all trusteeship functions of the UN were to be exercised by the Security Council.

In fact, there exists only one strategic area agreement—that concluded between the UN and the US government on the Pacific islands mandated to Japan after World War I. Most of the general provisions of the other trusteeship agreements are included in it, but the right of accessibility to the area is curtailed, and supervision by the UN is made dependent on US security requirements. The US is also authorized to close certain areas for security reasons.

The Role of the Administering Authorities

Administering countries were given full legislative, administrative, and judicial powers over the territories entrusted to them. If they so desired, they could administer the trust territory in conjunction with one of their own colonies. Thus, the trust territory of Ruanda-Urundi was united administratively with the Belgian Congo, and Australia established an administrative union between the trust territory of New Guinea and its own dependency, Papua. However, UN trusteeship territories were never considered to be under the sovereignty of the administering authorities, which governed them only on behalf of the UN.

The Work of the Trusteeship Council

In essence, the work of the Council consists in the exercise of the powers specifically granted to it by the Charter for the purpose of supervising the operation of the trusteeship system and ensuring that the administering authority is carrying out its obligations as laid down by the trusteeship agreement.

The work of the Trusteeship Council has diminished progressively as, one by one, the 11 trust territories either achieved independence or, on being granted self-determination, chose to unite with another independent state.

In November 1993, Palau, the last remaining Trusteeship Territory succeeded in passing a referendum approving a Compact of Free Association with the United States. In January, 1994, at its sixty-first session, the Council requested the United States, in consultation with the Government of Palau, the last remaining Trusteeship Territory, to agree on a date on or about October 1, 1994 for the full entry into force of the Compact of Free Association.

The council considered that the United States had satisfactorily discharged its obligations under the terms of the Trusteeship Agreement and that it was appropriate for that Agreement to be terminated with effect from the date referred to above, as agreed upon by the two Governments.

At that session the Trusteeship Council also amended its rules of procedure 1 and 2, which were replaced by the following:

"The Trusteeship Council shall meet as and where occasion may require, by decision of the Trusteeship Council, or by decision of its President, or at the request of a majority of its members, or at the request of the General Assembly, or at the request of the Security Council acting in pursuance of the relevant provisions of the Charter."

The Trusteeship Council suspended operation on 1 November 1994 after Palau became independent. The Council amended its rules of procedure to drop the obligation to meet annually and agreed to meet as occasion required—by its decision or the decision of its president, or at the request of a majority of its members or the General Assembly or the Security Council. As of spring 2000, the Council remained suspended but there had been no decision by the General Assembly to dissolve it.

THE INTERNATIONAL COURT OF JUSTICE

The International Court of Justice was established at the San Francisco Conference in 1945. It is a successor to and resembles the Permanent Court of International Justice created at the time of the League of Nations, but its competence is wider, because membership in the League did not automatically require a nation to join the Permanent Court. The International Court, however, is a principal organ of the UN, so that all UN members automatically become parties to its statute, which, modeled on that of the Permanent Court, was adopted as an integral part of the Charter. By joining the UN, each country binds itself, in the words of the Charter, "to comply with the decision of the International Court of Justice in any case to which it is a party." If any party to a case violates this obligation, the other party "may have recourse to the Security Council, which may, if it deems necessary, make recommendations or decide upon measures to be taken to give effect to the judgment."

The Charter further provides that nonmembers of the UN may become parties to the statute of the court "on conditions to be determined in each case by the General Assembly upon the recommendation of the Security Council." Two such countries—Nauru and Switzerland—have become parties to the statute in this way.

The rules under which the court is constituted and by which it functions are laid down in the statute and detailed in rules adopted by the court itself. The seat of the court is the Peace Palace at The Hague in the Netherlands, but it can meet elsewhere if it so desires. The judges are bound "to hold themselves permanently at the disposal of the Court."

The court is funded from the regular budget of the UN, to whose members its services are otherwise free of charge.

JUDGES OF THE COURT

The court consists of 15 independent judges, known as "members" of the court. They are elected "from among persons of high moral character" without consideration of nationality, except that no two judges of the same nationality may serve concurrently. They must be persons possessing the qualifications required in their respective countries for appointment to the highest judicial offices or be jurists of recognized competence in international law. No judge of the International Court of Justice may exercise any political or administrative function or engage in any professional occupation. When engaged in the business of the court, judges enjoy diplomatic privileges and immunities. A newly elected judge must "make a solemn declaration in open court that he will exercise his powers impartially and conscientiously." A judge cannot be dismissed except by a unanimous decision of the other judges that "he has ceased to fulfill the required conditions." No such dismissal has ever occurred.

As in any court, a judge may disqualify himself from sitting on a particular case. The statute enumerates certain conditions under which this disqualification is obligatory—for example, if a judge was previously involved in the case as a member of a commission of inquiry.

SIGNIFICANCE OF NATIONALITY OF JUDGES

The statute declares specifically that a judge has the right to sit on a case in which his own country is a party. Furthermore, any country that is a party to a case before the court may add a person to sit as judge on that case if there is not already a judge of its nationality on the court. If there are "several parties in the same interest," they may add only one judge to the bench. Such ad hoc judges are chosen by the respective states themselves and may, or may not, be nationals of the states choosing them.

NOMINATION AND ELECTION OF JUDGES

Two international conferences at The Hague, in 1899 and 1907, contemplated the establishment of a permanent international court, but the conferees were unable to agree on a system for electing judges. They did agree, however, on a convention establishing a Permanent Court of Arbitration. That convention provides that each country that is a party to it shall name four jurists as arbitrators who will be available to consider a concrete matter for international arbitration. When the Permanent Court of International Justice was established after World War I, a solution was found for the difficult problem of electing judges. The legal experts named as potential arbitrators under the Hague convention were given the right to nominate candidates, and the League of Nations elected the judges from among these nominees. This system has in essence been preserved by the UN. To ensure that candidates are not mere government nominees, they are proposed by the groups of jurists already established in the Permanent Court of Arbitration or by similar groups specially constituted in countries not members of that court; no national group may nominate more than four persons, and only two of those may bear the nationality of the group.

The list of candidates so nominated then goes to the UN. To be elected to a judgeship on the court, a candidate must obtain an absolute majority in the Security Council and the General Assembly, both bodies voting independently and simultaneously. If more than one candidate of the same nationality obtains the required votes, the eldest is elected. On these occasions, Nauru and Switzerland, the two nonmembers of the UN that are parties to the statute of the court, vote in the General Assembly. In electing judges to the court, delegates are requested to bear in mind that "the main forms of civilization" and "the principal legal systems of the world" should be represented at all times on the international tribunal.

TERMS OF JUDGESHIPS

Judges are elected for nine years. To stagger the expiration of terms, the terms of five of the judges named in the first election (1946) expired at the end of three years, and the terms of five others at the end of six years, as determined by lot. Hence, five judges are now elected every three years. Reelection is permissible and frequently occurs. Every three years, the court elects its president and vice-president from among the judges. Unless reelected, judges chosen to fill a casual vacancy serve only for the remainder of their predecessor's term.

The composition of the court as of 6 February 2000 was as follows (terms expire on 5 February of the year given in parentheses):

Mohammed Bedjaoui, Algeria (2006)
Carl-August Fleischhauer, Germany (2003)
Gilbert Guillaume, France (2009)

Géza Herczegh, Hungary (2003)
Rosalyn Higgins, United Kingdom (2009)
Shi Jiuyong, China (2003)
Pieter H. Kooijmans, Netherlands (2006)
Abdul G. Koroma, Sierra Leone (2003)
Shigeru Oda, Japan (2003)
Gonzalo Parru-Aranguren, Venezuela (2009)
Raymond Ranjeva, Madagascar (2009)
José Francisco Rezek, Brazil (2006)
Thomas Buergenthal, United States (2006)
Awn Shawkat Al-Khasawneh, Jordan, (2009)
Vladlen S. Vereshchetin, Russian Federation (2006)

Normally, all judges sit to hear a case, but nine judges (not counting an ad hoc judge) constitute a quorum. The statute of the court makes provision for the formation of chambers for summary procedure, for particular categories of cases, or for an individual case. A Chamber for Environmental Matters were established by the court in July 1993. Since 1945, four cases were referred to a chamber—in 1982, 1985, 1987, and 1993. A judgment delivered by a chamber is considered as rendered by the court.

PROCEDURE OF THE COURT

All questions are decided by a majority vote of the judges present. If the votes are equal, the president has the casting, or deciding, vote. The judgments have to be read in open court and are required to state the reasons on which they are based and the names of the judges constituting the majority. Any judge is entitled to append to the judgment a personal opinion explaining his or her concurrence or dissent. All hearings are public unless the court decides, whether at the request of the parties or otherwise, that the public should not be admitted.

Judgments are final and without appeal. An application for revision will be considered by the court only if it is based on the discovery of some decisive fact that at the time of the judgment was unknown to both the court and the party seeking revision. Should a dispute arise concerning the meaning or scope of a judgment, the court shall interpret it at the request of any party.

In order to simplify and expedite recourse to it, the court amended its Rules of Court in 1972. A completely overhauled set of rules, incorporating those amendments, was adopted in 1978.

COMPETENCE AND JURISDICTION OF THE COURT

Only states can be parties in cases before the court. Hence, proceedings may not be instituted by or against an individual, corporation, or other entity that is not a state under international law. However, if certain rules are satisfied, a state may take up a case involving one of its nationals. Thus, the Nottebohm Case (Liechtenstein v. Guatemala), in which a judgment was rendered on 6 April 1955, involved a claim by Liechtenstein in regard to injuries sustained by a German-born, naturalized citizen of Liechtenstein as a result of certain measures that Guatemala had taken during World War II.

All countries that are parties to the statute have automatic access to the court and can refer any case they wish to the court. In addition, the Security Council may recommend that a legal dispute be referred to the court.

Under the Charter, nations are not automatically obliged to submit their legal disputes for judgment. At the San Francisco Conference, it was argued by some that the court should be given compulsory jurisdiction and that UN members should bind themselves to accept the court's right to consider legal disputes between them. This proposal would have meant that if one member filed a case against another member, the court would auto-

matically, and without reference to the second member concerned, have the right to try the case. The proposal was rejected because some delegates feared that such a provision might make the statute unacceptable to their countries. Moreover, it was generally felt that since the disputants in an international court are sovereign states, they should not be summoned against their will to submit to the court's jurisdiction. Thus, the court cannot proceed to adjudicate a case unless all parties to the dispute have consented that it should do so. Such consent comes about mainly in one of the following three ways.

1. There can be a specific agreement between the parties to submit a dispute to the court. This is the simplest method and the one employed in several recent cases. Since the creation of the court, 10 cases have been brought before it in this way.

2. There can be specific clauses contained in treaties and conventions. Many treaties and conventions expressly stipulate that disputes that may arise under them, such as a claim by one country that a treaty has been violated by another country, will be submitted to the court for decision. More than 430 treaties and conventions, including peace treaties concluded after World War II, contain clauses to this effect, a fact which attests to the readiness of countries to agree in advance to accept judicial settlement.

3. There can be voluntary recognition in advance of the compulsory jurisdiction of the court in specified types of disputes. Article 36 of the statute states that all parties to the statute "may at any time declare that they recognize as compulsory ipso facto and without special agreement, in relation to any other state accepting the same obligation, the jurisdiction of the Court in all legal disputes concerning: (a) the interpretation of a treaty; (b) any question of international law; (c) the existence of any fact which, if established, would constitute a breach of an international obligation; (d) the nature or extent of the reparation to be made for the breach of an international obligation."

Such declarations may be made for only a limited period if desired and with or without any conditions, or they may state that they will become operative only when a particular country or number of countries accept the same obligation. The most far-reaching reservation that has been attached to a declaration is the condition that the court must not adjudicate any dispute that the country itself determines to be an essentially domestic matter. In effect, this reservation leaves the country free to deny the court's jurisdiction in most cases in which it might become involved. In general, the practical significance of many of the declarations is severely limited by the right to make conditions. As of March 2000, declarations recognizing the compulsory jurisdiction of the court had been made by 62 states, with a number of them excluding certain categories of dispute.

The jurisdiction of the court therefore comprises all legal disputes which the parties to the statute refer to it and all matters specifically provided for in the UN Charter or in treaties and conventions in force. In the event of a dispute as to whether the court has jurisdiction, the statute provides that the matter shall be decided by the court. Article 38 of the statute requires that in deciding the disputes submitted to it, the court shall apply the following: (1) international conventions establishing rules recognized by the contesting states; (2) international custom as evidence of a general practice accepted as law; (3) the general principles of law recognized by civilized nations; and (4) judicial decisions and teachings of the most highly qualified publicists of the various nations as a subsidiary means for determining the rules of law. In certain cases, however, if the parties concerned agree, the court may decide a case *ex aequo et bono*—that is, by a judgment in equity taken simply on the basis of what the court considers is right and good.

ADVISORY OPINIONS

The Charter provides that the General Assembly and the Security Council may request the court to give an advisory opinion on any legal question and that other UN organs and specialized agencies, when authorized by the General Assembly, may also request advisory opinions on legal questions arising within the scope of their activities. In such cases, the court does not render a judgment but provides guidance for the international body concerned. Thus, advisory opinions by their nature are not enforceable, and, although the bodies may receive them with respect, they may not necessarily find it politic to act on them. In some cases, however, the requesting body will be committed to abide by the court's decision.

EXTRAJUDICIAL FUNCTIONS OF THE COURT

Many international conventions, treaties, and other instruments confer upon the International Court of Justice or its president the function of appointing umpires or arbitrators in certain eventualities. Furthermore, even when no treaty provision to this effect exists, the court or individual judges may be requested to carry out functions of this nature.

Review of the Role of the Court

In 1970, citing the relative lack of activity of the court, nine member states sponsored a General Assembly agenda item on a review of the role of the court. In an explanatory memorandum, they noted that the situation at that time was "not commensurate with either the distinction of the judges or the needs of the international community." Proposals for remedying the situation included a revision of the court's statute and rules of procedure, the appointment of younger judges and/or shorter terms of office, and wider acceptance of the court's compulsory jurisdiction.

The subject was debated at four subsequent sessions of the General Assembly, culminating in the adoption in 1974 of a resolution designed to strengthen the role of the court. The recommendations included the possible insertion of clauses in treaties that would provide for submission to the court of disputes arising from differences in their interpretation or application; acceptance of the compulsory jurisdiction of the court with as few reservations as possible; and greater recourse to the court by UN organs and specialized agencies for advisory opinions.

SURVEY OF COURT PRACTICE

Since the court's inauguration in 1946, states have submitted more than 100 legal disputes to it, and international organizations have requested 24 advisory opinions.

LEGAL DISPUTES

Of the cases submitted to the court by states, some were withdrawn by the parties or removed from the list for some other reason. In still others, the court found that, under its statute, it lacked jurisdiction. The remaining 69 cases on which the court has rendered judgment encompassed a wide range of topics, including sovereignty over disputed territory or territorial possessions, the international law of the sea, and commercial interests or property rights either of states or of private corporations and persons. (Examples of these types of disputes are given in the case histories below.)

Many of the cases, including some that fall into the three categories just described, involve differences in interpretations of specific bilateral or multilateral treaties and other legal instruments. Thus, in the case of the rights of US citizens in Morocco (France v. US), the court found, on 27 August 1952, that the prohibition of certain imports into Morocco had violated US treaty rights.

However, it rejected the US claim that its citizens were not subject in principle to the application of Moroccan laws unless they had received the US's prior assent.

ADVISORY OPINIONS

The 24 advisory opinions requested by the General Assembly, Security Council, or authorized specialized agencies likewise have dealt with a variety of matters. The court, on 16 October 1975, rendered an opinion in response to a request made by the General Assembly at its 1974 session. The question concerned Western Sahara, which was passing from Spanish administration. Morocco, Mauritania, and Algeria, all bordering states, took conflicting positions on ties of sovereignty that might have existed before the territory came under Spanish administration. The court concluded that no ties of territorial sovereignty between Western Sahara and the Kingdom of Morocco or the Mauritanian entity had existed. In the decolonization of the territory, therefore, the principle of self-determination through the free expression of the will of its people should apply in accordance with the relevant General Assembly resolution.

Another opinion concerned the question of whether the costs of the peacekeeping operations in the Middle East and the Congo could, within the scope of Article 17 of the Charter, be regarded as expenses of the organization to be financed by contributions of member states, as assessed by the General Assembly. In its opinion, issued on 20 July 1962, the court concluded that the expenses of both operations could be regarded as expenses of the UN within the meaning of Article 17 of the Charter.

Recent advisory opinions were rendered in July 1996 in response to a request made by the World Health Organization on the Legality of the Use by a State of Nuclear Weapons in Armed Conflict; and a request made by the UN General Assembly on the Legality or Use of Nuclear Weapons.

CASES PENDING

As of March 2000, 24 cases were pending:

1. Maritime Delimitation and Territorial Questions between Qatar and Bahrain (Qatar v. Bahrain)

2–3. Questions of Interpretation and Application of the 1971 Montreal Convention arising from the Aerial Incident at Lockerbie (Libyan Arab Jamahiriya v. United Kingdom; Libyan Arab Jamahiriya v. United States of America)

4. Oil Platforms (Islamic Republic of Iran v. United States of America)

5. Application of the Convention on the Prevention and Punishment of the Crime of Genocide (Bosnia and Herzegovina v. Yugoslavia)

6. Gabcikovo-Nagymaros Project (Hungary/Slovakia)

7. Land and Maritime Boundary between Cameroon and Nigeria (Cameroon v. Nigeria)

8. Sovereignty over Pulau Ligitan and Pulau Sipadan (Indonesia/Malasia)

9. Ahmadou Sadio Diallo (Republic of Guinea v. Democratic Republic of Congo)

10. LaGrand (Germany v. United States of America)

11–18. Legality of Use of Force (Yugoslavia v. Belgium; Yugoslavia v. Canada; Yugoslavia v. France; Yugoslavia v. Germany; Yugoslavia v. Italy; Yugoslavia v. Netherlands; Yugoslavia v. Portugal; Yugoslavia v. United Kingdom)

19–21. Armed activities on the territory of the Congo (Democratic Republic of Congo v. Burundi; Democratic Republic of Congo v. Uganda; Democratic Republic of Congo v. Rwanda)

22. Application of the Convention on the Prevention and Punishment of the Crime of Genocide (Croatia v. Yugoslavia)

23.   Aerial Incident of 10 August 1999 (Pakistan v. India)
24.   Maritime Delimitation between Nicaragua and Honduras in the Caribbean Sea (Nicaragua v. Honduras)

SOME CASE HISTORIES OF DISPUTES SUBMITTED TO THE COURT

Disputes over Territorial Claims and Territorial Possessions

In the Case Concerning Sovereignty over Certain Frontier Land (Belgium v. Netherlands), the court traced developments that had begun before the 1839 separation of the Netherlands from Belgium, and in its judgment, on 20 June 1959, it decided that sovereignty over the disputed plots belonged to Belgium.

In a dispute regarding sovereignty over certain islets and rocks lying between the British Channel island of Jersey and the French coast, the Minquier and Ecrehos Islands Case, the UK and France invoked historical facts going back to the 11th century. The UK started its argument by claiming title from the conquest of England in 1066 by William, Duke of Normandy. France started its argument by pointing out that the dukes of Normandy were vassals of the king of France and that the kings of England after 1066, in their capacity as dukes of Normandy, held the duchy in fee from the French kings. The court decided, on 17 November 1953, that "the sovereignty over the islets and rocks of the Ecrehos and Minquier groups, insofar as these islets and rocks are capable of appropriation, belongs to the United Kingdom."

In 1980, in a case brought by the United States concerning the seizure of its embassy in Teheran and the detention of its diplomatic and consular staff, the court held that Iran must release the hostages, hand back the embassy and make reparations. However, before the court fixed the amount of reparation, the case was withdrawn following agreement reached between the parties.

In the first frontier dispute between two African states, by a special agreement Burkina Faso and Mali submitted to a chamber of the court in October 1983 the question of the delimitation of part of the land frontier between them. In January 1986, the court ordered interim measures of protection in order to restore peace between the two states following armed hostilities at the end of 1985. The court gave its final judgment in December 1986, establishing the coordinates for the delimitation of the frontier.

In 1984, Nicaragua alleged that the United States was using military force against it and intervening in its internal affairs. The United States denied that the court had jurisdiction. After written and oral proceedings, the court found, however, that it had jurisdiction and that Nicaragua's application was admissible. The United States refused to recognize either this ruling or the subsequent 1986 judgment in which the court determined that the United States had acted in breach of its obligations toward Nicaragua, must desist from the actions in question, and should make reparation. The request by Nicaragua that the court determine the form and amount of reparation was withdrawn in 1991.

In a case between Libya and Chad, the two countries submitted to the court a territorial dispute relating to the Aozou Strip in the Sahara. Libya's claim as made in the case extended far to the south of that strip of land. The court, in a judgment of 3 February 1994, found wholly in favor of Chad. After an agreement on the implementation of the judgment had been concluded between the two parties, Libyan forces, monitored by an observer force deployed by the Security Council, withdrew from the Aozou strip by 31 May 1994.

Disputes Relating to the Law of the Sea

The Corfu Channel Case (UK v. Albania), the first case decided by the court, was brought before it at the suggestion of the Security Council. On 22 October 1946, two UK destroyers passing through the Corfu channel off the Albanian coast struck mines whose explosion caused the death of 46 seamen and damage to the ships. The British thereupon mineswept the channel. Albania claimed that it had not laid the mines. The court found Albania "responsible under international law for the explosions . . . and for the damage and loss of human life that resulted therefrom" and determined the compensation due to the UK at £843,947, equivalent to approximately US$2.4 million at that time. The court also found that the British mine-sweeping activities in Albanian territorial waters had violated international law. The unanimous rejection by the court of the British claim that the action was justified under the principle of "self-protection" constituted the first judicial finding that the use of force for self-help is in certain circumstances contrary to international law.

In 1981, Canada and the US submitted to a chamber of the court a question as to the course of the maritime boundary dividing the continental shelf and fisheries zones of the two countries in the Gulf of Maine area. In its judgment of 12 October 1984, the chamber of the court established the coordinates of that boundary. On 3 June 1985, the court delivered a judgment in a dispute relating to the delimitation of the continental shelf between Libya and Malta that had been referred to the court in 1982 by means of a special agreement specifically concluded for that purpose. On 14 June 1993, the court delivered a judgment in a maritime delimitation dispute between Denmark and Norway.

Disputes Involving Commercial Interests and Property Rights

The Anglo-Iranian Oil Co. Case grew out of a law passed by Iran on 1 May 1951, terminating the concessions of the Anglo-Iranian Oil Co. and expropriating the company's refinery at Abadan, the largest in the world. On 5 July, the court ordered important "interim measures" enjoining the two governments to refrain from any action that might aggravate the dispute or hinder the operation of the company. The company was to continue under the same management as before nationalization, subject to such modification as agreed to by a special supervisory board, which the court requested the two governments to set up. A year later, however, on 22 July 1952, the court, in its final judgment, ruled that it lacked jurisdiction and lifted the "interim measures." The court found that the 1933 agreement, which gave the Iranian concession to the Anglo-Iranian Oil Co. and which the UK claimed had been violated by the act of nationalization, was merely a concessionary contract between Iran and a foreign corporation. The court ruled that the interpretation of such a contract was not one of the matters in regard to which Iran had accepted the compulsory jurisdiction of the court. The controversy was settled by negotiations in 1953, after the Mossadegh regime in Iran had been replaced by another government.

The Barcelona Traction Case (Belgium v. Spain) arose out of a 1948 adjudication by a provincial Spanish law court of the bankruptcy of a company incorporated in Canada with subsidiaries operating in Barcelona. Belgium was seeking reparation for damages alleged to have been sustained by Belgian shareholders in the company as a result of the Spanish court's adjudication, which Belgium claimed was contrary to international law. The court, on 5 February 1970, found that the Belgian government lacked the standing to exercise diplomatic protection of Belgian shareholders in a Canadian company with respect to measures taken against that company in Spain.

(The complete text of all of the Court's decisions—from 1946 up to the present date—can be accessed at the ICJ's web site at www.icj-cij.org/icjwww/idecisions.htm.)

THE SECRETARIAT

CHARTER REQUIREMENTS

The charter lays down very few requirements governing the establishment of the sixth main organ of the UN—the Secretariat. Such requirements as are specified, in Chapter XV, may be conveniently listed under the following headings.

Composition. The charter states simply: "The Secretariat shall comprise a Secretary-General and such staff as the Organization may require."

Appointment of Staff. With regard to the Secretary-General, the charter stipulates that the person to hold the position "shall be appointed by the General Assembly upon the recommendation of the Security Council." In other words, the Security Council first must agree on a candidate, who then must be endorsed by a majority vote in the General Assembly. The other members of the Secretariat are to be appointed by the Secretary-General "under regulations established by the General Assembly." The charter stipulates that the "paramount consideration" in the employment of staff "shall be the necessity of securing the highest standards of efficiency, competence, and integrity." However, to this consideration is added an important rider—namely, that "due regard shall be paid to the importance of recruiting the staff on as wide a geographical basis as possible."

Functions of the Secretariat. The duties of the general staff are not specified beyond an instruction that an appropriate number shall be permanently assigned to the Economic and Social Council and the Trusteeship Council and, "as required, to other organs of the United Nations." With respect to the functions of the Secretary-General, the charter states only that he shall be "the chief administrative officer of the Organization," shall "act in that capacity" at all meetings of the General Assembly and the three councils, and shall also perform "such other functions as are entrusted to him by these organs." Apart from these general requirements, the charter accords the Secretary-General one specific duty and one specific power: to make an annual report to the General Assembly on the work of the organization, and he has the right to bring to the attention of the Security Council any matter that "in his opinion may threaten the maintenance of international peace and security."

The single restriction on the Secretariat is that "in the performance of their duties the Secretary-General and the staff shall not seek or receive instructions from any government or from any other authority external to the Organization," and that "they shall refrain from any action which might reflect on their position as international officials responsible only to the Organization." As a corollary to this injunction, the charter puts member nations under the obligation to "respect the exclusively international character of the responsibilities of the Secretary-General and the staff and not to seek to influence them in the discharge of their responsibilities."

APPOINTMENT OF THE SECRETARY-GENERAL

Since the charter does not specify the qualifications for Secretary-General and the term of office, these decisions had to be made by the first General Assembly, in January 1946. It was agreed that, in making its recommendations to the General Assembly, the Security Council should conduct its discussions in private and vote in secret, for the dignity of the office required avoidance of open debate on the qualifications of the candidate. The General Assembly also decided that the term of office would be five years (the Secretary-General of the League of Nations was elected for 10 years) and that the Secretary-General would be eligible for reappointment.

The permanent members of the Security Council have tacitly agreed that the Secretary-General should not be a national of one of their own countries.

STRUCTURE AND COMPOSITION OF THE SECRETARIAT

The Secretariat services the other organs of the UN and administers the programs and policies laid down by them. As the scope and range of UN activities have widened, the staff of the Secretariat has increased in number and its organizational pattern has increased in complexity. The major elements of the Secretariat, variously designated as offices, departments, programs, conferences, and the like, are headed by officials of the rank, but not necessarily the title, of undersecretary-general or assistant secretary-general. In 1987 there were 48 officials at those two levels in the Secretariat.

As the United Nations grew from its original 51 members in 1945 to 188 members in 2000, the Secretariat necessarily changed and evolved. Between 1945 and 1994 major reform of the Secretariat's structure was undertaken five times: 1953–56; 1964–66; 1974–77; 1985–86; and 1992–94. The latest round of restructuring was requested by the General Assembly in numerous resolutions beginning in 1988 (41/213; 44/200; 45/254; 46/232, and 47/212A). Secretary-General Boutros Boutros-Ghali began the restructuring process upon his entry into office in January 1992. In 1991 there were 48 high-level posts (1 director general, 26 undersecretary-generals, 20 assistant secretary-generals) reporting directly to the Secretary-General, by the 1996–1997 biennium that number had been reduced to 21 undersecretary-generals and 15 assistant secretary-generals for a total of 36. In October 1996, the activities of the Secretariat were organized in the following departments:

The Department of Political Affairs (DPA). The functions of five previous offices and units were integrated into the DPA. The department oversees the organization's efforts in preventive diplomacy and peacemaking, collects and analyzes information to alert the General Assembly and Security Council of impending crises, and carries out mandates handed down by the General Assembly and Security Council. DPA provides secretariat services to both bodies. It also provides electoral assistance to countries requesting help in strengthening the democratic process.

The Department of Peacekeeping Operations (DPKO). This department supervises the operations of the United Nations peacekeeping missions around the world. The work of the United Nations in this area has grown exponentially in size and complexity since the end of the cold war. In December 1991, peacekeeping missions involved approximately 11,000 troops and 4,000 civilian personnel with a combined budget of us$500 million. At its peak in 1995 (when UN peacekeeping personnel were heavily deployed in the former Yugoslavia), the Department of Peacekeeping Operations was supervising approximately 70,000 military and civilian personnel, whose annualized budgets approached US$3 billion. In the reorganization, the Field Operations Division, which had been part of the Department for Administration and Management, was transferred to its main client, the Department of Peacekeeping Operations. The annual budget was subsequently reduced to about US$1 billion.

The Department of Humanitarian Affairs (DHA). From September 1992 to April 1996, the UN launched 64 consolidated inter-agency appeals for humanitarian assistance seeking some US$11 billion in relief programs. To handle the increasing number of emergencies the organization's membership requested it to manage, the Secretary-General created the Department of Humanitarian Affairs, incorporating the functions of the UN Disaster Relief Office (UNDRO) and 11 other units of the Secretariat. Two new units were created: the Complex Emergencies Branch and the Inter-Agency Support Unit. The DHA works to improve the delivery of humanitarian assistance to victims of disasters and other emergencies. It also acts as an advocate for humanitarian activities being considered by intergovernmental bodies. It was designed to provide quick needs assessments, field situation analyses, and early negotiations on access to emergency situations. A major feature of this department is interagency coordination that allows all the organizations of the UN system to make consolidated appeals for humanitarian assistance and to better track contributions from donor governments, UN agencies, and nongovernmental organizations.

The Department for Policy Coordination and Sustainable Development (DPCSD). This department provides support for the Economic and Social Council and the General Assembly's Second Committee (economic and financial matters) and Third Committee (social, humanitarian, and cultural matters). It is responsible for the follow-up to the long-term mandates on promoting sustainable development (known as Agenda 21) handed down by the UN Conference on Environment and Development. It also incorporates the activities of the previously Vienna-based Centre for Social Development and Humanitarian Affairs and the Rome-based World Food Council secretariat. One of DPCSD's main jobs is to promote cooperation with the many nongovernmental organizations that wish to contribute to the work of the organization in economic, social and environmental fields.

The Department of Economic and Social Information and Policy Analysis (DESIPA). This department provides support to the Statistical and Population Commissions of ECOSOC. It is the focal point for economic and social analysis of information about population and statistics. It handles technical cooperation activities in the areas of statistics and population. In addition, it makes projections and identifies emerging issues requiring attention by the international community. DESIPA serves as the lead unit in economic and social information and cooperates closely with the World Bank and the International Monetary Fund (IMF).

The Department of Development Support and Management Services (DDSMS). This department has a two-part mandate. It acts as an executing agency for development projects in the fields of natural resources and energy planing, governance and public management, financial management and accounting, focussing attention on the needs of the least developed countries and the countries of the former Soviet Union (often referred to as "economies in transition"). Its second mandate is to be the focal point for implementing technical cooperation management services.

The Department of Public Information (DPI). Under the reorganization, the Dag Hammarskjöld Library and the publishing services of the organization were transferred from the Office of Conference Services to DPI. The department, which creates press releases, publications, and radio and video programs publicizing the work of the organization, also took on the activities that had been handled by the former Office of the Spokesman for the Secretary-General. Many of DPI's field offices were integrated into the field offices of the UN Development Programme (UNDP) for substantial savings. DPI's work was facilitated by the installation of an electronic mail system connecting peacekeeping missions, information centers and UNDP offices—increasing headquarters' contact with its far-flung staff.

The Department of Administration and Management (DAM). This department has four offices: the Office of Programme Planning, Budget and Accounts; the Office of Human Resources Management; the Office for Conference and Support Services; and the Financial Management Office.

The Office of Internal Oversight Services (OIOS). In August 1993, the Secretary-General announced the creation of a new Office of Inspections and Investigations, headed by an assistant secretary-general, which would incorporate various former units of the DAM dealing with audit, management advisory services, evaluation, and monitoring. In July 1994, the General Assembly strengthened the office, and changed its name to the Office of Internal Oversight Services (resolution A/218B [29 July 1994]). The General Assembly stipulated that the head of the new office, at the level of undersecretary-general, should be an expert in the fields of accounting, auditing, financial analysis and investigations, management, law, or public administration. It further stipulated that the individual should serve only one five-year term, and that the post would not be subject to geographical distribution limits. The watchdog office was given wider independence to investigate possible fraud and abuse within the organization. It is assisted in its task by the Integrated Management Information System (IMIS), a major hardware and software upgrade that allows greater monitoring and audit capabilities through electronic audit trails. The creation of this office had long been sought by industrialized countries concerned that their contributions to the United Nations were being wasted by fraud and abuse.

Each of the above departments is headed by an undersecretary-general, with the exception of the Department for Political Affairs (DPA) which is headed by two undersecretaries-general whose responsibilities are divided geographically.

The Office of Legal Affairs (OLA). This office advises the organization and the Secretary-General on legal matters. For example, the OLA has provided advice on numerous activities related to the International Criminal Tribunals for the former Yugoslavia and for Rwanda. Under the 1992 reorganization, it also assumed responsibility for the Office for Ocean Affairs and Law of the Sea. The OLA also provides a range of advice and assistance on issues relating to treaty law and technical aspects of treaties.

Besides the above departments, the Centre for Human Rights, formerly a division, had its activities greatly expanded by a series of new mandates by the General Assembly, ECOSOC, the Commission on Human Rights, and expert groups in the human rights field. It is the principal entity of the UN Secretariat dealing with human rights issues, and is responsible for supervising the ratification and implementation of the international human rights agreements. The Secretary-General, in his 1993 report (A/48/428), stated that the activities of the Centre for Human Rights were evolving from standard-setting to furthering the implementation of a universal culture of human rights. The center is responsible for following up the recommendations of the Second World Conference on Human Rights held in Vienna in June 1993. Recognizing this, the 47th session of the General Assembly authorized additional financial resources for the center. The center is headed by an assistant secretary-general who reports directly to the Secretary-General.

Directly below the ranks of undersecretary-general and assistant secretary-general are directors of main subdepartments and chiefs of specific bureaus within the major organizational units. Below them is the professional staff: personnel with qualifications

ORGANIZATIONAL STRUCTURE OF THE UNITED NATIONS SECRETARIAT

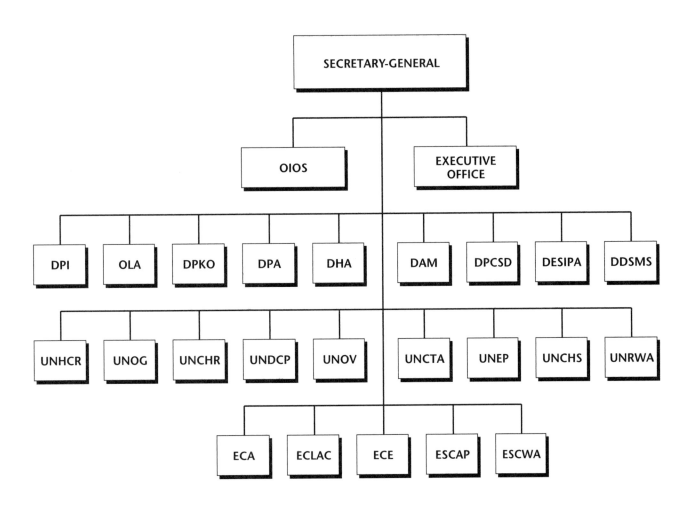

LISTING OF KEY ORGANIZATIONAL UNITS

OIOS	Office of Internal Oversight Services
DPI	Department of Public Information
OLA	Office of Legal Affairs
DPKO	Department of Peace-keeping Operations
DPA	Department of Political Affairs
DHA	Department of Humanitarian Affairs
DAM	Department of Administration and Management
DPCSD	Department for Policy Coordination and Sustainable Development
DESIPA	Department for Economic and Social Information and Policy Analysis
DDSMS	Department for Development Support and Management Services
UNHCR	Office of the United Nations High Commissioner for Refugees
UNOG	United Nations Office at Geneva
UNCHR	United Nations Centre for Human Rights

UNDCP	United Nations International Drug Control Programme
UNOV	United Nations Office at Vienna
UNCTAD	United Nations Conference on Trade and Development
UNEP	United Nations Environment Programme
UNCHS	United Nations Centre for Human Settlements
UNRWA	United Nations Relief and Works Agency for Palestinian Refugees in the Near East
ECA	Economic Commission for Africa
ECLAC	Economic Commission for Latin America and the Caribbean
ECE	Economic Commission for Europe
ESCAP	Economic and Social Commission for Asia and the Pacific
ESCWA	Economic and Social Commission for Western Asia

as administrators, specialists, technical experts, statisticians, translators, editors, interpreters, and so on. Staff in the category of general services include administrative assistants, clerical workers, secretaries, typists, and the like. Manual workers, such as building maintenance staff, are separately classified.

Personnel at the professional level and above are recruited in the various member countries of the UN and, when serving outside their own country, are entitled to home-leave travel, repatriation grants, and related benefits. General service personnel include a number of nationalities, but they are recruited locally and are not selected according to any principle of geographical representation. The majority of general service staff employed at UN headquarters are US citizens.

Organizational Distribution of Staff
In 2000, the global work force stood at 8,700 posts, down from 12,205 in 1984–85. Some posts currently are being kept vacant as a result of the General Assembly's decision to increase vacancy rates.

Problems of Staff Appointment According to Equitable Geographical Distribution
All UN senior staff members are appointed by the Secretary-General under regulations established by the General Assembly. Some of the appointments, such as the UN High Commissioner for Refugees, are subject to confirmation by the General Assembly. Staff recruitment, in general, is handled by the Office of Personnel, salary scales and other conditions of employment being determined by the General Assembly.

UN member governments attach great importance to having a fair proportion of their nationals employed in the Secretariat. The 1962 General Assembly recommended that in applying the principle of equitable geographical distribution, the Secretary-General should take into account members' financial contributions to the UN, the respective populations of the member countries, the relative importance of posts at different levels, and the need for a more balanced regional composition of the staff at the director level. It further recommended that in confirming permanent contracts (UN staff are initially hired on the basis of one-year contracts), particular account should be taken of the need to reduce underrepresentation of some member states. By the end of June 1996, the proportion of posts subject to geographical distribution stood at 35.1%.

The 1975 General Assembly reaffirmed previously defined aims for UN recruitment policy and mentioned the following specifically: development of an international civil service based on the highest standards of efficiency, competence, and integrity; equitable geographic distribution, with no post, department, or unit to be regarded as the exclusive preserve of any member state or region; the recruitment of a greater number of qualified women for professional and senior-level posts; and the correction of imbalances in the age structure of the Secretariat.

One of the United Nations' most disturbing lapses relates to the status of women within the organization's own secretariat. The equality of men and women is a principle enshrined in the UN charter. However, while more than half of the Secretariat's general service (nonprofessional) posts are filled by women, until the 1990s, few women were appointed to the highest levels of management. No woman has even been seriously considered for the position of Secretary-General. The General Assembly called in 1978 for an increase in the number of women in posts at the professional level to 25% of total staff. The Secretary-General reported in 1987 that the number of women in the professional and higher categories had increased to 25.7% of the total, com-

pared to 17.9% in 1977. In 1985, at the end of the United Nations Decade for Women, the number of women in professional posts (designated as P-1, P-2, P-3, P-4, P-5, D-1 and D-2) had risen to 29%. However, women held only 8% of the highest administrative posts (director level, including assistant secretary-general and undersecretary-general; designated D-1 and D-2). In response, the General Assembly raised its goal for women to 35% of all professional level posts, with 25% in the senior, D-level posts by 1995. Some of the United Nations' semiautonomous subsidiary bodies already achieved progress in equitable gender representation in their own secretariats. The United Nations Population Fund (UNFPA) reported in 1992 that 43% of its professional posts were occupied by women and set a goal of 50% of professional posts to be filled by women by the year 2000. UNICEF, which had women in 24.6% of its professional posts in 1986, increased that level to 35% in 1992. By June 1996, women accounted for 17.9% of the high level posts, and had received 40.3% of promotions within the last year. In 1992, in an effort to further strengthen the position of all women in the Secretariat, the first guidelines on sexual harassment were issued.

The International Civil Service Commission, established by the General Assembly in 1972, is responsible for making recommendations to that body for the regulation and coordination of service within the UN, the specialized agencies, and other international organizations that are part of the UN system. The commission is composed of 15 independent experts, appointed in their individual capacities for four-year staggered terms.

THE EVOLVING ROLE OF THE SECRETARIAT
The UN's administrative arm has developed largely in accordance with the demands made upon it. In the process, it has evolved a distinctive character of its own, in keeping with its status as a constitutionally defined organ of the world body.

The Secretary-General has played the most significant part in shaping the character of the Secretariat. As chief administrative officer, the Secretary-General has wide discretionary powers and latitude to administer as he thinks fit. As Eleanor Roosevelt, a former chairman of the UN Commission on Human Rights, noted in 1953, the Secretary-General, "partly because of the relative permanence of his position (unlike the president of the General Assembly who changes every year) and partly because of his widely ramified authority over the whole UN organization, tends to become its chief personality, its embodiment and its spokesman to the world."

Each Secretary-General strives to develop and maintain the positive functions of the Secretariat. Although each has had his own views on the role of the office, all have shared the belief that the Secretariat is the backbone of the UN system. The most eloquent statement of that belief was probably made by Dag Hammarskjöld in an address at the University of California in 1955: ". . . the United Nations is what member nations made it, but within the limits set by government action and government cooperation, much depends on what the Secretariat makes it." In addition to the Secretariat's function of providing services and facilities for governments in their capacity as members of the UN, he said, the Secretariat also "has creative capacity. It can introduce new ideas. It can, in proper forms, take initiatives. It can put before member governments findings which will influence their actions." Stressing the fact that members of the Secretariat serve as international officials rather than as government representatives, Hammarskjöld concluded that "the Secretariat in its independence represents an organ, not only necessary for the life and proper functioning of the body, but of importance also for its growth."

THE SECRETARY-GENERAL

From the outset, the secretary-general of the UN has played an important role in helping to settle crises that have troubled nations since the end of World War II. In practice, the role has gone far beyond what might be anticipated from a reading of the terse Charter provisions for the office. Yet the role has been developed precisely through a skillful exploitation of the potentialities inherent in those provisions.

The deliberative organs of the UN are political bodies intended to function as forums where the interests of governments can be represented and reconciled. The secretary-general and the Secretariat embody the other aspect of the UN: the organization is also intended to be a place where people may speak not for the interests of governments or blocs but as impartial third parties. The secretary-general is consistently working in a political medium but doing so as a catalytic agent who, in person or through special missions, observers, and mediators, uses his influence to promote compromise and conciliation.

Under the Charter, the secretary-general has the right to bring to the attention of the Security Council any matter that, in his opinion, might threaten international peace and security. This right goes beyond any power granted the head of an international organization before the founding of the UN. The Charter requires that he submit to the General Assembly an annual report on the work of the organization. In this report, he can state his views and convey his voice to the world's governments. The secretary-general's role has also been considerably enhanced by exploiting the Charter provision that he shall perform "such other functions" as are entrusted to him by the main organizational units of the United Nations.

THE ROLE OF THE UN SECRETARY-GENERAL

In 1986, then Secretary-General Pérez de Cuéllar was invited to give the Cyril Foster Lecture at Oxford University. His thoughts on the institution of the secretary-general in an era of international evolution deserve attention.

First, he suggested that a secretary-general must avoid two extremes: "On one side is the Scylla of trying to inflate the role through too liberal a reading of the text [of the Charter]: of succumbing, that is, to vanity and wishful thinking. On the other is the Charybdis of trying to limit the role to only those responsibilities which are explicitly conferred by the Charter and are impossible to escape: that is, succumbing to modesty, to the instinct of self-effacement, and to the desire to avoid controversy. Both are equally damaging to the vitality of the institution. I submit that no secretary-general should give way to either of them."

Pérez de Cuéllar stated that he used the annual report to the General Assembly as a way to initiate action and galvanize efforts in other parts of the UN system. He pointed out that the secretary-general sometimes remains the only channel of communication between parties in conflict, and therefore must be able to improvise in the context of "good offices" missions. A disciple of "quiet diplomacy," Pérez de Cuéllar said that the secretary-general must not only be impartial, but must be perceived to be so. He observed that a secretary-general needs enormous patience; he does not have the option of being frustrated or discouraged. He suggested that the secretary-general must "try to understand the roots of insecurity, the fears and resentments and the legitimate aspirations which inspire a people or a state to take the position they do."

He delineated four priority areas for attention by the world body: (1) disarmament, and particularly, nuclear disarmament; (2) human rights; (3) "the shaming disparity of living standards between those who live in the developed world—the North—and their less fortunate brethren in the developing world—the South"; and (4) the world response to natural and man-made disasters.

In closing, Pérez de Cuéllar set forth his own essential requirements for a secretary-general:

The Secretary-General is constantly subjected to many and diverse pressures. But in the last analysis, his office is a lonely one. He cannot stand idle. Yet helplessness is often his lot. The idealism and hope of which the Charter is a luminous expression have to confront the narrow dictates of national policies. The Secretary-General's efforts must be based on reason but, behind many a government's allegedly logical position, there are myths and silent fears. The voice of the Charter is often drowned by clashes and conflicts between states. If the Secretary-General is to rise above these contradictions in international life, two qualities are essential.

One is faith that humanity can move—and indeed is moving—towards a less irrational, less violent, more compassionate, and more generous international order . . . .

The other essential quality is to feel that he is a citizen of the world. This sounds [like] a cliché, but the Secretary-General would not deserve his mandate if he did not develop a sense of belonging to every nation or culture, reaching out as best he can to the impulse for peace and good that exists in all of them. He is a world citizen because all world problems are *his* problems; the Charter is his home and his ideology, and its principles are his moral creed.

The role of the secretary-general has varied with the individual and with the time and circumstances. This chapter contains an outline account of the initiatives taken by the seven secretaries-general in various international crises and areas of conflict. Additional discussion of some of the main areas of conflict may be found in the chapter on International Peace and Security.

THE SECRETARIES GENERAL

The first secretary-general, Trygve Lie of Norway, was appointed for a five-year term on 1 February 1946. On 1 November 1950, he was reappointed for three years. He resigned on 10 November 1952 and was succeeded by Dag Hammarskjöld of Sweden on 10 April 1953. On 26 September 1957, Hammarskjöld was appointed for a further five-year term beginning on 10 April 1958. After Hammarskjöld's death in a plane crash in Africa on 17 September 1961, U Thant of Burma was appointed secretary-general on 3 November 1961, to complete the unexpired term. In November 1962, U Thant was appointed secretary-general for a five-year term beginning with his assumption of office on 3 November 1961. On 2 December 1966, his mandate was unanimously renewed for another five years. At the end of his second term, U Thant declined to be considered for a third. In December

1971, the General Assembly appointed Kurt Waldheim of Austria for a five-year term beginning on 1 January 1972. In December 1976, Waldheim was reappointed for a second five-year term, which ended on 31 December 1981. He was succeeded by Javier Pérez de Cuéllar of Peru, who was appointed by the Assembly in December 1981 for a five-year term beginning on 1 January 1982. He was reappointed for a second five-year term beginning on 1 January 1987. In late 1991, Pérez de Cuéllar expressed his wish not to be considered for a third term. On 3 December 1991, the General Assembly appointed Boutros Boutros-Ghali of Egypt to a five-year term beginning on 1 January 1992. On 17 December 1996, Kofi Annan of Ghana was appointed to a five-year term that began on 1 January 1997.

Trygve Lie

Born in Oslo, Norway, 1896; died in Geilo, Norway, 30 December 1968. Law degree from Oslo University. Active in his country's trade union movement from the age of 15, when he joined the Norwegian Trade Union Youth Organization. At 23, became assistant to the secretary of the Norwegian Labor Party. Legal adviser to the Norwegian Trade Union Federation (1922–35). Elected to the Norwegian Parliament (1935). Minister of justice (1935–39). Minister of trade, industry, shipping, and fishing (1939–40). After the German occupation of Norway in 1940 and until the liberation of Norway in 1945, he was, successively, acting foreign minister and foreign minister of the Norwegian government in exile in London. A prominent anti-Nazi, he rendered many services in the Allied cause during World War II. For example, he was instrumental in preventing the Norwegian merchant marine, one of the world's largest, from falling into German hands. Reelected to Parliament in 1945. Headed the Norwegian delegation to the San Francisco Conference. Secretary-General, 1946–1952.

Dag Hjalmar Agne Carl Hammarskjöld

Born in Jönkönpirg, Sweden, 1905; died in a plane accident while on a peace mission near Ndola, Northern Rhodesia (now Democratic Republic of the Congo), 17 September 1961. Studied at Uppsala and Stockholm universities; Ph.D., Stockholm, 1934. Secretary of Commission on Unemployment (1930–34). Assistant professor of political economy, Stockholm University (1933). Secretary of the Sveriges Riksbank (Bank of Sweden, 1935–36); chairman of the board (1941–45). Undersecretary of state in the Swedish ministry of finance (1936–45). Envoy extraordinary and financial adviser to the ministry of foreign affairs (1946–49). Undersecretary of state (1949). Deputy foreign minister (1951–53). Delegate to the Organization for European Economic Cooperation (OEEC; 1948–53). Vice-chairman of the Executive Committee of the OEEC (1948–49). Swedish delegate to the Commission of Ministers of the Council of Europe (1951–52). Hammarskjöld was a member of the Swedish Academy, which grants the Nobel prizes, and vice-president of the Swedish Tourist and Mountaineers' Association. Secretary-General, 1953–1961.

U Thant

Born in Pantanaw, near Rangoon, Burma (now Myanmar), 1909; died in New York, 25 November 1974. Educated at University College, Rangoon. Started career as teacher of English and modern history at Pantanaw High School; later headmaster. Active in development and modernization of Burma's educational system. Author and free-lance journalist. Books include a work on the League of Nations (1932), *Democracy in Schools* (1952), and *History of Post-War Burma* (1961). After Burma's independence, became Burma's press director (1947), director of broadcasting (1948), and secretary in the ministry of information (1949–53). Chief adviser to his government at many international conferences. Member of Burma's delegation to the 1952 General Assembly. In 1957, moved to New York as head of Burma's permanent delegation to the UN. Secretary-General, 1961–1971.

Kurt Waldheim

Born in Sankt Andrä-Wördern, Austria, 21 December 1918. Studied at the Consular Academy of Vienna and took an LL.D. at the University of Vienna. Member of the delegation of Austria in negotiations for Austrian State Treaty, London, Paris, and Moscow (1945–47). First secretary of Austria's legation to France (1948–51). Counselor and head of personnel division, ministry of foreign affairs, Vienna (1951–55). Permanent observer of Austria to the UN (1955–56). Minister, embassy to Canada, Ottawa (1956–58), and ambassador (1958–60). Director-general, political affairs, ministry of foreign affairs, Vienna (1960–64). Ambassador and permanent representative of Austria to the UN (1964–68 and 1970–71). Austrian minister of foreign affairs (1968–70). Unsuccessful candidate for the presidency of Austria in 1971. UN Secretary-General, 1972–1981. Guest Professor of Diplomacy, Georgetown University, Washington, DC, 1982–84. Author of *The Austrian Example,* on Austria's foreign policy in 1973; *Building the Future Order,* in 1980; *In the Eye of the Storm,* 1985.

In 1986, during his second campaign for the Austrian presidency, information about Waldheim's record as a German Army lieutenant in World War II was reported for the first time in the international press. Despite his previous assertions that he had been wounded at the Russian front in 1941 and then returned to Vienna to study law, it was discovered he had served as a lieutenant in the high command of Army Group E, whose commander, General Alexander Loehr, was later hanged for atrocities. The reports indicated that Waldheim had served in Yugoslavia and Greece, a fact that he had hitherto concealed, at a time when reprisals, deportations, and other war crimes were being carried out by the German Army. In 1987, the US Justice Department, on the basis of an examination of US files and of the records of the War Crimes Commission in the UN archives, placed Waldheim on a watch list, which is used to bar entry to the US for people linked to war crimes.

An international commission of historians appointed by Waldheim, after his election to the presidency of Austria in 1986, reported in February 1988 that it had found evidence that Waldheim was aware of war crimes during his service in the Balkans and had concealed his record but had found no evidence that he himself had committed any crime. The commission's report created a national crisis in the government of Austria and deeply divided the Austrian people. A national poll showed that, while the majority of people did not wish him to resign (as many prominent intellectuals and politicians were loudly insisting), most indicated that they would not vote for him again. Waldheim himself insisted that the commission cleared him of the charge of committing war crimes.

However, the debate over which countries did (or did not) know the facts about Waldheim's war service before or during his tenure as secretary-general continued to surface in the press periodically. There was general agreement that public knowledge of the real nature of Waldheim's war service would have disqualified him for consideration for the post of secretary-general. In August 1994, Representative Carolyn B. Maloney, Democrat of Manhattan, introduced the War Crimes Disclosure Act, H.R. 4995, with the intention of forcing the Central Intelligence Agency to disclose parts of the Waldheim dossier which it has withheld, citing national security interests.

Waldheim served as president of Austria for one term, from 1986 to 1992. In July 1994, Pope John Paul II, a long-time friend of Waldheim's, awarded him the Knighthood of the Order of Pius "for outstanding service as secretary-general of the United Nations." The honor is awarded to Catholics or non-Catholics for outstanding services to the church or society, and is largely symbolic.

Javier Pérez de Cuéllar

Born in Lima, Peru, 19 January 1920. Graduated from the law school of Catholic University, Lima (1943). Joined Peruvian ministry of foreign affairs (1940) and the diplomatic service (1944). Served as secretary at Peruvian embassies in France, the United Kingdom, Bolivia, and Brazil. Returned to Lima (1961) as director of legal and personnel departments, ministry of foreign affairs. Served as ambassador to Venezuela, USSR, Poland, and Switzerland. Member of Peruvian delegation to the 1st General Assembly (1946) and of delegations to the 25th through 30th sessions (1970–75). Permanent representative of Peru to the UN (1971–75). Served as UN secretary-general's special representative in Cyprus (1975–77); UN undersecretary-general for special political affairs (1979–81); and secretary-general's personal representative in Afghanistan (1981). After resigning from the UN, he returned to the ministry of foreign affairs and voluntarily separated from the service of his government on 7 October 1981. UN Secretary-General, 1982–1991. In 1992 UNESCO named him chairman of its World Commission on Culture and Development. The lawyer and career diplomat retired in the late 1990s. He is a former professor of diplomatic law at the Academia de Guerra Aérea del Peru. Author of *Manual de derecho diplomático (Manual of International Law)*, 1964.

Boutros Boutros-Ghali

Born in Cairo, Egypt, 14 November 1922. Graduated from Cairo University in 1946 with a Bachelor of Law. Received his Ph.D. in international law in 1949 from Paris University. From 1949–77 he was Professor of International Law and International Relations and head of the Department of Political Science at Cairo University. Boutros-Ghali was a Fulbright Research Scholar at Columbia University in 1954–55. He served as director of the Centre of Research of The Hague Academy of International Law from 1963–1964, and was a visiting professor at the Faculty of Law of Paris University from 1967–68. In 1977 he became Egypt's Minister of State for Foreign Affairs, and was present at the Camp David Summit Conference during the negotiations that led to the Camp David accords between Egypt and Israel in 1978. He continued as Minister of State for Foreign Affairs until 1991, when he became Deputy Prime Minister of Foreign Affairs. He became a member of the Egyptian parliament in 1987 and was part of the secretariat of the National Democratic Party since 1980. From 1980–92 he was a member of the Central Committee and Political Bureau of the Arab Socialist Union. From 1970–91 he was a member of the UN's International Law Commission. His professional affiliations include membership in the Institute of International Law, the International Institute of Human Rights, the African Society of Political Studies and the Académie des Sciences Morales et Politiques (Académie Française, Paris). He founded the publication *Al Ahram Iktisadi* and was its editor from 1960 to 1975. Boutros-Ghali has authored more than 30 books and over 100 articles on international affairs, international law, foreign policy, diplomacy, human rights, and economic and social development. UN Secretary-General, 1992–1996.

Kofi Annan

Born in Kumasi, Ghana, on 8 April 1938. Studied at the University of Science and Technology in Kumasi, Ghana, and in 1961 completed his undergraduate work in economics at Macalester College in St. Paul, Minnesota. During 1961–62, he undertook graduate studies in economics at the Institut universitaire des hautes études internationales in Geneva. Having worked with the UN for over 30 years in various capacities, he is considered the first Secretary-General to rise from within the organization. His first assignment with the United Nations was in 1962 as an Administrative Officer and Budget Officer at the World Health Organization (WHO) in Geneva. As a Sloan Fellow in 1971–72 at the Massachusetts Institute of Technology, he received a Master of Science in Management. He returned to Ghana from 1974 to 1976 and was the Managing Director of the Ghana Tourist Development Company, serving on both its board and on the Ghana Tourist Control Board. In the UN, he held the position of Deputy Director of Administration and Head of Personnel in the Office of the UN High Commissioner for Refugees during 1980–83, Director of the Budget in the Office of Financial Services during 1984–87, and then as Assistant Secretary-General in the Office of Human Resources Management and Security Coordinator for the UN system during 1987–90. From 1990 to 1992 he served as Assistant Secretary-General for Program Planning, Budget and Finance and Controller of the UN. After the invasion of Kuwait by Iraq in 1990, he was sent to Iraq to facilitate the repatriation of over 900 international staff, and became engaged in negotiations for the release of Western hostages. He also helped bring attention to the situation of the 500,000 Asians stranded in Kuwait and Iraq. He also headed the UN team that negotiated the possible sale of Iraqi oil to buy humanitarian aid. In 1992 he was appointed Assistant Secretary-General for Peacekeeping Operations, and became Under-Secretary-General in the same department in March 1993. He also served as a Special Representative of the Secretary-General to the former Yugoslavia and as Special Envoy to the North Atlantic Treaty Organization (NATO) during the transitional period that followed the signing of the Dayton Peace Agreement. Began term as UN Secretary-General, January 1997.

DEVELOPMENTS UNDER TRYGVE LIE, 1946–1952

Trygve Lie had not yet been in office three months when he took the initiative of advising the Security Council on the Secretariat's interpretation of the Charter. The Council was considering its first case, the Iranian complaint against the USSR. The secretary-general delivered a legal opinion that differed sharply from that of the Security Council. The Council did not accept his interpretation, but it upheld his right to present his views. After setting this precedent, Lie submitted legal opinions on other matters.

During Lie's first term as secretary-general, East-West tension charged the UN atmosphere. As the world situation became increasingly threatening, the political role of the secretary-general expanded. Lie took definite stands on three issues, each of which earned him the dislike of some permanent members of the Security Council. The issues were Chinese representation, a plan for the general settlement of the cold war, and UN military action in the Korean War.

Chinese Representation. By the end of 1949, a number of states, including the USSR and the United Kingdom—permanent members of the Security Council—had recognized the mainland government, the People's Republic of China. In January 1950, the USSR representatives, having failed to obtain the seating of the representatives of the People's Republic, began boycotting UN meetings at which China was represented by delegates of the Republic of China, based on Taiwan. In private meetings with delegations, Lie tried to solve the impasse. He adduced various reasons, including a ruling of the International Court of Justice, for the thesis that nonrecognition of a government by other governments should not determine its representation in the UN.

Trygve Lie's Twenty-Year Peace Plan. Lie developed an extraordinary initiative during the first half of 1950. In a letter to the Security Council dated 6 June 1950, approximately two weeks before the outbreak of the Korean War, he said: "I felt it my duty to suggest a fresh start to be made towards eventual peaceful solution of outstanding problems." In his *Twenty-Year Program for Achieving Peace Through the United Nations*, Lie proposed new international machinery to control atomic energy and check the competitive production of armaments and also proposed the establishment of a UN force to prevent or stop localized outbreaks of violence.

Armed with these proposals and other memoranda, including the one on Chinese representation, Lie journeyed first to Washington, then to London, to Paris, and finally to Moscow. He held conversations not only with foreign ministers and high-ranking diplomats but also with US President Harry S Truman, British Prime Minister Clement Attlee, French President Vincent Auriol, and Soviet Premier Joseph Stalin. Lie's reception was cordial in Moscow, warm in Paris, and friendly in London, but cool in Washington.

The international picture changed abruptly, however, with the outbreak of the Korean War. The attitude of a number of governments toward Lie changed dramatically as well.

The Korean War. An outstanding example of a secretary-general taking a stand on an issue was Lie's intervention in the emergency meeting of the Security Council on 24 June 1950. He unequivocally labeled the North Korean forces aggressors because they had crossed the 38th parallel, declared that the conflict constituted a threat to international peace, and urged that the Security Council had a "clear duty" to act. After the Council (in the absence of the Soviet delegate) had set in motion military sanctions against North Korea, Lie endorsed this course of action and rallied support from member governments for UN military action in Korea. These moves brought him into sharp conflict with the USSR, which accused him of "slavish obedience to Western imperialism" and to the "aggression" that, in the Soviet view, the US had committed in Korea.

As the Korean conflict grew more ominous with the intervention of the People's Republic of China, Lie played an active role in getting cease-fire negotiations underway in the field. At the same time, he fully identified himself with military intervention in Korea on behalf of the UN.

Extension of Lie's Term as Secretary-General. Lie's first term as secretary-general was to expire on 31 January 1951. In the Security Council, the USSR vetoed a resolution recommending him for a second term and subsequently announced that it would accept anyone other than Lie who was acceptable to the other members of the Council. The US announced that it would veto anyone but Lie. The Council was unable to recommend a candidate for the office of secretary-general to the General Assembly, a situation unforeseen in the Charter. A resolution in the Assembly to extend Lie's term by three years, beginning on 1 February 1951, was carried by 46 votes to 5, with 8 abstentions. The negative votes were cast by the Soviet bloc.

The USSR maintained normal relations with Lie until the expiration of his original term on 31 January 1951. Thereafter, it stood by its previous announcement that the extension of the term was illegal and that it would "not consider him as secretary-general." By the fall of 1951, however, its nonrecognition policy toward Lie subsided. However, other complications were facing Lie, and on 10 November 1952, he tendered his resignation to the General Assembly.

DEVELOPMENTS UNDER DAG HAMMARSKJÖLD, 1953–1961

Hammarskjöld's activities in the political field were more numerous and far-reaching than Lie's had been. Both the General Assembly and the Security Council repeatedly relied on his initiative and advice and entrusted important tasks to him.

The 1954 General Assembly set a precedent when it asked the secretary-general to seek the release of 11 US fliers held prisoner by mainland China. The Assembly resolution left the course of action entirely to his judgment. After various preparations, Hammarskjöld flew to Peking (now Beijing) for personal negotiations with that government, and the 11 fliers were released. This success greatly increased the readiness of the Assembly to rely on the secretary-general as a troubleshooter.

The Suez Crisis. Grave responsibilities were entrusted to the secretary-general by the General Assembly in connection with the establishment and operation of the UN Emergency Force (UNEF). On 4 November 1956, at the height of the crisis resulting from British, French, and Israeli intervention in Egypt, the secretary-general was requested to submit a plan within 48 hours for the establishment of a force "to secure and supervise the cessation of hostilities." The Assembly approved his plan and, at his suggestion, appointed Major-General E. L. M. Burns, Chief of Staff of the UN Truce Supervision Organization, as the chief of UNEF. The Assembly authorized the secretary-general to take appropriate measures to carry out his plan, and an advisory committee of seven UN members was appointed to assist him. Hammarskjöld flew to Egypt to arrange for the Egyptian government's consent for UNEF to be stationed and to operate in Egyptian territory. He was given the task of arranging with Egypt, France, Israel, and the United Kingdom the implementation of the cease-fire and an end to the dispatch of troops and arms into the area and was authorized to issue regulations and instructions for the effective functioning of UNEF.

Hammarskjöld's Views on Developing the Role of Secretary-General. Even before the Middle East crisis of 1956, Hammarskjöld had pointed to the need for the secretary-general to assume a new role in world affairs. On his reelection to a second term, Hammarskjöld told the General Assembly that he considered it to be the duty of the secretary-general, guided by the Charter and by the decisions of the main UN organs, to use his office and the machinery of the organization to the full extent permitted by practical circumstances. But he then declared: "I believe it is in keeping with the philosophy of the Charter that the secretary-general be expected to act also *without such guidance,* should this appear to him necessary in order to help in *filling a vacuum* that may appear in the systems which the Charter and traditional diplomacy provide for the safeguarding of peace and security." (Italics added.) In other words, inaction or a stalemate either at the UN or outside of it may be justification for the secretary-general to act on his own.

Thus, in 1958, Hammarskjöld took an active hand in the Jordan-Lebanon crisis. After a resolution for stronger UN action failed to carry in the Security Council, he announced that he would nevertheless strengthen UN action in Lebanon and "accept the consequences" if members of the Security Council were to disapprove; none did. In the fall of 1959, the USSR made it known that it did not favor a visit by the secretary-general to Laos and, in particular, the assignment of a special temporary "UN ambassador" there. Yet Hammarskjöld did go to Laos to orient himself on the situation in that corner of Southeast Asia, and he assigned a high UN official as the head of a special mission to Laos. In March 1959, Hammarskjöld sent a special representative to help Thailand and Cambodia settle a border dispute. He acted at their invitation without specific authorization by the Security Council or the General Assembly. The dispute was settled.

In his report to the 1959 Assembly, he said: "The main significance of the evolution of the Office of the Secretary-General . . . lies in the fact that it has provided means for smooth and fast action . . . of special value in situations in which prior public debate on a proposed course of action might increase the difficulties . . . or in which . . . members may prove hesitant. . . ."

The Congo Crisis. By far the greatest responsibilities Hammarskjöld had to shoulder were in connection with the UN Operation in the Congo (now Zaire).

On 12 and 13 July 1960, respectively, President Joseph Kasavubu and Premier Patrice Lumumba of the newly independent Congo each cabled the secretary-general, asking for UN military assistance because of the arrival of Belgian troops and the impending secession of Katanga. At Hammarskjöld's request, the Security Council met on the night of 13 July. He gave his full support to the Congo's appeal and recommended that the Council authorize him to "take the necessary steps" to set up a UN military assistance force for the Congo, in consultation with the Congolese government and on the basis of the experience gained in connection with the UNEF in the Middle East. The Security Council so decided.

Since the Congo operation thus initiated was of much greater dimensions than the UNEF operation, the responsibilities imposed upon the secretary-general were correspondingly heavier, for, although the Security Council and the General Assembly guided Hammarskjöld, he himself had to make extraordinarily difficult decisions almost daily, often on highly explosive matters that arose as a result of serious rifts within the Congolese government and many other factors.

Various member governments, including the USSR and certain African and Western countries, criticized Hammarskjöld for some actions that the UN took or failed to take in the Congo. At times, he had to face the possibility that some country that had contributed military contingents to the UN force would withdraw them.

When it became known in February 1961 that Lumumba, who had been deposed by Kasavubu early in September 1960 and later detained by the Léopoldville authorities, had been handed over by them to the Katanga authorities and subsequently murdered, Hammarskjöld declared that the UN was not to blame for the "revolting crime." However, several delegates claimed that he should have taken stronger measures to protect Lumumba.

The "Troika" Proposal. The USSR had asked for Hammarskjöld's dismissal long before the assassination of Lumumba. Premier Khrushchev, as head of the Soviet delegation to the 1960 General Assembly, accused Hammarskjöld of lacking impartiality and of violating instructions of the Security Council in his conduct of the UN operation in the Congo. He also proposed a basic change in the very institution of the secretary-general, arguing that since the secretary-general had become "the interpreter and executor of decisions of the General Assembly and the Security Council," this one-man office should be replaced by a "collective executive organ consisting of three persons, each of whom would represent a certain group of states"—namely, the West, the socialist states, and the neutralist countries; the institution of a "troika," he declared, would guarantee that the UN executive organ would not act to the detriment of any of these groups of states.

Hammarskjöld rejected the accusations against his impartiality, declared that he would not resign unless the member states for which the organization was of decisive importance or the uncommitted nations wished him to do so, and received an ovation from the overwhelming majority of the delegations. He also stated that to replace the one-man secretary-general by a three-man body would greatly alter the character and limit the scope of the UN.

Outside the Soviet bloc there had been little support for the "troika" proposal, but some "subtroika" proposals were advanced. Hammarskjöld in turn suggested that his five top aides, including a US and a Soviet citizen, advise the secretary-general on political problems. Discussions of the question were interrupted by his death.

Death of Dag Hammarskjöld. Because of dangerous developments in the Congo, Hammarskjöld flew there in September 1961. On the night of 17 September, the plane carrying him from Léopoldville to a meeting with the Katanga secessionist leader at Ndola, Northern Rhodesia, crashed in a wooded area about 16 km (10 mi) west of Ndola airport. Hammarskjöld and all 15 UN

civilian and military personnel traveling with him, including the crew, were killed. The exact cause of the tragedy has not been determined. An investigation commission appointed by the General Assembly reported several possibilities: inadequate technical and security preparations for the flight, an attack on the plane from the air or the ground, sabotage, or human failure by the pilot.

DEVELOPMENTS UNDER U THANT, 1961–1971

U Thant's approach to his office was different from that of Hammarskjöld, whose dynamic conception of the secretary-general's political role had aroused such opposition in the Soviet bloc. Thant did not take the same initiatives as his predecessor, but he consistently sought to use the prestige of his office to help settle disputes. Moreover, both the General Assembly and the Security Council assigned him to mediate extremely delicate situations. In his annual reports, he put forth proposals on basic issues, such as disarmament and economic and social cooperation and many of his suggestions were adopted.

An early example of a successful initiative taken by U Thant was in connection with the long-standing dispute between Indonesia and the Netherlands over the status of West Irian. The territory, formerly known as West New Guinea, had belonged to the Dutch East Indies, and Indonesia now claimed it as its own. In December 1961, fighting broke out between Dutch and Indonesian troops. Appealing to both governments to seek a peaceful solution, the secretary-general helped them arrive at a settlement. That settlement, moreover, brought new responsibilities to the office of the secretary-general: for the first time in UN history, a non-self-governing territory was, for a limited period, administered directly by the world organization.

The Cyprus Operation. Intercommunal clashes broke out in Cyprus on Christmas Eve 1963 and were followed by the withdrawal of the Turkish Cypriots into their enclaves, leaving the central government wholly under Greek Cypriot control. A "peace-making force" established under British command was unable to put an end to the fighting, and a conference on Cyprus held in London in January 1964 ended in disagreement. In the face of the danger of broader hostilities in the area, the Security Council on 4 March 1964 decided unanimously to authorize U Thant to establish a UN Peacekeeping Force in Cyprus (UNFICYP), with a limited three-month mandate to prevent the recurrence of fighting, to help maintain law and order, and to aid in the return to normal conditions. The force was to be financed on the basis of voluntary contributions. The Council also asked the secretary-general to appoint a mediator to seek a peaceful settlement of the Cyprus problem. The report of U Thant's mediator, Galo Plaza Lasso, was transmitted to the Security Council in March 1965 but was rejected by Turkey. Plaza resigned in December 1965, and the function of mediator lapsed.

Another crisis occurred in November 1967, but threatened military intervention by Turkey was averted, largely as a result of US opposition. Negotiations conducted by Cyrus Vance for the US and José Rolz-Bennett on behalf of the secretary-general led to a settlement. Intercommunal talks were begun in June 1968, through the good offices of the secretary-general, as part of the settlement. The talks bogged down, but U Thant proposed a formula for their reactivation under the auspices of his special representative, B. F. Osorio-Tafall, and they were resumed in 1972, after Thant had left office.

The India-Pakistan War of 1965 and Conflict of 1971. Hostilities between India and Pakistan broke out in Kashmir in early August 1965 and soon spread along the entire length of the international border from the Lahore area to the sea. At the behest of the Security Council, whose calls on 4 and 6 September for a cease-fire had gone unheeded, U Thant visited the subcontinent from 9 to 15 September. In his report to the Council, the secretary-general proposed certain procedures, including a possible meeting between President Ayub of Pakistan and Prime Minister Shastri of India, to resolve the problem and restore the peace.

The Council, on 20 September, demanded a cease-fire and authorized the secretary-general to provide the necessary assistance to ensure supervision of the cease-fire and withdrawal of all armed personnel. For this purpose, U Thant strengthened the existing UN Military Observer Group in India and Pakistan (UNMOGIP), stationed in Kashmir, and established the UN India-Pakistan Observation Mission (UNIPOM) to supervise the cease-fire and withdrawal of troops along the border outside Kashmir.

At a meeting organized by Soviet Premier Kosygin in January 1966 in Tashkent, USSR, the leaders of India and Pakistan agreed on the withdrawal of all troops; this withdrawal was successfully implemented under the supervision of the two UN military observer missions in the area. UNIPOM was disbanded in March 1966, having completed its work.

Following the outbreak of civil strife in East Pakistan in March 1971 and the deterioration of the situation in the subcontinent that summer, U Thant offered his good offices to India and Pakistan and kept the Security Council informed under the broad terms of Article 99 of the Charter. When overt warfare broke out in December, the Security Council appealed to all parties to spare the lives of innocent civilians. Pursuant to a decision by the Council, U Thant appointed a special representative to lend his good offices for the solution of humanitarian problems after the cease-fire of 18 December 1971, which was followed by the independence of Bangladesh.

U Thant's Stand on the Vietnam War. Throughout his tenure, U Thant was deeply concerned with the question of Vietnam. By tacit consent, the question was never formally debated in the General Assembly and only cursorily touched upon in the Security Council. Until the opening of the Paris peace talks in 1968, the secretary-general was unremitting in his efforts to persuade the parties in the conflict to initiate negotiations on their own. In 1966, he put forward a three-stage proposal to create the conditions necessary for discussion, but it was ignored by the US.

After the Paris talks began, U Thant deliberately refrained from making any public statements on Vietnam "in order to avoid creating unnecessary difficulties" for the parties. He broke this silence only once, on 5 May 1970, when he expressed his deep concern "regarding the recent involvement of Cambodia in the war."

U Thant's Second Term. U Thant's second term of office was dominated by the protracted Middle East crisis that arose in the aftermath of the Six-Day War in 1967. His quick action in removing UNEF troops from the Suez area at the request of the United Arab Republic just before that war began occasioned much criticism and some misunderstanding.

Of the two other major political conflicts during the period 1967–70, the civil war in Nigeria and the Soviet invasion of Czechoslovakia on 20 August 1968, only the latter was debated at the UN. The political aspects of the Nigerian situation were never raised in either the General Assembly or the Security Council out of deference to the African countries themselves, whose main objective was to keep external intervention to a minimum. However, as the troops of the Federal Republic of Nigeria began to penetrate more deeply into the eastern region (which had announced its secession from Nigeria and proclaimed itself an independent state under the name of Biafra), the various humanitarian organs of the UN became increasingly concerned about the plight of the people there. Accordingly, in August 1968, the secretary-general took the initiative of sending a personal representative to Nigeria to help facilitate the distribution of food and medicine.

At the request of its six Western members, the Security Council decided to debate the situation in Czechoslovakia, despite the protests of the USSR. On 23 August 1968, 10 members voted for a resolution condemning the Soviet action, which the USSR vetoed. Another resolution, requesting the secretary-general to send a representative to Prague to seek the release of imprisoned Czechoslovak leaders, was not put to a vote. In view—as one UN text puts it—of the "agreement reached on the substance of the problem during the Soviet-Czechoslovak talks held in Moscow from August 23 to 26," no further action was taken by the Council. However, it is worth noting that U Thant was among the first world figures to denounce the invasion publicly. At a press briefing on 21 August at UN headquarters, he expressed unequivocal dismay, characterizing the invasion as "yet another serious blow to the concepts of international order and morality which form the basis of the Charter of the United Nations . . . and a grave setback to the East-West détente which seemed to be re-emerging in recent months."

DEVELOPMENTS UNDER KURT WALDHEIM, 1972–1981

Two overriding concerns shaped Waldheim's secretary-generalship: concern for the preservation of the peace and concern for the evolution of world economic arrangements that would effect a more equitable distribution of the world's wealth. Two other issues were also of special concern to Waldheim: the financial position of the UN and terrorism. The financial position of the UN had been rendered precarious by the practice of some member states, including the USSR, France, and the US, of withholding or threatening to withhold their share of UN funds for activities that they questioned. When Waldheim took office, the crisis had become an emergency, and he dealt with it vigorously throughout his tenure. In September 1972, he placed the question of terrorism on the agenda of the General Assembly against the wishes of many member states. It was the first time a secretary-general had ever placed a substantive item on the Assembly's agenda.

Peacemaking. In 1972, on his own authority, Waldheim undertook a number of missions on behalf of peace. Visiting Cyprus, he temporarily calmed the Turkish community's concern over reported arms shipments to the Greek-dominated government. He visited the island again in 1973 in pursuit of reconciliation. After the hostilities in 1974, he was able to bring Greek and Turkish leaders together for negotiations, and he presided over the Geneva talks regarding Cyprus.

Waldheim's efforts to conciliate in the Vietnam War were rebuffed by both sides in 1972. He then tried, without success, to end the war through action by the Security Council. He visited the two Yemens to try to mediate a border dispute in 1972, and in the same year, he tried to mediate between India and Pakistan.

In the long-standing Arab-Israeli dispute, Waldheim made many efforts toward a satisfactory settlement and organized the UN Emergency Force as a buffer between the armies of Egypt and Israel at the request of the Security Council in October 1973.

Striving for a New International Economic Order. The sixth special session of the Assembly, in the spring of 1974, and the seventh special session, in September 1975, resulted in a number of decisions and proposals for bridging the gap between the rich and the poor nations and building a "new international economic order." The seventh special session was, in Waldheim's words, "a major event, even a turning point, in the history of the United Nations and showed a new and highly promising capacity of the organization to achieve practical results through consensus and through negotiation."

Financial Status of the UN. Waldheim acted both to reduce the costs of running the UN and to bring in contributions from member nations.

The US contribution to the UN, historically the highest single assessment, by the early 1970s stood at 31.5% of the budget. In October 1973, the US Congress reduced the US share to 25% of the UN budget; 116 other nations also had their contributions reduced by the UN. The difference was made up by increasing the assessments of Japan, China, and 10 other members and by admitting to membership the two Germanys. Waldheim helped to bring these changes about, fostering the notion that any country paying more than 25% of the UN's expenses could wield excessive influence.

Terrorism. Incidents of terrorism increased in the early 1970s. In September 1972, during the XXth Olympiad in Munich, 11 Israeli athletes were killed by Palestinians of the Black September group. Waldheim expressed himself strongly about the event and put the question of terrorism on the agenda of the 1972 General Assembly. A number of Arab and African countries took exception to his initiative, arguing that attention should be focused on the causes of terrorism. Although the Assembly had earlier condemned aerial hijacking, the resolution that it adopted on terrorism did not condemn the practice but called for a study of its causes. After OPEC officials were attacked by terrorists in 1975, the sentiment for more ample UN action against terrorism grew among third-world countries.

Waldheim's Second Term. Waldheim entered his second term of office in January 1977 with few illusions about the United Nations. To some extent, he wrote, it was still in search of its identity and its true role: "It tends to react rather than foresee, to deal with the effects of a crisis rather than anticipate and forestall that crisis." The history of the UN since its founding, he wrote, "has essentially been the story of the search for a working balance between national sovereignty and national interests on the one hand and international order and the long-term interests of the world community on the other." He said he was not discouraged, however, and he urged governments—particularly the major powers—to turn away from the age-old struggle for spheres of influence and to honor and respect their obligations and responsibilities under the Charter.

In 1978, Waldheim called for an effort to improve and streamline the workings of the UN, beginning with the General Assembly, the agenda of which should be reviewed, he said, and items of lesser interest removed. He noted that the Assembly had grown in three decades from a body of 50 members with an agenda of 20 items to a gathering of some 150 members and an agenda of more than 130 items.

Waldheim traveled extensively in East Asia in early 1979 and again in 1980 to get a firsthand view of developments in that area, particularly Indo-China, where, in the aftermath of the Vietnam war, there was an exodus of refugees, by land and sea, from that country. With the tide of these and other refugees from Laos and Kampuchea rising daily, Waldheim convened a meeting in Geneva in June 1979 to help alleviate the problem.

In May 1979, pursuing a "good offices" mission in Cyprus, Waldheim convened a high-level meeting calling for a resumption of intercommunal talks. The talks were subsequently resumed but broke down shortly thereafter. Waldheim again exerted his best efforts beginning in late 1979, as did the UN itself, in search of solutions to unexpected crises touched off by the Soviet invasion of Afghanistan and the taking of US diplomatic personnel as hostages in Iran. From the outset, his efforts were directed at freeing the hostages and settling relations between Iran and the US, and, for this purpose, he went to Tehran himself, as did a UN commission of inquiry. Waldheim noted that the war between Iran and Iraq, which began in September 1980, had resisted all efforts, both within and outside the UN, at finding a peaceful solution. He offered his own good offices for this purpose and appointed Olof Palme, former Swedish prime minister, as his special representative. In regard to the Afghanistan crisis, he appointed Javier Pérez de Cuéllar of Peru as his personal representative.

DEVELOPMENTS UNDER JAVIER PÉREZ DE CUÉLLAR, 1982–1991

Secretary-General Pérez de Cuéllar presided over the United Nations during one of the most remarkable decades in the political history of the world. During his tenure, the stalemate imposed on the United Nations by the rivalries of the Cold War came to an end. The political map of Europe, which had remained stable for more than 40 years since the end of WWII, was completely redrawn when the Soviet Union collapsed in 1989. East and West Germany were united and the Berlin Wall was reduced to rubble. Historic achievements in bilateral arms control and disarmament negotiations lowered the level of confrontation between the West and the East for the first time since the dawn of the nuclear era. A new atmosphere of consensus enabled the Security Council to begin providing the kind of leadership envisioned for it by the founders of the organization, as enshrined in the UN Charter. Long-standing political problems in Namibia, Cambodia, and Latin America were resolved with success by United Nations peacekeeping missions, and the evolution of the organization's activities in helping organize and monitor free and fair elections in new democracies began. The winds of change were also blowing strongly in South Africa, where the *apartheid* system was beginning to crumble after more than 30 years of condemnation by the United Nations.

The story of Pérez de Cuéllar's 10-year term as secretary-general straddles this historic evolution of the world scene at the *fin de siécle*. Upon leaving office in December 1991, in his report on the work of the United Nations, he set forth his own feelings about his experience as secretary-general:

"Peace has won victories on several fronts. . . . New vistas are opening for States to work together in a manner they did not do before. The earlier posture of aloofness and reserve towards the Organization has been replaced by more ardent participation in its endeavors. An era of law and justice may not be around the corner but the United Nations has defined the direction. . . . Today there are far more solid grounds for hope than there are reasons for frustration and fear. The hope arises both from the enduring relevance of the philosophy of the Charter and from the vastly strengthened credentials of the Organization. My credo is anchored in that philosophy and it will remain so. With its return from the doldrums, and with its role no longer peripheral, the United Nations has come nearer to the vision of its Charter. Everyone who contributed to the process is entitled to a measure of exultation and I, for my part, to a feeling of fulfillment. I profoundly appreciate the confidence placed in me through this testing phase of international affairs. I close on that note of faith and gratitude."

The situation had been very different when Pérez de Cuéllar first took office, in 1982. In his first report to the General Assembly, in September 1982, on the work of the organization, Pérez de Cuéllar commented on the inability of the UN to play an effective and decisive role in its capacity to keep the peace and serve as a forum for negotiations. The Falkland Islands crisis and the invasion of Lebanon by Israel, both major events of 1982, were clear examples of the failure of the international community, and its organization, to use the mechanisms of diplomacy to prevent international conflict. Countries seemed unwilling or reluctant to use the United Nations' peacekeeping mechanisms to help them resolve their difficulties without resorting to violence. Time after time, he said, "we have seen the Organization set aside or rebuffed, for this reason or for that, in situations in which it should and could have played an important and constructive role." He saw this trend as dangerous for the world community and for the future and criticized the tendency of governments to resort to confrontation, violence, and even war in pursuit of what were perceived as vital interests.

Another clear indication of the organization's lack of stature was the crippling budgetary problems caused by some member states' continuing practice of withholding part or all of their assessed contributions, placing the work of the entire organization in a constant state of uncertainty. Clearly, at the beginning of his term, the United Nations stood in need of a rebirth.

The Middle East

The Iran-Iraq War. In regard to the prolonged war between Iran and Iraq, which had started in 1980 and taken an enormous toll in human lives, Pérez de Cuéllar considered it to be his overriding responsibility under the Charter not only to seek an end to the conflict but also, until that goal was achieved, to try, under international humanitarian rules, to mitigate its effects in such areas as attacks on civilian population centers, use of chemical weapons, treatment of prisoners of war, and safety of navigation and civil aviation. On four occasions between 1984 and 1986, he dispatched specialists to investigate charges of the use of chemical weapons, initially against Iranian forces but later injuring Iranian civilians and Iraqi forces as well. In 1984 and 1985, two UN teams investigated allegations of violations of promises by the two countries to cease deliberate attacks on purely civilian population centers, and in January 1985, the secretary-general dispatched a fact-finding mission to Iran and Iraq to investigate the treatment of prisoners of war and civilian detainees. He himself visited Tehran and Baghdad in April 1985 to discuss proposals he had drawn up to initiate movement toward a comprehensive settlement of the war, and he continued to search for new approaches to this goal.

In July 1987, the Security Council unanimously adopted a resolution (598/1987) asking the secretary-general to send UN observers to verify and supervise a cease-fire between Iran and Iraq and withdrawal to internationally recognized boundaries. Pérez de Cuéllar was also asked by the Council to explore the question of entrusting to an impartial body the task of inquiring into responsibility for the conflict. Subsequent discussions with the two governments in their capitals reaffirmed his conviction that his good offices could be used to facilitate the restoration of peace and stability in the region. On 20 August 1988, the fighting stopped and UN military observers took up the challenge of monitoring compliance with the cease-fire. The secretary-general and his representative continued a "good offices" mission to build confidence and lay the basis for a lasting peace in the region.

The Gulf War. In August 1990, Iraq invaded Kuwait with 100,000 troops and took complete control of the small, underdefended country within 48-hours. In the four months following the invasion the Security Council responded with historic speed and unanimity. It passed 12 resolutions condemning the invasion, invoking Chapter VII of the Charter to impose economic sanctions on Iraq, and addressing aid to refugees and Iraq's taking of hostages. Pérez de Cuéllar remarked in his 1990 annual report that the council "has established that such actions, which are in direct contravention of the principles of the Charter and international law, cannot be committed with impunity." On 29 November 1990, after three weeks of debate, the Security Council passed Resolution 678 "authorizing Member States cooperating with the Government of Kuwait, unless Iraq on or before January 15, 1991, fully implements . . . the foregoing resolutions, to use all necessary means to implement Security Council Resolution 660 and all subsequent relevant resolutions to restore international peace and security in the area."

With the phrase "all necessary means," a new chapter in the history of the UN began. A 680,000-strong multi-national military force, led by 410,000 United States troops, was authorized by this resolution to impose the Security Council's will upon Iraq and restore the national sovereignty of Kuwait. On 16 January 1991, the allies began a six-week aerial bombardment of Iraq and Kuwait in preparation for a land attack on Kuwait. On 25 February, the ground attack began. Twelve days later the allied forces had decisively defeated Iraq's army of occupation, decimating it and pushing surviving units back into Iraq. Iraqi casualties were estimated in the hundreds of thousands. The United States lost 309 lives, some in pre-combat incidents. On 6 April, Iraq's parliament officially accepted the terms of Resolution 687, which it characterized as "unjust."

Resolution 687 had established a 200-kilometer-long demilitarized zone along the Iraq-Kuwait border, extending 10 kilometers into Iraq and five kilometers into Kuwait, to be patrolled by the UN Iraq-Kuwait Observer Mission (UNIKOM). The secretary-general reported that UNIKOM's 1,400 troops from 36 countries had been fully deployed on 9 May 1991.

In his 1991 report on the work of the organization, Pérez de Cuéllar pointed out that the experience of the Gulf action, moving as it did into areas undefined by the charter, suggested the need for "collective reflection on questions relating to the future use of the powers vested in the Security Council under Chapter VII. In order to preclude controversy, these questions should include the mechanisms required for the Council to satisfy itself that the rule of proportionality in the employment of armed force is observed and the rules of humanitarian law applicable in armed conflicts are complied with." He also warned that the use of Chapter VII measure should not be "overextended," since the imposition of mandatory economic sanctions necessarily created hardships for third-party nations (nations not party to the conflict, but who have important economic partnerships with the sanctioned state).

The Arab-Israeli Conflict. In mid-1982, Israeli forces moved into Lebanese territory, bypassing the UN Interim Force in Lebanon (UNIFIL). In August of that year, at the request of Lebanon and with the authorization of the Security Council, Pérez de Cuéllar deployed military observers to monitor the violence in and around Beirut. He also put forward proposals for expanding the role of UNIFIL—deploying the force, with elements of the Lebanese army and internal security forces, in areas vacated by Israeli forces as they withdrew from Lebanon, and working out arrangements to ensure that southern Lebanon became a zone of peace under the sovereignty and authority of the Lebanese government. These proposals were not accepted by Israel.

Pérez de Cuéllar also attempted to pursue the long-standing goal of convening a peace conference on the Middle East, holding numerous consultations with the parties involved. In December 1987, the diplomatic stalemate was shaken by a massive Palestinian uprising, the *intifadah,* in the Israeli-occupied territories that forced the Palestine National Council (the PLO's parliament in exile) to formally recognize Israel. However, the Israeli government declined to reciprocate. Yasser Arafat, the head of the PLO, was asked to address an emergency session of the Security Council, which had to be held in Geneva, since it was feared the United States would deny him an entry-visa. At that session, the United States vetoed the dispatch of a UN mission to the occupied territories to monitor the treatment of Palestinians by Israeli security forces.

In 1990 and 1991, the United States took the lead in trying to reconvene a peace conference. In October 1991, US Secretary of State James Baker made history by convening in Madrid the first-ever direct negotiations between all parties to the conflict. A key group interested in the talks were the former Palestinians, who since 1967 had been residing in territories under the control of Israels and were represented by the PLO. Since the Israelis had insisted on their exclusion from the Madrid talks, little progress was made. In December 1991, the General Assembly repealed its

Resolution 3379 (1975) which had equated Zionism with racism. This was only the second time in the history of the UN that the General Assembly had voted to rescind a resolution.

Afghanistan

The secretary-general and his personal representative, Diego Cordovez, acting as mediator, were continuously involved, until early 1988, in discussions and consultations aimed at negotiating a settlement of the situation in Afghanistan that had been brought about by Soviet military intervention in that country in late 1979 and had affected neighboring countries, particularly Pakistan, to which many Afghan refugees had fled. The negotiations revolved around four points: agreement on noninterference and nonintervention; the voluntary return of refugees; international guarantees on the settlement, to be given by the US and the USSR; and the withdrawal of foreign troops.

The General Assembly supported these efforts and appealed to all states and national and international organizations to extend humanitarian relief assistance to alleviate the hardships of the Afghan refugees, in coordination with the UN high commissioner for refugees.

The negotiation efforts met with success in early April 1988, when agreement was reached on a treaty under which the USSR would withdraw its 115,000 troops from Afghanistan, Pakistan and Afghanistan would cease all interference in each other's internal affairs, Afghan refugees would be given a safe return to their country, and Afghanistan would become a neutral and nonaligned state guaranteed by the USSR and the US. A small UN military observer team (UNGOMAP) was to be sent to Afghanistan to monitor compliance with the treaty, which was signed in Geneva on 14 April by Afghanistan, Pakistan, the USSR, and the US. The USSR withdrew its troops in February 1989, however fighting continued, and rebel forces continued to receive aid from the United States and Pakistan. The USSR, for its part, continued to prop up the Marxist government in Kabul. UNGOMAP's mandate ran out in March 1990 and the secretary-general replaced it with a smaller high-level Office of the Secretary-General in Afghanistan and Pakistan, funded out of the UN's regular budget. This office's purpose was to advise the secretary-general on the military and political situation in order to assist him in finding a settlement.

Central America

In Central America, Pérez de Cuéllar and the secretary-general of the Organization of American States extended, in November 1985, a joint offer of services to the five Central American countries concerned—Costa Rica, El Salvador, Guatemala, Honduras, and Nicaragua—as well as to those of the Contadora Group, bringing to their attention the resources that the two organizations could provide, separately and together, to facilitate resolution of the region's problems and complement the Contadora process. The two leaders visited the area in January 1986 in an effort to reactivate the negotiating process. Pérez de Cuéllar welcomed the proposal of President Oscar Arias Sánchez of Costa Rica for a peace plan, put forward in February 1987 and agreed to that August in Guatemala City by the five Central American countries. He agreed to serve as a member of the International Committee for Verification and Follow-up created by the Guatemala agreement and offered to extend any additional assistance that would be appropriate under the UN Charter.

As a result of this initiative, the countries concerned joined in a framework agreement, Esquipulas II, which gave the UN a mandate to verify the commitments made by the parties to each other. In 1989, the secretary-general established the UN Observer Mission (ONUVEN) to supervise the electoral process in Nicaragua. It was the first time the UN had been directly involved in electoral supervision. The UN Observer Group in Central America

(ONUCA) was charged with overseeing the demobilization of the Contra guerrillas in Nicaragua. In December 1989, the secretary-general brought together the five Central American presidents in order to resume a dialogue between the government of El Salvador and the FMLN guerrillas. By July 1990, the San José Human Rights Accord was concluded, in which the government of El Salvador agreed to have its compliance monitored by a UN mission (UN Observer Mission in El Salvador—ONUSAL). After 20 months of negotiations, on his very last day in office, Pérez de Cuéllar witnessed the signing of a cease-fire agreement in the 12-year civil war in El Salvador, on 31 December 1991.

The success of the United Nations in monitoring the elections in Nicaragua encouraged Haiti to request the organization to monitor its elections in December 1990. The General Assembly granted the request, and created the UN Observer Group for Verification of Elections in Haiti, known by its French acronym, ONUVEH. Jean-Bertrand Aristide was elected president in elections declared by the United Nations to be free and fair. However, in September 1991, President Aristide was overthrown by a military coup, creating an intransigent problem for Pérez de Cuéllar's successor.

Cambodia

Hostilities between Cambodia (at that time Kampuchea) and Vietnam had broken out in 1978. The United Nations became deeply involved in a humanitarian mission to assist refugees in the conflict along the border of Thailand and Cambodia. In January 1989, the revitalized Security Council began to take a more active role in the 11-year-old civil war. The secretary-general's special representative, Under Secretary Rafeeuddin Ahmed, played an essential role in the negotiating the framework for a settlement leading to a specific blueprint for the restoration of peace. In August 1989 the Paris Conference on Cambodia was convened, but was suspended within a month. Meetings in New York and Paris in 1990 finally secured the agreement of all the parties to the framework agreement developed by the Security Council. The agreement was signed on 23 October 1991, and two more UN missions were created: the UN Transitional Authority in Cambodia (UNTAC), and the UN Advance Mission in Cambodia (UNAMIC). The scale and cost of the mandate for these missions was unprecedented. It included repatriation of refugees from the Thai border camps, cantonment of all military forces and demobilization of 70% of these troops, registration of voters, supervision of elections for a Constituent Assembly, and supervision of the process of drafting and ratifying a new constitution.

Namibia

The change in the players on the world stage led to the resolution of this long-standing issue, nearly twenty-five years after the General Assembly first denounced South Africa's attempted annexation of South West Africa (now Namibia), and a dozen years after the Security Council laid out the settlement plan for its independence. The Security Council's resolution 435 of 1978 had called for a cease-fire in Namibia, the abolition of apartheid laws, the withdrawal of South Africa from Namibia, the election of a constituent assembly, and the establishment of the United Nations Transitional Assistance Group (UNTAG) to oversee free and fair elections. However, the presence of Cuban troops in Namibia in support of the liberation movement, the South West Africa Peoples' Organization (SWAPO), created another stalemate between East and West. In 1988, the change in the political climate between the two superpowers produced an agreement that led to the withdrawal of the Cuban troops and the implementation of UNTAG. The transition began in April 1989 and 97% of the registered voters participated in elections in November. On 21 March 1990, Namibia became an independent state, with SWAPO leader Sam Nujoma as its president. UNTAG withdrew from Nambia in March 1990. As Pérez de Cuéllar reported in 1990, "UNTAG turned out to be something far more than its somewhat pedestrian name implied. It established the workability of democratic procedures even in a terrain which at first looked most unpromising. It also proved the executive ability of the United Nations in successfully managing a complex operation which brought together 8,000 men and women from more than 100 nations . . . ."

Apartheid

The dramatic events that led to the dismantling of the apartheid system and the birth of a new South African nation are chronicled in the chapter on International Peace and Security. However, it was during Pérez de Cuéllar's tenure as secretary-general that the General Assembly held its 16th Special Session (12–14 December 1989) devoted to the question of apartheid. On 11 February 1990, South African President F.W. de Klerk released Nelson Mandela after 27 years of imprisonment. In response to the assembly's Resolution S-16/1, the secretary-general sent a high-level mission to South Africa in June 1990 to investigate the progress that had been made toward dismantling *apartheid*. By the end of his tenure, the process of change that would bear fruit in 1994, was firmly established.

Other Major Developments

Besides the problems of international peace and security listed above, the secretary-general's reports to the General Assembly made it clear he observed a growing appreciation in the international community of the need for cooperative action on a number of problems that transcend country borders and defy the ability of states to solve them independently. The recognition of the HIV/AIDS pandemic, its link to the plague of drug abuse and drug trafficking, and the concomitant links to international terrorism and organized crime all urgently required the attention of the world organization.

It was in the final years of Pérez de Cuéllar's tenure that the stage was set for what he called a new evolution in global society, in which humankind would make international covenants, not only between individuals and nations, but also between humankind and the environment: the 1987 Montreal Protocol on Substances that Deplete the Ozone Layer came into force in 1989; the Basel Convention on the Control of Transboundary Movements of Hazardous Wastes and Their Disposal was adopted in March 1989; the Second World Climate Conference was held in late 1990; and in February 1991, the first negotiations by the International Negotiating Committee on a framework convention on climate change began. Those negotiations would lead to the historic UN Conference on Environment and Development (UNCED), held in Rio de Janeiro in 1992 and dubbed the "Earth Summit." It was during the final years of the 1980s that an entirely new concept for the UN's work was developed: sustainable development.

DEVELOPMENTS UNDER BOUTROS BOUTROS-GHALI 1992–1996

Secretary-General Boutros Boutros-Ghali took office in an air of general euphoria over the accomplishments of the United Nations in the post-Cold War era. However, his first two years in office witnessed the proliferation of intractable and appalling regional conflicts in Haiti, Somalia, the former Yugoslavia and Rwanda, among others. The multiplicity and savagery of these conflicts cast a pall on the much hoped-for "new world order" which the end of the Cold War had inspired.

Soon after Boutros-Ghali's inauguration, in January 1992, the Security Council met in its first-ever summit session, at which the heads of states of all the members of the council convened in New York, in person. On 31 January 1992, they requested that the sec-

retary-general submit to the Security Council "an analysis and recommendations on ways of strengthening and making more efficient within the framework and provisions of the Charter the capacity of the United Nations for preventive diplomacy, for peacemaking and for peacekeeping." Boutros-Ghali's *An Agenda for Peace* set forth an analysis of the world organization's new situation at a time of global transition with respect to international peace and security. This document is more fully explained in the chapter on International Peace and Security.

In May 1994, Boutros-Ghali responded to a 1992 request of the General Assembly to submit a similar report on development under the agenda item "Development and International Economic Cooperation." He declared that development was not only a fundamental human right, but also the most secure basis for peace. Although the UN had accomplished remarkable achievements in many areas, it was undeniable that after decades of efforts to assist the developing world, the poorest nations were falling even further behind, strangled by debt and social upheaval. Boutros-Ghali said that, although concerns had been expressed that the United Nations put greater emphasis on peacekeeping than development, the numbers of staff and the regular budgetary allocations did not support this fear. He posited that development could not proceed without a fundamental basis in peace, and went on to describe the ideal evolution of a peacekeeping/humanitarian aid operation into a situation of sustainable development.

Boutros-Ghali further maintained that protection of the environment was another fundamental concept for development. "In the developing world, ecological pressure threatens to undermine long-term development. Among many countries in transition, decades of disregard for the environment have left large areas poisoned and unable to sustain economic activity in the long term. Among the wealthiest nations, consumption patterns are depleting world resources in ways that jeopardize the future of world development," observed Boutros-Ghali. The concept of "sustainable development," as elaborated by UNCED in 1992, had to be strengthened as a guiding principle of development. Social justice and democracy were posited as the other pillars of a successfully developing country.

Haiti

Elected in UN-supervised elections in December 1990 and deposed by a military coup in September 1991, Haiti's President Jean-Bertrand Aristide turned to the United Nations and the Organization of American States for assistance. In its Resolution 46/7 (September 1991), the General Assembly strongly condemned the "attempted illegal replacement of the Constitutional President of Haiti" and demanded that President Aristide be restored to power. It requested that the secretary-general cooperate with the Organization of American States (OAS) to restore the legally elected government in Haiti. A trade embargo and a halt to bilateral assistance were imposed on the illegal government, but there was little progress in negotiations. In December 1992, the secretary-general appointed Dante Caputo as Special Envoy for Haiti. The OAS also endorsed Caputo in January 1993. In its Resolution 47/20B (20 April 1993), the General Assembly mandated a joint UN/OAS International Civilian Mission to Haiti (known by its French acronym, MICIVIH) to be deployed throughout Haiti to report on the human rights situation there. On 16 June 1993, the Security Council imposed sanctions on Haiti. In July, talks were held on Governors Island, New York, and an agreement reached on specific measures relating to the return of President Aristide. In August 1993, the Security Council passed a resolution (862/1993) approving the dispatch of an advance team to prepare the way for the UN Mission in Haiti (UNMIH) which would supervise the transition. On 25 August 1993, the Haitian parliament ratified President Aristide's appointment of Robert Malval as prime minister-delegate during the transition period, as provided by the Governors Island Agreement. The Security Council then suspended the sanctions against Haiti.

On 27 September, the Security Council approved the deployment of UNMIH. However, on 11 October, armed civilians (known as "attachés") prevented the mission from debarking upon its arrival in Haiti. The attachés were known to be terrorizing the population through assassinations, attacks on the offices of the prime minister, and a general strike against UNMIH. It was also reported that police had facilitated, and in some cases participated in, these actions.

It became apparent that the military government was reneging on its promises under the Governors Island Agreement. On 13 October 1993, the Security Council reimposed its oil and arms embargo. That same month, most of the personnel of MICIVIH were evacuated, leaving a small administrative team to report on the alarming violence and violations of human rights being perpetuated, particularly against supporters of President Aristide.

In May 1994, the Security Council imposed expanded sanctions on Haiti, including a ban on commercial air travel. On 31 August 1994, the Security Council, in its resolution 940 (1994), authorized the use of a multinational force similar to the one used to repel Iraq from Kuwait. Specifically, the Security Council authorized UN members to: "form a multinational force under unified command and control and, in this framework, to use all necessary means to facilitate the departure from Haiti of the military leadership, consistent with the Governors Island Agreement, the prompt return of the legitimately elected President and the restoration of the legitimate authorities of the Government of Haiti, and to establish and maintain a secure and stable environment that will permit implementation of the Governors Island Agreement, on the understanding that the cost of implementing this temporary operation will be borne by the participating Member States." By the same resolution, the Security Council approved the eventual deployment of the 6,000-strong UNMIH force to assist with the restoration of democracy in Haiti.

The multinational force succeeded in landing in Haiti without significant bloodshed, pursuant to a last-minute negotiation headed by former United States President Jimmy Carter at the request of current President Bill Clinton. By October 1994 President Aristide was able to safely return to Haiti. On 16 November 1995 the Security Council commended UNMIH on the substantial progress it had made towards fulfilling its mandate as set out in Resolution 940 in 1994. After a phased reduction of the military and civilian police personnel, 4,000 military and 300 civilian police remained in the mission area by February 1996.

Somalia

The downfall of Somalia's President Siad Barre in January 1991 resulted in a power struggle and clan warfare in many parts of Somalia. In November 1991, the fighting intensified causing widespread death and destruction, and forcing hundreds of thousands of civilians to flee their homes. Almost 4.5 million people in Somalia—over half the estimated population—were threatened by severe malnutrition. It was estimated that as many as 300,000 people had died since November and at least 1.5 million were at immediate risk. The United Nations had instituted humanitarian operations in Somalia, but due to the deteriorating situation, it had been obliged to withdraw its personnel from the country.

In early 1992, Under Secretary-General for Political Affairs, James O.C. Jonah led a team to Somalia for talks aimed at bringing about a cessation of hostilities and securing access by the international relief community to civilians caught in the conflict. During that visit, unanimous support was expressed by all faction leaders for a United Nations role in bringing about national reconciliation. On 23 January 1992, the Security Council (Resolution 733/1992) urged all parties to cease hostilities, called for an embargo on military equipment, and requested the secretary-gen-

eral to contact all parties involved in the conflict. In February, the secretary-general obtained the agreement of the two main factions in Mogadishu to an immediate cease-fire and on 3 March 1992, Interim President Ali Mahdi and General Mohamed Farah Aidid signed an "Agreement on the Implementation of a Cease-fire." The agreement also included acceptance of a United Nations security component for convoys of humanitarian assistance and deployment of 20 military observers on each side of Mogadishu to monitor the cease-fire.

On 24 April 1992, the Security Council adopted resolution 751 (1992) and established a UN Operation in Somalia (UNOSOM). The total strength of UNOSOM was eventually established at 4,219 troops to protect the representatives of the six main UN organizations at work in Somalia coordinating humanitarian efforts (FAO, UNDP, UNICEF, UNHCR, WFP and WHO). In addition, more than 30 non-governmental organizations were working in Somalia as "implementing partners" of the UN. However, in October the security situation deteriorated, as some factions refused to agree to the deployment of UN troops to assure delivery of humanitarian aid to people in great need. According to some estimates, as many as 3,000 persons a day were dying of starvation, while warehouses remained stocked with food supplied by the humanitarian agencies. On 3 December 1992, the Security Council unanimously adopted Resolution 794 (1992) authorizing the use of "all necessary means to establish as soon as possible a secure environment for humanitarian relief operations in Somalia." A Unified Task Force (UNITAF), led by United States troops, was deployed in Mogadishu on 9 December 1992.

On 3 March 1993, the secretary-general recommended the Security Council establish a new force, UNOSOM II, to take over from UNITAF, which had deployed approximately 37,000 troops in southern and central Somalia. The secretary-general appointed Admiral Jonathan T. Howe (Ret.) of the United States as his new Special Representative for Somalia to oversee the transition from UNITAF to UNOSOM II. A Conference on National Reconciliation in Somalia was convened on 15 March 1993 in Addis Ababa, Ethiopia. It was attended by the leaders of 15 Somali political movements and representatives of regional organizations. After two weeks of intensive negotiations, the 15 Somali leaders signed an Agreement for disarmament and security, rehabilitation and reconstruction, restoration of property and settlement of disputes, and transitional mechanisms.

UNOSOM II took over from UNITAF on 4 May 1993, and proceeded to fulfill its mandate to disarm the Somali factions who were terrorizing the people and obstructing humanitarian activities. This provoked the hostility of a few clan leaders. On 5 June, 25 Pakistani soldiers were killed, 10 were missing and 54 were wounded in a series of ambushes and armed attacks against UNOSOM II troops throughout Mogadishu. The Security Council reaffirmed that the secretary-general was authorized to take all necessary measures against those responsible for armed attacks, and on 12 June 1993, UNOSOM II initiated decisive military action in south Mogadishu.

On 3 October 1993, United States Rangers, deployed in support of UNOSOM II, but not under UN command, launched an operation in south Mogadishu aimed at capturing a number of key aides of General Aidid who were suspected of complicity in the 5 June attack, as well as subsequent attacks on UN personnel and facilities. Two US helicopters were shot down by Somali militiamen using automatic weapons and rocket-propelled grenades. While evacuating the detainees, the Rangers came under concentrated fire, and 18 US soldiers were killed and 75 wounded. The bodies of the US soldiers were subjected to humiliating treatment. Following these events, the US both reinforced its Quick Reaction Force in Somalia and announced its intention to withdraw its forces from Somalia by 31 March 1994.

On 9 October 1993, General Aidid's faction declared a unilateral cessation of hostilities against UNOSOM II, but the situation remained tense. It was reported that the major factions were rearming in anticipation of renewed fighting. UNOSOM II's mandate to force the factions to disarm was unenforceable.

In February 1994, the leaders of the two main Somali factions met in Nairobi and signed a Declaration of National Reconciliation on 24 March, committing themselves to repudiate any form of violence. A National Reconciliation Conference was scheduled for 15 May 1994; however, this conference was postponed. By March 1995, UNOSOM II withdrew from Somalia. In August 1995 a wide range of Somali factions held consultations at Nairobi, Kenya and agreed to work out a common political platform and to start a process of national reconciliation. General Aidid rejected the calls for national reconciliation, and intense fighting broke out against the militia of Ali Mahdi. Aidid's forces occupied Baidoa and Hoddur, and a stalemate between faction leaders continued into 1996.

The Former Yugoslavia

In June 1991, the Republics of Croatia and Slovenia declared themselves independent from Yugoslavia. Fighting broke out when Serbs living in Croatia, supported by the Yugoslavian Army, opposed this move. European Community efforts to end hostilities were unsuccessful. On 25 September 1992, the United Nations Security Council unanimously adopted resolution 713 (1991) calling on all states to implement an arms embargo to Yugoslavia. Then Secretary-General Pérez de Cuéllar appointed former US Secretary of State Cyrus Vance as his personal envoy for Yugoslavia. Vance undertook several missions to Yugoslavia and discussed with the parties the feasibility of deploying a UN peacekeeping operation. An unconditional cease-fire was signed on 2 January 1992, and the Security Council approved the dispatch of a group of 50 military liaison officers to Yugoslavia to use their good offices to promote maintenance of the cease-fire. However, some political groups in Yugoslavia objected to the UN plan for a peacekeeping mission. Nevertheless, on 21 February 1992, the Security Council established the United Nations Protection Force (UNPROFOR) as an interim arrangement to create conditions of peace and security required for the negotiation of an overall settlement of the Yugoslav crisis.

On 30 April 1992, the secretary-general deployed 40 military observers to the Mostar region of Bosnia and Herzegovina in response to the deteriorating security situation there. However, fighting between Bosnian Muslims and Croats on one side, and Bosnian Serbs on the other, intensified. UNPROFOR, which had established its headquarters in Sarajevo, the capital, was obliged to relocate to Zagreb, the capital of Croatia.

A situation tragically similar to that in Somalia quickly developed. UN humanitarian convoys could not reach civilians trapped in the conflict. The Security Council, in its resolution 770 (1992) once again invoked Chapter VII of the Charter and called on states to "take nationally or through regional agencies or arrangements all measures necessary" to facilitate the delivery of humanitarian assistance to Sarajevo and other parts of Bosnia and Herzegovina. The situation continued to deteriorate and the Security Council declared a "no-fly zone" to prevent the bombing of Sarajevo and other villages. On 13 March 1993 three unidentified aircraft dropped bombs on two villages, the first time that the "no-fly zone" had been violated since its declaration. On 31 March the Security Council extended its ban on flights, and authorized NATO to enforce the no-fly zone. Between the establishment of the no-fly zone and April 1994, 1,620 violations of the ban on flights over Bosnian airspace were registered. On 28 February 1994, NATO fighters in the airspace of Bosnia and Herzegovina shot down four of six jets which had defied the international ban on military flights and ignored two warnings.

On 27 April 1994, the Security Council increased the strength of UNPROFOR to 33,891. Negotiations for a resolution of the crisis in the former Yugoslavia continued in July 1994.

The General Framework Agreement for Peace in Bosnia and Herzegovina (The Dayton Agreement)

Following a mortar attack on Sarajevo's Makale commercial district on 28 August 1995, the North Atlantic Treaty Organization (NATO) conducted air strikes against Bosnian Serb positions near Sarajevo. The air strikes were authorized by the United Nations Peace Forces, and deterred any further attacks on safe areas. By October 1995, a country-wide cease-fire was in place, arranged by a delegation from the United States. The cease-fire included civilian provisions, such as humane treatment of detained persons, freedom of movement, and the right of displaced persons to return to their homes.

On 21 November 1995, a series of agreements to restore peace in Bosnia and Herzegovina concluded in Dayton, Ohio. The General Framework Agreement for Peace in Bosnia and Herzegovina (known as the Dayton Agreement) was initialed by the governments of the Republic of Bosnia and Herzegovina, the Republic of Croatia, and the Federal Republic of Yugoslavia. During the talks, several non-NATO countries, such as the Russian Federation, agreed to participate in the implementation of the Bosnian peace plan. The United Nations was not officially represented during the talks.

The economic sanctions against the Federal Republic of Yugoslavia and the Bosnian Serb party were suspended following the signing of the Dayton Agreement. In his 1996 annual report, Secretary-General Boutros Boutros-Ghali indicated that "the value of sanctions as a means of conflict resolution was amply demonstrated in the former Yugoslavia, where the conclusion of peace accords has been facilitated by the effective implementation of a sanctions regime."

After the signing of the Dayton Agreement, it seemed possible to solve the problem of repatriation for the estimated two million Bosnian refugees and displaced persons. The UN High Commissioner for Refugees (UNHCR) was designated as the agency in charge of planning and carrying out the repatriation of the Bosnians who wanted to return. However, by June 1996, only 70,000–80,000 refugees and internally displaced persons had returned to their homes.

Cambodia

The UN Transitional Authority in Cambodia (UNTAC) successfully undertook its mission to conduct elections and repatriate more than 360,000 refugees. Its 21,000 military, police, and civilian personnel were fully deployed by mid-1992. Elections were held in May 1993, and 96% of the eligible population, nearly 4.7 million people, registered to vote. Despite concerns about disruption by the National Army of Democratic Kampuchea, which had withdrawn from the process, a six-week election campaign in which 20 political parties took part was successfully held. On 10 June, the secretary-general's special representative declared his view that the elections had been free and fair. The newly elected Constituent Assembly held its inaugural meeting on 4 June 1993 to begin its task of drafting and adopting a new constitution. The four Cambodian political parties that won seats in the election agreed to join in an interim administration for the remainder of the transitional period. UNTAC's mandate terminated in November 1993. A small Military Liaison Team remained in the country for six months as observers. The liaison team's mandate expired on 15 May 1994, and they were replaced by three military officers assisting the secretary-general's special representative in Cambodia.

DEVELOPMENTS UNDER KOFI ANNAN, 1997–

Secretary-General Kofi Annan came to power at a time of differences between the UN and the US government concerning financial matters. At the end of 1996, the US was US$376.8 million in arrears, but the government was reluctant to pay the debt because of the belief that the UN had not been thrifty with its budget. The US held the position that the UN should be reduced in size, but Annan took a strong stand against further budget and staff cuts. Nevertheless, Annan took action to reform the UN. In 1998, the organization announced it stood "poised, finally, to undertake sweeping structural change." The then 185 member states gave strong backing to a plan to overhaul the organization, making it more efficient and responsive to the world scene in the post–cold war era. The secretary-general was credited with mobilizing the General Assembly behind the "ambitious program" while member states were lauded for not allowing individual concerns to "override their common recognition that strategic changes were essential to ensure the relevance and vibrancy of the organization in meeting current global challenges." Reforms included consolidation of some offices and revisions to the charter to allow for further streamlining.

The Annan-led reform efforts helped strengthen relations between the UN and its headquarters host country, the United States, which by the time the reorganization was announced was more than US$1 billion in arrears to the international body. President Clinton praised the reform and issued strong statements of support for the new secretary-general. Further, the US President promised to work out a plan with Congress to pay the nation's debt to the UN. Faced with losing its vote and influence in the organization (at the end of 1999), the US later made good on the promise, which, combined with initiatives to ensure zero-growth budgets, relieved the international body's long-standing financial crisis.

However, relations between the US and the UN were strained over US military action (including the Clinton administration's attacks on suspected terrorist bases in Afghanistan in August 1998, and US-British bombings of Iraqi targets in May 2000) and inaction: Faced with wars on several fronts in Africa, in mid-May 2000, Kofi Annan said that the UN peacekeeping efforts needed the kind of military help that the United States was unwilling to provide. The US had offered only to transport troops from other countries to confront the crisis in Sierra Leone, where hundreds of UN peacekeepers were being held hostage.

Indeed, Sierra Leone was one of four peacekeeping missions added in 1999 alone. The others were in Kosovo, East Timor, and the Democratic Republic of the Congo (formerly Zaire). In a press statement about the emerging situation in Africa, Annan called for a "new style of peacekeeping force for a different age." The secretary-general described it as one needing "rapid-reaction contingents" who would be on-call from countries with well-trained and well-equipped troops, ready to move fast to pave the way for peacekeeping forces. He also cited the need for better intelligence and more intelligence sharing, admitting the UN was "completely sleeping on the issue of intelligence." While world health, the environment, the status of women, and nuclear non-proliferation were the emphasis of the UN's program at the turn of the 21st century, the peacekeeping initiatives continued to take center stage—posing formidable hurdles for the UN leadership.

INTERNATIONAL PEACE AND SECURITY

The first purpose of the UN, as stated in Article 1 of its charter, is the maintenance of international peace and security. To this end, the organization is required "to take effective collective measures for the prevention and removal of threats to the peace, and for the suppression of acts of aggression or other breaches of the peace, and to bring about by peaceful means . . . adjustment or settlement of international disputes or situations which might lead to a breach of the peace." The UN has undertaken this heavy responsibility with varying levels of success over the years. However, in the nuclear era, international security in the absence of an organization like the United Nations is unimaginable. More than 1,580 UN peacekeepers died in the service of international peace and security between 1945 and 1998. In recognition of their invaluable contribution to world peace, the United Nations peacekeeping forces were awarded the Nobel Peace Prize in 1988.

BASIC CHARTER PROVISIONS

The basic provisions of the charter defining the functions of the Security Council and the General Assembly are summarized here, but fuller accounts will be found in the chapters on those bodies, which complement the present chapter.

1. *Relative Powers of the Security Council and the General Assembly.* Under Article 24 of the charter, the Security Council has "primary responsibility" in questions of peace and security. It is invested with special powers enabling it to decide, on behalf of the entire UN membership, to take collective action when peace is threatened (Articles 39–42) and is empowered to negotiate agreements with individual members of the UN for the provision of armed forces necessary to maintain international security and to determine how many members shall participate in any collective action undertaken (Articles 43–48).

The General Assembly, on the other hand, is empowered only to consider and make recommendations, either to the Security Council or to particular states, on matters pertaining to peace and security. Moreover, under Articles 11 and 12, it may discuss but may not make actual recommendations on any special dispute between nations that is currently under consideration by the Security Council. However, though the Assembly is not expressly empowered to take action, neither is it expressly prohibited from doing so. In the only charter provision touching on the subject, paragraph 2 of Article 11—which is the focus of conflicting interpretation in the long-standing constitutional controversy on the financing of certain General Assembly-sponsored peacekeeping operations—the actual wording is as follows: "Any such question [of international peace and security] on which action is necessary shall be referred to the Security Council by the General Assembly either before or after discussion."

2. *Bringing a Dispute or Serious Situation Before the UN.* Although the charter firmly establishes the primacy of the Security Council over the General Assembly in matters of peace and security, it does not stipulate that disputes or serious situations must be discussed in the Security Council before they are discussed by the General Assembly. A dispute may be brought before the UN in a variety of ways specified in the charter without order of preference. One or more of the disputing parties may bring the matter before the Security Council voluntarily, or the council itself may choose to exercise its constitutional right to investigate a dispute at its own discretion; or any UN member, whether or not it is involved in the dispute, may propose the matter for discussion by the General Assembly; or a non-UN member that is a party to the dispute may—under certain conditions—bring it to the attention of the General Assembly; or the Security Council may ask the General Assembly to discuss the matter.

Despite these liberal provisions, the charter does not stipulate that all political disputes between states should be brought before the UN. Article 33, for example, enjoins UN members "first of all" to seek a solution to their differences on their own initiative (though if they fail to take this initiative, the Security Council is empowered to call upon them to do so). Only after their efforts to achieve a peaceful settlement have proved fruitless are the disputing parties obliged by the charter to refer the matter to the Security Council. Again, the UN was never intended by its founders to be regarded as the sole international agency for dealing with political disputes. Thus, Article 52 states that nothing in the charter "precludes the existence of regional arrangements or agencies for dealing with such matters relating to the maintenance of international peace and security as are appropriate for regional action" and that members participating in such regional arrangements or agencies "shall make every effort to achieve pacific settlement of local disputes through such regional arrangements or by such regional agencies before referring them to the Security Council."

POLITICAL BACKGROUND TO THE UN'S PEACEKEEPING ACTION

The UN's efforts to preserve international peace and security are the most contentious aspect of its entire work, because of the inherently political nature of its role and the fact that both the Security Council and the General Assembly are essentially political bodies, not courts of law that apportion blame and impartially hand down judgments drawn from a set of established legal codes. Their task in disputes brought before them is to find a compromise solution that is at once satisfactory to all parties, based on the political realities of the world situation and consistent with the principles of the charter. In this way, each local dispute brought before the UN automatically becomes a dispute involving the entire membership, as nations express differing views on the appropriate action to be taken by consensus of the membership.

The involvement of the general membership in all disputes is precisely what the founders of the UN intended—as a means of ensuring collective international responsibility for political solutions that are both just and realistic. However, in order to provide a counterweight to the unavoidable taking of sides, they established the principle of unanimity among the great powers by bestowing the right of veto on the permanent members of the Security Council. The workability of this principle in practice presupposed a basic measure of cooperation among the great powers. As events turned out, however, unanimity among the great powers proved to be a chimera. Within a year of the signing of the charter, the world was in the throes of the cold war, and the United States and USSR were engaged in a power struggle. The effects of this unexpected political development on the UN's work in maintaining international peace and security were immediate and devastating. Each dispute between the smaller nations that came before the UN was subsumed under the developing power struggle between the giants. As a result, between 1945 and 1990, the Security Council was deadlocked again and again by 279 vetoes. Furthermore, the charter requirements for agreement on the provision of armed forces for the UN could not be met.

Whereas the USSR looked to the Security Council and the veto as its power instrument in the UN, the United States looked to the support of the majority vote in the General Assembly. In order to circumvent the Soviet veto in the Security Council, and being at that time confident of majority support for most of its substantive policy objectives, the United States spearheaded a drive to turn the General Assembly into a body for action in periods of international crisis. This drive culminated in the adoption in 1950 of the Uniting for Peace Resolution, which empowered the General Assembly to undertake collective measures for maintaining or restoring peace when the Security Council found itself unable to act in times of emergency (for the terms of the resolution, see the chapter on the General Assembly). It was the United States, represented by Secretary of State Dean Acheson, that originated the proposal for the resolution. Although some of the small nations expressed reservations about certain clauses, most of them were eager to participate more fully in the UN's peace and security responsibilities. Only India and Argentina abstained in the vote, and only the Soviet bloc voted against the resolution, branding it as illegal and contrary to the charter.

The Uniting for Peace Resolution has been invoked in three major crises: the Korean War, the Suez crisis, and the Congo crisis (discussed under Case Histories below). In all three instances, the Security Council found itself deadlocked, and General Assembly action was deemed essential by the majority of members. Nevertheless, despite its proven usefulness as an instrument of restoring peace in these instances, the resolution seems unlikely to be invoked in future disputes. Certain countries questioned the legality of the resolution and of the General Assembly's action taken under it, and they felt justified on these grounds in refusing to contribute to the costs of the Suez and Congo peacekeeping operations.

At the end of the 1980s, the demise of the Soviet Union and the cold war dramatically changed this state of affairs. Within a few short years the entire Soviet bloc was dissolved and a new era of cooperation between the United States and the Russian Federation raised hopes that the Security Council would begin to fulfill the function foreseen for it by the organization's founders. However, the political vacuum created by the collapse of the East-West stalemate was followed by an eruption of intransigent, deadly regional conflicts and civil wars, particularly in Africa and Eastern Europe. While 13 operations were established between 1948 and 1988, 40 new operations have been authorized since 1988. At its peak in 1995, total deployment of UN military and civilian personnel reached almost 70,000 from 77 countries. By the end of 1996, 16 peacekeeping operations were severely taxing the ability and political will of member states to respond with personnel and financial contributions. And in 2000, the number of current peacekeeping missions was holding steady at 15.

TYPES OF ACTION TAKEN BY THE UN

The UN has two main responsibilities with respect to the political disputes that are brought before it by states: helping the parties concerned to arrive at a peaceful settlement of the issue that caused the dispute, and maintaining the peace if animosities threaten to erupt into violence or restoring the peace if hostilities have already broken out.

An Agenda for Peace

In response to the profoundly altered global political situation, on 31 January 1992, the Security Council met in a historic summit session attended by 13 heads of state and two foreign ministers. At that session, the Security Council requested Secretary-General Boutros Boutros-Ghali to prepare an analysis and recommendations on ways to strengthen UN peacekeeping efforts. In June 1992 the Secretary-General submitted *An Agenda for Peace*. This important document challenged member states to adapt their world organization to the new international situation with more effective and rational peacekeeping procedures. The document began by defining four types of peace-related activities:

Preventive Diplomacy. Defined as action to prevent disputes from arising and to prevent existing disputes from escalating into conflicts. The Secretary-General listed a number of different actions that constituted preventive diplomacy: confidence building (exchange of military missions, opening channels for the exchange of information, and providing monitoring for regional arms reduction agreements), fact-finding missions, early warning from regional organizations with observer status at the United Nations, preventive deployment of a UN force before hostilities occur, and the establishment of demilitarized zones.

Peacemaking. Action to bring hostile parties to agreement through peaceful means like those outlined in Chapter VI of the UN Charter, namely: negotiation, enquiry, mediation, conciliation, arbitration, judicial settlement or appealing to regional organizations.

The Secretary-General suggested that the International Court of Justice remained an underused resource for peaceful settlement of international disputes. He recommended that member states that had not accepted the general jurisdiction of the International Court of Justice, do so before the end of the UN Decade of International Law in the year 2000. Another tool for peacemaking was the imposition of economic sanctions under Article 41 of the charter. The main difficulty with this tool was compensating member states that would find their own economies crippled by the imposition of sanctions on an offending state.

Peacekeeping. Defined as the deployment of a UN force to the field, usually with the consent of the parties to the conflict. Peacekeeping could involve military, police, and civilian personnel. The UN pioneered this new form of military deployment during the early conflicts in the Middle East and the Congo. Peacekeeping troops serve at the request of all the parties to a conflict, for example, to monitor implementation of a cease-fire, or to prevent shipments of weapons across borders. They may also serve to monitor a demilitarized zone and provide a buffer between combatants. Peacekeeping forces, however, are only lightly armed and authorized to use force only in self-defense. By its very nature, peacekeeping implies an even-handed treatment of all the parties in a conflict.

Peace Enforcement. Although not officially defined as a separate concept in *An Agenda for Peace*, the Secretary-General did propose the creation, under Article 43 of the charter, of forces which could respond quickly and forcefully to imminent or outright aggression. In fact, the UN had sometimes been called upon to send forces to restore a cease-fire. In the Secretary-General's proposal, these troops would be maintained and specially trained by the armed forces of member states. When called upon, they would be more heavily armed than peacekeeping forces and authorized to use deadly force to stop combatants. The Secretary-General proposed that these special units would be on call for quick response to the early stages of an international crisis. In the post–cold war era, peace enforcement had already found expression in the Security Council's authorization of a multinational force (sanctioned by the UN but not, however, under UN administration) led by the United States to suppress Iraq's 1991 invasion of Kuwait.

However, the concept of peace enforcement remains controversial, as some experts and member countries maintain that there is no basis in the UN charter for an organization dedicated to international peace to settle disputes with military force. Under the charter, member states are meant to settle their disputes by peaceful means.

On the other hand, Article 43 of the charter provides for member states to make military forces available to the Security Council. In fact, it was originally envisioned that the United States alone would provide twenty divisions (over 300,000 troops), a very large naval force, 1,250 bombers, and 2,250 fighters. These provisions were never implemented due to lack of consensus.

In 1993, former Undersecretary-General Brian Urquhart, who participated in the management of 15 peacekeeping operations during his 40-year tenure at the United Nations, proposed the creation of an elite UN-trained military force made up of international volunteers, not soldiers seconded from national forces. Urquhart suggested that such a volunteer force would give the Security Council the ability to back up preventive diplomacy with immediate peace enforcement. "Clearly, a timely intervention by a relatively small but highly trained force, willing and authorized to take combat risks and representing the will of the international community, could make a decisive difference in the early stages of a crisis," said Urquhart in the journal "Foreign Policy." Urquhart suggested that such a force might have been used effectively, for example, during the attempted deployment of the UN Mission in Haiti (UNMIH). When the United States naval ship carrying the first deployment of troops arrived at Port au Prince in October 1993, the ship was prevented from landing by a disorganized and violent demonstration of armed civilians at the port. By August 1994, the escalating crisis in Haiti had led the Security Council to authorize a multinational force, similar to that used in the Iraq-Kuwait crisis, to restore the democratically elected government of Haiti. The escalation might have been prevented if UNMIH had been enabled to carry out its mandate.

Peace Building. Defined as "action to identify and support structures which will tend to strengthen and solidify peace in order to avoid a relapse into conflict."

The UN had already begun to develop the concept of "peace building" as early as 1990, when the UN Observer Group in Central America supervised Nicaraguan elections which were certified to be "free and fair" by the UN Observer Mission to Verify the Electoral Process in Nicaragua (ONUVEN).

Since then the demand for UN electoral assistance has grown enormously. Before 1992, the UN supervised elections in Haiti, Namibia, and Nicaragua. However, between January 1992 and June 1994, the United Nations received 56 requests for electoral assistance. The organization's Electoral Assistance Unit was established in 1992 and operates within the Department of Peacekeeping Operations. It provided assistance to 53 of those states. Following is a list of member states requesting and receiving assistance during this period: Albania, Argentina, Azerbaijan, Brazil, Burundi, Cameroon, Central African Republic, Chad, Colombia, Congo, Djibouti, El Salvador, Equatorial Guinea, Eritrea, Estonia, Ethiopia, Gabon, Ghana, Guinea, Guinea-Bissau, Guyana, Kenya, Latvia, Lesotho, Liberia, Madagascar, Malawi, Mozambique, Namibia, Netherlands Antilles, Nicaragua, Niger, Panama, Paraguay, Peru, Philippines, Romania, Russia, Rwanda, Senegal, Seychelles, Sierra Leone, South Africa, Swaziland, Togo, Uganda, and Western Sahara. The Electoral Assistance Unit is supported by the UN Trust Fund for Electoral Observation, a voluntary fund which, in 1994, was supported by contributions from Austria, Denmark, Iceland, Ireland, Norway, Sweden, Switzerland, and the United Kingdom.

From June 1994 to December 1996, the Electoral Assistance Unit received requests and provided varying amounts of assistance to the following countries: Algeria, Armenia, Azerbaijan, Bangladesh, Benin, Burkina Faso, Cambodia, Chad, Comoros, Côte d'Ivoire, Democratic Republic of the Congo (formerly Zaire), Croatia, Djibouti, East Timor, El Salvador, Equatorial Guinea, Fiji, Gabon, Gambia, Ghana, Guinea, Guinea-Bissau, Guyana, Haiti, Honduras, Indonesia, Kyrgyzstan, Lesotho, the Former Yugoslav Republic of Macedonia, Madagascar, Malawi, Mali, Mexico, Mozambique, Namibia, Nepal, Netherlands Antilles, Nicaragua, Niger, Nigeria, São Tomé and Principe, South Africa, Tanzania, Uganda, Ukraine, Uzbekistan, Yemen, and Zambia.

Besides building peace by strengthening a country's democratic infrastructure, the Secretary-General also included the following activities under the concept of peace building: clearing land-mines so that agriculture and transportation may be resumed safely; disarming the warring parties; taking custody of and destroying weapons; repatriating refugees; training security personnel; educational and cultural exchanges; and joint projects to develop agriculture, improve transportation, or utilize shared natural resources.

The Cost of Waging Peace

In *Renewing the United Nations System* (Dag Hammarskjöld Foundation, 1994), co-authors Brian Urquhart and Erskine Childers (former senior adviser to the UN Director General for Development and International Cooperation) cite the following figures: "By early 1993 the UN was deploying four times the number of troops, 70 times more police and over 100 times the number of civilian personnel as in 1987, at nearly 10 times the annual cost. As of 30 April 1994 the UN had contributions from 66 countries of 65,838 troops, 2,400 military observers, and 1,307 civilian and police personnel, with possible further deployments (and costs) evolving almost weekly relative to situations like those in Haiti, Rwanda and the former Yugoslavia. The projected costs of peace-keeping rose from some US$600 million in 1991 to an estimated US$2.3 billion for 1993."

In fact, in May 1994, the Secretary-General was unable to obtain 5,500 troops from African nations to protect refugees and international aid workers caught in the bloody Rwandan civil war. He attributed this to donor fatigue among the countries that frequently assign troops to UN operations.

As the world has increasingly turned to the UN to deal with conflicts, the cost of peacekeeping has risen accordingly. The annual cost of all peacekeeping operates in 1995 amounted to about US$3.0 billion. However, global military expenditures in the 1990s amount to around US$1 trillion per year. Of course, these monetary figures do not adequately take into account the tragic price paid in human death and suffering during war. UN peacekeeping equipment and personnel cost about US$1.6 billion in 1996, down from US$2.8 billion in 1995, which reflected the cost of UN peacekeeping in the former Yugoslavia. In 1997, the cost was about US$1 billion.

Most UN peacekeeping operations are not financed from the organization's regular budget, but from special accounts established by the organization to fund each particular operation. Each member is then assessed for a share of the mission's estimated cost. Special assessments for peacekeeping are divided into three categories. The five permanent members of the Security Council pay about 22 percent more than the regular scale of assessments because of their greater influence over Security Council decisions (by virtue of holding the power of veto). Other developed industrial states pay the same share for peacekeeping as they pay for the regular budget. Wealthier developing countries pay one-fifth of their regular budget share for peacekeeping. The poorest nations (least developed countries, or LDCs) pay one-tenth of their regular share. There are certain inequities to this arrangement. For example, 15 "developing" states with per capita GNPs of $5,000 or more still are assessed only one-fifth of their regular budget assessment for peacekeeping (United Arab Emirates, Kuwait, Qatar, Brunei, Singapore,

Bahamas, Israel, Cyprus, Barbados, Bahrain, Saudi Arabia, Malta, Greece, Libya, and Oman).

A recurrent and critical problem for UN peacekeeping has been the consistent shortfall in the payment of members' assessed contributions. As of February 1998, member states owed the UN a total of US$1.6 billion in current and back peacekeeping dues.

Since 1945, 110 nations have contributed personnel at various times; 77 were providing peacekeepers in August 1998. In the mid 1990s, the top contributors of personnel to ongoing peacekeeping missions were Pakistan, the Russian Federation, Bangladesh, India, and Brazil. The small island nation of Fiji has taken part in virtually every UN peacekeeping operation, as has Canada.

For the above reasons, the Secretary-General suggested in his *Agenda for Peace* that contributions to UN peacekeeping operations be financed from defense budgets, rather than from foreign affairs budgets. Other innovative proposals in the agenda included obtaining standing commitments from member states as to the numbers and kinds of skilled personnel they can offer the United Nations as new operations arise; new arrangements for training peacekeeping personnel, including indispensable civilian and police staff; stockpiling basic peacekeeping equipment (vehicles, communications equipment, generators, etc.); and air and sea lift capacity to be provided by member states either free of cost or at lower than commercial rates.

Genesis of a Peacekeeping Mission

Many missions are planned in response to a crisis, so the steps in mounting them happen more or less simultaneously. When more time is available, the following sequence of events is usually adhered to:

- Mediation. The Secretary-General may be instructed to dispatch field survey missions, or may choose to send his own special representative to help achieve a political settlement.
- Initial Design. The mission concept is presented to the Security Council for its preliminary approval.
- Security Council Directive. The Security Council directs the Secretary-General to report back within a specified amount of time with a plan for the mission that includes its size, structure, duties, and timeline.
- Mission Design. Units of the Department of Peacekeeping Operations put together a plan for the mission.
- Security Council approval obtained.
- Creation and verification of the mission budget.
- Submission of the budget to the Fifth Committee (Financial).
- Fifth Committee submits the budget to the General Assembly for approval.
- Assessment letters are sent to the member states.

Until approved by the General Assembly, the Secretary-General cannot make contractual commitments for equipment, transport, or other services in excess of a US$10 million annual spending authority for special circumstances. The length of the approval process creates a devastating time lag when an international crisis develops that requires a timely response.

Chronology of Peacekeeping Operations

Between 1945 and 1999, there were 53 UN peacekeeping or observer missions. The following is a list of the UN peacekeeping operations, arranged in chronological order. Unless otherwise noted, figures are accurate as of April 2000. For more background on the conflicts and the countries receiving UN peacekeeping missions, please refer to the country entries in Volumes I through IV of this encyclopedia.

UNTSO-United Nations Truce Supervision Organization

Duration: June 1948 to present.
Headquarters: Government House, Jerusalem.
Strength: 153 military observers.
Fatalities: 28.
Mandate: Initially to supervise the original truce of 1948; in 1949, following the conclusion of armistice agreements between Israel and its Arab neighbors (Egypt, Jordan, Lebanon, and Syria), its responsibility became to assist the parties in supervising the application and observance of those agreements. However, over the years, its activities and responsibilities have expanded to cover a number of UN-supervised emergency situations in Israel, Syria, and Lebanon.
Composition: UNTSO's military observers come from 19 contributing countries: Argentina, Australia, Austria, Belgium, Canada, Chile, China, Denmark, Estonia, Finland, France, Ireland, Italy, Netherlands, New Zealand, Norway, Russian Federation, Slovakia, Slovenia, Sweden, Switzerland, and United States.
Annual cost: approximately US$23 million.

UNMOGIP-United Nations Military Observer Group in India and Pakistan

Duration: January 1949 to present.
Location: The cease-fire line between India and Pakistan in the state of Jammu and Kashmir.
Strength: 44 military observers.
Fatalities: 6.
Mandate: To observe developments pertaining to the strict observance of the cease-fire of 17 December 1971 and report to the Secretary-General.
Composition: UNMOGIP's military observers come from eight countries: Belgium, Chile, Denmark, Finland, Italy, Republic of Korea, Sweden, and Uruguay.
Annual cost: approximately US$8.3 million.

UNEF I-First United Nations Emergency Force

Duration: November 1956 to June 1967.
Location: Initially the Suez Canal sector and the Sinai peninsula; later, along the Armistice Demarcation Line in the Gaza area and the Egyptian side of the international frontier in the Sinai peninsula..
Strength: At peak: 6,073; at end: 3,400.
Fatalities: 107.
Mandate: To secure and to supervise the cessation of hostilities, including the withdrawal of the armed forces of France, Israel, and the United Kingdom from Egyptian territory, and to serve as a buffer between the Egyptian and Israeli forces.
Composition: Brazil, Canada, Colombia, Denmark, Finland, India, Indonesia, Norway, Sweden, and Yugoslavia.
Total cost: approximately US$214 million.

UNOGIL-United Nations Observation Group in Lebanon

Duration: June 1958 to December 1958.
Location: Beirut, Lebanon.
Strength: 591 military observers (maximum).
Fatalities: None.
Mandate: To ensure that there was no illegal infiltration of personnel or supply of arms across the Lebanese border.
Composition: Forces from 21 countries.
Total cost: approximately US$3.7 million.

UNOC-United Nations Operation in the Congo

Duration: July 1960 to June 1964.
Location: Leopoldville (now Kinshasa), Republic of Congo (now Zaire).
Strength: Peak: 19,828.
Fatalities: 250.

Mandate: Initially, to ensure withdrawal of Belgian forces and assist the government in maintaining law and order; later, to maintain territorial integrity and independence of the Congo and to prevent the occurrence of civil war.

Composition: Argentina, Brazil, Canada, Denmark, Ethiopia, Ghana, Guinea, India, Indonesia, Ireland, Italy, Liberia, Malaysia, Mali, Morocco, Netherlands, Nigeria, Norway, Pakistan, Sudan, Sweden, Tunisia, Yugoslavia.

Total cost: approximately US$400 million.

UNSF-United Nations Security Force in West New Guinea (West Irian)

Duration: October 1962 to April 1963.

Location: Hollandia, West Irian (now Jayaphra, Indonesia).

Strength: 1,576.

Fatalities: None.

Mandate: To maintain peace and security in the territory under the UN Temporary Executive Authority established by agreement between Indonesia and the Netherlands while the administration of the territory was transferred to Indonesia.

Composition: Canada, Pakistan, United States.

Total cost: approximately US$26.4 million (cost borne by Netherlands and Indonesia).

UNYOM-United Nations Yemen Observations Mission

Duration: July 1963 to September 1964.

Location: Sana'a, Yemen.

Strength: 25 military observers; 114 members of a reconnaissance unit; 50 members of an air unit.

Fatalities: None.

Mandate: To observe and certify the implementation of the disengagement agreement between Saudi Arabia and the United Arab Republic (now Egypt and Syria).

Composition: Canada, Yugoslavia.

Total cost: approximately US$1.8 million (cost borne by Saudi Arabia and Egypt).

UNFICYP-United Nations Peacekeeping Force in Cyprus

Duration: March 1964 to present.

Location: Cyprus.

Strength: 1,242 troops and support personnel, and 230 international and civilian police.

Fatalities: 165.

Mandate: To prevent a recurrence of fighting between Turkish-backed Cypriots and Greek-backed Cypriots; to contribute to the maintenance and restoration of law and order.

Composition: The operational elements of UNFICYP are provided by Argentina, Australia, Austria, Canada, Finland, Hungary, Ireland, Nepal, Netherlands, Slovenia, and the United Kingdom. There are also 34 international civilian personnel and 381 locally recruited staff.

Annual cost: approximately US$45.6 million.

DOMREP-Mission of the Representative of the Secretary-General in the Dominican Republic

Duration: May 1965 to October 1966.

Location: Santo Domingo, Dominican Republic.

Strength: Two military observers.

Fatalities: None.

Mandate: To observe the situation and to report on breaches of the cease-fire between the two *de facto* authorities.

Composition: None.

Total cost: US$275,831 (through UN regular budget).

UNIPOM-United Nations India-Pakistan Observation Mission

Duration: September 1965 to March 1966.

Location: Lahore, Pakistan, and Amritsar, India (deployed along the India/Pakistan border between Kashmir and the Arabian Sea).

Strength: 96 military observers (maximum).

Fatalities: None.

Mandate: To supervise the cease-fire along the India/Pakistan border (except the State of Jammu and Kashmir where UNMOGIP operates) and the withdrawal of all armed personnel to the positions held before 5 August 1965.

Composition: Australia, Belgium, Brazil, Burma, Canada, Chile, Denmark, Ethiopia, Finland, Ireland, Italy, Nepal, Netherlands, New Zealand, Nigeria, Norway, Sweden, Sri Lanka, Venezuela.

Total cost: US$1,713,280.

UNEF II-Second United Nations Emergency Force

Duration: October 1973 to July 1979.

Location: Suez Canal sector and later the Sinai peninsula.

Strength: Peak: 6,973; end: 4,000.

Fatalities: 55.

Mandate: To supervise the cease-fire between Egyptian and Israeli forces; later, to supervise the redeployment of those forces and act as a buffer between them.

Composition: Australia, Austria, Canada, Finland, Ghana, Indonesia, Ireland, Nepal, Panama, Peru, Poland, Senegal, Sweden.

Total cost: approximately US$446.5 million.

UNDOF-United Nations Disengagement Observer Force

Duration: June 1974 to present.

Location: Syrian Golan Heights.

Strength: 1,037 troops, assisted by approximately 80 military observers.

Fatalities: 31.

Mandate: To maintain the cease-fire between Israel and Syria; supervise the disengagement of Israeli and Syrian forces; supervise the areas of separation and limitation.

Composition: Originally composed of Austrian and Peruvian infantry units and Canadian and Polish logistic elements. Currently composed of contingents from Austria, Canada, Japan, Poland, and Slovakia.

Annual cost: approximately US$35.4 million.

UNIFIL-United Nations Interim Force in Lebanon

Duration: March 1978 to present.

Location: Southern Lebanon.

Strength: 4,550 troops and approximately 50 military observers; 450 local and international civilian staff.

Fatalities: 193.

Mandate: To confirm the withdrawal of Israeli forces from southern Lebanon; restore international peace and security; assist the government of Lebanon in ensuring the return of its effective authority in the area.

Composition: Troops provided by Fiji, Finland, France, Ghana, India, Ireland, Italy, Nepal, and Poland.

Annual cost: approximately US$148.9 million.

UNGOMAP-United Nations Good Offices Mission in Afghanistan and Pakistan

Duration: April 1988 to March 1990.

Location: Kabul, Afghanistan, and Islamabad, Pakistan.

Strength: 50 military observers.

Fatalities: None.

Mandate: To assist in monitoring the implementation of the 1988 peace settlement between Afghanistan and Pakistan.

Composition: Austria, Canada, Denmark, Finland, Fiji, Ghana, Ireland, Nepal, Poland, and Sweden.

Total cost: approximately US$14 million.

UNIIMOG-United Nations Iran-Iraq Military Observer Group

Duration: August 1988 to February 1991.

Location: The 740-mile border between Iran and Iraq (headquarters in both Baghdad, Iraq, and Teheran, Iran).

Strength: 400 military personnel; 93 local staff.

Fatalities: 1.

Mandate: To verify, confirm, and supervise the cease-fire and withdrawal of troops.

Composition: Argentina, Australia, Austria, Bangladesh, Canada, Denmark, Finland, Ghana, Hungary, India, Indonesia, Ireland, Italy, Kenya, Malaysia, New Zealand, Nigeria, Norway, Peru, Poland, Senegal, Sweden, Turkey, Uruguay, Yugoslavia, Zambia.

Total cost: approximately US$178 million.

UNAVEM I-United Nations Angola Verification Mission I

Duration: January 1989 to June 1991.

Location: Luanda, Angola.

Strength: Peak: 70 military observers; 22 international staff; 15 local staff.

Fatalities: None.

Mandate: To monitor the withdrawal of Cuban troops from Angola.

Composition: Algeria, Argentina, Brazil, Congo, Czechoslovakia, India, Jordan, Norway, Spain, Yugoslavia.

Total cost: approximately US$16.4 million.

UNTAG-United Nations Transition Assistance Group

Duration: April 1989 to March 1990.

Location: Windhoek, Namibia.

Maximum strength: Approximately 4,500 military personnel; 1,500 police; 2,000 civilian personnel; 1,000 election observers.

Fatalities: 19.

Mandate: To monitor and supervise the Namibia independence plan, including supervision of elections to a Constituent Assembly.

Composition: Argentina, Australia, Austria, Bangladesh, Canada, Denmark, Finland, Ghana, Hungary, India, Indonesia, Ireland, Italy, Kenya, Malaysia, New Zealand, Nigeria, Norway, Peru, Poland, Senegal, Sweden, Turkey, Uruguay, Yugoslavia, Zambia.

Total cost: approximately US$368.5 million.

ONUCA-United Nations Observer Group in Central America

Duration: November 1989 to January 1992.

Location: Costa Rica, El Salvador, Guatemala, Honduras, and Nicaragua (headquarters in Tegucigalpa).

Strength: Peak: 1,195; end: 338.

Fatalities: None.

Mandate: Initially, to verify the compliance of the five Central American countries with their security undertakings (the Esquipulas II Agreement, 1987) to cease aid to insurrectionist movements in the region and not to allow their territory to be used for attacks on other states; later, to monitor the demobilization of the Nicaraguan resistance (the "Contras").

Composition: Argentina, Brazil, Canada, Colombia, Ecuador, India, Ireland, Spain, Sweden, Venezuela.

Total cost: approximately US$89 million.

UNIKOM-United Nations Iraq-Kuwait Observation Mission

Duration: April 1991 to present.

Location: The demilitarized zone along the boundary between Iraq and Kuwait.

Strength: 195 military observers and 908 support personnel, and some 200 international and local civilian staff. Due to repeated Iraqi incursions, in 1993 UNIKOM's mandate was expanded to include taking action against such incursions.

Fatalities: 2.

Mandate: To monitor the Khawr 'Abd Allah waterway between Iraq and Kuwait and the demilitarized zone; deter violations of the boundary; observe any hostile action; and, as expanded by Security Council resolution 806 (1993), to resist attempts to prevent it by force from discharging its duties.

Composition: Argentina, Austria, Bangladesh, Canada, China, Denmark, Fiji, Finland, France, Germany, Ghana, Greece, Hungary, India, Indonesia, Ireland, Italy, Kenya, Malaysia, Nigeria, Pakistan, Poland, Romania, Russian Federation, Senegal, Singapore, Sweden, Thailand, Turkey, United Kingdom, United States, Uruguay, and Venezuela.

Annual cost: approximately US$54 million.

UNAVEM II-United Nations Angola Verification Mission II

Duration: June 1991 to February 1995.

Location: Angola.

Strength: 350 military observers, 126 police observers, 400 electoral observers, 80 international civilian staff and 155 local staff.

Fatalities: 3.

Mandate: Initially, monitor the cease-fire between the Angolan Government and UNITA, until general elections were held in 1992; observe the elections scheduled for September 1992. When fighting broke out again after the elections, UNAVEM II's mandate was expanded to include monitoring the new cease-fire between the government and UNITA. However, the political situation continued to deteriorate, until in 1993 UNAVEM II had to evacuate 45 of its 67 monitoring locations. Its mandate was extended three months at a time, as it had become an essential factor in a continuous UN effort to facilitate the resumption of negotiations and support humanitarian activities in the country. Following the signing of 20 November 1994 by the Government of Angola and UNITA of the Lusaka Protocol, UNAVEM II verified the initial stages of the peace agreement.

Composition: Military and police personnel are contributed by Argentina, Brazil, Congo, Guinea-Bissau, Hungary, India, Ireland, Jordan, Malaysia, Morocco, Netherlands, Nigeria, Norway, Slovak Republic, Spain, Sweden, and Zimbabwe.

Total cost: US$175.8 million.

ONUSAL-United Nations Observer Mission in El Salvador

Duration: July 1991 to April 1995.

Location: El Salvador.

Strength: Approximately 380 military observers, 8 medical officers, 631 police observers; there was also a provision for some 140 civilian international staff and 180 local staff.

Fatalities: 5.

Mandate: Initially, to verify compliance with the San José Agreement on Human Rights by the government of El Salvador and the Frente Farabundo Marti para la Liberación Nacional (FMLN); monitor the human rights situation in El Salvador; investigate specific cases of alleged human rights violations; promote human rights in the country; make recommendations for the elimination of violations; and report on these matters to the Secretary-General. Subsequent to final peace agreements which were signed in 1992, ONUSAL's mandate was expanded to include verification of the cease-fire and separation of forces; and monitoring the maintenance of public order while a new National Civil Police force was set up. Finally, ONUSAL's mandate was expanded to observe national elections for the presidency, the legislative assembly, mayors, and municipal councils in March 1994.

Composition: ONUSAL military observers are provided by

Brazil, Canada, Colombia, Ecuador, India, Ireland, Spain, Sweden, and Venezuela. Police observers come from Austria, Brazil, Chile, Colombia, France, Guyana, Italy, Mexico, Spain, and Sweden.

Total cost: approximately US$107 million.

MINURSO-United Nations Mission for the Referendum in Western Sahara

Duration: April 1991 to present.

Location: Western Sahara.

Strength: 191 military observers, 25 military support personnel, 79 civilian police officers, supported by international and local staff.

Fatalities: 4.

Mandate: To verify a cease-fire between the government of Morocco and the Frente Popular para la Liberación de Saguia el-Hamra y de Rio de Oro (Frente Polisario); monitor the confinement of Moroccan and Frente Polisario troops to designated locations; ensure release of all political prisoners or detainees; oversee exchange of prisoners of war; implement a repatriation program; identify and register qualified voters; organize and ensure a free referendum to enable the people of Western Sahara to exercise their right to self-determination, to choose between independence and integration with Morocco. Updated mandate was only through May 2000.

Composition: Military observers and support personnel are provided by Argentina, Austria, Bangladesh, Belgium, China, Egypt, El Salvador, France, Ghana, Greece, Guinea, Honduras, Hungary, India, Ireland, Italy, Kenya, Malaysia, Nigeria, Norway, Pakistan, Poland, Portugal, Republic of Korea, Russian Federation, Sweden, United States, Uruguay, and Venezuela.

Annual cost: approximately US$52.1 million.

UNAMIC-United Nations Advance Mission in Cambodia

Duration: October 1991 to March 1992.

Location: Cambodia.

Strength: 1,504 military and civilian personnel.

Fatalities: None.

Mandate: To immediately deploy a small advance mission to assist the Cambodian parties to maintain a cease-fire while preparations were made for the larger UNTAC force. UNAMIC consisted of civilian and military liaison staff, a military mine-awareness unit, and logistics and support personnel. Its mandate was expanded in January 1992 to include training Cambodians in mine-clearing.

Composition: Algeria, Argentina, Australia, Austria, Bangladesh, Belgium, Canada, China, France, Germany, Ghana, India, Indonesia, Ireland, Malaysia, Netherlands, New Zealand, Pakistan, Poland, Russian Federation, Senegal, Thailand, Tunisia, United Kingdom, United States, And Uruguay.

Total cost: See UNTAC, below.

UNPROFOR-United Nations Protection Force

Duration: March 1992 to December 1995.

Location: Bosnia and Herzegovina, Croatia, the Federal Republic of Yugoslavia (Serbia and Montenegro), and the former Yugoslav Republic of Macedonia.

Strength: 38,599 military personnel, 684 UN military observers, 803 civilian police, 2,017 international civilian staff, and 2,615 local staff.

Fatalities: 167.

Mandate: In the wake of the end of the cold war, fighting broke out among ethnic and religious factions in the former Yugoslavia. In January 1992, Secretary-General Boutros Boutros-Ghali sent 50 military liaison officers to Yugoslavia to promote maintenance of cease-fire by facilitating communication. In February, although some political groups in Yugoslavia were still

expressing objections to a UN plan for a peace-keeping operation, the Security Council established UNPROFOR for an initial period of 12 months to create the conditions of peace and security required for the negotiation of an overall settlement of the Yugoslav crisis. UNPROFOR's operational mandate extends to five republics of the former Yugoslavia, as indicated above. In the rapidly deteriorating situation, its mandate has been enlarged in all five republics to include such things as security at Sarajevo airport; protection of humanitarian convoys; monitoring of a "no-fly zone" banning all military flights in the airspace of Bosnia and Herzegovina; border control; the creation of "safe areas" to protect civilians from armed attack. UNPROFOR monitored the implementation of a cease-fire agreement signed by the Bosnian government and Bosnian Croat forces in February 1994. UNPROFOR also monitored the arrangements for a cease-fire negotiated between the Bosnian government and Bosnian Serb forces which became effective on 1 January 1995.

Composition: Military and/or civilian police personnel are provided by Argentina, Australia, Bangladesh, Belgium, Brazil, Canada, Colombia, Czech Republic, Denmark, Egypt, Finland, France, Ghana, Ireland, Jordan, Kenya, Luxembourg, Nepal, Netherlands, New Zealand, Nigeria, Norway, Poland, Portugal, Russian Federation, Slovak Republic, Spain, Sweden, Switzerland, Tunisia, Ukraine, United Kingdom, United States, and Venezuela.

Total cost: Approximately US$4.6 billion.

UNTAC-United Nations Transitional Authority in Cambodia

Duration: March 1992 to September 1993.

Location: Cambodia.

Strength: (Peak) 22,000 military and civilian personnel.

Fatalities: 78.

Mandate: To monitor and help implement the Paris Agreements signed in 1991 between the various political entities in Cambodia. The mandate included aspects relating to human rights, the organization and conduct of free and fair general elections, military arrangements, civil administration, the maintenance of law and order, the repatriation and resettlement of the Cambodian refugees, and rehabilitation of essential Cambodian infrastructure. During its mission the Security Council requested UNTAC to play many roles, including human rights oversight and investigation of allegations of human rights abuses during the transitional period; implementing a legal framework for the electoral process; stabilizing the security situation; and ensuring a neutral political environment conducive to free and fair elections. After elections were held in May 1993 and a newly elected Constituent Assembly began work on 14 June 1993, a withdrawal schedule for UNPROFOR was established, leaving a smaller contingent of military police officers and medical units to continue the work of mine clearance and training.

Composition: UNTAC military and/or civilian police personnel were provided by Algeria, Argentina, Australia, Austria, Bangladesh, Belgium, Brunei Darussalam, Bulgaria, Cameroon, Canada, Chile, China, Colombia, Egypt, Fiji, France, Germany, Ghana, Hungary, India, Indonesia, Ireland, Italy, Japan, Jordan, Kenya, Malaysia, Morocco, Namibia, Nepal, Netherlands, New Zealand, Nigeria, Norway, Pakistan, Philippines, Poland, Russian Federation, Senegal, Singapore, Sweden, Thailand, Tunisia, United Kingdom, United States, and Uruguay.

Total cost: The total cost of both UNAMIC and UNTAC for the period was approximately US$1,621 million.

ONUMOZ-United Nations Operation in Mozambique

Duration: December 1992 to December 1994.

Location: Mozambique.

Strength: 6,625 troops and military personnel, 354 military observers and 1,144 civilian police; there were also some 355 international staff and 506 local staff; in addition, during the polling, ONUMOZ sent out about 900 electoral observers.

Fatalities: 24.

Mandate: To help implement the General Peace Agreement signed in 1992 in Rome, after 14 years of devastating civil war between the Republic of Mozambique and the Resisténcia Nacional Moçambicana (RENAMO). ONUMOZ's mandate included four important elements: political, military, electoral, and humanitarian. ONUMOZ military wing would monitor and verify the cease-fire, the separation of forces of the two parties, their demobilization and the collection, storage, and destruction of weapons. It would authorize security arrangements for vital infrastructures and provide security for United Nations and other international activities. ONUMOZ's Electoral Division would monitor and verify all aspects and stages of the electoral process. ONUMOZ's humanitarian component would function as an integrated component of ONUMOZ to make available food and other relief for distribution to soldiers in the assembly area. After successful presidential and legislative elections in October 1994, and the installation of Mozambique's new Parliament and President, ONUMOZ's mandate ended on 9 December 1994.

Composition: The military component includes 302 military observers and some 6,250 infantry and support personnel from Argentina, Bangladesh, Botswana, Brazil, Canada, Cape Verde, China, Czech Republic, Egypt, Guinea-Bissau, Hungary, India, Italy, Japan, Malaysia, Netherlands, Portugal, Russian Federation, Spain, Sweden, Uruguay, and Zambia.

Total cost: Approximately US$471 million.

UNOSOM I-United Nations Operation in Somalia I

Duration: April 1992 to March 1993.

Location: Somalia.

Strength: Originally 50 military observers; expanded to include 3,500 security personnel, and further expanded to include 719 personnel in logistical units; there were also some 200 international staff.

Fatalities: 8.

Mandate: To monitor a cease-fire in the capital, Mogadishu; provide protection for UN personnel, equipment, and supplies at the seaports and airports; escort deliveries of humanitarian supplies from there to distribution centers in the city and its immediate environs.

Composition: Observers were sent from Australia, Austria, Bangladesh, Belgium, Canada, Czechoslovakia, Egypt, Fiji, Finland, Indonesia, Jordan, Morocco, New Zealand, Norway, Pakistan, and Zimbabwe.

Total cost: Approximately US$42.9 million.

UNOSOM II-United Nations Operation in Somalia II

Duration: March 1993 to March 1995.

Location: Somalia.

Strength: 28,000 military personnel and 2,800 civilian staff.

Fatalities: 147.

Mandate: To establish a secure environment throughout the whole of Somalia; provide assistance to the Somali people in rebuilding their economy and social and political life; help reestablish the country's institutional structure; monitor that all factions continued to respect the various agreements; prevent resumption of violence and, if necessary, take appropriate action against any faction that violated the cessation of hostilities; maintain control of heavy weapons; seize small arms of all unauthorized elements; secure and maintain security at all ports, airports, and lines of communications; protect personnel, installations, and equipment belonging to the UN and other international organizations; take forceful action to neutralize armed elements that attacked or threatened to attack such facilities; assist in repatriation of refugees; continue the program of mine clearance begun

under UNISOM I. UNISOM II also sought to assist the Somali people in rebuilding their economy and society, based on a democratic government. In February 1994, after several violent incidents and attacks on UN soldiers, the Security Council revised the mandate to exclude use of coercive methods. UNISOM II was withdrawn in March 1995.

Composition: Military personnel are provided by Australia, Bangladesh, Belgium, Botswana, Canada, Egypt, France, Germany, Greece, India, Ireland, Italy, Kuwait, Malaysia, Morocco, Nepal, New Zealand, Nigeria, Norway, Pakistan, Republic of Korea, Romania, Saudi Arabia, Sweden, Tunisia, Turkey, United Arab Emirates, United States, and Zimbabwe.

Note: The United States forces deployed in Mogadishu to support UNOSOM I and UNOSOM II were not under United Nations command or authority. The Unified Task Force (UNITAF) spearheaded by the United States was deployed in Mogadishu on 9 December 1992 and included military units from Australia, Belgium, Botswana, Canada, Egypt, France, Germany, Greece, India, Italy, Kuwait, Morocco, New Zealand, Nigeria, Norway, Pakistan, Saudi Arabia, Sweden, Tunisia, Turkey, United Kingdom, and Zimbabwe.

Total cost: Approximately US$1,643 million.

UNOMUR-United Nations Observer Mission in Uganda-Rwanda

Duration: June 1993 to September 1994

Location: Uganda side of the Uganda-Rwanda border.

Strength: 81 military observers, 17 international staff, and 7 locally recruited personnel.

Fatalities: None.

Mandate: To verify that no lethal weapons and ammunitions are transported across the border from Uganda into northern Rwanda. The tragic slaughter in Rwanda in April 1994 prevented UNOMUR from fully implementing its mandate. However, the Observer Mission played a useful role immediately after the conclusion of the Arusha Peace Agreement.

Composition: Military observers were provided by Bangladesh, Botswana, Brazil, Canada, Hungary, Netherlands, Senegal, and Zimbabwe.

Total cost: (From inception to December 1993): US$2.3 million; US$8 million net.

UNOMIG-United Nations Observer Mission in Georgia

Duration: August 1993 to present.

Location: Georgia.

Strength: Authorized: 102 military observers supported by international and local civilian staff.

Mandate: To verify compliance with a cease-fire agreed to on 27 July 1993 between the government of Georgia and separatists in its northwestern region, Abkhazia. It would also investigate reports of cease-fire violations and attempt to resolve such incidents; and report to the Secretary-General about such violations. Before UNOMIG could be fully deployed, the cease-fire broke down, and, in accordance with the instructions of the Security Council resolution 858 (1993), deployment was halted. In May 1994, the Georgian and Abkhaz sides agreed to a cease-fire and separation of forces. UNOMIG then was to monitor the implementation of that agreement, and to verify the exit of troops and military equipment from the security zone. In December 1996, a human rights office was opened in Abkhazia to investigate reported or alleged violations.

Composition: Albania, Austria, Bangladesh, Czech Republic, Denmark, Egypt, France, Germany, Greece, Hungary, Indonesia, Jordan, Korea, Pakistan, Poland, Russian Federation, Sweden, Switzerland, Turkey, United Kingdom, United States, and Uruguay.

Annual cost: US$31 million.

UNOMIL-United Nations Observer Mission in Liberia

Duration: September 1993 to September 1997.

Location: Liberia.

Strength: 92 military personnel during electoral period (July 1997).

Mandate: To verify the Cotonou Peace Agreement signed in Cotonou, Benin, between the parties to the Liberian conflict that broke out in 1990 when the Liberian president, Samuel Doe, was overthrown, causing a complete breakdown of law and order. The UNOMIL was created at the invitation of the Economic Community of West African States (ECOWAS), which has taken various initiatives to peacefully settle the conflict, including the establishment of its own military observer group, ECOMOG. UNOMIL was to work with ECOMOG in implementing the Cotoneau Peace Agreement. ECOMOG has primary responsibility for the implementation of the agreement's provisions, and UNOMIL's role is to monitor the implementation procedures to verify their impartial application.

Composition: The military component was composed of personnel from Austria, Bangladesh, Belgium, China, Congo, Czech Republic, Egypt, Guinea-Bissau, Hungary, India, Jordan, Kenya, Malaysia, Nepal, Pakistan, Poland, Russian Federation, Slovakia, Sweden, and Uruguay.

Total cost: Approximately US$81.4 million.

UNMIH-United Nations Mission in Haiti

Duration: September 1993 to June 1996

Location: Haiti.

Strength: 1,200 troops and military support personnel, and 300 civilian police; there was also a provision for about 160 international staff, 180 local staff, and 18 UN volunteers.

Fatalities: 6.

Mandate: Pending the creation of a new police force, assist the government in monitoring the activities of those members of the armed forces involved in carrying out police functions; provide guidance and advice; monitor the conduct of police operations; ensure that legal requirements are fully met. However, the advance unit of UNMIH was prevented from landing at Port au Prince on 11 October 1993. After the Haitian Constitutional government was restored in October 1994, UNMIH assisted the democratic Haitian government in securing stability, training the Haitian armed forces, and creating a separate police force. UNMIH also helped the legitimate constitutional government to organize free and fair elections for the summer of 1995.

Composition: Djibouti, France, Mali, Netherlands, Pakistan, Russian Federation, Togo, Trinidad and Tobago, and United States.

Total cost: Estimated at US$315.8 million.

UNAMIR-United Nations Assistance Mission for Rwanda

Duration: October 1993 to March 1996.

Location: Rwanda.

Strength: 2,548 military personnel, 60 police officers, 110 international civilian staff, and 61 locally recruited civilian staff.

Fatalities: 26.

Mandate: In the context of the Arusha peace agreement concluded in August 1993 between the government of Rwanda and the Rwandese Patriotic Front (RPF), UNAMIR originally was to contribute to the establishment and maintenance of a climate conducive to the secure installation and subsequent operation of the transitional government; assure the security of the capital city, Kigali; monitor a cease-fire agreement, including establishing an expanded demilitarized zone and demobilization procedures; monitor the security situation leading up to elections; assist with mine clearance. UNAMIR would also investigate alleged non-compliance with provisions of the peace agreement and provide security for the repatriation of Rwandese refugees. It would also

escort and protect humanitarian activities. After renewed fighting in April 1994, UNAMIR's mandate was altered to permit intermediary action between warring parties, and to provide security for refugees and civilians at risk. After the cease-fire and installation of the new government, UNAMIR was adjusted to ensure stability and security in the northwestern and southwestern regions of Rwanda, to monitor and encourage the return of displaced persons, and support humanitarian aid, and national reconciliation.

Composition: At its peak strength UNAMIR was to be composed of 2,217 formed troops and 331 military observers provided by Argentina, Austria, Bangladesh, Belgium, Canada, Congo, Ecuador, Egypt, Fiji, Ghana, Malawi, Mali, Nigeria, Pakistan, Russian Federation, Senegal, Tanzania, Togo, Tunisia, Uruguay, and Zimbabwe.

Total cost: Estimated at US$437.4 million.

UNASOG-United Nations Aozou Strip Observer Group

Duration: May 1994 to June 1994.

Location: Aozou Strip, Republic of Chad.

Strength: 9 military observers and 6 international staff.

Fatalities: None.

Mandate: Established to verify the departure of the Libyan administration and forces from the Aozou Strip in accordance with the decision of the International Court of Justice. UNASOG accomplished its mandate after both Chad and Libya declared the withdrawal complete.

Total cost: US$67,471.

UNMOT-United Nations Mission of Observers in Tajikistan

Duration: December 1994 to present (Under liquidation as of May 2000.)

Location: Tajikistan.

Strength: 18 military observers, supported by international and local civilian staff.

Mandate: Established to monitor the implementation of the agreement between the Tajik government and the opposition on a temporary cease-fire along the Tajik-Afghan border, and to investigate reports of violations and report them to the UN and to the Joint Commission. UNMOT also is to serve as a political liaison and coordinate services that help the efficient deployment of humanitarian assistance by the international community.

Composition: Austria, Bulgaria, Czech Republic, Denmark, Jordan, Poland, Ukraine, and Uruguay.

Total cost: US$18.7 million.

UNAVEM III-United Nations Angola Verification Mission III

Duration: February 1995 to June 1997.

Location: Angola.

Strength: 283 military observers, 7,869 troops and other military personnel, and 288 civilian police as of 30 June 1997.

Mandate: On 1 February 1995 the Secretary-General recommended to the Security Council that UNAVEM III take over from UNAVEM II to help adversarial parties in Angola restore peace and achieve national reconciliation. UNAVEM III was to provide mediation between the government and the UNITA party, to monitor and confirm the provision of legitimate government administration throughout Angola, and promote national reconciliation. UNAVEM III also was to control and verify the elimination of forces, monitor the cease-fire, and ensure the neutrality of the Angolan National Police.

Composition: Algeria, Bangladesh, Brazil, Bulgaria, Congo, Egypt, France, Guinea Bissau, Hungary, India, Jordan, Kenya, Malaysia, Mali, Namibia, Netherlands, New Zealand, Nigeria, Norway, Pakistan, Poland, Portugal, Republic of Korea, Romania, Russian Federation, Senegal, Slovak Republic, Sweden, Tanzania, Ukraine, Uruguay, Zambia.

Fatalities: 32.
Total cost: More than US$800 million.

UNCRO-United Nations Confidence Restoration Operation
Duration: March 1995 to January 1996.
Location: Croatia.
Strength: 6,581 troops, 194 military observers and 296 civilian police, supported by international and locally recruited staff.
Fatalities: 16.
Mandate: UNCRO replaced UNPROFOR in Croatia, and was established to carry out the functions planned in the cease-fire agreement of March 1994 and the economic agreement of December 1994. UNCRO also monitored and reported the crossing of military personnel, supplies, equipment, and weapons over international borders between Croatia and Bosnia and Herzegovina, and Croatia and the Federal Republic of Yugoslavia (Serbia and Montenegro) at the border crossings. The mandate also facilitated the delivery of humanitarian aid to Bosnia and Herzegovina through the territory of Croatia, and monitored the demilitarization of the Prevlaka peninsula.
Cost: See UNPROFOR, above.

UNPREDEP-United Nations Preventive Deployment Force
Duration: March 1995 to February 1999.
Location: The Former Yugoslav Republic of Macedonia
Strength: 1,040 troops, 35 military observers, and 26 civilian police, 203 local and civilian staff.
Mandate: UNPREDEP was established on 31 March 1995 to replace UNPROFOR, but the mandate was basically the same: to monitor and report any developments in the border areas that could affect confidence and stability in the Former Yugoslav Republic of Macedonia.
Composition: Argentina, Bangladesh, Belgium, Brazil, Canada, Czech Republic, Denmark, Egypt, Finland, Ghana, Indonesia, Ireland, Jordan, Kenya, Nepal, New Zealand, Nigeria, Norway, Pakistan, Poland, Russian Federation, Sweden, Switzerland, Turkey, Ukraine, and United States.
Fatalities: 4.
Total cost: Approximately US$200 million.

UNMIBH-United Nations Mission in Bosnia and Herzegovina
Duration: December 1995 to present.
Location: Bosnia and Herzegovina.
Strength: 1,646 civilian police and 5 military support personnel; 1,800 international and local civilian staff.
Mandate: The Security Council established the UN International Police Task Force (IPTF) in December 1995 in accordance with the peace agreement signed by the leaders of Bosnia and Herzegovina, Croatia, and the Federal Republic of Yugoslavia (Serbia and Montenegro). The IPTF monitors law enforcement facilities and activities, advises and trains law enforcement personnel, assesses threats to public order, advises authorities in Bosnia and Herzegovina on operating effective civilian law enforcement agencies, and accompanies law enforcement personnel in some responsibilities.
Composition: Argentina, Austria, Bangladesh, Bulgaria, Canada, Chile, Denmark, Egypt, Estonia, Fiji, Finland, France, Germany, Ghana, Greece, Hungary, Iceland, India, Ireland, Italy, Jordan, Malaysia, Nepal, Netherlands, Nigeria, Norway, Pakistan, Poland, Portugal, Romania, Russian Federation, Senegal, Singapore, Spain, Sweden, Switzerland, Thailand, Tunisia, Turkey, Ukraine, United Kingdom, and United States.
Annual cost: US$178.2 million.

UNMOP-United Nations Mission of Observers in Prevlaka
Duration: January 1996 to present.
Location: Prevlaka peninsula, Croatia.

Strength: 27 military observers.
Mandate: With the termination of UNCRO's mandate in January 1996, UNMOP became a continuation of the mission to monitor the demilitarization of the Prevlaka peninsula.
Composition: Argentina, Bangladesh, Belgium, Brazil, Canada, Czech Republic, Denmark, Finland, Ghana, Indonesia, Ireland, Jordan, Kenya, Nepal, New Zealand, Nigeria, Norway, Pakistan, Poland, Portugal, Russian Federation, Sweden, Switzerland, and Ukraine.
Annual cost: Included in UNMIBH, above.

UNTAES-United Nations Transitional Administration in Eastern Slavonia
Duration: January 1996 to January 1998.
Location: Eastern Slavonia, Baranja, and Western Sirmium, Croatia.
Strength: A total of 2,847 personnel, consisting of 2,346 troops, 97 military observers, and 404 civilian police as of 21 October 1997.
Mandate: UNTAES was set up with both military and civilian components. The military part supervised and assisted in the demilitarization of the region, monitored the return of refugees in cooperation with the UNHCR, and contributed to maintaining the peace by its continuing presence. The civilian part was to set up a temporary police force, monitor the prison system, promote the return of refugees, and to organize and verify elections.
Composition: Argentina, Austria, Bangladesh, Belgium, Brazil, Czech Republic, Denmark, Egypt, Fiji, Finland, Ghana, Indonesia, Ireland, Jordan, Kenya, Lithuania, Nepal, Netherlands, New Zealand, Nigeria, Norway, Pakistan, Poland, Russian Federation, Slovak Republic, Sweden, Switzerland, Tunisia, Ukraine, and United States.
Annual cost: US$285.8 million. Total cost not available.

UNSMIH-United Nations Support Mission in Haiti
Duration: July 1996 to July 1997.
Location: Haiti.
Strength: 225 civilian police and 1,300 military personnel funded for a total of some 1,525 military personnel on 10 July 1997. The mission was supported by international and local civilian staff. A number of UN Volunteers also participated in the mission.
Mandate: UNSMIH was established to help the government of Haiti in the professionalization of the police and to assist in the creation and training of an effective national police force.
Composition: Civilian police personnel: Algeria, Canada, France, India, Mali, Togo, United States. Military personnel: Canada, Pakistan.
Total cost: US$57.2 million (estimate).

MINUGUA-United Nations Verification Mission in Guatemala
Duration: January to May 1997.
Location: Guatemala.
Strength: Mission total of 188 uniformed personnel, comprising145 military observers and 43 civilian police.
Mandate: The peacekeeping mission within the larger civilian and humanitarian MINUGUA mission was established by the Security Council in resolution 1094 (1997) on 20 January 1997 for a three-month period to verify agreement on the cease-fire between the government of Guatemala and the Unidad Revolucionaria Naciónal Guatemalteca (URNG), which was signed at Oslo on 4 December 1996.
Total cost: US$4.6 million (estimated).

MONUA-United Nations Mission of Observers in Angola
Duration: July 1997 to February 1999.

Location: Angola.

Strength: 240 personnel all ranks; consisting of 222 troops, 12 military observers, and 6 civilian police monitors; and supported by international and locally recruited civilian staff as of May 1999.

Fatalities: 14 (as of 31 December 1998).

Mandate: MONUA was set up to assist the Angolan parties in consolidating peace and national reconciliation, enhancing confidence-building and creating an environment conducive to long-term stability, democratic development, and rehabilitation of the country.

Composition: Bangladesh, Bolivia, Brazil, Egypt, Ghana, India, Jordan, Pakistan, Poland, Portugal, Romania, Russian Federation, Senegal, Uruguay, Zambia, and Zimbabwe.

Total cost: Approximately us$225.6 million.

UNTMIH-United Nations Transition Mission in Haiti

Duration: August to November 1997.

Location: Haiti.

Strength: 250 civilian police personnel and 50 military personnel.

Mandate: To assist the government of Haiti by supporting and contributing to the professionalization of the Haitian National Police (HNP).

Composition: Argentina, Benin, Canada, France, India, Mali, Niger, Senegal, Togo, Tunisia, and United States.

Total cost: us$20.6 million.

MIPONUH-United Nations Civilian Police Mission in Haiti

Duration: December 1997 to March 2000.

Location: Haiti.

Strength: 300 civilian police personnel, including a special police unit, supported by a civilian establishment of some 72 international and 133 local personnel and 17 United Nations Volunteers.

Mandate: MIPONUH's main task was to assist the Government of Haiti in the professionalization of the Haitian National Police. MIPONUH, which succeeded the previous United Nations Missions in Haiti in December 1997, placed special emphasis on assistance at the supervisory level and on training specialized police units.

Composition: Argentina, Benin, Canada, France, India, Mali, Niger, Senegal, Togo, Tunisia, and United States.

Total cost: Not available.

UNPSG-United Nations Civilian Police Support Group

Duration: January 1998 to October 1998.

Location: Croatia's Danube region (Eastern Slavonia, Baranja, ·and Western Sirmium).

Strength: As of 30 September 1998, mission total: 114 police, supported by about 200 international and local civilian staff.

Mandate: UNPSG took over policing tasks on 16 January 1998 from UNTAES after that mission's mandate expired. The function of UNPSG was to continue monitoring the performance of the Croatian police in the Danube region, particularly with respect to the return of displaced persons, for a single nine-month period.

Composition: Argentina, Austria, Denmark, Egypt, Fiji, Finland, Indonesia, Ireland, Jordan, Kenya, Lithuania, Norway, Poland, Russian Federation, Sweden, Switzerland, Ukraine, and United States.

Total cost: Approximately us$30 million.

MINURCA-United Nations Mission in the Central African Republic

Duration: April 1998 to February 2000.

Location: Central African Republic.

Strength: Maximum authorization: 1,350 troops; 25 civilian police.

Mandate: Assisted in maintaining and enhancing security and stability in Bangui and immediate vicinity and in maintaining law and order there; supervised and controlled storage, and monitored the final disposition of weapons retrieved in disarmament exercise; ensured security and freedom of movement of UN personnel; assisted in capacity-building efforts of the national police; provided advice and technical support regarding conduct of legislative elections.

Composition: Benin, Burkina Faso, Cameroon, Canada, Chad, Côte d'Ivoire, Egypt, France, Gabon, Mali, Portugal, Senegal, Togo, and Tunisia.

Annual cost: us$33.3 million.

UNOMSIL-United Nations Mission of Observers in Sierra Leone

Duration: July 1998 to October 1999.

Location: Sierra Leone.

Strength: Military component as of 30 July 1999: 51, consisting of 49 military observers and 2 troops, supported by a 2-person medical team. Civilian component as of 4 June 1999: 53, consisting of 29 international civilian personnel and 24 locally recruited staff.

Mandate: UNOMSIL's military element was to monitor the military and security situation; monitor the disarmament and demobilization of former combatants concentrated in secure areas of the country. UNOMSIL's civilian element was to advise, in coordination with other international efforts, the government of Sierra Leone and local police officials on police practice, training, re-equipment and recruitment; advise on the reform and restructuring of Sierra Leone's police force and monitor progress; report on violations of international humanitarian law and human rights in Sierra Leone and assist the government in its efforts to address the country's human rights needs.

Composition: Bangladesh, Croatia, the Czech Republic, Denmark, Egypt, France, India, Indonesia, Jordan, Kenya, Kyrgyzstan, Malaysia, Nepal, New Zealand, Norway, Pakistan, Russian Federation, Sweden, Thailand, the United Republic of Tanzania, United Kingdom, Uruguay, and Zambia.

Annual cost: us$40.7 million.

UNMIK-United Nations Interim Administration Mission in Kosovo

Duration: June 1999 to present.

Location: Kosovo province of Yugoslavia.

Strength: About 1,957 personnel of UN and partner organizations on the ground, including about 1,297 UN civilian staff. Plus 3,159 civilian police deployed in all five regions of the province and at four border crossings as of 27 April 2000.

Mandate: In the wake of the Kosovar conflict, in which the Yugoslav government used hard-handed tactics to control an independence movement in the southern province, the UN Security Council set up UNMIK. Unprecedented in its scope, UNMIK encompasses the activities of three non-UN organizations under the UN's overall jurisdiction. UNMIK's mandate is to provide an interim civil administration (UN-led), take leadership in humanitarian affairs (UNHCR-led), spearhead reconstruction including rebuilding the infrastructure (EU-led), and reestablish institutions (OSCE-led). A NATO-led force is to provide an international security presence.

Annual cost: us$456.4 million.

UNTAET-United Nations Transitional Administration in East Timor

Duration: October 1999 to present.

Location: East Timor.

Strength: Military component, 8,241; civilian police component, 1,113.

Mandate: As Portugal gave up its claim to East Timor in 1975, Indonesian troops moved in; the half-island territory has been ruled by Indonesia since. At elections on 30 August 1999, the people of East Timor voted for independence. UNTAET was established to administer the territory and exercise legislative and executive authority during the transition period. UNTAET consults and works in close cooperation with the East Timorese people.

Composition: Argentina, Australia, Austria, Bangladesh, Bolivia, Bosnia and Herzegovina, Brazil, Canada, Cape Verde, Chile, China, Denmark, Egypt, Fiji, France, Gambia, Ghana, Ireland, Italy, Jordan, Kenya, Korea (Republic of), Malaysia, Mozambique, Nepal, New Zealand, Niger, Nigeria, Norway, Pakistan, Papua New Guinea, Philippines, Portugal, Russian Federation, Senegal, Singapore, Slovenia, Spain, Sri Lanka, Sweden, Thailand, Turkey, Ukraine, United Kingdom, United States, Uruguay, Zambia, and Zimbabwe.

Annual cost: US$386.3 million.

UNAMSIL-United Nations Mission in Sierra Leone

Duration: October 1999 to present.

Location: Sierra Leone.

Strength: As of May 2000, 10,707 military personnel, including 254 military observers. Other personnel include some 28 civilian police, and 234 international and 104 local civilian personnel.

Mandate: UNAMSIL is to cooperate with the government and the other parties in implementing the Lome Peace Agreement and to assist in the implementation of the disarmament, demobilization, and reintegration plan. On 7 February 2000, the Council revised the mandate of the Mission and expanded its size.

Composition: Bangladesh, Bolivia, Canada, China, Croatia, Czech Republic, Denmark, Egypt, France, Gambia, Ghana, Guinea, India, Indonesia, Jordan, Kenya, Kyrgyzstan, Malaysia, Mali, Namibia, Nepal, New Zealand, Nigeria, Norway, Pakistan, Russian Federation, Senegal, Slovakia, Sweden, Thailand, United Kingdom, United Republic of Tanzania, Uruguay, Zambia, and Zimbabwe.

Annual cost: US$265.8 million.

MONUC-United Nations Organization Mission in the Democratic Republic of the Congo

Duration: 30 November 1999 to present.

Location: Democratic Republic of the Congo and the subregion, including Namibia, Rwanda, Uganda, Zambia, and Zimbabwe .

Strength: 126 military observers, and 73 international and 50 local civilian personnel.

Mandate: After Democratic Republic of the Congo and five regional states signed the Lusaka Cease-fire Agreement in July 1999, the UN Security Council (in November 1999) set up MONUC to maintain liaison with the parties and carry out other tasks, incorporating UN personnel authorized in earlier resolutions. On 24 February 2000, the Council expanded the mission's mandate and size.

Composition: Algeria, Bangladesh, Benin, Bolivia, Canada, Denmark, Egypt, France, Ghana, India, Kenya, Libya, Mali, Nepal, Pakistan, Poland, Romania, Russian Federation, Senegal, South Africa, Sweden, Tanzania, Ukraine, United Kingdom, Uruguay, and Zambia.

Annual cost: US$199 million.

SOME CASE HISTORIES OF UN ACTION

The cases are arranged in order of the dates when the disputes were first brought before the UN.

The Middle East

Establishment of Israel. In April 1947, the General Assembly, at a special session, established a Special Committee on Palestine to make recommendations for the future status of the British mandate. The resulting partition plan, which divided Palestine into an Arab and a Jewish state, with an international regime for the city of Jerusalem, was adopted by the General Assembly in November of the same year. A UN Palestine Commission was established to carry out the recommendations, and the Security Council was requested to implement the plan. The date for termination of the British mandate and withdrawal of British troops was 1 August 1948. However, violent fighting broke out between the Arab nations and the Jewish community in Palestine. The Security Council thereupon established a Truce Commission consisting of Belgium, France, and the United States, while the General Assembly authorized a UN Mediator for Palestine to replace the Palestine Commission.

On 14 May 1948, the Jewish state of Israel was proclaimed. Almost immediately, the Arab nations instituted full-scale armed action. Following a four-week truce at the request of the Security Council, hostilities were renewed on 8 July. This time, the Security Council, invoking Chapter VII of the charter, ordered the governments concerned to desist from further military action and proclaimed a cease-fire.

Through the UN mediator, Count Folke Bernadotte, the Security Council then established a UN Truce Supervision Organization (UNTSO) of military observers from different countries, with headquarters in Jerusalem, and assigned it the task of patrolling the frontiers. Fighting continued, however, and Count Bernadotte was assassinated in September 1948. During its regular session in the fall of 1948, the General Assembly established a three-member Conciliation Commission (France, Turkey, and the US) to negotiate a settlement and also established the UN Relief for Palestine Refugees (later replaced by UNRWA). Following negotiations with the acting UN mediator, Ralph Bunche, in the first half of 1949, Israel, Egypt, Jordan, Lebanon, and Syria signed armistice agreements. The agreements provided for mixed armistice commissions to check on their implementation. UNTSO continued in operation to observe the cease-fire and is still in existence, investigating complaints of armistice violations and reporting to the Security Council. The Conciliation Commission also continues to function, still trying to fulfill its mandate from the General Assembly to assist the parties concerned to negotiate a final settlement of all issues.

The Suez Crisis. In July 1956, Egypt nationalized the Suez Canal. In September, after Egypt's rejection of the London Conference plan for international control of the canal, France and the United Kingdom informed the Security Council that Egypt's attitude was endangering the peace. Israel invaded Egypt's Gaza Strip the following month, and a Security Council resolution calling for a cease-fire and the withdrawal of Israeli troops was vetoed by France and the United Kingdom. France and the United Kingdom began armed intervention in the area, and thereafter the situation was handled exclusively by the General Assembly under the Uniting for Peace Resolution. In November 1956, the General Assembly established the UN Emergency Force (UNEF) to secure and supervise cessation of hostilities. Since Israel would not permit UNEF contingents on territory under its control, the force was stationed on the Egyptian side of the demarcation line. Withdrawal of British and French forces was completed by December 1956 and of Israeli forces by March 1957. The canal was cleared by April of the same year, and Egypt declared it open to international traffic (Israeli ships were barred, however).

The Six-Day War, 1967. By the mid-1960s, the tension between Israel and the Arab countries had begun to manifest itself in frequent and sometimes major hostilities across the various armistice borders. On 18 May 1967, the United Arab Republic (UAR), which two days earlier had begun deploying troops to the armistice demarcation line in the Sinai peninsula, officially requested Secretary-General U Thant to withdraw all UNEF units from the area. After consultations with the UNEF Advisory Committee, U Thant ordered the withdrawal of the force that evening.

U Thant's prompt compliance with the UAR's request aroused severe criticism in Israel and other quarters. His view was that both legal and practical considerations required him to act without delay. In subsequent reports, he pointed out that UNEF was not an enforcement operation ordered by the Security Council but a peacekeeping operation dependent on the consent of the host country. His unilateral decision to disband the force was, however, probably the most controversial of his career as Secretary-General. Some of his critics challenged the legal validity of his stand, while many others believed that he could have used his office to try to persuade the UAR at least to agree to a postponement of its request for UNEF's withdrawal, which they felt only helped pave the way for the crisis that followed.

The UAR occupied the fortress Sharm el-Sheikh, which commands the Strait of Tiran at the mouth of the Gulf of Aqaba. On 22 May 1967, it declared the gulf closed to Israeli ships and to other ships bound for Israel with strategic goods. Israel found its sole direct access to the Red Sea blockaded and considered the blockade, together with the military agreement that the UAR had recently signed with Jordan, a justified *casus belli*. Regarding the assurances of help that it had received from Western countries in the course of concentrated diplomatic activity intended to avert the impending war as insufficient, it simultaneously attacked the UAR, Jordan, and Syria on 5 June. Within three days, it had deeply penetrated the territory of each country.

The Security Council, in emergency session, demanded a cease-fire on 6 June 1967. Israel announced that it would accept a cease-fire provided that the other parties accepted it. Jordan announced acceptance on 7 June, the UAR on 8 June, and Syria on 9 June, and a cease-fire accordingly took effect on 10 June. Violations of the cease-fire, especially along the Israel-Syria border, continued until 13 June, when Secretary-General U Thant was able to report the "virtual cessation" of all military activity. By then, Israel had voluntarily withdrawn its forces from much of the territory that it had occupied but had retained control of several areas regarded as essential to its security—namely, the whole of the UAR's Sinai peninsula up to the Suez Canal, including Sharm el-Sheikh and the Gaza Strip; the Jordanian part of the city of Jerusalem and the West Bank area of the Jordan River; and the Golan Heights, in Syrian territory overlooking the Sea of Galilee. On 14 June, the Security Council adopted a resolution calling upon Israel to ensure the "safety, welfare and security" of the inhabitants of the occupied areas and upon the "governments concerned" scrupulously to respect the humanitarian principles governing the treatment of prisoners of war contained in the 1949 Geneva Convention.

An emergency special session of the General Assembly, held from 19 June to 21 July 1967, failed to produce a resolution that might serve as the frame of reference for a settlement. The division of opinion between the supporters of the Arabs, including the Soviet bloc and several African and Asian countries, and the supporters of the Israeli position, including the United States and several Western countries, was too deep to be bridged. However, the General Assembly did adopt, by a vote of 99 in favor with 20 abstentions, a resolution declaring invalid Israel's proclamation on 28 June that Jerusalem would thenceforward be a unified city under Israeli administration.

Resolution 242. For many months, the Security Council was equally unsuccessful in the attempt to devise an acceptable formula for establishing permanent peace in the area. Finally, on 22 November 1967, after weeks of quiet diplomacy and closed discussions, it adopted Resolution 242, which provided the basis of

UN efforts to achieve a definitive settlement. The resolution, based on a British draft, establishes certain principles for a peaceful settlement without going into contentious specifics or prescribing priorities. The principles include withdrawal of Israeli forces from occupied areas (the text deliberately avoided requesting withdrawal from "all" occupied areas, in view of Israel's declaration that it would not give up certain strategic places, including Jordanian Jerusalem); an end to states of belligerency; respect for the rights of all states in the area to peaceful existence; and an affirmation of the need to guarantee free navigation through international waterways, settle the long-standing Palestine refugee problem, and guarantee the territorial integrity and political independence of the countries involved. All parties—except, initially, Syria—accepted the formula.

The October War, 1973. Full-scale hostilities broke out again in the Suez Canal and Israel-Syria sectors on 6 October 1973. The Security Council met four times without considering any draft resolutions and on 12 October decided to reconvene at a later date after consultations. It did so on 21 October at the request of the United States and the USSR and the next day adopted Resolution 338, which called for the immediate cessation of all military activities. It also decided that negotiations between the concerned parties for a just and durable peace should begin at once. China did not participate in this or other votes on the question. Israel, Syria, and Egypt agreed to comply, each stating conditions.

A second UN Emergency Force (UNEF II) was established by the Security Council on 25 October 1973. Its personnel were to be drawn from member states, with the exception of the permanent members of the council, and its eventual strength was to be 7,000. As the force was assembled, it took up stations in zones of disengagement between Israel and Egypt.

A peace conference on the Middle East was convened in December 1973 in Geneva under the auspices of the UN and the co-chairmanship of the United States and the USSR. The work of the conference came to fruition at kilometer 101 on the Cairo-Suez road on 18 January 1974, when the chief of staff of the Egyptian Armed Forces and the chief of staff of the Israel Defense Forces signed an Agreement on Disengagement of Forces, with the UNEF commander as witness. The agreement came into effect on 25 January 1974.

It was not until 31 May 1974, in Geneva, that Syria and Israel signed an Agreement on Disengagement, which called for the creation of a UN Disengagement Observer Force (UNDOF) and specified that it did not represent a peace agreement but a step toward peace. On the same day, after the signing, the Security Council adopted a resolution jointly sponsored by the United States and the USSR that set up UNDOF. China and Iraq did not participate in the vote. The strength of UNDOF was to be 1,250, its components to be drawn from members of the UN that were not permanent members of the Security Council. In 2000, UNDOF comprised some 1,000 troops, provided by Austria, Canada, Japan, Poland, and Slovakia, deployed between the Israeli and Syrian forces on the Golan Heights.

Developments in Lebanon. On 15 March 1978, following a Palestinian commando raid in Israel, Israeli forces invaded southern Lebanon. On 19 March, the Security Council called on Israel to cease its military action against Lebanese territory and decided to establish a UN Interim Force in Lebanon (UNIFIL) to confirm the withdrawal of Israeli forces and assist the Lebanese government in ensuring the return of its effective authority in the area.

The mandate of the 6,000-man UNIFIL has been extended by the Security Council since then. Perhaps its greatest crisis occurred on the morning of 6 June 1982, when Israeli forces, comprising two mechanized divisions with air and naval support, moved into Lebanese territory, bypassing positions occupied by UNIFIL. The Israeli invasion was followed by a few days of intensive exchanges of fire with PLO and Syrian forces and by Israeli air attacks on targets in the Beirut area. In subsequent days and weeks, the Security Council met numerous times to demand a cease-fire, withdrawal of Israeli forces, and respect for the rights of the civilian population.

UNIFIL's mandate was enlarged to extend protection and humanitarian assistance to the population of the area; an international survey mission was established to assess the situation on the spot; a UN observer group was deployed in and around Beirut to ensure that a cease-fire was fully observed by all concerned; and, at Lebanon's request, a 4,000-man multinational force, composed of contingents from France, Italy, and the United States (and later the United Kingdom), was deployed in the Beirut area. The force was withdrawn in 1984.

In May 2000, UNIFIL comprised some 4,550 troops, provided by Fiji, Finland, France, Ghana, India, Ireland, Italy, Nepal, and Poland. It has continued to assist the Lebanese government in ensuring the return of its effective authority in southern Lebanon.

The Question of Palestinian Rights. Concurrently with its consideration of the situation in the Middle East and of the role of peacekeeping forces in the region, the UN has been concerned with the question of Palestinian rights. In 1968, the General Assembly established the Special Committee to Investigate Israeli Practices Affecting the Human Rights of the Population of the Occupied Territories, which reports annually to it, and in 1974, it reaffirmed "the inalienable rights of the Palestinian people" to unhindered self-determination, national independence, and sovereignty. The General Assembly recognized the Palestinian people as a principal party in the establishment of a just and durable peace in the Middle East, and it invited the PLO to participate as an observer in its work and in UN conferences.

In 1975, the General Assembly established the Committee on the Exercise of the Inalienable Rights of the Palestinian People and asked it to recommend a program for the implementation of those rights. The committee recommended that a timetable be established by the Security Council for the complete withdrawal of Israeli forces from the areas occupied in 1967. The evacuated areas, with all properties and services intact, would be taken over by the UN, which, with the cooperation of the League of Arab States, would subsequently hand them over to the PLO as the representative of the Palestinian people. The General Assembly has endorsed the committee's recommendations at successive sessions since 1976, but the Security Council has not acted on them.

An International Conference on the Question of Palestine, held in Geneva in the summer of 1983, adopted a declaration on Palestine and a program of action for the achievement of Palestinian rights, which was later endorsed by the General Assembly. The conference also called for the convening of an international conference on the Middle East, a proposal which the General Assembly endorsed.

At its 1987 session, the General Assembly reaffirmed its conviction that "the question of Palestine is the core of the conflict in the Middle East and that no comprehensive, just and lasting peace in the region will be achieved without the full exercise by the Palestinian people of its inalienable national rights and the immediate, unconditional and total withdrawal of Israel from all the Palestinian and other Arab occupied territories." The General Assembly again called for the convening of an international peace conference on the Middle East under the auspices of the UN and at the invitation of the Secretary-General, with the participation of the five permanent members of the Security Council and all the parties to the Arab-Israeli conflict, including the PLO.

Korea

At the end of World War II, the Allied powers agreed that Soviet troops would accept the Japanese surrender north of the 38th parallel in Korea and that United States forces would accept it south of that line. The two occupying powers established a joint commission to set up a provisional government for the country, but the commission could not come to an agreement, and the United States brought the matter to the General Assembly in September 1947. In November, the General Assembly created a Temporary Commission on Korea to facilitate nationwide elections. However, since the commission was denied access to northern Korea, it was only able to supervise elections in the southern half of the country. These elections took place in May 1948, and in August, the United States transferred governmental and military functions to the duly elected government of the Republic of Korea (ROK). Meanwhile, a separate government was established in the north. In December 1948, the General Assembly, over the objection of the USSR, established a seven-member UN Commission on Korea (UNCOK) to replace the Temporary Commission and to seek reunification.

On 25 June 1950, both UNCOK and the United States informed the Security Council that the Democratic People's Republic of Korea (DPRK) had attacked the ROK that morning. The council met on the same day and (the USSR being absent at the time in protest against a council decision on Chinese representation) declared the attack to be a breach of the peace. It called for a cease-fire, withdrawal of DPRK forces to the 38th parallel, and the assistance of member states to the ROK. As the fighting continued, the Security Council, on 27 June, recommended that UN members furnish assistance to the ROK to repel the attack and restore peace and security. On the same day, the United States announced that it had ordered its own air and sea forces to give cover and support to the South Korean troops. On July 7, the Security Council voted to recommend that states make forces available to a UN Unified Command under the United States. (It should be noted that although the council had used the language of Chapter VII of the charter—"breach of the peace," etc.—it did not specifically invoke the chapter itself or use its constitutional power thereunder to order all states to comply with its decision.) In all, 16 nations supplied troops: Australia, Belgium, Canada, Colombia, Ethiopia, France, Greece, Luxembourg, Netherlands, New Zealand, Philippines, Thailand, Turkey, South Africa, the United Kingdom, and the US; the ROK also placed its troops under the UN Command.

On 1 August 1950, the USSR returned to the Security Council (having by then been absent for six months) and declared that all the actions and decisions that had previously been taken by the council were illegal. On 6 November, the USSR vetoed a resolution proposed by the United States. As a result of the ensuing deadlock, the General Assembly virtually took over the handling of the entire situation (the Security Council even agreeing unanimously, on 31 January 1951, to remove the item from its agenda). The legalistic device by which the General Assembly voted itself competent to continue with collective measures that under the charter are the exclusive preserve of the Security Council was the Uniting for Peace Resolution.

Even before the Security Council became deadlocked, the General Assembly had considered an agenda item entitled "The Problem of the Independence of Korea." Under this item, it established the Commission for the Unification and Rehabilitation of Korea (UNCURK) to replace UNCOK. Then, on 6 November 1950, events were given a new twist when the People's Republic of China entered the war on the side of the DPRK. The General Assembly promptly added the agenda item entitled "Intervention of the Central People's Government of the People's Republic of China in Korea." Under this item, the General Assembly established the UN Korean Reconstruction Agency (UNKRA) and a three-member Cease-fire Group that included the president of the General Assembly to determine a basis for ending hostilities. Following China's refusal to cooperate, the General Assembly, in February 1951, adopted a resolution that that government had engaged in aggression. It also established a

Good Offices Committee and an Additional Measures Committee to supplement the Cease-fire Group. Truce negotiations began in July 1951, but fighting continued until 1953, when an armistice agreement was signed on 27 July. A year later, the General Assembly called for the political conference that had been provided for in the armistice agreement. The conference was held between April and June 1954, but it failed to resolve problems and negotiate reunification of the country. UNKRA ceased operations in 1960, and UNCURK was dissolved by a consensus vote of the 1973 General Assembly.

On 18 November 1975, the General Assembly adopted two resolutions—one with Western support, the other with that of the Communist states—which were to some extent conflicting but which both favored dissolution of the UN Command at an early date. The first resolution called for negotiations among the DPRK, the ROK, China, and the United States. The second called for negotiations between the DPRK and the United States. The DPRK declared that it would not participate in negotiations with the ROK.

As of mid-1987, the following countries were still represented on the UN Command: Australia, Canada, Philippines, ROK, Thailand, United Kingdom, and United States.

In his 1987 report to the General Assembly on the work of the UN, Secretary-General Pérez de Cuéllar stated that there had been, during the previous year, a series of proposals emanating from both North and South Korea for the resumption of talks on overcoming the contentious issues between the two sides and that he had had continuing contacts with both sides in an effort to assist in reducing the causes of tension between them and enhancing the prospect of a negotiated settlement.

Kashmir

Kashmir (officially, Jammu and Kashmir) was originally one of the princely states of British India. Under the partition plan and the Indian Independence Act of 1947, it became free to accede to either India or Pakistan, on both of which it borders. On 1 January 1948, India reported to the Security Council that tribesmen were invading Kashmir with the active assistance of Pakistan. After the invasion had begun, the maharajah of Kashmir had requested accession to India and India had accepted on the understanding that, once normal conditions were restored, the question of accession would be settled by a plebiscite. Pakistan declared that Kashmir's accession to India was illegal.

The Security Council, after asking the parties to mediate, called for withdrawal of Pakistani nationals, reduction of Indian forces, and arrangement of a plebiscite on Kashmir's accession to India. A UN Commission for India and Pakistan (UNCIP) was sent to mediate in July 1948. By 1949, UNCIP had effected a cease-fire and was able to state that principles on a plebiscite had been accepted by both governments. In July 1949, agreement was reached on a cease-fire line, and UNCIP appointed a group of military observers to watch for violations. However, it was unable to reach agreement on terms for the demilitarization of Kashmir prior to a plebiscite.

In March 1951, after several attempts at further negotiation had failed, the Security Council decided to continue the observer group—now called the UN Military Observer Group in India and Pakistan (UNMOGIP)—to supervise the cease-fire within Kashmir itself. Despite continued mediation, the differences between the parties remained. The Security Council repeatedly considered the matter without achieving appreciable progress.

In August 1965 there was a sudden outbreak of serious hostilities. UNMOGIP reported clashes between the regular armed forces of both India and Pakistan, and fighting continued into September, although the Security Council had twice called for a cease-fire. Following a report that fighting had spread to the international border between India and West Pakistan, the coun-

cil, on September 20, requested that both sides issue orders for a cease-fire within two days and withdraw their forces to their previously held positions. The cease-fire was accepted by both states, but continuous complaints of violations were made by each side. Accordingly, the Council requested Secretary-General U Thant to increase the size of UNMOGIP and to establish the UN India-Pakistan Observation Mission (UNIPOM) on the India-West Pakistan border.

On 5 November 1965, the Security Council urged that a meeting between the parties be held as soon as possible and that a plan for withdrawal containing a time limit for execution be developed. U Thant appointed a representative to meet with authorities of both countries on the question. On 17 February 1966, he informed the council that a plan and rules for withdrawals had been worked out. He also stated that, on 10 January, the prime minister of India and the president of Pakistan had agreed at Tashkent, where they had met at the initiative of the USSR, that their respective forces would be withdrawn to their original positions by 25 February. Thus, though the crisis remains quiescent, the conflict itself is unresolved, and UNMOGIP is still in operation, with some 40 military observers stationed in the area.

In 1971, another conflict between the two countries broke out, this time in connection with the civil strife in East Pakistan, which later became the independent state of Bangladesh. As nearly 10 million refugees streamed into neighboring India, tension increased in the subcontinent. U Thant conveyed his serious concern to the president of Pakistan and the prime minister of India and, with the consent of the host governments, set up two large-scale humanitarian programs. One of these, with the UN high commissioner for refugees as the focal point, was for the relief of the refugees in India. The other was for assistance to the distressed population in East Pakistan. U Thant's actions were subsequently unanimously approved by the General Assembly.

On 20 July 1971, the Secretary-General drew the attention of the president of the Security Council to the steady deterioration of the situation in the region, which he described as a potential threat to peace and security. He noted that humanitarian, economic, and political problems were involved, and he indicated that the UN should play a more forthright role to avert further deterioration. In October of that year, he offered his good offices to the governments of India and Pakistan, but India declined. Clashes broke out between the two countries, and on 3 December, U Thant notified the Security Council under Article 99 of the charter that the situation in the region constituted a threat to international peace and security.

After a cease-fire had put an end to the fighting on 17 December 1971, the Security Council adopted a resolution demanding the strict observance of the cease-fire until withdrawal of all armed forces to their previous positions should take place. The council also called for international assistance to relieve the suffering and for the appointment of a special UN representative to lend his good offices for the solution of humanitarian problems. During 1972, the refugees, with UN assistance, returned to their homeland. The UN relief operation helped pave the way for the rehabilitation of the shattered economy of Bangladesh, which became a member of the UN in 1974.

In 2000 UNMOGIP consisted of 44 military observers from eight countries: Belgium, Chile, Denmark, Finland, Italy, Norway, Sweden, and Uruguay.

The Congo (Zaire)

One week after the Democratic Republic of the Congo (formerly Zaire), a former Belgian colony, had become independent on 30 June 1960, troops of the Force Publique mutinied against the Belgian officers, demanding higher pay and promotions. As violence and general disorder spread rapidly throughout the country, Belgium rushed troops to the area to protect its extensive mining interests. On 11 July, Katanga, the richest province of the country by virtue of its Belgian-controlled copper mines, proclaimed its secession from the new state. On the following day, President Kasavubu and Prime Minister Patrice Lumumba appealed for UN military assistance "to protect the national territory against acts of aggression committed by Belgian metropolitan troops."

In a series of meetings, the Security Council called for the withdrawal of Belgian troops and authorized Secretary-General Hammarskjöld to provide the Congolese government with such military and technical assistance as might be necessary until the national security forces, through the efforts of the government with UN assistance, might be able, in the government's opinion, to meet their tasks fully.

Within two days, contingents of a UN force provided by a number of countries, including Asian and African states, began to arrive in the Congo, followed by UN civilian experts to help ensure the continued operation of essential services. Over the next four years, the task of the UN Operation in the Congo (UNOC) was to help the Congolese government restore and maintain the political independence and territorial integrity of the country, maintain law and order, and to put into effect a wide and long-term program of training and technical assistance.

At its peak strength, the UN force totaled nearly 20,000 officers and men. The instructions of the Security Council to the force were strengthened early in 1961 after the assassination of Lumumba in Katanga. The force was to protect the Congo from outside interference, particularly by evacuating foreign mercenaries and advisers from Katanga and preventing clashes and civil strife, by force if necessary as a last resort.

Following the reconvening of the Congolese parliament in August 1961 under UN auspices, the main problem was the attempted secession, led and financed by foreign elements, of the province of Katanga, where secessionist gendarmes under the command of foreign mercenaries clashed with UN forces. Secretary-General Hammarskjöld died on 17 September 1961, when his plane crashed on the way to Ndola (in what is now Zambia), where talks were to be held for the cessation of hostilities.

In February 1963, after Katanga had been reintegrated into the national territory of the Congo, a phasing out of the force was begun, aimed at its termination by the end of that year. At the request of the Congolese government, however, the General Assembly authorized the stay of a reduced number of troops for a further six months. The force was completely withdrawn by 30 June 1964. Civilian aid continued in the largest single program of assistance undertaken by the UN up to that time, with some 2,000 experts at work in the nation.

Cyprus

Cyprus was granted independence from British rule in 1960 through agreements signed by the United Kingdom, Greece, and Turkey. Under these agreements, Cyprus was given a constitution containing certain unamendable provisions guaranteeing specified political rights to the Turkish minority community. The three signatory powers were constituted guarantors of Cyprus's independence, each with the right to station troops permanently on the island.

The granting of independence had been preceded by a prolonged conflict between the Greek and Turkish communities on the future status of Cyprus. The Greek Cypriots, comprising 80 percent of the total population, originally had wanted some form of union with Greece, thereby provoking a hostile reaction among the Turkish Cypriots, who countered by demanding partition. Each side was supported in its aims by the country of its ethnic origin. Independence did nothing to alleviate dissension on the island. Both sides were dissatisfied with the constitution that had been granted them, but their aims were diametrically opposed. The Turks wanted partition or a type of federal govern-

ment, whereas the Greeks wanted a constitution free of outside controls and of provisions perpetuating the division between the two communities.

After three years of continuous tension, the Cyprus government, under Greek Cypriot president Makarios, complained to the Security Council on 27 December 1963 that Turkey was interfering in its internal affairs and committing acts of aggression. Against a background of mounting violence on the island, the council considered the matter but did not immediately take any peacekeeping action.

With the consent of Cyprus, British troops had been trying to restore order during the crisis. However, in mid-February 1964, the United Kingdom informed the Security Council that its efforts to keep the peace would have to be augmented. Accordingly, on 4 March 1964, the council unanimously authorized the establishment of the UN Peacekeeping Force in Cyprus (UNFICYP) for a three-month period and at the same time requested Secretary-General U Thant to designate a UN mediator to promote a substantive settlement. UNFICYP became operational on 27 March 1964, with a mandate to prevent the recurrence of fighting, help maintain law and order, and promote a return to normal conditions.

A coup d'état on 15 July 1974 by Greek Cypriot and Greek elements opposed to President Makarios forced him to flee the country. This was quickly followed by military intervention by Turkey, whose troops subsequently established Turkish Cypriot control over the northern part of Cyprus. Four days after a cease-fire went into effect on 16 August 1974, the UN high commissioner for refugees was asked to coordinate humanitarian assistance in Cyprus, where more than 200,000 persons had been dislocated as a result of the hostilities.

Concurrently with the functioning of UNFICYP, the UN has been active in promoting a peaceful solution and an agreed settlement of the Cyprus problem. This task, first entrusted to a mediator, has been carried out since 1968 through the good offices of the Secretary-General. Within that framework, a series of intercommunal talks between representatives of the Greek and Turkish Cypriot communities, as well as high-level meetings, were held, beginning in 1974, in an effort to reach a just and lasting solution. The intercommunal talks were discontinued after the Turkish Cypriot authorities, on 15 November 1983, proclaimed a "Turkish Republic of Northern Cyprus," a step which the Security Council called legally invalid. Secretary-General Pérez de Cuéllar met separately with representatives of the two sides in an effort to resume the negotiating process. Settlement talks headed by the UN continued in the 1990s.

UNFICYP has continued its task of supervising the cease-fire and maintaining surveillance over the buffer zone between the cease-fire lines. In 2000, the force numbered 1,242 troops and support personnel, and 230 civilian police.

Apartheid in South Africa

The racial policy of apartheid practiced by the South African government not only violated the political and human rights of its African citizens, it also destabilized the entire southern African region. The government of South Africa's policies towards the independence of surrounding African nations, the flight of South African freedom fighters to those countries, and the possibility that the technologically advanced government of South Africa might acquire nuclear capabilities, led the United Nations to consider apartheid in South Africa as a real threat to international peace and security. More than four decades of effort by the United Nations bore fruit in April 1994, when Nelson Mandela was elected president of South Africa in democratic elections open to South African citizens of all races.

The racial policies of the government of South Africa were a major concern of the UN since its earliest years. Over more than four decades, the General Assembly and the Security Council called for measures by the international community aimed at bringing about the end of apartheid, an Afrikaans word meaning "separateness," and at enabling the Africans of South Africa, who outnumber the whites by more than 4 to 1, to exercise political, economic, and all other rights in their country. In the words of a 1982 General Assembly resolution, the goal of the UN with regard to South Africa was "the total eradication of apartheid and the establishment of a democratic society in which all the people of South Africa as a whole, irrespective of race, color, sex or creed, will enjoy equal and full human rights and fundamental freedoms and participate freely in the determination of their destiny."

The question of South Africa's racial policies was first raised in the General Assembly in 1946, when India complained that the South African government had enacted legislation discriminating against South Africans of Indian origin. The General Assembly expressed the view that the treatment of Indians in South Africa should conform with South Africa's obligations under agreements concluded between that country and India and its obligations under the UN Charter.

The wider question of racial conflict in South Africa arising from that government's apartheid policies was placed on the General Assembly's agenda in 1952. On that question and on India's original complaint, the South African government maintained that the matter was essentially within its domestic jurisdiction and that, under the charter, the UN was barred from considering it.

The Security Council took up the question for the first time in 1960, following an incident at Sharpeville on 21 March in which South African police fired on peaceful demonstrators protesting the requirement that all Africans carry "passes"; 69 people were killed and 180 wounded. The council stated that the situation in South Africa had led to international friction and, if continued, might endanger international peace and security. The council called on the South African government to abandon its policy of apartheid, which it termed "a crime against the conscience and dignity of mankind."

In order to keep the racial policies of South Africa under review, the General Assembly decided, in 1962, to establish the Special Committee Against Apartheid. The committee, composed of 18 members, was subsequently given a wider mandate to review all aspects of South Africa's policies of apartheid and the international repercussions of those policies.

The committee's work included the following activities: holding of meetings and hearings; the sending of missions to member states to gain support for the struggle against apartheid; the organization of international conferences, special sessions, and seminars; and the implementation of the resolutions of the General Assembly and the Security Council, particularly by promoting sports, cultural, consumer, and other boycotts and, with the UN Center Against Apartheid, cooperating with governments, intergovernmental organizations, trade unions, women's organizations, religious leaders, student and youth movements, and antiapartheid groups in mobilizing international public opinion in support of action against apartheid.

The General Assembly also established, in 1965, the UN Trust Fund for South Africa, which, through voluntary contributions, made grants to organizations for legal aid to persons persecuted under South Africa's apartheid laws, relief to such persons and their families, and relief for refugees from South Africa. In 1967, the General Assembly established the UN Educational and Training Program for Southern Africa, which granted scholarships to students from South Africa and Namibia for study and training abroad.

Arms Embargo and Other Sanctions. A voluntary arms embargo against South Africa was instituted by the Security Council in 1963. Noting that some of the arms supplied to South Africa were being used to further its racial policies and repress the African people, the council called on all states to stop the sale and shipment of arms, ammunition of all types, and military vehicles to South Africa. Subsequently, in 1970, the Security Council condemned violations of the arms embargo and called on all states to strengthen and implement it unconditionally; withhold the supply of all vehicles, equipment, and spare parts for use by South African military and paramilitary forces; revoke all licenses and patents granted for South African manufacture of arms, aircraft, or military vehicles; prohibit investment or technical assistance for arms manufacture; and cease military cooperation with South Africa.

Both the Security Council and the General Assembly condemned the shooting, on 26 June 1976, of Africans, including schoolchildren, demonstrating in the township of Soweto.

The following year, the Security Council made the arms embargo against South Africa mandatory, the first time that such action had been taken against a member state under Chapter VII of the charter, which provides for enforcement action in the face of threats to international peace and security. Concerned that South Africa was at the threshold of producing nuclear weapons, the Security Council also decided that states should refrain from any cooperation with South Africa in the manufacture and development of such weapons. It established a committee to keep under constant review the implementation by states of the mandatory arms embargo.

Meanwhile, the General Assembly, in 1970, urged states to terminate diplomatic and other official relations with South Africa, as well as economic and all other types of cooperation, as an expression of international rejection of South Africa's policy of apartheid, which the General Assembly called "a crime against humanity." In 1973, the General Assembly adopted the International Convention on the Suppression and Punishment of the Crime of Apartheid (see the section on Racial Discrimination in the chapter on Human Rights).

In 1974, the General Assembly rejected South Africa's credentials and recommended that South Africa be totally excluded from participation in all international organizations and conferences held under UN auspices until it abandoned its policies of apartheid.

The International Conference on Sanctions Against South Africa, held in Paris in May 1981, called for further international action to isolate South Africa, including the imposition, under Chapter VII of the charter, of sanctions "as the most appropriate and effective means to ensure South Africa's compliance with the decisions of the United Nations." The need for sanctions, including disengagement of transnational corporations operating in South Africa and disinvestment in companies doing business with South Africa, remained the focal point of UN efforts to end that country's policies of apartheid.

Other measures included a sports boycott, embodied in the International Declaration Against Apartheid in Sports, which was adopted by the General Assembly in 1977, and the International Convention Against Apartheid in Sports, which was adopted in 1985 and came into force on 4 April 1988.

Other Action. Other action taken by the UN in support of the African majority of South Africa and against that country's policies of apartheid included:

- condemnation of South Africa's policy of destabilization in southern Africa through its armed incursions into neighboring independent African states that support and assist the efforts of the African majority of South Africa;
- rejection of South Africa's policy of establishing "homelands" as "independent" entities within South Africa where Africans are forced to resettle;
- recognition of the African liberation movements of South

Africa—the African National Congress of South Africa (ANC) and the Pan Africanist Congress of Azania (PAC), both banned by South Africa—as "the authentic representatives of the overwhelming majority of the South African people"; and support for persons imprisoned or detained in South Africa for their opposition to apartheid.

The Final Stages. In April 1989, the Special Committee against Apartheid and the Intergovernmental Group to Monitor the Supply of Shipping of Oil and Petroleum Products to South Africa met in New York and recommended that the Security Council impose a mandatory oil embargo. It also recommended that pending action by the Security Council, all oil-producing, shipping, and handling states should enact legislation to stop the flow of oil to South Africa.

On 12–14 December 1989, the General Assembly held a Special Session on Apartheid and its Destructive Consequences in South Africa. It adopted by consensus a historic declaration which listed the steps that the South African regime should take to restore political and human rights in that country. It suggested guidelines for negotiations and for drawing up a new constitution based on the principles of the United Nations Charter and the Declaration of Human Rights. The declaration called upon all South Africans, as a matter of urgency, to join together to negotiate an end to the apartheid system and agree on all the measures necessary to transform their country into a nonracial democracy.

In February 1990, in a dramatic development, most political prisoners in South Africa, including Nelson Mandela, deputy president of the ANC, were released, and the ANC, PAC, and the South African Communist Party were recognized by the government. On 22 June 1990, Nelson Mandela addressed the General Assembly, thanking the United Nations for its efforts to secure his release and that of other South African political prisoners. He urged the UN and individual governments to continue the sanctions which they had imposed on South Africa. In May 1990, the government of South Africa and the ANC adopted the Groote Schurr Minute, which granted indemnity to political exiles and refugees, and paved the way for their return to South Africa. In August 1990, both parties agreed to the Pretoria Minute under which the government undertook to review emergency and security matters, while the ANC suspended armed actions.

On 1 February 1991, South African president F.W. de Klerk announced that the basic laws of apartheid would be repealed during that session of Parliament. He also issued a Manifesto for the New South Africa, stating that the new nation should be based on justice. The basic laws of apartheid were repealed on 5 June 1991, and later that month a peace summit was held by religious and business leaders, and some of the major parties to political violence. As a result, a preparatory committee, including the government and the ANC, was established and became known as the National Peace Initiative. In August 1991, the National Peace Initiative released a draft national peace accord. Also in August, the government and the office of the UN High Commissioner for Refugees (UNHCR) agreed on a plan for the voluntary repatriation of an estimated 40,000 South african refugees and political exiles.

In spite of the commencement of formal negotiations on constitutional reforms in December 1991, not all political parties participated and violence in the townships continued to escalate. In June 1992, 50 people died in the Boipatong massacre and the ANC suspended its participation in the talks until the government took more decisive action to put an end to the violence.

In July 1992, several political players in South Africa were invited to come and apprise the Security Council of the situation in their country. Subsequently, the Security Council authorized the Secretary-General to appoint a special representative to go to South Africa to find out first hand what was going on in the country, so that it could be determined how the international community could assist in bringing an end to the violence and create conditions for a peaceful transition in South Africa. As a result of this mission, the Security Council adopted Resolution 772 (1992) authorizing the Secretary-General to deploy the UN Observer Mission in South Africa (UNOMSA), charged with the task of assisting with strengthening the structures set up under the 1991 peace accords. The resolution also invited other international organizations such as the Organization of African Unity (OAU), the Commonwealth and the European Union to consider deploying their own observers in coordination with the United Nations. The first group of 50 UNOMSA observers was deployed in September 1992. It was widely agreed by all parties in South Africa that the presence of international observers greatly helped to reduce political tension, limit violence, and improve the climate for the negotiation process.

In April 1993, a new negotiating framework, the Multiparty Negotiating Council (MPNC) brought together 26 parties and was the most representative gathering in the history of South Africa. After several months of protracted negotiations, in November 1993, the MPNC adopted a number of constitutional principles and institutions to guide the country during a transitional period lasting until 27 April 1999. This interim constitution set forth plans for elections of a Constitutional Assembly that would draft a new national constitution. In response to all the positive developments, on 8 October 1993, in its Resolution 48/1 (1993), the 184-member General Assembly unanimously ended its 31-year ban on economic and other ties with South Africa in the areas of trade, investment, finance, travel, and transportation. Member states were asked to lift the sanctions they had imposed over the years under numerous UN resolutions and decisions. On 15 October 1993, the Nobel Peace Prize was awarded to South African president F.W. de Klerk and ANC president Nelson Mandela.

Although incidents of violence continued, and some parties to the negotiations threatened to withdraw from the election process, the elections were held successfully from 26–28 April 1994. At the request of the South African Transitional Executive Committee, the Security Council increased the UNOMSA contingent to approximately 1,800 during the election period. Another approximately 900 international observers from foreign governments and international organizations also were deployed across the country to observe the balloting. The UNOMSA observers determined whether voters enjoyed free access to voting stations, whether the secrecy of the vote had been guaranteed, and that ballot boxes had been properly sealed, protected, and transported. It also witnessed the counting of the ballots and the communication of the results to South Africa's Independent Electoral Commission, the body responsible for organizing, administering, and monitoring all aspects of the elections to verify that they were free and fair.

A New Era Dawns. On 27 April 1994 the new six-color flag of a South Africa liberated from apartheid was unfurled at United Nations headquarters in New York. On 10 May 1994, Nelson Rolihlala Mandela was inaugurated as the new president of the Republic of South Africa. On 25 May 1994, the Security Council lifted the mandatory arms embargo it had imposed on South Africa in 1977. On 21 June 1994, the General Assembly, in its Resolution 48/258 (1994), declared that the mandate of the Special Committee against Apartheid had been successfully concluded, and terminated its existence. By the same resolution, it removed the agenda item on the elimination of apartheid from the agenda of its next (49th) session. On 23 June 1994, South Africa was welcomed back to full participation in the work of the General Assembly, after 20 years of banishment.

ARMS REGULATION AND DISARMAMENT

Only days after the signing of the Charter, the world entered the nuclear age. On 6 and 9 August, 1945, respectively, atomic bombs destroyed the Japanese cities of Hiroshima and Nagasaki. The newly formed UN was thus confronted with unprecedented military and political problems. The Charter had envisaged arms limitation and disarmament elements in the progressive establishment of an international security system. It empowered the General Assembly to consider "principles governing disarmament and the regulation of armaments" and assigned to the Security Council the task of formulating plans to establish an appropriate system of controls for the "regulation of armaments," to be submitted to the members of the UN. However, the revolutionary changes brought about by the discovery of atomic power gave the need for disarmament greater immediacy and an enhanced place in the sphere of international politics and security. The UN has reacted progressively to this unfolding of events while the peoples of the world have begun to live under the threat of nuclear annihilation.

Fifty years after the founding of the organization, the tensions that dominated the international political situation during the Cold War period eased, significant progress was achieved in the field of disarmament, and new opportunities opened for the international community to achieve security at lower levels of arms. At the same time, new challenges confronted the members of the UN as the focus of tensions among nations turned from the international to the regional and local level.

In the course of the past five decades, the UN has used a variety of methods, techniques, and approaches in the search for disarmament.

INITIAL EFFORTS

Under Article II of the UN Charter, the General Assembly is empowered to consider "principles governing disarmament and the regulation of armaments" and to recommend action to be taken by member states or the Security Council or both. The General Assembly has undertaken this kind of consideration at every one of its regular sessions since it first met in 1946. The General Assembly's very first resolution, adopted on 24 January 1946, addressed the question of disarmament. It sought the elimination of atomic weapons and other weapons of mass destruction and the assurance that, from then on, atomic energy would be used only for peaceful purposes, and it established the Atomic Energy Commission. In a resolution adopted in December 1946, the General Assembly recognized the connection between the questions of disarmament and of international peace and security.

In 1947, the Security Council set up the Commission for Conventional Armaments in order to regulate armaments and armed forces under an international system of control and inspection, and it called upon the two commissions to take immediate action.

Despite the urgency of the matter, the two commissions did not make much progress. In 1952, the General Assembly, in an attempt to break the impasse, consolidated them into a single 11-member Disarmament Commission, which was entrusted with the task of preparing proposals for the regulation, limitation, and balanced reduction of all armed forces and armaments, by stages, in a coordinated, comprehensive program.

The early debates in the Disarmament Commission ended inconclusively in October 1952. In November, the first hydrogen bomb, with a force that dwarfed that of the Hiroshima-type atomic bomb, was tested by the United States at Eniwetok (now Enewetak), in the Pacific. The following August, a hydrogen bomb was exploded by the USSR.

A subcommittee of the Disarmament Commission, set up by the General Assembly in 1953 and consisting of representatives of Canada, France, the USSR, the United Kingdom, and the US, held a number of meetings, but by the autumn of 1955, efforts aimed at drawing up a comprehensive disarmament plan ended in deadlock. The subcommittee's efforts to consider partial disarmament measures also came to a stalemate over the next two years. In 1957, the General Assembly enlarged the Disarmament Commission from 11 to 25 nations. It was again enlarged, in 1959, to comprise all members of the UN, but it convened only one further time, in 1965.

In 1959, the General Assembly unanimously adopted the first resolution ever to be sponsored by all member states. In it, the General Assembly declared that it was "striving to put an end completely and forever to the armaments race," and it stated that "the question of general and complete disarmament is the most important facing the world today." The resolution aimed at having all proposals and suggestions made during the General Assembly debate transmitted to the Disarmament Commission "for thorough consideration."

Substantive differences in the approach taken to disarmament by the Western powers and the USSR emerged during the subsequent period. A Ten-Nation Committee on Disarmament, based on equal East-West representation, was set up in 1960 outside the framework of the UN to discuss general and complete disarmament but became deadlocked on issues of partial or general measures. As a result, the UN began to pursue disarmament efforts in two ways. While the ultimate goal remained, as it has ever since, "general and complete disarmament under effective international control," measures that would bring about partial disarmament were viewed as integral to that goal and not as hindrances to its achievement. It was felt that devoting parallel, and at times even primary, attention to "collateral" measures designed to reduce tension and build confidence would facilitate the complex task of achieving general and complete disarmament. The immediate hopes and expectations of the majority of nations centered on two such measures: the discontinuance of nuclear-weapon tests and the prevention of the spread of nuclear weapons. By the mid-1960s, the elaboration of partial disarmament measures within the UN began to overshadow all-embracing, long-range efforts.

In 1961, John I. McCloy of the United States and Valerian A. Zorin of the USSR, representing their respective nations in formal disarmament talks, submitted to the General Assembly a Joint Statement of Agreed Principles of Disarmament Negotiations. These eight principles, which were unanimously endorsed by the General Assembly, dealt with: (1) the stated goal of negotiations—a program ensuring that disarmament was to be "general and complete" and was to be accompanied by reliable procedures for the maintenance of peace; (2) the reduction of non-nuclear weapons and facilities to such levels as might be agreed to be necessary for the maintenance of internal order and the provision of personnel for a UN peacekeeping force; (3) an agreed elaboration of the main elements of the disarmament program; (4) implementation of the program in agreed stages, which were to have specified time limits; (5) balance so that at no stage could any state or group maintain an advantage; (6) the need for international control under an international disarmament organization to be created within the framework of the UN; (7) the need during and after disarmament to strengthen institutions for maintaining world peace; and (8) the need to achieve and implement the widest possible agreement in the shortest possible time.

At the same time, the General Assembly also endorsed an agreement to set up, in place of the Ten-Nation Committee, an Eighteen-Nation Committee on Disarmament. When the committee first met in Geneva in early 1962, one member, France, decided not to participate, explaining that it hoped that it might be possible later for the disarmament problem to be discussed among the powers that could contribute effectively to its solution. At the outset, the committee decided to organize so as to permit simultaneous work on general and complete disarmament, confidence-building (collateral) measures, and the discontinuance of nuclear-weapon tests.

In 1969, the committee's membership was enlarged to 26, and its name changed to the Conference of the Committee on Disarmament (CCD). The General Assembly requested the CCD, as the multilateral negotiating body, to work out, while continuing its negotiations on collateral measures, a comprehensive program to deal with the cessation of the arms race and general and complete disarmament under effective international control. In 1975, the CCD was further enlarged, to 31 members, with France still declining to take its seat.

The scant results and continuing difficulties in disarmament negotiations, among other things, led, also in 1969, to the General Assembly's adoption of a resolution declaring the 1970s as a Disarmament Decade. The 1980s and 1990s were also later declared as disarmament decades.

SPECIAL SESSIONS OF THE GENERAL ASSEMBLY ON DISARMAMENT

First Special Session, 1978

By 1976 it was clear that no real progress had been made to halt the arms race. World military expenditure was estimated at many times more than the amount spent globally on health, education, and economic development. While the nuclear-weapon powers were the major competitors in the arms race, military spending by countries outside the two main military alliances was also rising. Since the end of the Second World War, many millions of people have been killed by conventional weapons in more than 100 wars, most of them fought in the developing areas of the world.

In 1976, the General Assembly, deploring the "meagre achievements" up to that time of the first Disarmament Decade in terms of truly effective agreements, decided, primarily at the initiative of developing countries, to hold a special session in 1978 devoted entirely to disarmament. The aim of the session was to set a new course in international affairs, turn states away from the nuclear and conventional arms race, and obtain agreement on a global strategy for disarmament.

The first special session on disarmament, held at UN headquarters from 23 May to 1 July 1978, was the largest, most representative meeting of nations ever convened to consider the question of disarmament endeavors, the international community of states as a whole achieved a consensus on a comprehensive disarmament strategy, which was embodied in the Final Document adopted at the session.

The Final Document stressed the central role and primary responsibility of the UN in the field of disarmament and placed disarmament issues in a more comprehensive perspective than had ever been done before. It reaffirmed the fundamental importance of disarmament to international peace and security and stated that "disarmament and arms limitation agreements should provide for adequate measures of verification satisfactory to all parties." It contained specific measures intended to strengthen the machinery dealing with disarmament within the UN system. Composed of four parts—an introduction, a declaration, a program of action, and a section on machinery—the Final Document set out goals, principles, and priorities in the field of disarmament.

The *Introduction* stated that while the final objective should continue to be general and complete disarmament under effective international control, the immediate goal was the elimination of the danger of a nuclear war and the implementation of measures to halt and reverse the arms race.

The *Declaration* stated that "the increase in weapons, especially nuclear weapons, far from helping to strengthen international security, on the contrary weakens it, . . . heightens the sense of insecurity among all states, including the non-nuclear-weapon states, and increases the threat of nuclear war." It further stated that "genuine and lasting peace can only be created through the effective implementation of the security system provided for in the Charter of the United Nations and the speedy and substantial reduction of arms and armed forces." It emphasized that, in the adoption of disarmament measures, the right of each state to security should be kept in mind and that, at each stage of the disarmament process, "the objective should be undiminished security at the lowest possible level of armaments and military forces."

The *Program of Action* listed priorities and measures that states should undertake as a matter of urgency in the field of disarmament. Priorities included nuclear weapons; other weapons of mass destruction, including chemical weapons; and conventional weapons, including any that might be deemed to be excessively injurious or to have indiscriminate effects. The program called for agreements or other measures to be "resolutely pursued on a bilateral, regional and multilateral basis with the aim of strengthening peace and security," and it recommended that measures be taken and policies pursued to strengthen international peace and security and to build confidence among states. The urgency of preventing the proliferation of nuclear weapons and of halting nuclear tests was stressed. The program called for full implementation of the 1967 Treaty of Tlatelolco, prohibiting nuclear weapons in Latin America, and recommended steps to put into effect the proposals for the establishment of other nuclear-weapon-free zones. Other measures included prohibition of the development, production, and stockpiling of chemical weapons; limits on the international transfer of conventional weapons; agreed reduction of military budgets; and further study of the question of verification. The program also listed measures to be undertaken to mobilize world public opinion on behalf of disarmament.

The final section, on *Machinery,* noted the urgency of revitalizing the disarmament machinery and outlined the consensus reached on the strengthening or establishment of appropriate forums, of suitably representative character, for disarmament deliberations and negotiations, as well as for other activities to be undertaken, including research.

Acting on the recommendations of the special session, the General Assembly established, as a specialized, subsidiary deliberative body, a revitalized Disarmament Commission composed of all UN members. It was assigned the mandate of making recommendations on disarmament problems as requested by the General Assembly, and to follow up the relevant decisions and recommendations of the special session on disarmament.

The special session recognized the continued need for a single multilateral negotiating forum on disarmament and recognized that the Committee on Disarmament in Geneva should continue to fulfil this role and to carry on the work of its predecessors—the Ten-Nation Committee on Disarmament (1959–60), the Eighteen-Nation Committee on Disarmament (1962–69) and the Conference of the Committee on Disarmament (1969–78). Known as the Conference on Disarmament since 1984, it has a membership of 38 countries, including the five nuclear-weapon states and most of the militarily powerful states of the world's regions. In 1994, in recognition of the changed international situation after the Cold War, the conference reviewed the idea of expanding its membership.

Other results of the General Assembly's first special session included the establishment of a program of fellowships on disarmament; an increased flow of information on disarmament to governments, nongovernmental organizations, the media, and the general public; and the designation of the week beginning 24 October (UN Day) to be observed each year as Disarmament Week (see also under Studies, Research, Information, and Training below).

In order to enable the UN to fulfil its role in the field of disarmament and to carry out the tasks assigned to it, the special session took steps to strengthen the role of the section of the UN Secretariat handling disarmament affairs, the Centre for Disarmament Affairs. The centre's main tasks include maintaining a database on conventional armaments transfers, supporting ongoing deliberations and negotiations in New York, Geneva, and elsewhere, fostering regional confidence and security building initiatives, and disseminating information to sources outside the UN.

In 1979, the General Assembly declared the 1980s as the Second Disarmament Decade, stating that its goals should remain consistent with the ultimate objective of general and complete disarmament. The basic goals of the Second Disarmament Decade were set out as follows: halting and reversing the arms race; conclusion of agreements on disarmament according to the objectives and priorities of the 1978 Final Document; strengthening international peace and security in keeping with the UN Charter; and reallocating resources from military to development purposes, particularly in favor of developing countries.

In the four years following the first special session, the international situation in fact deteriorated: numerous events beyond effective UN influence evolved in such a way as to hinder international arms-limitation efforts, particularly in the early 1980s, when military expenditures increased and a lack of confidence permeated disarmament discussions and affected negotiations. After some initial progress, negotiations stalled on virtually every important disarmament issue, and the 1978 Program of Action remained substantially unimplemented.

Second Special Session, 1982

The second special session of the General Assembly devoted to disarmament was held at UN headquarters from 7 June to 10 July 1982. Given the international tension and armed conflicts prevailing at that time, the atmosphere did not bode well for the reaching of further accords on sensitive, substantive issues then relating to the perceived national security interests of states.

At the time of the first special session in 1978, the General Assembly had reaffirmed the goal of general and complete disarmament, a concept that had received considerable attention even before that in the framework of the UN. The emphasis placed on general and complete disarmament slowly gave way to another approach, known as the comprehensive program of disarmament. The intent of the approach was to elaborate a program which would place partial measures of disarmament into a carefully considered plan, setting out objectives, priorities, and timeframes, with a view to the achievement of disarmament on a progressive basis.

A main agenda item of the session—to elaborate the strategy of the 1978 Program of Action into a Comprehensive Program of Disarmament—was not achieved. Thus, the General Assembly did not agree, as it had in 1978, on a formula for specific action. In the Concluding Document of the session, however, the General Assembly unanimously reaffirmed the validity of the Final Document of the first special session on disarmament. It expressed its profound preoccupation over the danger of war, particularly nuclear war, and urged member states to consider as soon as possible proposals for ensuring prevention of such a war. The General Assembly also stressed again the need for strengthening the central role of the UN in the field of disarmament, for implementing the security system provided for in the Charter of the UN, and for enhancing the effectiveness of the multilateral negotiating body, the Committee on Disarmament.

The committee and then the Conference on Disarmament continued to negotiate the draft comprehensive program of disarmament until 1989. At the end of the conference's session that year, it was agreed to suspend work on the program until the circumstances were more propitious for progress.

Among the other decisions of the second special session was the launching of a World Disarmament Campaign to increase public awareness of disarmament issues (see also under Studies, Research, Information, and Training below). The General Assembly also decided to convene a third special session on disarmament (subsequently scheduled to be held in 1988 at UN headquarters).

Third Special Session, 1988

The third special session took place in 1988 against the background of a considerably improved international climate. The progress that had been recorded in some important fields of disarmament, in particular nuclear disarmament, was welcomed throughout the debates during the session.

The 1987 *Treaty between the former Soviet Union and the United States on the Elimination of Their Intermediate-Range and Shorter-Range Missiles* (INF Treaty); the achievements of the 1986 Stockholm Conference on Confidence- and Security-Building Measures and Disarmament in Europe; and the 1986 *South Pacific Nuclear Free Zone Treaty* (Treaty of Rarotonga) were indicative of the favorable trends in arms control and disarmament.

The progress reported on the negotiations that had begun before the commencement of the special session, between the former Soviet Union and the United States, on a treaty on the reduction and limitation of strategic offensive arms (START) (see below), as well as progress made in the Conference on Disarmament on the complete elimination of chemical weapons, also were highly welcomed. All this notwithstanding, member states were unable to adopt by consensus a final document setting the pace and direction for future negotiations.

In December 1995, the General Assembly decided to convene a Fourth Special Session devoted to disarmament in 1997. However, as the Disarmament Commission completed its 1998 session, it had not come to agreement on the objectives and agenda of the proposed fourth special session, then pushed back to 1999. In December 1999, the General Assembly decided anew to convene the fourth session on disarmament and requested the Secretary-General to seek the views of the member states on the objectives, agenda, and timing. In April 2000, there still was no consensus by the General Assembly on the objectives.

DISARMAMENT MACHINERY

General Assembly

The General Assembly, as the main deliberative body of the UN, takes up questions concerning disarmament and related international security matters at each of its annual sessions, through its First Committee, and makes recommendations. In the late 1980s and into the 1990s, some 25–30% of the resolutions adopted by the General Assembly have been concerned with disarmament and related international security matters; many of these resolutions give mandates to the Disarmament Commission or make requests to the Conference on Disarmament (formerly the Committee on Disarmament) to take into consideration various ideas or questions under negotiation. Both the Disarmament Commission and the Conference on Disarmament report to the General Assembly each year.

Disarmament Commission

The revitalized Disarmament Commission established after the first special session of the General Assembly on disarmament is composed of all members of the UN. It provides a deliberative forum for consideration of specific disarmament issues when the General Assembly is not in session. A subsidiary organ of the General Assembly, it meets annually at UN headquarters for approximately four weeks, usually in spring, to make recommendations to the General Assembly on specific disarmament problems and to follow up mandates given to it.

Conference on Disarmament

As a result of its first special session on disarmament, the General Assembly mandated the Committee on Disarmament to fulfil the role of a single multilateral negotiating forum and to carry on the work of earlier committees. It enlarged the membership of the committee to 40 countries, including all five nuclear-weapon states (China, France, the USSR, the United Kingdom, and the US). Redesignated the Conference on Disarmament at the end of 1983, it meets in Geneva for approximately six months each year, usually when the General Assembly is not in session. Its Secretary-General is appointed, upon consultation, by the Secretary-General of the UN and also serves as that individual's personal representative.

The Conference on Disarmament has a unique relationship with the UN. It defines its own rules of procedure and develops its own agenda, taking into account the recommendations made by the General Assembly. It agreed on a permanent agenda of 10 items in 1979, and from those items it chooses an annual agenda and fixes its program of work for the year. Its work in plenary meetings and also in subsidiary bodies dealing with specific items is conducted by consensus, since international agreements, if they are to be effective, must be generally acceptable.

MAIN ACHIEVEMENTS

Multilateral Agreements

After World War I, intense efforts were made to translate the 1874 Brussels Declaration and the subsequent Hague Conventions into a ban on chemical weapons and "the use of projectiles, the sole object of which is the diffusion of asphyxiating or deleterious gases." Although a total ban is still to be attained, one of the first achievements, in 1925, was the Protocol for the Prohibition of the Use in War of Asphyxiating, Poisonous or Other Gases, and of Bacteriological Methods of Warfare, generally referred to as the Geneva Protocol. It bans "the use in war of asphyxiating, poisonous or other gases and of all analogous liquids, materials or devices," as well as "the use of bacteriological methods of warfare." The Geneva Protocol, with 110 states parties in 1987, is the point of departure in current efforts toward a ban on the production, possession, and stockpiling of chemical weapons and helped establish the convention banning bacteriological weapons in 1972 (see below).

Concerted efforts by the UN and by governments since 1945 at both the multilateral and bilateral levels, as well as on a regional basis, have led to a body of important agreements, trea-

ties, and conventions committing their parties to various arms limitation and disarmament measures. The multilateral instruments concluded so far are given below (the number of states parties is shown in parentheses after each title).

- The 1959 *Antarctic Treaty* (37) provides for the demilitarization of Antarctica and is the first treaty to put into practice the concept of the nuclear-weapon-free zone, later applied to Latin America and the South Pacific, as well as to the seabed and outer space. It prohibits any military maneuvers, weapon tests, building of installations, or disposal of radioactive wastes in the Antarctic region.

- The 1963 *Treaty Banning Nuclear Weapon Tests in the Atmosphere, in Outer Space and Under Water* (Partial Test-Ban Treaty) (115) bans all nuclear weapon tests in the three environments designated but does not ban underground tests. Since 1963, the General Assembly has repeatedly urged conclusion of a comprehensive treaty banning all nuclear tests, including those conducted underground.

- The 1967 *Treaty on Principles Governing the Activities of States in the Exploration and Use of Outer Space, Including the Moon and Other Celestial Bodies* (Outer-Space Treaty) (87) bans nuclear and other weapons of mass destruction from the earth's orbit and prohibits the military use of celestial bodies and the placing of such weapons on those bodies.

- The 1967 *Treaty for the Prohibition of Nuclear Weapons in Latin America* (Treaty of Tlatelolco) (31) creates the first nuclear-weapon-free zone in a densely populated area and is the first arms-limitation agreement to provide for control and verification by an international organization, the Agency for the Prohibition of Nuclear Weapons in Latin America, as well as through the safeguards system of the International Atomic Energy Agency (IAEA).

- The 1968 *Treaty on the Non-Proliferation of Nuclear Weapons* (Non-Proliferation Treaty) (138) aims at preventing the spread of nuclear weapons to non-nuclear-weapon states, at guaranteeing all countries access to nuclear technology for peaceful purposes, and at promoting the process of nuclear disarmament. The treaty defines a nuclear-weapon state as one that had manufactured and exploded a nuclear weapon or other nuclear explosive device prior to 1 January 1967. With the broadest adherence of all treaties, it has helped so far to maintain the number of nuclear-weapon states at five.

- The 1971 *Treaty on the Prohibition of the Emplacement of Nuclear Weapons and Other Weapons of Mass Destruction on the Sea-Bed and the Ocean Floor and in the Subsoil Thereof* (Sea-Bed Treaty) (79) bans the placement of nuclear and other weapons of mass destruction and facilities for such weapons on or under the seabed outside a 12-mile coastal zone.

- The 1972 *Convention on the Prohibition of the Development, Production and Stockpiling of Bacteriological (Biological) and Toxin Weapons and on Their Destruction* (109) is the first international agreement providing for actual disarmament, that is, the destruction of existing weapons.

- The 1977 *Convention on the Prohibition of Military or Any Other Hostile Use of Environmental Modification Techniques* (64) prohibits the use of techniques that would have widespread, long-lasting, or severe effects in causing such phenomena as earthquakes, tidal waves, and changes in weather and climate patterns.

- The 1979 *Agreement Governing Activities of States on the Moon and Other Celestial Bodies* (9) goes further than the 1967 Outer-Space Treaty in prohibiting the use of the moon and other celestial bodies for military purposes.

- The 1981 *Convention on Prohibitions or Restrictions on the Use of Certain Conventional Weapons Which May Be Deemed to Be Excessively Injurious or to Have Indiscriminate Effects*

(63) restricts or prohibits the use of mines and booby traps, incendiary weapons, and fragments not readily detectable in the human body. These rules range from a complete ban on the use of such weapons to restrictions on their use in conditions that would cause incidental loss of life or injury to civilians or damage to civilian objects.

- The 1985 *South Pacific Nuclear-Free-Zone Treaty* (Treaty of Raratonga) (9), exemplifies a positive regional limitation measure. Its geographical limits are contiguous with those of the two other major zonal treaties, the Treaty of Tlatelolco and the Antarctic Treaty, the three instruments covering a significant portion of the earth's surface.
- The 1990 *Treaty on Conventional Armed Forces in Europe* (CFE Treaty) (22), was a considerable post-Cold War breakthrough achieved at a summit meeting of the Conference on Security and Cooperation in Europe (CSCE). It was adopted in Paris in November 1990. The treaty entered into force on 9 November 1992, after it was signed by the original 22 participating states, joined by seven of the new republics formed from the former Soviet Union. It established limits for five categories of weapons within its area of application, which stretches from the Atlantic to the Urals. Chosen for limitation were those categories of weapons systems that would eliminate disparities in force levels and the capability of launching surprise attack or large-scale offensives. The treaty was the first in Europe to provide for the actual reduction of conventional weapons. As called for in the treaty, negotiations among the states party to the CFE Treaty soon began, aimed at limiting the personnel strength of armed forces. Known as the *CFE-1A Agreement*, it was signed in July 1992 at the summit meeting of the CSCE at Helsinki.
- The 1993 *Convention on the Prohibition of the Development, Production, Stockpiling and Use of Chemical Weapons and their Destruction* (Chemical Weapons Convention) (68), is the first disarmament agreement that would eliminate an entire category of weapons. Such chemical weapons exist in large quantities, are possessed by many countries, and have been used in combat even in recent years. The convention was ratified by 65 countries and entered into force on 29 April 1997.

Bilateral Agreements

Over the same period, bilateral negotiations between the USSR/ Russian Federation and the United States have produced a number of agreements between the two powers, including those described below.

- The 1972 *Treaty on the Limitation of Anti-Ballistic Missile Systems* (ABM Treaty and part of the SALT I agreements) restricts in general the development of sea-based, air-based, space-based, or mobile land-based antiballistic missile (ABM) systems and specifically limits development of ABM systems to two sites with no more than 100 launchers each. By a protocol of 1974, the deployment of ABM systems is further limited to a single area, with no more than 100 launchers.
- The 1972 *Interim Agreement on Certain Measures with Respect to the Limitation of Strategic Offensive Arms* (commonly regarded as SALT I) establishes limitations for a five-year period—with a provision for extension—on the number of launchers of strategic weapons.
- Under the 1973 *Agreement on the Prevention of Nuclear War*, the two parties agree to make the removal of the danger of nuclear war and of the use of nuclear weapons an objective of their policies and to make all efforts toward guaranteeing stability and peace.
- The 1974 *Treaty on the Limitation of Underground Nuclear-Weapon Tests* (Threshold Test-Ban Treaty) establishes a nuclear threshold by prohibiting underground nuclear-weapon tests having a yield exceeding 150 kilotons.
- The 1976 *Treaty on Underground Nuclear Explosions for Peaceful Purposes* prohibits the carrying out of any individual nuclear explosion for peaceful purposes having a yield exceeding 150 kilotons or any group explosion with an aggregate yield exceeding 1,500 kilotons, and it includes on-site verification procedures.
- The 1979 *Treaty on the Limitation of Strategic Offensive Arms* (SALT II) establishes limits on the number and types of strategic nuclear-delivery vehicles.
- The 1974, 1976, and 1979 treaties have not come into force, but each party has agreed to adhere to their substantive provisions as long as the other party does likewise.
- The 1987 *Treaty between the Two States on the Elimination of Their Intermediate Range and Shorter-Range Missiles* (INF Treaty) provides for the elimination of an entire class of nuclear weapons with a range between 55 and 5,500 kilometers (3,410 miles). The treaty entered into force on 1 June 1988 and its provisions were implemented before the 1 June 1991 date set by the treaty.
- The 1991 *Treaty on the Reduction and Limitation of Strategic Offensive Arms* (START Treaty) places limits on the two sides' strategic nuclear forces, i.e., inter-continental ballistic missiles (ICBMs). This treaty established an unprecedented reduction of 35% to 40% of the states' overall nuclear forces at the time and created an elaborate system for verification of compliance.
- The 1993 *Treaty on Further Reduction and Limitation of Strategic Offensive Arms* (START II), once implemented, will bring about deep reductions in the overall levels of ICBMs, submarine-launched ballistic missiles (SLBMs), nuclear armed heavy bombers and nuclear air-launched cruise missiles (ACLMs). The agreement is not yet ratified, as its terms provide that it cannot enter into force before the START Treaty.

MAJOR ISSUES AND DISARMAMENT NEGOTIATION EFFORTS

The Threat of Nuclear Weapons

When the first atomic bombs were exploded on 6 and 9 August 1945, their immense destructive power confronted the world with military and political problems of unprecedented magnitude.

The catastrophic consequences of the use of nuclear weapons would not be confined to the nuclear adversaries but would threaten civilization on a global scale. According to a 1984 World Health Organization (WHO) report on the effects of nuclear war on health and health services, as many as 10,000 megatons of nuclear bombs could be exploded globally in an all-out nuclear war—90% of them in Europe, Asia, and North America and 10% in Africa, Latin America, and Oceania. As a result, half of the world's population could instantly become war victims. About 1.5 billion people could die and 1.1 billion could be injured. In addition, millions of immediate survivors of an attack would die of radiation effects, disease, cold temperatures, and starvation over the following few years. Thus, the greatest threat to humanity comes from nuclear arsenals, whose total destructive power has reached a level equivalent to more than 1 million Hiroshima bombs. Yet, each of the nuclear powers, albeit with expressed reluctance, considers it essential, either as a strategy or a necessary policy of credible deterrence of war, to possess operational nuclear weapons as long as the others have them.

A 1988 UN study on the climatic and potential physical effects of nuclear war concluded that a major nuclear war would entail the high risk of a global environmental disruption. A 1990 UN report captured the sense of the turning point in history brought about by the development of nuclear weapons. According to that report, nuclear weapons represented a historically new form of weaponry, which, by their multiple and far-reaching effects, provided a means of warfare whose mass destructive potential was unparalleled in human experience. Nuclear technology had made it possible to release more energy in one microsecond from a single nuclear weapon than all the energy released by conventional weapons used in all wars throughout history. The same expert group estimated that, by 1990, the arms race had led to the gradual deployment on land and on the high seas of some 50,000 nuclear warheads. They also estimated that the world stockpile of nuclear weapons was equivalent to some 13,000 million tons of TNT, and that its explosive capacity was 1 million times the explosive energy of the Hiroshima atomic bomb.

In 1945, only the United States had developed the technology to produce nuclear weapons, but by 1949, the USSR had also developed a nuclear-weapon capability, followed by the United Kingdom in 1952, France in 1960, and China in 1964. Throughout the Cold War era, the United States and the former Soviet Union, among the five nuclear-weapon states, held the vast majority of nuclear weapons and the most advanced delivery systems. Indeed, the UN, in a consensus document adopted at the first special session of disarmament in 1978, recognized the special responsibility that these two states bore with respect to nuclear disarmament.

Over the years, concerns have been expressed in UN forums that some non-nuclear-weapon states might develop nuclear-weapon programs (the issue of so-called "threshold" states). After the end of the war in the Persian Gulf in April 1991, it came to light that some of the concerns expressed, at least in the case of Iraq, were warranted. In 1993–94 the defiance of the Democratic Peoples' Republic of Korea (DPRK) touched off an international crisis. The DPRK refused to allow access to IAEA inspectors charged with monitoring peaceful nuclear facilities (see chapter on IAEA). These developments challenged the UN, especially its Security Council, and the IAEA to unprecedented action.

With the dissolution of the Soviet Union at the end of 1991, its nuclear weapons were left on the territories of four of the newly independent states: Belarus, Kazakhstan, Russian Federation, and Ukraine. This state of affairs created a new set of challenges to the international community in the control of nuclear weapons.

Over the years, many measures have been proposed in the UN and other multilateral forums to limit, reduce, and eliminate nuclear weapons and their delivery systems; to assure non-nuclear-weapons states that nuclear weapons will not be used or even threatened to be used against them; to prevent the spread of nuclear weapons to non-nuclear-weapons states; to bring about a halt to all nuclear testing; to ensure the non-use of nuclear weapons; to bring about the cessation of the production of nuclear weapons as well as the production of fissionable material for weapons purposes; to restrict the deployment of nuclear weapons by nuclear-weapon states, and to foster cooperation in the peaceful uses of nuclear energy.

With the close of the Cold War era, a turning point in international political history had been reached and the dramatic international events that occurred had direct repercussions in the area of nuclear disarmament. Bilateral negotiations between the Russian Federation and the United States led to several agreements which, when fully implemented, will result in unprecedented reductions in the nuclear forces of both sides.

These developments served to codify the end of the Cold War and helped to pave the way for further control over the nuclear arsenals of the two major nuclear-weapon states, as well as to encourage the other three declared nuclear-weapon states towards further efforts in the field of nuclear weapons.

In a further sign that the international situation had significantly progressed, the conference decided to begin multilateral negotiations in January 1994 on a comprehensive nuclear test ban treaty. During the regular session of the General Assembly in 1993, the two major powers expressed interest in reaching agreement on a cessation of the production of fissionable material for weapons purposes.

Bilateral Nuclear Arms Reduction Agreements

Although the United Nations did not take part in the historic bilateral negotiations between the former USSR and the United States from 1969 to 1993, member states of the UN have responded with encouragement to the initiatives of the two major powers and have appealed to them to conduct their negotiations with the utmost determination to prevent nuclear war, reduce nuclear arsenals, prevent an arms race in outer space—a long-standing UN objective—and halt the arms race. Other nuclear-weapon states have declared that they would join the process of reducing nuclear weapons once the major powers have reduced theirs. In this context, it is appropriate to review here the sequence of events that brought these negotiations to such a salutary conclusion and their far-reaching implications for global security.

The SALT Treaties

The Strategic Arms Limitation Talks (SALT), which the former Soviet Union and the United States initiated in 1969, led in their first phase to the signing on 26 May 1972 in Moscow of two agreements: the *Treaty on the Limitation of Anti-Ballistic Missile Systems* (ABM Treaty), subsequently amended by a protocol of 3 July 1974, and the *Interim Agreement on Certain Measures With Respect to the Limitation of Strategic Offensive Arms*, with a protocol attached. Both the ABM Treaty and the Interim Agreement entered into force on 3 October 1972.

By signing the ABM Treaty, the United States and the former Soviet Union undertook not to develop, test, or deploy mobile land-based, sea-based, air-based, or space-based ABM systems. They also agreed to limit ABM systems to two sites with no more than 100 launchers at each site. In that way, they would not build nationwide ABM systems, which each side viewed as destabilizing. In 1974, the treaty was amended by a protocol which limited each side to one ABM deployment area only. The former Soviet Union chose to maintain its ABM system in the area centered on its capital, Moscow, and the United States chose to maintain its system in an intercontinental ballistic missile (ICBM) deployment area in North Dakota. Subsequently, the United States decided not to deploy its ABM system.

The second phase of the talks (SALT II) began in November 1972 and ended in June 1979 with the signing in Vienna of the *Treaty on the Limitation of Strategic Offensive Arms*, a protocol which was an integral part of the treaty, and a *Joint Statement of Principles and Basic Guidelines for Subsequent Negotiations on the Limitation of Strategic Arms*. The treaty, designed to remain in force to the end of 1985, defined and identified specific weapons and included numerous detailed limitations on the testing, deployment, modernization and replacement, and conversion of particular weapons systems. A Standing Consultative Commission was set up by the two countries in 1972 to deal with any questions or doubts about compliance with SALT II. Although SALT II was not immediately ratified by either party, each side declared its intention to abide by the provisions of the treaty as long as the other did. The US Senate approved the treaty in 1996; Russian lawmakers ratified it in April 2000, which was considered a major victory for Russian President-elect Vladimir Putin, whose party joined with more moderate forces against communists opposed to the treaty.

The INF Treaty

Early in the 1980s, the United States and the former Soviet Union opened two new sets of negotiations, one on intermediate-range nuclear forces (INF) and one on the reduction of strategic arms (START). After their discontinuation in December 1983, owing to the strained political situation between the two sides on the question of intermediate forces in Europe, the two powers agreed in January 1985 to hold negotiations on the complex questions concerning space and nuclear arms—both strategic and intermediate range—in order to work out an agreement for preventing an arms race in space and terminating it on earth, at limiting and reducing nuclear arms, and at strengthening strategic stability. This process led first to the signing in December 1987 in Washington of the *Treaty between the Two States on the Elimination of Their Intermediate-Range and Shorter-Range Missiles* (INF Treaty). It provided for the elimination of an entire class of nuclear weapons, namely, those nuclear forces with a range of between 500 and 5,500 kilometres. (Nuclear weapons with a range of more than 5,500 kilometres were considered to be strategic, while those with a range of less than 500 kilometres belonged to the category of tactical nuclear weapons.) The treaty entered into force on 1 June 1988. The INF Treaty is considered the first nuclear disarmament treaty, as it brought about the first actual reductions in the nuclear weapons of the two major powers. It also was considered an important turning point with respect to the strict verification schedule that it established, which included mutual arrangements for on-site inspections. Its provisions were fully implemented before June 1991, the date set by the treaty.

The START Treaties

In parallel to the negotiations being conducted on intermediate nuclear force, a complex series of talks were also held on reducing significantly the two sides' strategic nuclear weapons, in particular inter-continental ballistic missiles (ICBMs). These negotiations were finalized by the signing, at a summit meeting between President Bush and President Gorbachev in Moscow on 31 July 1991, of the *Treaty on the Reduction and Limitation of Strategic Offensive Arms* (START Treaty). The main objective of the treaty was to increase stability in the nuclear relationship between the former USSR and the United States. The interrelated limits and sublimits on the two sides' strategic nuclear forces established by the treaty amounted to an unprecedented reduction of 35% to 40% of their overall nuclear forces at the time. Furthermore, an elaborate system, including a full range of notifications, inspections, and permanent monitoring, was adopted for the verification of compliance with the terms of the treaty.

At the same time as efforts were being carried forward to ratify the START Treaty and to deal with the problems raised by the dissolution of the former Soviet Union, the Russian Federation and the United States intensified their negotiations on their strategic nuclear weapons. As a result, on 3 January 1993, President Bush and President Yeltsin signed the *Treaty on Further Reduction and Limitation of Strategic Offensive Arms* (START II). The treaty, once implemented, will bring about deep reductions in the overall number of nuclear warheads of the two sides including in their levels of inter-continental ballistic missiles (ICBMs), submarine-launched ballistic missiles (SLBMs), nuclear armed heavy bombers and nuclear air-launched cruise missiles (ACLMs).

Entry into force of the START I Treaty was complicated by the breakup of the USSR in 1989. The Russian Federation ratified the treaty on condition that the new republics of Belarus, Kazakhstan, and Ukraine also ratify the treaty and join the Nuclear Non-Proliferation Treaty (NPT). The START I Treaty was ratified by the United States Senate (1 October 1992), the Russian parliament (4 November 1992), the Belarus parliament (4 February 1993), the Kazakhstan parliament (2 July 1992), and the Ukrainian parliament (3 February 1994). Belarus joined the NPT on 22 July 1993. Kazakhstan joined the NPT on 14 February 1994. As of 1 August 1994, the government of Ukraine had stated that it would join the NPT, but had not yet done so. The treaty will come into force when that final condition is met and a formal exchange of treaty documents takes place.

The START II treaty provides that, in a two-phased process, the Russian Federation will reduce the number of its strategic nuclear weapons to 3,000 and the United States to 3,500, by the year 2003.

Unilateral Initiatives

In addition to the joint efforts of the two major powers to reduce the level of nuclear confrontation between them, a broad set of unilateral nuclear initiatives was announced by President Bush on 27 September and by President Gorbachev on 5 October 1991, which affected the entire spectrum of nuclear weapons of the United States and the former Soviet Union. The broad unilateral initiatives announced the destruction by both sides of their tactical nuclear weapons throughout the world, as well as other significant moves with respect to their nuclear forces. At the same time, President Gorbachev declared a one-year moratorium on nuclear weapons testing.

Upon the dissolution of the former Soviet Union at the end of 1991, its nuclear arsenal, which was subject to the reductions and limitations agreed under the START Treaty, passed into the jurisdiction of four newly formed states: Belarus, Kazakhstan, the Russian Federation, and Ukraine. To address the questions raised by the new situation, the four states, together with the United States, signed on 23 May 1992 in Lisbon, a protocol to the 1991 START Treaty. In the document, the four states, as successor states of the former USSR, agreed to assume the obligations of the former Soviet Union under the treaty, including working out arrangements among themselves to comply with the limits and restrictions contained in the treaty. While the Russian Federation assumed the status of nuclear-weapon state inherited from the former USSR, Belarus, Kazakhastan, and Ukraine committed themselves to adhere to the non-proliferation treaty as non-nuclear-weapon states in the shortest possible time.

Cessation of Nuclear Testing

It is widely considered that a comprehensive test ban would inhibit the proliferation of nuclear weapons. It would make it difficult, if not impossible, for the nuclear-weapon states to develop new weapon designs and would place constraints on the refinement of existing ones. On the other hand, nuclear-weapon states, including the US, tend to regard at least some form of testing as necessary so long as their security is at all dependent on a strategy of nuclear deterrence.

The question of the discontinuance of nuclear testing has been discussed in the General Assembly since 1945. An estimated 1,622 nuclear-test explosions were detonated between 16 July 1945 and 31 December 1986—815 by the US, 597 by the USSR, 140 by France, 40 by the United Kingdom, 29 by China, and 1 by India, which stated that its nuclear test was an experiment strictly for peaceful purposes.

Despite ongoing unilateral and international efforts to ban nuclear testing, it continued in the 1990s. Notably, in early October 1995, France (despite its assurances that it would not) conducted a nuclear test on Fangataufa Atoll in the Pacific. The blast triggered a wave of protest throughout the region. Ongoing tests by nuclear-weapons states prompted the General Assembly on 12 December 1995 to issue a statement saying it "strongly deplored all current nuclear testing and strongly urged the immediate cessation of all such testing" and had adopted a resolution by a vote of 85 in favor to 18 against, with 43 abstentions, commending those nuclear-weapon states observing testing moratoriums and urging them to continue the moratoriums pending the entry into force of a comprehensive nuclear test-ban treaty. In spring 1998, India and Pakistan, whose dispute over the Kashmir region continued, each conducted underground nuclear tests, causing scientists to move the hands of the infamous Doomsday Clock closer to midnight (the point of annihilation). These events highlighted the urgency of reaching consensus on nuclear non-proliferation and testing and underscored the role of the UN in bringing the parties to the table.

Partial Test Ban Treaty

Late in 1958, the nuclear powers (then the USSR, the United

Kingdom, and the US) began negotiations in Geneva on the discontinuance of nuclear-weapon tests. Although they accomplished nothing definitive, related and subsequent efforts in the General Assembly and the Eighteen-Nation Committee on Disarmament and, finally, further negotiations led to the signing in Moscow on 5 August 1963 of the *Treaty Banning Nuclear Weapons Tests in the Atmosphere in Outerspace and under Water* (Partial Test-Ban Treaty). The treaty prohibits any nuclear explosions for weapons testing or for any other purpose in the atmosphere or beyond its limits, including outer space; or under water, including territorial waters or high seas. Its prohibitions also extend to nuclear explosions in any other environment if such an explosion produces radioactive debris outside the territorial limits of the state under whose jurisdiction or control the explosion is conducted. Further to the main provisions of the treaty, which did not prohibit the testing of nuclear devices underground, the parties to the treaty also confirmed their intention to seek an end to all testing of nuclear weapons and to continue negotiations towards that end, and declared their desire to end radioactive contamination of the environment.

The treaty was the first international agreement to regulate nuclear arms worldwide, and it has been recognized as an important instrument in reducing international tensions and decreasing radioactive pollution. It also helped to create a climate in which negotiations on other nuclear-arms limitation agreements, notably the *Treaty on the Non-Proliferation of Nuclear Weapons*, were able to take place.

France and China did not become parties to the treaty, but France announced in 1974 that it would not conduct any further atmospheric tests.

Bilateral Agreements on Nuclear Testing

In 1963, the nonaligned states in particular made strenuous efforts to persuade the USSR and the United States to extend the Partial Test Ban Treaty to include a ban on underground tests. Disagreement about verification prevented such an extension. Even after the Partial Test Ban Treaty came into effect, extensive underground testing continued, particularly by the USSR and the United States.

Two bilateral treaties, between the former Soviet Union and the United States, placed limits on their underground nuclear tests. These were the 1974 *Treaty on the Limitation of Underground Nuclear Weapon Tests* (known as the threshold test-ban treaty) and the 1976 *Treaty on Underground Nuclear Explosions for Peaceful Purposes*. Each party agreed not to test explosives yielding more than the 150-kiloton limit. Because of difficulties with the verification provisions and technology associated with the two treaties, they remained unratified for many years, although the two powers complied with their provisions. Following three years of bilateral negotiations from November 1987 to 1 December 1990 on nuclear testing verification and yield measurement methodology, the two powers exchanged instruments of ratification of the two treaties. The verification arrangements set out in conjunction with those two treaties were unprecedented in their openness and transparency, and helped to set the stage for even greater cooperation between the two major powers in agreements on the reduction of their nuclear-weapon arsenals.

Comprehensive Test Ban Treaty

The question of the complete cessation of all nuclear-weapon tests or of all nuclear explosive tests has been considered as a separate issue in UN bodies since 1963 and is the subject of many General Assembly resolutions. Between 1977 and 1980, the USSR, the United Kingdom, and the United States also undertook trilateral negotiations on a comprehensive test-ban treaty but again did not succeed in completing one. Questions of how to verify compliance with a ban on nuclear-weapon tests, how to treat nuclear explosions for peaceful purposes under the conditions of a ban, and whether to seek to ban all nuclear explosions

have presented difficulties both in the Conference on Disarmament, which has been the main focus of efforts since 1980, and in the bilateral discussions that commenced in July 1986 between the USSR and the US. The two powers have discussed the questions of more precise verification, methodologies for measuring the yield of permitted explosions, conditions for ratifying the 1974 and 1976 treaties, and the possibility of lower thresholds for underground explosions leading to a comprehensive ban.

In an effort to add impetus to the ongoing efforts, the USSR halted all nuclear explosions for an 18-month period, from August 1985 to February 1987. The United States did not reciprocate because it believed that such an unverifiable measure was not a substitute for a negotiated, binding treaty.

At the 1995 Non-Proliferation Treaty Review and Extension Conference, the first measure agreed to was the completion of a Comprehensive Nuclear-Test-Ban Treaty (CTBT) no later than 1996. On 24 September 1996, the CTBT was opened for signature. As of 20 April 2000, it had been signed by 155 states, including all five nuclear-weapon states, and ratified by 51 states. However, the treaty had not yet entered into force since not all the states whose ratification is required for its entry into force had done so, including the United States, which rejected ratification in fall 1999.

Unilateral Actions Towards an End to Nuclear Testing

With the end of the Cold War and the improvement in international political climate, important political strides towards the achievement of a comprehensive nuclear test ban were registered. In the early 1990s the number of underground nuclear tests being conducted by the nuclear-weapon states began to decrease considerably. In October 1991, the former Soviet Union declared a unilateral moratorium on nuclear tests, which was extended by the Russian Federation indefinitely. In April 1992 France suspended its nuclear testing. In October 1992 the United States enacted a law which not only declared a unilateral moratorium on its nuclear tests, but also directed that after September 1996, the United States government could no longer conduct nuclear tests. The United Kingdom, which has conducted for several decades its nuclear-weapon tests at the nuclear testing site in the United States, has respected the declared moratorium of the United States and has not conducted any nuclear tests since November 1991. However, China conducted its nuclear tests in October 1993 and in June 1994. In 1995, France announced that it wanted to conduct a final series of eight nuclear weapons tests in the South Pacific, and the government of New Zealand, Australia, Marshall Islands, Federated States of Micronesia, Western Samoa, and the Solomon Islands sought to intervene.

Prevention of Nuclear Proliferation

In the early years of the atomic era, it was widely assumed that only a few highly industrialized nations would be able to afford to manufacture nuclear weapons. However, by the mid-1960s, advancing technology and simplification of nuclear production processes, particularly for electric-power generation, had led to the categorization of some 20 nations, including relatively small ones, as countries possessing a nuclear capability; there are now some 30 so-called "threshold" states. The fear of horizontal nuclear proliferation has thus spawned much discussion in the General Assembly. During 1965 and 1966, the greater part of the General Assembly's debates on disarmament was devoted to this issue, especially with the emergence of China as a nuclear-weapon power.

In 1967, the United States and the USSR, after prolonged negotiations, put forward identical draft non-proliferation treaties in the Eighteen-Nation Committee on Disarmament, and in 1968, after further negotiation, a final joint draft was commended overwhelmingly by the General Assembly as the *Treaty on the Non-Proliferation of Nuclear Weapons*. The treaty came into force in March 1970. By May 2000, it had been ratified by

182 countries, including the five declared nuclear-weapon states: China, France, the Russian Federation, the United Kingdom, and the United States. Though the treaty had received a great deal of support as reflected by the number of ratifications to it, challenges to its objectives remained.

The Non-Proliferation Treaty (NPT) prohibits the spread of nuclear weapons, employing the safeguards system of the IAEA to provide assurance against any diversion or misuse of nuclear materials by non-nuclear-weapon states. It also contains provisions for promoting the peaceful uses of nuclear energy; for making nuclear equipment, materials, and information available on a nondiscriminatory basis to non-nuclear-weapon states for peaceful purposes; and for the pursuit of negotiations relating to the cessation of the nuclear-arms race and to nuclear and general disarmament. All the non-nuclear-weapon parties to the treaty must accept safeguards, through separate agreements, with the IAEA. The safeguards system provides for international inspection of all their nuclear installations. Several states that are not parties to the treaty have also signed safeguards agreements with the IAEA covering all or most of their installations.

Following the disintegration of the former Soviet Union at the end of 1991, the nuclear weapons left on its former territory had fallen under the jurisdiction of Belarus, Kazakhstan, the Russian Federation, and Ukraine. While the Russian Federation assumed the treaty obligations of the former Soviet Union, in a special agreement, the Lisbon Protocol, Belarus, Kazakhstan, and Ukraine had agreed to become non-nuclear-weapon states party to the NPT. As of 1 November 1993, only Belarus had complied with that commitment. In addition, several other states not party to the treaty, among them Argentina, Brazil, India, Israel, and Pakistan, have extensive nuclear programs and facilities, the great majority subject to non-treaty nuclear safeguards agreements with the IAEA. Their lack of participation reflects one of the main criticisms of the treaty, that is, they believe that its organization and structure is discriminatory, dividing the international community into nuclear haves and have-nots.

In the wake of the war in the Persian Gulf, the UN Special Commission (UNSCOM), appointed to eliminate Iraq's capability to use weapons of mass destruction, uncovered the existence of a clandestine nuclear weapons program in that country. This revelation further challenged the NPT regime and in particular the inspection procedures employed by the IAEA.

Six conferences have been held to review the operation of the treaty—in 1975, 1980, 1985, 1990, 1995, and 2000. In accordance with the terms of the treaty, a conference is to be held 25 years after its entry into force to decide whether it shall continue in force indefinitely or shall be extended for an additional fixed period or periods. Since the treaty's entry into force, the parties and the General Assembly have called in various contexts for universal adherence to the treaty as the best means of further strengthening the non-proliferation regime.

Some of the aspects that are of crucial importance to the extension of the NPT and the strengthening of the non-proliferation regime revolve around the issue of efforts being made towards the cessation of the nuclear arms race and nuclear disarmament. In that connection, the question of the achievement of a comprehensive nuclear test ban treaty has taken on paramount importance for many non-nuclear-weapon states. In addition, the issue of the granting of guarantees to non-nuclear-weapon states that nuclear weapons will not be used against them would make an important contribution to the reinforcement of the NPT structure. Many states have for years supported the call for the nuclear-weapon states to cease production of fissionable material for weapons purposes, which they consider would contribute significantly in a qualitative manner to the ending of the nuclear arms race.

Notwithstanding the above caveats, the Non-Proliferation Treaty remains effective as the cornerstone of an international non-proliferation structure that has grown to embrace the overwhelming majority of countries of the world.

Nuclear-Weapon-Free Zones

The establishment of nuclear-weapon-free zones in various parts of the world has long been considered a possible means for curbing horizontal nuclear proliferation and enhancing peace and security for non-nuclear-weapon states on a regional basis.

Outer Space

The 1967 *Treaty on Principles Governing the Activities of States in the Exploration and Use of Outer Space, including the Moon and Other Celestial Bodies*, while not strictly belonging to that body of law which bans nuclear weapons from a particular area, is relevant nonetheless to the concept of nuclear-free zones. Among other things, it provides that states parties will not place any objects carrying nuclear weapons or any weapon of mass destruction in orbit around the earth, install these weapons on celestial bodies, or station them in outer space.

The Seabed

The 1972 *Treaty on the Prohibition of the Emplacement of Nuclear Weapons and Other Weapons of Mass Destruction on the Sea-Bed and the Ocean Floor and in the Subsoil Thereof* provides that states parties undertake not to place on or under the seabed, beyond the outer limit of a 12-mile coastal zone, any nuclear or other weapons of mass destruction or any facilities for such weapons.

Antarctica

The 1959 *Antarctic Treaty* was the first international agreement to provide for the absence of nuclear weapons in a specified area by having established a demilitarized zone in the Antarctic. Under the terms of the treaty, Antarctica is to be used exclusively for peaceful purposes. All military activity, nuclear explosions, or disposal of radioactive waste in the area are prohibited. The provisions of this treaty appear to have been scrupulously observed.

Latin America and the Caribbean

The *Treaty for the Prohibition of Nuclear Weapons in Latin America and the Caribbean* (Treaty of Tlatelolco), signed on 14 February 1967 at Tlatelolco, Mexico, was the first treaty establishing a nuclear-weapon-free zone in a densely populated area. It is also the first regional agreement to establish its own system of international verification and a permanent supervisory organ, the Agency for the Prohibition of Nuclear Weapons in Latin America (known by its Spanish acronym OPANAL), which was set up in June 1969. States parties to the treaty agree to use any nuclear material or facilities under their jurisdiction exclusively for peaceful purposes and to prohibit the presence of nuclear weapons in their territories, under any circumstances. They also agree not to engage in, encourage, authorize, directly or indirectly, or in any way participate in, the testing, use, manufacture, production, possession, or control of any nuclear weapon. The treaty's verification system includes the requirement that safeguards agreements be concluded with IAEA in respect of all the nuclear activities undertaken by the parties. Annexed to the treaty are two Additional Protocols. Under Additional Protocol I, France, the Netherlands, the United Kingdom, and the United States agree to guarantee nuclear-weapon-free status to those territories for which they are, *de jure* or *de facto*, internationally responsible. In August 1972, the protocol was signed by France, thus giving it full force as all four countries had now signed. Under Additional Protocol II, nuclear-weapon states pledge to respect fully the denuclearization of Latin America and not to use or threaten to use nuclear weapons against parties to the treaty. By 1979, all five nuclear-weapon states had become parties to it.

The South Pacific

The states party to the 1986 *South Pacific Nuclear Free Zone Treaty* (Treaty of Rarotonga) have undertaken not to manufacture or acquire any nuclear explosive device; to control the export of fissionable material; to ensure that their nuclear activities are exclusively for peaceful and nonexplosive purposes and are conducted under strict safeguards; to ban the testing of nuclear explosive devices in the South Pacific; to prohibit the stationing of nuclear explosive devices in their territories; and to prevent the dumping at sea, in the region, of nuclear waste.

The treaty has three protocols, which are integral to its purposes. Protocol 1 obliges France, the United Kingdom, and the United States to apply the terms of the treaty in respect of the territories for which they are responsible in the region, especially with regard to prohibitions on the manufacture, stationing, and testing of any nuclear explosive device. The three states have not signed this protocol. Protocol 2 commits the five nuclear-weapon states not to use or threaten to use any nuclear explosive device against parties to the treaty. This protocol has been agreed to by China and the Russian Federation. Protocol 3 commits the five nuclear-weapon states not to test any nuclear explosive device anywhere within the zone covered by the treaty. China and the Russian Federation have ratified this protocol.

Proposals for Nuclear-weapon-free Zones

In addition to those areas and zones mentioned above, where there has been success in elaborating treaties prohibiting the use of nuclear weapons, the General Assembly has also discussed, with varying degrees of success, proposals for creating nuclear-weapon-free zones in many other regions of the world. Although these discussions have covered a number of geographic zones, including the Balkans, the Mediterranean, and Northern Europe, most proposals have dealt in particular with Central Europe, the African continent, the Middle East, and South Asia.

Security Assurances to Non-nuclear-weapon States

Since the conclusion of the NPT in 1968, the non-nuclear-weapon states have repeatedly insisted that their promise not to acquire nuclear weapons should be met with an assurance that nuclear weapons would not, under any circumstances, be used against them. On 19 June 1968, the Security Council recognized that aggression using nuclear weapons, or the threat of doing so, against a non-nuclear-weapon state would warrant immediate action by the Security Council, above all its nuclear-weapon state permanent members. The Security Council also reaffirmed the provision of the UN Charter that declares that a state, if the victim of an armed attack, has a right to act in individual or collective self-defense until such time as the Security Council could take action to maintain peace and security.

At the 1978 special session on disarmament, four of the five nuclear-weapon states individually declared their intention not to use, or threaten to use, nuclear weapons against non-nuclear-weapon states, which met the conditions outlined in their respective declarations. At that session also, China reiterated the declaration it made when it conducted its first nuclear test—that it would never use nuclear weapons against a non-nuclear-weapon state. The nuclear-weapon states have refined and reasserted their respective security guarantees several times since then.

Since 1979, the Conference on Disarmament has considered proposals for effective international arrangements that would assure non-nuclear-weapon states against the use, or threat of use, of nuclear weapons. Non-nuclear-weapon states have expressed the view that further assurances, in legally binding form, are necessary in order to effectively guarantee their security against nuclear attack. The Western nuclear-weapon states and their allies have been of the view that, in order to receive such negative security assurances, states must have demonstrated a commitment not to acquire nuclear weapons, by forming part of a nuclear-weapon-free zone or by adhering to the Nuclear Non-Proliferation Treaty. Those non-nuclear-weapon states that are party to the NPT considered the issue of pivotal importance to the outcome of the 1995 NPT Conference.

Prohibition of the Production of Fissionable Material

An approach to nuclear disarmament which has received much international attention over the years has been to stop the production of fissionable material for weapons purposes.

The United States submitted proposals on this subject to the Eighteen-Nation Committee on Disarmament and the General Assembly during the 1960s, which included plans for inspection of certain types of nuclear reactors and separation plants; the dismantling of a number of nuclear weapons by both the United States and the former Soviet Union, to be carried out in the presence of observers; and the transfer or conversion of fissionable material to industries or forms in which it could be used for peaceful purposes.

In 1992 the United States announced a unilateral cessation of its national production of plutonium and highly enriched uranium for nuclear weapons. Among the nuclear-weapon states, both the Russian Federation and the United States have recently expressed support for reaching an international agreement to halt the production of weapons-grade fissionable material in the interests of non-proliferation. In 1993, the General Assembly adopted without a vote a resolution recommending negotiation in the most appropriate international forum of a non-discriminatory, multilateral, and internationally and effectively verifiable treaty banning the production of material for nuclear weapons or other nuclear explosive devices.

The dissolution of the Soviet Union and the fact that nuclear weapons are now on the territories of four of the successor states, as well as the vast amount of nuclear material that will need to be removed and monitored owing to the disarmament process of the two major powers, represent challenges which the non-proliferation movement must overcome.

OTHER WEAPONS OF MASS DESTRUCTION

In 1946, the General Assembly envisaged not only the elimination of atomic weapons, but also of all other major weapons of mass destruction. The dangers of such weapons to humanity cannot be underestimated. Even in World War I, "first-generation" chemical agents caused some 1.3 million casualties, of which over 100,000 were fatal. In 1948, the Commission for Conventional Armaments, in setting out the limits of its jurisdiction, also defined weapons of mass destruction as including, besides atomic explosive weapons, radioactive material weapons, lethal chemical and biological weapons, and any weapons developed in the future with comparable destructive effects.

Chemical and Biological Weapons

As mentioned earlier, the powerful sense of outrage generated by the use of chemical weapons during the First World War resulted in the signing of the Geneva Protocol of 1925 banning the use, but not the production, possession, or stockpiling, of chemical or bacteriological weapons. As a consequence, possession and acquisition, particularly of chemical weapons, has continued and, indeed, in recent years has proliferated. Many parties to the Geneva Protocol have included reservations or statements with their signatures that open the door to the possible retaliatory use of such weapons.

The protocol also did not provide for mechanisms to verify compliance or for procedures to deal with violations. Recognizing the shortcomings of the protocol, the international community continued its quest for a complete ban on chemical and biological weapons. Although treated as a single issue previously, it was agreed in 1971 to separate consideration of chemical and biological weapons in the hope that an early ban on biological weapons could be achieved.

Biological Weapons

The *Convention on the Prohibition of the Development, Production and Stockpiling of Bacteriological (Biological) and*

Toxin Weapons and on Their Destruction entered into force on 26 March 1975 and was hailed as a first step towards a comprehensive ban on biological weapons.

The convention prohibits the development, production, stockpiling, acquisition, or retention of microbial or other biological agents, or toxins whatever their origin or methods of production, of types and in quantities that have no justification for prophylactic, protective, or other peaceful purposes. It also prohibits weapons, equipment, or means of delivery designed to use such agents or toxins for hostile purposes or in armed conflict. The agents, toxins, weapons, equipment, and means of delivery held by states that became party to the convention should be destroyed or diverted to peaceful purposes not later than nine months after the entry into force of the convention for that state. Furthermore, any state party that finds that any other state party is not complying with the provisions of the convention may lodge a complaint with the Security Council.

In 1986, states parties decided to initiate a set of confidence-building measures in the form of a voluntary exchange of information and data. The information to be exchanged included data on high-risk research centers and laboratories; outbreaks of infectious diseases; publication of results of biological research; and the promotion of contacts among scientists in biological research.

In 1991, the states parties established an Ad Hoc Group of Governmental Experts to identify and examine potential verification measures from a scientific and technical standpoint. A majority of states parties have requested a special conference to review the results of the expert group.

In December 1996, the Fourth Review Conference of States Parties to the Biological Weapons Convention held a two-week session. The conference supported intensified work by an ad hoc group to design a verification protocol for the international treaty. The conference expressed hope that the group would reach agreement on a draft protocol to be considered by a special conference of states parties to the convention as soon as possible and before the Fifth Review Conference, which was scheduled for not later than 2001.

Chemical Weapons

In 1966, with the adoption of its first resolution on the question of chemical and bacteriological (biological) warfare, the General Assembly commenced a long process of international discussions and negotiations on issues relevant to the question. The adoption of the resolution reflected growing international awareness of the dangers involved with the possible use of such weapons of mass destruction.

The question of chemical and biological weapons was treated as a single issue requiring a unified approach before 1971. After agreement had been reached on the Biological Weapons Convention in 1972, attention turned more to the chemical weapons aspect and numerous proposals were put forward in the multilateral negotiating body in Geneva, including the complete texts of drafts conventions. In 1980, the Conference on Disarmament began working toward a convention on chemical weapons, but progress was evident only late in the decade. The former Soviet Union and the United States, the only states that had admitted to possessing stockpiles of chemical weapons, began a series of bilateral contacts that led to agreement between them on sensitive issues of verification of implementation of a convention, including the question of challenge and on-site inspection.

The actual use of chemical weapons during the war between Iraq and the Islamic Republic of Iran in the 1980s, confirmed by an investigative team appointed by the Secretary-General, focussed greater international attention on the need to reach early agreement on the prohibition of these weapons. In 1991, the war in the Persian Gulf and the possibility that chemical weapons might again be used added even greater urgency to the efforts to rid the world of chemical weapons as soon as possible.

The *Convention on the Prohibition of the Development, Production, Stockpiling and Use of Chemical Weapons and on Their Destruction* was opened for signature on 13 January 1993 in Paris, France. The required number of ratifications (65) was completed in October 1996 and the treaty entered into force 29 April 1997, by which time a total of 87 countries had ratified it, including the US (which ratified it 24 April 1997). Russia was among those countries that had yet to sign on. One year later, a total of 108 states were party to the convention. By that time the Organization for the Prohibition of Chemical Weapons (OPCW), headquartered in The Hague, Netherlands, had already worked with nine cooperating states that provided the OPCW with information on past or existing chemical weapons programs. The OPCW had completed almost 200 inspections and witnessed the destruction of approximately 1,000 tons of nerve agents in its first year. By May 2000, 135 countries had ratified the chemical weapons convention, with the most recent additions being Malaysia, Federal Republic of Yugoslavia, Colombia, and Kazakhstan.

The convention is considered a genuine disarmament measure in that it provides for the elimination of an entire category of weapons of mass destruction. Its importance lies in the fact that these weapons exist in large quantities, have been used in combat in the past, and are believed to be possessed by a large number of countries. Further, the verification system provided for under the convention is the most comprehensive to have been formulated for a multilateral agreement in the field of disarmament.

By the terms of the convention, states parties undertake never, under any circumstances, to use chemical weapons, nor to develop, produce, otherwise acquire, stockpile, or retain chemical weapons, or transfer them, directly or indirectly, to anyone. They also commit themselves never to engage in any military preparations to use chemical weapons nor to assist, encourage, or induce, in any way, anyone to engage in any activity prohibited under the convention. Within a period of 10 years, each state party undertakes to destroy chemical weapons and production facilities that it may own or possess, or that are located in any place under its jurisdiction or control, as well as all chemical weapons it has abandoned on the territory of another state party. The convention also bans the use of riot control agents as a method of warfare.

The states parties are required to submit detailed declarations on any chemical weapons they might possess, on old and abandoned chemical weapons they might have on their territory, and on any related chemical weapons production facilities, as well as on the plans and implementation of the destruction of such. They have agreed to a comprehensive and graduated system of routine inspections for international monitoring of the implementation of their obligations under the convention. Also provided for is a system of short-notice, challenge inspections, by which each state party may request an international inspection team to monitor any facility or location in the territory of another state party, which is obliged to allow the inspection, for the purpose of clarifying and resolving any questions concerning possible non-compliance. An inspected state party may protect activities and installations that it considers unrelated to the inspection request.

New Weapons of Mass Destruction

The question of new weapons of mass destruction has been under consideration since the mid-1970s in the General Assembly and the Conference on Disarmament, which have stated that effective measures should be taken to prevent the emergence of such weapons. The former USSR and other nations supported a general agreement precluding laboratory development of weapons of mass destruction, as well as specific agreements as relevant possibilities are identified; other states feel that meaningful, verifiable agreements are practical only for specific, emergent weapons or systems.

A list of specific types of potential weapons of mass destruction presented by the former USSR in 1979 included the following: radiological weapons, using radiological materials, a possibility already foreseen in 1948; particle-beam weapons, using charged or neutral particles to affect biological targets; and infrasonic "acoustic radiation" weapons and electromagnetic weapons operating at certain radio frequencies, either of which could have injurious effects on human organs.

Radiological Weapons

At the 1976 session of the General Assembly, the United States proposed an instrument prohibiting radioactive weapons. This proposal led to bilateral negotiations with the USSR and the submission in 1979 of an agreed joint initiative for consideration by the then Committee on Disarmament.

Since 1980, the multilateral negotiating body has considered proposals for reaching agreement on a convention to prohibit the development, production, stockpiling, or use of radiological weapons. Some nonaligned and neutral states of the Conference on Disarmament, while recognizing the potential danger of the development of radiological weapons, considered that a military attack on a civilian nuclear power installation represented a more dangerous risk of mass destruction caused by the release of radiological substances. The former Soviet Union and the United States felt this idea altered the basic concept and content of the joint initiative.

Finding an acceptable way to cover both a ban on radiological weapons in the traditional sense and a prohibition of attacks against peaceful nuclear facilities has since been the main problem in efforts to negotiate a radiological weapons convention. This question has remained on the agenda of the Conference on Disarmament and the General Assembly, but differences of view concerning the question of the prohibition of attacks against nuclear facilities have persisted, and no progress has been made.

PROTECTING THE ENVIRONMENT FROM MILITARY ACTIVITY

In recent history, the world has viewed with mounting concern the specter of deliberate destruction of the environment as a method of warfare. The damage inflicted on the environment during the war in the Persian Gulf in 1991 and 1992 led to the inclusion of a new item on the agenda of the General Assembly, entitled "Exploitation of the environment as a weapon in times of armed conflict and the taking of practical measures to prevent such exploitation."

Prohibition of Environmental Modification

In July 1974, following a summit meeting between the United States and the USSR, the two powers advocated measures to preclude the use of environmental modification techniques for hostile military purposes. This proposal led to consideration of the question in the General Assembly and the Conference of the Committee on Disarmament and the opening for signature on 18 May 1977 of the Convention on the Prohibition of Military or Any Other Hostile Use of Environmental Modification Techniques. The convention entered into force in 1978. In essence, the convention bolsters existing provisions in international law protecting the environment by outlawing environmental modification techniques that would cause widespread, long-lasting, or severe effects to another state. During the process that led to the convention, many states decided it too narrowly defined the scope of the techniques to be banned. By 1994, the convention had acquired only 55 signatures. And in 1995, at the behest of the First Committee, the General Assembly approved a resolution urging member nations to sign the now-stalled treaty.

The convening of the UN conference in Rio de Janeiro in 1992 and the specter of oil wells set ablaze and a massive oil spill in the Persian Gulf during the Gulf War of 1991–92 intensified the debate over the environmental consequences of war. Some of the states parties to the convention made it known that they would ask the Secretary-General of the UN, as depositary (the holder of the legal, certified copies of the treaty), to convene a consultative committee of experts to provide views on the scope and application of the provisions of the convention. The states parties also have confirmed that the use of herbicides as an environmental modification technique was a method of warfare that fell within the scope of the prohibition of the convention if such use upset the ecological balance of a region, thus causing widespread, long-lasting, and severe effects.

CONVENTIONAL WEAPONS

It is a painful reality that, throughout the nuclear era and the cold war, and now in the post-cold war world, all armed conflicts—almost every one of them in developing countries—have been fought with conventional weapons. More than 20 million people have died in those wars. Every year, armed conflicts are waged in some 30 locations on the planet, all fought with conventional weapons. Conventional weapons and armed forces account for some four-fifths of global military expenditures and for approximately 80% of the world arms trade.

Thus, while consideration of nuclear questions has dominated disarmament debates in the UN and other forums, the problems posed by the conventional arms race and arms transfers have come increasingly to the fore, particularly in the 1980s. In the disarmament forums at the UN, discussions of the issue of conventional disarmament have focussed on four main elements: (a) limitations on conventional weapons themselves; (b) transparency in international arms transfers and the establishment of a UN Register on Conventional Arms; (c) the regional approach and the building of military confidence and security among states; and (d) the strengthening of international humanitarian and disarmament law with respect to inhumane weapons, including the question of land mines.

In 1986, "conventional disarmament" was considered as a separate item on the agenda of the General Assembly for the first time, and, as a result, in 1987 it appeared on the agenda of the Disarmament Commission, indicating an increasing acceptance of the view that nuclear and conventional disarmament should proceed simultaneously.

When the question of prohibiting the use of certain conventional weapons, such as napalm and other incendiaries, was first raised in the General Assembly in the late 1960s, there were numerous proposals for banning various weapons, such as mines and booby traps, that also were deemed to cause unnecessary suffering or have indiscriminate effects. Considerable work, including some under the auspices of the International Committee of the Red Cross and of diplomatic conferences on protocols to the Geneva Convention of 1949 relating to humanitarian law in armed conflicts, was done in the late 1960s and the 1970s. As noted above, in 1980, a UN conference at Geneva adopted the *Convention on Prohibitions or Restrictions on the Use of Certain Conventional Weapons Which May Be Deemed to Be Excessively Injurious or to Have Indiscriminate Effects*; the convention was opened for signature in 1981 and came into force in December 1983.

UN Register of Conventional Arms

On 1 January 1992 the *UN Register of Conventional Arms* was officially established and the first reports on arms transfers during 1992 were due to be received by the UN Centre for Disarmament Affairs by 30 April 1993. In October of 1993, the Secretary-General presented a consolidated report on the first year of operation of the register to the General Assembly, which brought the information presented by states into the public domain. Information was received from 87 states, including most of the major supplier countries, on arms imports and exports in seven categories of heavy conventional weapons—battle tanks, armored combat vehicles, large calibre artillery systems, combat aircraft, attack helicopters, warships, and missiles and missile launchers. Submissions to the register, which are on a voluntary basis, are to be made by 30 April of each year. Upon the request of the General Assembly, the Secretary-General convened a group of experts in 1994 to examine the continuing operation of the register and its further development. In that connection, many states asserted that the information shared should include information on military holdings, on procurement through national production, and on weapons of mass destruction. They believed that these additions to the register would help to attract wider universality in reporting.

The establishment of the Register of Conventional Arms by the UN was a ground-breaking endeavor. The exchange of information enacted by means of the register has the potential to foster confidence among states and create an atmosphere more conducive to self-restraint and real measures of disarmament. The successful further development and operation of the register could provide the member states of the UN with an effective instrument of preventive diplomacy.

Also in relation to openness and transparency in military matters, the Disarmament Commission completed its work on guidelines and recommendations for objective information on military matters, which were endorsed by the General Assembly. Also in 1992, the Conference on Disarmament took up for the first time an item dealing with conventional weapons under a new agenda item entitled "Transparency in armaments." It continued consideration of the item in 1993 and 1994 in the framework of a subsidiary body of the conference, and presented a report to the General Assembly on its work in 1993.

Inhumane Weapons

Early international humanitarian laws dealt with the effects of inhumane conventional weapons. The St. Petersburg Declaration of 1868 recognized that the object of warfare would not be served by the use of weapons that uselessly aggravate the suffering of disabled soldiers. The "dum-dum" bullet, developed a few years later, was banned by the 1899 Hague Conference as contrary to the St. Petersburg Declaration. Principles enunciated in the St. Petersburg Declaration of 1868 and the Hague Conferences of 1899 and 1907 were repeated in the Geneva Conventions of 1949, prohibiting the employment of weapons, projectiles, and material and methods of warfare of a nature to cause superfluous injury or unnecessary suffering. Between 1974 and 1977, two protocols were negotiated to the Geneva Conventions, but were not considered effective at adopting any prohibitions or restrictions on conventional weapons.

In 1977, the General Assembly decided to convene a UN conference with the aim of reaching an agreement on prohibitions or restrictions of use of certain conventional weapons. The UN Conference, held at Geneva in 1979 and 1980, adopted the convention, which entered into force on 2 December 1983. Annexed Protocol I prohibits the use of any weapons that injure with fragments that are not detectable by X-rays. Protocol II prohibits or sets out restrictions on the use of mines (excluding anti-ship mines), booby-traps, and other delayed action devices. Protocol III prohibits or outlines restrictions on the use of incendiary weapons, that is, weapons designed with the primary purpose of setting fire to objects or causing injury by means of fire.

Among other items of discussion with respect to the review of the convention, the vast toll in civilian life and bodily injury, together with the devastation of societies and economies in post-conflict situations caused by the massive and indiscriminate use of land mines, has been receiving greater international attention. In 1993, the General Assembly called upon all states to adopt a moratorium on the export of antipersonnel land mines. In a

related resolution, the General Assembly requested the Secretary-General to prepare a report on the problems caused by the increasing presence of mines and other unexploded devices resulting from armed conflicts and on the manner in which the United Nations' contribution to the solution of problems relating to mine clearance could be strengthened.

As part of Secretary-General Kofi Annan's reform, the United Nations Mine Action Service (UNMAS) was created to coordinate the mine-related activities of 11 UN departments and agencies. Wholly funded by the Voluntary Trust for Assistance in Mine Action, UNMAS spearheaded the development of the Mine Action and Effective Coordination: The United Nations Policy, a document that serves as the basis for the coordinated, system-wide approach to mine action. While UNMAS focused its efforts on removing existing land-mines, the 1997 Convention on the Prohibition of the Use, Stockpiling, Production and Transfer of Anti-Personnel Mines and on Their Destruction aimed to eliminate, or at least reduce the number of, new land-mines. The convention entered into force March 1999.

CONFIDENCE-BUILDING MEASURES

Regional Confidence-Building

The objective of confidence-building measures is to contribute toward reducing or eliminating the causes for mistrust, fear, tensions, and hostilities, which are significant factors behind the international arms buildup. A UN study on confidence-building measures, issued in 1981, represented an attempt to clarify and develop the concept of confidence-building and to provide guidelines to governments for introducing and implementing confidence-building measures and promoting public awareness of the concept so as to advance negotiations and enhance peace and security. In that same year, the General Assembly invited all states to consider the possible introduction of confidence-building measures in their particular regions and, where possible, to negotiate among themselves in keeping with conditions and requirements prevailing in the respective regions. In fact, multilateral negotiations on these issues had been under way since the early 1970s.

The Vienna Talks on the Mutual Reduction of Forces and Armaments and Associated Measures in Central Europe, which commenced in 1973 among the member countries of NATO and the Warsaw Pact, were aimed at enhancing stability in the central region of the two alliances and in Europe as a whole while reducing armed forces and equipment but maintaining undiminished security. After decades of unsuccessful efforts in that framework, the two sides agreed to close down the talks in 1989 to pursue efforts in the context of a new set of talks on conventional force reductions within the security pillar of the Conference on Security and Cooperation in Europe (CSCE), ongoing since the adoption of the 1975 Helsinki Act.

The CSCE, held in Geneva and Helsinki from 1972 to 1975 and involving 33 European countries, as well as Canada and the US, further developed the concept of confidence-building measures on a non-UN regional basis; its Final Act, issued at Helsinki in August 1975, included provisions on security, human rights, and scientific cooperation. The final Stockholm Document, adopted in September 1986, constituted the first security agreement for Europe among the 35 states participating in the conference that adopts militarily significant, politically binding, and verifiable confidence-building measures. Under its terms, the CSCE states agreed to a new set of standards on the notification and observation of certain military activities, and, most important, they agreed upon verification of compliance by means of mandatory on-site inspection arrangements.

Reviewed during 1977–78 in Belgrade and again from 1980 to 1983 in Madrid, the conference led to the Stockholm Conference on Confidence- and Security-Building Measures and Disarmament in Europe, held from 1984 to 1986, with the same states participating.

In Vienna in 1989, at the same time that negotiations between the two military alliances were initiated on conventional armed forces in Europe, a new set of negotiations began on confidence- and security-building measures (CSBMs) among all the CSCE participating states. The talks led to the adoption of the Vienna Document of 1990, which incorporated and expanded the provisions of the Stockholm Document. Among its provisions are an exchange of military information among its parties on the command structure of their military forces, plans for the deployment of major weapon and equipment systems, and the military budget plans for the forthcoming year. The CSCE held a summit meeting in Paris immediately following the adoption of the Vienna CSBM document and adopted the Charter of Paris. Among other results, the participating CSCE states decided to establish a Crisis Prevention Centre in Vienna, which became essentially the operational component of the CSBM document.

In order to consolidate further the achievements of the 1990 Charter of Paris, the CSCE held a summit meeting in 1992. It issued an important document relating to confidence-building entitled the *Helsinki Document–1992–The Challenges of Change*, adopted unanimously by its full membership. In Helsinki, the states parties decided *inter alia* to start a new negotiation on arms control, disarmament, and confidence- and security-building; established a new CSCE Forum for Security Cooperation; and strengthened the Conflict Prevention Centre set up in Vienna.

In the interest of improving openness and transparency, and facilitating monitoring and compliance with existing or future arms control agreements and to strengthen the capacity for conflict resolution and crisis management in the CSCE, a *Treaty on Open Skies* was signed in March 1992 by 24 of the CSCE participating states. Covering an area from Vancouver to Vladivostok, the treaty allows observation flights by a state party over the territory of other state parties.

The UN has contributed to the process of confidence-building in a number of ways. The Secretary-General has assisted states parties to arms limitation agreements, at their request, in exchanges of information. This is the case for the newly formed Register of Conventional Arms, for the maintenance of an international system for standardized reporting of military expenditures, for the biological weapons convention as well as for the seabed treaty.

The Secretary-General also has contributed to confidence-building within regions by stimulating informal discussions of regional and global disarmament issues at seminars and conferences organized under the auspices of the Centre for Disarmament Affairs. Further, in order to promote cooperation among regional states towards arms limitation and disarmament, the UN has established three regional centers as follows: UN Regional Centre for Peace and Disarmament in Africa (Lomé, Togo); UN Regional Centre for Peace and Disarmament in Asia and the Pacific (Kathmandu, Nepal), and the UN Regional Centre for Peace, Disarmament and the Development in Latin America and the Caribbean (Lima, Peru). The centers focus their activities on dissemination of information, training, and regional meetings.

Zones of Peace

The 1971 Declaration of the Indian Ocean as a Zone of Peace is considered annually by an ad hoc Committee on the Indian Ocean, which has proposed the convening of a conference of the regional states. There also have been proposals for zones of peace and cooperation in various other regions, including the Mediterranean and the South Atlantic.

ECONOMIC AND SOCIAL CONSEQUENCES OF THE ARMS RACE

Since the 1950s, the General Assembly has appealed for the reduction of military spending and has suggested that the money thus saved be redeployed for economic and social development activities. A 1981 UN expert study on the relationship between disarmament and development saw a triangular relationship between disarmament, security, and development and concluded that the world could either continue to pursue the arms race or move toward a more sustainable international and political order; it could not do both. A 1982 expert study on the economic and social consequences of the arms race and of military expenditures concluded that UN mechanisms for peaceful settlement of disputes should be strengthened, that the use of the world's finite resources for military ends should be discouraged, and that there should be extensive diversion of these resources from military applications to socioeconomic development.

Conference on Disarmament and Development

In 1984, the General Assembly decided to convene an International Conference on the Relationship Between Disarmament and Development. The conference, which took place at UN headquarters in August–September 1987, considered ways and means of enhancing security and of releasing additional resources for development purposes through disarmament measures.

In particular, the conference called upon the UN to make greater efforts to promote collective knowledge of the nonmilitary threats to international security; to establish an improved and comprehensive database on global and national military expenditures; to continue to analyze the impact of global military expenditures on the world economy and the international economic system; to monitor trends in military spending, and to facilitate an international exchange of views and experience in the field of conversion from military to civilian production. To carry out the above work, a high-level task force was set up within the UN Secretariat. The Secretary-General reports each year to the General Assembly on the efforts carried out in this regard.

The improvement in the East-West relations in the late 1980s and the beginning of significant reductions in armed forces and armaments in the 1990s drew considerable attention to the issue of conversion of weapons, weapons testing and production facilities, and redeployment of armed forces. At its 44th session in 1989, the General Assembly, for the first time, adopted a resolution dealing with the subject of conversion of military resources.

Beginning with the 1990 international conference in Moscow on Conversion: Economic Adjustments in an Era of Arms Reduction, a number of similar conferences on different aspects of conversion of military resources to civilian production have been organized by the Centre for Disarmament Affairs and other interested UN bodies in cooperation with various host countries. The conference in Moscow was followed by an international conference on International Cooperation in Peaceful Uses of Military Industrial Technology in Beijing, China, in 1991. This was followed by yet another international conference on aerospace complex conversion held in Moscow in 1992.

The UN Institute for Disarmament Research (UNIDIR) submitted to the General Assembly at its 47th session in 1992, through the Secretary-General, a study entitled *Economic aspects of disarmament: disarmament as an investment*. It found that on the cost side disarmament required a fundamental reallocation of resources from military to civilian production, which could result in major problems of unemployment or underemployment of labor, capital, and other resources. Economic dividends of disarmament were likely to be small in the short term, it concluded. In the long term, however, disarmament would lead to significant benefits in the civilian sector through the production of goods and services made possible through the reallocation of resources from the military sector. Thus, in its economic aspects, the report said, disarmament was like an investment process involving short-run costs and long-run benefits.

Reduction of Military Budgets

Proposals for the reduction of military budgets, based on the conviction that such measures would facilitate the disarmament process and help release resources for economic and social development, were made in the General Assembly during the 1950s and 1960s. Throughout the 1970s and 1980s, the General Assembly pursued this question on two tracks. There were those states that pressed for the identification and elaboration of principles for freezing and reducing military budgets, while other states favored an effort by the General Assembly to broaden participation in the standardized reporting system.

During the same period, the General Assembly initiated a series of expert studies and established an Ad Hoc Panel on Military Budgeting, aimed at arriving at a generally acceptable conceptual definition of military budgets and the development of a standardized system of measuring and reporting the military expenditures of states.

An international system for the standardized reporting of military expenditures was introduced in pursuance of resolution 35/142 B of 17 December 1980. A 1982 study reaffirmed that the reporting instrument was a practical method for monitoring and reporting on military expenditures and strongly recommended its continuous use. On the basis of national reports on military expenditures received, the Secretary-General has submitted annually to the General Assembly a document on the operation of the reporting system. The General Assembly also has continued to recommend that member states use the reporting instrument to forward annually to the Secretary-General military expenditures for the latest fiscal year for which data are available.

The Disarmament Commission also considered the reduction of the military budgets from 1979 until 1989. Despite the progress and refinement made on the reporting system, basic differences in approach to the problem of reducing military budgets remained. In the 1986 session of the Disarmament Commission, provisional agreement was achieved on a text embodying a set of principles to govern the action of states in freezing and reducing military budgets. However, there was disagreement on the use of the standardized reporting instrument. The item has not been on the agenda of the Disarmament Commission since 1990.

In 1992, the General Assembly endorsed a set of guidelines and recommendations for objective information on military matters as adopted by the Disarmament Commission at its 1992 session. The "Guidelines" are intended *inter alia* to encourage openness and transparency on military matters, to facilitate the process of arms limitation, reduction, and elimination, as well as to assist verification of compliance with obligations undertaken by states in these fields.

STUDIES, RESEARCH, INFORMATION, AND TRAINING

Studies and Research

Since the early 1960s, the UN has prepared studies on disarmament issues mandated by the General Assembly, usually with the assistance of experts and consultants. The purpose of these studies is to assist the negotiating process through analysis of specific questions, as well as to provide information in order to facilitate better understanding of the issues.

The *UN Institute for Disarmament Research* (UNIDIR), which was established in October 1980 as an autonomous institution within the UN framework, conducts independent research on disarmament problems, aimed at encouraging disarmament by expanding accessible information on proposals and concepts. Located in Geneva, UNIDIR is funded principally by voluntary contributions from governments and public and private organizations.

The *Advisory Board on Disarmament Studies* functions as the board of trustees of UNIDIR. Its other major functions include advising on programs for disarmament studies and research and on implementation of the UN Disarmament Information Programme. It may also advise the Secretary-General of the UN on specific disarmament and related questions.

Information

The Department for Disarmament Affairs (DDA) was created during the UN's late 1990s reform efforts to coordinate the UN's activities in this area. As part of this effort, the DDA issues the *UN Disarmament Yearbook* and a variety of other publications. Its web site www.un.org/Depts/dda keeps track of news and developments in disarmament, including the latest treaty ratifications as well as pertinent UN resolutions and decisions. A listing of publications and databases is also available at the web site www.un.org/Depts/dda/MDI.htm

Training

A disarmament fellowships program for young diplomats and public officials from various countries, particularly developing countries, was established by the General Assembly at its first special session on disarmament. The program is aimed at preparing students for work with their governments in the field of disarmament and at enhancing and broadening diplomatic expertise. Disarmament fellows are trained each year under the auspices of the Department for Disarmament Affairs.

PEACEFUL USES OF OUTER SPACE

In October 1957, the USSR launched the first *Sputnik* into orbit around the earth. In the following year, the General Assembly for the first time debated the question of outer space. Two items were proposed for inclusion on the agenda: "The Banning of the Use of Cosmic Space for Military Purposes, the Elimination of Foreign Bases on the Territories of Other Countries, and International Cooperation on the Study of Cosmic Space," proposed by the USSR; and a "Program for International Cooperation in the Field of Outer Space," proposed by the US. The very titles of these items indicate the differences that initially existed between the two powers in regard to an international accord on the uses of outer space. The USSR proposed that the first order of business should be a ban on armaments in space but wished to link this goal with the dismantling of US overseas military bases. The US preferred to avoid the disarmament issue altogether in this connection and wished merely to emphasize that it was the common aim of mankind to ensure the use of outer space for peaceful purposes. This disagreement provoked a series of disputes over the composition and terms of reference of the special UN body that should be established to deal with outer space problems. The USSR wanted a body with East-West parity, while the US preferred a body more broadly geographical in representation.

Owing to these differences, the 1958 General Assembly merely set up an 18-member ad hoc committee to deal with questions of outer space. It included only three member states from the Soviet bloc, which, because of the composition of the committee, declared that they would not take part in its work. The committee eventually was reduced to 13 participants.

After intensive negotiations, the 1959 General Assembly set up the permanent 24-nation Committee on the Peaceful Uses of Outer Space. Its membership was increased to 28 in 1962, 37 in 1973, 47 in 1977, and 53 in 1980. In 1998, membership was expanded to 61. In 1962, the committee organized itself into two subcommittees of the whole, one to deal with scientific and technical cooperation and the other with the task of evolving outer space law. The committee has also set up working groups of the whole to deal with navigation satellites, direct broadcasting satellites, remote sensing satellites, and the use of nuclear power sources in outer space.

DEVELOPMENTS IN SCIENTIFIC AND TECHNICAL COOPERATION

Scientific and technical cooperation within the framework of the UN grew out of General Assembly action on the basis of recommendations of the committee and has increased over the years. It covers various fields of activity, including the following.

Exchange of Information. The UN Secretariat produces annual reports on national and cooperative international projects. Since 1961, a growing number of countries and international organizations have provided the committee with information on space activities and programs.

Public Registry of Launchings of Space Vehicles. An essential requirement for international cooperation in outer space development is that launchings of space vehicles, together with scientific data on the results of such launchings, be made public. In 1961, the General Assembly decided unanimously that the UN "should provide a focal point" for such information and requested the Secretary-General to open a public registry for this purpose. The information is transmitted to the Committee on the Peaceful Uses of Outer Space for review and is then placed in the registry.

The Russian Federation and the US regularly supply appropriate data, as do Australia, Canada, China, France, Germany, India, Italy, Japan, the UK, and the European Space Agency (ESA).

Cooperation with Specialized Agencies and Other International Organizations. By the terms of its 1961 resolution on outer space, the General Assembly requested the WMO to submit reports to the Committee on the Peaceful Uses of Outer Space on the international cooperation required in weather research. In the following year, it endorsed steps taken under WMO auspices that resulted in the establishment of the World Weather Watch, incorporating meteorological satellites into its operational system. The same resolution also requested the ITU to submit reports on cooperation required to develop effective space communications. In the ensuing years, this cooperative effort embraced other agencies and international organizations having special interests in matters related to outer space, including UNEP, FAO, UNESCO, ESA, the International Telecommunications Satellite Organization (INTELSAT), and the International Maritime Satellite Organization (INMARSAT).

Education and Training. The General Assembly has emphasized the need to train personnel from countries not yet advanced in space activities. The secretariat distributes a periodically revised directory of information taken from UN documents and carries out an educational program on space applications. The program creates an awareness of the potential of space applications for development, especially in developing countries, through technical advisory services, seminars, and workshops and the administration of fellowships offered by member states and international organizations for education and training.

Under the United Nations Programme on Space Applications, the latest efforts are being directed towards the development and enhancement of knowledge and skills in the discipline through the establishment and operation of centers for space science and technology education at the regional level.

INTERNATIONAL SPACE YEAR AND THE UNITED NATIONS CONFERENCE ON ENVIRONMENT

In 1989, the General Assembly recommended that more attention be paid to all aspects related to the protection and preservation of the outer space environment, especially those potentially affecting the earth's environment. In the same year, the General Assembly also endorsed the designation of the year 1992 as International Space Year and its use as a vehicle for promotion of international cooperation, which should be carried out for the benefit and in the interests of all states, with particular emphasis on the needs of developing countries.

Numerous programs were carried out in support of International Space Year and culminated in 1992. "Mission to Planet Earth," which was a central focus of the International Space Year, saw scientists worldwide using space technologies to assess such threats to the earth's environment as global warming, deforestation, and ozone depletion. Subsequently, the General Assembly recommended that the United Nations should actively encourage the continuation of activities initiated for International Space Year and promote broader involvement in those activities by more nations.

Reflecting the growing concern of the international community on environmental security, the United Nations Conference on Environment and Development took place also in 1992 at Rio de Janeiro. Such concern for the protection of environment also was a focus of the activities for International Space Year. The following year, the Secretary-General suggested in his report that it might also be time to examine ways to formalize international cooperation in the utilization of space systems and space technology for environmental purposes, particularly the implementation of the programs recommended in Agenda 21. The product of the Rio conference, Agenda 21 lays out a detailed program of action to be taken by the United Nations, other international organizations, national governments, and intergovernmental organizations. In response to the request by the Committee on the Peaceful Uses of Outer Space, which was subsequently endorsed by the General Assembly, the Secretary-General prepared an analytical report on the role that the committee could play in view of the decisions and recommendations of the United Nations Conference on Environment and Development.

UN CONFERENCES ON OUTER SPACE

Originally recommended by the General Assembly in 1959, the first UN Conference on the Exploration and Peaceful Uses of Outer Space was held in August 1968 in Vienna, with 78 states and a large number of international organizations attending. The conference examined the practical benefits to be derived from space research and the opportunities for international cooperation available to nations without space capability, with special reference to the needs of the developing countries. The participants submitted some 200 papers dealing primarily with space applications. They reviewed 10 years of space research in practical applications—in communications, meteorology, navigation, and education—and practical benefits, as well as economic and legal questions pertaining to international cooperation.

In August 1982, the Second UN Conference on the Exploration and Peaceful Uses of Outer Space (called UNISPACE 82) was held in Vienna, with 94 state participants and 45 observers representing intergovernmental and nongovernmental organizations. The conference dealt with the entire gamut of space sciences, technologies, and applications from scientific, technical, political, economic, social, and organizational points of view. It also considered the legal implications of issues on the agenda and discussed growing international concern relating to military activities in outer space.

The report of the conference, adopted by consensus, dealt with questions relating to the prevention of an arms race in space, the needs and possibilities for technology transfer, coordination in the use of the geostationary orbit, remote sensing of earth resources from space, the use of direct-broadcasting satellites, space transportation and space platform technologies, protection of the near-earth environment, the role of the UN, and other matters. The recommendations of the conference were seen as an agenda for nations and organizations to follow in carrying out space activities.

The Third United Nations Conference on the Exploration and Peaceful Uses of Outer Space (UNISPACE III) was held in Vienna, Austria (headquarters of OOSA since 1993), on 19–30 July 1999. The program included technical and space generation forums as well as a space exhibition and global conferences. The key objective was to create a blueprint for the peaceful uses of outer space in the 21st century. At the time of the conference there were five UN treaties covering a range of space activities. At a UNISPACE III plenary meeting, the Vienna Declaration on Space and Human Development and its related Action Plan were adopted. The Dec-

laration and Plan were the outcome of the coordinated work of attendees, including representatives of governments, intergovernmental bodies, civil society, and, for the first time, the private sector, to create a practical framework for cooperation and action to protect the planet and prepare for the "space millennium." The program involves using space applications for human security, protecting the outer space environment, increasing developing countries' access to space science and its related benefits, raising public awareness of the importance of the peaceful use of outer space, strengthening the UN's space activities, and promoting international cooperation.

Recommendations included creating a voluntary United Nations fund (to be called the UNISPACE III Implementation Fund); proclaiming a World Space Week in early October; encouraging improved access by states to the International Space Station; supporting regional centers for space science and technology education set up under the auspices of the UN; and exploring the legal aspects of space debris, the use of nuclear power sources in space, intellectual property rights for space-related technologies, and ownership and access to the resources of celestial bodies.

DEVELOPMENT OF INTERNATIONAL LAW ON OUTER SPACE

The early work of the legal subcommittee of the Committee on the Peaceful Uses of Outer Space was marked by disputes that delayed progress on the development of outer space law. The majority of members stressed the dangers of spectacular scientific advances without corresponding legal obligations and safeguards.

In originally proposing the formulation of an international legal code on outer space, the General Assembly had recommended that such a code be based, insofar as possible, on the existing body of international law (including the UN Charter) and the principle of freedom of space exploration for all states. But the USSR and the US differed on certain fundamental issues from the time that the question was first debated in the General Assembly in 1959. The most important difference was on the relation between the prevention of armaments in space and disarmament on earth.

The breakthrough in this quasi-procedural deadlock first came as part of the general East-West détente that followed the partial nuclear test-ban treaty signed in August 1963. During its 1963 session, the General Assembly was able to adopt by acclamation two important measures relating to restricting the use of outer space to peaceful purposes. The first was a resolution calling upon all states to refrain from placing in orbit objects carrying nuclear weapons or other weapons of mass destruction. The second was a resolution embodying a Declaration of Legal Principles Governing the Activities of States in the Exploration and Use of Outer Space. Though not an agreement with binding force, as the USSR had wished, it was regarded as the forerunner to a full legal treaty.

The *Treaty on Principles Governing the Activities of States in the Exploration and Use of Outer Space, Including the Moon and Other Celestial Bodies*, which the General Assembly unanimously acclaimed in 1966 and which came into force on 10 October 1967, was based on drafts submitted individually by both the US and the USSR. The 17 articles of the treaty state that the exploration and use of outer space shall be carried out for the benefit of all countries and shall be the province of all mankind, that outer space and celestial bodies are not subject to national appropriation by claim of sovereignty or any other means, and that exploration shall be carried on in accordance with international law. Parties to the treaty undertake not to place in orbit any objects carrying nuclear weapons, install such weapons on celestial bodies, or otherwise station them in outer space. The moon and other celestial bodies shall be used by all parties exclusively for peaceful purposes, and military bases or maneuvers on celestial bodies shall be forbidden. States shall regard astronauts as envoys of mankind in outer space and shall render them all possible assistance in case of accident, distress, or emergency landing. Parties launching objects into outer space are internationally liable for damage caused by such objects or their component parts. The principle of cooperation and mutual assistance shall be followed in space exploration. Harmful contamination of the moon and other celestial bodies shall be avoided. All stations, installations, equipment, and space vehicles on the moon and other celestial bodies shall be open for inspection to representatives of other states on a reciprocal basis.

Under the 1967 *Agreement on the Rescue of Astronauts, the Return of Astronauts, and the Return of Objects Launched into Outer Space,* which came into force on 3 December 1968, contracting parties agree to procedures for assistance to spacecraft personnel in the event of an accident or emergency landing and for the return of space objects.

The 1971 *Convention on International Liability for Damage Caused by Space Objects,* which came into force on 1 September 1972, provides a procedure for the presentation and settlement of claims.

Under the 1974 *Convention on Registration of Objects Launched into Outer Space,* which came into force on 15 September 1976, a central register of objects launched into space was established and is maintained by the UN Secretary-General, with mandatory registration, as well as notification to the Secretary-General of voluntary markings of such objects. Assistance is provided to states requesting help in the identification of hazardous objects or those causing damage.

The *Agreement Governing Activities of States on the Moon and Other Celestial Bodies,* adopted by the General Assembly on 5 December 1979, describes the moon and its natural resources as the common heritage of mankind, and it reserves the moon for exclusively peaceful purposes. It bars the emplacement of nuclear or other weapons of mass destruction on the moon and also prohibits the placing in orbit, or in any other trajectory to or around the moon, of objects carrying such weapons and the establishment of military bases, the testing of any type of weapons, and the conduct of military activities on the moon.

The General Assembly has adopted three more sets of principles based on the work of the Committee on the Peaceful Uses of Outer Space. The *Principles Governing the Use by States of Artificial Earth Satellites for International Direct Television Broadcasting,* adopted in 1982, condition the establishment of direct-broadcasting satellite services on the prior consent of receiving states. The *Principles Relating to Remote Sensing of the Earth from Outer Space,* adopted in 1986, provide for international cooperation and participation in remote sensing; they specify that such activities will be permitted without the consent of the states being sensed but that the latter will have the right to receive data and information concerning their resources.

Finally, after many years of difficult debate and negotiation within the Committee, the General Assembly adopted in 1992 the *Principles Relevant to the Use of Nuclear Power Sources in Outer Space.* They provide guidelines and criteria for safe use of nuclear power sources in outer space, including the requirement that a safety review be made prior to launching of any nuclear power source and that results of such review be made public through the Secretary-General of the United Nations, who should also be notified of any re-entry of radioactive materials to the earth.

Reflecting the changes in the international political and security environment, which provide new possibilities for the utilization of space technology to promote international peace, there were more constructive discussions within the committee in the 1990s on the enhancement of international cooperation in various aspects. The committee and its Legal Subcommittee continued their considerations on the matters relating to the definition and delimitation of outer space and to the character and utilization of the geostationary orbit and on legal framework for sharing the benefits of space exploration by all states.

LAW OF THE SEA

The earth is essentially a liquid planet, with more than 70% of its surface covered by water. Although geographically divided and labeled as continents, islands, seas, and oceans, the earth, when viewed from outer space, appears as one large body of water interspersed with lesser land masses. The world's oceans thus provide a common link for the more than 110 nations whose shorelines are washed by their waters. Despite these universal characteristics, however, this last earthly frontier had become an arena for disputes over such matters as fishing rights and varying claims of national jurisdiction, exploitation of deep sea mineral resources, responsibility for the protection of the environment, the right of innocent passage of ships, and free access to the sea for landlocked countries.

For centuries the doctrine that governed ocean space and resources was "freedom of the seas"; coastal state claims were restricted within narrow limits. The first change in this regime came with the emergence of the doctrine of the continental shelf, spurred by the development of offshore oil and gas fields. The US, in 1945, was the first to proclaim jurisdiction over the natural resources of its continental shelf "beneath the high seas" (that is, beyond US territorial limits). Other nations were quick to follow suit, many of them seeking to extend their jurisdiction over fisheries. In order to clarify accepted norms and codify state practice, the UN, in 1958, convened the First Conference on the Law of the Sea. Working on the basis of drafts prepared by the International Law Commission (see the chapter on International Law), the conference adopted the Convention on the Continental Shelf, thus establishing the new doctrine in international law. The conference adopted three other conventions—on the territorial sea and contiguous zone, the high seas, and fishing and conservation of living resources. A further attempt made in 1960, at the Second Conference on the Law of the Sea, failed to define the limits of the territorial sea.

A sense of urgency was again given to problems connected with the deep seas in 1967, when Malta warned the General Assembly that there was a danger that advanced, industrialized countries who were so equipped might wish to appropriate the ocean floor for their national use, not only to develop its immense resources but also for defense and other purposes. Malta's delegate, Arvid Pardo, remarked that the "dark oceans" were "the womb" of life: life had emerged from the protecting oceans. Man was now returning to the ocean depths, and his penetration "could mark the beginning of the end for man, and indeed for life as we know it . . . it could also be a unique opportunity to lay solid foundations for a peaceful and increasingly prosperous future for all peoples."

Reacting to the Maltese call for international solutions, the General Assembly set up the Committee on the Peaceful Uses of the Seabed and the Ocean Floor Beyond the Limits of National Jurisdiction, called the Seabed Committee, to study various aspects of the problem and to indicate practical means to promote international cooperation. The principal results of the committee's work were embodied in a Declaration of Principles, adopted by the General Assembly in 1970, proclaiming that the seabed and ocean floor and its resources beyond the limits of national jurisdiction "are the common heritage of mankind" and that no nation should exercise sovereignty or rights over any part of the area. The declaration also called for the establishment of an international regime to govern the exploration and exploitation of the sea's resources for the benefit of mankind.

Recognizing that the problems of ocean space are interrelated and need to be considered as a whole, the General Assembly also decided, in 1970, to convene a new UN Conference on the Law of the Sea to prepare a single comprehensive treaty. The Seabed Committee, in preparation for the conference, thus had to deal not only with the international seabed area but also with such issues as the regime of the high seas, the continental shelf and territorial sea (including the question of limits), fishing rights, preservation of the marine environment, scientific research, and access to the sea by landlocked states.

THIRD LAW OF THE SEA CONFERENCE
The Third UN Conference on the Law of the Sea opened at UN headquarters in New York in December 1973 with a brief organizational session. Its real work commenced the following year in Caracas, Venezuela, with the important decision to proceed on the basis of a negotiated "package deal"—meaning no one provision or section would be formally approved until all others were in place. This informal approach was dictated not only by the interdependence of the issues involved but also by the need to produce ultimately an overall balance that could command the widest support. The first informal text, as the agreed basis for negotiations, was prepared in 1975. It was followed by a series of revisions.

UN CONVENTION ON THE LAW OF THE SEA
The final text of the UN Convention on the Law of the Sea (UNCLOS) was approved by the conference at UN headquarters on 30 April 1982, by a vote of 130 in favor, with 4 against (Isreal, Turkey, US, and Venezuela) and 17 abstentions. Following the signing of the Final Act of the conference in Jamaica on 10 December 1982, the UNCLOS entered into force on 16 November 1994. As of May 2000, 133 nations were keeping parties while 25 other states had signed the treaty and were completing the ratification process.

The UNCLOS created three international institutions dealing with specific areas of the Law of the Sea: the International Seabed Authority (ISBA), the International Tribunal for Law of the Sea (ITLOS), and the Commission on the Limits of the Continental Shelf (CLCS).

THE CONTENTIOUS ISSUE OF DEEP SEA MINING
Although the United States had been a leader in the international community's effort to develop an overall legal framework for the oceans in the Third United Nations Conference on the Law of the Sea, deep divisions arose between developing and developed nations over the establishment of an international organization to regulate the exploration of deep sea mining in international waters (Part XI of the Treaty). These divisions were so deep that the United States and other industrialized countries declined to formally sign the treaty, although endorsing the consensus that had been reached by the conference on other areas covered by the treaty.

On the economic and commercial front, the industrialized nations sought a more market-oriented regime. They objected to provisions for mandatory technology transfer, production limitations from the seabed, what they perceived as onerous financial obligations on miners, and the establishment of a subsidized international public enterprise that, it was postulated, would compete unfairly with other commercial enterprises.

In July 1990, the Secretary-General of the UN undertook informal consultations aimed at achieving universal participation in UNCLOS. Fifteen meetings were convened in the period 1990 to 1994, resulting in major amendments to the seabed mining portion of UNCLOS. In early 1993, the Clinton administration in the US decided to take a more active role in the reform effort, deciding that the merit of actively participating would not be to find an answer to every future question regarding the uses of the oceans, but to create a framework and channel discussions of new issues along lines more acceptable to the industrialized nations.

The Agreement Relating to the Implementation of Part XI of the United Nations Convention on the Law of the Sea (hereafter referred to as the "agreement") concluded on 3 June 1994. The agreement avoids establishing a detailed regime anticipating all phases of activity associated with mining of the deep seabed. However, it sets forth economic and commercial principles consistent with a free market philosophy to form the basis for developing rules and regulations at such time as commercial mining develops in international waters.

The agreement retains the institutional outlines of Part XI of the treaty, but scales back the structure and links the activation and operation of institutions to the actual development of concrete interest in seabed mining.

The agreement limits assistance to land-based producers of minerals to adjustment assistance financed out of a portion of royalties from future seabed mining. It also replaces the production control regime of Part XI by the application of GATT principles on subsidization. The agreement further replaces the detailed financial obligations imposed on miners by a future system for recovering economic rents based on systems applicable to land-based mining, and provides that it be designed to avoid competitive incentives or disincentives for seabed mining.

At the conclusion of the informal consultations, only the Russian Federation made a statement reserving its position, since some of its proposals had not been incorporated into the agreement. It was then decided to convene a resumed 48th session of the General Assembly from 27–29 July 1994 for the purpose of adopting and opening for signature the agreement, at which time most of the abstaining industrialized nations signed the treaty. It entered into force on 28 July 1996 having received 40 ratifications.

Provisions of UNCLOS

The convention covers almost all human uses of the seas—navigation and overflight, resource exploration and exploitation, conservation and pollution, fishing, and shipping. Its 321 articles and nine annexes constitute a guide for behavior by nations in the world's oceans, defining maritime zones, laying down rules for drawing boundaries, assigning legal duties and responsibilities, and providing machinery for settlement of disputes. Some of the main provisions of the convention are the following.

Territorial Sea. Coastal states would exercise sovereignty over their territorial sea of up to 22.2 km (12 naut mi) in breadth, but foreign vessels would be allowed "innocent passage" through those waters for purposes of peaceful navigation.

Straits Used for International Navigation. Ships and aircraft of all countries would be allowed "transit passage" through straits used for international navigation, as long as they proceeded without delay and without threatening the bordering states; states

alongside the straits would be able to regulate navigation and other aspects of passage.

Archipelagic States. Archipelagic states, consisting of a group or groups of closely related islands and interconnecting waters, would have sovereignty over a sea area enclosed by straight lines drawn between the outermost points of the islands; all other states would enjoy the right of passage through sea lanes designated by the archipelagic states.

Exclusive Economic Zone. Coastal states would have sovereign rights in a 370-km (200-naut mi) exclusive economic zone with respect to natural resources and certain economic activities and would also have certain types of jurisdiction over marine science research and environmental protection; all other states would have freedom of navigation and overflight in the zone, as well as freedom to lay submarine cables and pipelines. Landlocked and other geographically disadvantaged states would have the opportunity to participate in exploiting part of the zone's fisheries when the coastal state could not harvest them all. Highly migratory species of fish and marine mammals would be accorded special protection.

Continental Shelf. Coastal states would have sovereign rights over the continental shelf (the national area of the seabed) for the purpose of exploring and exploiting it; the shelf would extend at least 370 km (200 naut mi) from shore and 648 km (350 naut mi) or more under specified circumstances. Coastal states would share with the international community part of the revenue that they would derive from exploiting oil and other resources from any part of their shelf beyond 370 km (200 naut mi). A Commission on the Limits of the Continental Shelf would make recommendations to states on the shelf's outer boundaries.

High Seas. All states would enjoy the traditional freedoms of navigation, overflight, scientific research, and fishing on the high seas; they would be obliged to adopt, or cooperate with other states in adopting, measures to conserve living resources.

Islands. The territorial sea, exclusive economic zone, and continental shelf of islands would be determined in accordance with rules applicable to land territory, but rocks that could not sustain human habitation or economic life would have no economic zone or continental shelf.

Enclosed or Semienclosed Seas. States bordering enclosed or semi-enclosed seas would be expected to cooperate on management of living resources and on environmental and research policies and activities.

Landlocked States. Landlocked states would have the right of access to and from the sea and would enjoy freedom of transit through the territory of transit states.

International Seabed Area. A "parallel system" would be established for exploring and exploiting the international seabed area. All activities in this area would be under the control of an International Seabed Authority, to be established under the convention. The authority would conduct its own mining operations through its operating arm, called the "Enterprise," and would also contract with private and state ventures to give them mining rights in the area, so that they could operate in parallel with the authority. The first generation of seabed prospectors, called "pioneer investors," would have guarantees of production once mining was authorized.

Marine Pollution. States would be bound to prevent and control marine pollution from any source and would be liable for damage caused by violation of their international obligations to combat marine pollution.

Marine Scientific Research. All marine scientific research in the exclusive economic zone and on the continental shelf would be subject to the consent of the coastal state, but coastal states would in most cases be obliged to grant consent to foreign states when the research was to be conducted for peaceful purposes.

Development and Transfer of Marine Technology. States would be bound to promote the development and transfer of marine technology "on fair and reasonable terms and conditions," with proper regard for all legitimate interests, including the rights and duties of holders, suppliers, and recipients of technology.

States would be obliged to settle their disputes over the interpretation or application of the convention by peaceful means. They would have to submit most types of disputes to a compulsory procedure entailing decisions that would be binding on all parties. Disputes could be submitted to an International Tribunal for the Law of the Sea, to be established under the convention; to the International Court of Justice; or to arbitration. Conciliation also would be available, and, in certain circumstances, submission to conciliation might be compulsory.

International Acceptance

The new legal regime for the seas is now firmly established throughout the world: by September 1998, 133 states had established 12-nautical-mile territorial limits and 106 states had declared exclusive economic zones. Nineteen states had declared fishing zones of 200 nautical miles. Most such national legislation is derived directly from the provisions of the convention. The General Assembly is concerned with ensuring maximum conformity in state practice and each year examines the status of the convention and reviews developments relating to its application.

ECONOMIC AND SOCIAL DEVELOPMENT

Article 55 of the charter, on international economic and social cooperation, calls on the UN to promote higher standards of living, full employment, and conditions of economic and social progress and development. The fostering of economic and social development, however, was only one of several objectives specified in the charter, and no special emphasis was accorded to it. The League of Nations and the early ILO were concerned primarily with defensive or protective action, such as the protection of countries against diseases that might cross international frontiers, prevention of international traffic in women and children and in illicit drugs, and protection of workers against unfair and inhumane conditions of labor. Such early action in the economic and social fields was taken in a climate of thought that hardly recognized the concept of economic and social development.

Toward the middle of this century, however, the concept took root as a major objective of international cooperation, and the primary goal of the UN and the specialized agencies in the economic and social fields came to be promoting the development of the less developed countries.

THE RICH AND THE POOR NATIONS
The UN's preoccupation with development is tied to the division of its membership between rich and poor nations, a division that the Secretary-General has frequently characterized as a leading long-term threat to world peace and security.

In 1945, when the UN was established, this sharp dichotomy could not be drawn. The wealth of Europe had been wasted by the ravages of war. Only the US could claim to be rich, and even the US, with the depression of the 1930s still a fresh memory, could not be confident of lasting prosperity. What made the challenge of development central to the thinking of every aspiring country was the rapidity with which the countries of Western Europe recovered their prosperity and went on to attain higher levels of economic and social well-being than they had ever experienced. Meanwhile, economic expansion continued apace in the more prosperous countries that had not been directly hurt by the war—the US, Canada, Australia, and New Zealand. And within a few years, in Asia, the miracle of Japan's recovery and growth was matching Europe's postwar record.

Nothing comparable occurred among the colonial peoples and former colonial peoples. Tropical Asia, Africa, and Latin America had been cultivated in preceding generations largely as appendages to industrial Europe and North America—on the one hand, supplying essential primary commodities not commonly found in the temperate regions and, on the other hand, serving as profitable markets for consumer goods produced in the temperate regions. The peoples of these economically underdeveloped areas made rapid political progress in the postwar era. Significant economic progress also was recorded in a number of these countries, so that by the late 1950s, it was considered not only tactful but also proper to refer to them as "developing" rather than "underdeveloped" nations. As a group, however, the developing countries were far outdistanced in economic growth by the temperate zone industrialized countries, which were finding the postwar era the most propitious in history for their development. Before the UN had completed its first 15 years, it was abundantly evident that a very disturbing gap had opened up between the industrialized and the developing nations and that, despite very substantial foreign aid efforts, the gap was growing broader year by year.

SCOPE OF THE UN'S WORK
The international community was not slow to recognize the political and economic dangers inherent in such an imbalance of national wealth. As early as 1946, when "recovery" rather than "development" dominated UN thinking on economic matters, the General Assembly requested the Economic and Social Council to study ways and means of furnishing advice to nations desiring help in developing their resources. As a result, the UN, in cooperation with the specialized agencies of the UN system, began its first programs of technical assistance.

This chapter describes the principles and goals of the UN development effort. It also discusses some of the factors influencing development, such as science and technology, the role of transnational corporations, and the use of natural resources, and it summarizes the work of the regional commissions. Programs of technical cooperation undertaken by the UN and its related organizations are described in the chapter on Technical Cooperation Programs, and social and humanitarian programs in the chapter on Social and Humanitarian Assistance. The work of the specialized agencies in supporting economic and social development is described in the separate chapters on those agencies.

FIRST UN DEVELOPMENT DECADE
The first UN Development Decade was launched by the General Assembly in December 1961. It called on all member states to intensify their efforts to mobilize support for measures required to accelerate progress toward self-sustaining economic growth and social advancement in the developing countries. With each developing country setting its own target, the objective would be a minimum annual growth rate of 5% in aggregate national income by the end of the decade.

The economically advanced states were asked to pursue policies designed to enable the developing countries to sell more of their products at stable and remunerative prices in expanding markets in order to finance more of their economic development, and to follow policies designed to ensure developing countries an equitable share of earnings from extraction and marketing of their natural resources by foreign capital. Industrialized states were also called on to pursue policies that would lead to an increase in the flow of developmental resources and stimulate the lflow of private capital to developing countries on mutually acceptable terms. The General Assembly recommended that the flow of international capital and assistance to developing countries should be about 1% of the combined national incomes of the economically advanced countries.

Throughout the decade of the 1960s, however, the growth rate in the economically advanced market economies accelerated, and the gap between the per capita incomes of the developing countries and those of the developed countries widened. Two-thirds of the world's population living in the less developed regions of the world still had less than one-sixth of the world's income. In 1962, annual per capita income in those regions averaged $136, while that of the economically advanced market economies in North America and Western Europe averaged $2,845 and $1,033, respectively.

In a report issued in 1969, Secretary-General U Thant noted that the slower progress in development had been accompanied by the emergence or aggravation of major imbalances that imperiled future growth. Without greater progress in food production and the more effective control of communicable diseases, the necessary conditions for steady economic and social development could hardly be said to have been created. At the same time, the Secretary-General pointed out, the experience of a few countries had demonstrated that "given a favorable constellation of circumstances and policies, an adequate and sustained pace of development can be achieved," and acceptance of development as a fundamental objective had gradually wrought a desirable change in attitudes and modes of action on the part of developing countries. Public decisions were no longer made solely in response to expediency, and policies and programs previously decided upon in relative isolation were gradually being integrated and harnessed to a common purpose. At the international level, the Secretary-General noted, the institutional machinery for the review and advancement of international policies had been considerably strengthened by the creation of such bodies as the UN Conference on Trade and Development and the Committee for Development Planning.

The first UN Development Decade ended in December 1970 with one of its major goals, the attainment of a 5% growth rate, unattained in the developing countries. During the period 1960–67, those countries achieved an annual rate of increase in their total domestic product of about 4.6%, but, because of the population increase, the increase in their per capita gross product was only about 2%. The General Assembly concluded that one of the reasons for the slow progress was the absence of a framework of international development strategy.

SECOND UN DEVELOPMENT DECADE
At its 25th session, in 1970, the General Assembly adopted a resolution outlining an international development strategy for the second UN Development Decade—the 1970s. The main objectives of the plan were to promote sustained economic growth, particularly in the developing countries; ensure a higher standard of living, and facilitate the process of narrowing the gap between the developed and developing countries. The General Assembly declared that the developing countries bore primary responsibility for their development but that their efforts would be insufficient without increased financial assistance and more favorable economic and commercial policies on the part of the developed countries.

Under the goals and objectives of the second decade, the General Assembly stated that the average annual rate of growth in the gross product of the developing countries as a whole should be at least 6%, with the possibility of attaining a higher rate in the second half of the decade. Such a rate of growth would imply an average annual expansion of 4% in agricultural output and 8% in manufacturing output.

The General Assembly also stated that it was essential to bring about a more equitable distribution of income and wealth in order to promote social justice and efficiency of production; to raise the level of employment substantially; to achieve a greater degree of income security; to expand and improve facilities for education, health, nutrition, housing, and social welfare; and to safeguard the environment. Thus, qualitative and structural changes in society should go hand in hand with rapid economic growth, and existing disparities—regional, sectoral, and social—should be substantially reduced. The General Assembly believed that developing countries must bear the main responsibility for financing their development. To this end, they were asked to pursue sound fiscal and monetary policies and to remove institutional obstacles through the adoption of appropriate legislative and administrative reforms. At the same time, each economically advanced country was called upon to endeavor to provide annually to developing countries financial resource transfers of a minimum net amount of 1% of its gross national product (GNP). A major part of financial resource transfers to the developing countries should be provided in the form of official development assistance.

Progress achieved during the first half of the decade was reviewed by the General Assembly in 1975. It noted that the gap between the developed and the developing countries had increased alarmingly during the first half of the decade, but it found the generally gloomy picture lightened by one element—the developing countries had emerged "as a more powerful factor, as a necessary consequence of the new and growing perception of the reality of interdependence." The General Assembly also found that some of the aggregate targets set in the strategy for the decade had been met or exceeded, "owing mainly to the developing countries' own efforts and, to a certain extent, to external factors such as the commodity boom" (a short-lived rise in commodity prices between 1972 and 1974). Those aggregates, however, did not reflect the variation in achievement among developing countries, for many countries did much worse than the average. A major area of shortfall was in agriculture, where less than half the target rate of 4% annual growth was realized by the developing countries as a whole.

The General Assembly further noted that the net flow of financial resources from developed countries in the form of official development assistance had decreased in real terms and as a percentage of GNP. At the same time, the burden of debt-service payments of developing countries had continued to increase in relation to their export earnings.

NEW INTERNATIONAL ECONOMIC ORDER
In September 1973, in Algiers, the Arab petroleum-exporting countries discussed the possible uses of oil as a political weapon. When a new Arab-Israeli conflict broke out on 6 October, the Arab countries reduced the flow of oil to Europe and Japan and suspended exports to the US, the Netherlands, and Portugal. The embargo against the US was lifted in March 1974, that against the Netherlands in July 1974, and that against Portugal after a new regime instituted a policy leading to independence for African territories under Portuguese administration in 1974 and 1975. However, the measures taken by the petroleum-exporting countries marked a turning point for the world economy. Members of the Organization of Petroleum-Exporting Countries (OPEC) undertook a long-term study of the collective fixing of oil prices and increased them periodically thereafter.

On 31 January 1974, President Boumedienne of Algeria requested a special session of the General Assembly to consider the question of all raw materials and relations between developed industrial and developing states. Within two weeks, 70 nations endorsed his proposal.

Sixth Special Session of the General Assembly. The special session, held in April–May 1974, adopted a declaration and program of action on the establishment of a new international economic order. The declaration and program of action called for a fundamental change in the international economic order, in the absence of which the gap between developing and developed countries would only continue to widen. Such a change would require the industrial countries to make adjustments in their policies and economies for the benefit of the poorer countries, which in turn were determined to control their own resources.

The program of action called for efforts to link the prices of exports of developing countries to the prices of their imports from developed countries. It suggested the formation of producers' associations, orderly commodity trading, increased export income for producing developing countries, and improvement in their terms of trade. It also looked to the evolution of an equitable relationship between the prices of raw materials, primary commodities, and semimanufactured goods exported by developing countries and the raw materials, primary commodities, food, manufactured and semimanufactured goods, and capital equipment imported by them.

In the declaration, UN member states proclaimed their determination to work urgently for "the establishment of a new international economic order based on equity, sovereign equality, interdependence, common interest, and cooperation among all states, irrespective of their economic and social systems, which shall correct inequalities and redress existing injustices, make it possible to eliminate the widening gap between the developed and the developing countries and ensure steadily accelerating economic and social development in peace and justice for present and future generations."

Though the program and declaration were adopted without a vote and enthusiastically supported by almost all developing and socialist countries, most Western European and other industrialized states with market economies entered reservations, often very far-reaching. They warned against constraints to the flow of trade that might result from the establishment of producers' associations and argued that nationalization should be carried out in accordance with the existing rules of international law.

Charter of Economic Rights and Duties of States. At its regular session in 1974, the General Assembly adopted a charter of Economic Rights and Duties of States. The charter affirmed that every state has the right to exercise freely full permanent sovereignty over its wealth and natural resources, to regulate foreign investment within its national jurisdiction, and to nationalize, expropriate, or transfer the ownership of foreign property. The charter provided that appropriate compensation should be paid in cases of nationalization and that any controversies should be settled under the domestic laws of the nationalizing states unless all states concerned agree to other peaceful means. It also set forth the right of states to associate in organizations of primary producers in order to develop their national economies.

Seventh Special Session of the General Assembly. The General Assembly held a seventh special session devoted to development and international cooperation in September 1975. The polemical atmosphere in which the program and declaration on the new international economic order and the charter on the economic rights and duties of states had been adopted was replaced by a pragmatic approach. Negotiations were carried on chiefly in private meetings between "contact groups" representing the developing countries and the Western European and other states with market economies. Since the market economy states were the buyers of approximately three-quarters of the exports of the developing countries, agreement between the two groups was essential to significant progress. At the close of the session, Secretary-General Kurt Waldheim declared that it had been "about *change* rather than the smoother management of the status quo."

The results of the special session were embodied in a resolution that proposed a large number of initiatives and was unanimously adopted by the General Assembly. It reaffirmed the target, originally defined in the strategy for the second Development Decade, of 1% of the GNP of developed countries to be devoted to official assistance to the developing countries, and it called for the accumulation of buffer stocks of commodities in order to offset market fluctuations, combat inflationary tendencies, and ensure grain and food security.

In 1979, the General Assembly called for the launching, at the third special session on development in 1980, of a round of global and sustained negotiations on international economic cooperation for development. The negotiations, however, failed to achieve the hoped-for progress at the special session held in September 1980, but at the regular session that year, an international development strategy for the third UN Development Decade was adopted.

THIRD UN DEVELOPMENT DECADE

In the new international development strategy adopted by the General Assembly for the third UN Development Decade, beginning on 1 January 1981, governments pledged themselves, individually and collectively, to fulfill their commitment to establish a new international economic order based on justice and equity. They agreed to subscribe to the goals and objectives of the strategy and to translate them into reality by adopting a coherent set of interrelated, concrete, and effective policy measures in all sectors of development.

The strategy set forth goals and objectives for an accelerated development of the developing countries in the period 1981–90, including the following: (1) a 7% average annual rate of growth of gross domestic product (GDP); (2) a 7.5% annual rate of expansion of exports and an 8% annual rate of expansion of imports of goods and services; (3) an increase in gross domestic savings to reach about 24% of GDP by 1990; (4) a rapid and substantial increase in official development assistance by all developed countries, to reach or surpass the target of 0.7% of GNP of developed countries; (5) a 4% average annual rate of expansion of agricultural production; and (6) a 9% annual rate of expansion of manufacturing output. Other goals and objectives of the strategy included the attainment, by the year 2000, of full employment, of universal primary school enrollment, and of life expectancy of 60 years as a minimum, with infant mortality rates no higher than 50 per 1,000 live births.

The strategy also set out a series of policy measures—in international trade, industrialization, food and agriculture, financial resources for development, international monetary and financial issues, science and technology for development, energy, transportation, environment, human settlements, disaster relief, and social development, as well as in technical cooperation, including cooperation among developing countries themselves, and special measures for the least-developed countries and for geographically disadvantaged countries, such as island and landlocked developing countries.

In fact, the 1980s was a terrible decade for the economies of developing countries. By 1990 only five donor countries had met the UN's target of donating 0.7% of their GNP to development: Norway, the Netherlands, Denmark, Sweden, and France. Canada and Germany had achieved a level of 0.4% of their GNP. The United States, which had never agreed to the UN target, had given 0.2% of its GNP. Intransigent recession in the industrialized world, declining commodity prices, rising interest rates, trade barriers, and crippling international debt meant human suffering for the vast majority of the world's population. By 1990 4.2 billion of the world's 5.3 billion people lived in developing countries. Overall growth in these nations shrank to about 3% annually, and per capita growth to 1%, compared to averages of 5.5% in the 1960s and 3% in the 1970s. Lending by the IMF and World Bank group of institutions often came with requirements for "restructuring" that carried a heavy price in terms of human sacrifice. Debt-laden developing countries found themselves spending vastly more on debt service than on social services.

This dismal result was illustrated by the fact that the number of countries designated by the General Assembly as "least developed" had grown from 24 in 1972 to 47 in 1991.

FOURTH UN DEVELOPMENT DECADE

In 1990, the General Assembly concluded that its goals for the Third UN Development Decade had not been attained. It set new priorities and goals for the growth of the developing member nations with its International Development Strategy (IDS) for the Fourth United Nations Development Decade (1991–2000). Within one year of its passage, however, the former USSR had dissolved, forever changing the landscape of international economic relations. Many of the assumptions on which the IDS had been based were upset by the historic forces that were thus set in motion.

In September 1990, the Second United Nations Conference on the Least Developed Countries set targets for official development assistance (ODA) to those nations. The General Assembly, through the new IDS, urged industrialized countries to reach or surpass those targets. It also recommended that developing countries try to raise their rate of industrialization by 8–10% and increase their annual food production by 4%.

The General Assembly set forth six goals for the new IDS that amounted to an early manifestation of a new philosophy of "sustainable" development that would be vigorously developed at the historic UN Conference on Environment and Development (UNCED), two years later. The goals of the IDS were:

1. To speed up the pace of economic growth in the developing countries;
2. To devise a development process that meets social needs, reduces extreme poverty significantly, develops and uses people's capacity and skills, and is environmentally sound and sustainable;
3. To improve the international systems of money, finance, and trade;
4. To strengthen and stabilize the world economy and establish sound macroeconomic management practices, nationally and internationally;
5. To strengthen international cooperation for development;
6. To make a special effort to deal with the particular problems of the least developed countries.

The philosophy for the new IDS was based on the principle that, because the developed countries have the greatest influence on the international economic environment, they have a special responsibility for the success of development efforts. It also recognized that speeding up development would require strenuous efforts by developing countries to increase domestic savings, raise investment and investment returns, hold down inflation, exercise monetary and fiscal discipline, maintain realistic exchange rates, and allocate resources more efficiently.

Improving the state of international trade was paramount for any development plan. The Uruguay Round of the GATT talks were stalled and protectionism was on the rise in the developed nations. The strategy proposed that the following actions be taken to accelerate international trade in the 1990s:

1. Stand by the commitment made in 1986 to halt and reverse protectionism;
2. Liberalize trade and improve developing countries' access to all markets by reducing or removing tariff barriers;
3. Free up trade in tropical products and products based on natural resources;
4. Bring trade in textiles under the normal rules of GATT;
5. Substantially reduce agricultural subsidies and other protective policies;
6. Implement and improve the generalized system of preferences under which some developing countries' exports are admitted to industrialized countries at reduced rates or duty-free;
7. Ensure that regional economic arrangements and trade blocs conform with GATT rules;
8. Make sure that GATT contracting parties adhere strictly to the agreement's rules and principles.

Other provisions of the IDS included establishing more stable commodity markets, obtaining concessional terms for the transfer of technology to developing countries, and finding agreement on a way that the intellectual property system (which protects ownership of copyrights, trademarks, industrial designs, and patents) can promote development while protecting intellectual property. It also recommended that work on international rules and standards to govern the exchange of technological information (the code of conduct on the transfer of technology), which had come to a halt at the end of the 1980s, should be completed.

The underlying causes of economic stagnation also were decried. The IDS called for the eradication of poverty, hunger, adult illiteracy, lack of basic education for women, and runaway population growth in developing countries, and noted the catastrophic deterioration of the environment by shortsighted development projects.

In 1992, the Secretary-General gave the General Assembly a guardedly optimistic report on the progress of the IDS to that point. The developed market economies themselves had grown by only about 1% in 1991. Although a recovery had begun in 1992, it was considered to be weak. There was concern that the urgent needs of the newly independent countries of the former USSR, often referred to as "economies in transition," would divert assistance from developing countries. Per capita incomes remained stagnant or declined in all the developing regions, except South and East Asia and China. The debt crisis of the developing countries had not worsened, but little progress had been made in terms of debt relief and forgiveness. However, some of the Latin American countries had again become creditworthy.

The *1993 Report on the World Social Situation*, commissioned by the General Assembly to review the implementation of the Declaration on Social Progress and Development made 20 years earlier, also was cautiously optimistic. It noted the positive direction of reform in the United Nations system towards coordination between various UN agencies with operations in the same countries. "Although the major development goals, proclaimed more than 20 years ago in the Declaration on Social Progress and Development, have not changed significantly, the priorities, approaches and emphases have been reviewed and renewed, as the understanding of the forces behind development have deepened. Thus, emphasis is now on assisting the recipient countries to strengthen their institutional capacity to sustain the development process" the report said. In other words: helping them learn how to help themselves.

In October 1999, as the Second Committee began consideration of sustainable development and economic cooperation in the year 2000, it reviewed a report evaluating the implementation of the commitments and policies agreed on in the IDS. The report concluded that though there were improvements in the 1990s, economic growth had not accelerated in all developing countries. The Uruguay Round had led to progress being made with the betterment of the global trading system, but the international financial system had not been stabilized. Nor had there been a marked improvement in international development cooperation. The world's least developed countries had seen "negligible" economic and social advancement during the decade. For future purposes, the report went on to differentiate between growth, which may carry with it negative social consequences, and development, which means more than simply increased purchasing power (as reflected in gross domestic product per capita). According to the report, development also pertains to education, health, and environmental standards, as well as to social (including gender) equity. For this reason, "the spotlight is now shifting from a focus on macroeconomic challenges to a number of institutional preconditions, including good governance, transparency and accountability, decentralization and participation and social security," said the UN report. Acceptable and viable development strategies in the new millennium would have to take into account the prevailing circumstances in developing countries, which could not be expected to keep pace with industrialized, developed societies in the North.

The economic and social initiatives of the 1990s had highlighted that neither growth nor development necessarily eliminates poverty, which was one of the key objectives of IDS. The UN concluded that sustainable development, of both urban and rural human settlements, was directly linked to the alleviation of poverty, which became the focus of economic and social development at the dawn of the 2000s. At the October 1999 meeting of the Second Committee, the Group of 77 developing countries and China presented draft resolutions for the first United Nations Decade for the Eradication of Poverty (which technically began in 1997 and extended through 2006). On 9 December 1999 the General Assembly voted to implement the Decade and called on all nations to formulate and implement "outcome-oriented national strategies and programs" and set time-bound targets for poverty reduction. The Assembly further called on developed countries to strengthen their efforts to achieve the agreed target of 0.7% of their gross national product for overall official development assistance, and within that target to "earmark 0.15% to 0.20% of their gross national product for the least developed countries." Acknowledging the information age, the Assembly resolution highlighted the importance of strengthening the cooperation between developed and developing nations in order to "promote capacity-building and facilitate access to and transfer of technologies and corresponding knowledge."

THE EARTH SUMMIT—AGENDA 21

The United Nations Conference on Environment and Development (UNCED), popularly dubbed the "Earth Summit," brought together 117 heads of state and government in Rio de Janeiro, Brazil, on 3–14 June 1992. The product of this historic meeting, an 800-page document called "Agenda 21," set forth global measures to protect the planet's environment while guaranteeing sustainable economic growth. An important statement of the basic principles of sustainable development, *The Rio Declaration on Environment and Development,* was adopted by acclamation. The conference also spawned a new functional commission of ECOSOC, the Commission on Sustainable Development, which has a mandate to monitor international treaties on the environment, provide policy direction, and coordinate action within the United Nations system to achieve the goals of Agenda 21.

In addition to Agenda 21, two important conventions on the environment were opened for signature and received widespread endorsement: the Global Warming Convention, which set guidelines for regulating emissions of gases believed to cause global warming, was signed by 153 nations; and the Biodiversity Convention, which committed signatory nations to protection of endangered species and cooperation on genetic and biological technology, was signed by representatives of 150 countries. The Biodiversity Convention became legally binding in December 1993, after 30 countries had ratified it. Two important documents setting forth the principles behind the concept of sustainable development also were widely adopted at the Earth Summit: the Statement on Forest Principles, recommending preservation of world forests and monitoring of development impact on timberlands; and the Declaration on Environment and Development, a statement of principles that emphasized the coordination of economic and environmental concerns.

More than two years were spent preparing for the Earth Summit and drafting the documents that would achieve widespread international acceptance. However, many controversial propositions had to be deleted or scaled down in the final documents to achieve the final consensus. For example, negotiators removed or excluded specific targets on pollution controls, resource protection, and financial aid to developing countries that restrain their economic development in order to protect their natural resources. Developing countries had sought to establish a "green fund" to support their efforts to implement environmentally sustainable development. However, the G-7 group of industrialized countries

succeeded in specifying that such development funds would be channeled through the World Bank's Global Environment Facility (GEF), effectively retaining control of funding in the hands of the industrialized world. The European Community had recommended a tax on fossil fuels in industrialized nations, but, opposition from oil-producing countries killed this provision. Also deemphasized in the final documents were references to population control. Passages referring to contraception were completely deleted at the insistence of an odd coalition that included the Holy See (Vatican), Roman Catholic countries, and Moslem countries.

The sense of urgency that brought 35,000 accredited participants and 117 heads of state to Rio de Janeiro for the Earth Summit is perhaps well summed up by the UNCED secretary-general, Canadian Maurice Strong: "The Earth Summit must establish a whole new basis for relations between rich and poor, North and South, including a concerted attack on poverty as a central priority for the 21st Century. We owe at least this much to future generations, from whom we have borrowed a fragile planet called Earth."

At the Earth Summit+5 meeting held in June 1997 in New York City, the objectives were to revitalize and energize commitments to sustainable development, to recognize failures and identify their causes, to recognize achievements (there were many Agenda 21 success stories that were highlighted during the event), to define priorities for the post-97 period, and to raise the profile of issues addressed insufficiently by Rio. In addition to assessing progress since the last meeting and outlining areas requiring urgent action, attendees called for greater cooperation and adherence among intergovernmental organizations and developed a program of work for the Commission on Sustainable Development for the years 1998–2002. The program included a comprehensive review of the program of action for the sustainable development of Small Island Developing States (SIDS), developing integrated management and planning of land resources, and developing strategic approaches to freshwater management.

THE 1994 AGENDA FOR DEVELOPMENT

The 47th General Assembly requested the Secretary-General to consult with member states and prepare an "agenda for development." After obtaining submissions from member states, agencies of the UN system and public and private sources worldwide, he presented his report to the 49th General Assembly in 1994. Entitled *Development and International Economic Cooperation: An Agenda for Development,* this wide-ranging document summarized the basic tenets of the experience gained during the UN's 50 years of development work. The agenda was intended to offer guidelines for thought and action by member states.

One reason put forward for creating such a document was that with the end of the cold war, funding development projects as a mechanism for establishing spheres of influence also had ended. The fundamental social, political, and economic changes that had altered the map of Europe and provided a new atmosphere of consensus at the United Nations, also threatened to bewilder and exhaust the potential donors to UN programs for development. Some quarters had even suggested that the UN was expending more for its many new peacekeeping operations than for development. The Secretary-General produced statistics in an annex to the agenda that demonstrated that this was not the case, even exempting the funds expended by the specialized agencies.

Several major themes of the agenda set forth a new underlying philosophy regarding international development programs.

1. National governments bear the major responsibility for development. However, the United Nations' vast experience and global reach made it a unique resource for the developing nations. The United Nations could act as facilitator and communicator, but it could not substitute for the commit

ment of individual states and their domestic and international partners.

2. However, national governments could no longer be assumed to be paramount economic agents. The internationalization of trade and the ascendance of the market system worldwide meant that governments must, however, provide a regulatory framework for effective operation of a competitive market system. They must also invest in human capital by ensuring that social safety nets are in place.

3. Economic growth should promote full employment and poverty reduction, not just economic growth as an end in itself. If, despite national economic improvement, great poverty continued in a nation, no development effort could be sustainable.

4. No mechanism exists by which the major economies could be induced to make globally beneficial structural change in their own economies, or to adopt more globally responsible economic, fiscal, and monetary policies. This single point represents a sea change in philosophy from the "new international economic order" of the 1970s.

5. UNCED's historic Agenda 21 demonstrated that the environment had finally been recognized by the international community as a resource for development that must be nurtured and protected. Governments had the responsibility to provide the leadership and regulatory structure to protect their natural environment. Successful development required policies that incorporate environmental considerations. The Secretary-General pointed out that pioneering efforts were being made to make local inhabitants incentive partners rather than simply collateral beneficiaries of sustainable development programs. As the keyword and rallying cry of the Earth Summit, "sustainability" must be the guiding principle of development, to be achieved by a true partnership of governments, international organizations, and nongovernmental organizations; a true partnership between humanity and nature.

6. No development could be considered sustainable in the presence of poverty, disease, illiteracy, great unemployment, discrimination against women, armed conflict, or lack of social integration; the manifestations of social integration being discrimination, fanaticism, intolerance, and persecution.

7. Democracy and development are processes (not events) that are fundamentally linked because people's participation in the decision-making processes that affect their lives gives legitimacy to governments and their development programs.

In his conclusions, the Secretary-General admitted that, over the years, absence of clear policy guidance from the General Assembly and the lack of effective policy coordination by ECOSOC had resulted in an overall lack of focus in the UN development system. The fundamental changes under way included the restructuring of development efforts to be channeled through UNDP resident coordinators, by means of the development of one comprehensive "country strategy note." This alone would bring about better (if not perfect) coordination and more rational use of available funds.

However, the Secretary-General also noted the growth of other obstructions to the urgent need for social and economic development in the developing countries: "At present the UN mechanism is caught in a confining cycle. There is a resistance to multilateralism from those who fear a loss of national control. There is a reluctance to provide financial means to achieve agreed ends from those who lack conviction that assessments will benefit their own interests. And there is an unwillingness to engage in difficult operations by those who seek guarantees of perfect clarity and limited duration. Without a new and compelling collective vision, the international community will be unable to break out of this cycle."

DEVELOPMENT PLANNING

Almost all the organizations in the UN family contribute in one way or another to development planning—by helping to evolve and introduce new planning methods, by assisting governments in establishing realistic growth targets, and by trying to ensure that overall plans take account of the needs of the different sectors of society.

Within the UN, problems relating to development planning are the concern of the Economic and Social Council's Committee for Development Planning. The 24-member committee, established in 1966, is a consultative body that meets annually to consider problems encountered in implementing development plans.

The UN Secretariat provides an account of the state of the world economy through its annual publication of the *World Economic and Social Survey*, which has appeared every year since 1948. Since 1990 UNDP has stimulated debate about the concept of human-centered development through the publication of the annual *Human Development Report*, written by an independent team of development specialists and published by Oxford University Press. Statistical data, considered indispensable for economic and social development planning, also appears in a number of UN publications, including the *Statistical Yearbook*, *Demographic Yearbook*, *Yearbook of National Accounts Statistics*, *Yearbook of International Trade Statistics*, *World Energy Supplies*, *Commodity Trade Statistics*, *Population and Vital Statistics Report*, and *Monthly Bulletin of Statistics*.

WORLD FOOD COUNCIL (WFC)

The world food situation in the early 1970s was marked by extreme food shortages in many developing countries in Africa and parts of Southeast Asia, by a general lack of progress in the world fight against hunger and malnutrition, and by very slow progress in the creation of a system of internationally coordinated cereal reserves to meet crop shortfalls and other abnormal situations.

It was against this background that the General Assembly decided, in 1973, to convene a conference to deal with global food problems. The UN World Food Conference, held in Rome in November 1974, called for the creation of a 36-member ministerial-level World Food Council to review annually major problems and policy issues affecting the world food situation and to bring its political influence to bear on governments and UN bodies and agencies alike.

Each year up through 1992 the WFC met in plenary session at the invitation of one of its member states. The council, as a subsidiary body of the UN General Assembly, reports annually to it through the Economic and Social Council.

At first, the WFC's approach to solving world food problems was to encourage the adoption of national food strategies by developing countries. Under this plan, each country would assess its present food situation, including needs, supply, potential for increasing food production, storage, processing, transport, distribution, marketing, and the ability to meet food emergencies. In the early 1980s, this concept was taken over by the World Bank.

In 1989, at its 15th session held in Cairo, Egypt, the WFC delineated a Programme of Co-operative Action with four main goals for UN member countries within the next decade: the elimination of starvation and death caused by famine; a substantial reduction of malnutrition and mortality among young children; a tangible reduction in chronic hunger; and the elimination of major nutritional-deficiency diseases. The Programme of Co-Operative Action contained proposals for immediate action to be taken on food-for-work programs in rural areas where employment opportunities are not available and measures to make specific food items affordable to the poor. Over the longer term, the WFC recommended projects to create production and employment opportunities in rural and urban areas; community initiative projects designed to enable the communities themselves to identify and implement projects; vocational training schemes; retraining schemes; food stamp schemes. In the area of nutrition, the WFC recommended the implementation on an emergency basis of supplementary feeding programs for children; primary health care programs, including programs to improve sanitation and drinking water; family planning programs; nutritional education programs; and support to food and nutrition programs undertaken by WHO, UNICEF, and other international agencies.

At its 16th session in 1990, held in Bangkok, Thailand, the council observed that most countries had not yet set specific goals and targets to implement its call to action. However, by 1991 those goals had been adopted by all UN member states as part of the International Development Strategy for the Fourth United Nations Development Decade.

The WFC also considered the coordination of the activities of some 35 international agencies that have programs significantly related to hunger problems. The WFC observed that its own role was that of providing a central, undivided focus on hunger and recommended the creation of an inter-secretariat consultative mechanism among the four Rome-based food organizations (FAO, IFAD, WFC, and WFP). In 1991, meeting in Helsingor, Denmark, it reiterated this support. It noted with concern the great financial difficulties facing these international organizations.

The 18th session of the WFC met in 1992 in Nairobi, Kenya. Its report to the General Assembly noted that although most developing regions made some headway during the 1980s in reducing hunger and malnutrition, this was not the case for the peoples of Africa where disastrous droughts and civil disturbances had caused widespread starvation in recent years. The council praised the IFAD Special Programme for Sub-Saharan African Countries Affected by Drought and Desertification. In response to the disastrous problems of Africa, the WFC called for a "New Green Revolution," and the intensified transfer of technology to accomplish such a revolution. It recommended that substantial increases in investments in research, extension, and training were needed, particularly in Africa.

In 1992 the WFC also noted the problems of millions of people in Eastern Europe and the Commonwealth of Independent States (formerly the USSR) in gaining access to adequate food as a result of the dislocation of their economies.

In the context of the efforts of the General Assembly to streamline the activities of the United Nations, the WFC considered its future role within the framework of the restructuring process. With disarming frankness, the council stated: "We agree that the council has fallen short of achieving the political leadership and coordination role expected from its founders at the 1974 World Food Conference." It concluded that, in a rapidly changing world, the continuation of the status quo for the World Food Council and the United Nations as a whole was not possible. It established an ad hoc committee to review the mandate and future role of the WFC, which met in New York on 14–15 September 1992 and submitted its report to the 47th Session of the General Assembly (1992). However, the committee could not reach agreement on what the council's future role should be. Views ranged from abolishing it to strengthening it and integrating its mandate with another intergovernmental body. With this the committee referred the matter to the General Assembly, which requested the council members to continue attempts to agree on appropriate measures to be taken. After informal meetings from January to May 1993, the council reported to the General Assembly that "Council members are agreed on a set of principles to guide the United Nations response to global food and hunger problems, but disagreements continue to exist concerning the most effective institutional response to these principles."

In 1993 no formal WFC session was held, nor were any substantive documents prepared by the WFC secretariat. In fact, in December 1993, the secretariat in Rome was abolished as a result of the restructuring of the United Nations. Responsibility for servicing any future meetings of the WFC was given to the newly formed Department for Policy Coordination and Sustainable Development (DPCSD) in New York.

In November 1993 the president of the World Food Council held informal consultations with other WFC ministers of agriculture during the biennial FAO Conference in Rome about the possibility of scheduling the next (19th) session of the council. The consultations were inconclusive and the future of the WFC was not taken up at the General Assembly's 48th regular session in light of these ongoing discussions.

At a General Assembly plenary meeting on 26 May 1996 it was recommended that the World Food Council be discontinued and its functions absorbed by the Food and Agriculture Organization (FAO) and World Food Program (WFP). To eliminate duplicative and overlapping efforts, this recommendation was heeded and the WFC was dissolved. The move was generally hailed as a sign that the Assembly was rededicating itself to better use of its resources. As the FAO and WFP became heirs to the World Food Council's initiatives, the restructuring was also viewed as a reinforcement of ECOSOC's development-related activities. (For more information on the UN's ongoing work to combat hunger around the globe, please see the chapter on the Food and Agriculture Organization.)

SCIENCE AND TECHNOLOGY FOR DEVELOPMENT

A major event of the first UN Development Decade was the UN Conference on the Application of Science and Technology for the Benefit of the Less Developed Countries, held in Geneva in 1963. The conference focussed world attention on the practical possibilities of accelerating development through the application of advances in science and technology and on the need for reorienting research toward the requirements of the developing countries.

A second conference, the UN Conference on Science and Technology for Development, held in Vienna in 1979, adopted a program of action (the Vienna Programme) designed to put science and technology to work for the economic development of all countries, particularly the developing countries. It recommended the creation by the General Assembly of a high-level intergovernmental committee on science and technology for development, open to all member states, and the establishment of a voluntary fund to be administered by UNDP.

The Geneva Conference was a predominantly technical or pragmatic conference at which developed countries provided developing countries with state-of-the-art reports on developed-country technologies. By contrast, the Vienna Conference reflected the 1970s discussions between developed and developing countries over a more equal access of the latter to the world's science and technology. Thus science and technology were placed within the context of international diplomacy. The result, the Vienna Programme of Action was a compromise that did not fully meet the expectations of the developing countries.

The Vienna Programme of Action was divided into three target areas: strengthening the science and technology capacities of developing countries; restructuring the existing pattern of international scientific and technological relations; and strengthening the role of the UN system in the field of science and technology and the provision of increased financial resources.

Endorsing the recommendations of the Vienna conference, the General Assembly decided to establish an Intergovernmental Committee on Science and Technology for Development (ISTD), to be open to all states, and to create within the UN Secretariat a Center for Science and Technology for Development (CSTD) to provide substantive support to the committee and to coordinate activities within the UN system. In 1982, the General Assembly established the UN Financing System for Science and Technology for Development to finance a broad range of activities intended to strengthen the endogenous scientific and technological capacities of developing countries. In 1986, it transferred the responsibilities and resources of the financing system to a newly created UN Fund for Science and Technology for Development, administered by UNDP. In 1992, this new voluntary fund amounted to US$1.56 million and had funded six policy meetings in Cape Verde, Jamaica, Pakistan, Togo, Uganda, and Vietnam.

In 1989, on the tenth anniversary of the Vienna Conference, the General Assembly expressed its disappointment with the implementation of the Vienna Programme. As part of the effort to rationalize and reform the entire United Nations system, in April 1992, the General Assembly decided to transform the ISTD into a functional commission of ECOSOC, the Commission on Science and Technology for Development. The activities of the Centre for Science and Technology for Development were incorporated into the new Department of Economic and Social Development, within its Division of Science, Technology, Energy, Environment and Natural Resources.

Major objectives of the commission, which held its first session in April 1993, included:

(a) Assisting ECOSOC in providing science and technology policy guidelines and recommendations to member states, in particular developing countries;
(b) Providing innovative approaches to improving the quality of coordination and cooperation in the area of science and technology within the United Nations system, with a view to ensuring optimum mobilization of resources;
(c) Providing expert advice to other parts of the UN system.

The commission also requested that the Secretary-General prepare proposals to improve the coordination of the different bodies in the UN system, including the World Bank, which are involved in science and technology activities.

Developments, such as the United Nations Conference on Environment and Development in 1992—which had substantial science and technology components—and changing attitudes within intergovernmental bodies regarding the role of government and the private sector in view of the end of the cold war, led to the need for a major restructuring of the United Nations in the economic and social sector (including science and technology). While the General Assembly confirmed the continued validity of the Vienna Programme of Action in its resolution on science and technology for development in December 1993, its objectives were merged with the Technology Programme of the UN Conference on Trade and Development (UNCTAD). UNCTAD thus became responsible for science and technology within the United Nations system. Major program elements of the revised work program include:

(a) Endogenous capacity-building and resource mobilization in the area of science and technology for development;
(b) Technology assessment and information services;
(c) Issues related to investment and technology transfer.

The Commission on Science and Technology also decided to adopt themes for study by working groups during the two-year periods between its sessions. For 1993–95, these included technology for small-scale economic activities to address the basic needs of low-income populations, the gender implications of science and technology for developing countries, and the science and technology aspects of work being considered by the Commission

on Sustainable Development. The commission also considered studying a variety of other issues, including the role of technology in military conversion, the effect of new and emerging technologies on industrialization, and the role of information technologies in developing countries.

In October 1998, it was recommended that the membership of the Commission on Science and Technology for Development, along with three other subsidiaries of the Economic and Social Council, be reconstituted. The commission's membership was subsequently reduced from 53 to 33, with the following geographic distribution: eight members from African states; seven from Asian states; six from Latin America and the Caribbean; four from Eastern Europe; and eight from Western European and other states. The body remains a functional commission of the Council, with members holding office for four years.

At its Fourth Session, held in May 1999 in Geneva, the focus was on science and technology partnerships and networking for national capacity-building; particular attention was paid to biotechnology and energy. During the meeting, the commission discussed the concept of global entitlement to knowledge, the changing role of the state in the development of science and technology, and the role of networking and partnership in a multi-disciplinary approach to science and technology. In summarizing the proceedings, the moderator concluded that since sustainable development can be thought of as composed of economic growth, social equity, and an adequate use of the environment, and since government is viewed as a "key articulator" of these, the role of science and technology in the near future should be to establish reliable frameworks for consistent communication, effective forecasting, and the dissemination of knowledge.

Transnational Corporations

Since the end of World War II, the role of multinational or transnational corporations in international commerce has been growing, but information on their activities has been fragmentary and often closely held. Many of these corporations are household names. They conduct a large portion of their business outside their host country, often recruiting management from their overseas subsidiaries and recruiting shareholders around the world. Some of these corporations command resources greater than those of most governments represented at the UN. In 1989, estimated sales by foreign affiliates of transnationals worldwide were US$4.5 trillion. In comparison, world exports were only US$3 trillion. The relationship of transnational corporations with developing countries frequently has been troubled, but they can provide capital, managerial expertise, and technology that are all urgently required for development and often would be hard to come by in any other way.

In 1972, the Economic and Social Council requested the Secretary-General to appoint a group of eminent persons to study the impact of transnational corporations on development and international relations. The group of 20 economists, government officials, and corporation executives from all parts of the world met in 1973 and heard testimony from 50 witnesses in public hearings—a procedure new to the UN. Its report, issued in 1974, recommended the creation of a permanent commission on transnational corporations under the Economic and Social Council and an information and research center in the UN Secretariat.

In December 1974, the council established an intergovernmental Commission on Transnational Corporations as a standing committee (not a functional commission) to furnish a forum within the UN system regarding such corporations; promote an exchange of views about them among governments, intergovernmental organizations, business, labor, and consumers; assist the council in developing the basis for a code of conduct on the activities of transnational corporations; and develop a comprehensive information system on their activities.

The 48-member commission meets annually. At its second session, held in Lima in March 1976, it gave priority to the elaboration of a code of conduct and recommended that the Economic and Social Council establish an Intergovernmental Working Group on a Code of Conduct. The code was to be the first multilaterally agreed framework governing all aspects of the relations between states and transnational corporations, with standards to protect the interests of both the host countries and investors in those countries. The working group held a number of negotiating sessions between 1977 and 1982. Negotiations continued in meetings of a special session of the commission, open to all states.

In April 1991, the commission approved a text authorizing the preparation of recommendations on encouraging TNCs to cooperate in efforts to protect and enhance the environment in all countries for submission to the UN Conference on Environment and Development (UNCED) in 1992. The commission agreed that the following issues should be addressed: internationally agreed standards; improving management and regulation of industrial processes; transferring environmentally sound technologies to developing countries on favorable terms; using environment and development accounting and reporting methods; international environmental management; preventive measures to minimize risks to human life, property, and the environment; and the question of reparations for damage. It directed its secretariat, the Center on Transnational Corporations, to prepare its submission to UNCED. However, in early 1992, the center's functions were absorbed into a new department of the Secretariat and eventually transferred altogether to UNCTAD (see below).

At its 1994 Substantive Session, the commission recommended to ECOSOC that it be integrated into the institutional machinery of the UN Conference on Trade and Development (UNCTAD). ECOSOC decided to transmit this recommendation to the General Assembly for action.

An Intergovernmental Group of Experts on International Standards of Accounting and Reporting, established by the Economic and Social Council in 1982, reviews issues that give rise to divergent accounting and reporting practices of transnational corporations and identifies areas where efforts at harmonization appear necessary.

The four other priorities for the commission's program of work were: establishment of an information system to advance understanding of the nature of transnational corporations and their effects on home and host countries; research into the effects of their operations; technical assistance; and work leading to a more precise definition of the term *transnational corporations.*

The UN Center on Transnational Corporations was established by the Economic and Social Council in 1974 as part of the UN Secretariat. The functions of the center were to develop a comprehensive information system on the activities of transnational corporations, using data from governmental, corporate, and other sources; to analyze and disseminate the information to all governments; to provide technical assistance and strengthen the capacity of host countries (especially developing countries) in their dealings with transnational corporations; and to carry out political, legal, economic, and social research, particularly research to help in devising a code of conduct. By 1985, the center had established that the 350 largest transnational corporations (half of which were based in the United States) had combined sales of US$2.7 trillion, a sum which was larger than the combined GNP of all the developing countries, including China.

In 1990 ECOSOC requested the Center on Transnational Corporations to undertake a survey of corporate environmental management to document the most advanced practices as models for companies that had not yet created environmental programs and to submit the results to UNCED. The "Benchmark Corporate Environmental Survey," was submitted to the UNCED preparatory meeting in August 1991. Twenty percent of the 163 firms surveyed responded. The center recommended UNCED consider the following recommendations in preparing its Agenda 21: increased international cooperation to better inform TNCs of the impact of their operations on the greenhouse phenomenon; include TNCs in the consultative process surrounding climate change studies; treat dioxins and PCBs as international, not just local, pollution problems; transnational affiliates in developing countries should handle toxic wastes according to the same rules as in developed countries; TNCs should create safety zones around their facilities to lessen the potential impact of accidents; the oceans should be protected from land-based pollution; TNCs should sponsor programs to save wetlands and rainforests and protect biodiversity; TNCs should help develop a code of conduct on biotechnology. The center also pointed out that environmental rules and regulations differed from country to country. The companies that responded to the survey were interested in the UN setting international guidelines, although many of them were unaware of the existence of current international guidelines.

In 1992, as part of the comprehensive restructuring of the UN secretariat, the functions of the center were incorporated into a new unit: the Transnational Corporations and Management Division of the Department of Economic and Social Development. In May 1993, the General Assembly transferred responsibility for the transnational program again to the secretariat of UNCTAD.

In 2000, the UNCTAD Advisory Service on Investment and Technology, based on the joint work of the secretariat Divisions on Transnational Corporations and Investment and on Science and Technology, was working to help developing countries expand "their enterprise sector in conjunction with wider national trade, technology, and investment strategies." UNCTAD provided analysis of the role of the largest transnational corporations (TNCs) in foreign direct investment (viewed as critical to development) and emphasized that TNCs must exercise social responsibility in order to support sustainable development.

NATURAL RESOURCES AND ENERGY

The importance of natural resources for economic development was emphasized in 1970 when the Economic and Social Council established the Committee on Natural Resources. The committee develops guidelines for advisory services to governments, reviews arrangements to coordinate UN activities in natural resources development, and evaluates trends and issues concerning natural resources exploration and development, as well as prospects for selected energy, water, and mineral resources.

During the 1970s, the Committee on Natural Resources played an important role in focusing world attention on the status of the global stock of water resources to meet human, commercial, and agricultural needs. As a result of an initiative of the committee, the UN Water Conference was convened in 1977 in Mar del Plata, Argentina. The conference adopted an action plan to guide international efforts to effectively manage, develop, and use water resources. To give impetus to the Mar del Plata Action Plan, the General Assembly, in 1980, launched the International Drinking Water Supply and Sanitation Decade (1981–90).

In 1973, the General Assembly established the UN Revolving Fund for Natural Resources Exploration, which began operation in 1975. The fund, financed from voluntary contributions, is intended to provide additional risk capital for mineral exploration in developing countries. In 1981, the fund was authorized to extend its exploration activities to geothermal energy.

During the 1970s, with the rise in and volatility of costs for petroleum, affecting the economies of all countries, particularly those of the poorer countries, and the growing awareness that known supplies of petroleum would, in the long run, be unable to meet global requirements, more attention was focussed on new and renewable sources of energy. This led to the General Assembly's decision to convene, in Nairobi in August 1981, the UN Conference on New and Renewable Sources of Energy. The conference examined alternative forms of energy, including solar, biomass, geothermal, and ocean energy; wind power; hydropower; fuelwood and charcoal; peat; and the use of draft animals for energy purposes. It adopted the Nairobi Program of Action for the Development and Utilization of New and Renewable Sources of Energy as a blueprint for national and international action. The Nairobi Program identified five broad areas for concentrated action: energy assessment and planning; research, development, and demonstration; transfer, adaptation, and application of mature technologies; information flows; and education and training.

Endorsing the Nairobi Program later that year, the General Assembly set up an interim committee to launch immediate implementation and, in 1992, established the Committee on the Development and Utilization of New and Renewable Sources of Energy, open to the participation of all states as full members. Later in 1992, in response to the requirements of implementing UNCED's Agenda 21, this committee was combined with the energy portion of the Committee on Natural Resources and Energy, and became a new standing committee of ECOSOC: the Committee on New and Renewable Sources of Energy and on Energy for Development. The Committee on Natural Resources now concentrates mainly on water and mineral resources. Each committee has a membership of 24 government-nominated experts who are elected by ECOSOC.

The first session of the new Committee on New and Renewable Resources and Energy met in New York from 7–18 February 1994. The Secretary-General reported to the committee that in 1990 new and renewable energy sources accounted for 17.7% of the total energy consumption. The drop in oil prices during the 1980s had led to a decline in investment in renewable energy resources, but growing concern for the fragile state of the world's environment lent urgency to efforts to find alternatives to burning fossil fuels and wood, which were contributing to the threat of global warning.

At its first session, the committee noted that the Nairobi Program had led to progress in the application of large-scale technologies, such as hydropower and geothermal energy, and had helped bring to maturity solar energy and wind technologies. However, the overall impact of these new technologies remained insignificant. The committee identified four domains for action by member states: more efficient use of energy and energy-intensive material; increased use of renewable sources of energy; more efficient production and use of fossil fuels; and fuel substitution from high carbon to low carbon-based fuels. It also called for integrated national action programs for developing energy systems; for removing subsidies on conventional sources of energy; establishing support for new, environmentally sound technologies; and finding ways to use wasted energy, such as waste heat from industrial processes. Its report to ECOSOC also recommended the establishment of regional "centers of excellence" to provide training, technology support, and resource data.

Another positive development in this field in the 1990s was the increasing recognition by the World Bank and the International Monetary Fund (IMF) that energy conservation makes good economic and environmental sense. Public outcry over displacement of local populations by big dams and destruction of rain forests for grazing projects funded by the World Bank had led it to institute an environmental assessment on every project it undertook. In 1992 the IMF also began to study the impact of its policies on its member nations' environment. The bank also branched out into supporting new sources of energy, for example by lending Mauritius us$15 million to support a program to generate 10–20% of that nation's future energy needs by burning sugar-cane waste product readily available in that country.

Addressing another important area in the energy field—the use of nuclear energy for the economic and social development of developing countries—the General Assembly, in 1977, set in motion arrangements for an international conference on the subject. The first global effort in this field, the UN Conference for the Promotion of International Cooperation in the Peaceful Uses of Nuclear Energy, was held in Geneva in 1987. Although unable to reach agreement on principles acceptable to all, the participants at the conference exchanged views and experience on topics ranging from the production of electricity to the various applications of nuclear techniques in food and agriculture, medicine, hydrology, research, and industry.

The first session of the newly reconstituted Committee on Natural Resources was held in early 1993. Its second session met in New York in early 1994. In the 1990s the focus of the Committee on Natural Resources became the implementation of the recommendations of Agenda 21, particularly measures to promote the more rational and sustainable use of natural resources. In the chairman's summary of the meeting, he noted that mineral and water resources had to be seen as finite and valuable resources, and that their production and consumption affected other constituents of the environment. Therefore, a holistic approach was required to the planning and management of natural resources within the geographical boundaries of each country and also in the consideration of the global impact of national policies or measures. A continued call was made for integrated approaches to water and land management. The committee emphasized the need to consider natural resources as a whole, rather than by individual sectors, such as agriculture and industry.

The committee also noted that the fundamental importance of mineral resources to economic development and quality of life had not been adequately reflected in Agenda 21. It recommended that the need to ensure the sustainable supply of minerals should be a key issue for deliberations on Agenda 21.

The committee's discussion on mineral resources was influenced by the impact of privatization of state mineral enterprises on people in the developing countries and economies in transition. While there seemed to be a new trend toward closer understanding between these countries and transnational corporations, the committee stated that governments should promote measures to reduce destruction of the environment from private mining operations. It also recommended that governments promote measures to encourage better use of existing resources through recycling and substitution.

In 1998 the Committee on New and Renewable Sources of Energy and on Energy for Development and the Committee on Natural Resources were merged into one expert body—the Committee on Energy and Natural Resources for Development, which serves as a subsidiary body of ECOSOC. The new committee, which meets biennially for two weeks, is made up of two subgroups of 12 experts each; one sub-group deals with energy and the other with water resources. The geographical distribution of the 24 members is: six members from African States; five from Asia; four from Latin American and the Caribbean; three from Eastern Europe; and six from Western European and other states. The term of office is four years.

The reconstituted committee met for the first time in April 1999, during which it worked to prepare a draft paper for the next, eighth, session of the Commission on Sustainable Development. The committee had before it various reports from the Secretary-General, including: a report on environmentally sound and efficient fossil energy technologies, which highlighted the need to increase efficiency of fossil energy use, improve environmental compatibility of fossil technologies, and shift to fossil fuels with lower environmental impacts, such as natural gas; the report on renewable sources of energy, which emphasized wind energy and stressed the importance of continued research and development in this area; the report on rural energy policies, which stated that service to rural areas remains inadequate (of the estimated 3.1 billion people in rural areas, approximately 2 billion had no access to electricity); the report on energy and transportation, which reviewed global transportation trends in both developed and developing nations; and the report on spatial planning of land (including minerals) and water resources, which identified emerging issues and highlighted the finite nature of the earth's resources.

REGIONAL COMMISSIONS

The five regional commissions—serving Europe, Asia and the Pacific, Latin America and the Caribbean, Africa, and Western Asia—have been established by the Economic and Social Council in recognition of the fact that many economic and social problems are best approached at the regional level. The commissions work to raise the level of economic and social development activity in their respective regions, as well as to maintain and strengthen relations among countries within and outside regions. All actions taken by the commissions are intended to fit within the framework of overall UN economic and social policies. The commissions also are empowered, with the agreement of the governments concerned, to make recommendations directly to member governments and to the specialized agencies.

The commissions are subsidiary organs of the Economic and Social Council, to which they report annually. The secretariats of the commissions—each headed by an executive secretary with the rank of undersecretary-general—are integral parts of the UN staff, and their budgets form part of the regular UN budget.

An important part of the work of all the regional commissions is the preparation of regional studies and surveys, particularly annual economic and social surveys that are published at the headquarters of each commission. Supplementing these are bulletins and periodicals covering a wide range of subjects—such as agriculture, population, transportation and communications, energy, industry, and housing and construction—that are widely used as sources of information by governments, business and industry, educational institutions, other UN organs, and the press.

In the early 1990s, under pressure from both developing and industrialized countries to reform and rationalize the scattered development activities of the United Nations system, Secretary-General Boutros Boutros-Ghali proposed that the activities of all United Nations organs be coordinated. In December 1992, the General Assembly adopted his proposal with its historic Resolution A/47/199 that stressed the need for development activities to "be streamlined and rationalized, especially in the interrelated areas of programming, execution, decentralization, monitoring and evaluation, thus making the UN system more relevant and responsive to the national plans, priorities and objectives of developing countries, and more efficient in its delivery systems." Under this plan, many of the functions carried out by various committees and boards of the specialized agencies and UN funds were transferred away from headquarters (in New York, or, in the case of the specialized agencies, Geneva or Vienna), to the regional commissions (headquartered in major cities of each region) and the office of the UNDP resident coordinator in the specific countries that were to be served by development programs. As this strategy developed, the role of the regional commissions became more and more central to the work of the United Nations system.

Economic Commission for Europe (ECE)

The Economic Commission for Europe (ECE), with headquarters in Geneva, was established in 1947 to help mobilize concerted action for the economic reconstruction of postwar Europe and to increase European economic activity among countries both within and outside the region. To these goals was added that of providing governments with economic, technological, and statistical information. Begun as an experiment at a time when severe postwar shortages of some commodities and surpluses of others made economic cooperation in Europe a necessity, ECE soon became the only multilateral forum to deal with cooperation between Eastern and Western Europe. The ECE provides a systematic means of intergovernmental cooperation among the countries of Europe, the United States, Canada, Israel, and the republics of the former Soviet Union.

ECE priority objectives include the development of trade, scientific and technical cooperation, improvement of the environment, and long-term planning and projections as a basis for formulation of economic policy. Through meetings of policymakers and experts, publication of economic analyses and statistics, and study tours and exchanges of technical information, the commission provides a link between governments having different economic and social systems and belonging to different subregional organizations.

Plenary meetings of the commission are held annually; its subsidiary organs meet throughout the year.

ECE works closely with a number of specialized agencies, particularly the ILO and FAO; with other intergovernmental organizations; and with nongovernmental organizations, which ECE has consulted frequently for their expertise in particular subjects.

The analytical work of the ECE provides both a macro- and micro-economic picture of the state of the region. It publishes statistical bulletins and special reports on the state of markets in industry, timber, and human settlements. It has also published guides for the management of joint ventures, privatization and conditions for foreign direct investment.

The network of committees and working parties mentioned above carries on the ECE's technical cooperation work. The ECE has formulated regionwide strategies and legal instruments in the fields of environment and transportation. One of its most significant accomplishments is the establishment of a standard for electronic data interchange (the UN/EDIFACT or United Nations Electronic Data Interchange for Administration, Commerce and Transport). This international standard for communication between networks of computers paves the way for the development of paperless international trade in the twenty-first century.

The events of 1989–91, during which the entire face of Europe changed beyond recognition, provided enormous challenges for the ECE. War in the former Yugoslavia and the resulting economic sanctions and displacement of 3 million people made a somber picture. The ECE provided technical cooperation to the countries of Eastern Europe in transition to a market economy. By 1994, these countries made up fully one-half of its expanded membership. Hundreds of workshops on transition issues were conducted by the ECE in these countries in 1994 and 1995. The program of workshops was supplemented by the introduction of regional advisory services in each of the ECE's major fields of activity.

Membership. As of September 1999, the following countries were members of ECE: Albania, Andorra, Armenia, Austria, Azerbaijan, Belarus, Belgium, Bosnia and Herzegovina, Bulgaria, Canada, Croatia, Cyprus, Czech Republic, Denmark, Estonia, Finland, France, Georgia, Germany, Greece, Hungary, Iceland, Ireland, Israel, Italy, Kazakhstan, Kyrgyzstan, Latvia, Liechtenstein, Lithuania, Luxembourg, Malta, Monaco, Netherlands, Norway, Poland, Portugal, Republic of Moldova, Romania, Russian Federation, San Marino, Slovakia, Slovenia, Spain, Sweden, Switzerland, Tajikistan, the Former Yugoslav Republic of Macedonia, Turkey, Turkmenistan, Ukraine, United Kingdom, United States, Uzbekistan, and Yugoslavia.

Economic and Social Commission for Asia and the Pacific (ESCAP)

The Economic and Social Commission for Asia and the Pacific (ESCAP), with headquarters in Bangkok, Thailand, and a Pacific Operations Center based in Port Vila, Vanuatu, serves a region that contains more than half the world's population. It was established in 1947 as the Economic Commission for Asia and the Far East to promote reconstruction and economic development of the region. Its name was changed in 1974 to reflect equal concern with economic growth and social progress and to clarify its geographic scope. The commission meets annually.

ESCAP's activities help identify common problems and facilitate cooperation for economic and social development at the regional level. It provides technical assistance and advisory services to governments on request, carries out research on regional issues, and acts as a clearinghouse of information.

One of ESCAP's most significant meetings in the 1990s was the Fourth Asian and Pacific Population Conference (Bali, August 1992). The conference was cosponsored by ESCAP and UNFPA, in recognition of the fact that population issues were inextricably linked to the cycles of poverty and the struggle for development. The conference adopted the Declaration on Population and Development (known as the "Bali Declaration"). By this declaration, ESCAP's member countries set goals for themselves to adopt strategies to attain replacement-level fertility (around 2.2 children per woman) by the year 2010 or sooner. They also agreed to reduce the level of infant mortality to 40 per thousand live births or lower by the same time.

In the late 1990s, with more than 50 years of experience, ESCAP described itself as a regional think tank and acknowledged that its ultimate challenge lay in bringing some 830 million of the region's poor into the economic mainstream, "enabling everybody to achieve a better standard of life as envisaged in the Charter of the United Nations."

Membership. As of 1999, the 51 member states of ESCAP were: Afghanistan, Armenia, Australia, Azerbaijan, Bangladesh, Bhutan, Brunei Darussalam, Cambodia, China, Democratic People's Republic of Korea, Fiji, France, India, Indonesia, Islamic Republic of Iran, Japan, Kazakhstan, Kiribati, Kyrgyzstan, Lao People's Democratic Republic, Malaysia, Maldives, Marshall Islands, Micronesia (Federated States of), Mongolia, Myanmar, Nauru, Nepal, Netherlands, New Zealand, Pakistan, Palau, Papua New Guinea, Philippines, Republic of Korea, Russian Federation, Samoa, Singapore, Solomon Islands, Sri Lanka, Tajikistan, Thailand, Tonga, Turkey, Turkmenistan, Tuvalu, United Kingdom of Great Britain and Northern Ireland, United States of America, Uzbekistan, Vanuatu, and Vietnam. It also had nine associate members: American Samoa, Guam, New Caledonia, Cook Islands, Hong Kong (China), Niue, French Polynesia, Macao (China), and Northern Mariana Islands.

Economic Commission for Latin America and the Caribbean (ECLAC)

The Economic Commission for Latin America and the Caribbean (ECLAC), with headquarters in Santiago, Chile, was established in 1948 as the Economic Commission for Latin America. In 1983, it formally incorporated the Caribbean region into its name. ECLAC's aim is to help the governments of the region promote the economic development of their countries and improve living standards. To this end, it collaborates with the governments of the region in the investigation and analysis of regional and national economic problems, and provides assistance in the formulation of development plans. It organizes and convenes regional intergovernmental meetings on topics in the field of economic and social development. ECLAC conducts research, executes studies, disseminates information, provides technical assistance, participates in seminars and conferences, and gives training courses.

ECLAC's initial stress on economic growth and trade was later complemented with emphasis on employment, income distribution, and other social aspects of development. In recent years, the commission has expanded its activities to include research in such areas as the environment, the development and transfer of technology, and the role of transnational corporations.

In 1999, ECLAC had divisions and units dealing with the following: planning and operations; economic development; social development; international trade and finance development; production, productivity, and management; statistics and economic projections; environment and human settlements; and natural resources and infrastructure. It also had a documents and publications division. ECLAC also has two sub-regional headquarters (in Mexico and Port of Spain), and offices in Bogota, Brasilia, Buenos Aires, Montevideo, and Washington, D.C.

ECLAC meets biennially; a committee of the whole carries on intersessional work.

Two other organizations are part of the ECLAC system: the Latin American and Caribbean Institute for Economic and Social Planning (ILPES) in Santiago, Chile; and the Latin American Demographic Center (CELADE), also in Santiago. ILPES was established in 1962 and undertakes research and provides training and advisory services, as well as furthering cooperation among the planning services of the region. CELADE was established in 1957, but became an integral part of the commission in 1975. It collaborates with governments in formulating population policies and provides demographic estimates and projections, documentation, data processing, and training facilities.

The commission carries out its work in close cooperation with UNDP, the International Trade Center (UNCTAD/GATT), UNESCO, the International Maritime Organization (IMO), UNICEF, and the International Telecommunications Union (ITU).

Membership. As of 1999, ECLAC had 41 members: Antigua and Barbuda, Argentina, Bahamas, Barbados, Belize, Bolivia, Brazil, Canada, Chile, Colombia, Costa Rica, Cuba, Dominica, Dominican Republic, Ecuador, El Salvador, France, Grenada, Guatemala, Guyana, Haiti, Honduras, Italy, Jamaica, Mexico, Netherlands, Nicaragua, Panama, Paraguay, Peru, Portugal, Saint Kitts and Nevis, Saint Lucia, Saint Vincent and the Grenadines, Spain, Suriname, Trinidad and Tobago, United Kingdom of Great Britain and Northern Ireland, United States of America, Uruguay, and Venezuela. It also had seven associate members: Anguilla, Aruba, British Virgin Islands, Montserrat, Netherlands Antilles, Puerto Rico, and United States Virgin Islands.

Economic Commission for Africa (ECA)

The Economic Commission for Africa, with headquarters in Addis Ababa, Ethiopia, was established in 1958. It was the first intergovernmental organization in Africa whose geographical scope covered the whole of a continent in which economic and social conditions differed widely and where many countries and dependent territories were among the poorest in the world. ECA's chief objective is the modernization of Africa, with emphasis on both rural development and industrialization. Its work has been marked by a sense of urgency and a determination to match the rapid pace of African political progress with economic and social progress. In carrying out its functions, ECA works closely with the Organization of African Unity and various organizations of the UN system.

The commission's sessions are held annually at the ministerial level and are known as the Conference of Ministers.

The approach of ECA is primarily at the level of its four subregions: North Africa, Eastern and Southern Africa, Central Africa, and West Africa. ECA members have made it clear that the subregional approach is to be regarded as a necessary first step and that pan-African economic integration remains the goal. For that reason, five multinational programming and operational centers were established: in Tangier, Morroco, for North Africa; in Niamey, Niger, for West Africa; in Lusaka, Zambia, for Eastern and Southern Africa; in Yaounde, Cameroon, for Central Africa; and a fifth center for the countries of Rwanda, Burundi, and Zaire in Gisenyi, Rwanda.

Work priorities for the 1990s and beyond included the broadened concept of food security and poverty alleviation through sustainable development with emphasis on capacity building; the promotion of economic cooperation among African countries and between African and other developing countries; the physical integration of the continent in line with the goals of the UN Transport and Communications Decade for Africa (1991–2000); and greater control and sovereignty over natural resources and environment. In the field of industrial development, ECA implemented the UN Second Industrial Development Decade in Africa (IDDA) by strengthening the technological and entrepreneurial capabilities of African countries. Special attention was paid to subregional and regional cooperation in small-scale cottage and rural industries and to highly advanced technology.

In 1992 ECA issued a technical publication evaluating the impact of the 1992 European economic integration measures on African agriculture. The publication discussed the various factors underlying the European single market. The publication underscored the need for galvanizing the cooperation of African nations in the face of moves to strengthen economic integration in other regions, notably Europe and North America. ECA also consulted with the OAU and the African Development Bank on the establishment and functioning of an African Economic Community (AEC).

ECA supervised the African Training and Research Centre for Women, which assisted ECA member states in improving the socioeconomic conditions of African women and enhancing their participation in development. ECA pursued its efforts to establish a regional Federation of African Women Entrepreneurs and a Bank for African Women to support women's entrepreneurial activities. ECA developed a Pan-African Development Information System that provides training, advisory services, data base development, and network-building, and produces studies and publications for ECA member states, institutions, and nongovernmental organizations.

Beginning in July 1995, ECA embarked on major institutional and managerial reforms, resulting in a new strategic focus, which it defined by five core programs and two cross-cutting themes. The core programs were facilitating economic and social policy analysis; ensuring food security and sustainable development; strengthening development management; harnessing information for development; and promoting regional cooperation and integration. The themes were: fostering leadership and empowerment for women in Africa and enhancement of ECA capacities (with regard to information and technology, staff training, communication, and public awareness of programs through the mass media).

Membership. As of 1999, the following countries were members of ECA: Algeria, Angola, Benin, Botswana, Burkina Faso, Burundi, Cameroon, Cape Verde, Central African Republic, Chad, Comores, Côte d'Ivoire, Democratic Republic of the Congo, Djibouti, Egypt, Eritrea, Ethiopia, Gabon, Gambia, Ghana, Guinea, Guinea-Bissau, Equatorial Guinea, Kenya, Lesotho, Liberia, Libya, Madagascar, Malawi, Mali, Mauritania, Mauritius, Morocco, Mozambique, Namibia, Nigeria, Republic of the Congo, Rwanda, São Tomé and Principe, Senegal, Seychelles, Sierra Leone, Somalia, South Africa, Sudan, Swaziland, Togo, Tunisia, Uganda, United Republic of Tanzania, Zambia, and Zimbabwe.

Economic and Social Commission for Western Asia (ESCWA)

A regional economic commission for the Middle East was first proposed in 1947–48. A commission that would include the Arab nations and Israel proved to be out of the question, however, and in 1963, the UN Economic and Social Office in Beirut (UNESOB) was set up. For 11 years, UNESOB assisted governments in economic and social development and provided them with consultants in such fields as community development, demography, industrial development planning, and statistics.

In 1972, Lebanon revived the issue of a regional commission for the area, and in August 1973, the Economic and Social Council established the Economic Commission for Western Asia to supersede UNESOB. In 1984, it was renamed the Economic and Social Commission for Western Asia (ESCWA) to reflect the importance of the social aspect of its activities.

The commission began operations on 1 January 1974, with provisional headquarters in Beirut. As defined by the resolution establishing the commission, its task is to initiate and participate in measures for facilitating concerted action for the economic reconstruction and development of Western Asia, for raising the region's level of economic activity, and for maintaining and strengthening the economic relations of countries of the region both among themselves and with other countries of the world.

ESCWA undertakes or sponsors studies of economic and social issues in the region, collects and disseminates information, and provides advisory services at the request of countries of the region on ESCWA's fields of activities. Much of ESCWA's work is carried out in cooperation with other UN bodies. The commissions conducts industrial studies for individual countries in conjunction with UNIDO. It cooperates with FAO in regional planning, food security, and management of agricultural resources. UNDP supports ESCWA's work on household surveys in Western Asia and the Arab Planning Institute in Kuwait. Work is also undertaken with UNFPA and UNIFEM in population and women's programs, with ILO in statistical surveys on labor, with AGFUND in rural development, with UNCTAD in development planning and maritime transport training, with UNEP in integrating environmental aspects (particularly control of desertification) into development programs, and with OIC in natural resources, industry, and trade issues.

The sessions of the commission (held every two years) are attended by representatives of member states and bodies, UN bodies and specialized agencies, regional and intergovernmental organizations, and other states attending as observers.

In 1992, the commission called for the establishment of an Arab and international interagency coordinating committee on environment and development to promote the goals of the UN Conference on Environment and Development's (UNCED) Agenda 21.

In May 1994, during the Commission's seventeenth ministerial session in Amman, ESCWA member states voted to move the permanent headquarters to Beirut. The 8-story UN house was built in the Beirut Central District for this purpose.

ESCWA maintains close liaison with other UN organs and specialized agencies and with intergovernmental organizations in the region, such as the League of Arab States and the Arab Fund for Economic and Social Development.

In 1976, ESCWA decided to move its operations to Amman, Jordan, for one year because of the conflict in Lebanon. Later the same year, it decided to accept the offer of the government of Iraq for Baghdad to be the site of its permanent headquarters. It moved to Baghdad in 1982, only to relocate to Amman during the Gulf War between Iraq and Kuwait in 1991. ESCWA had established six working committees by the late 1990s; they were: statistical, social development, energy, water resources, transport, and liberalization of foreign trade and economic globalization.

Membership. As of 1999, there were 13 members of ESCWA: Bahrain, Egypt, Iraq, Jordan, Kuwait, Lebanon, Oman, Palestine (Palestine Liberation Organization), Qatar, Saudi Arabia, Syria, United Arab Emirates, and Yemen.

TECHNICAL COOPERATION PROGRAMS

The International Development Strategy for the third UN Development Decade called for a renewed emphasis on technical cooperation and a significant increase in the resources provided for this purpose. It recognized that technical cooperation contributes to the efforts of developing countries to achieve self-reliance by facilitating and supporting investment, research, and training, among other things.

UN programs of technical cooperation may be grouped in three categories: (1) the UN regular program, financed under the portion of the UN regular budget set aside for technical cooperation activities; (2) activities funded by the UN Development Programme (UNDP); and (3) extrabudgetary activities financed by contributions provided directly to the executing agencies by multilateral funding organizations within or outside the UN system, other than UNDP, and by contributions from governments and nongovernmental organizations.

To consolidate the responsibilities and resources within the UN Secretariat in support of technical cooperation activities, the UN General Assembly in March 1978 set up the Department of Technical Cooperation for Development (DTCD). In 1993, under further restructuring of the United Nations, this became the Department for Development Support and Management Services (DDSMS).

DDSMS provides technical and managerial support and advisory services to member states of the UN, relevant research, and parliamentary services to expert groups and intergovernmental bodies. It has a twofold mandate: (i) it acts as an executing agency for programs and projects relating to institution-building and human resource development in areas such as development policies and planning, natural resources and energy planning, governance and public management, and financial management and accounting; (ii) it acts as a focal point for the provision of management services and implementation functions for technical cooperation.

UNITED NATIONS DEVELOPMENT PROGRAMME (UNDP)

Since its earliest days, the UN system has been engaged in a growing effort that has two main thrusts. The first, and most important, is supporting the vigorous drive of the world's developing countries to provide their own people with the essentials of a decent life—including adequate nutrition, housing, employment, income, education, health care, consumer goods, and public services. The second aim, which is closely related, is to help these countries increase their output of commodities, raw materials, and manufactured items, which the world increasingly needs, as well as to ensure them a fair return.

The United Nations Development Programme (UNDP) is the UN's major arm—and the world's largest channel—for international technical cooperation for development provided on a grant basis. Working with the government of nearly every country—and with more than 30 international agencies—UNDP supports the development efforts of 175 countries and territories in Africa, Asia and the Pacific, Latin America and the Caribbean, the Arab states, and Europe and the Commonwealth of Independent States. Under the overall framework of "sustainable human development," the programs it supports focus primarily on building national capacities to eliminate poverty, protect and regenerate the environment, create employment, and empower women. The ultimate goal is to improve the quality of human life.

Evolution of UNDP

Although UNDP came into formal existence only in January 1966, it really began 20 years earlier, for it grew out of two long-established UN institutions.

In 1948, the UN General Assembly (GA) had decided to appropriate funds under its regular budget to enable the UN Secretary-General to supply teams of experts, offer fellowships, and organize seminars to assist national development projects at the request of governments. About the same time, many of the specialized agencies had begun to undertake similar projects. However, no sooner had the Regular Programs of Technical Assistance, as they were called, begun to operate than it became apparent that the money that could be spared from the regular budget would not meet demand. In 1949, the General Assembly set up a separate account for voluntary contributions toward technical assistance and decided to make it a central account to finance the activities not only of the UN itself but also of the specialized agencies. Machinery was established for distributing financial resources and coordinating projects, and the whole enterprise was called the Expanded Programme of Technical Assistance (EPTA), to distinguish it from the UN's technical assistance financed under the regular budget. The venture proved remarkably successful. Ten years after it had begun operations, EPTA was financing technical assistance in some 140 countries and territories. Between 1950 and 1960, the number of governments contributing funds had grown from 54 to 85, and the total annual contributions had risen from $10 million to $33.8 million.

In 1958, the General Assembly felt that it would be desirable to broaden the scope of UN technical assistance to include large-scale preinvestment surveys and feasibility studies on major national development projects that would lay the groundwork for subsequent investment of capital. These surveys and studies involved a much greater financial outlay than the kind of technical assistance then being undertaken, and the General Assembly decided to set up a new institution that would be run along lines similar to those of EPTA. Thus, the Special Fund was established to act as a multilateral channel for voluntary contributions to preinvestment projects, and as a coordinating center for the work of the various UN agencies. The Special Fund began operations in 1959; within three years, 86 governments had pledged over $110 million.

In January 1964, the Secretary-General formally proposed to the Economic and Social Council that EPTA and the Special Fund be merged into a single enterprise. The advantages to be derived from the merger were a pooling of resources, a simplification of procedures, improvement in overall planning, elimination of duplication, reduction in administrative costs, and a general strengthening of UN development aid. By August 1964, the Council had adopted recommendations for the merger, but because of the stalemate at the 1964 General Assembly, no action could be taken until the following year. On 22 November 1965, the General Assembly unanimously voted to consolidate the two operations, effective 1 January 1966, as the United Nations Development Programme.

Structure and Organization

Administrator and Executive Board. UNDP is headed by an administrator, appointed by the UN Secretary-General and confirmed by the General Assembly, who is responsible to a 36-nation Executive Board for all aspects of program operations. The board—representing every geographical region and both contributor and program countries—reports to the General Assembly through the Economic and Social Council. In addition to setting overall policy guidelines, the Executive Board examines and approves the volume of assistance allocated to each country over successive five-year cycles and must similarly approve all country programs. (The Executive Board began its work in 1994, replacing the 48-nation UNDP/UNFPA Governing Council, which had a similar composition and function. The Governing Council's decision-making almost always took place by "consensus" rather than by recorded voting.)

Regional Bureaus. Regional bureaus, located at UN headquarters, cover Africa, Asia and the Pacific, Latin America and the Caribbean, and the Arab states. There is also a Division for Europe and the Commonwealth of Independent States. These offices serve as the administrator's principal links with the program countries. Together with bureaus or divisions for strategic planning, program policy and evaluation, program development and support, and finance and administration, they furnish UNDP's country-based Resident Representatives with day-to-day operational support.

Resident Representatives. Resident Representatives heading 128 program country offices function as field-level leaders of the UN development system. They are responsible for seeing that UNDP-assisted country programs are carried out effectively and efficiently. They act as chief liaison officers between government planning authorities and the executing agencies, help blueprint all activities from formulation to follow-up, and are responsible for ensuring that personnel, equipment, and facilities are utilized to best advantage.

Resident Representatives and other staff in UNDP's country offices also perform a variety of non-project-related development activities that make a significant contribution to UNDP's goals, and to the needs of its national partners. These include engaging in policy dialogue with national officials and providing them with development planning advice; furnishing technical advisory and general problem-solving services, often at the request of concerned sectoral ministries; assisting in mobilizing investment from both internal and external sources, as well as with follow-up investment advice and services; acting as a focal point for government needs in emergencies caused by natural or man-made disasters; assisting in the formulation, management, and evaluation of UNDP country programs; and, upon request, participating in the coordination of external assistance from other sources and in the preparation of well-balanced, effective national development programs.

Training and other support is offered on issues of special concern: UNDP's Division for Gender in Development helps to ensure that programs consider women's needs and interests; the Division for Nongovernmental Organizations promotes increased participation of NGOs and community groups in development activities; the Environment and Natural Resources Group ensures that the environmental impact of all programs is weighed; the Short-Term Advisory Services program sends skilled advisers to provide top-level technical and managerial advice in such sectors as agriculture, transportation, and industry.

Functions and Guiding Principles

The nature of UNDP and its activities has changed over the years.

In part, this has been in response to the evolving requirements and interests of the program countries. The changes also have reflected global concerns for particular development problems and issues.

In the early 1970s, UNDP had to demonstrate its ability to replace a basic structure, which had served it well in its formative stages, with a "second generation" mechanism designed to determine the nature of UNDP's market with greater discrimination, and to deliver the required product with more efficiency. The cumulative impact of a number of intensive inquiries into development and development assistance—by the Pearson Commission, the UN Committee for Development Planning, Sir Robert Jackson's study of the capacity of the UN development system, and by some of the major donor countries individually—helped to fashion a new look for UNDP. The various studies agreed on needs for more deliberate matching of country requests for assistance with available resources; the introduction of forward and coordinated planning and programming; more careful and appropriate project design; and greater quality, timeliness, and efficiency of implementation.

The consideration of these matters by the UNDP Governing Council in 1970 produced a consensus on the future of UNDP that was endorsed by the General Assembly in the same year, translated into organizational and procedural changes in 1971, and brought substantially into effect during the next few years. The pivotal change was the introduction of "country programming." This involved the forward programming of UNDP assistance at the country level for periods of up to five years, identification of the role UNDP inputs would play in specified areas related to a country's development objectives, and the phasing of these inputs. Country programming, together with a similar approach to regional, interregional, and global activities, is designed to achieve the most rational and efficient utilization of resources.

A necessary counterpart to the introduction of UNDP country programming was administrative reform. The most important change involved decentralization—a substantial shift of power and responsibility for effective UNDP technical cooperation at all stages away from headquarters and into the program countries, where the UNDP Resident Representatives often play a lead role in UN development system activities within a country. Guidelines for the selection of these officials imply that, first and foremost, they should be effective managers, for it is they who cooperate directly with the governments to ensure the smooth functioning of development programs. In addition, they must intervene to help ensure more efficient implementation and more effective use of the results of project assistance. Upon request, they must be ready to play a vital part in the coordination of assistance from other sources with that provided by UNDP. In fact, under the restructuring of the UN development system mandated by the General Assembly, most UNDP Resident Representatives also are designated by the UN Secretary-General as Resident Coordinators of all UN operational assistance for development.

In 1975, UNDP further revised its programming principles to include "new dimensions" in technical cooperation, designed primarily to foster greater self-sufficiency among developing countries by relying more heavily on their own skills and expertise for development activities. Accordingly, UNDP redefined its role in technical cooperation to stress results achieved, rather than inputs required from the industrialized nations.

Seen from this perspective, the purpose of technical cooperation is to promote increasing autonomy with regard to the managerial, technical, administrative, and research capabilities required to formulate and implement development plans in the light of options available.

In the 1990s, UNDP made other changes that had a substantial impact on its programming, as well as on development thinking in general. In 1990 the Governing Council directed UNDP to focus its activities on six themes: poverty eradication and grass roots participation; environment and natural resources management; technical cooperation among developing countries (TCDC); management development; transfer and adaptation of technology; and women in development. UNDP has also adopted a "program approach," whereby funding is provided for comprehensive programs with integrated components rather than distinct, separate projects. This enables UNDP to deliver assistance that is more focused and has greater impact and sustainability.

Another change has been UNDP's promotion of "human development," which puts people at the center of development, enlarging their choices and creating opportunities through which they can realize their potential and express their creativity. Human development does not measure a country's progress solely by its Gross National Product, but takes into account such factors as its people's access to health services, level of education, and purchasing power. Since 1990 UNDP has stimulated debate about this concept through the publication of an annual Human Development Report, written by an independent team of development specialists and published by Oxford University Press. Since then, a growing number of countries have received UNDP assistance in incorporating human development concerns into planning and the allocation of budgets.

Linking human development with its traditional emphasis on building self-reliance, UNDP has now embraced the concept of "sustainable human development" as the guiding principle underlying all its work. As defined by UNDP's administrator, James Gustave Speth, who took office in July 1993:

> "Sustainable human development is development that not only generates economic growth but distributes its benefits equitably; that regenerates the environment rather than destroying it; that empowers people rather than marginalizing them. It gives priority to the poor, enlarging their choices and opportunities and providing for their participation in decisions affecting them. It is development that is pro-poor, pro-nature, pro-jobs and pro-women. In sum, sustainable human development stresses growth, but growth with employment, environment, empowerment and equity."

Within this framework, UNDP has identified three priority goals: (1) strengthening international cooperation for sustainable human development and serving as a substantive resource on how to achieve it; (2) building developing countries' capacities for sustainable human development; and (3) helping the United Nations become a powerful, unified force for sustainable human development.

From its inception, UNDP has been called upon to make its assistance available to all countries where it can be effective in helping to meet priority needs, provided that those countries are members of the UN or one of its affiliated agencies. This broad frame of reference is essential for protecting two of UNDP's most valuable assets—its universality and its large measure of freedom from political problems and pressures.

Planning and Programming

In the planning and programming of UNDP assistance, the largest role is played by the developing countries themselves. The process involves three basic steps.

First, an estimate is made of the core financial resources expected to be available to UNDP over a five-year period. This estimate is then divided up into Indicative Planning Figures (IPFs) for each country assisted, and for regional, interregional, and global programs. The IPFs are approved, and adjusted from time to time, by UNDP's Executive Board.

Second, with its IPF as a guide, each government draws up a "country program," outlining its priorities for UNDP assistance

and allocating its share of UNDP resources among those priorities. Country program formulation—in which the UNDP's Resident Representative and locally based officials of other UN agencies usually participate—takes a number of factors into account. Among these are a country's overall development plans, the domestic resources that it can call upon for carrying out those plans, and the assistance expected from external sources other than UNDP. Each country program is then submitted to the Executive Board for approval.

The third step involves preparation of individual project requests—again usually in consultation with advisers from the UN system. These requests delineate each project's main objectives, its duration, its cost, and the respective responsibilities of the government and the UN system.

Allocation of Funds

UNDP IPFs for 1972–76, the first programming cycle, were largely determined by applying the same percentage of total UNDP resources actually committed to each country from 1967 through 1971 to the total of projected UNDP resources for the years 1972 through 1976.

Completely new criteria were established by the Governing Council for the 1977–81 "second cycle." Of the country programming resources expected to be available during those years, 92.5% was allocated largely on the basis of a formula involving each country's population and its per capita gross national product (GNP)—with this second factor being given somewhat greater weight in calculating each country's allocation.

Under the new criteria, about 13% of total resources was devoted to regional programs aimed at fostering development cooperation among neighboring countries or at achieving economies by making expertise available to several governments from a single regional base. There was also a separate IPF for global and interregional programs, such as "breakthrough" research on high-yielding strains of staple food grains.

On an overall basis, during the third cycle (1982–86), countries with per capita GNPs of $500 a year or less received 80% of total UNDP funding, as compared with 52% in the 1977–81 period and 40% in the 1971–76 period.

In 1985, the Governing Council decided that for the fourth programming cycle (1987–91), countries with 1983 per capita GNPs of $750 or less a year were to receive 80% of IPF resources, reflecting UNDP's emphasis on assisting the poorer countries.

In the fifth programming cycle (1992–96) countries with yearly per capita GNPs of $750 or less received 87% of national IPF resources.

Implementation in the Field

UNDP is primarily a funding, programming, monitoring, and coordinating organization. Over the years, the bulk of the field work it has supported has been carried out by UN agencies and regional commissions, and by regional development banks and funds. Increasingly, UNDP is also calling upon national institutions and nongovernmental organizations for project execution.

The executing agencies, as they are called, perform three major functions. They serve as "data banks" of development knowledge and techniques in their respective specialties. They help governments plan the individual sectors in their country programs for UNDP assistance. As a rule, they recruit the international experts, purchase the equipment, and procure the specialized contract services needed for project execution.

The choice of a particular agency to implement any given project is made by UNDP in consultation with the government of the developing country. Though a single agency is always in charge of a particular project, often two or more collaborate in providing the services required.

Through its Office for Project Services, UNDP directly implements those activities that are not carried out by other executing agencies, providing a full range of management services, including procurement and finance.

The progress of field work is monitored through periodic reviews, involving UNDP country office staffs, government officials, and experts of the executing agencies. A modern computer-based management information system provides a continuous flow of operational data from the field. When required, special missions are sent to program countries to evaluate project work.

Systematic efforts are made to stimulate follow-up investments on surveys, feasibility studies, and other appropriate projects. These activities—which often begin at very early stages of project implementation—involve cooperation with all likely and acceptable sources of development finance—internal and external, public and private.

In a larger sense, however, most projects have a "built-in" follow-up component because they are deliberately planned to create permanent institutions or facilities that will be taken over by national personnel. Thus, many projects—particularly in training, applied research, and development planning—not only continue but also significantly expand their work after UNDP support ends.

Typically, some 5,000 projects, ranging from two to five years in duration, have been under way in any given year. Since 1993, however, UNDP has been making a deliberate attempt to sharpen its focus. It became more selective in what it would finance, concentrating in particular on capacity-building initiatives that gave priority to the poor, to creating employment, to advancing women, and to regenerating the environment. The largest share of UNDP core resources in both 1994 and 1995 went to Latin America and the Caribbean, followed by Asia and the Pacific, Africa, the Arab states, and Europe.

Total expenditures for technical cooperation activities by UNDP in 1994 were US$1,036.5 million, covering not only direct country programs but also the costs of UNDP program planning, management, and coordination by 133 offices worldwide and at UNDP headquarters in New York, and project implementation services by 31 executing agencies.

Voluntary contributions between 1994 and 1997 were distributed as follows: good governance, 28%; public resource management for sustainable human development, 25%; poverty eradication and livelihoods for the poor, 23%; environmental resources and food security, 22%. The remaining 2% was allocated to other programs.

Financing and Expenditures

UNDP is financed in several ways. First, the developing countries themselves pay a large share of the costs of their UNDP-assisted projects. Their funds are used for the salaries of local personnel, construction and maintenance of project buildings and facilities, and the purchase of locally available supplies and services. Second, almost every member of the UN and its associated agencies makes a yearly voluntary contribution to UNDP's core resources. Third, cost-sharing contributions make up a growing portion of UNDP's income. These are resources provided in convertible currency by program country governments, or by another country or organization to share in the costs of particular programs. In 1994 it became clear that the biennial budget would have to be reduced further to keep administrative costs in line with declining core program resources. Between 1992 to 1995 US$53.6 million was cut from the administrative budget, primarily through a 26% staff reduction at headquarters and 8% at the country level. Between 1992 and 1997, UNDP reduced its administrative budget by 19% in real terms and decreased total regular staff by nearly 15%. Regular staffing at headquarters was decreased by 31%. As of the late 1990s, a zero-growth budget policy was in

effect and resources were being deployed from headquarters to the country offices.

In 1996 voluntary contributions by member countries to UNDP's core resources amounted to US$852.26 million.

Major contributors to UNDP's core resources in 1996
(US$ millions)

COUNTRY	VOLUNTARY CONTRIBUTION
Japan	$110.11
Netherlands	98.09
Denmark	97.85
Germany	88.53
Norway	77.77
Sweden	69.24
United States	51.00
Switzerland	43.41
United Kingdom	36.92
Canada	31.94
Italy	21.82
Belgium	21.15
France	18.41
Australia	14.11
Austria	14.00
Finland	12.79
Spain	9.98

UNDP expenditures in 1995 by region and by economic or social sector were as follows:

UNDP Estimate of Field Program Expenditures by Region, 1995
(US$ millions)

REGION	EXPENDITURE
Africa	$195.9
Asia and the Pacific	214.0
Latin America and the Caribbean	457.3
Arab states	64.4
Europe and the Commonwealth of Independent States	26.0
Global and Interregional	50.0
TOTAL	$1,007.6

Associated Programs

The UNDP administrator also is responsible for several associated funds and programs:

United Nations Capital Development Fund provides limited amounts of "seed financing" for such social infrastructure as low cost housing, water supply systems, rural schools, and hospitals; and for such "grass roots" productive facilities as agricultural workshops, cottage industry centers, cooperatives, and credit programs.

United Nations Sudano Sahelian Office works with 22 countries across the Sudano Sahelian belt of Africa, from Senegal to Somalia, designing projects in such areas as deforestation control, sand dune stabilization, and rangeland management; mobilizing resources to carry them out; and implementing them in cooperation with other UN agencies.

United Nations Development Fund for Women provides direct assistance to innovative and potentially replicable projects involving women, including those to reduce workload and increase income; helps to raise women's status in society; and works to ensure their involvement in mainstream development activities. (see UNIFEM).

UN Revolving Fund for Natural Resources Exploration helps underwrite searches for economically useful mineral deposits that developing countries could not otherwise carry out because of the high risk factor involved.

United Nations Volunteers program, established by the General Assembly in 1971, is administered by UNDP from its Geneva, Switzerland, office. Volunteers from 115 professions serve in both UNDP and UN-assisted projects, as well as in development programs carried out directly by host governments. Recruited globally, they are sent to a country only at the request, and with the approval, of the host government. Volunteers serve for two years and receive a monthly allowance to cover necessities. The average age of UNV specialists is 39, with an average of 10 years' experience in their field of specialization. The actual age ranges from the mid-20s to the 60s and 70s, as retirees are welcomed for their experience. In the first 20 years of the UNV's existence, its specialists completed 6,000 assignments.

The skills most in demand for UNV specialists are: agriculture, agronomy, animal husbandry, appropriate technology, audiovisual arts, business management, cartography, community development, computer programming, construction trades, data processing, demography, development administration, disaster preparedness, economics, education, electronics, employment for the disabled, engineering, environment, export promotion, fisheries, forestry, handicrafts, HIV/AIDS prevention, home economics, horticulture, logistics, marketing/trade promotion, medicine, nursing/midwifery, printing/bookbinding, public administration, public health, social work, statistics, teacher training, teaching English language, teaching math/science, technical trades/skills, urban/regional planning, vehicle/fleet maintenance, veterinary science, vocational training, women in development, and youth work.

In 2000, more than 3,400 men and women of more than 140 nationalities were serving in developing countries as vounteer specialists and field workers. UNV professionals work alongside their host country peers in four main areas: technical cooperation; community-based initiatives for self-reliance; humanitarian relief and rehabilitation; and support to electoral and peace-building processes.

UN CONFERENCE ON TRADE AND DEVELOPMENT (UNCTAD)

The first UN Conference on Trade and Development, which met in Geneva in the spring of 1964, recommended the establishment of a permanent UN body to deal with trade in relation to development. The General Assembly, noting that international trade was an important instrument for economic development and that there was a widespread desire among developing countries for a comprehensive trade organization, decided to establish UNCTAD as one of its permanent organs in December 1964.

The main purpose of UNCTAD is to promote international trade, particularly that of developing countries, with a view to accelerating economic development. UNCTAD is one of the principal instruments of the General Assembly for deliberation and negotiation in respect to international trade and international economic cooperation. It formulates principles and policies on international trade, initiates action for the adoption of multilateral trade agreements, and acts as a center for harmonizing trade and development policies of governments and regional economic groups. The 1992 conference reaffirmed UNCTAD's functions to be policy analysis, intergovernmental deliberation, consensus building, negotiation of international agreements, monitoring, implementation, follow-up, and technical cooperation.

UNCTAD has 188 member states and has granted observer status to a number of organizations. There have been 10 sessions of UNCTAD at approximately four-year intervals: Geneva (1964); New Delhi (1968); Santiago (1972); Nairobi (1976); Manila (1979); Belgrade (1983); Geneva (1987); Cartagena de Indias, Colombia (1992); Midrand, South Africa (1996); and Bangkok, Thailand (2000).

At the ninth session of UNCTAD, in May 1996, UNCTAD's new mandate sought to deal with:

- the interests of developing countries;
- competition and its relation to the law and the environment in developing countries;
- support for small and medium-sized enterprises;
- and to consolidate the Trade Point Network.

The outcome of the ninth session was a comprehensive agreement by the member governments of UNCTAD on the treatment of development and a concrete program of work, to be implemented by UNCTAD before the next general session in 2000.

In his closing statement of UNCTAD-X, Secretary-General Rubens Ricupero concluded that to date global integration had affected only a dozen developing countries. He called for "real reciprocity," a new international order that would remove massive barriers to trade in agriculture, textiles and clothing; give developing countries recognition for their efforts in promoting economic solidarity—to "strengthen the move towards positive economic integration"; and transform existing international economic institutions so that they can "bridge the interests of both developed and developing countries."

Structure

The continuing work of the organization is carried out between sessions by the Trade and Development Board (TDB), UNCTAD's executive body, established by the General Assembly. The TDB implements conference decisions and initiates studies and reports on trade and related development problems. The TDB reports annually to the General Assembly through the Economic and Social Council. It also serves as the preparatory body for sessions of the conference.

The Trade and Development Board has several standing committees that review trends and make recommendations in specific areas, including the Commission on Trade in Goods, Services, and Commodities; the Commission on Investment, Technology and Related Financial Issues; and the Commission on Enterprise, Business Facilitation and Development.

Secretariat

The UNCTAD secretariat is located at Geneva. It provides service to the conference, the TDB, and its subsidiary bodies. The Secretary-General of UNCTAD is appointed by the Secretary-General of the UN and confirmed by the General Assembly.

In May 1993 the UN General Assembly assigned the UNCTAD secretariat responsibility for servicing two subsidiary bodies of the Economic and Social Council: the Commission on Transnational Corporations and the Commission on Science and Technology for Development (see the section on "Economic and Social Development").

The UNCTAD secretariat also provides technical assistance to developing countries in connection with the Uruguay Round of multilateral trade negotiations which took place under the auspices of the General Agreement on Tariffs and Trade (GATT).

Export Promotion and Marketing

Export promotion and marketing are the responsibility of the International Trade Center in Geneva, which is operated jointly by UNCTAD and GATT. The center focuses attention on export market opportunities and helps developing countries to train personnel in marketing and export-promotion techniques and to set up the institutions and programs necessary to build up modern export-promotion services.

Commodities

In 1980, the Agreement Establishing the Common Fund for Commodities was adopted by the UN Negotiating Conference on a Common Fund. International agreements also have been concluded for nine commodities—cocoa, coffee, tin, olive oil, sugar, natural rubber, wheat, jute and jute products, and tropical timbers. The fund came into operation in September 1989.

At its 1976 session in Nairobi, UNCTAD adopted an Integrated Program for Commodities aimed at setting prices for the primary commodities of developing countries that would take into account world inflation, monetary changes, and the cost of manufactured imports. As part of the program, the Nairobi session agreed that steps would be taken to negotiate a common fund for the financing of buffer stocks that would be held or sold as conditions required, thus helping to end the wide fluctuation in commodity prices that has plagued developing countries dependent on these products as exports.

The eighth session of UNCTAD in 1992 recognized the need to formulate an effective international commodity policy for the 1990s. Commodity markets remained extremely depressed and most of the commodity agreements achieved by UNCTAD in the 1980s had lapsed. In 1993 UNCTAD began to develop a microcomputer-based commodity analysis and information system (MICAS), which provides comprehensive, up-to-date information on all aspects of commodity use, production, trade, and consumption. The system assists developing countries in managing their economies and competing more effectively in world markets.

Preferential Tariffs for Developing Countries
UNCTAD adopted the General System of Preferences (GSP) in 1968, giving preferential tariff treatment in developed countries to manufactured goods exported by developing countries. By 1999, operating programs gave preferential treatment to more than US\$70 billion worth of exports a year from more than 100 developing countries. However, the conference recognized that the more advanced developing countries benefited most from the system, and in 1992 efforts were undertaken to include more agricultural products and some "sensitive" industrial products.

Shipping
UNCTAD initiated the development of the 1978 UN Convention on the Carriage of Goods by Sea (called the Hamburg Rules). By July 1993, the Hamburg Rules had received 21 ratifications and entered into force on 1 November 1993.

The Convention on a Code of Conduct for Liner Conferences (1974) provides for the national shipping lines of developing countries to participate on an equal basis with the shipping lines of developed countries. This convention became effective in 1983. In 1991 the conference reviewed this convention and adopted guidelines towards its more effective implementation. Technical and structural changes in liner shipping since 1974 were taken into account. By July 1993 there were 77 contracting parties to the convention.

The UN Convention on International Multimodal Transport of Goods (1980) establishes a single liability organizational structure for the international carriage of given consignments of goods entailing use of more than one mode of transport. By July 1993 it had received seven ratifications (entry into force requires 30 contracting parties).

The UN Convention on Conditions for Registration of Ships (1986) introduces new standards of responsibility and accountability for the world shipping industry and defines the elements of the genuine link that should exist between a ship and the state whose flag it flies. By July 1993 nine ratifications had been received (entry into force requires 40 contracting parties accounting for 25% of the world's tonnage).

UNCTAD also provides technical cooperation and specialized training projects financed in part by UNDP. Training courses cover multimodal transport, improving port performance, and the use of the Advance Cargo Information System (ACIS) to enable shipping lines and railway companies to track the movement of cargo.

Other Multilateral Agreements and Conventions
The Set of Multilaterally Agreed Equitable Principles and Rules for the Control of Restrictive Business Practices (1980) establishes international means for the control of restrictive business practices, including those of transnational corporations, adversely affecting international trade, in particular the trade and economic development of developing countries.

Negotiations were begun in 1978 on an International Code of Conduct on the Transfer of Technology. The provisions of the proposed code fall into two broad groups: those concerning the regulation of the transfer of technology transactions and of the conduct of parties to them, and those relating to steps to be taken by governments to meet their commitments to the code. In 1991 consultations were held on setting up an intergovernmental group of experts to prepare ground for the resumption of negotiations on the code of conduct.

As a result of these consultations, the Trade and Development Board acknowledged that it was impossible at that time to obtain consensus on the outstanding issues for a draft code of conduct. In 1993 the Trade and Development Board established an Ad Hoc Working Group on Interrelationship between Investment and Technology Transfer to examine and encourage new initiatives on investment and technology policies that would facilitate technology transfer. This group adopted a work program aimed at examining issues of investment flows, transfer of technology and competitiveness, technological capacity-building in developing countries, and transfer and development of environmentally sound technologies. In light of the ongoing work of this group, the Secretary-General of UNCTAD recommended to the General Assembly in 1993 that further consultations on the code of conduct take place after the completion of the activities of the Ad Hoc Working Group.

UNCTAD also elaborated the Modes Clauses on Marine Hull and Cargo Insurance, which assists the insurance markets in developing countries to produce their own insurance policy clauses and conditions. UNCTAD also has prepared minimum standards for shipping agents that serve as guidelines for national authorities and professional associations establishing standards.

Debt Relief
In the area of money and finance, UNCTAD devotes particular attention to the debt problems of developing countries and has negotiated measures of debt relief for the poorer among those countries, as well as a set of agreed guidelines for dealing with future debt problems. At its 1987 session in Geneva, UNCTAD recommended a number of policy approaches and measures to deal with debt problems, resources for development, and related monetary issues; commodities; international trade; and the problems of the least developed countries—all aimed at revitalizing development, growth, and international trade in a more predictable and supportive environment through multilateral cooperation.

UNCTAD and the World Bank developed a joint program to extend technical cooperation to developing countries in the field of debt management. UNCTAD is responsible for the software component of the project. The assistance is based on the development and distribution of the Debt Management and Financial Analysis System (DMFAS), software designed to enable debtor countries to analyze data, make projections, and plan strategies for debt repayment. UNCTAD trains operators to use the software. It also provides training for senior officials in raising their awareness of institutional reforms that might be necessary for effective debt management.

Least Developed Countries (LDCs)

In 1993 47 countries were classified as least developed countries (LDCs). UNCTAD has taken a lead role in mobilizing support for LDCs by organizing two UN conferences on LDCs. The first, held in Paris in 1980, adopted the Substantial New Program of Action (SNPA), which defined measures to be taken by LDCs to promote their own development. The second, also held in Paris, in 1990, reviewed the implementation of the SNPA and strengthened the program.

UNCTAD has given political impetus to the setting of official development assistance at 0.7% of the GNP of donor countries. It also has recommended improvement of International Monetary Fund's compensatory financing facility for export earnings shortfalls of developing countries and the creation of special drawing rights for LDCs.

The eighth session of UNCTAD in 1992 requested that detailed analyses be made of the socioeconomic situations and domestic policies of the LDCs, their resource needs, and external factors affecting their economies. The ninth session of UNCTAD in 1996 adopted the Midrand Declaration, which called for greater partnership between developed, developing, and the least developed countries.

Trade in the 21st Century

The 1992 conference identified four priority areas to be analyzed.

1. *New International Partnership for Development.* To assist developing countries and countries in transition to market economies increase their participation in the world economy.
2. *Global Interdependence.* Emphasis to be placed on the international implications of macroeconomic policies, the evolution of international trading, monetary and financial systems, effective management at the international level, and the consequences of enlarged economic spaces and regional integration processes.
3. *Paths to Development.* The conference called for studies of national development experiences with a view to deriving useful lessons to inform future action. The studies would include consideration of general economic management and the relationships between economic progress and market orientation.
4. *Sustainable Development.* The interaction between trade and environmental policies was to be considered. The promotion and implementation of environmentally sound technologies as elaborated at the UN Conference on Environment and Development in 1992 were stressed.

The 1992 conference also discussed trade efficiency and the use of electronic data interchange to reduce the cost of transactions. In July 1995, UNCTAD organized a World Symposium on Trade Efficiency in Columbus, Ohio. The symposium was subtitled "New Technologies for Efficient Global Trade; UNCTAD's Tradepoint Network." The symposium will unite trade ministers, chief executives, and senior officials in focussing on new technologies in the fields of banking, insurance, transport, telecommunications, and information for trade. The promotion of international standards for electronic commerce will be a key component of the symposium. The symposium also will launch a worldwide process of alleviating technical and procedural barriers that prevent poorer countries from fully participating in world trade. UNCTAD is developing a Trade Point Network of 100 operational trading points to facilitate this process. At the end of 1999, 114 countries were participating in UNCTAD's Trade Point Program.

WORLD FOOD PROGRAM (WFP)

The World Food Program, which the UN sponsors jointly with the Food and Agriculture Organization (FAO), began operations in 1963. It has since grown from a small experimental program to become the largest multilateral food distributor in the world. In 1998, more than 75 million people received direct assistance through WFP emergency operations and development projects.

Between 1946 and 1960, several attempts were made to establish an international body to regulate international trade and to deal with surpluses produced by food exporting countries. None of these attempts were successful, mainly because some countries objected to interference in their trade relations. In 1955, a study called, "Uses of Agricultural Surpluses to Finance Economic Development in Under-developed Countries," provided the breakthrough. The report posited that agricultural surpluses could finance additional investment in developing countries without competing with the sales of domestic products or with imports from other countries.

At the 1961 FAO Conference, George McGovern, the head of the US delegation, formally proposed establishing a multilateral program with a fund of US$100 million in commodities and cash, to which the US was willing to contribute US$40 million. This initiative led the FAO and the UN to establish the World Food Program on a three-year experimental basis (January 1963 to December 1965).

WFP uses food commodities, cash, and services contributed by UN member states to back programs of social and economic development, as well as for emergency relief. At the request of governments, WFP provides food aid for development projects to increase agricultural production, rehabilitate roads and other vital infrastructure, protect the environment and improve health and education. WFP food assistance also provides basic sustenance for refugees and other victims of disasters. The aim of the WFP is to apply food aid in ways that will eventually make the recipients self-sufficient in obtaining or producing food. The success of the program's work should ultimately be judged by the number of people who, over time, are able to feed themselves.

In the first three decades of its existence, the program invested approximately US$14 billion (43 million tons of food aid) to combat hunger and to promote economic and social development in the developing world. More than 1,600 development projects and 1,200 emergency operations were assisted by the WFP during that period. However, in the mid-1990s, emergency operations dominated the WFP's work. In 1998 alone, WFP delivered 2.8 million metric tons of emergency food aid to nearly 75 million people in 80 countries.

WFP supplies for development purposes are used in a variety of ways. Early projects included a land-settlement project in Bolivia, the development of nomadic sheep husbandry in Syria, resettling nomads in Egypt, land reclamation and development in Morocco, and land settlement in Tanzania. Other projects contributed directly to the development of human resources by providing food for school children, expectant and nursing mothers, hospital patients, and adults attending education centers.

The program gave special attention to creating employment and income through food-for-work programs. In Bangladesh, a vulnerable-group development project, begun in 1975, continues to provide training in health, literacy, and income-generation for women. Similar projects were started in Bolivia and Mexico, while major land-development programs commenced in Egypt, Sudan, Korea, and China. The largest single dairy project ever undertaken, "Operation Flood," in India, increased milk production by 50% and benefitted 30 million people.

Early in its operations, recipient governments had a major problem in covering the non-food costs of a project, including transport storage and other expenses. The early success of the program (28 formal requests for aid in May 1963 rose to 193 requests by November 1964) led donor countries to increase their contributions to cover these costs. Indeed, the WFP's ability to quickly transport large quantities of food, at short notice, to remote areas of the world, is one of its most important areas of expertise.

In 1973 a worldwide food shortage created a serious lack of resources, and the WFP governing body was unable to approve any new projects that year. The number of existing recipients and the size of their rations also were cut. Despite these measures there was a shortfall of 160,000 tons of commodities. A concerted effort was made to find new funds, and in 1974 King Faisal of Saudi Arabia offered US$50 million, the largest cash donation ever made. This marked a turning point because the donation came from a nonindustrial developing country that was, and still is, a net importer of food commodities. It also marked an important change in the nature of donations, away from the idea of surplus disposal and toward a wider sharing of responsibility for those in need.

In 1975 the UN General Assembly established the International Emergency Food Reserve (IEFR), to be placed at the disposal of WFP. This reserve, which receives contributions from all governments, has a minimum annual target of 500,000 tons, enabling WFP to quickly respond to emergency situations.

In 1988 donor commitments for development activities reached a high point of US$778 million, which represented two-thirds of WFP resources. By 1993 this trend had reversed and emergency situations were consuming more than 60% of WFP's resources. Part of this increase is directly attributable to the program's new relationship with the UN body that supervises refugee relief. In January 1992, the UN High Commissioner for Refugees (UNHCR) worked out an agreement giving the WFP the responsibility to procure and deliver food commodities to UNHCR-managed refugee feeding operations.

In the last 30 years, WFP has witnessed the graduation of former food-aid recipients to the status of potential donors. The Republic of Korea, Singapore, Venezuela, Greece, Hungary, and Mexico are all former recipients who now boast growing economies. The program has also developed ways to use its cash contributions creatively. For example, by buying more food in developing countries for relief and development activities it has encouraged and expanded trade between developing countries. In 1993 the WFP was the largest UN purchaser of goods in developing countries.

WFP has its headquarters in Rome and development projects in 80 countries worldwide; the WFP staff numbers more than 5,000, over half of whom are employed on a temporary basis. Permanent staff members (numbering 2,116 in 1998) were employed at headquarters (586 people) and in the field (1,530 people). It is administered by an executive director. Its governing body is the 36-member Bureau of the Executive Board. Half of the members of the board are elected by ECOSOC, the other half by the FAO Council. In 2000, the members of the executive board elected by ECOSOC were: Congo (Republic of), Finland, France, Haiti, Hungary, Indonesia, Iran (Islamic Republic of), Japan, Mexico, Morocco, Norway, Pakistan, Russian Federation, Sierra Leone, Swaziland, Sweden, United Kingdom, and Yemen. Executive board members elected by the FAO Council were Australia, Bangladesh, Burundi, Canada, China, Cuba, Egypt, El Salvador, Germany, Lesotho, Madagascar, Netherlands, Peru, Romania, Saudi Arabia, Spain, Sudan, and United States of America.

In 1998, WFP had US$1.348 billion in expenditures, of which US$647 million went for food commodity purchases. Of the food expenditures, 60% was purchased from developing countries. The remaining expenditures were in the categories of transport costs (US$291 million); other transport-related and project costs (US$300 million); and administration (US$110 million, or 8.1%).

UNITED NATIONS POPULATION FUND (UNFPA)

The UN has been concerned with population questions since its earliest years, establishing the Population Commission in 1947 as one of the functional commissions of the Economic and Social Council. The early work of the UN on population questions concentrated on the improvement of demographic statistics, which were lacking for many areas of the world, and then began to focus on the application of statistical data in analytical studies and in the preparation of worldwide population estimates and projections. The first *Demographic Yearbook* was published by the UN Statistical Office in 1948.

In the 1960s, however, the extraordinarily rapid rate at which the world's population was growing became an urgent concern (between 1950 and 1960, the world population increased from 2.5 billion to over 3 billion, and by 2000 it had doubled—reaching 6 billion). In a resolution adopted in 1966, the General Assembly authorized the UN to provide technical assistance in population matters, and the following year, the General Assembly established a Trust Fund for Population Activities, renamed in 1969 the United Nations Fund for Population Activities (UNFPA), to provide additional resources to the UN system for technical cooperation activities in the population field. In 1972, the fund was placed under the authority of the General Assembly, which designated the Governing Council of UNDP as its administering body. By its resolution number 1763(LIV) of 18 May 1973, the Economic and Social Council of the United Nations defined the mandate of UNFPA, and, in 1979, the General Assembly affirmed that the UNFPA was a subsidiary organ. In 1987, the fund's name was changed to the United Nations Population Fund, but the acronym UNFPA was retained. In 1993, the General Assembly transformed the Governing Council of UNDP into the UNDP/UNFPA Executive Board, which will provide intergovernmental support to and supervision of the UNFPA in accordance with overall policy guidance of the General Assembly and ECOSOC of the United Nations.

The first World Population Conference, held in Bucharest in 1974, adopted a World Population Plan of Action (WPPA) that stressed the relationship between population factors and overall economic and social development. The General Assembly affirmed that the plan was "an instrument of the international community for the promotion of economic development" and urged that assistance in the population field should be expanded, particularly to UNFPA, for the proper implementation of the plan.

The International Conference on Population, held in Mexico City in August 1984, reaffirmed the validity of the WPPA and adopted recommendations for its further implementation. Target mortality rates were adjusted, and emerging issues, such as migration, urbanization, computerized data processing, and aging of populations, were addressed. Also considered was the need for an intersectoral approach to population and development, for policies that respect individual and family rights, and for improvement in the status of women, including their increased participation in all aspects of development.

The third decennial conference, the International Conference on Population and Development, was held in Cairo, 5–13 September 1994. The Programme of Action adopted at the Cairo conference recommended that population concerns be fully integrated into development planning, in order to meet the needs and improve the quality of life of present and future generations. The program builds upon the considerable international awareness and knowledge that has developed since the Bucharest and Mexico City conferences regarding the linkages among population issues, sustained economic growth, and sustainable development. The program also addresses the reproductive health and educational needs of individuals, especially of girls and women, and calls for increased investment in the social sectors, from donor agencies and recipient governments alike.

UNFPA supports a broad range of population activities. Nearly half of the fund's assistance is used for maternal and child health care and family planning programs. Another 20% is used for population and family planning communication and education. UNFPA also supports developing countries in their efforts to collect and analyze population data, conduct population censuses, formulate population policies, and undertake research on fertility, mortality, and migration and their relationship to development, as well as on linkages between population and sustainable development. The fund supports special programs concerning women, youth, the aged, AIDS, and population and development. UNFPA is the leading source of population assistance within the United Nations system. The fund's resources come from voluntary contributions from governments.

UNFPA's Work

A major component of UNFPA's work is disseminating information based on its data and analysis of population trends. In the *State of the World Population 1999* report, UNFPA called the dawn of the 21st century a time of choices and it urged governments to action. With global population quadrupling during the 20th century, surpassing 6 billion in 1999, UNFPA stated that how fast the next billion people are added, what the effect will be on natural resources and the environment, and the quality of life will depend on policy and funding decisions that are made over the next 5 to 10 years. The population report pointed to the issue of below replacement-level reproduction in some 60 countries, which, UNFPA predicted, would put pressures on these developed nations to provide support and medical care for the elderly. Meanwhile, HIV/AIDS is taking a higher toll in some parts of the world (particularly sub-Saharan Africa) than it is elsewhere, lowering life expectancy and "erasing decades of progress in child mortality" in these regions. Finally, the report highlighted unbalanced consumption patterns around the globe, concluding that it will combine with continued population growth to cause environmental damage—including the collapse of fisheries, shrinking forests, rising temperatures, and the extinction of numerous plant and animal species. In summary, UNFPA warned that unless nations rededicate themselves to combating issues of overpopulation, continuing poverty, gender discrimination, threats such as HIV/AIDS, environmental changes, and shrinking (relative to the population) resources, the benefits of lower fertility that were realized in the second half of the 20th century would be wiped out. UNFPA urged governments to commit action and funding to the 20-year Program of Action endorsed by the world's governments in 1994 at the International Conference on Population and Development.

In its *World Population 1999* report, UNFPA focused on global women's issues and youth at risk. In both areas the organization called for stepped-up educational and health programs. UNFPA stated that despite progress, far too many women are denied education, contraception, and decent health care, and that violence against women is "endemic in all countries." The report went on to say that hundreds of millions of women continue to suffer needlessly from gender-based violence, unwanted pregnancies, unsafe abortions, and poor health. Similarly, UNFPA stated that "today's young people are frequently at risk of unwanted pregnancy, HIV/AIDS and other sexually transmitted diseases, sexual exploitation, and alienation from parents and communities." The organization warned that ignoring the issues confronting women and youth incurs high costs—"in ill health, wasted opportunities, and social disruption." According to UNFPA, studies have shown that family life education should begin early to help young people through the years when they are beginning to be interested in sex. Further, the benefits of education for girls

and women had been well-documented during the 1900s, yet in 1999 in developing countries, girls comprised two-thirds of the 130 million children not attending school. The call for schooling was seen to have the double benefit of educating young women and postponing childbirth.

While UNFPA releases the report annually, the 1999 document was expected to have far-reaching influence in that it was issued as the world turned its attention to considering the next millennium, in a year when a critical population threshold (6 billion) was crossed, and it was to be followed, in 2000, by several conferences that were expected to use the 1999 report as the basis for discussion and program development. Among the major conferences on the UN's 2000 docket were Beijing+5 Review (New York, 5–9 June 2000), the World Summit for Social Development and Beyond (Geneva, Switzerland, 26–30 June 2000), and Millennium Summit: The Role of the United Nations in the 21st Century (New York, 6–8 September 2000).

Budget and Organization

Regular income in 1998 totaled US$277 million, a decrease of 5.3% from 1997. Pledges to UNFPA's general resources in 1998 totaled US$269.2 million, US$18.1 million less than in 1997, a decrease of 6.3%. At year end, cumulative pledges through 1998 totaled about US$4.5 billion from a cumulative total of 172 donors. Total (provisional) programmable resources for 1998 were US$305.1 million, compared to US$306.8 million in 1997. Project expenditures in 1998 totaled US$216.6 million, as compared with US$214.4 million in 1997. The 1998 figure included US$174.7 million for country programs and US$41.9 million for inter-country (regional and inter-regional) programs.

UNFPA publishes a range of products in a variety of media. Public service announcements are broadcast on national and international television networks around the world. The definitive publication is the annual *The State of World Population*, a comprehensive demographic study of patterns in population growth and distribution. UNFPA also publishes the annual *AIDS Update,* which highlights assistance provided by UNFPA for HIV/AIDS prevention and control activities undertaken in line with national AIDS policies and programs and within the global strategy of the Joint and Co-sponsored UN Program on HIV/AIDS.

UN ENVIRONMENT PROGRAM (UNEP)

In the course of the twentieth century, and especially after World War II, the increase in the earth's population and the advance of technology, with concomitant changes in patterns of production and consumption, led to pressure on the environment and threats to its stability that were new in human history. For a long time, the implications of these phenomena were largely ignored. In the decade of the 1960s, however, problems such as soil erosion; air, water, and marine pollution; the need for conservation of limited resources; and desiccation of once-fertile zones became acute enough to awaken the consciousness of governments and people in all parts of the world, but especially in the industrialized countries, to the urgency of the situation. The UN responded with the decision of the 1968 General Assembly to convene a world conference on the human environment.

The first UN Conference on the Human Environment was held in Stockholm in June 1972. The conference was a focus for, rather than the start of, action on environmental problems. At its conclusion, the participants, representing over 90% of the world's population, adopted a declaration and a 109-point plan of action for the human environment that became the blueprint for a wide range of national and international programs. The broad intent of the action plan was to define and mobilize "common effort for the preservation and improvement of the human environment." The preamble to the declaration conveys the urgency, magnitude, and complexity of that task.

Later in 1972, on the basis of the conference's recommendations, the General Assembly created the UN Environment Program (UNEP), to monitor significant changes in the environment and to encourage and coordinate sound environmental practices. With headquarters in Nairobi, Kenya, UNEP is the first global UN agency to be headquartered in a developing country. Its mission is to provide leadership and encourage partnership in caring for the environment by inspiring, informing, and enabling nations and peoples to improve their quality of life without compromising that of future generations.

Twenty years after its inception, UNEP's mandate was reaffirmed and strengthened in 1992 at the UN Conference on Environment and Development (UNCED), held in Rio de Janeiro, Brazil. Out of that conference came an ambitious plan of action—Agenda 21—with an emphasis on integrating development and environment into all United Nations program areas.

The UNEP secretariat is headed by an executive director who is elected by the UN General Assembly for a four-year term, upon the recommendation of the Secretary-General. UNEP's professional staff in 1997 numbered around 250. Besides its Nairobi headquarters, UNEP maintains regional offices in Africa, Europe, Asia and the Pacific, Latin America and the Caribbean, West Asia, and North America.

UNEP's Governing Council is composed of 58 states elected by the General Assembly for four-year terms on the basis of equitable geographic representation (16 African seats, 13 Asian seats, 10 Latin American and Caribbean seats, 6 seats for Eastern European states, 13 seats for Western European and other states). The Governing Council generally meets every two years.

In 2000, the following states had representatives on the Governing Council: Antigua and Barbuda, Argentina, Austria, Bahamas, Belarus, Belgium, Benin, Botswana, Brazil, Burkina Faso, Burundi, Cameroon, Canada, China, Colombia, Comoros, Cuba, Denmark, Egypt, Equatorial Guinea, France, The Gambia, Germany, Hungary, India, Indonesia, Iran (Islamic Republic of), Italy, Jamaica, Japan, Kazakhstan, Libya, Malawi, Marshall Islands, Mexico, Netherlands, New Zealand, Nigeria, Norway, Pakistan, Poland, Republic of Korea, Republic of Moldova, Russian Federation, Samoa, Saudi Arabia, Senegal, Slovakia, Sudan, Suriname, Syrian Arab Republic, Thailand, Turkey, Uganda, United Kingdom of Great Britain and Northern Ireland, United States of America, Venezuela, and Zimbabwe.

The Council's functions and responsibilities include promoting international cooperation in the field of environment and recommending policies to that end, providing general policy guidance for environmental programs within the UN system, keeping the world environmental situation under review so as to ensure that emerging problems requiring international assistance receive adequate consideration by governments, promoting the contribution by international scientific and other professional communities to knowledge about the environment and the technical aspects of UN environmental programs, keeping under review the impact of national and international development policies, and reviewing and approving the utilization of the resources of the Environment Fund.

The Environment Fund was set up under the authority of the Governing Council to finance wholly or partly the costs of new environmental initiatives within the UN system. It is made up of voluntary contributions. Altogether 142 countries made at least one voluntary contribution to the Environment Fund over the period 1973–98. Eleven countries maintained their regular annual contributions over the whole period, thus ensuring continuous support and implementation of the UNEP program. Still, 95% of the total contributions to the fund came from just 20 countries. Payments to the Environment Fund in 1998–99 were expected to reach US$93 million. By September 1999, 45 countries had contributed about US$35.48 million to the Environment Fund.

For its first 20 years, UNEP's policy, as set by the Governing Council, has been focused on the three broad areas of environmental assessment, environmental management, and international environmental law. Many parts to the program evolved under these three themes. There was the environmental monitoring capacity built up in the Global Environment Monitoring System (GEMS), and the establishment of a computer-based store of data in the International Register of Potentially Toxic Chemicals (IRPTC). More computer-based capability was developed to show how both natural and human resources are distributed in the Global Resource Information Database (GRID). Another key information system is INFOTERRA, UNEP's international network for the retrieval of global environmental information. It is a worldwide network with national focal points in 178 countries, providing governments, industry, and researchers with access to a vast reservoir of environmental data and information gathered from about 6,800 institutions and experts in more than 1,000 priority subject areas.

Environmental management and legal instruments were developed. The most successful example of international environmental law can be seen in the instruments used to protect the ozone layer: the 1985 Vienna Convention and the 1987 Montreal Protocol. Expert groups convened by UNEP, with the World Meteorological Organization (WMO), the scientific community, and industry, led to the development of the Vienna Convention for the Protection of the Ozone Layer, which was adopted in March 1985. In September 1987 the Montreal Protocol on Substances that Deplete the Ozone Layer was signed, setting limits for the production and consumption of chloro-fluorocarbons (CFCs) and halons. The Montreal Protocol came into force on 1 January 1989 and was amended in London in June 1990, in Copenhagen in 1992, and in Vienna in 1995 after research showed that ozone depletion was even more severe than previously feared. Industrialized countries succeeded in phasing out the production and consumption of halons by 1 January 1994, and were well on the way to the phase-out of chlorofluorocarbons by the end of 1995. The consumption of CFCs in industrialized countries decreased from about 1,000,000 tons in 1987 (when the Protocol was signed) to about 13,000 tons in 1996. Developing countries, although mandated to begin phase-out only in 1999, began making progress before that time. A multilateral fund, involving UNEP, UNDP, and the World Bank, was established to help developing countries meet the costs of complying with the revised protocol and to provide for the necessary transfer of technology. By 1997, the fund had already disbursed US$365 million to developing countries for transition to ozone-safe technology.

The Mediterranean Action Plan has been the model as UNEP's Regional Seas Programme has spread. Today, nearly 140 countries take part in Regional Seas Programmes catalyzed and coordinated by UNEP. Action Plans cover the Mediterranean, the Kuwait region, the Red Sea, the Caribbean, the Atlantic coast of West and Central Africa, the Eastern African seaboard, the Pacific coast of South America, the islands of the South Pacific, the East-Asian region, the South Asian region, the Black Sea, the North-West Pacific and the South-West Atlantic. An Action Plan for the Caspian Sea is being developed. Coordination is provided through the UNEP Water Branch.

UNEP provides the secretariat for the Convention on International Trade in Endangered Species of Wild Fauna and Flora (CITES), which entered into force in 1975 and prohibits or regulates trade in some 30,000 endangered species. The protection of endangered species under the CITES Convention has seen successful international cooperation to stamp out trade in rare plants and animals.

UNEP also provides the secretariat for the Convention on the Conservation of Migratory Species of Wild Animals (CMS), which came into force in 1983. UNEP supports the World Conservation Monitoring Center (WCMC), which assesses the distribution and abundance of the world's species. Action plans for African elephants and rhinos, Asian elephants and rhinos, primates, cats, and polar bears have been published by UNEP and IUCN.

UNEP also has contributed to the drawing up of global conventions on hazardous waste, climate change, biodiversity, and desertification and of international guidelines, including those on international trade in chemicals, protection of marine environment from land-based activities, environmental impact assessment and shared natural resources.

In March 1989, the Basel Convention on the Control of Transboundary Movements of Hazardous Wastes and their Disposal, drafted by UNEP, was adopted by 116 governments and the European Community. The convention entered into force on 5 May 1992. Its immediate target is to impose strict controls on the international movement of hazardous wastes and eventually to reduce their production. As of January 1997, 100 countries acceded or had signaled their intention to accede to the convention.

In June 1992, the Convention on Biological Diversity was signed during the UN Conference on Environmental and Development in Rio de Janeiro. The convention was prepared by an Intergovernmental Negotiating Committee, set up by UNEP's Governing Council and assisted by UNEP, FAO, UNESCO, and IUCN. Its main aims are to conserve biological diversity and to ensure that its benefits to mankind are shared equitably. UNEP also supports the International Board for Plant Genetic Resources (IBPGR), which has established a network of gene banks in 30 countries to house the world's 40 base collections. More than 100 countries collaborate and more than 500,000 plant species have been collected, evaluated, and deposited.

A joint venture between UNEP, UNDP, and the UN Sudano-Sahelian Office is assisting 22 Sudano-Sahelian countries to fight desertification. In spite of these efforts, implementation of the Plan of Action to Combat Desertification has been slow. UNEP's Plan of Action to Combat Desertification has been succeeded by the Convention to Combat Desertification, wich entered into force in 1996. UNEP's activities in desertification control now focus on achieving strong support and effective implementation of the convention.

UNEP, along with the World Meteorological Organization (WMO), established the Intergovernmental Panel on Climate Change to provide scientific assessments on the magnitude, timing, and potential environmental and socioeconomic consequences of climate change and realistic response strategies. Negotiations begun in early 1991 led to the formulation of the United Nations Framework Convention on Climate Change, which was signed by 154 governments in Rio de Janeiro during the 1992 United Nations Conference on Environment and Development. It entered into force on 21 March 1994.

The organization also is responsible for UN activities involving freshwater. Among regional initiatives are the Action Plan for Latin America and the Caribbean and the program for environmentally sound management of inland waters in the Zambezi Basin.

UNEP, along with UNDP and the World Bank, administers the US$2 billion Global Environment Facility (GEF), and is responsible for GEF's Scientific and Technical Advisory Panel (STAP). GEF was established as a three-year pilot in 1991 to oversee funding for global environment protection in the areas of climate change, biodiversity, international waters, and ozone depletion. In 1992, a restructuring process began that resulted in agreement on fundamentally altered institutional arrangements for the facility, now known as GEFF II. UNEP will play the primary role in catalyzing the development of scientific and technical analysis and in advancing environmental management in

GEF-financed activities. It also will be responsible for establishing and supporting the Scientific and Technical Advisory Panel as an advisory body to the GEF. The UNDP is responsible for technical assistance activities and capacity building. The World Bank, the GEF Trust Fund's repository, plays the primary role in ensuring the development and management of investment projects while also mobilizing private sector resources that are consistent with GEF objectives and national sustainable development strategies. The GEF provides the interim funding mechanism for the conventions on climate change and biological diversity, until parties to those conventions agree on a permanent arrangement.

UNCED and Agenda 21 marked a new beginning for the world community as a whole. Agenda 21 reaffirmed UNEP's role as the principal environment body in the UN system and expanded UNEP's role to encompass a vast range of world environmental needs and problems, with an emphasis on regional delivery.

Five years later, at the nineteenth session of the Governing Council of UNEP in 1997, as part of the ongoing reform process of the United Nations system, UNEP's Governing Council adopted the Nairobi Declaration, again asserting the role and mandate of UNEP as the leading global environmental authority and calling for assurances of financial stability for the implementation of its agenda.

Specifically, the Nairobi Declaration set out the following as core elements of the focused mandate of a revitalized UNEP:

- To analyze the state of the global environment and assess global and regional environmental trends;
- To further the development of its international environmental law aiming at sustainable development;
- To advance the implementation of agreed international norms and policies;
- To strengthen its role in the coordination of environmental activities in the United Nations system in the field of environment;
- To promote greater awareness and facilitate effective cooperation among all sectors of society and actors involved in the implementation of the international environmental agenda;
- To provide policy and advisory services in key areas of institution building to Governments and other relevant institutions.

UNEP's integrated work program emphasizes relationships between socio-economic driving forces, environmental changes, and impacts on human well-being. Equipped with a stronger regional presence and marked by a process of continuous monitoring and assessment of its implementation, UNEP's program of work focuses on the following areas: sustainable management and use of natural resources; sustainable production and consumption; a better environment for human health and well-being; and globalization of the economy and the environment.

In 2000, the fifth special session of the UNEP Governing Council and the subsequent 20th session of the Governing Council elaborated UNEP's areas of concentration, which included environmental monitoring, assessment, information, and research (including early warning); enhanced coordination of environmental conventions and development of environment policy instruments; freshwater; technology transfer and industry; and support to Africa. To support these initiatives, UNEP initiated a restructuring that was expected to trim administration costs while developing the Nairobi facility as a critical UN administrative office.

UN CENTER FOR HUMAN SETTLEMENTS (HABITAT)

UN concern with the problems of human settlements, particularly with the deteriorating quality of living conditions in developing countries and the need to link urban and regional development programs with national development plans, led to the convening of the first international conference on the question in Vancouver,

Canada, in May–June 1976. The declaration and plan of action adopted by Habitat: UN Conference on Human Settlements (Habitat I) represented an important commitment on the part of governments and the international community to improve the quality of life for all people through human settlements development. The plan of action contained 64 recommendations for national action concerning settlement policies and planning; provision of shelter, infrastructure, and services; land use and land tenure; the role of popular participation; and effective institutions and management.

Habitat I also recommended the strengthening and consolidation of UN activities in a single organization concerned exclusively with human settlements. Acting on this recommendation, the General Assembly established in 1978 the UN Center for Human Settlements (Habitat, also UNCHS), with headquarters in Nairobi, Kenya, to serve as a focal point for human settlements action and to coordinate human settlements activities within the UN system.

The center provides technical assistance to governments; organizes expert meetings, workshops, and training seminars; issues print, audio visual, and electronic publications; and disseminates information worldwide. In 1993 the center had under execution 257 technical cooperation programs and projects in over 90 countries, with an overall budget in excess of US$42 million for the year.

In 1982, the General Assembly proclaimed 1987 as the International Year of Shelter for the Homeless. The objectives were to improve the shelter situation of the poor and disadvantaged at both individual and community levels, particularly in developing countries, and to demonstrate means of continuing those efforts as ongoing national programs beyond 1987.

Beginning in 1986, the tenth anniversary of Habitat I, World Habitat Day has been observed each year on the first Monday in October. As lead agency in the UN system for coordinating activities related to the Global Strategy for Shelter to the Year 2000, the center continues to work toward its goal of facilitating adequate shelter for all by that date.

The Habitat II Conference met in Istanbul, Turkey, in 1996, 20 years after Habitat I. Subtitled "A Summit for Cities," the UN Conference on the Future of Cities has as its goal making the world's cities, towns, and villages healthy, safe, just, and sustainable. The two central themes were "sustainable human settlements in an urbanizing world" and "adequate shelter for all."

The follow-up conference was scheduled for June 2001; "Istanbul+5: Reviewing and Appraising Progress Five Years after Habitat II" was slated as a special session of the UN General Assembly. All member states were invited to prepare a report on national and local implementation of the Habitat Agenda, reflecting the views of the government and of its partners.

UN RESEARCH INSTITUTE FOR SOCIAL DEVELOPMENT (UNRISD)

The UN Research Institute for Social Development (UNRISD) was created in 1963 as an autonomous agency within the UN system. It engages in multidisciplinary research on the social dimensions of contemporary problems affecting development. Its work is guided by the conviction that, for effective development policies to be formulated, an understanding of the social and political context is crucial. The institute attempts to provide governments, development agencies, grass roots organizations, and scholars with a better understanding of how development policies and processes of economic, social, and environmental change affect different social groups.

Working through an extensive network of national research centers, UNRISD aims to promote original research and strengthen research capacity in developing countries.

The UNRISD program for the 2000–03 period included work in the following areas: social policy and development; democracy and human rights; identities, conflict and cohesion; civil society and social movements; technology and society.

In 1996, UNRISD conducted the War-Torn Societies Project, which focused on post-conflict rebuilding and rehabilitation. The project sought to identify novel and integrated policy responses to the complex interactions between peacekeeping, relief, rehabilitation, and development activities.

The UNRISD Internship Program provides a limited number of graduate students from around the world the opportunity to gain valuable experience in an international research institute setting. Interns are selected on the basis of their academic experience and interests. Students selected for the unpaid internships spend a minimum of two months at UNRISD assisting project coordinators in developing project proposals, compiling annotated bibliographies, organizing research seminars, translating correspondence, and carrying out various tasks in the Reference Centre. As part of its mandate, UNRISD issues newsletters, books, and other publications, some of which are available online at http://www.unrisd.org/engindex/publ.htm.

By 2000, the institute had approximately 30 staff members at its headquarters in Geneva, and is financed entirely by voluntary contributions.

UN INSTITUTE FOR TRAINING AND RESEARCH (UNITAR)

In 1963, the General Assembly requested the Secretary-General to establish a UN Institute for Training and Research as an autonomous body within the framework of the UN. UNITAR commenced functioning in March 1965. It is headed by an executive director and has a board of trustees appointed by the UN Secretary-General in consultation with the president of the General Assembly and the president of the Economic and Social Council. UNITAR originally had its headquarters in New York and a European office in Geneva. In 1993 UNITAR's headquarters was transferred to Geneva. It maintains a liaison office in New York to coordinate training activities.

The mandate of UNITAR is to enhance the effectiveness of the UN in attaining its major objectives—particularly the maintenance of peace and the promotion of economic and social development—through training and research. Its functions include ensuring liaison with UN organizations and strengthening cooperation with academic institutions; conducting training programs in multilateral diplomacy and international cooperation for diplomats accredited to the United Nations and national officials; and carrying out a wide range of training programs in social and economic development. In addition, UNITAR responds to ad hoc requests for training. For example, in 1993 UNITAR received requests for programs from UNDP, UNEP, and other UN bodies.

In the late 1990s, UNITAR offered courses in the following areas: debt, economic, and financial management; foreign economic relations; international affairs management; international migration policy; peacemaking and preventive diplomacy; applications of environmental law; chemicals and waste management; climate change; decentralized cooperation; and information and communication technologies.

In a typical year, UNITAR designs and conducts some 70 different training programs on five continents for the benefit of more than 3,000 national staff and government officials. In the early 1990s training programs in diplomacy, negotiation, foreign affairs management, and debt and financial management were developed for newly independent countries in Europe and Central Asia; countries in transition in Africa, Asia, and Europe; and for the Palestinian negotiating team.

The institute's research program originally concentrated on three main areas: UN institutional issues, peace and security issues, and economic and social issues. After restructuring in

1992, basic research on training was conducted only if extrabudgetary funds were provided.

UNITAR is supported by voluntary contributions from governments, intergovernmental organizations, foundations, and other nongovernmental organizations.

UN UNIVERSITY (UNU)

In 1969, Secretary-General U Thant proposed that a UN university be established. The Founding Committee was set up two years later, and in December 1973, the General Assembly approved a charter for the university. The following spring, the UNU Council, composed of academic leaders and prominent persons from 24 countries, was appointed. Members of the university council serve in their individual capacities rather than as representatives of governments. UNU commenced operations in September 1975. For 17 years the university maintained its headquarters in a high-rise office building in Tokyo. In 1992 it moved to a new building in the Shibuya district of Tokyo constructed and made available by the government of Japan. The university maintains a liaison office in New York.

UNU is an autonomous organ of the General Assembly. It is jointly sponsored by the UN and UNESCO, whose Secretary-General and Director General, respectively, together appoint the rector and members of the university council. Its charter guarantees academic freedom and emphasizes the primacy of scholarly excellence over any other considerations—for example, choices of programs and personnel—in determining its activities.

Like traditional universities, UNU is concerned with the advancement of knowledge. Unlike traditional universities, however, it has no students of its own, no faculty, and no campus. It is a completely new institution: an international community of scholars engaged in research, postgraduate training, and the dissemination of knowledge to help solve, in the words of its charter, "pressing global problems of human survival, development and welfare." It operates through worldwide networks of academic and research institutions and individual scholars who work together on projects concerned with such problems as peace, development, the environment, science, and technology. The UNU's areas of concentration are: peace and governance; environment; science and technology; and development.

The academic activities of the university are carried out primarily through a network of its research and training centers: UNU World Institute for Development Economics Research (UNU/WIDER), Helsinki, Finland; UNU Institute for New Technologies (UNU/Intech), Maastricht, the Netherlands; UNU International Institute for Software Technology (UNU/IIST), Macau; UNU Institute for Natural Resources in Africa (UNU/INRA), at University of Ghana, Legon; UNU Institute of Advanced Studies (UNU/IAS) in Tokyo; UNU Programme for Biotechnology in Latin America and the Caribbean (UNU/BIOLAC) in Planta Baja, Venezuela; UNU International Leadership Academy (UNU/ILA) in Amman, Jordan; UNU International Network on Water, Environment and Health (UNU/INWEH) in Hamilton, Ontario, Canada; UNU Food and Nutrition Programme for Human and Social Development at Cornell University in Ithaca, New York (US); UNU Geothermal Training Programme (UNU/GTP) in Reykjavik, Iceland; and The Initiative on Conflict Resolution and Ethnicity (INCORE) in Londonderry, Northern Ireland, UK.

Between 1976 and 1996, some 1,450 UNU fellows received postgraduate training through the university's network. Fellows are selected after recommendation from their home institutions, which must be working in an area of concern to the university, and must be committed to returning to work at those institutions.

The UNU Press publishes scholarly works on the United Nations system in the areas of peace studies, regional studies, technology and development, human and social development, international law, food and nutrition, energy technology, and nat-

ural resources and environment. The UNU Press publishes one periodical, *The Food and Nutrition Bulletin*, issued quarterly. UNU publications are distributed in North America by UNIPUB based in Lanham, Maryland.

UNU is supported by voluntary contributions from governments, foundations, and individuals. Its principal source of support is investment income from an endowment fund that ensures academic freedom and financial independence. The annual budget in 2000 was approximately US$36 million.

UNIVERSITY FOR PEACE

The University for Peace was established in 1980 in San Jose, Costa Rica, to promote postgraduate studies and research on peace. A General Assembly resolution called on member states, NGOs, and intergovernmental bodies, as well as interested individuals and organizations, to contribute to the university's Trust Fund.

In 2000, the University for Peace (nicknamed UPAZ) was in the process of major change and transition in which its programs, priorities, and administrative practices were being reviewed and a new strategy and program was being developed. At the time, its programs included Culture for Peace and Democracy in Central America; Natural Resources and Peace; Communications for Peace; Human Rights and Education for Peace; International World Center of Research and Information for Peace (in Montevideo, Uruguay); Gandhi Television Center for Communication and Peace; Radio for Peace International; and CEDIPAZ, a center for documentation and information for peace as well as the UPAZ library.

INTERNATIONAL RESEARCH AND TRAINING INSTITUTE FOR THE ADVANCEMENT OF WOMEN (INSTRAW)

The United Nations International Research and Training Institute for the Advancement of Women (INSTRAW) was established by the Economic and Social Council in conformity with an earlier decision of the General Assembly, which was based on a recommendation made by the World Conference of the International Women's Year held in Mexico City from 19 June to 2 July 1975. In 1984, INSTRAW's statute, submitted by INSTRAW's Board of Trustees, its governing body, was approved by *Economic and Social Council resolution 1984/124* and then by *General Assembly resolution No. 39/249.* INSTRAW is the only autonomous research and training vehicle at the international level in order to contribute to the advancement and mobilization of women in development, to raise awareness of women's issues worldwide, and to better assist women to meet new challenges and directions. INSTRAW has been based in Santo Domingo since 1983, at the invitation of the Government of the Dominican Republic.

INSTRAW and its work are governed by the Board of Trustees, which is composed of eleven members nominated by Member States and appointed by the Economic and Social Council, based on their personal capacity and the principle of equitable geographical distribution. A representative of the Secretary-General, the Director of the Institute, a representative of each of the Regional Commissions of the Economic and Social Council, and a representative of the Host Country are *ex officio* members of the Board of Trustees. The Institute and its work are funded by voluntary contributions received from States, inter-governmental organizations, non-governmental organizations, and private sources. The main responsibilities and tasks of the Board of Trustees are: to formulate principles, policies, and guidelines for the activities of the Institute; to consider and approve the work program and budget proposals of the Institute on the basis of recommendations submitted by the Director of the Institute; to make necessary or desirable recommendations for the operation of the

Institute; and to report periodically to the Economic and Social Council and to the General Assembly.

INSTRAW's research and training programs are aimed at placing issues relevant to the advancement of women into the economic and political decision-making process. It does this by holding national training workshops and conducting joint research and training programs and projects in collaboration with specialized United Nations agencies, the Commission on the Status of Women, United Nations Focal Points for Women, and especially, regarding data and statistics, with the Statistical Division of the United States Secretariat. INSTRAW's training program, supported by data and its research findings, aims at developing training materials that will include women in the development process, especially in developing countries.

Two billion people in remote rural areas and urban slums of the developing world—half of whom are women—lack safe drinking water and even rudimentary sanitation facilities. Because of the critical need to address the question of water for human survival, INSTRAW produced in 1986, and updated in 1991, a training package on "Women, Water Supply and Sanitation," which has been the focus of ten national, regional, and international training seminars organized by the Institute from 1987 to 1994 in some African, Asian, and Latin American countries. The package illustrates the importance of women's participation on all aspects of water resources, including agriculture, human resources development and water resources management. INSTRAW's modular training program is crucial due to negative effects that water and sanitation problems have on a large number of the world's population.

Considering the importance of waste disposal for reasons of health and environmental sanitation, INSTRAW prepared an additional module to include in the "Women, Water Supply and Sanitation" package, aimed at sensitizing the decision makers on the needs and ways of including women in waste management schemes. Produced in 1994, the new training module of "Women and Waste Management" has been used in Namibia (first ever training seminar ever conducted in Namibia), Guyana, and Ecuador (where five national follow-up seminars were conducted with a total of 159 participants), with an average of 40 participants in each country. This training module presents an integrated approach to environmental sanitation and provides practical guidelines and checklists for integrating women at the designing, implementation, operation and maintenance, monitoring, and evaluation phases. The module provides numerous examples of successful community waste management and other initiatives in the area of environmental sanitation around the world.

The multimedia training package, "Women and New and Renewable Sources of Energy" (NRSE), was first developed by INSTRAW in 1989 (and updated in 1995). The main objective is to contribute with a new approach in the organization of NRSE systems by including women's needs as well as their participation in the planning, technical operations, maintenance, assessment, and implementation of environmentally sound NRSE programs and projects.

INSTRAW produced in 1995 a modular training package in "Women, Environmental Management and Sustainable Development." It was developed for senior officials of Ministries of Environment, Natural Resources, Planning, Women's Affairs, Education, Health; development planners and provincial or local authorities in charge of environmental programs and projects; engineers in charge of designing new technologies; university professors, trainers and managers of national training institutes and educational institutions training staff on various aspects of women, environmental management, and sustainable development, and representatives of nongovernmental and women's organizations involved in environmental projects.

In 1995, INSTRAW produced a training package on "Gender Statistics and Policy." The most important feature of this training package is that it is designed to provide statisticians and development planners with hands-on exercises on the actual use of existing data in policy designs. This package contains a pre-workshop module, which is designed to familiarize the users with gender issues and their relevance to National policy goals, better preparing them for the actual training; illustration of how gender-specific statistics and indicators affect policy goals/targets; computerized statistical policy models which visually describe direct impact of certain variables on target policy indicators. This module includes statistical models that can be adapted at the national level.

During 1993, INSTRAW adapted existing computer models in order to assist policy makers in understanding the relationship between certain sectoral policies and the advancement of women. This was completed in collaboration with the Population Division of the former Department of Economic and Social Development. The two models, entitled "Urban Women in Development Model" and "Rural Women in Development Model" are designed as teaching tools and conceptual framework that can serve as a basis for recognizing the multisectoral approach needed to ensure equitable participation of women and men in development. The models come with an instruction manual, sample exercises, and a computer diskette containing the program information.

The United Nations leadership in recognizing women's equal rights as prerequisite for their full participation in sustainable development is not as well known as it deserves to be. INSTRAW attempted to address this situation in the first module of the "Gender Training Portfolio," published in 1993. This Portfolio is designed to describe and disseminate information on women/gender and development for use in a variety of situations. As the world works toward the goal of sustainable development, people become more aware of the interaction of gender relations in development planning and its effect on the status of women worldwide. INSTRAW's aim is to promote the sharing and effective utilization of such knowledge to positively influence development policies nd help make them more responsive to the needs of both women and men.

UNITED NATIONS DEVELOPMENT FUND FOR WOMEN (UNIFEM)

In 1976, the UN General Assembly established the Voluntary Fund for the United Nations Decade for Women. The fund was created to provide direct support for women's projects and to promote the inclusion of women in the decision-making processes of mainstream development programs. In 1985 the New York-based organization formally joined the UN family of agencies as UNIFEM.

UNIFEM reports directly to the administrator of UNDP. It is overseen by a five-member Consultative Committee representing UN member states from the world's five principal regional groups. The committee approves large projects and advises on the use of the fund's resources. UNIFEM is administered by a director.

In order to support efforts of the women of the developing world to achieve their objective for economic and social development and for equality, and by so doing to improve the quality of life for women and men alike, the fund supports microprograms run by women in developing countries. For example, UNIFEM estimates that although women grow, process, and market between 50% and 80% of the food consumed in developing countries, governments rarely record these inputs or support them with financial credit. UNIFEM's programs include: training women in improved agricultural techniques; transfer of appropriate food technologies such as grinding mills, graters, oil presses, solar driers, and fish smokers; obtaining for women increased access to credit for seeds, fertilizers, and equipments; and support for microenterprises. UNIFEM works with the UN High Commisioner for Refugees (UNHCR) in assisting African refugees. At any one time it manages a portfolio of approximately 150 projects and has supported over 750 projects in 100 developing countries.

In 1991 UNIFEM collaborated on the publication of *The World's Women 1970–90: The Trends and Statistics*. Co-authored by the UN Statistical Office, UNICEF, and UNFPA, this publication gathered statistics and interpreted trends on women, families, and households; women in public life and leadership; the status of education and training for women; health and child-bearing; housing, human settlements, and the environment; and women's work and the economy.

Financing is provided by the governments of both industrialized and developing countries, by nongovernmental organizations, foundations, corporations, private individuals, and from UNIFEM's growing number of national committees.

SOCIAL AND HUMANITARIAN ASSISTANCE

International disaster relief, the special problems of children, refugees, the elderly, youth, the disabled, and families are all subjects for which member states have directed the UN to provide international leadership and expert guidance. The global nature of trade in illicit narcotic drugs and the internationalization of criminal activities were social ills that became so destabilizing at the end of the twentieth century that member states requested their international organization to implement innovative global programs to maintain security and social justice.

INTERNATIONAL DISASTER RELIEF

Background

The international community is faced with the growing challenge of preventing, mitigating the effects of, and providing humanitarian assistance to affected populations in crises that require rapid and effective response. The 1990s saw a dramatic increase in "complex emergencies" that often involved ethnic and civil strife. In mid-1994 more than 30 million people in 29 countries were in dire need of emergency assistance. Severe drought threatening over 20 million people in sub-Saharan Africa added an additional element of suffering to that already faced by millions in Burundi, Liberia, Rwanda, Somalia, southern Sudan, and Zaire. A study released at the World Conference on Natural Disaster Reduction, convened by the General Assembly in May 1994, showed that the previous three decades had seen a steady and rapid increase in the number of significant natural disasters—and in the numbers of people affected.

Office of the United Nations Disaster Relief Coordinator (UNDRO)

Beginning in 1965, proposals were put forward in the General Assembly to increase the UN's ability to help people stricken by disasters, but it was the disasters of 1970 that brought international concern for emergency relief to a head. In 1971, the General Assembly established the Office of the United Nations Disaster Relief Coordinator (UNDRO), with headquarters in Geneva.

UNDRO was not designed to assume all the responsibilities of meeting disasters from its own resources. Its principal function is that of catalyst and coordinator of donors of aid and services. Its data bank and independent telecommunications system, supplemented by the worldwide UN system, give it the capacity to define the specific needs arising from a disaster and to respond rapidly by identifying potential sources of relief. It directs and mobilizes aid emanating from the UN system and coordinates aid from other sources.

UNDRO's mandate also includes assisting governments in preventing disasters or mitigating their effects by contingency planning, in association with similarly concerned voluntary organizations. It promotes the study, prevention, control, and prediction of natural disasters and gathers and disseminates information relevant to disaster relief.

Between its inception in 1972 and 1987, UNDRO helped coordinate relief and raise money for emergency aid in more than 380 major disasters.

The Department of Humanitarian Affairs (DHA)

In December 1991, the General Assembly, by its Resolution 46/182, recognized the need to strengthen coordination for rapid response to humanitarian emergencies. Over the years ad hoc arrangements had sprung up in many of the UN departments and specialized agencies to deal with emergency relief. Sometimes these arrangements were found to be working at cross-purposes or competing for financial support from the same potential donors. The General Assembly requested the Secretary-General to designate an emergency relief coordinator, supported by a secretariat, to ensure that the entire UN system was better prepared for, and more capable of rapid and coherent response to national disasters and other humanitarian emergencies. The resolution also stipulated guiding principles of humanity, neutrality and impartiality for the provision of humanitarian assistance. It also stressed respect for the sovereignty, territorial integrity and national unity of states.

In April 1992, the Secretary-General established the Department of Humanitarian Affairs, incorporating UNDRO, various UN units that had been dealing with specific emergency programs, and the secretariat for the International Decade for Natural Disaster Reduction. The Secretary-General appointed an Emergency Relief Coordinator to head the new department. The DHA has its headquarters in New York and an office in Geneva.

Resolution 46/182 gave the DHA three tools to speed up the response of the international community to emergencies: the Inter-Agency Standing Committee (IASC) to formulate and coordinate policy; the Central Emergency Revolving Fund (CERF) as a quick source of emergency funding; and the Consolidated Appeals Process (CAP), which assesses the needs of a critical situations and prepares a comprehensive interagency response strategy.

With UN reforms in the late 1990s, the Office for the Coordination of Humanitarian Affairs (OCHA) was established to manage complex emergencies (through the Consolidated Appeals Process), natural disasters, and other humanitarian crises. OCHA replaced the Department of Humanitarian Affairs (DHA). In 1997, the New York and Geneva offices of OCHA were staffed by 50 regular budget posts and 87 extra-budgetary posts; additionally, there were 51 staff members working in the field. Its 1997 budget was US$42.4 million. As the successor organization to DHA, OCHA took over management and coordination of DHA's programs including IASC, CERF, and CAP.

The IASC is chaired by the Emergency Relief Coordinator and is composed of the executive heads of the following UN organizations: the United Nations Development Programme (UNDP); the Office of the UN High Commissioner for Refugees (UNHCR); the UN Children's Fund (UNICEF); the World Food Program (WFP); the World Health Organization (WHO), and the Food and Agriculture Organization of the UN (FAO). Other humanitarian organizations such as the International Committee of the Red Cross (ICRC), the International Federation of Red Cross and Red Crescent Societies (IFRC), and the International Organization for Migration (IOM) also take part in the IASC. Representatives of relevant nongovernmental organizations (NGOs) are invited to participate.

In addition to coordinating overall policy on humanitarian assistance, the IASC addresses issues such as: access to victims, security of personnel and relief supplies, ensuring humanitarian imperatives in conflict situations, examining special needs arising from application of UN sanctions, demobilization of combatants, de-mining, resource mobilization, assistance to internally displaced persons, field coordination of international humanitarian responses, and ensuring transition from relief to development.

The Central Emergency Revolving Fund (CERF) of US$50 million was created under the terms of Resolution 46/182 as a cash-flow mechanism for use by operational organizations, especially during the critical initial stages of emergencies. The CERF is financed by voluntary contributions and managed by the Department of Humanitarian Affairs. Agencies draw on the CERF and repay the advances they receive as donors respond to their own fundraising efforts. From its establishment in 1992 until the end of 1997, the CERF was utilized on 51 occasions, providing operational humanitarian organizations with a total of about US$128 million.

The Consolidated Appeals Process (CAP), coordinated and monitored by OCHA, is an interagency exercise by which UN system organizations and other humanitarian organizations assess the full range of requirements for responding to emergencies. The CAP helps the international community to identify the most critical needs of affected people and to determine the most appropriate ways to provide assistance. This process enables donors and agencies to concentrate their efforts where they are needed most and eliminates wasteful competition among agencies for donor funds. From 1995 through May 2000, appeals were launched for countries including Afghanistan, Albania, Angola, Bosnia and Herzegovina, Burundi, Congo, Democratic Republic of the Congo, Croatia, Eritrea, Ethiopia, Guinea-Bissau, Indonesia, Iraq, Democratic People's Republic of Korea, Lebanon, Liberia, the Former Yugoslav Republic of Macedonia, Rwanda, Sierra Leone, Somalia, Sudan, Tajikistan, Uganda, United Republic of Tanzania, and Yugoslavia. Appeals are often made by region as well—including for the Caucasus, Great Lakes Region of Africa, and Southeastern Europe (including the Kosovo province of Yugoslavia).

OCHA's work takes place where the fields of international security, political affairs, and humanitarian concerns converge. An important responsibility entrusted to OCHA involves humanitarian diplomacy in efforts to prevent emergencies and in negotiation with parties to conflicts aimed at ensuring access to those in need. OCHA's staff is involved in policy planning and early warning functions, emergency operational support and relief coordination, and disaster mitigation. The OCHA maintains close contact with the UN Departments of Political Affairs and Peacekeeping Operations in order to coordinate the security, political, and humanitarian aspects of complex emergencies.

New Initiatives

To help manage its efforts, OCHA set up Relief Web, available at http://www.reliefweb.int. The Internet site provides up-to-date information on complex emergencies and natural disasters collected from over 170 sources. Users from over 150 countries access an average of 200,000 documents each month. In addition, OCHA runs the Humanitarian Early Warning System (HEWS), which identifies crises with humanitarian implications. Through analysis of field-based information and the evaluation of trends, HEWS informs decision-makers at headquarters about the likelihood and extent of crises. An extensive database of information for more than 100 countries supports this activity. The Integrated Regional Information Network (IRIN), at Nairobi, was set up in 1995 to analyze and synthesize data on developments in Africa's Great Lakes region. It issues daily reports and thematic studies for over 2,000 primary subscribers in more than 50 countries.

IRIN at Abidjan was set up in 1997 and began providing similar reports covering West Africa. IRIN coverage was expected to be expanded in the late 1990s to cover southern Africa, Central Asia and the Caucasus region, as well as the Balkans.

International Decade for Natural Disaster Reduction

Between 1960 and 1990 deaths from natural disasters rose by a factor of 10, with 90% of casualties occurring in developing countries ill prepared to respond to natural disasters. Although the World Meteorological Organization has shown that each dollar spent on disaster preparedness is equivalent to 100 dollars spent after a disaster, no mechanisms existed to transfer the huge body of knowledge on disaster preparedness and prevention from the industrialized countries to developing countries. For example, an earthquake of 6.6 magnitude on the Richter scale in California in January 1994 caused fewer than 100 deaths. An earthquake of 6.4 magnitude in India's Maharashtra State in September 1993 caused 10,000 deaths. Most of the deaths in the Indian tragedy were caused by the collapse of homes while people slept. By contrast, California has long been a proving ground for earthquake-resistant architectural innovations.

In 1989, the General Assembly declared the 1990s the International Decade for Natural Disaster Reduction to reduce loss of life and property damage resulting from natural disasters. It established a high-level council of 10 internationally renowned personalities, a scientific and technical committee of 24 scientists from around the world, and approximately 120 national committees to promote the decade and the formulation of disaster preparedness programs. 13 October was declared "International Day for Natural Disaster Reduction," and observed by public gatherings and publicity to raise awareness of the need to implement disaster preparedness.

In May 1994, the World Conference on Natural Disaster Reduction was convened in Yokohama, Japan. Representatives from 147 countries and 37 nongovernmental organizations and observers from UN specialized agencies participated in the conference, which both reviewed implementation of the General Assembly's recommendations during the first half of the decade and adopted the "Guidelines for Natural Disaster Prevention, Preparedness and Mitigation," also called the "Yokohama Strategy." It noted that the first half of the decade had seen some improvement in the field of disaster response, but that the goals for disaster prevention and preparedness had not received wide publicity.

The conference document stated that, while natural phenomena that cause disasters are outside human control, vulnerability of populations was a result of human activity (or nonactivity). In its "Strategy for the Year 2000 and Beyond," the conference called for a global culture of prevention and a policy of self-reliance in each vulnerable country and community. Other elements of the strategy included education and training in disaster prevention, strengthening research and development for disaster reduction and mitigation, and improving awareness in vulnerable communities through more active use of media. Finally the conference called on all countries to express the political commitment to reduce their vulnerability by means of legislation and policy decisions at the highest levels to mobilize domestic resources, develop risk assessment programs, and emergency plans and to design projects for subregional, regional, and international cooperation. It also recommended an improvement in communications capabilities on natural disasters among countries for preparedness and early warning systems.

Man-made Humanitarian Disasters

Perhaps the thorniest problem for OCHA (then the DHA) was the increase in and complexity of humanitarian disasters caused by internal civil strife in places like Angola, the former Yugoslavia, and Rwanda. In the largest exodus ever known, 2 million people in Rwanda abandoned their homes in one week during the resumption of a civil war and the organized slaughter of thousands of civilians in that country in the summer of 1994. The exodus overwhelmed the capacity of international aid organizations to deal with the crisis, and thousands of people died of cholera, dysentery, and other diseases in makeshift camps hurriedly set up along Rwanda's border with other countries. In August 1994, the UN agencies appealed to member states for us$470 million to respond to the disaster. The initial response to the appeal yielded us$137 million. In his report to the 49th General Assembly on "Strengthening of the coordination of emergency humanitarian assistance" (A/49/177), the Secretary-General stated:

"Complex emergencies are presenting serious new challenges to humanitarian organizations and others involved in providing relief assistance. Disregard for fundamental humanitarian principles, serious violations of humanitarian law and threats to the safety and protection of relief personnel have underscored the need for enhancing awareness of all involved in complex emergencies—including the Security Council—of humanitarian concerns and objectives and for appropriate measures to protect humanitarian mandates in conflict situations. *While the new generation of multifaceted United Nations operations require close interaction between the political, military and humanitarian dimensions, it is important, at the same time, to ensure that the humanitarian component can preserve its unique identity by maintaining neutrality and impartiality.*" (emphasis added).

In this connection, the IASC established a set of guidelines for humanitarian missions in conflict situations:

(a) The need for humanitarian relief assistance to be undertaken in accordance with the principles of impartiality, neutrality, and humanity;

(b) Reaffirmation of free, safe, and unimpeded access for humanitarian assistance and the role of humanitarian diplomacy in that regard;

(c) The need for greater collaboration with nongovernmental organizations engaged in humanitarian relief;

(d) The need to ensure security and protection of all relief personnel;

(e) The need to apprise the Security Council fully on relevant humanitarian issues that should be appropriately reflected in its decisions on complex emergencies;

(f) The importance of shielding humanitarian assistance against the effects of sanctions, particularly in relation to vulnerable groups.

United Nations Sahelian Office (UNSO)

Another UN undertaking in disaster relief developed in response to the desiccation of the Sudano-Sahelian zone of West Africa. Many years of drought in Burkina Faso, Chad, Mali, Mauritania, Niger, and Senegal had, by 1973, resulted in a crisis and the threat of mass starvation in the region. In May, the Secretary-General, acting under resolutions of the General Assembly and the Economic and Social Council, designated FAO as the "focal point" of an emergency operation of the UN system to provide and transport rations, seeds for sowing, animal feed, and vaccines to victims in the six countries. The following month, the UN Sahelian Office (UNSO) was created to promote medium- and long-term recovery in cooperation with the Permanent Interstate Committee on Drought Control in the Sahel, known by its French acronym CILSS and composed of eight affected states—Burkina

Faso, Cape Verde, Chad, Gambia, Mali, Mauritania, Niger, and Senegal.

In 1977, UNSO's mandate was expanded to assist the UN Environment Programme (UNEP) in implementing the Plan of Action to Combat Desertification in the Sudano-Sahelian Region. Within its desertification program, UNSO serves 22 countries. In addition to the member states of CILSS, these are Benin, Cameroon, Djibouti, Ethiopia, Ghana, Guinea, Guinea-Bissau, Kenya, Nigeria, Somalia, Sudan, Tanzania, Togo, and Uganda. UNSO mobilizes general and earmarked contributions to promote sustainable management of the natural resources in arid and semi-arid lands. It helps governments plan and coordinate natural resource management and implement field projects on soil and water conservation and integrated land management.

UN CHILDREN'S FUND (UNICEF)

The UN International Children's Emergency Fund (UNICEF) was established by the General Assembly on 11 December 1946 to provide emergency relief assistance in the form of food, medicine, and clothing to the children of postwar Europe and China. In December 1950, the General Assembly extended the life of the fund for three years, changing its mandate to emphasize health and nutrition programs of long-range benefit to children of developing countries. In October 1953, the General Assembly decided that UNICEF should continue its work as a permanent arm of the UN system, and charged the organization to emphasize programs giving long-term benefit to children everywhere, particularly those in developing countries who are in the greatest need. The organization's name was changed to the UN Children's Fund, but the acronym "UNICEF" was retained. The UNICEF Executive Board reaffirmed its mandate in January 1996, when it adopted a statement on the mission of UNICEF saying that UNICEF "is guided by the Convention on the Rights of the Child and strives to establish children's rights as enduring ethical principles and international standards of behaviour towards children."

In 1959 the General Assembly unanimously adopted the Declaration of the Rights of the Child, affirming the right of children to special protection and opportunities and facilities for healthy, normal development.

Following a global study of the needs of children in 1961, UNICEF increased the scope and flexibility of its approach to children to include projects that promote the role of children as an invaluable "human resource" in national development, thus making it possible to provide aid for education.

UNICEF was awarded the Nobel Peace Prize in 1965.

In November 1989, the General Assembly voted to transform the rights and obligations under the 1959 Declaration into the Convention on the Rights of the Child, the most comprehensive treaty ever to address the individual rights of children and set universally accepted standards for their children. The convention entered into force as international law in September 1990. In 2000, UNICEF reported that the convention had been ratified by every country in the world except two, and "therefore uniquely places children center-stage in the quest for the universal application of human rights."

As the only United Nations agency devoted exclusively to the needs of children, UNICEF promotes the full implementation of the Convention on the Rights of the Child by 1995. UNICEF also participated in the World Conference on Human Rights in Vienna in June 1993, speaking out forcefully on behalf of children and against violation of their rights.

UNICEF also participated in the International Conference on Population and Development in Cairo, Egypt, in September 1994; the World Summit for Social Development in Copenhagen, Denmark, in March 1995; the Fourth World Conference on Women in Beijing, China, in September 1995; the Habitat II World Assembly of Cities and Local Authorities in Istanbul, Turkey, in

June 1996; and the World Congress against Commercial Sexual Exploitation of Children in Stockholm, Sweden, in August 1996, strongly promoting measures for child survival, protection, and development. UNICEF was one of the host organizations and core participants of Beijing+5, the first follow-up meeting to the watershed Fourth World Conference on Women (1995). Convened in June 2000 in New York City, Beijing+5 (also called Women 2000) was set up to review progress and establish action plans for the next five years. More than 150 countries and thousands of non-governmental organizations participated in programs at UN headquarters. UNICEF focused on four key themes at the event: gender equality starts early; women's rights and girls' rights are independent (laws and structures that protect women also need to be made to protect girls); children's rights cannot be achieved without girls' rights; and community partnerships are needed to end violence and prevent HIV/AIDS. In support of women's issues, UNICEF funded a news web site, http://www.womenswire.org, to publicize areas of concern and advance public understanding of the issues.

Purposes and Scope of Work

Combining humanitarian and development objectives, UNICEF's primary goal is to help children of the poorest and least developed countries. It helps them directly, by supporting government programs to improve child health, nutrition, education, and social services, and indirectly, by serving as child advocate, appealing to governments and to the consciences of individuals worldwide to find and commit the resources required to protect and prepare children adequately.

UNICEF's mandate from the General Assembly's 1946 resolution for "strengthening . . . the permanent child health and welfare programs of the countries receiving assistance" has been developed and continuously adapted to current conditions. It places strong emphasis on community participation in the development and operation of services for children and has increasingly focused on community-based action. As a funding agency—as distinct from a specialized agency—UNICEF is able to work with various ministries and nongovernmental organizations, maintaining an intersectoral approach to community action in meeting the needs of children.

In 1976, UNICEF adopted an approach to the provision of basic health and welfare services, the key element of which was community participation. This new approach resulted from experiences in economically and politically diverse developing countries showing that services are likely to be not only cheaper but also more effective when community members are involved, because they mobilize hitherto unused abilities within the community and the services can be run at recurrent costs that the country and community can afford. Integration of women into the establishment of community-based services is especially important, since their participation can have a significant impact on the quality of life for their children.

UNICEF gives priority to the establishment of long-term programs and places special emphasis on the use of national expertise wherever feasible.

UNICEF cooperates with developing countries in several ways: it assists in the planning and extension of services benefiting children and in the exchange of experience between countries; it provides funds to strengthen the training and orientation of national personnel, complementing, wherever possible, the work of specialized agencies; and it delivers technical supplies, equipment, and other aid for extending services.

In September 1990, the Convention on the Rights of the Child entered into force, less than one year after its adoption by the General Assembly. That month, UNICEF organized the World Summit for Children, attended by representatives from more than 159 countries, including 71 heads of state or government. It pro-

duced a Declaration and a Plan of Action, which recognized the rights of the young to "first call" on nations' resources and set goals for the year 2000, including:

1. A reduction of the 1990 infant and under-five child mortality rates by one third or to 50 to 70 per 1,000 live births respectively, whichever is lower;
2. A reduction by half of the 1990 maternal mortality rate;
3. A reduction by half of the 1990 rate for severe malnutrition among children under the age of five;
4. Universal access to safe drinking water and to sanitary means of excreta disposal, and
5. Universal access to basic education and completion of primary education by at least 80% of school-age children.

In September 1996, the Secretary-General of the UN reported to the General Assembly that significant progress was made toward the World Summit goals in some 90 countries in the previous 6 years. Over 150 countries had drawn up National Programs of Action (NPAs) to implement the goals.

Recognizing that survival and development of children is intricately linked to the status of women in developing countries, the Executive Board, at its annual meeting in May 1994, requested the executive director to give high priority to UNICEF efforts to develop gender-sensitive indicators in each sectoral area of development and to set gender-specific goals in national programmes of action. UNICEF supports gender equalit, organized participation of women at all levels, and capacity-building and mobilization of youth for a more gender-equitable society.

At the Fourth World Conference on Women in Beijing, China, in September 1995, UNICEF advocated more attention and resources to girls' education and the linkage between goals for girls and women. It drew attention to the complementary objectives of the Convention on the Rights of the Child and the Convention on the Elimination of All Forms of Discrimination against Women.

As a result of the Beijing conference, UNICEF identified the following areas of concern or emphasis: women and poverty; education and training of women; women's health, including safe motherhood and reproductive health (including HIV/AIDS); violence against women, including family violence and harmful traditional practices (such as female genital mutilation), sexual abuse, and exploitation and trafficking in women and girls; women and armed conflict; women in power and decision-making; institutional mechanisms for the advancement of women; human rights of women; women and the media; and women and the environment.

Organization

UNICEF is an integral part of the UN, with semiautonomous status. The Executive Board, which is the governing body of UNICEF, meets once a year to establish policy, review programs, and approve expenditures. It also holds regular sessions between the annual formal meetings. The Executive Board has 36 members, elected for a three-year term with the following regional allocation of seats: eight African states, seven Asian states, four Eastern European states, five Latin American and Caribbean states, and 12 Western European and other states (including Japan). The board year runs from 1 January to 31 December. In 2000, board members whose terms would expire at the end of the year were: Antigua and Barbuda, Azerbaijan, Bangladesh, Comoros, Congo, Finland, Greece, Japan, Kazakhstan, Libyan Arab Jamahiraya, South Africa, Spain, Sudan, Turkey, United Kingdom of Great Britain and Northern Ireland, and Yemen; board members whose terms would expire 31 December 2001 were: Canada, China, Denmark, Guyana, Pakistan, Paraguay, Russian Federation, Ukraine, and Zimbabwe; and board members whose terms would expire 31 December 2002 were: Bolivia, Côte d'Ivoire, Guinea, India, Islamic Republic of Iran, Italy, Netherlands, Romania, Sweden, Trinidad and Tobago, and United States.

The executive director of UNICEF is appointed by the UN Secretary-General in consultation with the Executive Board. The administration of UNICEF and the appointment and direction of staff are the responsibility of the executive director, under policy directives laid down by the Executive Board, and under a broad authority delegated to the executive director by the Secretary-General. The executive director as of 2000 was Carol Bellamy; she was reappointed to a second term in 1999, and would serve to April 2005.

UNICEF has a network of country and regional offices serving 133 countries and territories. UNICEF maintains headquarters offices in New York, Geneva, Brussels, Tokyo, Florence (site of the International Child Development Centre, available at http://www.unicef-icdc.org), Copenhagen, and Huningue (France). Eight regional offices serve Latin America and the Caribbean, Central and Eastern Europe (including Commonwealth of Independent States and Baltic States), East Asia and the Pacific, Eastern and Southern Africa, Middle East and North Africa, South Asia, and West and Central Africa.

In 2000, UNICEF employed a total staff of 5,594 people, 86% of which were in the field.

In 1985, only 27% of international professional posts were filled by women. By 1996, that figure had been raised to 40%. In 2000, UNICEF reported that it endorsed its own policy of gender equality and empowerment of women and girls by mobilizing and organizing women for participation in its programs. The organization paid particular attention to ensuring that women, both in its offices and in the field, were in decision-making roles that would help guide UNICEF's work.

UNICEF is supported by 37 National Committees, mostly in the industrialized countries, whose more than 100,000 volunteer members raise money through various activities, including the sale of greeting cards. The committees also undertake advocacy, education for development, and information activities. About 30% ($331 million, including $40 million for emergencies) of the organization's 1995 budget was contributed through the National Committees.

In 2000 the National Committees maintained offices in Andorra, Australia, Austria, Belgium, Bulgaria, Canada, Czech Republic, Denmark, Estonia, Finland, France, Germany, Greece, Hong Kong, Hungary, Ireland, Israel, Italy, Japan, Latvia, Lithuania, Luxembourg, Netherlands, New Zealand, Norway, Poland, Portugal, Republic of Korea, San Marino, Slovakia, Slovenia, Spain, Sweden, Switzerland, Turkey, United Kingdom, and United States.

Cooperation with Other Agencies

UNICEF collaborates closely with the specialized agencies, including the International Labour Organization (ILO), Food and Agriculture Organization (FAO), the United Nations Education, Scientific and Cultural Organization (UNESCO), and World Health Organization (WHO), as well as with the units of the UN Secretariat concerned with services benefiting children. It also works with the funding agencies and programs of the UN system—such as United Nations Development Programme (UNDP), United Nations Population Fund (UNFPA), World Food Programme (WFP), the World Bank, International Fund for Agricultural Development (IFAD), and United Nations Environment Programme (UNEP)—to exchange information, discuss policies of cooperation affecting the situation of children, and explore potential program collaboration.

Close working relations are maintained with the UN Department of Humanitarian Affairs (DHA) and with the United Nations High Commissioner for Refugees (UNHCR) in emergency relief and aid to refugees, respectively. UNICEF also works with regional development banks and the regional economic and social commissions and with bilateral aid agencies.

Of particular importance is UNICEF's cooperation and collaboration in programs with nongovernmental organizations (NGOs), both national and international. The NGO Committee on UNICEF comprises over 100 international professional and voluntary groups involved with children and either directly or indirectly, through concern with aspects of social development. A roster of international and national correspondent organizations is continuing to grow, particularly from developing countries. Some 400 organizations participate in activities and share information through UNICEF/NGO liaison offices in New York and Geneva. Many of these organizations have become important supporters of UNICEF by providing a channel for advocacy on behalf of children and by participating in fund-raising and in UNICEF programs.

Financing

UNICEF's work is accomplished with voluntary contributions from both governments and nongovernmental sources. Total income for 1998 was us$966 million. Contributions from governments and intergovernmental organizations accounted for 62% (us$603 million) of this income; 33% (us$319 million) was from nongovernmental and private sources; and 5% (us$44 million) was derived from a variety of other sources. The United States remained the largest donor to UNICEF, providing a total of us$162 million. Sweden and Norway were the next largest government donors. The largest nongovernment donor nation was Japan with us$76,490. Germany and the Netherlands were the next largest nongovernment donors. (For other top donor nations, see the following table.) Additionally, the United Nations Foundation, Inc., established in 1997 by American businessman Ted Turner with a us$1 billion grant, approved more than us$18 million in funds for UNICEF in 1998.

Top Donors to UNICEF 1998
(in thousands of US dollars)

NATION	CONTRIBUTIONS	COMMITTEES
AUSTRALIA	13,902	6,589
AUSTRIA	2,797	2,629
BELGIUM	4,155	7,630
CANADA	23,660	5,569
CHINA	1,160	NA
DENMARK	37,689	2,019
FINLAND	14,290	2,218
FRANCE	10,120	30,597
GERMANY	6,672	47,362
GREECE	NA	4,258
HONG KONG	NA	6,573
IRELAND	3,758	NA
ITALY	12,860	22,092
JAPAN	38,748	76,490
KOREA, REPUBLIC OF	NA	2,738
NETHERLANDS	44,700	41,060
NEW ZEALAND	1,888	NA
NORWAY	71,406	NA
PORTUGAL	NA	3,316
SPAIN	1,797	22,581
SWEDEN	75,066	2,051
SWITZERLAND	14,130	15,856
UNITED KINGDOM	38,557	15,025
UNITED STATES	161,530	21,600

NA=not available

Expenditure

UNICEF's total expenditure in 1998 amounted to us$882 million, of which 89% went directly to programs and 11% was spent on administration and other charges. Expenditure by program sector was as follows:

UNICEF Program Expenditure by Sector, 1998
(in millions of US dollars)

SECTOR	EXPENDITURE
Child health	282
Water and environmental sanitation	97
Child nutrition	53
Community and family-based services for children and women	115
Education and early childhood development	123
Planning, advocacy, and support	212
TOTAL	882

PROGRAMS

Through its extensive field network in developing countries UNICEF undertakes, in coordination with governments, local communities, and other partners, programs in health, nutrition, education, water and sanitation, the environment, women in development, and other activities that improve the well-being of children. Emphasis is placed on community-based programs in which people participate actively and are trained in such skills as health care, midwifery, and teaching.

UNICEF facilitates the exchange of programming experience among developing countries, and encourages governments to undertake a regular review of the situation of their children and to incorporate a national policy for children in their comprehensive development plans. It also places emphasis on national capacity building and the use of national expertise wherever possible.

UNICEF provides assistance on the basis of mutually agreed priorities for children in collaboration with the governments concerned. Priority is given to the world's most vulnerable—almost all its resources are therefore invested in the poorest developing countries, with the greatest share going to children under five years old. As of 1999, UNICEF maintained programs in 161 countries: 46 in sub-Saharan Africa; 32 in Latin America; 33 in Asia; 18 in the Middle East and North Africa; and 16 in Central and Eastern Europe and Central Asia.

Health
Immunization

In cooperation with the World Health Organization (WHO), UNICEF supports the expanded Program on Immunization that each year prevents an estimated 3 million child deaths from six diseases—diphtheria, measles, poliomyelitis, tetanus, tuberculosis, and whooping cough. In October 1991, both agencies announced that their goal of protecting 80% of the world's children before their first birthday had been achieved (compared to less than 5% in 1975, when the program was launched). UNICEF and WHO made an effort to raise immunization coverage for the six diseases to this level in all countries, eliminate neonatal tetanus, poliomyelitis and substantially reduce measles deaths and cases by the end of 1995. As a result, a large majority of countries have reached the immunization coverage goal of 80% for all antigens except tetanus toxoid; polio has been eradicated in many countries; major progress has been made towards elimination of neonatal tetanus; and measles mortality and morbidity have been reduced in some regions. In 1998 alone, UNICEF purchased US$86 million worth of vaccines—the largest single commodity purchased.

Oral rehydration therapy

UNICEF works closely with WHO to control diarrheal dehydration, which is the single largest cause of death among children under five years of age in the developing world. UNICEF-assisted programs for the control of diarrheal diseases promote the manufacture and distribution of prepackaged salts—oral rehydration salt (ORS)—or homemade solutions. The use of oral rehydration therapy (ORT) has significantly increased from 17% in 1985 to 85% at present, and is believed to prevent more than 1.5 million deaths each year.

Acute respiratory infections (ARI)

ARI, in particular pneumonia, are the single biggest cause of child mortality in the world and account for over 2 million deaths among children under five years of age in developing countries. UNICEF has adopted a comprehensive approach to control ARI, including helping countries to develop national plans and infrastructures; decentralizing activities to substantial level; training health workers; supporting access to essential drugs and appropriate technological devices; and helping with monitoring and communication.

Safe motherhood

In the 1990s it was estimated that more than a half million women die every year from causes related to pregnancy and childbirth. In cooperation with WHO, UNICEF worked to reduce maternal mortality by 50% by the year 2000, to improve prenatal care, and to ensure safe delivery for all pregnant women and access by all couples to family planning services. It also focuses on information, education, and communication on birth-spacing, responsible parenthood, and discouraging early marriage and early pregnancy.

HIV/AIDS

By 1996, 2.6 million children (400,000 in new infections in 1996) had been infected with the human immunodeficiency virus (HIV), 90% of whom lived in sub-Saharan Africa. A report by the Joint United Nations Programme on HIV/AIDS (UNAIDS) indicated that the majority of the 2.7 million newly infected adults in 1996 were under 25 years old, nearly half of them women. It is estimated that in 1996, 22.6 million people were HIV-infected worldwide.

UNICEF works closely with governments and supports prevention programs such as youth health and development promotion; school-based interventions; sexual and reproductive health promotion; family and community care; and mass communication and mobilization. It also helps AIDS-infected families and AIDS orphans.

UNICEF participates in UNAIDS, cosponsored by the UN Development Fund (UNDF), UN Population Fund (UNFPA), UN Educational, Scientific and Cultural Organizations (UNESCO), World Health Organization (WHO), and the World Bank.

Nutrition

In 1996, 174 million children were malnourished as a result of frequent bouts of diarrhea and other illnesses, bottle-feeding of infants and poor weaning practices, low birth-weight, infrequent feeding and micronutrient deficiencies. On average, over 50% of young child deaths in developing countries are associated with malnutrition. In 2000, UNICEF's statistics showed that 30% of the world's children were moderately to severely underweight and 11% were wasting. UNICEF fights malnutrition by empowering communities; protecting and promoting breastfeeding and appropriate child feeding practices; controlling the three main forms of micronutrient deficiencies—iron, iodine, and vitamin A; improving nutrition information system; and helping countries to reach consensus as to the causes of malnutrition. It aims to achieve universal salt iodization to prevent iodine deficiency disorders, and to eliminate vitamin A deficiency.

UNICEF participated in the International Conference on Nutrition held in Rome in December 1992 and contributed to the formulation of the World Declaration on Nutrition and the Plan of Action for Nutrition adopted by the conference. The declaration identified children under five years of age as the group most affected by malnutrition.

Breastfeeding

In coordination with WHO, UNICEF launched in June 1991, a "baby-friendly hospital initiative" to promote breastfeeding. The initiative aims at empowering women to breastfeed by ending the distribution of free and low-cost supplies of infant formula in hospitals and maternity facilities. As of 1996, 8,120 hospitals and maternity facilities had become "baby-friendly" by implementing the "Ten Steps to Successful Breastfeeding" recommended by UNICEF and WHO. Baby-friendly hospitals encourage mothers to initiate breastfeeding immediately after birth and to continue exclusive breastfeeding, and they do not accept free and low-cost formula from companies.

Water supply and sanitation

Statistics for the period 1990–98 showed that 28% of the world's population living in developing nations did not have access to safe drinking water. During the same period, an astonishing 66% of urban and rural populations in developing countries were without access to adequate sanitation.

To meet the goals of universal access to safe drinking water and to sanitary means of excreta disposal, and elimination of guinea worm disease by the end of the decade, UNICEF allocates a large portion of its income to this sector (for the amount see section on expenditure). In addition to provision of effective low-cost water supply and sanitary services, UNICEF promotes hygiene education and environmental protection. UNICEF is working to eliminate the water-borne guinea worm disease (dracunculiasis).

Basic education

In its 1999 Annual Report, UNICEF stated that nearly a billion people would enter the 21st century unable to read a book or sign their names and that two-thirds of them were women. The total included more than 130 million school-age children, 73 million of them girls, who were growing up in the developing world without access to basic education. UNICEF works to improve access to primary education and to reduce drop-out rates. It gives priority to the education of girls, with the aim of reducing gender disparities. At the Habitat II in Instabul, Turkey in June 1996, UNICEF advocated for the inclusion of children's concerns in the Global Action Plan adopted by the assembly.

At the Fourth World Conference on Women in Beijing in 1995, UNICEF made a successful effort to include girls' education in the Platform for Action adopted by the conference. Also at the conference, UNICEF promised to more than double its resources to basic education during the 1990s, with special attention to girls' education. The organization was to report on its progress at the Beijing+5 conference, in New York in June 2000.

Urban basic services

Almost half of the developing world's urban dwellers are children whose vulnerability has increased with the rapid growth of towns and cities amid economic and environmental crisis and recurring conflict. UNICEF revised its policy in 1993 by focusing on poverty reduction, primary environmental care, rehabilitation, and preventive approaches for urban children in especially difficult circumstances. It also provides advocacy and technical support and emphasizes the need for concerted effort at all levels—national, subnational, and community.

Children in especially difficult circumstances

Around the world, millions of children are at special risk because of acute poverty, wars, natural calamities, disabilities, and other circumstances. Children in such situations often become separated from their relatives, left without the protection and security families provide and vulnerable to terrible forms of exploitation and abuse.

Over 250 million children in the world work, many of them are at risk from hazardous exploitative labor, in factories, in domestic services, on the streets, or in degrading conditions of sexual exploitation. An estimated one million children are believed to work as prostitutes. UNICEF supports special projects for children affected in these ways, by helping provide education, reuniting families, and counseling to help heal trauma. It vigorously advocates against the exploitation of children by working with governments international organizations, and non-governmental organizations to protect child rights as set forth in the Convention on the Rights of the child. At the World Conference against Commercial Exploitation of Children that convened in Stockholm in August 1996, UNICEF strongly called for the immediate end to commercial exploitation of children everywhere in the world.

Emergency relief and rehabilitation

Although most UNICEF activities focus on the "silent" emergencies that claim 12 million children's lives every year, natural disasters and armed conflicts constitute the main "loud" emergencies that challenge the organization's resources. In any emergency situation, UNICEF works closely with other UN agencies and many nongovernmental organizations (NGOs).

Removal of Land Mines

The scale of the land mine problem almost defies imagination. Due to the persistence of armed conflicts throughout the world, it is estimated that there are more than 110 million land mines in 68 countries around the world, or one mine for every 20 children in the world today. An estimated 25,000 people are killed or maimed every year by land mines—90% of these victims are civilians and 5,000–6,000 are children. The region with the highest concentration of land mines is Africa, in countries such as Angola, Mozambique, and Somalia, but land mines are also destroying the lives of children in Asia, Central America, the Middle East, and Central and Eastern Europe.

UNICEF strongly advocates for a total ban of the production, marketing, and use of land mines and supports land mine awareness programs. In November 1995, UNICEF executive board director Carol Bellamy announced UNICEF's commitment to not deal with companies manufacturing or selling land mines.

Debt swaps

Since 1989, UNICEF has assisted in the conversion of foreign debt in developing countries to funds that supplement UNICEF's ongoing contributions to child survival and development in basic education, primary health care, and water and sanitation. The essential feature of the program is that the government concerned agrees to spend local currency on programs for children rather than using its scarce foreign exchange to service the debt.

Major UNICEF Publications

The State of the World's Children (annual).
The Progress of Nations (annual, first appeared 1993). Ranks the nations of the world according to their achievements for children in health, nutrition, and education, as well as progress in the field of family planning and in women's development.
UNICEF Annual Report

OFFICE OF UN HIGH COMMISSIONER FOR REFUGEES (UNHCR)

The UN Relief and Rehabilitation Administration (UNRRA) was established on 9 November 1943, to bring material aid to war-stricken areas of the world. Through its services, some 6 million displaced persons were repatriated. The constitution of a successor agency, broader in scope, the International Refugee Organization (IRO), was approved by the General Assembly on 15

December 1946. In addition to the relief and repatriation assistance provided by UNRRA, the IRO was charged with the protection of refugees and displaced persons and with resettlement responsibilities. The IRO Preparatory Commission became operative on 30 June 1947; by 31 December 1951, when IRO's operational activities ceased, more than 1 million persons had been resettled.

As part of a series of initiatives designed to address refugee problems following the dissolution of the IRO, the General Assembly, in December 1949, agreed on the necessity of setting up a body primarily responsible for the international protection of refugees and the search for durable solutions to their plight. As a consequence, the Office of the UN High Commissioner for Refugees (UNHCR) was established as of 1 January 1951 for a limited period of three years. It was soon evident, however, that international assistance was needed, and as new situations that created refugees have continued to arise, UNHCR's mandate has been renewed by the General Assembly for successive periods of five years.

UNHCR was awarded the Nobel Peace Prize in 1954 and again in 1981.

Organization

The UN High Commissioner for Refugees is elected by the General Assembly on the nomination of the Secretary-General and follows policy directives given by the General Assembly. The Executive Committee of UNHCR meets annually to review activities in the fields of protection and material assistance, approve assistance projects to be included in the next year's annual program, and provide overall guidance. The high commissioner reports to the committee on the implementation of special tasks that he may have been called upon to carry out—often at the request of the Secretary-General—and on the administration of special trust funds. In July 1994, ECOSOC recommended that the General Assembly increase the membership of the Executive Committee to 50 states. In 1998, the Executive Committee had been extended to 53 member countries.

UNCHR headquarters are in Geneva, Switzerland. As of 1998, the organization had 274 offices in 122 countries and a worldwide staff of 5,617, of whom more than 80% were at work in the field.

In 1998, 22.7 million people in over 140 countries fell under the concern of the UNHCR.

Financing

The financial arrangements made at the creation of UNHCR reflected the fundamental difference between it and the IRO. The IRO's budget was separate from that of the UN, while a very limited amount of the basic administrative costs of UNHCR is covered by the regular UN budget, since UNHCR is an integral part of the Secretariat, rather than a specialized agency. Its substantive activities in the field of protection and material assistance, however, depend entirely on voluntary contributions.

At the outset, UNHCR was not allowed to appeal to governments for funds without the express authorization of the General Assembly. The first funds of any magnitude put at the high commissioner's disposal came from the Ford Foundation in 1952 in the form of a grant of us$2.9 million (later increased to us$3.1 million) for a pilot program of projects intended to promote the local settlement of some 100,000 refugees in Europe through such measures as low-rent housing, small loans, vocational training, and rehabilitation of the handicapped. Subsequently, in 1954, the General Assembly authorized the high commissioner to appeal to governments for a four-year us$16 million program oriented toward permanent solutions and modeled on the Ford experimental undertaking. The target was eventually reached

through us$14.5 million in contributions by governments and over us$2 million by private organizations.

Clearing refugee camps in Europe was the main objective of UNHCR at this time, and the funds needed to finish this task were raised to a large extent through World Refugee Year (1959/60), a campaign that extended to 100 countries and areas.

In 1957, UNHCR's capacity to react effectively to unexpected situations was enhanced when the General Assembly authorized the high commissioner to establish an emergency fund not to exceed us$500,000. This innovation grew out of the experience of 1956, when some 200,000 refugees from Hungary crossed into Austria and Yugoslavia within a matter of weeks, prompting the high commissioner to appeal for funds for the emergency. By 1993, the emergency fund's ceiling was raised to us$25 million, with up to us$8 million available for a single emergency in a given year.

With the exception of a very limited subsidy from the United Nations regular budget (which is used exclusively for administrative costs), UNHCR's assistance programs are funded by voluntary contributions from governments, intergovernmental and nongovernmental organizations, and individuals. These so-called "voluntary funds" finance all UNHCR assistance programs worldwide. UNHCR's annual voluntary funds expenditure rose rapidly during the last decades of the 1900s, surpassing an annual budget of more than us$1 billion for a fifth consecutive year in 1998. The 1999 budget also surpassed the billion-dollar mark; the us$1.17 billion budget was revised to cover the Kosovo emergency.

The High Commissioner's Responsibilities

The high commissioner's primary responsibility is international protection. In addition, he promotes durable solutions to the problems of refugees through voluntary repatriation, local integration, or resettlement in another country. Whatever the field of activity, he and his staff are always guided by humanitarian and strictly nonpolitical considerations. UNHCR's ability to adhere to this policy over the years since its inception in 1951 has led the General Assembly to extend the scope of its material assistance activities, in many cases to persons who do not necessarily meet the definition of refugees contained in the high commissioner's statute. This definition describes refugees as persons who, owing to well-founded fear of being persecuted for reasons of race, religion, nationality, membership of a particular social group, or political opinion, are outside their country of nationality and are unable or unwilling, because of such fear, to avail themselves of the protection of that country. In recent years, UNHCR has increasingly been called on to help not only refugees but also persons uprooted by man-made disasters and displaced either outside or within their country of origin. However, UNHCR's competence does not extend to refugees already receiving help from another UN organization, notably the Arab refugees from Palestine who are cared for by UNRWA (see separate section, farther on).

From its outset, UNHCR's work was intended to be undertaken jointly with other members of the international community. UNHCR draws on the expertise of other United Nations organizations in matters such as food production (FAO), health measures (WHO), education (UNESCO), child welfare (UNICEF), and vocational training (ILO). It also cooperates closely with the World Food Programme in providing basic food supplies to refugees, and with the World Bank and the International Fund for Agricultural Development (IFAD) in implementing projects that aim to promote self-reliance. Over the decades, the most sustained and devoted service to the cause of refugees has been provided by nongovernmental organizations (NGOs). Over 200 NGOs cooperate in UNHCR's relief and legal assistance programs. In 1993, the Nansen Medal, awarded for outstanding service to the cause of refugees, recognized the valuable collaboration of one such NGO, Médecins sans Frontières (Doctors without Borders).

Since refugees no longer enjoy the protection of the countries they have fled, they must rely on the international community to provide it. The main vehicle for international protection is the 1951 Convention Relating to the Status of Refugees and its 1967 protocol, which lays down minimum standards for the treatment of refugees by countries that have acceded to it. By July 1999, 137 states were party to either the convention or its protocol.

One of the most important provisions of the 1951 convention is that refugees must not be sent back to a country where they may face persecution on grounds of race, political opinion, religion, nationality, or membership in a particular social group (the principle of *non-refoulement*). The convention also defines the rights of refugees in the country of asylum with respect to such matters as the right to work, education, access to courts, and social security. Moreover, it provides for the issuance of travel documents by the country of residence to compensate for the fact that refugees are not in a position to use their national passports.

By its statute and under the 1951 convention, UNHCR is given specific responsibility for supervising the application of the provisions of the convention. It is also available to supply technical advice to governments on appropriate legal and administrative measures to give effect to the stipulations of the convention.

Another important legal instrument concerning refugees is the Convention Governing the Specific Aspects of Refugee Problems in Africa, adopted by the Organization of African Unity in 1969. This convention, which came into force on 20 June 1974, emphasizes that the granting of asylum is a peaceful and humanitarian act that should not be regarded as unfriendly by any member state. A similar provision can be found in the Declaration on Territorial Asylum adopted by the General Assembly in December 1967 (see the section on Other Declarations in the chapter on Human Rights).

Asylum is the key aspect of the protection work of the high commissioner's office. A conference of plenipotentiaries convened by the General Assembly in 1977 "to consider and adopt a convention on territorial asylum" failed to achieve its objectives, and the absence of such a convention remains a gap in the legal basis for the protection of asylum-seekers.

In 1975, UNHCR undertook new duties in the field of protection on a provisional basis, following the entry into force on 13 December of the 1961 Convention on the Reduction of Statelessness. Under the terms of the convention, stateless persons may apply to national authorities to have nationality accorded to themselves or to their children or may ask UNHCR's assistance in presenting a claim.

MATERIAL ASSISTANCE ACTIVITIES

UNHCR's material assistance activities include emergency relief, assistance in voluntary repatriation or local integration, and resettlement through migration to other countries, as well as social services.

Africa

UNHCR's involvement in Africa dates from 1957, when thousands of people fled from the fighting in Algeria to Morocco and Tunisia. Working in conjunction with the League of Red Cross Societies, UNHCR provided both immediate and long-term assistance and helped to organize the repatriation of some 200,000 refugees in 1962, after the cessation of hostilities.

By 1967 there were an estimated 750,000 refugees in Africa, many of them victims of the struggles for independence in Guinea-Bissau, Angola, and Mozambique. In 1974–75, UNHCR

assisted in repatriating many of these refugees to their newly independent countries. A large-scale repatriation and rehabilitation program involving some 200,000 refugees and displaced persons in Zimbabwe was coordinated by UNHCR in 1980, and a major repatriation to Chad was completed in 1982.

By the early 1990s, Africa harbored over 6 million refugees, or around one-third of the global refugee population. During the previous decade, refugee situations persisted or erupted in the Horn of Africa, West Africa, and southern Africa. In some cases, such as for Mozambican refugees in Malawi and in the Horn, these situations were exacerbated by drought.

A number of refugees were able to return home, notably Namibians, Ethiopians, and Ugandans in the Sudan, and Somalis in Ethiopia. The repatriation of some 1.7 million Mozambicans got under way in mid-1993. In the Horn, a cross-border approach was put into action aimed at creating conditions conducive to the voluntary repatriation of refugees and safe return of internally displaced persons. This approach has been characterized by the use of "quick impact projects" (QIPs). QIPs entail the execution of small-scale projects, such as the repair and reconstruction of essential facilities; the provision of livestock, seed, and processing machinery; and the establishment of small-scale businesses. The projects are designed to bridge the gap between relief and development by helping returnees and their communities regain self-sufficiency. In certain areas such as North-West Somalia and Mozambique, however, repatriation has been bedeviled by the presence of land-mines in the areas of return.

In 1993, violent upheavals in the central African state of Burundi drove some 580,000 persons to seek refuge in neighboring countries. The following year, bloodshed engulfed neighboring Rwanda, creating, by May 1994, over 800,000 refugees. UNHCR launched emergency assistance programs to cope with refugees from both situations.

Principal origins of major refugee populations as of 1999 included: 2,648,000 Rwandan refugees in Iran, Pakistan, and India; 631,000 Iraqi refugees in Iran, Syria, Saudi Arabia, and Western European countries; 597,000 refugees from Bosnia and Herzegovina in Yugoslavia, Germany, Croatia, Sweden, and Switzerland; 525,000 Somali refugees in Ethiopia, Kenya, Yemen, and Djibouti; 517,000 Burundi refugees in Tanzania, Democratic Republic of the Congo, Rwanda, and Zambia; 487,000 Liberian refugees in Guinea, Côte d'Ivoire, Ghana, and Sierra Leone; 351,000 Sudanese in Uganda, Democratic Republic of the Congo, Ethiopia, Kenya, and Central African Republic; 342,000 Croatian refugees in Yugoslavia and Bosnia and Herzegovina; 328,000 refugees from Sierra Leone in Guinea, Liberia, and The Gambia; and 317,000 Vietnamese in China, France, Sweden, and Switzerland. The 3.2 million Palestinians who were covered under the mandate of UNRWA (UN Relief and Works Agency for Palestine Refugees in the Near East) are not included in these figures. Statistics of refugees seeking asylum in developed countries (where they may have acquired citizenship) are not reported in these figures.

Southwest Asia, North Africa, and the Middle East

In August 1974, following events in Cyprus, the high commissioner was designated to coordinate humanitarian relief for 241,300 people who had been uprooted and displaced. In the absence of a political settlement, aid is still being channeled to the island.

Events in Afghanistan in the late 1970s and the 1980s provoked a tremendous exodus from the country. Despite the unprecedented repatriation of 1.5 million Afghans in 1992, at the beginning of 1995 over 2.7 million Afghans remained in exile (1.6 million in Iran and 1.5 million in Pakistan). Hopes for their continued repatriation were stymied by a resurgence of fighting in Afghanistan in April 1992. In that year, Afghanistan itself became a country of asylum when some 60,000 Tajiks escaping from their country's civil war found sanctuary in northern Afghanistan. By 1995, there were still some 18,800 Tajik refugees in Afghanistan.

In 1991, the Gulf War led to a situation of mass displacement, creating, by May 1991, some 1.4 million refugees in Iran and 400,000 on the border with Turkey. UNHCR mounted a massive emergency assistance program for these groups, as well as for internally displaced Kurds in northern Iraq. By the end of 1991, most of the Iraqis in Iran and on the Turkish border had returned home.

UNHCR estimated the funding cost for major special and emergency programs in South West Asia, North Africa, and the Middle East in 1997 at US$25 million.

Asia and Oceania

In May 1971, the high commissioner was appointed "focal point" for UN assistance to millions of Bengali refugees from East Pakistan (later Bangladesh) in India. More than US$180 million in cash, goods, or services was channeled through this focal point, mainly for emergency relief in India but also for the repatriation operation that began early in 1972, following the creation of Bangladesh. The operation involved the transfer of non-Bengalis from Bangladesh to Pakistan and of Bengalis from Pakistan to Bangladesh. By the time it was concluded in July 1974, 241,300 people had been moved, nearly all by air, across the subcontinent in either direction.

Another major crisis erupted in mid-1978, when nearly 200,000 refugees from the Arakan state of Burma flooded into Bangladesh. UNHCR was again designated as coordinator of UN assistance. Following an agreement concluded with the Burmese government in July 1978, repatriation began in November of that year. The UNHCR program included assistance to the returnees once they were back in their country of origin.

Early in 1975, the conflict that for almost three decades had involved Vietnam, Cambodia, and Laos came to an end with changes of regime in the three countries of Indochina. Since that time, over 2.8 million Vietnamese, Cambodians, and Lao have left their homes and sought asylum in neighboring countries. These mass movements reached their peak in 1979, when some 393,560 people arrived by boat or overland in various asylum countries throughout the region, and in early 1980, when additional large numbers of Kampucheans moved into the border area with Thailand to escape hostilities in their own country.

UNHCR has undertaken to provide temporary assistance for Indochinese in various countries of Southeast Asia, to ask governments to extend permanent resettlement opportunities, and to facilitate voluntary repatriation where feasible. In addition, large numbers of displaced persons in the Thai-Kampuchean border area have been assisted by other UN agencies and the ICRC. By the beginning of 1994, some 2.7 million Indo-Chinese Refugees and displaced persons had been resettled, repatriated, or integrated locally, while around 88,000 remained in camps throughout the region.

Under the terms of a memorandum of understanding concluded with the Vietnamese government in May 1979, UNHCR has been coordinating a program of orderly departure from Vietnam. A further coordinating role has been played by UNHCR in the funding of a major program to combat piracy against refugee boats and other vessels in the South China Sea. In 1995, there were an estimated 341,600 Vietnamese refugees, mostly seeking asylum in China or Hong Kong.

The Comprehensive Plan of Action for Indo-Chinese Refugees (CPA) was adopted in June 1989 with the objective of discouraging clandestine departures; assuring access to status determination procedures for all asylum-seekers; providing resettlement opportunities for bona fide refugees; and ensuring a safe and dignified repatriation for those not determined to be refugees. The CPA had the effect of dramatically reducing the numbers of Lao and Vietnamese asylum-seekers; the number of Vietnamese asylum-seekers, for example, dropped from 71,364 in 1989 to a mere 55 in 1992.

The repatriation of Cambodians from Thailand, which began in March 1992, resulted in the return home of some 387,000 refugees, or nearly the whole caseload in Thailand. Returnees and the communities receiving them were assisted, in some cases, by means of QIPs (see the section on Africa, above), to consolidate their reintegration.

In 1991–92, around 250,000 mainly Muslim refugees fled Myanmar to Bangladesh. At the request of the government of Bangladesh, UNHCR began assisting this group in February 1992. At the beginning of 1995, there were some 203,900 refugees from Myanmar seeking asylum, mostly in Thailand and Bangladesh.

Some 140,000 Sri Lankan Tamils sought safety from their country's communal violence in the Indian State of Tamil Nadu. Since 1992, some 40,000 of them have been repatriated. In Sri Lanka, UNHCR assists both the returnees and internally displaced persons.

UNHCR estimated funding costs for major special and emergency programs in Asia and Oceania for 1997 amounted to US$42.6 million.

Latin America and the Caribbean

Originally, Latin America was a primary resettlement area for European refugees. However, the events in Chile in September 1973 involved UNHCR in major assistance measures for Latin American refugees. UNHCR had to contend first with the problem of several thousand refugees of various nationalities in Chile, providing relief, care, and maintenance and helping establish "safe havens" where they could live until their resettlement could be arranged.

In addition to ongoing assistance to Chilean refugees, UNHCR was called on to assist an increasing number of Nicaraguans in Costa Rica, Honduras, and Panama in late 1978. By 1979, the number of Nicaraguan refugees receiving such assistance had risen to 100,000. However, following the change of government in Nicaragua in July 1979, voluntary repatriation began, and UNHCR launched a special program to facilitate both the return itself and the rehabilitation of returnees through assistance in areas such as agriculture, health, and housing.

In the early 1980s, Central America became an area of increasingly grave concern to UNHCR. By the end of 1980, 80,000 refugees from El Salvador had sought refuge in neighboring countries. The International Conference on Central American Refugees (CIREFCA), which was convened in May 1989, proved to be of considerable help in facilitating a convergence towards durable solutions for uprooted populations. The move towards democratization in the region, the success of regional peace initiatives, and the CIREFCA process resulted in a reduction in refugee numbers as a result of attainment of durable solutions. In Haiti, however, the overthrow of the country's democratically elected president in September 1991 led to an exodus of Haitians seeking asylum in the region. Despite UNHCR's plea to governments in the region to uphold the principle of *non-refoulement*, Haitian asylum-seekers continued to be interdicted on the high seas. Beginning in 1992, political violence prompted many Guatemalans to go into exile. At the start of 1995, UNHCR was assisting over 42,000 Guatemalan refugees who had gone to neighboring Mexico. About 10,000 Guatemalans per year have returned as the situation became conducive to repatriation.

UNHCR estimated the funding cost of major special and emergency programs in the Americas and the Caribbean for 1997 at US$9.9 million.

Europe

When UNHCR came into existence in 1951, it inherited responsibility for some 120,000 persons still living in refugee and displaced persons' camps, mainly in the Federal Republic of Germany, Austria, Italy, and Greece. The great majority of these persons had been uprooted during World War II, primarily through the Nazi policies of removing people from occupied territories for forced labor and forcibly shifting populations for racial reasons. Particularly deplorable was the situation of the children born in the camps. Clearance of those camps was long delayed, mainly for lack of funds. Eventually, some 100,000 people, refugees since World War II, were settled as a result of UNHCR's programs.

New movements of refugees have, however, continued to occur. One of the largest of these was the result of the Hungarian crisis in 1956. The high commissioner was called on, in October 1956, to coordinate the activities of governments and voluntary organizations on behalf of the 200,000 Hungarians who sought refuge in Austria and Yugoslavia. From October 1956 until the end of 1959, about 180,000 Hungarian refugees arrived in Austria, and 19,000 in Yugoslavia. The total movement involved 203,100 persons. Of these, 18,000 eventually chose to return to Hungary, 9,600 elected to remain in Austria, 65,400 went to other European countries, and 107,400 emigrated overseas; the whereabouts of 2,700 are unknown.

In November 1991, UNHCR received a mandate from the United Nations Secretary-General to act as the lead United Nations agency to provide protection and assistance to those affected by conflict in the former Yugoslavia, then estimated at half a million people. By the beginning of 1995, there were 843,000 refugees from the former Yugoslavia seeking asylum, mostly in Croatia, Serbia, and Germany. There also were 1,282,000 internally displaced persons in Bosnia-Herzegovina and 307,000 in Croatia.

The war between Armenia and Azerbaijan in the early 1990s created some 663,100 displaced Azeris and some 299,000 refugees from Azerbaijan seeking asylum in Armenia at that time, and 201,500 refugees from Armenia seeking asylum in Azerbaijan. The military conflict in Georgia created around 280,000 refugees and displaced persons. UNHCR, in coordination with the United Nations Department of Humanitarian Affairs and other UN agencies, operated emergency response programs in all three countries. In May 1996, UNHCR convened a regional conference to address the problems of refugees, displaced persons, and returnees in the countries of the Commonwealth of Independent States (CIS). UNCHR estimated at that time there were 2.4 million refugees and internally displaced persons in the CIS countries.

During 1997, UNHCR estimates the funding for major special and emergency programs in Europe at us$314.3 million.

UN RELIEF AND WORKS AGENCY FOR PALESTINE REFUGEES IN THE NEAR EAST (UNRWA)

The plight of Palestine refugees has been a serious concern of the UN ever since the Arab-Israeli War of 1948. When a cease-fire came into effect early in 1949, hundreds of thousands of Arabs who lived in the territory that is now Israel were stranded on the other side of the armistice line from their homes. The Arab states claim that the refugees were driven out by the Israelis or fled in fear of reprisals. Israel, on the other hand, asserts that the Arab states told the Arab population to evacuate the area temporarily so that their armies could more easily drive the Israelis into the sea. (For the political background, see the section on the Middle East in the chapter on International Peace and Security.)

The refugees were given emergency relief at first by the ICRC, the League of Red Cross Societies, and the American Friends Service Committee, using money and supplies provided by the temporary UN Relief for Palestine Refugees, established in December 1948. In December 1949, the General Assembly created a special agency, the United Nations Relief and Works Agency for Palestine Refugees in the Near East (UNRWA), to provide relief and works projects in collaboration with the local governments. In the following year, the General Assembly extended UNRWA's mandate to June 1952 and instructed it to carry out development projects that would enable the refugees to be absorbed into the economy of the region. As originally conceived, UNRWA was a large-scale but definitely temporary operation, to be terminated by the end of 1952. The General Assembly accordingly asked Israel and its neighbors to secure "the permanent reestablishment of the refugees and their removal from relief." In carrying out programs of resettlement, however, all parties concerned, including UNRWA, were to act without prejudice to the rights of those refugees who "wished to return to their homes and live in peace with their neighbors." These were to "be permitted to do so at the earliest practicable date"; those who chose not to do so were to be compensated for their losses.

These goals were not achieved by 1952 and have not been met since then. Large-scale development projects to induce the refugees to leave the camps and enable them to become self-supporting in their host countries were approved by the General Assembly but never realized. Since 1952, UNRWA's mandate has been repeatedly extended.

For more information on UNRWA, see the chapter on International Peace and Security.

YOUTH

Concern for youth has been expressed within the UN system ever since its inception and particularly since the adoption by the General Assembly in 1965 of the Declaration on the Promotion Among Youth of the Ideals of Peace, Mutual Respect and Understanding Between Peoples. In that declaration, the General Assembly stressed the importance of the role of youth in today's world, especially its potential contribution to development, and proposed that governments give youth an opportunity to take part in preparing and carrying out national development plans and international cooperation programs.

Other recommendations made to member states by the General Assembly relate to the preparation of youth, through education, for full participation in all aspects of life and development; health policies and programs to ensure that young people are able to take advantage of opportunities open to them; the adoption of all possible means to increase employment for youth; the opening up of channels of communication between the UN and youth organizations; and measures aimed at promoting human rights and their enjoyment by youth.

The World Youth Assembly, held at UN headquarters in July 1970, was the first international youth convocation organized by the UN. It brought together some 650 young people to express their views on issues relating to world peace, development, education, and the environment and to discuss ways in which they could support the UN.

In 1979, the General Assembly decided to designate 1985—the twentieth anniversary of the 1965 Declaration—as International Youth Year, with the three themes of participation, development, and peace. The objectives of the year were to bring about widespread awareness of the situation of young people and of their problems and aspirations, and to engage them in the development process. International Youth Year resulted in the endorsement by the General Assembly of guidelines for strategies and activities in favor of youth at the national, regional, and international levels in coming years.

In observance of the tenth anniversary of International Youth Year, in 1995, the General Assembly devoted a plenary meeting to the subject of youth to set forth goals for a world youth program of actions towards the year 2000 and beyond. Its principal objective was to provide a global framework for national and regional action. The plan of action was drafted by the UN secretariat following the submission of proposals by member states, organizations of the UN system, and nongovernmental organizations.

A trust fund established for International Youth Year and renamed the UN Youth Fund is used to support projects involving young people in the development of their countries.

AGING AND THE ELDERLY

In the 75 years between 1950 and the year 2025, the world elderly population is projected to increase from 8% to 14% of the total global population, or 1.2 billion persons. While the total world population will have grown by a factor of a little more than three, the elderly will have grown by a factor of six and the very old by a factor of 10. The developing countries are projected to age more quickly in the coming decades, and are concerned by two factors: a weak institutional infrastructure for accommodating the elderly, and the uncertainty that families will be able to continue providing traditional care for the elderly.

In 1948, Argentina first presented a draft declaration on old age rights to the General Assembly, which referred it to ECOSOC. ECOSOC requested the Secretary-General to draft a report on the matter, and in 1950 he submitted a report entitled "Welfare of the Aged: Old Age Rights." However, the rapid change in the world's population structure was not evident in 1950, and an interval of 20 years elapsed before Malta tabled another initiative on the agenda of the General Assembly in 1969. This initiative was followed throughout the 1970s and led to the convening of the World Assembly on Aging in 1982.

In 1973, the General Assembly considered a comprehensive report that noted the demographic increase in the absolute and relative size of the older populations of the world (a trend that was expected to continue because of medical advances and decreases in birth and death rates) and estimated that the number of persons 60 years of age or over throughout the world would double between 1970 and the year 2000. The General Assembly recommended guidelines to governments in formulating policies for the elderly, including development of programs for the welfare, health, and protection of older people and for their retraining in accordance with their needs, in order to maximize their economic independence and their social integration with other segments of the population.

In 1978, the General Assembly decided to convene a world assembly for the purpose of launching "an international action program aimed at guaranteeing economic and social security to older persons," as well as opportunities for them to contribute to national development. The General Assembly later decided that the conference should also consider the interrelated issue of the aging of whole populations.

The World Assembly on Aging, held in Vienna in July–August 1982, was attended by representatives of more than 120 countries. It adopted an international plan of action, both to help the aging as individuals and to deal with the long-term social and economic effects of aging populations. Recommendations contained in the plan of action covered (1) the need to help the elderly lead independent lives in their own family and community for as long as possible, instead of being excluded and cut off from all activities of society; (2) the importance of giving the elderly a choice in regard to the kind of health care they receive and the importance of preventive care, including nutrition and exercise; (3) the need to provide support services to assist families, particularly low-income families, to continue to care for elderly relatives; and (4) the need to provide social-security schemes, to assist the elderly in finding (or returning to) employment, and to provide appropriate housing. The plan of action also included recommen-

dations for meeting the needs of particularly vulnerable persons, such as elderly refugees and migrant workers.

The Commission for Social Development, which is entrusted with reviewing implementation of the plan of action every four years, noted in 1985 that by the year 2025, more than 70% of persons over 60 years of age would live in developing countries. In 2025, experts estimate that the elderly population of the world will number 1.2 billion, six times more than the 200 million elderly worldwide in 1950. The commission listed priorities for action, including the creation of national committees on aging, coordinated planning, strengthening of information exchange, training, research, and education programs.

In 1988, the UN established the International Institute on Aging in Valetta, Malta, to conduct training, research, collection and publication of data, and technical cooperation in the field of aging. In 1990, the General Assembly designated 1 October as the International Day for the Elderly. In 1991, the General Assembly adopted a set of 18 United Nations "Principles for Older Persons" clustered under five themes: independence, participation, care, self-fulfillment, and dignity. The principles mandate that older persons should have the opportunity to work and to determine when to leave the work force; remain integrated in society and participate actively in the formation of policies that affect them; have access to health care to help them maintain the optimum level of physical, mental, and emotional well-being; be able to pursue opportunities for their full development; and be able to live in dignity and security.

In 1992, the General Assembly gave its patronage to the privately-created Banyan Fund Association's World Fund for Aging, in Torcy, France, which assists developing countries, at their request, in activities aimed at formulating and implementing policies and programs on aging. Also in 1992, the General Assembly devoted four special plenary meetings in October to a conference on aging. It issued a Proclamation on Aging (resolution A/47/5), which reaffirmed its previous resolutions and established the year 1999 as the International Year of the Elderly "in recognition of humanity's demographic coming of age and the promise it holds for maturing attitudes and capabilities in social, economic, cultural and spiritual undertakings, not least for global peace and development in the next century." In its Resolution 47/86, the General Assembly adopted a set of global targets on aging for the year 2001 as a practical strategy for countries to provide for the needs of the elderly.

The United Nations Trust Fund for Aging became operational in 1983, and supports training, income-generation, policy-formulation, and needs assessments projects. Governments, nongovernmental organizations, private organizations, and individuals can contribute to the fund, which is managed by the director general of the United Nations Office at Vienna. By January 1991, the United Nations Trust Fund for Aging had disbursed over US$1 million in seed money grants to 42 projects.

DISABLED PERSONS

Under the charter principles of the dignity and worth of the human being and the promotion of social justice, the General Assembly has acted to protect the rights of disabled persons. In 1971, it adopted the Declaration on the Rights of Mentally Retarded Persons, and in 1975, the Declaration on the Rights of Disabled Persons (see the section on Other Declarations in the chapter on Human Rights). In 1976, the General Assembly decided to proclaim 1981 as International Year of Disabled Persons, and it called for a plan of action for the year at the national, regional, and international levels.

The year's purpose, and its theme, was the promotion of "full participation and equality," defined as the right of disabled persons to take part fully in the life and development of their societies, to enjoy living conditions equal to those of other citizens, and

crime prevention and mobilizing support from member states. It coordinates the activities of the UN's regional and interregional institutes on crime prevention and criminal justice. It also is responsible for preparing for UN crime congresses.

The Crime Prevention and Criminal Justice Branch

This branch of the UN Secretariat, headquartered in Vienna, is the UN's central repository of technical expertise in matters of crime prevention, criminal justice, criminal law reform, and major criminological concern. It prepares studies and reports for the quinquennial congresses and for the Commission on Crime Prevention and Criminal Justice. The branch collects and analyzes statistics and provides technical assistance to member states and regional institutes. It prepares periodic country-by-country surveys of crime trends and criminal justice policies. The branch issues two regular publications: *The International Review of Criminal Policy*, a journal of applied criminology published annually since 1952, and the *Criminal Justice Newsletter*, which disseminates information on United Nations activities in the field, published twice a year.

The Criminal Justice Branch also works closely with various regional centers, a research institute and an international computer information network. The international standards proposed by the UN are meant as springboards to for appropriate national action. Differences in history, culture, economic structures, and governmental institutions dictate against a wholesale adoption of UN guidelines and standards. Regional centers can take into account the differing cultures and traditions of geographically linked countries and can better guide and harmonize national policies.

The *United Nations Interregional Crime and Justice Research Institute (UNICRI)* is based in Rome. It was founded in 1968, in response to concerns voiced by the 1965 Stockholm crime conference, under the name United Nations Social Defence Research Institute. UNICRI is housed in the heart of the old section of Rome, in an edifice built at the order of Pope Innocent X as a model prison for the replacement of dungeons used in the Middle Ages. The Italian government modernized the building's interior and made it available to UNICRI.

UNICRI carries out field research in conjunction with local institutions and experts. The institute is often charged with specific research projects in preparation for international crime congresses. It also holds international seminars and workshops. Its experts execute technical cooperation missions to assist member countries in implementing specific projects. It has a small but highly specialized library on criminology, penology, and related fields of law, sociology, and psychology. It also maintains a collection of United Nations and Council of Europe documents concerning criminal justice affairs. It publishes major research papers and an annual catalog of relevant research from around the world. UNICRI has computerized its *World Directory of Criminological Institutes*, and it has created the software and user manual for a computerized international expert roster. It has taken the lead in developing a UN global information network (see UNCJIN, below). UNICRI is financed by the UN Social Defense Trust Fund, a voluntary fund maintained by donations from governments and other sources.

The *African Regional Institute for the Prevention of Crime and the Treatment of Offenders (UNAFRI)* was established in January 1987, in temporary quarters at Addis Ababa, Ethiopia. It is now based in Kampala, Uganda. It organizes training courses and research and brings together criminal justice officials and development planners from all over Africa. It has conducted a feasibility study on the establishment of a regional, computerized information network to link up with the United Nations Criminal Justice Information Network (UNCJIN) (see below). UNAFRI operates under the auspices of the Economic Commission for Africa with financial assistance from the United Nations Development Program.

The *Asian and Far East Institute for the Prevention of Crime and the Treatment of Offenders (UNAFEI)* was established in 1961 and is based in Tokyo, Japan. It provides facilities for training courses and sends its staff to countries within the region to conduct classes in cooperation with host governments. UNAFEI publishes a regular newsletter and studies such as *Forms and Dimensions of Criminality in Asian Countries, Alternatives to Imprisonment in Asia,* and *Criminal Justice in Asia—the Quest for an Integrated Approach*. Although UNAFEI was initially a joint venture between the United Nations and the government of Japan, financial assistance from the UN was discontinued in 1970. The director of UNAFEI is assigned by the government of Japan in consultation with the UN.

The *European Institute for Crime Prevention and Control (HEUNI)* was established in 1981 in an agreement between the United Nations and the government of Finland. It is based in Helsinki. Its funds are provided by the government of Finland with assistance from other governments. HEUNI conducts training seminars and holds expert meetings to study regional issues in depth. Its expert meetings are often convened in order to offer a European perspective on draft documents of UN criminal justice policy. HEUNI has been actively involved with plans for a global UN information system on crime and criminal justice. Its publications include: *Criminal Justice Systems in Europe, The Role of the Victim of Crime in European Criminal Justice Systems,* and *Non-Custodial Alternatives in Europe.*

The *Latin American Institute for the Prevention of Crime and the Treatment of Delinquency (ILANUD)* was established in 1975 and is based in San José, Costa Rica. ILANUD devises practical strategies taking into account UN recommendations in criminal justice. It organizes regular training courses, workshops, seminars, and conferences for personnel in the criminal justice systems of Latin American governments. In 1987 it established an Agrarian Justice Program that aimed at improving procedures governing agricultural production. ILANUD also implemented a computerized data base in its documentation center. ILANUD was established with financial assistance from the United Nations, but now is supported mainly by the government of Costa Rica.

In 1989, the Criminal Justice Branch the *United Nations Criminal Justice Information Network (UNCJIN)* began operating under the auspices of the Criminal Justice Branch. UNCJIN is a computer network accessible by modem and gopher technology on the Internet. The UNCJIN gopher was resident on the computer system of the State University of New York at Albany. UNCJIN is funded in part by the United States Bureau of Justice Statistics, the State University of New York at Albany, and the Research Foundation of the State University of New York. UNCJIN's goal is to establish a worldwide network to disseminate and exchange information concerning criminal justice and crime prevention issues. Information available through the UNCJIN is constantly evolving and expanding. UNCJIN data and documents (many in PDF, portable document format) are available on their web site at http://www.uncjin.org/. In 2000 it included: criminal justice profiles of more than 120 countries; basic constitutional documents of countries; summaries of the latest United States Supreme Court decisions; international criminal justice statistics from the UN World Crime Surveys; United States Bureau of Justice Statistics reports; the entire CIA Factbook; and an annotated list of publication outlets in criminal justice and criminology. One can also search the on-line library catalogs of major criminal justice and law libraries around the world, examine all the major United Nations rules and guidelines on criminal justice, and access to other UN online resources.

UN Congresses on Prevention of Crime and Treatment of Offenders

Participants in UN crime congresses include criminologists, penologists, and senior police officers as well as experts in criminal law, human rights, and rehabilitation. Representatives of UN member states and of intergovernmental and nongovernmental organizations also attend. Eight crime congresses were held between 1955 and 1990. The tenth congress was scheduled to be held in Vienna, Austria, in 2000.

The *first congress*, held in Geneva in 1955, was attended by delegates from 51 governments and representatives from the ILO, UNESCO, WHO, the Council of Europe, and the League of Arab States. The topics of the first congress reflected the pressing concerns of Europeans recovering from the turmoil of World War II. Many delegates had experienced brutality and deprivation while incarcerated in their own countries by the occupying Fascist powers. It adopted 95 standard minimum rules for the Treatment of Prisoners, which set out what is accepted to be good general principle and practice in the treatment of prisoners and are also intended to guard against mistreatment. An additional rule, adopted in 1977, provides that persons arrested or imprisoned without charge are to be accorded the same protection as persons under arrest or awaiting trial and prisoners under sentence. The success of the Standard Minimum Rules paved the way for many other international models, standards, norms, and guidelines touching on every aspect of criminal justice. The prevention of juvenile delinquency was also considered at the congress, since so many children were growing up abandoned or orphaned.

The *second congress*, held in London in 1960, was attended by representatives of 70 governments and delegates from 60 nongovernmental organizations. In all, there were 1,131 participants. The second congress dealt with a wider range of issues than the first congress. It considered the growing problem of juvenile delinquency, as well as questions of prison labor, parole, and after-care. The addition of new member states to the United Nations required the expansion of the largely European perspective that dominated the first congress. The congress analyzed crime and criminal justice in relation to overall national development. Experts warned that economic improvement alone was not a one-way street leading away from crime. Tumultuous economic growth could lead to a greater prevalence of crime.

The *third congress*, held in Stockholm in 1965, addressed the ambitious theme of "Prevention of Criminality." Topics on the agenda included a continuation of the discussion on social change and criminality; social forces and the prevention of crime; community-based preventive action; measures to curtail recidivism; probation policies; and special preventive and treatment programs for young adults. A total of 1,083 participants, representatives of 74 governments and 39 nongovernmental organizations, attended the third congress. The influence of the increasing numbers of developing member nations made itself felt in 1965. The congress asserted that developing nations should not restrict themselves to mechanically copying criminal justice institutions developed in Western countries.

The *fourth congress*, held in Tokyo in 1970, was the first to take place outside of Europe. Although the number of participants declined slightly, to 1,014, the number of governments represented rose to 85. The fourth congress was convened under the slogan "Crime and Development," reflecting the dramatic increase in the number of developing countries who had become members of the UN during the 1960s. It stressed the need for crime control and prevention measures (referred to as "social defense policies") to be built into development planning. The third congress expanded the theme of community-based prevention, noting the successful utilization of civic involvement in the

host nation, Japan. The congress also investigated the nation-by-nation implementation of the Standard Minimum Rules for the Treatment of Prisoners, relying on results of a questionnaire submitted to member states before the opening of the congress.

The *fifth congress*, held in Geneva in 1975, the number of nations represented increased to 101 and the participation of the specialized agencies was augmented by the presence of Interpol and the Organisation for Economic Cooperation and Development (OECD). The congress's theme was "Crime Prevention and Control: the Challenge of the Last Quarter of the Century." Among the many topics considered were:

- changes in the form and dimension of criminality at national and transnational levels;
- crime as a business and organized crime;
- the role of criminal legislation, judicial procedures, and other forms of social control in the prevention of crime;
- the addition of crime-prevention activities to the traditional law enforcement roles of police;
- the implementation of the Standard Minimum Rules for the Treatment of Offenders;
- the economic and social consequences of crime;
- alcohol and drug abuse;
- victim compensation as a substitute for retributive criminal justice.

The fifth congress was responsible for two documents that rank in importance with the standard minimum rules: the "Declaration on the Protection of All Persons from Being Subjected to Torture and Other Cruel, Inhuman or Degrading Treatment or Punishment," which was adopted by the General Assembly by its resolution 3452(XXX); and the "Code of Conduct for Law Enforcement Officials," which has been called a Hippocratic oath for police professionals. The code was adopted by the General Assembly in 1979. The declaration on torture was given binding legal form in 1984, when the General Assembly adopted a convention on the same subject (see the section on Other International Human Rights Conventions in the chapter on Human Rights).

The *sixth congress*, held in Caracas in 1980, was the first UN crime congress to be hosted by a developing nation and the first held in the western hemisphere. Delegations from 102 nations, the ILO, WHO, the Council of Europe, Interpol, the League of Arab States, the Organization for African Unity, and the Pan-Arab Organization for Social Defence attended. The congress's theme was "Crime Prevention and the Quality of Life." It considered the following matters:

- new trends in crime and appropriate prevention strategies;
- the application of juvenile justice measures;
- offenses by the powerful, who quite often stand beyond the effective reach of the law;
- deinstitutionalization of correction measures;
- the role of UN guidelines and standards in criminal justice;
- capital punishment;
- the importance of international cooperation.

A working group of experts from Latin America and the Caribbean contributed an innovative approach on the classification of crimes. It suggested that the scope of criminal law statutes should be broadened to include willful actions harmful to the national wealth and well-being—destruction of the ecology, or participation in drug trafficking, or trafficking in persons. By way of corollary, the working group recommended a decrease in the number of statutes covering petty crimes or crimes that had little socially destructive effect.

The *seventh congress*, held in Milan in 1985, adopted the

Milan Plan of Action as a means of strengthening international cooperation in crime prevention and criminal justice. The plan was approved later the same year by the General Assembly, which also approved international instruments and principles adopted by the Milan Congress. These were the UN Standard Minimum Rules for the Administration of Juvenile Justice (the Beijing Rules), the Declaration of Basic Principles of Justice for Victims of Crime and Abuse of Power, Basic Principles on the Independence of the Judiciary, and a Model Agreement on the Transfer of Foreign Prisoners.

The Beijing Rules aim at promoting juvenile welfare to the greatest possible extent, thereby minimizing the necessity of intervention by the juvenile justice system. The rules set minimum standards for the handling of juvenile offenders, enumerate the rights of juveniles, and include principles for adjudication and disposition of juvenile offenses and for institutional and noninstitutional treatment of juvenile offenders.

The Declaration of Basic Principles of Justice for Victims of Crime and Abuse of Power defines "victims" as persons who, individually or collectively, have suffered harm, including physical or mental injury, emotional suffering, economic loss, or substantial impairment of their fundamental rights, through acts or omissions that are in violation of criminal laws or constitute violations of internationally recognized norms relating to human rights. It sets forth the rights of such victims and their families to restitution, compensation, and social assistance.

The Basic Principles on the Independence of the Judiciary stipulate that the judiciary shall have jurisdiction over all issues of a judicial nature and that judges shall decide matters before them impartially, without any restrictions, improper influences, or interference. The right of everyone to be tried by ordinary courts or tribunals is reaffirmed.

The Model Agreement on the Transfer of Foreign Prisoners is aimed at promoting the social resettlement of offenders by facilitating the return of persons convicted of crimes abroad to their country of nationality or residence to serve their sentence at the earliest possible stage.

The Milan Congress also considered questions relating to human rights in the administration of justice and to the prevention of juvenile delinquency and domestic violence.

The *eighth congress* was held in Havana, Cuba, from 27 August to 7 September 1990. The congress was attended by 1,400 participants from 127 countries, five intergovernmental organizations, and 40 nongovernmental organizations. Its overall theme was "International cooperation in crime prevention and criminal justice for the twenty-first century." The congress considered five topics: (1) crime prevention and criminal justice in the context of development; (2) criminal justice policies in relation to problems of imprisonment, other penal sanctions, and alternative measures; (3) effective national and international action against organized crime, terrorist criminal activities; (4) prevention of juvenile delinquency and protection of the young; and (5) United Nations norms and guidelines in crime prevention and criminal justice.

The eighth congress adopted a number of new instruments and resolutions that the General Assembly promptly approved. These included model treaties on extradition, mutual assistance in criminal matters, the transfer of proceedings in criminal matters, and the supervision of offenders conditionally sentenced or conditionally released. Other instruments passed were:

- A model treaty for the prevention of crimes against a peoples' cultural heritage;
- Basic Principles on the Use of Force and Firearms by Law Enforcement Officials;
- Basic Principles on the Role of Lawyers;
- Guidelines on the Role of Prosecutors;
- United Nations Standard Minimum Rules for Non-custodial Measures (the Tokyo Rules);
- Basic Principles for the Treatment of Prisoners;
- Guidelines for the Prevention of Juvenile Delinquency (the Riyadh Guidelines); and
- Rules for the Protection of Juveniles Deprived of Their Liberty.

The conference also adopted resolutions on computerization, prevention of urban crime, protection of the environment, corruption in government, racketeering and illicit trafficking in narcotic drugs and psychotropic substances, computer-related crimes, measures against drug addiction, organized crime and terrorism, domestic violence, and the instrumental use of children in criminal activities. The congress also requested that guidelines be prepared on the management of prisoners infected with human immunodeficiency virus (HIV) and those with acquired immunodeficiency syndrome (AIDS).

The eighth congress called for the elaboration of an effective international crime and justice program to assist countries in combating problems of national and transnational crime. An important outcome was the creation of the Commission on Crime Prevention as a functional commission of ECOSOC.

Substantive topics at the ninth congress (in 1995) included the fight against transnational organized crime; the elimination of violence against women; improvements in the administration of justice and the rule of law; migration and crime; technical cooperation and coordination of activities. Agenda items at the tenth congress (2000) included promoting the rule of law and strengthening the criminal justice system; international cooperation in combating transnational crime; effective crime prevention: keeping pace with new developments; and offenders and victims: accountability and fairness in the justice process. Workshops were to be conducted on combating corruption; relating crimes to the Computer Network; women in the criminal justice system; and community involvement in crime prevention. Focal issues in 1999–2000 were terrorism prevention, global program against corruption, the global program against trafficking in human beings, and the global studies on organized crime.

INTERNATIONAL COOPERATION FOR NARCOTIC DRUGS CONTROL

"...Let us resolve that at this special session of the General Assembly, words lead to action and that this action leads to success. Drug abuse is a time bomb ticking away in the heart of our civilization. We must now find measures to deal with it before it explodes and destroys us."

—Secretary-General Javier Pérez De Cuéllar

Remarks to the 17th Special Session of the General Assembly, 20 February 1990

Until the end of the 19th century, trade in narcotics was considered a legitimate business. Misuse of addiction-producing substances—opium, coca leaf, and Indian hemp—was thought to be the result of ingrained habits in particular areas of the world. The problem was considered a domestic one. However, modern technology and the expansion of transport and world trade introduced a new dimension. An increasing number of alkaloids and derivatives were being produced from opium and coca leaves and easily distributed. In addition, a large number of psychotropic substances (depressors of the central nervous system such as barbiturates, stimulants of the central nervous system such as amphetamines, and hallucinogens such as lysergic acid diethylamide, or LSD) were developed and their consumption increased enormously; hence, problems once considered local became global.

The UN exercises functions and powers relating to the worldwide control of narcotic drugs in accordance with a number of international treaties concluded since 1912, when the first International Opium Convention was signed at The Hague. By 1994, the majority of countries were parties to one or more of the treaties. The international control system is based on the cooperation of the states that are bound by these treaties in controlling the manufacture and sale of drugs within their jurisdiction. The treaties stipulate that these states are bound to adopt appropriate legislation, introduce necessary administrative and enforcement measures, and cooperate with international control organs as well as with each other.

Narcotics Control Under the League of Nations

The League of Nations Covenant provided that League members should "entrust the League with the general supervision over agreements with regard . . . to the traffic in opium and other dangerous drugs." The first League Assembly created an Advisory Committee on Traffic in Opium and Other Dangerous Drugs to assist and advise the League's Council in its supervisory tasks in the field. The League established a Permanent Central Board, later renamed the Permanent Central Narcotics Board, to supervise the control system introduced by the second International Opium Convention, which came into force in 1928. The board was composed of independent experts, to whom League members were required to submit annual statistics on the production of opium and coca leaves and on the manufacture, consumption, and stocks of narcotic drugs and quarterly reports on the import and export of narcotic drugs. Specific governmental authorizations were required for every import and export of narcotic drugs.

The Convention for Limiting the Manufacture and Regulating the Distribution of Narcotic Drugs, signed at Geneva in 1931, created a new technical organ, also composed of independent experts, the Drug Supervisory Body. The aim of the 1931 convention was to limit world manufacture of drugs to the amount actually needed for medical and scientific purposes.

The Convention for the Suppression of the Illicit Traffic in Dangerous Drugs, signed at Geneva in 1936, called for severe punishment of illicit traffickers in narcotics and extradition for drug offenses.

A protocol signed on 11 December 1946 (and which entered into force on 10 October 1947) transferred to the United Nations the functions previously exercised by the League of Nations under the pre-World War II narcotics treaties.

The United Nations and International Drug Control
Historical Background

The functions of the League's Advisory Committee were transferred to the United Nations Commission on Narcotic Drugs (CND), established in 1946 as a functional commission of the Economic and Social Council. Over the years a number of bodies were created to carry out the work of the United Nations in the field of narcotics control, including the International Narcotics Board (INCB), the Division of Narcotic Drugs (part of the United Nations Secretariat), and the United Nations Fund for Drug Abuse Control (UNFDAC). In addition, several specialized agencies, notably the World Health Organization (WHO) and the United Nations Educational, Scientific and Cultural Organization (UNESCO), also were called on to contribute to the war on illegal drugs.

By mid-1980s the General Assembly recognized that, while several important treaties had been elaborated (see under The Treaty System below), the system had not produced the desired result. Illicit traffic in drugs had achieved crisis proportions all over the world, threatening the stability of governments and regional peace and security in Africa, Southeast Asia, Latin America, and the Caribbean. In 1984, the General Assembly requested the CND to elaborate a new treaty to explicitly treat the problem

of illegal drug trafficking. In 1985 the General Assembly decided to convene an International conference on Drug Abuse and Illicit Trafficking in Vienna in June 1987. That Conference adopted a Declaration and a Comprehensive Multidisciplinary Outline of Future Activities in Drug Abuse Control.

However, the 1987 annual report of INCB revealed that drug-trafficking syndicates now held enough financial power to challenge the elected authorities of some South American countries. In addition, the spread of Acquired Immune Deficiency Syndrome (AIDS) and the HIV virus had assumed pandemic proportions, due in large part to the sharing of infected needles by drug abusers. The INCB noted that international drug traffic was financed and organized by criminal organizations with international links and with accomplices in financial circles who helped "launder" money obtained through the drug trade. Member states proclaimed 26 June 1988 as the first International Day Against Drug Abuse, to begin to focus public attention on the worldwide scope of the problem.

In February 1988, a plenipotentiary conference of the United Nations member states was convened in Vienna. It adopted the 1988 United Nations Convention Against Illicit Trafficking in Narcotic Drugs and Psychotropic Substances (see under The Treaty System below), which was immediately ratified by 43 nations. However, for lack of sufficient ratifications and accessions, the convention did not come into effect until December 1990.

The Global Programme of Action Against Drug Abuse

In November 1989, the General Assembly expressed its alarm at the slow pace of accessions holding up the entry into force of the 1988 convention. To consolidate international efforts, the General Assembly held a four-day special session (its seventeenth special session) in February 1990 to adopt a Political Declaration (A/RES/S-17/2) affirming the determination of the international community to band together to fight drug trafficking. In its declaration the General Assembly recognized the links between drug trafficking and the economic and social conditions of the countries producing drugs. It also voiced its concern about the link between drug trafficking and international terrorism, and the threat posed by transnational crime organizations that corrupted elected governments. The member states resolved to "protect mankind from the scourge of drug abuse and illicit trafficking in narcotic drugs and psychotropic substances...." They reaffirmed their commitment to support the international effort to eradicate drug trafficking both financially and by bringing national laws into line with the various United Nations treaties on narcotics control. The document also noted that international cooperation in restraining drug trafficking should be conducted in accordance with the principles of national sovereignty embodied in the United Nations charter. The General Assembly concluded the document by adopting a Global Programme of Action and declaring the period 1991–2000 the United Nations Decade Against Drug Abuse.

The 100-paragraph Global Programme of Action contained proposals for worldwide cooperation to stem the rising tide of drug abuse. Some of its provisions were based on the Multidisciplinary Outline mentioned above, and included:

- Raising national priorities for drug abuse prevention and reduction programs;
- Commissioning an analysis of the social causes generating drug demand;
- Providing UN financial support to prevent drug abuse by children, and the use of children in the drug trade in developing countries;
- Having the UN act as a global information clearinghouse on treatment and rehabilitation of drug addicts;
- Using high resolution satellite imagery and aerial photography

(with the agreement of producing countries) to identify illegal narcotic cultivation;

- Convening an international conference to elaborate ways to prevent the diversion of the chemicals and substances used to process the raw materials of illicit drugs;
- Developing international mechanisms should be developed to prevent drug money laundering and to confiscate funds and property acquired with drug money;
- Promoting through the UN the exchange of information among states on the flows of drug money; coordinating anti-drug operation training.

On 15 February 1990, just before the General Assembly's special session, the United States, Bolivia, Colombia, and Peru met in Cartagena, Colombia, and signed the Cartagena Declaration, agreeing to cooperate to stem the flow of drugs to the United States. The four countries, representing the world's largest consumer (the United States) and the largest suppliers of illicit cocaine, agreed to wage a war on drugs on three fronts: demand reduction, consumption reduction, and supply reduction. The United States agreed to financially support alternative development to replace the coca-growing economy in Peru and Bolivia and to fund emergency social programs. The multilateral cooperation begun at the Cartagena summit was extended in 1992 at a summit held in San Antonio, Texas, to include Mexico in the international struggle against drug trafficking organizations.

1990 World Ministerial Summit

The government of the United Kingdom, in association with the United Nations, organized a three-day World Ministerial Summit to Reduce the Demand for Drugs and to Combat the Cocaine Threat. The summit was held in London from 9–11 April 1990, and was attended by 650 delegates, most at the ministerial level, from 124 countries. The summit adopted the London Declaration committing the nations to giving higher priority to prevention and reduction of illicit drug demand at national and international levels. The London summit produced a consensus that, whereas producing countries had previously felt that drug abuse did not threaten their own populations, developing countries now realized that drug abuse had become a worldwide phenomenon cutting across national boundaries, class, race and income levels.

Some of the London Declaration's provisions include:

- Drug abuse prevention and treatment should be part of national health, social, education, legal and criminal justice strategies;
- Drug education should be developed at all school stages;
- Prevention programs in the workplace should be developed and implemented;
- Mass media campaigns against drugs should be used;
- The United Nations Fund for Drug Abuse Control (later the United Nations International Drug Control Program, see below) should be provided the funds to devise a strategy for the Andean sub-region, where most of the world's coca is grown and illicitly processed into cocaine.
- Nations that had not yet done so should ratify or accede to the 1988 United Nations Convention Against Illicit Traffic in Narcotic Drugs and Psychotropic Substances, and, in the meanwhile, they should try to apply its terms provisionally.

In October 1993, China, Laos, and Myanmar (referred to as the "Golden Triangle") signed a Memorandum of Understanding, expanding existing cooperation on drug control, in cooperation with the UNDCP. The countries aimed to eliminate opium poppy cultivation through economic and social development programs; curb traffic in narcotic drugs and essential chemicals used in manufacturing drugs; and implement programs to reduce the demand for illicit drugs.

Despite the growing alarm of nations, the phenomenon of illicit drug trafficking and drug abuse continued to rise. The 1994 report of the INCB stated that the worldwide drug menace had broken past geographic limits and outgrown its traditional classification as a criminal or social issue and penetrated the spheres of international politics and world economics. Drug organizations had become illegal transnational corporations. In 1994 the CND concluded that UNDCP should, once again, review existing international drug control instruments and activities in order to identify ways to strengthen the system and make appropriate changes. In June 1994, the International Conference on Preventing and Controlling Money Laundering and the Use of the Proceeds of Crime was held in Italy (see Crime Prevention and Criminal Justice, above).

UN Bodies Concerned With Narcotics Control

The United Nations International Drug Control Programme

In December 1990, the General Assembly requested that the Secretary-General merge the various units of the organization that were concerned with drug control into a single, integrated program. In 1991, the United Nations International Drug Control Programme (UNDCP) integrated the functions of the Division of Narcotic Drugs, UNFDAC, and the secretariat for the INCB. Headquartered in Vienna, UNDCP is charged with the responsibility of coordinating and leading United Nations drug control activities. UNDCP is headed by an executive director. The program publishes a quarterly *Bulletin on Narcotics* as well as information letters, scientific notes, and publications on drug abuse control activities. UNDCP's budget comes from both the UN regular budget (US$16.4 million for 1996–97) and from the voluntary Fund of UNDCP (US$152.4 million for 1996–97).

UNDCP's *Treaty Implementation and Policy Development* monitors and ensures the implementation of the various conventions, decisions, and resolutions entrusted to the United Nations (see The Treaty System below). This division provides secretariat services to the expert meetings, the CND, INCB, ECOSOC, and the General Assembly as required.

The *Division for Operational Activities* manages UNDCP technical cooperation programs worldwide. It assists governments and other institutions in the development and implementation of national, subregional, and regional programs to reduce illicit cultivation, production, manufacture, traffic and abuse of drugs.

The *Technical and Advisory Services Branch* provides technical expertise to CND, expert groups, and INCB. It assists in identifying and formulating technical cooperation projects that will be managed by the Division for Operational Activities. The Technical and Advisory Services Branch keeps a roster of international specialists on drug-related subjects and stays in contact with research institutions and universities for the latest findings in the field of drug abuse.

The Commission on Narcotic Drugs (CND)

The Commission on Narcotic Drugs is the main policy-making body within the United Nations system for all issues pertaining to international drug abuse control. It analyzes the world drug abuse situation and develops proposals to strengthen international efforts. It is one of the functional commissions of the Economic and Social Council. In addition, it prepares such draft international conventions as may be necessary; assists the council in exercising such powers of supervision over the application of international conventions and agreements dealing with narcotic drugs as may be assumed by or conferred on the council; and considers what changes may be required in the existing machinery for the international control of narcotic drugs and submits proposals thereon to the council. In addition, the commission has special functions under the 1961 Single Convention on Narcotic Drugs (see under The Treaty System, below), such as placing drugs under international control and making recommendations for the implementation of the aims and provisions of the convention, including programs of scientific research and the exchange of scientific or technical information. The commission also reviews implementation of the Global Programme of Action, provides policy guidance to UNDCP, and monitors its activities. The commission meets annually in regular or in special sessions.

The International Narcotics Control Board (INCB)

The International Narcotics Control Board is responsible for promoting compliance with the provisions of drug control treaties. It was created by the 1961 Single Convention on Narcotic Drugs as a successor to the Permanent Central Board and the Drug Supervisory Body. The members of the board are not government representatives but experts acting in their private, individual capacities. The board has important functions to perform under the treaties. It watches over statistics of drug production, manufacture, trade, and consumption and also over the estimates needed for the coming year that states are required to furnish to it; if a state does not send estimates, the board makes them itself. The board may request any state to explain a condition that in its view indicates an improper accumulation of narcotic drugs. It may even recommend, in case of difficulties created by a country for the international control, that other states stop the shipment of drugs to that country. A most effective means of ensuring compliance is publicity: the reports of the board (and of other international bodies) ensure that the public is made aware of any situation that may contribute to the spread of drug abuse.

Other United Nations Bodies Cooperating with UNDCP

The *United Nations Interregional Crime and Justice Research Institute (UNICRI)* was formerly known as the United Nations Social Defence Research Institute. UNICRI carried out a four-year research study funded by UNDCP on the interaction between criminal behavior and drug abuse and on control measures adopted in individual countries. It conducts research, surveys, and workshops on the criminal aspects of drug abuse for UNDCP. UNICRI is more fully described above, under Crime Prevention and Criminal Justice.

The *International Labour Organisation (ILO)* carries out activities on drug-related problems in the workplace and on the vocational rehabilitation of recovering drug addicts. WHO and UNDCP prepared a multi-media resource kit to assist enterprises in developing solutions to those problems.

The *World Health Organization (WHO)* carries out activities related to drug dependence and other drug control activities assigned to it by international drug control treaties. WHO plays an integral role in determining which substances should be placed under international control, in accordance with the provisions of the 1961 Single Convention on Narcotic Drugs and the 1971 Convention on Psychotropic Substances. WHO's Global Programme on Drug Dependence cooperates with member states in the prevention, treatment, and management of drug addiction. WHO also develops guidelines and manuals for teachers and health professionals.

The *United Nations Educational, Scientific and Cultural Organization (UNESCO)* focuses on the prevention of drug abuse through public education and awareness. UNESCO works with media organizations in producing radio and television programs. With the support of UNDCP, UNESCO is carrying out research projects on drug use and prevention in Africa, Asia and the Pacific, and Latin America and the Caribbean.

The *International Maritime Organization (IMO)* is concerned with the transportation of illicit drugs by ships. IMO has compiled guidelines on the prevention of drug smuggling on ships engaged in international traffic. The guidelines set out security precautions, methods of concealments, actions to be taken when drugs are discovered, identification of addicts, and cooperation with customs.

The *International Civil Aviation Organization (ICAO)* seeks to counteract the shipment of illicit drugs by air. It develops technical specifications and guidance material for civil flights, and suggests measures to ensure that commercial carriers are not used to transport illicit drugs.

The *Universal Postal Union (UPU)* has carried out studies to establish international measures covering the shipment of illicit drugs through the mails.

The *Food and Agriculture Organization of the United Nations (FAO)* manages several multidisciplinary programs financed by UNDCP. FAO covers the agricultural aspects of the drug crisis. Its programs are aimed at raising the income level of farmers, and thereby reducing the incentive to cultivate narcotic crops. It has participated in UNDCP-financed projects in Bolivia, Myanmar, and Pakistan. FAO and UNDCP are studying the potential of remote sensing techniques and satellite imagery (already in use by FAO to predict droughts and other international crop statistics) in the detection of illicit crops.

The *United Nations Development Programme (UNDP)* incorporates drug abuse control programs into its development projects in Asia and the Pacific, and Latin America and the Caribbean. UNDP's resident coordinators and resident representatives work closely with the UNDCP in countries where serious drug problems exist.

The *United Nations Children Fund (UNICEF)* focuses on the world's 100 million street children, who are often drug abusers and/or drug sellers. UNICEF has programs in Latin America and the Caribbean to strengthen families and provide services to children in need. UNAIDS works with countries to help prevent the spread of HIV and help those already afflicted with the virus. The virus can infect drug abusers who share syringe needles.

The Treaty System

One of the tasks of the UN in drug control is to adapt international treaty machinery to changing conditions. Six agreements have been drawn up under United Nations auspices.

The Paris Protocol of 1948. The prewar international conventions on narcotics applied to all addictive products of three plants—the opium poppy, the coca bush, and the cannabis plant—and to products belonging to certain chemical groups known to have addictive properties. By the end of World War II, however, a number of synthetic narcotics not belonging to the defined chemical groups had been developed. A protocol signed in Paris on 19 November 1948 authorized WHO to place under international control any new drug not covered by the previous conventions that was or could be addictive. The Paris protocol came into force on 1 December 1949.

The Opium Protocol of 1953. Despite earlier international treaties on opium, its production continued and found its way into illicit channels. The Commission on Narcotic Drugs first proposed an international opium monopoly, with production quotas and a system of international inspection. It was impossible, however, to obtain agreement on such important questions as the price of opium and inspection rights.

A compromise was worked out by the United Nations Opium Conference, held in New York in May–June 1953, and was embodied in a Protocol for Limiting and Regulating the Cultivation of the Poppy Plant, the Production of, International Trade in, and Use of Opium. Under this protocol, only seven states—Bulgaria, Greece, India, Iran, Turkey, the USSR, and Yugoslavia—were authorized to produce opium for export. Producing states were required to set up a government agency to license opium poppy cultivators and designate the areas to be cultivated. Cultivators were to deliver all opium immediately after harvesting to this agency, the only body with the legal right to trade in opium. The Permanent Central Narcotics Board, under the protocol, was empowered to employ certain supervisory and enforcement measures and, with the consent of the government concerned, to carry out local inquiries. The protocol came into force in December 1964.

The Single Convention on Narcotic Drugs, 1961. On 30 March 1961, a conference at United Nations headquarters adopted and opened for signature the Single Convention on Narcotic Drugs, 1961. This convention, which came into force on 13 December 1964, was a milestone in international narcotics control.

The first objective of the convention—codification of existing multilateral treaty law in this field—was almost achieved. The second goal—simplification of the international control machinery—was achieved: the Permanent Central Board and the Drug Supervisory Body were combined as the International Narcotics Control Board, as described earlier. The third goal was extension of control to cover cultivation of plants grown for narcotics. The treaty continued controls on opium, including national opium monopolies and the obligation of governments to limit production to medical and scientific purposes. Provisions dealing with medical treatment and rehabilitation of addicts were quite new as treaty obligations. Opium smoking, opium eating, coca-leaf chewing, hashish (cannabis) smoking, and the use of cannabis for nonmedical purposes were prohibited. The convention required states that are parties to it to take special control measures for particularly dangerous drugs, such as heroin and ketobemidone. Earlier treaty provisions, requiring (1) that exports and imports of narcotic drugs be made only on government authorization from both sides, (2) that governments report on the working of the treaty, and (3) that they exchange, through the Secretary-General, laws and regulations passed to implement the treaty, were retained. Provisions for controlling the manufacture of narcotic drugs and the trade and distribution of narcotic substances also were continued, together with measures for controlling new synthetic drugs.

The Convention on Psychotropic Substances, 1971. During the 1960s there was increasing concern over the harmful effects of such drugs as barbiturates, amphetamines, LSD, and tranquilizers. WHO and the Commission on Narcotic Drugs recommended that governments take legislative and administrative control measures.

On the basis of a draft drawn up by the Commission on Narcotic Drugs, in close collaboration with WHO, a plenipotentiary conference for the adoption of a protocol on psychotropic substances met in Vienna in 1971, with 71 states represented. On 21 February 1971, it adopted and opened for signature the Convention on Psychotropic Substances, 1971. The convention has been in force since 1976.

The 1971 convention was a major step in the extension of international drug control. It contains a number of prohibitive measures for hallucinogens that present a high risk of abuse and have no therapeutic application. Special provisions regarding substances such as LSD prescribe, among other things, prohibition of their use except for research authorized and supervised by governments.

The requirement of licenses for manufacture, trade, and distribution, the supervision of these activities, and the repression of acts contrary to laws and regulations are applied to all of the drugs enumerated in the 1971 convention. Governments may limit or prohibit the import (and export) of any psychotropic drug. With this regulatory system, governments can protect themselves against unwanted drugs. Psychotropic drugs used in therapy but with great abuse potential, such as sleeping pills, are controlled by requiring medical prescriptions and by supervision of export-import activity. International trade in the most dangerous stimulants—the amphetamines—is subject to a more stringent authorization system. Strict record-keeping of drug movements and statistical reports to the International Narcotics Control Board are also required.

A humane provision in the treaty requires that "all practicable measures for the prevention of abuse, the early identification, treatment, education, after-care, rehabilitation, and social reintegration of persons involved" be taken and that "either as an alternative to conviction or punishment or in addition to conviction or punishment, such abusers shall undergo measures of treatment, education, after-care, rehabilitation, and social reintegration."

The Protocol Amending the 1961 Single Convention on Narcotic Drugs, 1972. A plenipotentiary conference adopted, on 25 March 1972, amendments to strengthen the international narcotics control system and to include new concepts and means.

The International Narcotics Control Board was increased from 11 to 13 members, to serve for five years instead of three. Technical measures included in the protocol concern limitation of the production of opium, seizure and destruction of illicitly cultivated opium poppies, and the option of the board to recommend technical or financial assistance to governments. The protocol, like the 1971 Convention, provides for after-care and rehabilitation of drug abusers. Also, drug offenders are made extraditable in any extradition treaty. The protocol came into force on 8 August 1975.

Convention Against Illicit Trafficking in Narcotic Drugs and Psychotropic Substances, 1988. In recognition of the increasing difficulty faced by law enforcement and other government agencies in coping with the expansion of illicit drug trafficking, the General Assembly, in 1985, requested the Commission on Narcotic Drugs to prepare a new convention covering areas not adequately regulated by existing treaties.

In 1988, the United Nations convened a conference in Vienna that was attended by representatives of 106 nations. The conference adopted the new convention, which was immediately ratified by 43 nations. The convention entered into force on 11 November 1990.

World leaders met in New York 8–10 June 1998 in a special session of the UN General Assembly to adopt a worldwide plan to substantially reduce drug demand and supply by the year 2008. The session addressed guiding principles on reducing demand for illicit drugs, eradication of illicit crops and alternative development, amphetamine-type stimulants (stated as a priority requiring urgent action), money laundering, controlling precursor chemicals (intermediate substances used to manufacture drugs), and judicial cooperation to promote drug control. By November 1999, 153 states had ratified the 1988 convention.

The 34-article convention addresses the issues of tracing, freezing, and confiscating proceeds and property derived from drug trafficking. Courts may seize bank, financial, or commercial records, without the imposition of bank secrecy laws. The convention also provides for extradition of major drug traffickers, mutual legal assistance between states on drug-related investigations, and transfer of proceedings for criminal prosecution. The convention also commits states to eliminate or reduce illicit demand for narcotic drugs and psychotropic substances. One of the most important provisions of the treaty, Article 12, sets forth two tables of substances used to manufacture illicit drugs and agrees to implement controls on the manufacture and shipment of such substances. In essence, Article 12 imposed the same controls on the chemicals used to manufacture illicit drugs as are imposed on the raw materials like opium and cocaine. The substances controlled by the convention included ephedrine, ergometrine, ergotamine, lysergic acid, 1-phenyl-2-proanone, pseudoephedrine, acetic anhydride, acetone, anthranilic acide, ethyl ether, phenylacetic acide, and piperidine.

Narcotic Drugs Under International Control

Opium and Its Derivatives. Opium, the coagulated juice of the poppy plant *Papaver somniferum L.*, was known to the Sumerians living in lower Mesopotamia in 3000 BC. It was used by the Greeks and Arabs for medicinal purposes and was probably introduced into China by the Arabs in the ninth or tenth century. The opium poppy can be grown in most of the habitable parts of the world and is often cultivated for its beautiful flowers or its seeds, which are a valuable food. As an addictive drug, opium was originally eaten or drunk as an infusion. The practice of smoking opium is only a few hundred years old.

The best-known derivatives of opium are morphine, codeine, and diacetylmorphine, more commonly called heroin. While morphine and codeine have valuable medicinal properties, heroin has no medical uses for which less dangerous analgesics cannot be substituted, and upon the recommendation of the Commission on Narcotic Drugs, its manufacture has been banned in most countries. A number of drugs are derived from morphine or are compounded with it, including ethylmorphine and benzylmorphine. Some morphine derivatives, such as apomorphine, are not addictive in themselves.

The most important drugs in national and international illicit traffic are still opium and its derivatives, in particular morphine and heroin. As a result of effective international controls, there has been little diversion of opium or opiates from legitimate channels into the illicit trade. There is, however, illicit production of opium in some countries. From these supplies, clandestine factories manufacture morphine that is converted into heroin. Opium contains as an average 10% of morphine, which is made into diacetylmorphine or heroin in equal weight by relatively simple methods. Clandestine factories have been moving closer to the opium-producing areas. Morphine can be extracted from poppy capsules whether or not the opium has been extracted; at least 30% of licit morphine comes from this process. When Turkey, in 1974, resumed cultivation of the opium poppy, which had been stopped two years earlier, it decided not to produce opium but to use the "poppy-straw method" for extraction of morphine. About 90% of the licit morphine is used to make codeine, whereas 90% of illicit morphine is used to make heroin. An effective way of eradicating heroin is to stop illicit poppy cultivation. This is the intent of the international treaties and also of crop substitution undertaken in several countries with the support of the UNDCP.

Coca Leaf and Cocaine. Coca leaves grow on an evergreen shrub, *Erythroxylon coca,* native to the mountainous western region of South America. The leaves are the raw material for the manufacture of cocaine. The leaves themselves have been chewed by some of the Andean peoples for centuries to help combat hunger and overcome the fatigue and exhaustion caused by the high altitude.

The Commission on Narcotic Drugs concluded that coca-leaf chewing is a dangerous habit and constitutes a form of addiction. In 1954, the Economic and Social Council recommended that the countries concerned should gradually limit the cultivation and export of coca leaf to medical, scientific, and other legitimate purposes and should progressively abolish the habit of coca-leaf chewing. At the same time, it was recognized that there was little chance of eliminating coca-leaf addiction unless the living conditions of those among whom the habit was widespread could be improved and that the problem must be attacked on this front as well.

Coca leaves are used to make licit cocaine, the production of which has declined to about one ton a year, but they are also used for the illicit market that supplies increasing quantities of this dangerous drug to North America, Western Europe, and other regions.

A new, more addictive, and more deadly form of cocaine called "crack" is an inexpensive, potent form of the base drug in crystalline form. It is usually smoked, giving a quick, intense high, which lasts only a few minutes. "Crack" is harmful to the brain, heart, lungs, and nervous system and produces serious psychological effects.

Cannabis (Marijuana). The plant *Cannabis sativa,* or the crude drug derived from it, is known under almost 200 different names—marijuana, hashish, Indian hemp, charas, ganji, kif, bhang, and maconha, to name a few. Widely used as an intoxicant by millions of people for at least 4,000 years, it can be grown in most parts of the inhabited world. Depending on the soil and cultivation, the plant grows to a height of one to 20 feet. The narcotic resin is found in the flowering tops.

Cannabis is used as a narcotic in many parts of Africa, the Middle East, and the Americas. Because the plant grows wild and is easy to cultivate illicitly, traffickers have little difficulty in obtaining cannabis. Statistics on users are not available, but their number must run well in the millions.

Synthetic Narcotic Drugs. A number of synthetic substitutes, especially for morphine, are widely used. They were placed under control by the 1948 protocol. They may and do give rise to abuse but in a relatively limited way, and there is little, if any, illicit traffic in them. The most widely known are pethidine and methadone.

Psychotropic Substances. Psychotropic substances placed under international control by the 1971 convention are listed, like narcotic drugs, in treaty schedules that may be modified from time to time by the Commission on Narcotic Drugs. They have widely different characteristics, and, according to complex criteria having to do with the dangers they present to the individual and society, they have been placed in four schedules with decreasing severity of control. In Schedule I are found mainly hallucinogens, such as LSD, mescaline, and psilocine. All are made by synthesis, but the last two are also found in plants, the peyotl cactus and the hallucinatory mushroom, respectively. Schedule II contains mainly drugs of the amphetamine type that stimulate the central nervous system. They have limited therapeutic value but are widely abused, especially by young people who inject them intravenously, possibly causing psychoses. In Schedule III are found mainly the most powerful depressants of the central nervous system—barbiturates used as hypnotics (sleeping pills) by a very large number of consumers everywhere. These drugs, if used without therapeutic necessity, produce a form of addiction that can be extremely dangerous. Barbiturates are often used in association with heroin, with alcohol (with an especially dangerous interaction), and even with stimulants. Schedule IV has some barbiturate depressants and a number of tranquilizers. These constitute a very large body of medicaments supposed to eliminate anxiety and nervousness. Large quantities of such drugs as meprobamate and diazepam are consumed without therapeutic need and may alter mood and behavior.

Methamphetamines, amphetamines and other stimulants are covered by the 1971 convention. In November 1996 UNDCP declared that the global rise in the abuse of amphetamine-type stimulants was likely to be a major drug problem in the 21st century. By 2000, the prediction had already been borne out. These stimulants have the potential to pose more health problems to society than heroin or cocaine because they are simple to produce ad the necessary precursor materials are readily accessible. Phenyl-2-propanone (P2P) is an immediate precursor that can be easily synthesized into methamphetamine. Amphetamine-type stimulants are usually taken orally or injected. Crystalline d-methamphetamine hydrochloride, commonly referred to as "ice" or "crystal meth," is ingested by smoking.

HUMAN RIGHTS

In the Preamble to the Charter, "the peoples of the United Nations" express their determination "to reaffirm faith in fundamental human rights, in the dignity and worth of the human person, in the equal rights of men and women and of nations large and small." Article 1 of the Charter states that one of the purposes of the UN is to promote and encourage "respect for human rights and for fundamental freedoms for all without distinction as to race, sex, language, or religion." In Article 56, "all Members pledge themselves to take joint and separate action in cooperation with the Organization for the achievement" of this purpose. The Charter vests responsibility for assisting in the realization of human rights and fundamental freedoms in three of the principal organs: the General Assembly, the Economic and Social Council, and the Trusteeship Council. The Charter also provides for the establishment of commissions for the promotion of human rights as subsidiary bodies of the Economic and Social Council. As early as 1946, two such commissions were created: the Commission on Human Rights and the Commission on the Status of Women.

THE INTERNATIONAL BILL OF RIGHTS

At the San Francisco Conference, a proposal to embody an international bill of rights in the Charter itself was put forward but was not pursued because it required more detailed consideration. The idea of establishing an international bill of rights, however, was regarded as inherent in the Charter. Even before the Charter was ratified and had entered into force and before the UN as an organization was established, steps were taken toward this goal. The Preparatory Commission of the UN and its Executive Committee, meeting in the fall of 1945, both recommended that the work of the Commission on Human Rights should be directed, in the first place, toward the formulation of an international bill of rights. The General Assembly agreed with these recommendations in January 1946. Accordingly, when the terms of reference of the Commission on Human Rights were laid down in February 1946, "an international bill of rights" was the first item on its work program.

When the Commission on Human Rights and its drafting committee started work on this ambitious project, it turned out that there was disagreement among the members about the form that the draft bill of rights should take. Some members thought the bill should be a "declaration" or "manifesto" that would be proclaimed by a resolution of the General Assembly. Others urged that it take the form of an international treaty, which, in addition to being approved by the General Assembly, would have to be opened for signature and for ratification or accession by governments and would be binding only on those governments that had ratified it or acceded to it. The relevant report of the drafting committee records that it was agreed by those who favored the declaration form that the declaration should be accompanied or followed by one or more conventions. It was also agreed by those who favored the convention form that the General Assembly, in recommending a convention to member nations, might make a declaration wider in content or more general in expression. As a consequence, drafts of a "declaration" and of a "convention" were prepared, and studies were undertaken for the creation of international supervisory and enforcement machinery, called "measures of implementation."

Eventually, the decision emerged that the international bill of rights should not be produced by one single, comprehensive, and final act but should consist of two or more international instruments, namely, a declaration and a convention (or covenant), and measures of implementation. Later, it was decided that there should be not one but two covenants—one on civil and political rights and the other on economic, social, and cultural rights—and that the provisions on the measures of implementation should be embodied in the texts of the covenants. The latter decision was modified somewhat in 1966, when the provisions regulating one specific aspect of the implementation arrangements, the right of petition (communication), were included in a separate optional protocol.

The Universal Declaration of Human Rights

The Universal Declaration of Human Rights was prepared by the Commission on Human Rights in 1947 and 1948 and adopted and proclaimed by the General Assembly on 10 December 1948 by a vote of 48 in favor, none against, with 6 abstentions. Two representatives were absent. One of them stated later that, if he had been present, he would have voted in favor.

The Universal Declaration consists of a preamble and 30 articles. It proclaims—and in this regard it differs from the traditional catalog of the rights of man that are contained in various constitutions and fundamental laws of the 18th and 19th centuries and the first decades of the 20th century—not only civil and political rights but also rights that were eventually regulated in the International Covenant on Economic, Social and Cultural Rights.

The declaration proclaims, in Article 1, that all human beings are born free and equal in dignity and rights and, in Article 2, that everyone is entitled to all the rights and freedoms set forth in the declaration "without distinction of any kind, such as race, color, sex, language, religion, political or other opinion, national or social origin, property, birth or other status" and that "no distinction shall be made on the basis of the political, jurisdictional or international status of the country or territory to which a person belongs, whether it be independent, trust, non-self-governing or under any other limitation of sovereignty."

In Articles 3 to 21, the declaration deals with the traditional civil and political rights, including the right to life, liberty, and security of person; freedom from slavery and servitude; freedom from torture or cruel, inhuman, or degrading treatment or punishment; equality before the law and equal protection of the law; freedom from arbitrary arrest, detention, or exile; the right to be presumed innocent until proved guilty; the right to protection against arbitrary interference with one's privacy, family, home, or correspondence and to protection against attacks upon one's honor and reputation; freedom of movement and residence; the right to leave any country, including one's own; the right to seek and enjoy in other countries asylum from persecution; the right to a nationality and the right to change one's nationality; the right of men and women of full age to marry, without any limitation due to race, nationality, or religion; freedom of thought, conscience, and religion; the right to own property and not to be arbitrarily deprived of it; freedom of opinion and expression; the right to peaceful assembly and association; the right to take part in the government of one's country; and the right to equal access to public service.

Economic, social, and cultural rights (Articles 23 to 27) are introduced by Article 22, which states generally that "everyone, as a member of society, has the right to social security" and is entitled to the realization of "economic, social and cultural rights indispensable for his dignity and the free development of his personality." The article implies, however, that those economic, social, and cultural rights are not everywhere and immediately achievable. It states that the "realization" of these rights is to be brought about "through national effort and international cooperation and in accordance with the organization and resources of each state."

The declaration affirms everyone's right to work, to free choice of employment, to just and favorable conditions of work, and to protection against unemployment. It affirms the right of everyone to equal pay for equal work; to "just and favorable remuneration"; to form and join trade unions; to "a standard of living adequate for the health and well-being of himself and of his family"; and to "rest and leisure, including reasonable limitation of working hours and periodic holidays with pay." It also proclaims "the right to security in the event of unemployment, sickness, disability, widowhood, old age or other lack of livelihood in circumstances beyond [one's] control." Everyone has the right to education, which "shall be free, at least in the elementary and fundamental stages" and compulsory on the elementary level. The declaration affirms everyone's right "freely to participate in the cultural life of the community, to enjoy the arts and to share in scientific advancement and its benefits."

Article 28 asserts that "everyone is entitled to a social and international order in which the rights and freedoms set forth in this Declaration can be fully realized." In the exercise of individual rights and freedoms, everyone shall be subject only to such limitations as are determined by law. Such limitations, according to Article 29, shall be "solely for the purpose of securing due recognition and respect for the rights and freedoms of others and of meeting the just requirements of morality, public order, and the general welfare in a democratic society." Article 30 states that nothing in the declaration may be interpreted as implying for any state, group, or person "any right to engage in any activity or to perform any act aimed at the destruction of any of the rights and freedoms" set forth in the declaration.

The Universal Declaration of Human Rights was adopted, not in the form of an international convention that, when ratified, is legally binding on the states that are parties to it, but in the form of a resolution of the General Assembly, as "a common understanding" of the rights and freedoms that member states have pledged themselves to respect and observe and as "a common standard of achievement for all peoples and all nations." In the view of most of those who were instrumental in its preparation and adoption, the declaration was not meant to be a "binding" instrument. However, as soon as the declaration was adopted, it began to be used as a code of conduct and as a yardstick to measure the compliance by governments with the international standards of human rights.

In countless allegations of human rights violations that it has been called upon to examine, the UN has had recourse to the declaration, whether it was dealing with allegations of forced labor, with discrimination in non-self-governing and trust territories, with customs and practices inconsistent with the dignity of women, or with other violations of human rights. The declaration also has played an important role in the activities of specialized agencies, such as the ILO, UNESCO, and ITU, and in regional organizations, such as the OAS, the Council of Europe, and the OAU.

The declaration has thus acquired a validity beyond that originally contemplated in 1948. The international community, both the states that had been instrumental in its creation and those that later achieved independence, used the declaration for the purpose of fulfilling an assignment greater and more far-reaching than that originally carved out for it. Today, the declaration has acquired the status of customary international law and is valid for all states that have ratified it.

The International Covenants on Human Rights

The Commission on Human Rights, the Economic and Social Council, and the General Assembly devoted 19 years (1947–66) to the preparation of the International Covenants on Human Rights. One problem that created a considerable amount of controversy, particularly in the early years, was whether the treaty that would give legal effect to the rights and freedoms set forth in the Universal Declaration of Human Rights should regulate only those rights that traditionally have been guaranteed in national constitutions or catalogs of rights and are known as "civil and political rights" or whether the treaty should also set forth "economic, social and cultural rights."

As already indicated, it was eventually decided that there should be two covenants dealing with the two sets of provisions, respectively. The principal reason for having two separate instruments regulating the two groups of rights was the fundamentally different character of the rights concerned, which led some even to question whether "economic, social and cultural rights" are, technically, rights at all—in the sense of enforceable and justiciable rights. The different character of these rights made it necessary to provide for a difference in the type of international obligations to be undertaken by states that are parties to one or the other, or both, of the two covenants. Another reason for establishing two different covenants was thought to be the necessity to adjust the arrangements for international supervision—the "measures of implementation"—to the different character of the rights.

In the International Covenant on Civil and Political Rights, each state party undertakes to *respect* and to *ensure* to all individuals within its territory and subject to its jurisdiction the rights recognized in that covenant. In the International Covenant on Economic, Social and Cultural Rights, each state party undertakes only to *take steps*, individually and through international assistance and cooperation, to the maximum of its available resources, *with a view to achieving progressively* the full realization of the rights recognized in that covenant. Subject to certain exceptions and modifications, the International Covenant on Civil and Political Rights imposes upon states parties the obligation to maintain defined standards. The states parties to the International Covenant on Economic, Social and Cultural Rights assume the obligation to promote an objective—the achievement of human rights.

By and large, the two covenants between them cover the rights proclaimed in the Universal Declaration of Human Rights, as they have been described above, but there are considerable differences between the Universal Declaration and the covenants.

The provisions of the Universal Declaration proclaiming that everyone has a right to own property and that everyone has the right to seek and to enjoy in other countries asylum from persecution have no counterpart in the covenants. On the other hand, the covenants deal with a number of questions in regard to which the declaration contains no provision. An example is the provision of both covenants that all peoples have the right to self-determination "by virtue of which they freely determine their political status and freely pursue their economic, social, and cultural development."

The International Covenant on Civil and Political Rights, but not the declaration, protects aliens against expulsion, entitles everyone not to be compelled to testify against himself or herself or to confess guilt, provides for a right to compensation for miscarriage of justice, and also provides that no one shall be liable to be tried or punished again for an offense for which he or she has already been finally convicted or acquitted. The covenant prohibits any propaganda for war and any advocacy of national, racial, or religious hatred. It provides for the protection of ethnic, religious, and linguistic minorities. The declaration does not contain corresponding provisions.

The International Covenant on Economic, Social and Cultural Rights contains provisions on the right to work and to enjoy just and favorable conditions of work; the right to form and join trade unions and, subject to the law of the land, the right to strike; the right to social security, including social insurance and the protection of the family; the right to an adequate standard of living and freedom from hunger; the right to the enjoyment of the highest attainable standards of physical and mental health; the right to education; and the right to take part in cultural life.

The International Covenant on Economic, Social, and Cultural Rights and the International Covenant on Civil and Political Rights are legally binding human rights agreements. Both were adopted by the General Assembly in 1966 and entered into force ten years later, making many of the provisions of the Universal Declaration of Human Rights effectively binding. As of May 2000, 142 states were party to the Covenant on Economic, Social, and Cultural Rights; and 144 states were party to the Covenant on Civil and Political Rights.

Measures of Implementation

The states parties to the Covenant on Economic, Social and Cultural Rights undertake to submit to the Economic and Social Council reports on the measures that they have adopted and the progress made in achieving the observance of the rights recognized in that covenant. Until 1986, the Economic and Social Council entrusted the task of examining such reports to a working group. Since then, this task has been carried out by the Committee on Economic, Social and Cultural Rights, an eight-member group of experts elected by the council to serve in their personal capacity. The committee submits to the council a summary of its consideration of the reports of states parties and makes suggestions and recommendations of a general nature.

Under the International Covenant on Civil and Political Rights, a Human Rights Committee was established to consider reports submitted by states parties on measures taken to implement the covenant's provisions and also to consider communications alleging violations under the Optional Protocol, which provides for consideration of communications from individuals who claim to be victims of violations of any rights set forth in the covenant. However, only claims against states parties to the protocol can be considered. The Optional Protocol entered into force 23 March 1976, and as of May 2000, 95 states were party to it. The Second Optional Protocol to the International Covenant on Civil and Political Rights, which aims to abolish the death penalty, was adopted by the General Assembly 15 December 1989 and entered into force roughly two years later, when 10 states had ratified it. As of May 2000, 43 states were party to it.

Apart from the right of individual complaint under the specific procedure of the Optional Protocol, thousands of letters and reports alleging human rights violations are received each year by the UN. Communications containing complaints of violations of human rights are summarized and sent confidentially to the members of the Commission on Human Rights and its Subcommission on Prevention of Discrimination and Protection of Minorities; copies of the complaint also are sent to the member states named. The identity of the writers is not disclosed unless they have consented to disclosure. Any replies from the government are forwarded to the commission and subcommission.

The subcommission, if it finds that the communications appear to reveal "a consistent pattern of gross and reliably attested violations" of human rights, may refer the situation to the commission, which, in turn, can decide to carry out a thorough study of the situation or to name an ad hoc committee to investigate it. All these procedures are confidential and are dealt with in private meetings until a report, if any, is made by the Commission on Human Rights to the Economic and Social Council.

The Commission on Human Rights and its subcommission also consider in public session each year the question of violations of human rights and fundamental freedoms, including racial discrimination and apartheid, in various countries and territories. For example, since 1967, an ad hoc working group of experts of the commission has reported regularly on allegations of ill-treatment of opponents of apartheid and other racist policies, and on the treatment of political prisoners and detainees, in South Africa and Namibia.

Since 1968, the commission has been considering the question of the violation of human rights in the territories occupied by Israel as a result of the 1967 hostilities in the Middle East, including violations of the 1949 Geneva Convention concerning the protection of civilian persons in time of war.

In 1975, the commission established a five-member working group to study the human rights situation in Chile. The group visited Chile in 1978 and submitted a report to the General Assembly and the commission. After the completion of the group's mandate, the commission appointed a special rapporteur in 1979 to continue to study the situation. The commission has also requested that studies or reports be prepared by special rapporteurs or by the Secretary-General on the human rights situation in Afghanistan, Bolivia, El Salvador, Equatorial Guinea, Guatemala, Iran, and Poland.

In addition, the commission and its subcommission have studied specific phenomena of particularly serious violations of human rights. Thus, working groups have been established—on southern Africa, on enforced or involuntary disappearances, on slavery, and on indigenous populations—and special rapporteurs have been appointed to examine the question of summary or arbitrary executions and questions concerning torture, religious intolerance, and the use of mercenaries.

OTHER HUMAN RIGHTS CONVENTIONS

The UN and two of the specialized agencies, the ILO and UNESCO, have prepared and put into force a number of conventions in the human rights field that, while not as comprehensive as the International Bill of Rights, deal with important specific rights. (Conventions on racial discrimination and on the status of women are discussed in separate sections below.)

Prevention and Punishment of Genocide

In 1948, the General Assembly adopted the Convention on the Prevention and Punishment of the Crime of Genocide. The convention entered into force in 1951. As of May 2000, it had been acceded to or ratified by 130 states. Under the convention, genocide means any of the following acts committed with intent to destroy in whole or in part a national, ethnic, racial, or religious group as such: (a) killing members of the group; (b) causing serious bodily or mental harm to members of the group; (c) deliberately inflicting on the group conditions of life calculated to bring about its physical destruction in whole or in part; (d) imposing measures intended to prevent births within the group; and (e) forcibly transferring children of the group to another group. One result of the convention is that the states parties place it beyond doubt that genocide (and conspiracy, incitement, and attempt to commit it and complicity in it), even if perpetrated by a government in its own territory against its own citizens, is not a matter essentially within the domestic jurisdiction of states but one of international concern. States parties confirm that genocide, whether committed in time of peace or in time of war, is a crime under international law that they undertake to prevent and to punish. Any contracting party can call upon UN organs to intervene.

Freedom of Association

The Freedom of Association Convention of 1948 (in force since 1950) was the first major achievement of the joint efforts of the UN and the ILO in the field of international legislation on human rights problems. By this convention, states parties undertake to give effect to the right of workers and employers, without distinction whatsoever, to establish and join organizations of their own choosing without previous authorization. In exercising the rights provided for in the convention, workers and employers and their respective organizations, like other persons or organized groups, shall respect the law of the land. However, the law of the land shall not be such as to impair, nor shall it be so applied as to impair, the guarantees provided in the convention.

Under the Right to Organize and Collective Bargaining Convention of 1949 (in force since 1951), workers shall enjoy adequate protection against acts of antiunion discrimination in their employment, particularly in respect to acts calculated to make the employment of a worker subject to the condition that the worker shall not join a union or shall relinquish trade union membership.

Freedom of Information

Out of the very ambitious legislative program of the UN and the specialized agencies to guarantee through international instruments the right set forth in Article 19 of the Universal Declaration of Human Rights to seek, receive, and impart information and ideas through any medium and regardless of frontiers, only the Convention on the International Right of Correction has been adopted. At a UN Conference on Freedom of Information held in 1948, two additional conventions in this field were drafted—a general Convention on Freedom of Information and a Convention on the International Transmission of News—but these have not yet been opened for signature and ratification, although the General Assembly has approved the latter convention.

The idea underlying the Convention on the International Right of Correction, which was opened for signature in 1953 and has been in force since 1962, is the attempt to transfer to the international level an institution that has been part of national law in a great number of countries. In the convention, the contracting states agree that in cases where a contracting state contends that a news dispatch capable of injuring its relations with other states or its national prestige or dignity, transmitted from one country to another by correspondents or information agencies and published or disseminated abroad, is false or distorted, it may submit its version of the facts (called a communiqué) to the contracting states within whose territories such dispatch has been published or disseminated. The receiving state has the obligation to release the communiqué to the correspondents and information agencies operating in its territory through the channels customarily used for the release of news concerning international affairs for publication.

Protection of Refugees and Stateless Persons

In the Convention Relating to the Status of Refugees of 1951 (in force since 1954, with a protocol of 1967) and the Convention Relating to the Status of Stateless Persons of 1954 (in force since 1969), far-reaching provisions for the protection of refugees and stateless persons were enacted. Two principles are the basis of both conventions: (1) there shall be as little discrimination as possible between nationals on the one hand and refugees or stateless persons on the other, and (2) there shall be no discrimination based on race, religion, or country of origin at all among refugees and stateless persons.

In 1961, a conference of plenipotentiaries adopted the Convention on the Reduction of Statelessness, which entered into force in 1975.

Abolition of Slavery, the Slave Trade, and Forced Labor

The fight against slavery has been an international concern since the beginning of the 19th century. In more recent times, under the auspices of the League of Nations, the Slavery Convention of 1926 was enacted, by which the contracting parties undertook to prevent and suppress the slave trade and to bring about "progressively and as soon as possible" the complete abolition of slavery in all its forms. Under UN auspices, the Supplementary Convention on the Abolition of Slavery, the Slave Trade, and Institutions and Practices Similar to Slavery was adopted in 1956 and has been in force since 1957. Under the convention, states parties undertake to bring about, also "progressively and as soon as possible," the complete abolition or abandonment not only of slavery but also of other objectionable practices, such as debt bondage and serfdom.

By the Convention Concerning the Abolition of Forced Labor, adopted by the International Labor Conference in 1957 and in force since 1959, states parties undertake to suppress and not to make use of any form of forced or compulsory labor as a means of political coercion or education or as a punishment for holding or expressing political views or views ideologically opposed to the established political, social, or economic system; as a punishment for having participated in strikes; or as a means of racial, social, national, or religious discrimination.

Equality in Employment and Occupation

By the Convention on Discrimination in Employment and Occupation, adopted by the International Labor Conference in 1958 (in force since 1960), each state party undertakes to declare and pursue a national policy designed to promote, by methods appropriate to national conditions and practices, equality of opportunity and treatment with respect to employment and occupation, with a view to eliminating discrimination. The fulfillment of the obligations undertaken by this convention is subject to the supervisory arrangements that apply under the constitution of the ILO.

Equality in Education

In 1960, the General Conference of UNESCO adopted the Convention Against Discrimination in Education (in force since 1962). Like the Discrimination (Employment and Occupation) Convention, the Convention Against Discrimination in Education prohibits any distinction, exclusion, limitation, or preference based on race, color, sex, language, religion, political or other opinion, national or social origin, economic condition, or birth that has the purpose or effect of impairing equality of treatment in education. The establishment or maintenance of separate educational systems or institutions for pupils of the two sexes is not prohibited, provided that these systems or institutions offer equivalent access to education and provide teaching staffs meeting the same standards of qualification. A special protocol adopted in 1962 institutes a Conciliation and Good Offices Commission to be responsible for seeking a settlement of any disputes that may arise between the states parties to the convention.

Non-Applicability of Statutory Limitations to War Crimes and Crimes Against Humanity

In 1968, the General Assembly adopted the Convention on the Non-Applicability of Statutory Limitations to War Crimes and Crimes Against Humanity. The convention, in force since 1970, provides that no statutory limitation shall apply to war crimes and crimes against humanity, irrespective of the date of their commission. It also revises and extends the concepts of war crimes and crimes against humanity as they were defined in 1945 in the Charter of the International Military Tribunal and were applied and interpreted by the tribunal. The states parties to the 1968 convention undertake to adopt all necessary domestic measures with a view to making possible the extradition of persons who have committed such crimes.

War Crimes Records. Records of the International Military Tribunal (Nuremberg) and the International Military Tribunal for the Far East (Tokyo) are in the UN Archives in New York. Also deposited there are the records of various national military tribunals that were submitted to the UN War Crimes Commission established in London by a meeting of Allied and Dominion representatives in October 1943, two years before the UN was created. The following 17 countries were members of the commission: Australia, Belgium, Canada, China, Czechoslovakia, Denmark, France, Greece, India, Luxembourg, Netherlands, New Zealand, Norway, Poland, UK, US, and Yugoslavia. The commission's primary task was to collect, investigate, and record evidence of war crimes and to report to the governments concerned those instances where the material available appeared to disclose a prima facie case. The commission took no part in the detention of persons listed or in the prosecution of the cases. It ended its work in March 1948 and deposited its records in the UN Archives with the stipulation that access to the records be limited to requests by governments for information on specific individuals. Following consultations among representatives of the former members of the commission in September/October 1987, its chairman recommended to the UN Secretary-General that the files be opened to governments for research into and investigation and prosecution of war crimes and to individuals, with the permission of the government of which they are nationals or permanent residents, for research into the history and work of the commission and into war crimes.

Prevention and Punishment of Crimes Against Internationally Protected Persons

In 1973, the General Assembly adopted the Convention on the Prevention and Punishment of Crimes Against Internationally Protected Persons, Including Diplomatic Agents. The convention, in force since 1977, aims at preventing the commission of acts of terrorism against heads of state, heads of government, ministers of foreign affairs, representatives of states, and officials of international organizations, as well as members of their families who accompany them or form part of their households. Each state party to the convention agrees to make murder, kidnapping, or other attacks upon the person or liberty of an internationally protected person or a violent attack upon his official premises, private accommodations, or means of transport a punishable crime. States agree to cooperate in the prevention of these crimes and in the prosecution and punishment of offenders.

Prevention of Torture and Other Cruel, Inhuman, or Degrading Treatment or Punishment

In 1975, the General Assembly proclaimed the Declaration on the Protection of All Persons from Being Subjected to Torture and Other Cruel, Inhuman or Degrading Treatment or Punishment. The declaration spells out in greater detail the provisions of the Universal Declaration of Human Rights and the International Covenant on Civil and Political Rights that no one may be subjected to torture or to cruel, inhuman, or degrading treatment or punishment.

The declaration was given binding legal form in 1984, when the General Assembly adopted the Convention Against Torture and Other Cruel, Inhuman or Degrading Treatment or Punishment. In the convention, which came into force on 26 June 1987, torture is defined as any act by which severe physical or mental pain is intentionally inflicted by, at the instigation of, or with the acquiescence of someone acting in an official capacity, whether to obtain information or a confession; to punish, intimidate, or coerce; or for reasons based on discrimination. It does not include

pain or suffering arising only from, inherent in, or incidental to lawful sanctions. States parties undertake to prevent torture in their jurisdictions and ensure that it is legally punishable. No exceptional circumstances, such as war, the threat of war, internal political instability, or any other emergency, may be invoked to justify torture, nor can a torturer be excused by virtue of having acted under orders. The convention provides for extradition of persons believed to have committed acts of torture and for protection and compensation for torture victims. As of May 2000, 119 states were party to this convention.

Convention on the Rights of the Child

In November 1989, the General Assembly adopted the Convention on the Rights of the Child, based on the draft proposed by the Commission on Human Rights in March of that year. The convention, which came into force in September 1990, had 191 states party to it as of May 2000. The convention recognizes and protects a wide range of civil rights and liberties. It acknowledges the importance of a secure and healthy family or alternative environment; provides for education, leisure, and cultural activities; and states that children in emergencies are entitled to special protection and that children who are in conflict with the law must be guaranteed basic rights. The convention also stipulates that children should be protected from any form of exploitation.

In accordance with article 43 of the Convention, a Committee on the Rights of the Child was established in February 1991. The committee meets twice a year to consider periodic reports submitted by states which give details of their effective implementation of the provisions of the convention. The committee submits to the General Assembly, through the Economic and Social Council, a report on its activities every two years.

International Convention on the Protection of the Rights of All Migrant Workers and Members of their Families

In December 1990, the General Assembly adopted a convention that takes into account the importance and extent of the migration phenomenon, which involves millions of people and affects a large number of states in the international community. In particular, the convention stipulates that all migrant workers and members of their families have the same right to equality with nationals of the state where they are engaged in remunerated activity. The convention will enter into force when 20 states have accepted it; as of May 2000, 12 states were party to it.

REGIONAL HUMAN RIGHTS INSTRUMENTS

The work of the UN in the human rights field, for which the provisions of the Charter have been the point of departure, has also inspired important developments in the protection of human rights on the regional level by the Council of Europe, the Organization of American States, and the Organization of African Unity.

The European Convention on Human Rights

Under the auspices of the Council of Europe, the European Convention on Human Rights was signed in 1950 and entered into force in 1953. The convention is based on an early draft of what is now the International Covenant on Civil and Political Rights. It was concluded by the governments of European countries "to take the first steps for the collective enforcement of certain of the rights stated in the Universal Declaration of Human Rights." It was subsequently supplemented by five additional protocols. As far as the substantive provisions are concerned, the European Convention and the International Covenant on Civil and Political Rights cover, more or less, the same ground, although there are a number of important differences between the two instruments.

The European Convention established two internal organs "to ensure the observance of the engagements undertaken by the High Contracting Parties in the present Convention"—that is, the

European Commission on Human Rights and the European Court of Human Rights. Any party to the convention has the right to refer to the commission any alleged breach of the convention by another party. The commission may also receive petitions from any person, nongovernmental organization, or group of individuals claiming to be the victim of a violation, by one of the parties, of the rights set forth in the convention and in the relevant protocols. The exercise of this power by the commission is subject to the condition that the state against which the complaint is directed has recognized this competence of the commission.

If the commission does not succeed in securing a friendly settlement on the basis of respect for human rights as defined in the convention, it draws up a report on the facts and states its opinion as to whether the facts found disclose a breach by the state concerned of its obligations under the convention. The final decision is taken either by the Committee of Ministers of the Council of Europe, a political organ, or, if it has jurisdiction and the matter is referred to it, by the European Court of Human Rights.

The European Social Charter

The European Social Charter is the European counterpart to the International Covenant on Economic, Social and Cultural Rights. The provisions of the European Social Charter, however, are more specific and detailed. It has established a reporting procedure. The reports are examined by a committee of independent experts, which submits its conclusions to a governmental social subcommittee. The Consultative Assembly of the Council of Europe is consulted. In the final stage, the Committee of Ministers may make any recommendation that it considers necessary to any contracting party in the areas of economic, social, and cultural rights.

The American Convention on Human Rights

In 1948, several months before the adoption by the General Assembly of the Universal Declaration of Human Rights, the Ninth International Conference of American States, meeting in Bogotá, adopted the American Declaration of the Rights and Duties of Man. This declaration was followed in 1969 by the signing in San José, Costa Rica, of the American Convention on Human Rights. The convention, in force since 1978, is a very comprehensive instrument, similar to both the European Convention on Human Rights and the International Covenant on Civil and Political Rights. The organs of implementation of the Pact of San José are the Inter-American Commission on Human Rights (corresponding to the European Commission and to the Human Rights Committee under the International Covenant on Civil and Political Rights) and the Inter-American Court of Human Rights. While the right of petition of individuals is optional under the European Convention and the International Covenant on Civil and Political Rights, in the inter-American system, every state party accepts the right of petition automatically.

The African Charter on Human and Peoples' Rights

In 1981, the Assembly of Heads of State and Government of the Organization of African Unity, meeting in Nairobi, Kenya, adopted the African Charter on Human and Peoples' Rights. The charter, which came into force on 21 October 1986, provides for an African Commission on Human and Peoples' Rights, composed of 11 members elected by the assembly, to promote and protect the rights set forth in the charter. The provisions of the charter are similar to those of the Universal Declaration of Human Rights but with special reference to African traditions of rights and freedoms, including the right to self-determination and the right of peoples to dispose of their wealth and natural resources.

THE FIGHT AGAINST RACIAL DISCRIMINATION

The idea of the equality of races emerged as the one that, more than any other, has dominated the thoughts and actions of the post–World War II period. The aim of racial equality has permeated the lawmaking and the standard-setting activities of the UN family of organizations and also the day-to-day work of many of its organs. The Charter, the Universal Declaration of Human Rights, and the two International Covenants on Human Rights prohibit discrimination on the grounds of race or color, as do the conventions against discrimination in employment and occupation and in education that have already been described.

The Declaration on the Elimination of All Forms of Racial Discrimination

In 1963, the General Assembly proclaimed the Declaration on the Elimination of All Forms of Racial Discrimination, which affirms that discrimination between human beings on the grounds of race, color, or ethnic origin is an offense to human dignity, a denial of Charter principles, a violation of the rights proclaimed in the Universal Declaration of Human Rights, and an obstacle to friendly and peaceful relations among peoples.

The International Convention on the Elimination of All Forms of Racial Discrimination

In 1965, the General Assembly adopted the International Convention on the Elimination of All Forms of Racial Discrimination which entered into force in January 1969. As of May 2000, it had been acceded to or ratified by 156 states. Under the convention, states parties undertake not only to condemn racial discrimination and pursue a policy of eliminating it in all its forms but also to prohibit and bring to an end, by all appropriate means, including legislation as required by circumstances, racial discrimination by any individual, group, or organization. States parties undertake to declare it an offense punishable by law to disseminate ideas based on racial superiority or hatred or that are an incitement to racial discrimination. They also commit themselves to declare illegal and prohibit organizations that promote and incite racial discrimination and to recognize participation in such organizations as an offense punishable by law. The convention provides for the establishment of international supervisory machinery similar to that laid down in the International Covenant on Civil and Political Rights but contains tighter provisions.

Under the convention, an 18-member Committee on the Elimination of Racial Discrimination was established, which, like the Human Rights Committee provided for in the International Covenant on Civil and Political Rights, has the function of considering reports by states and allegations by a state party that another state party is not giving effect to the provisions of the convention. States parties to the convention also may recognize the competence of the Committee on the Elimination of Racial Discrimination to receive and consider petitions (communications) from individuals or groups of individuals. In the last instance, the International Court of Justice can be apprised of disputes with respect to the interpretation and application of the convention.

The International Convention on the Suppression and Punishment of the Crime of Apartheid

In 1973, the General Assembly adopted the International Convention on the Suppression and Punishment of the Crime of Apartheid which entered into force in July 1976. At 31 December 1993, it had been acceded to or ratified by 99 states. The convention provides that international responsibility for the crime of apartheid shall apply to individuals, members of organizations and institutions, and representatives of a state, whether residing in the state in which the acts are perpetrated or elsewhere. Persons charged can be tried by any state party to the convention. A three-member group of the Commission on Human Rights meets each year to review progress in implementing the convention.

The International Declaration and the International Convention Against Apartheid in Sports

The International Declaration Against Apartheid in Sports, adopted by the General Assembly in 1977, calls on states to take all appropriate action to cease sporting contacts with any country practicing apartheid and to exclude or expel any such country from international and regional sports bodies.

The International Convention Against Apartheid in Sports, adopted by the General Assembly in 1985, gave the provisions of the declaration a binding legal form. It entered into force in April 1988. As of May 2000, it had been acceded to or ratified by 58 states.

Other Action to Combat Racism and Racial Discrimination

In 1972, the General Assembly decided to launch a Decade for Action to Combat Racism and Racial Discrimination, to begin on 10 December 1973, the 25th anniversary of the Universal Declaration of Human Rights, and in 1973, the General Assembly approved a comprehensive and ambitious program for the decade. Among its goals were the following: to promote human rights for all without distinction of any kind on grounds of race, color, descent, or national or ethnic origin, especially by eradicating racial prejudice, racism, and racial discrimination; to arrest any expansion of racist policies; to identify, isolate, and dispel the fallacious and mythical beliefs, policies, and practices that contribute to racism and racial discrimination; and to put an end to racist regimes.

While there was not necessarily complete unanimity in the General Assembly on every phrase and formulation of the relevant decisions on the decade adopted in 1972, 1973, and 1974, there was a general consensus in support of its goals. However, at the 1975 session of the General Assembly, a resolution was adopted by which the General Assembly determined that "Zionism is a form of racism and racial discrimination." The resolution was adopted by 72 votes to 35, with 32 abstentions. Among those strongly opposed were the nine members of the European Economic Community, as well as the US, Canada, Australia, and New Zealand, and other states of Western Europe, Latin America, and Africa. Many of these states declared that the resolution radically changed the concept of the decade and would therefore change their attitude toward it.

The midpoint of the decade was marked by a world conference held in Geneva in August 1978. The conference adopted recommendations for comprehensive mandatory sanctions against the racist regimes of southern Africa, elimination of all discriminatory laws and practices, adoption of laws to punish dissemination of ideas based on racial superiority or hatred, and promotion of the rights of indigenous peoples and migrant workers. In 1979, the General Assembly adopted a program for the remaining four years of the decade, and in 1982, it decided that a second conference would be held in 1983.

The Second World Conference to Combat Racism and Racial Discrimination, held in Geneva in August 1983, was attended by representatives of 128 states, as well as of UN organs and specialized agencies and of intergovernmental and nongovernmental organizations. The conference adopted a declaration and a program of action in which it noted that "in spite of the efforts of the international community during the Decade, at the national, regional and international levels, racism, racial discrimination and apartheid continue unabated and have shown no sign of diminishing." The program of action contained practical suggestions on matters such as action to combat apartheid; education, teaching, and training; dissemination of information and the role of the mass media in combating racism and racial discrimination;

measures for the promotion and protection of the human rights of minority groups, indigenous peoples, and migrant workers who are subject to racial discrimination; recourse procedures for victims of racial discrimination; implementation of the International Convention on the Elimination of All Forms of Racial Discrimination and other related international instruments; national legislation and institutions; seminars and studies; action by nongovernmental organizations; and international cooperation.

On the recommendation of the conference, the General Assembly proclaimed the Second Decade to Combat Racism and Racial Discrimination, on 22 November 1983, and called for renewed and intensified efforts and for implementation of the program of action approved by the conference.

In 1997, the General Assembly decided to convene the Third World Conference against Racism, Racial Discrimination, Xenophobia, and Related Intolerance, which was scheduled for August and September 2001 in South Africa. The conference was to focus on action-oriented and practical steps to eradicate racism, including measures of prevention, education, and protection, as well as the provision of effective remedies. The World Conference was viewed as important opportunity to "create a new world vision for the fights against racism in the 21st century."

THE WORK OF THE UN RELATING TO THE STATUS OF WOMEN

The work of the UN relating to the status of women, aimed at achieving equal rights for men and women, is an important part of the UN's efforts to promote and to encourage respect for human rights and fundamental freedoms. The organ given the main responsibility in this field is the Commission on the Status of Women, a functional commission of the Economic and Social Council, established in 1946. Almost all the achievements of the UN in this matter are due to the initiative and work of the commission.

The Convention on the Political Rights of Women

The Convention on the Political Rights of Women, adopted in 1952 and in force since 1954, represented the culmination of the endeavors of generations of fighters for women's rights. It provides that women shall be entitled to vote in all elections, that they shall be eligible for election to all publicly elected bodies, and that they shall be entitled to hold public office and to exercise all public functions on equal terms with men and without any discrimination.

The Convention on the Nationality of Married Women

The Convention on the Nationality of Married Women, adopted in 1957 and in force since 1958, provides that neither the celebration nor the dissolution of marriage between a national and an alien, nor the change of nationality by the husband during marriage, shall automatically affect the nationality of the wife.

The Convention on Consent to Marriage, Minimum Age for Marriage, and Registration of Marriages

The Convention on Consent to Marriage, Minimum Age for Marriage, and Registration of Marriages, adopted in 1962 and in force since 1964, provides that no marriage shall be legally entered into without the full and free consent of both parties, such consent to be expressed by them in person after due publicity and in the presence of the authority competent to solemnize the marriage. States parties to the convention are committed to take legislative action to specify a minimum age for marriage. All marriages shall be registered in an official register by a competent authority.

In a recommendation on the same subjects as those of this convention, adopted in 1965, the General Assembly stated that the minimum age shall be not less than 15 years.

The Declaration on the Elimination of Discrimination Against Women

In 1967, the General Assembly solemnly proclaimed the Declaration on the Elimination of Discrimination Against Women. The declaration states that discrimination against women, denying or limiting as it does their equality of rights with men, is fundamentally unjust and constitutes an offense against human dignity. Work was started on a convention to put the principles of the declaration into binding legal form.

The Convention on the Elimination of All Forms of Discrimination Against Women

On 18 December 1979, the General Assembly adopted the Convention on the Elimination of All Forms of Discrimination Against Women. The convention came into force in September 1981; as of May 2000, 165 states had ratified the convention.

Under the convention, states parties undertake to adopt all appropriate measures to abolish existing laws, regulations, customs, and practices that are discriminatory against women and to establish legal protection of the rights of women on an equal basis with men. The convention contains detailed provisions concerning equal rights for women in voting and holding public office and in education, employment, and health care. It provides for equality before the law and for the elimination of discrimination against women in all matters relating to marriage and family relations.

The convention established a Committee on the Elimination of Discrimination Against Women to periodically examine reports by states parties on measures that they have taken to implement the convention. The 23-member committee meets annually to consider the reports, which are due within one year of ratification or accession to the convention and every four years thereafter. The committee makes recommendations and observations to states parties on the basis of its consideration of the reports.

International Women's Year

In 1972, the General Assembly proclaimed the year 1975 as the International Women's Year. In 1974, the Economic and Social Council decided to convene an international conference to examine to what extent the organizations of the UN system had implemented the recommendations for the elimination of discrimination against women made by the Commission on the Status of Women since its establishment and to launch an international action program aimed at achieving the integration of women as full and equal partners with men in the total development effort, eliminating discrimination on grounds of sex, and achieving the widest possible involvement of women in strengthening international peace and eliminating racism and racial discrimination.

The World Conference of the International Women's Year took place in June/July 1975 in Mexico City. It was the most representative meeting on women's issues held to date, bringing together more than a thousand representatives, about 70% of them women, from more than 130 countries. The conference adopted the "Declaration of Mexico on the Equality of Women and Their Contribution to Development and Peace, 1975"; a world plan of action for implementation of the objectives of the International Women's Year; regional plans of action; and a great number of decisions on concrete problems. In the Declaration of Mexico, the conference affirmed its faith in the objectives of the International Women's Year—equality, development, and peace.

UN Decade for Women

Later in 1975, the General Assembly endorsed the proposals of the Mexico conference and proclaimed the period 1976–85 as the UN Decade for Women: Equality, Development, and Peace. The General Assembly called for the decade to be devoted to effective and sustained action to implement the world plan of action, and it decided to convene in 1980, at the midpoint of the decade, another world conference to review and evaluate the progress made.

The second world conference, held in Copenhagen in July 1980, adopted a program of action for the second half of the decade, 1980–85, to promote the three objectives of equality, development, and peace, with special emphasis on the sub-theme—employment, health, and education. It called for specific action to ensure that the objectives of the world plan were met by the end of the decade.

The program of action was endorsed later in 1980 by the General Assembly, which decided to convene in 1985 a world conference to review and appraise the achievements of the decade.

1995 Fourth World Conference on Women

The Fourth World Conference on Women was held in Beijing, from 4–15 September 1995, subtitled "Action for Equality, Development and Peace." At preparatory meetings in 1994, the Secretary-General said a turning point had been reached in the cause of women worldwide. The conference represented a vital continuation of the work on development issues begun during the United Nations Conference on the Environment and Development (UNCED) in June 1992 and the World Conference on Human Rights held in Vienna in June 1993, and tied in with the International Conference on Population and Development, held in Cairo (5–13 September 1994) and the World Summit for Social Development, held in Copenhagen (11–12 March 1995).

Besides receiving reports from virtually all UN organizations on their programs relating to the status of women, the conference addressed gender issues in the context of a new vision of the 21st century as one in which gender equality would be achieved. It will also focused on the problems of rural women and the need to facilitate access to resources so that they can improve their lives and, in turn, the lives of their families and communities.

The first follow-up meeting to the Fourth World Conference on Women was convened in June 2000 in New York City: Beijing+5 (also called Women 2000) was set up to review progress and establish action plans for the next five years. More than 150 countries and thousands of non-governmental organizations were to attend sessions at the UN headquarters.

The Nairobi Forward-Looking Strategies

The World Conference to Review and Appraise the Achievements of the UN Decade for Women was held in Nairobi, Kenya, in July 1985, attended by representatives of 157 states, as well as observers from specialized agencies and other organizations. The major achievement of the conference was the adoption, by consensus, of the Nairobi Forward-Looking Strategies for the Advancement of Women to the Year 2000. Measures recommended included technical cooperation, training and advisory services, institutional coordination, research and policy analysis, participation of women in activities at the international and regional levels, and dissemination of information on goals and objectives for the advancement of women.

The Declaration on the Participation of Women in Promoting International Peace and Cooperation

The Declaration on the Participation of Women in Promoting International Peace and Cooperation was adopted by the General Assembly in 1982. It states that women and men have an equal and vital interest in contributing to international peace and cooperation and that, to this end, women must be enabled to exercise their right to participate in the economic, social, cultural, civil, and political affairs of society on an equal footing with men.

OTHER DECLARATIONS IN THE HUMAN RIGHTS FIELD

The Declaration of the Rights of the Child

In 1959, the General Assembly adopted the Declaration of the Rights of the Child, which proclaims that every child, without distinction or discrimination on account of race, color, sex, language, religion, political or other opinion, national or social origin, property, birth, or other status, whether of the child or of the child's family, shall enjoy special protection and be given opportunities and facilities to develop physically, mentally, morally, spiritually, and socially in a healthy and normal manner and in conditions of freedom and dignity. Every child shall be entitled from birth to a name and nationality and shall enjoy the benefits of social security. The child who is physically, mentally, or socially handicapped shall be given the special treatment, education, and care required by his or her particular condition. Every child is entitled to receive education that shall be free and compulsory, at least in the elementary stages. Every child shall be protected against all forms of neglect, cruelty, and exploitation and from practices that may foster racial, religious, or any other form of discrimination.

The Declaration on the Granting of Independence to Colonial Countries and Peoples

The Declaration on the Granting of Independence to Colonial Countries and Peoples, adopted by the General Assembly in 1960, declares that the subjection of peoples to alien subjugation, domination, and exploitation constitutes a denial of fundamental human rights, is contrary to the Charter, and is an impediment to the promotion of world peace and cooperation. The declaration proclaims that all peoples have the right to self-determination.

In 1961, the General Assembly established a Special Committee on the Situation with Regard to the Implementation of the Declaration. (See also the chapter on Independence of Colonial Peoples.)

The Declaration on Territorial Asylum

The Declaration on Territorial Asylum, adopted by the General Assembly in 1967, supplements Article 14 of the Universal Declaration of Human Rights and provides that asylum granted by a state, in the exercise of its sovereignty, to persons entitled to invoke Article 14 of the Universal Declaration, including persons struggling against colonization, shall be respected by all other states. It rests with the state granting asylum to evaluate the grounds for asylum. Where a state finds difficulty in granting or continuing to grant asylum, states individually or jointly or through the UN shall consider, in the spirit of international solidarity, appropriate measures to lighten the burden on that state. No person entitled to invoke Article 14 of the Universal Declaration shall be subjected to measures such as retention at the frontier or, if he has already entered the territory in which he seeks asylum, expulsion or compulsory return to any state where he may be subjected to persecution.

The Declaration on Social Progress and Development

In 1969, the General Assembly solemnly proclaimed the Declaration on Social Progress and Development, which sets forth the principles, objectives, means, and methods to eliminate obstacles to social progress, particularly inequality, exploitation, war, colonialism, and racism. The declaration shows the close connections between social development policies and endeavors to promote respect for human rights. Article 1 provides that all peoples and all human beings, without distinction as to race, color, sex, language, religion, nationality, ethnic origin, family or social status, or political or other conviction, shall have the right to live in dignity and freedom and to enjoy the fruits of social progress and should, on their part, contribute to it.

The Declaration on Principles of International Law Concerning Friendly Relations and Cooperation Among States

On 24 October 1970, the 25th anniversary of the entry into force of the Charter, the General Assembly adopted the Declaration on Principles of International Law Concerning Friendly Relations and Cooperation Among States in Accordance with the Charter of the United Nations. One of the principles thus proclaimed is that states "shall cooperate in the promotion of universal respect for, and observance of, human rights, and fundamental freedoms for all, and in the elimination of all forms of racial discrimination and all forms of religious intolerance."

The Declaration on the Rights of Mentally Retarded Persons

The Declaration on the Rights of Mentally Retarded Persons, adopted in 1971, proclaims that the mentally retarded person has, to the maximum degree of feasibility, the same rights as other human beings: the right to proper medical care and physical therapy, education, training, rehabilitation, and guidance; the right to economic security and to perform productive work; and the right, when necessary, to a qualified guardian and to protection from exploitation, abuse, and degrading treatment. Whenever mentally retarded persons are unable to exercise all their rights in a meaningful way or if it should become necessary to restrict or deny them, the procedure used must contain proper safeguards against abuse.

The Declaration on the Protection of Women and Children in Emergency and Armed Conflicts

In 1974, the General Assembly proclaimed the Declaration on the Protection of Women and Children in Emergency and Armed Conflicts. The declaration states that attacks on civilians, "especially on women and children, who are the most vulnerable members of the population," shall be prohibited and condemned and that states involved in armed conflicts shall make all efforts "to spare women and children from the ravages of war."

The Declaration on the Rights of Disabled Persons

The Declaration on the Rights of Mentally Retarded Persons was confirmed and expanded by the Declaration on the Rights of Disabled Persons, adopted in 1975. The term "disabled person" means any person unable to ensure by himself or herself wholly or partly the necessities of a normal individual and/or social life, as a result of a deficiency in his or her physical or mental capacities. While the formulation of some of the rights set forth in the Declaration on the Rights of Disabled Persons occasionally differs from that contained in the earlier instrument, there are no differences as regards the principles and purposes, except that the later declaration applies also to persons who are physically, not mentally, handicapped.

The Declaration on the Use of Scientific and Technological Progress in the Interests of Peace

In 1975, the General Assembly adopted the Declaration on the Use of Scientific and Technological Progress in the Interests of Peace and for the Benefit of Mankind. The declaration provides that all states shall promote international cooperation to ensure that the results of scientific and technological developments are used in the interests of strengthening international peace and security, freedom, and independence and that they are also used for economic and social development and the realization of human rights and freedoms. The declaration calls on all states to help prevent the use of scientific and technological developments to limit or interfere with the enjoyment of the human rights of the individual.

The Declaration on the Elimination of All Forms of Religious Intolerance

The Declaration on the Elimination of All Forms of Intolerance and of Discrimination Based on Religion and Belief, prepared by the Commission on Human Rights and adopted by the General Assembly in 1981, states that everyone shall have the right of freedom of thought, conscience, and religion and that no one shall be subject to discrimination on the grounds of religion or other beliefs.

The Declaration on the Human Rights of Individuals Who Are Not Nationals of the Country in Which They Live

In 1985, the General Assembly adopted the Declaration on the Human Rights of Individuals Who Are Not Nationals of the Country in Which They Live. The declaration defines the term "alien" as any individual who is not a national of the state in which he or she is present. It declares that all aliens shall enjoy a wide range of civil rights, as well as the right to safe and healthy working conditions, fair wages, and equal remuneration for work of equal value; the right to join trade unions and other associations; and the right to health protection, medical care, social security, education, rest, and leisure. No alien shall be deprived of his or her lawfully acquired assets, and aliens shall be free at any time to communicate with the consulate or diplomatic mission of the state of which they are nationals.

The Declaration on the Right to Development

The Declaration on the Right to Development was adopted by the General Assembly in 1986. In the declaration, the right to development is proclaimed as an inalienable human right by virtue of which every person and all peoples are entitled to participate in, contribute to, and enjoy economic, social, cultural, and political development, in which all human rights and fundamental freedoms can be fully realized. The right to development also implies the full realization of the right of peoples to self-determination, including their inalienable right to exercise full sovereignty over all their natural wealth and resources.

Declaration on the Rights of Persons belonging to National or Ethnic, Religious and Linguistic Minorities

In December 1992, the General Assembly reaffirmed that one of the basic aims of the United Nations was to promote and encourage respect for human rights and fundamental freedoms for all, without distinction as to race, sex, language, or religion. The Declaration on the Rights of Persons belonging to National or Ethnic, Religious and Linguistic Minorities invites states to protect the identity of minorities within their respective territories, in particular through appropriate legislation.

Declaration on the Protection of All Persons from Enforced Disappearance

In December 1992, the General Assembly also adopted the Declaration on the Protection of All Persons from Enforced Disappearance, which urges states to contribute by all means to the prevention and eradication of this gross offense to human dignity and flagrant violation of human rights. Acts of enforced disappearance should be considered offenses under criminal law punishable by appropriate penalties that take into account their extreme seriousness. The victims of acts of enforced disappearance, and their families, have the right to obtain redress and adequate compensation, including complete rehabilitation.

INDEPENDENCE OF COLONIAL PEOPLES

Since the creation of the UN, more than 80 territories that were formerly under foreign rule have become sovereign states and members of the UN. In this radical transformation of the world's political map, the UN has played a significant role that stems from the basic precepts of its charter as laid down in Article 1, which states that one of the purposes of the UN is to "develop friendly relations among nations based on respect for the principle of equal rights and self-determination of peoples, . . ." Chapters XI, XII, and XIII of the charter are devoted specifically to measures that are designed to promote the welfare of dependent peoples.

In its efforts to implement these measures, the UN has dealt with two types of territories: (1) former colonial territories administered by designated member states as UN trust territories pending independence, and (2) non-self-governing dependencies or colonies of UN member states. Since the UN powers and responsibilities differ considerably in regard to the two categories of territories, this chapter has been divided into two sections.

TRUST TERRITORIES
The main features of the trusteeship system are outlined in the chapter on the Trusteeship Council. What follows here is a brief description of the territories originally placed under UN trusteeship in 1946.

Trust Territories That Have Achieved Independence
Three types of countries became part of the UN's trusteeship system: (1) territories still administered by a nation under a League of Nations mandate, (2) territories detached from enemy states as a result of the Second World War, and (3) territories voluntarily placed under the system by states responsible for their administration. All 11 territories that were placed under the trusteeship system in 1946 have since achieved the goals of the charter, either as independent states or as parts of independent states.

Following is a list of the territories that have achieved independence. The territories are listed under their administering powers.

Australia
Nauru (coadministered with New Zealand and the United Kingdom). The territory became independent on 31 January 1968, in accordance with a 1965 General Assembly resolution setting this date as the target for accession to independence.

New Guinea. The trust territory of New Guinea was administered by Australia together with the non-self-governing territory of Papua until the two were united and became the independent state of Papua New Guinea in 1975.

Belgium
Ruanda-Urundi under Belgian administration. In a special session convened in June 1962, the General Assembly approved separate independence for the two territories, which were established on 1 July 1962 as the Republic of Rwanda and the Kingdom of Burundi.

France
Togoland. In 1958, with the agreement of France, the UN supervised elections, and the territory became the independent state of Togo on 27 April 1960.

Cameroons. Following a notification in 1958 by its legislative assembly of the desire of the territory to become independent and acting upon the recommendation of the Trusteeship Council, the General Assembly, in agreement with France, resolved that on 1 January 1960 trusteeship status would end and the territory would become independent as Cameroon.

Italy
Somaliland. In union with the dependency of British Somaliland, the territory became the sovereign state of Somalia on 1 July 1960.

New Zealand
Western Samoa. In agreement with the administering authority, the UN conducted a plebiscite in May 1961, following which the territory attained independence on 1 January 1962.

United Kingdom
Togoland. To ascertain the freely expressed wishes of the people as to their political future, the UN, in agreement with the United Kingdom, conducted a plebiscite in 1956. As a result of the plebiscite, the territory united in March 1957 with the former Gold Coast to form the independent state of Ghana.

Cameroons. Both the northern and southern sectors of the territory were administered as part of the federation of Nigeria, a British dependency. Following a plebiscite held under UN supervision in March 1961, the northern sector became part of newly independent Nigeria on 1 June 1961. Following a similar plebiscite, the peoples of the southern sector joined the newly independent state of Cameroon on 1 October 1961.

Tanganyika. Following negotiations between the United Kingdom and African leaders, the territory attained independence on 9 December 1961. It united with Zanzibar in 1964 to become the United Republic of Tanzania.

United States
Trust Territory of the Pacific Islands. By the end of 1975, only the Trust Territory of the Pacific Islands remained under the UN trusteeship system. It was administered by the United States under an agreement approved by the Security Council. Because it is a "strategic" trust territory, it was under the ultimate authority of the Security Council rather than the General Assembly. (See the chapter on the Trusteeship Council.)

The Pacific Islands, collectively known as Micronesia, include the former Japanese-mandated islands of the Marshalls, the Carolines, and the Northern Marianas (except Guam, which was ceded to the United States by Spain in 1898). In 1975, a covenant for political union with the United States was approved by the people of the Northern Marianas. In February 1976, the United States Congress gave final approval for granting commonwealth status to the Northern Marianas. The Commonwealth Covenant with the Northern Marianas came into force on 3 November 1986.

In a referendum held on 12 July 1978, Kosrae, Ponape, Truk, and Yap—in the Caroline archipelago—approved and ratified a draft constitution for a proposed Federated States of Micronesia. The four districts subsequently held elections, and the Congress of the Federated States of Micronesia was inaugurated on 10 May 1979. The Compact of Free Association with the Federated

States of Micronesia also came into force on 3 November 1986.

On 21 December 1978, the Marshall Islands Constitutional Convention approved a draft constitution, and in a referendum held on 1 March 1979, the voters of those islands adopted it by a substantial majority. Legislative power in the Marshall Islands was vested in the Nitijela (legislature); the first general election under the new constitution took place on 10 April 1979. The Compact of Free Association with the Marshall Islands came into force on 21 October 1986.

On 2 April 1979, the Constitutional Convention of Palau adopted a draft constitution, which was approved by a referendum on 9 July. Elections were held on 4 November 1980, and the new constitution came into force on 1 January 1981. However, since its constitution required a 75% majority for the approval of the Compact of Free Association with the United States, Palau was unable to obtain approval for the compact in seven different referendums over the next 10 years.

In November 1992, Palau held a constitutional amendment referendum and changed the requirement for approval to simple majority (50% plus 1). Thereafter, the eighth plebiscite was held in November 1993 and the compact was approved by 68 per cent of Palauans voting in favor. In January 1994, the United States informed the Trusteeship Council that its government and the government of Palau intended to implement the compact as soon as practicable. Planning for the smooth transition to Palau's new status was under way. In late 1994 the two countries implemented the Compact of Free Association and with it came the official end of Palau's status as a trusteeship territory.

Non-self-governing Territories

The delegates attending the 1945 San Francisco Conference, at which the UN was founded, included many spokesmen for anticolonialist sentiment. As a result of their efforts and generous proposals by Australia and the United Kingdom (which possessed the world's largest colonial empire at the time), the charter incorporates a pledge on the part of the colonial powers to assume certain obligations toward the peoples of their dependencies.

Charter Declaration on Non-self-governing Territories

The pledge takes the form of a declaration regarding non-self-governing territories that is embodied in Article 73, Chapter XI, of the charter. Under Article 73, all UN members "which have or assume responsibilities for the administration of territories whose peoples have not yet attained a full measure of self-government recognize the principle that the interests of the inhabitants of these territories are paramount, and accept as a sacred trust the obligation to promote to the utmost, within the system of international peace and security established by the present Charter, the well-being of the inhabitants of these territories, . . ." This general obligation is then divided into five specific obligations: (a) to "ensure, with due respect for the culture of the peoples concerned, their political, economic, social, and educational advancement, their just treatment, and their protection against abuses"; (b) to "develop self-government, to take due account of the political aspirations of the peoples, and to assist them in the progressive development of their free political institutions, according to the particular circumstances of each territory and its peoples . . ."; (c) to "further international peace and security"; (d) to "promote constructive measures of development . . ."; and (e) to "transmit regularly to the Secretary-General for information purposes, subject to such limitations as security and constitutional considerations may require, statistical and other information of a technical nature relating to economic, social, and educational conditions in the territories for which they are respectively responsible. . . ."

Today, when so many of these people have claimed and won their independence, the obligations contained in the declaration may not seem very far-reaching. For example, nothing is said about preparing non-self-governing territories for actual independence—indeed, the word "independence" appears nowhere in the declaration. Although due account is to be taken of the "political aspirations of the peoples," all that is explicitly acknowledged is the obligation to develop "self-government," which does not necessarily imply independence.

However, the validity of the declaration must be considered in the context of its era. Few people at the San Francisco Conference foresaw how intense or universal the desire of colonial peoples for full political sovereignty would be. All told, the obligations included in the declaration probably represented the maximum that reasonably could be expected from colonial countries at that time. Moreover, in the circumstances then prevailing, the agreement by the colonial nations, under paragraph (e) of Article 73, to submit information to an international body concerning their own territories—in effect, to yield up a degree of their sovereignty—was a considerable concession.

TERRITORIES COVERED BY THE DECLARATION

The somewhat unwieldy term "non-self-governing territory" was chosen primarily because it was broad enough to include the various constitutional designations given by administering powers to their dependencies—colony, protectorate, and so on—as well as all stages of political development short of actual self-government or independence. The declaration includes all those territories "whose peoples have not yet attained a full measure of self-government." However, the precise meaning of the phrase "a full measure of self-government" was not specified in the charter, an omission that left the door open for subsequent dispute and controversy.

At the outset, it was considered the responsibility of the eight colonial powers that were UN members to identify the dependencies they regarded as non-self-governing within the meaning of Article 73 of the charter. At its first working session, in 1946, the General Assembly adopted a resolution enumerating 74 non-self-governing territories that the administering countries had identified as falling within the provisions of the declaration. The eight colonial countries were Australia, Belgium, Denmark, France, the Netherlands, New Zealand, the United Kingdom, and the United States. The combined population of their dependencies—which ranged from tiny Pitcairn Island, with a population of 100 persons, to the Netherlands Indies, with 73 million—was estimated at 215 million. The dependencies of Spain and Portugal could not be included in the 1946 list, since these two colonial powers were not UN members at the time. (For the non-self-governing territories listed by the General Assembly in 1946 and subsequently, see Table 1.)

THE ROLE OF THE UN

The charter does not assign any particular task to the UN with respect to non-self-governing territories. It does not even specify what should be done with the information transmitted to the Secretary-General. Hence, the General Assembly has considered itself free to define its own functions.

Since, even in the very beginning, the majority of UN members were vehemently anticolonial, the immediate task that the General Assembly set for itself was to induce the colonial countries by every means in its power to fulfill their obligations under the charter declaration. Judging from the disputes and controversies that arose even as early as 1946, it seems safe to assume that this development was totally unforeseen by the colonial countries at the time of the San Francisco Conference.

Although the General Assembly lacks the power to enforce its recommendations, the colonial powers had no wish to see themselves recorded as being in constant opposition in majority decisions. Consequently, they fought from the start to maintain the right to take the initiative in affairs concerning their own territories and to prevent the UN from expanding its role in colonial matters. However, they were fighting a losing battle against an irreversible trend of world opinion; in effect, the story of the UN's role has essentially been one of increasing involvement in the process of decolonization.

Disputes over the Transmission of Information

The first dispute that arose between the colonial powers and the other UN members concerned the General Assembly's desire to discuss the reports that had been submitted on the various territories. Some of the colonial governments, particularly Belgium, contended that the mere submission of reports fulfilled the charter's requirements under paragraph (e) of Article 73. Disregarding these protests, the 1947 General Assembly set up a special committee to report on the information received. In 1949, this committee was established as the Committee on Information from Non-Self-Governing Territories, composed of an equal number of administering and nonadministering countries. In the same year, the General Assembly adopted a standard questionnaire, which the administering powers were expected to answer in annual reports. The questionnaire covered virtually every aspect of the social, economic, and educational conditions in the territories. However, because of the controversies discussed below, the committee received reports on only 56 of the 74 territories.

Cessation of Information

By 1949, some of the administering powers had unilaterally interpreted paragraph (e) of Article 73 to mean that when they themselves considered a territory to have attained self-government, they no longer needed to submit reports on it to the UN. On this basis, the United Kingdom ceased sending information on Malta after its first report in 1946. Likewise, France, after 1946, stopped sending reports on certain of its territories, including Guadeloupe, Martinique, and New Caledonia, that it regarded as overseas departments with rights equal to those of the metropolitan departments of France or as having reached a requisite stage of "internal autonomy." Nor did the United States send reports on the Panama Canal Zone after 1946 (though this decision may have been made because Panama itself contested classification of the Canal Zone as a non-self-governing territory). Concerned about these developments, the 1949 General Assembly, over the opposition of the colonial powers (the United States abstaining), decided that it was "within the responsibility of the General Assembly to express its opinion on the principles which have guided or which may in future guide the Members concerned in enumerating the territories for which the obligation exists to transmit information under Article 73 (e) of the Charter."

The General Assembly, in 1952, established a special committee to draw up a list of criteria of self-government and, at its next session, voted itself competent to decide on the basis of this list whether reports were due on a given territory. Since that time, the General Assembly has formally approved the cessation of reports on a number of territories, finding that they had "attained a full measure of self-government." However, in each case the administering power in question had already announced, prior to that approval, that it would no longer transmit information on these territories. The territories and the dates of General Assembly approval were as follows: from 1953 to 1955, Puerto Rico (United States), Greenland (Denmark), Suriname and Curaçao (Netherlands); in 1959, Alaska and Hawaii (United States); in 1965, the Cook Islands (New Zealand); and in 1974, Niue (New Zealand).

It should be noted, however, that so long as a territory is not actually independent, the General Assembly considers that it has the right to reopen the question of the territory's status at any time. Thus, although France ceased transmitting information on New Caledonia in 1947, the General Assembly decided on 2 December 1986 that New Caledonia was a non-self-governing territory within the meaning of Chapter XI of the charter and it was again included in the list of such territories.

In 1967, the United Kingdom announced that since a number of its small Caribbean dependencies—namely, Antigua, Dominica, Grenada, St. Kitts-Nevis-Anguilla, and St. Lucia—had achieved the status of associated states with a "full measure of self-government," it would no longer submit reports on those territories. The General Assembly did not, however, accept the territories' new status as constituting full self-government and continued to consider them as non-self-governing. (All the associated states except Anguilla subsequently attained independence, and the United Kingdom resumed transmission of information regarding Anguilla in 1984.) A similar situation arose with respect to Brunei, in 1972, when the United Kingdom informed the Secretary-General that the territory had attained full internal self-government and that, consequently, the United Kingdom considered the transmission of information about it to be no longer appropriate. (Brunei became independent in 1984.)

Refusal to Transmit Information

Until the General Assembly began to assert a competence in the matter, the inclusion of a territory in the list of non-self-governing territories to which Article 73 applies was at the discretion of the administering power concerned. For instance, in 1946, the United Kingdom did not include Southern Rhodesia in the list of dependent territories under its administration because the territory was self-governing but subsequently changed its position after the unilateral declaration of independence by the white-majority regime in 1965.

When Spain and Portugal became UN members in 1955, they also refused to transmit information on their overseas territories, maintaining that these were not colonial possessions but "overseas provinces." Spain retreated from this position in 1960, to the "satisfaction" of the General Assembly, and began to submit reports. However, Portugal maintained its stand until 1974, when an internal upheaval brought about a change of government.

These differences concerning the obligation to transmit information under Article 73 (e) led the Assembly in 1960 to adopt a resolution that defined a "full measure of self-government" to mean one of three specific conditions: (1) emergence of the territory as a sovereign independent state, (2) free association with an independent state, or (3) integration with an independent state, both (2) and (3) to be the result of a free and voluntary choice of the people concerned and the people to possess certain specified rights and safeguards in their new status. Unless one of these three conditions pertained, the General Assembly asserted, the administering power had an obligation to transmit information on any territory that is "geographically separate and is distinct ethnically and/or culturally from the country administering it."

THE 1960 ASSEMBLY DECLARATION ON THE ENDING OF COLONIALISM

Throughout the 1950s, the various disputes with colonial powers over the transmission of information on non-self-governing territories took place against a background of steady decolonization. Whether gracefully granted or bitterly fought for, sovereignty was achieved by a growing number of former colonial dependencies. In 1946, at the first working session of the General Assembly, only a handful of members had memories of recent foreign rule: India, the Philippines, and the four Arab countries that had been League of Nations mandate territories (Iraq, Jordan, Lebanon, and Syria). By 1959, eight Asian countries (Burma, Cambodia, Ceylon, Indonesia, Laos, Malaya, Nepal, and Pakistan) and two African countries (Ghana and Guinea) had become sovereign independent states. As these nations joined the UN, many of them after years of struggle against their former masters or with humiliating memories of the indignities of foreign rule, anticolonialist sentiment became increasingly bitter and significantly influenced the tone of the debates in the General Assembly. Wholeheartedly supported by the Soviet-bloc nations, the newly independent nations began a drive to put a speedy end to colonialism altogether, thus going far beyond anything specifically spelled out in the charter.

The 1960 General Assembly proved to be decisive for the triumph of the anticolonialist forces in the UN. At the opening of that session, 16 new African states and Cyprus became members, thereby bringing the total number of African and Asian nations to 44 out of a total UN membership of 100. In addition, members of the Afro-Asian Group, as it was called, knew that they could count on the support of the Soviet bloc, many Latin American countries, and the Scandinavian countries. By the end of the session, they had drafted the text of a Declaration on the Granting of Independence to Colonial Countries and Peoples that was designed to serve as the UN's basic framework for its work in colonial matters, complementing the charter declaration.

Main Provisions of the Declaration

Whereas the charter declaration had been a gentlemanly agreement among masters to look after the welfare of their subjects, the General Assembly declaration, in effect, was an assertion of the right of these subject peoples to be subjects no longer. Written from the viewpoint of the colonial peoples themselves, the declaration in its preamble recognizes "the passionate yearning for freedom in all dependent peoples"; the existence of "increasing conflicts resulting from the denial . . . of the freedom of such peoples, which constitute a serious threat to world peace"; and "the important role of the United Nations in assisting the movement for independence in Trust and Non-Self-Governing Territories." The declaration then lists seven provisions: (1) the subjection of peoples to alien domination "is contrary to the Charter of the United Nations and is an impediment to the promotion of world peace and cooperation"; (2) "all peoples have the right to self-determination"; (3) inadequacy of preparedness "should never serve as a pretext for delaying independence"; (4) all armed action or repressive measures against dependent peoples "shall cease in order to enable them to exercise peacefully and freely their right to complete independence"; (5) "immediate steps shall be taken . . . to transfer all powers to the peoples of those territories, without any conditions or reservations"; (6) any attempt to disrupt the national unity and territorial integrity of a country "is incompatible with the purposes and principles of the Charter"; and (7) all states "shall observe faithfully and strictly" the provisions of the Charter, the Universal Declaration of Human Rights, and "the present Declaration" on the basis of equality, noninterference in the internal affairs of states, and respect for the sovereign rights of all peoples.

Although the phrase "colonial powers" does not appear, the declaration was clearly and firmly directed against those countries. Nevertheless, such was the force of anticolonial sentiment that no colonial power cared to record a negative vote. Accordingly, on 14 December 1960, the Declaration on the Granting of Independence to Colonial Countries and Peoples was adopted 89–0, with only nine abstentions (Australia, Belgium, the Dominican Republic, France, Portugal, South Africa, Spain, the United Kingdom, and the United States).

Establishment of the Special Committee

A year after the adoption of the declaration, the USSR took the initiative by asking the General Assembly to discuss the problem of implementing it. The ensuing debate led to the creation of a 17-member Special Committee on the Situation with Regard to the Implementation of the Declaration on the Granting of Independence to Colonial Countries and Peoples. Because of the importance attached to its work, seven additional members were added in the following year. Since that time, the composition of the Special Committee (in its early days called "the Special Committee of 24") has changed slightly when certain countries have withdrawn for various reasons, to be replaced by countries representing the same geopolitical grouping as the outgoing members. Originally, the committee included three colonial or administering powers—Australia, the United Kingdom, and the United States—but France, Spain, and the two most recalcitrant administering countries, Portugal and South Africa, were never members. In later developments, both the United Kingdom and the United States suspended their cooperation. Thus, the committee's deliberations have always been anticolonialist in tone.

In 1963, the committee's functions were expanded to include the work of the 1947 Committee on Information from Non-Self-Governing Territories, which was dissolved. At the same time, the General Assembly gave the committee the right to apprise the Security Council of any developments in any territory that it had examined that might threaten international peace and security. (Normally, subsidiary bodies do not have this right but must act through the General Assembly.) In addition, the General Assembly empowered the committee to examine information on the trust territories, as well as on non-self-governing territories—although the Trusteeship Council continued to exercise its normal functions until the graduation of the last trusteeship territory in 1994. The committee was also empowered to send visiting missions to dependent territories. Hence, since 1963, the committee has been the General Assembly's chief executive arm in colonial matters.

Besides considering problems connected with individual colonial territories, the committee debates topics of a more general nature assigned to it by the General Assembly—for example, the role played by foreign economic and military interests that are impeding the attainment of independence or exploiting the natural resources of the territories that rightfully belong to the indigenous inhabitants. The committee has been particularly active in the dissemination of information on colonial problems and in mobilizing international support and assistance for the colonial peoples and their efforts to achieve self-determination and independence.

In 1988, the General Assembly declared the decade 1990–2000 the Decade for the Eradication of Colonialism. In 1991, it approved a plan of action for the Special Committee which it hoped would achieve the total elimination of colonialism by the year 2000. The plan of action called for the Special Committee to, among other things: formulate specific proposals for the elimination of the remaining manifestations of colonialism, and to report its findings each year to the General Assembly; to make concrete suggestions to the Security Council about developments in colonial territories that threaten international peace and security; to pay special attention to small territories, and dispatch visiting missions to those territories to gather information firsthand; and to continue to collect, prepare, and disseminate studies and articles on the problems of decolonization, including continuation of the periodical *Objective: Justice* and the special series called *Decolonization*.

In January, 1986, the United Kingdom informed the Special committee's chairman that it would no longer take part in the Committee's work, since, in its own opinion, all the remaining territories under its administration had chosen to remain in close association with the United Kingdom. However, the United Kingdom agreed to continue to fulfill its obligations under the charter and to transmit information to the committee under Article 73e. The UK also reiterated to the Fourth Committee in 1990 that it would respect the wishes of the people of any of its 10 remaining territories, no matter what the size of their population.

In February 1992, the United States suspended its cooperation with the Special Committee, claiming that it had focused on an outmoded agenda instead of new approaches aimed at addressing the needs of the few remaining non-self-governing territories.

In 2000, the following 24 countries were represented on the Special Committee: Antigua and Barbuda, Bolivia, Chile, China, Congo, Côte d'Ivoire, Cuba, Ethiopia, Fiji, Grenada, India, Indonesia, Iran, Iraq, Mali, Papua New Guinea, Russian Federation, Saint Lucia, Sierra Leone, Syrian Arab Republic, Tunisia, United Republic of Tanzania, Venezuela, and Yugoslavia.

PROGRESS OF DECOLONIZATION

In the 10 years following the adoption of the declaration on the ending of colonialism (1960 to 1970), 27 territories (with a total population of over 53 million) attained independence. Some 44 territories (with a population of approximately 28 million) remained under foreign rule or control, however, and the General Assembly's work in hastening the process of decolonization was far from completed. In Africa, an ever-widening confrontation had emerged between the colonial and white-minority regimes and the roughly 18 million Africans in Portuguese Guinea (now Guinea-Bissau), Angola, Mozambique, Cape Verde, and São Tomé and Príncipe; in Southern Rhodesia, which was legally still a British possession; and in the old League of Nations mandate territory of South West Africa, officially designated as Namibia by the UN. Resisting all efforts by the UN to bring an end to white-minority rule by peaceful means, these regimes refused to change despite pressures brought upon them both by the international community and by the demands of the African peoples of the territories.

This refusal had led to the emergence of African national liberation movements within the territories and to a series of armed conflicts that were seen by independent African states as a menace to peace and stability and as the potential cause of a bloody racial war engulfing the whole of Africa. Armed conflict, beginning in 1960 in Angola, had, in fact, spread to all the Portuguese-controlled territories on the African mainland and, as the African liberation movements gained strength and support, had developed into full-scale warfare in Angola, Portuguese Guinea, and Mozambique, engaging large Portuguese armies and putting a serious strain on Portugal's economy.

In Southern Rhodesia and Namibia, armed struggle for liberation was slower to develop, but despite the essential differences in the problems presented by these territories, the General Assembly—partly in response to a growing collaboration between South Africa, Portugal, and the white-minority regime in Southern Rhodesia—had come to view them as aspects of a single consuming issue of white-minority rule versus black-majority rights.

The strategy advocated by the Afro-Asian Group, supported by the Soviet-bloc countries and many others, for rectifying the situation in these territories was essentially to obtain recognition and support for their African national liberation movements and to seek the application, through a Security Council decision made under Chapter VII of the charter, of mandatory enforcement measures, including full economic sanctions and military force as circumstances warranted. However, in each case, except partially in that of Southern Rhodesia, the use of mandatory enforcement measures was decisively resisted by two permanent members of the Security Council, the United Kingdom and the United States, which, together with several other Western nations, felt that they could not afford to embark upon a policy of confrontation with the economically wealthy white-minority regimes of southern Africa.

Despite this resistance, the African and Asian nations continued to maintain the spotlight of attention on issues of decolonization. Year after year, one or another of the cases mentioned above was brought before the Security Council. Each session of the General Assembly, and of the Special Committee on decolonization, was the scene of lengthy and often acrimonious debates. This constant pressure led to greater recognition and status for the national liberation movements of the territories in Africa and brought about widespread condemnation and isolation of the white regimes. In 1971, for the first time, a mission of the Special Committee visited the liberated areas of Guinea-Bissau at the invitation of the African liberation movement concerned and found that the liberation movement had established an effective administration.

In 1972, the General Assembly affirmed for the first time that "the national liberation movements of Angola, Guinea-Bissau and Cape Verde, and Mozambique are the authentic representatives of the true aspirations of the peoples of those territories" and recommended that, pending the independence of those territories, all governments and UN bodies should, when dealing with matters pertaining to the territories, ensure the representation of those territories by the liberation movements concerned. In the following year, the General Assembly extended similar recognition to the national liberation movements of Southern Rhodesia and Namibia.

On 25 April 1974, largely as a result of internal and external pressures resulting from its colonial wars, a change of regime occurred in Portugal that had major repercussions on the situation in its African territories. The new regime pledged itself to ending the colonial wars and began negotiations with the national liberation movements. By the end of 1974, Portuguese troops had been withdrawn from Guinea-Bissau and the latter had become a UN member. This was followed by the independence and admission to UN membership of Cape Verde, Mozambique, and São Tomé and Príncipe in 1975 and Angola in 1976.

Southern Rhodesia (now Zimbabwe)

The problem of Southern Rhodesia, which in 1977 had a population of almost 7 million, of whom 6.5 million were Africans, was not resolved until the end of the decade.

Southern Rhodesia had been given full internal self-government by the United Kingdom in 1923, although under a constitution that vested political power exclusively in the hands of the white settlers. Hence, the United Kingdom did not include this dependency in its original 1946 list of non-self-governing territories and did not transmit information on it to the UN. Although, by the terms of the 1923 constitution, the United Kingdom retained the residual power to veto any legislation contrary to African interests, this power was never used, and no attempt was made to interfere with the white settlers' domination of the territorial government.

UN involvement in the question of Southern Rhodesia began in 1961, when African and Asian members tried, without success, to bring pressure to bear upon the United Kingdom not to permit a new territorial constitution to come into effect. While giving Africans their first representation in the Southern Rhodesian parliament, the 1961 constitution restricted their franchise through a two-tier electoral system heavily weighted in favor of the European community.

In June 1962, acting on the recommendation of the Special Committee, the General Assembly adopted a resolution declaring Southern Rhodesia to be a non-self-governing territory within the meaning of Chapter XI of the charter, on the grounds that the vast majority of the people of Southern Rhodesia were denied equal political rights and liberties. The General Assembly requested the United Kingdom to convene a conference of all political parties in Rhodesia for the purpose of drawing up a new constitution that would ensure the rights of the majority on the basis of "one-man, one-vote." However, the United Kingdom continued to maintain that it could not interfere in Rhodesia's domestic affairs. The 1961 constitution duly came into effect in November 1962.

On 11 November 1965, the government of Ian Smith unilaterally declared Southern Rhodesia independent. The United Kingdom, after branding the declaration an "illegal act," brought the matter to the Security Council on the following day, and a resolution was adopted condemning the declaration and calling upon all states to refrain from recognizing and giving assistance to the "rebel" regime. On 20 November, the council adopted a resolution condemning the "usurpation of power," calling upon the United Kingdom to bring the regime to an immediate end, and requesting all states, among other things, to sever economic relations and institute an embargo on oil and petroleum products. In 1968, the Security Council imposed wider mandatory sanctions against Southern Rhodesia and established a committee to oversee the application of the sanctions. The General Assembly urged countries to render moral and material assistance to the national liberation movements of Zimbabwe, the African name for the territory.

On 2 March 1970, Southern Rhodesia proclaimed itself a republic, thus severing its ties with the United Kingdom. After Mozambique became independent in 1975, guerrilla activity along the border with Southern Rhodesia intensified; the border was then closed, further threatening the economy of Southern Rhodesia, already hurt by UN-imposed sanctions.

In 1977, Anglo-American proposals for the settlement of the Southern Rhodesian problem were communicated to the Security Council by the United Kingdom. The proposals called for the surrender of power by the illegal regime, free elections on the basis of universal suffrage, the establishment by the United Kingdom of a transitional administration, the presence of a UN force during the transitional period, and the drafting of an independence constitution. The proposals were to be discussed at a conference of all political parties in Southern Rhodesia, white and African. However, the regime rejected the idea of such a conference. Attempts by the regime in 1978 and early 1979 to draft a new constitution giving some political power to Africans but maintaining effective control by the white minority failed, and the struggle by forces of the liberation movement, called the Patriotic Front, intensified.

In August 1979, British prime minister Margaret Thatcher stated at the Conference of Commonwealth Heads of State and Government that her government intended to bring Southern Rhodesia to legal independence on a basis acceptable to the international community. To this end, a constitutional conference was convened in London on 10 September, to which representatives of the Patriotic Front and the Rhodesian administration in Salisbury were invited. On 21 December, an agreement was signed on a draft independence constitution and on transitional arrangements for its implementation, as well as on a cease-fire to take effect on 28 December. Lord Soames was appointed governor of the territory until elections, which took place in February 1980 in the presence of UN observers. On 11 March, Lord Soames formally appointed Robert G. Mugabe, whose party had received the majority of seats in the House of Assembly, as prime minister. The independence of Zimbabwe was proclaimed on 18 April 1980, and on 25 August, Zimbabwe became a member of the UN.

Remaining Colonial Issues

The 17 remaining dependent territories are almost all small islands scattered about the globe. Their tiny populations and minimal economic resources render it almost impossible for them to survive as viable, fully independent states. Table 2 sets forth all the former non-self-governing territories that have become independent or joined neighboring independent states.

Although the administering powers joined with the rest of the UN membership in asserting that the peoples of these small territories have an inalienable right to the exercise of self-determination, the leaders of the drive to end colonialism have doubted the genuineness of the preparations for achieving this goal. As evidence to justify their skepticism, the African and Asian nations pointed out that military bases were established in some of the small territories, which they declared "incompatible with the purposes and principles of the Charter." Moreover, in the case of territories that the administering powers have declared their intention of preparing for self-governing status rather than for full independence, the majority of UN members feel that the General Assembly should be granted an active role in ascertaining the wishes of the inhabitants and furnished with more comprehensive information on conditions prevailing in the territories. The General Assembly has approved numerous resolutions requesting the administering states to allow UN missions to visit the remaining non-self-governing territories to ascertain, firsthand, the wishes of the inhabitants, but has met with little cooperation.

Two of the territories that have been brought under the General Assembly's surveillance through the Special Committee are United Kingdom possessions in which the issue of decolonization is complicated by conflicting claims of sovereignty by other nations—the Falkland Islands (Malvinas), also claimed by Argentina, and Gibraltar, also claimed by Spain.

In regard to another territory, East Timor, the administering power, Portugal, informed the General Assembly in 1977 that developments in the territory had prevented it from carrying out its responsibilities or exercising its authority. On 5 May 1999, Portugal and Indonesia (the latter had been ruling East Timor for 23 years) signed three agreements at UN Headquarters to enable the people of East Timor to decide if they wanted wide-ranging autonomy under Indonesian rule. Indonesia agreed to take the constitutional steps necessary to terminate its links with East Timor if the special autonomy option were rejected in the popular consultation. On 30 August, the East Timorese voted for freedom, sparking unrest on the half-island territory. The UN responded by approving a peacekeeping mission, which stepped in on 26 October 1999 to take control during the transition and guide East Timor toward independence from Indonesia. With regard to Western Sahara, Spain informed the Secretary-General in 1976 that it had terminated its presence in the territory and considered itself henceforth exempt from any international responsibility in connection with its administration. Both territories, however, continued to be listed by the General Assembly as non-self-governing.

The Special Committee annually reviews the list of territories to which the declaration on decolonization is applicable. In 1986, France, the administering power of New Caledonia, refused to recognize the competence of the committee over the territory or to transmit to the UN the information called for under Article 73 (e) of the charter. France has, however, asserted that it will respect the wishes of the majority of the people of New Caledonia, in accordance with the provisions of the Matignon Agreement agreed to by all the parties in 1988. Under the terms of that agreement, a national referendum on self-determination was to take place between 1 March and 31 December 1998. As of 2000, New Caledonia remained under French control, sending parliamentary representatives to Paris. Though it is subject to French laws, special legislation is required to introduce laws in the areas of education, health, and labor.

The Problem of Namibia (South West Africa)

The status of South West Africa (officially designated as Namibia by the General Assembly in June 1968), a pre-World War I German colony that was administered by South Africa under a League of Nations mandate beginning in 1920, has preoccupied the General Assembly almost from the first moment of the UN's existence. In 1946, South Africa proposed that the Assembly approve its annexation of the territory. Fearing that the South African government would seek to extend its apartheid system to South West Africa, the General Assembly did not approve the proposal and recommended instead that the territory be placed under the UN trusteeship system. In the following year, South Africa informed the General Assembly that while it agreed not to annex the territory, it would not place it under trusteeship. Although South Africa had reported on conditions in the territory in 1946, it declined to submit further reports, despite repeated requests from the General Assembly.

In 1950, the International Court of Justice, in an advisory opinion requested by the General Assembly, held that South Africa continued to have international obligations to promote to the utmost the material and moral well-being and social progress of the inhabitants of the territory as a sacred trust of civilization, and that the UN should exercise the supervisory functions of the League of Nations in the administration of the territory. South Africa refused to accept the court's opinion and continued to oppose any form of UN supervision over the territory's affairs.

In October 1966, the General Assembly, declaring that South Africa had failed to fulfill its obligations under the League of Nations mandate to ensure the well-being of the people of the territory and that it had, in fact, disavowed the mandate, decided that the mandate was therefore terminated, that South Africa had no other right to administer the territory, and that thenceforth the territory came under the direct responsibility of the UN. In May 1967, the General Assembly established the UN Council for South West Africa (later renamed the UN Council for Namibia) to administer the territory until independence "with the maximum possible participation of the people of the territory." It also decided to establish the post of UN Commissioner for Namibia to assist the council in carrying out its mandate. Later in the same year, in the face of South Africa's refusal to accept its decision and to cooperate with the UN Council for Namibia, the General Assembly recommended that the Security Council take measures to enable the UN Council for Namibia to carry out its mandate.

In its first resolution on the question, in 1969, the Security Council recognized the termination of the mandate by the General Assembly, described the continued presence of South Africa in Namibia as illegal, and called on South Africa to withdraw its administration from the territory immediately. In the following year, the Security Council explicitly declared for the first time that "all acts taken by the government of South Africa on behalf of or concerning Namibia after the termination of the mandate are illegal and invalid." This view was upheld in 1971 by the International Court of Justice, which stated, in an advisory opinion requested by the Security Council, that "the continued presence of South Africa in Namibia being illegal, South Africa is under obligation to withdraw its administration from Namibia immediately and thus put an end to its occupation of the territory." South Africa, however, again refused to comply with UN resolutions on the question of Namibia, and it continued to administer the territory.

To secure for the Namibians "adequate protection of the natural wealth and resources of the territory which is rightfully theirs," the UN Council for Namibia enacted a Decree for the Protection of the Natural Resources of Namibia in September 1974. Under the decree, no person or entity may search for, take, or distribute any natural resource found in Namibia without the council's permission, and any person or entity contravening the decree "may be held liable in damages by the future government of an independent Namibia." The council also established, in the same year, the Institute for Namibia (located in Lusaka, Zambia, until South Africa's withdrawal from Namibia) to provide Namibians with education and training and equip them to administer a future independent Namibia.

In 1976, the Security Council demanded for the first time that South Africa accept elections for the territory as a whole under UN supervision and control so that the people of Namibia might freely determine their own future. It condemned South Africa's "illegal and arbitrary application . . . of racially discriminatory and repressive laws and practices in Namibia," its military buildup, and its use of the territory "as a base for attacks on neighboring countries."

In the same year, the General Assembly condemned South Africa "for organizing the so-called constitutional talks at Windhoek, which seek to perpetuate the apartheid and homelands policies as well as the colonial oppression and exploitation of the people and resources of Namibia." It decided that any independence talks regarding Namibia must be between the representatives of South Africa and the South West Africa People's Organization (SWAPO), which it recognized as "the sole and authentic representative of the Namibian people." In 1977, the General Assembly declared that South Africa's decision to annex Walvis Bay, Namibia's main port, was "illegal, null, and void" and "an act of colonial expansion," and it condemned the annexation as an attempt "to undermine the territorial integrity and unity of Namibia."

At a special session on Namibia in May 1978, the General Assembly adopted a declaration on Namibia and a program of action in support of self-determination and national independence for Namibia. Expressing "full support for the armed liberation struggle of the Namibian people under the leadership of the SWAPO," it stated that any negotiated settlement must be arrived at with the agreement of SWAPO and within the framework of UN resolutions.

The UN Plan for Namibian Independence. In July 1978, the Security Council met to consider a proposal by the five Western members of the council—Canada, France, the Federal Republic of Germany, the United Kingdom, and the United States—for a settlement of the Namibian question. The proposal comprised a plan for free elections to a constituent assembly under the supervision and control of a UN representative, assisted by a UN transition assistance group that would include both civilian and military components. The council took note of the Western proposal and requested the Secretary-General to appoint a special representative for Namibia. In September 1978, after approving a report by the Secretary-General based on his special representative's findings, the council, in Resolution 435 (1978), endorsed the UN plan for the independence of Namibia, and it decided to establish, under its authority, the UN Transition Assistance Group (UNTAG) to ensure the early independence of Namibia through free and fair elections under UN supervision and control.

The Secretary-General's report stated that the implementation of the UN plan would be carried out in three stages: (1) cessation of all hostile acts by all parties; (2) the repeal of discriminatory or restrictive laws, the release of political prisoners, and the voluntary return of exiles and refugees; and (3) the holding of elections after a seven-month pre-electoral period, to be followed by the entry into force of the newly adopted constitution and the consequent achievement of independence by Namibia.

Since 1978, the General Assembly has continually reaffirmed that Security Council Resolution 435 (1978), in which the council endorsed the UN plan for the independence of Namibia, is the only basis for a peaceful settlement. It has condemned South Africa for obstructing the implementation of that resolution and other UN resolutions, for "its manoeuvres aimed at perpetuating its illegal occupation of Namibia," and for its attempts to establish a "linkage" between the independence of Namibia and "irrelevant, extraneous" issues, such as the presence of Cuban troops in Angola. In furtherance of the objective of bringing to an end South Africa's occupation of Namibia, the General Assembly has called upon all states to sever all relations with South Africa, and it has urged the Security Council to impose mandatory comprehensive sanctions against South Africa. The General Assembly also has continued to authorize the UN Council for Namibia, as the legal administering authority for Namibia, to mobilize international support for the withdrawal of the illegal South African administration from Namibia, to counter South Africa's policies against the Namibian people and against the UN, to denounce and seek the rejection by all states of South Africa's attempts to perpetuate its presence in Namibia, and to ensure the nonrecognition of any administration or political entity installed in Namibia, such as the so-called interim government imposed in Namibia on 17 June 1985, that is not the result of free elections held under UN supervision and control.

In April 1987, the Secretary-General reported to the Security Council that agreement had been reached on the system of proportional representation for the elections to be held in Namibia as envisaged in Council Resolution 435 (1978). Thus, he noted, all outstanding issues had been resolved, and the only reason for the delay in the emplacement of UNTAG and an agreement on a cease-fire was South Africa's unacceptable precondition that the Cuban troops be withdrawn from Angola before the implementation of the UN plan for Namibian independence.

In December 1988, after eight months of intense negotiations brokered by the United States, Angola, Cuba, and South Africa signed agreements on the withdrawal of Cuban troops from Angola and the achievement of peace in south-western Africa. On 16 January 1989 the Security Council officially declared that Namibia's transition to independence would begin on 1 April 1989 (Security Council Resolution 628/1989). The council also authorized sending the UNTAG to Namibia to supervise the transition (Security Council Resolution 629/1989).

In one short year, from 1 April 1989 to 21 March 1990, the 8,000-member UNTAG force established 200 outposts, including 42 regional or district centers and 48 police stations. During the transition the UN High Commissioner for Refugees (UNHCR) had supervised the repatriation of 433,000 Namibian exiles who had been scattered throughout 40 countries. UNTAG supervised the registration of more than 700,000 voters, more than 97% of whom cast ballots in the historic election from 7–11 November 1989 that marked the end of Namibia's colonial history. The Special Committee also dispatched a visiting mission to observe and monitor the election process. In that election Sam Nujoma, head of SWAPO, was elected the country's first president. The mission reported to the Special Committee that the people of Namibia had, in accordance with Security Council resolution 435 (1978), exercised their inalienable right to self-determination by choosing their representatives to a constituent assembly that was charged with drafting a constitution for an independent Namibia.

In March 1990, Secretary-General Perez de Cuéllar administered the oath of office to the new Namibian president at a historic celebration. In a moving show of good faith, President F.W. DeKlerk of South Africa took part in the inauguration ceremony. Nelson Mandela, then leader of South Africa's African National Congress party and only recently released from prison in South Africa, also attended, as did hundreds of dignitaries from 70 countries.

On 23 April 1990 Namibia became the 159th member of the United Nations.

Table 1

Non-Self-Governing Territories, Listed by the General Assembly in 1946 and Subsequent Years, That Have Become Independent States or Joined Neighboring Independent States

Australia

Cocos (Keeling) Islands (integrated with Australia)

Papua (now part of Papua New Guinea)

Belgium

Belgian Congo (now Democratic Republic of the Congo)

France

Comoros

French Equatorial Africa (now Central African Republic, Chad, Congo, and Gabon)

French Somaliland (now Djibouti)

French West Africa (now Burkina Faso, Côte d'Ivoire, Dahomey, Guinea, Mali, Mauritania, Niger, and Senegal)

Indochina (now Kampuchea, Laos, and Vietnam)

Madagascar

Morocco

New Hebrides (Anglo-French condominium; now Vanuatu)

Tunisia

Netherlands

Netherlands Indies (now Indonesia)

Suriname

West New Guinea (West Irian; now part of Indonesia)

New Zealand

Cook Islands (self-governing in free association with New Zealand)

Niue (self-governing in free association with New Zealand)

Portugal

Angola

Cape Verde

Goa (united with India)

Mozambique

Portuguese Guinea (now Guinea-Bissau)

Sâo Tomé and Principe

Spain

Fernando Poo and Rio Muni (now Equatorial Guinea)

Ifni (returned to Morocco)

United Kingdom

Aden (now part of Yemen)

Antigua (now Antigua and Barbuda)

Bahamas

Barbados

Basutoland (now Lesotho)

Bechuanaland (now Botswana)

British Guiana (now Guyana)

British Honduras (now Belize)

British Somaliland (now Somalia)

Brunei (now Brunei Darussalam)

Cyprus

Dominica

Ellice Islands (now Tuvalu)

Fiji

Gambia

Gilbert Islands (now Kiribati)

Gold Coast (now Ghana)

Grenada

Jamaica

Kenya

Malaya (now Malaysia)

Malta

Mauritius

Nigeria

New Hebrides (Anglo-French condominium; now Vanuatu)

North Borneo (now part of Malaysia)

Northern Rhodesia (now Zambia)

Nyasaland (now Malawi)

Oman

St. Kitts and Nevis

St. Lucia

St. Vincent and the Grenadines

Sarawak (now part of Malaysia)

Seychelles

Sierra Leone
Singapore
Solomon Islands
Southern Rhodesia (now Zimbabwe)
Swaziland
Trinidad and Tobago
Uganda
Zanzibar (now part of Tanzania)
United Nations
Namibia (formerly South West Africa)[1]
United States
Trust Territory of the Pacific Islands (Federated States of Micronesia, Marshall Islands, Palau (in free association with the United States))

1. In 1966, the General Assembly terminated South Africa's mandate over South West Africa and placed the territory under the direct responsibility of the UN. In 1968, the General Assembly declared that the territory would be called Namibia, in accordance with its people's wishes. Until independence, the legal administering authority for Namibia was the UN Council for Namibia.

Table 2

Remaining Non-Self-Governing Territories Listed by the General Assembly, as of 2000

France[2]
New Caledonia
New Zealand
Tokelau Islands
Portugal
East Timor[3]
Spain
Western Sahara[4]
United Kingdom
Anguilla
Bermuda
British Virgin Islands
Cayman Islands

Falkland Islands (Malvinas)
Gibraltar
Montserrat
Pitcairn Island
St. Helena
Turks and Caicos Islands
United States
American Samoa
Guam
United States Virgin Islands

2. On 2 December 1986, the General Assembly decided that New Caledonia was a non-self-governing territory within the meaning of Chapter XI of the UN Charter.

3. On 20 April 1977, Portugal informed the Secretary-General that effective exercise of its sovereignty of the territory had ceased in August 1975 and that the only information that could be transmitted would concern the first months of 1975. In subsequent years, Portugal further informed the Secretary-General that conditions prevailing in East Timor continued to prevent it from assuming its responsibilities for the administration of the territory.

4. Spain informed the Secretary-General on 26 February 1976 that as of that date, it had terminated its presence in the territory of the Sahara and deemed it necessary to place the following on record: "Spain considers itself henceforth exempt from any responsibility of an international nature in connection with the administration of the territory in view of the cessation of its participation in the temporary administration established for the territory." On 5 December 1984, and in many subsequent resolutions, the General Assembly reaffirmed that the question of Western Sahara was a question of decolonization, which remained to be resolved by the people of Western Sahara. In August 1988 the Kingdom of Morocco and the Frente Popular para la Liberación (Polisario Front) agreed in principle to the proposals put forward by Secretary-General Perez de Cuéllar and the Organization of African Unity. By its Resolutions 658 (1990) and 690 (1991) the Security Council adopted a settlement plan for Western Sahara that included a referendum for self-determination by the people of the country. In September 1991, the UN achieved a cease-fire in Western Sahara between the factions. In 1993, however, talks were still continuing between the parties on the final arrangements for the referendum.

INTERNATIONAL LAW

The idea of developing international law through the restatement of existing rules is not of recent origin. In the last quarter of the eighteenth century, Jeremy Bentham proposed a codification of the whole of international law. Since his time, numerous attempts at codification have been made by private individuals, by learned societies and by governments. Enthusiasm for the "codification movement"—the name sometimes given to such attempts—generally stems from the belief that written international law would remove the uncertainties of customary international law by filling existing gaps in the law, as well as by giving precision to abstract general principles whose practical application is not settled.

MODERN ANTECEDENTS OF THE INTERNATIONAL LAW COMMISSION

The intergovernmental effort to promote the codification and development of international law made an important advance with the resolution of the assembly of the League of Nations of 22 September 1924, envisaging the creation of a standing organ called the Committee of Experts for the Progressive Codification of International Law, which was to be composed so as to present the "main forms of civilization and the principal legal systems of the world." This committee, consisting of 17 experts, was to prepare a list of subjects "the regulation of which by international agreement" was most "desirable and realizable" and thereafter to examine the comments of governments on this list and report on the questions which "were sufficiently ripe," as well as on the procedure to be followed in preparing for conferences for their solutions. This was the first attempt on a worldwide basis to codify and develop whole fields of international law rather than simply regulating individual and specific legal problems.

After certain consultations with governments and the League Council, the League Assembly decided, in 1927, to convene a diplomatic conference to codify three topics out of the five that had been considered to be "sufficiently ripe," namely: (1) nationality; (2) territorial waters; and (3) the responsibility of states for damage done in their territory to the person and property of foreigners. Delegates from 47 governments participated in the Codification Conference which met at The Hague, from 13 March to 12 April 1930. Unfortunately, nationality was the only subject for which an international instrument was agreed on. No further experiment in codification was made by the League of Nations after 1930, but on 25 September 1931, the League Assembly adopted an important resolution on the procedure of codification, the main theme of which was the strengthening of the influence of governments at every stage of the codification process.

PROVISIONS OF THE UNITED NATIONS CHARTER

Article I of the UN Charter calls for the adjustment or settlement of international disputes by peaceful means in conformity with the principles of justice and international law. In Article 13, the charter also requires the General Assembly to "initiate studies and make recommendations for the purpose of . . . encouraging the progressive development of international law and its codifica-

tion." To help it fulfill this mandate, the General Assembly set up two law commissions.

The International Law Commission was established in 1947 as a permanent subsidiary organ with its own separate statute. It began meeting in 1949 and since that time has completed a significant body of work.

At its 1966 session, the General Assembly established another commission with the specific object of promoting the harmonization and unification of international law in the field of trade. The UN Commission on International Trade Law (UNCITRAL) held its first meeting in 1968.

INTERNATIONAL LAW COMMISSION

Like the judges of the International Court of Justice, the 34 (originally 15) members of the International Law Commission are not representatives of governments. Instead, they are chosen in their individual capacity "as persons of recognized competence in international law" and with due consideration to representation of "the main forms of civilization" and "the principal legal systems of the world." No two members of the commission may be nationals of the same country. They are elected for five-year terms by the General Assembly, from a list of candidates nominated by UN member states.

The members of the International Law Commission do not serve in a full-time capacity on the International Law Commission and need not give up their other professional activities. Until 1997, they met each year, normally in Geneva, for a session of approximately 12 weeks. In 1997, the General Assembly authorized the commission to hold its 50th session in two parts: the first to be held in Geneva from 27 April to 12 June 1998, and the second in New York, from 27 July to 14 August 1998. In 1998 the commission was authorized to convene one 12-week session in 1999, which was held in Geneva. Geneva was again the site in 2000, but the General Assembly saw fit to divide the commission's work into two parts for this, its 52nd session. The various topics under consideration are usually assigned to individual members, who then serve as special rapporteurs on the item concerned, carry out the necessary studies between sessions, and submit reports to the commission at its annual sessions.

Functions

Although the UN Charter does not lay down any principles for determining a desirable "progressive development" of international law, Article 1 of the Statute of the International Law Commission provides that the "Commission shall have for its object the promotion of the progressive development of international law and its codification." From the outset the discussions in the International Law Commission and the General Assembly have made very clear the main considerations involved. The traditional legal norms prevailing at the time of the San Francisco Conference were inherited from an era when world politics was dominated by a handful of Western European nations. As a consequence, international law itself reflected the values and interests of those nations. In essence, therefore, what has been required is an adjustment of the entire international legal order so as to take account of the interests and traditions of a much broader community of nations.

Article 15 of the Statute of the International Law Commission defines "progressive development" as the preparation of draft conventions on subjects which have not yet been regulated by international law, or in regard to which the law has not yet been sufficiently developed in the practice of states. It defines "codification" as meaning the more precise formulation and systemization of rules of international law in fields where there already has been extensive state practice, precedent, and doctrines.

Progressive Development. Under the Statute of the International Law Commission, proposals for the progressive development of international law are not formulated by the commission, but are referred to it by the General Assembly, or by members of the United Nations and other authorized agencies. On the other hand, the commission itself may select topics for codification.

Progressive development of international law is a conscious effort towards the creation of new rules of international law, whether by means of the regulation of a new topic or by means of the comprehensive vision of existing rules. Accordingly, the drafters of the statute considered that when the commission is engaged in the progressive development of any branch of law, the consummation of the work could be achieved only by means of an international convention. Thus the statute contemplates that the commission prepares a draft convention, and the General Assembly then decides whether steps should be taken to bring about the conclusion of an international convention.

Codification. On the other hand, when the commission's task is one of codification (the mere precise formulation and systematization of existing customary law), the statute envisages two other possible conclusions to its work: (a) simple publication of its report; and (b) a resolution of the General Assembly, taking note of or adopting the report. The statute also lays down the specific steps to be taken by the commission in the course of its work on progressive development and on codification.

Methods of Work

The commission follows essentially the same method for both progressive development and codification. A "special rapporteur" is appointed for each topic; an appropriate plan of work is formulated; where desirable, governments are requested to furnish the texts of relevant laws, decrees, judicial decisions, treaties, and diplomatic correspondence; the special rapporteur submits reports; the commission approves a provisional draft based on those reports in the form of articles, with a commentary setting forth precedents, any divergence of views, and alternative solutions considered. The provisional draft is issued as a commission document and submitted to the General Assembly, and also to governments for their written observations. On the basis of comments received from governments, together with any comments made in the debates of the Sixth Committee of the General Assembly, the special rapporteur submits a further report, recommending the changes in the provisional draft that seem appropriate. The commission then, on the basis of that report and the comments, adopts a final draft. The final draft is submitted to the General Assembly with a recommendation regarding further action.

Special Assignments. The General Assembly has from time to time requested the International Law Commission to examine particular texts or to report on particular legal problems. For example, at the specific request of the General Assembly, the commission dealt with the following topics: draft declaration on the rights and duties of states (1949); formulation of the Nürnberg principles (1950); questions of international criminal jurisdiction (1950); the question of defining aggression (1951); reservations to multilateral conventions (1951); draft code of offenses against the peace and security of mankind (1951 and 1954); extended participation in general multilateral treaties concluded under the auspices of the League of Nations (1962); ques-

tion of the protection and inviolability of diplomatic agents and other persons entitled to special protection under international law (1972); and review of the multilateral treaty-making process (1979). The commission's reports on some of these topics were presented in the form of draft articles with commentaries. Conclusions reached on some other topics did not lend themselves to draft articles.

Scope of the Commission's Work

The General Assembly does not assign all legal issues with which it is concerned to the International Law Commission. Thus, the legal aspect of an agenda item that relates to another sphere of the General Assembly's work is often handled by a special committee set up to study that particular subject. This is the case, for example, with the legal aspects of the peaceful uses of outer space and with many matters of human rights and economic and social development. On occasion, too, the General Assembly has established a special committee to consider certain legal topics that directly affect the conduct of nations in the area of international peace and security and are therefore highly political. Thus, the agenda item entitled "Consideration of principles of international law concerning friendly relations and cooperation among states in accordance with the Charter of the United Nations" was assigned to a special 31-member committee. After eight years of discussion, the committee completed a draft declaration, as requested, in time for the commemorative session to celebrate the UN's 25th anniversary in 1970. The declaration embodies seven principles: the nonuse of force, peaceful settlement of disputes, nonintervention, sovereign equality, the duty to cooperate, equal rights and self-determination, and fulfillment of obligations under the charter.

Another example of a legal topic having a strongly political character is the definition of aggression. The International Law Commission originally was asked to draw up a definition of aggression. The task was taken over by the General Assembly only after the commission had failed to reach agreement. A special committee of the General Assembly drafted the text of the Definition of Aggression, which was adopted by the General Assembly in 1974.

Another special committee of the General Assembly drafted the International Convention on the Taking of Hostages, which was adopted in 1979, and still another prepared the draft of what became, after being approved by the General Assembly in 1982, the Manila Declaration on the Peaceful Settlement of International Disputes. A special committee, originally established by the General Assembly in 1977, completed a draft Declaration on the Enhancement of the Effectiveness of the Principle of Refraining from the Threat or Use of Force in International Relations, which the General Assembly approved in 1987. The General Assembly also has established an ad hoc committee to recommend practical measures for elimination of the problem of international terrorism. The committee, in 1979, submitted its final report and recommendations to the General Assembly, which welcomed the results achieved. In 1980, the General Assembly established an ad hoc committee on the drafting of an international convention against the recruitment, use, financing, and training of mercenaries. The committee completed its work in 1989. In the same year, the General Assembly adopted a convention on the subject. In 1993, the General Assembly entrusted an ad hoc committee with the task of elaborating an international convention dealing with the safety and security of United Nations and associated personnel, with particular reference to responsibility for attacks on such personnel. The ad hoc committee held its first session in March–April 1994.

Topics Selected for Codification

At its first session, in 1949, the commission considered 25 topics for possible study. It selected 14 of these for codification. The list was only provisional, and it was understood that changes might be made after further study by the commission or in compliance with the wishes of the General Assembly. The list, however, still constitutes the commission's basic long-term program of work.

Topics on which the commission has completed its work and submitted final drafts or reports to the General Assembly include the following: rights and duties of states; ways and means for making the evidence of customary international law more readily available; formulation of Nürnberg principles; the question of international criminal jurisdiction; reservations to multilateral conventions; the question of defining aggression, nationality, including statelessness; law of the sea; arbitral procedure; diplomatic intercourse and immunities; extended participation in general multilateral treaties concluded under the auspices of the League of Nations; law of treaties; special missions; relations between states and international organizations; succession of states in respect of treaties; question of protection and inviolability of diplomatic agents and other persons entitled to special protection under international law; the most-favored-nation clause; succession of states in respect of matters other than treaties; question of treaties concluded between states and international organizations or between two or more international organizations; status of the diplomatic courier and the diplomatic bag not accompanied by diplomatic courier; and jurisdictional immunities of states and their property.

The Sixth Committee itself sometimes functions as a codification body. On two occasions, with regard to the topics "Special Missions" and "Draft Convention on the Prevention and Punishments of Crimes against Diplomatic Agents and other Internationally Protected Persons," the Sixth Committee was assigned the finalization of the relevant conventions. The General Assembly subsequently adopted both conventions.

In 1994, the General Assembly, on the recommendation of the Sixth Committee, established an ad hoc committee to elaborate an international convention dealing with the safety and security of UN personnel. The committee's task was to consolidate, in a single document, the set of principles and obligations contained in existing treaties as well as to codify customary international law. The Sixth Committee also convened in New York in 1995 a United Nations Congress on Public International Law as part of the activities of the UN Decade for International Law (1990–1999).

Extended Participation in Multilateral Treaties Concluded Under the Auspices of the League of Nations

The commission's conclusions on the question of extended participation in multilateral treaties concluded under the auspices of the League of Nations were submitted to the General Assembly in 1963. On the basis of those conclusions, the General Assembly decided that it was the appropriate organ of the UN to exercise the functions of the League Council with respect to 21 general multilateral treaties of a technical and nonpolitical character concluded under the auspices of the former world body.

Law of Treaties

The most far-reaching task undertaken by the International Law Commission has been its work on the law of treaties—the laws governing the way in which treaties are to be negotiated, adopted, altered, and abrogated. The commission, which began work on this project in 1949, finally completed it in 1966, after 18 sessions. Throughout this period, the commission regularly submitted provisional draft articles to the General Assembly's Sixth Committee and to individual governments for comment. Accordingly, the final draft of 75 articles adopted by the commission and submitted to the General Assembly's 1966 session included many revisions. At a conference that met in two sessions

in Vienna in 1968 and 1969, the Vienna Convention on the Law of Treaties was adopted. It came into force in 1980.

During the preparation of the draft articles on the law of treaties, the commission considered whether the articles should apply not only to treaties between states but also to treaties concluded by other entities, particularly by international organizations. The commission decided to confine its work to treaties between states, but following adoption of the Vienna Convention on the Law of Treaties, it took up, in consultation with the principal international organizations, the question of treaties concluded between states and international organizations or between two or more international organizations.

At a conference that met in Vienna in 1986, the Vienna Convention on the Law of Treaties Between States and International Organizations or Between International Organizations was adopted.

Law of the Sea

In accordance with its 1949 program, the commission worked for a number of years on the codification of the law of the sea. Following a request of the 1954 General Assembly, the commission grouped together the articles that it had previously adopted and submitted a final draft on the law of the sea in 1956. The General Assembly called a special conference on the law of the sea at Geneva in 1958. At that conference, four conventions were adopted: (1) the Convention on the High Seas, which came into force on 30 September 1962; (2) the Convention on the Continental Shelf, on 24 April 1964; (3) the Convention on the Territorial Sea and the Contiguous Zone, on 10 September 1964; and (4) the Convention on Fishing and Conservation of the Living Resources of the High Seas, on 20 March 1966. (See also the chapter on the Law of the Sea.)

Reduction of Statelessness

In 1954, the commission prepared two drafts, one for a convention on the elimination of statelessness and another, which would impose fewer obligations on states, on the reduction of statelessness. General Assembly discussions showed that the first and more sweeping draft had no chance of acceptance. Even the measures on which countries would have to agree in order to reduce the number of stateless persons raised so many problems that two special conferences were eventually required, one in 1959 and one in 1961, to arrive at a Convention on the Reduction of Statelessness. It came into force in 1975.

Diplomatic and Consular Relations

In 1959, the commission adopted final draft articles on diplomatic intercourse and immunities. The General Assembly endorsed the drafts and convened an international conference, which met in Vienna in 1961 and adopted the Vienna Convention on Diplomatic Relations and two optional protocols, one concerning acquisition of nationality and the other compulsory settlement of disputes. The convention adapts to twentieth century requirements the rules for diplomatic intercourse formulated by the 1815 Congress of Vienna, which since that time have essentially governed diplomatic relations. It came into force on 24 April 1964.

Final draft articles on consular relations were submitted by the commission to the General Assembly in 1961. On the basis of these drafts, an international conference, held in Vienna in 1963, adopted the Vienna Convention on Consular Relations and two protocols. It came into force in 1967.

Special Missions

In 1968 and 1969, the General Assembly considered the question of a draft convention on special missions on the basis of draft articles prepared by the commission. On 8 December 1969, the

General Assembly adopted the Convention on Special Missions and an optional protocol concerning the compulsory settlement of disputes. The convention, which came into force on 21 June 1985, provides rules applying to forms of ad hoc diplomacy—itinerant envoys, diplomatic conferences, and special missions sent to a state for limited purposes—that are not covered by the Vienna conventions of 1961 and 1963 relating to diplomatic and consular relations among states.

Protection of Diplomats
In 1973, the General Assembly adopted the Convention on the Prevention and Punishment of Crimes Against Internationally Protected Persons, Including Diplomatic Agents, on the basis of draft articles prepared by the commission. The convention's preamble states that crimes against diplomatic agents and other internationally protected persons, jeopardizing their safety, create a serious threat to the maintenance of normal international relations necessary for cooperation among states. It came into force on 20 February 1977.

Relations Between States and International Organizations
On the basis of draft articles prepared by the commission, the Vienna Convention on the Representation of States in Their Relations with International Organizations of a Universal Character was adopted in 1975 by an international conference.

Succession of States
Work on the subject of the succession of states was begun by the commission in 1962. Succession of states deals with cases in which dependent territories gain independence, as well as those involving the transfer of territory and the union, dissolution, and separation of states. In 1967, the commission divided the subject into three subtopics: succession in regard to treaties; in regard to matters other than treaties; and in regard to membership of international organizations.

Subsequently, two conferences were convened by the General Assembly to consider the subject on the basis of drafts prepared by the commission. The first conference, held in April 1977 and resumed in August 1978, adopted the Vienna Convention on Succession of States in Respect of Treaties. The second, which met in March–April 1983, adopted the Vienna Convention on Succession of States in Respect of State Property, Archives and Debts. In 1999 the commission adopted draft articles on the nationality of natural persons in relation to the succession of states.

Jurisdictional Immunities of States and Their Property
The commission completed its work on this topic in 1991 and recommended that the General Assembly convene an international conference to examine the 22 draft articles and conclude a convention. The Sixth Committee examined the draft articles in a working group in 1992 and 1993 in order to resolve differences of views on some of the substantive issues raised.

TOPICS PENDING BEFORE THE GENERAL ASSEMBLY

Diplomatic Protection
The commission completed its work on the topic of the diplomatic courier in 1989 and recommended that the General Assembly convene an international conference of plenipotentiaries to examine the draft articles and conclude a convention on the subject. The Sixth Committee of the General Assembly considered the issue in 1990, 1991, and 1992 and decided to return to it at its 49th session in 1995. The 50th session of the General Assembly in 1996 invited governments to submit comments regarding the commission's suggestion to include diplomatic protection as a topic.

Proposed Court to Cover Serious Crimes Punishable Under International Law
In 1992 the UN General Assembly requested that the Commission elaborate a Draft Statute for an International Criminal Court, which could prosecute persons for serious crimes under international law. The commission completed the draft statute in 1994, and included crimes under general international law such as genocide, aggression, serious violations of humanitarian law, crimes against humanity, unlawful seizure of aircraft, apartheid, and hostage taking. In 2000, the draft statute continued to be under consideration.

Current Topics
The following items were on the agenda of the commission at its 52nd session (in 2000): state responsibilities; reservations to treaties; international liability for injurious consequences arising out of acts not prohibited by international law; unilateral acts of states; and diplomatic protection.

UN COMMISSION ON INTERNATIONAL TRADE LAW (UNCITRAL)
Like the International Law Commission, UNCITRAL is a permanent subsidiary organ of the General Assembly, which elects its members, observing the principle of balance among the geographical regions and the main economic and legal systems of the world.

In contrast to the International Law Commission, whose members serve in their individual capacities, the UN Commission on International Trade Law (UNCITRAL) is composed of the representatives of 36 (originally 29) states. Members serve six-year terms and are eligible for reelection. States not members of UNCITRAL, representatives of United Nations organs (the IMF and the World Bank), and some other international organizations (for example, the Inter-American Development Bank and the Organization of African Unity) may attend its sessions as observers.

The commission holds one regular session a year. As of 1 June 1998, the members of UNCITRAL (and the years their memberships expire) were: Algeria (2001), Argentina (2004, alternating annually with Uruguay, starting in 1998), Australia (2001), Austria (2004), Botswana (2001), Brazil (2001), Bulgaria (2001), Burkina Faso (2004), Cameroon (2001), China (2001), Colombia (2004), Egypt (2001), Fiji (2004), Finland (2001), France (2001), Germany (2001), Honduras (2004), Hungary (2004), India (2004), Iran (Islamic Republic of) (2004), Italy (2004), Japan (2001), Kenya (2004), Lithuania (2004), Mexico (2001), Nigeria (2001), Paraguay (2004), Romania (2004), Russian Federation (2001), Singapore (2001), Spain (2004), Sudan (2004), Thailand (2004), Uganda (2004), United Kingdom of Great Britain and Northern Ireland (2001), United States (2004), and Uruguay (2004, alternating annually with Argentina, beginning in 1999).

Between sessions, working groups designated by the commission meet on specific topics such as electronic commerce, international contract practices, arbitration, and insolvency law.

Functions
A clear understanding of the respective rights and obligations of buyers, sellers, and other commercial parties facilitates the flow of trade from one country to another. When the laws of countries in this field are at variance, impediments may arise. In establishing UNCITRAL, the UN recognized that there was a need for it to play a more active role in removing or reducing legal obstacles to international trade.

UNCITRAL is charged with the task of seeking to resolve differences in national laws by providing texts that may become the basis of international conventions or other agreements. The 1966

General Assembly resolution establishing UNCITRAL invests it with seven specific functions in the furtherance of "progressive harmonization and unification of the law of international trade": coordinating the work of international organizations active in this field; promoting wider participation in existing international conventions, preparing new international conventions; promoting the means of ensuring the uniform interpretation and application of international conventions, collecting and disseminating information on national legislation and legal development in the field of international law; maintaining a close collaboration with UNCTAD; and maintaining liaison with other concerned UN organs and specialized agencies.

The Work of UNCITRAL

The commission draws up its own program of work, subject to the approval of the General Assembly. It selects topics that are both intrinsically capable of unification and ripe for final settlement by virtue of a sufficiently close convergence in their treatment among bodies of national law. Three topics have been given priority: the international sale of goods, international payments, and commercial arbitration.

The first treaty elaborated under the auspices of UNCITRAL was the Convention on the Limitation Period on the International Sale of Goods, adopted in 1974 and called the "Limitation Convention." The convention fixes at four years the period of time in which parties to a contract for the international sale of goods may sue under the contract, and it regulates various matters in regard to the commencement, prolongation, and termination of that period.

Other treaties elaborated by UNCITRAL include the UN Convention on the Carriage of Goods by Sea, adopted at Hamburg, Germany, in 1978 (the "Hamburg Rules"), which entered into force in 1992; the UN Convention on Contracts for the International Sale of Goods, adopted in 1980 (the "United Nations Sales Convention"); the 1988 Convention on International Bills of Exchange and International Promissory Notes (the "UNCITRAL Bills and Notes Convention"); the 1991 United Nations Convention on the Liability of Operators of Transport Terminals in International Trade (the "United Nations Terminal Operators Convention"); and the 1995 United Nations Convention on Independent Guarantees and Stand-by Letters of Credit.

A growing area of work for UNCITRAL in the 1990s was model laws, which become the basis or guidelines for national legislation. Model laws have been issued on international credit transfers (in 1992); procurement of goods, construction, and services (1994); electronic commerce (1996); and cross-border insolvency (1997).

UNCITRAL also conducts a substantial training and technical assistance program, designed to disseminate information concerning UNCITRAL legal texts to government officials, legislators, practicing lawyers, judges, traders, and academics.

UNIVERSAL DECLARATION OF HUMAN RIGHTS

On 10 December 1948 the General Assembly of the United Nations adopted and proclaimed the Universal Declaration of Human Rights. Following this act, the Assembly called upon all member countries to publicize the text of the Declaration and "to cause it to be disseminated, displayed, read and expounded principally in schools and other educational institutions, without distinction based on the political status of countries or territories." The full text of the final authorized version follows. The UN celebrated the declaration's 50th anniversary in 1998 with a special program of events at its headquarters.

PREAMBLE

Whereas recognition of the inherent dignity and of the equal and inalienable rights of all members of the human family is the foundation of freedom, justice and peace in the world,

Whereas disregard and contempt for human rights have resulted in barbarous acts which have outraged the conscience of mankind, and the advent of a world in which human beings shall enjoy freedom of speech and belief and freedom from fear and want has beep proclaimed as the highest aspiration of the common people,

Whereas it is essential, if man is not to be compelled to have recourse, as a last resort, to rebellion against tyranny and oppression, that human rights should be protected by the rule of law,

Whereas it is essential to promote the development of friendly relations between nations,

Whereas the peoples of the United Nations have in the Charter reaffirmed their faith in fundamental human rights, in the dignity and worth of the human person and in the equal rights of men and women and have determined to promote social progress and better standards of life in larger freedom,

Whereas Member States have pledged themselves to achieve, in co-operation with the United Nations, the promotion of universal respect for and observance of human rights and fundamental freedoms,

Whereas a common understanding of these rights and freedoms is of the greatest importance for the full realization of this pledge,

Now, Therefore,

THE GENERAL ASSEMBLY
proclaims

THIS UNIVERSAL DECLARATION OF HUMAN RIGHTS

as a common standard of achievement for all peoples and all nations, to the end that every individual and every organ of society, keeping this Declaration constantly in mind, shall strive by teaching and education to promote respect for these rights and freedoms and by progressive measures, national and international, to secure their universal and effective recognition and observance, both among the peoples of Member States themselves and among the peoples of territories under their jurisdiction.

Article 1
All human beings are born free and equal in dignity and rights They are endowed with reason and conscience and should act towards one another in a spirit of brotherhood.

Article 2
Everyone is entitled to all the rights and freedoms set forth in this Declaration, without distinction of any kind, such as race, colour, sex, language, religion, political or other opinion, national or social origin, property, birth or other status. Furthermore, no distinction shall be made on the basis of the political, jurisdictional or international status of the country or territory to which a person belongs, whether it be independent, trust, non-self-governing or under any other limitation of sovereignty.

Article 3
Everyone has the right to life, liberty and security of person.

Article 4
No one shall be held in slavery or servitude; slavery and the slave trade shall be prohibited in all their forms.

Article 5
No one shall be subjected to torture or to cruel, inhuman or degrading treatment or punishment.

Article 6
Everyone has the right to recognition everywhere as a person before the law.

Article 7
All are equal before the law and are entitled without any discrimination to equal protection of the law All are entitled to equal protection against any discrimination in violation of this Declaration and against any incitement to such discrimination.

Article 8
Everyone has the right to an effective remedy by the competent national tribunals for acts violating the fundamental rights granted him by the constitution or by law.

Article 9
No one shall be subjected to arbitrary arrest, detention or exile.

Article 10
Everyone is entitled in full equality to a fair and public hearing by an independent and impartial tribunal, in the determination of his rights and obligations and of any criminal charge against him.

Article 11
(1) Everyone charged with a penal offense has the right to be presumed innocent until proved guilty according to law in a public

trial at which he has had all the guarantees necessary for his defense.

(2) No one shall be held guilty of any penal offense on account of any act or omission which did not constitute a penal offense, under national or international law, at the time when it was committed Nor shall a heavier penalty be imposed than the one that was applicable at the time the penal offense was committed.

Article 12

No one shall be subjected to arbitrary interference with his privacy, family, home or correspondence, nor to attacks upon his honor and reputation Everyone has the right to the protection of the law against such interference or attacks.

Article 13

(1) Everyone has the right to freedom of movement and residence within the borders of each state.

(2) Everyone has the right to leave any country, including his own, and to return to his country.

Article 14

(1) Everyone has the right to seek and to enjoy in other countries asylum from persecution.

(2) This right may not be invoked in the case of prosecutions genuinely arising from non-political crimes or from acts contrary to the purposes and principles of the United Nations.

Article 15

(1) Everyone has the right to a nationality.

(2) No one shall be arbitrarily deprived of his nationality nor denied the right to change his nationality.

Article 16

(1) Men and women of full age, without any limitation due to race, nationality or religion, have the right to marry and to found a family They are entitled to equal rights as to marriage, during marriage and at its dissolution.

(2) Marriage shall be entered into only with the free and full consent of the intending spouses.

(3) The family is the natural and fundamental group unit of society and is entitled to protection by society and the State.

Article 17

(1) Everyone has the right to own property alone as well as in association with others.

(2) No one shall be arbitrarily deprived of his property.

Article 18.

Everyone has the right to freedom of thought, conscience and religion; this right includes freedom to change his religion or belief, and freedom, either alone or in community with others and in public or private, to manifest his religion or belief in teaching, practice, worship and observance.

Article 19

Everyone has the right to freedom of opinion and expression; this right includes freedom to hold opinions without interference and to seek, receive and impart information and ideas through any media and regardless of frontiers.

Article 20

(1) Everyone has the right to freedom of peaceful assembly and association.

(2) No one may be compelled to belong to an association.

Article 21

(1) Everyone has the right to take part in the government of his country, directly or through freely chosen representatives.

(2) Everyone has the right of equal access to public service in his country.

(3) The will of the people shall be the basis of the authority of government; this will shall be expressed in periodic and genuine elections which shall be by universal and equal suffrage and shall be held by secret vote or by equivalent free voting procedures.

Article 22

Everyone, as a member of society, has the right to social security and is entitled to realization, through national effort and international co-operation and in accordance with the organization and resources of each State, of the economic, social and cultural rights indispensable for his dignity and the free development of his personality.

Article 23

(1) Everyone has the right to work, to free choice of employment, to just and favorable conditions of work and to protection against unemployment.

(2) Everyone, without any discrimination, has the right to equal pay for equal work.

(3) Everyone who works has the right to just and favorable remuneration ensuring for himself and his family an existence worthy of human dignity, and supplemented, if necessary, by other means of social protection.

(4) Everyone has the right to form and to join trade unions for the protection of his interests.

Article 24

Everyone has the right to rest and leisure, including reasonable limitation of working hours and periodic holidays with pay.

Article 25

(1) Everyone has the right to a standard of living adequate for the health and well-being of himself and of his family, including food, clothing, housing and medical care and necessary social services, and the right to security in the event of unemployment, sickness, disability, widowhood, old age or other lack of livelihood in circumstances beyond his control.

(2) Motherhood and childhood are entitled to special care and assistance All children, whether born in or out of wedlock, shall enjoy the same social protection.

Article 26

(1) Everyone has the right to education. Education shall be free, at least in the elementary and fundamental stages Elementary education shall be compulsory Technical and professional education shall be made generally available and higher education shall be equally accessible to all on the basis of merit.

(2) Education shall be directed to the full development of the human personality and to the strengthening of respect for human rights and fundamental freedoms It shall promote understanding, tolerance and friendship among all nations, racial or religious groups, and shall further the activities of the United Nations for the maintenance of peace.

(3) Parents have a prior right to choose the kind of education that shall be given to their children.

Article 27

(1) Everyone has the right freely to participate in the cultural life of the community, to enjoy the arts and to share in scientific advancement and its benefits.

(2) Everyone has the right to the protection of the moral and material interests resulting from any scientific, literary or artistic production of which he is the author.

Article 28

Everyone is entitled to a social and international order in which the rights and freedoms set forth in this Declaration can be fully realized.

Article 29

(1) Everyone has duties to the community in which alone the free and full development of his personality is possible.

(2) In the exercise of his rights and freedoms, everyone shall be subject only to such limitations as are determined by law solely for the purpose of securing due recognition and respect for the rights and freedoms of others and of meeting the just requirements of morality, public order and the general welfare in a democratic society.

(3) These rights and freedoms may in no case be exercised contrary to the purposes and principles of the United Nations.

Article 30

Nothing in this Declaration may be interpreted as implying for any State, group or person any right to engage in any activity or to perform any act aimed at the destruction of any of the rights and freedoms set forth herein.

ADDRESSES OF THE PRINCIPAL UNITED NATIONS ORGANIZATIONS

United Nations Headquarters
One United Nations Plaza
New York, NY 10017
212/963 1234

Centre for Human Rights
UN Office at Geneva
Palais des Nations
CH-1211 Geneva 10
Switzerland

**Economic and Social Commission
   for Asia and the Pacific (ESCAP)**
United Nations Building
Hajadamnern Avenue
Bangkok 10200
Thailand
66/2/282 9161-200

**Economic and Social Commission
   for Europe (ECE)**
Palais des Nations
CH-1211 Geneva 20
Switzerland
41/22/917 1234

**Economic and Social Commission
   for Western Asia (ESCWA)**
PO Box 927115
AMMAN
Jordan
962/6/694 351

Economic Commission for Africa (ECA)
PO Box 3001
Addis Ababa
Ethiopia
251/1/51 72 00

**Economic Commission for Latin America
   and the Caribbean (ECLAC)**
Casila 179 D
Santiago
Chile
56/2/210 2000

**The Food and Agriculture Organization
   of the United Nations (FAO)**
Via delle Terme di Caracalla
00100 Rome
Italy
39/6/57971

FAO
Suite 300
1001 22nd Street NW
Washington, D.C. 20437
202/653-2400

International Atomic Energy Agency (IAEA)
Vienna International Centre
P.O. Box 100
A-1400 Vienna
Austria
43/1/23600

International Civil Aviation Organization (ICAO)
999 University Street
Montreal, PQ H3C 5H7
Canada
514/954 8219

International Court of Justice
Peace Palace
2517 KJ
The Hague
The Netherlands
31/70 392 44 41

International Labour Organization (ILO)
4, route des Morillons
CH-1211 Geneva 22
Switzerland
41/22/799 61 11

International Labour Organization (ILO)
1828 L Street NW
Suite 801
Washington, D.C. 20036
202/653-7652

International Labour Organization (ILO)
220 East 42nd Street
Suite 3101
New York, NY 10017
212/697-0150

ILO Publications Center
49 Sheridan Ave.
Albany, NY 12210
518/436-9686 x 123

International Maritime Organization (IMO)
4 Albert Embankment
London SE1 7SR
United Kingdom
44/71/735 7611

International Monetary Fund (IMF)
700 19th Street NW
Washington, D.C. 20431
202/623 7000

International Narcotics Control Board (INCB)
Vienna International Center
PO Box 500
A-1400 Vienna
Austria
43/1/211 310

International Telecommunication Union (ITU)
Place des Nations
CH-1211 Geneva 20
Switzerland
41/22/730 51 11

International Criminal Tribunal
    for the Former Yugoslavia
PO Box 13888
2501 EW - The Hague
Netherlands
31/70/344 53 47

International Fund for Agricultural Development (IFAD)
Via del Serafico 107
I-00142 Rome
Italy
39/6/54591

International Fund for Agricultural Development (IFAD)
1889 F Street NW
Washington, D.C. 20006
202/289-3812

Office for Outer Space Affairs
Vienna International Centre
PO Box 500
A-1400 Vienna
Austria
43/1/211 31 - 4951

UN Commission on International Trade Law (UNCITRAL)
International Centre
PO Box 5500
A-1400 Vienna
Austria
43/1/211 31 4060

UN Conference on Trade and Development (UNCTAD)
Palais des Nations
CH-1211 Geneva 10
Switzerland
41/22/734 60 11

UN Conference on Trade and Development (UNCTAD)
United Nations Headquarters
Room S-927
New York, NY 10017
212/963-6896

UN Crime Prevention & Criminal Justice Branch
UN International Center
A-1400 Vienna
Austria
43/1/211 310

UN Department of Public Information (UNDPI)
United Nations
Room 1027A
New York, NY 10017
212/963 6830

UN Development Fund for Women (UNIFEM)
304 East 45th Street
Room FF-616
New York, NY 10017
212/906-6925

UN High Commissioner for Refugees (UNHCR)
Centre William Rappard
154 rue de Lausanne
CH-1202 Geneva
Switzerland
41/22/739 81 11

UN High Commissioner for Refugees (UNHCR)
Room S-931
United Nations
New York, NY 10017
212/963-6200

UN Industrial Development Organization (UNIDO)
PO Box 300
Vienna International Centre
A-1400 Vienna
Austria
43/1/21131

UN Institute for Training and Research (UNITAR)
Place des Nations
CH-1211 - Geneva 10
Switzerland
41/22/798 5850

UN International Research Training Institute
    for the Advancement of Women (INSTRAW)
PO Box 21747
Santo Domingo
Dominican Republic
809/685 2111

UN Interregional Crime and
    Justice Research Institute (UNICRI)
Via Giulia 52
I-00186 Rome
Italy
39/6/687 7437

UN Relief and Works Agency
    for Palestine Refugees (UNRWA)
Vienna International Centre
PO Box 700
A-1400 Vienna
Austria
43/1/211 310

UNRWA Headquarters
P.O. Box 61
Gaza City
Gaza Strip
97/27/677 7333

UN Educational, Scientific
    and Cultural Organisation (UNESCO)
7 Place de Fontenoy
B.P. 3.07 Paris
F-75700 Paris
France
33/1/45 68 10 00

UNESCO
Room DC2-0934
Two United Nations Plaza
New York, NY 10017
212/963-5974

UN Childrens' Fund (UNICEF)
Three United Nations Plaza
New York, NY 10017
212/326 7000

United Nations Centre
for Human Settlements (UNHCHS - Habitat)
PO Box 30030
Nairobi
Kenya
254/2/621234

United Nations Development Program (UNDP)
One United Nations Plaza
New York, NY 10017
212/906 5000

United Nations Environment Programme (UNEP)
P.O. Box 30552
Nairobi
Kenya
254/2/333 930

United Nations Environment Programme (UNEP)
United Nations
Room DC2-0816
New York, NY 10017
212/963-8138

United Nations Fund for Population Activities (UNFPA)
220 East 42nd St
New York, NY 10017
212/297-5000

United Nations International
Drug Control Programme (UNDCP)
Vienna International Centre
PO Box 500
A-1400 Vienna
Austria
43/1/211 31 4115

United Nations Office at Vienna (UNOV)
Vienna International Center
P.O. Box 500 (Wagrammer Strasse 5)
A-1400 Vienna
Austria
43/1/211 310

United Nations Research Institute
for Social Development (UNRISD)
Palais des Nations
CH-1211 Geneva 10
Switzerland
41/22/798 84 00

United Nations University (UNU)
Toho Seimei Building
15-1 Shibuya 2-chome, Shibuya-ku
TOKYO 150
Japan
81/3/3499 2811

United Nations University (UNU)
United Nations
Room DC2-1462-1470
New York, NY 10017
212/963 6387

Universal Postal Union (UPU)
Union postale universelle
Weltpoststrasse 4
3000 Berne 15
Switzerland
41/31/350 31 11

World Bank
1818 H Street NW
Washington, D.C. 20433
202/477 1234

World Food Program (WFP)
Via Cristoforo Colombo, 426
I-00145 Rome
Italy
39/6/57971

World Food Program (WFP)
United Nations
Room DC1-1027
New York, NY 10017
212/963 8364

World Health Organization (WHO)
20 avenue Appia
1211 Geneva 27
Switzerland
41/22/791 21 11

World Health Organization (WHO)
Room DC2-0956
United Nations
New York, NY 10017
212/963 6000
World Health Organization

Regional Office for Africa (AFRO)
P.O. Box No.6
Brazzaville/Congo
Tel: +242 83 38 60 or 64
World Health Organization

Regional Office for the Americas (AMRO)
525, 23rd Street, NW
Washington, D.C. 20037
USA
Tel: +1 202 861 3200
World Health Organization

Regional Office for the Eastern Mediterranean (EMRO)
P.O. Box 1517
Alexandria - 21511
Egypt
Tel: +203 48 202 23 or 48 202 24 or 48 300 90
World Health Organization

Regional Office for Europe (EURO)
8, Scherfigsvej
DK -2100 Copenhagen 0
Tel: +45 39 17 17 17
World Health Organization

Regional Office for South-East Asia (SEARO)
World Health House
Indraprastha Estate
Mahatma Gandhi Road
New Delhi 110002
India
Tel: +91 11 331 7804 or 11 331 7823

World Health Organization
Regional Office for the Western Pacific (WPRO)
P.O. Box 2932
1099 Manila
Philippines
632 521 84 21

World Intellectual Property Organization (WIPO)
34 Chemin des Columbettes
CH-1211 Geneva 20
Switzerland
41/22/730 91 11

World Meteorlogical Organization (WMO)
41 Avenue Giuseppe-Motta
CH-1211 Geneva 20
Switzerland
41/22/730 81 11

World Trade Organization (WTO)
Centre William Rappard
154 Rue de Lausanne
1211 Geneva 21
Switzerland
41/22/739 51 11

ADDRESSES OF UNITED NATIONS INFORMATION CENTERS AND SERVICES

Centers and Services in Africa

Center: United Nations Information Center
Gamel Abdul Nassar/Liberia Roads
Post Office Box 2339
Accra, Ghana
Services to: Ghana
Sierra Leone

Center: United Nations Information Service
Economic Commission for Africa
Africa Hall
Post Office Box 3001
Addis Ababa, Ethiopia
Services to: Ethiopia

Center: United Nations Information Centre
19, avenue Chahid El Ouali
Mustapha Sayed
Boîte Postale 823
Algiers, Algeria
Services to: Algeria

Center: United Nations Information Centre
22, rue Rainitovo, Antsahavola
Boîte Postale 1348
Antananarivo, Madgascar
Services to: Madagascar

Center: United Nations Information Centre
Avenue Foch
Case Ortf 15
Boîte Postale 13210
Brazzaville, Congo
Services to: Congo

Center: United Nations Information Centre
117, avenue de la Poste
Boîte Postale 2160
Bujumbura, Burundi
Services to: Burundi

Center: United Nations Information Centre
1 Osiris Street
Tagher Building (Garden City)
Boîte Postale 262
Cairo, Egypt
Services to: Egypt
Saudi Arabia
Yemen

Center: United Nations Information Centre
72, boulevard de la République
Boîte Postale 154
Dakar, Senegal
Services to: Cape Verde
Côte d'Ivoire
Gambia
Guinea
Guinea-Bissau
Mauritania
Senegal

Center: United Nations Information Centre
Matasalamat Building, 1st Floor
Samora Machel Avenue
Post Office Box 9224
Dar es Salaam, Tanzania
Services to: Tanzania

Center: United Nations Information Centre
Dolphin House, Ground Floor
123 L. Takawira Street
Post Office Box 4408
Harare, Zimbabwe
Services to: Zimbabwe

Center: United Nations Information Centre
United Nations Compound
University Avenue
Post Office Box 1992
Khartoum, Sudan
Services to: Somalia
Sudan

Center: United Nations Information Centre
Bâtiment Deuxième République
Boulevard du 30 Juin
Boîte Postale 7248
Kinshasa, Zaire
Services to: Zaire

Center: United Nations Information Centre
17 Kingsway Road, Ikoyi
Post Office Box 1068
Lagos, Nigeria
Services to: Nigeria

Center: United Nations Information Centre
107, Boulevard due 13 Janvier
Boîte Postale 911
Lomé, Togo
Services to: Benin
Togo

Center: United Nations Information Centre
Post Office Box 32905
Lusaka, Zambia
Services to: Botswana
Malawi
Swaziland
Zambia

Center: United Nations Information Centre
Corner Kingsway and Hilton Hill Road
Post Office Box 301
Maseru 100, Lesotho
Services to: Lesotho

Center: United Nations Information Centre
LBDI Building
Tubman Boulevard
Post Office Box 274
Monrovia, Liberia
Services to: Liberia

Center: United Nations Information Centre
United Nations Office
Post Office Box 34135
Nairobi, Kenya
Services to: Kenya
Seychelles
Uganda

Center: United Nations Information Centre
218 Rue de la Gare, Secteur No. 3
Boîte Postale 135
Ouagadougou 01, Burkina Faso
Services to: Burkina Faso
Chad
Mali
Niger

Center: United Nations Information Centre
Angle Charia Ibnouzaid et Zankat
Boîte Postale 601
Rabat, Morocco
Services to: Morocco

Center: United Nations Information Centre
Muzzafar Al Aftas Street
Hay El-Andolous 2
Post Office Box 286
Tripoli, Libyan Arab Jamahiriya
Services to: Libyan Arab Jamahiriya

Center: United Nations Information Centre
61, Boulevard Bab-Benat
Boîte Postale 863
Tunis, Tunisia
Services to: Tunisia

Center: United Nations Information Centre
Immeuble Kamden, Rue Josef Clère
Boîte Postale 836
Yaoundé, Cameroon
Services to: Cameroon
Central African Republic
Gabon

Center: Centres and Services in the Americas
United Nations Information Centre
Casilla de Correo 1107
Asunción, Paraguay
Services to: Paraguay

Center: United Nations Information Centre
Junín 9140, 1er piso
1113 **Buenos Aires**, Argentina
Services to: Argentina
Uruguay

Center: United Nations Information Centre
Edificio Naciones Unidas
Plaza Isabel la Católica
Apartado Postal 686
La Paz, Bolivia
Services to: Bolivia

Center: United Nations Information Centre
Mariscal Blas Cerdeña 450, San Isidro
Apartado Postal 14-0199
Lima, Peru
Services to: Peru

Center: United Nations Information Centre
Bolonia, de Plaza España
Apartado Postal 3260
Managua, Nicaragua
Services to: Nicaragua

Center: United Nations Information Centre
Presidente Mazaryk 29, 7° Piso
México 11570, D.F.
México
Services to: Dominican Republic
Mexico

Center: United Nations Information Centre
Urbanización Obarrio
Apartado Postal 6-9083 El Dorado
Panama City, Panama
Services to: Panama

Center: United Nations Information Centre
16 Victoria Ave.
Post Office Box 130
Port of Spain, Trinidad
Services to: Antigua and Barbuda
Bahamas
Barbados
Belize
Dominica
Grenada
Guyana
Jamaica
Netherlands Antilles
Saint Kitts and Nevi
Saint Lucia
Saint Vincent and the Grenadines
Suriname
Trinidad and Tobago

Center: United Nations Information Centre
Palacio Itamaraty
Avenida Marechal Floriano 196
20060 **Rio de Janeiro**, RJ, Brasil
Services to: Brazil

Center: United Nations Information Centre
Edificio Escalón, 2° Piso
Apartado Postal 2157
San Salvador, El Salvador
Services to: El Salvador

Center: United Nations Information Centre
Calle 72, No. 12-65, Piso 2
Apartado Aéreo 058964
Santa Fé de Bogotá 2, Colombia
Services to: Colombia
Ecuador
Venezuela

Center: United Nations Information Service
Edificio Naciones Unidas
Avenida Dag Hammarskjöld
Casilla 179-D
Santiago, Chile
Services to: Chile

Center: United Nations Information Centre
1889 F Street, NW
Washington, D.C. 20006
United States
Services to: United States

Centres and Services in Asia and Oceania

Center: United Nations Information Centre
197 Ataturk Bulvari
P.K. 407
Ankara, Turkey
Services to: Turkey

Center: United Nations Information Service
Amiriya, Airport Street
Post Office Box 27
Baghdad, Iraq
Services to: Iraq

Center: United Nations Information Service
United Nations Building
Rajadamnern Avenue
Bangkok 10200, Thailand
Services to: Cambodia
Hong Kong
Lao People's Dem. Republic
Malaysia
Singapore
Thailand
Viet Nam

Center: United Nations Information Centre
Apartment No. 1, Fakhoury Building
Monté Bain Militaire
Post Office Box 4656
Beirut, Lebanon
Services to: Jordan
Kuwait
Lebanon
Syrian Arab Republic

Center: United Nations Information Centre
202-204 Bauddhaloka Mawatha
Post Office Box 1505
Colombo 7, Sri Lanka
Services to: Sri Lanka

Center: United Nations Information Centre
House 25, Road 11
General Post Office Box 3658
Dhaka 100, Bangladesh
Services to: Bangladesh

Center: United Nations Information Centre
House No. 26, 88th Street, Ramna 6/3
Post Office Box 1107
Islamabad, Pakistan
Services to: Pakistan

Center: United Nations Information Centre
Gedung Dewan Pers, 5th Floor
32-34 Jalan Kebon Sirih
Jakarta 1001, Indonesia
Services to: Indonesia

Center: United Nations Information Centre
Shah Mahmoud Ghazi Watt
Post Office Box 5
Kabul, Afghanistan
Services to: Afghanistan

Center: United Nations Information Centre
Pulchowk, Patan
Post Office Box 107
Pulchowk, **Kathmandu**, Nepal
Services to: Nepal

Center: United Nations Information Centre
House No. 131, Road 2803
Segaya 328
Post Office Box 26004
Manama, Bahrain
Services to: Bahrain
Qatar
United Arab Emirates

Center: United Nations Information Centre
Post Office Box 7285 (ADC)
MIA Road, Pasay City
Metro Manila, Philippines
Services to: Papua New Guinea
Philippines
Solomon Islands

Center: United Nations Information Centre
55 Lodi Estate
New Delhi 110003, India
Services to: Bhutan
India

Center: United Nations Information Centre
2nd Floor, Suite 1, 125 York Street
Post Office Box 4045
Sydney, N.S.W. 2001
Australia
Services to: Australia
Fiji
Kiribati
Nauru
New Zealand
Samoa
Tonga
Tuvalu
Vanuatu

Center: United Nations Information Centre
Avenue Boharest Maydan
Argantine No. 74
Post Office Box 15875-4557
Teheran, Iran
Services to: Iran

Center: United Nations Information Centre
Shin Aoyama Building Nishika
22nd Floor
1-1 Minami Aoyama 1-chome
Minato-ku, **Tokyo** 107
Japan
Services to: Japan

Center: United Nations Information Centre
6 Natmauk Road
Post Office Box 230
Yangon, Myanmar
Services to: Myanmar

Centres and Services in Europe

Center: United Nations Information Centre
36 Amalia Avenue
GR-105
58 **Athens**, Greece
Services to: Cyprus
Greece
Israel

Center: United Nations Information Centre
Svetozara Markovica 58
Post Office Box 157
Belgrade, Yugoslavia YU-11001
Services to: Albania
Yugoslavia

Center: United Nations Information Centre
and Liaison Office with the
European Economic Community
Avenue de Broqueville 40
1200 **Brussells**, Belgium
Services to: Belgium
Luxembourg
Netherlands

Center: United Nations Information Centre
16 Aurel Vlaic Street
Post Office Box 1-701
Bucharest, Romania
Services to: Romania

Center: United Nations Information Centre
37 H.C. Andersens Boulevard
DK-1553 **Copenhagen** V, Denmark
Services to: Denmark
Finland
Iceland
Norway
Sweden

Center: United Nations Information Service
United Nations Office at Geneva
Palais des Nations
1211 **Geneva** 10, Switzerland
Services to: Bulgaria
Poland
Switzerland

Center: United Nations Information Centre
Rua Latino Coelho No. 1
Edificio Aviz, Bloco A-1, 10°
1000 **Lisbon**, Portugal
Services to: Portugal

Center: United Nations Information Centre
20 Buckingham Gate
London SW1E 6LB
United Kingdom
Services to: Ireland
United Kingdom

Center: United Nations Information Centre
Avenida General Perón, 32-1
Post Office Box 3400
28080 **Madrid**, Spain
Services to: Spain

Center: United Nations Information Centre
4/16 Ulitsa Lunacharskogo
Moscow 121002, Russian Federation
Services to: Belarus
Russian Federation
Ukraine

Center: United Nations Information Centre
1, rue Miollis
75732, **Paris** Cedex 15, France
Services to: France

Center: United Nations Information Centre
Panska 5
11000 **Prague** 1, Czech Republic
Services to: Czech Republic
Slovak Republic

Center: United Nations Information Centre
Palazzetto Venezia
Piazza San Marco 50
00186 **Rome**, Italy
Services to: Holy See
Italy
Malta

Center: United Nations Information Service
United Nations Office at Vienna
Services to: Austria and Germany

Center: Vienna International Centre
Wagramerstrasse 5
Post office Box 500
A-1400 **Vienna**, Austria
Services to: Hungary

UNITED NATIONS ONLINE DATABASES

Readers with access to a computer and modem may be able to access online sources of information about the United Nations via the internet. Current United Nations press releases, resolutions, and documents and breaking information on the UN's international conferences are maintained on the Internet www.un.org/News. Many UN databases are accessible over the Internet www.un.org/databases.

Although the following databases were developed for use by United Nations personnel and are not available free on the internet, a qualified researcher may be able to obtain online access to the following resources by making arrangements with the contact listed.

Database of United Nations Databases and Information Services (DUNDIS)
Subject: Databases; information services; information systems; UN system.
Contact: ACCIS Secretariat
Palais des Nations
1211 GENEVA 10
41/22/798 85 91

United Nations Press Release Retrieval System (UNPRESS)
Subject: Press releases on economic development; emergency relief; environment; international trade; law; natural resources; politics; population; science and technology; social conditions.
Contact: Senior Information Officer
Department of Public Information
United Nations
United Nations Plaza
NEW YORK, NY 10017
212/963 4176

Agenda Item File
Subject: ECOSOC; international relations; political problems; Trusteeship Council; UN; UN General Assembly; UN Secretariat; UN Security Council; UN system.
Contact: Chief, Technical Operations and Publications Service
Dag Hammarskjöld Library
United Nations Plaza
NEW YORK, NY 10017
212/963 7436 879

External Materials File (CATFILE)
Subject: Economic development; human rights; international law; international relations; political problems; population; public administration; social development; UN; UN system.
Contact: Chief, Technical Operations and Publications Service
Dag Hammarskjöld Library
United Nations Plaza
NEW YORK, NY 10017
212/963 7436 879

Resolutions File (RESFILE)
Subject: Economic development; ECOSOC; international relations; political problems; Trusteeship Council; UN; UN General Assembly; UN Secretariat; UN Security Council; UN system.
Contact: Chief, Technical Operations and Publications Service
Dag Hammarskjöld Library
United Nations Plaza
NEW YORK, NY 10017
212/963 7436 879

United Nations Documents File (DOCFILE)
Subjects: Economic development; ECOSOC; international relations; political problems; Trusteeship Council; UN; UN General Assembly; UN Secretariat; UN Security Council; UN system.
Contact: Chief, Technical Operations and Publications Service
Dag Hammarskjöld Library
United Nations Plaza
NEW YORK, NY 10017
212/963 7436 879

WORLD HEALTH ORGANIZATION COMPUTERIZED DATABASES

The following scientific databases are available either online or on diskette to qualified individuals, as indicated. For each database, specific information is presented, including: the type of data stored in the database; the principal areas of interest or specific subject content of the data; the user groups for whom the database, or parts of it, are used; the form in which the database, or parts of it, is made available; and the name of online services which provide online access to the data from the database. If the online file name in which the data is found is different from the database name given at the beginning of the entry, the file name is given. Finally, contact information is provided. This list was accurate as of September 1994.

AFRO/CDC - Morbidity/Mortality AFRO
Database type: Factual; numeric.
Subject scope: Morbidity; mortality.
Availability: UN system organizations; external users with restrictions.
Distribution media: Diskette; magnetic tape; printout.
Contact: Dr. Nguyen-Khanh
WHO/AFRO
PO Box 6
BRAZZAVILLE
Republic of Congo
Telephone: 242/83 38 60
Telefax: 242/83 18 79

AFRO/CEIS - Immunization AFRO

Database type: Numeric.

Subject scope: Immunization.

Availability: UN system organizations; external users with restrictions.

Printed products: Information system: summary for WHO/AFRO.

Distribution media: Diskette; printout.

Contact: Dr. Arevshatian
     WHO/AFRO
     PO Box 6
     BRAZZAVILLE
     Republic of Congo

Telephone: 242/83 38 60

Telefax: 242/83 18 79

AFRO/PHS - Health Indicators in AFRO

Database type: Factual; numeric.

Subject scope: Health indicators.

Availability: UN system organizations; external users with restrictions

Distribution media: Diskette; printout.

Contact: Dr. Nguyen-Khanh
     WHO/AFRO
     PO Box 6
     BRAZZAVILLE
     Republic of Congo

Telephone: 242/83 38 60

Telefax: 242/83 18 79

Antimalaria Activities Status

Database type: Factual; numeric.

Subject scope: Malaria.

Availability: UN system organizations; external users.

Printed products: Weekly epidemiological record; WHO health statistics quarterly.

Contact: Director, Control of Tropical Diseases
     WHO
     20, avenue Appia
     1211 GENEVA 27
     Switzerland

Telephone: 41 22/791 21 11

Telefax: 41 22/791 07 46

Breast Feeding

Database type: Bibliographic; numeric.

Subject scope: Breast feeding.

Contact: Maternal and Child Health
     Division of Family Health
     WHO
     20, avenue Appia
     1211 GENEVA 27
     Switzerland

Telephone: 41 22/791 21 11

Telefax: 41 22/791 07 46

Catalogue of WHO/WPRO Library (WPROLIB)

Database type: Bibliographic.

Subject scope: Chronic diseases; economic development; environment; food; health; infectious diseases; medicine; nutrition; primary health care; public health; social development.

Availability: UN system organizations; external users with restrictions.

Printed products: Recent acquisitions list; various bibliographies.

Contact: Librarian
     WPRO Library
     PO Box 2932
     United Nations cor Taft Avenues
     MANILA
     Philippines

Telephone: 63 2/521 8421

Telefax: 63 2/521 1036

Communicable Disease Data Base

Database type: Numeric.

Subject scope: Disease transmission; epidemiology; infectious diseases.

Availability: UN system organizations; external users: data is made available on demand to health workers, especially for research and planning.

Printed products: Annual review of communicable diseases; CAREC surveillance report.

Distribution media: Printout.

Contact: Statistician
     PAHO/CAREC
     PO Box 164
     16-18 Jamaica Boulevard
     Federation Park
     PORT-OF-SPAIN
     Trinidad & Tobago

Telephone: 500 809/24261; 23404; 23745

Decade Monitoring

Database type: Numeric.

Subject scope: Sanitation; water supply.

Availability: UN system organizations; external users.

Printed products: International drinking water supply and sanitation decade status reports: 1980, 1983, 1985.

Distribution media: Diskette; printout.

Contact: Manager, CWS
     Division of Environmental Health
     WHO
     20, avenue Appia
     1211 GENEVA 27
     Switzerland

Telephone: 41 22/791 21 11

Telefax: 41 22/791 07 46

Directory of Current Medical and Health-related Periodicals Published in the Western Pacific Region of WHO
Database type: Bibliographic; numeric.
Subject scope: Health; medicine; serials.
Availability: UN system organizations; external users.
Printed products: Directory of current medical and health-related periodicals published in the Western Pacific region of WHO.
Contact: Librarian
WPRO Library
PO Box 2932
United Nations cor Taft Avenues
MANILA
Philippines
Telephone: 63 2/521 8421
Telefax: 63 2/521 1036

Directory of On-going Research in Cancer Epidemiology Data Base
Database type: Full text.
Subject scope: Cancer; epidemiology; research.
Availability: UN system organizations; external users: directory distributed free to contributors; for sale through Oxford University Press.
Printed products: Directory of on-going research in cancer epidemiology.
Distribution media: Diskette (indexes); printout.
Contact: Unit of Descriptive Epidemiology
IARC
150, cours Albert Thomas
69372 LYON
France
Telephone: 33 7/7273 8485
Telefax: 33 7/7273 8575

Directory of Selected Medical and Health-related Libraries in the Western Pacific Region of WHO
Database type: Referral.
Subject scope: Health; information services; libraries.
Availability: UN system organizations; external users.
Printed products: Directory of selected medical and health-related libraries in the Western Pacific region of WHO.
Contact: Librarian
WPRO Library
PO Box 2932
United Nations cor Taft Avenues
MANILA
Philippines
Telephone: 63 2/521 8421
Telefax: 63 2/521 1036

ECO-Line
Subject scope: Environmental legislation; pesticides; pollution; toxic substances; toxicology.
Availability: UN system organizations; external users with restrictions.
Printed products: ECO-bibliograflas/ECO-bibliographies; ECO-boletin de adquisiciones bibliograficas/ECO-bibliographic acquisitions bulletin; ECO-library catalog; ECO-publications catalog.
Distribution media: Diskette; printout.
Contact: Head Librarian
ECO
Apartado Postal 37-473
06696 MEXICO CITY D.F.
Mexico

EURODOC
Database type: Bibliographic; referral.
Subject scope: Health; health services.
Availability: UN system organizations; WHO Member States.
Distribution media: Online; printout.
Online hosts: Health Documentation Service.
Contact: Librarian, WHO/EURO
8 Scherfigsvej
2100 COPENHAGEN 0
Denmark
Telephone: 45 31/29 01 11
Telefax: 45 31/18 11 20

Global Oral Epidemiology Data Bank
Database type: Bibliographic; full text; numeric; referral.
Subject scope: Dentistry; periodontal diseases.
Availability: UN system organizations; external users with restrictions: data is provided by printout on receipt of requests indicating countries' entities and age groups for which data is needed.
Distribution media: Diskette; printout.
Contact: Chief, ORH
WHO
20, avenue Appia
1211 GENEVA 27
Switzerland
Telephone: 41 22/791 34 90
Telefax: 41 22/791 07 46

Health for All Global Indicators
Database type: Numeric.
Subject scope: Health indicators.
Availability: UN system organizations; external users.
Printed products: Health situation report.
Distribution media: Diskette; printout.
Contact: Chief, HST/GSP
WHO
20, avenue Appia
1211 GENEVA 27
Switzerland
Telephone: 41 22/791 21 11
Telefax: 41 22/791 07 46

Health Legislation
Database type: Bibliographic; full text; referral.
Subject scope: AIDS; environmental legislation; health; human nutrition; legislation; occupational hygiene; pharmaceuticals; tobacco.
Availability: UN system organizations; external users.
Printed products: International digest of health legislation (English and French editions).
Contact: Chief, HLE
WHO
20, avenue Appia
1211 GENEVA 27
Switzerland
Telephone: 41 22/791 21 11
Telefax: 41 22/791 07 46

Health Legislation Notification System Data Base (EURO-HLE)

Database type: Full text; referral.

Subject scope: Health; legislation.

Availability: UN system organizations; external users (online); yearly report: free of charge to WHO Headquarters, the other WHO Regional Offices and Member States.

Printed products: Report.

Distribution media: Online; printout.

Online hosts: WHO-NET.

Contact: Regional Officer for Health Legislation, Health Legislation Unit
WHO/EURO
8 Scherfigsvej
2100 COPENHAGEN 0
Denmark

Telephone: 45 31/29 01 11

Telefax: 45 31/18 11 20

Health Statistics—Mortality

Database type: Numeric.

Subject scope: Health statistics; mortality.

Availability: UN system organizations; external users.

Printed products: World health statistics annual.

Distribution media: Magnetic tape.

Contact: Chief, HST/GSP
WHO
20, avenue Appia
1211 GENEVA 27
Switzerland

Telephone: 41 22/791 21 11

Telefax: 41 22/791 07 46

Health Statistics—Population & Live Births

Database type: Numeric.

Subject scope: Birth rate; demographic statistics; health statistics.

Availability: UN system organizations; external users.

Printed products: World health statistics annual.

Contact: Chief, HST/GSP
WHO
20, avenue Appia
1211 GENEVA 27
Switzerland

Telephone: 41 22/791 21 11

Telefax: 41 22/791 07 46

HQ/FHE—Health of Women

Database type: Bibliographic; numeric.

Subject scope: Health; women.

Availability: UN system organizations; external users: selected users in developing countries.

Printed products: Coverage of maternity care; Maternal mortality rates.

Distribution media: Printout.

Contact: Division of Family Health
WHO
20, avenue Appia
1211 GENEVA 27
Switzerland

Telephone: 41 22/791 21 11

Telefax: 41 22/791 07 46

HQ/NUT—Nutritional Status

Database type: Factual; numeric.

Subject scope: Nutrition.

Contact: Chief, Division of Family Health
WHO
20, avenue Appia
1211 GENEVA 27
Switzerland

Telephone: 41 22/791 21 11

Telefax: 41 22/791 07 46

HQ/NUT—Physical Growth of Children

Database type: Bibliographic; numeric.

Subject scope: Children; nutrition.

Contact: Nutrition
Division of Family Health
WHO
20, avenue Appia
1211 GENEVA 27
Switzerland

Telephone: 41 22/791 21 11

Telefax: 41 22/791 07 46

Immunization Articles

Database type: Bibliographic.

Subject scope: Immunization.

Availability: UN system organizations; external users.

Printed products: Listing of EPI articles by subject/author.

Distribution media: Diskette; printout.

Contact: Expanded Programme on Immunization
WHO
20, avenue Appia
1211 GENEVA 27
Switzerland

Telephone: 41 22/791 41 67

Telefax: 41 22/791 07 46

Immunization Cold Chain Products

Database type: Full text; numeric.

Subject scope: Immunization; refrigeration; vaccination.

Availability: UN system organizations; external users.

Printed products: Product information sheets.

Contact: Technical Officer, EPI
WHO
20, avenue Appia
1211 GENEVA 27
Switzerland

Telephone: 41 22/791 21 11

Telefax: 41 22/791 07 46

Immunization Coverage Surveys

Database type: Numeric.

Subject scope: Immunization.

Availability: UN system organizations; external users.

Printed products: EPI information system.

Distribution media: Diskette; printout.

Contact: Expanded Programme on Immunization
WHO
20, avenue Appia
1211 GENEVA 27
Switzerland

Telephone: 41 22/791 41 67

Telefax: 41 22/791 07 46

Immunization Demographic Data

Database type: Numeric.
Subject scope: Immunization.
Availability: UN system organizations; external users.
Printed products: EPI information system.
Distribution media: Diskette; printout.
Contact: Expanded Programme on Immunization
    WHO
    20, avenue Appia
    1211 GENEVA 27
    Switzerland
Telephone: 41 22/791 41 67
Telefax: 41 22/791 07 46

Immunization Morbidity

Database type: Numeric.
Subject scope: Immunization.
Availability: UN system organizations; external users.
Printed products: EPI information system.
Distribution media: Diskette; printout.
Contact: Expanded Programme on Immunization
    WHO
    20, avenue Appia
    1211 GENEVA 27
    Switzerland
Telephone: 41 22/791 41 67
Telefax: 41 22/791 07 46

Immunization Programme Reviews

Database type: Factual.
Subject scope: Immunization.
Availability: UN system organizations; external users.
Printed products: EPI information system.
Distribution media: Diskette; printout.
Contact: Expanded Programme on Immunization
    WHO
    20, avenue Appia
    1211 GENEVA 27
    Switzerland
Telephone: 41 22/791 41 67
Telefax: 41 22/791 07 46

International Nonproprietary Names for Pharmaceutical Substances Data Base

Database type: Full text; referral.
Subject scope: Pharmaceuticals; terminology.
Availability: UN system organizations; external users: data provided free of charge on tape provided by request.
Printed products: International nonproprietary names (INN) for pharmaceutical substances (Cumulative List No. 7).
Distribution media: Magnetic tape; printout.
Contact: Chief, PHA
    DMP
    WHO
    20, avenue Appia
    1211 GENEVA 27
    Switzerland
Telephone: 41 22/791 21 11
Telefax: 41 22/791 07 46

Latin American Literature in the Health Sciences (LILACS)

Database type: Bibliographic.
Subject scope: Health; medical research; medical sciences.
Printed products: Index medicus latinoamericano (IMLA).
Distribution media: CD-ROM; magnetic tape; printout.
Contact: A.L. Packer
    Latin American Health Sciences Information Center
    R. Botucatu 862
    04023 SAO PAULO
    Brazil
Telephone: 55 11/549 2611

Leprosy Cases on Multidrug Treatment

Database type: Factual; numeric.
Subject scope: Leprosy.
Availability: UN system organizations.
Contact: LEP Unit
    WHO
    20, avenue Appia
    1211 GENEVA 27
    Switzerland
Telephone: 41 22/791 26 46
Telefax: 41 22/791 07 46

Low Birthweight/Perinatal Mortality

Database type: Bibliographic; numeric.
Subject scope: Maternal and child health.
Availability: UN system organizations; external users.
Distribution media: Diskette; printout.
Contact: Maternal and Child Health
    Division of Family Health
    WHO
    20, avenue Appia
    1211 GENEVA 27
    Switzerland
Telephone: 41 22/791 21 11
Telefax: 41 22/791 07 46

Malaria Cases

Database type: Factual; numeric.
Subject scope: Malaria.
Availability: UN system organizations; external users.
Printed products: Weekly epidemiological record; WHO health statistics quarterly.
Contact: Director, Control of Tropical Diseases
    WHO
    20, avenue Appia
    1211 GENEVA 27
    Switzerland
Telephone: 41 22/791 21 11
Telefax: 41 22/791 07 46

Management Information System for the Special Programme for Research and Training in Tropical Diseases (MISTR)

Database type: Bibliographic; factual; referral.

Subject scope: Development projects; research projects; tropical diseases.

Availability: UN system organizations; external users with restrictions.

Printed products: Management summary report; List of TDR funded projects.

Distribution media: Diskette; magnetic tape; online; printout.

Online hosts: ICC.

Contact: Management Officer (Information), TDR
WHO
20, avenue Appia
1211 GENEVA 27
Switzerland

Telephone: 41 22/791 21 11; 791 37 74

Telefax: 41 22/791 07 46

PAHO Document Retrieval System On-line (PAHOINFO)

Database type: Bibliographic; full text.

Subject scope: Health; health planning; health services; medical education.

Availability: UN system organizations; external users.

Printed products: PAHO disaster update; PAHO nutrition; PAHO-MEET; PAHODOC; PAHOSTC; TABCONT.

Distribution media: COM; magnetic tape; online.

Online hosts: DIALOG; MDC; PAHO, file: BIRS FILE; U.S. National Library of Medicine.

Contact: Chief, HBL
Regional Office for the Americas (AMRO)
525, 23rd Street, N.W.
WASHINGTON, D.C. 20037
USA

Tel: 1 202 861 3200

Fax: 1 202 223 5971

Pharmaceuticals Section/(UN Consolidated List of Products Whose Consumption and/or Sale Have Been Banned, Withdrawn, Severely Restricted or Not Approved by Governments)

Database type: Factual; full text.

Subject scope: Pharmaceuticals; regulations.

Availability: UN system organizations; external users with restrictions.

Printed products: Pharmaceuticals section/(UN consolidated list of products whose consumption and/or sale have been banned, withdrawn, severely restricted, or not approved by governments).

Distribution media: Magnetic tape; printout.

Contact: Chief, PHA
DMP
WHO
20, avenue Appia
1211 GENEVA 27
Switzerland

Telephone: 41 22/791 21 11

Telefax: 41 22/791 07 46

REPIDISCA Data Base

Database type: Bibliographic.

Subject scope: Environmental engineering; sanitation; waste management; water pollution; water supply.

Availability: UN system organizations; external users.

Printed products: REPINDEX.

Distribution media: CD-ROM; magnetic tape.

Contact: Manager, REPIDISCA
WHO
Casilla 4337-Lima 100
Los Pinos 259
Urbanizacion Camacho
LIMA 3
Peru

Telephone: 51 14/35 41 35

Reported AIDS Cases

Database type: Numeric.

Subject scope: AIDS.

Contact: Global Programme on AIDS
WHO
20, avenue Appia
1211 GENEVA 27
Switzerland

Telephone: 41 22/791 21 11

Telefax: 41 22/791 07 46

WHO Library Information System (WHOLIS)

Database type: Bibliographic.

Subject scope: Health; health economics; public health; WHO.

Availability: UN system organizations; external users with restrictions.

Distribution media: Diskette; printout.

Contact: Head, Technical Services
HLT
WHO
20, avenue Appia
1211 GENEVA 27
Switzerland

Telephone: 41 22/791 20 73

Telefax: 41 22/791 07 46

WHO Terminology Information System (WHOTERM)

Database type: Factual.

Subject scope: Health; medicine; terminology.

Availability: UN system organizations.

Printed products: Glossaries; list of terms.

Distribution media: Diskette.

Contact: Chief, Technical Terminology Service
WHO
20, avenue Appia
1211 GENEVA 27
Switzerland

Telephone: 41 22/791 24 58; 791 24 55

Telefax: 41 22/791 07 46

World Health Statistics Data Base
Database type: Numeric.
Subject scope: Causes of death; demographic statistics; diseases; health personnel; health statistics; hospitals; infectious diseases; mortality.
Availability: UN system organizations; external users with restrictions: for national health authorities and government research institutes data is readily available.
Printed products: World health statistics annual; World health statistics quarterly.
Distribution media: Diskette; magnetic tape; printout.
Contact: Chief, HST/GSP
 WHO
 20, avenue Appia
 1211 GENEVA 27
 Switzerland
Telephone: 41 22/791 21 11
Telefax: 41 22/791 07 46

WPRO/CRP-Collaborating Centers in WPRO
Database type: Referral.
Subject scope: Health centres.
Availability: Agency staff.
Distribution media: Diskette.
Contact: WPRO
 PO Box 2932
 United Nations Cor Taft Avenues
 MANILA
 Philippines
Telephone: 63 2/521 8421
Telefax: 63 2/521 1036

WPRO/HSO-Indicators WPRO
Database type: Numeric.
Subject scope: Health indicators.
Availability: UN system organizations; external users with restrictions.
Printed products: Country health information profile; Western Pacific region data bank on socioeconomic and health indicators.
Distribution media: Printout.
Contact: WPRO
 PO Box 2932
 United Nations Cor Taft Avenues
 MANILA
 Philippines
Telephone: 63 2/521 8421
Telefax: 63 2/521 1036

UNITED NATIONS DEPOSITORY LIBRARIES

Listed below are the libraries where United Nations publications and other documents are available. Specific information on holdings is available by contacting the library directly. Many of the US depository libraries also have web sites. Up-to-date URLs may be looked up at www.un.org/MoreInfo/Deplib/usa.htm.

LIBRARIES IN THE UNITED STATES

California
Los Angeles Public Library, Los Angeles
Stanford University Libraries, Stanford
University of California, General Library, Berkeley
University of California, University Research Library, Los Angeles

Colorado
University of Colorado at Boulder

Connecticut
Yale University Library, New Haven

District of Columbia
Library of Congress, Washington, D.C.

Florida
Florida State University, Robert M. Strozier Library, Tallahassee
Nova Southeastern University Law Library, Fort Lauderdale

Hawaii
University of Hawaii Library, Honolulu

Illinois
Library of International Relations, Chicago
Northwestern University Library, Evanston
Documents Library, University of Illinois, Urbana

Indiana
Indiana University Library, Government Publications, Bloomington
Indiana University, School of Law Library, Indianapolis

Iowa
University of Iowa Library, Iowa City

Kansas
University of Kansas Libraries, Lawrence

Maryland
Johns Hopkins University, The Milton S. Eisenhower Library, Baltimore

Massachusetts
Harvard College Library, Cambridge
Boston Public Library

Michigan
University of Michigan, Harlan Hatcher Graduate Library, Ann Arbor

Minnesota
University of Minnesota, Wilson Library, Minneapolis

Nevada
University of Nevada Library, Reno

New Jersey
Princeton University Library, Princeton
Seaton College, Walsh Library, South Orange

New Mexico
Farmington Public Library, Farmington

New York
Columbia University Law Library, New York
Cornell University, Olin Library, Ithaca
Council on Foreign Relations, New York
New York Public Library, Science, Industry and Business Library, New York
New York University, Elmer Holmes Bobst Library, New York
St. John's University, Rittenberg Law Library, Jamaica

North Carolina
University of North Carolina, Davis Library, Chapel Hill

Ohio
Cleveland Public Library, Cleveland

Pennsylvania
University of Pennsylvania, Van Pelt-Dietrich Library, Philadelphia
University of Pittsburgh, Hillman Library

Rhode Island
Brown University, The John D. Rockefeller, Jr. Library, Providence

Tennessee
Vanderbilt University Library, Nashville

Texas
University of Texas, Perry-Castañeda Library, Austin

Utah
University of Utah, Marriott Library, Salt Lake City

Virginia
University of Virginia, Alderman Library, Charlottesville

Washington
University of Washington Libraries, Seattle

LIBRARIES IN PUERTO RICO

Puerto Rico
Universidad de Puerto Rico, Biblioteca General, Rio Piedras
Pontificia Universidad Católica de Puerto Rico, Biblioteca de Derecho, Ponce

LIBRARIES IN THE U.S. VIRGIN ISLANDS

St. Thomas
Virgin Islands Division of Libraries, Archives and Museum

LIBRARIES IN CANADA

Alberta
University of Alberta, The Library, Edmonton

British Columbia
University of British Columbia Library, Vancouver

Manitoba
Legislative Library, Winnipeg

New Brunswick
University of New Brunswick, Harriet Irving Library, Fredericton

Nova Scotia
Dalhousie University Library, Halifax

Ontario
Queens University, Documents Library, Mackintosh-Corry Hall, Kingston
University of Ottawa, Bibliothèque Morrisset, Ottawa
University of Toronto Library, Toronto

Québec
McGill University, McLennan Library, Montreal
Université de Montréal, Bibliothèque des Sciences Humaines et Sociales, Montréal
Université Laval, Bibliothèque, Québec

Saskatchewan
University of Saskatchewan, Murray Memorial Library, Saskatoon

Staff of the United Nations System

ORGANIZATION	FINANCED FROM REGULAR BUDGETS			EXTRA-BUDGETARY (VOLUNTARY FUNDS)			TOTAL	
	Prof.	G.S.	Total	Prof.	G.S.	Total	Prof.	G.S.
United Nations[1]	3,265	5,829	9,094	1,604	3,198	4,802	4,869	9,027
UNHCR	106	179	285	643	1,198	1,841	749	1,377
UNITAR	—	1	—	10	8	18	10	9
UNRWA	51	2	53	67	7	74	118	9
ITC	1		1	181	192	373	182	192
ICSC	18	22	40	—	—	—	18	22
ICJ	19	28	47	—	—	—	19	28
UNU	—	—	—	36	65	101	36	65
UNDP	—	—	—	1,571	5,033	6,604	1,571	5,033
UNICEF	—	—	—	1,179	2,623	3,802	1,179	2,623
ILO	678	1,012	1,690	695	692	1,387	1,373	1,704
FAO	1,051	2,062	3,113	1,608	1,649	3,257	2,659	3,711
UNESCO	808	1,406	2,214	248	341	589	1,056	1,747
WHO	1,269	2,350	3,619	564	1,208	1,772	1,833	3,558
ICAO	248	350	598	231	223	454	479	573
UPU	62	84	146	25	1	26	87	85
ITU	240	395	635	135	99	234	375	494
WMO	104	124	228	78	72	150	182	196
IMO	88	146	234	34	47	81	122	193
WIPO	114	237	351	4	18	22	118	255
UNIDO	355	665	1,020	305	458	763	660	1,123
IAEA	684	958	1,642	15	108	123	699	1,066
TOTALS	9,161	15,850	25,011	9,233	17,240	26,473	18,394	33,090

Grand Total UN System: 51,484

[1]These figures include staff for the central UN Secretariat in New York, Geneva, Vienna, the five Regional Commissions and many other units around the world, as of the end of 1990.
Note: "Prof." denotes professional grade positions; "G.S." denotes general service positions. "Regular Budget" positions are considered long-term worldwide civil service positions and are funded by legally binding assessments made upon all members of an organization; "Extra-budgetary" denotes positions for special development and humanitarian programs, which are funded by voluntary contributions from member governments. (Source: *Renewing the United Nations System* by Erskine Childers with Brian Urquhart, Dag Hammarskjöld Foundation, Sweden, 1994. Reprinted with permission.)

BIBLIOGRAPHY

The following is a selected list of titles for further reading about the United Nations. If no publisher is attributed, the book is published by the United Nations and available through the annual *United Nations Publications Catalog* www.un.org/Pubs/catalog.htm. UN publicatios may be ordered from: the Sales Section, 2 United Nations Plaza, Room DC2-853, Dept. 421, New York, NY 10017, (800) 253-9646; or from Bernan Associates (formerly UNIPUB), 4611-F Assembly Drive, Lanham, MD 20706, (800) 274-4888. In Europe, UN publications may be obtained from United Nations Publications, Sales Office and Bookshop, CH-1211 Geneva 10, Switzerland, 41(22) 734-1473.

GENERAL INFORMATION

A Global Agenda: Issues before the 46th General Assembly of the United Nations, John Tessitore, Susan Woolfson, editors, UN Association of the USA, University Press of America, 1992.

A Global Agenda: Issues before the 47th General Assembly of the United Nations, John Tessitore, Susan Woolfson, editors, UN Association of the USA, University Press of America, 1993.

About the United Nations, a series of VHS videos and texts providing insight into the issues facing the world organization today. Includes: *Human Rights, Environment and Development, Palestine, Literacy, Africa Recovery, Peace-Keeping*, and *Decolonization, 1991–1992.*

Acronyms and Abbreviations Covering the United Nations System and Other International Organizations, 1981. Contains the acronyms and abbreviations of approximately 825 titles within the UN system, in English, French, Russian, Spanish, Chinese, and Arabic.

Anarchy or Order: Annual Reports 1982–1991, by Javier Pérez de Cuéllar. A chronological assessment of the work of the organization during his tenure. 1991.

Basic Facts About the United Nations, annual.

International Institutions at Work, Paul G. Taylor, St. Martin's Press, 1988.

Peace by Pieces—United Nations Agencies and Their Roles: a Reader and Selective Bibliography, Robert N. Wells, Jr., Scarecrow Press, Metuchen, NJ, 1991, .

Programme budget for the biennium 1994–95, General Assembly, UN, 22 February 1994, A/RES/48/231.

Report of the Secretary General on the Work of the Organization, United Nations, annual.

Resolutions and Decisions Adopted by the General Assembly, United Nations, annual.

UN Chronicle, bi-monthly.

United Nations, Divided World, 2nd edition, Adam Roberts and Benedict Kingsbury, editors, Clarendon Press, 1993.

United Nations Yearbook, irregular.

Who's Who in the United Nations and Related Agencies, Detroit: Omnigraphics, 1992.

HISTORY OF THE UNITED NATIONS

A Dangerous Place, Daniel P. Moynihan, New York: Little Brown, 1978.

A Life in Peace and War, Brian Urquhart, New York: Harper & Row, 1987.

Hammarskjöld, Brian Urquhart, New York: Knopf, 1972.

Ralph Bunche: An American Life, Brian Urquhart, New York: W.W. Norton, 1993.

The Structure of the United Nations General Assembly: An Organizational Approach to Its Work, 1974–1980s, Blanche Finley, Kraus International Publications, 1988.

The US, the UN, and the Management of Global Change, New York: New York University Press, 1983.

The United Nations at Forty: A Foundation to Build On, 1985.

THE FUTURE OF THE UNITED NATIONS

A World in Need of Leadership: Tomorrow's United Nations (Development Dialogue 1990: 1–2), Erskine Childers with Brian Urquhart, Dag Hammarskjöld Foundation, Uppsala, 1990.

Future Role of the United Nations in an Interdependent World, 1989.

Global Outlook 2000, 1990.

Renewing the United Nations System, Erskine Childers with Brian Urquhart, Dag Hammarskjöld Foundation, Uppsala, 1994.

Third Generation World Organization, 1989.

Towards a More Effective United Nations, (Development Dialogue, 1991: 1–2), Erskine Childers with Brian Urquhart, Dag Hammarskjold Foundation, Uppsala, 1991.

DISARMAMENT

Concepts of Security Disarmament, 1986.

Disarmament, Environment and Development and their Relevance to the Least Developed Countries, 1991.

International Law of Disarmament and Arms Control, 1991.

Study on Conventional Disarmament, 1945–1985, 1985.

The United Nations and Disarmament, 1945–1985, 1985.

United Nations Disarmament Yearbook, annual.

PEACEFUL USES OF OUTER SPACE

Maintaining Outer Space for Peaceful Uses, 1985.

Prevention of an Arms Race in Outer Space: A Guide to the Discussions in the Conference on Disarmament, 1991.

Report of the Committee on the Peaceful Uses of Outer Space, 1991.

Space Activities of the United Nations and International Organizations, 1992.

INTERNATIONAL PEACE AND SECURITY

An Agenda for Peace, Boutros Boutros-Ghali, United Nations, June 1992, DPI/1247.

The Blue Helmets: A Review of UN Peace-Keeping, 2nd edition, United Nations, 1990.

Reference Paper: The United Nations and the Situation in the Former Yugoslavia, UNDPI document, March 1994, DPI/1312/Rev.2.

The Evolution of UN Peacekeeping: Case Studies and Comparative Analysis, William Durch, editor, New York: St. Martins Press, 1993.

The United Nations and Collective Management of International Conflict, 1986.

United Nations Peace-keeping Update: May 1994, UNDPI document, DPI/1306/Rev.3, June 1994.

ENVIRONMENT AND SUSTAINABLE DEVELOPMENT

Climate Change and Transnational Corporations: Analysis and Trends, 1992.

Global Partnership for Environment and Devleopment: A Guide to Agenda 21, 1992.

UNEP 1992 Annual Report: Twenty Years Since Stockholm, 1993.

State of the World Environment, 1991.

Sustainable Development and the Environment, UNDP.

ECONOMIC DEVELOPMENT

Conclusions on Accounting and Reporting by Transnational Corporations, 1988.

Development Update, UN Department of Public Information (UNDPI), United Nations, (bi-monthly).

Handbook of International Trade and Development Statistics 1991, 1992.

Industry and Development: A Global Report 1991/1992, 1991.

International Development Strategy and Establishment of a New International Economic Order: Third Regional Appraisal, 1981.

International Trade Statistics, annual.

International Development Strategy for the Fourth United Nations Development Decade (1991-2000), UN Dept. of Public Information, DPI/1107, 1991.

INSTRAW Report, annual.

The Least Developed Countries Report, UNCTAD, annual.

Paris Declaration and Programme of Action for the Least Developed Countries for the 1990s, 1992.

Report of the Commission on Science and Technology for Development, annual.

Source, (Magazine of the UNDP/World Bank Water and Sanitation Program), UNDP.

Trade and Development Report, UNCTAD, annual.

Transnational Corporations and the Transfer of New and Emerging Technologies to Developing Countries, 1990.

UNCTAD Review, biennial.

United Nations Development Programme: Compendium of Ongoing Projects, 1991.

United Nations University Annual Report.

UNU Press Publications to 1993.

World Economic Survey, annual.

World Statistics in Brief, annual.

SOCIAL DEVELOPMENT

Accelerating the Development Process: Challenges for National and International Policies in the 1990s, 1991.

Aging and Urbanization, 1991. Presents the reports and recommendations of the UN International Conference on Aging Populations in the Context of Urbanization.

An Agenda for Development, by Secretary General Boutros Boutros-Ghali, 1994.

Child Mortality in Developing Countries, 1991.

Crisis or Reform: Breaking the Barriers to Development, 1984.

Development for People: Goals and Strategies for the Year 2000, 1989.

Human Development Report 1993, UNDP, Oxford University Press.

The Least Developed Countries, 1990 Report, 1991.

The State of World Population, UNFPA, annual.

The World's Women, 1970–1990: Trends and Statistics, 1991.

UNFPA Annual Report.

UNFPA Publications & Audio Visual Guide, annual.

United Nations Demographic Yearbook, 42nd Issue, 1990, 1991.

Vienna International Plan of Action on Aging, UNDPI document, 1983, DPI/932.

Women: Challenges to the Year 2000, 1992.

World Survey on the Role of Women in Development, 1989.

World Food Programme 1993 Food Aid Review.

World Food Programme Journal, periodical.

HUMANITARIAN AFFAIRS AND DISASTER RELIEF

Images of Exile: 1951–1991, UNHCR, 1991. A visual record of the work of the UN High Commissioner for Refugees between 1951 and 1991.

Mitigating Natural Disasters: Phenomena, Effects and Options, 1991.

INTERNATIONAL CRIME AND ILLICIT TRAFFIC IN NARCOTIC DRUGS

Combating Drug Abuse and Related Crime, 1984.

Commission on Narcotic Drugs—Cumulative Index, 1987–1990, 1991. Covers all national laws and regulations on narcotic drugs and psychotropic substances which governments have communicated to the UN Secretariat during 1987–1990.

Eighth United Nations Congress on the Prevention of Crime and the Treatment of Offenders, 1991.

Report of the Commision on Crime Prevention and Criminal Justice, annual ECOSOC document.

Report of the Commission on Narcotic Drugs, annual ECOSOC document.

Report of the International Conference on Drug Abuse and Illicit Trafficking, June 1987, 1987.

The United Nations and Crime Prevention and Criminal Justice, UNDPI document, June 1990, DPI/1045.

The United Nations and Drug Abuse Control, UN International Drug Control Programme, United Nations (UNDPI), 1992.

United Nations Convention Against Illicit Traffic in Narcotic Drugs and Psychotropic Substances, 1991.

APARTHEID

Assembly accepts credentials of South African representatives after 24 years; deletes item on elimination of apartheid from its Agenda, UNDPI document, GA/8682.

Elimination of Apartheid and Establishment of a United Democratic and Non-racial South Africa, General Assembly document, 21 June 1994, A/48/L.58.

Progress Made in the Implementation of the Declaration on Apartheid and its Destructive Consequences in Southern Africa, Secretary General, General Assembly document, September 1991, A/45/1052.

Recent Developments on the Issue of Apartheid in South Africa (III); Upcoming Milestone: Democratic Parliamentary Elections, UNDPI document, March 1994, DPI/1469.

South Africa's Democratic Elections: The UN's Observer Role, UNDPI document, March 1994, DPI/1469.

INDEPENDENCE OF COLONIAL PEOPLES

Decolonization and World Peace, Brian Urquhart, University of Texas Press, Austin, 1989.

Decolonization: The Task Ahead; Profiles of 18 Trust and Non-Self-Governing Territories, United Nations, April 1991, DPI/1109.

HUMAN RIGHTS

Human Rights Committee: Its Role in the Development of the International Covenant on Civil and Political Rights, Dominic McGoldrick, Clarendon, Oxford University Press, 1991.

United Nations Actions in the Field of Human Rights, 40th Anniversary, 1989.
Universal Declaration of Human Rights.
Yearbook on Human Rights.

INTERNATIONAL LAW
International Court of Justice Bibliography, 1991.
International Court of Justice Reports and Judgments, Advisory Opinions and Orders, 1992.
Multilateral Treaties Deposited with the Secretary-General, annual.
The Law of the Sea: A Select Bibliography 1991, 1992.
The Law of the Sea: Multilateral Treaties Relevant to the United Nations Convention on the Law of the Sea, 1985.
United Nations Commission on International Trade Law Yearbook, annual.
United Nations Treaty Series. Treaties and international agreements entered into by UN member states.
Yearbook of the International Law Commission.

REGIONAL DEVELOPMENT
Economic and Social Survey for Asia and the Pacific, annual.
Economic Bulletin for Asia and the Pacific, semi-annual.
Economic Bulletin for Europe, issued periodically.
Economic Commission for Europe (ECE) Annual Report .
Economic and Social Commission for Asia and the Pacific (ESCAP), annual report.
Economic Survey of Europe, annual.
Economic Survey of Latin America and the Caribbean, annual.
Report of the Executive Secretary of ESCWA, annual.
Report of the Economic Commission for Africa (ECA), annual.
Report of the Economic Comission for Latin America and the Caribbean (ECLAC), annual.
Regional Cooperation: Report of the Secretary General, annual ECOSOC document.
Statistical Yearbook for Asia and the Pacific.
Statistical Yearbook for Latin America and the Caribbean.
Survey of Economic and Social Conditions in Africa, annual.

THE UNITED NATIONS

RELATED AGENCIES

AGENCIES OF THE UNITED NATIONS SYSTEM

The following organizations are often called part of the United Nations "family." The previous chapters have been concerned with the organs, programs, or funds of the United Nations that are directly governed by the General Assembly and/or the Security Council, and which have the Secretary General as their executive head. The following organizations all have their own separate member states, governing bodies, executive heads, and secretariats. While these organizations are bound to the UN by legal agreements, they are not governed directly by UN organs.

Most organizations in the system are related to the United Nations through legal agreements executed pursuant to Articles 57 and 63 of the Charter. A key purpose of these special agreements, as stated in Article 58, was coordination of activities in the pursuit of economic, social, and cultural objectives. However, some provisions have never been fully implemented.

The Specialized Agencies
The ILO, FAO, UNESCO and WHO all had predecessor organizations in the League of Nations but were re-established as part of the UN system between 1946–1994. UNIDO became a full specialized agency in 1985. Voting in the main governing bodies of these agencies is on the same one-nation-one-vote principle as in the United Nations.

Technical Agencies
Among this group are the very first truly international organizations, such as the International Telecommunications Union (ITU) and the Universal Postal Union (UPU), which were both established over a century ago. This group of agencies has a very specific focus, and countries are often represented by the head of the national ministry in charge of the relevant area, such as weather, telecommunications, postal service, intellectual property.

However, the International Atomic Energy Association (IAEA) was established in 1956 by the United Nations General Assembly, and is legally bound directly to the General Assembly. The other specialized and technical agencies report to the United Nations through the Economic and Social Council (ECOSOC).

GATT/WTO
The World Trade Organization (WTO) is the successor to the General Agreement on Tariffs and Trade (GATT), and serves as the legal and institutional foundation of the multilateral trading system. The WTO helps to legally determine how governments frame and carry out domestic trade legislation and regulations. The WTO also serves as a forum on which international trade relations can develop through collective debate, negotiation, and adjudication.

The Bretton Woods Institutions
The IMF and the World Bank Group are structured very differently from the specialized agencies. These agencies were established under the charter of the United Nations at a special conference held at Bretton Woods, New Hampshire in 1944. The World Bank Group comprises five separate organizations: the IBRD, the IDA, the IFC, MIGA, and the ICSD. Members of the IBRD can choose which of the four remaining organizations they wish to join.

One of the most fundamental differences between the UN and the Bretton Woods institutions is that voting in these organizations is governed according to the number of shares held by each member state. Therefore, the wealthier countries have more voting power.

IFAD, while not a Bretton Woods institution, is a more recent addition to the specialized agency family that deals with capital funding operations. It raises money through replenishments. Its governing council is made up of three groups of countries—industrialized, oil-producing, and other developing countries. Each group has equal voting rights.

THE AGENCIES IN CHRONOLOGICAL ORDER—WITH EFFECTIVE DATES OF ESTABLISHMENT
Universal Postal Union 1 July 1875
International Labor Organization 11 April 1919
International Telecommunication Union 1 January 1934
Food and Agriculture Organization
of the United Nations 16 October 1945
International Bank for Reconstruction
and Development 27 December 1945
International Monetary Fund 27 December 1945
United Nations Educational, Scientific
and Cultural Organization 4 November 1946
International Civil Aviation Organization 4 April 1947
General Agreement on Tariffs and Trade 1 January 1948
World Health Organization 7 April 1948
World Meteorological Organization 23 March 1950
International Finance Corporation 24 July 1956
International Atomic Energy Agency 29 July 1957
International Maritime Organization 17 March 1958
International Development Association 24 September 1960
World Intellectual Property Organization 26 April 1970
International Fund for
Agricultural Development 30 November 1977
United Nations Industrial
Development Organization 1 January 1986
World Trade Organization1 January 1995

The arrangement of articles on the United Nations related agencies follows the order of the chart on the Structure of the United Nations System shown in the first chapter. Each article is structured in the following sections: Background, Creation, Purposes, Membership, Structure, Budget, Activities, Bibliography.

THE INTERNATIONAL ATOMIC ENERGY AGENCY (IAEA)

BACKGROUND: The UN came into existence at the beginning of the atomic age. Man's success in harnessing atomic energy has made the UN's objectives not only important but even indispensable. The primary purpose of the UN is to prevent war. A major war involving the use of atomic weapons would be not simply catastrophic but very probably suicidal. The second objective of the UN is to promote the economic and social welfare of peoples throughout the world. Atomic energy promises to contribute greatly to worldwide prosperity. Although "atoms for peace" has been a continuing concern of the UN itself, and although a number of organizations of the UN family, such as FAO and WHO, have been concerned with specific aspects of peaceful uses of atomic energy, it was not until 1957 that a special organization, the International Atomic Energy Agency, came into being for the express purpose of accelerating and enlarging the contribution of atomic energy to peace, health, and prosperity throughout the world.

CREATION

Addressing the UN General Assembly in December 1953, US president Dwight D. Eisenhower called for the establishment of an international atomic energy organization to "serve the peaceful pursuits of mankind." The president said that he hoped the atomic powers, through such an organization, would dedicate "some of their strength to serve the needs rather than the fears of mankind."

President Eisenhower stated that the USSR "must, of course, be one" of the countries principally involved in the proposed organization. Accordingly, as a first step, the US State Department in the spring and summer of 1954 submitted a series of memoranda to the USSR suggesting the principles that should be incorporated in the statute of such an agency. It was, however, impossible for the two powers to reach agreement at that time. The USSR maintained that the issues of disarmament and peaceful uses of atomic energy were inseparable and that agreement on a general prohibition of nuclear weapons would have to precede the creation of the agency. The US countered with the argument that effective international control of nuclear weapons would have to precede their prohibition, and it announced that it was prepared to go ahead with international negotiations even without the participation of the USSR.

In the summer of 1954, the US issued invitations to seven other countries, including both "atomic powers" and important uranium-producing states—Australia, Belgium, Canada, France, Portugal, South Africa, and the UK—to meet with it in Washington, D.C., to prepare a draft statute for the proposed agency. In September, the USSR reversed its previous position. It announced its willingness to separate the issues of disarmament and peaceful uses of atomic energy and to accept the eight-power draft statute as a basis for further negotiations and guidance.

In December 1954, the General Assembly unanimously adopted an "Atoms for Peace" resolution expressing the hope that the International Atomic Energy Agency would be established "without delay" in order to assist "in lifting the burdens of hunger, poverty and disease." An international conference on the statute was convened at UN headquarters in New York on 20 September 1956, with the participation of 81 nations, including some, such as the Federal Republic of Germany, that were not yet members of the UN itself. After adopting a number of amendments, proposed for the most part by the atomic "have-not" powers, the conference unanimously adopted the statute as a whole on 26 October 1956.

On 29 July 1957, the statute came into force after 26 states had deposited instruments of ratification, and the International Atomic Energy Agency officially came into existence. The first General Conference of the IAEA was held in Vienna in October 1957, at which time it was decided to make Vienna the permanent headquarters site of the agency. The address of the IAEA is Wagramer Strasse 5, P.O. Box 100, A-1400 Vienna, Austria.

Additionally, the IAEA maintains field and liaison offices in Canada, Geneva, New York, and Tokyo; operates laboratories in Austria and Monaco; and supports a research center in Trieste, Italy, which is administered by the United Nations Educational and Scientific Organization (UNESCO).

PURPOSES

According to the statute of the IAEA, the agency "shall seek to accelerate and enlarge the contribution of atomic energy to peace, health and prosperity throughout the world. It shall ensure, so far as it is able, that assistance provided by it or at its request or under its supervision and control is not used in such a way as to further any military purpose."

The IAEA acts as a clearinghouse for the pooling and coordination of experience and research in the peaceful uses of nuclear power. It helps its member countries acquire the necessary skills and materials to share in the benefits of the atomic age. In practice, the IAEA has been particularly concerned with bringing the advantages of atomic energy to underdeveloped regions.

The IAEA is obliged under its statute to "ensure, so far as it is able," that all the activities in which it takes part are directed exclusively to civilian uses. A second important task of the IAEA, then, is to establish a system of supervision and control to make certain that none of the assistance programs that it fosters and none of the materials whose distribution it supervises are used for military purposes. This aspect of the work assumed significance far beyond its primary objective when the Treaty on the Non-Proliferation of Nuclear Weapons came into force in March 1970, since the IAEA is the body responsible for the necessary control system under that treaty.

MEMBERSHIP

Any member of the UN or of any of the specialized agencies that signed the statute within 90 days after 26 October 1956 thereby became a charter member of the IAEA upon ratification of the statute. Other countries, even if not members of the UN or any of the specialized agencies, may be admitted by the General Conference of the IAEA upon recommendation of the Board of Governors.

As of 1 December 1999 the IAEA had 130 members. Honduras applied for membership and was approved by the General Council, but had not yet deposited an instrument of acceptance of the statute.

STRUCTURE

The three organs of the IAEA are the General Conference, the Board of Governors, and the secretariat, headed by a Director-General.

General Conference

The General Conference consists of all members, each having one vote. It meets once a year at IAEA headquarters in Vienna. Special sessions may be convened by the director-general at the request of the Board of Governors or a majority of the IAEA members. The General Conference elects 22 of the 35 members of the Board of Governors for a period of two years. It considers the board's annual report and approves reports for submission to the UN and agreements with the UN and other organizations. It approves the budget recommended by the board and the appointment of the director-general. The General Conference may discuss any matter concerning the IAEA and may make recommendations to the Board of Governors or to any of the member states.

Board of Governors

The 35-member Board of Governors is the body actually vested with "the authority to carry out the functions of the Agency in accordance with (the) Statute." The board generally meets five times each year. It is composed as follows: the outgoing Board of Governors designates for membership on the board the 13 members most advanced in the technology of atomic energy and the production of source materials and the member most advanced in the technology of atomic energy and the production of source materials in two of the following areas in which none of the aforesaid 13 is located—North America, Latin America, Western Europe, Eastern Europe, Africa, the Middle East and South Asia, Southeast Asia and the Pacific, and the Far East.

The General Conference also elects to membership of the Board of Governors the following: (1) 20 members, with due regard to geographical representation, so that the board at all times will include in this category 5 representatives of Latin America, 4 representatives of Western Europe, 3 representatives of Eastern Europe, 4 representatives of Africa, 2 representatives of the Middle East and South Asia, 1 representative of Southeast Asia and the Pacific, and 1 representative of the Far East; (2) in addition, 1 further member from among the members of the following areas: the Middle East and South Asia, Southeast Asia and the Pacific, and the Far East; (3) and 1 further member from among the members in the following areas: Africa, the Middle East and South Asia, and Southeast Asia and the Pacific.

Member States represented on the IAEA Board for 1999–2000 were Algeria, Argentina, Australia, Austria, Belarus, Bolivia, Brazil, Canada, Chile, China, Cuba, Egypt, Finland, France, Germany, Greece, India, Indonesia, Japan, Jordan, Republic of Korea, Nigeria, Norway, Poland, Russian Federation, Saudi Arabia, Singapore, Slovakia, South Africa, Sudan, Sweden, Syrian Arab Republic, United Kingdom of Great Britain and Northern Ireland, United States of America, and Uruguay.

Director-General and Secretariat

The staff of the IAEA is headed by a director-general, appointed by the Board of Governors with the approval of the General Conference for a term of four years. The statute describes the director-general as "the chief administrative officer of the Agency," but it closely limits his independent powers by providing that he "shall be under the authority and subject to the control of the Board of Governors." The director-general is responsible for "the appointment, organization, and functioning of the staff."

The first director-general, who held the post from 1957 to 1961, was Sterling Cole of the US, a former congressman. Dr. Sigvard Eklund, a Swedish physicist and administrator, served as director-general from 1961 to 1981. He was succeeded by Dr. Hans Blix of Sweden, a former foreign minister, who was reappointed in 1993 for a fourth four-year term. On 1 December 1997, Blix was succeeded by Dr. Mohamed El-Baradei (of Egypt) as Director General. El-Baradei has been a senior member of the Secretariat since 1984. He heads a staff of about 2,100 from some 95 countries.

Position in the UN System

The IAEA is an autonomous international organization occupying its own position in the UN family of organizations. Under the relationship agreement between the UN and the IAEA, the IAEA is recognized as being "responsible for international activities concerned with the peaceful uses of atomic energy." One of the statutory objectives of the IAEA is to ensure that none of the assistance it gives to member states is "used in such a way as to further any military purpose," and the IAEA has a staff of inspectors to report violations of this rule. In case of noncompliance, the agency's Board of Governors reports to the Security Council and the General Assembly of the UN.

IAEA has established strong cooperation arrangements with many of the key UN development agencies in order to advance the contribution of nuclear science and technology in the fields of agriculture, human health, industry, environmental protection, and other sectors. Principal partners in are the Food and Agriculture Organization (FAO), the United Nations Development Programme (UNDP), the World Health Organization (WHO), the United Nations Environment Programme (UNEP), the World Meteorological Organization (WMO), the International Fund for Agricultural Development (IFAD), the United Nations Educational, Scientific and Cultural Organization (UNESCO), and the United Nations Industrial Development Organization (UNIDO). The agency also develops cooperative arrangements with multilateral development banks, bilateral donors, and non-governmental organizations and institutes such as the Inter-American Nuclear Energy Commission, the Agency for the Prohibition of Nuclear Weapons in Latin America, the League of Arab States, the OAU, the Nuclear Energy Agency of the OECD, and the European Atomic Energy Community. Finally, the IAEA maintains contact with 19 nongovernmental organizations having consultative status with it.

BUDGET

The IAEA is financed by regular and voluntary contributions from member states. For 1998, the IAEA General Conference approved a regular budget of us$221.4 million. The target for voluntary contributions to finance the IAEA program of technical cooperation was about us$71.5 million for 1998.

ACTIVITIES

A. Assistance to Member States

The initial program of the IAEA, unanimously adopted by the 1957 General Conference, emphasized activities that could be undertaken while the IAEA's experience and resources were still relatively limited. High priority was given "to those activities which will give the maximum possible benefit from the peaceful applications of atomic energy in improving the conditions and raising the standard of living of the peoples in the underdeveloped areas."

In the light of these considerations, two of the IAEA's major objectives are to help member states prepare for the eventual use of nuclear power and to encourage them in the wider use of radioisotopes. Although it cannot undertake actual programs of development for its members, it can assist them in initiating and carrying out such programs. By the 1990s IAEA was active in assisting its developing members in an impressive number of fields:

Basic human needs

- water resources development
- agriculture (mutation breeding, fertilizer and soil nutrition, pest control, use of agrochemicals)
- livestock (reproduction, health, nutrition)
- health care (radiation therapy, nuclear medicine and diagnostics)

Industrial applications

- nondestructive testing
- hydrology (silt movements, geothermal studies)
- radiation processing (surface coating, radiation sterilization, food preservation, sterilization of medical products)
- isotopic tracers for industry
- nuclear gauging for industry (paper, steel, food processing, mining industries)
- radioisotope and radiopharmaceutical production
- research reactor design and use

Electricity generation

- geology, mining and processing of nuclear raw materials
- fuel element fabrication
- metallurgy and materials testing
- power reactor design
- reactor electronics instrumentation and control
- reactor engineering and quality assurance
- electricity system planning

Support activities

nuclear centers and laboratories
- nuclear safety (regulation, safety standards, radiation protection, waste management, safety assessment)
- physics (atomic, nuclear, high-energy and solid-state physics)
- chemistry (nuclear, radio, radiation, and nuclear analytical chemistry)

Technical Cooperation

The IAEA has been providing technical assistance to developing member countries since 1959, in the form of expert services, equipment, and training, with the objective of facilitating technology transfer in various fields related to nuclear energy. The major fields in which assistance is provided are nuclear safety, the application of isotopes and radiation in agriculture, and nuclear engineering and technology. Other important areas for assistance are general atomic energy development, nuclear physics and chemistry, prospecting for and mining and processing of nuclear materials, and the application of isotopes and radiation in industry and hydrology, in medicine, and in biology.

Financial support for the IAEA's technical cooperation programs comes mainly from its own voluntary technical assistance and cooperation fund; other sources are extrabudgetary donations and contributions in kind from member states and UNDP. In 1997, there were 1,124 technical cooperation projects (254 in Africa, 250 in East Asia and the Pacific, 105 in West Asia, 236 in Europe, and 279 in Latin America); of these, 262 projects, or about 23%, were completed during the year. For 1998, the IAEA again planned involvement in more than 1,000 projects in nearly 100 countries. To support this effort, the agency approved program funding as follows: US$17.6 million for projects in Africa; US$14.2 million in East Asia and the Pacific; US$8.2 million in West Asia; US$20.1 million in Europe; and US$13.4 million in Latin America. In addition, US$4.5 million was approved for interregional projects and US$1.1 million for global projects.

Provision of Materials

Under the IAEA statute, any member desiring to set up an atomic energy project for peaceful purposes "may request the assistance of the Agency in securing special fissionable and other materials."

The IAEA acts, on request, as an intermediary in arranging the supply of reactor fuel and specialized equipment from one member state to another. Argentina, Finland, Japan, Mexico, Norway, Pakistan, Uruguay, and Zaire, among other countries, have been beneficiaries of such arrangements. Small quantities of special fissionable materials have also been supplied to a number of countries for research purposes.

Training of Technical Personnel

The IAEA's training program has retained its importance, not only because the need for trained staff is pressing but also because less elaborate preparations are required for assistance of this kind than for technical assistance operations involving the provision of expert services and demonstration equipment.

To meet the shortage of scientific and technical workers, the IAEA has initiated a fivefold program:

1. *Fellowships.* Fellowships are awarded in all subjects involving the peaceful uses of atomic energy, such as nuclear physics; the production, handling, and application of isotopes in agriculture, industry, medicine, biology, and hydrology; nuclear chemistry; the planning, construction, and operation of research and power reactors; health physics; and radiological protection.

2. *Assignment of experts and consultants.* The program provides for scientists and engineers to give advice and in-service training to developing countries on various subjects.

3. *Survey of available facilities in member states.* The IAEA collects detailed information from its member states about their training and research programs, training facilities, and the experts that they are prepared to make available to the IAEA. It is thus in a position to act as an international clearinghouse for training in atomic energy and to promote technical cooperation among developing countries.

4. *Training courses.* Regional and interregional courses have been organized on such subjects as the application of isotopes and radiation in medicine, nuclear instrumentation for laboratory technicians, the use and maintenance of nuclear and related electronic equipment, radiological and safety protection, physics, the utilization of research reactors, nuclear-power projects and other high-technology subjects, the preparation and control of radiopharmaceuticals, and uranium prospecting and ore analysis.

5. *Expanded training programs.* A number of developing countries, faced with the need to introduce nuclear power, require special assistance in the training of their key staff; the agency has therefore initiated an expanded training program on nuclear-power project planning, implementation, and operation. Special training courses contribute to the development

of efficient legal and organizational infrastructures for nuclear-power programs, including instruction in quality assurance and safety aspects. In addition, on-the-job training is arranged on subjects for which no formal courses are available.

In 1998 IAEA conducted 14 interregional and 146 regional training courses in 58 countries; more than 2,000 people participated in these courses. The total program cost for the year was US$9.3 million.

B. Exchange of Information

While its assistance programs are directed primarily to the needs of economically developing areas, the IAEA's program of conferences and exchange of information is designed to benefit all of its members—even the most technically advanced.

The International Nuclear Information System (INIS), set up by the agency in 1970, provides worldwide coverage of the literature dealing with all aspects of peaceful uses of atomic energy and is the first fully decentralized computer-based information system. Countries and organizations participating in the INIS collect and process all the relevant literature within their geographic areas and send it to the IAEA. In Vienna, the information is checked, merged, and further processed, and the resulting output is distributed to individuals and organizations around the world. The major products of the system are the magnetic tape service, the *INIS Atomindex,* and the direct availability of the INIS data base on-line from the IAEA computer in Vienna. The magnetic tapes and the on-line service, available to member states and participating organizations only, contain bibliographic descriptions, subject indexing, and abstracts and are utilized for current selective dissemination of information and retrospective searching. The *INIS Atomindex,* an international nuclear abstract journal, is published twice a month and is available to the public on a subscription basis. An additional service is the provision on microfiche of texts of all nonconventional literature submitted to the system. In 2000, INIS membership included 103 countries and 19 international organizations; it reported on over 1,700,000 documents. Beginning in 1992 the INIS data base was made available to INIS member states on CD-ROM disks.

The IAEA also cooperates with FAO in the provision of a similar information system for agriculture, known as *AGRIS.*

A second important information service of the IAEA concerns nuclear data—numerical and associated information on neutron cross-sections, related fission, capture, and scattering parameters of neutron-induced reactions, as well as other nuclear physical constants. The IAEA maintains an efficient system for collection of these data and, together with three other regional centers, in France, the Russian Federation, and the US, issues *CINDA,* an index to the literature on microscopic neutron data. It also compiles *WRENDA,* the world request list for nuclear-data measurements needed both for the development of fission and fusion reactors and for nuclear-material safeguards.

The IAEA plays a leading role in promoting the dissemination of scientific and technical information by organizing each year 15 to 20 conferences, symposia, and seminars and a large number of smaller technical meetings. The IAEA has organized major international meetings dealing with specific aspects of the peaceful uses of nuclear energy. For example, some important 2000 meetings included: International Conference on the Safety of Radioactive Waste Management (Córdoba, Spain); International Symposium on the Uranium Production Cycle and the Environment, (Vienna); 18th IAEA Fusion Energy Conference (Sorrento, Italy); International Symposium on Nuclear Techniques in Integrated Plant Nutrient, Water, and Soil Management (Vienna); International Symposium on Radiation Technology in Emerging Industrial Applications (Beijing); International Conference of

National Regulatory Authorities with Competence in the Safety of Radiation Sources and the Security of Radioactive Materials (Buenos Aires); Seminar on Nuclear Science and Technology for Diplomats (Vienna); Seminar on Nuclear Law; and Latin America International Seminar on Implementation of Systems to Prevent and Detect Unauthorized Uses of Nuclear and Radioactive Materials (Vienna).

C. Research

The International Center for Theoretical Physics, in Trieste, set up by the IAEA in 1964, brings together specialists from developing and developed countries to carry out research and to enable scientists from developing countries to keep abreast of progress without having to leave their own countries permanently or for long periods. Fellowships are awarded to candidates from developing countries for training and research, and an international forum is provided for personal contacts. Associate memberships are awarded by election to enable distinguished physicists to spend one to three months every year at the center. Senior and junior positions are offered by invitation, and a federation scheme is designed to forge a partnership with institutions in developing countries. Assistance has been given by Italy and by the university and city of Trieste. Further aid has come from the Ford Foundation and from UNESCO, which in 1970 undertook joint management of the center.

The IAEA has three laboratories: a small one at its headquarters in Vienna, the main laboratory at Seibersdorf (20 miles from Vienna), and one at Monaco for research on the effects of radioactivity in the sea. The laboratories undertake work in agriculture, hydrology, medicine, physics, chemistry, low-level radioactivity, and environment.

A research contract program has been established with various institutions in member states. The subjects include nuclear power and reactors; physics and chemistry; radioisotope and radiation applications in agriculture, food technology, industry, and medicine; water resources development; protection of humans against ionizing radiation; radiation biology; medical and biological radiation dosimetry; health physics and radiation protection; environmental contamination; and waste treatment and disposal.

To keep abreast of scientific developments, members of the IAEA's scientific staff visit institutions in member states and conduct various studies. The IAEA has made a survey of research trends in the sterilization of food and drugs by ionizing radiation, a problem of considerable interest to both developed and developing countries.

D. Nuclear Power

Nuclear power is already an important source of electrical generation, particularly in industrialized countries, and technically and economically ripe for an even larger application worldwide. As of May 1997, there were 444 nuclear power plants in operation worldwide and 35 additional plants under construction.

In response to the interest of developing countries in nuclear power, the IAEA has played an increasing role in objective nuclear-power planning studies for individual member states. Energy planning methodologies have been developed and made available. The IAEA has cooperated with interested member states in applying these methodologies to specific country cases and in assessing the economic role of nuclear power in meeting increasing requirements for electricity. IAEA efforts to help strengthen infrastructures for the planning, implementation, and operation of nuclear-power projects take the form of interregional and national training courses; technical assistance projects, often in cooperation with the World Bank; advisory missions to interested countries; and the publication of guidebooks.

The IAEA started to collect operating experience data from

nuclear-power plants in the late 1960s and has now established a Power Reactor Information System (PRIS), which monitors the performance of the nuclear-power plants in operation in the world. In addition to performance indices and data on energy production, the system contains information about full and partial plant outages affecting plant operation and about power-reactor operating experience in the world. Periodic publications by the IAEA make this information available to planners and operators in member states. In 1995, a new version, called PRIS-PC, was made available online for direct access through the public telephone network. Internet access became available at the end of 1996.

As an increasing number of countries are interested in the use of nuclear plants for heat-only production and cogeneration (for example, desalination combined with electricity generation), the IAEA periodically reviews progress in this area. In addition, scientific meetings on nuclear power are organized to discuss such matters as economic competitiveness of nuclear power, integration of nuclear-power plants in electric grids, operating experience, introduction of small and medium power reactors, development of fast-breeder and high-temperature reactors, and fusion technology.

E. Nuclear Safety

Although each state is responsible for nuclear safety with regard to nuclear activities within its own territory, nuclear safety is a field in which international cooperation can be very helpful, particularly in developing safety standards and providing assistance. The IAEA's activities in the field of nuclear safety include plant siting and design, the transport of radioactive waste, emergency planning and preparedness, and decommissioning. The IAEA also began work on an historic Nuclear Safety Convention in 1991, the text of which was finalized at a major international conference held in Vienna in June 1994. (See Nuclear Law below.)

The IAEA maintains a 24-hour Emergency Response System (ERS) staffed by 30 emergency duty officers. In 1992 the system underwent its second comprehensive exercise to test procedures developed in support of the conventions on early nuclear accidents signed as a result of the 1986 Chernobyl incident (see below). In addition to periodic comprehensive tests, the communication systems used for notifications and requests for assistance are tested at least once a day.

Regulations for the safe transport of nuclear material were developed by the IAEA in 1961. These were followed by Basic Safety Standards for Radiation Protection, which have been extensively revised in accordance with the new system of dose limitation recommended by the International Commission on Radiological Protection. The revised safety standards, carried out jointly with the ILO, WHO, and the Nuclear Energy Agency of the OECD, mark an important milestone in establishing international standards for radiation protection. In 1992 IAEA published the first in a series of radioactive waste management research abstracts.

The IAEA's Nuclear Safety Standards program provides member states with internationally acceptable safety codes and guides on the many aspects of safety associated with nuclear-power plants. The program, which deals with protection against the harmful effects of ionizing radiations, is based on experience in safety practices gained by countries advanced in nuclear technology. Two types of safety documents—codes of practice and safety guides—are being developed in the areas of government organization, siting, design, operation, and quality assurance of nuclear-power plants. For each area there is a code of practice and a number of related safety guides. The codes outline basic objectives and minimum requirements that must be fulfilled to provide an adequate safety level. The safety guides recommend procedures and acceptable technical solutions to implement the requirements and achieve the objectives of the codes.

In recognition of the increasing emphasis on operational safety, the IAEA initiated the Operational Safety Review Team program in 1983 to assist regulatory authorities in the review of operating nuclear-power plants. The program provides an opportunity for member states to benefit from outside expertise and experience. An Operational Safety Review Team is composed of about 10 experts, including IAEA staff, to cover subject areas common to all reactor types, and consultants to cover those areas that are reactor-specific. Experts from developing countries have frequently been included. The reviews, which take up to three weeks, help provide an international frame of reference for regulatory and operating personnel and also provide the IAEA with valuable insights in regard to updating its regular and technical assistance programs.

Additional highlights of IAEA safety activities are: work on the management of severe accidents and on emergency response; the man-machine interface; probabilistic safety assessment; and advanced safety technology. There is also a nuclear incident reporting system and an International Nuclear Event Scale System (INES). ASSET Missions assess, upon invitation, safety significant events involving nuclear power plants. In recent years, there has been a greater emphasis on evaluation and assistance to improve the safe operation of Eastern European nuclear reactors.

As the number of reactor years of operation increases, the feedback of experience is becoming a valuable means of enhancing safety and reliability. Systematic reporting and evaluation of safety-related events can make it possible to identify necessary plant modifications and develop improved plant procedures. To facilitate the exchange of experience, both the Nuclear Energy Agency of the OECD and the IAEA have established incident reporting systems to collect and examine details of events submitted by national organizations. National coordinators screen accounts of all events, passing on to the OECD and the IAEA the most important data.

Response of the IAEA to the Chernobyl Accident

In response to the accident that occurred in the fourth unit of the Chernobyl nuclear-power station in the USSR on 26 April 1986, resulting in loss of life, injuries, and considerable radioactive releases, the IAEA's Board of Governors met to elaborate proposals for expanded international cooperation in nuclear safety and radiological protection. Through a group of experts who convened in July–August 1986, it prepared drafts of two international conventions on nuclear accidents; at a post-accident review meeting convened by the IAEA in late August, about 600 experts from 62 countries and 21 international organizations discussed a comprehensive report presented by the USSR delegation. In September 1986, a special session of the IAEA's General Conference, attended by delegates from 94 countries and 27 national and international organizations, adopted the two draft conventions: the Convention on Early Notification of a Nuclear Accident and the Convention on Assistance in the Case of a Nuclear Accident or Radiological Emergency. The two conventions were immediately signed by more than 50 countries. By April 1999, the Early Notification Convention had 84 parties. The Accident Assistance Convention had 79 parties. In 1989, the IAEA and many other sister organizations embarked on the International Chernobyl Project, to assess the measures taken to enable people to live safely in areas affected by radioactive contamination. It involved more than 200 experts from 23 countries and marked the beginning of ongoing cooperation between intergovernmental organizations regarding nuclear safety.

In March 1994, an international expert safety assessment team examined the safety situation at Chernobyl, at the invitation of the Ukrainian government. It concluded that there were numerous safety deficiencies in the two units of the plant that remain operational. The team determined that the shelter enclosing the destroyed reactor was experiencing accelerated deterioration. The IAEA recommended to the government of Ukraine that an urgent

Members of the IAEA
(as of 1 December 1999)

Afghanistan	Ecuador	Liberia	Russian Federation
Albania	Egypt	Libyan Arab Jamahiriya	Saudi Arabia
Algeria	El Salvador	Liechtenstein	Senegal
Angola	Estonia	Lithuania	Sierra Leone
Argentina	Ethiopia	Luxembourg	Singapore
Armenia	Finland	Madagascar	Slovakia
Australia	France	Malaysia	Slovenia
Austria	Gabon	Mali	South Africa
Bangladesh	Georgia	Malta	Spain
Belarus	Germany	Marshall Islands	Sri Lanka
Belgium	Ghana	Mauritius	Sudan
Benin	Greece	Mexico	Sweden
Bolivia	Guatemala	Moldova, Republic of	Switzerland
Bosnia and Herzegovina	Haiti	Monaco	Syrian Arab Republic
Brazil	Holy See (Vatican)	Mongolia	Thailand
Bulgaria	Hungary	Morocco	The Former Yugoslav Republic of
Burkina Faso	Iceland	Myanmar	Macedonia
Cambodia	India	Namibia	Tunisia
Cameroon	Indonesia	Netherlands	Turkey
Canada	Iran	New Zealand	Uganda
Chile	Iraq	Nicaragua	Ukraine
China	Ireland	Niger	United Arab Emirates
Colombia	Israel	Nigeria	United Kingdom
Congo, Democratic Republic of	Italy	Norway	United Republic of Tanzania
the	Jamaica	Pakistan	United States
Costa Rica	Japan	Panama	Uruguay
Côte d'Ivoire	Jordan	Paraguay	Uzbekistan
Croatia	Kazakhstan	Peru	Venezuela
Cuba	Kenya	Philippines	Viet Nam
Cyprus	Korea, Republic of	Poland	Yemen
Czech Republic	Kuwait	Portugal	Yugoslavia
Denmark	Latvia	Qatar	Zambia
Dominican Republic	Lebanon	Romania	Zimbabwe

meeting on the situation at the Chernobyl reactor be held, to which the government agreed. At that meeting, the Ukrainian government pleaded severe economic hardship and an impending shortage of energy as a reason to delay closing the damaged plant. It asserted that, with international financial assistance, safety conditions at the plant could be improved. The government also asserted that the output of the Chernobyl station was a least-cost alternative for energy supply in the immediate future. Five new nuclear plants in planning and under construction would not be operational until 1999 at the earliest, and would cost more than US$2 billion to complete. Although a majority of the experts at that meeting wished to see the operation at Chernobyl discontinued, the meeting concluded that no simple, one-step solution to this dangerous problem existed.

F. Radioactive Waste Management

Safe management of radioactive wastes produced in all the stages of the nuclear fuel cycle is essential for the growth of nuclear power. The IAEA has been active since its establishment in all aspects of this field, including the publication of *Safety Series* and *Technical Reports,* which give guidelines and recommendations; the holding of seminars, symposia, and conferences; and the arranging of study tours for the benefit of member states. Major areas currently being studied by the IAEA are underground disposal, waste handling and treatment, and environmental aspects of waste disposal.

Safety standards and codes of practice have been prepared on the management of wastes produced by users of radioactive materials; the management of wastes from the mining and milling of uranium and thorium ores; the disposal of wastes in shallow ground, rock cavities, and deep geological formations; and criteria for underground disposal of wastes.

G. Nuclear Law

From its inception, the IAEA has been faced with the need for international coordination and harmonization of the principles governing third-party liability in the event of nuclear damage. The absence of special legislation might leave injured victims without redress. Great difficulties might arise if different nations were to incorporate different principles and procedures in their legislation concerning third-party liability.

Some steps toward worldwide harmonization of compensation for damage arising from nuclear operations were taken through the adoption of two international conventions: the Brussels Convention on the Liability of Operators of Nuclear Ships (1962) and the Vienna Convention on Civil Liability for Nuclear Damage (1963). These two conventions set the minimum standards concerning the liability of the operator of a nuclear installation or a nuclear ship in the event of accidents occuring during the international transport of nuclear materials.

Another convention was adopted in 1971: the Convention on Civil Liability in the Field of Maritime Carriage of Nuclear Matter, which came into force on 15 July 1975. This convention exonerates shipowners from liability under international maritime law in the case of nuclear damage falling within the purview of the Paris Convention on Third Party Liability in the Field of Nuclear Energy (1960), which came into force in 1968, or the Vienna Convention on Civil Liability for Nuclear Damage (1963), which came into force in 1977, whenever the carriage of nuclear material is involved; it thus eliminates what was previously a serious impediment to sea transport of such material. A joint protocol relating to the application of the Vienna Convention and the Paris Conventions entered into force on 27 April 1992.

The Convention on the Physical Protection of Nuclear Material was adopted on 26 October 1979 at a meeting of governmental representatives held at IAEA headquarters. The convention, which came into force on 9 February 1987, is designed to ensure that the prescribed levels of physical protection are applied to potentially hazardous nuclear materials during international transport.

As already noted, two conventions on nuclear accidents were adopted at a special session of the IAEA's General Conference in September 1986, in the aftermath of the Chernobyl accident in April of that year: the Convention on Early Notification of a Nuclear Accident, which came into force on 27 October 1986; and the Convention on Assistance in the Case of a Nuclear Accident or Radiological Emergency, which came into force on 27 February 1987.

In 1991, in recognition of the interdependence of nations in the nuclear fuel cycle, the General Conference supported the idea of an international nuclear safety convention. A draft convention elaborated by legal and technical experts from more than 50 countries was submitted to the General Conference at that time. In June 1994, delegations from 83 member states and four international organizations met in Vienna to consider and adopt the final text of the International Nuclear Safety Convention. The main features of the convention are the establishment of a reporting system on the implementation by contracting states of the obligations of the convention; the assurance of a proper legislative and regulatory framework to govern the safety of nuclear installations; general safety considerations to reinforce the priority of safety; sufficient financial and human resources; quality assurance; radiation protection, and emergency preparedness. The Nuclear Safety Convention came into force on 24 October 1996. The first review meeting was held in April 1999 in Vienna; it was attended by 45 of the 50 states that had by then ratified the convention.

In conjunction with the increasing number of states embarking on nuclear programs, there has also been a growing awareness of the necessity for establishing both a proper legislative framework and specialized regulations for the licensing and control of nuclear installations. The IAEA has provided advisory services to several developing countries in the framing of statutory and regulatory provisions in such areas as the establishment of competent bodies on atomic energy; radiation and environmental protection; transport of radioactive materials; licensing of nuclear installations; nuclear liability; and nuclear merchant ships.

H. Safeguards

The basic science and technology of nuclear energy are the same for both peaceful and military purposes. Therefore, the IAEA statute requires the agency "to establish and administer safeguards" to ensure that materials, services, equipment, facilities, and information that the IAEA makes available are not used "in such a way as to further any military purpose." Such safeguards may also be applied, "at the request of the parties, to any bilateral or multilateral arrangement, or, at the request of a state, to any of that state's activities in the field of atomic energy."

Under the IAEA safeguards system, which was first developed by the Board of Governors on the basis of these statutory provisions in 1961 and has been continuously revised to cover all major aspects of the fuel cycle, the IAEA exercises its control either over assistance provided directly by it or under its auspices, or over items placed voluntarily under IAEA safeguards by any state or group of states—for instance, over reactors, their fuel, and fuel-reprocessing plants.

A major development greatly affecting the significance of the IAEA's work was the coming into force in 1970 of the Treaty on the Non-Proliferation of Nuclear Weapons (NPT), under which states without nuclear weapons and party thereto agreed to accept IAEA safeguards on all their peaceful nuclear activities.

The objective of safeguards applied under agreements concluded in connection with the NPT is the timely detection of diversion of significant quantities of nuclear material from peaceful nuclear activities for the manufacture of nuclear weapons or other nuclear explosive devices or for purposes unknown, and the deterrence of such diversion by the risk of early detection. This objective is achieved by the independent verification of the findings of the national system of accountancy and control of nuclear materials, which a state without nuclear weapons must establish and maintain under the agreement. IAEA verification is accomplished by material accountancy, containment, and surveillance, including inspections, whose number, intensity, and duration must be kept to the minimum consistent with the effective implementation of safeguards.

The NPT was made permanent in 1995. As of June 1999, it had 187 state parties. With several complementary regional treaties (including the Treaty for the Prohibition of Nuclear Weapons in Latin America, also called the Treaty of Tlatelolco; and the South Pacific Nuclear Free Zone, or Rarotonga Treaty), the NPT provides the foundations of legally binding non-proliferation commitments by countries around the world.

The (1991) discovery of a clandestine nuclear weapons development program in Iraq after the Gulf War, however, demonstrated the limitations of the IAEA safeguards system to detect possible undeclared nuclear activities. This discovery—along with the emergence of new countries with new security perceptions at the end of the Cold War, and the 1996 report that the Democratic People's Republic of Korea was not in compliance with its obligations under the NPT safeguards agreement—was viewed as a call to action by IAEA member states. By mid-1997 a strengthened safeguards system was put in place to provide the international community with early warning about the possible diversion or clandestine production of nuclear materials that could be used for weapons purposes. At that time, the IAEA stated that the strength of the safeguards system depended on three interrelated elements: the extent to which the IAEA is aware of the nature and locations of nuclear and nuclear-related activities; the extent to which IAEA inspectors have physical access to relevant locations for the purpose of providing independent verification of the exclusively peaceful intent of a state's nuclear program; and the will of the international community, through IAEA access to the United Nations Security Council, to take action against States that are not complying with their non-proliferation commitments.

The IAEA also applies safeguards to some of the peaceful nuclear activities in five nuclear-weapon states—China, France, the Russian Federation, the United Kingdom, and the United States—under voluntary offer agreements.

In spite of the hundreds of safeguards in place at nuclear facilities worldwide, as the 21st century dawned, a group of "threshold" states (including India, Israel, and Pakistan) challenged the safeguards system. These are states that have not joined NPT nor have they accepted "comprehensive" IAEA safeguards, but have well-developed nuclear programs and the technological capability to build nuclear explosive devices.

BIBLIOGRAPHY

INIS Atomindex. Bimonthly.
International Atomic Energy Agency Bulletin. Quarterly.
IAEA Bulletin. Quarterly.
Meetings on Atomic Energy. Quarterly.
Nuclear Fusion Journal. Monthly.
Nuclear Safety Review. Issued annually.
Safety Series. Manuals on the safe handling and transport of radioactive materials, monitoring of personnel, and disposal of radioactive wastes.
(For more information on IAEA publications, visit their web site http://www.iaea.org/worldatom/Books/ and http://www.iaea.org/worldatom/Periodicals/.)

THE INTERNATIONAL LABOR ORGANIZATION (ILO)

BACKGROUND: The ILO is the only major organization originally part of the League of Nations system that has existed from the founding of the League in 1919 down to the present day. Its name is actually too narrow, for it is an organization neither of nor for labor alone. As the late James T. Shotwell, president emeritus of the Carnegie Endowment for International Peace, pointed out long ago, the ILO might more accurately have been termed an International Organization for Social Justice. Furthermore, as the organization's responsibilities have widened, it has given increasing attention to measures designed to help raise general standards of living. Its work now even includes activities such as productivity training courses for management personnel and high government. Michel Hansenne, Director General of the ILO from 1989 to 1999, said, "Employment—the best possible employment for all—has always been, and will remain, the principal objective of our Organization, whose mission is to link economic growth, social justice and the creation and distribution of wealth."

CREATION

The International Labor Organization (ILO) was created by the 1919 Peace Conference that followed World War I. Its original constitution, which formed part of the Treaty of Versailles, established it on 11 April 1919 as an autonomous organization associated with the League of Nations.

A statement made in the constitution's preamble—"Conditions of labor exist involving such injustice, hardship, and privation to large numbers of people as to produce unrest so great that the peace and harmony of the world are imperilled"—was not mere rhetoric. World War I had shaken many countries to their foundations. The revolution in Russia had succeeded. All over the world there was labor unrest, and the conviction of the need to improve the lot of working people was by no means limited to labor itself. Organized labor, however, had been especially active during the war in demanding that the peace treaty include recognition of the rights of labor and that labor be given a voice in international matters. The American Federation of Labor (AFL) and other powerful trade-union bodies demanded in particular an international organization of labor that would wield "tremendous authority."

At the 1919 Paris Peace Conference, the president of the AFL, Samuel Gompers, was chairman of the conference's Commission on Labor Legislation. The Peace Conference, instead of establishing an international organization of labor, created an organization in which labor, employers, and governments were to be represented on an equal footing. As so constituted, the ILO was, and still is, unique among international governmental organizations—the only one in which private citizens, namely representatives of labor and of employers, have the same voting and other rights as are possessed by governments.

The ILO's principal function was to establish international labor and social standards through the drafting and adoption of international labor conventions. Prior to the existence of the ILO, only two international labor conventions had been adopted: one, designed to protect the health of workers in match factories, prohibited the use of white phosphorus, a poison, in the manufacture of matches; the other prescribed modest restrictions on night work by women. Neither of these was widely ratified. By contrast, more than 182 international labor conventions and 190 recommendations have been adopted by the ILO since 1919. International labor standards are used as a benchmark by which the rights and conditions of human beings have been measured.

PURPOSES

The aims and objectives of the ILO were set forth in the preamble to its constitution, drawn up in 1919. The preamble declares that "universal and lasting peace can be established only if it is based upon social justice." Hence, the basic objective of the organization is to help improve social conditions throughout the world. The following examples of concrete measures "urgently required" are specifically mentioned in the preamble: regulation of the hours of work, including the establishment of a maximum working day and week; regulation of the labor supply; prevention of unemployment; provision of an adequate living wage; protection of the worker against sickness, disease, and injury arising out of his employment; protection of children, young persons, and women; provision for old age and injury; protection of the interests of workers when employed in countries other than their own; recognition of the principle of equal remuneration for work of equal value; and recognition of the principle of freedom of association.

International action in these matters is required, the preamble makes clear, because "the failure of any nation to adopt humane conditions of labor is an obstacle in the way of other nations which desire to improve the conditions in their own countries." Finally, in agreeing to the ILO constitution, the member governments declare in the preamble that they are "moved by sentiments of justice and humanity as well as by the desire to secure the permanent peace of the world."

Meeting in Philadelphia in 1944, the International Labor Conference adopted a declaration that rephrased and broadened the "aims and purposes" of the ILO and "the principles which should inspire the policy of its members." President Roosevelt stated that the Declaration of Philadelphia, as it was called, summed up the aspirations of an epoch that had known two world wars and that it might well acquire a historical significance comparable to that of the US Declaration of Independence. The declaration, which was incorporated into the amended constitution of the ILO, affirms that labor is not a commodity; that freedom of expression and association are essential to sustained progress; that poverty anywhere constitutes a danger to prosperity everywhere; and that the war against want must be carried on not only with unrelenting vigor within each nation but also by "continuous and concerted international effort in which the representatives of workers and employers, enjoying equal status with those of Governments, join with them in free discussion and democratic decision with a view to the promotion of the common welfare."

The Declaration of Philadelphia recognizes the "solemn obligation" of the ILO to further among nations of the world programs that will achieve the following:

- full employment and the raising of standards of living;
- employment of workers in the occupations for which they are best suited and where they can make their greatest contribution to the common well-being;
- facilities for training and the transfer of labor, including migration for employment and settlement;
- policies in regard to wages and earnings, hours, and other conditions of work calculated to ensure a just share of the fruits of progress to all and a minimum living wage to all employed and in need of such protection;
- effective recognition of the right of collective bargaining, the cooperation of management and labor in the continuous improvement of productive efficiency, and the collaboration of workers and employers in the preparation and application of social and economic measures;
- extension of social security measures to provide a basic income to all in need of such protection and comprehensive medical care;
- adequate protection for the life and health of workers in all occupations;
- child welfare and maternity protection;
- adequate nutrition, housing, and facilities for recreation and culture; and
- assurance of equality of educational and vocational opportunity.

Since 1994 the ILO has been involved in a process of modernizing and strengthening its labor standards system.

MEMBERSHIP

Originally, ILO membership was identical with League of Nations membership, since adherence to the League carried with it participation in the ILO. However, several countries that were not members of the League were admitted to the ILO, notably the US, which joined in 1934. In 1946, the ILO became the first specialized agency associated with the UN. The constitution of the ILO now provides that any nation that is a member of the UN can become a member of the ILO by unilaterally notifying the Director General that it accepts the obligations of the ILO constitution. Other nations may be admitted to ILO membership by a two-thirds vote of the International Labor Conference.

The ILO constitution originally made no provision for the expulsion of a member. However, two amendments adopted by the International Labor Conference in 1964 would have empowered the ILO membership, by a two-thirds vote, to expel or suspend any member that had been expelled or suspended by the UN or that had been found by the UN to be flagrantly and persistently pursuing by its legislation a policy of racial discrimination. The amendments were adopted in response to South Africa's policy of apartheid. These amendments never came into force for lack of ratifications. However, in 1972, the conference adopted another Instrument of Amendment about expulsions, which came into force on 1 November 1974.

A state may withdraw from the ILO by formal notification of its intent to do so, such withdrawal to be effective two years after ILO receives the notification. Germany, one of the original members, withdrew in 1935. South Africa notified the organization of its intent to withdraw before the amendments that could have led to its expulsion were adopted. Its withdrawal became effective on

11 March 1966. South Africa rejoined the ILO on 26 May 1994. Albania withdrew in 1967. Vietnam withdrew in 1985, but rejoined in 1992. Fourteen other countries withdrew their membership at various times (11 of them during the World War II period), but all sooner or later rejoined the organization. The rules that govern original admission to membership also apply to readmission.

In November 1975, the US filed a two-year notice of intent to withdraw, stating at the same time that it did not desire or expect to leave the ILO but hoped to help the ILO "return to basic principles." US Secretary of State Henry Kissinger said that the ILO had been "falling back" in four fundamental areas: workers' and employers' groups in the ILO falling under the domination of governments; an "appallingly selective" concern for human rights; "disregard of due process" in condemning member states "which happen to be the political target of the moment"; and "increasing politicization of the organization." The notice of intent to withdraw was allowed to run its course, thereby ending US membership in the ILO in November 1977. On the return of the US to membership in February 1980, President Jimmy Carter said: "As a member of the ILO and with the support of other countries, the United States will seek to ensure that the ILO continues to serve the interests of the world's working men and women by promoting more and better jobs while protecting human rights and dignity."

As of January 2000, the ILO had 174 members.

STRUCTURE

The principal organs of the ILO are the International Labor Conference, the Governing Body, and the International Labor Office, headed by a Director General.

International Labor Conference

The International Labor Conference is the organization's policy-making and legislative body, in which every member state is represented. It holds one session a year at ILO headquarters in Geneva.

Each member country sends to the International Labor Conference a national delegation consisting of four delegates. Two represent the government, one represents the country's employers, and one represents the country's workers. Alternates and advisers may be sent as well. Each delegate has one independent vote. Discussing this system of tripartite representation in 1959, the Director General noted that the ILO is "the only intergovernmental agency in whose work nongovernment delegates take part on an equal footing with government representatives as a matter of constitutional right. Representatives of employers' and workers' organizations are included in its policy-making, standard-setting, and executive machinery and participate, with full voting rights, in all these aspects of its work."

The government, employers', and workers' representatives to the conference act in many respects as three separate groups, functioning somewhat as political parties function in a national legislature: the three groups meet separately for informal discussions of strategy; they hold caucuses; and, voting separately, they elect the government, the employers', and the workers' delegates to the Governing Body and to tripartite committees. If the tripartite system is to function as intended, it is essential that employers' and workers' delegates be true representatives of their respective groups. The ILO constitution provides that governments must appoint these delegates in agreement with the "most representative" organizations of employers or workers "if such organizations exist."

Governing Body

The Governing Body is the executive council of the ILO. It is composed of 56 titular members (14 representing employers, 14

Members of the ILO

(as of 26 January 2000)

Afghanistan	Denmark	Lao People's Democratic Republic	St. Kitts and Nevis
Albania	Djibouti	Latvia	St. Lucia
Algeria	Dominica	Lebanon	St. Vincent and the Grenadines
Angola	Dominican Republic	Lesotho	San Marino
Antigua and Barbuda	Ecuador	Liberia	Sâo Tomé and Principe
Argentina	Egypt	Libyan Arab Jamahiriya	Saudi Arabia
Armenia	El Salvador	Lithuania	Senegal
Australia	Equatorial Guinea	Luxembourg	Seychelles
Austria	Eritrea	Macedonia, Former Yugoslav	Sierra Leone
Azerbaijan	Estonia	Republic of	Singapore
Bahamas	Ethiopia	Madagascar	Slovakia
Bahrain	Fiji	Malawi	Slovenia
Bangladesh	Finland	Malaysia	Solomon Islands
Barbados	France	Mali	Somalia
Belarus	Gabon	Malta	South Africa
Belgium	Gambia	Mauritania	Spain
Belize	Georgia	Mauritius	Sri Lanka
Benin	Germany	Mexico	Sudan
Bolivia	Ghana	Moldova, Republic of	Suriname
Bosnia and Herzegovina	Greece	Mongolia	Swaziland
Botswana	Grenada	Morocco	Sweden
Brazil	Guatemala	Mozambique	Switzerland
Bulgaria	Guinea	Myanmar	Syrian Arab Republic
Burkina Faso	Guinea-Bissau	Namibia	Tajikistan
Burundi	Guyana	Nepal	Tanzania, United Republic of
Cambodia	Haiti	Netherlands	Thailand
Cameroon	Honduras	New Zealand	Togo
Canada	Hungary	Nicaragua	Trinidad and Tobago
Cape Verde	Iceland	Niger	Tunisia
Central African Republic	India	Nigeria	Turkey
Chad	Indonesia	Norway	Turkmenistan
Chile	Iran, Islamic Republic of	Oman	Uganda
China	Iraq	Pakistan	Ukraine
Colombia	Ireland	Panama	United Arab Emirates
Comoros	Israel	Papua New Guinea	United Kingdom
Congo	Italy	Paraguay	United States
Congo, Democratic Republic of	Jamaica	Peru	Uruguay
the	Japan	Philippines	Uzbekistan
Costa Rica	Jordan	Poland	Venezuela
Côte d'Ivoire	Kazakhstan	Portugal	Vietnam
Croatia	Kenya	Qatar	Yemen
Cuba	Korea, Republic of	Romania	Yugoslavia
Cyprus	Kuwait	Russian Federation	Zambia
Czech Republic	Kyrgyzstan	Rwanda	Zimbabwe

representing workers, and 28 representing governments) and 66 deputy members (19 representing employers, 19 representing workers, and 28 representing governments).

Members of the Governing Body are elected by the corresponding groups in the International Labor Conference, except that 10 of the government representatives are appointed by countries that do not participate in the election of the other government representatives since these 10 countries are entitled to permanent seats as "states of chief industrial importance." The 10 governments permanently represented on the Governing Body are Brazil, China, France, Germany, India, Italy, Japan, the Russian Federation, the United Kingdom, and the United States of America. The remaining government members, elected for three years by the 1999 conference were from Africa—Algeria, Burkina Faso, Chad, Ethiopia, Ghana, Namibia; from the Americas—Canada, Guatemala, Peru, Trinidad and Tobago, Venezuela; from Asia—Islamic Republic of Iran, Republic of Korea, Malaysia, Saudi Arabia; and from Europe—Croatia, Slovakia, Switzerland.

The 14 employers' representatives on the governing body, elected for three years by the 1999 conference, included leading industrialists from Argentina, Australia, Brazil, France, Germany,

Japan, Kenya, Norway, Pakistan, Saudi Arabia, Senegal, Tunisia, United Kingdom, and United States.

The 14 members of the workers' group, elected in 1999 for three years, were ranking trade union officials from Australia, Brazil, Canada, Congo, Germany, Japan, Malaysia, Czech Republic, United States, Sweden, Tunisia, United Kingdom, Venezuela, and Zimbabwe.

Under amendments to the ILO constitution adopted by the International Labor Conference in 1986—to become effective when ratified or accepted by two-thirds of the members, including 5 of the 10 permanent members of the Governing Body—the members of the Governing Body will be increased to 112 (56 representing governments, 28 representing employers, and 28 representing workers) and the 10 permanent seats will be eliminated. As of 2000, this amendment had not yet entered into force.

Meeting several times a year, the Governing Body coordinates and in many ways shapes the work of the organization. It draws up the agenda for each session of the International Labor Conference; while the conference is empowered to change this agenda, it rarely does. The Governing Body appoints the Director-General of the International Labor Office. It examines the proposed budget submitted to it each year by the Director-General and approves it for adoption by the conference. The Governing Body also is responsible for convening the scores of other conference and committee meetings held under ILO auspices every year in various parts of the world and decides what action ought to be taken on their resolutions and reports.

International Labor Office and Director-General

The International Labor Office in Geneva, headed by the Director-General, is the ILO's headquarters and its permanent secretariat. In April 2000, its staff consisted of about 1,900 persons from more than 110 countries in Geneva and in 40 field offices.

During World War II, when for a time Switzerland was entirely surrounded by Axis forces, the International Labor Office and a skeleton staff were temporarily moved to Montreal, where, thanks to the hospitality of the Canadian government and McGill University, the office was able to continue its more urgent work.

The International Labor Office services the sessions of the conference, the Governing Body, and the various subsidiary organs and committees. It prepares the documents for these meetings; publishes periodicals, studies, and reports; and collects and distributes information on all subjects within the ILO's competence. As directed by the conference and the Governing Body, it carries out ILO operational programs that have been decided on in various fields.

The ILO has had nine Directors General—Albert Thomas, France, 1919–32; Harold Butler, UK, 1932–38; John G. Winant, US, 1939–41; Edward J. Phelan, Ireland, 1941–48; David A. Morse, US, 1948–70; Wilfred Jenks, UK, 1970–73; Francis Blanchard, France, 1973–89; Michel Hansenne, Belgium, 1989–99; Juan Somavia, Chile, 1999 to present.

THE ISSUE OF INDEPENDENT WORKER AND EMPLOYER REPRESENTATION

Since its early days, the ILO has been troubled by a basic constitutional issue: can the organization, without violating its own principles, countenance the seating of workers' and employers' delegates from countries where workers' and employers' organizations are not free from domination or control by the government?

Challenges to the Credentials of Workers

When, in the early 1920s, a member of the Italian Fascist labor corporations appeared at Geneva to take his seat as the workers' member of the Italian delegation to the ILO, his credentials were challenged, though unsuccessfully, by the workers' group, which maintained that he was not a true spokesman for Italian labor. Every session of the conference from 1923 to 1938 saw the credentials of one or more workers' delegates challenged on the grounds that these delegates did not represent an independent labor point of view. Among them were workers' delegates from Austria, Bulgaria, Germany, Greece, Italy, Latvia, Lithuania, and Poland. In all cases, however, the delegates were seated.

Since World War II, the conference has on several occasions actually refused to seat a workers' delegate whose credentials had been challenged. In 1945, it refused to seat the workers' delegate chosen by the Perón regime in Argentina on the ground that workers' organizations in Argentina did not at that time enjoy freedom of association, action, or speech. In 1950, it refused to seat the workers' delegate appointed by the government of Venezuela on the ground that the delegate could not have been nominated in agreement with the country's most representative workers' associations since the government had at that time dissolved all trade unions. Challenges to the credentials of Argentinian and Venezuelan workers' delegates on other occasions were overruled by the credentials committee, however, as was a 1955 challenge to the credentials of the Chilean workers' delegate.

The Question of Employers' Delegates from Communist Countries

Much greater difficulties arose in the past over the seating of employers' delegates from former communist countries. When the first employers' delegate from the USSR, Mr. Kaoulin of the People's Commissariat of Water Transport, appeared at the 1936 maritime conference, the employers' group acquiesced in his seating but requested an examination of the constitutional questions involved. A study duly carried out by the International Labor Office concluded that the ILO constitution did not require an employer to be a private person and that in countries where the state was the chief employer, it was for the state to choose the employers' delegate. The employers' group at the conference voted unanimously to reject this interpretation.

At the 1945 International Labor Conference, held in Paris shortly after the end of World War II, two constitutional amendments were proposed that aimed at increasing the size of the national delegations so as to give representation to both the public and private sectors of the economy. Both proposed amendments were, for a variety of reasons, rejected by the conference. The employers' group, however, issued a declaration stating that if the USSR, which had withdrawn from the ILO in 1940, were to resume membership, "it would naturally appoint as employers' delegates a representative of the socialized management of the USSR."

At the 1953 conference, the employers' group challenged the credentials of the Czechoslovakian employers' delegate and, when the USSR did rejoin the organization in 1954, challenged those of the Soviet employers' delegate as well. On both occasions, the group was overruled by the credentials committee, which held that the delegates in question performed executive and managerial functions corresponding to those normally exercised by employers under other economic systems.

When the Governing Board met in November 1954, it was sharply divided on the question of employers' delegates from countries with nationalized economies. In hopes of facilitating a compromise, it appointed a special fact-finding committee, headed by Sir Arnold McNair, former president of the International Court of Justice, to report on the "extent of the freedom of employers' and workers' organizations" in ILO member countries "from government domination or control." The lengthy report, which the committee submitted in February 1956, was based on a study of the situation in 59 countries, including five in the Soviet bloc.

The report recognized at the outset that the unique feature of the ILO—cooperation among representatives of government, employers, and workers—could only be meaningful if the latter represented their constituents in the true sense of the word and had the right "to speak and vote freely without government control." On the other hand, the report noted, major changes had occurred in the economic structure of many countries since 1919, with governments participating in their countries' economic and social life in a wide variety of new ways. The ILO had long maintained that the principle of freedom of association is violated if the right to organize is subject to government authorization. However, the report found, the constitutions of no less than 21 ILO countries subjected the right of association to statutory regulation.

The Hungarian uprising of 1956 had sharp repercussions in the ILO, which were reflected in the credentials dispute. The Governing Body expressed solidarity with the Hungarian workers "who were struggling to secure their fundamental rights," and the 1957 International Labor Conference rejected the credentials of the employers' and workers' delegates appointed by the Kádár government, which had, in effect, restored the Hungarian status quo ante. In 1958 and 1959, the conference took the unprecedented step of not only rejecting the credentials of the Hungarian workers' and employers' delegates, but also refusing admission to the government delegates.

In the meantime, various attempts were made to find a general solution to the problem that would satisfy all concerned, including the Western employers' delegates. Involved in the problem was the fact that, under the International Labor Conference rules, each group—government, employers, and workers—could refuse to seat delegates whose credentials it did not accept. In 1959, acting on a plan proposed by a tripartite committee headed by Roberto Ago of Italy, the ILO established a five-member Appeals Board composed of persons of "internationally recognized independence and impartiality" to rule on such matters.

The demise of the Soviet bloc in the late 1980s heralded the arrival of a new era of consensus. Now that so many formerly communist governments no longer adhere to a managed economy, challenges to credentials are much less significant.

BUDGET

The ILO's activities are financed by a biennial budget fixed by the International Labor Conference and raised from the governments of member states according to a scale of contributions approved by the conference. The scale ranges from 0.01% for 86 least developed countries (LDCs) to 4.21% for the Russian Federation, 8.93% for Germany, 15.43% for Japan, and 25% for the US. In addition, the ILO receives for its technical assistance programs a share of the funds raised from voluntary government contributions to UNDP.

A net expenditure budget of US$481.05 million was adopted for 1998–99.

ACTIVITIES

A. International Labor Standards

One of the principal achievements of the ILO has been the formulation of an extensive international labor code through the drafting and adoption of various standard-setting conventions and recommendations. The first international convention adopted was the 1919 Hours of Work Convention, establishing the eight-hour day and the six-day week in industry.

A convention is similar to an international treaty and is subject to ratification. Recommendations do not require ratification. They serve as guidelines for national policy.

By 2000, the various sessions of the International Labor Conference had built up the edifice of the international labor code through the adoption of 182 conventions and 190 recommendations, covering such questions as the following:

- employment and unemployment: employment services, national development programs, and provisions for unemployment;
- various aspects of conditions of work: wages, hours, weekly rest periods, annual holidays with pay, and allied topics;
- employment of children and young persons: minimum age of admission to employment, medical examination for fitness for employment, vocational training and apprenticeship, and night work;
- employment of women: maternity protection, night work, and employment in unhealthy work;
- industrial health, safety, and welfare;
- social security;
- industrial (i.e., management-labor) relations;
- labor inspection;
- social policy in nonmetropolitan areas and concerning indigenous and tribal populations;
- protection of migrants; and
- trade unionism and collective bargaining.

At first, the effort to build up minimum labor and social standards that would be internationally valid was considered by many as utopian. In these fields, international action used to be virtually unknown. But the freely accepted conventions and recommendations and the ILO machinery of mutual supervision have helped to improve working conditions and management-labor relations, protect the fundamental rights of labor, promote social security, and lessen the frequency and intensity of labor conflicts.

The international labor code is continually being revised and extended, not only to broaden its scope but also to keep pace with advancing concepts of social and economic welfare. The following conventions represent the heart and soul of the organization's commitment to its mandate to social justice:

Selected ILO Conventions

NUMBER	NAME
No. 29	Forced Labor Convention (1930)
No. 87	Freedom of Association and Protection of the Right to Organize (1948)
No. 98	Right to Organize and Collective Bargaining Convention (1949)
No. 100	Equal Remuneration Convention (1951)
No. 105	Abolition of Forced Labor Convention (1957)
No. 111	Discrimination (Employment and Occupation) Convention (1958)
No. 122	Employment Policy Convention (1964)
No. 135	Workers' Representatives Convention (1971)
No. 141	Rural Workers' Organizations Convention (1978)
No. 144	Tripartite Consultation (International Labor Standards) Convention (1976)
No. 151	Labor Relations (Public Service) (1978)
No. 155	Occupational Safety and Health Convention (1981)
No. 169	Indigenous and Tribal Peoples Convention (1989)
No. 174	Prevention of Major Industrial Accidents Convention (1993)
No. 182	Worst Forms of Child Labor Convention (1999)

Other important conventions are, for example, the 1960 convention and a recommendation on the protection of workers against ionizing radiations. These instruments, in essence, provide for the establishment of maximum permissible doses and amounts of radioactive substances that may be taken into the body. Appropriate radiation levels are fixed for workers over 16. Under these international instruments, workers under 16 are prohibited from working in direct contact with ionizing radiations.

In pursuit of ILO efforts to help extend the scope of social security coverage throughout the world and eliminate discrimination based upon nationality, the 1962 International Labor Conference adopted a convention on the equal treatment of nationals and non-nationals in social security. Under this convention, a ratifying country shall give to nationals of other ratifying countries, within its territory, equal treatment with its own nationals under its social security legislation. Countries may accept the obligations of the convention in any or all of the following types of social security: medical care, sickness benefits, maternity benefits, unemployment benefits, and family allowances.

The adoption of protective standard measures against occupationally caused cancer was taken up at the 1974 session of the International Labor Conference. Two international agreements were drawn up, aimed at limiting the use and the adverse effects of carcinogenic (cancer-causing) substances and strengthening protective measures to be used against them.

In 1983, a convention was adopted on the rights of handicapped people, aimed at increasing employment opportunities for the disabled. In 1986, a convention to protect workers against serious risks from the use of asbestos was adopted.

The following recommendations are representative of the ILO's work during the last two decades of the 20th century.

No. 175 Safety and Health in Construction Recommendation (1988)
No. 176 Employment Promotion and Protection against Unemployment Recommendation (1988)
No. 177 Chemicals Recommendation (1990)
No. 178 Night Work Recommendation (1990)
No. 179 Working Conditions in Hotels, Restaurants and Similar Establishments (1991)
No. 180 Protection of Workers' Claims in the Event of the Insolvency of Their Employer (1992)
No. 181 Prevention of Major Industrial Accidents (1993)
No. 184 Home Work Recommendation (1996)
No. 188 Private Employment Agencies Recommendation (1997)

For a complete listing of ILO conventions, visit their Internet site www.ilo.org. Recommendations are also listed at the site.

B. Obligation of Members after Adoption of International Labor Standards

The ILO, it should be borne in mind, is not a world lawgiver. The International Labor Conference cannot pass legislation that by itself is binding on any country. However, ingenious arrangements have been written into the ILO constitution to make sure that conventions and recommendations adopted by the International Labor Conference are not regarded as mere pious pronouncements. Member governments must report back to the ILO on the measures they have taken to bring the ILO convention or recommendation before their competent legislative authorities, and they must also keep the ILO informed of decisions made by those authorities.

Supervision of Application of Ratified Conventions

Once a convention has been ratified and has come into force, every country that ratified it is obligated to take all necessary measures to make its provisions effective.

By ratifying a convention, a country automatically agrees to report every year to the International Labor Office on how the convention is being applied in its territory. These reports are much more than a formality. For each convention, the Governing Body formulates a number of questions that include requests for information on the results of labor inspection, relevant court decisions, and statistics on the number of persons covered. Copies of each annual report prepared by a government are to be sent to the country's most representative employers' and workers' organizations, and the report, as finally submitted to the ILO, has to state whether the government has received any comments from them on the practical implementation of the convention in question.

These annual reports on the application of ratified conventions are first considered by a committee of independent experts and then by an employer-worker-government committee, which in turn reports to the full International Labor Conference. The object of this whole system of supervision is to enable the conference to determine what progress has been made in implementing the standards set forth in the conventions. On the basis of the intelligence it receives, the conference may, if it feels this to be necessary, make "observations" to governments, that is, suggest to them ways in which they may overcome discrepancies between the provisions of the conventions that they have ratified and existing national laws or practices.

The effectiveness of this supervisory machinery depends, naturally, on the cooperation of member governments in submitting their annual reports. On the whole, an increasing number of governments have been living up to their obligations in this respect. If required reports are not forthcoming or if the reports submitted by certain countries are not really informative, the ILO supervi-

sory committees express their dissatisfaction in polite but quite unmistakable terms. These criticisms are included in the printed reports of the committees and may occasion debates in the conference itself, thus giving the matter further publicity.

The ILO constitution provides two other procedures that may be followed to induce governments to carry out the provisions of conventions that they have ratified. First, workers' or employers' organizations may make representations to the International Labor Office if they believe that any government, even their own, has failed to live up to a convention that it has ratified. If the government concerned fails to provide a satisfactory answer to the allegation, the Governing Body may decide to publish the allegation and, if one has been submitted, the government reply. Second, any ILO member government may file a complaint against any other member for alleged noncompliance with a ratified convention. The ILO constitution provides that, in this event, a commission of inquiry shall examine the matter, report on its findings, and recommend such remedial steps as it thinks proper. The fact that the ILO constitution provides for specific machinery to take up such complaints itself has contributed to the observance of ratified international labor conventions on the part of member governments.

In his report to the 81st ILC in 1994, Director-General Michel Hansenne reported that in the preceding 30 years, close to 2,000 cases of progress were recorded by supervisory bodies. "That means 2,000 situations in which national legislation and policy have been brought into line with the requirements of ratified Conventions," said the Director-General.

Reports on Recommendations and Unratified Conventions

Recommendations adopted by the International Labor Conference, unlike the conventions that it adopts, are not international treaties and are not subject to ratification. Hence, these recommendations can never be binding on a member government in the sense that the provisions of a ratified convention are binding. Nevertheless, the recommendations constitute an important part of the international labor code, and, since 1948, the Governing Body of the ILO has had the right to ask member governments periodically to what extent they have given or intend to give effect to conventions not ratified and to recommendations. In such case, the governments also have to state the reasons that have so far prevented or delayed the ratification of conventions and the modification of national law and practices according to recommendations.

Ratifications

The number of ratifications that a given convention has received is not, in itself, an accurate measure of its acceptance or impact. The fact that a convention has not been ratified by a particular country does not necessarily mean that that country has not met the standards prescribed in the convention. The UK, for example, advised the ILO that it did not intend to propose parliamentary ratification of the convention requiring a minimum 24-hour weekly rest period for commercial and office workers. It explained that such workers in the UK were already assured a rest period of at least that length through established custom and that it was not the policy of the government to intervene in matters that had already been satisfactorily settled by the parties concerned.

New Zealand, which in many ways has pioneered in labor legislation, waited until 1938 to ratify the eight-hour-day, six-day-week convention of 1919. At the same time, New Zealand also ratified the more restrictive 40-hour-week convention of 1935 and, in fact, remained for 18 years the only country ratifying it. Ratifications may be withheld for various reasons by a country for a number of years, after which a number of ratifications may be approved at once. Thus, in 1962 alone, Peru ratified 31 different international labor conventions.

Very often, countries do not ratify conventions on subjects

that they feel do not concern them. The various maritime conventions, for example, are primarily of interest to nations with sizable merchant marine fleets. Occasionally, however, countries as a matter of principle ratify conventions on conditions quite alien to them. Thus, Switzerland ratified the 1957 Convention on the Abolition of Forced Labor on the recommendation of the Swiss Federal Council, which called for ratification because of the convention's humanitarian significance, although "forced labor in any of the forms mentioned in the Convention has never existed in Switzerland."

For a growing number of workers in an increasing number of countries, wages, working conditions, vacations, and so-called fringe benefits are being determined not through government legislation but through collective bargaining. The international standards embodied in the ILO's conventions, even though they may not show on the statute books, frequently serve as guides for labor-management agreements. The widening impact of ILO standards owes much to the various arrangements that have been worked out to make the provisions of the international labor code more widely known to employers' and workers' organizations.

The significance of the sharply increased rate at which governments have been ratifying ILO conventions since 1960 is very great. Ratification, particularly in a developing country, regularly signifies a step forward.

C. The ILO as a Promoter of Human Rights
Freedom of Association

World War II stimulated the growth of trade unions and increased their responsibilities. In many countries, labor was recognized as an equal partner in the effort that won the war. Nevertheless, in various parts of the world, the position of unions was far from secure, and in many countries, such a basic freedom as the worker's right to join a union of his choice was respected neither in law nor in practice.

In 1948, the International Labor Conference adopted the Convention on Freedom of Association and the Right to Organize, and in 1949, it adopted the Convention on the Right to Organize and Collective Bargaining. These conventions stipulate that all workers and employers shall possess the right to establish and join organizations of their own choosing without having to obtain government authorization. Such organizations shall have the right to function freely and without interference from public authorities; they may be dissolved or suspended only by normal judicial procedure and never by administrative authority. Workers must be protected against discrimination on the grounds of union membership or activities; thus, a worker may not be discharged because he joins or is active in a union. Employers and workers must not interfere in the establishment or operation of one another's organizations; this provision outlaws such devices as employer-dominated unions. By June 1994, the first of the two conventions had been ratified by 108 countries and the second by 121.

The ILO Committee on Freedom of Association (CFA) has recorded a dramatic rise in the numbers of complaints lodged under this convention: before 1990 a total of 61 complaints were received; 49 complaints were received in 1990 alone. In total, the CFA handles hundreds of cases each year. Cases are received even when the government concerned has not ratified the ILO's freedom of association convention.

The ILO has been particularly concerned with safeguarding the rights enumerated in these two conventions. It has made full use of its regular procedure to ascertain whether all member states have presented the conventions to the appropriate domestic authorities for ratification and to supervise the implementation of the conventions by states that have ratified them. In addition, the International Labor Conference has conducted reviews concerning the extent to which member states, whether bound by the conventions or not, have put their provisions into effect.

In 1969, a special review was made, in connection with the 50th anniversary of the ILO, of the problems and prospects of ratification of 17 key conventions. Special bodies were set up to deal with complaints against governments for violation of trade-union rights: a committee of the Governing Body, known as the Committee on Freedom of Association, composed of government, employer, and worker representatives; and the quasi-judicial Fact-Finding and Conciliation Commission, composed of nine independent persons serving as individuals. The Fact-Finding and Conciliation Commission is authorized to make on-the-scene investigations, but it cannot consider a case unless the government concerned gives its consent. Japan, in 1964, was the first to do so; Greece was the second, in 1965. The government-employer-worker Committee on Freedom of Association, however, not being a semi-judicial body, may consider complaints whether or not the government concerned gives its consent.

Feeling that fuller factual information was needed about conditions in various countries affecting freedom of association, the ILO Governing Body decided in 1958 to inaugurate a worldwide survey to be carried out through on-the-spot studies. The first country to invite such a survey was the US; the second was the USSR. An ILO survey mission visited both countries in 1959. At the invitation of the governments of Sweden, the United Kingdom, Burma, and Malaya, surveys on freedom of association in those countries were made in 1960 and 1961.

The Committee on Freedom of Association considered complaints of infringements of trade union rights in Poland following the proclamation of martial law in that country in December 1981 and in response to measures taken against the Solidarity trade union. In November 1982, the Governing Body urged the Polish government to lift martial law; it noted with deep concern that the government had dissolved all existing trade unions, including Solidarity, and deplored the fact that fundamental provisions of the new Polish labor law did not conform with ILO principles of freedom of association and collective bargaining. A commission of inquiry set up by the ILO in 1983 reported in the following year that Poland had infringed trade union rights laid down in two ILO conventions to which it was a party, and it rejected Poland's objection to its inquiry.

Forced Labor

Before World War II, ILO's efforts in regard to forced labor, including the adoption of the 1930 Convention on Forced Labor and the 1936 Convention on Recruiting of Indigenous Workers, were directed primarily toward stamping out abuses in non-self-governing territories. A convention adopted in 1939 prescribed that contracts for the employment of indigenous labor must always be made in writing, and an accompanying recommendation called for regulation of the maximum period of time for which an indigenous worker could bind himself under contract. Another convention adopted in 1939 required all penal sanctions exacted against indigenous labor for breach of contract to be progressively abolished "as soon as possible"; when applicable to juvenile workers, the sanctions against breach of contract were to be abolished without delay.

After World War II, emphasis shifted from protection against exploitation in colonial areas to the abolition of systems of forced labor wherever they occur, as part of the promotion of human rights. The first step in this broader attack was an impartial inquiry into the nature and extent of forced labor, including prison labor, gang labor, labor service, and the like. A joint UN-ILO committee studied the existence in the world of systems of forced or "corrective" labor as a means of political coercion or as punishment for political views. In 1953, the committee reported that it had found two principal forms of forced labor existing in fully self-governing countries: one used mainly as a means of political coercion or political punishment, and the other used mainly for economic reasons.

In 1957, the International Labor Conference, by a vote of 240 to 0, with 1 abstention, adopted the Convention on the Abolition of Forced Labor. The convention outlaws any form of forced or compulsory labor (a) as a means of political coercion or education or as punishment for political or ideological views, (b) as a means of obtaining labor for economic development, (c) as a means of labor discipline, (d) as punishment for participation in strikes, or (e) as a means of racial, social, national, or religious discrimination. The convention, one of the farthest-reaching adopted by the ILO, has been in force since 17 January 1959.

Discrimination in Employment and Occupation

The Convention on Discrimination in Employment and Occupation, adopted by the International Labor Conference in 1958, constitutes another effort to promote the principle of equal rights. The convention defines such discrimination as any distinction, exclusion, or preference based on race, color, sex, religion, political opinion, national extraction, or social origin that impairs equal access to vocational training, equal access to employment and to certain occupations, or equal terms and conditions of employment. Measures affecting a person justifiably suspected of being engaged in activities prejudicial to the security of the state are not to be deemed discrimination, provided such a person is guaranteed the right of appeal. Furthermore, special measures of protection or assistance required because of sex, age, disablement, family responsibility, or social or cultural status are not to be considered discriminatory, but workers' and employers' organizations must in certain cases be consulted on such measures.

Every state ratifying the convention thereby undertakes to declare and pursue a national policy designed to promote, by methods appropriate to national conditions and practice, equality of opportunity and treatment in respect of employment and occupation, with a view to eliminating discrimination. This goal is to be accomplished through cooperation with employers' and workers' organizations, through legislation, and through educational programs. Ratifying states also agree to pursue nondiscriminatory public employment policies and to ensure the observance of such policies by public vocational guidance, training, and placement services.

D. Maritime Questions

The problems of merchant sailors differ in many respects from those of other workers. When plans for an international labor organization were being worked out in 1919, world seafarers' organizations urged the creation of a separate "permanent general conference for the international regulation of maritime labor" and of a separate "supervisory office for maritime labor." Although it was eventually decided to include maritime questions as falling within the purview of the ILO, special ILO machinery was established to deal with them, including special maritime sessions of the International Labor Conference and a Joint Maritime Commission.

Maritime sessions of the International Labor Conference are periodic full-scale sessions of the conference devoted exclusively to maritime questions. The first such conference was held in 1920. Since then, some 50 conventions and recommendations concerning seafarers have been adopted, pertaining to conditions of employment, health and safety, welfare, and social security. Together, these conventions and recommendations form the International Seafarers' Code, which is binding on all subscribing countries.

The Joint Maritime Commission keeps questions regarding the merchant marine under review on a year-to-year basis. Since it began its work in 1920, the commission has been enlarged several times, mainly to provide wider geographical representation.

Conditions of Employment

The first of the ILO's maritime conventions, adopted in 1920, forbids the employment of children under 14 at sea, except on family-operated vessels. A convention adopted in 1936 raises the minimum age to 15. A convention adopted in 1926 prescribes the standard form and content of seafarers' articles of agreement or employment contracts, signing procedures, and the conditions under which such contracts may be terminated.

At the 1987 maritime session of the International Labor Conference, a number of conventions and recommendations were adopted, some of which revised and updated earlier instruments. A 1926 convention guaranteeing repatriation of seafarers was broadened to take into account developments in the shipping industry. The new instrument lists the circumstances under which repatriation rights shall apply, including cessation of employment, illness, shipwreck, and bankruptcy of the shipowner. Another revision of previous instruments was adopted on seafarers' welfare at sea and in port. States ratifying it will undertake to ensure that cultural and recreational facilities and information services are provided in appropriate ports and on board ship. A convention on health protection and medical care aims at providing seafarers with care comparable to that which is generally available to workers ashore.

Social Security for Seafarers

The first step toward social insurance for seafarers was taken by a 1920 convention which required a shipowner to pay two months' wages to crew members of a lost or foundered vessel.

Three conventions affecting seafarers were adopted at the 1976 maritime session: continuity of employment, annual leave with pay, and merchant shipping (minimum standards). The third convention provides that a state which has ratified the convention and in whose port a ship calls may take account of a complaint or evidence that the ship does not conform to the standards of the convention.

A new convention adopted in 1987 revised a number of existing instruments dealing with social security and insurance against illness; it requires ratifying states to provide seafarers with social security protection not less favorable than that enjoyed by shore workers for which the state has legislation in force. Member states would be bound to apply either minimum standards, as specified in the Social Security (Minimum Standards) Convention, or superior standards, as laid down in other ILO instruments.

The standards set by these conventions, even when not ratified by many countries, have an influence on collective agreements, national statutes, and regulations.

E. Technical Cooperation

Member states have always been able to count on the direct cooperation of the ILO. The expression "technical assistance" is to be found in an ILO report as early as 1930. ILO officials who were then sent on consultative missions to governments were the precursors of today's experts.

Depending on priority programs established by governments, the activities of consultants have become an increasingly integral feature of national development plans. Among these priorities are the development of human resources, the raising of living standards, and the promotion of full employment. The ILO works actively with the authorities to set up and put into effect concrete cooperative projects. These tasks range from brief preliminary missions to major projects, such as the setting up of networks of vocational training or management development centers, to the establishment of full-scale rural development programs.

A cooperative project is deemed a success when it can be fully taken over by the national counterparts of the country concerned after the ILO experts have left. To encourage this trend, the ILO has made it possible for national officials to complete their training overseas. Many cooperative projects also provide for study grants and the organization of training courses and seminars. The supply of specialized equipment for certain services is another form of ILO aid—for example, equipment to set up vocational training centers.

The international technical cooperation effort is financed in part by UNDP. Some of the industrialized countries also make funds available to the ILO for cooperative projects.

In the budget for the 1998–99 biennium, a total of US$139 million was allocated for technical cooperation and field programs. The ILO concentrates its efforts on activities that produce maximum long-term results, such as the creation of institutions of various kinds or of training centers for trainers. It also seeks to enlist the aid of employers and workers in the technical cooperation effort.

Technical cooperation is linked to action promoting adherence to international labor standards, such as aid in the area of labor legislation and administration. This policy improves workers' conditions while taking into account the realities of the situation in the country concerned.

Unemployment and Underemployment

The ILO considers help to member states in the struggle against unemployment to be one of its major responsibilities. Much work has been carried out in this area. Guided by international labor standards, and often with the practical aid of the ILO, many countries have taken steps to ease the lot of the unemployed, to organize employment bureaus, and to develop vocational training facilities. However, these measures are far from enough to solve the immense unemployment problem facing the world today.

A coherent set of measures is needed to solve the unemployment and underemployment problem: development of rural areas, as well as urban industrialization; training of citizens in modern employment techniques; and taking a census of the active population and concentrating the development effort on the sectors and techniques calculated to absorb the maximum number of workers. In short, employment does not automatically flow from economic expansion unless it is geared to a policy designed to promote employment systematically. The International Labor Conference recognized this point when, in 1964, it adopted a convention and a recommendation on unemployment policy; the promotion and planning of employment are now an integral part of the development effort.

Faced with the unemployment crisis, the ILO launched the World Employment Program in 1969. This program was the starting point in the ILO's efforts to help combat unemployment and underemployment.

It was in keeping with the recognition that growing world poverty required new initiatives that the World Employment Conference was held in 1976. The resulting declaration of principles and program of action called the world's attention to the need for full employment and an adequate income for every inhabitant in the shortest possible time.

The ILO-developed concept of basic needs is paramount to the effort to get to the root of poverty. Basic needs include two elements: certain minimum requirements of a family for private consumption—adequate food, shelter, and clothing are obviously included, as would be certain household equipment and furniture; and essential services provided for the community at large, such as safe drinking water, sanitation, public transportation, and health and education facilities.

The program of the 1976 conference emphasized that strategies and national development plans and policies should include explicitly, as a priority objective, the promotion of employment and the satisfaction of the basic needs of each country's population. The people should participate in making the decisions that affect them through organizations of their own choice. The concept of freely chosen employment is an integral part of a basic needs strategy. Among measures to be taken by governments to meet the target of creating sufficient jobs for all in developing countries by the year 2000 are ratification of selected ILO conventions; selection of development projects with a view to their employment and income distribution potential; and implementation of active labor market policies, with consideration given to social policies designed to increase the welfare of working people, especially women, the young, and the aged.

ILO operational activities and advisory missions remain important elements of the program. Regional employment teams in Asia, Africa, and Latin America provide technical advisory services and training courses in response to requests from a large number of countries.

Technical cooperation projects in the fields of employment planning, personnel planning, and labor-market information range from multiexpert, long-term projects to short-term consultancies and special advisory missions.

ILO technical advisory missions for special public works programs not only help governments define and, where appropriate, expand the scope of special public works programs and determine the technical feasibility of projects and organizational and staffing needs, but also assist in the preparation of technical cooperation components and in management reviews of ongoing programs.

At the 78th Session of the ILC in 1991, Director General Michel Hansenne raised the issue of the "working poor," the approximately 300 million people around the world who work in jobs that fall into what is called the "informal sector." Almost one-third of the world's gross domestic product is believed to be contributed by these millions working on the fringes of the recognized labor market. Such activities range from small manufacturing enterprises to a single person selling rolled cigarettes on a street corner. Generally, products of the informal sector require a low level of capital investment, technology, and skills. Low productivity or low wages imply that very long hours have to be worked to achieve a subsistence income.

The ILO initiatives focussed on the informal sector are the Regional Employment Program for Latin America and the Caribbean (PREALC) and the Jobs and Skills Program for Africa (JASPA). These initiatives include gathering data, providing training and technical cooperation, promoting income-generating projects for specific vulnerable groups, studying ways to open traditional apprenticeship and training for production schemes to women, and examining case studies of regulatory barriers.

Development of Human Resources

In an age when production techniques and structures are rapidly changing, simultaneously with a rapid increase in the world's active population, the entire concept of labor and vocational training must be viewed in a new light.

Many trades for which young people are being prepared will undergo radical transformation, and the qualifications that workers hold today will be obsolete without frequent refresher courses. Moreover, there will be a steady increase in the number of workers switching from one sector to another—for example, from agriculture to industry or from industry to commerce.

Any modern conception of developing human resources must take these factors into account by extending and diversifying vocational training facilities: apprenticeships, technical training and education, advanced training, and refresher courses. Vocational guidance must be developed not only to aid young people to make a wise choice of a career but also to retrain adult workers for different jobs. A coherent policy aimed at utilizing human resources must, therefore, include measures that make it possible for the worker to continue education and training, depending on the person's aptitudes and the opportunities in the labor market.

Vocational training is one of the key elements of ILO's technical cooperation program. Hundreds of projects have been mounted on all continents, some designed to create or strengthen national vocational training systems and others aimed at specific sectors of the economy: specialized industries, agriculture, handicrafts, commerce, the hotel trade, and tourism, among others.

The ILO also cooperates in projects for management development and is active in the field of vocational rehabilitation. Its long-standing interest in handicapped people was expressed anew in 1983 with the adoption of a recommendation and a convention recognizing the importance that it attaches to the formulation and implementation of coherent national policies. The convention emphasizes collective participation—notably that of the representatives of employers' and workers' organizations and of the disabled themselves—in determining needs and developing vocational rehabilitation services at national as well as community levels.

The ILO's International Training Centre at Turin trained 66,000 men and women froom 172 countries from 1965 through 1999.

Social Institutions

The ILO's efforts to foster social justice in order to improve working and living conditions and to encourage balanced economic and social development would be wasted if there were no social structures promoting large-scale participation.

To assist governments, employers' associations, and trade unions in building or consolidating the necessary institutions and mechanisms, the ILO is active in such fields as labor law and administration, labor relations, workers' education, promotion of cooperatives, and rural institutions.

The ILO's work in standard-setting has had a formative effect on social legislation and labor law throughout the world. The ILO also has supplied expert advice to countries requesting it on the measures needed to bring their legislation up to the level of international labor standards or to solve certain social problems. Many developing countries have sought ILO help in establishing or codifying their labor and social legislation. To ensure that the legislation is effectively applied, a country must have a labor administration that includes the necessary services. To meet this need and to help labor ministries play an active role in designing a development policy, the ILO has mounted an increasing number of projects in this field.

The ILO has always been keenly concerned with labor-management relations and with the relations among trade unions, employers' organizations, and governments. When such relations are cordial, they foster a climate conducive to economic and social progress. When they are unsatisfactory, they can impede united national development. The ILO considers labor relations to be good when they are based on the full recognition of freedom of association, in law and in practice, and when they permit labor, management, and government representatives to handle common problems.

Here again, technical cooperation is an extension of the action designed to set up standards and guidelines. ILO help is increasingly being sought in the field of industrial relations. Bipartite ILO missions comprising trade-union and management experts from industrialized countries have been sent to developing nations to encourage the establishment of a healthy working relationship between workers and employers. Study courses and seminars have been organized in various parts of the world.

Adequate training of workers' representatives is a prerequisite if they are to play an effective role in economic and social life. The trade unions themselves are aware of this fact and are increasing their own training programs accordingly. To assist them in this task, the ILO established a workers' education program to enable trade unions and workers' education bodies to develop their services and to provide workers and their representatives with the social and economic training they need. ILO efforts have been directed to such objectives as the training of unionists to help them take part in the planning and execution of development policies, the encouragement of cooperative action, and the organization of union research and information services.

As part of this program, the ILO has organized seminars, study courses, and technical discussions, often on a regional basis. An average of 50 courses of this type, including discussions on such matters as population and family planning, are held each year in different parts of the world. There is also a publications program, consisting of handbooks, booklets, bulletins, and educational material, in addition to a film and filmstrip lending library.

Since its earliest days, the ILO has played an important role in developing the cooperative movement. Its range of activities in this field has grown with the introduction of the cooperative system in many developing countries. The governments of these countries recognize that cooperatives provide an instrument that can facilitate social and economic advancement. With their built-in system of controls and internal management, their freely elected councils, and public discussion of their programs, cooperatives can be compared to grass-roots civics classes, giving their members a true sense of responsibility and involvement in national development. They are a unifying agent in bringing men and women together for constructive tasks, and they contribute to training for leadership. Above all, cooperatives are a key factor in rural development, for both production and marketing.

The creation of processing cooperatives in rural areas for handling produce, as well as the organization of cooperatives for small enterprises and handicraft workshops, can aid progress toward industrialization. Whatever form they take, cooperatives raise living standards and increase employment opportunities. At the request of the governments, and with the financial support of UNDP, ILO experts are helping countries set up or develop cooperative movements.

The interregional project for the production of materials and techniques for cooperative management training ended in 1990 after 13 years of operation. The terminal evaluation considered the project to have achieved results of high quality and relevance, with almost 200,000 people having been trained in more than 60 countries.

Enterprise and Cooperative Development

A major program to promote the establishment and effective operation of enterprises in the formal and informal sectors, in both rural and urban areas, was implemented in 1991. The Entrepreneurship and Management Development Program seeks to develop managerial resources at various levels and in various sectors of the economy in an environment characterized by rapid change.

Projects in operation focus on four major areas: strengthening national institutional mechanisms to monitor and manage productivity improvement; developing small and microenterprises; assisting structural adjustment processes; and strengthening management development institutions.

F. Problems of Key Industries

During World War II, and even earlier, it was felt that a gap existed in the structure of the ILO: special machinery was needed for the detailed and continuing study of specific industries by people with a thorough practical knowledge of their particular problems. Acting on a plan prepared by British Minister of Labor and National Services Ernest Bevin, submitted in 1943 by the UK government, the Governing Body established seven ILO industrial committees in 1945 "to provide machinery through which the special circumstances of the principal international industries [could] receive special and detailed consideration." By 1946, industrial committees had been created to deal with the problems of the following key industries: inland transport; coal mines; iron and steel; textiles; petroleum; building, civil engineering, and public works; and chemicals. In 1994 a total of 12 industrial committees were active: the Inland Transport; Coal Mines; Iron and Steel; Metal Trades; Textiles; Building, Civil Engineering, and Public Works; Chemical Industries; Committee on Work on Plantations; Advisory Committee on Salaried Employees and Professional Workers; Hotel, Catering and Tourism; Forestry and Wood Industries; Food and Drink Industries.

Other ILO committees that deal with special problems of international significance include the Advisory Committee on Salaried Employees and Professional Workers, the Permanent Agricultural Committee, and the Committee on Work on Plantations. The ILO has also established Asian, African, and inter-American advisory committees, which provide information on special regional problems. The ILO industrial committees are, in effect, small-scale specialized international labor conferences.

Resolutions adopted by these committees may call for further action on the part of the ILO. They may also be designed for the guidance of employers' associations and trade unions in their collective bargaining, and they may contain suggestions addressed to the UN, to other specialized agencies, or to governments. The following are a few examples of subjects concerning which important resolutions or recommendations have been adopted:

Inland transport: prevention of accidents involving dock labor; inland transport working conditions in Asia and Africa; automatic coupling of railway cars; transport and handling of dangerous goods; limitation of loads carried by one person; marking of weights on loads; and interport competition;

Coal mines: principles for incorporation in a coal miners' charter; coal miners' housing; productivity in coal mines; safety in coal mines; and the social consequences of fuel and power consumption trends;

Iron and steel: regularization of production and employment at a high level; dismissal pay and payment for public holidays; and cooperation at the industry level;

Metal trades: regularization of production and employment at a high level; and long-term estimates of raw material requirements;

Textiles: disparities in wages in the textile industries of different countries;

Building, civil engineering, and public works: reduction of seasonal unemployment in the construction industry; social aspects of the world timber situation and outlook; and national housing programs;

Work on plantations: the place of the plantation in the general economy of the countries concerned; living and working conditions as related to plantation productivity; and the need for international action on commodity regulation; and

Salaried employees and professional workers: rights of the inventor who is an employee; migration of salaried and professional workers; hygiene in shops and offices; employment problems of musicians, actors, and other public performers; employment conditions of teachers; professional problems of journalists; problems involved in collective bargaining for white-collar and professional workers; wages and working conditions of hospital and health-service staff; and wages and working conditions of civil servants.

G. Other Activities

The Occupational Safety and Health Information Center (CIS)

In 1976, the ILO launched the International Program for the Improvement of Working Conditions and Environment (PIACT), aimed at giving governments and employers' and workers' organizations help in drawing up and implementing programs for the improvement of working conditions and environment. The various means of action included standard-setting; technical cooperation, including the sending of multidisciplinary teams to member states at their request; tripartite meetings, particularly meetings of industrial committees, regional meetings, and meetings of

experts; action-oriented research and studies; and gathering and dissemination of information, particularly through the International Occupational Safety and Health Information Center.

The International Occupational Safety and Health Information Center (CIS) has as its objective to collect and disseminate world information that can contribute to the prevention of occupational accidents and diseases. The center is assisted by 70 national centers representing all continents. The CIS also offers on-line compact disc and microcomputer databases.

The conditions in which men and women work are at the very heart of the ILO's mandate. Despite the progress achieved, the working conditions of a great many workers remain arduous or give rise to new problems as a result of technological developments. In this arena the ILO is concerned with the safety and healthfulness of the working environment, working time, organization and content of work, working conditions and choice of technology, and working and living environment.

In 1991, with the assistance of a grant from the German government, the International Program on the Elimination of Child Labor (IPEC) was launched. More than 80 projects with government institutions, trade unions, employers' organizations, and non-governmental organizations (NGOs) were implemented in at least 12 countries.

International Health Hazard Alert System

A new approach to dealing with newly discovered or suspected occupational hazards, which spread very quickly around the world, is the ILO's International Health Hazard Alert System, established in 1977. When a new hazard is discovered, an alert is sent out by the ILO to the participating countries for their assessment and reply. For example, the communication concerning possible health hazards in the use of carbonless copy papers was widely disseminated in several countries. In 1993 the Health Hazard Alert System circulated requests to member states for up-to-date information on major occupational health hazards and their prevention.

Tripartite Declaration Concerning Multinational Enterprises and Social Policy

The 1977 Tripartite Declaration Concerning Multinational Enterprises and Social Policy applies to the fields of employment, training, conditions of work and life, and industrial relations. Already operational in the ILO, where it will continue to affect its purposes, it was foreseen as the employment and labor chapter of the proposed UN Code of Conduct on Transnational Corporations that has been the subject of prolonged debate. In the early 1990s the General Assembly decided to discontinue work on this subject. However, the matter of a code of conduct for transnational corporations continues to be raised. In 1996, UNCTAD Secretary-General Rubens Ricupero stated it would be particularly important "within the context of how to establish a balance between the rights and obligations of the countries that are the source of investments and the countries that receive the investments." The declaration stresses the positive contributions that multinational enterprises can make to economic and social progress and aims at minimizing and resolving the difficulties that their various operations may create. The principles are commended to governments and employers' and workers' organizations of home and host countries and to the multinational enterprises themselves for their voluntary observance.

The subject areas covered by the declaration conform to the areas of substantive competence of the ILO within the overall program of the UN. There are 22 ILO conventions and 27 recommendations referenced in the declaration. The declaration is universal in scope; it is addressed to all of the parties in the ILO's tripartite structure; it ascribes a leading role to multinational enterprises when they operate in developing countries; and, finally, it is voluntary.

BIBLIOGRAPHY

Conditions of Work Digest. Legal, policy, and program information on significant issues and emerging trends in the field of conditions of work and quality of working life. Annotated bibliographies, guides to information sources. Worldwide coverage.

International Labour Review. Notes and comments on the social and labor situation in the world and articles based on recent ILO and other research into economic and social topics of international interest affecting labor. Notes on new books published or received by the ILO. Six issues per year.

LABORDOC. (database) Machine-readable version of International Labour Documentation, available for interactive and retrospective on-line searching through several information hosts. Offers worldwide coverage of labor questions, especially industrial relations, labor law, employment, working conditions, vocational training, labor related aspects of economics, social development, rural development, and technological change.

Official Bulletin, Series A. Information on activities of the ILO, texts adopted by the ILC, and other official documents. Three issues per year. *Series B.* Reports of the Committee on Freedom of Association of the Governing Body and related material. Three issues per year.

The World Employment Report. Reviews the global employment situation. Biennial.

World Labour Report. Reviews significant recent events and policy experiences in: human rights at work; employment; labor relations; social protection and working conditions. Yearly.

Yearbook of Labour Statistics. A comprehensive survey of annual data from all parts of the world relating to total and economically active population, employment, unemployment, hours of work, wages, labor cost, strikes, and lockouts.

All publications may be ordered from the Secretariat in Geneva, or, in North America, from the ILO Publications Center, 49 Sheridan Avenue, Albany, NY 12210. The ILO catalog of publications is available online at www.ilo.org/public/english/support/publ/index.htm.

THE FOOD AND AGRICULTURE ORGANIZATION OF THE UNITED NATIONS (FAO)

"To the millions who have to go without two meals a day the only acceptable form in which God dare appear is food."

Mahatma Gandhi

BACKGROUND: Hunger is still the most urgent problem confronting the greater part of humanity. Hundreds of millions of the world's inhabitants are seriously and chronically undernourished. Not only is their diet quantitatively insufficient, but it is qualitatively insufficient as well, lacking the protein essential to health and vigor. In 1999 it was estimated that more than 800 million people did not have enough to eat.

CREATION

From the mid-19th century, reflecting a growing recognition of the interdependence of nations in agriculture and associated sciences, international conferences were held at which there were exchanges of knowledge relating to biology, biochemistry, crop diversification, and animal health. However, it was not until 1905 that these individually valuable but unrelated efforts were coordinated with the founding of the International Institute of Agriculture (IIA).

One of the institute's aims, which were necessarily modest because of public and governmental apathy, was "to get the farmer a square deal." The words were those of David Lubin, a prosperous California dry-goods dealer, born in a Polish ghetto, who almost single-handedly founded the institute. Depressed by the plight of his farmer customers during the agricultural crisis of the 1890s, he bought and managed his own fruit farm in order to study their problems. Rebuffed in his adopted country, he toured the chancelleries of Europe, preaching the importance of a healthy agriculture as a requisite of a healthy international society. Finally, Lubin found a sympathetic listener in King Victor Emmanuel III of Italy. Under his patronage, the institute started functioning in Rome in 1908 as a center for the dissemination of farming news, trends, prices, statistics, and techniques. Though lacking the capacity to initiate or directly assist projects in the field, the IIA's experience as a "head office" for the collection, collation, analysis, and dissemination of data formed a useful platform for the later launching of FAO's similar but wider reaching activities in agriculture.

The League of Nations did not directly concern itself with agriculture, but work done under its auspices in the relatively new field of nutrition proved of great practical significance. Ironically, Nazi Germany, although a sardonic critic of the League, was the first country to base its wartime rationing system on the scientific standards of diet drawn up by the League for heavy workers, expectant mothers, children, and others. Soon, other countries did the same, often with striking results. In the UK, for example, the meager and often uninteresting but balanced diet dictated by the ration card actually led to an improvement in the nation's nutritional health.

FAO was the end product of a series of conferences held during World War II. In 1941, the US Nutrition Conference for Defense, attended by 900 delegates, resolved that it should be a goal of the democracies to conquer hunger, "not only the obvious hunger that man has always known, but the hidden hunger revealed by modern knowledge of nutrition." In line with President Franklin D. Roosevelt's call in 1942 for the Four Freedoms, the Australian economist Frank McDougal proposed the creation of a "United Nations program for freedom from want of food" and urged the president that food be the first economic problem tackled by the UN system being proposed for establishment when the war ended.

President Roosevelt convened the UN Conference on Food and Agriculture at Hot Springs, Virginia, in May and June 1943. The first UN conference, antedating the San Francisco Conference by two years, it established an Interim Commission on Food and Agriculture, headed by Lester B. Pearson of Canada. The commission drew up a draft constitution for FAO, thus paving the way for the first FAO Conference, held in Quebec in October 1945 and attended by 44 nations and a number of observers. On 16 October 1945, 34 nations signed the constitution that brought FAO into existence. By the end of the conference, the new organization, headed by British nutritionist Sir John Boyd Orr, had 42 member nations.

PURPOSES

As expressed in the preamble to the FAO constitution, member states are pledged to promote the common welfare through separate and collective action to raise levels of nutrition and standards of living, improve the efficiency of the production and distribution of all food and agricultural products, better the conditions of rural populations, and thus contribute toward an expanding world economy and ensure humanity's freedom from hunger. Specifically, FAO is charged with collecting, evaluating, and disseminating information relating to nutrition, food, and agriculture and associated areas, including fisheries, marine products, forestry, and primary forestry products.

FAO is committed to promoting and, where appropriate, recommending national and international action with respect to the following: (a) scientific, technological, social, and economic research relating to nutrition, food, and agriculture; (b) improvement of education and administration relating to nutrition, food, and agriculture and the spread of public knowledge of nutritional and agricultural science and practice; (c) conservation of natural resources and the adoption of improved methods of agricultural production; (d) improvement of the processing, marketing, and distribution of food and agricultural products; (e) adoption of policies for the provision of adequate agricultural credit, national and international; and (f) adoption of international policies on agricultural commodity arrangements. The FAO also plays a major role in dealing with food and agricultural emergencies such as drought, famine, plant diseases, and insect plagues.

Other functions of FAO are to furnish such technical assistance as governments may request; to organize, in cooperation with the governments concerned, such missions as may be needed to assist them in fulfilling obligations arising from their acceptance of the recommendations of the UN Conference on Food and Agriculture and of its constitution; and, generally, to take all necessary and appropriate action to implement the purposes of the organization as set forth in the preamble.

MEMBERSHIP

The 45 countries represented on the interim commission were entitled to original membership. The Russian Federation retains the entitlement to original membership previously held by the USSR, to be made effective at any time through the ratification of FAO's constitution.

Any nation may withdraw after four years. Among the countries that have withdrawn and later rejoined are Czechoslovakia (withdrew 1950, rejoined 1969), Poland (withdrew 1951, rejoined 1957), Hungary (withdrew 1952, rejoined 1967), and South Africa (withdrew 1964, rejoined 1993). Taiwan withdrew in 1952.

As of November 1999, FAO had 180 member nations. In addition, Puerto Rico was an associate member. The European Economic Community was a member organization.

STRUCTURE

The principal organs of FAO are the FAO Conference, the FAO Council, and the secretariat, headed by a Director General.

FAO Conference

The supreme body of FAO is the all-member FAO Conference, which holds its regular biennial sessions in Rome in odd-numbered years. The conference determines the policy of FAO and adopts its budget. It makes recommendations relating to food, agriculture, fisheries, forestry, and related matters to member nations and to other international organizations. It approves conventions and agreements for submission to member governments. It may establish commissions, working parties, and consultative groups and may convene special conferences. It periodically elects the Director General, as well as the member nations to be represented on the FAO Council. Each FAO member has one vote in the conference.

FAO Council

The FAO Council, consisting of 49 member nations elected by the FAO Conference for three-year terms on a rotating basis (one-third of the membership stands down each year), meets at least once a year, under an independent chairman, as an interim governing body between meetings of the conference.

Director General and Secretariat

Under the supervision of the conference and the Council, the Director General has full power and authority to direct the work of FAO. Edouard Saouma of Lebanon was Director General from 1975 to 1993. Dr. Jacques Diouf of Senegal began a six-year term

as Director General in January 1994. Reelected for a second term, he heads a staff of more than 4,300, including more than 2,000 persons working in various development projects in the field.

Headquarters and Regional Offices. FAO headquarters were in Washington, DC, until 1951. Since then, they have been located in Rome on extraterritorial grounds near the Colosseum and the Baths of Caracalla. The headquarters building was planned originally by the government of Mussolini, but construction was halted by World War II. Completed after the war, it was leased by the Italian government for the "permanent use and occupancy" of FAO at an annual rental of US\$1.

Growth in staff and activities over the years created a need for more work space. Aside from additions to the main complex, office space was for some time rented away from the headquarters building. In 1993, the Italian government completed a major expansion of headquarters facilities, bringing all FAO staff together at the Terme di Caracalla address for the first time in 32 years.

Aside from headquarters in Rome, which also serves as the European regional office, FAO has regional offices for Africa in Accra, Ghana; Asia and the Pacific in Bangkok, Thailand; Latin America and the Caribbean in Santiago, Chile; and the Near East in Cairo, Egypt. There are also five liaison offices—in Geneva (Switzerland); Washington, DC, and New York; Brussels (Belgium); and Yokohama (Japan).

The Organization

The FAO comprises eight departments: Economic and Social Policy, Agriculture, Fisheries, Forestry, Sustainable Development, Technical Cooperation, Administration and Finance, and General Affairs and Information. The Technical Cooperation and Sustainable Development Departments were created in 1994 through a process of restructuring to respond more effectively to evolving needs among the organization's member nations.

BUDGET

FAO's biennial internal budget, or Regular Programme, covers internal operations, including the maintenance of the highly qualified staff who conduct field work, advise governments on policy and planning, and service a wide range of development needs. The Regular Programme is financed by contributions from member nations. It covers the costs of the organization's secretariat, its Technical Cooperation Programme, and part of several special action programs. The budget for the 2000–01 biennium was US\$650 million; this represented a zero nominal growth budget (which was effectively a cut of US\$14.9 million when inflation and other cost increases were taken into account).

The Technical Cooperation Program (TCP) was initiated in 1976. It enables the organization to provide speedy assistance to, for instance, a country when disasters affect its food and agricultural situation; practical and vocational training to complement training financed from trust funds and other sources; and short-term, small-scale supplementary technical assistance and policy advice that can be immediately useful to a country's food and agricultural situation. The amount of funds allocated to TCPs has been increasing in each FAO budget; funds rose to US\$91.5 million in 2000–01 from US\$77.4 million in 1992–93.

The Field Programme implements FAO's development strategies and provides assistance to governments and rural communities. Projects are usually undertaken in cooperation with national governments and other agencies. Nearly half of Field Programme finances come from national trust funds and just over 40% is provided by the United Nations Development Program. FAO contributes about 10% from the Regular Programme budget through its Technical Cooperation Programme. An increasing amount of money comes from donor countries that ask FAO to carry out part of their aid activities for them. Many of these countries also assign and finance young technicians to work in FAO projects.

ACTIVITIES

FAO collects, analyzes and disseminates information, provides policy and planning advice to governments, offers direct development assistance, and acts as an international forum for debate on food and agriculture issues.

Despite considerable progress in recent decades, the world still falls short of the goal of adequate food and nutrition for all. FAO estimates that more than 790 million people in the developing world are chronically undernourished, consuming too little food to meet even minimal energy and protein needs. Millions suffer from lack of essential micronutrients; their symptoms include blindness, vulnerability to infectious diseases, anemia, and mental retardation. Those most at risk include the poor, the elderly, refugees and displaced persons, drought-prone populations, and children. According to data gathered between 1987 and 1998, two out of five children in the developing world are stunted, one in three is underweight, and one in 10 is wasted. FAO advocates equitable, participatory rural development as the key to eradication of poverty, the first and foremost cause of undernutrition and food insecurity.

Widespread hunger and malnutrition are not simply problems of inadequate food production; they are the most critical and cruel elements of poverty. Farmers in the developing world are discouraged from increasing food production by the lack of purchasing power among rural and urban populations as much as by a lack of technical assistance or inputs such as improved seeds and fertilizers. People go hungry because they do not have the money to buy food, rather than because local farmers cannot produce more. The fight against world hunger is a major part of the battle against world poverty. Building up a country's agriculture provides both food for the hungry and jobs for the rural populace; it contributes to the overall prosperity of the nation.

Food Security

The goal of eradicating hunger and malnutrition and ensuring food security for all is central to FAO's mandate. Following the serious depletion of world grain reserves caused by poor harvests in 1972, FAO saw the need to develop an international system to maintain minimum world food security and offset the effects of crop failures. The organization made a proposal under which all countries, be they developed or developing, would cooperate in building up national food reserves under a structure of international cooperation. Special efforts were called for to increase the self-reliance of developing countries. The proposal was endorsed by the World Food Conference held in Rome in November 1974, and FAO was requested to prepare an International Undertaking on World Food Security. In 1976, the organization established the Food Security Assistance Scheme to carry out the work of the International Undertaking.

In 1983, FAO's Committee on World Food Security adopted a broader concept of world food security, with the ultimate objective of ensuring that all people at all times have both physical and economic access to the food they need, and in 1986, the FAO Council endorsed a World Food Security Compact, which provides a clearly defined moral basis for action by governments, organizations, and individuals directed toward securing food supplies for all. The compact urged developing countries to promote domestic food production as the first line of defense and to reexamine, and if necessary revise, national policies to ensure adequate incentives to farmers, particularly small-scale producers. It recommended that governments of developing countries prepare to maintain food security in times of shortage by such measures as early-warning systems and emergency food reserves and to promote rural development that helps increase the purchasing power of the poor. Developed countries, both importers and exporters, were asked to consider world as well as national interests when setting policies concerning food production, stocks, imports, and prices. They were encouraged to continue providing emergency food aid to less fortunate countries, as well as to assist in increasing agricultural production in those countries, and to help low-income countries to secure imports of food, fertilizers, and other agricultural inputs in times of difficulty. They were also requested to take into account, in negotiations on trade questions, the fact that the food security of many developing countries depends on their ability to export agricultural and other products in order to meet the cost of food imports.

The World Food Security Compact called on nongovernmental organizations to help stimulate public interest in food-security issues, thereby facilitating additional action by governments, and it called for a commitment to food security on the part of individuals throughout the world. The individual was called upon not only to work for his own food security and that of his family but also to recognize that he has "a sacred obligation" to concern himself with the food security of those less fortunate than himself. "Failure to provide succor when it is needed," the compact stated, "is a betrayal of man's duty to his fellow men."

In 1992, the International Conference on Nutrition (ICN) was convened at FAO headquarters in Rome. Organized jointly by FAO and WHO, the conference brought together almost 1,400 delegates from 159 countries and the EEC to address ways of channeling greater resources to the eradication of hunger and malnutrition worldwide. The ICN addressed eight important nutritional issues: preventing micronutrient deficiencies; preventing and managing infectious diseases; improving household food security; promoting healthy diets and lifestyles; enhancing the capacity for care; improving food quality and safety; assessing, analyzing, and monitoring nutrition situations; and incorporating nutrition objectives in development policies. Attention was drawn to the fact that, though enough food is produced yearly to provide an adequate diet for all, the distribution of these resources is very uneven.

FAO's activities are increasingly focused on food security as a question of household access to food as much as of overall food availability. In this context, proper identification of vulnerable groups is fundamental. FAO is developing, at national and subregional levels, an Aggregate Household Food Security Index. The conceptual basis for the index was approved by the FAO Council in 1993. Once fully developed, it will serve as a tool to help monitor food security trends worldwide. In November 1996, the FAO hosted 194 heads of state or government at a World Food Summit to discuss and combat world hunger. Leaders pledged to reduce the number of hungry people to 400 million by 2015. But according to the State of Food Insecurity in the World 1999, the rate of progress (a reduction of 8 million undernourished people a year) means there is no hope of meeting the goal. Further, there is not uniform progress throughout the world: In the first half of the 1990s, only 37 countries achieved a reduction in the number of undernourished, totaling 100 million people; while across the rest of the developing world, the number of hungry people actually increased by almost 60 million.

Information for Agriculture

Among its information functions, FAO provides technical information for specialists through an active publishing program in the form of statistical yearbooks, periodicals, technical reports, scientific monographs, training materials, and other studies of agriculture worldwide (see Bibliography). Most of these publications are translated from their original language into at least one of the organization's other official languages: Arabic, Chinese, English, French, and Spanish.

FAO's David Lubin Memorial Library serves as a coordinating center for the Worldwide Network of Agricultural Libraries (AGLINET). It houses over 1 million items covering agriculture, statistics, economics, food and nutrition, forestry, fisheries, and rural development. The library's computerized facilities supply on-demand bibliographies to field projects, individuals, and institutions in FAO's member nations.

FAO's filmstrips and its radio, television, and video programs cover a wide range of topics from improved farming techniques to animal husbandry, aquaculture, and soil conservation. Translation of these materials into local languages is encouraged in order to reach small farmers and extension workers unable to use one of the five official languages. In addition, the organization provides users with access to over 40 databases on agriculture, fisheries, and forestry, as well as satellite-based information on climate that is crucial to monitoring and responding in a timely fashion to signs of drought, crop failure, and insect plagues.

Every decade, FAO sponsors a worldwide agricultural census, continuing and expanding the first world census carried out by the International Institute of Agriculture in 1930.

FAO has made considerable efforts to identify future demands on agriculture and how these demands might be met, based on the results of data collection and analysis, policy reviews, and practical knowledge of agricultural development. In 1969, FAO published a provisional World Plan for Agricultural Development, an attempt to analyze the major issues that would confront world agriculture in the 1970s and early 1980s. Building on this base, FAO submitted to the FAO Conference in 1979 a study entitled *Agriculture: Toward 2000*. The study's main purpose was to provide a framework for the analysis of options and consideration of policy issues relevant to the development of world agriculture until the end of the century. The study was global in scope, but the major emphasis was on developing countries. Approximately 90 developing countries, which, excluding China, together accounted for over 98% of the population of the developing countries, were studied individually.

In 1993, the FAO Conference launched *Agriculture: Towards 2010*, the revised and updated version of a study originally published by FAO in 1987. Designed to address how the future may unfold, rather than how it ought to develop, the document analyzes trends in food security, nutrition, and agricultural development to determine the most likely outcomes by the year 2010. Among the success stories, it foresees that world agricultural growth, although lower than in the past, will continue to outpace population increases. Also, the majority of people in the developing countries are expected to experience improvement in their per capita food availability and nutritional situation. At the policy level, the study notes a growing awareness of—and greater capabilities to respond to—the need to increase agricultural sustainability. Trade agreements are also seen as becoming more liberal and less trade-distorting, even though the progress may not be smooth.

Yet despite these favorable predictions, many problems are foreseen as remaining, especially for the less developed nations. Significant chronic undernutrition will continue to prevail in many countries and will likely affect significant proportions of the population in entire regions such as sub-Saharan Africa. According to the study, if present trends continue, sub-Saharan Africa will replace South Asia as the global area with the highest number of chronically undernourished people—close to 300 million by the year 2010. Though improvements will be made in South Asia, that region will still have 200 million undernourished.

The pressures on agriculture, on forest and fisheries resources, and on the environment will continue to build. Coupled with this, there will be few prospects for expansion of the main agricultural exports of the developing countries. The study presents detailed assessments of land resources potential for future crop production in the developing countries. These assessments are accompanied and sustained by maps illustrating the dominant land classes for each major geographical area. Aside from providing projections, the study proposes to assist planning at the national and international level, making recommendations designed to aid people and governments in taking early action to reverse negative trends. While doing so, it calls for continued vigilance and preparedness to deal with newly emerging problems.

To help in assessing potential food availability, FAO and UNESCO published in 1978 the Soil Map of the World. By combining the data in the Soil Map with inputs on climate and population, institutes undertaking global studies on climate change, agricultural production, and soil degradation can make efficient projections. In 1992, FAO completed a digitized version of the Soil Map in a form that allows it to be used as an input into climate change models. The data was also updated and the symbols were modified to make it accessible to nonspecialists. The Soil Map is part of FAO's Geographic Information System (GIS), which also provides data on vegetation cover and other aspects of land use.

The locust and grasshopper menace that periodically threatens Africa has given urgency to FAO's efforts to improve its Rome-based Global Information and Early Warning System for Food and Agriculture. The system, established in 1975 to monitor the world's food supply, sounds the alarm when food security is threatened. FAO prepares monthly, quarterly, and annual reports that provide comprehensive, up-to-date analyses of the world food situation and identify countries threatened by shortages. The reports also serve as a guide to potential donors and help avoid food crises.

FAO's Remote Sensing Center collects and interprets data and helps establish data-receiving stations, particularly in Africa; these stations can interpret information on precipitation, soil moisture, and biomass in order to forecast harvests and can transmit the information to national early-warning systems. ARTEMIS, FAO's Africa Real Time Environmental Monitoring Information System, uses high frequency environmental satellite data to produce, at regular intervals, images indicating the rainfall situation and the development of vegetation at continental scales. In combination with data from other sources, ARTEMIS enables specialists to make assessments of crop growing conditions, detect droughts at an early stage, and locate potential breeding grounds for desert locusts. ARTEMIS is an important tool for the GIEWS.

Research and Technical Information. FAO has stressed the importance of agricultural research in developing countries, where the shortage of trained personnel for research remains a major problem. Its Research and Technology Development Division, established in 1984, helps developing countries make the best use of their research resources and assists in the transfer of the fruits of research and technology to developing countries.

The Information System for the Agricultural Sciences and Technology (AGRIS) and the Current Agricultural Research Information System (CARIS) are two worldwide networks coordinated by FAO in support of research and development programs in food and agriculture. As of April 1999, 161 national and 31 regional multinational centers were reporting information to AGRIS. CARIS links 137 developing countries and 19 regional international centers, enabling them to exchange information on their current research activities.

FAO operates the world's most comprehensive bank of agricultural information and statistics. Called AGROSTAT, it brings together FAO's major data files, including data compiled since 1961 on annual supplies and utilization of crops, livestock, and fishery and forest products, as well as on producer prices, population, and other topics. AGROSTAT PC provides an electronic version of FAO's AGROSTAT yearbooks. Other important statistical information maintained by FAO's technical divisions include the Fisheries Statistical Database (FISHDAB), the Globefish Databank and Electronic Library, the Forest Resources Information System (FORIS), and the Geographic Information System (GIS).

To meet increasing demand for agricultural data, FAO has prepared the World Agricultural Information Centre (WAICENT). WAICENT gives governments, institutions, universities, and individuals easy, economical access to information from over 40 FAO databases. Users can access the composite database employing a variety of methods including diskette, CD-ROM, computer networks, and telephone lines.

Advice to Governments
One of FAO's important mandates is to provide member nations with advice on agricultural and food topics. This involves a very broad range of technical, policy, and planning support, principally aimed at building awareness towards key issues, generating appropriate action, and helping countries to develop their own capacities. The recent restructuring of FAO's Policy Formulation, Investment Centre, and Field Operations divisions into a Technical Cooperation Department is intended to provide a consolidated base at headquarters for the provision of direct assistance to member nations in policy, investment, and implementation of field operations.

FAO's Food Security Assistance Scheme (FSAS) helps member countries formulate comprehensive food security program. A fundamental aspect of the FSAS methodology is the use of national multidisciplinary teams of experts in program planning and implementation. This approach contributes to accurate diagnosis of problems, realistic formulation of solutions, capacity building at the national level and anchoring of programs within the national institutional framework.

FAO's Investment Centre helps developing countries construct sound development programs and projects for funding by multilateral organizations, linking the interests of governments and donors to forge viable partnerships. During project identification, the center carefully assesses the development priority of investment proposals, working closely with local staff to promote self-sufficiency and to complement national expertise. This is followed by detailed project preparation for consideration by financing institutions.

The prime source of funding for FAO-assisted investment projects is the World Bank, particularly the IDA, but the Investment Centre also cooperates with most of the principal multilateral financing institutions, including the International Fund for Agricultural Development (IFAD) and regional development banks. Rural poverty alleviation is especially important in projects formulated in conjunction with IFAD.

FAO assists governments in using pesticides safely and rationally through the International Code of Conduct on the Distribution and Use of Pesticides. The code includes a clause for Prior Informed Consent (PIC), which establishes a mechanism for information exchange, enabling importing countries to decide whether they want to receive pesticides that have been banned or severely restricted because of threats to human health or the environment.

The Codex Alimentarius (a joint commission of FAO and WHO) is an international code of food standards. It is designed to guide the world's food industry and to protect the health of consumers by establishing definitions and requirements for foods, assisting in their harmonization, and, in doing so, facilitating international trade.

The Codex Alimentarius also responds to changes or trends in food production. For example, in 1999 it set up the Ad Hoc Intergovernmental Task Force on Foods Derived from Biotechnology, which met for the first time in March 2000 to "develop standards, guidelines, or other principles, where appropriate" for these products. The task force, whose members include government representatives from Codex Alimentarius member countries, scientists, consumer and industry organizations and international non-governmental organizations, was given a four-year mandate by FAO and WHO. FAO is involved in a continuous process of consultation with its member governments, providing information, advice, and technical assistance that can help them make the best choices in promoting sustainable rural development.

Development Assistance
To promote sustainable agriculture and contribute to development that will provide long-term solutions to the fundamental problems of poverty and hunger, FAO gives practical help to developing countries through a wide range of technical assistance projects. The organization encourages an integrated approach, with environmental, social, and economic considerations included in the formulation of development projects. By encouraging people's participation, FAO aims to draw on local expertise and ensure a cooperative approach to development.

Emergency Assistance and Rehabilitation
FAO's Office for Special Relief Operations (OSRO) began operations in 1973 in response to the disastrous drought in 1972–73 in the semiarid countries on the southern edge of the Sahara Desert. In 1975, following an improvement in the Sahel situation, FAO's work was extended to cover emergencies elsewhere. The emphasis in these operations is on speedy approval and delivery of assistance. When disaster strikes a country, the FAO representative assesses needs in close collaboration with local authorities and with other UN agencies. At the request of the government, emergency missions are organized by FAO to assess in detail the damages and losses and to prepare assistance projects for consideration by multilateral and bilateral agencies. Most emergency projects are funded by governments, nongovernmental organizations, and UN agencies. In many cases, FAO, through its Technical Cooperation Program, offers an immediate source of funding for special relief operations. Supplies and equipment provided include seeds, fertilizers, pesticides, and livestock supplies and equipment, as well as logistical support. Disaster-prone countries may also receive preventive assistance to cope with calamities.

Through its Agricultural Rehabilitation Program for Africa, conceived in 1984 at the height of the Ethiopian famine, FAO helped channel some US$194 million into 25 countries to supply farmers with seeds and fertilizers, repair irrigation systems, and rebuild cattle herds.

Since the early 1950s, FAO has coordinated the campaign against the destructive desert locust, which intermittently swarms in the Middle East, Africa, and other regions. Campaigns were almost continuous until 1963, when the pest was brought under control. There have, however, been serious outbreaks of swarms since then, particularly between 1967 and 1970, and in 1978 in desert areas in India.

In 1986, FAO led the battle against the grasshopper and locust plagues that threatened to devastate crops in all parts of Africa. The Emergency Center for Locust Operations (ECLO), established at FAO headquarters, directed what was to become a US$50 million continent-wide campaign that helped save more than 90% of crops in the Sahel alone. FAO monitored breeding areas with satellite imagery, implemented projects carrying out spraying missions, sent pest-control experts to advise African authorities, and helped set up coordinating committees of government and donor representatives in the most directly threatened countries. More than 40 donors, including both developed and developing countries, UN agencies, and nongovernmental organizations, contributed to the fight in 13 countries. The center was deactivated in the spring of 1989 when locusts were brought under control in some 40 countries in Africa, the Near East, and Southwest Asia. In late 1992, with the reappearance of the desert locust on the coastal plains around the Red Sea, the ECLO was immediately brought back into full operation.

FAO continues to strengthen its ability to prevent and respond to emergencies caused by pests and diseases, placing special emphasis on locusts and rinderpest.

INCREASING FOOD AND AGRICULTURAL PRODUCTION

FAO devotes a large share of the resources of its field and regular programs each year to increasing the output of crops, livestock, food fish, and forest products.

Crop Production and Protection

FAO's work in crop production includes collecting, conserving, and evaluating genetic resources; improving seed quality, production, and distribution; increasing crop output; and preventing losses before harvest. Particularly important in developing countries is the supply of high-quality food-crop seed to small farmers, who are responsible in some countries for more than 90% of domestic food production. National seed services and centers often are crucial for the supply of seeds to farmers, and much of FAO's seed development work is concerned with building up these national institutions.

Many countries give high priority to cash crop production, and urban populations often have easier access to imported cereals, including wheat, than to traditional staples, such as cassavas, breadfruit, sweet potatoes, yams, and plantains. The danger of these trends is twofold: increased dependency on food imports and lagging production of traditional crops often used in rural communities as insurance against food scarcity and famine. FAO activities to combat these trends range from training sessions for extension staff to pilot projects, such as helping women's groups to start home vegetable gardens and working on ways to improve processing and storage of perishable vegetables. FAO also has helped develop varieties of wheat and barley suited to arid conditions, as well as more nutritive varieties.

Requests for technical assistance in horticulture are a constant on the FAO agenda. FAO projects cover, for example, citrus production in the Mediterranean, date palm production in the Near East and the Mediterranean, protected cultivation of vegetables in the Near East and North Africa, promotion of tropical fruit-tree production in humid and subhumid areas, and improved vegetable production in tropical semiarid and humid regions.

FAO has played a pivotal role in international crop protection activities for over four decades. The International Plant Protection Convention (IPPC) was vested in FAO in 1951. In order to strengthen FAO's role as coordinator, an IPPC secretariat was created in 1992–93. FAO's general objective in this field is to reduce or if possible prevent crop losses caused by pests. Specific objectives include reducing the spread of pests across national borders and promoting Integrated Pest Management (IPM), which consists of a "best mix" of natural control methods with a need-only-based use of selective pesticides (see Pest Control). In cooperation with the World Health Organization, FAO is conducting studies on the effects of pesticide residues on humans.

Plant diseases remain one of the major checks on crop production. The easiest and most economical way of coping with plant parasites is to breed varieties that are resistant to them. FAO-supported research has been aimed at breeding varieties with durable or long-term resistance. FAO recently established a Plant Genetic Resources Information and Seed Exchange Unit, which disseminates technical information and exchanges seeds and planting material samples for experimental purposes. The main beneficia-

ries are national and international research centers, plant breeders, and FAO field projects. On a national level, FAO advises governments on seed production and legislation.

Examples of FAO activities aimed at increasing crop output include:

- Integrated Pest Management (IPM) programs account for the majority of the FAO's field projects. IPM involves farmers and field staff from national and local governments and from nongovernment institutions. Insofar as it has provided farmers with better training, it has had socioeconomic benefits beyond plant protection.

- Since the early 1950s, FAO has coordinated the campaign against the destructive desert locust, which intermittently swarms in the Middle East, Africa, and other regions (see Emergency Assistance and Rehabilitation). FAO's Emergency Center for Locust Operations is fundamental in conducting these campaigns.

- The Global Information and Early Warning System (see Information for Agriculture) also contributes to crop protection, warning against potential difficulties and disasters.

- The Global System on Plant Genetic Resources supports international and regional networks for *in situ* and *ex situ* conservation under the auspices of FAO. The system also promotes evaluation, management, and enhanced use of plant genetic resources (PGR), and prepares periodic reports on the state of the world's PGR. The Commission on Genetic Resources for Food and Agriculture (CGRFA) coordinates the Code of Conduct for Biotechnology applied in the conservation and use of PGR, as well as work on farmers' rights and support for an international fund for PGR.

- FAO's agricultural research program strengthens countries' capabilities to generate and develop appropriate technology for crop protection and production. Special attention is given to traditional technologies and their use by farmers, as well as the role of rural women and the constraints they face.

- The Joint FAO/IAEA Division of Nuclear Techniques in Food and Agriculture operates a laboratory at Seibersdorf, near Vienna. The division's program is based on two fundamental approaches. Under the first, the movements and transformations of isotopically labeled chemical compounds of importance in relation to soils, water, air, plants, and livestock are studied. This information is used to improve management of soils and water, nutrition of plants and animals, and the safety of agrochemical use. The second approach uses ionizing radiation to induce mutations for selection of useful traits in plants, to sterilize insects for control purposes, and to improve the safety and preservation of food.

- FAO provides information on crops through a global database of crop environmental requirements, with data for hundreds of species.

Animal Production and Health

Livestock often forms a key component of the "production systems approach" promoted by FAO in agricultural development schemes. The approach is based on the principle that the production of different commodities is often linked and that increased production of one may result in increased output of another. In India, for example, the production of food grain increased markedly in villages where dairy cooperatives function. Milk sales provide the small farmer with the cash income to purchase fertilizers, improved seeds, and irrigation water essential for increased grain yields. Thus, increased milk production has led to significant improvements in farm output and living standards. This approach also is being applied to sheep, goat, poultry, and rabbit production.

FAO's International Dairy Development Program is designed

to help low-income countries modernize the complex chain linking milk producers and consumers. It helps coordinate efforts aimed at improving all aspects of the dairy industry, from farmers' organizations and veterinary services to processing plants and marketing channels. The program is aimed at assisting in the planning, coordination, and implementation of model projects for integrated dairy development, with the full participation of small-scale milk producers, the firm commitment of cooperating governments, and the active involvement of donors, and at making dairying a more effective force in rural development through its socioeconomic impact in rural areas and its contribution to nutrition.

FAO also works to improve livestock feeding and management by reducing to a minimum the amount of grain consumed by animals and making maximum use of pasture and fodder, crop residues, and agro-industrial by-products. An FAO database entitled *Tropical Feeds* offers concise and updatable information on over 500 tropical feed materials in published form and on diskette. This information is updated regularly.

Rapidly expanding human populations are increasing the demand for agricultural products—among them livestock—and in response, production is being intensified. To help foresee and forestall possible negative side effects of intensified production and enhance positive ones, FAO is conducting studies on the influence of livestock development practices on the natural resource base. These studies involve livestock feed quality, use of biomass for animal fodder, avoidance of overgrazing, manure management, animal waste disposal, domestic animal genetic diversity, plant and animal wildlife diversity, and integration of cropping and livestock systems.

FAO has joined hands with animal welfare organizations to initiate joint activities that will promote humane treatment of slaughter animals while heightening the quality of meat products and by-products. The organization also has helped boost the efficiency of village-level meat processing by developing modular designs for slaughtering and processing facilities. The designs employ affordable, easily available materials and modules that can be selected and adapted by users according to their needs. Use of the facilities helps reduce losses and limit contamination while increasing employment—particularly for rural women—as well as income for small producers.

Disease continues to check animal production in most developing countries. FAO focuses concerted attention on animal health involving the control of important diseases such as foot-and-mouth, rinderpest, swine fever, Rift-valley fever, trypanosomiasis, and Newcastle disease. In 1994 FAO established the Emergency Prevention System (EMPRES) for Transboundary Animal and Plant Pests and Diseases in order to minimize the risk of animal disease emergencies. Veterinary policy development and education also are stressed.

FAO and the International Atomic Energy Agency (IAEA) have established a laboratory to promote nuclear-based methodology and related molecular techniques for diagnosis of livestock diseases. Accurate diagnosis is fundamental to disease control and eradication. The laboratory cooperates closely with national and international organizations to promote standardization and transfer of techniques designed specifically for the difficult conditions often experienced in less advanced countries. Priority is being given to the diseases of greatest importance such as rinderpest, trypanosomiasis, and foot-and-mouth disease.

In 1993, FAO and UNEP first published the *World Watch List for Domestic Animal Diversity* to document the state of global livestock genetic diversity. Monitoring, describing, and characterizing existing breeds constitute a vital part of conservation, allowing people to understand each species' status, as well as its members' unique qualities and potential. The *World Watch List* is

the voice of the Global Early Warning System for Animal Genetic Resources in helping prevent erosion and encouraging a more effective use of farm animal genetic diversity. The second edition (published in 1995) covered 28 avian and mammalian species of farm animals and more than 120 species of their wild relatives.

Fisheries

In the 1970s, the concepts of national sovereignty over marine resources off the shores of coastal countries began to emerge. FAO assumed a key role in helping member nations to develop priorities and build up capacities to assess, allocate, exploit, and manage fisheries resources through a comprehensive Programme of Assistance in the Development and Management of Fisheries in Exclusive Economic Zones.

To respond to the demands arising from this situation, FAO convened a World Conference on Fisheries and Development in 1984. The conference was the largest of its sort ever assembled, bringing together representatives of nearly 150 countries and over 60 international organizations to confront the fundamental problems and potential of world fisheries as a vital source of food, employment, and income. Principles and guidelines for fisheries management were endorsed by the conference to cover the contribution of fisheries to national economic, social, and nutritional goals; improved national self-reliance in fisheries management and development; national management and optimum use of fish resources; the special role and needs of small-scale fisheries; international trade in fish and fishery products; investment in fisheries; and international cooperation in fisheries management and development.

FAO's fisheries policy is based on the five programs of action endorsed by the conference: fisheries planning, management, and development; small-scale fisheries; aquaculture; international trade in fish and fishery products; and the use of fish in alleviating undernutrition.

To aid in fisheries management, FAO collects statistics, monitors fishing trends in the world fishing fleet, collects biological information on resources, and assists member countries in the areas of fishery analysis, research, and management.

A network of regional fishery bodies established under the auspices of FAO provides an important framework for coordinating fisheries development and management. The first of these regional fishery bodies, the Indo-Pacific Fisheries Commission (IPFC), and now called the Asia-Pacific Fishery Commission (ASFC), was established in 1948. There are now nine regional bodies as well as three other FAO and UN bodies—the Advisory Committee on Fisheries Research (ACFR), Coordinating Working Party on Fishery Statistics (CWP), Group of Experts on the Scientific Aspects of Marine Environmental Protection (GESAMP) and the joint commission (with IMO, UNESCO, WMO, WHO, IAEA, and UNEP). Within the FAO framework, these commissions work to facilitate and secure the long-term sustainable development and utilization of the world's fisheries and aquaculture. As part of this effort, the FAO publishes the State of World Fisheries and Aquaculture, the only worldwide watch on fishery resources; runs the Species Identification and Data Programme; and maintains FishBase, a global information system on fishes (which can be accessed at www.fishbase.org). The FAO fisheries departments has also been instrumental in assisting developing nations in mapping their Exclusive Economic Zones (EEZs) in order to better manage their coastlines and resolve disputes.

National fish inspection and quality assurance programs have been upgraded in several countries. This is an area of some urgency because of more stringent health and sanitary requirements imposed in recent years by major importing countries, such as the United States and Japan.

In March 1999, during an international conference held by the FAO in Rome, representatives of some 120 countries expressed their growing concern about "over-fishing of the world's major marine fishery resources, destructive and wasteful fishing practices, and excess capacity." There are too many vessels or vessels with too much harvesting power in a growing number of fisheries. This leads to fewer fish in the sea for reproduction. In response, the FAO developed the Plan of Action on Fishing Capacity to achieve "an efficient, equitable and transparent management of fishing capacity." The FAO urged states to limit existing levels of fishing and progressively reduce fishing capacity. Between 2003 and 2005 each country supporting the international Plan of Action is to develop a national plan to manage fishing capacity and, if necessary, reduce it. According to the UN agency, only 6% of all major marine fisheries are under-exploited, 20% moderately exploited, 50% fully exploited, 15% overfished, 6% depleted, and 2% recovering.

The 1999 Plan of Action on Fishing Capacity was part of the FAO's ongoing effort to promote activities that protect the world's oceans, which are now recognized as a natural resource that must be preserved. Earlier (in 1994), the FAO prepared the technical guidelines for fishing operations as part of its Code of Conduct for Responsible Fishing. The code is intended to address unregulated fishing and to counteract negative effects on marine ecosystems.

As capture fisheries reach their peak, aquaculture is helping to fill gaps in supply. FAO promotes aquaculture development in rural communities as a valuable source of animal protein as well as of income and export earnings. The organization is supporting the development of a system to report aquaculture data separately from catch statistics, while concentrating on fish nutrition and breeding strain selection.

Reliable market information is a key ingredient of successful trade development for fish and fish products. The Fish Marketing Information System set up by FAO establishes contacts between buyers and sellers, provides price and market information, and offers technical assistance and advice on post-harvest aspects of fisheries including handling, processing, equipment selection, and quality.

Forestry

The importance of forests has become increasingly recognized, especially for people in developing countries. One problem is that more than 250 million rural people throughout the world practice some form of shifting cultivation. They slash and burn trees against a backdrop of rapidly disappearing forests. FAO has a number of community forestry projects aimed at settling shifting cultivators or integrating their activities into rural development plans.

Another problem is that wood, which is the major source of energy in developing countries, is in chronically short supply and women and children often have to walk many miles a day to gather it. With inadequate, and expensive, fuel supplies, many people are unable to cook their food properly, and lack of fuelwood can lead directly to malnutrition and disease. As the people harvest whatever woodland is available, the trees disappear, to be replaced by rangelands or deserts. In Nepal, for example, the loss of soil-protecting trees used mainly for fuelwood and animal fodder has led to landslides in the foothills and the loss of lives, homes, and crops. The situation is being improved, however, through projects to restore and manage the watersheds and to bring the population together in community forestry development, including the establishment of plantations of quickly maturing trees to provide fodder and fuelwood.

FAO's Tropical Forests Action Programme is fundamental in contributing to the objectives set forth in UNCED's Agenda 21 (developed at 1992's Earth Summit). The program is a major international undertaking uniting 90 partners in the battle to combat deforestation and to promote the conservation and sus-

tainable development of tropical forests. Together, the partners are following an international strategy to integrate forestry into farming systems, develop waste forest industries, increase supplies of fuelwood, and conserve tropical forest ecosystems while helping countries solve social and economic problems.

FAO's Forest Resources Assessment 1990 Project analyzed satellite images and existing survey data of 179 countries to assess deforestation between 1981 and 1990. The next periodic report will be Global Forest Resources Assessment 2000; it will constitute the most ambitious assessment to date and include new parameters on ecological aspects of forests, sustainable forest management, and non-wood goods and services. These assessments provide the factual information to frame international discussion on forestry: the reports detail the location and extent of forest resources, as well as highlight the net changes in extent, quantity, and quality over time.

The organization has carried out a wide variety of studies to develop participatory approaches and mechanisms for the management, production, and utilization of renewable natural resources—and of forests in particular—by rural people. FAO's Forests Trees and People Programme promotes self-reliance of rural groups in the sustainable management of forest resources.

Other forestry priorities include planning and policy formulation, national resources assessment, fire prevention and control, tree planting, conservation of genetic resources, plantation development, seed improvement, and development of harvesting and wood industries. Wildlife conservation and utilization also receive attention.

IMPROVING HANDLING AND DISTRIBUTION

Inadequate distribution of agricultural products causes waste of precious outputs and hinders agricultural development by reducing farmers' economic returns. FAO is involved at every stage in the distribution chain, from prevention of food losses in storage to attempts to bring about more equitable international trade. Programs deal with reduction of post-harvest losses, development of marketing skills, and promotion of trade terms that will help producers and exporters get a fair return.

Prevention of Post-Harvest Losses

In 1978, FAO began operations of its Action Program for the Prevention of Food Losses (PFL), designed primarily to reduce post-harvest losses of staple foods. The program focuses particular attention on women, major actors in the post-harvest system, through specific training activities and promotion of suitable technologies. Activities range from the development of adequate facilities for handling, drying, and storage to research on post-harvest practices that will protect harvests while reducing or avoiding the use of pesticides. For instance, FAO has successfully helped the Pacific Island nations develop control measures that will allow them to discontinue the use of ethylene dibromide, a pesticide banned by the major importers of fresh fruits and vegetables produced by the island countries.

Marketing

Poor marketing of local agricultural products often seriously impedes distribution and trade. Assistance is given to people involved in marketing from the grass-roots level to the senior management of marketing boards, as well as to officials responsible for marketing policy, legislation, and infrastructure. Direct assistance to marketing boards is aimed primarily at strengthening their management capacity and systems. FAO's field projects also support development of rural marketing centers and strengthening of the role of cooperatives.

In the 1990s, FAO developed the computerized version of FAO Agri-Market. This computer software program helps governments develop and perfect their price information systems, particularly during the transition from centrally planned to market-based economies. The organization also produces Marketing Extension Training Series videos focusing on techniques to be used by extension officers in providing marketing support to farmers.

Commodities and Trade

FAO's work on commodities and trade covers three main areas: commodity and trade policy, early warning, and food security.

In commodity policies and trade, FAO plays a lead role in the development of agricultural commodity projections. FAO's Intergovernmental Commodity Groups debate on developments in national policies, particularly those relating to protectionism, to analyze problems in commodity development and develop programs of work and projects.

FAO's Global Information and Early Warning System is housed in the Commodities and Trade Division (see Information for Agriculture). The preparation of information for the GIEWS entails continuous fielding of crop and food supply assessment missions to individual countries. GIEWS collects and analyzes a great variety of information from member nations, the private sector, and organizations active in the food, agriculture, and rural sectors, primarily in developing countries. When there are indications of unsatisfactory conditions, GIEWS intensifies its monitoring, most often involving on-the-spot missions to affected countries.

In the area of food security, FAO relies on national teams and workshops to derive and internalize realistic policy conclusions. The growing realization that food security is as much a question of household access to food as overall food availability has led to the development of composite indices of household food security in countries worldwide. These serve as a tool to governments in addressing the needs of vulnerable groups. The Food Security Assistance Scheme (see Advice to Governments) supports member nations in the formulation of comprehensive national food security programs.

SUSTAINABLE AGRICULTURAL RESOURCES DEVELOPMENT

In November 1991, the FAO Conference launched the International Cooperative Framework for Sustainable Agriculture and Rural Development. The SARD framework, as it has come to be known, supports the integration of sustainability criteria in the programs and activities of the organization. Guidelines for achieving SARD were set down in the Den Bosch Declaration at a major international conference organized by FAO and the Netherlands in 1991. Preparations for the Den Bosch Conference also contributed to FAO's input to the UN Conference on Environment and Development in 1992.

FAO helps member countries plan and implement environmentally positive projects through sustainability assessment and review of policies and plans in the agriculture and related natural resources sectors. Assessment and preparation of investment projects by FAO's Investment Centre focus on sustainability criteria. At the same time, FAO is the "task master" for the "land cluster" of Agenda 21: water resources, forests, fragile mountain ecosystems, and sustainable agriculture and rural development. The organization also chairs two UN sub-committees to coordinate the implementation of Agenda 21 chapters on oceans and water resources.

To meet growing needs for food, FAO advocates equitable, participatory rural development as the key to eradication of poverty, the first and foremost cause of undernutrition. At the same time, FAO's approach includes fine-tuning programs and projects to the continuing challenges of balancing increased production with environmental and sustainability concerns.

To improve linkages between agricultural research and exten-

sion, the FAO set up the Virtual Extension Research Communication Network (VERCON). The Internet-accessible network http://www.fao.org/waicent/vercon.htm consists of a number of collaborating research and extension institutions.

Land and Water Management

Among the most basic of resources for agriculture, water and soil are quickly reaching their limits. As burgeoning populations demand more food, the realization of the finiteness of resources, and of the need to manage them carefully, becomes increasingly acute. The effects of soil and water degradation are especially severe in the developing countries, and in particular among the rural poor who have the most limited access to these vital resources. FAO has initiated many research projects to help farmers in developing nations make the most of the resources available to them.

FAO helps national and nongovernmental institutions and organizations study the effects of erosion on soil productivity, develop methods for soil reclamation, improve management of arid and semi-arid soils, disseminate appropriate tillage techniques, and monitor soil micro-organisms and bacteria as well as waterlogging and salinity. The organization also helps rural communities combat deforestation and concomitant soil degradation, developing knowledge and self-reliance that makes them more efficient managers of the resources under their custody.

On the information side, in addition to providing data on soil use for scientists, FAO's digitized version of the Soil Map of the World (see Information for Agriculture) has been modified to make it accessible to nonspecialists. FAO contributes to technical seminars and general policy conferences on various aspects of soil and water management. For instance, the organization played a key role in the International Conference on Water and the Environment held in Dublin in 1992. The Dublin Statement emphasized water's economic value, and warned that this resource cannot be taken for granted.

The FAO maintains two computer programs designed as tools for increasing the efficiency of water use in agriculture. AQUASTAT is a global database on water use in agriculture and rural development. Though irrigation is the major issue, AQUASTAT provides information on such diverse aspects as drainage, environmental impact of water resources development, and water balance to users worldwide. The other computer-based system, SIMIS (Scheme Irrigation Management Information System), was developed to help reduce losses in irrigation systems. Many complex and shifting factors must be considered in irrigation schemes. Designed to be adaptable to diverse local situations in the developing world, the SIMIS system covers a range of irrigation management topics, from human resources administration, to information on climate, crops, soils, and machinery, to accounting codes. SIMIS can process information on one or several projects, making rapid and precise calculations to assess needs and possibilities while streamlining routine activities such as billing and registration.

Through the International Action Plan on Water and Sustainable Agricultural Development, FAO has launched programs in numerous member nations to help them manage water resources efficiently and meet the water needs of rural people.

A joint FAO/IAEA/SIDA research program uses neutron moisture meters to measure how water is used by crops and crop varieties. The study has shown that some varieties of cereals, for example, are up to three times more efficient in water use than others. The possibility of choosing water-efficient varieties provides farmers in water-scarce areas with welcome relief.

Nutrient Management

After land and water, fertilizers are the most important input for increasing agricultural yield. Increased efficiency in fertilizer use can cut farmers' costs while helping to protect the environment, increase yields, and heighten consumer satisfaction. One of the Agenda 21 missions spearheaded by FAO is the achievement of increased food production through improvements in plant nutrition systems. In 1993, the organization renamed its Fertilizer Programme to reflect essential changes in approach. The new Plant Nutrition Programme focuses on the application of Integrated Plant Nutrition Systems (IPNS).

Under the program, FAO promotes IPNS activities at the farm level for sustainable nutrient management based on a comprehensive vision of the cropping cycle. The objective is to help farmers establish the best association of biological (manure, crop residues), mineral, and naturally occurring (soil) nutrients to achieve a balanced supply while controlling losses and enhancing labor productivity.

Breeding research for improved plant nutrition concentrates on selecting and incorporating traits that will enhance a variety's nutrient uptake and utilization. In addition, the Plant Nutrition Programme helps governments develop sound policies and strategies at the national level, encouraging them to adapt or create institutions and organizations for the regulation of nutrient production, supply, and use.

Pest Control

FAO has numerous programs and projects aimed at reducing and rationalizing use of potentially harmful pesticides. The International Code of Conduct on the Distribution and Use of Pesticides (see Advice to Governments) identifies potential hazards and sets standards for those engaged in the regulation, distribution, and use of pesticides—governments, industry, traders, and users—to increase safety, efficacy, and economy.

FAO focuses its field work in plant protection on the application of the IPM strategy (see Crop Production and Protection) at the farm level, encouraging governments to support farmers who seek to improve production using these integrated methods. In Asia, over half a million rice growers have been able to minimize pesticide use and raise profits using techniques learned in IPM field schools. FAO has organized study tours to help plant protection specialists from countries in Africa, Latin America, and the Near East learn from the Asian experience. During the last two decades of the 20th century, pesticide use, combined with crop intensification practices and the use of fertilizers, substantially increased rice yield by farmers in developing countries.

PROMOTING RURAL DEVELOPMENT

Agrarian Reform and Rural Development

The World Conference on Agrarian Reform and Rural Development (WCARRD), sponsored by FAO in cooperation with other agencies of the UN system, was held at FAO headquarters in Rome in 1979. It was attended by more than 100 ministers and deputy ministers and some 1,400 other delegates from 145 countries. The conference approved a Declaration of Principles and a Program of Action to provide a framework for the reorientation of development policy and strategy toward greater participation and equity for rural people in the development process. FAO is the UN's lead agency for the implementation of the WCARRD program of action. Much of the work involves field projects to promote agrarian reform, land tenure improvement, and land settlement.

FAO helped to establish three regional centers to assist countries in the implementation of the program of action, and more generally, to coordinate activities in the area of integrated rural development at national level. The Centre on Integrated Rural Development for Asia and the Pacific (CIRDAP) is located in Dakha, Bangladesh; the Centre on Integrated Rural Development for Africa (CIRDAFRICA) is located in Arusha, Tanzania; and

the Centre for Agrarian Reform and Rural Development for the Near East (CARDNE) is located in Amman, Jordan.

Activities related to rural development form an integral and permanent part of FAO's mainstream program. Every four years, the secretariat assists governments in the preparation of progress reports on implementation of the WCARRD program of action. FAO has organized intergovernmental consultations on WCARRD follow-up in Africa, Asia and the Pacific, and Latin America and the Caribbean. Interagency and Expert Consultations have been convened by FAO regional offices. Finally, at the request of member countries, FAO has fielded high-level WCARRD follow-up missions to assist governments in reviewing national rural development and agrarian reform strategies.

This support is especially crucial in the context of the transition from central planning and control to market orientation being undergone by numerous countries.

Aid to Small Farmers

Close to half of the world's population lives in the rural areas of the developing countries. The majority of these people can be considered poor, they have very small agricultural holdings from which to derive their existence. It is often difficult for small farmers to make their voices heard in the social, economic, and political power structures.

FAO has numerous programs devoted to helping small farmers, taking into consideration the smallholders' needs, motivations, capabilities, risks, and resources, and how these factors affect the production and marketing of produce or its use by the farm family. Governments are encouraged to consider the rural poor in their policies and planning, providing the necessary inputs at the right time, in reasonable quantities, and at acceptable prices. Emphasis is also placed on building collective strength among farmers for identifying and finding solutions to their problems and preparing production plans on the basis of their particular needs and priorities. Farmer self-help organizations are assisted in planning and managing their credit requirements, and improved access to credit is stressed.

The Role of Women

Women play a crucial role in agricultural development, yet they are perhaps the least integrated of the players in the development process. FAO recognizes the vital importance of the full integration of women, and has developed a Plan of Action for the Integration of Rural Women into the Development Process. The plan outlines four principal areas of activity, focusing on the civil status, economic, social, and decision-making spheres of rural women. The plan of action outlines activities in each of these spheres to remove existing barriers to women and foster their potential. FAO's approach involves implementation of projects directed exclusively at women, as well as support for the concerns of women in all FAO's projects and activities.

Nutrition

FAO plays a key role in helping countries improve nutrition, promote healthy diets, and ensure access to safe food. Prime areas of interest include food quality control; handling, processing, and storage; household food security; forestry, fisheries, crop production, and local foods; and nutrition monitoring, assessment, planning, education, and information.

In 1992, the organization cosponsored with WHO the International Conference on Nutrition (see Food Security). The conference adopted a Declaration and Plan of Action for Nutrition. The countries at the conference composed a World Declaration on Nutrition and pledged their adherence to a plan of action for the coming decades. The World Declaration reaffirmed that "poverty and lack of education, which are often the effects of underdevelopment, are the primary causes of hunger and under-

Members of FAO
(as of November 1999)

Afghanistan
Albania
Algeria
Angola
Antigua and Barbuda
Argentina
Armenia
Australia
Austria
Azerbaijan
Bahamas
Bahrain
Bangladesh
Barbados
Belgium
Belize
Benin
Bhutan
Bolivia
Bosnia and Herzegovina
Botswana
Brazil
Bulgaria
Burkina Faso
Burundi
Cambodia
Cameroon
Canada
Cape Verde
Central African Republic
Chad
Chile
China
Colombia
Comoros
Congo
Congo, Democratic Republic of the
Cook Islands
Costa Rica
Côte d'Ivoire
Croatia
Cuba
Cyprus
Czech Republic
Denmark
Djibouti
Dominica
Dominican Republic
Ecuador
Egypt
El Salvador
Equatorial Guinea
Eritrea
Estonia
Ethiopia
European Economic Community (Member Organization)
Fiji
Finland
France
Gabon

Gambia
Georgia
Germany
Ghana
Greece
Grenada
Guatemala
Guinea
Guinea-Bissau
Guyana
Haiti
Honduras
Hungary
Iceland
India
Indonesia
Iran, Islamic Republic of
Iraq
Ireland
Israel
Italy
Jamaica
Japan
Jordan
Kazakhstan
Kenya
Kiribati
Korea, Democratic People's Republic of
Korea, Republic of
Kuwait
Kyrgyz Republic
Laos
Latvia
Lebanon
Lesotho
Liberia
Libyan Arab Jamahiriya
Lithuania
Luxembourg
Madagascar
Malawi
Malaysia
Maldives
Mali
Malta
Marshall Islands
Mauritania
Mauritius
Mexico
Moldova
Mongolia
Morocco
Mozambique
Myanmar
Namibia
Nepal
Netherlands
New Zealand
Nicaragua
Niger
Nigeria

Niue
Norway
Oman
Pakistan
Palau
Panama
Papua New Guinea
Paraguay
Peru
Philippines
Poland
Portugal
Puerto Rico (Associate Member)
Qatar
Romania
Rwanda
St. Kitts and Nevis
St. Lucia
St. Vincent and the Grenadines
Samoa
San Marino
Sâo Tomé and Principe
Saudi Arabia
Senegal
Seychelles
Sierra Leone
Slovakia
Slovenia
Solomon Islands
Somalia
South Africa
Spain
Sri Lanka
Sudan
Suriname
Swaziland
Sweden
Switzerland
Syria
Tajikistan
Tanzania
Thailand
The Former Yugoslav Republic of Macedonia
Togo
Tonga
Trinidad and Tobago
Tunisia
Turkey
Turkmenistan
Uganda
United Arab Emirates
United Kingdom
United States of America
Uruguay
Vanuatu
Venezuela
Vietnam
Yemen
Yugoslavia
Zambia
Zimbabwe

nutrition." It emphasized the need to identify the groups most in need, targeting nutritional resources first and foremost to alleviating their lot. It also stressed that food should not be used as a tool for political pressure. The importance of building knowledge among vulnerable groups through nutrition education was highlighted, as was the need for better preparedness for food emergencies resulting from civil strife and natural disasters.

The plan of action provides guidelines for governments, acting in partnership with NGOs, the private sector, local communities, families and households, and the international community. It contains recommendations on policies, programs, and activities identified through the intensive ICN consultative process and brings together a wide range of expert opinion from around the world. The 159 nations that participated in the ICN committed themselves to developing national nutrition plans with attainable goals and measurable targets. In the continuing follow-up to the ICN, FAO is assisting many governments in preparing national plans of action for nutrition. To support the process, the document "Guidelines for Developing National Plans of Action for Nutrition" was distributed to member governments.

Many FAO nutrition projects work towards improving knowledge of nutrition within households, and particularly among women. Awareness of the need to improve the frequency and quality of meals is built up through participatory, pilot-family programs concentrating on nutrition education and home gardening. Households are encouraged either to grow the foods they need to fill their dietary gaps or to use income from home gardens to purchase vitamin-and-mineral-rich fruits and vegetables they cannot easily cultivate.

FAO has produced country nutrition profiles for 100 developing countries to provide a concise view of their food and nutrition status, agricultural production, and economic and demographic situation. Country profiles are used by governments and institutions for planning and training. FAO advocates incorporating nutritional information in early warning networks to supplement agricultural production data.

The Codex Alimentarius (see Advice to Governments) contributes to raising nutritional status by developing international standards, codes of practice, and other recommendations for food quality to protect consumer health and encourage fair trading practices in the food trade. As of 2000, 162 countries were members of the Codex Alimentarius Commission.

FAO's World Food Survey, published about once a decade, provides as complete a picture as possible of the world food and nutrition situation. It includes food balance sheets for almost all countries and, increasingly, household food-consumption surveys for developing countries.

BIBLIOGRAPHY

Unless otherwise noted, all titles are published by the FAO. For a complete listing of available publications, visit their web site http://www.fao.org/icatalog/inter-e.htm.

Animal Health Yearbook.

Commodity Review and Outlook. Annual.

Fertilizer Yearbook.

FAO Plant Protection Bulletin. Quarterly.

Production Yearbook.

Trade Yearbook.

The State of Food and Agriculture. Annual.

Unasylva: An International Journal of Forestry and Forest Products. Quarterly.

World Agriculture: Towards 2010, An FAO Study. John Wiley & Sons, 1995.

Yearbook of Fishery Statistics.

Yearbook of Forest Products.

THE UNITED NATIONS EDUCATIONAL, SCIENTIFIC AND CULTURAL ORGANIZATION (UNESCO)

BACKGROUND: "Since wars begin in the minds of men," the preamble to the UNESCO constitution states, "it is in the minds of men that the defenses of peace must be constructed." As also stated in the preamble, "the great and terrible war which has now ended was a war made possible by the denial of the democratic principles of the dignity, equality and mutual respect of men and by the propagation, in their place, through ignorance and prejudice, of the doctrine of the inequality of men and races." World War II was too recent an event when UNESCO was created for its founders to forget that fact. UNESCO's purpose as a member of the UN family of organizations is "to contribute to peace and security by promoting collaboration among the nations through education, science and culture in order to further universal respect for justice, for the rule of law and for the human rights and fundamental freedoms which are affirmed for the peoples of the world, without distinction of race, sex, language or religion, by the Charter of the United Nations."

CREATION

Occasional attempts at international cooperation in educational, scientific, and cultural matters were made before World War I, but no machinery existed to promote these efforts on a worldwide scale. Even the League of Nations Covenant, when it was drawn up after the war, failed to mention international cooperation in these matters. However, thanks in great part to the efforts of the Belgian delegate Henri La Fontaine, a League of Nations Committee on Intellectual Cooperation was formed. Composed of 12 eminent persons, the committee met for the first time in the summer of 1922 under the chairmanship of the French philosopher Henri Bergson. Among those who served on the committee were Marie Curie, Gilbert Murray, and Albert Einstein. The intellectual atmosphere that prevailed in the committee was a lofty one, but at the same time the committee established precedents in practical matters that have proved useful to UNESCO. Thus, the 40-odd national committees on intellectual cooperation whose creation this committee promoted were a precedent for the national commissions now operating in over 173 countries to further the work of UNESCO. The International Institute of Intellectual Cooperation, established with the aid of the French government and located in Paris, began work early in 1926 and provided a permanent secretariat for the committee.

The League was thus provided with a technical body to promote international activity and was active in many fields, especially those of interest to scholars, professionals, learned societies, librarians, and the like. Numerous conferences and symposia were held under the auspices of the International Institute in Paris. Among the topics taken up by these conferences as the world situation became more menacing were the psychological causes of war and methods of promoting peaceful change as a substitute for war.

More intensive international cooperation in the field of educational problems began during World War II itself. A Conference of Allied Ministers of Education was convened in London in November 1942 to consider how the devastated educational systems of the countries under Nazi occupation could be restored after the war. The first meeting of the conference was attended by representatives of eight governments in exile and the French National Committee of Liberation. The conference met at frequent intervals throughout the war, with the participation of a growing number of representatives of other allied governments. The United States delegation to the April 1944 meeting of the conference included J. William Fulbright, then congressman and later senator from Arkansas, and the poet Archibald MacLeish, at that time Librarian of Congress, who was later to participate in the drafting of UNESCO's constitution.

It was decided at San Francisco that one of the objectives of the UN should be to promote international cultural and educational cooperation. Addressing the closing plenary session, President Truman declared: "We must set up an effective agency for constant and thorough interchange of thoughts and ideas, for there lies the road to a better and more tolerant understanding among nations and among peoples."

The conference creating UNESCO was convened by the United Kingdom and France in London in November 1945. It was decided that the new organization should deal not only with the transmission of existing knowledge but also with the pursuit of new knowledge. Hence, the encouragement of natural and social sciences through international cooperation was one of the principal tasks assigned UNESCO. UNESCO's constitution was adopted by the London conference after only two weeks of discussion and went into effect on 4 November 1946, when 20 states had deposited instruments of acceptance with the United Kingdom government.

PURPOSES

UNESCO's functions, as prescribed in its 1945 constitution, are as follows:

(a) to collaborate in the work of advancing the mutual knowledge and understanding of peoples through all means of mass communication;

(b) to give fresh impulse to popular education and to the spread of culture by collaborating with members, at their request, in the development of educational activities; by instituting collaboration among the nations to advance the ideal of equality of educational opportunities without regard to race, sex, or any distinctions, economic or social; and by suggesting educational methods best suited to prepare the children of the world for the responsibilities of freedom; and

(c) to maintain, increase, and diffuse knowledge by ensuring the conservation and protection of the world's heritage of books, works of art, and monuments of history and science; by encouraging cooperation among the nations in all branches of intellectual activity, including the international exchange of persons active in the fields of education, science, and culture and the exchange of publications, objects of artistic and scientific interest, and other materials of information; and by initiating methods of international cooperation calculated to give the people of all countries access to the printed and published materials produced by any of them."

Since UNESCO's constitution specifically emphasizes the need to preserve "the independence, integrity and fruitful diversity of the cultures and educational systems" of the member states, the organization cannot impose any particular standard either on all its members or on any of them, and it is "prohibited from intervening in matters . . . within their domestic jurisdiction."

MEMBERSHIP

Any UN member may join UNESCO. Other states may be admitted to UNESCO membership upon the recommendation of the organization's Executive Board and the approval of its General Conference by a two-thirds majority. Austria, Hungary, and Japan joined UNESCO years before entering the UN.

Under a United Kingdom-proposed amendment to the constitution adopted in 1951, territories or groups of territories not responsible for their international relations can be admitted as associate members upon application of member states or other authorities responsible for their international relations. Associate members do not have the right to vote.

A state may withdraw from UNESCO by notifying the organization's director-general of its intention to do so; the withdrawal takes effect as of the end of the respective calendar year. South Africa withdrew as of 31 December 1956. Czechoslovakia, Hungary, and Poland suspended their participation in UNESCO activities in 1952 but returned as active participants in 1954. Portugal withdrew in 1972 but returned in 1974. In November 1974, a vote dominated by Arab and Communist delegations excluded Israel from UNESCO's European regional group and withheld aid from it on the ground that it persists "in altering the historic features" of Jerusalem during excavations—an allegation not sustained by UNESCO's archaeological expert.

At the end of 1984, the United States withdrew from UNESCO, stating that "trends in the policy, ideological emphasis, budget, and management of UNESCO were detracting from the organization's effectiveness." One year later, the United Kingdom and Singapore withdrew. In February 1994, the *New York Times* reported that the United States State Department had recommended that the US rejoin UNESCO, which had cut its staff by nearly 1,800 people and changed its stand on the controversial New World Information and Communications Order (NWICO). In late 1995, plans by the Clinton administration to rejoin UNESCO were postponed due to budgetary constraints. Until its departure, the United States had been responsible for 25% of UNESCO's budget. As of 2000, the United States had not rejoined.

As of 2000, UNESCO had 188 members and 5 associate members.

STRUCTURE

UNESCO is an autonomous organization affiliated with the UN through a relationship agreement signed in 1946. Its three principal organs are the General Conference, the Executive Board, and the secretariat, headed by a director-general.

General Conference

All UNESCO members have the right to be represented in the General Conference, which determines UNESCO's policies and decides on its major undertakings. Each member state has one vote in the conference but may be represented by five delegates. The constitution of UNESCO requires that member governments are to consult with national educational, scientific, and cultural bodies before selecting these delegates; in countries where UNESCO commissions have been established, these too are to be consulted.

From 1946 through 1952, the General Conference met every year. Since then it has met generally every two years. As a rule, the conference takes place in Paris, but it has also met in Mexico City, Beirut, Florence, Montevideo, New Delhi, Nairobi, Belgrade, and Sofia.

Decisions of the General Conference are made by a simple majority vote, except for certain constitutionally specified matters that require a two-thirds majority, such as amending the UNESCO constitution or adopting an international convention. Member nations are not automatically bound by conventions adopted by the General Conference, but the UNESCO constitution requires them to submit such conventions to their appropriate national authority for ratification within one year. The same applies to recommendations, which the General Conference is empowered to adopt by simple majority vote.

Executive Board

Elected by the General Conference, the Executive Board is one of three constitutional organs of UNESCO and consists of 58 member states serving a four-year term. It supervises the execution of UNESCO's program. It meets at least twice a year. Before the General Conference convenes, the Executive Board reviews the budget estimates and work program for the following two-year period, as prepared by the director-general. It submits these with its recommendations to the General Conference and prepares the agenda for the conference.

Originally, the UNESCO constitution provided that "although the members of the Executive Board are representatives of their respective governments, they shall exercise the powers delegated to them by the General Conference on behalf of the Conference as a whole." Until 1993, the members of the board were not member states, but personalities designated by name. UNESCO's constitution only designated that the General Conference should "endeavor to include persons competent in the arts, the humanities, the sciences, education and the diffusion of ideas." In 1993, the General Conference changed this criteria. Since that time, the member states of the Executive Board are requested to appoint a person qualified in one or more of the fields of competence of UNESCO and with the necessary experience and capacity to fulfill the administrative and executive duties of the board. The General Conference, in electing member states to the Executive Board, must also take into account the diversity of cultures and balanced geographical distribution.

Following a constitutional amendment adopted by the General Conference in 1972, board members are elected for four years and are not immediately eligible for a second term. At each session, the General Conference elects members to succeed those whose terms end with that session. A system of electoral groups of member states, governing only elections to the Executive Board, was established in 1968.

Director-General and Secretariat

The secretariat carries out UNESCO's programs. It is headed by a director-general, nominated by the Executive Board and elected by the General Conference. The staff members are appointed by the director-general. Julian Huxley of the United Kingdom was UNESCO's first director-general. Federico Mayor Zaragoza of Spain was elected director-general in November 1987, succeeding Amadou-Mahtar M'Bow of Senegal, who had held the post since 1974. At the 1993 General Conference, Mr. Mayor was elected for a second six-year term. Koichiro Matsuura of Japan was appointed Director-General at the General Conference on 12 November 1999.

Headquarters. UNESCO's first headquarters were in the Hotel Majestic, in Paris, a building which, ironically, had served as the headquarters for the German army during its occupation of France. In 1958, the organization's headquarters were transferred to a 3-hectare (7.5-acre) site, located at 7 place de Fontenoy, donated to UNESCO by the government of France.

UNESCO headquarters originally consisted of a conference building, a secretariat building, and a building for the permanent delegations assigned to UNESCO. In 1965, a new building constructed around underground patios was added, and in 1970 and 1977, two supplementary buildings. The buildings were designed and approved by several leading architects. Works by contemporary artists are an integral part of the headquarters.

Field Offices

UNESCO has been criticized by the United States since the 1980s for the concentration of its staff at its headquarters office in Paris, rather than in the field. A 1992 report by the US State Department said that 73% of UNESCO's total staff of 2,697 persons were located in Paris. The same report also conceded that, despite this fact, 44% of the organization's regular and extra-budgetary resources were spent in the field. This disparity, however, may simply reflect the vastly different nature of UNESCO's mandate, as opposed to the mandate of technically-oriented specialized agencies. In 1999, UNESCO had a staff of 2,382, of which 1,717 worked in the headquarters and 665 in more than 70 field offices. The percentage of staff working in the field had not markedly changed since 1980, though the number of field offices had increased.

In Africa, UNESCO offices are located in Luanda, Angola; Porto Novo, Benin; Ouagadougou, Burkina Faso; Bujumbura, Burundi; Yaounde, Cameroon; Bangui, Central African Republic; Brazzaville, Congo; Kinshasa, Democratic Republic of the Congo; Abidjan, Côte d'Ivoire; Addis Ababa, Ethiopia; Libreville, Gabon; Accra, Ghana; Conakry, Guinea; Nairobi, Kenya; Bamako, Mali; Maputo, Mozambique; Windhoek, Namibia; Abuja, Nigeria; Kigali, Rwanda; Dakar, Senegal; Pretoria, South Africa; Dar es Salaam, United Republic of Tanzania; Lusaka, Zambia; and Harare, Zimbabwe.

In the Arab world, UNESCO offices are located in Cairo, Egypt; Amman, Jordan; Beirut, Lebanon; Rabat, Morocco; Ramallah, West Bank (Palestine)—liaison office; Doha, Qatar; and Tunis, Tunisia.

In Asian and the Pacific, UNESCO offices are located in Dhaka, Bangladesh; Phnom Penh, Cambodia; Beijing, China; New Delhi, India; Jakarta, Indonesia; Tehran, Iran; Almaty, Kazakhstan; Kuala Lumpur, Malaysia; Kathmandu, Nepal; Islamabad, Pakistan; Apia, Samoa; Bangkok, Thailand; Tashkent, Uzbekistan; and Hanoi, Vietnam.

In Europe and North America, UNESCO offices are located in Vienna, Austria; Sarajevo, Bosnia and Herzegovina; Quebec, Canada; Venice, Italy; Bucharest, Romania; Moscow, Russian Federation; Geneva, Switzerland; and New York and Washington, DC, United States—liaison offices.

In Latin America and the Caribbean, UNESCO offices are located in Buenos Aires, Argentina; Bridgetown, Barbados; La Paz, Bolivia; Brasilia, Brazil; Santiago, Chile; San Jose, Costa Rica; Havana, Cuba; Santo Domingo, Dominican Republic; Quito, Ecuador; San Salvador, El Salvador; Guatemala City, Guatemala; Port-au-Prince, Haiti; Kingston, Jamaica; Mexico City, Mexico; Panama City, Panama; Asunción, Paraguay; Lima, Peru; Port of Spain, Trinidad and Tobago; Montevideo, Uruguay; and Caracas, Venezuela.

National Commissions for UNESCO

The UNESCO constitution requests every member state to associate "its principal bodies interested in educational, scientific, and cultural matters with the work of the Organization, preferably by the formation of a National Commission. . . ." By 2000, 188 member states had established such broadly representative national commissions to collaborate with UNESCO in attaining its objectives. These commissions are not official UNESCO organs, but they provide a vital link between UNESCO and the public at large. They advise their governments and the delegations that attend the UNESCO General Conference on pertinent matters and serve as liaison agencies and information outlets.

The various national commissions vary greatly in size and composition. Often the country's minister of education is the commission's president, and its members may include high government officials, leaders in the fields of education, science, and the arts, and representatives of professional organizations. Through meetings, publications, broadcasts, contests, and exhibitions, the commissions stimulate public interest in specific UNESCO projects. National UNESCO commissions of several countries often meet for regional conferences. National commissions are frequently given contracts to translate UNESCO publications and to handle printing and distribution of these translations.

Cooperation with Nongovernmental Organizations

The constitution of UNESCO states that "a peace based exclusively upon the political and economic arrangements of governments would not be a peace which could secure the unanimous, lasting and sincere support of the peoples of the world" and that "peace must therefore be founded, if it is not to fail, upon the intellectual and moral solidarity of mankind."

In order to attain that objective, the founders of UNESCO sought ways of associating the peoples of the world as closely as possible in the preparation and implementation of the organization's aims and programs. Thus, from its inception, UNESCO has sought the collaboration of international nongovernmental organizations (NGOs). The NGOs with which UNESCO cooperates have activities and interests paralleling those of the organization, ranging from specialized or scholarly organizations (of teachers, scientific researchers, philosophers, sociologists, journalists, writers, and legal experts) to mass organizations (trade unions, cooperatives, women's associations, and youth movements) and denominational organizations.

UNESCO consults and cooperates with NGOs so as to receive the broadest possible assistance from them in the preparation and implementation of its programs, thus strengthening international cooperation in the fields of education, science, and culture.

BUDGET

For the biennium 2000–01, the General Conference approved a regular budget of US$544,367,250, which represented zero nominal growth. At the same time, the organization has increased financing for its programs while reducing administrative costs. US$168,209,480 was for Education; US$132,281,242 was for Natural, Social and Human Sciences; US$65,868,437 was for Culture; US$50,081,787 was for Communication, Information and Informatics; US$31,573,301 was for Transdisciplinary Project Towards a Culture of Peace; US$28,851,464 was for Transverse Activities; US$33,750,770 was for Participation Program; and US$33,750,770 was for Information and Dissemination Services.

UNESCO's budget is financed through contributions assessed against member states on a sliding scale. For the biennium 2000–01, these assessments ranged from a minimum of 0.01% of the total amount to 25% (Japan).

UNESCO receives funds from other specialized agencies of the UN system—mainly UNDP, UNFPA, UNEP and the World Bank—and regional banks for operational assistance to member states. For the 2000–01 biennium, it was estimated that these funds, when added to funds from other sources, would make a grand total of US$250 million in extrabudgetary resources devoted to operational projects.

ACTIVITIES

UNESCO's work is carried out principally in the fields of education, the natural sciences, the social and human sciences, culture, and communication.

At the 27th session of the General Conference (1993), a broad consensus emerged on the need to concentrate efforts on two of the objectives common to the United Nations system as a whole—the consolidation of peace and the promotion of sustainable human development. The General Conference also underlined the importance of UNESCO's role in promoting international intellectual cooperation, that is, acting as an international "think tank."

The Organization's Constitution outlines UNESCO's fundamental mission of promoting access to, and the transfer and sharing of knowledge. UNESCO's continued role of offering guidance, advice, and assessment when needed calls for strengthening activities in the following areas: anticipating and preparing innovative strategies, gathering and circulating reliable information on the present situation and probable trends in the Organization's fields of competence; and encouraging political leaders at the highest level to make firm commitments.

UNESCO's recent actions have been largely determined by commitments made at the major intergovernmental conferences it has recently convened—solely or jointly with other UN agencies—or in which it has participated, in particular the World Conference on Education for All, held in Jomtien, Thailand, in March 1990 and the United Nations Conference on Environment and Development (UNCED), held in Rio de Janeiro, Brazil, in June 1992.

The increasingly global nature and growing complexity of the problems in today's world call for a multidisciplinary or transdisciplinary approach in many of UNESCO's activities. A good example is the interdisciplinary project "Environment and population education and information for human development," conceived following the Rio Conference and aimed at the adoption of an integrated approach in order to achieve a development that is people-centered, equitable, and sustainable.

UNESCO's transdisciplinary Action Programme to Promote a Culture of Peace was created in 1993 to initiate activities in favor of the consolidation of peace following conflict. This involves reconstituting social infrastructures, fostering national reconciliation, reintegrating displaced persons, constructing a basis for a democratic citizenship, helping to create endogenous capabilities and ensuring the broadest possible involvement of the population in development efforts.

Since the fall of the Berlin Wall in 1989, UNESCO has been at the forefront of UN and international action in Central and Eastern Europe. The 26th Session of the General Conference (1991) called for UNESCO "to establish intersectoral coordination to support the introduction of democratic reforms" and "to establish close cooperation for carrying out this activity with international intergovernmental and non-governmental organizations, funds and other bodies" in support of Central and eastern Europe and in the newly independent states of the former Soviet Union. It

was decided that the many existing activities in the region could be better focused if they were brought together under a single program, and the Programme for Central and Eastern European Development (PROCEED) was created.

Finally, the Organization's action in recent years has been focused on satisfying the needs of three priority target groups—the least developed countries, the UNESCO member states of Africa, and women.

A. Education

UNESCO's largest sectoral activity, education, is the field for constant but changing endeavor. From originally helping to reconstruct educational systems in war-torn Europe and carrying out isolated, modest projects elsewhere, UNESCO has progressed to large-scale undertakings, such as literacy campaigns, rural development, science teaching, educational planning and administration, and teacher training.

UNESCO's major education activities have focused on basic education, the renewal of educational systems and educational advancement and policy.

In activities following up the 1990 World Conference on Education for All, UNESCO has assisted member states in diagnosing basic learning needs, setting national education-for-all (EFA) objectives, and devising effective strategies to move towards EFA.

In cooperation with UNFPA, UNESCO organized the International Congress on Population Education and Development (Istanbul, April 1993) which adopted the Istanbul Declaration and Action Framework for Population Education on the Eve of the Twenty-first Century.

Emergency assistance programs and reconstruction operations in the field of education were carried out in such countries as Afghanistan, Albania, Angola, Bosnia and Herzegovina, Cambodia, Croatia, Iraq, Lebanon, Mozambique, Slovenia, and Somalia. Following the international meeting on "Peace, the day after," held in Granada, Spain in December 1993, activities aimed at the rebuilding of Palestinian educational and cultural institutions were initiated.

The Scheme of Humanitarian Assistance for Refugee Education (SHARE) responds specifically to the needs of refugee children. The program goes beyond the urgent but short-term goal of providing shelter, food, and medicines, to develop a coherent policy of refugee education in cooperation with local and national authorities. After initial experiences in Cambodia, Somalia, and Afghanistan, SHARE activities were also carried out in Slovenia and Croatia.

UNESCO also promotes studies and teaching in the fields of drugs, population, and the environment. In cooperation with WHO, the Organization has elaborated a joint prototype curriculum for AIDS education in schools and disseminated documents and guidelines to support AIDS education programs in member states.

The UNITWIN/UNESCO Chairs Programme was launched in 1991 to strengthen cooperation between universities through twinning arrangements and promote the development of interuniversity networks in order to facilitate the exchange of knowledge and improve teacher training. As of 30 September 1999, there were 63 UNITWIN networks.

The World Education Report, a biennial first published in 1991, presents a broad but concise analysis of major trends and policy issues in education, including many tables, graphs, and a unique set of statistics—"World Education Indicators"—which give a country-by-country summary of key aspects of education in over 160 countries.

In January 1993, UNESCO set up the International Commission on Education for the Twenty-First Century, under the Chairmanship of Jacques Delors, President of the Commission of the European Community, to study and reflect on the challenges facing education in the coming years, and to make recommendations that can serve as an agenda for renewal, innovation, and action for policy-makers. The Commission focused its reflection on one central question—what kind of education is needed for what kind of society of tomorrow?—in its report at the end of 1995.

The Associated Schools Project (ASP), an international network set up to experiment with ways and means for enhancing the role of education in preparing young people to live in a world community, was launched in 1953. As of 1999, it included over 5,600 educational institutions in 162 countries, which conduct pilot projects to enhance education for a culture of peace. ASPnet schools focus on any of four main themes of study: World Concerns and the United Nations system, Human Rights and Democracy, Intercultural Learning, and Environmental Issues.

Closely linked with the Associated Schools Project, often carrying out joint projects in crucial fields such as literacy work and the environment, are the 5,000 UNESCO associations, centers and clubs, the first of which was founded in 1947. Found in some 120 countries, with members from all age groups, they are set up in schools, universities, as associations or as permanent centers and, since 1981, are grouped together as part of the World Federation of UNESCO Clubs, Centers and Associations (WFUCA).

In specific educational areas, UNESCO's work is supported by three separate institutes which conduct research and training programs. The International Bureau of Education (IBE), located in Geneva, serves as an international center for studies and publications on comparative education. The Institute for Educational Planning (IIEP), in Paris, organizes an annual nine-month training program for education planners and administrators, and offers training courses in the planning, financing and management of education. The Institute for Education (UIE), located in Hamburg, focuses on adult and non-formal education, within the framework of lifelong learning.

B. The Natural Sciences

UNESCO is the only organization within the UN system to have a mandate for the basic sciences. This mandate implies UNESCO's commitment to the promotion of multilateral, international, and regional cooperation for the training of specialists from developing countries in university science education and basic research in the four core areas of basic science, namely mathematics, physics, chemistry, and biology. Projects to be implemented in these and allied, interdisciplinary areas are selected for the impact they will have on strengthening national capacities, enabling access to current scientific information, human resources development, and their real or potential impact on sustainable development.

One of the main accomplishments of the Rio Conference on Environment and Development was Agenda 21, an international program of action for global sustainable development into the 21st century. Because of its broad mandate and long experience, UNESCO is implicated in many aspects of UNCED follow-up, with particular emphasis on Agenda 21 and the conventions on biological diversity and climate change.

In UNESCO's Natural Sciences sector, priority is therefore being given to implementing the recommendations of Agenda 21 by promoting multidisciplinary scientific programs which combine training, information and research and which are at the interface between environment and development. Special attention is also being accorded to the promotion of teaching (especially at the university level) and research in the basic sciences and engineering.

Environment and development problems have been a major focus of the Organization's work for the past 50 years. Beginning with the Arid Zone Programme in 1951, numerous UNESCO programs have been launched to address research, education, training, and policy needs related to specific environment and development issues, such as water resources management and the conservation of biological diversity and ecological systems such as islands, tropical forests, and arid lands.

The activities of the Intergovernmental Oceanographic Commission (IOC), with 124 countries participating, primarily center around narrowing down the uncertainties about the role of the ocean in climate and global systems. In response to Agenda 21, the IOC adopted new strategies and action plans, especially in the field of oceanography.

IOC has developed global and regional ocean science programs related to living and non-living resources, and marine pollution research and monitoring, and enhanced the efficiency of the International Tsunami Warning System in the Pacific. It also organizes training and assistance and provides information, together with WMO, to coastal and island member states on events in the oceans and adjacent seas through a quarterly "Products Bulletin of the Integrated Global Ocean Services System," a precursor of the Global Ocean Observing System (GOOS).

The International Hydrological Decade, another intergovernmental program, was launched by UNESCO in 1965. In 1975 it became a long-term endeavor, the International Hydrological Programme (IHP). Now in its fourth phase (1990–95), the IHP is actively involved with some 150 countries in the development of scientific bases for the rational management of water resources. The objectives of IHP-IV have been divided into three sub-programs: Hydrological research in a changing environment; Management of water resources for sustainable development; and Education, training, the transfer of knowledge and public information.

UNESCO's first *World Science Report* was produced in 1993. Through updated editions, it aims to provide an understanding of the present state of science around the world, including the ways in which scientific research is organized and how it works.

Under the "Diversitas" program, in cooperation with the International Union of Biological Sciences (IUBS) and the Special Committee on Pollution and the Environment (SCOPE) of the International Council of Scientific Unions (ICSU), UNESCO is promoting worldwide coordinated research on, and inventories and the monitoring of, biological diversity.

A Biotechnological Information Exchange System (BITES) has also been developed.

The Man and the Biosphere (MAB) Programme was launched in 1971 as an international program of applied research on the interactions between man and his environment. The program aims to provide the scientific knowledge and trained personnel to manage natural resources in a rational and sustained manner, giving priority to work in the field at the local level, within general frameworks for scientific cooperation at the international level. Based on a network of 128 MAB national committees, the program monitors the international biosphere reserve network, composed (as of January 2000) of 368 sites located in 91 countries, and has developed a number of problem-oriented research programs involving specialists from developing countries.

The International Geological Correlation Programme is a joint environmental activity between UNESCO and the International Union of Geological Sciences (IUGS), whose objectives are increasing knowledge of geological processes through correlation studies of many locations around the world, developing more effective ways of finding and assessing energy and mineral resources, and improving research methods and techniques. The transfer of traditional and new technologies, such as computerized information handling (GIS, DAS and PANGIS) and remote sensing analysis (e.g. GARS) to developing countries is privileged.

C. The Social and Human Sciences

UNESCO encourages the development of the social and human sciences at the international and regional levels by promoting training and research activities, as well as international exchanges.

In the fields of peace, human rights, and democracy, UNESCO's activities are aimed at the promotion and protection of human rights, consolidation of peace and democracy, as well as at the prevention and elimination of all forms of discrimination by means of research and education, dissemination of information and publications, and organization of meetings in cooperation with governments, intergovernmental and non-governmental organizations. UNESCO's activities in this field have led to the elaboration of important international instruments.

The emergence of multicultural and multiethnic societies, urbanization, and globalization are the transformation processes at the heart of the Management of Social Transformations Programme (MOST), established by the 1993 General Conference to foster policy-relevant, interdisciplinary and comparative social science research in three fields—the management of multiethnic societies, cities as arenas of accelerated social transformations, and coping locally and regionally with transnational phenomena.

The International Bioethics Committee, composed of specialists in biology, genetics, medicine, law, philosophy, and the social and human sciences, was set up to meet the ethical concern arising from progress in life sciences.

Within the framework of a UNESCO/UNFPA project, research is conducted on socio-cultural factors affecting demographic change.

UNESCO has an extensive program on the improvement of women's condition, stressing the principle of equality between men and women and against all forms of discrimination. This program provided input for the Fourth UN World Conference on Women: Action for Equality, Development and Peace (Beijing, September 1995).

The organization's youth program deals with the analysis of problems and dissemination of information concerning youth, enrollment of young people in the service of international cooperation, development and peace, and action on behalf of disadvantaged young people. To counteract splintering of various and scattered information sources and networks on youth and to help implement youth policies from global to local levels, in 1991 UNESCO set up the INFOYOUTH Network, a clearing house and information service for members states and partners.

D. Culture

UNESCO's main cultural activities are devoted to safeguarding the cultural heritage, preserving and fostering respect for cultural identities and diversity, and promoting creative and intellectual expression. Almost two thousand projects were launched worldwide in the context of the World Decade for Cultural Development (1988–97), including projects on the "Maya World," "Espaces du Baroque," "Slave Route" and "Iron Road." "The Silk Roads: Routes of Dialogue" project continues to assess the findings of four expeditions carried out in previous years and a joint UNESCO/World Tourism Organization project for cultural tourism on the Silk Roads in Central Asia was launched in 1993.

Safeguarding of Cultural Heritage

Under the terms of its constitution, UNESCO was entrusted with the task of "ensuring the preservation and protection of the world heritage of works of art and monuments of historic or scientific interest."

Training activities aimed at strengthening the application of the 1954 Hague Convention for the Protection of Cultural Property in the Event of Armed Conflict and the 1970 Convention on the Means of Prohibiting and Preventing the Illicit Import, Export and Transfer of Ownership of Cultural Property continue to be an important part of UNESCO's activities in this field.

UNESCO's activities in safeguarding the world's cultural heritage are best known through its campaigns to mobilize international support. The first such campaign was devoted to safeguarding the monuments of Nubia, in Egypt, and led to the successful reconstruction of the Temple of Abu Simbel, a us$40 million undertaking. Another project, successfully brought to a conclusion in 1983, was the restoration of Borobudur in Indonesia. A second Egyptian campaign was devoted to the creation of museums in Aswan and Cairo. As of 30 November 1999, the World Heritage List in Danger included 27 sites around the world, including two in the United States—Everglades National Park and Yellowstone.

The growing determination of member states to preserve their national cultural heritage has led to an increase in museum development and in activities to preserve historical monuments and sites, works of art, and other cultural property. UNESCO's contribution in this field has consisted mainly in the provision of consultant services, equipment, supplies, and financial assistance to individual projects throughout the world. Improving the training of specialists in the conservation, preservation, and presentation of cultural heritage has involved the provision of lecturers and fellowships for international, regional, and subregional training projects.

UNESCO's activities have also resulted in the adoption of a number of conventions and recommendations, such as the International Convention Concerning the Protection of the World Cultural and National Heritage—called the World Heritage Convention—adopted by the General Conference in 1972. The convention provides, for the first time, a permanent legal, administrative, and financial framework for international cooperation. It also relates sectors that had previously been considered very different—the protection of cultural heritage and that of natural heritage—and introduces the concept of "world heritage," transcending political and geographical boundaries. The convention aims to foster a greater awareness among all peoples of the irreplaceable value of world heritage and the perils to which it is exposed. It is intended to complement, assist, and stimulate national endeavors without either competing with or replacing them. By May 2000, the convention had been ratified or accepted by 160 member states. The World Heritage Committee has thus far included 630 cultural and natural sites on the World Heritage List and has regularly approved financial support for technical cooperation through the World Heritage Fund.

Under its research, study, and information exchange activities, UNESCO has contributed to the advancement and spread of specialized knowledge concerning heritage preservation. It has issued a series of technical manuals on such subjects as museums, underwater archaeology, preserving and restoring monuments and historic buildings, the man-made landscape, conservation standards for works of art in transit and on exhibition, and conservation of stone. In response to the need for more elementary and accessible practical guidance, particularly in developing countries, a new series of technical handbooks was launched in 1975. The quarterly, *Museum,* published since 1948, is an international forum of information and reflection on museums of all kinds.

Study and Dissemination of Cultures

An important part of UNESCO's activities in the field of culture focus on cultural identity, including the preparation of general histories and works on various geocultural areas.

By 1999, the UNESCO publications catalog listed more than 1,000 titles in English, French, Spanish, Russian, Chinese, and Arabic, published under its own imprint or co-published. The organization publishes some 160 new titles each year and has distributors in 122 countries. For young readers, the World Heritage series is a bestseller with over 1.3 million copies printed in English, French, and Spanish. Large-scale international projects involving specialists from different countries have resulted in major works such as *The General History of Africa, History of*

Humanity, History of Civilizations of Central Asia, History of Latin America, and *History of the Caribbean.*

Cultural Development

The Universal Declaration of Human Rights asserts that everyone has the right to participate freely in the cultural life of society. This principle implies the right of people in different societies to share in the cultural heritage of the world community, and it implies that culture cannot be the privilege of an elite few but must be regarded as a dimension of human life. In this spirit, since the end of the 1960s, UNESCO has attached increased importance to cultural policies and activities related to cultural development. The principles governing UNESCO's activities in the field of culture stress the strengthening of the cultural dimension of development, that is, viewing culture not only in itself but also in relation to certain key areas of development, such as educational systems (including the cultural content of education and the adaptation of teaching models to local culture), the environment, science, and communication.

In 1970 the Intergovernmental Conference on Institutional, Administrative, and Financial Aspects of Cultural Policies, held in Venice, examined the role of public authorities in defining and achieving the objectives of cultural development and acknowledged for the first time the responsibility of governments to provide and plan for the cultural needs of society by implementing appropriate cultural policies. The Venice conference was followed by a series of regional conferences on cultural policies. Discussions at these meetings reflected a need to locate humanity and culture at the heart of the development process, rather than considering development as only economic progress.

The World Conference on Cultural Policies, held in Mexico City in 1982, took stock of the experience acquired in policies and practices in the field of culture and gave new impetus to the worldwide action carried out under UNESCO's auspices. The conference unanimously adopted the Mexico City Declaration on Cultural Policies, which proclaimed the guiding principles for promoting culture and strengthening the cultural dimension of development.

The World Commission on Culture and Development, under the Chairmanship of former UN Secretary-General Javier Pérez de Cuéllar was set up in December 1992 to focus on interrelations between culture and development in general and cultural policies and development models in particular. The Commission, composed of 12 members and five honorary members, presented its final report at the end of 1995 to the UN General Assembly and UNESCO's General Conference. The Commission's work is centered around five fundamental questions: the impact of cultural and socio-cultural factors on development; the impact of social and economic development on culture; the relationship between culture and models of development; the influence of cultural development on individual and collective well-being; and the role of cultural activities and artistic creativity in development and international cooperation.

E. Communication, Information, and Informatics

UNESCO is enjoined by its constitution to "collaborate in the work of advancing the mutual knowledge and understanding of peoples, through all means of mass communication." It is also authorized to recommend international agreements to facilitate "the free flow of ideas by word and image" and to encourage the international exchange of persons active in intellectual affairs and the exchange of "publications, objects of scientific interest, and other materials of information."

New World Information and Communication Order (NWICO)

In the 1970s, developing countries began to express their concern that the world's news media were predominantly Western-controlled. Major syndicated newspapers, press agencies like UPI,

Reuters and Agence France Presse, the US networks, the BBC, and the ORTF of France, were seen to be innately biased in their reporting on third world countries. It was felt that those organizations were able to greatly influence public opinion both in their own nations and in the developing countries themselves. The new nations of the UN system called for a New World Information and Communication Order (NWICO) which would allow them greater access to the sources of global information. At that time, UNESCO considered it a constitutional responsibility, and one especially pertinent to communication, to contribute to the removal of imbalances and inequalities in the capacity to produce, disseminate, and receive messages, and to eliminate the obstacles to a wider and better balanced flow of information.

In 1976, following a decision of the General Conference inviting UNESCO to undertake a review of all the problems of communication in contemporary society in the context of technological progress and recent developments in international relations, an international commission was appointed to study communication problems. The commission's recommendations were published by UNESCO in 1980 under the title *Many Voices, One World.* The General Conference considered the commission's report in 1980 and proposed 11 considerations on which a New World Information and Communication Order could be based. It also urged UNESCO "to contribute to the clarification, elaboration and application of the concept of a New World Information and Communication Order."

In 1978 the General Conference adopted the Declaration on Fundamental Principles Concerning the Contribution of the Mass Media to Strengthening Peace and International Understanding, to the Promotion of Human Rights and to Countering Racialism, Apartheid and Incitement to War. This declaration raised alarm in Western media organizations and governments. The declaration was interpreted as implying controls on press freedom. In later debates some Soviet countries proposed the licensing of journalists. However these proposals were never adopted, and no program of action based on them was ever put into action.

In the belief that high tariffs were an obstacle to the free flow of information, a UNESCO Working Group on Telecommunication Tariffs, established in 1979, recommended special tariffs under a Development Press Bulletin Service and a Conventional Press Bulletin Service to be applied to developing and developed countries, respectively.

The 1980 General Conference urged UNESCO "to contribute to the clarification, elaboration and application of the concept of a New World Information and Communication Order." However, the acrimonious public debate about NWICO had already damaged UNESCO's image in the West, and prompted the United States Congress to insert provisos in its 1982–83 appropriation for UNESCO stating that the funds would be withheld: "if that organization implements any policy or procedure the effect of which is to license journalists or their publications, to censor or otherwise restrict the free flow of information within or among countries, or to impose mandatory codes of journalistic practice or ethics."

Although the General Conference's espousal of NWICO was not cited in the United States' 1984 decision to withdraw from UNESCO (see Membership), concern over the "politicization" it represented was emblematic of the suspicion with which the Western countries (in particular the United States and the United Kingdom) regarded Soviet influence in the developing world. Now that developing nations greatly outnumbered industrialized nations, it was perceived that programs of action could be passed in UNESCO that were contrary to the interests of the West.

In 1989 the General Conference decided, by general agreement, to adopt a "New Strategy" in communication. The objective of this new strategy is "to render more operational the concern of the Organization to ensure a free flow of information at international as well as national levels, and its wider and better balanced dissemination, without any obstacle to the freedom of expression, and to strengthen communication capacities in the developing countries, so that they can participate more actively in the communication process." This last goal is implemented through UNESCO's International Program for the Development of Communication.

In February 1990, UNESCO organized an informal meeting of East-West media representatives to learn more about the needs of an independent press in Eastern Europe and how it could help to meet them. Since then, a number of regional seminars have been held to secure international support for strengthening press freedom and diversity.

The Windhoek and Other Declarations

In April 1991, UNESCO and the United Nations convened a round table for media professionals in Windhoek, Namibia. Participants assessed the situation of the press in Africa and, on 3 May, adopted the Windhoek Declaration, which declared that "independence, pluralism and diversity" were essential for the media in democracy. The United Nations declared May 3rd, the anniversary of the signing of the Windhoek Declaration, as International Press Freedom Day. UNESCO Director-General Federico Mayor declared in a speech to the World Press Freedom Committee in 1992: "UNESCO is fully committed to the advance of press and media freedom. This means leaving codes of journalistic ethics and similar issues in the new and emerging democratic systems strictly within the purview of the press and media professionals themselves." As a follow-up to the Windhoek Declaration, similar regional meetings were held in Almaty, Kazakhstan, in 1992 and in Santiago, Chile, in 1994.

Other similar declarations have been made since Windhoek, notably the Alma Ata Declaration (Kazakhstan, 1992) on promoting independent and pluralistic media in Asia; the Sana'a Declaration (Yemen, 1996) on promoting independent and pluralistic media in the Arab world; and the Sofia Declaration (Bulgaria, 1997), which declared that the move toward democracy in Central and Eastern European states would promote a climate that would foster independent and pluralistic media.

Communication Technologies for Development

UNESCO has been particularly concerned with the problem of disparities in communication existing between the developed and developing countries, which the great strides in communication technologies have only served to emphasize. In this field, UNESCO relies on three programs for the implementation of its activities: the International Programme for the Development of Communication (IPDC), the General Information Programme (known by its French acronym, PGI), and the Intergovernmental Informatics Programme (IIP).

One of the most important ways of improving information flow is by building up the resources of developing countries. The International Programme for the Development of Communication (IPDC), set up in 1980, aims to strengthen the resources of developing countries in terms of both personnel and equipment, to facilitate production and dissemination of news and other programming, thereby diminishing the imbalances that exists in the flow of information. At the 17th session of the IPDC Intergovernmental Council in March 1997, the Council concentrated on the questions of the role, crisis, and problems of media in societies in transition and the role of press freedom and independence of media in democracy. At its 18th session, held in Paris in March 1998, the IDPC decided that its fellowship program would particularly promote young journalists.

The General Information Programme (PGI) was launched in 1976 to assist member states, particularly in the developing world, to increase their capacity to gather, organize, diffuse and utilize information. The PGI assists member states in establishing

national information policies. It also helps governments recognize the value of public records as a strategic resource for public administration through the Records and Archives Management Program (RAMP). It provides access to knowledge and technical know-how in the treatment of information and research, by training specialists and coordinating information systems in developing countries. It also undertakes the "Memory of the World" project, aimed at safeguarding library collections and archives.

UNESCO's Intergovernmental Informatics Programme (IIP) carries out regional and national activities in its priority areas of training, computer networking, software production, informatics research and development, and national informatics strategies. Among the projects approved by the IIP Bureau in the 1990s were the "Computer network for the countries of the Maghreb—MaghrebNet" and the "Strengthening of the Regional Informatics Network for Eastern Europe—RINEE."

In the 1990s, the Organization reinforced its program in favor of independent and pluralist media, notably through the International Freedom of Expression Exchange Network (IFEX). UNESCO encourages movements towards the liberalization of media in Africa, Asia (including Central Asia), and Central and Eastern Europe, by assisting member states in restructuring their broadcasting systems, preparing appropriate legislation, and training media specialists.

Infrastructural projects supported by the United Nations, UNHCR and professional organizations for peace-building have been carried out in Cambodia, South Africa, and the former Yugoslavia.

Other Activities in Communications

Many of UNESCO's activities in the field of communications involve extensive data collection, analysis, and dissemination. The *World Communication Report*, a reference tool which focuses on trends in information and communication technologies and their impact on the work of media professionals and on society at large, was published in 1989; an updated version was published in 1996.

An agreement with the International Telecommunication Union (ITU) came into effect in 1993 and a joint study on telecommunication tariffs in the field of education, science, and culture was completed.

UNESCO also prepared the booklet *Island Agenda*, which analyzes the problems facing small island states and the way in which UNESCO's expertise in education, science, culture, and communication can be used to catalyze sustainable development.

In preparation for the Fourth World Conference on Women in Beijing in September 1995, UNESCO organized regional workshops on the theme of women in the media.

F. Agreement on the Importation of Educational, Scientific, and Cultural Materials

The states that are parties to the Agreement on the Importation of Educational, Scientific, and Cultural Materials and its protocol, adopted by the General Conference of UNESCO at Florence in 1950 and at Nairobi in 1976, respectively, exempt all the following materials from customs duties and any other importation charges: books, newspapers, and periodicals; various other categories of printed or duplicated matter; manuscripts, including typescripts; music; geographical, hydrographic, and astronomical maps and charts, irrespective of language and destination; works of art (paintings, drawings, and sculpture) and antiques, defined as articles more than 100 years old; visual and auditory materials, such as films, filmstrips, microfilms, sound recordings, glass slides, models, wall charts, and posters of an educational, scientific, or cultural character; and scientific instruments and apparatus, under the conditions that they be intended exclusively for educational purposes or pure scientific research, that they be consigned to public or private institutions

Members of UNESCO
(as of 2000)

Afghanistan	Dominican Republic	Lithuania	Senegal
Albania	Ecuador	Luxembourg	Seychelles
Algeria	Egypt	Madagascar	Sierra Leone
Andorra	El Salvador	Malawi	Slovakia
Angola	Equatorial Guinea	Malaysia	Slovenia
Antigua and Barbuda	Eritrea	Maldives	Solomon Islands
Argentina	Estonia	Mali	Somalia
Armenia	Ethiopia	Malta	South Africa
Australia	Fiji	Marshall Islands	Spain
Austria	Finland	Mauritania	Sri Lanka
Azerbaijan	France	Mauritius	Sudan
Bahamas	Gabon	Mexico	Suriname
Bahrain	Gambia	Micronesia	Swaziland
Bangladesh	Georgia	Moldova, Republic of	Sweden
Barbados	Germany	Monaco	Switzerland
Belarus	Ghana	Mongolia	Syrian Arab Republic
Belgium	Greece	Morocco	Tajikistan
Belize	Grenada	Mozambique	Thailand
Benin	Guatemala	Myanmar	The Former Yugoslav
Bhutan	Guinea	Namibia	Republic of Macedonia
Bolivia	Guinea-Bissau	Nauru	Togo
Bosnia and Herzegovina	Guyana	Nepal	Tonga
Botswana	Haiti	Netherlands	Trinidad and Tobago
Brazil	Honduras	New Zealand	Tunisia
Bulgaria	Hungary	Nicaragua	Turkey
Burkina Faso	Iceland	Niger	Turkmenistan
Burundi	India	Nigeria	Tuvalu
Cambodia	Indonesia	Niue	Uganda
Cameroon	Iran	Norway	Ukraine
Canada	Iraq	Oman	United Arab Emirates
Cape Verde	Ireland	Pakistan	United Kingdom
Central African Republic	Israel	Palau	United Republic of Tanzania
Chad	Italy	Panama	Uruguay
Chile	Jamaica	Papua New Guinea	Uzbekistan
China	Japan	Paraguay	Vanuatu
Colombia	Jordan	Peru	Venezuela
Comoros	Kazakhstan	Philippines	Vietnam
Congo	Kenya	Poland	Yemen
Congo, Democratic Republic of	Kiribati	Portugal	Yugoslavia
the	Korea, Democratic People's	Qatar	Zambia
Cook Islands	Republic of	Romania	Zimbabwe
Costa Rica	Korea, Republic of	Russian Federation	
Côte d'Ivoire	Kuwait	Rwanda	ASSOCIATE MEMBERS
Croatia	Kyrgyzstan	St. Kitts and Nevis	Aruba
Cuba	Lao People's Democratic Republic	St. Lucia	British Virgin Islands
Cyprus	Latvia	St. Vincent and the Grenadines	Cayman Islands
Czech Republic	Lebanon	Samoa	Macau
Denmark	Lesotho	San Marino	Netherlands Antilles
Djibouti	Liberia	São Tomé and Principe	
Dominica	Libyan Arab Jamahiriya	Saudi Arabia	

approved by the importing country as entitled to exemption from customs duty, and that instruments or apparatus of equivalent scientific value not be manufactured in the importing country. Books and other publications for the blind and other materials of an educational, scientific, or cultural character for the use of the blind are also exempt.

G. The UNESCO Coupon Program

UNESCO coupons are a type of international money order permitting persons living in countries with foreign-exchange restrictions to purchase from abroad books and many other articles of a scientific or cultural nature.

A person living in a country that participates in the UNESCO coupon plan who wishes to obtain from another participating country an item covered by the plan buys the required UNESCO coupons, pays for them in local currency at the official UN rate, and mails them abroad without having to go through any formal-

ities. To redeem the coupons, the seller sends them to Bankers Trust Company in New York (for the Americas), the Japan Society for the Promotion of Science in Tokyo (for Asia and the Far East), or to UNESCO's headquarters in Paris (for Europe and Africa). They are redeemed in the seller's national currency at the official UN exchange rate, after the deduction of a handling charge.

H. Encouragement of International Exchanges

As a means of promoting education, research, and international understanding, UNESCO aids and encourages various forms of exchange between its member states. It acts as a clearinghouse for governments, as well as international organizations, on all questions of exchange; administers its own program of fellowships and exchange of experts; and promotes study, training, and teaching abroad with the cooperation of governments and organizations. The principal publication issued by the exchange service is

Study Abroad, a trilingual publication issued every two years, listing opportunities for subsidized higher education and training abroad through a wide variety of fellowships, scholarships, and educational exchange programs of nearly 3,000 awarding agencies in some 120 different countries and territories.

I. Cooperative Action Program

UNESCO's Cooperative Action Program (Co-Action) enables individuals and groups to make direct contributions to community development projects such as schools, libraries, and vocational institutions for the disabled in developing countries. An illustrated catalog of selected Co-Action projects describing some of the priority needs and estimated costs is issued by UNESCO.

Direct "people-to-people" relationships are established between donors and recipients that often develop into lasting friendships. In addition, the program has a special appeal for school groups.

THE WORLD HEALTH ORGANIZATION (WHO)

BACKGROUND: In taking the pulse of global health in 1974, WHO member states concluded that despite vaccines, antibiotic drugs, and a host of extraordinary advances in medical technology, the world was far from healthy. There was a "signal failure," the 27th World Health Assembly concluded, to provide basic services to two-thirds of the world's population, particularly to rural inhabitants and the urban poor, who, despite being the most needy and in the majority, were the most neglected. That assessment—made 24 years after WHO's establishment—led to a reorientation of WHO's outlook and to the adoption of the goal of "health for all by the year 2000" through the approach of primary health care. Although WHO's great achievement remained the eradication of smallpox, the HIV/AIDS pandemic and a virulent resurgence of preventable diseases like malaria and tuberculosis posed grave challenges to the goal of "health for all" as the 21st century dawned. The main task of WHO since its founding has been to work to ensure that people everywhere have access to health services that will enable them to lead socially and economically productive lives.

CREATION

During the 19th century, waves of communicable diseases swept Europe, accompanying the growth of railways and steam navigation. Yet the first international sanitary conference, attended by 12 governments, was not held until 1851. An international convention on quarantine was drawn up, but it was ratified by only three states. Progress was slow.

The limited objectives of the nations participating in these early conferences also militated against the success of international health efforts. International public health did not come of age until the 20th century. The first international health bureau with its own secretariat was established by the republics of the Americas in 1902—the International Sanitary Bureau. The name was changed in 1923 to the Pan American Sanitary Bureau.

The idea of a permanent international agency to deal with health questions was seriously discussed for the first time at the 1874 conference, but it was not until 1903 that the establishment of such an agency was recommended. By that time, scientific discoveries concerning cholera, plague, and yellow fever had been generally accepted. The agency, known as the Office International d'Hygiène Publique (OIHP), was created in December 1907 by an agreement signed by 12 states (Belgium, Brazil, Egypt, France, Italy, the Netherlands, Portugal, Russia, Spain, Switzerland, the UK, and the US). The OIHP was located in Paris, and its first staff consisted of nine persons. Originally a predominantly European institution, the OIHP grew to include nearly 60 countries and colonies by 1914.

World War I left in its wake disastrous pandemics. The influenza wave of 1918–19 was estimated to have killed 15 to 20 million people, and in 1919, almost 250,000 cases of typhus were reported in Poland and more than 1.6 million in the USSR. Other disasters also made heavy demands on the OIHP, which found itself overburdened with work.

Early in 1920, a plan for a permanent international health organization was approved by the League of Nations. United official action to combat the typhus epidemic then raging in Poland was urged by the League's Council. The OIHP, however, was unable to participate in an interim combined League-OIHP committee. This was partly because the US, which was not a member of the League, wished to remain in the OIHP but could not if the OIHP were absorbed into a League-connected agency. The OIHP existed for another generation, maintaining a formal relationship with the League of Nations.

The OIHP's main concern continued to be supervision and improvement of international quarantine measures. Smallpox and typhus were added to the quarantinable diseases by the International Sanitary Convention in 1926. Also adopted were measures requiring governments to notify the OIHP immediately of any outbreak of plague, cholera, or yellow fever or of the appearance of smallpox or typhus in epidemic form.

The League of Nations established a permanent epidemiological intelligence service to collect and disseminate data worldwide on the status of epidemic diseases of international significance. The Malaria Commission was founded and adopted a new international approach: to study and advise on control of the disease in regions where it existed rather than to work out the conventional precautions needed to prevent its spread from country to country. The annual reports of the League's Cancer Commission on such matters as results of radiotherapy in cancer of the uterus became an important source of international information on that disease. Other technical commissions included those on typhus, leprosy, and biological standardization.

Most of the work of the OIHP and the League's health units was cut short by World War II, although the *Weekly Epidemiological Record* continued. Fear of new postwar epidemics prompted the Allies to draw up plans for action. At its first meeting in 1943, the newly created United Nations Relief and Rehabilitation Administration (UNRRA) put health work among its "primary and fundamental responsibilities."

At its first meeting, in 1946, the UN Economic and Social Council decided to call an international conference to consider the establishment of a single health organization of the UN. The conference met in New York and on 22 July adopted a constitution for the World Health Organization, which would carry on the functions previously performed by the League and the OIHP.

WHO did not come into existence until 7 April 1948, when its constitution was ratified by the required 26 UN member states. In the meantime, UNRRA was dissolved, and a WHO Interim Commission carried out the most indispensable of UNRRA's health functions. The first WHO assembly convened in June 1948.

Among the severe problems that beset the Interim Commission was a cholera epidemic in Egypt in 1947. Three cases were reported on 22 September; by October, 33,000 cases were reported in widely separated areas on both sides of the Red Sea and the Suez Canal. Urgent calls for vaccine were sent out by the Interim Commission within hours after the first three cases were reported, and by means of a history-making cholera airlift, 20 million doses of vaccine were flown to Cairo from the US, USSR, India, and elsewhere, one-third of them outright gifts. The cholera epidemic claimed 20,472 lives in Egypt by February 1948. During the epidemic the number of countries ratifying WHO's constitution increased by almost 50%.

PURPOSES

WHO's main functions can be summed up as follows: to act as a directing and coordinating authority on international health work, to ensure valid and productive technical cooperation, and to promote research.

The objective of WHO is the attainment by all peoples of the highest possible level of health. Health, as defined in the WHO Constitution, is a state of complete physical, mental, and social well-being and not merely the absence of disease or infirmity. In support of its main objective, the organization has a wide range of functions, including the following:

- To act as the directing and coordinating authority on international health work;
- To promote technical cooperation;
- To assist Governments, upon request, in strengthening health services;
- To furnish appropriate technical assistance and, in emergencies, necessary aid, upon the request or acceptance of Governments;
- To stimulate and advance work on the prevention and control of epidemic, endemic, and other diseases;
- To promote, in cooperation with other specialized agencies where necessary, the improvement of nutrition, housing, sanitation, recreation, economic or working conditions, and other aspects of environmental hygiene;
- To promote and coordinate biomedical and health services research;
- To promote improved standards of teaching and training in the health, medical and related professions;
- To establish and stimulate the establishment of international standards for biological, pharmaceutical, and similar products, and to standardize diagnostic procedures;
- To foster activities in the field of mental health, especially those activities affecting the harmony of human relations.

WHO also proposes conventions, agreements, and regulations and makes recommendations about international nomenclature of diseases, causes of death, and public health practices. It develops, establishes, and promotes international standards concerning foods and biological, pharmaceutical, and similar substances.

MEMBERSHIP

UN members can join WHO by unilateral, formal notification to the UN secretary-general that they accept the WHO constitution. A non-UN member may be admitted if its application is approved by a simple majority vote of the World Health Assembly. Territories or groups of territories "not responsible for the conduct of their international relations" may be admitted as associate members upon application by the authority responsible for their international relations.

As of 2000, WHO had 191 member states.

STRUCTURE

The principal organs of WHO are the World Health Assembly, the Executive Board, and the secretariat, headed by a director-general.

World Health Assembly

All WHO members are represented in the World Health Assembly. Each member has one vote but may send three delegates. According to the WHO constitution, the delegates are to be chosen for their technical competence and preferably should represent national health administrations. Delegations may include alternates and advisers. The assembly meets annually, usually in May, for approximately three weeks. Most assemblies have been held at WHO headquarters in Geneva. A president is elected by each assembly.

The World Health Assembly determines the policies of the organization and deals with budgetary, administrative, and similar questions. By a two-thirds vote, the assembly may adopt conventions or agreements. While these are not binding on member governments until accepted by them, WHO members have to "take action" leading to their acceptance within 18 months. Thus, each member government, even if its delegation voted against a convention in the assembly, must act. For example, it must submit the convention to its legislature for ratification. It must then notify WHO of the action taken. If the action is unsuccessful, it must notify WHO of the reasons for nonacceptance.

In addition, the assembly has quasi-legislative powers to adopt regulations on important technical matters specified in the WHO constitution. Once such a regulation is adopted by the assembly, it applies to all WHO member countries (including those whose delegates voted against it) except those whose governments specifically notify WHO that they reject the regulation or accept it only with certain reservations.

WHO is empowered to introduce uniform technical regulations on the following matters:

1. sanitary and quarantine requirements and other procedures designed to prevent international epidemics;
2. nomenclature with respect to disease, causes of death, and public health practices;
3. standards with respect to diagnostic procedures for international use;
4. standards with respect to safety, purity, and potency of biological, pharmaceutical, and similar products in international commerce; and
5. advertising and labeling of biological, pharmaceutical, and similar products in international commerce.

The assembly, at its first session in 1948, adopted World Health Regulation No. 1, *Nomenclature with Respect to Diseases and Causes of Death*. This regulation guides member countries in compiling statistics on disease and death and, by providing for a standardized nomenclature, facilitates their comparison. World Health Regulation No. 2 deals with quarantinable diseases.

Each year, the assembly doubles as a scientific conference on a specific topic of worldwide health interest, selected in advance. These technical discussions are held in addition to other business. They enable the delegates, who as a rule are top-ranking public health experts, to discuss common problems more thoroughly than formal committee debates would permit. Governments are asked to contribute special working papers and studies to these discussions and, if practicable, to send experts on the matters to be discussed with their delegations.

Executive Board

The World Health Assembly may elect any 32 member countries (the only rule being equitable geographical distribution) for three-year terms, and each of the countries elected designates one person "technically qualified in the field of health" to the WHO Executive Board. The countries are elected by rotation, one-third of the membership being replaced every year, and may succeed themselves. Board members serve as individuals and not as representatives of their governments.

The Executive Board meets twice a year, for sessions of a few days to several weeks, but it may convene a special meeting at any time. One of its important functions is to prepare the agenda of the World Health Assembly. The WHO constitution authorizes the board "to take emergency measures within the functions and financial resources of the Organization to deal with events requiring immediate action. In particular, it may authorize the director-general to take the necessary steps to combat epidemics and to participate in the organization of health relief to victims of a calamity."

Director General and Secretariat

The secretariat comprises the technical and administrative personnel of the organization. It is headed by a director-general, appointed by the World Health Assembly. The first director-general of WHO was Dr. Brock Chisholm of Canada. He was succeeded in 1953 by Dr. Marcolino G. Candau of Brazil and in 1973 by Dr. Halfdan T. Mahler of Denmark. Dr. Mahler served WHO for 15 years and was declared Director-General Emiritus upon his retirement in 1988. Dr. Hiroshi Nakajima of Japan was elected Director General in 1988 and re-elected to a second five-year term in 1993. Dr. Gro Harlem Brundtland succeeded him on 21 July 1998.

WHO is staffed by some 3,800 health and other experts in both professional and general service categories, working at headquarters and in the regional offices. WHO has six regional offices, each covering a major geographic region of the world. These are located in Alexandria for the Eastern Mediterranean area, in Manila for the Western Pacific area, in New Delhi for the Southeast Asia area, in Copenhagen for Europe, in Brazzaville for the African area, and in Washington, DC, where the directing council of the Pan American Health Organization acts as the regional committee of WHO in the Americas.

While all work of direct assistance to individual member governments is decentralized to the regional offices, the Geneva headquarters is where the work of the regions is coordinated and worldwide technical services are organized, including collection and dissemination of information. The headquarters cooperates with the UN, the other specialized agencies, and voluntary organizations and is responsible for medical research.

WHO assistance is given in response to a request from a government. Member governments meet annually in regional committees to review and plan WHO activities for their areas. Requests are consolidated by the regional directors and forwarded to the director-general, who incorporates regional programs and their estimated costs into the overall WHO draft program and budget. The program and budget, after review by the Executive Board, are submitted to the World Health Assembly.

BUDGET

For 1949, the first year of WHO's existence, its regular budget amounted to us$5 million. A regular working budget of us$842,654,000 was approved by the World Health Assembly for the 2000–01 biennium, unchanged from the previous two budgets. WHO estimated that extrabudgetary contributions would bring the total budget for the biennium to us$1.8 billion. WHO reported that among programs supported were the following: Tropical disease control and research programs; malaria prevention and control; Global AIDS Programme; programs for environmental health in the developing world (combating, for

example, the pollution problems that encourage water-borne diseases like cholera); programs in human reproduction research; eradication of poliomyelitis; immunization programs; control of a resurgence of tuberculosis; WHO's programs to fight hunger and malnutrition. WHO's emergency and humanitarian relief operations also received additional funds, reflecting the increased demands by the world community on all UN organizations to respond to natural and man-made disasters.

ACTIVITIES

Under the global "health for all" strategy, WHO and its member states have resolved to place special emphasis on the developing countries. Nevertheless, the benefits of WHO's international health work are reaped by all countries, including the most developed. For example, all nations have benefited from their contributions to the WHO programs that led to the global eradication of smallpox and to better and cheaper ways of controlling tuberculosis.

Prevention is a key word in WHO. The organization believes that immunization, which prevents the six major communicable diseases of childhood—diphtheria, measles, poliomyelitis, tetanus, tuberculosis, and whooping cough—should be available to all children who need it. WHO is leading a worldwide campaign to provide effective immunization for all children in cooperation with UNICEF.

Provision of safe drinking water and adequate excreta disposal for all are the objectives of the International Drinking Water Supply and Sanitation Decade proclaimed by the UN General Assembly in 1980 and supported by WHO.

WHO is also active in international efforts to combat the diarrheal diseases, killers of infants and young children. The widespread introduction of oral rehydration salts, together with improved drinking water supply and sanitation, will, it is hoped, greatly reduce childhood mortality from diarrhea.

WHO's program for primary health care comprises eight essential elements:

1. education concerning prevalent health problems and the methods of preventing and controlling them;
2. promotion of food supply and proper nutrition;
3. maintenance of an adequate supply of safe water and basic sanitation;
4. provision of maternal and child health care, including family planning;
5. immunization against the major infectious diseases;
6. prevention and control of locally endemic diseases;
7. appropriate treatment of common diseases and injuries; and
8. provision of essential drugs.

These eight elements were defined in the Declaration of Alma-Ata, which emerged from the International Conference on Primary Health Care, held in Alma-Ata, USSR, in 1978.

A. Disease Research, Control and Prevention

UNAIDS Programme

The Acquired Immune Deficiency Syndrome (AIDS) pandemic is an international health problem of extraordinary scope and urgency. The mission of UNAIDS is to mobilize an effective, equitable, and ethical response to the pandemic. It strives to raise awareness, stimulate solidarity, and unify worldwide action. UNAIDS works with countries to develop programs to prevent HIV transmission and reduce the suffering of people already affected. It provides technical and policy guidance to governments, other United Nations agencies, and non-governmental organizations. It also promotes and supports research to develop new technologies, interventions, and approaches to AIDS prevention and care. Its inception in 1988 was first as the Global Programme on AIDS. UNAIDS combines the efforts of six other UN system organizations, including UNDP, the World Bank, UNICEF, UNFPA, WHO, and UNESCO. Since January 1996, the joint and co-sponsored UN Programme on HIV/AIDS, or UNAIDS, has been operational to better coordinate fund raising and prevention efforts.

WHO estimated in 2000 that more than 47 million people had been infected with the human immunodeficiency virus (HIV), which causes AIDS, since the epidemic came to public attention in the 1980s. WHO and UNAIDS estimated that by the end of 1999, 33.6 million people were living with HIV/AIDS worldwide. It was also estimated that during 1999, 5.6 million people (including 570,000 children under the age of 15) became infected. By the end of 1999, it was estimated that a total of 16.3 million adults and children have died because of HIV/AIDS since the beginning of the epidemic. In 1999, approximately 20% of these deaths occurred among children and 51% were among women. Of the 5.6 million people infected with HIV in 1999, 3.8 million lived in Sub-Saharan Africa, the region that has been hardest hit by AIDS/HIV.

The disease is caused by a virus which destroys the body's innate capacity to withstand disease (the immune system). As the immune system is weakened, infected persons can no longer resist diseases which cause diarrhea, fatigue, severe weight loss, and skin lesions. Eventually, the AIDS-related illnesses cause death. Persons become infected with the HIV virus by contact with body fluids like semen (during sexual intercourse) or blood (if they receive contaminated blood during a transfusion). Intravenous drug users who share hypodermic needles have been shown to be at great risk for contracting HIV. HIV cannot be transmitted by air or simple touch. The insidious nature of the disease contributed to its silent explosion into the world population, since infected persons do not show signs of infection for as many as six to ten years.

AIDS was already an international epidemic (a "pandemic") by the time it was first recognized in 1981. In late 1983, WHO held the first international meeting on AIDS in Geneva. In February 1987, WHO established its Special Programme on AIDS in order to develop a global strategy for AIDS control, obtain financial resources, and begin implementation of the program. In 1988, the Executive Board renamed it the Global Programme on AIDS (GPA). Today it is known as UNAIDS Programme. The main objectives of the global strategy are:

- to prevent HIV infections;
- to reduce the personal and social impact of HIV infection; and
- to mobilize and unify national and international efforts against AIDS.

The global strategy was updated in 1992 to place increased emphasis on:

- health care for AIDS patients;
- treatment for sexually transmitted diseases;
- improving the status of women in developing countries in order to reduce the risk of infection;
- providing more frank information about AIDS;
- planning for the socio-economic impact of the pandemic;
- overcoming stigmatization and discrimination directed at persons infected with HIV/AIDS.

A World Summit of Ministers of Health on Programmes for AIDS Prevention was held in London in January 1988. The summit proclaimed 1 December as Worlds AIDS Day. In 1989 the World Health Assembly resolved to make World AIDS Day the annual focus for worldwide efforts against AIDS. That same year, WHO established a Global Commission on AIDS to provide the

Director General with broad policy and scientific guidance from eminent experts representing a wide variety of disciplines. By the end of 1991, AIDS programs had been established in every WHO member country.

Tuberculosis

In April 1993, WHO declared a tuberculosis (TB) global emergency. WHO said that 35 years of neglect by governments, and a linkage to the HIV/AIDS pandemic, had led to a resurgence of the bacillus that causes tuberculosis. In New York City, the incidence of TB rose 150% between 1980 and 1993, prompting WHO to declare a global TB epidemic. The link between HIV/AIDS and tuberculosis, which were fueling each other, was so pronounced that by 1994 WHO called the phenomenon a co-epidemic. The breakdown in health services, the spread of HIV/AIDS, and the emergence of strains of TB that are multidrug-resistant contributed to the worsening impact of the disease. As of 2000, the global epidemic was growing and becoming more dangerous: Tuberculosis was killing 2 million people a year. Health experts estimated that between 2000 and 2020, nearly one billion people would be newly infected, 200 million people would get sick, and 35 million would die from TB if the disease was not controlled.

Tuberculosis is an age-old killer, traces of which have been found in the lungs of 3,000-year-old Egyptian mummies. It is caused by a bacillus that infects the lungs, forming knobby lesions called "tubercles." Up until the 20th century it was commonly called "consumption." Today the bacillus responsible for TB is called *Mycobacterium tuberculosis*. The first diagnostic test was discovered in 1905 and the first vaccine was created in France in 1921. The first antibiotic effective against TB, streptomycin, was discovered in 1944 in the United States. By 1960, chemotherapy for TB was so effective, sanitoria in mountain areas which had been used for more than a century to care for TB patients were closed. TB was presumed dead, at least in the industrialized world: public health measures for TB control were dismantled, and funding for research fell to a trickle. However, multidrug-resistant (MDR) strains began to flourish as patients being treated with antibiotics neglected to completely finish a course of treatment. In New York City, MDR strains accounted for only 7% of all TB strains in the early 1980s. By 1992, more than one-third of the strains tested were resistant to one drug, and almost one-fifth were resistant to the two main drugs.

WHO contends that the rise of tuberculosis in the industrialized world is linked not only to HIV/AIDS, but also to inadequate funding of international programs to combat tuberculosis in the developing world. The organization has insisted that it will be impossible to control TB in the industrialized countries unless it is sharply reduced in Africa, Asia, and Latin America.

The WHO Tuberculosis Programme aims to cut the annual death toll from TB from 3 million deaths in 1992 to 1.6 million by 2002. WHO predicts that about US$100 million needs to be spent each year to provide medicines, microscopes, and a modest infrastructure enabling poor countries to undertake successful tuberculosis programs. WHO reports that in the developing world, a complete cure could cost as little as US$13 per patient. However, the treatment of a patient with a multidrug-resistant strain of TB in New York City could cost US$180,000 per patient.

As of 2000, WHO targets were to detect 70% of new infectious TB cases and to cure 85% of those detected. Six countries had achieved these targets by 1998. But WHO stated that governments, non-governmental organizations, and civil society must continue to act to improve TB control in order to reach these targets worldwide.

The Tropical Disease Research Programme

The UNDP/World Bank/WHO Special Programme for Research

and Training in Tropical Diseases (TDR) was set up in 1975 to target malaria, schistosomiasis (bilharzia or "snail fever"), leishmaniasis, African trypanosomiasis (sleeping sickness), American trypanosomiasis (Chagas disease), lymphatic filariasis (which leads to elephantiasis), onchocerciasis (river blindness), and leprosy. Almost 500 million people, nearly all of them in developing countries, suffer from these diseases, which can cause terrible anguish, deformity, and death. At the same time, they cause considerable economic losses and frequently interfere with development projects (particularly water projects such as dams and irrigation schemes, and planned and unplanned forestry).

The death toll from the diseases—particularly among children from malaria in Africa—is expected to double by 2010, possibly reaching four million lives a year, unless radical solutions are found. Population increase, the spread of parasite resistance, mass migrations, environmental disturbance, and disruption of control programs through economic devastation, civil unrest, and wars, all contribute to the tropical disease problem.

TDR has a mandate to:

1. Develop new methods of preventing, diagnosing, and treating tropical diseases, methods that would be applicable, acceptable, and affordable by developing countries, require minimal skills or supervision, and be readily integrated into the health services of these countries.

2. Strengthen—through training in biomedical and social sciences and through support to institutions—the capability of developing countries to undertake the research required to develop and apply these new methods.

In this work, TDR collaborates closely with WHO's Division of Control of Tropical Diseases (CTD), and with many other WHO programs and outside bodies concerned with tropical disease research and control.

TDR acts to some extent like a research council, supporting investigator-initiated projects selected by peer-review, and to some extent as a pro-active agency commissioning the research required to reach its objectives. A quarter of TDR's funds goes to research capability strengthening (RCS) in developing countries. This RCS work is being increasingly combined with the performance of needed research: "training by doing."

Over the eighteen years of TDR's existence, a large number of drugs, diagnostic techniques, vector control agents, and other products have been developed, and in conjunction with national and international control programs there has been considerable success in applying these to reduce (or potentially reduce) the burden of some of the tropical diseases—notably leprosy, onchocerciasis, and Chagas disease. The other diseases still pose major problems, either globally or regionally.

TDR's research targets, and the appropriate management and decision-making structure to reach those targets was thoroughly reviewed in 1992–93. A new structure, which gives the program greater focus on priority targets and more flexibility to identify and respond to the practical health and control needs of populations, has been in operation since 1 January 1994.

In the new structure, TDR's research is divided into three basic functional areas: "strategic research," "applied field research," and "product research and development."

Strategic research. TDR defines "strategic research" (SR) as basic research, usually on the diseases, the parasites that cause them, or the vectors that carry them, aimed at a specified long-term goal in tropical disease control—such as the genetic engineering of the mosquito to make it unable to carry malaria. The amount of strategic research supported by TDR is decreasing, but not vanishing; important opportunities must always be grasped, subject to the availability of funds.

Applied field research. The research, development, and even introduction of a new tool does not automatically lead to

improved control. Experience has shown that the ultimate success of TDR's efforts to control tropical diseases depends on social and economic factors in the endemic communities and on control programs' awareness of people's needs, perceptions, and wishes. Thus applied field research must develop cost-effective and sustainable control strategies which are based on a thorough understanding of social and economic factors, on the needs of the people in the endemic communities as identified by them, and on the availability and use of health facilities. AFR addresses a multitude of practical community-level and health-system control questions which will help effectively apply the products of earlier research and will provide new appropriate directions for research. About a dozen AFR Task Forces were organized in areas including operations research in Chagas disease and onchocerciasis, women and tropical disease, the use of bed nets, an integrated approach to the sick child of tropical diseases, and health financing.

Product research and development. TDR's product research and development (PRD) covers the process of transforming scientific knowledge into usable disease control products, through Phase I-IV field trials, registration, and the negotiation of production at an affordable price. The Product Development Unit focuses most resources on a short list of a few such projects, such as artemisinin derivatives, tumor necrosis factor antagonists, transmission-blocking vaccines for malaria, and the codelivery of praziquantel and albendazole for helminth infections.

TDR's particular strength is that, as part of the United Nations system, it enjoys a world view of the tropical disease scene and the standing conferred by a lack of partisan or profit-making motivation. These assets explain in large measure TDR's rapid success in creating an international network of over 5000 scientists, which gives it access to a broad range of expertise and scientific disciplines.

Through its WHO connection, TDR has ready access to programs and units working in related fields and—most importantly, with its new focus on the field and on national control programs—to WHO's 191 Member States. TDR can call on government support in endemic regions in order to engage populations and facilities in multi-center field trials rapidly and at very low cost.

Leprosy

Leprosy, also known as Hansen's disease, has been a serious public health problem in the developing countries. But the widespread use of multidrug therapy (MDT) has reduced the disease burden dramatically. In the last 15 years of the 20th century, 10 million leprosy patients were cured, the prevalence rate dropped by 85%, and the number of countries where leprosy remained a public health problem dropped from 122 to 24. Once the prevalence rate at the global level is reduced to less than one case per 10,000 persons, health experts believe there will be a natural interruption of transmission over time and future generations will not contract the disease.

At the end of the 20th century, the prevalence rate at the global level was 1.4 cases per 10,000 people. Approximately 804,000 new cases were detected during 1998 and 820,000 cases were on the register at the end of the year. It was estimated that about 2.5 million patients would be detected between 2000 and 2005.

In the late 1990s, leprosy remained a public health problem in 24 countries situated mainly in the inter-tropical belt of the world. Of the 24, it was estimated that 12 (Cameroon, Chad, Congo, Côte d'Ivoire, Ethiopia, Gabon, Gambia, Guinea-Bissau, Mali, Papua New Guinea, Paraguay, Sierra Leone) would meet the elimination goal in the year 2000 if strategies were intensified and accelerated. WHO reported that special efforts would be needed to eliminate leprosy in 12 other countries: Angola, Brazil, Central African Republic, Democratic Republic of the Congo,

India, Indonesia, Guinea, Madagascar, Mozambique, Myanmar, Nepal, and Niger. Together these 12 countries represented 90% of the prevalence in the world in 1999.

In order to eradicate leprosy, WHO stated that political commitments needed to be strengthened in countries where leprosy remained a public health problem. Additionally, it said that strong leadership by ministries of health was absolutely necessary, particularly in some of the major endemic countries. Finally, the organization estimated that US$100 million was needed for the period 2000–05, of which US$54 million had been pledged through 1998.

Malaria

In the late 1990s, WHO reported that malaria was a public health problem in more than 90 countries, inhabited by a total of some 2.4 billion people or roughly 40% of the world's population. At the time, worldwide prevalence of the disease was estimated to be between 300 and 500 million clinical cases a year, with more than 90% of the cases occurring in sub-Saharan Africa. Of those contracting the disease, an estimated one million die each year, with the majority of deaths occurring among young African children. WHO stated that other high-risk groups were pregnant women, and non-immune travelers, refugees and other displaced persons, and workers entering endemic areas.

Malaria has been a priority for WHO since its founding in 1948. Control activities are coordinated by WHO's Programme on Communicable Diseases (CDS). The four basic technical elements of WHO's global control strategy are: provision of early diagnosis and prompt treatment for the disease; planning and implementation of selective and sustainable preventive measures; early detection for the prevention or containment of epidemics; and, strengthening local research capacities to promote regular assessment of malaria situations, in particular the ecological, social and economic determinants of the disease.

In 1992, WHO convened a Ministerial Conference on Malaria in Amsterdam which was attended by health leaders from 102 countries and representatives of United Nations bodies and nongovernmental organizations. The conference endorsed a global malaria control strategy. WHO planned to implement control programs in 90% of the countries affected by the disease no later than 1997. The target was to reduce mortality by at least 20% between 1995 and 2000.

WHO has published many books in support of its fight against malaria, including: *A Global Strategy for Malaria Control, Basic Malaria Microscopy, Parasitic Diseases in Water Resources Development,* and books in many languages on the diagnosis and treatment of malaria.

Smallpox

The eradication of smallpox is among the finest achievements of WHO, which coordinated the international effort to combat this disease. It is the first time in history that a human malady has ever been totally eliminated. This became feasible because the virus causing the disease was transmitted only by direct human contagion; there were no animal reservoirs or human "carriers." Victims of the disease were immune to further attacks, while successful vaccination at three-year intervals gave essentially complete protection.

Eradication was based on a twofold strategy of surveillance-containment and vaccination. Rapid detection of cases, their immediate isolation, and the vaccination of anyone with whom the patient could have come in contact during the infective period, lasting about three weeks after the onset of rash, prevented further transmission. Implementation of these procedures, coupled with the basic immunity level attributable to routine immunization, resulted in the eradication of smallpox everywhere in the world.

Although a global program of eradication was initiated in 1959, it was not until 1967, when a special WHO budget with increased bilateral and multilateral support was prepared, that a definitive target date of 10 years was set for global eradication. By the end of 1977, this goal was achieved.

In 1967, 131,776 cases of smallpox were reported from 43 countries, 31 of which were classified as smallpox-endemic; however, the actual number of cases was estimated to have been between 10 million and 15 million, among whom possibly 1.5 to 2 million died. Since that time, WHO has convened many international commissions which certified smallpox eradication in 79 recently endemic countries. The global eradication of the disease was declared by the World Health Assembly in 1980. By 1985, all WHO member states had discontinued routine smallpox vaccination, and no country required smallpox vaccination certificates from international travelers.

By 1993, the complete nucleotide sequence of the genomes of several strains of the virus had been determined, fulfilling the requirements set in 1990 for the final destruction of the remaining stock of variola virus. On 9 September 1994, an expert committee agreed that the destruction of the remaining clinical specimens of variola virus should take place on 30 June 1995, after confirmation by the May 1995 meeting of the World Health Assembly. The committee also recommended that 500,000 doses of smallpox vaccine be kept by WHO in case of an emergency and that the vaccine seed virus be maintained in the WHO Collaborating Centre on Smallpox Vaccine in Bilthoven, Netherlands.

Cholera

In 1961, cholera caused by *Vibrio cholerae 01 El Tor* began to spread from its endemic locations and gradually invaded practically all countries in the Western Pacific and Southeast Asia regions, most of which had been free from cholera for many years. Cholera continued to spread westward, reaching Pakistan, Afghanistan, Iran, and Uzbekistan (USSR) in 1965 and Iraq in 1966. In 1969 and 1970, it created great problems in the Middle East, North and West Africa, and Europe and has since spread to most countries of Africa, becoming endemic in many of them. Its spread has been facilitated by the fact that most of the persons who come in contact with *El Tor vibrio* become mild cases or carriers of the disease. Between 1984 and 1990, reported cases of cholera had increased from 28,893 to 70,084, a 142% increase. By 1991, cholera had completed its spread around the globe and appeared in Latin America for the first time in this century. Extensive epidemics also recurred in Africa. In 1991, reports received by WHO indicated that 594,694 people contracted cholera, and of that number, 19,295 people died, more than in the previous five years combined.

Numerous field and laboratory studies showed that the control measures were not sufficiently effective. The anticholera vaccines in use, when tested in controlled field trials, were shown to protect at most about half the persons vaccinated and for less than six months. Some vaccines provided no protection at all.

In view of these findings, WHO intensified its research activities in improving treatment and vaccines; it also worked to reinforce the ability of governments to face the problem of cholera within the framework of control programs directed against diarrheal diseases in general.

A simple and inexpensive oral-rehydration treatment, proven effective in the 1970s for all acute diarrhea, has made cholera treatment substantially easier. As most of the cases of *El Tor vibrio* cholera cannot be differentiated from other diarrheal diseases on clinical grounds, WHO has developed a comprehensive and expanded program for the control of all diarrheal diseases, including cholera.

In April 1991, WHO created a Global Task Force on Cholera to strengthen global control efforts and improve preparedness. A new strain *Vibrio cholerae O139* emerged in the period 1992–93, causing new epidemics and largely replacing *El Tor vibrio*. Reinforced efforts around the globe brought the disease under control during the 1990s: In 1998, the number of new cases dropped to 293,121, of which 10,586 died; in 1999, the raw figures decreased again—to 206,531 reported cases and 8,181 deaths (with the death rate, about 3% of cholera cases, remaining constant).

Other communicable diseases

WHO continues to monitor and sponsor research on influenza, viral hepatitis, arthropod-borne viruses, yellow fever, Japanese encephalitus, bubonic plague, meningitis, Legionellosis, and streptococcal infections.

Diseases Transmissible Between Animals and Man (Zoonoses) and Related Problems

Since its inception, WHO has been developing veterinary public health programs in cooperation with its member states. In the 1970s, WHO's veterinary public health program was reoriented toward more direct collaboration with member states in the development of national and intercountry programs in which zoonoses and food-borne disease control receive the highest priority. This action was justified because these diseases have become increasingly prevalent in many countries mainly as a result of the following factors: the greatly expanded international and national trade in live animals, animal products, and animal feedstuffs, which facilitates the spread of infection; the growth of urbanization, coupled with the increased numbers of domestic and half-wild animals living in close association with city populations, which exposes more people to zoonoses; and changing patterns of land use, such as irrigation, together with new systems of animal farming, which may lead to changes in the ecology that disseminate and increase animal reservoirs of zoonoses.

The 1978 World Health Assembly adopted a resolution on "prevention and control of zoonoses and food-borne diseases due to animal products" in which member states were invited to formulate and implement appropriate country-wide programs for the control of zoonoses; to strengthen cooperation between national veterinary and public health services in improving the surveillance, prevention, and control of these diseases; and to collaborate further in ensuring the appropriate development of zoonoses centers. The resolution also requested the director-general of WHO to continue development of national, regional, and global strategies and of methods for the surveillance, prevention, and control of zoonoses, and to promote the extension of the network of zoonoses centers in all regions so that the necessary support could be provided to country health programs dealing with these diseases.

WHO cooperates with member states in planning, implementing, and evaluating their national zoonoses and food-borne disease control programs. WHO centers, such as those in Athens (Mediterranean Zoonoses Control Center) and Buenos Aires (Pan American Zoonoses Control Center), play an increasing role in direct collaboration with countries and in organizing intercountry technical cooperation.

Global Epidemiological Surveillance

In the *Weekly Epidemiological Record*, WHO publishes notes on communicable diseases of international importance and information concerning the application of international health regulations. In the past, the publication was chiefly a summary of the weekly or daily notifications of diseases under the regulations, with declarations of infected areas or of freedom from infection when attained. It then became the vehicle for timely reports, narrative summaries, and interpretative comments on a variety of communicable disease topics. Annual, semiannual, or quarterly summaries are published on major trends in diseases and on special programs, such as those on malaria and AIDS. Data from special surveillance programs, such as the global influenza program, the European program for salmonella, and dengue-hemorrhagic fever surveillance, are summarized and published at appropriate intervals. The *Weekly Epidemiological Record* also communicates important changes in international health regulations and policies of member states.

Global Programme for Vaccines and Immunization

Immunization, one of the most powerful and cost-effective weapons of disease prevention, remains tragically underutilized. Preventable diseases such as neonatal tetanus and poliomyelitis, which have been virtually eliminated in most of the developed world, continue to take a heavy toll in developing countries. Measles, whooping cough, diphtheria, and tuberculosis are serious health threats to children in developing countries, causing blindness, deafness, and even death. In 1993, WHO reported that 8 million children were dying annually in developing countries from viral and bacterial illnesses, and 900 million were becoming severely ill.

The Expanded Programme on Immunization (EPI). In 1974, with the help of UNICEF, UNDP, national donor agencies, and voluntary agencies, WHO initiated the Expanded Programme on Immunization, with the goal of providing immunizations for all children of the world by 1990.

In 1974, it was estimated that immunization coverage in the developing world was less than 5%. By 1987, coverage of children in developing countries in their first year of life with one dose of BCG and measles vaccines and three doses of DPT and poliomyelitis vaccines was reported to be between 45% and 55%. That level of immunization coverage was preventing over 1 million deaths and almost 200,000 cases of paralytic poliomyelitis a year in the developing world. In its coordinating role, WHO gave priority to the managerial training of health workers and the development of cold-chain systems in order to provide for the establishment of vaccine delivery mechanisms capable of achieving high coverage of susceptible populations with vaccines known to be safe and effective. WHO estimated that in 1990 alone, immunization programs reached more than 100 million infants each year, and saved 3.2 million children annually from measles, neonatal tetanus and pertussis. However, approximately 2.1 million children were still dying each year from the preventable diseases included in the EPI. Little progress had been made in extending coverage to hard-to-reach populations, and coverage in Africa had even begun to decline.

In 1993, WHO, UNICEF, UNDP, the World Bank, and the Rockefeller Foundation founded the *Children's Vaccine Initiative (CVI)*. The Initiative undertook the research and development of a heat-stable oral poliomyelitis vaccine, a single-dose tetanus toxoid vaccine, and an improved measles vaccine which could be given earlier in life. In 1994, the EPI and the Children's Vaccine Initiative were merged into the *Global Programme for Vaccines and Immunization (GPV)*, which also took over the activities of the WHO/UNDP Programme for Vaccine Development. The GPV was established to sustain the accomplishments of the EPI and the CVI, to achieve the goals for immunization and disease control set by the World Health Assembly and the World Summit for Children, and to add new and improved vaccines as they become available.

By 1999 the Global Programme for Vaccines and Immunization became the Department of Vaccines and Biologicals. Based on World Health Assembly targets, three major objectives were defined for the department: (1) innovation, including facilitating the development of new vaccines, simplifying immunization, and accelerating the introduction of new or improved vaccines (pneumococcal, Hib, rotavirus, and hepatitis B vaccines were given top priority); (2) establishing immunization systems, including increasing coverage to 90%, strengthening the system for epidemiological surveillance, and assuring the safety of vaccines; and

(3) accelerated disease control through the eradication of polio by 2000, reducing measles cases by 90%, eliminating neonatal tetanus, and eliminating vitamin-A deficiency.

B. Prevention and Control of Noncommunicable Diseases

Cancer

Cancer, a noncommunicable disease, has been ranked as the second or third main cause of death globally among persons who survive the first five years of life. Contrary to the general belief that cancer occurs mainly in the industrialized world, it is estimated that more than half of all cancer patients today are in developing countries. By the year 2015, the annual figure is expected to reach 15 million cases, and by 2000, 20 million new cases. Some 70% of these are expected to occur in developing countries, which, as of the late-1990s, together had less than 5% of the resources for cancer control. Dramatic increases in life expectancy, combined with changes in lifestyles, were expected to lead to global epidemics of cancer and other chronic, non-communicable diseases. In 1997 alone, cancer claimed more than 6 million lives, or 12% of all deaths worldwide, and these figures continued to rise through the end of the decade.

Cancer Strategies for the New Millennium, an international conference, was convened in London in October 1998. It was attended by more than 100 professionals from 26 countries. At the event, WHO Cancer Programme chief Karol Sikora said action was needed from national governments working in close partnership with the private sector. WHO announced plans to work to reduce the global incidence of cancer by five million per year and reduce mortality by six million per year by 2020. "It's imperative that the private sector play its part since resources have become over-stretched and the lives of millions of people are seriously at risk. Together, we can make a difference," said Sikora. WHO Director-General Dr. Gro Harlem Brundtland added that these goals were attainable given new strategies that are aimed at an integrated approach to cancer prevention, early detection, curative treatment, and palliative care. At the core of these strategies is the "cancer priority ladder," which provides internationally accepted priorities for developing effective national control program. The steps of the ladder include tobacco control, a curable cancer program, a healthy eating program, effective pain control, referral guidelines, clinical care guidelines, nurse education, a national cancer network, clinical evaluation, a clinical research program, a basic research program, and an international aid program. WHO said it would support such efforts by offering to its 191 member states a comprehensive program of expertise, channeled through national ministries of health and health departments.

The International Agency for Research on Cancer, located in Lyons, France, is associated with WHO and conducts research on identification of carcinogenic factors in the environment, as well as lifestyle factors in cancer development.

Cardiovascular Diseases

The MONICA Project. WHO coordinated the Monitoring of Trends and Determinants of Cardiovascular Diseases (MONICA) which was established in 1979 and became operational in 39 collaborating centers located in 26 countries in October 1984. The MONICA project was the largest collaborative epidemiological study of these diseases ever carried out. It followed 25 million people between 25 and 64 years of age over a 10-year period, collecting data on coronary deaths, non-fatal heart attacks, coronary risk factors, and coronary care. By 1993, the main results from the MONICA study were: cross-sectional comparisons of risk factor levels; relations between various risk factors; five-year trends in risk factors; acute coronary care; medical services; cross-sectional comparisons of incidence rates for stroke; and management of stroke around the world. Several optional studies are being carried out in connection with MONICA on nutrition, anti-oxidant vitamins, polyunsaturated fatty acids, physical activity and psychosocial studies, and drug monitoring.

The MONICA data center was established at the National Public Health Institute in Finland, and prepared the data collection instruments and methodology for the study. It receives and analyzes the data collected. In 1993 the MONICA study entered its final stage of data collection. The final results of the study were made available in 1998 and were made accessible online at www.ktl.fi/monica.

Substance Abuse

Tobacco Use. Cigarette smoking is one of the principal preventable causes of premature mortality and ill health, particularly in industrialized countries but also in developing countries, where it is spreading. According to WHO estimates in early 2000, there are 4 million deaths a year from tobacco, a figure expected to rise to about 10 million by the 2020s or early 2030s. By that date, based on smoking trends, tobacco was predicted to be the leading cause of disease burden in the world, causing about one in eight deaths. 70% of those deaths were expected to occur in developing countries. Smoking has been shown to be linked with circulatory complications in women using oral contraceptives, cause lower body weight in newborns of smoking mothers, decrease male and female fertility, and be associated with cancers of organs other than the lungs. Passive smoking causes a higher frequency of upper respiratory tract infections in children exposed to tobacco smoke. In adults, it is associated with a significantly higher risk of lung cancer among exposed nonsmokers. Tobacco chewing causes cancer of the mouth.

Tobacco use is considered as a dependence disorder in WHO's International Classification of Diseases. WHO has taken the lead in international action to stem the spread of smoking and its harmful health consequences. It collaborates with numerous national smoking and health associations around the world, as well as with nongovernmental organizations and other UN agencies. WHO collaborating reference centers assist in analyses of toxic components of cigarettes. Seminars and conferences muster scientific knowledge and political support.

In 1988, the World Health Assembly declared 31 May as a "World No Tobacco Day" to focus public attention and recognize contributions to healthy life-style free from tobacco use. In 1989 the WHA approved a plan of action on a program called "Tobacco or Health." The program promoted national tobacco control programs; provided advocacy and information services; and acted as a clearinghouse for activities in the field.

To improve the global response to tobacco as an important health issue, in July 1998, WHO Director-General Dr. Gro Harlem Brundtland established the Tobacco Free Initiative (TFI). The long-term mission of global tobacco control is to reduce smoking prevalence and tobacco consumption in all countries and among all groups, thereby reducing the burden of disease caused by tobacco. In support of this mission, the stated goals of the TFI are to: strengthen global support for evidence-based tobacco control policies and actions; build new partnerships and reinforce existing partnerships for action; heighten awareness of the social, human and economic harm of tobacco in all sectors of society, and the need to take comprehensive actions at all levels; accelerate national, regional, and global strategic planning, implementation and evaluation; commission policy research to support rapid, sustained, and innovative actions; mobilize adequate resources to support action; integrate tobacco into the broader agenda of health and development; and facilitate the development of an effective Framework Convention for Tobacco Control and related protocols. In achieving these goals, WHO stated that TFI would build strong internal and external partnerships with each WHO cluster and regional and country offices, and with a range of organizations and institutions around the world. WHO has also been instrumental in heightening awareness of World No-Tobacco Day (May 31 each year).

Alcohol and Drug Abuse. WHO is the executing agency for the United Nations Fund for Drug Abuse Control. In collaboration with the International Narcotics Control Board and the United Nations Division of Narcotic Drugs, WHO has prepared guidelines on drug-abuse reporting systems that give special attention to data on health, to complement the law enforcement data that are traditionally gathered. In 1991, WHO held an Interregional Meeting on Alcohol-Related Problems in Tokyo, which recommended a number of actions to reduce alcohol dependence in member states. In the 1992/93 biennium, the Abuse Trends Linkage Alerting System (ATLAS) was set up to gather health-related data from a variety of sources in order to assist in mobilizing efforts to reduce demand for dependence-producing substances. In 1993, WHO supplied global data on substance abuse for the World Bank's publication of *World Development Report 1993: Investing in Health.*

To better lead the fight against substance abuse, WHO established a Substance Abuse Department (SAB), which promotes the agency's "health for all" concept by working to reduce the incidence and prevalence of substance abuse. In the 1990s SAB began developing programs, coordinating research, and working with existing health departments and other organizations to curtail demand for alcohol and drugs (psychoactive substances). SAB placed emphasis on intervention research on the effects of urbanization and drug abuse among young people; developing a global database of model program and best practices; strengthening country capacity to reduce alcohol abuse; and reducing HIV/AIDS-associated risks and consequences of substance abuse.

C. Primary Healthcare and Health Building

Family Health

"Health for all" requires that special attention be paid to specific population groups whose health and welfare have profound social, demographic, and economic implications for society. The health of mothers and children is particularly important because of the special biological and psychosocial needs inherent in the rapid process of human growth, needs which must be met in order to ensure the survival and healthy development of the fetus and the child, as well as to maintain the health and development of the mother. The health of young people is also important, since the energy and idealism of youth are important resources that can be channeled to the benefit of their societies.

WHO assists governments in the application of preventive, curative, and rehabilitative measures aimed at promoting and protecting the health of women and children and at strengthening the role of all family members in health care and child rearing. WHO's primary approaches are the following: (1) to identify the extent and nature of the major health needs of mothers, children, and young people; (2) to develop and adapt methods for the promotion of healthy behavior and the protection of women, children, and adolescents during vulnerable periods of rapid physiological and social changes, particularly relating to reproduction; (3) to provide technical guidance in the planning, management, and evaluation of preventive and curative programs of maternal and child health, including family planning; (4) to introduce and adapt training approaches for improving knowledge and skills in interpersonal and group communication and counseling, the health rationale for family planning, and innovative maternal and child health/family planning technologies; (5) to disseminate information on the health needs of women, children, and adolescents and on new ways of addressing those needs; (6) to identify and support research in basic clinical and applied aspects of pediatrics, adolescent medicine, gynecology and obstetrics, social psychology, and health systems; (7) to collaborate in the activities of national and international organizations concerned with maternal and child health/family planning and young people; and (8) to contribute to the development of intersectoral policies and programs.

In 1992, the World Health Assembly established the Global Commission for Women's Health (GCWH). The commission is composed of eminent persons from different professional fields and acts as an advisory body to the Directory General, providing independent scientific and technical advice on policies and strategies relating to women's health. The commission meets once a year.

At the commission's fifth meeting, in February 1997, US First Lady Hillary Rodham Clinton joined the GCWH in setting out a comprehensive agenda on the issue of maternal morbidity: According to WHO, the annual global estimated toll is close to 600,000 deaths (one woman dying every minute of every day) and eight million cases of disability from pregnancy-related causes. The GCWH dedicated itself to future advocacy to ensure that the tragedy of women dying in childbirth was not ignored. The First Lady noted WHO's progress in women's health made since 1995's Beijing World Conference on Women. The Platform for Action, adopted by the Beijing Conference, highlighted the need to ensure universal access to appropriate, affordable and quality health care and services for women and girls as one of the 12 critical areas of concern requiring urgent attention by governments and the international community.

The agenda for women's health was expected to be furthered at the Beijing+5 conference, Women 2000:Gender Equality, Development and Peace for the Twenty-first Century, held June 2000 in New York City. Among the topics to be discussed at the forum were death during childbirth, HIV/AIDS and other sexually transmitted diseases, women in control of their own fertility, and malnutrition.

Reproductive Health

In 1993, the WHO Global Policy Council approved the following definition of reproductive health to provide a basis for action in this field. "Within the framework of WHO's definition of health as a state of complete physical, mental and social well-being, and not merely the absence of disease or infirmity, reproductive health addresses the reproductive processes, functions, and system at all stages of life. Reproductive health implies that people are able to have a responsible, satisfying, and safe sex life and that they have the capability to reproduce and the freedom to decide if, when, and how often to do so. Implicit in this last condition are the right of men and women to be informed of and to have access to safe, effective, affordable, and acceptable methods of fertility regulation of their choice, and the right of access to appropriate health care services that will enable women to go safely through pregnancy and childbirth and provide couples with the best chance of having a healthy infant."

Nutrition

In addition to developing criteria and norms for assessing nutritional status, WHO strives to strengthen the capacities of countries to assess and evaluate their nutritional problems and associated factors and to develop and implement sectoral strategies to deal with the causes of those problems. Increasing the awareness of the world community of those problems for which solutions have been designed and tested has resulted in a significant increase in national programs to control iodine-deficiency disorders and vitamin A deficiency. At the same time, improvements in factors that have an influence on nutrition, such as disease prevention and management, food production, and education, have resulted in a decreased prevalence of undernutrition.

The International Conference on Nutrition, held in Rome in December 1992, was the culmination of more than two years' joint effort by WHO and FAO to promote awareness of the extent and seriousness of nutritional and diet-related problems. The conference was attended by more than 1,300 people representing 159 governments and some 160 international and non-governmental organizations. The conference adopted the *World Declaration and Plan of Action for Nutrition* which declared its determination to eliminate hunger and reduce all forms of malnutrition, and called on the United Nations to declare an International Decade of Food and Nutrition. It was estimated at the conference that 780 million people in developing countries do not have access to enough food to meet their basic daily needs. It reaffirmed the right of women and adolescent girls to adequate nutrition. The conference set ambitious goals of eliminating famine and famine-related deaths by the end of the decade and substantially reducing starvation and widespread chronic hunger, especially among children, women, and the aged. It also called for the total elimination of inadequate sanitation and poor hygiene, including unsafe drinking water. Governments were urged to promote national plans of action based on the strategies developed at the conference and to allocate the financial and human resources needed to implement the necessary programs. In its report, the conference referred to the nutritional goals set by the Fourth United Nations Development Decade and the World Summit for Children.

In 1995, WHO reported that 31% of the world's children under the age of five who live in developing countries were underweight. A 1994 report urged member nations to implement the International Code of Marketing of Breast-milk Substitutes, adopted by the WHA in 1981, to protect women in developing world from being manipulated into feeding their infants breast-milk substitutes, a practice which had been shown to put infants at risk. A wide range of illnesses and nutrition-related disorders are prevented by breast-feeding children. WHO considers direct advertising of infant formula to mothers with infants in the first four to six months of life singularly inappropriate. The 1994 report stated that large sums were being spent misguidedly to provide breast-milk substitutes to the countries of Central and Eastern Europe within the context of food aid programs. The report noted that an adequate diet is more crucial in infancy than at any other time of life because infants have a high nutritional requirement in relation to body weight. Faulty nutrition during the first months has been proved to influence future health and development.

At the end of the century, WHO reported that overall progress in reducing protein-energy malnutrition among infants and young children was "exceedingly slow," and that the year-2000 goal of a 50% reduction in 1990 prevalence levels would not be met. This projected goal aimed at reducing global malnutrition by only 14.3% (89.8 million) in malnourished children under 5 years of age. In the year 2000, WHO reported an estimated 26.7% of the world's children under age 5 (149.6 million children) were still malnourished when measured in terms of weight for age. Nevertheless, this clearly represented significant progress when compared with the 31% who were underweight in 1995 and the 37.4% (accounting for 175.7 million children) who were malnourished in 1980.

Rehabilitation of the Disabled

Since the early 1950s, WHO has had a program for rehabilitation of the disabled. The program was initially set up to increase awareness of the problems faced by war veterans and to stimulate governments to provide increased services for this group.

During the 1970s, the program was reoriented to promote rehabilitation in developing countries. A new policy was accepted by the World Health Assembly in 1976, making rehabilitation part of primary health care services. WHO then developed a whole series of teaching-training materials to be used at the community level. All of this material has been published in a manual entitled *Training in the Community for People with Disabilities*.

The basic idea governing the program is that training for disabled people can be successfully given by family members, under the guidance and supervision of a local health worker. Referral services are needed for some 30%, mostly for short-term interventions. The program stresses the importance of involving the family and community in rehabilitation.

New plans concentrate on development of the personnel needed for providing community-based rehabilitation services at the community and district levels. The aim is to broaden the population coverage so that most people with disabilities will have access to at least the essential services.

Occupational Health

WHO's Occupational Health Program has four main aims: (1) health protection of the underserved working populations who constitute the bulk of the economically productive persons in developing countries; (2) strengthening of general health services through the application of occupational health technologies and approaches; (3) workers' participation in their health care delivery systems; and (4) development of occupational health science, technology, and practice.

The program incorporates identification and control of "work-related diseases," recognition of neuro-behavioral changes from occupational exposure to health hazards, control of occupational impairment in reproductive functions and other delayed effects and of adverse occupational psychosocial hazards, and the application of ergonomics as a factor in health promotion. WHO cooperates with countries in the development of their institutional framework for the health care of working people. Special attention is given to occupational health concerns of employed women, children, the elderly, migrant workers, and other groups.

Environmental Health

Safe drinking water, proper community sanitation (sewage disposal systems), rural and urban development, and housing standards are among the priorities of WHO's environmental health program. Many of WHO's projects in this area are carried out in collaboration with other United Nations agencies, including UNICEF, the World Bank, UNDP, and FAO.

Beginning in 1986, WHO sponsored a series of international consultations on cost recovery in community water supply and sanitation. Its *Guidelines for Drinking-water Quality* have been applied in developing countries. WHO has studied the technical aspects of wastewater reuse in agriculture and collaborated with UNEP, the World Bank, and FAO in formulating guidelines and defining strategies for safe wastewater reuse in agriculture.

WHO is also concerned with prevention and control of environmental pollution, and has produced technical manuals on the disposal of hazardous waste. The WHO/ILO/UNEP International Programme on Chemical Safety (IPCS) was established in 1980. It provides information on the risks to human health and the environment of potentially toxic chemicals, and guidance in the safe use of chemicals. The IPCS was designated by UNCED as the nucleus for international cooperation on environmentally sound management of toxic chemicals.

In 1991, WHO set up a Global Environmental Technology Network (GETNET) to link specialists in environmental management technology. In 1993 GETNET was expanded to include 340 members in 87 countries.

In 1992, the WHO Commission on Health and the Environment published *Our Planet, Our Health*, one of several documents that served as the basis of WHO's contribution to the United Nations Conference on Environment and Development (the Earth Summit) held in Rio de Janeiro in June 1992. The WHA endorsed a new global strategy for health and environment based on the Commission's recommendations.

In the interest of helping member states pursue programs of sustainable development and healthy environments, WHO set up the Protection of the Human Environment (PHE) program and web site http://www.who.int/peh/. To organize its efforts, the WHO has distinguished between environmental threats to human health that are "traditional hazards" (those associated with lack of development) and threats that pose "modern hazards" (those associated with unsustainable development). Traditional hazards, which are related to poverty and lack of development, include lack of access to safe drinking-water; inadequate basic sanitation in the household and community; food contamination with pathogens; indoor air pollution from cooking and heating; inadequate solid waste disposal; occupational injury hazards in agriculture and cottage industries; and natural disasters, including floods, droughts, and earthquakes. Modern environmental hazards, which are related to excessive development (development without regard to adequate health and the environment and which requires the unsustainable consumption of natural resources) include water and air pollution; hazardous waste accumulation and disposal; chemical and radiation hazards; deforestation and land degradation; climate change; and depletion of the ozone layer.

WHO's environmental health activities include risk assessment and research, which help provide evidence for legislators to formulate laws and standards. In this work, WHO collaborates with national health and environment authorities. WHO also supports analysis of the current environmental situation and trends to assist in the development of international initiatives to combat hazards that cross national boundaries.

Mental Health

WHO's Mental Health Department has as its major task the improvement of care for the mentally ill. In 1996, WHO estimated that at least 1,500 million people worldwide suffer at any given time from some kind of neuropsychiatric disorder, including mental, behavioral, and substance abuse disorders. The vast majority of these people are believed to suffer from depression, anxiety disorders, schizophrenia, dementia, and epilepsy. One-third may be affected by more than one neuropsychiatric ailment and three-quarters of those affected live in developing countries.

In the 1990s World Health Organization substantially expanded its investment in mental health; the Department of Mental Health represented one of its major arms for this purpose. The mission of the department is to mainstream mental health within the UN system and the health sector of its member states; to increase parity between physical and mental health, and between the rights of those affected by mental problems and those not affected; to design effective mental health policies promoting social cohesion; and to identify, disseminate, and implement cost-effective interventions.

A number of international collaborative studies have been sponsored and coordinated by WHO. These have focused on the form and course of mental disorders in different cultures, the development of prevention and treatment methods, the operation of mental health services, and psychosocial aspects of health and health care. International exchange of information is fostered through publications, training courses, seminars, and networks of collaborating research and training centers in some 40 countries.

The mental health program also includes projects concerned with the development of standardized procedures, diagnostic classifications, and statistics necessary for an improved mental health information system and collaboration in mental health research, and a major program concerned with the prevention and treatment of alcohol and drug dependence.

In the late 1980s WHO launched an Initiative of Support to People Disabled by Mental Illness, intended to facilitate the dissemination of information about good practice in community services for people with chronic mental illnesses. The initiative seeks to reduce the disabling effects of chronic mental illness and highlight social and environmental barriers which hinder treatment and rehabilitation. The Initiative sought to involve the patient in decisions affecting his or her care. The prerequisites to that involvement were considered to be: the right to be empowered; the right to representation; the right to have access to one's own medical records; the right to be free of stigmatizing labels.

In 1989, WHO began a major study to investigate the types and frequency of psychological problems in 14 countries. By 1992, it had screened 25,000 patients aged 18 to 65. The patients were classified in different categories according to the symptoms, and their progress was followed for a one-year period.

In December 1991, the United Nations General Assembly, in its resolution 46/119, approved the Principles for the Protection of Persons with Mental Illness and the Improvement of Mental Health Care. This gave mental health advocacy groups a tool to publicize their views on empowerment. The Initiative has produced publications, including *Schizophrenia: Information for Families*, which has been translated into 15 languages.

WHO considers the promotion of mental health—that is, the improvement of the position that mental health occupies in the scale of values of individuals, communities, and societies—as one of its fundamental tasks and as being essential for human development and the quality of life.

D. Pharmaceuticals

Pharmaceutical Products in International Commerce

Since 1964, WHO has studied ways of ensuring that all drugs exported from a country comply with its domestic drug quality requirements. A Certification Scheme on the Quality of Pharmaceutical Products Moving in International Commerce was adopted by the World Health Assembly in 1969, and a revised version in 1975. According to the scheme, in which about 124 countries are participating, the health authorities of the exporting countries provide a certificate that the product is authorized for sale in the exporting country and that the plant in which the product is produced is subject to regular inspection to ensure that it conforms to good practices of manufacture and quality control as recommended by WHO. Also under the scheme, the importing country may request from the authorities of the exporting country additional information on the controls exercised on the product. In addition to the product certificate issued by the competent authority of the exporting country, batch certificates, stating that the quality of the batch complies with quality specifications and indicating the expiration date and storage conditions, may be issued either by the competent authority of the exporting country or by the manufacturer.

International Biological Standardization

Biological substances cannot be characterized entirely by physical or chemical means. Their activity can be controlled only by tests in which laboratory animals, microorganisms, cell cultures, or antigen-antibody reactions are used. Such assays use biological reference materials which have previously been determined, usually under the form of an international unitage system, by calibration against appropriate international reference materials.

Much work in this field was done under League of Nations auspices. By 1945, 34 international biological standards had been established for such substances as antibiotics, antibodies, antigens, blood products and related substances, and hormones. Since then, WHO has enlisted the collaboration of more than 100 laboratories to conduct international collaborative studies, and there are now more than 200 international standards available to national control authorities throughout the world.

The work on biological standardization has expanded considerably and comprises a number of additional activities, including the establishment of international reference reagents, mainly for the purpose of diagnosis and identification. Furthermore, in order for manufacturers and national control authorities to achieve the production of biological substances which are safe and potent, international requirements on production and control have been prepared and are published in the *Technical Report Series,* released each year by the WHO Expert Committee on Biological Standardization. Such requirements are kept up to date in the light of developing technology. By the end of 1999, 48 sets of international requirements had been published. In addition, guidelines have been published on such subjects as the setting up of biological standards, the testing of kits used for the assay of biological substances, and the use of interferon therapy.

A complete list of international standards and international reference reagents is published by WHO in *Biological Substances.*

Pharmaceutical Quality Control

International Pharmacopoeia. Attempts to establish internationally agreed-upon specifications for therapeutic agents have been made since the 1850s. By 1910, limited agreements were reached concerning certain potent drugs. Since 1951, WHO has published the *International Pharmacopoeia,* which provides internationally acceptable standards for the purity and potency of pharmaceutical products moving in international commerce that are available for adoption by member states in accordance with the WHO constitution and resolutions of the World Health Assembly.

The first edition, consisting of two volumes and a supplement, was issued between 1951 and 1959. The second edition was published in 1967; a supplement was added in 1971 and additional monographs in 1972. Work on the third edition, started in 1975, aims to accommodate the needs of developing countries by offering sound standards for the essential drugs. Four volumes were issued in 1979, 1981, 1988, and 1994.

International Nonproprietary Names for Pharmaceutical Substances. Many pharmaceutical substances are known not only by their nonproprietary, generic, or scientific names but by various trade names as well. In order to identify each pharmaceutical substance by a unique, universally available nonproprietary name, WHO has set up a procedure to select international nonproprietary names for pharmaceutical substances. Such names are published regularly in the *WHO Chronicle.* By the end of 1987, over 5,400 names had been proposed and published in 48 lists. A ninth cumulative list was published in 1996, and includes over 6,500 names.

WHO Collaborating Center for Chemical Reference Substances. As a further service in the area of drug quality control, the WHO Collaborating Center for Chemical Reference Substances was established in Sweden, at the Apotekens Centrallaboratorium, in 1955. Its function is to collect, assay, and store international chemical reference substances and to make them available free to national and nonprofit laboratories and institutes and, for a nominal fee, to commercial firms. About 140 chemical reference substances needed for tests and assays described in the *International Pharmacopoeia* are available.

Good Practices in the Manufacture and Quality Control of Drugs. To assist member states with technical advice on adequate control processes in drug manufacture, the World Health Assembly, in 1969, recommended the requirements in a publication entitled *Good Practices in the Manufacture and Quality Control of Drugs.* A revised text was adopted in 1975 by the assembly. Today it is published in two volumes as *Quality Assurance of Pharmaceuticals: A Compendium of Guidelines and Related Materials.* The text contains requirements pertaining to personnel, premises, and equipment of manufacturing establishments and general hygienic and sanitation measures. Special requirements pertain to raw materials, manufacturing operations, and labeling and packaging of products. The organization and duties of a quality-control department and a quality-control laboratory are specified.

Essential Drugs. As early as 1975, the WHA had received reports of the experiences of a few countries who had adopted schemes of basic or essential drugs. The purpose was to help people in developing countries whose basic health needs could be met through the existing supply system by giving them access to the most necessary drugs. The WHA recommended that member states draw up national drug policies to ensure that the most essential drugs were available at a reasonable price, and to stimulate research and development to produce new drugs adapted to the real health requirements of developing countries. There was recognition that developing countries could not afford to waste scarce resources on drugs which either did not meet majority needs, or which were priced at a level which their societies could not afford.

In 1977, a WHO committee of experts met to determine how many drugs were really needed to ensure a reasonable level of healthcare for as many people as possible. It was determined that, in country after country, a surprisingly uniform picture of drug selection emerged. At the village health post or dispensary level, 10 to 15 drugs meet immediate needs. At the health center level, where the diagnostic and local facilities are better and the staff more highly trained, about 30 to 40 drugs will suffice for 80% to 90% of all complaints. District and provincial hospitals may need around 100 to 120 drugs, and the large referral and teaching hospitals the full range of 200 to 400. The committee's first *Model List of Essential Drugs* appeared in 1977 and contained some 200 items. By 1994 the list numbered 270 drugs. All of the drugs and vaccines on the list were of proven safety and efficacy, and possessed well understood therapeutic qualities. Most were no longer protected by patent and could be produced in quantity at reasonable cost. The *Model List* is revised every two years in order to respond to evolving needs and pharmaceutical advances. The list is not meant to be definitive, but to serve as a guideline for each country to pick and choose from in order to adopt a list of essential drugs according to its own priorities. The 11th edition was published in 1999.

In 1981, WHO launched its Action Programme on Essential Drugs to help narrow the list of drugs that would be essential for small medical units in developing countries. This program assists countries in developing their own legislation and methods of financing comprehensive drug programs. It also assists them in implementing the quality control monitoring regimes mentioned above. The Action Programme also provides support for training personnel in the areas of drug management and rational use. It supports national and regional seminars at which hundreds of health staff from countries throughout the world receive practical training. In the area of research, the program encourages research aimed at filling gaps in existing knowledge about the best means of selecting, procuring, and distributing drugs. This research seeks to discover how providers make decisions on which drugs to prescribe, or how and why patients use—or fail to use—medicines. This research has direct bearing on the ways in which vital medicines can be made available and accessible to the greatest number of people. More than 100 countries have adapted the Model List to match their own patterns of disease and financial resources.

E. Research Promotion and Development

Through its advisory committees on medical research—one for each of the six WHO regions and one at the global level—WHO provides guidelines for research planning, execution, and implementation in health programs directly linked to national priorities. The committees also offer an appropriate forum for the discussion of national and regional experiences and for the detailed formulation of scientific and technological policies in the field of health. Research programs and activities are developed in close coordination with medical research councils or analogous bodies, with particular emphasis on the strengthening of managerial capacities at all levels.

Members of the World Health Organization
(as of 2000)

Afghanistan	Dominica	Libyan Arab Jamahiriya	Senegal
Albania	Dominican Republic	Lithuania	Seychelles
Algeria	Ecuador	Luxembourg	Sierra Leone
Andorra	Egypt	Madagascar	Singapore
Angola	El Salvador	Malawi	Slovak Republic
Antigua and Barbuda	Equatorial Guinea	Malaysia	Slovenia
Argentina	Eritrea	Maldives	Solomon Islands
Armenia	Estonia	Mali	Somalia
Australia	Ethiopia	Malta	South Africa
Austria	Fiji	Marshall Islands	Spain
Azerbaijan	Finland	Mauritania	Sri Lanka
Bahamas	France	Mauritius	Sudan
Bahrain	Gabon	Mexico	Suriname
Bangladesh	Gambia	Micronesia (Federated States of)	Swaziland
Barbados	Georgia	Monaco	Sweden
Belarus	Germany	Mongolia	Switzerland
Belgium	Ghana	Morocco	Syria
Belize	Greece	Mozambique	Tajikistan
Benin	Grenada	Myanmar	Thailand
Bhutan	Guatemala	Namibia	The Former Yugoslav
Bolivia	Guinea	Nauru	Republic of Macedonia
Bosnia and Herzegovina	Guinea-Bissau	Nepal	Togo
Botswana	Guyana	Netherlands	Tonga
Brazil	Haiti	New Zealand	Trinidad and Tobago
Brunei Darussalam	Honduras	Nicaragua	Tunisia
Bulgaria	Hungary	Niger	Turkey
Burkina Faso	Iceland	Nigeria	Turkmenistan
Burundi	India	Niue	Tuvalu
Cambodia	Indonesia	Norway	Uganda
Cameroon	Iran	Oman	Ukraine
Canada	Iraq	Pakistan	United Arab Emirates
Cape Verde	Ireland	Palau	United Kingdom
Central African Republic	Israel	Panama	United Republic of Tanzania
Chad	Italy	Papua New Guinea	United States
Chile	Jamaica	Paraguay	Uruguay
China	Japan	Peru	Uzbekistan
Colombia	Jordan	Philippines	Vanuatu
Comoros	Kazakhstan	Poland	Venezuela
Congo	Kenya	Portugal	Vietnam
Congo, Democratic Republic of	Kiribati	Qatar	Western Samoa
the	Korea, Democratic People's	Republic of Moldova	Yemen
Cook Islands	Republic of	Romania	Yugoslavia
Costa Rica	Korea, Republic of	Russian Federation	Zambia
Côte d'Ivoire	Kuwait	Rwanda	Zimbabwe
Croatia	Kyrgyz Republic	St. Kitts and Nevis	
Cuba	Lao People's Democratic Republic	St. Lucia	ASSOCIATE MEMBERS
Cyprus	Latvia	St. Vincent and the Grenadines	Puerto Rico
Czech Republic	Lebanon	San Marino	Tokelau
Denmark	Lesotho	São Tomé and Principe	
Djibouti	Liberia	Saudi Arabia	

WHO's coordinating role in research calls for the development of a system for the exchange of scientific information and the enlistment of the collaboration of groups of scientists and research workers in various areas on solving key problems and developing methods for most effectively combining their efforts.

Over the years, more than 1200 institutions with the necessary expertise and facilities have been designated by WHO as "WHO Collaborating Centers." WHO also designates expert advisory panels. Financial assistance is sometimes provided by WHO through technical services agreements, partially offsetting the much larger expenses borne by the centers themselves.

In order to increase the research potential of member countries, WHO has developed a program to train research workers. The duration of grants varies, but as far as possible, they are made sufficiently long to permit the candidate to gain an adequate knowledge of methods and techniques and, very often, to carry out, under supervision, a specific piece of research.

Communication among scientists is also promoted. A scientist from one country is enabled to visit scientists in other countries for a period of up to three months, thus facilitating personal contact and the exchange of ideas.

WHO promotes meetings, symposia, seminars, and training courses in special techniques, bringing together scientists from various parts of the world. Reports of such meetings are circulated, when appropriate, to the scientific community.

F. Health Personnel Development

WHO's role in health personnel development is to collaborate with member states in their efforts to plan, train, deploy, and manage teams of health personnel made up of the numbers and types that are required (and that they can afford) and to help ensure that such personnel are socially responsible and possess appropriate technical, scientific, and management competence.

WHO is attempting to raise the political, economic, and social status of women as health care providers in the formal and informal health care system and in the community and to ensure that they receive the education, training, and orientation to enable them to expand the scope and improve the quality of the health care that they provide to themselves, each other, their families, and other members of the community.

Promotion of community-oriented educational programs with team and problem-based methods of teaching/learning is another approach. The programs are designed to prepare personnel to perform tasks directly related to identified service requirements of specific concern to the country. Appropriate teaching and learning materials, including those for self-teaching and audiovisual purposes, adapted to different cultures and languages, are promoted for all categories of health personnel.

Fellowships occupy an important place in WHO's program as one of the ways to provide opportunities for training and study in health matters which are not available in the fellow's own country and for the international exchange of scientific knowledge and techniques relating to health. WHO encourages the nomination, selection, and evaluation of fellows based on and determined by a member state's personnel development policy, in line with its national policy for health development, so that fellowships can contribute to the training of the type and amount of personnel needed to achieve the global target of "health for all." WHO awards fellowships preferably to candidates who will be directly involved in primary health care programs.

In many countries, however, the problem is no longer one of shortage of health professionals, but rather of establishing or maintaining the right balance between them to ensure that the necessary knowledge and skills are available. WHO is sponsoring studies to develop information systems and methods to help countries achieve this balance.

Nursing. The WHA, in 1992, recommended that each country develop a national action plan for nursing. A global advisory group on nursing and midwifery was established by the 45th WHA, and held its first meeting in 1992. It recommended that, as the largest group of health personnel in any country, nursing and midwifery be declared a priority area for WHO action. A WHO study group on nursing beyond the year 2000 convened in July 1993. It adopted the Nursing Declaration of Alma-Ata, which recognizes that a multiprofessional, multidisciplinary approach is needed to prepare healthcare providers to work in a rapidly changing environment. As a starting point, every health ministry was urged to establish a position of chief nurse, with appropriate staff and budget.

G. Public Information and Education for Health

To integrate health education and information for health, WHO established the Division of Public Information and Education for Health. Its major tasks, in close cooperation with all regions, are to work with governments in developing coordinated information/education programs aimed at promoting healthy behavior and increasing self-reliance among individuals and communities, and to work with technical units in planning, developing, and implementing an information/education component in their programs.

The need for promotion, advocacy, and greater public awareness of health issues is a recurring theme in virtually all WHO programs. WHO considers health education as the sum of activities that will encourage people who want to be healthy to know how to stay healthy, to do what they can individually and collectively to maintain health, and to seek help whenever it may be needed.

WHO has developed many computerized information resources over the years, including WHOLIS, the WHO library information system, which is available on diskette and on the Internet. WHODOC, a regular listing of new WHO publications and documents is also available on diskette and on the Internet. See United Nations Databases for a descriptive listing of WHO's computerized databases.

H. Health Legislation

While WHO is aware of the importance of health and related legislation to the delivery of personal and environmental health services in countries, it has no mandate to propose model legislation. On the other hand, it recognizes member states' need for relevant and timely information. WHO is mandated to maintain an awareness of all significant new laws and regulations in the field of health, and to disseminate information thereon as rapidly as possible. The main vehicle for information transfer is its *International Digest of Health Legislation* which is now issued only in an electronic form. A demand for information on HIV/AIDS legislation prompted WHO to develop a computerized database that covers relevant legislation as well as literature on the legal, ethical, and judicial aspects of AIDS. Data on other subjects, such as legislation to combat smoking, have also been computerized.

In February 1994, the First International Conference of Medical Parliamentarians was held in Bangkok, organized by the Asian Forum of Parliamentarians on Population Development and the International Medical Parliamentarians Organization in close cooperation with WHO. More than 80 medical parliamentarians from 33 countries attended the conference to discuss five specific areas: environmental health, population and development; narcotics drug abuse; organ transplantation; public health and development; and maternal and child health and AIDS. The conference adopted the Bangkok Declaration and Call for Action which set forth goals and priorities for the establishment of national legislation in the five subject areas.

The International Medical Parliamentarians Organization (IMPO) was admitted into official relations with WHO in 1995, joining the ranks of the numerous NGOs that have working relationships with WHO. In 1999, IMPO had individual members in more than 30 countries, including many developing nations.

BIBLIOGRAPHY

Bulletin of the World Health Organization. The principal scientific periodical of WHO; monthly.

International Travel and Health: Vaccination Requirements and Health Advice. Annual guide.

Pharmaceutical Newsletter. Monthly.

Weekly Epidemiological Record. Contains notifications and other information relating to diseases designated as "quarantinable" in the International Sanitary Regulations. For the guidance of national health administrations and quarantine services.

WHO Drug Information. A quarterly journal with reports on major drug regulatory action in different countries and information on medicinal products and selected essential drugs from WHO's Model List.

World Directory of Medical Schools. Country-by-country directory of more than 1,600 institutions.

(A complete listing of WHO publications and periodicals can be accessed and searched at the WHO web site www.who.int/.)

THE INTERNATIONAL CIVIL AVIATION ORGANIZATION (ICAO)

BACKGROUND: In December 1903, the first heavier-than-air craft, designed by the Wright brothers, managed to fly 37 m (120 ft) under its own power carrying one person. In 1998 scheduled airlines alone flew an estimated 2,630 billion passenger-kilometers. This figure was expected to rise to about 2,739 billion in 1999, 2,875 billion in 2000, and 3,038 billion in 2001. In 1999 it was estimated that scheduled airlines carried over 1.5 million passengers. Total operating revenues (passenger, cargo, mail) of the world's airlines had reached US$3.7 billion a year by 1958 and US$291 billion by 1997. Although in a number of countries regulation of domestic flights was established fairly soon, little was accomplished until 1944 to solve the multifarious technical, economic, and legal problems posed by international civil aviation.

CREATION

The first international civil aviation conference, held in 1910 and attended by European governments only, since transoceanic flight was then regarded as no more than a wild dream, was a failure. Almost another decade elapsed before an international convention, signed in Paris in 1919, created the International Commission for Air Navigation. The commission was to meet at least once a year and concern itself with technical matters. An international committee of jurists was also established, to concern itself with the intricate legal questions created by cross-border aviation. In 1928, a Pan-American convention on commercial aviation was adopted at a conference held in Havana to deal with problems then emerging as international flights became more frequent in the Western Hemisphere. Although some progress in obtaining agreement on international flight regulations had been made by the end of the 1930s, most nations still granted very few concessions to each other's airlines, and no agreement existed permitting foreign planes to fly nonstop over the territory of one country en route to another country.

The Chicago Conference of 1944

The tremendous development of aviation during World War II demonstrated the need for an international organization to assist and regulate international flight for peaceful purposes, covering all aspects of flying, including technical, economic, and legal problems. For these reasons, in early 1944, the US conducted exploratory discussions with its World War II allies, on the basis of which invitations were sent to 55 allied and neutral states to meet in Chicago in November 1944.

In November and December 1944, delegates of 52 nations met at the International Civil Aviation Conference in Chicago to plan for international cooperation in the field of air navigation in the postwar era. It was this conference that framed the constitution of the International Civil Aviation Organization—the Convention on International Civil Aviation, also called the Chicago Convention. This convention stipulated that ICAO would come into being after the convention was ratified by 26 nations. To respond to the immediate needs of civil aviation, a provisional organization was created and functioned for 20 months until, on 4 April 1947, ICAO officially came into existence.

In essence, the conference was faced with two questions: (1) whether universally recognized navigational signals and other navigational and technical standards could be agreed upon, and (2) whether international rules concerning the economics of air

transport could be established. One group of countries, led by the US, wanted an international organization empowered only to make recommendations regarding standard technical procedures and equipment. In its economic aspects, these countries believed, air transportation should be freely competitive. This policy would also best serve the interests of the "consumer nations" that had no international airlines of their own. Another group of countries, led by the UK, favored a stronger organization, which would have a great deal to say about the economics of civil aviation. It would be empowered to allocate the international routes that the airlines of different countries would be allowed to fly, regulate the frequency of flights, and fix rates. A radical proposal, advanced by New Zealand and supported by Australia, called for international ownership and operation of international air transport.

The Convention on International Civil Aviation finally adopted by the conference was something of a compromise between the American and British positions. The convention established for the first time an independent international body, the International Civil Aviation Organization, to supervise "order in the air," obtain maximum technical standardization for international aviation, recommend certain practices that member countries should follow, and carry out other functions. Countries ratifying or acceding to the convention thereby agreed in advance to conform to the greatest possible extent to ICAO-adopted civil aviation standards and to endeavor to conform to ICAO-adopted recommendations.

In the economic field, ICAO has no regulatory powers, but one of its constitutional objectives is to "prevent economic waste caused by unreasonable competition." In addition, under the convention, member states undertake to have their international airlines furnish ICAO with traffic reports, cost statistics, and financial statements showing, among other things, all receipts from operations and the sources of such revenues.

The Chicago Convention affirms every state's "complete and exclusive sovereignty over the airspace above its territory." It provides that nonscheduled flights may, subject to certain permissible conditions and limitations, be made by the civil aircraft of one country into or over the territory of another. Scheduled international air service, however, may be operated from one country into or over the territory of another country only with the latter's authorization, and member states are permitted to establish areas prohibited to foreign aircraft as long as these regulations are nondiscriminatory. Pilotless as well as conventional aircraft are covered by these provisions. The term *airspace* is not precisely defined, however, and with the development of rockets and long-range missiles, the problem of deciding where a country's airspace ends and where outer space begins has become a matter of practical concern. This problem has come under study by the UN Committee on the Peaceful Uses of Outer Space.

An important matter considered by the Chicago conference was the question of the exchange of commercial rights in international civil aviation. It was not possible to reach an agreement satisfactory to all states attending the conference. Hence, the question was covered not in the Convention on International Civil Aviation that serves as ICAO's constitution but in two supplementary agreements adopted by the conference: the International Air Services Transit Agreement and the International Air Transport Agreement. These two treaties do not form part of the ICAO constitution and are binding only on the ICAO member states that have ratified them.

The International Air Services Transit Agreement guarantees (1) the freedom of civil aircraft to fly over foreign countries and territories as long as they do not land, and (2) the freedom of civil aircraft to make nontraffic landings, for refueling or overhaul only, in foreign territory. The agreement thus established for the first time the principle of automatic right of transit and of emergency landing.

The International Air Transport Agreement, also known as the Five Freedoms Agreement, affirms, in addition to the two freedoms covered by the transit agreement, three other freedoms of the air: (3) freedom to transport passengers and cargo from an aircraft's homeland to other countries, (4) freedom to transport passengers and cargo from other countries to an aircraft's homeland, and (5) freedom to carry air traffic between countries other than the aircraft's homeland.

Because the Chicago Convention was adopted in December 1944, ICAO possesses a constitution older than the UN Charter. Countries were much slower in ratifying the Chicago Convention, however, than they were in ratifying the UN Charter. For this reason, ICAO did not come into being until 4 April 1947, 30 days after the convention had been ratified by the required 26 states.

PURPOSES

ICAO's aims and objectives, as stated in the Chicago Convention, are to foster the planning and development of international air transport so as to ensure the safe and orderly growth of international civil aviation throughout the world; encourage the arts of aircraft design and operation for peaceful purposes; encourage the development of airways, airports, and air navigation facilities for international civil aviation; meet the needs of the peoples of the world for safe, regular, efficient, and economical air transport; prevent economic waste caused by unreasonable competition; ensure that the rights of contracting states are fully respected and that every contracting state has a fair opportunity to operate international airlines; avoid discrimination between contracting states; promote safety of flight in international air navigation; and promote generally the development of all aspects of international civil aeronautics.

MEMBERSHIP

As of December 1998, ICAO had 185 member states.

STRUCTURE

The three main organs of ICAO are the assembly, the council, and the secretariat, headed by the Secretary General.

Assembly

The all-member assembly meets every three years. Every member state has one vote in the assembly, and decisions are made by a

simple majority vote unless otherwise specified by the Chicago Convention. Sessions have been held in many different cities.

The assembly makes policy recommendations, reviews the work of ICAO, offers guidance to other ICAO bodies, elects the council, and determines the budget. The assembly may amend the ICAO constitution by a two-thirds majority vote, and it has done so on several occasions. But amendments come into force for the states that ratify them only after they have been ratified by at least two-thirds of the ICAO member states as specified by the assembly. In other words, the assembly may feel that it would not be fair to introduce a particular innovation in international civil aviation unless certain states would abide by it. On the other hand, the assembly possesses a rather unusual prerogative to induce wide ratification of an amendment it has adopted: if a member state does not ratify a particular amendment within a given period of time, the assembly has the right to revoke that country's membership in ICAO. However, this provision (Article 94[b]) has never been invoked.

Council

The council is a permanent body, composed of 33 member states elected by the assembly for three-year terms. In selecting the membership of the council, the assembly is required by the Chicago Convention to give adequate representation to nations of major importance in air transport, to nations that provide the largest share of facilities for international civil air navigation, and to nations whose inclusion on the council will ensure broad geographical representation.

Assad Kotaite of Lebanon, president of the council since 1976, was reelected in November 1998. He was elected by acclamation for a ninth consecutive term as council president.

The council's powers are unusually broad, as compared with those of the executive councils of most other specialized agencies. It adopts international standards and recommended practices regarding civil air navigation and transport. It may act as arbiter between member states on disputes relating to the interpretation or application of the Chicago Convention and its annexes. It may investigate any situation that presents avoidable obstacles to the development of international air navigation. In general, it may take whatever steps are necessary to maintain the safety and regularity of operation of international air transport.

Secretary General and Secretariat

The ICAO secretariat is headed by a Secretary General, who is appointed by the council. The Secretary General appoints the staff of the ICAO secretariat and supervises and directs its activities. In March 2000 the Council appointed Renato Claudio Costa Pereira (of Brazil) as Secretary General for a second three-year term (beginning 1 August 2000).

ICAO headquarters are at 999 University Street, in the center of Montreal, occupying a 15-story tower with an adjoining complex offering complete conference facilities. ICAO maintains regional offices in Paris, Bangkok, Cairo, Mexico City, Nairobi, Lima, and Dakar to assist member states in providing aeronautical services.

BUDGET

The 1998 assembly approved the following budgets: 1999, us$52,578,000; 2000, us$53,765,000; 2001, us$55,174,000. Contributions by member states are assessed on a sliding scale determined by the assembly.

ACTIVITIES

A. International Standards and Recommended Practices

By joining ICAO—that is, by accepting the Chicago Convention—states undertake to collaborate in securing the highest practicable degree of uniformity in regulations, standards, procedures, and organization in all matters in which such uniformity will facilitate and improve air navigation. Hence, one of ICAO's chief tasks is to adopt such international standards and recommendations and to keep them up-to-date through modifications and amendments.

A standard, as defined by the first ICAO Assembly, is "any specification for physical characteristics, configuration, material, performance, personnel, or procedures, the uniform application of which is recognized as *necessary* for the safety or regularity of international air navigation and to which member states *will conform*." Standards may thus include specifications for such matters as the length of runways, the materials to be used in aircraft construction, and the qualifications to be required of a pilot flying an international route. A recommendation is any such specification, the uniform application of which is recognized as "*desirable* in the interest of safety, regularity, or efficiency of international air navigation and to which member states will *endeavor to conform.*"

Preparing and revising these standards and recommendations is largely the responsibility of ICAO's Air Navigation Commission, which plans, coordinates, and examines all of ICAO's activities in the field of air navigation. The commission consists of 15 persons, appointed by the council from among persons nominated by member states. If the council approves the text, it is submitted to the member states. While recommendations are not binding, standards automatically become binding on all member states, except for those who find it impracticable to comply and file a difference under Article 38 of the Chicago Convention.

Annexes to the Chicago Convention

The various standards and recommendations that have been adopted by ICAO are grouped into 18 annexes to the Chicago Convention. The aim of most of the annexes is to promote progress in flight safety, particularly by guaranteeing satisfactory minimum standards of training and safety procedures and by ensuring uniform international practices. The 18 annexes are the following:

1. Personnel Licensing—licensing of flight crews, air traffic controllers, and aircraft maintenance personnel.
2. Rules of the Air—rules relating to the conduct of visual and instrument flights.
3. Meteorological Services—provision of meteorological services for international air navigation and reporting of meteorological observations from aircraft.
4. Aeronautical Charts—specifications for aeronautical charts for use in international aviation.
5. Units of Measurement—dimensional systems to be used in air-ground communications.
6. Operation of Aircraft. Part I: International Commercial Air Transport; Part II: International General Aviation; Part III: International Operations–Helicopters. These specifications will ensure in similar operations throughout the world a level of safety above a prescribed minimum.
7. Aircraft Nationality and Registration Marks—requirements for registration and identification of aircraft.
8. Airworthiness of Aircraft—certification and inspection of aircraft according to uniform procedures.
9. Facilitation—simplification of customs, immigration, and health inspection regulations at international airports.
10. Aeronautical Telecommunications—standardization of communications equipment and systems and of communications procedures.
11. Air Traffic Services—establishment and operation of air traffic control, flight information, and alerting services.
12. Search and Rescue—organization and operation of facilities and services necessary for search and rescue.
13. Aircraft Accident Investigation—uniformity in the notification, investigation, and reporting of aircraft accidents.
14. Aerodromes—specifications for the design and equipment of aerodromes.
15. Aeronautical Information Services—methods for the collection and dissemination of aeronautical information required for flight operations.
16. Environmental Protection. Vol. I: Aircraft Noise—specifications for aircraft noise certification, noise monitoring, and noise exposure units for land-use planning; Vol. II: Aircraft Engine Emissions—standards relating to vented fuel and emissions certification requirements.
17. Security—specifications for safeguarding international civil aviation against acts of unlawful interference.
18. Safe Transport of Dangerous Goods by Air—specifications for the labeling, packing, and shipping of dangerous cargo.

B. Air Navigation

It is evident that air navigation covers an extremely broad spectrum of activities, ranging from short take-off and landing airplanes to supersonic transports, from security questions to the impact of aviation on the environment, from training and operating practices for pilots to the facilities required at airports.

ICAO's program regarding the environment provides a case in point. Growing air traffic and increased use of jet engines have heightened public awareness of the environmental impact of civil aviation. In 1968, ICAO instituted activities aimed at reducing aircraft noise. The first measures involved development of internationally agreed standards for the noise certification of aircraft (contained in Vol. I of Annex 16 to the Chicago Convention), which resulted in a quieter generation of jet aircraft.

Comparable studies of aviation's share in air pollution have resulted in the development of standards (Vol. II of Annex 16) relating to the control of fuel venting and of smoke and gaseous emissions from newly manufactured turbojet and turbofan engines for subsonic airplanes.

Concern about the continuing threat of violence against international civil aviation and its facilities, including the unlawful seizure and the sabotage of aircraft, led to adoption by the council of Annex 17 to the Chicago Convention, containing standards and recommended practices aimed at safeguarding international civil aviation against acts of unlawful interference. In addition, comprehensive guidance material on the subject has been developed. As part of its continuing effort to improve air safety, ICAO has adopted standards for the safe transport of dangerous goods by air. These form Annex 18 to the Chicago Convention. ICAO studies many other important subjects, such as all-weather operations, supersonic operations, application of space techniques to aviation, automated-data interchange systems, and visual aids.

C. Facilitation of International Air Transport

From the beginning of ICAO's history, the need to facilitate international air transport—to remove obstacles that would impede the free passage of aircraft, passengers, crew, baggage, cargo, and mail across international boundaries—was evident. This need is inherent in the speed of air travel itself; if, for example, customs, immigration, public health, and other formalities require one hour at each end of a transoceanic flight of six hours, the total duration of the trip is increased by 33%.

ICAO has therefore developed, over the years, a comprehensive facilitation program that is reflected in the international standards and recommended practices of Annex 9 to the Chicago Convention, as well as in the recommendations and statements of the ICAO Council and the Facilitation Division. Broadly speaking, the program aims at eliminating all nonessential documentary requirements, simplifying and standardizing the remaining forms, providing certain minimum facilities at international airports, and simplifying handling and clearance procedures. The program is concerned with such measures as liberalization of visa requirements and entry procedures for temporary visitors; the development of machine-readable passports and visas; speedy handling and clearance procedures for cargo, mail, and baggage; and the elimination, as far as possible, of requirements for documentation or examination in regard to transit traffic.

In addition to reducing procedural formalities, ICAO's efforts are aimed at providing adequate airport terminal buildings for passengers and their baggage and for air cargo, with all related facilities and services. Special attention is given to improving the accessibility of air transport to elderly and disabled passengers. The continuous growth in air traffic makes it necessary for airport administrations to review the adequacy of their facilities at regular intervals. When modifications in existing terminals or the building of new ones are contemplated, close coordination and cooperation between planners and users must be established from the earliest moment, even before any design is made. Proper airport traffic flow arrangements, with a sufficient number of clearance channels, baggage delivery positions, and cargo handling facilities, are necessary for the speedy processing of traffic through clearance control.

D. Regional Planning for Air Navigation

While worldwide uniformity is desirable for certain matters pertaining to civil aviation, others are best approached on a regional basis, since operating conditions vary a great deal from region to region. In the North Atlantic region, for example, long-range ocean flying predominates, whereas in Europe many international flights are short overland jumps. To deal with these different conditions and to facilitate detailed planning, ICAO has mapped out the following regions: Asia/Pacific, Middle East, Europe, Africa, Latin America and the Caribbean, South America, North Atlantic, and North America, which all have Planning and Implementation Regional Groups (PIRGs). At meetings held for each of them, detailed plans are drawn up for the facilities, services, and procedures appropriate to that region. The regional plans specify the air navigation facilities and services that are required, and the locations where they are required, for communications, air traffic control, search and rescue, meteorology, and so on. ICAO's plans for the nine regions are regularly revised or amended to meet the needs of increasing traffic and to take into account technical developments in civil aviation.

ICAO's regional offices are its principal agents in advising and assisting states in regard to implementation. The offices direct as much of their resources as possible to giving practical help, among other ways through frequent visits to states by members of the technical staff. In addition, ICAO allots funds for long-duration advisory implementation missions to help member countries overcome local deficiencies.

Shortcomings are taken up by the regional offices and the ICAO secretariat with the governments concerned. More complex cases may require study by the Air Navigation Commission and, if necessary, by the ICAO Council. The problem of eliminating deficiencies in navigational services and facilities is one that ICAO considers critical.

The major difficulties are lack of funds for facilities and services, a shortage of trained personnel, and administrative and organizational difficulties. ICAO has encouraged governments to upgrade their facilities through loans for capital expenditures, technical assistance, and other means. It also produces manuals and other documentation to assist states in setting up aviation training programs for flight and ground personnel and offers advice on maintenance and improvement of technical standards.

E. Jointly Operated or Financed Services

Under the Chicago Convention, every ICAO member state is required to provide air navigation facilities and services on its own territory. Navigational facilities and services must also be provided for air routes traversing the high seas and regions of undetermined sovereignty. The ICAO Council is constitutionally authorized at the request of a member state to "provide, man, maintain, and administer any or all of the airports and other air navigation facilities, including radio and meteorological services, required in its territory for the safe, regular, efficient, and economical operation of the international air services of the other contracting states." The council also may act on its own initiative to resolve a situation that might impair the "safe, regular, efficient, and economical operation" of international air services. Although ICAO has not yet undertaken the actual supervision of any nation's international air navigation facilities and services, two international agreements are in effect to furnish such services and facilities in parts of the North Atlantic region through so-called "joint-support" programs.

Under these joint-support agreements, the nations concerned provide services, facilities, or cash payments based on the use by their own aircraft of the routes involved. The two existing agreements are the Agreement on the Joint Financing of Certain Air Navigation Services in Greenland and the Faroe Islands and the Agreement on the Joint Financing of Certain Air Navigation Services in Iceland.

The vast majority of aircraft that utilize the special traffic-control, navigational, and meteorological services furnished from Iceland and Greenland for transatlantic crossings are neither Icelandic nor Danish. Hence, some 20 countries, including Iceland and Denmark, provide the funds necessary for the operation of these services.

ICAO administers these two agreements, the Secretary General having certain responsibilities and the ICAO Council having others. A special standing body, the Committee on Joint Support of Air Navigation Services, advises the council in these matters. The operation and costs of the services are constantly reviewed, and international conferences are held. In the early 1970s, charges for the use of the aeronautical facilities and services were imposed on all civil aircraft crossing the North Atlantic. These "user charges" covered only 40% of the costs allocable to civil aviation but were increased to 50% for the years 1975 to 1978, 60% for 1979 and 1980, 80% for 1981, and 100% thereafter.

F. Technical Assistance

In recognition of the importance of the airplane for international and domestic transport in countries where road and railway services are lacking, and as a means of aiding these countries in their social and economic development, ICAO has, from its inception, operated technical assistance programs through UNDP and other UN organs.

Assistance programs executed by ICAO fall into three main categories. UNDP obtains its funds from donor countries and allocates these funds among recipient countries in the form of country, intercountry, and interregional projects. The Funds-in-Trust program provides financial assistance for specific projects in the country receiving the technical assistance. The Associate Experts program provides experts from certain countries to work under ICAO guidance.

Each civil aviation project may include one or more of the following forms of assistance: experts to provide specialist advice to the civil aviation administration or national airline; fellowships to allow nationals to be trained abroad in civil aviation disciplines, often at civil aviation training centers that have been established through ICAO technical assistance; and equipment, such as radio navigational aids or communication facilities, to ensure safe and regular air service.

Fellowships have been awarded in many fields, including training as pilots, aircraft maintenance technicians, air traffic controllers, radio and radar maintenance technicians, communication officers, airport engineers, electronics engineers, air trans-

ICAO Contracting States
(as of December 1998)

Afghanistan
Albania
Algeria
Angola
Antigua and Barbuda
Argentina
Armenia
Australia
Austria
Azerbaijan
Bahamas
Bahrain
Bangladesh
Barbados
Belarus
Belgium
Belize
Benin
Bhutan
Bolivia
Bosnia and Herzegovina
Botswana
Brazil
Brunei Darussalam
Bulgaria
Burkina Faso
Burundi
Cambodia
Cameroon
Canada
Cape Verde
Central African Republic
Chad
Chile
China
Colombia
Comoros
Congo
Congo, Deomocratic Republic of
 the
Cook Islands
Costa Rica
Côte d'Ivoire
Croatia
Cuba
Cyprus
Czech Republic

Denmark
Djibouti
Dominican Republic
Ecuador
Egypt
El Salvador
Equatorial Guinea
Eritrea
Estonia
Ethiopia
Federated States of Micronesia
Fiji
Finland
France
Gabon
Gambia
Georgia
Germany
Ghana
Greece
Grenada
Guatemala
Guinea
Guinea-Bissau
Guyana
Haiti
Honduras
Hungary
Iceland
India
Indonesia
Iran, Islamic Republic of
Iraq
Ireland
Israel
Italy
Jamaica
Japan
Jordan
Kazakhstan
Kenya
Kiribati
Korea, Democratic People's
 Republic of
Korea, Republic of
Kuwait
Kyrgyzstan

Lao People's Democratic Republic
Latvia
Lebanon
Lesotho
Liberia
Libyan Arab Jamahiriya
Lithuania
Luxembourg
Madagascar
Malawi
Malaysia
Maldives
Mali
Malta
Marshall Islands
Mauritania
Mauritius
Mexico
Moldova, Republic of
Monaco
Mongolia
Morocco
Mozambique
Myanmar
Namibia
Nauru
Nepal
Netherlands
New Zealand
Nicaragua
Niger
Nigeria
Norway
Oman
Pakistan
Palau
Panama
Papua New Guinea
Paraguay
Peru
Philippines
Poland
Portugal
Qatar
Romania
Russian Federation
Rwanda

St. Lucia
St. Vincent and the Grenadines
Samoa
San Marino
Sâo Tomé and Principe
Saudi Arabia
Senegal
Seychelles
Sierra Leone
Singapore
Slovakia
Slovenia
Solomon Islands
Somalia
South Africa
Spain
Sri Lanka
Sudan
Suriname
Swaziland
Sweden
Switzerland
Syrian Arab Republic
Tajikistan
Thailand
The Former Yugoslav Republic of
 Macedonia
Togo
Tonga
Trinidad and Tobago
Tunisia
Turkey
Turkmenistan
Uganda
Ukraine
United Arab Emirates
United Kingdom
United Republic of Tanzania
United States
Uruguay
Uzbekistan
Vanuatu
Venezuela
Vietnam
Western Samoa
Yemen
Zambia

port economists, aeronautical information officers, aeronautical meteorologists, aviation medicine specialists, accident investigation experts, flight operations officers, airport fire officers, and instructors.

Major types of equipment provided include air traffic control, radar, and flight simulators; training aircraft; radio communication and radar systems; distance-measuring equipment; very high frequency omni radio ranges; instrument landing systems; nondirectional beacons; "navaid" flight-test units; airworthiness data-acquisition systems; language laboratories; audiovisual aids; visual approach slope indicator systems; and firefighting vehicles.

Major training institutions assisted by ICAO include civil aviation training centers in Egypt, Ethiopia, Gabon, Indonesia, Kenya, Mexico, Nigeria, Singapore, Thailand, Trinidad and Tobago, and Tunisia.

G. International Conventions Prepared Under ICAO

The increasing number of incidents of unlawful interference with civil aviation, beginning in the 1960s—aircraft hijacking, the placing of bombs on board aircraft, and attacks on aircraft, passengers, and crew members at airports—led to the adoption of three conventions.

- *The Tokyo Convention of 1963.* The Convention on Offenses and Certain Other Acts Committed on Board Aircraft does not define specific offenses, but it does have the virtue of ensuring that there will always be a jurisdiction (namely, that of the state of registry of the aircraft) in which a person who has committed an offense on board an aircraft can be tried. The convention also provides for the powers and duties of the aircraft commander and others respecting restraint and disembarkation of the suspected offender. It provides a detailed code of behavior for states in whose territory the suspected offender has disembarked and also stipulates the steps to be taken in the event of the hijacking of an aircraft.

- *The Hague Convention of 1970.* The Convention for the Suppression of the Unlawful Seizure of Aircraft defines the offense of unlawful seizure and provides for universal jurisdiction over, and arrest and custody of, the suspected offender. It also stipulates that prosecution or extradition of the suspected offender should take place without many restrictions.

- *The Montreal Convention of 1971.* The Convention for the Suppression of Unlawful Acts Against the Safety of Civil Aviation defines a number of acts of unlawful interference directed against international civil aviation. It provides for universal jurisdiction over the offender and, in general, contains rules for custody, extradition, and prosecution similar to those in the Hague Convention.

All three conventions are concerned with the preservation of the means of international communication and provide specifically that in the case of the unlawful seizure of an aircraft, any contracting state in which the aircraft or its passengers or crew are present shall facilitate the continuation of the journey of the passengers and crew as soon as practicable and shall return the aircraft and its cargo to the person lawfully entitled to possession.

The cooperative international action contemplated by the Tokyo, Hague, and Montreal conventions is intended to eliminate safe havens for hijackers and saboteurs.

Two additional international instruments in the field of aviation security have been developed under the auspices of ICAO.

- The *Protocol for the Suppression of Unlawful Acts of Violence at Airports Serving International Civil Aviation, Supplementary to the Convention for the Suppression of Unlawful Acts against the Safety of Civil Aviation*. The protocol was signed at Montreal on 24 February 1988 and came into force as of 6 August 1989. This protocol adds to the definition of "offence" given in the Montreal Convention of 1971, including actions that are likely to endanger airport safety. It establishes universal jurisdiction over the offender and applies the Montreal Convention's rules of custody, extradition, and prosecution.

- The *Convention on the Marking of Plastic Explosives for the Purposes of Detection*, opened for signature at Montreal in 1991 has not yet come into force. This convention requires that each state party prohibit and prevent the manufacture of unmarked plastic explosives. Four detection agents are defined in the convention's technical annex. The convention also requires each state party to prevent the movement of unmarked explosives out of its territory. It also provides for the destruction of certain kinds of existing stocks of plastic explosives.

Regime and Liability of Air Carriers

Much of ICAO's work has been devoted to keeping up-to-date the regime and limits of liability of air carriers in the case of death of, or injury to, passengers and in the carriage of cargo and postal items by air.

- The *Warsaw Convention of 1929*. The Convention on the Unification of Certain Rules Relating to International Carriage by Air, adopted during the early days of aviation, dominated the field of aviation passenger liability for almost half a century. It limits the liability, except in cases of gross negligence on the part of the carrier, to a maximum of 125,000 Poincaré gold francs (about us$10,000). The Hague Protocol of 1955 doubled the existing limits of liability. In 1971, by the Guatemala City Protocol, the rule of the Warsaw Convention based on presumption of fault yielded to *strict* liability, irrespective of fault. However, it will be some time before the 1971 protocol comes into force because at least 30 states, including five with major air traffic, must ratify it. An interesting feature of the Guatemala City Protocol is that although it provides for a limit of about us$100,000 per passenger, there is also provision for a domestic supplement if a state that is party to the protocol wishes to have a higher limit.

    In 1975, an International Conference on Air Law, convened under the auspices of ICAO, adopted new amendments to the Warsaw Convention, as amended by the Hague Protocol. Under the new provisions, the carrier is responsible for cargo damage, irrespective of fault. Another major change concerns the method of calculating the liability limits by turning from a solely gold monetary basis to a dual system, allowing countries that are members of the IMF to base passenger, baggage, and cargo liability on Special Drawing Rights, whereas countries not members of the IMF would declare liability limits in monetary units based on gold.

- The *Guadalajara Convention of 1961*. The Guadalajara Convention, supplementary to the Warsaw Convention, contains rules with regard to carriage performed by other than the contracting carrier, that is to say, by a carrier that had not issued the ticket to the passenger, or the air waybill to the consignor. In this case, both the contracting carrier and the actual carrier would be held jointly and severally liable under the Warsaw Convention or that convention as amended by the Hague Protocol.

- The *Rome Convention of 1952*. The Convention on Damage Caused by Foreign Aircraft to Third Parties on the Surface includes the principle of absolute liability of the aircraft operator for damage caused to third parties on the surface but places a limitation on the amount of compensation, expressed in Poincaré gold francs and calculated in relation to the aircraft concerned. However, a diplomatic conference convened in 1978 under ICAO auspices adopted a protocol for the amendment of the Rome Convention. The basic feature of the protocol is a substantial increase in the limits of liability and the expression of the limits in the Special Drawing Rights of the IMF.

- The *Geneva Convention of 1948*. The Convention on the International Recognition of Rights in Aircraft was prepared in order to promote the use of loans in financing the sale of aircraft by providing protection of the lender's rights in an aircraft whenever the aircraft is in the territory of another state that is party to the Geneva Convention.

Other legal subjects on ICAO's work program include the establishment of a legal framework for global navigation of satellite systems; expediting the ratification of Montreal protocols Nos. 3 and 4 of the "Warsaw System"; study of the instruments of the "Warsaw System"; liability rules that might be applicable to air traffic services providers; and the implication of the UN Convention on the Law of the Sea for the application of ICAO's Chicago Convention.

BIBLIOGRAPHY

Air Navigation Plans. For all nine ICAO regions of the world.

ICAO Journal. Provides a concise account of the activities of ICAO and features additional information of interest to contracting states and to the international aeronautical world. Issued ten times a year.

ICAO publications and audio visual training aids. Catalogs of reference materials from ICAO, including texts of conventions, procedures for air navigation services, technical publications, air transport studies, and videos on subjects such as air traffic control, airport emergency planning, aviation medicine, safety, and meteorology. Published annually. Catalogs are also accessible at the ICAO web site http://www.icao.org.

THE UNIVERSAL POSTAL UNION (UPU)

BACKGROUND: Every day, more than 1.1 billion letters are posted for delivery within national borders, accounting for more than 413 billion letters each year. In addition, each day, close to 24 million pieces of mail cross international boundaries, accounting for nearly 9 billion items posted in international service (over a third of them by developing countries) and are swiftly and safely delivered to their destinations. To handle this traffic, postal services employ some 5.9 million employees who work at or out of some 770,000 permanent post office outlets around the globe. The orderly and economical movement of international mail is made possible by the Constitution and Convention of the Universal Postal Union, the basic Acts under which the UPU operates. Since 188 countries now come under these Acts, the provisions affect virtually the entire world population. Under the Constitution, UPU member countries form a single postal territory for the reciprocal exchange of letter-post items, and freedom of transit is guaranteed throughout the entire territory of the Union.

CREATION

Although generally taken for granted, present-day postal service is of relatively recent origin. The use of postage stamps for pre-payment of postage was not introduced until 1840, when the UK established a unified postage charge, the famous penny rate, to be paid by the sender of a letter regardless of the distance it had to travel. Until that year, the postal fee based on distance was often very high and was not paid by the sender but by the addressee. If the addressee could not pay, the letter was returned. Gradually, other countries introduced adhesive stamps, and their use spread to international mail. In 1863, on the initiative of the US, representatives of 15 postal administrations met in Paris to consider the problem of standardizing international postal practices.

The decisive development came with the meeting of the first international Postal Congress at Bern in 1874, at the suggestion of the German government. The Bern Congress was attended by delegates from 22 countries: 20 European countries (including Russia), Egypt, and the US. The congress adopted a treaty concerning the establishment of a General Postal Union—commonly known as the Bern Treaty—signed on 9 October 1874. This was the forerunner of the series of multilateral Universal Postal Union conventions and came into force in the following year, when the union was formally established, on 1 July 1875, to administer its operative regulations.

The 1874 Convention provided for subsequent postal congresses to revise the convention in the light of economic and technical developments. The second congress, held in Paris in 1878, changed the name of the General Postal Union to the Universal Postal Union (UPU). Four more congresses were held prior to World War I: Lisbon, 1885; Vienna, 1891; Washington, 1897; and Rome, 1906. There were five congresses between the wars: Madrid, 1920; Stockholm, 1924; London, 1929; Cairo, 1934; and Buenos Aires, 1939. The first post–World War II congress met in Paris in 1947 and arranged for the UPU to be recognized as a specialized agency of the UN family in 1948. Other congresses met at Brussels, 1952; Ottawa, 1957; Vienna, 1964; Tokyo, 1969; Lausanne, 1974; Rio de Janeiro, 1979; Hamburg, 1984; Washington, 1989; and Seoul, 1994. The 22nd congress convened in Beijing in 1999.

PURPOSES

The basic objective of the union was stated in the 1874 Convention, reiterated in all successive revisions, and embodied in the constitution: "The countries adopting this Constitution comprise, under the title of the Universal Postal Union, a single postal territory for the reciprocal exchange of letter-post items." The 1924 congress added: "It is also the object of the Postal Union to secure the organization and improvement of the various international postal services." The 1947 congress added another clause: "and to promote the development of international collaboration in this sphere."

In recognition of the union's continued interest and newly assumed responsibilities in the field of development aid, the congress held in Vienna in 1964 enlarged the UPU's goals to include the provision of postal technical assistance to member states. Under the single-territory principle, all the union's member countries are bound by the constitution and convention to observe certain fundamental rules pertaining to ordinary mail. Ordinary mail under the Lausanne Convention includes letters, postcards, printed papers, small packets, and literature for the blind, such as books in Braille. Although the convention lays down basic postage rates for ordinary mail sent to addresses in UPU territory, variations are permitted within generous limits. Postal authorities of all member states are pledged to handle all mail with equal care, regardless of its origin and destination, and to expedite mail originating in other UPU countries on a level comparable to the best means of conveyance used for their own mail.

In the past, foreign mail was delivered to its destination without charge to the country where it was posted, and each country retained the postage collected on international mail. Since mid-1971, however, where there is an imbalance between mail sent and received, the postal administration of the country receiving the larger quantity is authorized to ask for repayment at a standard rate (fixed by the Postal Congress) to offset its excess costs. However, each country reimburses, at standard rates fixed by the Universal Postal Congress, all intermediary countries through which its mail passes in transit.

Freedom of transit—the basic principle of the union—is guaranteed throughout UPU territory. Specific regulations provide for the dispatch of mail and for the return of undeliverable mail to the sender. Certain articles, such as opium and other drugs and inflammable or explosive agents, are excluded from the international mails.

Four optional postal agreements supplement the convention. They cover parcel mail, money orders, giro (postal checks), and cash on delivery.

MEMBERSHIP

The original treaty allowed "overseas" countries to be admitted to the union subject to the agreement of administrations having postal relations with them. The 1878 congress decreed, however, that any country could accede directly to the union merely by unilateral declaration and communication of that declaration to the Swiss government. This system was revised by the Paris congress of 1947, which ruled that applications for membership in the union could be filed only by sovereign states and had to be channelled through the Swiss government. Approval is then required by at least two-thirds of the full membership. At the 1964 Vienna Congress, it was also decided that any member nation of the UN could accede directly to the UPU by a formal declaration addressed to the Swiss government. Since Washington Congress 1989, the government of the country concerned will address it directly to the Director General of the International Bureau, who will notify the member countries of the accession or consult with them on the application for admission, as the case may be.

Dependent territories were granted collective membership by a special postal conference held in Bern in 1876. Membership in the UPU as of 1999 had reached 190, including 188 independent states and two collective members of dependent territories.

RESTRICTED POSTAL UNIONS

Members of the UPU may establish restricted unions and make special agreements concerning the international postal service, provided always that they do not introduce provisions less favorable to the public than those provided for by the Acts of the UPU to which the member countries concerned are parties. Restricted unions are the Association of European Public Postal Operators (POSTEUROP), the Arab Permanent Postal Commission (APPC), the European Postal Financial Services Commission (CSFPE), the Regional Community for Posts and Telecommunications (RCPT), the Conference of Posts and Telecommunications Administrations of Central Africa (CAPTAC), the European Conference of Postal and Telecommunications Administrations (CEPT), the African Posts and Telecommunications Union (APTU), the Baltic Postal Union (BPU), the Postal Union of the Americas, Spain and Portugal (PUASP), the African Postal Union (APU), the Pan African Postal Union (PAPU), the Asian-Pacific Postal Union (APPU), the Nordic Postal Union (UPPN), and the South and West Asia Postal Union (SWAPU).

STRUCTURE

The permanent organs of the UPU are the Universal Postal Congress, the Council of Administration, the Postal Operations Council, and the International Bureau.

Universal Postal Congress

The Universal Postal Congress brings together the plenipotentiaries of all member countries and is the supreme authority of the Universal Postal Union. The congress meets in principle every five years. One of the major accomplishments of congresses held since the first Berne Congress in 1874 has been to allow UPU member countries to develop and integrate new products and services into the international postal network. In this way, such services as registered letters, postal money orders, international reply coupons, small packets, postal parcels, and expedited mail service, have been made available to the great majority of the world's citizens.

The congress' main function is legislative. However beginning in the late 1990s, the tendency was to increasingly delegate regulatory power to the two UPU councils, leaving the congress to focus on broad policy issues.

Members of the UPU

(as of May 1999)

Afghanistan	Gambia	Pakistan
Albania	Georgia	Panama
Algeria	Germany	Papua New Guinea
Angola	Ghana	Paraguay
Antigua and Barbuda	Greece	Peru
Argentina	Grenada	Philippines
Armenia	Guatemala	Poland
Australia and Australian territories	Guinea	Portugal (and Macau)
	Guinea-Bissau	Qatar
Austria	Guyana	Romania
Azerbaijan	Haiti	Russian Federation
Bahamas	Honduras	Rwanda
Bahrain	Hungary	St. Kitts and Nevis
Bangladesh	Iceland	St. Lucia
Barbados	India	St. Vincent and the Grenadines
Belarus	Indonesia	
Belgium	Iran	Samoa
Belize	Iraq	San Marino
Benin	Ireland	São Tomé and Princ- ipe
Bhutan	Israel	
Bolivia	Italy	Saudi Arabia
Bosnia and Herzegovina	Jamaica	Senegal
	Japan	Seychelles
Botswana	Jordan	Sierra Leone
Brazil	Kazakhstan	Singapore
Brunei Darussalam	Kenya	Slovakia
Bulgaria	Kiribati	Slovenia
Burkina Faso	Korea, Democratic People's Republic of	Solomon Islands
Burundi		Somalia
Cambodia	Korea, Republic of	South Africa
Cameroon	Kuwait	Spain
Canada	Kyrgyzstan	Sri Lanka
Cape Verde	Lao People's Demo- cratic Republic	Sudan
Central African Republic		Suriname
	Latvia	Swaziland
Chad	Lebanon	Sweden
Chile	Lesotho	Switzerland
China (including Hong Kong and Macao)	Liberia	Syrian Arab Republic
	Libyan Jamahiriya	Tajikistan
	Liechtenstein	Tanzania, United Republic of
Colombia	Lithuania	
Comoros	Luxembourg	Thailand
Congo	Madagascar	The Former Yugo- slav Republic of Macedonia
Congo, Democratic Republic of the	Malawi	
	Malaysia	
Costa Rica	Maldives	Togo
Côte d'Ivoire	Mali	Tonga
Croatia	Malta	Trinidad and Tobago
Cuba	Mauritania	Tunisia
Cyprus	Mauritius	Turkey
Czech Rep	Mexico	Turkmenistan
Denmark (including Faroe Islands and Greenland)	Moldova	Tuvalu
	Monaco	Uganda
	Mongolia	Ukraine
Djibouti	Morocco	United Arab Emirates
Dominica	Mozambique	United Kingdom
Dominican Republic	Myanmar	United Kingdom overseas territories
Ecuador	Namibia	
Egypt	Nauru	United States
El Salvador	Nepal	United States territories
Equatorial Guinea	Netherlands	
Eritrea	Netherlands Antilles and Aruba	Uruguay
Estonia		Uzbekistan
Ethiopia	New Zealand and New Zealand territories	Vanuatu
Fiji		Vatican
Finland		Venezuela
France and French overseas depart- ments and territories	Nicaragua	Vietnam
	Niger	Yemen
	Nigeria	Yugoslavia
	Norway	Zambia
Gabon	Oman	Zimbabwe

Independent countries whose situation with regard to the UPU has not yet been settled: Andorra, Marshall Islands, Micronesia (Federated States of), Palau
Territory in a special situation: East Timor

Council of Administration

The Council of Administration (CA), formerly called the Executive Council, consists of a chairman and 40 member countries and meets in principle each year at UPU headquarters in Berne. (The chairmanship of the Council of Administration is given automatically to the host country of the preceding Congress.) It ensures the continuity of the union's work between congresses, supervises union activities, and studies regulatory, administrative, legislative and legal issues of interest to the UPU. In order to ensure the agency's ability to react quickly to changes in the postal environment, the CA has been given the power to approve proposals from the Postal Operations Council for the adoption of regulations or new procedures until the next congress has decided on the matter. The CA can also take measures necessary to resolve urgent matters. The CA approves the annual budget and accounts of the UPU, as well as yearly updates of the UPU's Programme and Budget. It is also responsible for promoting and coordinating all aspects of technical assistance among member countries.

Postal Operations Council

The Postal Operations Council (POC), formerly called the Consultative Council for Postal Studies, is the technical and operational body of the UPU and consists of 40 elected member countries. It deals with the operational, economic, and commercial aspects of international postal services. At its first meeting after each Congress, the POC revises the regulations. It promotes the introduction of new postal products by collecting, analyzing, and making public the results of experiments with new products undertaken by some postal services. It also prepares and issues recommendations to member countries concerning standards for technological, operational, or other processes where uniformity of practice is essential. The POC's program focuses on helping postal services to modernize and upgrade their products, including not only letter post but also expedited mail service, postal parcels, and postal financial services.

The chairmanship of the Postal Operations Council for the period between congresses is decided through election by the council.

International Bureau

The International Bureau, established by the Treaty of Berne in 1874, is located in Berne and provides secretariat and support facilities for the UPU's bodies. It serves as liaison, provides information and consultation services, and promotes technical cooperation among UPU members. It also acts as a clearing house for the settlement of accounts between postal administrations for inter-administration charges related to the exchange of postal items and international reply coupons.

The International Bureau is responsible for ensuring the representation of the UPU in its external relations, notably with international organizations. However, it does not intervene in relations between postal administrations and their customers.

In the new UPU structure approved by the Seoul Congress (1994), the International Bureau took on a stronger leadership role in certain activities, including the application of Electronic Data Interchange (EDI) technology and monitoring the quality of postal service on a global scale. To carry out its activities, the International Bureau implemented modern management techniques including total quality management, a strategic planning process, and a performance evaluation system based on individual objectives.

BUDGET

Since 1992, the UPU has pursued zero real growth budgeting, maintaining its annual budget increases at or below the level of inflation. The 1996 budget was set at 35 million Swiss francs.

The UPU's budget expenses are financed jointly by member countries, based on a contribution class system. Upon admission to the UPU, new member countries are free to choose one of ten contribution classes ranging from one to 50 units. An additional contribution class of one-half unit is reserved for the least developed countries. There are at present five countries with the maximum of 50 contribution units.

ACTIVITIES

A. Clearing accounts for international services

The UPU acts as a central office for the international postal traffic carried on by its members. In principle, UPU member states retain the revenue they derive from the sale of postage stamps and from other fees and charges for foreign-bound mail. Administrations must, however, reimburse one another for the transportation of foreign mail in intermediate transit and for the imbalance between international mail sent and received (terminal dues). At the end of each year, the International Bureau draws up an annual general clearing account for transit and terminal charges, stating the balances due.

Every two years the International Bureau publishes a general clearing account for the international reply coupons that it supplies to facilitate payment of international correspondence. Some 165 countries now sell these coupons, and all countries must accept them as payment for postage.

B. Information services

The UPU acts as an international clearinghouse for postal information. At the request of postal administrations, the International Bureau circulates inquiries concerning the operation of the various postal systems and makes the replies available to all UPU members. Inquiries may concern domestic, as well as international, postal practices and cover subjects as diverse as the texts of propaganda permitted on letters and packages, mobile post offices on motorboats, the opening of new offices of exchange, introduction of summer time, and national regulations for the dispatch of radioactive substances.

The International Bureau publishes a number of international postal handbooks, including the following: *Postal Statistics* (internal and international); *List of Prohibited Articles* (prohibited from the mails); and the *Multilingual Vocabulary of the International Postal Service*, designed to ensure that terms used by different national postal services convey an identical meaning. The bureau also prepares an annotated edition of UPU legislation, which includes discussion of principles, opinions, decisions, and practices underlying current international postal procedures and the present organization of the union.

C. Arbitration and interpretation of international postal rules

If a difference of opinion on the interpretation of UPU legislation between two or more postal administrations cannot be resolved by direct negotiations, the matter is settled by in-house arbitration. The countries concerned may also designate a single arbitrator, such as the International Bureau of the UPU.

D. Revision of rules and adoption of guidelines for international services

The main function of the Universal Postal Congress, as noted above, is to study and revise the acts of the union on the basis of proposals put forward by member countries, the Council of Administration, and the Postal Operations Council. At the 22nd Congress, held in Beijing (August–September) 1999, the UPU outlined the following strategy for the years 2000 to 2004: ensure the provision of a universal postal service, allowing customers to send and receive goods and messages, from any point in the world to any other point; strengthen the quality of the international postal network, providing customers with reliable, secure and efficient postal services; increase the cost-effectiveness of the international postal network, providing customers with affordable postal services; respond effectively, through improved market knowledge and product development, to the needs and expectations of postal service customers; through postal reform and development, enable customers to draw maximum benefit from technological, economic, and regulatory changes in the postal environment; and strengthen and broaden cooperation and interaction among the stake-holders of the postal industry.

E. Technical assistance

The principle of technical assistance is contained in Article 1 of the UPU constitution; it was couched in general terms in order to give the union flexibility in the use of all forms of technical cooperation, present and future.

Requests for UPU assistance in technical cooperation matters cover all sectors: planning, organization, management, operations, training, and financial services. The aid provided comes in three forms: recruiting and sending experts, consultants, or volunteers; granting vocational training or further training fellowships for individual or group courses; and supplying equipment and training or demonstration aids.

The UPU executes country and intercountry projects covering all aspects of the postal services and the three components of experts, fellowships, and equipment. Projects common to several countries, which form a very important part of this program, make it possible to solve, economically and rationally, the problems that arise in a given region, especially by setting up intercountry postal training schools. These regional and interregional projects are carried out in conjunction with the restricted postal unions and the UN regional commissions.

In the 1990s, the UPU undertook a global Electronic Data Interchange (EDI) project. Through the development of computer applications that facilitate international mail processing and allow exchange of electronic data, postal services have the ability to track mail shipments from end to end and to provide customers with tracking information on time-certain products such as expedited mail service EMS. It is expected that within a few years, exchanges of postal data via EDI will become a common feature of the majority of postal services.

Funds from the UPU budget make it possible to provide additional assistance to that of UNDP—namely, in the form of short consultant missions of three months at most, at the request of the postal administration concerned. A noteworthy feature is that, for many missions, the consultants' countries of origin also share the cost of this form of technical cooperation by continuing to pay all or part of the salaries of their officials during the mission. At the same time, since 1991 the UPU also has funded integrated projects incorporating short-term consultants' missions, vocational training fellowships, and items of minor equipment. The UPU Special Fund, set up in 1966 and maintained by voluntary contributions from member countries, is mainly designed to finance training and to further training activities in the form of fellowships, equipment, and training courses or study cycles. Some developed countries provide the International Bureau with funds for the management of associate experts in order to supplement the staff of ongoing projects and to give young people with sufficient training the opportunity to improve their professional qualifications.

Lastly, under a resolution adopted by the Council of Administration in 1967, governments may avail themselves of technical assistance instead of payment, which they finance themselves from funds in trust; the International Bureau then undertakes to manage the projects implemented in this way. Of course, the UPU, through the International Bureau, continues to act as an intermediary, wherever expedient, for supplying assistance in kind to developing countries on the basis of offers from developed countries. It also has made a special effort in the field of vocational training by assessing the needs to be met and listing the facilities available in the various member countries. This effort is reflected in the establishment or reinforcement of national or multinational schools and the organization of study cycles for the further training of senior staff and of instructor-training courses; with this aid, a large number of postal administrations now have qualified postal instructors.

F. Postal Studies

The 1989 Washington Congress adopted the practice of having major UPU studies divided into specific sub-study areas. The major technical studies covered the following areas: the post and its markets (commercial strategies, delivery network and customer analysis, press and publishing, parcel-post products/services), development of rapid services (EMS and electronic mail), operations and quality of service (improvement of the postal system, monitoring, mail circulation standards), modernization (automation, coding, telematics, technology research), management (international accounting, productivity indices, security, decentralization), human resources (adapting to the demands of competition, training), and postal development.

UPU reports are published as the *Collection of Postal Studies*, which is available in four languages.

BIBLIOGRAPHY

Annual Report of the Work of the Union. Résumé and general review of UPU activities.

Collection of Postal Studies. A series of publications concerning topics studied by the UPU.

Union Postale. Quarterly. Parallel text in the seven languages of the union—Arabic, Chinese, English, French, German, Russian, and Spanish. Contains articles on postal services and information on UPU activities.

The Universal Postal Union. (brochure) A brief outline of UPU features.

THE INTERNATIONAL TELECOMMUNICATION UNION (ITU)

BACKGROUND: The International Telecommunication Union is the oldest of the intergovernmental organizations that have become specialized agencies related to the UN. In 1865, a convention establishing an International Telegraph Union was signed in Paris by the plenipotentiaries of 20 continental European states, including two extending into Asia—Russia and Turkey. Three years later, a permanent international bureau for the union was established in Bern, Switzerland. This bureau, which operated until 1948, was the forerunner of the present General Secretariat of the ITU. In 1885, at Berlin, the first regulations concerning international telephone services were added to the telegraph regulations annexed to the Paris convention. By the end of the nineteenth century, radiotelegraphy, or "wireless," had been developed, and for the first time it was possible to communicate directly between shore stations and ships at sea. Rival wireless companies frequently refused to accept one another's messages, however. In 1903, an international conference was called to consider the problem, and in 1906, in Berlin, 29 maritime states signed the International Radiotelegraph Convention, establishing the principle of compulsory intercommunication between vessels at sea and the land. The International Radiotelegraph Conference, which met in Washington in 1927, drew up for the first time a table of frequency allocations.

CREATION

Two plenipotentiary conferences were held in 1932 at Madrid—one covering telephone and telegraph and the other radiotelegraph communication. The two existing conventions were amalgamated into a single International Telecommunication Convention (the word *telecommunication* signifying "any transmission, emission or reception of signs, signals, writing, images and sounds, or intelligence of any nature by wire, radio, optical, or other electromagnetic systems"). The countries accepting the new convention, which came into force on 1 January 1934, formed the International Telecommunication Union.

The International Telecommunication Convention of 1932 has been revised six times. The Plenipotentiary Conference of the ITU, meeting in Atlantic City in 1947, radically changed the organization to keep up with developments in telecommunication: for example, a new permanent organ, the International Frequency Registration Board, was created to cope with the overcrowding of certain transmission frequencies; and an agreement was drawn up under which the ITU was recognized by the UN as the specialized agency for telecommunication. The convention was further modified in certain respects by plenipotentiary conferences in 1952, 1959, 1965, 1973, and 1982.

In 1989, the Plenipotentiary Conference held in Nice created a High-Level Committee to propose wide-ranging recommendations about the role of ITU in a world totally transformed by the convergence of telecommunications and computer technology and the globalization and privatization of telecommunications providers. An historic Additional Plenipotentiary Conference was convened in Geneva in December 1992 to adopt far-reaching structural changes to the union and a thoroughly revised constitution and convention. The new constitution officially entered into force on 1 July 1994. However, the structural changes were considered so important to maintaining the organization's relevance in the rapidly changing technological world that the new structure was implemented as of 1 March 1993. The Constitution has been amended at subsequent plenipotentiary conferences.

PURPOSES

The new Constitution of the International Telecommunication Union (Geneva, 1992) cites the following purposes for the union:

- to maintain and extend international cooperation between all members of the union for the improvement and rational use of telecommunications of all kinds;
- to promote and to offer technical assistance to developing countries in the field of telecommunications;
- to promote the development of technical facilities and their efficient operation;
- to promote the extension of the benefits of the new telecommunication technologies to all the world's inhabitants;
- to harmonize the actions of members in the attainment of these ends;
- to promote, at the international level, the adoption of a broader approach to telecommunications issues, an approach that includes other world and regional organizations and nongovernmental organizations concerned with telecommunications.

MEMBERSHIP

As of May 2000 ITU had 189 member nations. Although membership in the union itself is open only to sovereign states, the union's three sectors and their various conferences are open to telecommunications companies, scientific organizations, industrial groups, financing and development institutions, international and regional telecommunication organizations, and the United Nations itself as well as its specialized agencies. Indeed, the 1992 constitution makes it clear that the participation of private sector organizations in the union's work is encouraged. In the late 1990s, some 360 members (scientific and industrial companies, public and private operators, broadcasters, regional/international organizations) took part in ITU's ongoing standardization work.

STRUCTURE

The new structure of ITU combines the activities of its previous bodies into three "pillars" supporting the work mandated by the

Plenipotentiary Conference: the Radiocommunication Sector, the Telecommunication Standardization Sector, and the Development Sector. Each sector's work is directed by international and regional conferences, supported by a bureau under the administration of a director. The bureau directors are assisted by "Advisory Groups" that are open to representatives of national telecommunication administrations, authorized organizations, and study groups. The Plenipotentiary Conference also elects the ITU Council, which acts as an intersessional administrative body guiding the work of the organization in the four-year intervals between conferences. The organization's General Secretariat, headquartered in Geneva, is administered by a Secretary-General, assisted by a Deputy Secretary-General as well as the directors of Radiocommunication Bureau, Telecommunication Standardization Bureau, and the Telecommunication Development Bureau. Yoshio Utsumi of Japan was elected ITU Secretary-General by the Minneapolis Plenipotentiary Conference (October 1998).

Plenipotentiary Conference

The supreme body of the ITU is the Plenipotentiary Conference, in which each member has one vote. Previously, it met at intervals of five or more years—in Atlantic City in 1947, Buenos Aires in 1952, Geneva in 1959, Montreux in 1965, Torremolinos in 1973, Nairobi in 1982, and Nice in 1989. In 1992 the extraordinary Additional Plenipotentiary Conference met in Geneva to fundamentally revamp the organization. The first session of the Plenipotentiary Conference after the restructuring was held in Kyoto, Japan, in September 1994. The Plenipotentiary Conference convened in Minneapolis in 1998.

The Plenipotentiary Conference sets general policies for fulfilling the purposes of the union; receives reports on the organization's activities since the previous conference and takes decisions on those reports; establishes the budget in light of decisions taken by the ITU Council; fixes salary scales; elects member nations to the ITU Council; elects the secretary-general; the deputy secretary-general; the directors of the bureaus of the three sectors, and the members of the Radio Regulations Board; considers and adopts amendments to the constitution and the convention; concludes agreements between ITU and other organizations that may be concluded by the ITU Council. In general the conferences focus on long-term policy issues.

The ITU Council

The ITU Council (formerly called the Administrative Council) traces its history back to the New Jersey Plenipotentiary Conference of 1947. It is composed of 46 member nations elected by the plenipotentiary along a regional formula: the Americas have eight seats, Western Europe has eight seats, Eastern Europe has five seats, Africa has 13 seats, and Asia and Australasia has 12 seats. The council members hold office until the next plenipotentiary, at which time they may be reelected.

The ITU Council guides the work of the union between sessions of the plenipotentiary. It approves the budgets of the union and controls its finances. It is responsible for the coordination of ITU's work with other United Nations organizations.

The members of the ITU Council from 1999 to 2001 were: Region A (Americas): Argentina, Brazil, Canada, Cuba, Mexico, Saint Lucia, United States, Venezuela; Region B (Western Europe): Denmark, France, Germany, Italy, Portugal, Spain, Switzerland, United Kingdom; Region C (Eastern Europe): Bulgaria, Czech Republic, Poland, Romania, Russia; Region D (Africa): Algeria, Burkina Faso, Cameroon, Côte d'Ivoire, Egypt, Gabon, Kenya, Mali, Morocco, Senegal, South Africa, Tanzania, Tunisia; and Region E (Asia and Australasia): Australia, China, India, Japan, Korea (Republic of), Kuwait, Malaysia, Pakistan, Philippines, Saudi Arabia, Thailand, Vietnam.

The Radiocommunications Sector
World Radiocommunication Conferences

World Radiocommunication Conferences (WRCs) revises the radio regulations and any associated frequency assignment and allotment plans; addresses any radiocommunication matter of worldwide character; instructs the Radio Regulations Board and the Radiocommunication Bureau, and review their activities; and determines questions for study by the Radiocommunication Assembly and its study groups in preparation for future Radiocommunication Conferences. WRCs are normally convened every two or three years.

Radiocommunication Conferences and Assemblies

Every two to three years the Radiocommunication Conference and a Radiocommunication Assembly meet to review and revise the Radio Regulations on the basis of an agenda adopted by the ITU Council. Radiocommunication conferences are open to all ITU member administrations and to the United Nations and its specialized agencies, regional telecommunication organizations, and intergovernmental organizations operating satellite systems. In addition, telecommunication operators authorized by their country to participate in the work of the Radio Sector are admitted to the conferences.

The Radiocommunication Assemblies provide the technical basis for the work of the conferences. The assemblies create study groups of experts and decide on the priority, urgency, and timescale for study of specific issues. The study groups are made up of experts from both administrations and public/private sector entities.

Radiocommunication Bureau

World Radiocommunication Conferences (WRCs) revises the radio regulations and any associated frequency assignment and allotment plans; addresses any radiocommunication matter of worldwide character; instructs the Radio Regulations Board and the Radiocommunication Bureau, and review their activities; and determines questions for study by the Radiocommunication Assembly and its study groups in preparation for future Radiocommunication Conferences. WRCs are normally convened every two or three years.

Radio Regulations Board

The Radio Regulations Board is a part-time, 12-member body of experts that approves the rules of procedure to register radio frequency assignments and equitable utilization of the geo-stationary satellite orbit. It also investigates complaints by ITU members about frequency interference, and formulates recommendations to resolve such problems. It holds up to four meetings a year in Geneva. The board members, elected at the Plenipotentiary Conference, serve as custodians of international public trust and not as representatives of their respective member states or region, hence they cannot be part of national delegations at conferences. The Radio Regulations Board replaced the former five-member International Frequency Registration Board (IFRB), which was a full time body.

The Telecommunication Standardization Sector
World Telecommunication Standardization Assemblies

These assemblies are held every four years to approve, modify, or reject draft standards (called "Recommendations" because of their voluntary character). The conferences set the work program for the study groups that elaborate these recommendations. The Telecommunication Standardization Study Groups are groups of experts in which administrations and public/private sector entities participate. They focus on the standardization of telecommunication services, operation and performance of equipment, systems, networks, services, tariffs, and accounting methods.

Telecommunication Standardization Bureau

The bureau is headed by a director elected by the plenipotentiary. It prepares for assemblies and meetings and processes and publishes information received from administrations about the application of the International Telecommunication Regulations. This information includes international telephone routes, statistics, notifications, and operational bulletins. It also is responsible for updating the documents and data bases of the Telecommunication Standardization Sector.

The Telecommunication Development Sector
World and Regional Telecommunication Development Conferences
These conferences fix objectives and strategies for balancing worldwide and regional development in telecommunications. They serve as a forum for studying policy, organization, operation, regulatory, technical, and financial questions related to the needs of developing countries. A World Telecommunication Development Conference is held every four years and a number of Regional Telecommunication Development Conferences are held within that same period. The resolutions, decisions, recommendations, and reports of the conferences are submitted to the plenipotentiary. The development conferences direct the work of the Telecommunications Development Bureau. The conferences also set up study groups on issues specific to developing countries.

The Telecommunication Development Bureau
This body is the administrative arm of the Development Sector. Its duties and responsibilities cover a variety of functions including program supervision, technical advice, collection and processing of relevant information for publication in machine-readable and other formats. The bureau is headed by an elected director who organizes and manages the work of the Sector.

General Secretariat
The General Secretariat is at ITU headquarters in Geneva, Switzerland. It handles arrangements for ITU conferences and meetings and maintains liaison with member states and with the UN, the specialized agencies, and other international organizations. It also carries out the ITU's extensive publication program. It is headed by the secretary-general. Pekka Tarjanne of Finland was elected secretary-general by the Nice Plenipotentiary in 1989.

The Secretariat also organizes an international commercial telecommunications exhibition called TELECOM, held in Geneva every four years. It also cosponsors regional telecommunications exhibitions with member administrations (Asia TELECOM, Africa TELECOM, Americas TELECOM, and Europa TELECOM). These trade shows feature a comprehensive display of telecommunication equipment and services, including digital transmission, switching technologies, and digital networks. In conjunction with TELECOM, ITU sponsors a FORUM which deals with emerging trends in telecommunications technology, administration, management, financing, research, and equipment supply.

BUDGET
The ordinary budget includes expenditures pertaining to the ITU Council, the Geneva headquarters, and the various conferences and meetings. The technical cooperation special accounts budget includes administrative expenditure for technical assistance to developing nations and is financed by the UNDP. The publications budget includes production costs of all publications and is self-financed through sales.

At each Plenipotentiary Conference, member countries choose a class of contribution. The lowest classes are reserved for countries designated least developed countries by the United Nations. The ordinary budget is then divided by the number of units assigned to each member. However, regional radio conferences require additional contributions.

All other organizations (private enterprises, international organizations, etc.) that take part in the work of the union's three

sectors must also choose a contribution class; however, their units are 1/5th the value of the member countries' contributory unit. Separate contributions must be made for participation in any of the various conferences of the union.

The total budget for 2000–01 amounted to Swiss francs 332,621,000.

ACTIVITIES

Background
In the early 1980s ITU members recognized that advances in technology were fundamentally changing the nature of telecommunications and the very principles upon which the union was founded. These fundamental changes were behind the restructuring of the union, which was completed in 1994. An understanding of these changes is fundamental to understanding ITU's activities in the rapidly evolving world of telecommunications.

From 1900 to the 1980s telecommunication was generally understood to mean essentially the transmission of voice telephone signals. Governments and the telecommunications industry shared easily communicable goals: provide telephone service for every business and home and arrive at international technological standards that would allow telephone connections between all countries. Until the 1980s telecommunication equipment technology evolved comparatively slowly, allowing enough time for ITU's international bodies to set standards without inhibiting the progress of technology development. In the area of pricing (tariffs) there was widespread acceptance that densely populated areas would produce enough income for telephone companies to cover their expenses for providing coverage for remote, sparsely populated areas.

In the 1980s technological advances in the digitization of telephone signals, software control, component miniaturization, and sharply decreasing switching and transmission costs brought about an explosion in products and services that could now transmit not only voice, but also data, text, image, and video information. Telecommunications became less a stand-alone industry and more intimately connected with the computer industry. It could be said that the two technologies had "converged," fundamentally reshaping the way all kinds of information services could be delivered to people and businesses. Similarly, wired and "wireless" telecommunications also began to converge. Wireless systems (cellular telephones, for example) began to compete with existing networks at every level through terrestrial and satellite-based communications systems.

At the same time, the equipment supply industry was transformed by shorter innovation cycles and global marketing efforts. This drastically shortened the time available for consultation and adoption of international standards. Finally, the profitability ethic of the computer industry began to replace the universal coverage ethic of the telecommunications industry. Businesses began to demand cost-based pricing, which would reduce their costs in increasingly competitive global markets. However, the growth of cost-based pricing would effectively deny telecommunications to isolated or sparsely populated countries or regions, since they could never afford to pay enough to be as profitable as densely populated areas. In other words, the competitive environment produced "islands" of high telecommunication capability where profitable customers existed and "deserts" of low telecommunications capability where profitable returns could not be achieved.

This trend strengthened towards the end of the 1980s with the end of the cold war. An international consensus emerged that market-based economies were the most efficient way to deliver goods and services and promote economic growth. Previously, most of the world's countries had government-controlled telecommunications departments. In the new atmosphere of deregulation and privatization, many state-owned telecommunications departments would become state-owned corporations, and perhaps eventually private corporations. Telecommunications companies in industrialized countries found their main opportunity for growth was to change from offering only domestic services to offering services region-wide or even globally, competing with the domestic services of other nations.

ITU's secretary-general, Dr. Pekka Tarjanne, told an international gathering in Tokyo in 1994 that: "Today's ITU does not fully reflect the dramatic changes that have taken place in telecommunications. The Union remains largely the preserve of dominant carriers, with little active participation by new players in the telecommunications industry or by major users. This trend strongly suggests the need for greater private sector participation by the new players in the telecommunications industry. . . . How can non-governmental players be given a greater voice in ITU decision-making processes without infringing on the sovereign rights of nations?" The future evolution of the organization and its activities will revolve around this dilemma.

The activities of the organization were defined in the 1992 constitution as:

- allocating bands of the radio frequency spectrum, alloting radio frequencies, registering radio frequency assignments, and registering orbital positions in the geostationary-satellite orbit in order to avoid harmful interference between radio stations of different countries;
- coordinating efforts to eliminate harmful intereference between radio stations of different countries;
- facilitating worldwide standardization of telecommunications;
- delivering technical assistance to developing countries that want to create, develop, and improve their telecommunications systems;
- fostering collaboration among its members to establishing rates at levels as low as possible while ensuring efficient service;
- promoting measures that would save lives through the cooperation of telecommunications services; and

- promoting the establishment of preferential and favorable lines of credit from international financial and development organizations for extending telecommunications services to the most isolated areas in countries.

PUBLICATIONS
One of the most important duties of ITU headquarters is to collect and collate essential telecommunication data and to edit and publish the numerous documents essential for the day-to-day operation of the various telephone, telegraph, and broadcasting systems of the world. Among the documents regularly issued by the ITU are the *International Frequency List;* the quarterly *High Frequency Broadcasting Schedules;* yearly radio statistics; lists of coast, ship, and fixed stations; codes and abbreviations in general use; lists of radiolocation stations; an alphabetical list of call signs; summaries of international monitoring information; the *ITU Newsletter* (formerly the *Telecommunication Journal*) and similar publications, all generally issued in English, French, and Spanish editions, or in a single trilingual edition. Many of ITU's technical documents are available in electronic forms: online as part of ITUDOC, on CD-ROM discs, or on other computer-readable media.

Telecom Information Exchange Services (TIES) and ITUDOC
This on-line computer communication service is based at ITU headquarters for telecommunications-related information exchange. The system offers electronic mail, bulletin boards, document interchange, computer conferencing, and distributed access to ITU data bases such as global telecom services and tariffs, as well as notification of telecommunication information. It also contains a terminology infobase of 30,000 telecommunications terms in English, French, and Spanish.

ITUDOC allows users of the Internet to retrieve ITU documents and publications from a central computer server at ITU headquarters. It also allows participants in ITU's work to submit their contributions electronically.

ITU MEMBER COUNTRIES
(as of May 2000)

Afghanistan
Albania
Algeria
Andorra
Angola
Antigua and Barbuda
Argentina
Armenia
Australia
Austria
Azerbaijan
Bahamas
Bahrain
Bangladesh
Barbados
Belarus
Belgium
Belize
Benin
Bhutan
Bolivia
Bosnia and Herzegovina
Botswana
Brazil
Brunei Darussalam
Bulgaria
Burkina Faso
Burundi
Cambodia
Cameroon
Canada
Cape Verde
Central African Republic
Chad
Chile
China
Colombia
Comoros
Congo
Congo, Democratic Republic of the
Costa Rica
Côte d'Ivoire
Croatia
Cuba
Cyprus
Czech Republic
Denmark
Djibouti
Dominica
Dominican Republic
Ecuador
Egypt
El Salvador
Equatorial Guinea
Eritrea
Estonia
Ethiopia
Fiji
Finland
France
Gabon
Gambia
Georgia

Germany
Ghana
Greece
Grenada
Guatemala
Guinea
Guinea-Bissau
Guyana
Haiti
Honduras
Hungary
Iceland
India
Indonesia
Iran (Islamic Republic of)
Iraq
Ireland
Israel
Italy
Jamaica
Japan
Jordan
Kazakhstan
Kenya
Kiribati
Korea, Democratic People's Republic of
Korea, Republic of
Kuwait
Kyrgyzstan
Lao People's Democratic Republic
Latvia
Lebanon
Lesotho
Liberia
Libya
Liechtenstein
Lithuania
Luxembourg
Madagascar
Malawi
Malaysia
Maldives
Mali
Malta
Marshall Islands
Mauritania
Mauritius
Mexico
Micronesia
Moldova
Monaco
Mongolia
Morocco
Mozambique
Myanmar
Namibia
Nauru
Nepal
Netherlands
New Zealand
Nicaragua
Niger
Nigeria

Norway
Oman
Pakistan
Panama
Papua New Guinea
Paraguay
Peru
Philippines
Poland
Portugal
Qatar
Romania
Russian Federation
Rwanda
St. Lucia
St. Vincent and the Grenadines
Samoa
San Marino
Sâo Tomé and Principe
Saudi Arabia
Senegal
Seychelles
Sierra Leone
Singapore
Slovakia
Slovenia
Solomon Islands
Somalia
South Africa
Spain
Sri Lanka
Sudan
Suriname
Swaziland
Sweden
Switzerland
Syrian Arab Republic
Tajikistan
Tanzania
Thailand
The Former Yugoslav Republic of Macedonia
Togo
Tonga
Trinidad and Tobago
Tunisia
Turkey
Turkmenistan
Tuvalu
Uganda
Ukraine
United Arab Emirates
United Kingdom
United States
Uruguay
Uzbekistan
Vanuatu
Vatican
Venezuela
Vietnam
Yemen
Yugoslavia
Zambia
Zimbabwe

THE WORLD METEOROLOGICAL ORGANIZATION (WMO)

BACKGROUND: The practical uses of meteorology are to instruct, advise, and warn mankind about the weather. Thus, it can help prevent devastation caused by flood, drought, and storm; it can also assist the peoples of the world in best adapting their agriculture and industry to the climatic conditions under which they live.

For meteorology, international cooperation is indispensable. The reasons are expressed in the following words of President John F. Kennedy: ". . . there is the atmosphere itself, the atmosphere in which we live and breathe and which makes life on this planet possible. Scientists have studied the atmosphere for many decades, but its problems continue to defy us. The reasons for our limited progress are obvious. Weather cannot be easily reproduced and observed in the laboratory. It must, therefore, be studied in all of its violence wherever it has its way. Here, new scientific tools have become available. With modern computers, rockets and satellites, the time is ripe to harness a variety of disciplines for a concerted attack. . . . The atmospheric sciences require worldwide observation and, hence, international cooperation."

CREATION

Beginning in 1853, many of the world's leading maritime countries tried to establish an international system for collecting meteorological observations made by ships at sea.

The first international meteorological congress was held in Vienna in 1873; it led to the founding of the International Meteorological Organization, composed of directors of meteorological services from various countries and territories throughout the world. This body carried out ambitious programs to perfect and standardize international meteorological practices.

As transportation, communications, agriculture, and industry developed in the 20th century, they increasingly relied on meteorology, while meteorology itself relied to an increasing extent on advances in science and technology to perfect its methods of observing and predicting weather phenomena. Hence, the closest possible collaboration was called for between the International Meteorological Organization and other international bodies.

A conference of directors of national meteorological services met in Washington in 1947 under the auspices of the International Meteorological Organization and adopted the World Meteorological Convention, establishing the World Meteorological Organization as a UN specialized agency. On 23 March 1950, after 30 signers had ratified or acceded to the convention, it came into force. The first WMO congress opened in Paris on 19 March 1951.

PURPOSES

As set forth in the World Meteorological Convention, the purposes of the WMO are sixfold:

1. to facilitate worldwide cooperation in the establishment of networks of stations for meteorological, hydrological, and other geophysical observations and to promote the establishment and maintenance centers charged with the provision of meteorological and related services;
2. to promote the estabishment and maintenance of systems for rapid exchange of weather information;
3. to promote standardization of meteorological and related observations and ensure uniform publication of observations and statistics;

4. to further the application of meteorology to aviation, shipping, water problems, agriculture, and other human activities;
5. to promote activities in operational hydrology and cooperation between meteorological and hydrological services; and
6. to encourage research and training in meteorology and, as appropriate, to assist in coordinating the international aspects of such research and training.

MEMBERSHIP

Membership in the WMO is not limited to sovereign states; it may include territories that maintain their own meteorological services. Membership is open to any of the 45 states and 30 territories attending the 1947 conference in Washington that signed the convention or to any member of the UN with a meteorological service. Any of these automatically becomes a member of the WMO upon ratifying or acceding to the convention. Any other state, territory, or group of territories maintaining its own meteorological services may become eligible for membership upon approval of two-thirds of the WMO membership. As of June 1997, the WMO had 184 members.

STRUCTURE

The WMO is headed by a president and three vice-presidents, elected by the World Meteorological Congress. There is also an Executive Council and a secretariat.

World Meteorological Congress

The World Meteorological Congress is the supreme body of the organization and is composed of the delegates representing its member states and territories. (According to the World Meteorological Convention, the principal delegate of each member "should be the director of its meteorological service.") The congress, which meets every four years, determines changes in the constitution and functions of the various WMO bodies, adopts regulations covering meteorological practices and procedures, and determines general policies for carrying out the purposes of the organization and related matters. It also establishes the regional associations and technical commissions.

Each member of the congress has one vote. Election of individuals to serve in any capacity in the organization is by a simple majority of the votes cast; other questions are decided by two-thirds of the votes cast for and against. On certain subjects, only members that are states may vote.

Executive Council

The Executive Council has 36 members: the president and the three vice-presidents of the WMO; the presidents of the six regional associations; and 26 directors of meteorological services from the member countries, elected by the congress. Meeting at least once a year, the council carries out the activities of the organization and the decisions of the congress. Its own decisions are reached by a two-thirds majority.

Regional Associations

There are six regional associations: one each for Africa, Asia, South America, North and Central America, the Southwest Pacific, and Europe. The regional associations are composed of the WMO members whose meteorological networks lie in or extend into the respective regions. They meet when necessary and examine from a regional point of view all questions referred to them by the Executive Council. Each association has the responsibility for coordinating meteorological activity.

Technical Commissions

The technical commissions are composed of experts in meteorology. They study various meteorological problems and make recommendations to the executive committee and the congress. The WMO has established eight commissions for the following areas: basic systems; instruments and methods of observation; atmospheric sciences; aeronautical meteorology; agricultural meteorology; marine meteorology; hydrology; and climatology. Each commission meets every four years.

Secretary-General and Secretariat

The secretariat, in Geneva, completes the structure of the WMO. Its staff, under the direction of a Secretary-General, undertakes studies, prepares publications, acts as secretariat during meetings of the various WMO bodies, and provides liaison between the various meteorological services of the world. The Secretary-General is G. O. P. Obasi of Nigeria. He is assisted by a staff of about 250.

BUDGET

Contributions to the WMO's regular budget are assessed upon members by the congress. The maximum expenditure for the 1996–99 financial period, as aproved by the 12th World Meteorological Congress, was SFr255 million. The extrabudgetary resources projected to be available at the same time amount to SFr89.7 million. The extrabudgetary resources support scientific components of programs such as technical cooperation, education and training, improvement of the World Weather Watch, and some urgent environmental and climatological monitoring, research, and cooperative work. Extrabudgetary expenditures are funded through UNDP, the WMO Voluntary Cooperation Program, and funds-in-trust.

ACTIVITIES

A. World Weather Watch

The World Weather Watch (WWW) was established by the Fifth World Meteorological Congress, held in Geneva in 1967. Its purpose is to make available to each national meteorological service meteorological and related environmental information required in order to enjoy the most efficient and effective meteorological and related environmental services possible in both applications

and research. No other scientific discipline has such international interdependence. The WWW has three essential elements:

1. The Global Data-Processing System provides meteorological analyses and forecast products to all meteorological services. It is composed of three world meteorological centers, in Melbourne, Moscow, and Washington, DC; 26 regional meteorological centers; and more than 150 national meteorological centers.
2. The Global Observing System provides observational data from surface-based observing stations and platforms and from meteorological satellites of its space-based subsystem.
3. The Global Telecommunication System consists of telecommunication facilities and arrangements necessary for the rapid and reliable exchange of the observational data and processed products required by meteorological services. The system is organized into the main telecommunication network (the core of the system), six regional meteorological telecommunication networks, and national meteorological telecommunication networks that interconnect meteorological centers through approximately 240 data links.

The WWW also has two support functions:

1. WWW Data Management is concerned with the overall real-time management of data and product selection and presentation to recipients in appropriate standard formats and codes and with the monitoring of the data availability, quality, and operational status of the WWW system.
2. WWW Systems Support Activities make available to WMO members information on new WWW technology, operational experience, and proven methodology.

Also grouped under the WWW umbrella are WMO's satellite and emergency response activities. Emergency response activities involve the coordination and implementation of procedures and response mechanisms in case of nuclear accidents, as well as the Instruments and Methods of Observation Programme and the Tropical Cyclone Programme (TCP). The TCP, is designed to assist more than 50 countries in areas vulnerable to tropical cyclones to minimize destruction and loss of life by improving forecasting and warning systems, and disaster preparedness measures.

B. World Climate Programme

The World Climate Programme (WCP) established by the eighth WMO Congress in 1979 comprises four major component programs: the World Climate Applications and Services Programme (WCASP); the World Climate Data and Monitoring Programme (WCDMP); the World Climate Research Programme (WCRP); and the World Climate Impact Assessment and Response Strategies Programme (WCIRP).

The objectives of the WCP are:

1. facilitate the effective collection and management of climate data and the monitoring of the global climate system, including the detection and assessment of climate variability and changes;
2. foster the effective application of climate knowledge and information for the benefit of society and the provision of climate services, including the prediction of significant climate variations both natural and as a result of human activity;
3. assess the impacts of climate variability and changes that could markedly affect economic or social activities and advise governments thereon and contribute to the development of a range of socioeconomic response strategies that could be used by governments and community;

4. improve the understanding of climate processes for determining the predictability of climate, including its variability and change; identifying the extent of human influence on climate; and developing the capability for climate prediction.

WMO is directly responsible for WCASP and WCDMP and for the overall coordination of the WCP, but has joint responsibility with the International Council of Scientific Union (ICSU) and the Intergovernmental Oceanographic Commission (IOC) of UNESCO for the WCRP. UNEP is responsible for the WCIRP. Several other international organizations such as FAO, UNESCO, WHO, and UNDP are actively involved.

The close cooperation required for the WCP, which is complex and multidisciplinary, is achieved through interagency meetings and through the Climate Exchange Co-ordination Activities. Within the program, priority attention is given to the food, water, and energy sectors.

The World Climate Programme provides an interagency, interdisciplinary framework to address the full range of climate change issues, including research into the economic and social consequences of climate change. It is the major international program supporting the work of the Intergovernmental Panel on Climate Change, the process of implementation of the Framework Convention on Climate Change, and relevant to the implementation of Agenda 21, the seminal statement of the 1992 UN Conference on Environment and Development (the "Earth Summit").

The eleventh World Meteorological Congress decided that the WCP should be supported by the Global Climate Observing System (GCOS) as an essential activity associated with the World Climate Programme.

The basic objectives of the WCRP are to increase understanding of climate mechanisms and to determine to what extent climate can be predicted and the possible influence of man's activities on climate. Achieving these objectives requires input from many scientific disciplines. To assist in this, coordination and overall guidance is provided by the WMO/ICSU Joint Scientific Committee. The eleventh WMO Congress decided that UNESCO's Intergovernmental Oceanographic Commission (IOC) should be invited to join in WCRP. Continuing efforts are made at model development and global climate analysis, in particular the assessment of cloud prediction schemes and the representation of ocean-atmosphere interface fluxes in atmospheric general circulation models. Projects to assemble quality-controlled, consistent global climatological sets of sea-surface temperature and precipitation also have been established. Continual support is given to WCRP activities concerned with the study of climate forcing, including research on radiation codes used in climate models, aerosol sensitivity investigations and the global ozone research and monitoring projects.

C. Applications of Meteorology

The WMO's Aeronautical Meteorology Programme serves to further the application of meteorology to aviation. It is keyed to ensure, jointly with ICAO, the continuous development of regulatory and guidance material required for the provision of services to aviation in accordance with the operational requirements of aviation. It also contributes to the implementation and improvement of meteorological services necessary to ensure the safety, regularity, and efficiency of air transport.

The overall purpose of the WMO's Marine Meteorological Programme is the promotion of the required marine meteorological services over the high seas and coastal areas, including specialized ocean services and the application of marine climatological information for planning marine activities. The program also includes development of a comprehensive marine environmental monitoring service, a coordinated ocean data management system, and activities within the Integrated Global Ocean Services

System, a joint venture of the WMO and the Intergovernmental Oceanographic Commission.

The purpose of the Agricultural Meteorology Programme is to help WMO members develop the capability to provide the agricultural community with practical information—based on knowledge of the climate, recent weather, and short-, medium-, and long-term forecasts—that can be used to improve production, reduce risks and crop losses, decrease pollution by agricultural chemicals, diminish costs, and increase the efficiency of the use of energy in agriculture. In turn, these immediate goals can help members achieve self-sufficiency in food production and increase export earnings from agriculture. At the international and regional levels, the program helps to identify requirements for information in agricultural meteorology, assess the impact of weather and climate fluctuations on food production, and apply agrometeorological methods to improve land use, crop selection, and management practices.

D. Atmospheric Research and Environment Programme

The purpose of the Atmospheric Research and Environment Programme (AREP) is to contribute to the advancement of atmospheric sciences and to assist members in providing better meteorological services by fostering research in meteorology and related environmental fields. It also is aimed at ensuring that members have relevant information and guidance to make the best use of the results of research applied for the benefit of their national economies and quality of life. The transfer of technology is ensured through support, within available resources, for the participation of scientists from developing countries in AREP.

AREP has five main components: the Global Atmosphere Watch (GAW); the Programme on Short- and Medium-Range Weather Prediction Research; the Programme on Long-range Forecasting Research; the Tropical Meteorology Research Programme; and the Programme on Physics and Chemistry of Clouds and Weather Modification Research.

Global Atmosphere Watch (GAW). This worldwide system integrates most monitoring and research activities involving the measurement of atmospheric composition. It is intended to serve as an early warning system to detect further changes in the ozone layer and in long-range transport of pollutants, including acidity and toxicity of rain, as well as the atmospheric burden of aerosols. The instruments of these globally standardized observations and related research are the WMO Global Ozone Observing System (GOOS), operating about 140 stations in more than 60 countries, and the WMO Background Air Pollution Monitoring Network (BAPMoN), which has nearly 200 stations in more than 90 countries. GAW is the main contributor of data on chemical composition and physical characteristics of the atmosphere to the Global Environment Monitoring Systems (GEMS) of UNEP. GAW will be a main component of the Global Climate Observing System (GCOS). Through GAW, WMO collaborates with the UN Economic Commission for Europe (ECE) and is responsible for the meteorological part of the Monitoring and Evaluation of the Long-Range Transmission of Air Pollutants in Europe. In this respect WMO has arranged for the establishment of two Meteorological Synthethizing Centres (in Oslo and Moscow) that provide daily analysis of the transport of pollution over Europe. GAW also gives attention to atmospheric chemistry studies, prepares assessments, and encourages integrated environmental monitoring.

Weather Prediction Research Programs. These programs assist members in improving their weather services by exchanging the results of research on weather prediction. It accomplishes this goal by means of international conferences, technical reports, and progress reports on numerical weather prediction. The Programme on Short- and Medium-Range Weather Prediction Research aims at strengthening members' research with emphasis on improving the accuracy of short- and medium-range weather forecasting, including forecasting of local weather phenomena (particularly severe phenomena). The main objective of the Programme on Long-Range Forecasting Research is to foster members' research efforts in the development, introduction, and improvement of operational long-range weather forecasting systems.

Tropical Meteorology Research Programme. This program aims at the promotion and coordination of members' efforts into such important problems as monsoons, tropical cyclones, droughts in the arid zones of the tropics, rain-producing tropical weather systems, and the interaction between tropical and mid-latitutde weather systems. The goal is to be of economic benefit to tropical countries by improving members' forecasting abilities.

Physics and Chemistry of Clouds and Weather Modification Research Programme. This program encourages scientific research in physics and chemistry of clouds and its application to all fields where clouds have a major role. Examples include weather enhancement (rain making) and hail suppression. The program provides information on worldwide weather modification projects and guidance in the design and evaluation of experiments. It also studies the role of clouds in the transport, transformation, and dispersion of pollution.

E. Hydrology and Water Resources

The purpose of the WMO's Hydrology and Water Resources Programme is to promote worldwide cooperation in the assessment of water resources and their development through the coordinated establishment of hydrological networks and services, including data collection and processing, hydrological forecasting and warnings, and the supply of meteorological and hydrological data to be used for the design of projects. The five primary components of the program are: the Operational Hydrological Programme (OHP); Basic Systems, Including the Hydrological Operational Multipurpose Systems (HOMS); the Operational Hydrology Programme (OHP); Applications and Environment; and the Programme on Water-Related Issues.

The emphasis is on the operational hydrology program, and particularly its hydrological operational multipurpose subprogram, the main aim of which is to provide an efficient means and systematic institutional framework for transfer of operational hydrological technology to and between developing countries.

The program for applications and services in regard to water resources provides technical support for WMO activities dealing with environmental problems, such as the Tropical Cyclone Programme, the World Climate Programme, and WMO activities relating to droughts and desertification.

F. Education and Training

The Education and Training Programme is designed to support the scientific and technical programs of the WMO, as well as to assist in the development of the required personnel in the national meteorological and hydrological services of member countries.

Activities under the program include surveys of personnel training requirements; the development of appropriate training programs; the establishment and improvement of regional training centers; the organization of training courses, seminars, and conferences; and the preparation of training materials in the form of compendia of lecture notes, problem workbooks, and visual and audiovisual aids. The program also arranges individual training programs and provides fellowships. Training programs place several hundred specialists in advanced courses each year.

The program provides advice on education and training in meteorology and operational hydrology and on the availability of suitable training facilities. A training library is maintained. Films are provided on a loan basis to members on request.

The Panel of Experts on Education and Training serves as the focal point of the program.

G. Technical Cooperation

The WMO's technical cooperation activities—in the form of fellowships, expert missions, equipment, and assistance for group training, such as workshops and seminars—are carried out through UNDP, the Voluntary Cooperation Programme, trust-fund arrangements, and the regular budget of the organization. Assistance has been given in support of projects ranging from the establishment, organization, and operation of meteorological and hydrological services to the application of meteorology in increasing food production and assessing alternative energy sources.

WMO's Voluntary Cooperation Program (VCP) is maintained by contributions from members to the Voluntary Cooperation Fund and to the Equipment and Services Program. Although priority is given to the implementation of the World Weather Watch, the VCP also provides assistance and supports other WMO programs in such fields as agrometeorology, hydrology, and climate. It grants fellowships to nationals of developing countries.

Under trust-fund arrangements, countries make funds available through the WMO for technical cooperation activities either in the country providing the funds or in another country.

Activities under the WMO's regular budget represent only a very small percentage of the total assistance and are confined mainly to the awarding of fellowships and participation in group training.

H. WMO Regional Program

WMO provides support through three regional offices and two sub-regional offices. Regional offices are located in Bujumbura, Burundi (for Africa); Asunción, Paraguay (for the Americas); and at the Geneva, Switzerland, headquarters (for Asia and Southwest Pacific). Sub-regional office are in Lagos, Nigeria (for West Africa); and in San José, Costa Rica (for North America, Central America and the Caribbean). A third sub-regional office is in consideration for Asia and the Southwest Pacific.

The Regional Program helps bridge the gap between developed and developing countries and accelerates the implementation and operation of the World Weather Watch, operational hydrology, and Global Atmosphere Watch. The Regional Program also assists in implementing the recommendations made by the six Regional Associations and provides the necessary support to their presidents. It contributes to cooperation activities of regional intergovernmental bodies as well as to high-priority activities such as those relating to climate change, sustainable development, and protection of the environment resulting from UNCED and the UN Framework Convention on Climate Change.

BIBLIOGRAPHY

International Glossary of Hydrology
Manual on the Global Data Processing System
Manual on the Global Observing System
Manual on Marine Meteorological Services
Operational Hydrology Reports
Special Environmental Reports
Technical Regulations—Manual on Codes
WMO Annual Report.
WMO Bulletin. Summarizes the work of the WMO and of developments in international meteorology. Quarterly.
WMO Training Series
World Weather Watch—The Plan and Implementation Programme.
(The WMO Library carries 35,000 monographs and 200 periodicals on the topics of meteorology, climatology, hydrology, marine and agricultural meteorology, and related topics of pollution and environment.)

Members of the World Meteorological Organization
(as of June 1997)

Afghanistan
Albania
Algeria
Angola
Antigua and
 Barbuda
Argentina
Armenia
Australia
Austria
Azerbaijan
Bahamas
Bahrain
Bangladesh
Barbados
Belarus
Belgium
Belize
Benin
Bolivia
Bosnia and Herzegovina
Botswana
Brazil
British Caribbean Territories
Brunei Darussalam
Bulgaria
Burkina Faso
Burundi
Cambodia
Cameroon
Canada
Cape Verde
Central African
 Republic
Chad
Chile
China
Colombia
Comoros

Congo
Congo, Democratic
 Republic of the
Cook Islands
Costa Rica
Côte d'Ivoire
Croatia
Cuba
Cyprus
Czech Republic
Denmark
Djibouti
Dominica
Dominican Republic
Ecuador
Egypt
El Salvador
Eritrea
Estonia
Ethiopia
Fiji
Finland
France
French Polynesia
Gabon
Gambia
Georgia
Germany
Ghana
Greece
Guatemala
Guinea
Guinea-Bissau
Guyana
Haiti
Honduras
Hong Kong
Hungary
Iceland
India

Indonesia
Iran
Iraq
Ireland
Israel
Italy
Jamaica
Japan
Jordan
Kazakhstan
Kenya
Korea, Democratic
 People's Republic of
Korea, Republic of
Kuwait
Kyrgyzstan
Lao People's
 Democratic Republic
Latvia
Lebanon
Lesotho
Liberia
Libyan Arab Jamahiriya
Lithuania
Luxembourg
Madagascar
Malawi
Malaysia
Maldives
Mali
Malta
Mauritania
Mauritius
Mexico
Micronesia, Federated
 States of
Moldova
Monaco
Mongolia
Morocco

Mozambique
Myanmar
Namibia
Nepal
Netherlands
Netherlands Antilles and
 Aruba
New Caledonia
New Zealand
Nicaragua
Niger
Nigeria
Norway
Oman
Pakistan
Panama
Papua New Guinea
Paraguay
Peru
Philippines
Poland
Portugal
Qatar
Romania
Russian Federation
Rwanda
St. Lucia
São Tomé and
 Principe
Saudi Arabia
Senegal
Seychelles
Sierra Leone
Singapore
Slovakia
Slovenia
Solomon Islands
Somalia
South Africa
Spain

Sri Lanka
Sudan
Suriname
Swaziland
Sweden
Switzerland
Syrian Arab Republic
Tajikistan
Tanzania
Thailand
The Former
 Yugoslav Republic
 of Macedonia
Togo
Tonga
Trinidad and
 Tobago
Tunisia
Turkey
Turkmenistan
Uganda
Ukraine
United Arab
 Emirates
United Kingdom
United States
 of America
Uruguay
Uzbekistan
Vanuatu
Venezuela
Vietnam
Western Samoa
Yemen
Yugoslavia
Zambia
Zimbabwe

THE INTERNATIONAL MARITIME ORGANIZATION (IMO)

BACKGROUND: The seven seas, accounting for about two-thirds of the earth's surface, are the only truly international part of our globe. Except for a marginal belt a very few miles wide, touching on the shores of countries, the greater part of the world's oceans and maritime resources are the common property of all nations. Since ancient times, however, "freedom of the seas" has too often been a theoretical ideal rather than a reality. In each historic era, the great maritime powers tended to use their naval might to dominate the sea. Some of those powers, while serving their own interests, served the world as a whole, as in the great explorations of unknown continents. Many sought to use the waters for purely national interests, particularly in matters affecting straits and other narrow waterways. Private shipping interests, often supported by their national governments, have been even more competitive, and international cooperation in maritime matters has been very limited.

The need for an international organization to develop and coordinate international maritime cooperation was expressed by President Woodrow Wilson, who called for "universal association of the nations to maintain the inviolate security of the highway of the seas for the common and unhindered use of all the nations of the world." However, it was not until after the creation of the UN that such an organization came into being.

CREATION

The convention establishing the International Maritime Organization (originally called the Inter-Governmental Maritime Consultative Organization) was drawn up in 1948 by the UN Maritime Conference in Geneva, but it was 10 years before the convention went into effect. The conference decided that the IMO's success depended on participation by most of the nations with large merchant navies, and it specified that the organization would come into being only when 21 states, including seven having at least 1 million gross tons of shipping each, had become parties to the convention. On 17 March 1958, the convention went into effect. The first IMO Assembly met in London in January 1959. The relationship of the IMO to the UN as a specialized agency was approved by the UN General Assembly on 18 November 1958 and by the IMO Assembly on 13 January 1959.

PURPOSES

The purposes of the IMO, as set forth in the convention, are the following:

1. to facilitate cooperation among governments on technical matters of all kinds affecting shipping engaged in international trade;
2. to encourage the general adoption of the highest practicable standards in matters concerning maritime safety, efficiency of navigation, and the prevention and control of marine pollution;
3. to encourage the removal of discriminatory action and unnecessary restrictions by governments engaged in international trade, so as to promote the availability of shipping services to world commerce without discrimination;
4. to consider matters concerning unfair restrictive practices by shipping concerns; and
5. to consider any matters concerning shipping that may be referred to the IMO by any UN organ or specialized agency.

MEMBERSHIP

Any state invited to the 1948 Maritime Conference or any member of the UN may become a member of the IMO by accepting the 1948 convention. Any other state whose application is approved by two-thirds of the IMO membership becomes a member by accepting the convention. If an IMO member responsible for the international relations of a territory (or group of territories) declares the convention to be applicable to that territory, the territory may become an associate member of the IMO. As of April 2000 there were 158 IMO members and two associate members.

STRUCTURE

The IMO's structure comprises the Assembly, the Council, the Maritime Safety Committee, the Marine Environment Protection Committee, the Legal Committee, the Technical Cooperation Committee, and the secretariat, headed by a Secretary-General.

Assembly

The governing body of the IMO is the Assembly, composed of all IMO members. The Assembly determines the work program and votes on the budget to which all members contribute. It meets once every two years in regular sessions, but may also meet in extraordinary session if necessary.

Council

Between sessions of the Assembly, the Council performs all functions of the organization except that of recommending the adoption of maritime safety regulations, a prerogative of the Maritime Safety Committee. The Council also has an important policymaking role. Drafts of international instruments and formal recommendations must be approved by the Council before they can be submitted to the Assembly.

The Council is made up of 32 members elected by the Assembly for two-year terms: eight members represent states with the largest international shipping services; eight represent states with the largest international seaborne trade; and 16 represent states, not elected under the foregoing categories, that have special interests in maritime transport or navigation and whose presence in the Council will ensure representation of the world's major geographic areas. The Council normally meets twice a year. The members of the Council elected by the 21st Assembly in 1999 for 2000–01 were: (from the first category) China, Greece, Italy, Japan, Norway, Russian Federation, United Kingdom, United States; (from the second category) Argentina, Brazil, Canada, France, Germany, India, Netherlands, Sweden; and (from the last category) Australia, Bahamas, Cyprus, Egypt, Finland, Indonesia, Malta, Mexico, Morocco, Panama, Philippines, Republic of Korea, Singapore, South Africa, Spain, Turkey.

Committees

The Maritime Safety Committee is made up of all IMO member states. Its work is carried out mainly through nine sub-committees working in the following areas: bulk liquids and gases; carriage of dangerous goods, solid cargoes and containers; fire protection; radiocommunication and search and rescue; safety of navigation; ship design and equipment; stability and load lines and fishing vessels safety; standards of training and watch-keeping; flag state implementation.

The Marine Environment Protection Committee is responsible for all matters relating to the prevention and control of marine pollution from ships.

The Legal Committee, established in the aftermath of the *Torrey Canyon* disaster of 1967 to deal with the legal problems arising from that incident, is responsible for any legal matter within the scope of the IMO.

The Technical Cooperation Committee coordinates the work of the IMO in providing technical assistance in the maritime field, especially to developing countries.

The Facilitation Committee is a subsidiary body of the Council. It was established in May 1972 and deals with IMO's work in eliminating unnecessary formalities and "red tape" in international shipping.

Secretary-General and Secretariat

The secretariat consists of a Secretary-General, appointed by the Council with the approval of the Assembly, and an international staff of about 300. IMO headquarters are at 4 Albert Embankment, London, SE1, 7SR.

The Secretary-General is William A. O'Neil, of Canada, who was appointed to the position with effect of 1 January 1990.

BUDGET

The IMO Assembly approved a budget of £36.612 million for the 2000–01 biennium, the same as the previous biennium. Contributions to the IMO budget are based on a formula that is different from that used in other agencies. The amount paid by each member state depends primarily on the tonnage of its merchant fleet. In 1996 the top ten contributors to the IMO budget (and the percentage of the total budget) were Panama 15.8%; Liberia 10.17%; Japan 5.23%; Bahamas 4.36%; Greece 4.32%; USA 4.12%; Malta 3.96%; Cyprus 3.91%; Norway 3.86%; Singapore 3.31%.

ACTIVITIES

The IMO's general functions, as stipulated in its convention, are "consultative and advisory." It thus serves as a forum where members can consult and exchange information on maritime matters. It discusses and makes recommendations on any maritime question submitted by member states or by other bodies of the UN and advises other international bodies, including the UN itself, on maritime matters. Various other intergovernmental agencies deal with specialized maritime matters, such as atomic propulsion for ships (IAEA), health at sea (WHO), maritime labor standards (ILO), meteorology (WMO), oceanography (UNESCO), and ship-to-ship and ship-to-shore communications (ITU). One of the functions of the IMO is to help coordinate the work in these different fields.

The IMO is also authorized to convene international conferences when necessary and to draft international maritime conventions or agreements for adoption by governments. These conferences, and the conventions resulting from them, have been mainly concerned with two subjects of primary concern to the IMO: safety at sea and the prevention of marine pollution.

A. Safety at Sea

A conference convened by the IMO in 1960 adopted the International Convention on Safety of Life at Sea (SOLAS) to replace an earlier (1948) instrument. The convention covers a wide range of measures designed to improve the safety of shipping, including subdivision and stability; machinery and electrical installations; fire protection, detection, and extinction; lifesaving appliances; radiotelegraphy and radiotelephony; safety of navigation; carriage of grain; carriage of dangerous goods; and nuclear ships. A new convention, incorporating amendments to the 1960 agreement, was adopted in 1974 and entered into force in 1980. The SOLAS convention was updated with the SOLAS Protocol of 1978, which entered into force in 1981, and with the SOLAS Protocol of 1988, which entered into force in February 2000.

In 1966, an IMO conference adopted the International Convention on Load Lines (LL), which sets limitations on the draught to which a ship may be loaded, an important consideration in its safety. The convention was updated by the LL Protocol of 1988, which entered into force in February 2000. The 1969 International Convention on Tonnage Measurement of Ships is designed to establish a uniform system for tonnage measurement.

Two conventions were adopted in 1972, following IMO conferences: the Convention on the International Regulations for Preventing Collisions at Sea, which concerns traffic separation schemes; and the Convention for Safe Containers, which provides uniform international regulations for maintaining a high level of safety in the carriage of containers by providing generally acceptable test procedures and related strength requirements.

The International Convention on the International Maritime Satellite Organization, adopted in 1976, concerns the use of space satellites for improved communication, enabling distress messages to be conveyed much more effectively than by conventional radio.

Three additional conventions concern safety at sea: the 1977 Torremolinos Convention for the Safety of Fishing Vessels, which applies to new fishing vessels of 24 m (79 ft) in length or longer; the 1978 Convention on Standards of Training, Certification, and Watch-keeping for Seafarers, which aims to establish internationally acceptable minimum standards for crews; and the 1979 International Convention on Maritime Search and Rescue, which is designed to improve existing arrangements for carrying out search and rescue operations following accidents at sea.

In September 1994, a roll-on/roll-off (ro-ro) automobile ferry the *Estonia* capsized and quickly sank, killing over 900 people. Following the disaster, the IMO Maritime Safety Committee made major changes to the safety standards of ro-ro passenger ships, including amendments to the 1974 International Convention for the Safety of Life at Sea.

B. Prevention of Marine Pollution

The 1954 Oil Pollution Convention, for which the IMO became depositary in 1959, was the first major attempt by the maritime nations to curb the impact of oil pollution. Following a conference convened by the IMO, the 1954 convention was amended in 1962, but it was the wreck of the oil tanker *Torrey Canyon* in March 1967 that fully alerted the world to the great dangers that

Membership of IMO
(as of April 2000)

Albania	El Salvador	Libyan Arab Jamahiriya	Senegal
Algeria	Equatorial Guinea	Lithuania	Seychelles
Angola	Eritrea	Luxembourg	Sierra Leone
Antigua and Barbuda	Estonia	Madagascar	Singapore
Argentina	Ethiopia	Malawi	Slovakia
Australia	Fiji	Malaysia	Slovenia
Austria	Finland	Maldives	Solomon Islands
Azerbaijan	France	Malta	Somalia
Bahamas	Gabon	Marshall Islands	South Africa
Bahrain	Gambia	Mauritania	Spain
Bangladesh	Georgia	Mauritius	Sri Lanka
Barbados	Germany	Mexico	Sudan
Belgium	Ghana	Monaco	Suriname
Belize	Greece	Mongolia	Sweden
Benin	Grenada	Morocco	Switzerland
Bolivia	Guatemala	Mozambique	Syrian Arab Republic
Bosnia and Herzegovina	Guinea	Myanmar	Thailand
Brazil	Guinea-Bissau	Namibia	The Former Yugoslav Republic
Brunei Darussalam	Guyana	Nepal	of Macedonia
Bulgaria	Haiti	Netherlands	Togo
Cambodia	Honduras	New Zealand	Tonga
Cameroon	Hungary	Nicaragua	Trinidad and Tobago
Canada	Iceland	Nigeria	Tunisia
Cape Verde	India	Norway	Turkey
Chile	Indonesia	Oman	Turkmenistan
China	Iran, Islamic Republic of	Pakistan	Ukraine
Colombia	Iraq	Panama	United Arab Emirates
Congo	Ireland	Papua New Guinea	United Kingdom
Congo, Democratic Republic of	Israel	Paraguay	United Republic
the	Italy	Peru	of Tanzania
Costa Rica	Jamaica	Philippines	United States
Côte d'Ivoire	Japan	Poland	Uruguay
Croatia	Jordan	Portugal	Vanuatu
Cuba	Kazakhstan	Qatar	Venezuela
Cyprus	Kenya	Romania	Vietnam
Czech Republic	Korea, Democratic People's	Russian Federation	Yemen
Denmark	Republic of	Samoa	Yugoslavia
Djibouti	Korea, Republic of	St. Lucia	
Dominica	Kuwait	St. Vincent and	ASSOCIATE MEMBERS
Dominican Republic	Latvia	the Grenadines	Hong Kong
Ecuador	Lebanon	Sâo Tomé and Principe	Macau
Egypt	Liberia	Saudi Arabia	

the transport of oil posed to the marine environment. In 1969, two new conventions were adopted: the Convention on Intervention on the High Seas in Cases of Oil Pollution Casualties, which gives states the right to intervene in incidents on the high seas that are likely to result in oil pollution; and the Convention on Civil Liability for Oil Pollution Damage, which is intended to ensure that adequate compensation is available to victims and which places the liability for the damage on the shipowner.

Two years later, a conference convened by the IMO led to the adoption of the Convention for the Establishment of an International Fund for Compensation for Oil Pollution Damage. The fund, with headquarters in London, is made up of contributions from oil importers. If an accident at sea results in pollution damage which exceeds the compensation available under the Civil Liability Convention, the fund is made available to pay an additional amount.

These three conventions all deal with the legal aspects of oil pollution, but the continuing boom in the transportation of oil showed that more work needed to be done on the technical side as well. The problem of oil pollution—not only as a result of accidents but also through normal tanker operations, especially the cleaning of cargo tanks—was so great in some areas that there was serious concern for the marine environment.

In 1973, a major conference was convened by the IMO to discuss the whole problem of marine pollution from ships. The

result of the conference was the International Convention for the Prevention of Pollution from Ships, which deals not only with oil but also with other sources of pollution, including garbage, sewage, and chemicals. The convention greatly reduces the amount of oil that can be discharged into the sea by ships and bans such discharges completely in certain areas, such as the Black Sea and the Red Sea. It gives statutory support for such operational procedures as "load on top," which greatly reduces the amount of mixtures to be disposed of after tank cleaning, and for segregated ballast tanks.

A series of tanker accidents that occurred in the winter of 1976/77 led to demands for further action and to the convening of the Conference on Tanker Safety and Pollution Prevention in 1978. The most important measures adopted by the conference were incorporated in protocols to the 1974 Convention on Safety of Life at Sea and the 1973 Marine Pollution Convention.

The protocol to the 1973 convention greatly strengthened the provisions regarding oil pollution and at the same time was modified to incorporate the parent convention. It was amended in 1984, and further amendments were made in 1985 to Annex II, which deals with pollution by noxious liquid substances carried in bulk.

In 1989, a conference of leading industrial nations in Paris called upon IMO to develop further measures to prevent oil pollution from ships. In 1990 IMO adopted the International Convention on Oil Pollution Preparedness, Response and Co-operation (OPRC). The convention provides a global framework for international cooperation in combating major incidents or threats of marine pollutions. Parties to the convention will be required to establish measures for dealing with pollution incidents and ships and operators of offshore oil units will be required to have oil pollution emergency plans. The convention also calls for the establishment of stockpiles of oil spill-combating equipment, the holding of oil spill-combating exercises, and the development of detailed plans for dealing with pollution incidents. It entered into force in May 1995.

In addition, through its Maritime Environment Protection Committee, the IMO has been working on various other projects designed to reduce the threat of oil pollution—for example, the Regional Oil-Combating Center, established in Malta in 1976 in conjunction with UNEP. The Mediterranean is particularly vulnerable to pollution, and a massive oil pollution incident there could be catastrophic. The center's purpose is to coordinate anti-pollution activities in the region and to help develop contingency plans that could be put into effect should a disaster occur. The IMO has also taken part in projects in other regions, including the Caribbean and West Africa.

C. Other Maritime Questions

In 1965, the IMO adopted the Convention on Facilitation of Maritime Traffic, the primary objectives of which are to prevent unnecessary delays in maritime traffic, to aid in cooperation between states, and to secure the highest practicable degree of uniformity in formalities and procedures.

In association with the IAEA and the European Nuclear Energy Agency of the OECD, the IMO convened a conference in 1971, which adopted the Convention on Civil Liability in the Field of Maritime Carriage of Nuclear Matter.

The Convention on Carriage of Passengers and Their Luggage, adopted in 1974, establishes a regime of liability for damage suffered by passengers carried on seagoing vessels. It declares the carrier liable for damage or loss suffered by passengers if the incident is due to the fault or neglect of the carrier. The limit of liability is set at US$55,000 per carriage.

Another convention on liability, the 1976 Convention on Limitation of Liability for Maritime Claims, covers two types of claims: claims arising from loss of life or personal injury and claims arising from damage to ships, harbor works, or other property. To further clarify liability issues, in 1996 the IMO adopted the International Convention on Liability and Compensation for Damage in connection with the Carriage of Hazardous and Noxious Substances by Sea (called the HNS Convention); as of April 2000, it had not entered into force.

In addition to such conventions, whose requirements are mandatory for nations that ratify them, IMO has produced numerous codes, recommendations, and other instruments dealing with maritime questions. These do not have the legal power of conventions but can be used by governments as a basis for domestic legislation and for guidance. Some of the recommendations deal with bulk cargoes, safety of fishermen and fishing vessels, liquefied gases, dangerous goods, timber deck cargoes, mobile offshore drilling units, noise levels on board ships, and nuclear merchant ships.

Some codes, such as those dealing with the transport of bulk chemicals and liquefied gas, have been made mandatory through amendments to the International Convention on Safety of Life at Sea.

In 1988, IMO adopted the Convention for the Suppression of Unlawful Acts Against the Safety of Maritime Navigation, which entered into force in 1992. The main purpose of the convention is to ensure that appropriate action is taken against persons committing unlawful acts against ships and fixed platforms engaged in the exploitation of offshore oil and gas.

The International Convention on Salvage was adopted in 1989, and entered into force in July 1996. The convention is intended to replace an instrument adopted in Brussels in 1910. That convention incorporated the "no cure, no pay" principle that has been in existence for many years and is the basis of most salvage operations today. However, it did not take compensation into account. The new convention seeks to remedy this by making provisions for "special compensation" to be paid to salvers when there is a threat to the environment.

D. Technical Assistance and Training

While the adoption of conventions, codes, and recommendations has been the IMO's most important function, in recent years the agency has devoted increasing attention to securing the effective implementation of these measures throughout the world. As a result, the IMO's technical assistance activities have become more important, and in 1975 it established the Technical Cooperation Committee. The purpose of the technical assistance program is to help states, many of them developing countries, to ratify IMO conventions and to reach the standards contained in the conventions and other instruments.

Advisors and consultants employed by the IMO, in the field and at headquarters, deal with such matters as maritime safety administration, maritime legislation, marine pollution, training for deck and engineering personnel, the technical aspects of ports, and the carriage of dangerous goods.

Through its technical assistance program, the IMO is able to offer advice in these and other areas and to assist in the acquisition of equipment and the provision of fellowships. IMO relies almost exclusively on extra-budgetary sources for financing the International Technical Cooperation Program (TCP) and in the 1990s funding became a serious problem, in particular since the strategic reorientation of the united Nations Development program (UNDP), traditionally the core provider of TCP funding. For example, in 1990 approximately US$5.6 million was received from UNDP; by 1997 this support had dwindled to US$3.93 million. In 2000, IMO's funding partners for the TCP included international funding agencies, regional development banks, donor countries, recipient countries, the private sector (shipping and port industries), non-Governmental organizations involved in maritime and port activities, and individuals.

For the 2000–01 biennium, the total Technical Cooperation fund was approved at US$5,010,000. Of the total amount, 24% was allocated to global activities, 16% to regional coordination, 16% to projects in Africa, 13% to projects in Asia, 12% to projects in Latin America and the Caribbean, 10% to projects in Eastern Europe, and 9% to projects in the Arab and Mediterranean states.

The World Maritime University, in Malmö, Sweden, which was established under the auspices of the IMO and opened in 1983, provides advanced training for more than 100 maritime personnel annually—senior maritime teachers, surveyors, inspectors, technical managers, and administrators from developing countries. Funded by UNDP and by Sweden and other countries, the university offers two-year courses in maritime education and training, maritime safety administration, general maritime administration, and technical management of shipping companies, as well as field and other training. It is designed to help meet the urgent need of developing countries for high-level maritime personnel and to contribute to maintaining international standards for maritime safety and preventing pollution of the seas by ships. The university serves as the apex of an international system of training in the maritime field, collaborating with regional, sub-regional, and national maritime training institutions throughout the world. By 1999 the university had produced more than 1,500 graduates from over 130 countries.

BIBLIOGRAPHY

IMO News. Quarterly.

IMO—What It Is, What It Does. Descriptive leaflet.

(The IMO also publishes the texts of all its conventions, codes, and recommendations, as well as a number of specialized manuals and guides, such as the *Manual on Oil Pollution; Regulations on Subdivision and Stability of Passenger Ships; Merchant Ship Search and Rescue Manual; International Maritime Dangerous Goods Code; Pocket Guide to Cold Water Survival; and Noise Levels on Board Ships.*) A complete listing of current publications is available at the IMO web site http://www.imo.org/imo/pubs/pubstart.htm).

THE WORLD INTELLECTUAL PROPERTY ORGANIZATION (WIPO)

BACKGROUND: Intellectual property includes industrial property, such as inventions, trademarks, and designs, on the one hand, and the objects of copyright and neighboring rights on the other. Until a century ago, there were no international instruments for the protection of intellectual property. Legislative provisions for the protection of inventors, writers, dramatists, and other creators of intellectual property varied from country to country and could be effective only within the borders of states adopting them. It came to be widely recognized that adequate protection of industrial property encourages industrialization, investment, and honest trade. That the arts would be advanced by legal safeguards in favor of their practitioners had long been argued, but such safeguards were difficult to devise and enact into law. The Paris Convention of 20 March 1883 and the Bern Convention of 9 September 1886 represented initial steps toward systematic provision of the two sorts of international protection that led eventually to the creation of the World Intellectual Property Organization (WIPO).

CREATION

The 1883 Paris Convention established the International Union for the Protection of Industrial Property, also called the Paris Union. The convention is open to all states. Its most important functions have to do with patents for inventions and marks for goods and services.

The term industrial property is applied in its widest sense in the convention. In addition to inventions, industrial designs, trademarks, service marks, indications of source, and appellations of origin, it covers small patents called utility models in a few countries, trade names or the designations under which an industrial or commercial activity is carried on, and the suppression of unfair competition.

The convention states that members must provide the same protection of rights in industrial property to nationals of the other members as they provide to their own nationals. It permits foreigners to file for a patent that will apply in all member states within a year after first filing in the country of origin. Additionally, it defines conditions under which a state may license the use of a patent in its own territory—for example, if the owner of the patent does not exploit it there.

The 1886 Bern Convention established the International Union for the Protection of Literary and Artistic Works, also called the Bern Union. It also is open to all states. Its function is the protection of copyright, the main beneficiaries of which include authors of books and articles; publishers of books, newspapers, and periodicals; composers of music; painters; photographers; sculptors; film producers; and creators of certain television programs. Under the convention, each member state must accord the same protection to the copyright of the nationals of the other member states as it accords to that of its own nationals. The convention also prescribes some minimum standards of protection—for example, that copyright protection generally continues throughout the author's life and for 50 years thereafter. It includes special provisions for the benefit of developing countries.

In 1893, the secretariats of the Paris Union and the Bern Union were joined in the United International Bureaus for the Protection of Intellectual Property (BIRPI).

The World Intellectual Property Organization (WIPO) was established by a convention signed at Stockholm 14 July 1967 by 51 states. When the convention entered into force on 26 April 1970, WIPO incorporated BIRPI and perpetuated its functions. BIRPI still has a function for members of the Paris or Bern unions that have not yet joined WIPO.

WIPO became the fourteenth specialized UN agency, the first new one since 1961, when the General Assembly approved that status on 17 December 1974.

PURPOSES

The purposes of WIPO are twofold: (1) to promote the protection of intellectual property throughout the world through cooperation among states and, where appropriate, in collaboration with any other international organization; and (2) to ensure administrative cooperation among the unions.

Intellectual property comprises two main branches: *industrial property,* chiefly in inventions, trademarks, and industrial designs; and *copyright,* chiefly in literary, musical, artistic, photographic, and cinematographic works.

The WIPO Convention lists rights in intellectual property relating to literary, artistic, and scientific works; performances of artists; phonograms; broadcasts; inventions in all fields of human endeavor; scientific discoveries; industrial designs; trademarks; service marks; and commercial names and designations. The convention also offers protection against unfair competition and covers all other rights resulting from intellectual activity in the industrial, scientific, literary, or artistic fields.

As of 1999, WIPO administered the following 21 unions or treaties, listed in the chronological order of their creation:

1. *Industrial property (15):* the Paris Union (1883), for the protection of industrial property; the Madrid Agreement (1891), for the repression of false or deceptive indications of source on goods; the Madrid Union (1891), for the international registration of marks; the Hague Union (1925), for the international deposit of industrial designs; the Nice Union (1957), for the international classification of goods and services for the purpose of registration of marks; the Lisbon Union (1958), for the protection of appellations of origin and their international registration; the Locarno

Union (1968), establishing an international classification for industrial designs; the International Patent Cooperation (IPC) Union (1970), for the establishment of worldwide uniformity of patent classification; the Strasbourg Patent Classification Treaty (PCT) Union (1971), for cooperation in the filing, searching, and examination of international applications for the protection of inventions where such protection is sought in several countries; the Vienna Union (1973), establishing an international classification of the figurative elements of marks; the Budapest Union (1977), for the international recognition of the deposit of microorganisms for the purpose of patent procedure; the Nairobi Treaty (1981), on the protection of the Olympic symbol; the Washington (DC) Treaty (1989) on intellectual property in respect of integrated circuits; the Geneva Trademark Law Treaty (1994); and the Agreement on the Trade-Related Aspects of Intellectual Property Rights (TRIPS Agreement; 1995/96) between WIPO and the World Trade Organization.

2. *Copyright and neighboring rights (6):* the Bern Union (1886), for the protection of literary and artistic works; the Rome Convention (1961), for the protection of performers, producers of phonograms, and broadcasting organizations, jointly administered with the ILO and UNESCO; the Geneva Convention (1971), for the protection of producers of phonograms against unauthorized duplication of their phonograms; the Brussels Convention (1974), relating to the distribution of program-carrying signals transmitted by satellite; the WIPO Copyright Treaty (1996); and the WIPO Performances and Phonograms Treaty (1996).

Three additional treaties are to be administered by WIPO when they come into effect: the Vienna Agreement, on the protection of typefaces and their international deposit; the Geneva Treaty, on the international recording of scientific discoveries; and the Madrid Multilateral Convention, on the question of double taxation of copyright royalties.

MEMBERSHIP
Membership in WIPO is open to any state that is a member of any of the unions, is a member of the UN or any of the specialized agencies or the IAEA, is party to the Statute of the International Court of Justice, or is invited by the General Assembly of WIPO to become a party to the WIPO Convention. The 171 members of WIPO (W), 152 members of the Paris Union (P), and 137 members of the Bern Union (B) as of September 1999 are listed in the table on the next page.

STRUCTURE
The Paris and Bern unions each have an assembly consisting of the member states, meeting biennially. An executive committee elected by the General Assembly, consisting of one-fourth of the member states, meets annually. The other unions, in most cases, have an assembly but no executive committee.

WIPO itself has four organs: the General Assembly, the Conference, the Coordination Committee, and a secretariat called the International Bureau.

General Assembly
The General Assembly consists of all states party to the WIPO Convention that are also members of any of the unions. It meets biennially and has the highest authority of all the organs.

Conference
The Conference consists of all states party to the WIPO Convention, whether or not they are members of one or more of the unions. It meets biennially to discuss matters of general interest in the field of intellectual property, as well as to establish WIPO's program of technical legal assistance and the budget for that program.

Coordination Committee
The Coordination Committee meets annually. It consists of executive committee members of the Paris or the Bern union or both.

International Bureau
The International Bureau, located in Geneva, is the secretariat of the various governing bodies of WIPO and the unions. In 1999 it consisted of a staff of 690 people from 75 different countries, headed by a Director General. Arpad Bogsch, of the US, was elected to successive terms as Director General since the establishment of WIPO in 1974. In 1997 he was replaced by Kamil Idris of Sudan as Director General.

BUDGET
Until January 1994, the budget was entirely met from contributions of member states; from fees paid by applicants for international protection of inventions, international registration of trademarks and appellations of origin, and deposit of industrial designs; and from the sale of publications. Beginning with the 1994–95 biennium, the WIPO governing bodies instituted a system of unitary contributions. The advantages of the unitary contribution system are that it makes the administration of contributions simpler, and will be an incentive for states to join more unions, since adherence will not increase the amount of their contribution. In addition, the governing bodies adopted a new formula for contributions that was intended to significantly lower overall cost of contributions for developing countries. For the 2000–01 biennium the WIPO budget was SFR4,175,000, of which SFR3,595,000 was staffing costs and SFR580,000 was non-staffing.

ACTIVITIES

A. Assistance to Developing Countries
One of the main objectives of WIPO is to assist developing countries in the fields of both industrial property and copyright.

In the field of industrial property, WIPO's chief aims are the following: (1) to encourage and increase, in quantity and quality, the creation of patentable inventions in developing countries by their own nationals and in their own enterprises and thereby to increase their technological self-reliance; (2) to improve conditions for the acquisition of foreign patented technology; (3) to increase the competitiveness of developing countries in international trade through better protection of trademarks; and (4) to make it easier and cheaper for developing countries to locate the technological information contained in patent documents.

In the field of copyright, the main objectives are the following:

1. to encourage and increase the creation of literary and artistic works in developing countries by their own nationals and thereby to maintain their national culture in their own languages and corresponding to their own ethnic and social traditions and aspirations; and
2. to improve conditions for the acquisition of the right to use or enjoy the literary and artistic works in which copyright is owned by foreigners.

In order to attain these objectives, most developing countries need to create or modernize domestic legislation and governmental institutions, accede to international treaties, and have more specialists in the fields of industrial property and copyright.

WIPO's assistance consists mainly of advice, training, and the furnishing of documents and equipment. Advice is given by the staff of WIPO, by experts chosen by WIPO, or at international

Members of WIPO and of the Paris and Bern Unions
(W = WIPO, P = Paris, B = Bern)
(as of September 1999)

Albania,	W, P, B	Dominican Republic	, B	Laos,	W, P	St. Lucia,	W, P, B
Algeria	W, P, B	Ecuador,	W, P, B	Latvia,	W, P, B	St. Vincent and the	
Andorra,	W	Egypt,	W, P, B	Lebanon,	W, P	Grenadines,	W, P, B
Angola	W	El Salvador,	W, P, B	Lesotho,	W, P, B	Samoa,	W
Argentina	W, P, B	Equatorial Guinea,	W, P, B	Liberia,	W, P, B	San Marino,	W, P
Armenia	W, P	Eritrea,	W	Libyan Arab Jamahiriya,	W, P, B	Sao Tome and Principe,	W, P
Australia,	W, P, B	Estonia,	W, P, B	Liechtenstein,	W, P, B	Saudi Arabia,	W
Austria,	W, P, B	Ethiopia,	W	Lithuania,	W, P, B	Senegal,	W, P, B
Azerbaijan,	W, P, B	Fiji,	W, B	Luxembourg,	W, P, B	Sierra Leone,	W, P
Bahamas,	W, P, B	Finland,	W, P, B	Madagascar,	W, P	Singapore,	W, P, B
Bahrain,	W, P, B	France,	W, P, B	Malawi,	W, P, B	Slovakia,	W, P, B
Bangladesh,	W, P, B	Gabon,	W, P, B	Malaysia,	W, P, B	Slovenia,	W, P, B
Barbados,	W, P, B	Gambia,	W, P, B	Mali,	W, P, B	Somalia,	W, B
Belarus,	W, P, B	Georgia,	W, P, B	Malta,	W, P, B	South Africa,	W, P, B
Belgium,	W, P, B	Germany,	W, P, B	Mauritania,	W, P, B	Spain,	W, P, B
Benin,	W, P, B	Ghana,	W, P, B	Mauritius,	W, P, B	Sri Lanka,	W, P, B
Bhutan,	W	Greece,	W, P, B	Mexico,	W, P, B	Sudan,	W, P
Bolivia,	W, P, B	Grenada,	W, P	Moldova, Republic of,	W, P, B	Suriname,	W, P, B
Bosnia and Herzegovina,	W, P, B	Guatemala,	W, P	Monaco,	W, P, B	Swaziland,	W, P, B
Botswana,	W, P, B	Guinea,	W, P, B	Mongolia,	W, P, B	Sweden,	W, P, B
Brazil,	W, P, B	Guinea-Bissau,	W, P, B	Morocco,	W, P, B	Switzerland,	W, P, B
Brunei Darussalam,	W	Guyana,	W, P, B	Mozambique,	W, P	Tajikistan,	W, P
Bulgaria,	W, P, B	Haiti,	W, P, B	Namibia ,	W, B	Thailand,	W, B
Burkina Faso,	W, P, B	Holy See (Vatican),	W, P, B	Nepal,	W	The Former Yugoslav	
Burundi,	W, P	Honduras,	W, P, B	Netherlands,	W, P, B	Republic of Macedonia,	W, P, B
Cambodia,	W, P	Hungary,	W, P, B	New Zealand,	W, P	Togo,	W, P, B
Cameroon,	W, P, B	Iceland,	W, P, B	Nicaragua,	W, P	Trinidad and Tobago,	W, P, B
Canada,	W, P, B	India,	W, P, B	Niger,	W, P, B	Tunisia,	W, P, B
Cape Verde,	W, B	Indonesia,	W, P, B	Nigeria,	W, B	Turkey,	W, P, B
Central African Republic,	W, P, B	Iran, Islamic Republic of	, P	Norway,	W, P, B	Turkmenistan,	W, P
Chad,	W, P, B	Iraq,	W, P	Oman,	W, P, B	Uganda,	W, P
Chile,	W, P, B	Ireland,	W, P, B	Pakistan,	W, B	Ukraine,	W, P, B
China,	W, P, B	Israel,	W, P, B	Panama,	W, P, B	United Arab Emirates,	W, P
Colombia,	W, P, B	Italy,	W, P, B	Papua New Guinea,	W, P	United Kingdom,	W, P, B
Congo,	W, P, B	Jamaica,	W, B	Paraguay,	W, P, B	United Rep. of Tanzania,	W, P, B
Congo, (DRC)	W, P, B	Japan,	W, P, B	Peru,	W, P, B	United States of America,	W, P, B
Costa Rica,	W, P, B	Jordan,	W, P, B	Philippines,	W, P, B	Uruguay,	W, P, B
Côte d'Ivoire,	W, P, B	Kazakhstan,	W, P, B	Poland,	W, P, B	Uzbekistan,	W, P
Croatia,	W, P, B	Kenya,	W, P, B	Portugal,	W, P, B	Venezuela,	W, P, B
Cuba,	W, P, B	Korea, Democratic People's		Qatar,	W	Vietnam,	W, P
Cyprus,	W, P, B	Republic of,	W, P	Romania,	W, P, B	Yemen,	W
Czech Republic,	W, P, B	Korea, Republic of,	W, P	Russian Federation,	W, P, B	Yugoslavia,	W, P, B
Denmark,	W, P, B	Kuwait,	W	Rwanda,	W, P, B	Zambia,	W, P, B
Dominica,	W, P, B	Kyrgyzstan,	W, P, B	St. Kitts and Nevis,	W, P, B	Zimbabwe,	W, P, B

meetings convened by WIPO. Training may be individual (on-the-job) or collective (in courses, seminars, and workshops) and may take place in the interested developing country, in an industrialized country, or in another developing country. The resources for such activities are provided in WIPO's budget or from donor countries or organizations, particularly UNDP.

In 1998, more than 10,000 men and women from some 122 developing countries benefitted from the 179 courses, seminars, and other meetings held under WIPO's cooperation for development program. In addition, the International Bureau gave advice and assistance to officials from newly independent governments of the former Soviet Union in connection with the preparation and enactment of intellectual property laws, the establishment of industrial property offices, as well as adherence to WIPO-administered treaties. In particular, the International Bureau advised the Interstate Council on the Protection of Industrial Property (which groups nine states from the former Soviet Union: Armenia, Belarus, Kazakhstan, Kyrgyzstan, the Republic of Moldova, the Russian Federation, Tajikistan, Ukraine, and Uzabekistan) on a plan to set up a regional patent system under the proposed Eurasian Patent Convention.

B. Other Activities

In order to adapt the treaties administered by WIPO to changing circumstances and needs, a constant watch is kept to see whether they need to be revised. The Paris Convention, for example, has had six revisions, the last in Stockholm in 1967, and the Bern Convention has had five, the last in Paris in 1971. WIPO also keeps international classifications of patents, trademarks, and industrial designs under review in order to keep them up-to-date.

In addition, WIPO observes changes in international industrial, trade, and cultural relations that seem to call for adaptations not only in the treaties administered by WIPO but also in national laws, regional arrangements, contractual practices, and professional activities in the field of intellectual property.

Thus, for example, in the field of industrial property, WIPO is considering the possibilities of uniform provisions in national patent laws, particularly concerning the effects on the patentability of an invention or a public disclosure of the invention by the inventor prior to filing a patent application. It also advocates laws and treaty provisions that would give more efficient protection against the counterfeiting of goods and would protect the intellectual creators of microchips or integrted circuits and inventions in biotechnology, including genetic engineering.

In the field of copyright, WIPO has been engaged, in some cases jointly with UNESCO, in recommending laws for the protection of computer programs, for works created by employee-authors, for expressions of folklore, for more effective protection of authors and performers in connection with cable television, and for protection against piratical editions of books, phonograms, and videotapes and excessive unauthorized reproduction. WIPO is also studying the copyright law aspects of the rental of phonograms and videograms, of direct broadcast satellites, and of electronic libraries and the possibility of creating an international register of audiovisual works.

In 1993, WIPO established the WIPO Academy to conduct encounter sessions on current intellectual property issues at the policy level for government officials from developing countries. WIPO also awarded to three nationals from developing countries the first long-term scholarships to institutions in industrialized countries for intellectual property law studies.

The WIPO Arbitration Center was established in July 1994 to offer enterprises and individuals four dispute-settlement procedures: mediation, arbitration, expedited arbitration (for small-scale disputes), and a combined procedure of mediation and arbitration.

International Registrations

The International Patent Documentation Center, established in Vienna in 1972 under an agreement between WIPO and the government of Austria, puts on computer the principal bibliographic data of almost 1 million patent documents a year and permits the retrieval of the data required for various purposes by patent offices, industry, and research and development institutions. The financial and operational responsibility lies with the Austrian government, but WIPO assists the center in its contacts with the patent offices of the various countries.

The International Bureau of WIPO, in Geneva, maintains four registration services in the fields of patents, trademarks, industrial designs, and appellations of origin.

BIBLIOGRAPHY

Copyright. Monthly review of the Bern Union in English and French. Covers ratifications and contains texts of laws, court decisions, studies.

Industrial Property. Monthly review of the Paris Union in English and French. Covers ratifications and contains texts of laws, court decisions, studies.

International Designs Bulletin. Monthly review in English and French. Contains notifications and modifications concerning the international registration of industrial designs.

Model Laws for Developing Countries on Inventions, on Marks, Trade Names and Acts of Unfair Competition and on Designs. In English, French, and Spanish.

(WIPO also publishes the texts of conventions, treaties, and agreements on intellectual property; international classifications; and model laws. Many are available on the WIPO web site www.wipo.org/eng/main.htm).

THE INTERNATIONAL FUND FOR AGRICULTURAL DEVELOPMENT (IFAD)

BACKGROUND: The International Fund for Agricultural Development (IFAD) is the first international institution established exclusively to provide additional resources for agricultural and rural development in developing countries and to channel those resources to the poorest rural populations in Africa, Near East and North Africa, Asia, and Latin America and the Caribbean that suffer from chronic hunger and malnutrition.

CREATION

IFAD was one of the major initiatives of the World Food Conference, held in Rome in 1974, following two years of negotiations. The agreement establishing the fund was adopted by 91 governments on 13 June 1976 and was opened for signature or ratification on 20 December 1976, following attainment of the target of US$ 1 billion in initial pledges. The agreement came into force on 30 November 1977.

PURPOSES

The objective of the fund is to mobilize additional resources to be made available on concessional terms to help developing countries improve their food production and nutrition. The fund is unique in that its projects are focused exclusively on agricultural development, concentrating on the poorest sections of the rural populations in developing countries. It deals with all aspects of agriculture, including crops, irrigation, agricultural credit, storage, livestock, and fisheries.

The UN Social Summit in Copenhagen agreed in 1995 that each member country would devise a program to halve the incidence of 'dollar poverty' between 1995 and 2015. In 1996 OECD agreed to set their country-specific aid into the context of these national programs. Rural areas of developing countries contain over 75% of the world's dollar-poor. Therefore, policies for the reduction of rural poverty must make a large contribution if the poverty reduction target is to be achieved.

MEMBERSHIP

IFAD had a total of 161 member nations in March 1998, compared with 91 at the time of its establishment. In February 1997, all member states were reclassified as follows: Category I (developed countries) were reclassified as List A countries; Category II (oil-exporting developing countries) reclassified as List B countries; and Category III (other developing countries) reclassified globally as List C Countries. In March 1998 there were 22 List A countries, 12 List B countries, and 127 List C countries.

STRUCTURE

IFAD is a new kind of institution in the UN system. The governing bodies that supervise its operations reflect an innovative formula that brings together the interests of industrialized countries, each of the three categories having the same number of votes (600). As an action-oriented organization, the fund normally works by consensus rather than by voting.

The three main organs are the Governing Council, the Executive Board, and the secretariat, headed by a president.

As of October 1999, IFAD's professional staff numbered 132 and general service staff numbered 158.

Governing Council

The highest governing body of the fund is the Governing Council, which meets once a year and on which all members are represented by a governor and an alternate governor. The council adopts the fund's budget, approves the applications of new members, and elects the president of the fund and members of the Executive Board.

Executive Board

The Executive Board, composed of 18 members and 18 alternates, oversees the operations of the fund, including its investments and work program. The board holds three sessions a year.

President and Secretariat

The president of the fund, elected for four years, is responsible for its management. He is chairman of the Executive Board and heads the secretariat. Fawzi Al-Sultan of Kuwait was elected president of the fund in January 1993 and was reelected for a second term in 1997. The fund's headquarters are located at 107, Via del Serafico 00142 Rome, Italy.

BUDGET

During 1996–97, IFAD developed a strategy to streamline budget formulation. An internal reorganization made a considerable contribution to cost-effectiveness, reducing administrative costs by over 23% during the period 1993–97 (while the loan volume over the same period increased by approximately 20%). The approved budget for 2000 was US$55,392,000, including a contingency of US$400,000 plus a separate amount of US$141,000 for funding meetings of the Consultation to Review the Adequacy of the Resources Available to IFAD.

ACTIVITIES

A. Loans and Resources

The first project loans were approved by IFAD's Executive Board in April 1978. At the end of the three-year period, 1978–80, the fund's cumulative commitments amounted to nearly US$900 million in loans and grants for some 70 of its developing member states.

For the period 1981–83, IFAD expanded its operational program. By 1983, IFAD's total financial commitments since April 1978 exceeded US$1.4 billion for projects and programs in some

80 member countries in Africa, Near East and North Africa, Asia, and Latin America and the Caribbean. By mid-1987, IFAD had extended loans totalling US$2.3 billion to 89 developing countries to finance 204 projects. From 1978 to 1996, IFAD financed 461 projects in 110 countries, committing US$4.9 billion in loans and grants, of which 81% were made available to 83 low income, food-deficit countries. Loans were extended to lower income countries at highly concessional terms, repayable over 40 years, including a grace period of ten years and a 0.75% service charge per annum.

The first replenishment of IFAD resources was unanimously approved by the fund's Governing Council in January 1982. Member countries offered to provide contributions totalling US$1 billion for the period 1981–83, including US$620 million from List A (developed) countries, US$450 million from List B (oil-exporting developing) countries, and US$32 million from List C (other developing) countries.

In 1986, the Governing Council agreed on a second replenishment of IFAD's resources totalling US$488 million, of which List A countries pledged US$276 million; List B countries, US$184 million; and List C countries, US$28 million. In 1990, the Governing Council agreed on a third replenishment. Member countries offered to provide contributions totalling US$567 million of which List A countries pledged US$378 million; List B countries, US$124 million, and List C countries, US$65 million. A fourth replenishment, totalling US$470 million, began in February 1997. Of this, US$419 million was pledged as of 9 December 1999.

B. Lending Policies and Operations

IFAD loan operations fall into two groups: projects initiated by the fund and projects cofinanced with other financial and development institutions. IFAD-initiated projects are those for which the fund has taken the lead in project identification and preparation and in mobilizing additional resources from other financial agencies where necessary.

Most of IFAD's assistance has been provided on highly concessional terms—loans repayable over 50 years with a 10-year grace period and an annual service charge of 1%. About one-quarter of the loans are repayable over 20 years at 4% annual interest, while a few have been offered at 8% over 15–18 years. However, at its 17th session of January 1994, the Governing Council adopted a resolution which amended the lending terms and conditions for the first time since the fund's establishment.

In the future, those developing members countries having a Gross National Product (GNP) per capita of US$805 or less in 1992 prices, or which qualify for loans from the World Bank's "soft loan" agency, the International Development Association, will normally be eligible to receive loans from IFAD on highly concessional terms. Loans on highly concessional terms will be free of interest but will bear a service charge of 0.75% per annum and have a repayment period of 40 years, including a grace period of 10 years. The total amount of loans provided each year on highly concessional terms will be approximately two-thirds of the total lent annually by IFAD.

IFAD loans represent only a part of the total project costs; the governments concerned contribute a share. In most of the projects approved so far, IFAD also has cooperated with the World Bank (IBRD and IDA); the African, Asian, Inter-American, and Islamic development banks; the Arab Fund for Economic and Social Development; the Central American Bank for Economic Integration; the World Food Programme; the EEC; OPEC; and other multilateral and bilateral institutions.

IFAD, while seeking to preserve an appropriate balance in its regional allocations, also has attempted to respond to the special needs of the 74 low-income, food-deficit countries. Well over 80% of the fund's loans were channelled to these countries in the 1978–95 period. The regional shares of IFAD-supported projects approved between 1978–95 under both regular and special programs were: Africa (sub-Sahara), 41%; Asia and the Pacific, 26%; Latin America and the Caribbean, 16%; and Near East and North Africa, 16.4%.

Members of IFAD
(as of March 1998)

LIST A: DEVELOPED COUNTRIES

Australia	Greece	Portugal
Austria	Ireland	Spain
Belgium	Italy	Sweden
Canada	Japan	Switzerland
Denmark	Luxembourg	United Kingom
Finland	Netherlands	United States
France	New Zealand	
Germany	Norway	

LIST B: OIL-EXPORTING DEVELOPING COUNTRIES

Algeria	Iraq	Qatar
Gabon	Kuwait	Saudi Arabia
Indonesia	Libya	UAE
Iran	Nigeria	Venezuela

LIST C: OTHER DEVELOPING COUNTRIES

Afghanistan	Ethiopia	Pakistan
Albania	Fiji	Panama
Angola	Gambia	Papua N. Guinea
Antigua and Barbuda	Georgia	Paraguay
Argentina	Ghana	Peru
Armenia	Grenada	Philippines
Azerbaijan	Guatemala	Republic
Bangladesh	Guinea	Romania
Barbados	Guinea-Bissau	Rwanda
Belize	Guyana	Saint Lucia
Benin	Haiti	Saint Vincent
Bhutan	Honduras	Samoa
Bolivia	India	São Tomé and Principe
Bosnia and Herzegov-	Israel	Senegal
ina	Jamaica	Seychelles
Botswana	Jordan	Sierra Leone
Brazi	Kazakhstan	Solomon Islands
Burkina Faso	Kenya	Somalia
Burundi	Korea, Democratic	South Africa
Cambodia	People's Republic of	Sri Lanka
Cameroon	Korea, Republic of	St Kitts and Nevis
Cape Verde	Kyrgystan	Sudan
Central African	Laos	Suriname
Republic	Lebanon	Swaziland
Chad	Lesotho	Syrian Arab Republic
Chile	Liberia	Tajikistan
China	Madagascar	Tanzania, United
Colombia	Malawi	Republic of
Comoros	Malaysia	Thailand
Congo	Maldives	The Former Yugoslav
Congo, DRC	Mali	Republic of Mace-
Cook Islands	Malta	donia
Costa Rica	Mauritania	Togo
Côte d'Ivoire	Mauritius	Tonga
Croatia	Mexico	Trinidad and Tobago
Cuba	Moldova, Republic of	Tunisia
Cyprus	Mongolia	Turkey
Djibouti	Morocco	Uganda
Dominica	Mozambique	Uruguay
Dominican Republic	Myanmar	Vietnam
Ecuador	Namibia	Yemen
Egypt	Nepal	Yugoslavia
El Salvador	Nicaragua	Zambia
Equatorial Guinea	Niger	Zimbabwe
Eritrea	Oman	

In January 1986, IFAD, as the first international financial institution to respond to the socioeconomic crisis in sub-Saharan Africa, in the wake of the disastrous droughts and famines of 1983–85, launched the Special Programme for Sub-Saharan African Countries Affected by Drought and Desertification (SPA), with a target for resource mobilization of US$300 million. This target was outrun by contributions reaching US$322.8 million from five developing countries and the European Community.

The program aims to restore the productive capacity of small farmers, promote traditional food crops mainly grown by smallholders, and initiate small-scale water control schemes, in addition to recommending measures for environmental protection and providing assistance to governments in regard to policy.

By January 1993, a second phase of the program became effective. While it preserves the focus of the first phase, it extends its conceptual frame and operational scope. Specifically it carries environmental and soil conservation objectives from on-farm to off-farm (particularly in the common property resource domain), and addresses overall coping strategies of households and communities through economic diversification. The approved loan program for 1999 was US$437.3 million; the proposed amount for 2000 was US$446 million, the same real level of programming from the previous year, adjusted for projected inflation (by 2%).

Projects by Region under the Regular Programme for 2000
(in millions of US$)

REGION	NUMBER OF PROJECTS	AMOUNT
Africa	13	$1.64
Asia and the Pacific	7	1.38
Latin America and the Caribbean	5	0.76
Near East and North Africa	5	0.68
TOTAL	30	$4.46

In selecting an area of a country for assistance, IFAD determines whether the area is geographically or functionally isolated from the rest of the national economy; the extent to which its population has a lower average per capita income than the national average; the degree to which the area is food-deficient; whether it has relatively inadequate delivery systems and infrastructure in comparison with the rest of the country; and the proportion of poverty—for example, the proportion of landless—in comparison with other rural areas. In terms of impact, IFAD's projects, at full development, will help some 30 million poor rural households out of hunger and poverty.

C. Technical Assistance

IFAD provides grant financing for technical assistance in project preparation, institutional development, agricultural research, training, and other activities which support the fund's activities. The approved technical assistance grant program for 1999 was US$35.5 million; the proposed amount for 2000 was US$36.2 million, the same real level of programming from the previous year, adjusted for projected inflation (by 2%).

BIBLIOGRAPHY

IFAD Annual Report. Published in English, French, Spanish.
IFAD Update. Published twice yearly in English, French, Spanish.
Meeting Challenges in a Changing World.
Near East and North Africa Management Training in Agriculture
Rural Women in IFAD's Projects: The Key to Poverty Alleviation.
Working Together. A multifaceted field collaboration among FAO, IFAD, and WFP.

(IFAD also publishes booklets, brochures, manuals, and periodicals. A complete listing is available on the organization's web site http://www.ifad.org/pub/cat/cat.htm).

THE UNITED NATIONS INDUSTRIAL DEVELOPMENT ORGANIZATION (UNIDO)

BACKGROUND: Industrialization is one of the primary goals of the developing countries, to increase their share of world manufacturing output and decrease their dependence on imported goods and services and on their traditional raw-materials export economies. The United Nations Industrial Development Organization (UNIDO), the newest specialized agency of the UN, seeks to further that goal through its programs of technical cooperation with developing countries, designed to aid in the planning and implementation of industrial projects, the training of personnel in manufacturing and managerial skills, the transfer of technology and the provision of information, and the promotion of investment in industry in developing countries.

CREATION

UNIDO was established by the General Assembly in November 1966 as an autonomous organization within the UN to promote and accelerate the industrialization of developing countries and to coordinate the industrial development activities of the UN system.

The first General Conference of UNIDO was held in Vienna in 1971. The second General Conference, held in Lima in 1975, proposed the conversion of UNIDO into a specialized agency "in order to increase its ability to render assistance to developing countries in the most efficient ways." The conference also adopted the Lima Declaration and Plan of Action, which called for developing countries to reach the target of 25% of world industrial output by the year 2000.

In 1979, a conference of plenipotentiaries, meeting in Vienna, adopted a constitution for UNIDO, to become effective when at least 80 states had ratified it. This was achieved on 21 June 1985, and UNIDO's conversion into a specialized agency became effective on 1 January 1986.

PURPOSES

UNIDO's mandate from the General Assembly is to act as the central coordinating body for industrial activities within the United Nations system and to promote industrial development and cooperation at global, regional, national, and sectoral levels.

In the wake of the reorganization of the activities of the United Nations and its specialized agencies in the early 1990s, UNIDO identified five development objectives that provide a new conceptual framework for the organization's future programs:

- industrial and technological growth and competitiveness;
- human resource development;
- equitable development through industrialization;
- environmentally sustainable industrial development; and
- international cooperation in industrial investment and technology.

By applying its expertise at three levels—policy, institution, and enterprise—UNIDO acts as:

- the central coordinating agency for matters related to industrial development;

- a focal point for industrial technology;
- an honest broker for industrial cooperation;
- a center of excellence on industrial development issues; and
- a global source of industrial information.

MEMBERSHIP

As of 2000, UNIDO had a membership of 168, an increase of 20 countries since 1987. The growth in membership was mainly caused by the emergence of the newly independent nations of Central and Eastern Europe in the wake of the collapse of the Soviet Union. A few of the most industrialized countries chose to withdraw from UNIDO, claiming that the organization is inefficiently operated. In December 1995, the US decided to withdraw, followed by Germany in November 1996 and the United Kingdom in December 1996. The UK and Germany later rejoined, but as of 2000, the United States had not.

STRUCTURE

The four organs of UNIDO are the General Conference, the Industrial Development Board, the program and budget committee, and the secretariat, headed by a Director-General.

General Conference

UNIDO's strategies and policies in regard to industrial development are outlined at its General Conference, which meets every two years and is composed of representatives of all members. Since the organization's inception, the General Conference has met in 1971 (Vienna), 1975 (Lima), 1980 (New Delhi), 1984 (Vienna), 1985 (Vienna—UNIDO's transition to a specialized agency), 1987 (Bangkok), 1989 and 1991 (Vienna), 1993 (Yaoundé), 1995, 1997, and 1999 (Vienna).

Industrial Development Board

The Industrial Development Board consists of 53 members elected by the General Conference for four-year terms. The board reviews the implementation of the work program and the budget and makes recommendations to the General Conference on policy matters, including the appointment of the Director-General, when required. It meets once during General Conference years, and twice in other years.

As of 6 December 1999 the members of the Industrial Development Board were: Algeria, Argentina, Austria, Belarus, Belgium, Bulgaria, Burkina Faso, Chile, China, Colombia, Côte d'Ivoire, Croatia, Cuba, Ecuador, Egypt, Ethiopia, France, Germany, Ghana, Guatemala, India, Indonesia, Iran, Ireland, Italy, Japan, Kuwait, Lesotho, Libyan Arab Jamahiriya, Luxembourg, Madagascar, Mexico, Morocco, Nigeria, Norway, Pakistan, Peru, Poland, Portugal, Republic of Korea, Russian Federation, Saudi Arabia, Spain, Sri Lanka, Sudan, Sweden, Switzerland, Syrian Arab Republic, Thailand, Tunisia, Turkey, United Kingdom, Uruguay.

Program and Budget Committee

The program and budget committee is composed of 27 members elected for two-year terms. Member states meet once a year to assist the board in the preparation and examination of the work program, budget, and other financial matters.

As of 6 December 1999 the members were: Angola, Argentina, Austria, China, Côte d'Ivoire, Cuba, Ecuador, Egypt, France, Germany, Greece, Hungary, India, Italy, Japan, Democratic People's Republic of Korea, Mexico, Nigeria, Philippines, Russian Federation, Saudi Arabia, Slovakia, Sudan, Sweden, Tunisia, Turkey, United Kingdom.

Director-General and Secretariat

The Director-General of UNIDO, elected by the General Conference on 5 December 1997 for a four-year term was Carlos Alfredo Magariños of Argentina.

Prior to its conversion into a specialized agency, UNIDO was headed by an executive director appointed by the Secretary-General of the UN. The first two executive directors were Ibrahim Helmi Abdel-Rahman (1967–74) and Abd-El Rahman Khane (1975–85). Domingo L. Siazo, Jr., of the Philippines was the first Director General of UNIDO when it became a specialized agency in 1985. He served as Director General from 1985 to 1993, when he was succeeded by Mauricio de Maria y Campos of Mexico (to 1997).

As of 2000, UNIDO had a professional and staff of 603 at its Vienna headquarters, including engineers, economists, and technology and environment specialists.

Offices

UNIDO is headquartered in Vienna, Austria. It maintains liaison offices at UN headquarters in New York and at the UN office in Geneva. It also operates two "focal point" offices, in Sri Lanka and Ukraine. UNIDO maintains 29 field offices worldwide. UNIDO also runs the Centre for International Industrial Cooperation in the Russian Federation and nine Investment and Technology Promotion Offices (ITPOs)—in Bahrain, China, France, Greece, Italy, Japan, Republic of Korea, Poland, and Slovakia. Financed by the countries in which they are located, the ITPOs promote business contacts between industrialized and developing countries and economies in transition.

BUDGET

The regular program budget for the 2000–01 biennium was us$132.9 million, financed from assessed contributions of member states. Most costs of expert advice, equipment, and other forms of technical assistance, in partnership with and at the request of developing countries, are met by the UNDP, for which UNIDO is an executing agency. Special UNIDO projects use the Industrial Development Fund (IDF), established in 1976 with a "desirable funding level of us$50 million annually." In 1999, project approvals under the IDF amounted to us$22.4 million and trust funds totaled us$14.8 million. Project approvals under the Montreal Protocol program amounted to us$31.9 million. UNIDO annually awards about 200 contracts valued at about us$20 million. Spending on training in the form of fellowships,

study tours, and group training annually amounts to about us$14 million.

ACTIVITIES

Thirty-two integrated program were formulated and approved as of 31 December 1999, while 14 were being finalized or were under development, and ten more were foreseen for 2000.

A. Technical Cooperation

In 1999, UNIDO provided us$83.5 million worth of technical assistance. The 1999 amount was distributed as follows:

DISTRIBUTION BY GEOGRAPHICAL AREA	SHARE OF TOTAL (PERCENT)
Asia and the Pacific	39
Africa	18
Arab States (including the African Arab States)	9
Latin America and the Caribbean	11
Europe and Newly Independent States	7
Interregional and global	16

DISTRIBUTION BY PRODUCT COMPONENT	SHARE OF TOTAL (PERCENT)
Project personnel (experts)	65.4
Equipment	9.0
Fellowships and training	8.3
Subcontracts	12.4
Miscellaneous	4.8

UNIDO's objectives in technical cooperation are the following:

1. To elaborate programs and projects for the industrial development of developing countries, including special measures for the least developed countries;
2. To formulate policies and strategies for the development of UNIDO's operational activities, from different sources of finance and with particular focus on the country, subregion, and region concerned;
3. To prepare technical cooperation programs and formulate specific projects, in collaboration with other UN bodies and with governments, as well as through participation in round-table meetings or consultative groups;
4. To help improve the effectiveness of technical cooperation programs by assessing the progress made and the results achieved by projects at intermediate and final stages and by feeding back into the programming process the results of their impact; and
5. To maintain a program of UNIDO country directors that enhances the services rendered to the developing countries.

In seeking to industrialize their economies, developing countries face a wide spectrum of problems, ranging from preparation of national plans, development of sectoral programs, and elaboration of appropriate policies and strategies of industrial development, to concerns relating to the technical processes to be employed in manufacturing any specific product, preparation of preinvestment studies, organization of production facilities, training of personnel in new skills, management of factory operations, and establishment of an industrial infrastructure to support industrial enterprises and to mobilize financial resources for investment in industrial production.

UNIDO assists in addressing these problems by in-depth studies on specific priority problems of industrialization in particular countries, with consideration given to important concerns, such as the rehabilitation of troubled industries, international cooperation for small- and medium-sized industry development, institutional development for technology transfer and adaptation, and technical cooperation among developing countries.

UNIDO also works to increase the resources available for technical cooperation purposes, working with traditional as well

Members of UNIDO
(as of 2000)

Afghanistan	Chad	Germany	Lebanon	Pakistan	Switzerland
Albania	Chile	Ghana	Lesotho	Panama	Syrian Arab Republic
Algeria	China	Greece	Liberia	Papua New Guinea	Tajikistan
Angola	Colombia	Grenada	Libyan Arab	Paraguay	Tanzania, United
Argentina	Comoros	Guatemala	Jamahiriya	Peru	Republic of
Armenia	Congo	Guinea	Lithuania	Philippines	Thailand
Austria	Congo, Democratic	Guinea-Bissau	Luxembourg	Poland	The Former Yugoslav
Azerbaijan	Republic of the	Guyana	Madagascar	Portugal	Republic of
Bahamas	Costa Rica	Haiti	Malawi	Qatar	Macedonia
Bahrain	Côte d'Ivoire	Honduras	Malaysia	Romania	Togo
Bangladesh	Croatia	Hungary	Maldives	Russian Federation	Tonga
Barbados	Cuba	India	Mali	Rwanda	Trinidad and Tobago
Belarus	Cyprus	Indonesia	Malta	Sao Tome and Principe	Tunisia
Belgium	Czech Republic	Iran	Mauritania	Saudi Arabia	Turkey
Belize	Denmark	Iraq	Mauritius	Senegal	Turkmenistan
Benin	Djibouti	Ireland	Mexico	Seychelles	Uganda
Bhutan	Dominica	Israel	Moldova, Republic of	Sierra Leone	Ukraine
Bolivia	Dominican Republic	Italy	Mongolia	Slovakia	United Arab Emirates
Bosnia and	Ecuador	Jamaica	Morocco	Slovenia	United Kingdom
Herzegovina	Egypt	Japan	Mozambique	Somalia	Uruguay
Botswana	El Salvador	Jordan	Myanmar	Spain	Uzbekistan
Brazil	Equatorial Guinea	Kazakhstan	Namibia	Sri Lanka	Vanuatu
Bulgaria	Eritrea	Kenya	Nepal	St. Kitts and Nevis	Venezuela
Burkina Faso	Ethiopia	Korea, Democratic	Netherlands	St. Lucia	Vietnam
Burundi	Fiji	People's Republic of	New Zealand	St. Vincent and the	Yemen
Cambodia	Finland	Korea, Republic of	Nicaragua	Grenadines	Yugoslavia
Cameroon	France	Kuwait	Niger	Sudan	Zambia
Cape Verde	Gabon	Kyrgyzstan	Nigeria	Suriname	Zimbabwe
Central African	Gambia	Lao People's	Norway	Swaziland	
Republic	Georgia	Democratic Republic	Oman	Sweden	

as new funding sources, such as trust funds under which the developing countries themselves finance UNIDO technical assistance projects, and mobilizing the support of nongovernmental organizations.

Industrial Operations Technology
A common problem of developing countries is how best to exploit their natural resources and other comparative advantages in order to ensure a worthwhile share for themselves in world production and trade in manufactured products, including replacement of imported industrial products with locally manufactured ones. In order to increase industrial production in developing countries, UNIDO assists them, through the implementation of technical cooperation projects, in acquiring the technological base and know-how that will enable them to establish, expand, rehabilitate, and improve the efficiency and productivity of industrial facilities in the main branches of industry. It provides this help through direct assistance to manufacturing enterprises or through the establishment or strengthening of specialized technology centers servicing individual industrial sectors.

UNIDO also extends assistance in the efficient utilization of energy resources by industry, in the industrial-scale production of fuel and feedstock from renewable resources, and in promoting environmentally sustainable industrial development. Continued attention is given to the establishment of pilot and demonstration plants to accelerate the utilization of locally available raw materials, including industrial and agricultural wastes. Particular attention is given to technical assistance in chemical industries and in the production of capital goods, including equipment for telecommunications and transportation, especially in support of rural development and in the manufacture of pesticides, fertilizers, and agricultural equipment.

Industrial Institutions and Services
In order to increase industrial production, developing countries have to make extensive use of planning techniques and preinvestment studies and also need to establish and strengthen institutional infrastructures and support services and the skills required to set up and operate manufacturing enterprises. Institutional infrastructures are particularly critical in order to compensate, at least in part, for the absence of a long tradition of industrial development in most developing countries. There is a continuous demand for the establishment or strengthening of institutions dealing with standardization and quality control, industrial research, small-scale industries, and rural development. The lack of production, managerial, and entrepreneurial skills is frequently the greatest obstacle to industrial development.

Through its technical cooperation programs, UNIDO seeks to assist developing countries, particularly in the development of human resources, by identifying priority areas for industrial training and for the establishment of national institutes for research and development and for training and consultancy that may become centers for training of personnel, including training in management and in the preparation of preinvestment studies, project implementation, and operation of industrial enterprises. UNIDO extends assistance through fellowships, study tours, and group training programs.

B. Investment Promotion
Another major focus of UNIDO activities is the acceleration of investment in the private and public sectors of developing countries, in a manner consistent with their national plans and policies, and through the implementation of technical cooperation projects in the field of industrial investment.

Although there is a need for a massive flow of financial and technical resources from outside sources to implement projects necessary to achieve the targets of industrial growth laid down in the plans of developing countries, the lack of sound and well-prepared investment projects backed by suitable entrepreneurs has been a more serious obstacle to the flow of these needed resources than the lack of investment funds. Information is scarce regarding the sources of financing and the identification of enterprises that are suitable and willing to participate in manufacturing projects in developing countries or to redeploy their industrial plants to developing countries. At the same time, there is often a lack of awareness among development finance institutions and entrepreneurs in industrialized and selected developing countries of the possibilities for cooperation with project sponsors in developing countries.

UNIDO seeks to stimulate industrial development in developing countries by promoting cooperation between industrialists in both developed and developing countries in the generation, formulation, and promotion of investment projects through investment promotion services, access to information stored in computer data banks, and links with international, regional, subregional, and national development finance institutions.

UNIDO's Investment Promotion Resources Information System contains thousands of records on industrial investment project proposals, potential partners, development finance institutions, investment-related institutions, and project sponsors. UNIDO also maintains investment service offices in Athens, Vienna, Paris, Cologne, Seoul, Tokyo, Zurich, Warsaw, Washington, and Milan, which serve as a direct link to businesses and governments in developing countries and can be the "eyes and ears" of firms in industrialized countries interested in investment opportunities in developing countries.

C. Information and Consultations

Through its Industrial and Technological Information Bank, UNIDO seeks to accelerate the flow of information to developing countries, many of which lack access to such information and to technological trends and advances. It also assists in advancing the capacities of developing countries for acquisition of technology through workshops and advisory services and through its System of Consultations. At both the regional and interregional levels, UNIDO's System of Consultations is an instrument in promoting industrial cooperation among developing countries.

BIBLIOGRAPHY

UNIDO Annual Report. Also available as pdf files at UNIDO's web site.)

Industry and Development Global Report. Annual.

Industrial Development Reviews. Primary source of information on UNIDO activities in developing countries.

UNIDO Database of Industrial Statistics.

Industrial Development Abstracts Database.

THE WORLD TRADE ORGANIZATION (WTO)

BACKGROUND: The World Trade Organization (WTO) was established on 1 January 1995 as the legal and institutional foundation of the multilateral trading system. It provides the principal contractual obligations determining how governments frame and implement domestic trade legislation and regulations. And it is the platform on which trade relations among countries evolve through collective debate, negotiation and adjudication. The WTO is the embodiment of the results of the Uruguay Round trade negotiations and the successor to the General Agreement on Tariffs and Trade (GATT).

CREATION

The origin of the WTO can be traced back to the creation of the International Trade Organization at the 1944 Bretton Woods' Conference. While the terms of the ITO charter were being drafted and debated (a process which began in February of 1946 and lasted until their a final draft was produced in March 1948) and countries pondered whether they would join the organization, representatives from a group of 17 nations assembled in Geneva and concluded an interim agreement (GATT) to lower trade barriers and tariffs among themselves. The agreement, which was to take effect on 1 January 1948, was not meant to be a permanent trade body but rather a stopgap agreement to serve until the time that the ITO would be put in place.

However, when the Truman Administration decided not to submit the charter creating the ITO to the US Senate for ratification (since there were not enough votes in the Senate in favor of ratification) the plan to create the ITO was abandoned leaving the GATT Treaty in its place.

While the GATT functioned well enough, the leading members wished to replace it with a world-wide trade-regulating body like the WTO for a number of reasons. First, the GATT rules applied to trade only in merchandise goods. In addition to goods, the WTO covers trade in services and trade-related aspects of intellectual property (through the agreement on Trade-related Aspects of Intellectual Property Rights—TRIPs). Second, while GATT was a multilateral instrument, by the 1980s many new agreements of a plurilateral, and therefore selective nature had been added. The agreements which constitute the WTO are almost all multilateral and, thus, involve commitments for the entire membership. Third, The WTO dispute settlement system is faster, more automatic, and thus much less susceptible to blockages, than the old GATT system.

But beyond these practical and functional reasons for establishing the WTO, there were also more philosophical and symbolic reasons. The GATT was a set of rules, a multilateral agreement, with no institutional foundation, only a small associated secretariat which had its origins in the attempt to establish an International Trade Organization in the 1940s. By contrast, the WTO is a permanent institution with its own secretariat. Moreover, the GATT was applied on a "provisional basis" even if, after more than forty years, governments chose to treat it as a permanent commitment while the WTO commitments are fully and functionally permanent.

For the above reasons, the creation of a new, permanent trade body became one of the principal objectives about half-way through the GATT's Uruguay round, which ran from 1986 to 1994. A draft for the new international trade body, the WTO, was drafted and formally approved at the Ministerial Conference held in the ancient trade center of Marrakesh in July of 1994. Under the terms of the so-called "Final Act" signed there, the GATT was replaced by the WTO on 1 January 1995.

The Preamble of the Agreement Establishing the WTO states that members should conduct their trade and economic relations with a view to "raising standards of living, ensuring full employment and a large and steadily growing volume of real income and effective demand, and expanding the production of and trade in goods and services, while allowing for the optimal use of the world's resources in accordance with the objective of sustainable development, seeking both to protect and preserve the environment and to enhance the means for doing so in a manner consistent with their respective needs and concerns at different levels of development."

Furthermore, members recognize the "need for positive efforts designed to ensure that developing countries, and especially the least-developed among them, secure a share in international trade commensurate with the needs of their economic development."

To contribute to the achievement of these objectives, WTO Members have agreed to enter into "reciprocal and mutually advantageous arrangements directed to the substantial reduction of tariffs and other barriers to trade and to the elimination of discriminatory treatment in international trade relations."

As the successor to GATT, WHO celebrated the golden jubilee of the multilateral trading system in May 1998.

PURPOSES

The fundamental principles of the WTO are:

Trade without discrimination. Under the "most-favored nation" (MFN) clause, members are bound to grant to the products of other members no less favorable treatment than that accorded to the products of any other country. The provision on "national treatment" requires that once goods have entered a market, they must be treated no less favorably than the equivalent domestically-produced good.

Predictable and growing access to markets. While quotas are generally outlawed, tariffs or customs duties are legal in the WTO. Tariff reductions made by over 120 countries in the Uruguay Round are contained in some 22,500 pages of national tariff schedules which are considered an integral part of the WTO. Tariff reductions, for the most part phased in over five years, will result in a 40% cut in industrial countries' tariffs in industrial products from an average of 6.3% to 3.8%. The Round also increased the percentage of bound product lines to nearly 100%

for developed nations and countries in transition and to 73% for developing countries. Members have also undertaken an initial set of commitments covering national regulations affecting various services activities. These commitments are, like those for tariffs, contained in binding national schedules.

Promoting fair competition. The WTO extends and clarifies previous GATT rules that laid down the basis on which governments could impose compensating duties on two forms of "unfair" competition: dumping and subsidies. The WTO Agreement on agriculture is designed to provide increased fairness in farm trade. An agreement on intellectual property will improve conditions of competition where ideas and inventions are involved, and another will do the same thing for trade in services.

Encouraging development and economic reform. GATT provisions intended to favor developing countries are maintained in the WTO, in particular those encouraging industrial countries to assist trade of developing nations. Developing countries are given transition periods to adjust to the more difficult WTO provisions. Least-developed countries are given even more flexibility and benefit from accelerated implementation of market access concessions for their goods.

MEMBERSHIP

As of April 2000, there were 136 member nations of the WTO. There were 35 observer countries at this time, 30 of which had applied to join the WTO. All GATT signatory nations who signed the Final Act of the Uruguay Round in Marrakesh in July of 1994 automatically became original members of the WTO. In addition, several other countries who joined the GATT later in 1994 and signed the Final Act of the Uruguay Round and became original WTO members. When the WTO became effective on 1 January 1995, there were 76 original WTO members and another 50 nations at various stages in the membership process.

Aside from the original WTO members, any nation or "customs territory" having full autonomy in the conduct of its trade policies may accede to the WTO on terms agreed with WTO members. The process of a nonmember nation joining the WTO takes place in several stages. In the first stage of the accession procedures the applicant government is required to provide the WTO with a memorandum covering all aspects of its trade and economic policies having a bearing on WTO agreements. This memorandum becomes the basis for a detailed examination of the accession request in a working party.

Alongside the working party's efforts, the applicant government engages in bilateral negotiations with interested member governments to establish its concessions and commitments on goods and its commitments on services. This bilateral process, among other things, determines the specific benefits for WTO members in permitting the applicant to accede. Once both the examination of the applicant's trade regime and market access negotiations are complete, the working party draws up basic terms of accession.

Finally, the results of the working party's deliberations contained in its report, a draft protocol of accession, and the agreed schedules resulting from the bilateral negotiations are presented to the General Council or the Ministerial Conference for adoption. If a two-thirds majority of WTO members vote in favor, the applicant is free to sign the protocol and to accede to the Organization; when necessary, after ratification in its national parliament or legislature.

After becoming a member, many countries are represented in the WTO by permanent diplomatic missions in Geneva usually headed by a special Ambassador.

As a result of regional economic integration—in the form of customs unions and free trade areas—and looser political and geographic arrangements, some groups of countries act together in the WTO with a single spokesperson in meetings and negotiations.

The largest and most comprehensive grouping is the European Union and its 15 member states. The EU is a customs union with a single external trade policy and tariff. While the member states coordinate their position in Brussels and Geneva, the European Commission alone speaks for the EU at almost all WTO meetings. The EU is a WTO member in its own right as are each of its member states.

It is important to note that any country can withdraw at any time from the WTO.

STRUCTURE

The highest WTO authority is the Ministerial Conference which meets at least once every two years and is composed of representatives from all WTO signatories. The day-to-day work of the WTO, however, falls to a number of subsidiary bodies, principally the General Council, which is required to report to the Ministerial Conference. The General Council meets several times a year in the Geneva headquarters. Like the Ministerial Conference, the General Council is composed of representatives from all member nations. As well as conducting its regular work on behalf of the Ministerial Conference, the members of the General Council also convene as the Dispute Settlement Body (DSB) and as the Trade Policy Review Body. At the next level are the Goods Council, Services Council and Intellectual Property (TRIPS) Council, which report to the General Council.

Three other bodies are established by the Ministerial Conference and report to the General Council: the Committee on Trade and Development, the Committee on Balance of Payments and the Committee on Budget, Finance and Administration. The General Council formally established, in early 1995, a Committee on Trade and Environment, which presented a report on its work to the first meeting of the WTO Ministerial Conference in Singapore in December 1996. At the second Ministerial Conference in Geneva in 1998, ministers decided that the WTO would also study the area of electronic commerce, a task to be shared by existing councils and committees.

Each of the plurilateral agreements of the WTO—those on civil aircraft, government procurement, dairy products and bovine meat—have their own management bodies which report to the General Council.

The DSB itself also establishes subsidiary bodies for the resolution of trade disputes. One such set of bodies are called "panels." These panels are set up on an ad-hoc basis and last only long enough to hear the merits of a particular trade dispute between WTO members and reach a decision as to whether unfair trade practices are involved. After the DSB approves the formation of a panel, the WTO Secretariat will suggest the names of three potential panelists to the parties to the dispute, drawing as necessary on a list of qualified persons. If there is real difficulty in the choice, the Director-General can appoint the panelists. The panelists serve in their individual capacities and are not subject to government instructions.

The DSB also has the responsibility of establishing an Appellate Body to review decisions made by individual panels. The Appellate Body is modeled after the structure of the U.S. Federal Appeals Courts: the Appellate Body is composed of seven persons, three of which are assigned to each appeal from a panel's judgment. The members of the Appellate Body must be broadly representative of WTO membership, and are required to be persons of recognized standing in the field of law and international trade, and not affiliated with any government. Each member serves a four-year term.

The procedural operation of panels and the Appellate Body are described below under the heading of "Activities."

SECRETARIAT

The WTO Secretariat is located in Geneva. It has around 500 staff and is headed by a Director-General, and four Deputy Directors-General. Its responsibilities include the servicing of WTO delegate bodies with respect to negotiations and the implementation of agreements. It has a particular responsibility to provide technical support to developing countries, and especially the least-developed countries. WTO economists and statisticians provide trade performance and trade policy analyses while its legal staff assist in the resolution of trade disputes involving the interpretation of WTO rules and precedents. Other Secretariat work is concerned with accession negotiations for new members and providing advice to governments considering membership. Despite the increased responsibilities of the WTO when compared with the GATT, there has been no significant increase in administrative or other staffing levels.

BUDGET

As of 1999, the WTO budget was about 117 million Swiss francs with individual contributions calculated on the basis of shares in the total trade conducted by members. Part of the budget also goes to the International Trade Centre.

ACTIVITIES

A. Reviewing Member Nations' Trade Policies

Surveillance of the national trade policies of WTO member nations is a fundamentally important activity running throughout the work of the WTO. At the center of this work is the Trade Policy Review Mechanism (TPRM).

Reviews are conducted on a regular, periodic basis. The four biggest traders—the European Union, the United States, Japan and Canada—are examined approximately once every two years. The next 16 countries in terms of their share of world trade are reviewed every four years; and the remaining countries every six years, with the possibility of a longer interim period for the least-developed countries.

The review examines the overall trading practices of a WTO member rather than focusing on the legal compatibility of any particular trade policy or practice.

Reviews are conducted in the Trade Policy Review Body (TPRB)—established at the same level as the General Council. The TPRB conducts its review through the use of two documents: a policy statement prepared by the government under review, and a detailed report prepared independently by the WTO Secretariat. These two reports, together with the proceedings of the TPRB are published after the review meeting.

In addition to the TPRM, many other WTO agreements contain obligations for member governments to notify the WTO Secretariat of new or modified trade measures. For example, details of any new anti-dumping or countervailing legislation, new technical standards affecting trade, changes to regulations affecting trade in services, and laws or regulations concerning the TRIPs agreement all have to be notified to the appropriate body of the WTO. Special groups are also established to examine new free-trade arrangements (e.g. regional trade associations like NAFTA—The North American Free Trade Agreement) and the trade policies of acceding countries.

In 2000, new talks were slated to begin on agriculture and services.

B. Settling Trade Disputes

The WTO also functions to settle trade disputes between member nations. Indeed, one of the goals of the WTO is to dissuade members from taking unilateral action against perceived violations of the trade rules and to instead seek recourse in the multilateral dispute settlement system and to abide by its rules and findings.

Unlike the situation in a TPRM review, where a nation's overall trade policy is examined, a trade dispute between member nations usually involves the legality of a particular trade policy or practice. Which one member nation, the complainant, has called into question.

When any such trade dispute arises, the nations party to the dispute first engage in bilateral meetings between themselves (usually conducted by the nations' respective representatives in Geneva). If this fails the WTO Director-General, who, acting in an *ex officio* capacity, will try conciliation or mediation to settle the dispute.

If consultations and mediation fail to arrive at a solution after 60 days, the complainant can ask the Dispute Settlement Body (DSB) to establish a panel to examine the case. Generally, the DSB cannot refuse to establish a panel and must constitute the panel within 30 days of its establishment.

Each party to the dispute submits to the panel a brief on the facts and arguments in the case, in advance of the first substantive meeting. At that first meeting, the complainant presents its case and the responding party its defense. Third parties which notified their interest in the dispute may also present views. Formal rebuttals are made at the second substantive meeting.

The panel then submits an interim report, including its findings and conclusions, to the parties, giving them one week to request a review. The period of review is not to exceed two weeks, during which the panel may hold additional meetings with the parties. A final report is submitted to the parties and three weeks later, it is circulated to all WTO members.

If the panel decides that the measure in question is inconsistent with the terms of the relevant WTO agreement, the panel recommends that the member concerned bring the measure into conformity with that agreement. It may also suggest ways in which the member could implement the recommendation. Panel reports are adopted by the DSB 60 days after being issued, unless one party notifies its decision to appeal or a consensus emerges against the adoption of the report.

The WTO dispute settlement mechanism gives the possibility of appeal to either party in a panel proceeding. However, any such appeal must be limited to issues of law covered in the panel report and the legal interpretation developed by the panel. Appeals are heard by the standing Appellate Body established by the DSB.

An Appellate Body can uphold, modify or reverse the legal findings and conclusions of the panel. As a general rule, the appeal proceedings are not to exceed 60 days but in no case shall they exceed 90 days.

Thirty days after it is issued, the DSB adopts the report of the Appellate Body which is unconditionally accepted by the parties to the dispute—unless there is a consensus against its adoption.

After the DSB adopts the report of the panel or the Appellate Body, the DSB has the responsibility of implementing the decision. At a DSB meeting held within 30 days of the adoption of the panel or appellate report, the party against whom the panel or the Appellate Body has ruled, must state its intentions in respect of the implementation of the recommendations. If it is impractical to comply immediately, the member will be given a grace period (set by the DSB) to come into compliance. If it fails to act within this period, it is obliged to enter into negotiations with the complainant in order to determine a mutually-acceptable compensation—for instance, tariff reductions in areas of particular interest to the complainant.

If after 20 days, no satisfactory compensation is agreed, the complainant may request authorization from the DSB to suspend concessions or obligations against the other party. The DSB should grant this authorization within 30 days of the expiration of the grace period established by the DSB.

There is a peculiar component of the WTO structure, the

Member Nations
Nation / Date of Membership

Angola	1 December 1996	Germany	1 January 1995	Nicaragua	3 September 1995
Antigua and Barbuda	1 January 1995	Ghana	1 January 1995	Niger	13 December 1996
Argentina	1 January 1995	Greece	1 January 1995	Nigeria	1 January 1995
Australia	1 January 1995	Grenada	22 February 1996	Norway	1 January 1995
Austria	1 January 1995	Guatemala	21 July 1995	Pakistan	1 January 1995
Bahrain	1 January 1995	Guinea Bissau	31 May 1995	Panama	6 September 1997
Bangladesh	1 January 1995	Guinea	25 October 1995	Papua New Guinea	9 June 1996
Barbados	1 January 1995	Guyana	1 January 1995	Paraguay	1 January 1995
Belgium	1 January 1995	Haiti	30 January 1996	Peru	1 January 1995
Belize	1 January 1995	Honduras	1 January 1995	Philippines	1 January 1995
Benin	22 February 1996	Hong Kong, China	1 January 1995	Poland	1 July 1995
Bolivia	13 September 1995	Hungary	1 January 1995	Portugal	1 January 1995
Botswana	31 May 1995	Iceland	1 January 1995	Qatar	13 January 1996
Brazil	1 January 1995	India	1 January 1995	Romania	1 January 1995
Brunei Darussalam	1 January 1995	Indonesia	1 January 1995	Rwanda	22 May 1996
Bulgaria	1 December 1996	Ireland	1 January 1995	Saint Kitts and Nevis	21 February 1996
Burkina Faso	3 June 1995	Israel	21 April 1995	Saint Lucia	1 January 1995
Burundi	23 July 1995	Italy	1 January 1995	Saint Vincent and	
Cameroon	13 December 1995	Jamaica	9 March 1995	the Grenadines	1 January 1995
Canada	1 January 1995	Japan	1 January 1995	Senegal	1 January 1995
Central African Republic	31 May 1995	Jordan	11 April 2000	Sierra Leone	23 July 1995
Chad	19 October 1996	Kenya	1 January 1995	Singapore	1 January 1995
Chile	1 January 1995	Korea	1 January 1995	Slovak Republic	1 January 1995
Colombia	30 April 1995	Kuwait	1 January 1995	Slovenia	30 July 1995
Congo	27 March 1997	Kyrgyz Republic	20 December 1998	Solomon Islands	26 July 1996
Costa Rica	1 January 1995	Latvia	10 February 1999	South Africa	1 January 1995
Côte d'Ivoire	1 January 1995	Lesotho	31 May 1995	Spain	1 January 1995
Cuba	20 April 1995	Liechtenstein	1 September 1995	Sri Lanka	1 January 1995
Cyprus	30 July 1995	Luxembourg	1 January 1995	Suriname	1 January 1995
Czech Republic	1 January 1995	Macau, China	1 January 1995	Swaziland	1 January 1995
Democratic Republic		Madagascar	17 November 1995	Sweden	1 January 1995
of the Congo	1 January 1997	Malawi	31 May 1995	Switzerland	1 July 1995
Denmark	1 January 1995	Malaysia	1 January 1995	Tanzania	1 January 1995
Djibouti	31 May 1995	Maldives	31 May 1995	Thailand	1 January 1995
Dominica	1 January 1995	Mali	31 May 1995	Togo	31 May 1995
Dominican Republic	9 March 1995	Malta	1 January 1995	Trinidad and Tobago	1 March 1995
Ecuador	21 January 1996	Mauritania	31 May 1995	Tunisia	29 March 1995
Egypt	30 June 1995	Mauritius	1 January 1995	Turkey	26 March 1995
El Salvador	7 May 1995	Mexico	1 January 1995	Uganda	1 January 1995
Estonia	13 November 1999	Mongolia	29 January 1997	United Arab Emirates	10 April 1996
European Communities	1 January 1995	Morocco	1 January 1995	United Kingdom	1 January 1995
Fiji	14 January 1996	Mozambique	26 August 1995	United States	1 January 1995
Finland	1 January 1995	Myanmar	1 January 1995	Uruguay	1 January 1995
France	1 January 1995	Namibia	1 January 1995	Venezuela	1 January 1995
Gabon	1 January 1995	Netherlands	1 January 1995	Zambia	1 January 1995
Gambia	23 October 1996	New Zealand	1 January 1995	Zimbabwe	3 March 1995

Dispute Settlement Review Commission, that applies solely to the United States. The commission is composed of five appellate judges and is activated whenever a panel decision is made against the US. The commission analyzes the decision to determine whether it was unjustified, that is whether the panel exceeded its authority in making the decision or whether the panel went beyond the powers in the Uruguay round in making the decision. If the commission determines that three unjustified decisions occurred within any five year period a member of Congress can begin the process of removing the US from the WTO. It should be noted that since any member can withdraw at any time from the WTO, the existence of this commission does not explicitly enhance US power in the WTO. It was created primarily as a mechanism to assure the US Congress that the WTO would monitor itself against any anti-US bias and in fact the commission was established within the WTO to secure the support of Senator Robert Dole for US entry into the WTO.

C. Training and Technical Instruction to Developing Countries
The WTO Secretariat has also continued GATT's program of training courses. These take place in Geneva twice a year for officials of developing countries. Since their inception in 1955 and up to the end of 1994, the courses have been attended by nearly 1400 trade officials from 125 countries and 10 regional organizations. Beginning in 1991, special courses have been held each year in Geneva for officials from the former centrally-planned economies in transition to market economies.

The WTO Secretariat, alone or in cooperation with other international organizations, conducts missions and seminars and provides specific, practical technical cooperation for governments and their officials dealing with accession negotiations, implementing WTO commitments or seeking to participate effectively in multilateral negotiations. Courses and individual assistance is given on particular WTO activities including dispute settlement and trade policy reviews. Moreover, developing countries, especially the least-developed among them, are helped with trade and tariff data relating to their own export interests and to their participation in WTO bodies.

The WTO continues the GATT's participation in operating the International Trade Centre (which it operates jointly with World Bank's Economic Development Institute). The Centre responds to requests from developing countries for assistance in formulating and implementing export promotion programs as well as import operations and techniques. It provides information and advice on export markets and marketing techniques, and assists in establishing export promotion and marketing services and in training personnel required for these services. The Centre's help is freely available to the least-developed countries. Since the beginning, GATT/WHO has trained more than 1,700 officials from developing countries.

D. Participation in Global Economic Policy-Making

An important aspect of the WTO's mandate is to cooperate with the International Monetary Fund, the World Bank and other multilateral institutions to achieve greater coherence in global economic policy-making.

Although the original agenda (established at a GATT meeting in Punta del Este, Uruguay in 1986) made no mention of a world trade body, a draft for such an organization was put forth in 1991 and quickly gained interest among many members for establishing such an organization.

BIBLIOGRAPHY

Dispute Settlement Reports.

From GATT to the WTO: The Multilateral Trading System in the New Millennium, edited by the WTO Secretariat.

Reshaping the World Trading System, second edition.

WTO Agreement Series.

WTO Annual Report.

(A full listing of publications is available on the WTO web site http://www.wto.org/wto/publicat/publicat.htm.)

THE INTERNATIONAL MONETARY FUND (IMF)

BACKGROUND: The 1930s was a period not only of great political upheaval but also of grave financial and economic difficulty. The gold standard was largely abandoned, and currency exchange rates fluctuated wildly. Economic chaos was aggravated by a lack of coordination between governments that imposed controls on international financial transactions and engaged in ruthless economic warfare.

During World War II, most countries realized that they would emerge from the conflict with depleted economic resources just when they would have to confront a reconstruction effort of staggering dimensions. It was also known that the United Kingdom would emerge from the war as the world's principal debtor nation and the United States, whose productive capacity had greatly increased during the war, as the world's principal creditor nation.

CREATION

The United Kingdom, the United States, and their allies were convinced that international economic and financial cooperation through intergovernmental institutions was required to prevent a more serious recurrence of the economic and monetary chaos of the 1930s. Two plans were proposed almost simultaneously in 1943: a United States plan for an International Stabilization Fund, referred to as the White plan, after H. D. White, then assistant to the United States secretary of the treasury; and a British plan for an International Clearing Union, referred to as the Keynes plan, after the British economist John Maynard Keynes. Both plans called for international machinery to stabilize currencies and—a radical innovation—a prohibition against altering exchange rates beyond narrow limits without international approval. Both would have introduced a new international currency unit defined in terms of gold. The American plan called for participating nations to contribute to a relatively limited stabilization fund of about $5 billion, on which they would be permitted to draw in order to bridge balance-of-payments deficits. The British plan would have established a system of international clearing accounts, under which each member country could borrow up to its own quota limit, while its creditors would be credited with corresponding amounts, expressed in international currency units. Both plans were discussed with financial experts of other powers, including the Republic of China, the French Committee for Liberation, and the USSR. The International Monetary Fund as finally constituted resembled the United States-suggested stabilization fund. The proposal to establish a new international monetary unit was deferred for the time being.

The Bretton Woods Conference

A conference called by President Franklin D. Roosevelt and attended by delegates from all 44 United and Associated Nations was held from 1 to 22 July 1944 at Bretton Woods, New Hampshire. The Bretton Woods Conference produced the constitutions, or Articles of Agreement, of two agencies conceived as sister institutions: the International Monetary Fund (IMF) and the International Bank for Reconstruction and Development (IBRD).

The IMF came into existence on 27 December 1945, when 29 governments, responsible for 80% of the quotas to be contributed to the Fund, signed the IMF Articles of Agreement. An agreement with the UN, under which the IMF became a specialized agency, entered into force on 15 November 1947.

PURPOSES

The purposes of the IMF are the following:

1. to promote international monetary cooperation;
2. to facilitate the expansion and balanced growth of international trade and contribute thereby to the promotion and maintenance of high levels of employment and real income;
3. to promote exchange stability, maintain orderly exchange arrangements among member states, and avoid competitive currency depreciations;
4. to assist in establishing a multilateral system of payments of current transactions among members and in eliminating foreign-exchange restrictions that hamper world trade; and
5. to alleviate serious disequilibrium in the international balance of payments of members by making the resources of the Fund available under adequate safeguards, so as to prevent the members from resorting to measures that endanger national or international prosperity.

MEMBERSHIP

The original members of the IMF were the 29 nations whose governments had ratified the Articles of Agreement by 27 December 1945. Any other state, whether or not a member of the UN, may become a member of the IMF in accordance with terms prescribed by the Board of Governors. The IMF had 181 members as of 18 May 2000. (See membership list at the end of this section.) Membership in the IMF is a prerequisite to membership in the IBRD. A member may withdraw from the IMF at any time, and its withdrawal becomes effective on the day that a written notice to that effect is received by the Fund.

If a member state fails to fulfill its obligations under the IMF Articles of Agreement, the Fund may declare that country ineligible to use its resources. If, after a reasonable period has elapsed, the member state persists in its failure to live up to its obligations, the Board of Governors may require it to withdraw from membership.

The Third Amendment of the IMF's Articles of Agreement came into force on 11 November 1992. It allows for the suspension of voting and related rights of a member that persists in its failure to fulfill its obligations under the Articles.

STRUCTURE

The Fund has a Board of Governors, composed of as many governors as there are member states; 24 executive directors; and a managing director and staff.

Board of Governors

All powers of the IMF are vested in its Board of Governors, on which all member states are represented. Each member state appoints one governor and one alternate governor, who may vote when the principal governor is absent. A government customarily appoints its minister of finance, the president of its central bank, or another high-ranking official as its governor. For example, in May 2000, the United States governor was Secretary of the Treasury Lawrence H. Summers, and the alternate, Federal Reserve Board Chairman Alan Greenspan.

The principle that applies in most international bodies—one nation, one vote—does not apply in the IMF Board of Governors. Multiple votes are assigned to IMF member states, more votes being assigned to those subscribing larger quotas to the Fund's resources. Each member has 250 votes plus 1 additional vote for each SDR 100,000 of its quota. (The SDR is an international reserve asset created by the Fund. See section F.) The total number of votes of all IMF members was 2,142,907 on 18 May 2000, of which the United States held about 17.3%, Germany and Japan about 6% each, and the United Kingdom and France about 5% each.

Each governor is entitled to cast all the votes allotted to his country as a unit. On certain matters, however, voting power varies according to the use made of the Fund's resources by the respective member. IMF decisions are made by a simple majority of the votes cast, unless otherwise stipulated in the constitution. The Board of Governors regularly meets once a year. It may also be convened for other than annual meetings.

Except for such basic matters as admission of new members, quota changes, and the like, the Board of Governors delegates most of its powers to the Executive Directors of the Fund.

The Board of Governors has an advisory committee, the International Monetary and Financial Committee (IMFC), formerly known as the Interim Committee, which meets twice a year. Its composition reflects that of the Executive Board; each country that appoints, and each group that elects, an Executive Director, also appoints a member to the IMFC. These members are governors of the Fund, ministers, or others of comparable rank.

Executive Board

The 24 executive directors (and 24 alternates) of the IMF are responsible for the Fund's general operations, and for this purpose they exercise all the powers delegated to them by the Board of Governors. They "function in continuous session" at the Fund's headquarters and meet as often as business may require, usually several times a week.

Of the 24 executive directors, five are appointed by the countries having the largest quotas (United States, Japan, Germany, France, and the United Kingdom), and the other 19 are elected by regional groups of the remaining members. The IMF's managing director also serves as chairman of the Executive Board.

Managing Director and Staff

The managing director, who is chosen by the executive directors, is responsible for the conduct of the ordinary business of the Fund. He is appointed for a five-year term and may not serve concurrently as a governor or executive director of the IMF. The managing director chairs meetings of the executive directors but may vote only in case of a tie.

The permanent headquarters of the IMF are at 700 19th Street, N.W., Washington, DC 20431. As of 1 May 1999, the staff consisted of about 2,700 persons from 123 countries.

The IMF has a regional office for Asia and the Pacific, located in Tokyo.

BUDGETS

The approved administrative budget for the fiscal year ending 30 April 2000 was $575.8 million and a capital project budget of $47.3 million. The Fund's income considerably exceeds its administrative expenditures. This income is derived principally from charges on the Fund's transactions.

ACTIVITIES

A. Resources of the IMF

The Fund obtains its necessary financial resources from the accumulated subscriptions made by its members. How much a member government subscribes to the Fund's resources is determined by the quota assigned to that country. As mentioned above, the quota also determines the country's voting strength in the IMF. Furthermore, the quota, which is expressed in SDRs, determines the amounts that the country may draw from the Fund's currency pool, as well as the country's allocations of SDRs.

In determining a member's quota, the IMF considers relevant economic data, including the country's national income, its international reserves, and the volume of its imports and exports.

The method of payment for initial quota subscriptions or increases in quotas was modified when the Second Amendment to the Articles of Agreement went into effect in 1978. Under the original Articles, members were required to pay 25% of their quota in gold and the remainder in their own currencies. Following the Second Amendment, an amount not exceeding 25% of new members' initial quotas, or existing members' increases in quotas, is paid in reserve assets, while the remainder is paid in the members' own currencies.

The Fund is required by its constitution to review its members' quotas at regular intervals of not more than five years and to propose called-for adjustments in quotas. A member may also at any time request an adjustment of its own quota. All quota changes must be approved by an 85% majority of the total voting power.

Several reviews of the adequacy of members' quotas have led to general and selective increases of Fund quotas. A special review in 1958/59 resulted in a 60.7% increase in quotas, which was followed by a 30.7% general increase in 1965 and a further 35.4% general increase in 1970. The 1976 review of quotas was affected by developments in the international monetary system, including the quadrupling of oil prices. As a result of that review, total quotas were increased by 33.6%, to SDR 39 billion, reflecting a doubling of the collective share in total quotas of the major oil-exporting countries. The share of all other developing countries was maintained at its then existing level. The 1978 review provided for a 50.9% general quota increase for most members and additional special increases for 11 members. Consents to increases under this review raised total quotas to SDR 59.6 billion. The 1983 review increased quotas by 47.5%, to SDR 90 billion, and the quotas increased by 50.0% in November 1992 as a result of the Ninth General Review (in 1990).

The Tenth General Review in 1995 did not result in an increase. As of September 1996, total quotas amounted to SDR 145.3 billion (about US$210 billion). In September 1997, the IMF's Executive Board concluded the Eleventh General Review, which resulted in an agreement on an overall increase in quotas of 45%, to SDR 210 billion (about US$283 billion). The IMF stated that the increase reflected changes in the size of the world economy, the scale of potential payments imbalances, and the rapid globalization and liberalization of trade and payments. The quota increase became effective in January 1999.

The Fund is authorized under its Articles to supplement its resources by borrowing. In January 1962, a four-year agreement was concluded with 10 industrial members (the Group of 10)—subsequently joined by Switzerland as an associate and by Saudi Arabia under a special arrangement in 1983—by which they undertook to lend to the Fund to finance drawings by participants of the General Arrangements to Borrow (GAB) "if this should be needed to forestall or cope with an impairment of the international monetary system." These General Arrangements to Borrow have been renewed every four or five years, most recently in December 1997.

On 19 January 1983, the ministers of the Group of 10 agreed in principle to enlarge the GAB to SDR 17 billion, from approximately SDR 6.0 billion, and to permit the Fund to borrow under the enlarged credit arrangements to finance exchange transactions with members that are not GAB participants. In addition, the ministers agreed to authorize Swiss participation in the agreement. The amounts of credit arrangements (in millions of SDRs) are as follows: the United States, 4,250; the Deutsche Bundesbank of Germany, 2,380; Japan, 2,125; France, 1,700; the United Kingdom, 1,700; Saudi Arabia, 1,500; Italy, 1,105; Switzerland, 1,020; Canada, 892.5; the Netherlands, 850; Belgium, 595; and the Riksbank of Sweden, 382.5.

In January 1997, the IMF approved the New Arrangements to Borrow (NAB). The NAB combines with the GAB to provide supplementary resources to the IMF. The amount of the resources available to the IMF under the NAB (which became effective November 1998) and the GAB is SDR 34 billion (about US$46 billion), twice the amount of the GAB alone.

The Fund has also, in the past, supplemented its resources by borrowing, for example, for the oil facility for 1974 and 1975 and for the supplementary financing facility, whose resources of SDR 7,784 billion were borrowed from 14 members or institutions.

B. General Obligations of IMF Members

The economic philosophy of the Bretton Woods Agreement holds that monetary stability and cooperation and the unhampered movement of money, especially in payment of current international transactions, will promote national and international prosperity. This principle is reflected in certain general obligations that countries undertake by accepting the IMF's Articles of Agreement. The Articles favor stabilization measures to help overcome short-term balance-of-payments difficulties, and they discourage exchange controls under normal conditions. The Agreement also enables the Fund to help governments in short-term payments difficulties.

C. Consultations

Consultations with members are an essential component of the Fund's work and provide a major instrument for Fund surveillance of members' policies in several key areas.

Article IV of the Articles of Agreement, entitled "Obligations Regarding Exchange Arrangements," allows individual members considerable freedom in the selection of their exchange arrangements, but it also stipulates general obligations and specific undertakings.

In order to help the Fund ensure observance of these obligations through the exercise of "firm surveillance" over exchange-rate policies, members are required to consult with the Fund regularly under Article IV, in principle on an annual basis. These consultations provide an opportunity for detailed review of the economic and financial situation and the policies of members from both the national and international viewpoints. They also help the Fund deal expeditiously with members' requests for the use of Fund resources and for proposed changes in policies or practices that are subject to Fund approval. For the individual member, regular consultations provide the occasion for an external appraisal of policies and for discussion of any special difficulties that may arise from the actions of other members.

Members availing themselves of the transitional arrangements permitted under Article XIV of the Articles of Agreement to maintain multiple exchange rates or other restrictions on current international payments are required to consult annually with the Fund. Article VIII countries have accepted the obligation to avoid such practices. Consultations under Article IV include the regular consultations under Article VIII and Article XIV and are required for all members.

Between annual consultations, there is a supplemental surveillance procedure under which the managing director initiates an informal and confidential discussion with a member whenever he thinks that a modification in the member's exchange arrangements or exchange-rate policies or the behavior of the exchange rate of its currency may be important or may have important effects on other members.

Special consultations with selected countries also supplement regular consultations in connection with the periodic reviews of the world economic outlook undertaken by the Executive Board. The purpose of these consultations is to provide up-to-date knowledge of the economic situation in countries whose external policies are regarded as being of major importance to the world economy.

D. Transactions Between the Fund and Its Members
Use of Resources

Members of the Fund may draw on its financial resources to meet their balance-of-payments needs. As of 31 December 1999, the IMF had credits and loans outstanding to 93 countries for an amount of SDR 57.5 billion (or about US$75 billion). Financial assistance is made available under a number of policies and facilities. Member countries may, for example, use the reverse tranche and the credit tranche, or they may receive emergency assistance. The IMF has set up various facilities for specific purposes—the Compensatory and Contingency Financing Facility (CCFF); the Buffer Stock Financing Facility (BSFF); the Extended Fund Facility; and the Structural Adjustment Facility (SAF), which was superceded by the Enhanced Structural Adjustment Facility (ESAF). (For full descriptions of these policies and facilities, see farther on.).

For any drawing, a member is required to indicate to the Fund that the desired purchase is needed to stabilize its balance-of-payments or reserve position or to deal with adverse developments in its reserves.

When a member draws on the Fund, it uses its own currency to purchase the currencies of other member countries or SDRs held by the General Resources Account. Thus, a drawing results in an increase in the Fund's holdings of the purchasing member's currency and a corresponding decrease in the Fund's holdings of other currencies or SDRs that are sold. Within a prescribed time, a member must reverse the transaction (unless it is a reserve tranche purchase; see farther on) by buying back its own currency with SDRs or currencies specified by the Fund. Usually, repurchases are to be made within three to five years after the date of purchase. However, under the extended Fund facility, the period for repurchases is within four and a half to ten years, and under the supplementary financing facility, within three and a half to seven years. In addition, a member is expected normally to repurchase as its balance-of-payments or reserve position improves.

Reserve Tranche. The difference between a member's quota and the Fund's holdings of that member's currency is referred to as the member's reserve tranche. Purchases in the reserve tranche—a reserve asset that can be mobilized by the member with minimum delay—are subject to balance-of-payments need but not to prior challenge, economic policy conditions, or repurchase requirements. This drawing does not constitute a use of IMF credit, as its reserve position is considered part of the member's foreign reserves, and is not subject to an obligation to repay.

Credit Tranche. Credits under regular facilities are made available to members in tranches (segments) of 25% of quota. For first credit tranche drawings, members must demonstrate reasonable efforts to overcome their balance of payments difficulties. Upper credit tranche drawings (over 25%) are normally phased in relation to certain conditions or "performance criteria."

Policy on Emergency Assistance. The IMF provides emergency assistance to members to meet balance of payments needs arising from sudden and unforeseeable natural disasters and in post-conflict situations. Normally this takes the form of an outright purchase of up to 25% of quota, provided the member is cooperating with the IMF. For post-conflict cases, additional access of up to 25% of quota can be provided.

All requests for the use of the Fund's resources other than use of the reserve tranche are examined by the Fund to determine whether the proposed use would be consistent with the provisions of the Articles of Agreement and with Fund policies.

The criteria used by the Fund in determining whether its assistance should be made available are more liberal when the request is in the first credit tranche (that is, when the Fund holdings of a member's currency are above 100% but not above 125% of the member's quota) than when it is in the higher credit tranches (that is, when the Fund's holdings following the drawing exceed 125% of quota).

A member requesting a direct purchase expects to draw the full amount immediately after approval of the request; under a standby arrangement (SBA), a member may make the agreed drawing at any time during the period of the standby arrangement.

Requests for purchases in the higher credit tranches require substantial justification. Such purchases are almost always made under standby or similar arrangements. The amount available under a standby arrangement in the upper credit tranches is phased to be available in portions at specified intervals during the standby period, and the member's right to draw is always subject to the observance of certain key policy objectives described in the program or to a further review of the situation.

Compensatory and Contingency Financing Facility. In November 1987, the Executive Board began to examine the need to address external contingencies in Fund arrangements and the design of appropriate contingency financing mechanisms. These deliberations resulted in the establishment of the Compensatory and Contingency Financing Facility (CCFF) in August 1988. The CCFF incorporated existing facilities—the Compensatory Financing Facility (established in 1963), which provided financial assistance to members experiencing temporary export shortfalls, and the facility providing compensatory financing for excesses in cereal import costs that were largely attributable to circumstances beyond the members' control. The CCFF also introduced a new element—the external contingency mechanism (ECM). This mechanism gave members with fund arrangements the opportunity to protect themselves from unexpected, adverse external developments.

The compensatory element of the CCFF is designed to provide compensation to member countries experiencing shortfalls in export earnings and/or excesses in cereal import costs The eligibility criteria require that the shortfall/excess be temporary and stem from factors beyond the authorities' control, and that the member have a balance of payments need. In addition, where the member is experiencing balance of payments difficulties beyond the effects of the temporary shortfall/excess, the member is expected to cooperate with the Fund in an effort to address them. The export shortfall (cereal import excess) is calculated as the amount by which a member's export earnings (cereal import costs) for a 12-month period are below (above) their medium-term trend. Other provisions of the CCFF ensure that requests for compensatory financing are met in a timely fashion, in particular that a request cannot be made later than six months after the end of the shortfall year, and that the calculation for the shortfall year

may include up to 12 months of estimated data.

The Buffer Stock Financing Facility. In 1969 the BSFF was established to provide assistance to members in connection with their contributions to international buffer stocks of primary products, operating in the context of approved international commodity agreements (ICAs). The BSFF was the Fund's contribution to efforts to stabilize commodity prices, which were seen at the time as excessively volatile, with damaging consequences for the stability of export earnings of developing countries heavily dependent on commodity exports. The BSFF provides support in the context of those ICAs whose objective is the stabilization of international prices through market intervention by buffer stocks, and that satisfy certain participation requirements adopted by the United Nations Economic and Social Council, in particular that they are open to participation of both consuming and producing countries, and that they do not maintain artificially high prices through long-term restrictions of supply. The IMF had, as of December 1999, authorized the use of its resources in connection with buffer stocks of cocoa, tin, sugar, and natural rubber. At that time, all eligible commodity agreements had expired (he last to expire was the 1987 International Natural Rubber Agreement in December 1993): there were no agreements under which drawings under the BSFF could be made. But the Fund has recently been requested to consider whether the International Rubber Agreement (1995) was suitable for BSFF support.

Extended Facility. Under the extended facility, the Fund may provide assistance to members to meet their balance-of-payments deficits for longer periods and in amounts larger in relation to quotas than under the credit tranche policies. For example, a member might apply for assistance under the facility if it has serious payments imbalances relating to structural maladjustments in production, trade, and prices and if it intends to implement a comprehensive set of corrective policies for two or three years. Use of the facility might also be indicated by an inherently weak balance-of-payments position that prevents the pursuit of an active development policy.

Drawings under extended arrangements generally take place over periods of up to three years, although this may be extended to four years.

Structural Adjustment Facility. In response to the particularly difficult situation confronting the low-income members of the Fund, the Executive Board established in March 1986 a Structural Adjustment Facility (SAF) within the Fund's Special Disbursement Account. This facility provided concessional balance-of-payments assistance—in conjunction with the World Bank and other lenders—to low-income countries eligible for IDA loans that were facing protracted balance-of-payments problems and were undertaking comprehensive efforts to strengthen their balance-of-payments position.

In December 1987 the IMF established the Enhanced Structural Adjustment Facility (ESAF). As successor to the SAF, it is similar in objectivity, eligibility and program features, but differs in scope, terms of access, and funding sources. The ESAF was renewed and extended since its creation; in September 1996 the IMF decided to make it a permanent facility, as the centerpiece of the agency's strategy to help low-income countries. It also decided that the IMF's participation in the initiative to lower the debt of the heavily indebted poor countries (HIPCs) would be through special, more concessional ESAF operations. As of end-February 1999, a total of SDR 7.0 billion (about US$9.0 billion) had been disbursed under 79 ESAF arrangements to 51 developing countries. A total of SDR 1.8 billion (about US$2.5 billion) was disbursed under SAF arrangements. Altogether, as of September 1999, 56 countries had benefitted from the IMF's concessional assistance, affecting some 3.2 billion people, at least half of whom survive on less than US$1 a day. Some 80 countries were eligible for ESAF loans as of September 1999.

Conditionality

A country making use of the Fund's resources is generally required to implement economic policies aimed at achieving a viable balance-of-payments position over an appropriate period of time. This requirement is known as "conditionality," and it reflects the principle that balance-of-payments financing and adjustment must go hand in hand.

A comprehensive review of the guidelines for conditionality was undertaken in 1979. These guidelines include the use of consultation clauses in Fund-supported programs, the phasing of purchases, and the injunction that objective indicators for monitoring performance be limited only to those variables necessary to ensure achievement of the objectives of the programs. In addition, the guidelines emphasize the need to encourage members to adopt corrective measures at an early stage of their balance-of-payments difficulties; to recognize that in many cases adjustment will take longer than the period associated with standby arrangements; to provide for the adoption of a flexible approach for the treatment of external borrowing in adjustment programs; and to stress the necessity to pay due regard to the domestic social and political objectives, the economic priorities, and the circumstances of members, including the causes of their payments problems.

Within the context of the guidelines, Fund-supported programs emphasize a number of major economic variables, including certain financial aggregates, such as domestic credit, public sector financial needs, and external debt, as well as some key elements of the price system, including the exchange rate, interest rates, and, in exceptional cases, the prices of commodities that bear significantly upon public finances and foreign trade.

The Fund-supported corrective strategy provides for a reorientation of the economy toward sustained growth and avoids purely deflationary policies that may have a deleterious effect on investment and fail to encourage the required shift of resources to the external sector.

Charges for Use of Resources and Remuneration on Creditor Positions

The Fund applies charges for the use of its resources, except for reserve tranche purchases. A service charge of 0.5% is payable on purchases other than reserve tranche purchases. In addition, the Fund levies charges on balances of members' currencies resulting from purchases. The rate of charge on purchases in the four credit tranches and under the extended Fund facility, the compensatory financing facility, and the buffer-stock financing facility is determined at the beginning of each financial year on the basis of the estimated income and expense of the Fund during the year and a target amount of net income. The average rate of charge on the use of the Fund's ordinary resources as of 22 May 2000 was 5.09%, after adjustments for burden sharing, and an average rate of remuneration of 4.39%. Members that use the Fund's borrowed resources pay charges that reflect the Fund's borrowing costs plus a margin.

When the Fund's holdings of a member's currency are reduced below a specified level, the member acquires a creditor position in the Fund on which it earns remuneration (that is, interest). The Fund pays remuneration on creditor positions at a rate determined by a formula based on short-term market interest rates in the United States, the United Kingdom, Germany, France, and Japan.

E. Technical Assistance

Technical assistance is a major activity of the Fund. Staff officials are sent to member countries, sometimes for extended periods, to give advice on stabilization programs, the simplification of exchange systems, the modification of central banking machinery, the reform of fiscal systems and budgetary controls, or the preparation of financial statistics. The Fund collects and publishes a considerable number of statistics supplied by members. As part of its technical cooperation, the Fund established the IMF Institute in May 1964 to coordinate and expand its training program for staff members of finance ministries and central banks. The IMF estab-

lished the Joint Vienna Institute in the Fall of 1992. In May 1998, the IMF inaugurated its Singapore Regional Training Institute (STI). Additionally, the agency operates other regional training programs. Today, the IMF provides approximately 300 person-years of technical assistance annually to its member countries. In the late 1990s technical assistance projects grew larger and more complex, requiring multiple sources of financing to underwrite costs.

F. Special Drawing Rights (SDRs)

The SDR is an international reserve asset created by the Fund and allocated to its members as a supplement to existing reserve assets. The Fund has allocated a total of SDR 21.4 billion in six allocations.

The last allocation of SDRs in the third basic period was made on 1 January 1981, when a total of SDR 4,052 million was allocated to the 141 countries that were members of the Fund at that time. Similar amounts were allocated in each of the two previous years. The Fund allocates SDRs to its members in proportion to their quotas at the time of allocation. In deciding on the timing and amount of SDR allocations, the Fund considers whether there exists a global need to supplement existing reserve assets, and it takes into account the objectives of the Fund's Articles of Agreement, which call upon Fund members to collaborate with each other and with the Fund with a view to making the SDR the principal reserve asset of the international monetary system.

All 178 member countries of the Fund are participants in the SDR Department and are eligible to receive allocations. They may use SDRs in transactions and operations among themselves, with prescribed "other holders," of which there are now 15, and with the Fund itself. The SDR is the Fund's unit of account, and, increasingly, commercial transactions and private financial obligations are being denominated in SDRs.

Members with a balance-of-payments need may use SDRs to acquire foreign exchange in a transaction with designation—that is, one in which another member, designated by the Fund, provides currency in exchange for SDRs. The Fund designates members to provide currency on the basis of the strength of their balance-of-payments and reserve positions. However, a member's obligation to provide currency does not extend beyond the point at which its holdings are three times the net cumulative allocation that it has received. Fund members and "other holders" may also use SDRs in a variety of voluntary transactions and operations by agreement. They may buy and sell SDRs, both spot and forward, use SDRs in swaps and in settlement of financial obligations, or make donations (grants) with SDRs.

The valuation of the SDR is determined on the basis of a basket of five currencies. Since 1981, the currencies of France, Germany, Japan, United Kingdom, and United States have been included in the five-year reviews since these countries have the largest exports of goods and services. With the introduction of the euro on January 1, 1999, the currency amounts of the deutsche mark and French franc were replaced with the euro. The next review of the SDR valuation basket was scheduled to take place in late-2000, with any changes slated to take effect on January 1, 2001. The value of the SDR in U.S. dollar terms is calculated daily as the sum of the values in U.S. dollars of the specific amounts of four currencies (euro, U.S. dollar, Japanese yen, pound sterling), based on exchange rates quoted at noon at the London Market. On 24 May 2000, SDR 1 equaled US$1.31076. The SDR exchange rate is posted daily on the IMF web site http://www.imf.org/external/np/tre/sdr/sdr.htm.

G. Gold Sales by the Fund

The Fund's original Articles of Agreement required members to pay one-fourth of their quota subscription in gold. The establishment of the SDR in 1969 and the Second Amendment to the Articles of Agreement in 1978 virtually eliminated the monetary role of gold from the Articles, although gold still remains an important component in the reserve holdings of member countries. As a result of these developments, the Executive Board decided to sell off a portion of the Fund's gold holdings, beginning in 1976. In May 1980, the Fund completed a four-year gold sales program, through which 50 million oz, or one-third of the Fund's gold holdings at the beginning of the period, were sold. One-sixth of the gold (25 million oz) was sold to members at the former official price of SDR 35 an ounce. Another one-sixth was sold at auction for the benefit of developing countries. Some of the profits from these auctions were used to finance a trust fund, providing concessional balance-of-payments assistance to eligible developing countries. Repayments of these concessional loans form the basic funding for the structural adjustment facility.

BIBLIOGRAPHY

Annual Report of the Executive Board. Reviews the Fund's activities and surveys the world economy.

Annual Report on Exchange Arrangements and Exchange Restrictions.

Balance of Payments Statistics Yearbook.

Direction of Trade Statistics. Quarterly. Contains trade-by-country statistics of some 150 countries and summaries by geographic and monetary areas.

Government Finance Statistics Yearbook.

International Financial Statistics Yearbook. Contains statistics on all aspects of domestic and international finance (exchange rates, gold and foreign exchange holdings, money supply, bank assets, international trade, prices, production, interest rates, etc.).

World Economic Outlook: A Survey by the Staff of the International Monetary Fund. Published May 2000.

(The complete and searchable IMF catalog of publications is available online at http://www.imf.org/external/pubind.htm.)

IMF Members and Their Quotas
(as of 18 May 2000)

MEMBER	QUOTA
Afghanistan, Islamic State of	120.4
Albania	48.7
Algeria	1,254.7
Angola	286.3
Antigua and Barbuda	13.5
Argentina	2,117.1
Armenia	92.0
Australia	3,236.4
Austria	1,872.3
Azerbaijan	160.9
Bahamas	130.3
Bahrain	135.0
Bangladesh	533.3
Barbados	67.5
Belarus	386.4
Belgium	4,605.2
Belize	18.8
Benin	61.9
Bhutan	6.3
Bolivia	171.5
Bosnia and Herzegovina	169.1
Botswana	63.0
Brazil	3,036.1
Brunei Darussalam	150.0
Bulgaria	640.2
Burkina Faso	60.2
Burundi	77.0
Cambodia	87.5
Cameroon	185.7
Canada	6,369.2
Cape Verde	9.6
Central African Republic	55.7
Chad	56.0
Chile	856.1
China	4,687.2
Colombia	774.0
Comoros	8.9
Congo, Democratic Republic of the	291.0
Congo	84.6
Costa Rica	164.1
Côte d'Ivoire	325.2
Croatia	365.1
Cyprus	139.6
Czech Republic	819.3
Denmark	1,642.8
Djibouti	15.9
Dominica	8.2
Dominican Republic	218.9
Ecuador	302.3
Egypt	943.7
El Salvador	171.3
Equatorial Guinea	32.6
Eritrea	15.9
Estonia	65.2
Ethiopia	133.7
Fiji	70.3
Finland	1,263.8
France	10,738.5
Gabon	154.3
Gambia	31.1
Georgia	150.3

MEMBER	QUOTA
Germany	13,008.2
Ghana	369.0
Greece	823.0
Grenada	11.7
Guatemala	210.2
Guinea	107.1
Guinea-Bissau	14.2
Guyana	90.9
Haiti	60.7
Honduras	129.5
Hungary	1,038.4
Iceland	117.6
India	4,158.2
Indonesia	2,079.3
Iran, Islamic Republic of	1,497.2
Iraq	504.0
Ireland	838.4
Israel	928.2
Italy	7,055.5
Jamaica	273.5
Japan	13,312.8
Jordan	170.5
Kazakhstan	365.7
Kenya	271.4
Kiribati	5.6
Korea	1,633.6
Kuwait	1,381.1
Kyrgyz Republic	88.8
Lao People's Democratic Republic	39.1
Latvia	126.8
Lebanon	203.0
Lesotho	34.9
Liberia	71.3
Libya	1,123.7
Lithuania	144.2
Luxembourg	279.1
Macedonia, the Former Yugoslav Republic of	68.9
Madagascar	122.2
Malawi	69.4
Malaysia	1,486.6
Maldives	8.2
Mali	93.3
Malta	102.0
Marshall Islands	2.5
Mauritania	64.4
Mauritius	101.6
Mexico	2,585.8
Micronesia, Federated States of	5.1
Moldova	123.2
Mongolia	51.1
Morocco	588.2
Mozambique	113.6
Myanmar	258.4
Namibia	136.5
Nepal	71.3
Netherlands	5,162.4
New Zealand	894.6
Nicaragua	130.0
Niger	65.8
Nigeria	1,753.2
Norway	1,671.7

MEMBER	QUOTA
Oman	194.0
Pakistan	1,033.7
Palau	3.1
Panama	206.6
Papua New Guinea	131.6
Paraguay	99.9
Peru	638.4
Philippines	879.9
Poland	1,369.0
Portugal	867.4
Qatar	263.8
Romania	1,030.2
Russia	5,945.4
Rwanda	80.1
St. Kitts and Nevis	8.9
St. Lucia	15.3
St. Vincent and the Grenadines	8.3
Samoa	11.6
San Marino	17.0
São Tomé and Principe	7.4
Saudi Arabia	6,985.5
Senegal	161.8
Seychelles	8.8
Sierra Leone	103.7
Singapore	862.5
Slovak Republic	357.5
Slovenia	231.7
Solomon Islands	10.4
Somalia	44.2
South Africa	1,868.5
Spain	3,048.9
Sri Lanka	413.4
Sudan	169.7
Suriname	92.1
Swaziland	50.7
Sweden	2,395.5
Switzerland	3,458.5
Syrian Arab Republic	293.6
Tajikistan	87.0
Tanzania	198.9
Thailand	1,081.9
Togo	73.4
Tonga	6.9
Trinidad and Tobago	335.6
Tunisia	286.5
Turkey	964.0
Turkmenistan	75.2
Uganda	180.5
Ukraine	1,372.0
United Arab Emirates	611.7
United Kingdom	10,738.5
United States	37,149.3
Uruguay	306.5
Uzbekistan	275.6
Vanuatu	17.0
Venezuela	2,659.1
Vietnam	329.1
Yemen	243.5
Zambia	489.1
Zimbabwe	353.4

Executive Directors of the IMF and Voting Power
(as of 18 May 2000)

DIRECTOR	CASTING VOTES OF	VOTES BY COUNTRY	TOTAL VOTES	% OF FUND TOTAL
APPOINTED				
Karin Lissakers	United States	371,743	371,743	17.35
Yukio Yoshimura	Japan	133,378	133,378	6.22
Bernd Esdar	Germany	130,332	130,332	6.08
Jean-Claude Milleron	France	107,635	107,635	5.02
Stephen Pickford	United Kingdom	107,635	107,635	5.02
ELECTED				
Willy Kiekens (Belgium)	Austria	18,973		
	Belarus	4,114		
	Belgium	46,302		
	Czech Republic	8,443		
	Hungary	10,634		
	Kazakhstan	3,907		
	Luxembourg	3,041		
	Slovak Republic	3,825		
	Slovenia	2,567		
	Turkey	9,890	111,696	5.21
J. de Beaufort Wijnholds (Netherlands)	Armenia	1,170		
	Bosnia and Herzegovina	1,941		
	Bulgaria	6,652		
	Croatia	3,901		
	Cyprus	1,646		
	Georgia	1,753		
	Israel	9,532		
Macedonia Former Yugoslav Republic of		939		
	Moldova	1,482		
	Netherlands	51,874		
	Romania	10,552		
	Ukraine	13,970	105,412	4.92
Agustín Carstens _(Mexico)	Costa Rica	1,891		
	El Salvador	1,963		
	Guatemala	2,352		
	Honduras	1,545		
	Mexico	26,108		
	Nicaragua	1,550		
	Spain	30,739		
	Venezuela	26,841	92,989	4.34
Riccardo Faini (Italy)	Albania	737		
	Greece	8,480		
	Italy	70,805		
	Malta	1,270		
	Portugal	8,924		
	San Marino	420	90,636	4.23
Thomas A. Bernes (Canada)	Antigua and Barbuda	385		
	Bahamas	1,553		
	Barbados	925		
	Belize	438		
	Canada	63,942		
	Dominica	332		
	Grenada	367		
	Ireland	8,634		
	Jamaica	2,985		
	St. Kitts and Nevis	339		
	St. Lucia	403		
St. Vincent and the Grenadines		333	80,636	3.76
Olli-Pekka Lehmussaari (Finland)	Denmark	16,678		
	Estonia	902		
	Finland	12,888		
	Iceland	1,426		
	Latvia	1,518		

DIRECTOR	CASTING VOTES OF	VOTES BY COUNTRY	TOTAL VOTES	% OF FUND TOTAL
	Lithuania	1,692		
	Norway	16,967		
	Sweden	24,205	76,276	3.56
Gregory F. Taylor (Australia)	Australia	32,614		
	Kiribati	306		
	Korea	16,586		
	Marshall Islands	275		
	Micronesia	301		
	Mongolia	761		
	New Zealand	9,196		
	Palau	281		
	Papua New Guinea	1,566		
	Philippines	9,049		
	Samoa	366		
	Seychelles	338		
	Solomon Islands	354		
	Vanuatu	420	72,413	3.38
Sulaiman M. Al-Turki (Saudi Arabia)	Saudi Arabia	70,105	70,105	3.27
Kleo-Thong Hetrakul (Thailand)	Brunei Darussalam	1,750		
	Cambodia	1,125		
	Fiji	953		
	Indonesia	21,043		
Lao People's Democratic Republic		641		
	Malaysia	15,116		
	Myanmar	2,834		
	Nepal	963		
	Singapore	8,875		
	Thailand	11,069		
	Tonga	319		
	Vietnam	3,541	68,229	3.18
José Pedro de Morais, Jr. (Angola)	Angola	3,113		
	Botswana	880		
	Burundi	1,020		
	Eritrea	409		
	Ethiopia	1,587		
	Gambia, The	561		
	Kenya	2,964		
	Lesotho	599		
	Liberia	963		
	Malawi	944		
	Mozambique	1,386		
	Namibia	1,615		
	Nigeria	17,782		
	Sierra Leone	1,287		
	South Africa	18,935		
	Swaziland	757		
	Tanzania	2,239		
	Uganda	2,055		
	Zambia	5,141		
	Zimbabwe	3,784	68,021	3.17
A. Shakour Shaalan (Egypt)	Bahrain	1,600		
	Egypt	9,687		
	Iraq	5,290		
	Jordan	1,955		
	Kuwait	14,061		
	Lebanon	2,280		
	Libya	11,487		
	Maldives	332		
	Oman	2,190		
	Qatar	2,888		
	Syrian Arab Republic	3,186		
	United Arab Emirates	6,367		
	Yemen, Republic of	2,685	64,008	2.99

Executive Directors of the IMF and Voting Power—*cont.*

(as of 15 August 1996)

DIRECTOR	CASTING VOTES OF	VOTES BY COUNTRY	TOTAL VOTES	% OF FUND TOTAL	DIRECTOR	CASTING VOTES OF	VOTES BY COUNTRY	TOTAL VOTES	% OF FUND TOTAL
Aleksei V. Mozhin (Russia)	Russia	59,704	59,704	2.79		Benin	869		
Roberto F. Cippa (Switzerland)	Azerbaijan	1,859				Burkina Faso	852		
	Kyrgyz Republic	1,138				Cameroon	2,107		
	Poland	13,940				Cape Verde	346		
	Switzerland	34,835				Central African Republic	807		
	Tajikistan	1,120				Chad	810		
	Turkmenistan	1,002				Comoros	339		
	Uzbekistan	3,006	56,900	2.66		Congo, Republic of	1,096		
						Côte d'Ivoire	3,502		
Murilo Portugal (Brazil)	Brazil	30,611				Djibouti	409		
	Colombia	7,990				Equatorial Guinea	576		
	Dominican Republic	2,439				Gabon	1,793		
	Ecuador	3,273				Guinea	1,321		
	Guyana	1,159				Guinea-Bissau	392		
	Haiti	857				Madagascar	1,472		
	Panama	2,316				Mali	1,183		
	Suriname	1,171				Mauritania	894		
	Trinidad and Tobago	3,606	53,422	2.49		Mauritius	1,266		
						Niger	908		
Vijay L. Kelkar (India)	Bangladesh	5,583				Rwanda	1,051		
	Bhutan	313				São Tomé and Príncipe	324		
	India	41,832				Senegal	1,868		
	Sri Lanka	4,384	52,112	2.43		Togo	984	25,169	1.17
Abbas Mirakhor (Iran)	Algeria	12,797			TOTAL			2,140,761	99.89
	Ghana	3,940							
	Iran	15,222							
	Morocco	6,132							
	Pakistan	10,587							
	Tunisia	3,115	51,793	2.42					
Wei Benhua (China)	China	47,122	47,122	2.2					
Ana Maria Jul (Chile)	Argentina	21,421							
	Bolivia	1,965							
	Chile	8,811							
	Paraguay	1,249							
	Peru	6,634							
	Uruguay	3,315	43,395	2.03					

Alexandre Barro Chambrier (Gabon)

[1] Voting power varies on certain matters pertaining to the General Department with use of the Fund's resources in that Department.

[2] Percentages are of total votes (2,142,907) in the General Department and the Special Drawing Rights Department.

[3] The total number of votes as of 18 May, 2,140,761, does not include the votes of the Islamic State of Afghanistan and Somalia, which did not participate in the 1998 Regular Election of Executive Directors. The total votes of these members is 2,146.

[4] The total number of votes also does not include the votes of the Democratic Republic of the Congo and Sudan, which were suspended effective June 2, 1994 and August 9, 1993, respectively, pursuant to Article XXVI, Section 2(b) of the Articles of Agreement.

THE WORLD BANK GROUP

The World Bank Group comprises five organizations: the International Bank for Reconstruction and Development (IBRD), the International Development Association (IDA), the International Finance Corporation (IFC), the Multilateral Investment Guarantee Agency (MIGA), and the International Centre for the Settlement of Investment Disputes (ICSID).

INTERNATIONAL BANK FOR RECONSTRUCTION AND DEVELOPMENT (IBRD)

Background

As early as February 1943, United States Undersecretary of State Sumner B. Welles urged preparatory consultation aimed at the establishment of agencies to finance reconstruction and development of the world economy after WWII. The US and the UK took leading roles in the negotiations that were to result in the formation of the IBRD and the IMF. The IBRD is the main lending organization of the World Bank Group and, like its sister institution, the International Monetary Fund (IMF), was born of the Allies' realization during World War II that tremendous difficulties in reconstruction and development would face them in the postwar transition period, necessitating international economic and financial cooperation on a vast scale. The IBRD, frequently called the "World Bank," was conceived in July 1944 at the United Nations Monetary and Financial Conference in Bretton Woods, New Hampshire, US.

Purposes

Although one of the Bank's early functions was to assist in bringing about a smooth transition from wartime to peaceful economies, economic development soon became the Bank's main object. Today, the goal of the World Bank is to promote economic development that benefits poor people in developing countries. Loans are provided to developing countries to help reduce poverty and to finance investments that contribute to economic growth. Investments include roads, power plants, schools, and irrigation networks, as well as activities like agricultural extension services, training for teachers, and nutrition-improvement programs for children and pregnant women. Some World Bank loans finance changes in the structure of countries' economies to make them more stable, efficient, and market oriented. The World Bank also provides technical assistance to help governments make specific sectors of their economies more efficient and more relevant to national development goals.

Membership

The Bank's founders envisioned a global institution, the membership of which would eventually comprise all nations. Membership in the IBRD rose gradually from 41 governments in 1946 to 181 as of March 2000.

A government may withdraw from membership at any time by giving notice of withdrawal. Membership also ceases for a member suspended by a majority of the governors for failure to fulfill an obligation, if that member has not been restored to good standing by a similar majority within a year after the suspension. Only a few countries have withdrawn their membership from the Bank, and all but Cuba (withdrew in 1960) have rejoined.

Although the Soviet Union took part in the 1944 Bretton Woods Conference, and signed the final act establishing the IMF and the IBRD, it never ratified the Articles of Agreement or paid in the 20% of its subscribed capital that was due within 60 days after the Bank began operations. Had it joined, the Soviet Union would have been the Bank's third largest shareholder, after the United States and the United Kingdom. Over the next four decades, as the Bank grew in size and scope, it couldn't fulfill its founders' intentions of being a truly global institution due to the absence of the Soviet Union. Then, at the beginning of the 1990s, as political and economic change swept through the 15 republics of the USSR, the Soviet government indicated its interest in participating in the international financial system and sought membership in the IMF and World Bank. On 15 July 1991, Soviet President Mikhail Gorbachev formally applied for membership for the USSR in the IBRD and its three affiliates (IFC, IDA and MIGA). However, by December 1991, the USSR had ceased to exist. During 1992, the Russian Federation and 15 former Soviet republics (including the Baltic states) applied for membership and were accepted. Eleven of them also applied to IDA, 14 to IFC and 15 to MIGA. To accommodate these countries, the total authorized capital of the bank was increased.

A "graduating" country is one where lending is being phased out. As of 2000 there were 26 countries that had "graduated" from the IBRD. These include (with the fiscal year of their final loan): France (1947), Luxembourg (1948), Netherlands (1957), Belgium (1958), Australia (1962), Austria (1962), Denmark (1964), Malta (1964), Norway (1964), Italy (1965), Japan (1967), New Zealand (1972), Iraq (1973), Iceland (1974), Finland (1975), Israel (1975), Singapore (1975), Ireland (1976), Spain (1977), Greece (1979), Oman (1987), Bahamas (1989), Portugal (1989), Cyprus (1992), Barbados (1993), and Korea (1995).

Structure

Board of Governors

All powers of the Bank are vested in its Board of Governors, composed of one governor and one alternate from each member state. Ministers of Finance, central bank presidents, or persons of comparable status usually represent member states on the Bank's Board of Governors. The board meets annually.

The Bank is organized somewhat like a corporation. According to an agreed-upon formula, member countries subscribe to shares of the Bank's capital stock. Each governor is entitled to cast 250 votes plus 1 vote for each share of capital stock subscribed by his country.

Executive Directors

The Bank's Board of Governors has delegated most of its authority to 24 executive directors. According to the Articles of Agreement, each of the five largest shareholders—the United States, Japan, Germany, France and the United Kingdom—appoints one executive director. The other countries are grouped in 19 constituencies, each represented by an executive director who is elected by a group of countries. The number of countries each of these 19 directors represents varies widely. For example, the executive directors for China, the Russian Federation, and Saudi Arabia represent one country each, while one director speaks for 24 Francophone African countries and another director represents 21 mainly English-speaking African countries.

President and Staff

The president of the Bank, elected by the executive directors, is also their chairman, although he is not entitled to a vote, except in case of an equal division. Subject to their general direction, the president is responsible for the conduct of the ordinary business of the Bank. Action on Bank loans is initiated by the president and the staff of the Bank. The amount, terms, and conditions of a loan are recommended by the president to the executive directors, and the loan is made if his recommendation is approved by them.

According to an informal agreement, the president of the Bank is a US national, and the managing director of the IMF is a European. The president's initial term is for five years; a second term can be five years or less. Past presidents of the Bank include Robert S. McNamara (1968–81), A. W. Clausen (1981–86), Barber B. Conable (1986–91), and Lewis T. Preston (1991–95). James D. Wolfensohn became president on 1 June 1995. On September 27, 1999, Mr. Wolfensohn was unanimously reappointed by the Bank's Board of Executive Directors to a second five-year term as president beginning June 1, 2000. He is the third president in World Bank history to serve a second term. He heads a staff of more than 7,100 persons from over 130 countries.

The IBRD's headquarters are at 1818 H Street, N.W., Washington, DC 20433.

Budget

In June 1999, the executive directors approved a total administrative budget of US$1,445.1 million for fiscal year 2000.

Activities

A. FINANCIAL RESOURCES

Authorized capital. At its establishment, the IBRD had an authorized capital of US$10 billion. Countries subscribing shares were required to pay in only one-fifth of their subscription on joining, the remainder being available on call but only to meet the IBRD's liabilities if it got into difficulties. Moreover, not even the one-fifth had to be paid in hard cash at that time. The sole cash requirement was the payment in gold or US dollars of 2% of each country's subscription. A further 18% of the subscription was payable in the currency of the member country concerned, and although this sum was technically paid in, in the form of notes bearing no interest, it could not be used without the member's permission. In 1959, each member was given an opportunity to double its subscription without any payment. Thus, for countries joining the IBRD after the 1959 capital increase and for those subscribing to additional capital stock, the statutory provisions affecting the 2% and 18% portions have been applied to only one-half of their total subscriptions, so that 1% of each subscription that is freely usable in the IBRD's operations has been payable in gold or US dollars, and 9% that is usable only with the

consent of the member is in the member's currency. The remaining 90% is not paid in but is subject to call by the IBRD.

Financial Resources for Lending Purposes. The subscriptions of the IBRD's members constitute the basic element in the financial resources of the IBRD. Subscribed capital for fiscal year 1999 was about US$188.2 billion. The Bank also draws money from borrowings in the market and from earnings. In 1999, the Bank's outstanding borrowings were US$115.7 billion, raised in the capital markets of the world. The IBRD is able to raise large sums at interest rates little or no higher than are paid by governments because of confidence in the Bank engendered by its record of stability since 1947 and the investors' knowledge that if the IBRD should ever be in difficulty, it can call in unpaid portions of member countries' subscriptions. In connection with its borrowing operations, the Bank also undertakes a substantial volume of currency and interest rate swap transactions. These swaps have enabled the IBRD to lower its fund-raising costs and to expand its direct borrowing transactions to markets and currencies in which it otherwise would not have borrowed.

B. LENDING OPERATIONS

The IBRD lends to member governments, or, with government guarantee, to political subdivisions, or to public or private enterprises.

The IBRD's first loan, US$250 million for postwar reconstruction, was made in the latter part of 1947. Altogether, it lent US$497 million for postwar reconstruction, all to European countries. The IBRD's first development loans were made in the first half of 1948. As of 30 June 1999, the cumulative total of loans made by the Bank was over US$338.5 billion.

Loan Terms and Interest Rates. The IBRD normally makes long-term loans, with repayment commencing after a certain period. The length of the loan is generally related to the estimated useful life of the equipment or plant being financed. Since July 1982, IBRD loans have been made at variable rates. The lending rate on all loans made under the variable-rate system is adjusted semiannually, on 1 January and 1 July, by adding a spread of 0.5% to the IBRD's weighted average cost during the prior six months of a "pool" of borrowings drawn down after 30 June 1982. Since July 1989, only borrowings allocated to lending have been included in the cost of borrowings with respect to new loans and existing variable rate loans that are amended to apply the new cost basis. For interest periods beginning from 1 January through 30 June 2000, the variable lending rate was 5.46%. Before July 1982, loans were made at fixed rates, and, accordingly, the semiannual interest-rate adjustments do not apply to payments made on these older loans.

C. PURPOSES OF THE LOANS

The main purpose of the Bank's operations is to lend to developing member countries for productive projects in such sectors as agriculture, energy, industry, and transportation and to help improve basic services considered essential for development. The main criterion for assistance is that it should be provided where it can be most effective in the context of the country's specific lending programs developed by the Bank in consultation with its borrowers. In the late 1980s, the World Bank came under criticism that its policies, intended to encourage developing countries to restructure their economies in order to render them more efficient, were actually imposing too heavy a burden on the world's poorest peoples. This, and charges by environmentalists that World Bank lending had underwritten projects that were severely detrimental to the environment of developing countries, led to a re-thinking of the Bank's policies in the 1990s.

Implementing the Bank's Poverty Reduction Strategy. The fundamental objective of the World Bank is sustainable poverty reduction. Underpinning this objective is a two-part strategy for reducing poverty that was proposed in the World Development Report 1990. The first element is to promote broad-based economic growth that makes efficient use of the poor's most abundant asset, labor. The second element involves ensuring widespread access to basic social services to improve the well being of the poor and to enable them to participate fully in the growth of the economy. Progress in implementing the poverty-reduction strategy is clearly visible in Bank-wide statistics on new lending. At the September 1999 annual meetings of the World Bank Group and IMF, ministers agreed to link debt relief to the establishment of a poverty reduction strategy for all countries receiving World Bank/IMF concessional assistance.

Sector and Structural Adjustment Lending. Bank lending for sector adjustment and structural adjustment increasingly supports the establishment of social safety nets and the protection of public spending for basic social services.

In its assistance to countries that are preparing adjustment programs, the Bank works with them to (a) design the phasing of programs to accommodate the needs of the poor, (b) give priority to relative price changes in favor of the poor early in the reform process, (c) secure adequate resources for the provision of basic social services aimed at the poor, and (d) design social safety nets into economic-reform programs. These efforts better position of the poor to be major beneficiaries of the economic growth and associated employment opportunities that are facilitated by the implementation of adjustment programs.

Human Resource Development. Bank lending for human resource development has largely been committed for education, and its focus has been towards development of basic education. Lending for education increased from an average US$700 million during the 1980s to an average US$1,907 million during the first four years of the 1990s. In 1999 the amount climbed to US$2,014 million.

Bank lending for population, health, and nutrition has expanded even more rapidly. Average yearly lending to this sector during the 1980s was US$207 million, while lending during fiscal 1999 was US$1,726 million.

The Environment. The Bank has continued to support environmental protection efforts with loans totaling US$978 million in fiscal 1999, compared to US$404 million in fiscal 1990. But the full story cannot be told by stand-alone environmental projects. As of the late 1990s, half of all World Bank projects now have an environmental component of some kind.

In fiscal 1993 the World Bank undertook structural changes to respond to growing borrower demand for Bank assistance in environmental issues, and to the need for internal strengthening of monitoring and implementation. A Vice Presidency for Environmentally Sustainable Development was established. Three departments were placed under this vice presidency—the Environment Department, the Agriculture and Natural Resources Department, and the Transport and Urban Development Department.

The Global Environment Facility is a cooperative venture between the World Bank, the United Nations Development Programme, the United Nations Environment Programme, and national governments. The Facility provides grants to help developing countries deal with environmental problems that transcend boundaries, such as airborne pollution produced by smokestacks or hazardous waste dumped into rivers. The GEF gives priority to four objectives: limiting emissions of greenhouse gases; preserving biodiversity; protecting international waters; and protecting the ozone layer.

Private Sector Development. The promotion of private sector growth in developing member countries has always been central to the Bank's overall mission of fostering sustainable growth and reducing poverty. In December 1999, the Bank Group announced a restructuring to better align and expand its work related to the private sector. The reforms took effect 1 January 2000. The reorganization tightened the link between the Bank's public sector work and its private sector transactions in the developing world, which are made through the IFC. The World Bank helps governments to formulate policy frameworks that encourage a positive environment for business to function as the primary engine of growth while the IFC, the private sector arm of the Bank Group, provides advice and makes loans and equity investments in companies in developing countries. According to an IFC official the changes were in response to "one of the biggest challenges facing [the Bank's] client countries: How to create a favorable business environment and help finance small and medium enterprises." In addition to creating a new combined unit to coordinate Bank Group activities, help capitalize local financial institutions, and teach them the business of financing small and medium enterprises, the restructuring also involved the creation of joint World Bank-IFC departments, or product groups, for industries where there is a strong interface between public policy and private sector transactions. Three new industry groups, telecommunications/informatics, oil/gas/petrochemicals, and mining, include both policy and transaction capacity. Beyond the new industry groups, the principal advisory services focused on the private sector in both the World Bank and IFC are coordinated under single management.

D. OTHER ACTIVITIES

Technical Assistance. The Bank provides its members with a wide variety of technical assistance, much of it financed under its lending program. The volume of technical assistance in which the Bank is involved as lender, provider, or administrator rose sharply during the 1990s. In addition to loans and guarantees to developing countries, the World Bank carries out its mission by providing advice and assistance with telecommunications sector reform and national information infrastructure strategies. Special programs in this category include InfoDev and TechNet. The Information for Development Program (InfoDev) began in September 1995 with the objective of addressing the obstacles facing developing countries in an increasingly information-driven world economy. It is a global grant program managed by the World Bank to promote innovative projects on the use of information and communication technologies (ICTs) for economic and social development, with a special emphasis on the needs of the poor in developing countries. In recognition of the critical role that science and technology play in promoting economic growth and social progress, in July 1999 TechNet was created as a cross-cutting thematic group to promote knowledge and education in the areas of science and technology and informatics. TechNet acts as a clearinghouse and network for professionals inside and outside the Bank.

Interagency Cooperation. The Bank's overarching purpose is helping to reduce global poverty. To this end, the institution encourages the involvement of other development agencies in preparing poverty assessments and works closely with other UN agencies in preparing proposals to improve the quality of poverty-related data. At the country level, the Bank is broadening its efforts to coordinate work with UNDP, UNICEF, and the International Fund for Agricultural Development in specific countries on preparing or following up poverty assessments and planned human development assessments.

Coordination between the Bank and the UN system on poverty at the project level is extensive, particularly in the design of social funds and social action programs. Together with other UN agencies, the World Bank has taken the lead in mobilizing groups of donors, both multilateral and bilateral, to tackle specific areas of concern—for example, the Consultative Group on International Agricultural Research (CGIAR), which is cosponsored by the FAO, UNDP, and the World Bank. The Bank is an active partner in interagency activities which include the follow-up to the World Conference on Education for All and the World Summit for Children; the Safe Motherhood Inter-Agency Group; the Onchocerciasis (riverblindness) Control Programme; the Global

Programme for AIDS; and the Task Force for Child Survival. The Bank also has links with the United Nations at the political and policy making level in the work of the General Assembly and its related committees, and the Economic and Social Council.

The Economic Development Institute was the Bank's department responsible for such dissemination. Through seminars, workshops and courses, EDI enabled policy-makers to assess and use the lessons of development to benefit their own policies. On 10 March 1999, the World Bank unveiled the successor to the EDI, the World Bank Institute (WBI). The new learning entity also absorbed the World Bank's Learning and Leadership Center. The WBI drives the Bank's learning agenda, working in three main areas: training, policy services, and knowledge networks. WBI is located at the World Bank headquarters in Washington, DC. Many of its activities are held in member countries in cooperation with regional and national development agencies and education and training institutions. The Institute's distance education unit conducts interactive courses via satellite links worldwide. While most of WBI's work is conducted in English, it also operates in Arabic, Chinese, French, Portuguese, Russian and Spanish.

Economic Research and Studies. The Bank's economic and social research program, inaugurated in 1972, is undertaken by the Bank's own research staff and is funded out of its administrative budget. The research program is shaped by the Bank's own needs, as a lending institution and as a source of policy advice to member governments, and by the needs of member countries. Its main purposes are to gain new insights into the development process and the policies affecting it; to introduce new techniques or methodologies into country, sectoral, and project analyses; to provide the analytical bases for major Bank documents, such as the World Development Report; and to help strengthen indigenous research capacity in developing countries.

Total Loans by Region in Millions of US Dollars
(as of 30 June 1999)

REGION	AMOUNT
Africa	2,069
East Asia and Pacific	9,765
South Asia	2,562
Europe and Central Asia	5,286
Latin America and the Caribbean	7,737
Middle East and North Africa	1,576
TOTAL	28,995

Total Loans by Major Purpose in Millions of US Dollars
(as of 30 June 1999)

PURPOSE	AMOUNT
Agriculture	2,528
Education	2,014
Electric power and other energy	591
Environment	978
Finance	6,645
Industry	677
Mining	346
Multisector	4,294
Oil and gas	18
Population, health, and nutrition	1,726
Public sector management	1,083
Social protection	3,595
Telecommunications	228
Transportation	3,022
Urban development	605
Water supply and sanitation	645
TOTAL	28,995

INTERNATIONAL CENTRE FOR SETTLEMENT OF INVESTMENT DISPUTES (ICSID)

Developing countries depend heavily on foreign private capital to finance development. Such capital flows are sensitive to legal and political conditions in developing countries. The International Centre for Settlement of Investment Disputes is an autonomous institution founded in 1966 to promote increased flows of international investment by providing facilities for the conciliation and arbitration of disputes between governments and foreign investors. ICSID also provides advice, carries out research, and produces publications in the area of foreign investment law. Its publications include a semiannual law journal, *ICSD Review-Foreign Investment Law Journal,* and multivolume collections of *Investment Laws of the World* and *Investment Treaties.* As of March 2000, ICSID had 131 member countries and had tried 39 cases; 33 other cases were pending.. Parties involved have included the governments of more than 40 different nations, and disputes have dealt with investments in agriculture, banking, construction, energy, health, industry, mining, and tourism.

MULTILATERAL GUARANTEE INVESTMENT AGENCY (MIGA)

MIGA was established in 1988. Its main purpose is to promote the flow of foreign direct investment among member countries by insuring investments against non-commercial (political) risk, and by providing promotional and advisory services to help member countries create an attractive investment climate. MIGA offers four basic types of coverage:

Currency Inconvertibility. Protects against losses arising from an inability to convert local currency investment returns into foreign exchange for transfer outside the host country;

Expropriation. Protects against loss from acts by the host government that may reduce or eliminate ownership of, or control over, rights to the insured investment;

War and Civil Disturbance. Protects against losses arising from military action or civil disturbance that destroys or damages tangible assets of the project enterprise or interferes with its operations; and

Breach of Contract. Protects against losses from the investor's inability to obtain and/or enforce a decision or award against a host country that has repudiated or breached an investment contract.

The demand for MIGA's services has been strong. On 29 March 1999, MIGA's Council of Governors adopted a resolution for a capital increase for the agency of approximately US$850 million. In addition, US$150 million had been transferred to MIGA by the World Bank as operating capital. During fiscal 1999, MIGA issued a total of 72 guarantee contracts, totaling US$1,310,2. As of March 2000, 151 countries had completed membership requirements with an additional 15 countries in the process of becoming members.

THE INTERNATIONAL DEVELOPMENT ASSOCIATION (IDA)

Background

The world's poorer countries have gone heavily into debt to finance their development. The total outstanding debt of 90 such countries rose from US$51 billion in 1970 to an estimated US$485 billion in 1985. Annual interest and amortization charges on this debt had, by 1985, reached over US$100 billion. Many countries have long since arrived at the point where they can no longer afford to raise all the development capital that they are in a position to use at ordinary rates of interest and in the time span of conventional loans, IBRD loans included.

The International Development Association (IDA), an affiliate of the World Bank, was established in 1960 to promote economic development in the world's poorest countries—those that cannot afford to borrow from the IBRD. It is the largest single multilateral source of concessional lending to low-income countries. The following criteria are used to determine which countries are eligible to borrow IDA resources: relative poverty, defined as GNP per capita below an established threshold (as of January 2000, US$8,950; lack of creditworthiness to borrow on market terms and therefore a need for concessional resources to finance the country's development program; good policy performance, defined as the implementation of economic and social policies that promote growth and poverty reduction. In early 2000, 78 countries were eligible to borrow from the IDA. At the time, these countries were home to 2.3 billion people, comprising 53% of the total population of the developing nations, and 1.5 billion of these people survived on incomes of US$2 or less a day.

The IDA's loans are interest-free and repayable over very long terms, with extended grace periods. As a result, the IDA's resources, unlike the resources of a regular lending institution, must be regularly replenished through contributions if the agency is to continue in business.

Creation

The creation of an international agency such as the IDA was discussed in the UN at various times during the 1950s. A report drawn up in 1951 by a group of experts on financing and economic development referred to the need for an "international development authority." Although such proposals were at first opposed by the US, the IDA as it was finally launched was largely the result of US initiative. In 1958, the US Senate passed a resolution introduced by Senator A. S. ("Mike") Monroney calling for cooperative international action along these lines. On 1 October 1959, the IBRD's Board of Governors approved, without objections, a motion of US Secretary of the Treasury Robert Anderson that a new agency, under the name International Development Association, be established as an affiliate of the Bank.

The debate that preceded the Board's action revealed potential disagreements among members of the Bank on a number of points, such as the terms that the IDA should set for its loans, the permissible restrictions that countries subscribing to the IDA's capital could place on the use of funds supplied in their national currencies, and related matters. Rather than decide these matters itself, the Board of Governors asked the Executive Directors of the IBRD to draw up Articles of Agreement for the IDA, which would then be submitted to the Bank's member governments.

The IDA's Articles of Agreement were accordingly drafted by the Executive Directors of the IBRD and early in 1960 transmitted to the member governments of the Bank. The next step was for those governments desiring to join the IDA to take whatever legislative or other action might be required to accept membership and to subscribe funds.

The new lending association came into existence on 24 September 1960, when governments whose subscriptions to its capital aggregated US$650 million, or 65% of the projected one-billion-dollar goal, had accepted membership. The IDA started operations in November of that year.

Purposes

In the preamble to the Articles of Agreement, the signatory governments declare their conviction that mutual cooperation for constructive economic purposes, healthy development of the world economy, and balanced growth of international trade foster peace and world prosperity; that higher standards of living and economic and social progress in the less developed countries are desirable not only in the interest of the latter but also for the international community as a whole; and that achievement of these objectives would be facilitated by an increase in the interna-

tional flow of capital, public and private, to assist in the development of the resources of less developed countries.

As stated in its Articles of Agreement, the purposes of the IDA are "to promote economic development, increase productivity, and thus raise standards of living in the less-developed areas of the world included within the Association's membership, in particular by providing financing to meet their important developmental requirements on terms which are more flexible and bear less heavily on the balance of payments than those of conventional loans, thereby furthering the developmental objectives of the [IBRD] and supplementing its activities."

Membership

As of March 2000, IDA had 161 member countries, of which 78 were eligible to borrow. Between its founding in 1960 and 1999, IDA lent almost US$115 billion to over 100 countries. It lends, on average, about US$5–6 billion a year for different types of development projects. When a country's Gross National Product (GNP) exceeds IDA's eligibility threshold and it becomes creditworthy to borrow from IBRD, it is no longer eligible for IDA's interest-free credits. It may then borrow from IBRD at market rates. As of 2000, some countries, such as India and Indonesia, were eligible for a combination of financing from both IBRD and IDA. Such countries are known as "blend" borrowers. Countries that once borrowed from IDA but, as of 2000, were too prosperous to qualify included China, Costa Rica, Chile, and Egypt.

Structure

The IDA is administered by the same officers and staff who administer the affairs of the IBRD. The president of the Bank also serves as the president of the IDA, and the governors and the executive directors of the Bank serve in the same capacity in the IDA. As in the IBRD, a member's voting power in the IDA is roughly proportionate to its capital subscription.

Budget

Since the IDA relies entirely on the IBRD's staff and facilities for all its activities, it reimburses the Bank through a management fee for administrative expenses incurred on its behalf.

Activities

A. Financial Resources

The IDA's funds are obtained from three main sources: members' subscriptions; periodic "replenishments" provided by richer members and certain special contributions; and transfer of income from the IBRD and repayments on IDA credits.

While IBRD raises most of its funds on the world's financial markets, IDA is funded largely by contributions from the governments of the richer member countries. As of July 1999, their cumulative contributions since IDA's beginning totaled US$96 billion. Donors get together every three years to replenish IDA funds. The 12th replenishment finances projects over the three years beginning 1 July 1999. Funding for the 12th Replenishment will allow IDA to lend about US$22 billion, of which donors' contributions will provide a little over half.

The largest pledges to the 12th replenishment were made by the United States, Japan, Germany, France, United Kingdom, Italy and Canada. Some less wealthy nations also contribute to IDA. Turkey and Korea, for example, once borrowers from IDA, became donors. Other contributors to the 12th replenishment were Australia, Austria, Belgium, Denmark, Finland, Greece, Iceland, Ireland, Israel, Luxembourg, Netherlands, New Zealand, Norway, Portugal, Saudi Arabia, Spain, Sweden, and Switzerland. Argentina, Brazil, Czech Republic, Hungary, Mexico, Poland, Russia, the Slovak Republic, South Africa, and Venezuela, though all then eligible to borrow from IBRD, made contributions to IDA's 12th replenishment.

Aside from their contributions under replenishment agreements, a number of countries have agreed over the years to make voluntary increases and special contributions in excess of their normal shares. Since 1964, the IDA has received regular support from the IBRD through the transfer of some of its net income not needed for the Bank's own purposes. When combined with repayments by IDA borrowers and contributions from the World Bank's net income, the 10th replenishment will finance a total of about US$22 billion in development credits.

B. Terms of IDA Lending

IDA provides credits to its borrowers, interest-free with a 35- to 40-year final maturity and a 10-year grace period. Although IDA does not charge interest, it does charge a small administrative fee of 0.75% against the outstanding balance of credits to meet administrative expenses. There is also a commitment fee of 0.5% of 50 basis points, but this has been waived since fiscal year 1989. IDA's credits are thus highly concessional with a grant element of about 85%.

C. IDA Operations

While the IDA's financial terms are liberal, its economic and technical criteria for development credits are exactly the same as those applied by the IBRD in lending on conventional terms. Each credit must be justified by the borrowing country's economic position, prospects, and policies. Credits are extended only for high-priority purposes that, in the words of the IDA's Articles of Agreement, will "promote economic development, increase productivity, and thus raise standards of living in the less-developed areas of the world."

Since the IDA's resources have been considerably less than the need of developing countries for additional external finance on easy terms, they must be carefully rationed on the basis of need and prospects for their most effective use. Borrowing countries typically have per capita GNPs below an established threshold. In 1998, most eligible countries had incomes below US$400 per capita.

D. IDA'S Evolving Role

IDA has taken an active role in helping governments undertaking structural adjustment to protect and expand social and environmental programs. It supports rural development programs and projects which aim to increase agricultural productivity and ensure adequate food supplies. IDA also finances projects that give special attention to improving women's incomes and status in their communities. The Association has markedly increased its support for population, health, and nutrition projects.

Environmental concerns have been integrated into all aspects of IDA's operations. The Association is helping borrowers develop their own Environmental Action Plans to identify the policy changes and investments that are required for environmentally sustainable development.

In fiscal 1998, IDA disbursed US$5.7 billion; of this amount, 38% went to African countries, 34% to South Asia, 10% to East Asia and the Pacific, 10% to Eastern Europe and Central Asia, and the remainder (about 8%) to poor countries in North Africa and in Latin America.

1998 Top Ten Disbursement Recipients

NATION	US$ millions
India	801
China	596
Bangladesh	331
Vietnam	238
Côte d'Ivoire	215
Ghana	211
Pakistan	190
Uganda	243
Zambia	157
Tanzania	153

IDA is the largest single source of multilateral concessional funds. Its annual net disbursements of around US$6 billion are about 30% of net concessional multilateral disbursements, and 12% of Official Development Assistance. The Association also helps mobilize and coordinate aid from other multilateral organizations and donor countries. IDA's involvement is often a catalyst for other bilateral aid donors and regional development banks to participate in providing assistance. On average, for every dollar IDA commits, 50 cents of cofinancing is mobilized.

In the 1990s, IDA provided US$85.6 million to Bosnia for landmine clearing, housing repair, electric power reconstruction, public works and employment, and the demobilization and reintegration of former combatants.

THE INTERNATIONAL FINANCE CORPORATION (IFC)

Background

The International Finance Corporation is the member of the World Bank Group that promotes the growth of the private sector in less developed member countries. The IFC's principal activity is helping finance individual private enterprise projects that contribute to the economic development of the country or region where the project is located. The IFC is the World Bank Group's investment bank for developing countries. It lends directly to private companies and makes equity investments in them, without guarantees from governments, and attracts other sources of funds for private-sector projects. IFC also provides advisory services and technical assistance to governments and businesses.

Creation

Within a few years of the founding of the International Bank for Reconstruction and Development (IBRD), it became evident that sufficient provision had not been made for financing the development of the private sector in countries looking to the UN system for aid. The Bank's charter restrained it from making equity (capital stock) investments or from lending money, directly or indirectly, to a private company without a governmental guarantee. Yet "venture capital" was the very thing needed in many developing countries to get a variety of productive enterprises underway, and the amount of venture capital available through private banking and investment channels was inadequate.

The first public suggestion for an international institution to close this gap appeared in a report, "Partners and Progress," which Nelson Rockefeller (then chairman of the advisory board of the Point 4 Program) had submitted to President Harry S. Truman in 1951. The matter was taken up by the staff of the IBRD, and in 1952, the Bank submitted proposals for such an institution to the UN Economic and Social Council. Some members of the Council, including the UK and the US, voiced the fear that the proposed institution might deter the flow of private capital to the developing countries. They also objected in principle to an intergovernmental organization's having the right to purchase shares in private companies.

The majority of members of the Economic and Social Council, however, strongly endorsed the idea of an international financial institution to aid private sector development, and by late 1954, a compromise was worked out. The International Finance Corporation, as originally established, could lend money to private enterprises without government guarantees, but it was not empowered to make equity investments, though loans with certain equity features, such as stock options, were allowed. The 31 countries necessary to launch the IFC pledged their consent over the next 18 months, and the IFC formally came into existence on 14 July 1956 as a separate legal entity affiliated with the IBRD.

The IFC's early investments often included such features as stock options and other profit-sharing devices in lieu of direct equity financing, but the terms were complex and difficult to negotiate, and it soon became apparent to all concerned that IFC's effectiveness was severely circumscribed by the restriction on equity investment. Proposals to amend the charter so as to permit the IFC to hold shares were put to the Board of Directors and the Board of Governors and approved in 1961—with the support, this time, of both the UK and the US. The revision of IFC's charter in 1961 to permit investment in equities made it possible to broaden and diversify operations, as well as to simplify the terms of investment. With the demand for IFC's services steadily expanding, the Board of Directors amended the charter again in 1965 to permit the IFC to borrow from the IBRD up to four times its unimpaired subscribed capital and surplus.

Purposes

IFC's purpose is to foster economic growth by promoting private sector investment in its developing member countries. It accomplishes this by providing venture capital for productive private enterprises in association with local investors and management, by encouraging the development of local capital markets, and by stimulating the flow of private capital. The Corporation is designed to supplement, rather than replace, private capital. It plays an important catalytic role in mobilizing additional project funding from other investors and lenders, either in the form of cofinancing or through loan syndications, the underwriting of debt and equity securities issues, and guarantees. In addition to project finance and resource mobilization, IFC offers a full array of advisory services and technical assistance in such areas as capital market development, corporate restructuring, risk management, and project preparation and evaluation, and advises governments on creating an environment that encourages the growth of private enterprise and foreign investment.

Membership

Membership in the IFC is open to all members of IBRD. As of March 2000, IFC had 174 member states.

Structure

The structure of IFC is similar to that of the IBRD. IFC's Board of Governors consists of those governors of the Bank (IBRD) whose countries are also members of IFC. Its Board of Directors is composed of all the Executive Directors of the Bank. The annual meeting of the IFC Board of Governors is held in conjunction with the annual meeting of the Board of Governors of the IBRD. IFC headquarters are at 2121 Pennsylvania Ave. N.W., Washington, D.C.

The first president of the IFC was Robert L. Garner, formerly vice-president of the IBRD. Since 1961, the president of the Bank also has been the president of the Corporation. The immediate direction of the Corporation is the responsibility of the executive vice-president, Peter Woicke, whose term becam effective 1 January 1999. IFC has more than 800 staff from 99 countries.

ACTIVITIES

A. Financial Resources

IFC's investments are funded out of its net worth—the total of paid-in capital and retained earnings. Of the funding required for its lending operations, 80% is borrowed in the international financial markets through public bond issues or private placements; the remaining 20% is borrowed from the IBRD.

Earnings and Borrowings

IFC's net income for fiscal year 1999 was US$249 million; paid-in capital was US$2,300 million; retained earnings were US$3,000 million; and borrowings amounted to US$4,300 million. IFC may borrow from the IBRD for use in its lending operations as long as the Corporation's total borrowings do not exceed four times its unimpaired subscribed capital and surplus.

Disbursements

In 1999 IFC approved 255 new projects; total financing approved, including syndications and underwriting was US$5.3 billion. The total project costs of commitments was US$13.3 billion. Since its founding in 1956 and through 1999, IFC committed more than US$26.7 billion of its own funds and arranged US$17.9 billion in syndications and underwriting for 2,264 companies in 135 developing countries.

B. Investment Policies

Unlike the IBRD, IFC lends to private companies and does not accept guarantees from host-country governments. It also makes equity investments in developing-country businesses, and mobilizes additional loan and equity financing in the international financial markets. Because of the success of IFC's operations, its bond issues in the international markets have earned triple-A ratings from Moody's and Standard and Poor's.

IFC is the single largest source of direct financing for private sector projects in developing countries. Although IFC invests and lends on market terms, it does not compete with private capital. It finances projects unable to obtain sufficient funding on reasonable terms from other sources. Normally, IFC does not finance more than 25% of total project costs, so as to ensure that most of the project financing comes from private investors and lenders. And while IFC may buy up to 35% of the stock of a company, it is never the largest shareholder and does not take part in a firm's management. But since IFC does not accept government guarantees, it shares all project risks with its partners.

IFC finances the creation of new companies as well as the expansion or modernization of established companies in sectors ranging from agribusiness to manufacturing to energy to mining. A number of IFC projects involve building up the financial sectors of developing countries, for example by financing the creation of institutions such as investment banks and insurance companies.

IFC can provide loans, equity investments, and arrange quasi-equity instruments—in whatever combination is necessary to ensure that a project is soundly funded from the outset. The Corporation can provide additional financial support through contingent financing or full or partial guarantees of other sources of financing. In the past few years, IFC has made derivative products, such as currency and interest rate swaps, available to companies in developing countries. It has intermediated several such swaps for companies in Bolivia, Egypt, Ghana, and Mexico, helping them gain access to risk-management techniques commonly used by companies in industrialized countries but not normally available to companies in the developing world.

C. IFC Investments

The IFC's history has been marked by growth in the number and size of investments and by a continued search for new ways to assist its member countries. An improved policy environment in many of IFC's developing member countries has helped the Corporation to make a larger contribution to economic development. Helping companies in developing countries achieve a proper balance between debt and equity financing is a key IFC objective.

In addition to approving debt and equity financing for its own account, the Corporation approved the mobilization of US$1.8 billion in financing from other investors and lenders through loan syndications and the underwriting of securities issues. It also mobilized considerable cofinancing. The total costs of the projects approved during the year were estimated to be US$17 billion. Thus, for every US$1 of financing approved by IFC for its own account, other investors and lenders will provide US$7.

The efficient provision of services in such sectors as power, water, transportation, and communications is critical to successful private sector development. A growing number of IFC's member countries are opening these sectors, once the preserve of the state, to private investment and management.

The countries of Eastern and Central Europe and the former Soviet republics are a new focus of IFC's work. IFC's role includes financing private-sector projects and advising governments on creating a modern financial sector, selling off state-owned enterprises, and attracting foreign investment.

IFC advised governments officials in Russia and Ukraine on different techniques for privatizing state enterprises, and developed privatization programs that can be used as models by local authorities in both republics. It helped design and implement the auction of small enterprises in three regions in Russia—Nizhny Novgorod, Volgograd, and Tomsk—and in the city of L'viv, Ukraine, and produced a manual on the privatization of small enterprises.

In many developing countries small-scale entrepreneurs with promising ideas are often unable to get the financing or advice they need to start or expand businesses. IFC has set up project development facilities in Sub-Saharan Africa, Central America and the Caribbean, the South Pacific Islands, and Poland to help entrepreneurs prepare project proposals. Although these facilities do not themselves fund projects, they help entrepreneurs find loans and equity financing on reasonable terms. The Africa Enterprise Fund, established in 1989, is a special program devoted to financing small and medium-sized businesses in Sub-Saharan Africa.

Advisory Services and Technical Assistance

In the course of conducting project appraisals, IFC may provide considerable technical assistance to companies—for example, by helping them select a technical partner or a technology, identify markets for their products, and put together the most appropriate financial package. The Corporation also advises companies on financial restructuring, helping them reduce their debt.

IFC advises member governments on an array of issues, such as capital markets development. It helps governments create and put in place the regulatory, legal, and fiscal frameworks necessary for financial institutions to operate efficiently. IFC also provides advice on privatization and on restructuring state enterprises slated for privatization. The Foreign Investment Advisory Service, established by IFC and operated jointly with the Multilateral Investment Guarantee Agency and IBRD, advises governments on attracting direct foreign investment.

MIGA Shares and Voting Power
(as of March 2000)

MEMBER	SHARES	VOTING POWER NUMBER OF VOTES	% OF TOTAL	MEMBER	SHARES	VOTING POWER NUMBER OF VOTES	% OF TOTAL
Albania	58	235	0.18	Israel	654	831	0.62
Algeria	649	826	0.62	Italy	2,820	2,997	2.24
Angola	187	364	0.27	Jamaica	181	358	0.27
Argentina	1,254	1,431	1.07	Japan	7,037	7,214	5.38
Armenia	80	257	0.19	Jordan	97	274	0.20
Australia	1,713	1,890	1.41	Kazakhstan	209	386	0.29
Austria	775	952	0.71	Kenya	172	349	0.26
Azerbaijan	115	292	0.22	Korea, Republic of	449	626	0.47
Bahamas	138	315	0.24	Kuwait	930	1,107	0.83
Bahrain	77	254	0.19	Kyrgyz Republic	77	254	0.19
Bangladesh	340	517	0.39	Latvia	97	274	0.20
Barbados	68	245	0.18	Lebanon	142	319	0.24
Belarus	233	410	0.31	Lesotho	50	227	0.17
Belgium	2,030	2,207	1.65	Libya	549	726	0.54
Belize	50	227	0.17	Lithuania	106	283	0.21
Benin	61	238	0.18	Luxembourg	116	293	0.22
Bolivia	125	302	0.23	Macedonia, Former Yugoslav Rep. of	50	227	0.17
Bosnia and Herzegovina	80	257	0.19	Madagascar	100	277	0.21
Botswana	50	227	0.17	Malawi	77	254	0.19
Brazil	1,479	1,656	1.24	Malaysia	579	756	0.56
Bulgaria	365	542	0.40	Mali	81	258	0.19
Burkina Faso	61	238	0.18	Malta	103	280	0.21
Burundi	74	251	0.19	Mauritania	63	240	0.18
Cambodia	93	270	0.20	Mauritius	153	330	0.25
Cameroon	107	284	0.21	Micronesia	50	227	0.17
Canada	2,965	3,142	2.34	Moldova	96	273	0.20
Cape Verde	50	227	0.17	Mongolia	58	235	0.18
Chile	485	662	0.49	Morocco	348	525	0.39
China	3,138	3,315	2.47	Mozambique	97	274	0.20
Colombia	437	614	0.46	Namibia	107	284	0.21
Congo	65	242	0.18	Nepal	69	246	0.18
Congo, Democratic Republic of	338	515	0.38	Netherlands	3,822	3,999	2.98
Costa Rica	117	294	0.22	Nicaragua	102	279	0.21
Côte d'Ivoire	176	353	0.26	Nigeria	844	1,021	0.76
Croatia	187	364	0.27	Norway	699	876	0.65
Cyprus	104	281	0.21	Oman	94	271	0.20
Czech Republic	445	622	0.46	Pakistan	660	837	0.62
Denmark	718	895	0.67	Palau	50	227	0.17
Dominica	50	227	0.17	Panama	131	308	0.23
Dominican Republic	147	324	0.24	Papua New Guinea	96	273	0.20
Ecuador	182	359	0.27	Paraguay	80	257	0.19
Egypt	459	636	0.47	Peru	373	550	0.41
El Salvador	122	299	0.22	Philippines	484	661	0.49
Equatorial Guinea	50	227	0.17	Poland	764	941	0.70
Eritrea	50	227	0.17	Portugal	527	704	0.53
Estonia	65	242	0.18	Qatar	137	314	0.23
Ethiopia	70	247	0.18	Romania	555	732	0.55
Fiji	71	248	0.19	Russian Federation	3,137	3,314	2.47
Finland	600	777	0.58	Samoa	50	227	0.17
France	4,860	5,037	3.76	Saudi Arabia	3,137	3,314	2.47
Gambia	50	227	0.17	Senegal	145	322	0.24
Georgia	111	288	0.21	Seychelles	50	227	0.17
Germany	5,071	5,248	3.92	Sierra Leone	75	252	0.19
Ghana	245	422	0.31	Singapore	154	331	0.25
Greece	386	563	0.42	Slovak Republic	222	399	0.30
Grenada	50	227	0.17	Slovenia	102	279	0.21
Guatemala	140	317	0.24	South Africa	1,302	1,479	1.10
Guinea	91	268	0.20	Spain	2,265	2,442	1.82
Guyana	84	261	0.19	Sri Lanka	271	448	0.33
Haiti	75	252	0.19	St. Kitts And Nevis	50	227	0.17
Honduras	101	278	0.21	St. Lucia	50	227	0.17
Hungary	564	741	0.55	St. Vincent and the Grenadines	50	227	0.17
Iceland	90	267	0.20	Sudan	206	383	0.29
India	3,048	3,225	2.41	Swaziland	58	235	0.18
Indonesia	1,049	1,226	0.91	Sweden	1,049	1,226	0.91
Ireland	369	546	0.41	Switzerland	1,500	1,677	1.25

MIGA Shares and Voting Power (continued)
(as of March 2000)

MEMBER	SHARES	VOTING POWER NUMBER OF VOTES	% OF TOTAL	MEMBER	SHARES	VOTING POWER NUMBER OF VOTES	% OF TOTAL
Tanzania	141	318	0.24	Uruguay	202	379	0.28
Togo	77	254	0.19	Uzbekistan	175	352	0.26
Trinidad And Tobago	203	380	0.28	Vanuatu	50	227	0.17
Tunisia	156	333	0.25	Venezuela	1,427	1,604	1.20
Turkey	462	639	0.48	Vietnam	220	397	0.30
Turkmenistan	66	243	0.18	Yemen	155	332	0.25
Uganda	132	309	0.23	Zambia	318	495	0.37
Ukraine	764	941	0.70	Zimbabwe	236	413	0.31
United Arab Emirates	372	549	0.41				
United Kingdom	4,860	5,037	3.76	TOTAL	107,280	134,007	100%
United States	20,519	20,696	15.44				

Member countries of IBRD, IFC, IDA, MIGA and ICSID
(as of March 2000)

	IBRD	IDA	IFC	MIGA	ICSID
Afghanistan	X	X	X		X
Albania	X	X	X	X	X
Algeria	X	X	X	X	X
Angola	X	X	X	X	
Antigua and Barbuda	X		X		
Argentina	X	X	X	X	X
Armenia	X	X	X	X	X
Australia	X	X	X	X	X
Austria	X	X	X	X	X
Azerbaijan	X	X	X	X	X
Bahamas	X		X	X	X
Bahrain	X		X	X	X
Bangladesh	X	X	X	X	X
Barbados	X	X	X	X	X
Belarus	X		X	X	X
Belgium	X	X	X	X	X
Belize	X	X	X	X	
Benin	X	X	X	X	X
Bhutan	X	X			
Bolivia	X	X	X	X	X
Bosnia-Herzegovina	X	X	X	X	
Botswana	X	X	X	X	X
Brazil	X	X	X	X	
Brunei Darassalam	X				
Bulgaria	X		X	X	
Burkina Faso	X	X	X	X	X
Burundi	X	X	X	X	X
Cambodia	X	X	X	X	
Cameroon	X	X	X	X	X
Canada	X	X	X	X	
Cape Verde	X	X	X	X	
Central African Republic	X	X	X		X
Chad	X	X	X		X
Chile	X	X	X	X	X
China	X	X	X	X	X
Colombia	X	X	X	X	X
Comoros	X	X	X		X
Congo	X	X	X	X	X
Congo, Dem. Rep. of the	X	X	X	X	X
Costa Rica	X	X	X	X	X
Côte d'Ivoire	X	X	X	X	X
Croatia	X	X	X	X	X
Cyprus	X	X	X	X	X
Czech Republic	X	X	X	X	X
Denmark	X	X	X	X	X
Djibouti	X	X	X		
Dominica	X	X	X	X	
Dominican Republic	X	X	X		
Ecuador	X	X	X	X	X
Egypt	X	X	X	X	X
El Salvador	X	X	X	X	X
Equatorial Guinea	X	X	X	X	
Eritrea	X	X	X	X	
Estonia	X		X	X	X
Ethiopia	X	X	X	X	
Fiji	X	X	X	X	X
Finland	X	X	X	X	X
France	X	X	X	X	X
Gabon	X	X	X		X
Gambia	X	X	X	X	
Georgia	X	X	X	X	X
Germany	X	X	X	X	X
Ghana	X	X	X	X	X
Greece	X	X	X	X	X
Grenada	X	X	X	X	X
Guatemala	X	X	X	X	X
Guinea	X	X	X	X	X
Guinea-Bissau	X	X	X		
Guyana	X	X	X	X	X
Haiti	X	X	X	X	
Honduras	X	X	X	X	X
Hungary	X	X	X	X	X
Iceland	X	X	X	X	X
India	X	X	X	X	
Indonesia	X	X	X	X	X
Iran	X	X	X		
Iraq	X	X	X		
Ireland	X	X	X		X
Israel	X	X	X	X	X
Italy	X	X	X	X	X
Jamaica	X		X	X	X
Japan	X	X	X	X	X
Jordan	X	X	X	X	X
Kazakhstan	X	X	X	X	
Kenya	X	X	X	X	X
Kiribati	X	X	X		
Korea, Republic of	X	X	X	X	X
Kuwait	X	X	X	X	X
Kyrgyzstan	X	X	X	X	
Lao People's Dem. Rep.	X	X	X		

Member countries of IBRD, IFC, IDA, MIGA and ICSID (continued)
(as of March 2000)

	IBRD	IDA	IFC	MIGA	ICSID
Latvia	X	X	X	X	X
Lebanon	X	X	X	X	
Lesotho	X	X	X	X	X
Liberia	X	X	X		X
Libya	X	X	X	X	
Lithuania	X		X	X	X
Luxembourg	X	X	X	X	X
Macedonia, Former Yugoslav Rep. of	X	X	X	X	X
Madagascar	X	X	X	X	X
Malawi	X	X	X	X	X
Malaysia	X	X	X	X	X
Maldives	X	X	X		
Mali	X	X	X	X	X
Malta	X			X	
Marshall Islands	X	X	X		
Mauritania	X	X	X	X	X
Mauritius	X	X	X	X	X
Mexico	X	X	X		
Micronesia	X	X	X	X	X
Moldova	X	X	X	X	
Mongolia	X	X	X	X	X
Morocco	X	X	X	X	X
Mozambique	X	X	X	X	X
Myanmar	X	X	X		
Namibia	X		X	X	
Nepal	X	X	X	X	X
Netherlands	X	X	X	X	X
New Zealand	X	X	X		X
Nicaragua	X	X	X	X	X
Niger	X	X	X		X
Nigeria	X	X	X	X	X
Norway	X	X	X	X	X
Oman	X	X	X	X	X
Pakistan	X	X	X	X	X
Palau	X	X	X	X	
Panama	X	X	X	X	X
Papua New Guinea	X	X	X	X	X
Paraguay	X	X	X	X	X
Peru	X	X	X	X	X
Philippines	X	X	X	X	X
Poland	X	X	X	X	
Portugal	X	X	X	X	X
Qatar	X			X	
Romania	X		X	X	X
Russian Federation	X	X	X	X	
Rwanda	X	X	X		X
St. Kitts and Nevis	X	X	X	X	X
St. Lucia	X	X	X	X	X
St. Vincent and the Grenadines	X	X		X	
Samoa	X	X	X	X	X
São Tomé and Principe	X	X			
Saudi Arabia	X	X	X	X	X
Senegal	X	X	X	X	X
Seychelles	X		X	X	X
Sierra Leone	X	X	X	X	X
Singapore	X		X	X	X
Slovakia	X	X	X	X	X
Slovenia	X	X	X	X	X
Solomon Islands	X	X	X		
Somalia	X	X	X		X
South Africa	X	X	X	X	
Spain	X	X	X	X	X
Sri Lanka	X	X	X	X	X
Sudan	X	X	X	X	X
Suriname	X				
Swaziland	X	X	X	X	X
Sweden	X	X	X	X	X
Switzerland	X	X	X	X	X
Syria	X	X	X		
Tajikistan	X	X	X		
Thailand	X	X	X		
Togo	X	X	X	X	X
Tonga	X	X	X		X
Trinidad and Tobago	X	X	X	X	X
Tunisia	X	X	X	X	X
Turkey	X	X	X	X	X
Turkmenistan	X		X	X	X
Uganda	X	X	X	X	X
Ukraine	X		X	X	
United Arab Emirates	X	X	X	X	X
United Kingdom	X	X	X	X	X
United Republic of Tanzania	X	X	X	X	X
United States	X	X	X	X	X
Uruguay	X		X	X	
Uzbekistan	X	X	X	X	X
Vanuatu	X	X	X	X	
Venezuela	X		X	X	X
Vietnam	X	X	X	X	
Yemen	X	X	X	X	
Yugoslavia					X
Zambia	X	X	X	X	X
Zimbabwe	X	X	X	X	X

Executive Directors of the IFC and Voting Power
(on 8 March 2000)

DIRECTOR	CASTING VOTES OF	TOTAL VOTES	% OF TOTAL	DIRECTOR	CASTING VOTES OF	TOTAL VOTES	% OF TOTAL
APPOINTED				Pieter Stek (Netherlands)		86,262	3.6
Jan Piercy	United States	569,629	23.74		Armenia		
Satoru Miyamura	Japan	141,424	5.89		Bosnia And Herzegovina		
Helmut Schaffer	Germany	129,158	5.38		Bulgaria		
Jean-Claude Milleron	France	121,265	5.05		Croatia		
Stephen Pickford	United Kingdom	121,265	5.05		Cyprus		
					Georgia		
ELECTED					Israel		
Ruth Bachmayer (Austria)		125,221	5.22		Macedonia, Former Yugoslav Rep. of		
	Austria				Moldova		
	Belarus				Netherlands		
	Belgium				Romania		
	Czech Republic				Ukraine		
	Hungary						
	Kazakhstan			Andre Bugrov (Russian Fed.)		81,592	3.4
	Luxembourg				Russian Federation		
	Slovak Republic						
	Slovenia			Murilo Portugal (Brazil)		74,779	3.12
	Turkey				Brazil		
					Colombia		
Franco Passacantando (Italy)		98,866	4.12		Dominican Republic		
	Albania				Ecuador		
	Greece				Haiti		
	Italy				Panama		
	Malta				Philippines		
	Portugal				Suriname		
					Trinidad And Tobago		
B. P. Singh (India)		98,264	4.1				
	Bangladesh			Neil Hyden (Australia)		73,204	3.05
	Bhutan				Australia		
	India				Cambodia		
	Sri Lanka				Kiribati		
					Korea, Republic of		
Federico Ferrer (Spain)		97,375	4.06		Marshall Islands		
	Costa Rica				Micronesia, Fed. States of		
	El Salvador				Mongolia		
	Guatemala				New Zealand		
	Honduras				Palau		
	Mexico				Papua New Guinea		
	Nicaragua				Samoa		
	Spain				Solomon Islands		
	Venezuela				Vanuatu		
Terry O'leary (Canada)		92,944	3.87	Valeriano F. Garcia (Argentina)		64,144	2.67
	Antigua And Barbuda				Argentina		
	Bahamas				Bolivia		
	Barbados				Chile		
	Belize				Paraguay		
	Canada				Peru		
	Dominica				Uruguay		
	Grenada						
	Guyana			Matthias Meyer (Switzerland)		60,548	2.52
	Ireland				Azerbaijan		
	Jamaica				Kyrgyz Republic		
	St. Kitts And Nevis				Poland		
	St. Lucia				Switzerland		
	St. Vincent and the Grenadines				Tajikistan		
					Turkmenistan		
Ilkka Niemi (Finland)		86,693	3.61		Uzbekistan		
	Denmark						
	Estonia			James Hutagalung (Indonesia)		59,912	2.5
	Finland				Brunei Darussalam		
	Iceland				Fiji		
	Latvia				Indonesia		
	Lithuania				Lao People's Dem. Rep.		
	Norway				Malaysia		
	Sweden				Myanmar		
					Nepal		

Executive Directors of the IFC and Voting Power (continued)
(on 8 March 2000)

DIRECTOR	CASTING VOTES OF	TOTAL VOTES	% OF TOTAL	DIRECTOR	CASTING VOTES OF	TOTAL VOTES	% OF TOTAL
	Singapore				Kuwait		
	Thailand				Lebanon		
	Tonga				Libya		
	Vietnam				Maldives		
					Oman		
Godfrey Gaoseb (Namibia)		58,773	2.45		Qatar		
	Angola				Syrian Arab Republic		
	Botswana				United Arab Emirates		
	Burundi				Yemen		
	Eritrea						
	Ethiopia			Yahya Alyahya (Saudi Arabia)		30,312	1.26
	Gambia, The				Saudi Arabia		
	Kenya						
	Lesotho			Zhu Xian (China)		24,750	1.03
	Liberia				China		
	Malawi						
	Mozambique			Bassary Toure (Mali)		22,947	0.96
	Namibia				Benin		
	Nigeria				Burkina Faso		
	Seychelles				Cameroon		
	Sierra Leone				Cape Verde		
	South Africa				Central African Republic		
	Sudan				Chad		
	Swaziland				Comoros		
	Tanzania				Congo		
	Uganda				Congo, Dem. Rep. of		
	Zambia				Côte d'Ivoire		
	Zimbabwe				Djibouti		
					Equatorial Guinea		
Inaamul Haque (Pakistan)		46,016	1.92		Gabon		
	Algeria				Guinea		
	Ghana				Guinea-Bissau		
	Iran				Madagascar		
	Iraq				Mali		
	Morocco				Mauritania		
	Pakistan				Mauritius		
	Tunisia				Niger		
					Rwanda		
Khalid M. Al-saad (Kuwait)		34,079	1.42		São Tomé and Principe		
	Bahrain				Senegal		
	Egypt				Togo		
	Jordan						

SUPPLEMENTS

POLAR REGIONS

ANTARCTICA

Antarctica, the coldest and second-smallest continent (after Australia), is centered on the South Pole and is situated almost entirely within the Antarctic Circle at 66 1/2°s. Some 97% of the total area of about 13,924,000 sq km (5,376,000 sq mi) is covered by ice, and the continent contains about 90% of the world's ice and 70% of the fresh water. Antarctica is bounded by the South Atlantic, Indian, and South Pacific oceans. The nearest points of land are the southern tip of South America, South Georgia, the South Sandwich Islands, the South Orkney Islands, and the South Shetland Islands. All of these islands are located within the Antarctic Convergence, which encircles Antarctica at approximately 1,600 km (1,000 mi) from the coast and divides the cold Antarctic waters from the warmer waters of the three oceans, in a zone of perpetual turbulence.

Some 200 million years ago, Antarctica was joined to South America, Africa, India, and Australia in a large single continent, Gondwanaland; subsequent geological changes caused the breakup into separate continental masses. Recent geological studies and fossil finds indicate that Antarctica once had a tropical environment, but that its present ice sheet is at least 20 million years old.

The Transantarctic Mountains divide the continent into two parts: the larger East Antarctic ice sheet, with land mostly above sea level; and the smaller West Antarctic ice sheet, with land mostly below sea level. The highest point is the Vinson Massif (4,897 m/16,066 ft), in the Ellsworth Mountains of West Antarctica. The South Pole lies at an altitude of about 3,000 m (9,800 ft). The Antarctic ice sheet averages 2,160 m (7,090 ft) in depth and is 4,776 m (15,670 ft) deep at its thickest point. Glaciers form ice shelves along nearly half the coastline. The larger ice shelves—the Amery in the east, Ross in the south, and Ronne in the northwest—move seaward at speeds of from 900 to 1,300 m (2,950–4,250 ft) per year. Sea ice up to 3 m (10 ft) thick forms a belt about 500 km (300 mi) wide that encircles the continent in winter. Ice-free areas are located generally along the coast and include the dry valleys in southern Victoria Land and the Bunger Oasis in Wilkes Land. Largely ice-free areas where much scientific activity takes place are on the coast of the Antarctic Peninsula, and on Ross Island in McMurdo Sound.

The severity of the Antarctic cold varies with location and altitude. East Antarctica has the coldest climate; the Antarctic Peninsula in the west has the mildest, with summer temperatures generally remaining above freezing. The mean annual temperature of the interior regions is −57°C (−71°F); mean temperatures at the coastal McMurdo station range from −28°C (−18°F) in August to −3°C (27°F) in January. The world's record low temperature of −89.2°C (−128.6°F) was registered at what was the Soviet's Vostok station on 24 August 1960; highs of 15°C (59°F) have been measured on the northernmost Antarctic Peninsula. The interior is a vast desert, with annual precipitation averaging below 3 cm (1 in). The coastland is considerably more humid, with annual precipitation of about 25 cm (10 in) along the coasts of East Antarctica and the Antarctic Peninsula. Adélie Coast, in the southeast near the South Magnetic Pole, has recorded average wind speeds of 64 km/hr (40 mph), with gusts of nearly 320 km/hr (200 mph).

Because of its polar location, Antarctica has six months of continuous daylight from mid-September to mid-March, with the maximum 24 hours of light received at the summer solstice on 22 December; and six months of continuous darkness from mid-March to mid-September, with the winter solstice occurring on 22 June. In summer, the continent receives more solar radiation than even the Equator over a 24-hour period.

Although Antarctica has no native humans or large terrestrial mammals, it does have a varied marine life ranging from microscopic plankton to the largest whales and including about 100 species of fish. Land life includes bacteria, lichens, mosses, two kinds of flowering plants (in the ice-free areas), penguins, and some flying birds. Six types of seal—the crabeater, Weddell, elephant, leopard, fur, and Ross—thrive in Antarctica and together number about 32.7 million, with the crabeaters accounting for nearly 94% of the total. The once-numerous fur seals were reduced by uncontrolled slaughter (about 1 million were killed on South Georgia alone in 1820–22) to near extinction by 1870. This ended the Antarctic fur-sealing industry; since then, the number of fur seals has gradually increased, to more than 1 million, mostly on South Georgia. In 1972, the 12 nations active in the Antarctic signed the Convention for the Conservation of Antarctic Seals, which prohibits the killing of fur, elephant, and Ross seals, and sets annual quotas for the harvest of crabeater, leopard, and Weddell seals. The treaty entered into force in 1978, and as of 1987 had been ratified by 12 nations. In 1982, the Convention on the Conservation of Antarctic Marine Living Resources entered into force, assuring the protection of ecosystems found in the Antarctic waters; as of 1994, over 20 countries and the EC were parties to the treaty.

Exploitation by humans threatens the survival of the Antarctic whales—the sperm, blue, humpback, fin, minke, and sei—which decreased in number from more than 1,500,000 at the beginning of the 20th century to fewer than 700,000 by the mid-1980s. Since 1972, the International Whaling Commission (IWC) has set quotas by species on the taking of whales, and the survival of all species of Antarctic whales seemed assured by the early 1980s. In 1982, the IWC approved a moratorium on the commercial killing of all whales that began in 1985. However, Japanese fishermen caught 3,087 whales in 1985 and 2,769 in 1986. Japan promised to end commercial whaling in 1988 but announced plans to harvest 300 minke (nonendangered) whales in Antarctic waters for "research" purposes during the winter of 1987–88; these plans were criticized by the IWC. As recently s May 14, 1993 the IWC voted to uphold the ban on commerical whaling. Immediately after the IWC's decision Norway said it would withdraw its membership. Canada is a former member of the IWC but is generally adheres to IWC regulations and decisions.

Exploration

The ancient Greeks reasoned that there must be an "Antarctic" (opposite the Arctic) to balance the large land mass in the Northern Hemisphere, but it was not until the 19th century that definite proof was found that the continent existed. British Capt. James Cook had crossed the Antarctic Circle and circumnavigated the continent without sighting land (1772–75). In 1820, however, two other British mariners, William Smith and James

Bransfield, discovered and mapped the Antarctic Peninsula, which was also explored by the American sea captain Nathaniel Palmer and the Englishman James Weddell, who discovered the sea that bears his name. Russian Adm. Fabian von Bellingshausen sailed around Antarctica during his 1819–21 voyage and found Queen Maud Land and Peter I Island.

On 7 February 1821, US Capt. John Davis made the first known landing on the continent at Hughes Bay, in the northwest. Many other British and US sealers explored the area, including 11 shipwrecked Englishmen who spent the winter of 1821 on King George Island, in the South Shetlands. Palmer and Benjamin Pendleton led a pioneering expedition in 1828–30 that included James Eights, the first American scientist to visit Antarctica. In 1837, a French expedition under J. S. C. Dumont d'Urville discovered the Adélie Coast (named for his wife) in eastern Antarctica. A year later, Lt. Charles Wilkes of the US Navy sailed along the coast of eastern Antarctica for about 2,400 km (1,500 mi), thereby definitely establishing that Antarctica was a continent, not a cluster of islands. During his 1839–43 Antarctic voyage, British Capt. James C. Ross discovered Victoria Land and the sea and the ice shelf that were later named in his honor.

With the decline of the fur seal industry, Antarctic exploration was neglected for about 50 years, until Norwegian and Scottish whalers began operating in the area. A Norwegian whaling captain, Carl Anton Larsen, explored the east coast of the Antarctic Peninsula in 1892 and found the first fossils. Thus began a period of intensive exploration during which 9 countries sent 16 expeditions to Antarctica. Another Norwegian captain, Leonard Kristensen, landed at Cape Adare, on McMurdo Sound, in 1895. It was there that a British expedition, led by a Norwegian, Carsten Egeberg Borchgrevink, established a base in 1899; Borchgrevink became the first explorer to probe inland by sledge. Swedish, Scottish, Belgian, and French expeditions also arrived, and four British expeditions set up bases on Ross Island. From there, Sir Ernest Henry Shackleton sledged to within 156 km (97 mi) of the South Pole on 9 January 1909.

This feat encouraged five national expeditions to compete for the goal in 1911, and the competition narrowed to a "race to the pole" between Capt. Robert F. Scott and Roald Amundsen of Norway. Amundsen and four companions, with sledges and 52 dogs, left their base on the Ross Ice Shelf on 20 October, scaled 3,000-m (10,000-ft) glaciers in the Queen Maud Mountains, ascended to the icy plateau, and located the South Pole by celestial observation on 14 December. They returned to their base by late January 1912. Meanwhile, Scott's party of five explorers, who had left McMurdo Sound on 1 November, reached the pole on 18 January 1912, only to find that Amundsen had beaten them there by more than a month. Disheartened, they met with mishaps on the return journey and, weakened by food shortages and exhausted from man-hauling their sledges, they all perished on the ice in late March. Another expedition that ended badly was led in 1914–15 by Shackleton, who lost his ship *Endurance* in heavy pack ice in the Weddell Sea and, with five companions, made a perilous 1,300-km (800-mi) journey in an open whale boat to South Georgia Island, where he got help to rescue his stranded men. Shackleton died at South Georgia in 1922, while preparing another expedition.

Technological advances were applied to Antarctic exploration after World War I. An Australian, Sir Hubert Wilkins, in 1928 became the first man to fly an airplane along the Antarctic Peninsula. The following year, US Navy Adm. Richard Evelyn Byrd flew over the South Pole, with his Norwegian-American pilot Bernt Balchen; Byrd established the Little America base on the Ross Ice Shelf, and was the first explorer to coordinate airplanes, radios, aerial cameras, and other technological aids for the purpose of exploration. Another American, Lincoln Ellsworth, was the first to complete a transantarctic flight, from the Antarctic

Peninsula to the Ross Ice Shelf, in 1935. American, British, German, and Norwegian scientific expeditions did considerable aerial mapping of the continent throughout the 1930s; research in oceanography and marine biology by a British expedition resulted in the discovery of the Antarctic Convergence. The US expedition of 1939–41, headed by Byrd, established two continuing bases in the Antarctic, but the program ended with the outbreak of World War II.

Scientific Research

After the war, the US took the lead in conducting scientific research in Antarctica. The Navy's Operation Highjump (1946–47), the largest expedition ever made to the continent, involved 4,700 men, 13 ships, and 25 airplanes to map extensive coastal areas by aerial photography. The Antarctic Research Expedition (1947–48), headed by Finn Ronne, was a privately sponsored US expedition to the continent. A major joint international expedition (1949–52), mounted by the UK, Norway, and Sweden, initiated the use of geophysical methods on a large scale to determine the thickness of ice caps. The former USSR also mounted expeditions, in 1946–47 and 1951–52.

The greatest scientific undertaking involving the Antarctic was the International Geophysical Year (IGY) of 1957/58, in which 67 nations participated. The purpose of the IGY's Antarctic program was to study the effects of the continent's huge ice mass on global weather, the oceans, the aurora australis, and the ionosphere. More than 50 Antarctic stations were established by 12 countries: Argentina, Australia, Belgium, Chile, France, Japan, New Zealand, Norway, South Africa, the UK, the US, and the former USSR. The US built a supply base and airfield on Ross Island, a station at the South Pole that was provisioned by air, and four other stations. The former USSR had 4 bases, the UK 14, Argentina 8, and Chile 6. The South Pole was the terminus of three pole-to-pole observation chains along three meridians, and the US station at Little America analyzed meteorological reports from all over the world. Valuable information was gleaned from meteorological and seismic observations, studies of the upper atmosphere, magnetic measurements, and ice-sheet core drillings. The first surface transantarctic crossing, between the Weddell and Ross seas, was accomplished by the Commonwealth Transantarctic Expedition. After the IGY, very little of the continent remained to be explored.

An important result of the IGY's success was the continuation of significant research programs in Antarctica after 1958. Old stations were either closed or replaced with new buildings, and new stations were opened. The US constructed a year-round scientific village at McMurdo Sound, heated and lighted by a small atomic power plant that also used waste heat to distill seawater (the atomic reactor was replaced by diesel-powered units in 1972). Besides McMurdo Station, the US maintains two other year-round stations, at the South Pole and on Anvers Island, off the Antarctic Peninsula. Other countries maintaining year-round stations are the former USSR 7, Argentina 6, the UK 4, Chile 3, Australia 3, Japan 2, and 1 each by Brazil, China, the Federal Republic of Germany (FRG), France, India, Italy, New Zealand, Poland, and South Africa.

Transportation services are essential to Antarctic operations; for example, transportation expenses accounts for about half of the US's yearly expenditure in Antarctica The US, along with Argentina and New Zealand, routinely uses aircraft to carry both passengers and priority supplies to Antarctic stations. However, only four airfields can handle wheeled aircraft, those of Argentina, Chile, the former USSR, and the US. France reportedly built a fully equipped airport on the Adélie Coast. Air transport to other bases is by ski-equipped aircraft. The US has a fleet of transport airplanes which can carry large loads virtually anywhere in Antarctica. Transport between stations in the interior is provided mainly by tractor-trains and ski-equipped light aircraft. The longest surface supply route is from the former Soviet's Mirnyy station on the east coast to Vostok station in the interior, a distance of nearly 1,400 km (860 mi). Most nations operating in Antarctica rely on shipping for long-distance transportation and employ icebreakers to clear channels of pack ice. When conditions are favorable, ships offload cargo directly onto land or the ice shelf; when harbors are blocked by ice, tractors and helicopters carry passengers and cargo to shore.

Territorial Claims and International Cooperation

Seven nations have made separate territorial claims in Antarctica. Five of the claims begin at 60°s latitude and continue in the shape of a pie wedge to the South Pole. The exceptions are the claims of the UK, which start at 50°s in order to include the South Sandwich and South Georgia Islands of the Falkland chain; and of Norway, the northern and southern boundaries of which are undefined. The UK, the first nation to claim a "slice" of the continent (in 1908), was followed by New Zealand (1923), France (1924), Australia (1933), Norway (1939), Chile (1940), and Argentina (1943). The claims of Argentina and Chile overlap with each other and with that of the UK. Neither the US nor the former USSR has claimed any Antarctic territory, and neither recognizes the claims of other nations. Since international law requires "effective occupation" as the basis for ownership, and since no nation has met the criteria by sustaining such permanent occupation in Antarctica, these territorial claims have not been recognized by other countries, by the UN, or by any other international body.

In order to clarify the issue of territorial claims and to form a legal framework for the activities of nations in Antarctica, the 12 countries that had participated in the IGY signed the Antarctic Treaty on 1 December 1959: Argentina, Australia, Belgium, Chile, France, Japan, New Zealand, Norway, South Africa, the former USSR, the UK, and the US. All 12 had ratified the treaty by 23 June 1961, when it duly entered into force. Other nations that conduct Antarctic research are entitled to consultative membership; as of May 1989, seven countries—Poland (1977), Germany (1981), Brazil (1983), India (1983), China (1985), Uruguay (1985), and Italy (1987)—had attained consultative status. By that year, 23 countries in addition to the signatory nations had acceded to the terms of the treaty: Poland (1961), The Czech Republic (1962), Denmark (1965), the Netherlands (1967), Romania (1971), Brazil (1975), Bulgaria (1978), Germany (1979), Uruguay (1980), Papua New Guinea (1981), Italy (1981), Peru (1981), Spain (1982), China (1983), India (1983), Hungary (1984), Sweden (1984), Finland (1984), Cuba (1984), the Republic of Korea (1986), Austria (1987), the Democratic People's Republic of Korea (1987), and Ecuador (1987).

The Antarctic Treaty provides that "Antarctica shall be used for peaceful purposes only," and prohibits military bases, weapons testing (including nuclear explosions), and disposal of radioactive wastes. It seeks to foster freedom of scientific investigation and cooperation between nations, with the free exchange of scientific programs, observations, results, and personnel guaranteed. The treaty neither recognizes nor nullifies any preexisting territorial claims, but it does forbid any new claim or enlargement of any existing claim. The document specifies that contracting parties have the right to designate observers, and that such observers shall at all times have the right to inspect any station or installation. The treaty provides for the peaceful settlement of all disputes by the parties concerned or by the International Court of Justice. It also specifies periodic meetings between member states to exchange information and to enact measures in furtherance of treaty objectives; from 1961 to 1987, 14 consultative meetings were held. In 1991 the treaty was reviewed and renewed by 39 nations. The nations agreed to maintain the unique status of Ant-

arctica for another 50 years. The nations also agreed to establish regulations and guidelines with respect to Antarctica's mineral and natural resources.

Scientific research has continued under the provisions of the treaty, but the emphasis has shifted from short-term reconnaissance to long-term, large-scale investigations of Antarctic phenomena. Detailed study of the ice sheet has brought about increased understanding of global weather and climatic changes. The largest cooperative program completed to date has been the International Antarctic Glaciological Project (1971–81), conducted by Australia, France, the former USSR, the UK, and the US. The principal objectives are to measure precisely the East Antarctic ice sheet by means of core drillings through the ice to bedrock at several coastal and interior locations, and to make extensive aerial surveys of the area. Another collaborative project, Polar Experiment (POLEX)–South (1975–85), mounted by Argentina, the former USSR, and the US, expanded on existing national research programs on the atmosphere, ocean currents, and the ice sheet. The Dry Valley Drilling Project (1971–76), a joint project conducted by Japan, New Zealand, and the US, included geophysical exploration and bedrock drilling in the McMurdo Sound area. The Ross Ice Shelf Project, an ongoing US endeavor begun in 1973, has incorporated contributions from at least 12 other nations to measure the surface and under-ice topography, ice thickness, gravity, and seismic activity of the Ross Ice Shelf. Another US project, inaugurated in November 1983, involved the most intensive study yet of the relationship between the West Antarctica ice sheet and the global climate. A Soviet exploration project (1975–80) in the Filchner Ice Shelf of West Antarctica used aerial photography and geological surveys to evaluate the area's mineral resources. During the austral summers of 1983–86, international research resulted in significant discoveries of plant and animal fossils in Antarctica that provided new data on the geologic, climatic, and oceanic history of the Southern Hemisphere; enabled glaciologists to learn more about cycles of ice ages; and facilitated studies of Antarctic sea-ice algae and bacteria thought to be vital to the advancement of genetic engineering. In addition, a satellite link was established between the US and the McMurdo and South Pole stations. In the late 1980s, some of the most compelling research in Antarctica was focused on study of the springtime depletion of stratospheric ozone—a phenomenon popularly termed "the ozone hole"—allowing high levels of potentially harmful ultraviolet radiation to reach the earth's surface.

Resources

Estimates of Antarctica's mineral deposits are imprecise. A US Geological Survey study has concluded that the continent may contain some 900 major mineral deposits, but that only about 20 of these are likely to be found in ice-free areas. Two minerals, iron ore and coal, have been discovered in quantities that, were they accessible, would be commercially attractive. Small amounts of copper, chromium, platinum, nickel, gold, and hydrocarbons have also been found. Mineral exploration has been limited to comparatively small ice-free areas, but the Dufek Massif in the Pensacola Mountains of the Transantarctic Range shows the most potential for discovery of valuable metals. Offshore deposits of oil and natural gas show the greatest economic promise: traces of natural gas were discovered in a core taken from the Weddell Sea in 1972. However, the difficulty of operating in the harsh Antarctic climate, the inaccessibility of the deposits, and the high cost involved in mining and transportation make mineral exploitation of Antarctica unlikely for some time, if ever.

THE ARCTIC

The northernmost area of the earth's surface, the Arctic may be defined as all land and water within the Arctic Circle at 66°31′N.

However, the regional boundary may also be considered the 10°C (50°F) atmospheric isotherm for the warmest month (July), which extends well below the Arctic Circle in some places and coincides roughly with the tree line. The region, centered around the North Pole, includes the ice-covered Arctic Ocean basin, which is surrounded by the northern mainland and islands of North America and Eurasia, with outlets to the Bering Sea and the North Atlantic Ocean. The Arctic Ocean, with an area of about 14 million sq km (5.4 million sq mi), comprises nearly two-thirds of the total area. Principal land masses are the northern reaches of the former USSR, Scandinavia, Greenland, Canada, and Alaska.

Unlike Antarctica, the Arctic region has a year-round habitable climate at its fringes, a permanent population, and established territorial sovereignty over all land areas. The Arctic also is of great strategic importance because of its central location between North America and Eurasia; the northern tip of Canada lies only about 4,000 km (2,500 mi) from what was the Soviet city of Murmansk on the great circle route. As a consequence of such proximity, the Arctic region is the site of many radar stations maintained by Canada, the former USSR, and the US to monitor air traffic and to provide early warning of an air attack.

The continental shelf around the Arctic basin occupies more than half the ocean area, a much larger proportion than in any other ocean; the edge of the continental shelf near Franz Josef Land lies about 1,500 km (930 mi) from the Eurasian mainland. The landmasses that extend above the Arctic Circle exhibit three major types of landforms: rugged uplands and deep fjords formed by glaciation; swampy coastal plains and high ice plateaus covered by glacial deposits; and folded mountains, including the high peaks of the Canadian Rocky Mountains, Alaska's Brooks Range, and the rounded slopes of the Ural Mountains of the former USSR. Principal rivers flowing into the Arctic Ocean are the Mackenzie, in Canada, and the Ob', Yenisey, Lena, and Kolyma, in the former USSR. Major seas in the Arctic include the Chukchi, East Siberian, Laptev, Kara, Barents, Norwegian, Greenland, and Beaufort.

The Arctic Ocean remains frozen throughout the year (except for its fringes during summer) and is virtually icelocked from October to June. The vast Arctic ice pack expands from an average area of 7.8 million sq km (3 million sq mi) in summer to an average of 14.8 million sq km (5.7 million sq mi) during winter. The average thickness of the ice pack is estimated at 3–3.5 m (9.8–11.5 ft). Ice "islands" up to 60 m (200 ft) thick and 30 km (19 mi) wide break away from the moving ice pack off North America and float slowly in erratic circles before disintegrating or exiting to the North Atlantic. Smaller fragments called icebergs break off glaciers in Greenland and northeastern Canada and move southward via the East Greenland and Labrador currents into Atlantic shipping lanes. An estimated 1,000 icebergs each year cross 55°N, and nearly 400 reach the Grand Banks off Newfoundland. A few icebergs have traveled as far as 4,000 km (2,500 mi) over a three-year period and have been sighted as far south as Bermuda.

The most recent Ice Age climaxed about 15,000 years ago, when continental ice sheets covered most of the Northern Hemisphere. The retreat of the glaciers was stabilized some 8,500 years ago in Europe and 7,000 years ago in North America. The warming period that followed reached its maximum in historic times during AD 800–1000, making possible the Viking colonization of Arctic lands, and from the 1880s to the 1940s, when extensive Arctic exploration occurred. However, a minor cooling trend that began in the 1940s (and is expected to last well into the 1990s) has had severe effects in the Arctic, increasing the ice-covered area substantially and reducing the annual mean air temperatures by several degrees, thereby shortening the summer season along the Arctic coast of Eurasia by nearly a month.

The Arctic experiences alternating six-month periods of winter darkness and summer daylight, including 24 hours of daylight within the Arctic Circle during the summer equinox (hence the designation "land of the midnight sun"). The region is subject to long, cold winters and short, cool summers. The snow cover is relatively light, averaging 20–50 cm (8–20 in) and lasting for about 10 months over the frozen ocean. Air temperatures above the pack ice average –30°C (–22°F) in January and near 0°C (32°F) in July. Annual mean temperatures on land vary from –12°C (10°F) at Barrow, Alaska, and –16°C (3°F) on Resolute Island, in northern Canada, to 0°C (32°F) at Murmansk, in what was the western USSR. Annual mean temperatures in Greenland are low because of the island's high elevation and vast interior ice sheet; they range from –40°C (–40°F) in January to –10°C (14°F) in July, temperatures significantly colder than those of the North Pole. Total annual precipitation varies from 10 to 25 cm (4–10 in) on the Arctic ice pack to 45 cm (18 in) or more in Greenland.

A climate-dependent phenomenon is the presence of perennially frozen ground, or permafrost, which has impeded human use of land in the Arctic region. Permafrost, occurring wherever ground temperatures remain below freezing for two or more years, underlies most of the Arctic landmass of Alaska and Greenland, half of that in Canada and the former USSR, and parts of Scandinavia. It also has been found under coastal seabeds of the Arctic Ocean. The maximum thickness of permafrost has been measured at 500 m (1,640 ft) in Canada, 900 m (2,950 ft) in Alaska, and 1,500 m (4,920 ft) in the former USSR. Alternate freezing and thawing of the outer permafrost layer shortens the growing season during the summer and causes serious engineering problems for construction and mining operations in the Arctic region.

Vegetation on the Arctic tundra, or treeless plain, is limited to mosses, lichens, sedges, and a few flowering plants which blossom during the brief spring and summer seasons. The outer edges of the Arctic ice pack support a small number of animal species by providing an overhead platform for algae and plankton, which are eaten by fish that, in turn, serve as food for seals, walruses, and birds; the food chain is continued by foxes and polar bears which feed upon young seals. Altogether, the Arctic has about 20 species of land mammals, including the moose, caribou, reindeer, wolf, and squirrel. The arrival of migratory birds each spring increases the bird population enormously.

Principal fish are cod, herring, and capelin, a true Arctic fish; all of these have great commercial value, as do shrimp and crab. Since 15 October 1975, when Iceland extended its fishing zone to 200 nautical mi, all nations bordering the Arctic have done the same, and fish catch quotas are now under national management.

The ecological cycle of Arctic life has been damaged by human encroachment, but in recent years the natural environment has been increasingly protected by the five circumpolar countries (Canada, Denmark, Norway, the former USSR, and the US). In 1956, the former USSR prohibited hunting of the polar bear, and in 1973 the five nations agreed to protect the bear's habitat. During construction in the 1970s of the trans-Alaska oil pipeline from Prudhoe Bay on the Arctic coast to the port of Valdez on the Gulf of Alaska, the US government required contractors to clean up the work site and to restore displaced vegetation; drillers were directed to trap and remove spilled oil. The pipeline carrying hot oil was suspended above ground level to prevent the permafrost from thawing, and crossings under the pipeline were provided at intervals for caribou and moose migrations. The Alaska Native Claims Settlement Act (1971) set aside about one-fourth of the state's area for wilderness preserves, wildlife refuges, and national parks. To prevent or control oil spills in the Arctic Ocean, Canada in 1970 authorized a 161-km (100-mi) offshore pollution control zone north of the 60° line. The former USSR has established nature preserves on several islands off the Kola Peninsula, east of the Barents Sea, and on Wrangel Island. In 1973, Norway established nature reserves and national parks in its Svalbard territory in the Barents Sea, and the next year, Denmark designated the northeastern third of Greenland as a national park.

Settlement and Exploration

The Arctic region was settled some 10,000 to 12,000 years ago, after the last Ice Age, by peoples of Central Asia, probably of Mongoloid stock, who pursued animal herds northward in the wake of retreating glaciers. The ancestors of the Lapps migrated to northern Scandinavia and the Kola Peninsula, while further east diverse peoples settled along the Arctic coast. At about the same time, the forebears of the American Indians came from Asia via a land bridge across the Bering Strait or traveled along the Aleutian Islands to North America. It is believed that the Eskimos arrived in Alaska much later.

These migratory peoples adapted to the harsh Arctic environment by inventing snowshoes, the kayak, the igloo, and primitive tools. They fashioned clothing and tents of caribou or reindeer skins, perfected efficient hunting techniques, and evolved distinctive forms of social organization. Gradually, over the course of centuries, these hunter-gatherers made the transition to herding and trading; especially for the Indians and Eskimos of Canada and the US, however, intense contact with modern culture in the 20th century has meant abrupt change. In addition to Indians and Eskimos, principal indigenous Arctic population groups include the mixed Eskimo-Caucasian peoples of Greenland; the Lapps in Scandinavia; and the Samoyedic, Yakuts, Tungus-Manchurian, and Chukchi peoples of the former USSR. These aboriginal peoples constituted about half of the Arctic's total population.

The first explorers in Arctic waters were the Vikings (Northmen) from Scandinavia, who ventured into the North Atlantic as far as Greenland and the North American continent in the 10th and 11th centuries. It is generally accepted that the Norse chieftain Leif Ericson explored part of the northeastern North American mainland, which he called Vinland, although its actual location is disputed. During the 16th and 17th centuries, European explorers such as Martin Frobisher, William Baffin, and William Barents probed the Arctic Ocean for the fabled Northwest Passage around North America to the Orient. Arctic geographical landmarks have been named after them and for Vitus Bering, the Danish explorer who sailed in the service of Russia in 1728 through the strait that bears his name. In the late 18th century, while developing trade routes for English fur companies, Alexander Mackenzie and Samuel Hearne followed Canadian rivers to reach the Arctic coast. In 1819, William Parry sailed west through the northern Canadian islands as far as M'Clure Strait before being stopped by heavy pack ice. That year, Swedish explorer Nils Nordenskjöld became the first to complete the Northeast Passage along the Russian Arctic coast. The disappearance in 1845 of Sir John Franklin's expedition spurred further exploration and the mapping of many Canadian islands in the Arctic Ocean. Norwegian explorer Roald Amundsen successfully transited the Northwest Passage for the first time, from 1903 to 1906.

Amundsen's accomplishment shifted the emphasis of Arctic exploration to reaching the North Pole. American explorer Robert E. Peary came within 280 km (174 mi) of the goal in his 1905–06 expedition, and on 6 April 1909, he and his party, including four Eskimos, were the first men to reach the North Pole. In 1926, Adm. Richard E. Byrd, of Antarctic exploration fame, and his copilot Floyd Bennett were the first to fly over the pole, and Amundsen and Lincoln Ellsworth flew from Spitsbergen (now Svalbard) across the pole to Alaska. Much later, in 1958, the US atomic-powered submarine *Nautilus* was the first underwater vessel to navigate the North Pole, and in 1960, another US submarine, the *Skate*, became the first to surface at the pole. The Soviet icebreaker *Arktika* was the first surface vessel to reach it, in 1977.

Unresolved Arctic territorial disputes concern Norway's exclusive claim to the resources of the Svalbard continental shelf and conflicting Norwegian-Soviet claims in the Barents Sea. After the Antarctic Treaty was signed in 1959, hopes were raised for a similar agreement in regard to the Arctic, but the strategic importance of the Arctic region, its increasing economic value, and complex legal problems involving national sensitivities have thus far prevented the attainment of such an accord.

Arctic Development

The five nations with territories within the Arctic Circle have all developed the area's natural resources to some degree, but the former USSR has taken the lead both in populating the region and in exploiting its rich mineral deposits and other resources. The largest Arctic city is Murmansk, with a population of about 400,000, and there are some 30 other ex-Soviet cities and towns in the Arctic with more than 10,000 inhabitants. In contrast, the largest town on the North American mainland located north of the Arctic Circle is Inuvik, in Canada's Northwest Territories, with a population of about 3,000; Godthaab, the capital of Greenland, has less than 12,000 residents. The former USSR estimated the population of what it terms its "far north" (including areas in eastern Siberia as far south as 55°N) at about 4 million in the late 1970s. Of the total, about 65% lived in mining districts or coastal settlements based on fishing and military activities, 20% were concentrated in northern river valleys, and 15% were scattered in the hinterlands. Canada's Yukon Territory and Northwest Territories have over 40% of the country's land area but less than 1% of the total population. Alaska is the largest but second least populous of all the states of the US.

Beginning in the 1930s, with the establishment of the northern sea route to link coastal and river settlements, the Soviet government undertook the exceptionally costly task of fostering industrial development of the Arctic region. Because the harsh climate, the shortage of housing and amenities, and the low level of social services discouraged voluntary migration to the area, the Soviet government offered special resettlement inducements to workers, such as high wages and extensive fringe benefits. As a result, Soviet migration to the far north was nearly equal to the region's natural population increase between 1940 and 1970. However, labor turnover was rapid, with most new workers staying only one to three years. The most important economic activity was the mining of large nickel, copper, tin, platinum, cobalt, iron, and coal deposits. Eastern Siberia produced more than half the country's total output of nickel and much of the nation's copper, while the Kola Peninsula's apatite deposits provided at least two-thirds of the raw materials used to produce phosphate fertilizer. Eastern Siberia also produced about 90% of the former USSR's annual output of diamonds and tin. In addition, valuable oil fields and about two-thirds of proved Soviet natural gas reserves was located in western Siberia. Expansion of Soviet mining operations in the Arctic region continued into the 1980s and up until its collapse in the early 1990s.

The most significant economic development in the Arctic during the 1970s was the $4.5-billion trans-Alaska oil pipeline project and the exploitation of vast petroleum reserves (estimated at more than 10 billion barrels) at Alaska's Prudhoe Bay. Construction began on the 1,270-km (789-mi) pipeline to Valdez in 1974, and oil began to flow through the pipeline in 1977. Tens of thousands of American workers migrated to Alaska to take part in the project (earning the highest average wage rates in the US), and many stayed there after its completion, thereby contributing to Alaska's population increase of 32.4% during the decade. Coal reserves estimated at 5 trillion tons are located on Alaska's North Slope; coal is mined at Healy, between Anchorage and Fairbanks. Gold, copper, lead, zinc, tin, platinum, tungsten, and uranium have been mined in the past, and there are known reserves of silver, lead, nickel, cobalt, mercury, molybdenum, and asbestos. However, the remoteness of mining sites and the high production costs continued to hinder mineral development (except for oil) in the 1980s and early 1990s.

Valuable minerals produced in the Canadian Arctic include gold, silver, lead, zinc, copper, nickel, platinum, cadmium, and uranium. Canada also has proved oil reserves totaling 1.5 billion barrels in the Mackenzie River delta and offshore areas of the Beaufort Sea. Although Greenland also has considerable mineral resources, only lead, zinc, and coal were being mined in the early 1990s. The two largest iron mines in Scandinavia are situated in the vicinity of Kiruna, in Swedish Lapland, and in Norway, near the Soviet border. Both Norway and the former USSR operate coal mines in Svalbard, and both have explored for offshore oil beneath the Barents Sea.

Lack of adequate transportation facilities long hampered Arctic development. Since World War II, however, a network of air, water, and land routes has been developed, and modern technology has made most polar areas accessible. Scheduled flights from many airfields scattered throughout the region link cities and remote towns in Alaska, Canada, and the former USSR. In Greenland, where the rugged terrain makes the building of airstrips both difficult and costly, there is scheduled jet helicopter service. Air transport serves both military and civilian needs in Norway's polar region and links Svalbard with the mainland. Although water transport is seasonal because of ice-blocked channels in winter, large quantities of cargo generally move by ship. Several hundred Russian vessels, including icebreakers, ply the 2,800-km (1,740-mi) northern sea route between Novaya Zemlya and the Bering Strait, moving an estimated 4 million tons of cargo annually during 2–4 months of navigability.

The former USSR and Norway use waterborne shuttles to supply Svalbard and to convey coal to their respective home ports. Canada's shipping service for Hudson Bay, the Arctic islands, and the Mackenzie River delta is provided by the coast guard and by private companies. The Alaskan ports of Prudhoe Bay and Barrow are served by ships for a two-month period during late summer. Inland waterways provide important supply links in the Soviet Arctic and northwestern Canada.

Land routes in the Arctic are relatively undeveloped in the colder regions. However, there are four railroad lines in North America that penetrate the Arctic Circle. In addition to Alaska's heavily used Anchorage–Fairbanks line, there are three Canadian railroads, providing links to Churchill, on Hudson Bay; to Hay River, on the Great Slave Lake; and to Skagway, on the Alaskan border. Six Russian railroads serve the Arctic region, including the ports of Murmansk and Arkhangel'sk. Canada's two Arctic highways connect Inuvik with Dawson and with the Great Slave Lake towns of Hay River and Yellowknife. The most heavily traveled highway is Alaska's Arctic haul road between the Yukon River and Prudhoe Bay; this road was instrumental in hauling supplies and equipment to build the trans-Alaska oil pipeline. The Soviet Arctic has few roads, but the Murmansk area in the west connects with a well-developed Scandinavian road network.

Scientific Research

Scientific research in the Arctic region is directed mainly toward economic development and military applications. Research studies have dealt primarily with the Arctic's role in global air and water circulation and with such natural phenomena as pack ice, permafrost, geomagnetism, the aurora borealis, and other upper atmospheric conditions.

International cooperation has long played a vital role in Arctic research, dating back to the 1882/83 and 1932/33 International Polar Years. The most intensive multinational scientific study of the Arctic was accomplished during the International Geophysical Year (1957/58), in which some 300 Arctic stations were set up

to monitor polar phenomena. The US and the former USSR each launched two drifting stations on the pack ice to gather data on Arctic currents and the topography of the Arctic seabed. It was found that little marine life existed on the Arctic Ocean floor and that rocks were scattered in profusion on the ocean bottom. The land stations obtained detailed information on the aurora borealis, ionosphere, and polar magnetic field. During 1969–75, Canada and the US jointly conducted an Arctic ice experimental program involving manned and unmanned drifting stations to determine the dynamics of sea-ice movement within the polar environment.

Scientific efforts by the former USSR in the Arctic have exceeded the combined activities of all the other circumpolar nations. By the late 1970s, the former USSR operated at least 100 polar stations and more than a dozen specially equipped sea and air vehicles to collect data on weather, ocean currents, and sea ice, with the aim of maintaining shipping services over the northern sea route. Drifting ice stations maintained year-round make a variety of meteorological observations and conduct oceanographic and geophysical experiments. Each year, Russia mounts air expeditions to hundreds of sites along the ice pack, emplacing nearly two dozen automatic buoys to radio data on environmental conditions to the mainland.

US Arctic research centers mainly on Alaska but extends also to northern Canada, Greenland, and the Arctic Ocean. Civilian research is coordinated by the National Science Foundation (NSF), which awards funds for research to universities; the principal research centers are at Fairbanks and Barrow. Small outposts to gather weather information have been established at US military facilities in Alaska and at radar stations on the 4,800-km (3,000-mi) Distant Early Warning (DEW) line extending from Alaska to Greenland. In 1986/87, the NSF allocated approximately $19 million for Arctic research studies. In the same year, total US government outlay for Arctic research was approximately $93 million.

The US operates an average of one drifting ice station per year in the Arctic Ocean, supplemented by automatic data buoys. Ice reconnaissance flights are conducted, as well as ocean surveys by icebreakers and submarines in the Bering and Greenland seas. In the early 1980s, the NSF conducted a six-year project, called Processes and Resources of the Bering Sea Shelf (PROBES), to study the marine ecosystem of the Bering Sea in order to predict the environmental impact of both natural events and human activities. In 1987, the NSF initiated a follow-up program, Inner Shelf Transfer and Recycling (ISHTAR), conducted in the Bering and Chukchi seas to study the ways in which seasonal and annual variations in the northward transport of water influence life processes. In 1985, scientists from the National Oceanic and Atmospheric Administration (NOAA) embarked on a study of a 5,200-sq km (2,000-sq mi) polynya (open water in pack ice that is a source of heat in an extremely cold area) in the Bering Sea, hoping to assess its effects on weather patterns, wind behavior, and ocean currents. In the summer of 1981, the US cooperated with Denmark and Switzerland to obtain ice cores from the bottom of the Greenland ice sheet, which represents a record of the climate over the past 130,000 years. Other recent US programs include studies of the geology and geophysics of the Arctic basin and research in Alaska on so-called surging glaciers, which move forward at the unusually rapid rate of several miles a year.

Other circumpolar nations have concentrated their Arctic research on the land and continental shelf. Canada's ongoing Polar Continental Shelf Project, begun in 1959, makes intensive studies of the North American continental shelf, Arctic islands, and Arctic Ocean. From March to October of each year, Canada also conducts aerial surveys of sea ice in the Arctic Ocean, Baffin Bay, and Beaufort Sea. Norway's Polar Institute, in Oslo, supervises mapping and scientific surveys of Svalbard, Jan Mayen, and the Arctic Ocean. In Greenland, the US participates in geophysical and weather studies at Thule Air Base. Scientists from Russia, the UK, France, and other countries also conduct geological and biological research on the Danish dependency.

BIBLIOGRAPHY

Armstrong, Terrence, *et al. The Circumpolar North: A Political and Economic Geography of the Arctic and Sub-Arctic.* New York: Methuen, 1978.

Auburn, F. M. *Antarctic Law and Politics.* Bloomington: Indiana University Press, 1982.

Bonner, W. N., and R. J. Berry (eds.). *Ecology in the Antarctic.* New York: Academic Press, 1981.

Bush, W. M. *Basic Documents on Antarctica.* 2 vols. Dobbs Ferry, N.Y.: Oceana, 1982.

Federal Arctic Research. Springfield, Va.: Interagency Arctic Research Policy Committee, National Technical Information Service, 1985.

McWhinnie, Mary A. (ed.). *Polar Research: To the Present and the Future.* Boulder, Colo.: Westview Press, 1978.

Mirsky, Jeanette. *To the Arctic: The Story of Northern Exploration from Earliest Times to the Present.* Chicago: University of Chicago Press, 1970.

Parker, Bruce C. (ed.). *Environmental Impact in Antarctica.* Charlottesville: University Press of Virginia, 1978.

Polar Regions Atlas. Washington, D.C.: Central Intelligence Agency, 1978.

Porter, Eliot. *Antarctica.* New York: Dutton, 1978.

Pyne, Stephen J. *The Ice: A Journey to Antarctica.* Ames: University of Iowa Press, 1987.

Quigg, P. W. *A Pole Apart: The Emerging Issues of Antarctica.* New York: McGraw-Hill, 1982.

Ray, G. Carleton, and M. G. McCormick-Ray. *Wildlife of the Polar Regions.* New York: Abrams, 1981.

Sugden, David. *Arctic and Antarctic: A Modern Geographical Synthesis.* Totowa, N.J.: Barnes & Noble, 1982.

UN Economic Commission for Europe. *Human Settlements in the Arctic: An Account of the ECE Symposium on Human Settlements Planning and Development in the Arctic, Godthöab, Greenland, Aug. 18–25, 1978.* Elmsford, N.Y.: Pergamon, 1980.

WORLD TABLES

Table 1: World Demographic Indicators

COUNTRY	2000 POPULATION	2005 PROJECTION	DENSITY	% URBAN 1990	% URBAN 2000	%RATE OF CHANGE 1995-2000
Afghanistan	26,668,251	30,189,000	40		21.9	5.3
Albania	3,401,126	3,591,000	123	34	39.1	0.6
Algeria	31,787,647	35,118,000	13	43	59.3	2.3
Andorra	67,673	76,000	144		95.4	
Angola	11,486,729	13,104,000	10	21	34.2	3.3
Antigua and Barbuda	64,461	65,000	152		36.8	
Argentina	37,214,757	39,626,000	13	83	89.4	1.3
Armenia	3,396,184	3,352,000	135	66	70.0	0.2
Australia	18,950,108	19,729,000	2	86	84.7	1.1
Austria	8,148,007	8,194,000	98	65	64.7	0.6
Azerbaijan	7,955,772	8,172,000	91	53	57.3	0.8
Bahamas, The	287,548	306,000	29		88.5	
Bahrain	641,539	702,000	929		92.2	
Bangladesh	129,146,695	142,921,000	965	11	21.2	1.6
Barbados	259,248	261,000	618		50.0	
Belarus	129,146,695	142,921,000	965	11	21.2	1.6
Belgium	10,185,894	10,164,000	311	95	97.3	0.3
Belize	241,546	271,000	10		46.5	2.5
Benin	6,516,630	7,662,000	54	27	42.3	2.8
Bhutan	1,996,221	2,226,000			7.1	2.8
Bolivia	8,139,180	8,921,000	7	46	64.8	2.3
Bosnia and Herzegovina	3,591,618	3758000			43.1	3.9
Botswana	1,479,039	1,538,000	3	15	73.6	2.2
Brazil	173,790,810	182,837,000	20	66	81.3	1.2
Brunei Darussalam	330,689	370000	60		72.2	
Bulgaria	8,155,828	8,034,000	75	61	70.1	-0.5
Burkina Faso	11,892,029	13,566,000	39	9	18.5	2.8
Burundi	5,930,805	6,704,000	256	4	9.0	2.8
Cambodia (Kampuchea)	11,918,865	13,463,000	61	12	23.5	2.2
Cameroon	15,891,531	18,176,000	31	31	48.9	2.7
Canada	31,330,255	32,855,000	3	76	77.1	0.9
Cape Verde	411,487	438,000	102		62.2	
Central African Republic	3,515,657	3,905,000	6	35	41.2	2.1
Chad	7,760,252	8,846,000	6	19	23.8	2.8
Chile	15,155,495	15,716,000	20	81	84.6	1.4
China	1,256,167,701	1,296,200,000	133	20	34.3	0.9
Colombia	40,036,927	43,662,000	39	64	74.9	1.7
Comoros	580,509	676,000	238		33.2	
Congo (DROC)	51,987,773	60548000	21	29	30.3	2.6
Congo (ROC)	2,775,659	3702000	8	41	62.5	2.8
Costa Rica	3,743,677	4,084,000	69	43	51.9	2.1
Cote d'Ivoire	16,190,105	18,303,000	46	35	46.5	2.0
Croatia	4,681,015	4,671,000	82	50	57.7	-0.1
Cuba	11,139,412	11,314,000	101		77.9	0.4
Cyprus	759,048	817000	82		56.8	
Czech Republic	10,283,762	10,394,000	133	64	66.3	-0.1
Denmark	5,374,554	5,433,000	125	84	85.'7	0.2
Djibouti	454,294	516,000	28		83.3	
Dominica	63,944	61,000	98		71.0	

Table 1: World Demographic Indicators (Continued)

COUNTRY	2000 POPULATION	2005 PROJECTION	DENSITY	% URBAN 1990	% URBAN 2000	%RATE OF CHANGE 1995-2000
Dominican Republic	8,261,536	8,937,000	171	51	65.2	1.7
Ecuador	12,782,161	13,837,000	44	47	62.4	2.0
Egypt	68,494,584	74,636,000	62	44	45.9	1.9
El Salvador	5,925,374	6,383,000	292	42	46.6	2.2
Equatorial Guinea	477,763	542,000	15		48.2	2.5
Eritrea	4,142,481	4,958,000	38	14	18.7	3.7
Estonia	1,398,140	1,358,000	34	70	74.3	-0.1
Ethiopia	60,967,436	67,832,000	61	11	17.6	3.2
Fiji	823,376	878,000	45		42.3	1.6
Finland	5,164,825	5,178,000	17	60	65.0	0.3
France	59,128,187	59,625,000	107	73	75.6	0.3
Gabon	1,244,192	1,341,000	5		55.2	2.8
Gambia, The	1,381,496	1616000	122		32.5	2.3
Georgia	5,034,051	4,914,000	78	52	60.7	0.1
Germany	82,081,365	81860000	235	83	87.5	0.3
Ghana	19,271,744	21,128,000	81	31	38.4	2.8
Greece	10,750,705	10,921,000	82	58	60.1	0.3
Grenada	97,913	104,000			37.9	
Guatemala	12,669,576	14,423,000	100	37	40.4	2.8
Guinea	7,610,869	8,397,000	29	19	32.8	1.4
Guinea-Bissau	1,263,341	1,415,000	41		23.7	2.0
Guyana	703,399	709,000	4		38.2	1.0
Haiti	6,991,589	7,584,000	277	24	34.9	1.9
Honduras	6,130,135	6,750,000	55	35	46.9	2.8
Hungary	10,167,182	10,085,000	110	57	66.9	-0.6
Iceland	274,141	282,000	3		92.3	1.0
India	1,017,645,163	1,096,929,000	330	23	28.4	1.6
Indonesia	219,266,557	234,876,000	112	22	40.2	1.5
Iran	65,865,302	80,139,000	38	50	61.6	2.2
Iraq	23,150,926	29,366,000	51		76.8	2.8
Ireland	3,647,348	3,728,000	53	55	58.5	0.2
Israel	5,851,913	6,303,000	290	89	91.2	1.9
Italy	56,686,568	56,253,000	196	67	67.0	0.0
Jamaica	2,668,740	2,764,000	238	47	56.1	0.9
Japan	126,434,470	127,338,000	335	76	78.9	0.2
Jordan	4,700,843	5,403,000	51	60	74.2	3.3
Kazakhstan	16,816,150	16904000	6	54	61.7	0.1
Kenya	29,250,541	31,157,000	51	16	33.1	2.2
Kiribati	87,025	92,000	117		37.3	
Korea (DPRK)	21,687,550	23348000	192		62.8	1.6
Korea (ROK)	47,350,529	49490000	470	57	86.2	0.9
Kuwait	2,067,728	2,437,000	105	90	97.6	3.0
Kyrgyzstan	4,584,341	4,829,000	24	38	40.1	0.4
Laos	5,556,821	6,338,000	22	13	23.5	3.1
Latvia	2,326,689	2,222,000	39	68	74.3	-1.1
Lebanon	3,619,971	3,904,000	412	74	89.7	1.8
Lesotho	2,166,520	2,328,000	68	13	28.0	2.5
Liberia	3,089,980	3,750,000	31		47.9	8.6
Libya	5,114,032	7,315,000	3		87.6	3.3
Liechtenstein	32,410	34,000	200		22.7	

Table 1: World Demographic Indicators (Continued)

COUNTRY	2000 POPULATION	2005 PROJECTION	DENSITY	% URBAN 1990	% URBAN 2000	%RATE OF CHANGE 1995-2000
Lithuania	3,571,552	3,526,000	57	61	74.7	-0.3
Luxembourg	432,577	446,000	161		91.1	
Macedonia	2,035,044	2087000	79	53	62.0	0.7
Madagascar	15,294,535	17,559,000	25	18	29.5	3.1
Malawi	10,154,299	10,826,000	112	9	15.4	2.5
Malaysia	21,820,143	24,087,000	68	42	57.3	2.0
Maldives	310,425	364,000	874		28.3	
Mali	10,750,686	12,536,000	9	19	30.0	3.0
Malta	383,285	390,000	1180		90.5	
Marshall Islands	68,088	83,000	310		71.9	
Mauritania	2,660,155	3,089,000	2	27	57.7	2.5
Mauritius	1,196,172	1,265,000	571		41.3	1.1
Mexico	102,026,691	110,574,000	50	66	74.4	1.6
Micronesia	133,144		155		29.7	
Moldova	4,466,758	4,523,000	130	40	55.2	0.1
Monaco	32,231	33,000	1600		100.0	
Mongolia	2,654,572	2,834,000	2	52	63.5	2.1
Morocco	30,205,387	32924000	62	41	55.3	1.8
Mozambique	19,614,345	22,156,000	22	13	40.2	2.5
Myanmar (Burma)	48,852,098	52698000	68	24	27.7	1.8
Namibia	1,674,116	1,799,000	2	23	40.9	2.4
Nauru	10,704				100.0	
Nepal	24,920,211	28,173,000	160	7	11.9	2.5
Netherlands	15,878,304	16,144,000	463	88	89.3	0.5
New Zealand	3,697,850	3,868,000	14	83	86.9	1.1
Nicaragua	4,850,976	5,522,000	40	53	64.7	2.6
Niger	10,260,316	11,864,000	8	13	20.6	3.3
Nigeria	117,170,948	133,974,000	133	27	44.0	2.8
Norway	4,455,707	4,524,000	14	71	74.2	0.4
Oman	2,532,556	3,000,000	11		84.0	4.2
Pakistan	141,145,344	156,136,000	171	28	37.0	2.7
Palau	18,827		32		72.8	
Panama	2,821,085	3,030,000	37	50	57.7	1.6
Papua New Guinea	4,811,939	5,363,000	10	13	17.4	2.2
Paraguay	5,579,503	6,340,000	13	42	56.0	2.6
Peru	27,135,689	29,659,000	19	65	72.8	1.7
Philippines	80,961,430	89,056,000	252	37	58.6	2.0
Poland	38,644,184	39,258,000	127	58	65.6	0.1
Portugal	9,902,147	9,793,000	109	29	38.0	-0.1
Qatar	749,542	874,000	67		92.5	
Romania	22,291,200	22,304,000	98	49	58.2	-0.2
Russian Federation	145,904,542	144264000	9	70	77.7	-0.3
Rwanda	8,336,995	9,135,000	329	5	6.2	7.9
Saint Kitts and Nevis	43,441	47,000	113		34.1	
Saint Lucia	155,678	164,000	263		37.8	
Saint Vincent and the Grenadines	121,188	126,000	290		54.8	
Samoa	235,302	262,000	62		21.5	
San Marino	25,215	26,000			95.7	
Sao Tome and Principe	159,832	187,000	148		46.7	
Saudi Arabia	22,245,751	26,336,000	10	66	85.7	3.4

Table 1: World Demographic Indicators (Continued)

COUNTRY	2000 POPULATION	2005 PROJECTION	DENSITY	% URBAN 1990	% URBAN 2000	% RATE OF CHANGE 1995-2000
Senegal	10,390,296	12,235,000	47	36	47.0	2.7
Seychelles	79,672	82,000	175		58.5	
Sierra Leone	5,509,263	6,416,000	68	24	36.6	3.0
Singapore	3,571,710	3,751,000	5186	100	100.0	1.5
Slovakia	5,401,134	5,509,000	112	52	61.1	0.1
Slovenia	1,970,056	1,978,000	99	48	52.6	-0.1
Solomon Islands	470,000	545,000	15		19.7	3.2
Somalia	7,433,922	8,795,000	14		27.5	3.9
South Africa	43,981,758	46,221,000	34	48	50.4	2.2
Spain	39,208,236	39,334,000	79	73	77.6	0.1
Sri Lanka	19,355,053	20,418,000	290	22	23.6	1.0
Sudan	35,530,371	40,899,000	12		36.1	2.2
Suriname	434,093	446,000	3		52.2	1.2
Swaziland	1,004,072	1,101,000	57		35.7	2.8
Sweden	8,938,559	9,051,000	22	83	83.3	0.3
Switzerland	7,288,715	7,352,000	180	57	62.6	0.7
Syria	17,758,925	20,530,000	83	47	54.5	2.5
Taiwan	22,319,222	23325000				
Tajikistan	6,194,373	6,720,000	43	34	32.9	1.9
Tanzania	31,962,769	35,687,000	36	15	27.8	2.3
Thailand	61,163,833	63,794,000	120	17	21.6	0.8
Togo	5,262,611	6,255,000	82	23	33.3	2.7
Tonga	109,959	114,000	137		46.4	
Trinidad and Tobago	1,086,908	1,033,000	257		74.1	0.8
Tunisia	9,645,499	10,303,000	60	52	65.5	1.8
Turkey	66,620,120	71,663,000	82	44	75.3	1.6
Turkmenistan	4,435,507	4,791,000	10	47	45.5	1.9
Tuvalu	10,730	11,000			52.2	
Uganda	23,451,687	27,234,000	105	9	14.2	2.6
Ukraine	49,506,779	48,309,000	87	62	72.5	-0.4
United Arab Emirates	2,386,472	2,611,000	32		85.9	2.0
United Kingdom	59,247,439	58,136,000	244	89	89.5	0.1
United States	274,943,496	286,291,000	29	74	77.2	0.8
Uruguay	3,332,782	3,459,000	19	85	91.3	0.6
Uzbekistan	24,422,518	26,111,000	58	41	42.4	1.9
Vanuatu	192,848	212,000	15		20.0	
Vatican					100.0	
Venezuela	23,595,822	25,504,000	26	79	87.4	2.0
Vietnam	78,349,503	83442000	238	19	19.7	1.8
Yemen	17,521,085	20,807,000	31	20	38.0	3.7
Yugoslavia	11210243	11314000	104		59.9	0.5
Zambia	9,872,007	10,972,000	13	40	44.5	2.5
Zimbabwe	11,272,013	11,703,000	30	22	35.3	2.1

Table 2: World Agriculture

COUNTRY	LAND AREA (SQ MI) 1994	CROP LAND (1,000 HECTARES) 1994	% ECONOMICALLY ACTIVE POPULATION IN AGRICULTURE 1995	MEAT PRODUCTION (1,000 METRIC TONS) 1995	GRAINS OUTPUT (1,000 METRIC TONS) 1995	ROOTS AND TUBERS OUTPUT (1,000 METRIC TONS) 1995
Afghanistan	251,772	8,054	69.2	267	3,307	280
Albania	11,100	702	53.6	68	658	70
Algeria	919,591	8,043	24.1	490	2,194	720
Andorra	174	1	1.2	—	—	2
Angola	481,352	3,500	73.8	97	321	1,943
Antigua and Barbuda	171	—	11.0	1	—	—
Argentina	1,068,298	27,200	11.0	3,577	23,436	2,410
Armenia	11,500	573	15.3	37	259	400
Australia	2,978,133	47,196	4.5	3,270	26,560	1,152
Austria	32,375	1.513	6.5	872	4,476	724
Azerbaijan	33,400	2,000	30.3	82	939	200
Bahamas	5,382	10	5.1	5	—	1
Bahrain	263	2	1.7	13	—	—
Bangladesh	55,598	9,694	61.6	371	25,931	1,864
Barbados	166	16	6.4	15	2	3
Belarus	80,100	6,329	17.8	854	5,927	8,570
Belgium	12,780	667	2.5	1,666	2,256	2,076
Belize	8,865	57	30.5	10	38	4
Benin	43,483	1,880	59.7	66	648	2,447
Bhutan	18,147	134	94.0	8	106	56
Bolivia	424,162	2,380	44.6	325	1,110	1,044
Bosnia and Herzegovina	19,736	800	10.1	48	717	377
Botswana	224,606	420	39.3	67	46	9
Brazil	3,286,477	50,713	18.7	10,061	49,653	29,009
Brunei Darussalam	10,747	7	3.5	9	1	1
Bulgaria	42,822	4,219	11.0	346	5,739	476
Burkina Faso	105,869	3,565	92.4	105	2,492	75
Burma (Myanmar)	261,216	10,076	72.1	341	20,690	244
Burundi	10,745	1,180	90.9	25	269	1,326
Cambodia	69,900	3,838	72.8	130	1,867	60
Cameroon	183,568	7,040	68.0	190	1,260	2,080
Canada	3,851,794	45,500	2.5	3,117	49,693	3,774
Cape Verde	1,556	45	27.4	23	10	5
Central African Republic	240,533	2,020	78.3	71	112	718
Chad	495,753	3,256	80.8	98	963	528
Chile	292,259	4,250	17.2	745	2,804	907
China	3,705,392	95,782	71.3	53,016	416,796	152,813
Colombia	439,734	5,460	24.0	1,225	3,509	5,164
Comoros	838	100	75.2	2	21	66
Congo (ROC)	132,046	170	44.6	23	27	710
Congo (DROC)	905,564	7,900	66.1	244	1,697	18,358
Costa Rica	19,730	530	22.3	166	160	181
Côte d'Ivoire	124,502	3,710	57.1	140	1,685	4,761
Croatia	21,824	1,221	14.6	122	2,764	500
Cuba	42,803	3,370	15.7	235	181	652
Cyprus	3,571	143	10.0	87	144	223
Czech Republic	78,864	3,386	10.8	936	6,598	1,330
Denmark	16,637	2,374	4.4	1,906	8,698	1,480

Table 2: World Agriculture (Continued)

COUNTRY	LAND AREA (SQ MI) 1994	CROP LAND (1,000 HECTARES) 1994	% ECONOMICALLY ACTIVE POPULATION IN AGRICULTURE 1995	MEAT PRODUCTION (1,000 METRIC TONS) 1995	GRAINS OUTPUT (1,000 METRIC TONS) 1995	ROOTS AND TUBERS OUTPUT (1,000 METRIC TONS) 1995
Djibouti	8,958	—	76.8	8	—	—
Dominica	18,680	17	40.0	1	—	23
Dominican Republic	18,815	1,480	20.5	277	589	256
Ecuador	109,483	3,036	28.8	350	2,032	562
Egypt	386,660	3,500	33.1	965	17,182	1,734
El Salvador	8,124	730	32.4	94	893	107
Equatorial Guinea	10,831	230	73.1	—	—	82
Eritrea	48,000	519	79.1	26	153	109
Estonia	17,400	1,144	13.5	80	740	700
Ethiopia	471,776	11,012	85.4	578	8,245	2,018
Fiji	7,054	260	43.8	23	18	37
Finland	130,552	2,593	7.2	319	3,333	798
France	212,934	19,488	4.2	6,497	53,606	5,754
Gabon	103,348	460	45.4	28	28	396
Gambia	4,363	172	79.7	9	108	6
Georgia	26,900	1,127	24.9	121	554	250
Germany	137,819	12,015	3.0	5,748	39,870	10,382
Ghana	92,100	4,320	56.0	164	1,835	10,493
Greece	50,961	3,502	19.8	518	4,690	900
Grenada	133	11	24.0	1	—	4
Guatemala	42,042	1,910	50.6	156	1,516	79
Guinea	94,927	730	85.2)	37	773	801
Guinea—Bissau	13,946	340	84.3	16	201	65
Guyana	83,000	496	19.9	19	493	32
Haiti	10,714	910	65.7	67	373	772
Honduras	43,278	2,030	33.2	96	771	30
Hungary	35,919	4,974	13.6	968	11,042	1,151
Iceland	39,768	6	9.5	20	—	11
India	1,269,340	169,650	61.6	4,272	214,893	26,300
Indonesia	735,356	30,171	53.2	1,858	58,083	18,603
Iran	636,294	18,122	36.3	1,301	17,312	3,200
Iraq	169,236	5,750	11.5	172	2,845	420
Ireland	27,135	1,317	12.2	893	1,811	620
Israel	8,019	435	3.4	278	253	288
Italy	116,321	11,143	6.9	3,974	19,713	2,076
Jamaica	4,243	219	23.5	66	4	337
Japan	145,869	4,422	5.5	3,251	13,437	5,157
Jordan	34,444	405	14.7	112	127	90
Kazakhstan	1,048,900	34,978	21.1	1,302	10,583	1,950
Kenya	224,081	4,520	78.0	375	3,394	1,685
Kiribati	332	37	71.0	1	—	8
Korea (DPRK)	46,540	2,000	34.1	259	5,241	2,050
Korea (ROK)	38,232	2,055	13.5	1,427	6,923	848
Kuwait	6,880	5	1.3	60	2	1
Kyrgyzstan	76,600	1,420	31.2	177	782	431
Laos	91,429	900	77.3	68	1,491	223
Latvia	24,900	1,740	14.0	132	701	927
Lebanon	4,015	306	4.2	86	77	222
Lesotho	11,718	320	39.4	26	41	62

Table 2: World Agriculture (Continued)

COUNTRY	LAND AREA (SQ MI) 1994	CROP LAND (1,000 HECTARES) 1994	% ECONOMICALLY ACTIVE POPULATION IN AGRICULTURE 1995	MEAT PRODUCTION (1,000 METRIC TONS) 1995	GRAINS OUTPUT (1,000 METRIC TONS) 1995	ROOTS AND TUBERS OUTPUT (1,000 METRIC TONS) 1995
Liberia	37,741	375	70.1	17	50	523
Libya	679,359	2,170	6.1	119	318	127
Liechtenstein	61.8	4	2.4	—	—	127
Lithuania	25,200	3,046	17.9	377	2,500	1,594
Luxembourg	999	127	3.4	25	55	24
Macedonia	9,597	661	17.2	56	726	154
Madagascar	226,656	3,105	76.3	289	2,780	3,375
Malawi	45,745	1,700	86.3	41	1,778	576
Malaysia	127,317	7,604	22.9	944	2,169	530
Maldives	115	3	29.5	1	—	8
Mali	478,838	2,503	84.1	185	2,433	29
Malta	122	13	1.8	15	9	27
Marshall Islands	70	—	18.7	—	—	—
Mauritania	395,954	208	48.7	55	246	5
Mauritius	718	106	12.3	22	2	20
Micronesia	271	—	41.6	—	3	1
Mexico	756,062	24,730	24.2	3,473	25,344	1,252
Moldova	13,000	2,180	30.6	130	1,698	400
Monaco	1	—	—	—	—	—
Mongolia	604,827	1,320	27.6	223	261	52
Morocco	172,413	9,291	40.7	475	1,823	783
Mozambique	309,494	3,180	81.3	83	1,127	4,310
Namibia	317,873	662	45.1	70	60	190
Nauru	8	—	—	—	—	—
Nepal	54,363	2,354	93.3	179	5,450	981
Netherlands	14,413	948	4.2	2,916	1,590	7,363
New Zealand	104,629	3,800	10.1	1,281	855	282
Nicaragua	50,193	1,270	23.0	89	592	81
Niger	489,189	3,605	89.4	113	2,221	260
Nigeria	356,668	32,700	37.7	974	20,943	56,006
Norway	125,058	901	4.9	238	1,435	471
Oman	82,031	63	42.1	27	5	6
Pakistan	307,375	21,350	47.8	1,847	24,586	1,497
Palau	177	—	—	—	—	76
Panama	29,761	665	22.2	119	333	66
Papua New Guinea	178,703	415	77.6	53	3	1,267
Paraguay	157,046	2,270	34.8	383	1,133	2,708
Peru	496,224	4,140	33.0	682	2,142	3,369
Philippines	115,830	9,190	42.2	1,687	15,163	2,820
Poland	120,726	14,642	25.9	2,582	25,106	24,981
Portugal	35,672	2,900	14.3	637	1,306	1,477
Qatar	4,416	8	2.6	19	6	—
Romania	91,699	9,925	19.4	1,245	19,885	3,020
Russian Federation	6,591,100	132,302	12.4	5,946	61,795	37,300
Rwanda	10,170	1,170	91.3	25	151	1,534
Samoa	1,093	122	63.6	5	—	41
San Marino	23	1	2.1	—	—	—
São Tomé and Principe	372	41	40.4	1	4	11
Saudi Arabia	829,997	3,800	13.9	474	3,420	170

Table 2: World Agriculture (Continued)

COUNTRY	LAND AREA (SQ MI) 1994	CROP LAND (1,000 HECTARES) 1994	% ECONOMICALLY ACTIVE POPULATION IN AGRICULTURE 1995	MEAT PRODUCTION (1,000 METRIC TONS) 1995	GRAINS OUTPUT (1,000 METRIC TONS) 1995	ROOTS AND TUBERS OUTPUT (1,000 METRIC TONS) 1995
Senegal	75,954	2,350	74.2	153	1,059	68
Seychelles	175	7	12.0	2	—	—
Sierra Leone	27,699	540	66.8	20	338	105
Singapore	239	1	0.2	148	—	—
Slovakia	30,457	1,616	11.7	319	3,528	442
Slovenia	7,817	286	4.6	166	570	430
Solomon Islands	11,158	57	75.5	3	—	112
Somalia	246,201	1,020	74.1	154	285	44
South Africa	471,444	13,179	11.4	1,249	7,740	1,524
Spain	194,896	20,129	8.7	3,844	11,487	4,219
Sri Lanka	25,332	1,883	46.6	90	2,722	440
St. Kitts and Nevis	101	14	29.6	—	—	1
St. Lucia	238	18	22.9	2	—	12
St. Vincent and the Grenadines	150	11	25.7	—	1	18
Sudan	967,495	12,975	68.1	448	3,821	156
Suriname	63,039	68	20.0	6	220	7
Swaziland	6,703	191	33.6	20	79	8
Sweden	173,730	2,780	3.9	553	4,819	1,074
Switzerland	15,942	434	5.1	422	1,281	680
Syria	71,498	5,527	32.4	228	4,363	140
Taiwan	13,900	—	15.6	1,873	1,836	5,430
Tajikistan	55,200	860	37.6	65	251	140
Tanzania	364,900	3,500	83.2	295	4,617	6,670
Thailand	198,116	20,800	59.6	1,470	25,538	18,382
Togo	21,925	2,430	61.9	36	466	865
Tonga	289	48	70.0	2	—	101
Trinidad and Tobago	1,981	122	8.8	28	15	11
Tunisia	63,170	4,952	23.5	160	637	205
Turkey	300,946	27,771	50.7	1,181	28,163	4,750
Turkmenistan	188,400	1,480	36.0	116	1,249	11
Turks and Caicos Islands	166	1	—	—	—	—
Tuvalu	10	—	68.0	—	—	—
Uganda	91,073	6,800	83.3	218	2,080	5,246
Ukraine	233,000	34,357	18.2	2,294	32,429	14,729
United Arab Emirates	32,270	39	9.1	76	7	4
United Kingdom	94,548	5,989	2.1	3,453	21,987	6,445
United States	3,618,770	187,776	2.6	33,849	276,999	20,764
Uruguay	68,037	1,304	13.7	467	1,492	208
Uzbekistan	172,700	4,500	33.5	378	2,803	500
Vanuatu	4,707	144	61.1	9	1	50
Vatican	—	—	—	—	—	—
Venezuela	352,143	3,915	11.0	1,144	2,043	655
Vietnam	128,066	6,985	69.3	1,334	25,205	5,077
Yemen	203,850	1,545	56.8	136	825	200
Yugoslavia	39,424	4,085	26.5	891	8,388	931
Zambia	290,583	5,273	73.6	111	881	668
Zimbabwe	150,803	2,878	66.5	111	980	162

Table 3: World Income Indicators

COUNTRY	YEAR	GDP ($ MILLIONS)	% COMPOSITION OF GDP			PER CAPITA GDP ($)	% OF PER CAPITAL GDP SPENT ON			
			AGRICULTURE	INDUSTRY	SERVICES		FOOD	FUEL	HEALTH	EDUCATION
Afghanistan	1998	20,000	53	28	19	800				
Albania	1998	5,000	56	21	23	1,490	62	13	3	10
Algeria	1998	140,200	12	51	37	4,600				
Andorra	1995	1,200				18,000				
Angola	1998	11,000	13	53	34	1,000	36	8	3	18
Antigua and Barbuda	1998	503	4	13	83	7,900	30	17	15	15
Argentina	1998	374,000	7	37	56	10,300	52	18	3	15
Armenia	1998	9,200	35	30	35	2,700	24	9	2	16
Australia	1998	3,939,000	4	31	65	21,200	20	11	4	9
Austria	1998	184,500	1	31	68	22,700	51	16	9	2
Azerbaijan	1998	12,900	22	18	60	1,640	32	5	3	8
Bahamas, The	1998	5,630	3	5	92	20,100	32	8	1	6
Bahrain	1998	8,200	1	46	53	13,100	49	18	8	9
Bangladesh	1998	175,500	30	17	53	1,380				
Barbados	1998	2,900	6	15	79	11,200	36	15	7	10
Belarus	1998	175,500	30	17	53	1,380	17	8	3	1
Belgium	1998	236,000	2	27	71	23,400	27	5	3	13
Belize	1998	700	22	22	56	3,000	52	15	5	3
Benin	1998	7,600	34	14	52	1,300				
Bhutan	1998	19,000	38	38	24	1,000	37	11	9	14
Bolivia	1998	23,400	17	26	57	3,000				
Bosnia and Herzegovina	1998	5,800	19	23	58	1,720	24	12	2	7
Botswana	1998	5,250	4	45	51	3,600	22	18	15	34
Brazil	1998	1,035,200	14	36	50	6,100				
Brunei Darussalam	1998	5,400	5	46	49	17,000	30	17	8	11
Bulgaria	1998	33,600	26	29	45	4,100				
Burkina Faso	1998	11,600	35	25	40	1,000				
Burundi	1998	4,100	58	18	24	740				
Cambodia (Kampuchea)	1998	7,800	51	15	34	700	33	8	2	9
Cameroon	1998	29,600	42	22	36	2,000	14	10	4	21
Canada	1998	688,300	3	31	66	22,400				
Cape Verde	1998	581	8	18	74	14,500				
Central African Repub.	1998	5,500	53	21	26	1,640				
Chad	1998	7,500	39	15	46	1,000	17	24	20	15
Chile	1998	184,600	6	33	61	12,500				
China	1998	4,420,000	19	49	32	3,600				
Colombia	1998	254,700	19	26	55	6,600				
Comoros	1997	400	40	14	46	700				
Congo (DROC)	1998	34,900	59	15	26	710	34	12	3	3
Congo (ROC)	1998	3,900	10	59	31	1,500				
Costa Rica	1998	24,000	15	24	61	6,700	30	4	1	18
Cote d'Ivoire	1998	24,200	31	20	49	1,680	24	18	4	3
Croatia	1998	23,600	12	24	64	5,100				
Cuba	1998	17,300	7	37	56	1,560				
Cyprus	1997	10,000				13,000	24	14	5	12
Czech Republic	1998	116,700	5	34	61	11,300	16	11	3	17
Denmark	1998	124,400	4	27	69	23,300				
Djibouti	1998	530	3	20	77	1,200	33	11	3	6
Dominica	1997	216	20	16	64	3,300				

Table 3: World Income Indicators (Continued)

COUNTRY	YEAR	GDP ($ MILLIONS)	% COMPOSITION OF GDP			PER CAPITA GDP ($)	% OF PER CAPITAL GDP SPENT ON			
			AGRICULTURE	INDUSTRY	SERVICES		FOOD	FUEL	HEALTH	EDUCATION
Dominican Republic	1998	39,800	19	25	56	5,000				
Ecuador	1998	58,700	12	37	51	4,800	26	15	13	10
Egypt	1998	188,000	16	31	53	2,850	44	7	3	17
El Salvador	1998	17,500	15	24	61	3,000				
Equatorial Guinea	1997	660	46	33	21	1,500				
Eritrea	1998	2,500	18	20	62	660				
Estonia	1998	7,800	6	24	70	5,500	41	24	8	4
Ethiopia	1998	32,900	55	12	33	560				
Fiji	1998	5,400	19	22	59	6,700	35	19	2	13
Finland	1998	103,600	5	32	63	20,100	17	10	4	15
France	1998	1,320,000	2	28	70	22,600	22	9	3	8
Gabon	1998	7,700	8	67	25	6,400	40	9	3	7
Gambia, The	1998	1,300	23	13	64	1,000				
Georgia	1998	11,200	29	16	55	2,200	33	13	2	4
Germany	1998	1,813,000	1	33	66	22,100	14	7	2	10
Ghana	1998	33,600	41	14	45	1,800				
Greece	1998	143,000	9	23	68	13,400	32	14	5	14
Grenada	1998	340	10	15	75	3,500				
Guatemala	1998	45,700	24	21	55	3,800				
Guinea	1998	8,800	24	31	45	1,180	29	5	2	9
Guinea-Bissau	1998	1,200	54	11	35	1,000				
Guyana	1998	1,800	37	22	41	2,500				
Haiti	1998	8,900	42	14	44	1,300				
Honduras	1998	14,400	20	19	61	2,400				
Hungary	1998	75,400	3	30	67	7,400	25	17	6	20
Iceland	1998	6,060	13	24	63	22,400	16	8	3	10
India	1998	1,689,000	25	30	45	1,720				
Indonesia	1998	602,000	19	40	41	2,830	47	6	5	14
Iran	1998	339,700				5,000	20	32	12	8
Iraq	1998	52,300				2,400				
Ireland	1998	67,100	7	39	54	18,600	21	10	4	7
Israel	1998	101,900	2	17	81	18,100	23	11	2	6
Italy	1998	1,181,000	3	33	64	20,800	23	12	3	17
Jamaica	1998	8,800	7	42	51	3,300	24	3	1	9
Japan	1998	2,903,000	2	38	60	23,100	12	7	2	22
Jordan	1998	15,500	6	30	64	3,500	32	17	5	8
Kazakhstan	1998	52,900	11	33	56	3,100	37	20	9	6
Kenya	1998	43,900	29	17	54	1,550	31	21	2	8
Kiribati	1996	62	14	7	79	800				
Korea (DPRK)	1998	21,800	25	60	15	1,000				
Korea (ROK)	1998	584,700	6	43	51	12,600	18	7	5	14
Kuwait	1998	43,700	0	55	45	22,700				
Kyrgyzstan	1998	9,800	47	12	41	2,200	33	11	3	22
Laos	1998	6,600	51	21	28	1,260				
Latvia	1998	9,700	7	28	65	4,100	30	16	6	23
Lebanon	1998	15,800	4	23	73	4,500	31	10	7	9
Lesotho	1997	5,100	14	42	44	2,400				
Liberia	1998	2,800	30	36	34	1,000				
Libya	1998	38,000	5	55	40	6,700				
Liechtenstein	1998	730				23,000				

Table 3: World Income Indicators (Continued)

COUNTRY	YEAR	GDP ($ MILLIONS)	% COMPOSITION OF GDP			PER CAPITA GDP ($)	% OF PER CAPITAL GDP SPENT ON			
			AGRICULTURE	INDUSTRY	SERVICES		FOOD	FUEL	HEALTH	EDUCATION
Lithuania	1998	17,600	13	32	55	4,900	33	13	4	27
Luxembourg	1998	13,900	1	22	77	32,700	17	9	3	7
Macedonia	1998	2,100	20	39	41	1,050	33	15	6	9
Madagascar	1997	10,300	32	13	55	730	61	4	2	2
Malawi	1998	8,900	45	30	25	940	50	7	2	6
Malaysia	1998	215,400	13	46	41	10,300				
Maldives	1998	500	22	15	63	1,840				
Mali	1998	8,000	49	17	34	790	53	7	4	5
Malta	1998	5,000	3	26	71	13,000				
Marshall Islands	1998	91	15	13	72	1,450				
Mauritania	1998	4,700	26	31	43	1,890				
Mauritius	1998	11,700	8	29	63	10,000	21	13	3	13
Mexico	1998	815,300	6	26	68	8,300	30	4	2	7
Micronesia	1996	220				1,760				
Moldova	1998	10,000	30	29	41	2,200	31	11	3	15
Monaco	1996	800				25,000				
Mongolia	1998	5,800	31	35	34	2,250	56	9	8	14
Morocco	1998	107,000	14	33	53	3,200	33	16	5	15
Mozambique	1998	16,800	35	13	52	900				
Myanmar (Burma)	1998	56,100	59	11	30	1,200				
Namibia	1998	6,600	11	34	55	4,100				
Nauru	1993	100				10,000				
Nepal	1998	26,200	41	22	37	1,100	44	7	5	14
Netherlands	1998	348,600	2	28	70	22,200	17	7	2	13
New Zealand	1998	61,100	9	25	66	17,000	21	12	3	2
Nicaragua	1998	11,600	32	24	44	2,500				
Niger	1998	9,400	40	18	42	970				
Nigeria	1998	106,200	33	42	25	960	51	31	2	8
Norway	1998	109,000	2	30	68	24,700	16	11	5	4
Oman	1998	18,600	2	50	48	7,900	22	25	13	21
Pakistan	1998	270,000	24	26	50	2,000	45	19	6	5
Palau	1997	160				8,800				
Panama	1998	19,900	8	18	74	7,300	22	18	14	4
Papua New Guinea	1998	11,100	28	35	37	2,400				
Paraguay	1998	19,800	27	30	43	3,700				
Peru	1998	111,800	7	37	56	4,300	26	17	13	5
Philippines	1998	270,500	20	32	48	3,500	37	11	1	14
Poland	1998	263,000	5	27	68	6,800	28	19	6	1
Portugal	1998	144,800	4	36	60	14,600	29	7	2	19
Qatar	1998	12,000	1	49	50	17,100	22	11	5	13
Romania	1998	90,600	19	41	40	4,050	36	9	3	20
Russian Federation	1998	593,400	7	39	54	4,000	28	16	7	15
Rwanda	1998	5,500	36	24	40	690				
Saint Kitts and Nevis	1997	235	5	23	72	6,000	33	11	5	13
Saint Lucia	1997	625	11	32	57	4,100	40	11	4	17
Saint Vincent and the Grenadines	1998	289	11	17	72	2,400	27	8	2	13
Samoa	1997	470	40	25	35	2,100				
San Marino	1997	500				20,000				
Sao Tome and Principe	1998	164	23	19	58	1,100				

Table 3: World Income Indicators (Continued)

COUNTRY	YEAR	GDP ($ MILLIONS)	% COMPOSITION OF GDP			PER CAPITA GDP ($)	% OF PER CAPITAL GDP SPENT ON			
			AGRICULTURE	INDUSTRY	SERVICES		FOOD	FUEL	HEALTH	EDUCATION
Saudi Arabia	1998	186,000	6	53	41	9,000				
Senegal	1998	15,600	19	17	64	1,600	46	13	3	15
Seychelles	1997	550	4	15	81	7,000				
Sierra Leone	1998	2,700	52	16	32	530	47	9	3	13
Singapore	1998	91,700		28	72	26,300	15	5	3	14
Slovakia	1998	44,500	5	33	62	8,300	26	16	5	12
Slovenia	1998	20,400	5	35	60	10,300	27	14	4	16
Solomon Islands	1998	1,150				2,600				
Somalia	1998	4,000	59	10	31	600				
South Africa	1998	290,600	5	39	56	6,800				
Spain	1998	645,600	4	33	63	16,500	33	11	3	5
Sri Lanka	1998	48,100	18	31	51	2,500	43	7	4	8
Sudan	1998	31,200	33	17	50	930				
Suriname	1998	1,480	10	32	58	3,500				
Swaziland	1998	4,000	10	42	48	4,200	25	9	6	13
Sweden	1998	175,000	2	31	67	19,700	17	12	4	14
Switzerland	1998	191,800	3	31	66	26,400	19	9	3	18
Syria	1998	41,700	26	21	53	2,500				
Taiwan	1998	362,000	3	35	62	16,500				
Tajikistan	1998	6,000	25	35	40	990	48	10	0	14
Tanzania	1998	22,100	56	15	29	730	67	5	4	12
Thailand	1998	369,000	12	39	49	6,100	23	5	3	13
Togo	1998	8,200	32	23	45	1,670				
Tonga	1998	232	32	10	58	2,100				
Trinidad and Tobago	1998	8,850	2	44	54	8,000	20	23	5	13
Tunisia	1998	49,000	14	28	58	5,200	28	8	3	12
Turkey	1998	425,400	14	29	57	6,600	45	18	6	5
Turkmenistan	1998	7,000	18	50	32	1,630	32	14	6	18
Tuvalu	1995	7.8				800				
Uganda	1998	22,700	44	17	39	1,020				
Ukraine	1998	108,500	14	30	56	2,200	34	16	6	4
United Arab Emirates	1998	40,000	3	52	45	17,400				
United Kingdom	1998	1,252,000	2	31	67	21,200	14	9	3	3
United States	1998	8,511,000	2	23	75	31,500	13	9	4	6
Uruguay	1998	28,400	8	26	66	8,600	22	14	11	30
Uzbekistan	1998	59,200	26	27	47	2,500	34	13	4	7
Vanuatu	1997	240	23	13	64	1,300				
Vatican										
Venezuela	1998	194,500	4	63	33	8,500	30	17	16	13
Vietnam	1998	134,800	28	30	42	1,770	49	15	4	18
Yemen	1998	12,100	16	46	38	740	25	26	3	5
Yugoslavia										
Zambia	1998	8,300	23	40	37	880	52	8	2	11
Zimbabwe	1998	26,200	28	32	40	2,400	20	21	3	15

Table 4: World Education Indicators

COUNTRY	% OF POPULATION ILLITERATE				% OF POPULATION HAVING ATTENDED SCHOOL				
	YEAR	TOTAL	MALE	FEMALE	YEAR	NONE	PRIMARY	SECONDARY	TERTIARY
Afghanistan	2000	63.7	49.0	79.2	1979	89.0	6.5	1.1	3.0
Albania	1997	7							
Algeria	2000	36.7	24.9	48.7					
Andorra									
Angola	1998	58	44	72					
Antigua and Barbuda	1960	11	10	12					
Argentina	2000	3.1	3.1	3.1	1991	5.7	22.3	25.3	12.0
Armenia	1989	1	1	2					
Australia	1980	0	0	0					
Austria	1974	26			1991	0.0	0.0	94.0	6.1
Azerbaijan	1989	3	1	4	1990	3.5	25.4	57.7	13.5
Bahamas, The	2000	3.9	4.6	3.2	1991	38.4	26.2	25.1	10.3
Bahrain	2000	12.4	9.0	17.3	1981	70.4	16.7	7.4	1.3
Bangladesh	2000	59.2	48.3	70.5	1980	0.8	63.5	32.3	3.3
Barbados	1995	2.6	2	3.2	1981	70.4	16.7	7.4	1.3
Belarus	2000	59.2	48.3	70.5					
Belgium	1980	1			1991	13.0	64.3	14.9	6.6
Belize	1991	29.7	29.7	29.7	1992	78.5	10.8	8.2	1.3
Benin	2000	62.5	47.8	76.4					
Bhutan	2000	52.7	38.9	66.4	1992	23.5	20.4	15.2	9.9
Bolivia	2000	14.4	7.9	20.6					
Bosnia and Herzegovina					1993	20.4	44.1	19.8	1.4
Botswana	2000	22.8	25.6	20.2	1989	18.7	57.0	11.9	5.5
Brazil	2000	14.7	14.9	14.6	1981	32.1	28.3	30.1	9.4
Brunei Darussalam	2000	8.4	5.3	11.8	1992	4.7	12.5	35.7	15.0
Bulgaria	2000	1.5	0.9	2.0					
Burkina Faso	2000	77.0	66.8	86.9	1990	75.4	19.9	2.5	0.6
Burundi	2000	51.9	43.7	59.5	1993	30.5	47.0	16.2	1.0
Cambodia (Kampuchea)	1990	65	52	78					
Cameroon	2000	24.6	18.2	30.8	1991	1.0	4.0	34.3	21.4
Canada	1986	3							
Cape Verde	2000	26.5	15.7	34.7	1988	70.7	19.5	7.3	2.0
Central African Republic	2000	53.5	40.4	65.5					
Chad	2000	46.4	33.1	59.2	1992	5.8	48.0	33.9	12.3
Chile	2000	4.3	4.1	4.5	1990	29.3	34.3	34.4	2.0
China	2000	15.0	7.7	22.6	1993	11.9	27.3	13.3	10.4
Colombia	2000	8.2	8.2	8.2					
Comoros	2000	43.8	36.5	50.9	1984	52.4	30.3	14.6	1.3
Congo (DROC)	2000				1984	58.8	13.0	11.0	3.0
Congo (ROC)	2000	19.3	12.5	25.6					
Costa Rica	2000	4.4	4.5	4.3	1988		48.2	43.1	8.7
Cote d'Ivoire	2000	53.2	45.4	61.5	1991	10.2	43.6	39.5	6.4
Croatia	2000	1.7	0.6	2.7	1981	3.7	22.6	40.2	5.9
Cuba	2000	3.6	3.5	3.6	1992	5.1	13.0	34.2	17.0
Cyprus	2000	3.1	1.3	5.0	1991	0.3	31.4	58.6	8.5
Czech Republic		1			1991		38.7	3.4	19.6
Denmark	1980	1							
Djibouti	2000	48.6	35.0	61.6	1981	6.6	80.5	11.1	1.7
Dominica	1970	6	6	6					
Dominican Republic	2000	16.2	16.0	16.3					

Table 4: World Education Indicators (Continued)

COUNTRY	\% OF POPULATION ILLITERATE				\% OF POPULATION HAVING ATTENDED SCHOOL				
	YEAR	TOTAL	MALE	FEMALE	YEAR	NONE	PRIMARY	SECONDARY	TERTIARY
Ecuador	2000	8.1	6.4	9.8	1990	1.7	43.7	22.6	12.7
Egypt	2000	44.7	33.4	56.3	1986	64.1	16.5	14.8	4.6
El Salvador	2000	21.3	18.4	23.9	1992	37.2	46.0	9.8	6.4
Equatorial Guinea	2000	16.8	7.5	25.5					
Eritrea									
Estonia	1998	0	0	0	1989	2.2	39.0	45.1	13.7
Ethiopia	2000	61.3	56.1	66.6	1994	80.1	6.3	2.1	1.0
Fiji	2000	7.1	5.0	9.1	1986	10.9	35.9	24.9	4.5
Finland	1980	1			1990		49.4	35.3	15.4
France	1980	1	1	1	1990	0.6	51.1	36.9	11.4
Gabon	2000	29.2	20.2	37.8					
Gambia, The	2000	63.5	56.2	70.4					
Georgia	1995	36.8	26.3	46.7					
Germany	1977	1							
Ghana	2000	29.8	20.5	38.8					
Greece	2000	2.8	1.4	4.0	1991	5.7	12.7	6.7	8.7
Grenada	1970	2	2	2	1981	2.2	87.8	8.5	1.5
Guatemala	2000	31.3	23.8	38.9	1981	55.0	27.3	2.9	2.2
Guinea	2000	58.9	44.9	73.0					
Guinea-Bissau	2000	63.2	47.0	78.6	1979	91.1	7.5	0.6	0.1
Guyana	2000	1.5	1.0	1.9	1980	8.1	72.9	17.3	1.8
Haiti	2000	51.4	49.0	53.5	1986	59.5	30.5	9.3	0.7
Honduras	2000	27.8	27.5	28.0	1983	33.5	51.3	4.3	3.3
Hungary	2000	0.6	0.5	0.7	1990	1.3	24.3	33.6	10.1
Iceland	1976	0							
India	2000	44.2	31.4	57.9	1991	57.5	28.0	7.2	7.3
Indonesia	2000	13.0	8.1	17.9	1990	54.5	26.4	16.8	2.3
Iran	2000	23.1	16.3	30.0					
Iraq	1995	42	29.3	55	1987	52.8	21.6	11.6	4.1
Ireland	1981	2			1991	0.0	37.2	19.1	13.1
Israel	2000	3.9	2.1	5.7	1983	10.5	42.4	35.9	11.2
Italy	2000	1.5	1.1	1.9	1991	2.1	12.2	30.7	3.8
Jamaica	2000	13.3	17.5	9.3	1991	0.0	67.5	29.9	2.7
Japan	1970	1			1990	0.3	33.6	43.7	20.7
Jordan	2000	10.2	5.1	15.6					
Kazakhstan	1989	2	1	4	1989	7.7	29.2	50.7	12.4
Kenya	2000	17.5	11.0	24.0	1979	58.6	32.2	7.9	1.3
Kiribati									
Korea (DPRK)	1990	1	1	1					
Korea (ROK)	2000	2.2	0.8	3.6	1995	8.7	0.9	15.7	21.1
Kuwait	2000	17.7	15.7	20.1	1988	25.6	8.6	15.1	16.4
Kyrgyzstan	1989	3	1	4					
Laos	2000	38.2	26.4	49.5					
Latvia	2000	0.3	0.2	0.4	1989	0.6	18.5	46.3	13.4
Lebanon	2000	13.9	7.7	19.6					
Lesotho	2000	16.1	26.4	6.4					
Liberia	2000	46.6	30.1	63.2					
Libya	2000	20.2	9.1	32.4	1984	59.7	15.4	5.2	2.7
Liechtenstein	1981	0	0	0					
Lithuania	2000	0.5	0.3	0.6	1989	9.1	21.3	57.0	12.3

Table 4: World Education Indicators (Continued)

COUNTRY	% OF POPULATION ILLITERATE				% OF POPULATION HAVING ATTENDED SCHOOL				
	YEAR	TOTAL	MALE	FEMALE	YEAR	NONE	PRIMARY	SECONDARY	TERTIARY
Luxembourg	1980	0	0	0	1991		39.7	40.3	10.8
Macedonia					1994	28.0	30.6	6.7	
Madagascar	1990	20	12	27					
Malawi	2000	39.7	25.5	53.3	1987	55.0	31.8	2.7	0.4
Malaysia	2000	12.5	8.5	16.4	1996	16.7	13.0	19.4	6.9
Maldives	2000	3.7	3.7	3.6	1990	0.9	61.6	6.3	1.7
Mali	2000	59.7	52.1	66.8					
Malta	2000	7.9	8.6	7.2					
Marshall Islands	1980	7	0	12					
Mauritania	2000	60.1	49.4	70.5	1988	60.8	34.1	3.8	1.3
Mauritius	2000	15.7	12.3	19.0	1990	18.3	42.6	7.2	1.9
Mexico	2000	9.0	6.9	10.9	1990	18.8	28.6	12.7	9.2
Micronesia	1980	11	9	12					
Moldova	2000	1.1	0.4	1.7	1989	12.7	17.1	58.9	11.3
Monaco									
Mongolia	2000	0.7	0.8	0.7	1989	13.4	22.8	13.9	23.4
Morocco	2000	51.1	38.1	64.0					
Mozambique	2000	56.2	40.1	71.6	1980	81.0	18.1	0.8	0.1
Myanmar (Burma)	2000	15.3	11.0	19.4	1983	55.8	27.7	14.5	2.0
Namibia	2000	17.9	17.1	18.8	1991		49.1	43.8	4.0
Nauru									
Nepal	2000	58.6	40.9	76.2	1991	69.7	16.2	8.9	0.6
Netherlands	1979	1							
New Zealand	1980	1			1991	0.0	36.8	16.3	39.1
Nicaragua	2000	35.7	35.8	35.6					
Niger	2000	84.3	76.5	91.7					
Nigeria	2000	35.9	27.7	43.8					
Norway	1976	1			1994	0.0	0.0	37.3	18.7
Oman	2000	28.1	19.6	38.3	1996	71.7	11.5	5.9	11.1
Pakistan	2000	56.7	42.4	72.2	1990	73.8	9.7	5.8	2.5
Palau	1980	8	7	10					
Panama	2000	8.1	7.4	8.7	1990	11.7	20.2	12.6	13.2
Papua New Guinea	2000	24.0	16.3	32.3	1980	82.6	8.2	3.9	0.3
Paraguay	2000	6.7	5.6	7.8	1992	7.0	22.8	12.2	6.6
Peru	2000	10.1	5.3	14.6	1993	16.4	34.7	27.2	20.5
Philippines	2000	4.6	4.5	4.8	1995	3.8	20.8	17.3	22.0
Poland	2000	0.2	0.2	0.2	1988	1.5	5.6	47.8	7.9
Portugal	2000	7.8	5.2	10.0	1991	16.1	61.5	14.8	7.7
Qatar	2000	18.7	19.5	16.8	1986	53.5	9.8	10.1	13.3
Romania	2000	1.8	0.9	2.7	1992	5.4	24.4	63.2	6.9
Russian Federation	2000	0.6	0.2	0.8	1989		36.9	49.0	14.1
Rwanda	2000	33.0	26.3	39.4					
Saint Kitts and Nevis	1980	3	3	2	1980	1.1	29.0	66.6	2.3
Saint Lucia	1980	33	35	31	1991	0.0	75.5	21.2	3.4
Saint Vincent and the Grenadines	1970	4	4	4	1980	2.4	88.0	8.2	1.4
Samoa	1971	3	3	3					
San Marino	1976	4	3	5					
Sao Tome and Principe	1991	27	15	38	1981	56.6	18.0	4.6	0.3
Saudi Arabia	2000	23.0	15.9	32.8					
Senegal	2000	62.7	52.8	72.4					

Table 4: World Education Indicators (Continued)

COUNTRY	YEAR	% OF POPULATION ILLITERATE			YEAR	% OF POPULATION HAVING ATTENDED SCHOOL			
		TOTAL	MALE	FEMALE		NONE	PRIMARY	SECONDARY	TERTIARY
Seychelles	1971	42	14	40	1987	12.1	44.9	35.7	4.6
Sierra Leone	2000	63.7	49.3	77.4	1985	64.5	18.7	9.7	1.5
Singapore	2000	7.6	3.6	11.5	1995	14.3	11.2	36.9	7.6
Slovakia					1991	0.7	37.9	50.9	9.5
Slovenia	2000	0.3	0.3	0.4	1991	0.7	45.1	42.4	10.4
Solomon Islands									
Somalia	1990	76	64	86					
South Africa	2000	14.9	14.2	15.5	1995	13.0	17.1	26.7	8.8
Spain	2000	2.3	1.4	3.2	1991	65.3	65.3	25.5	8.4
Sri Lanka	2000	8.4	5.5	11.1	1981	15.9	48.9	34.1	1.1
Sudan	2000	42.9	31.7	54.0	1983	76.7	18.6	1.9	0.8
Suriname	2000	5.8	4.1	7.4					
Swaziland	2000	20.2	19.1	21.3	1986	42.0	24.0	13.2	3.3
Sweden	1979	1			1995		18.2	14.7	21.0
Switzerland	1980	1			1980		75.6	8.9	11.5
Syria	2000	25.6	11.7	39.6					
Taiwan	1998	6	7	21					
Tajikistan	2000	0.8	0.4	1.1	1989	9.8	13.0	65.5	11.7
Tanzania	2000	24.8	15.9	33.4	1988	0.0	89.7	7.8	2.0
Thailand	2000	4.4	2.8	6.0	1990	10.7	69.6	13.7	5.1
Togo	2000	42.9	27.8	57.4	1981	76.5	13.5	8.7	1.3
Tonga	1996	1.5	1.6	1.3	1986	9.6	34.6	51.1	2.8
Trinidad and Tobago	2000	1.8	1.0	2.5	1990	4.5	56.8	32.3	3.4
Tunisia	2000	29.2	18.6	39.9	1984	66.3	18.9	12.0	2.8
Turkey	2000	14.8	6.4	23.3	1993	30.6	6.6	21.9	21.9
Turkmenistan	1989	2	1	3					
Tuvalu					1991	0.8	71.4	16.2	7.0
Uganda	2000	32.7	22.3	42.9	1991	46.1	41.4	8.9	0.5
Ukraine	1989	2	0	3					
United Arab Emirates	2000	23.5	24.8	20.5					
United Kingdom	1978	1							
United States	1979	3	3	3	1994	0.6	8.2	44.6	46.5
Uruguay	2000	2.2	2.6	1.8	1996	3.4	53.6	31.7	10.1
Uzbekistan	1996	1	1	1					
Vanuatu	1979	47	43	52	1979	37.2	34.3	14.7	7.3
Vatican									
Venezuela	2000	7.0	6.7	7.3	1993	8.0	43.7	38.3	10.1
Vietnam	2000	6.7	4.3	9.0	1989	16.6	69.8	10.6	2.6
Yemen	2000	53.8	32.6	75.0					
Yugoslavia									
Zambia	2000	22.0	14.8	28.8	1993	18.6	54.8	12.9	1.5
Zimbabwe	2000	7.3	4.5	10.1	1992	22.3	53.2	19.4	4.9

Table 5: Current Account Indicators

COUNTRY	YEAR	EXPORTS	IMPORTS	BALANCE ON GOODS	SERVICES CREDIT	SERVICES DEBIT	BALANCE ON SERVICES	CURRENT ACCOUNT BLANCE
Afghanistan								
Albania	1998	208	812	-604	87	129	-43	-65
Algeria								
Andorra								
Angola	1996	5,095	2,041	3,055	268	2,423	-2,156	3,266
Antigua and Barbuda	1996	54	317	-263	368	155	213	-40
Argentina	1998	26,434	29,448	-3,014	4,660	9,045	-4,385	-14,697
Armenia	1998	229	806	-578	131	181	-51	-390
Australia	1998	55,839	61,232	-5,393	16,163	17,304	-1,141	-17,512
Austria	1998	62,826	66,480	-3,654	32,347	30,161	2,186	-4,609
Azerbaijan	1998	678	1,724	-1,046	332	701	-369	-1,365
Bahamas, The	1998	311	1,372	-1,061	1,581	958	623	-594
Bahrain	1998	3,270	3,199	71	769	740	29	-1,042
Bangladesh	1998	5,141	6,862	-1,721	724	1,253	-529	-190
Barbados	1998	257	901	-644	1,024	432	591	-57
Belarus	1998	7,123	8,482	-1,359	941	450	491	-862
Belgium	1998	153,160	145,599	7,561	36,814	34,258	2,556	12,111
Belize	1998	186	291	-105	141	99	42	-60
Benin	1997	424	577	-153	116	172	-56	-154
Bhutan								
Bolivia	1998	1,104	1,759	-655	253	441	-188	-673
Bosnia and Herzegovina								
Botswana	1998	2,061	1,983	78	255	522	-267	170
Brazil	1998	51,136	57,739	-6,603	7,631	16,676	-9,045	-33,829
Brunei Darussalam								
Bulgaria	1998	4,299	4,757	-458	1,255	1,120	135	-376
Burkina Faso	1994	216	344	-129	56	138	-82	15
Burundi	1997	87	98	-11	9	41	-33	4
Cambodia (Kampuchea)	1998	705	1,097	-391	110	189	-80	-224
Cameroon	1995	1,736	1,109	627	304	499	-194	90
Canada	1998	217,238	204,614	12,624	30,922	35,677	-4,755	-11,213
Cape Verde	1998	33	218	-186	86	91	-4	-58
Central African Republic	1994	146	131	15	33	114	-81	-25
Chad	1994	135	212	-77	55	199	-145	-38
Chile	1998	14,831	17,347	-2,516	4,122	4,236	-114	-4,139
China	1998	183,527	136,914	46,613	24,057	28,980	-4,923	29,325
Colombia	1998	11,363	14,008	-2,645	2,115	3,509	-1,394	-5,908
Comoros	1995	11	54	-42	35	50	-15	-19
Congo, (DROC)								
Congo, Republic of the	1997	1,744	803	941	56	565	-510	-252
Costa Rica	1998	5,547	5,791	-245	1,330	1,183	147	-460
Cote d'Ivoire	1998	4,575	2,705	1,870	550	1,474	-925	-313
Croatia	1998	4,613	8,774	-4,161	3,964	1,889	2,075	-1,543
Cuba								
Cyprus	1998	1,065	3,490	-2,426	2,957	1,138	1,819	-561
Czech Republic	1998	-26,383	28,976	-55,359	7,510	5,721	1,789	-1,108
Denmark	1998	47,829	44,382	3,447	14,835	15,496	-661	-2,419
Djibouti	1995	34	205	-172	151	87	64	-23
Dominica	1996	53	101	-48	61	45	16	-40

Table 5: Current Account Indicators (Continued)

COUNTRY	YEAR	EXPORTS	IMPORTS	BALANCE ON GOODS	SERVICES CREDIT	SERVICES DEBIT	BALANCE ON SERVICES	CURRENT ACCOUNT BLANCE
Dominican Republic	1998	4,981	7,597	-2,617	2,502	1,320	1,182	-336
Ecuador	1998	4,203	5,198	-995	804	1,211	-407	-2,169
Egypt	1998	4,403	14,617	-10,214	8,141	6,492	1,649	-2,566
El Salvador	1998	2,451	3,718	-1,267	290	549	-259	-84
Equatorial Guinea	1996	175	292	-117	5	185	-180	-344
Eritrea								
Estonia	1998	2,690	3,805	-1,115	1,480	910	570	-478
Ethiopia	1998	568	1,042	-474	431	419	13	134
Fiji	1998	393	612	-218	506	341	166	-55
Finland	1998	43,394	30,902	12,492	7,220	8,235	-1,015	7,561
France	1998	302,000	276,000	26,000	85,000	67,000	19,000	40,000
Gabon	1995	2,643	899	1,744	273	949	-677	100
Gambia, The	1997	120	207	-87	109	75	35	-24
Georgia	1998	300	1,060	-760	290	345	-55	-416
Germany	1998	539,990	460,950	79,040	83,420	126,400	-42,980	-3,440
Ghana	1998	1,813	2,346	-533	176	541	-365	-350
Greece	1997	5,576	20,951	-15,375	9,287	4,650	4,637	-4,860
Grenada	1996	25	148	-123	107	46	61	-58
Guatemala	1998	2,847	4,256	-1,409	640	792	-152	-1,039
Guinea	1998	693	572	121	111	390	-280	-119
Guinea-Bissau	1997	49	62	-14	8	26	-18	-30
Guyana	1995	496	537	-41	134	172	-38	-135
Haiti	1998	299	641	-341	180	381	-201	-38
Honduras	1998	2,017	2,340	-323	370	396	-26	-333
Hungary	1998	20,747	23,101	-2,354	4,910	4,000	910	-2,304
Iceland	1998	1,927	2,278	-351	947	965	-18	-469
India	1998	34,076	44,828	-10,752	11,691	14,540	-2,849	-6,903
Indonesia	1998	50,371	31,942	18,429	4,479	11,813	-7,334	3,972
Iran	1998	12,982	13,608	-626	1,315	2,581	-1,266	-1,897
Iraq								
Ireland	1998	65,032	41,651	23,381	6,717	20,062	-13,345	806
Israel	1998	22,972	26,197	-3,225	9,049	9,825	-776	-668
Italy	1998	242,572	206,941	35,631	67,549	63,379	4,170	19,998
Jamaica	1998	1,613	2,710	-1,097	1,770	1,260	510	-255
Japan	1998	374,000	252,000	122,000	62,000	112,000	-49,000	121,000
Jordan	1998	1,802	3,404	-1,602	1,825	1,784	41	14
Kazakhstan	1998	5,839	6,589	-750	897	1,128	-231	-1,201
Kenya	1998	2,013	3,029	-1,016	838	666	172	-363
Kiribati	1994	6	27	-21	18	17		1
Korea (DPRK)	1998	132,122	90,495	41,627	24,580	23,951	629	40,552
Korea (ROK)								
Kuwait	1998	9,614	7,714	1,900	1,762	5,483	-3,721	2,527
Kyrgyzstan	1998	535	756	-221	63	180	-118	-371
Laos	1998	342	507	-165	145	96	50	-150
Latvia	1998	2,011	3,141	-1,130	1,040	761	279	-713
Lebanon								
Lesotho	1998	193	866	-673	54	52	1	-280
Liberia								
Libya								
Liechtenstein								

Table 5: Current Account Indicators (Continued)

COUNTRY	YEAR	EXPORTS	IMPORTS	BALANCE ON GOODS	SERVICES CREDIT	SERVICES DEBIT	BALANCE ON SERVICES	CURRENT ACCOUNT BLANCE
Lithuania	1998	3,962	5,480	-1,518	1,109	869	241	-1,298
Luxembourg								
Macedonia	1998	1,318	1,715	-398	131	304	-173	-288
Madagascar	1998	538	693	-155	291	436	-145	-301
Malawi	1994	363	639	-276	22	234	-212	-450
Malaysia	1997	77,881	74,005	3,876	15,016	17,516	-2,500	-4,792
Maldives	1998	98	312	-214	329	99	231	-23
Mali	1997	560	551	10	82	345	-263	-178
Malta	1998	1,823	2,415	-592	1,240	827	413	-169
Marshall Islands								
Mauritania	1998	367	326	41	35	156	-121	79
Mauritius	1998	1,738	2,018	-280	974	730	245	35
Mexico	1998	117,459	125,374	-7,915	12,064	13,067	-1,003	-15,960
Micronesia, Federated States of								
Moldova	1998	644	1,043	-399	120	193	-73	-334
Monaco								
Mongolia	1998	462	524	-62	78	147	-69	-129
Morocco	1998	7,144	9,463	-2,319	2,827	1,895	932	-236
Mozambique	1998	248	782	-533	286	401	-115	-477
Myanmar (Burma)	1998	1,171	2,455	-1,284	543	445	99	-454
Namibia	1998	1,278	1,451	-173	327	457	-130	162
Nauru								
Nepal	1998	486	1,238	-753	565	196	369	-63
Netherlands	1997	166,967	147,974	18,993	51,755	45,999	5,756	27,684
New Zealand	1997	14,123	13,248	875	4,230	5,031	-801	-4,750
Nicaragua	1998	579	1,384	-804	182	272	-90	-607
Niger	1995	288	306	-18	33	152	-119	-152
Nigeria	1998	8,971	9,211	-240	884	4,166	-3,282	-4,244
Norway	1998	40,636	39,070	1,566	14,132	15,370	-1,238	-2,161
Oman	1997	7,631	4,649	2,982	18	1,166	-1,148	-57
Pakistan	1997	8,503	10,946	-2,443	1,678	2,707	-1,029	-1,792
Palau								
Panama	1998	6,325	7,696	-1,371	1,697	1,173	525	-1,212
Papua New Guinea	1998	1,773	1,078	695	318	794	-476	-29
Paraguay	1998	3,824	3,938	-114	489	562	-73	-106
Peru	1998	5,735	8,200	-2,465	1,753	2,294	-541	-3,800
Philippines	1998	29,496	29,524	-28	7,477	10,107	-2,630	1,287
Poland	1998	32,467	45,303	-12,836	10,920	6,704	4,216	-6,901
Portugal	1998	26,016	38,295	-12,279	8,606	7,031	1,575	-7,250
Qatar								
Romania	1998	8,302	10,927	-2,625	1,217	1,871	-654	-2,918
Russian Federation	1998	74,748	57,387	17,361	12,920	16,028	-3,108	2,262
Rwanda	1998	65	263	-198	47	219	-172	-143
Saint Kitts and Nevis	1994	29	98	-69	92	46	46	-26
Saint Lucia	1996	86	271	-184	270	143	127	-80
Saint Vincent and the Grenadines	1996	52	127	-75	94	56	38	-35
Samoa	1998	20	97	-76	62	29	33	20
San Marino								
Sao Tome and Principe								
Saudi Arabia	1998	39,772	27,535	12,237	4,421	17,098	-12,677	-12,880

Table 5: Current Account Indicators (Continued)

COUNTRY	YEAR	EXPORTS	IMPORTS	BALANCE ON GOODS	SERVICES CREDIT	SERVICES DEBIT	BALANCE ON SERVICES	CURRENT ACCOUNT BLANCE
Senegal	1997	905	1,176	-271	372	392	-20	-185
Seychelles	1997	115	303	-188	241	119	122	-63
Sierra Leone	1995	42	168	-127	87	92	-5	-127
Singapore	1998	110,379	95,702	14,677	18,327	17,997	330	17,614
Slovakia	1998	10,720	13,071	-2,351	2,292	2,276	16	-2,126
Slovenia	1998	9,096	9,870	-775	2,048	1,535	513	-4
Solomon Islands	1998	142	160	-18	55	55	1	8
Somalia								
South Africa	1998	29,534	27,216	2,318	5,295	5,471	-176	-1,936
Spain	1998	109,814	128,521	-18,707	49,070	27,884	21,186	-1,606
Sri Lanka	1998	4,735	5,302	-568	913	1,359	-446	-288
Sudan	1998	596	1,732	-1,137	16	204	-188	-957
Suriname								
Swaziland	1995	416	293	123	104	162	-58	73
Sweden	1998	85,179	67,547	17,632	17,952	21,721	-3,769	4,639
Switzerland	1998	93,859	92,871	988	26,683	15,406	11,277	24,547
Syria	1998	3,135	3,307	-172	1,795	1,481	314	59
Taiwan								
Tajikistan								
Tanzania	1998	590	1,365	-776	555	988	-433	-1,076
Thailand	1998	52,747	36,513	16,234	13,156	11,998	1,158	14,241
Togo	1994	328	366	-37	80	89	-9	-63
Tonga								
Trinidad and Tobago	1998	2,258	5,999	-3,741	67,137	255	66,882	-644
Tunisia	1998	5,725	7,875	-2,150	2,757	1,256	1,501	-675
Turkey	1998	31,220	45,552	-14,332	23,321	9,860	13,461	1,871
Turkmenistan	1997	774	1,005	-231	272	675	-403	-580
Tuvalu								
Uganda	1997	576	1,043	-467	165	693	-529	-388
Ukraine	1998	13,699	16,283	-2,584	3,922	2,545	1,377	-1,296
United Arab Emirates								
United Kingdom	1998	272,000	306,000	-34,000	99,000	79,000	20,000	
United States	1998	672,000	917,000	-245,000	262,000	181,000	81,000	-221,000
Uruguay	1998	2,832	3,594	-762	1,393	913	480	-400
Uzbekistan								
Vanuatu	1998	34	76	-42	116	45	71	5
Vatican								
Venezuela	1998	17,564	14,816	2,748	1,457	5,054	-3,597	-2,562
Vietnam								
Yemen	1998	1,501	2,201	-701	208	570	-362	-228
Yugoslavia								
Zambia								
Zimbabwe	1998	1,961	1,804	158	383	712	-329	-425

Table 6: Government Revenues and Expenditures

COUNTRY	YEAR	REVENUES ($ MILLIONS)	EXPEND. ($ MILLIONS)	DEFENSE	EDUCATION	HEALTH	SOCIAL SECURITY	HOUSING	INTEREST PAYMENTS
					% OF BUDGET EXPENDED ON				
Afghanistan									
Albania	1998	624	996	3.5	1.9	3.8	20.1	2.9	26.2
Algeria	1998	14,400	15,700			...			
Andorra	1993	138	177						
Angola	1992	928	2,500						
Antigua and Barbuda	1997	122.6	141.2						
Argentina	1998	56,000	60,000	4.5	5.7	2.3	52.3	2.4	12.8
Armenia	1998	322	424						
Australia	1998	90,730	89,040	7.0	7.6	14.8	35.5	1.2	6.1
Austria	1997	77,900	83,405	2.0	9.2	14.4	42.0	2.5	9.2
Azerbaijan	1999	869	992	11.1	3.2	0.8	33.1	...	1.9
Bahamas, The	1997	766	845	3.1	19.6	15.9	6.1	1.5	12.3
Bahrain	1999	1,500	1,900	17.3	13.2	9.0	4.3	3.5	3.7
Bangladesh	1997	3,800	50,500						
Barbados	1997	725.5							
Belarus	1998	939	966	4.5	4.1	3.2	36.3	...	2.4
Belgium	1997	213,813	225,097	...	...	...	...	...	16.5
Belize	1997	140	142	5.4	20.5	8.2	5.9	2.6	8.0
Benin	1995	299	445						
Bhutan	1998	146.5	146.8	...	10.9	11.1	...	2.6	1.9
Bolivia	1998	1,633	1,877	9.6	19.6	3.4	25.9	1.0	7.5
Bosnia and Herzegovina									
Botswana	1996	1,600	1,800	8.1	26.3	5.2	1.1	11.6	1.6
Brazil	1998	151,000	149,000	3.1	3.6	6.3	30.4	0.2	44.0
Brunei Darussalam	1995	2,500	2,600						
Bulgaria	1998	4,100	3,800	8.0	4.4	4.7	32.4	1.6	13.2
Burkina Faso	1995	277	492	14.0	17.3	6.9	...	0.8	8.3
Burundi	1998	126	165	26.1	13.9	2.6	5.8	...	7.5
Cambodia (Kampuchea)	1995	261	496						
Cameroon	1996	2,230	2,230	12.2	14.6	4.2	0.7	1.6	23.5
Canada	1998	121,300	112,600	6.1	3.3	4.6	42.9	1.5	18.4
Cape Verde	1996	188	228						
Central African Republic	1994	638	1,900						
Chad	1998	198	218						
Chile	1996	19,000	18,000	8.4	20.5	12.1	34.0	5.0	3.1
China	1997	59,506	72,600	13.6	2.0	0.2	0.2	0.1	...
Colombia	1998	11,800	17,000	14.4	21.0	8.8	10.8	5.3	17.4
Comoros	1997	48	53						
Congo (DROC)	1996	269	244	17.6	0.2	0.1	0.0	0.2	0.1
Congo (ROC)	1997	685	884						
Costa Rica	1991	1,100	1,340	...	16.8	22.1	20.5	0.3	19.9
Cote d'Ivoire	1997	2,300	2,600						
Croatia	1997	5,300	6,300	7.7	7.4	14.0	37.8	5.1	3.2
Cuba	1998	12,300	13,000						
Cyprus	1997	710.888	830.4	3.8	11.9	6.3	24.5	4.0	14.3
Czech Republic	1998	18,460	19,380	4.8	9.6	17.9	36.4	2.0	3.0
Denmark	1996	60,300	63,200	4.0	9.4	0.8	43.2	1.6	13.3
Djibouti	1997	156	175						
Dominica	1997	72	79.9						

Table 6: Government Revenues and Expenditures (Continued)

COUNTRY	YEAR	REVENUES ($ MILLIONS)	EXPEND. ($ MILLIONS)	% OF BUDGET EXPENDED ON					
				DEFENSE	EDUCATION	HEALTH	SOCIAL SECURITY	HOUSING	INTEREST PAYMENTS
Dominican Republic	1999	2,300	2,900	4.7	14.3	11.2	5.6	13.2	3.1
Ecuador	1999	5,100	5,100	13.1	18.4	11.2	1.9	0.6	23.2
Egypt	1997	20,000	20,800	9.4	14.8	3.3	0.5	5.3	19.7
El Salvador	1997	1,750	1,820	7.1	19.6	10.3	5.4	1.8	11.9
Equatorial Guinea	1996	47	43						
Eritrea	1996	226	453						
Estonia	1998	1,714	1,717	4.0	8.6	16.4	30.6	...	0.9
Ethiopia	1996	1,000	1,480	9.1	14.0	5.3	5.9	5.7	10.4
Fiji	1997	540.65	742.65	5.8	18.2	8.7	4.1	2.9	9.5
Finland	1997	39,656	42,646	4.6	10.1	3.4	39.1	3.2	11.2
France	1998	222,000	265,000	5.3	7.0	21.7	38.8	1.1	5.9
Gabon	1996	1,500	1,300						
Gambia, The	1996	88.6	98.2	4.3	12.3	7.0	3.0	4.6	16.7
Georgia	1998	364	568	9.1	4.9	4.0	17.7	1.0	20.6
Germany	1998	977,000	1,024,000	3.9	0.5	18.9	50.0	.5	7.1
Ghana	1996	1,390	1,470	4.9	22.0	7.0	7.1	2.8	16.6
Greece	1998	45,000	47,600	6.7	9.3	7.0	16.9	1.9	...
Grenada	1997	85.8	102.1	...	16.8	10.4	8.6	2.1	7.0
Guatemala	1998	1,868	2,113	15.2	19.0	10.6	...	...	10.0
Guinea	1995	553	652						
Guinea-Bissau	1999	817	923						
Guyana	1997	253.7	304.1						
Haiti	1997	323	363						
Honduras	1997	655	850						
Hungary	1998	11,200	13,200	2.3	8.6	6.0	29.9	1.5	17.5
Iceland	1996	1,900	2,100	...	10.1	24.1	23.6	0.7	10.2
India	1998	42,120	63,790	15.8	3.0	1.7	...	6.4	50.0
Indonesia	1998	35,000	35,000	5.3	6.9	2.3	5.0	13.9	14.6
Iran	1996	34,600	34,900	8.5	16.0	6.4	13.6	5.6	0.8
Iraq									
Ireland	1998	23,500	20,600	2.9	13.1	15.7	27.1	2.9	13.1
Israel	1998	55,000	58,000	17.8	13.4	13.9	25.2	3.3	12.6
Italy	1998	559,000	589,000						
Jamaica	1998	2,270	3,660						
Japan	1999	407,000	711,000	4.1	6.0	1.6	36.8	13.8	...
Jordan	1999	2,800	3,000	17.9	14.6	10.2	17.8	2.0	11.9
Kazakhstan	1998	2,900	4,200	5.1	4.8	7.7	38.1	...	4.3
Kenya	1997	2,600	2,700	5.9	20.2	6.0	...	3.4	26.2
Kiribati	1996	33.3	47.7						
Korea (DPRK)	1992	19,300	19,300						
Korea (ROK)	1997	100,400	100,500	16.7	20.5	0.8	10.8	2.3	2.9
Kuwait	1998	8,100	14,500	20.3	11.9	7.4	18.6	3.3	...
Kyrgyzstan	1996	225	308	6.5	22.3	12.8	13.0	5.0	...
Laos	1996	230.2	365.9						
Latvia	1998	1,330	1,270	2.6	5.3	11.0	40.8	1.4	2.1
Lebanon	1998	4,900	7,900	9.7	8.3	2.6	6.4	2.1	40.0
Lesotho	1996	507	487	6.5	26.7	9.3	...	...	4.3
Liberia									
Libya	1998	3,600	5,100						

Table 6: Government Revenues and Expenditures (Continued)

COUNTRY	YEAR	REVENUES ($ MILLIONS)	EXPEND. ($ MILLIONS)	DEFENSE	EDUCATION	HEALTH	SOCIAL SECURITY	HOUSING	INTEREST PAYMENTS
				\multicolumn{6}{c}{% OF BUDGET EXPENDED ON}			
Liechtenstein	1996	455	435						
Lithuania	1998	2,900	2,900	3.1	6.0	15.5	32.3	...	3.7
Luxembourg	1997	7,512	6,577	1.9	10.3	2.3	52.3	3.1	0.4
Macedonia	1996	1,060	1,000						
Madagascar	1996	477	706	5.1	11.3	5.8	2.6	2.9	29.3
Malawi	1993	530	674						
Malaysia	1996	22,600	22,000	11.1	22.8	6.3	7.2	7.3	12.0
Maldives	1998	166	184	11.7	14.6	11.3	2.8	5.3	4.8
Mali	1997	730	770						
Malta	1998	1,320	1,760	2.1	12.2	9.9	34.4	9.5	6.3
Marshall Islands	1995	80.1	77.4						
Mauritania	1996	329	265						
Mauritius	1996	824	1,000	0.9	16.9	8.3	20.6	5.9	12.6
Mexico	1998	117,000	123,000	3.5	22.1	3.4	18.1	3.4	13.7
Micronesia	1996	58	52						
Moldova	1998	536	594						
Monaco	1995	518	531						
Mongolia	1998	260	330	8.3	8.0	2.1	25.3	0.7	5.5
Morocco	1998	8,400	10,000	13.6	16.6	3.1	7.0	0.4	17.9
Mozambique	1997	402	799						
Myanmar (Burma)	1997	7,900	12,200	30.6	9.4	3.5	2.3	0.4	...
Namibia	1997	1,100	1,200						
Nauru	1996	23.4	64.8						
Nepal	1998	560	857	4.5	13.6	6.5	2.1	4.7	...
Netherlands	1999	163,000	170,000	3.9	10.0	14.8	37.4	1.5	9.1
New Zealand	1998	24,900	23,700	3.3	16.2	16.4	39.1	0.1	7.2
Nicaragua	1996	389	551	5.8	15.5	13.4	14.7	3.3	14.6
Niger	1998	370	370						
Nigeria	1998	13,900	13,900						
Norway	1997	67,000	66,000	6.8	6.9	4.5	38.4	0.5	5.0
Oman	1999	4,000	5,600	32.4	15.6	7.2	5.0	6.1	5.6
Pakistan	1999	11,250	13,800						
Palau	1997	52.9	59.9						
Panama	1997	2,400	2,400	5.0	18.3	18.7	20.5	5.1	12.5
Papua New Guinea	1997	1,500	1,350	3.3	17.6	8.9	.7	3.5	9.1
Paraguay	1995	1,250	1,660	10.7	22.1	7.3	16.2	0.4	6.0
Peru	1996	8,500	9,300						
Philippines	1998	14,500	12,600	7.9	20.3	3.2	2.5	0.5	16.6
Poland	1998	56,600	58,200	4.0	6.4	10.0	49.9	1.7	8.6
Portugal	1996	48,000	52,000	...	...	...	...	...	9.3
Qatar	1999	3,400	4,300						
Romania	1997	10,000	11,700	7.3	9.4	6.8	31.0	0.8	11.6
Russian Federation	1998	40,000	63,000	12.2	2.2	1.7	27.7	...	13.1
Rwanda	1996	231	319						
Saint Kitts and Nevis	1997	64.1	73.3	...	...	...	...	...	6.9
Saint Lucia	1998	141.2	146.7						
Saint Vincent and the Grenadines	1997	85.7	98.6	...	12.8	9.6	7.0	1.5	...
Samoa	1997	52	99						
San Marino	1995	320	320						

Table 6: Government Revenues and Expenditures (Continued)

| COUNTRY | YEAR | REVENUES ($ MILLIONS) | EXPEND. ($ MILLIONS) | % OF BUDGET EXPENDED ON | | | | | |
				DEFENSE	EDUCATION	HEALTH	SOCIAL SECURITY	HOUSING	INTEREST PAYMENTS
Sao Tome and Principe	1993	58	114						
Saudi Arabia	1999	32,300	44,000						
Senegal	1996	885	885						
Seychelles	1994	220	241	2.9	8.6	7.3	13.9	0.3	15.0
Sierra Leone	1997	96	150	9.9	13.3	9.6	2.3	0.8	18.2
Singapore	1998	16,300	13,600	28.9	18.8	6.7	1.8	5.2	4.2
Slovakia	1998	7,500	8,500	5.0	10.3	15.2	29.3	1.0	7.6
Slovenia	1996	8,480	8,530						
Solomon Islands	1997	147	168						
Somalia									
South Africa	1995	30,500	38,000	...	40.9	22.3	17.6	3.4	...
Spain	1995	113,000	139,000	3.2	3.7	5.6	38.5	0.4	12.4
Sri Lanka	1997	3,000	4,200	16.7	10.5	5.7	12.8	2.2	21.6
Sudan	1996	482	1,500						
Suriname	1997	393	403						
Swaziland	1997	400	450						
Sweden	1998	94,000	98,000	5.5	6.9	0.5	43.9	2.3	14.7
Switzerland	1998	32,660	34,890	5.2	2.3	19.7	50.5	0.7	3.2
Syria	1997	16,000	16,000	23.6	9.2	2.7	2.7	1.7	...
Taiwan	1998	40,000	55,000						
Tajikistan									
Tanzania	1999	700	1,000						
Thailand	1998	18,300	22,200	10.3	23.1	9.2	4.1	4.8	1.0
Togo	1997	232	252						
Tonga	1997	49	120						
Trinidad and Tobago	1997	1,590	1,540	1.8	13.7	8.4	14.3	8.9	17.7
Tunisia	1998	5,800	6,500	6.2	18.7	6.9	16.7	5.2	12.2
Turkey	1998	44,400	58,500	8.9	11.2	4.1	9.0	1.8	26.5
Turkmenistan	1996	521	548						
Tuvalu	1989	4.3	4.3						
Uganda	1996	869	985						
Ukraine	1997	18,000	21,000						
United Arab Emirates	1998	5,400	5,800	31.5	17.7	7.6	3.4	1.2	...
United Kingdom	1997	487,700	492,600	7.1	4.1	15.0	36.4	2.2	8.9
United States	1998	1,722,000	1,653,000	15.4	1.8	20.5	28.7	2.9	14.6
Uruguay	1997	4,000	4,300	3.9	7.0	5.8	61.4	1.5	4.7
Uzbekistan	1997	4,400	4,700						
Vanuatu	1996	94.4	99.8						
Vatican									
Venezuela	1996	11,990	11,480						
Vietnam	1996	5,600	6,000	...	13.5	3.9	11.8	...	3.3
Yemen	1998	2,300	2,600	18.8	21.8	4.4	...	1.6	8.8
Yugoslavia									
Zambia	1995	888	835	3.9	14.4	13.2	1.3	2.3	...
Zimbabwe	1997	2,500	2,900	7.1	24.2	8.1	18.2	4.4	19.9

Table 7: World Electronic Media Indicators, 1999

COUNTRY	PERSONAL COMPUTERS (PER 1000)	INTERNET HOSTS (PER 10,000)	RADIOS (PER 1000)	TELEVISIONS (PER 1000)	MOBILE PHONES (PER 1000)
Afghanistan	...	...	63	4	...
Albania	...	0.2	217	109	1
Algeria	5	0.0	241	105	1
Andorra	...	...	148	103	...
Angola	1	0.0	54	14	1
Antigua and Barbuda	...	...	...	434	...
Argentina	45	27.9	681	289	78
Armenia	5	1.9	224	218	2
Australia	412	477.9	1376	639	286
Austria	234	252.0	753	516	282
Azerbaijan	...	0.2	23	254	8
Bahamas, The	...	...	696	209	...
Bahrain	...	...	499	421	...
Bangladesh	...	0.0	50	6	1
Barbados	...	...	...	268	...
Belarus	...	0.8	296	314	1
Belgium	286	266.9	793	510	173
Belize	...	...	...	112	...
Benin	1	0.1	108	10	1
Bhutan	...	...	11.5	0	...
Bolivia	8	0.5	675	116	27
Bosnia and Herzegovina	...	1.4	248	41	7
Botswana	26	6.0	156	20	15
Brazil	31	18.5	444	316	47
Brunei Darussalam	...	...	859	523	...
Bulgaria	...	11.9	543	398	15
Burkina Faso	1	0.2	33	9	0
Burundi	...	0.0	71	4	0
Cambodia (Kampuchea)	1	0.1	127	123	6
Cameroon	...	0.0	163	32	0
Canada	330	423.0	1077	715	176
Cape Verde	...	...	...	17	...
Central African Republic	...	0.0	83	5	0
Chad	...	0.0	242	1	0
Chile	49	21.5	354	232	65
China	9	0.5	333	272	19
Colombia	28	7.5	581	217	49
Comoros	...	...	140	0	...
Congo, Democratic Republic of the (Zaire)	...	0.0	375	135	0
Congo, Republic of the	...	0.0	124	12	1
Costa Rica	40	10.4	271	387	28
Cote d'Ivoire	3.6	0.3	164	70	6
Croatia	112	25.9	336	272	41
Cuba	...	0.1	353	239	0
Cyprus (Greek and Turkish zones)	...	...	830	514	...
Czech Republic	98	85.6	803	447	94
Denmark	378	540.3	1141	585	364
Djibouti	...	...	77	37	...
Dominica	...	...	704	81	...

Table 7: World Electronic Media Indicators, 1999 (Continued)

COUNTRY	PERSONAL COMPUTERS (PER 1000)	INTERNET HOSTS (PER 10,000)	RADIOS (PER 1000)	TELEVISIONS (PER 1000)	MOBILE PHONES (PER 1000)
Dominican Republic	...	7.6	178	95	31
Ecuador	19	1.4	419	293	25
Egypt	10	0.3	324	122	1
El Salvador	...	1.2	464	675	18
Equatorial Guinea	...	...	...	8	...
Eritrea	...	0.0	91	14	0
Estonia	35	174.7	693	480	170
Ethiopia	...	0.0	195	5	0
Fiji	...	...	...	15	...
Finland	350	1116.8	1496	640	572
France	208	110.6	937	601	188
Gabon	8.6	0.0	183	55	8
Gambia, The	3	0.0	168	3	4
Georgia	...	1.6	555	473	11
Germany, Federal Republic of (FRG)	305	174.0	948	580	170
Ghana	2	0.1	238	99	1
Greece	52	59.6	477	466	194
Grenada	...	...	817	806	...
Guatemala	9	1.3	79	126	10
Guinea	3	0.0	47	41	3
Guinea-Bissau	...	0.1	44	...	0
Guyana	...	...	566	46	...
Haiti	...	0.0	55	5	0
Honduras	8	0.2	386	90	5
Hungary	59	93.1	689	437	105
Iceland	...	...	334	351	...
India	3	0.2	121	69	1
Indonesia	8	0.8	156	136	5
Iran	32	0.1	265	157	6
Iraq	...	0.0	229	83	0
Ireland	272	156.7	699	403	257
Israel	218	187.4	520	318	359
Italy	174	68.3	878	486	355
Jamaica	40	1.0	480	182	22
Japan	238	163.8	955	707	374
Jordan	9	1.2	287	52	12
Kazakhstan	...	1.4	384	231	2
Kenya	3	0.2	104	21	0
Kiribati	...	...	172	...	...
Korea, Democratic People's Republic of (DPRK)	...	...	147	53	0
Korea, Republic of (ROK)	157	55.5	1033	346	302
Kuwait	105	23.8	660	491	138
Kyrgyzstan	...	4.1	112	45	0
Laos	2	0.0	143	4	1
Latvia	...	50.9	710	492	68
Lebanon	40	7.0	906	352	157
Lesotho	...	0.1	49	25	5
Liberia	...	...	219	18	...
Libya	...	0.0	233	126	3
Liechtenstein	...	...	374	364	...

Table 7: World Electronic Media Indicators, 1999 (Continued)

COUNTRY	PERSONAL COMPUTERS (PER 1000)	INTERNET HOSTS (PER 10,000)	RADIOS (PER 1000)	TELEVISIONS (PER 1000)	MOBILE PHONES (PER 1000)
Lithuania	54	30.5	513	459	72
Luxembourg	...	...	532	232	...
Macedonia	...	4.4	200	250	15
Madagascar	2	0.1	192	21	1
Malawi	...	0.0	249	2	1
Malaysia	59	23.5	420	166	99
Maldives	...	...	91	24	...
Mali	1	0.0	54	12	0
Malta	...	...	493	783	...
Marshall Islands	...	...	...	...	...
Mauritania	6	0.0	151	91	0
Mauritius	88	4.6	368	226	53
Mexico	47	23.0	325	261	35
Micronesia, Federated States of	...	...	128	10	...
Moldova	7	2.4	740	297	2
Monaco	...	...	1024	745	...
Mongolia	6	0.0	151	63	1
Morocco (includes Western Sahara)	3	0.3	241	160	4
Mozambique	2	0.1	40	5	0
Myanmar (Burma)	...	0.0	95	7	0
Namibia	19	11.7	144	37	12
Nauru	...	...	374	...	...
Nepal	...	0.1	38	6	0
Netherlands	318	403.5	978	543	213
New Zealand	283	476.2	990	508	203
Nicaragua	8	2.2	285	190	4
Niger	1	0.0	69	27	0
Nigeria	6	0.0	223	66	0
Norway	374	754.2	915	579	474
Oman	21	2.9	598	595	43
Pakistan	4	0.2	98	88	1
Palau	...	...	478	85	...
Panama	28	3.0	299	187	29
Papua New Guinea	...	0.5	97	24	1
Paraguay	10	2.4	182	101	41
Peru	19	3.1	273	144	30
Philippines	16	1.3	159	108	22
Poland	44	40.9	523	413	50
Portugal	82	59.4	304	542	309
Qatar	...	...	268	274	...
Romania	11	9.0	319	233	29
Russian Federation	41	13.1	418	420	5
Rwanda	...	0.0	102	0	1
Saint Kitts and Nevis	...	...	576	219	...
Saint Lucia	...	...	668	167	...
Saint Vincent and the Grenadines	...	...	627	170	...
Samoa	...	...	323	26	...
San Marino	...	...	595	357	...
Sao Tome and Principe	...	...	207	...	...
Saudi Arabia	50	1.2	321	262	31

Table 7: World Electronic Media Indicators, 1999 (Continued)

COUNTRY	PERSONAL COMPUTERS (PER 1000)	INTERNET HOSTS (PER 10,000)	RADIOS (PER 1000)	TELEVISIONS (PER 1000)	MOBILE PHONES (PER 1000)
Senegal	12	0.3	142	41	2
Seychelles	...	...	628	151	...
Sierra Leone	...	0.1	253	13	0
Singapore	459	322.3	822	348	346
Slovakia	66	38.8	580	402	87
Slovenia	251	99.3	406	356	84
Solomon Islands	...	...	81	4	...
Somalia	...	...	40	16	...
South Africa	48	33.4	317	125	56
Spain	145	76.8	333	506	179
Sri Lanka	5	0.5	209	92	9
Sudan	2	0.0	271	87	0
Suriname	...	...	669	137	...
Swaziland	...	...	199	20	...
Sweden	362	581.5	932	531	464
Switzerland	422	371.4	1000	535	235
Syria	2	0.0	278	70	0
Taiwan	...	...	386	48	...
Tajikistan	...	0.2	142	285	0
Tanzania	2	0.1	279	21	1
Thailand	22	4.5	232	236	32
Togo	7	0.2	218	18	2
Tonga	...	...	600	18	...
Trinidad and Tobago	47	28.2	534	334	20
Tunisia	15	0.1	223	198	4
Turkey	24	8.1	180	286	53
Turkmenistan	...	0.6	276	201	1
Tuvalu	...	...	373	...	...
Uganda	2	0.1	128	27	1
Ukraine	14	4.6	884	490	2
United Arab Emirates	107	39.4	345	294	210
United Kingdom	263	271	1436	645	252
United States	459	1508.8	2146	847	256
Uruguay	92	38.3	607	241	60
Uzbekistan	...	0.1	465	275	1
Vanuatu	...	...	254	10	...
Vatican	...	...	...	...	...
Venezuela	43	4.0	468	185	87
Vietnam	7	0.0	107	47	2
Yemen	2	0.0	64	29	1
Yugoslavia (Serbia and Montenegro)	19	7.7	297	259	23
Zambia	...	0.5	121	137	1
Zimbabwe	9	1.2	93	30	4

Conversion Tables*

LENGTH
1 centimeter..0.3937 inch
1 centimeter...0.03280833 foot
1 meter (100 centimeters) ....3.280833 feet
1 meter ....1.093611 US yards
1 kilometer (1,000 meters) .... 0.62137 statute mile
1 kilometer .... 0.539957 nautical mile
1 inch ....2.540005 centimeters
1 foot (12 inches) ....30.4801 centimeters
1 US yard (3 feet) ....0.914402 meter
1 statute mile (5,280 feet; 1,760 yards) .... 1.609347 kilometers
1 British mile .... 1.609344 kilometers
1 nautical mile (1.1508 statute miles
or 6,076.10333 feet).................................. 1.852 kilometers
1 British nautical mile (6,080 feet)............................ 1.85319 kilometers

AREA
1 sq centimeter .... 0.154999 sq inch
1 sq meter (10,000 sq centimeters) .... 10.76387 sq feet
1 sq meter ....1.1959585 sq yards
1 hectare (10,000 sq meters)...........................2.47104 acres
1 sq kilometer (100 hectares)........................... 0.386101 sq mile
1 sq inch .... 6.451626 sq centimeters
1 sq foot (144 sq inches) .... 0.092903 sq meter
1 sq yard (9 sq feet) .... 0.836131 sq meter
1 acre (4,840 sq yards) .... 0.404687 hectare
1 sq mile (640 acres)....................................2.589998 sq kilometers

VOLUME
1 cubic centimeter ....0.061023 cubic inch
1 cubic meter
(1,000,000 cubic centimeters)...........................35.31445 cubic feet
1 cubic meter...1.307943 cubic yards
1 cubic inch ....16.387162 cubic centimeters
1 cubic foot (1,728 cubic inches) .... 0.028317 cubic meter
1 cubic yard (27 cubic feet) .... 0.764559 cubic meter

LIQUID MEASURE
1 liter... 0.8799 imperial quart
1 liter .... 1.05671 US quarts
1 hectoliter ....21.9975 imperial gallons
1 hectoliter ....26.4178 US gallons
1 imperial quart.......................................1.136491 liters
1 US quart .... 0.946333 liter
1 imperial gallon ....0.04546 hectoliter
1 US gallon ....0.037853 hectoliter

WEIGHT
1 Kilogram (1,000 grams) .... 35.27396 avoirdupois ounces
1 kilogram .... 32.15074 troy ounces
1 kilogram.........................2.204622 avoirdupois pounds
1 quintal (100 kg)..........................220.4622 avoirdupois pounds
1 quintal..........................1.9684125 hundredweights
1 metric ton (1,000 kg)...........................1.102311 short tons

1 metric ton ....0.984206 long ton
1 avoirdupois ounce .... 0.0283495 kilogram
1 troy ounce .... 0.0311035 kilogram
1 avoirdupois pound .... 0.453592 kilogram
1 avoirdupois pound............................. 0.00453592 quintal
1 hundred weight (cwt., 112 lb)............ 0.50802 quintal
1 short ton (2,000 lb) .... 0.907185 metric ton
1 long ton (2,240 lb) .... 1.016047 metric tons

ELECTRIC ENERGY
1 horsepower (hp) .... 0.7457 kilowatt
1 kilowatt (kw)....................................... 1.34102 horsepower

TEMPERATURE
Celsius (C) ....Fahrenheit-32 X 5/9
Fahrenheit (F) .... 9/5 Celsius + 32

BUSHELS

	LB	METRIC TON	BUSHELS PER METRIC TON
Barley(US)	48	0.021772	45.931
(UK)	50	0.022680	44.092
Corn (UK, US)	56	0.025401	39.368
Linseed (UK)	52	0.023587	42.396
(Australia, US)	56	0.025401	39.368
Oats (US)	32	0.014515	68.894
(Canada)	34	0.015422	64.842
Potatoes (UK, U&S)	60	0.027216	36.743
Rice (Australia)	42	0.019051	52.491
(US)	45	0.020412	48.991
Rye (UK, US)	56	0.025401	39.368
(Australia)	60	0.027216	36.743
Soybeans (US)	60	0.027216	36.743
Wheat (UK, US)	60	0.027216	36.743

BAGS OF COFFEE

	LB	KG	BAGS PER METRIC TON
Brazil, Columbia Mexico, Venezuela	132.28	60	16.667
El Salvador	152.12	69	14.493
Haiti	185.63	84.2	11.876

BALES OF COTTON

	LB	METRIC TON	BALES PER METRIC TON
India	392	0.177808	5.624
Brazil	397	0.180000	5.555
US (net)	480	0.217724	4.593
US (gross)	500	0.226796	4.409

PETROLEUM
One barrel = 42 US gallons = 34.97 imperial gallons = 158.99 liters = 0.15899 cubic meter (or 1 cubic meter = 6.2898 barrels).

*Includes units of measure cited in the text, as well as certain other units employed in parts of the English-speaking world and in specified countries.

Abbreviations and Acronyms

AD—Anno Domini
ADB—African Development Bank
AsDB—Asian Development Bank
AFL-CIO—American Federation of Labor–Congress of Industrial Organizations
AID—Agency for International Development [of the US]
AIDS—Acquired Immune Deficiency Syndrome
AM—before noon
AM—Amplitude modulation
ANZUS—Security Treaty of Australia, New Zealand, and the United States
Arch.—Archipelago
ASEAN—Association of Southeast Asian Nations
ASSR—Autonomous Soviet Socialist Republic
b.—born
BC—Before Christ
BCEAO—Central Bank of the West African States (Banque Centrale des États de l'Afrique de l'Ouest
BEAC—Bank of the Central African States (Banque des États de l'Afrique Centrale)
BENELUX—Benelux Economic Union (Belgium-Netherlands-Luxembourg Economic Union)
Bibliog.—bibliography
BIS—Bank for International Settlements
BLEU—Belgium-Luxembourg Economic Union
Br.—British
Brig.—brigadier
c.—circa (about)
C—Celsius
CACM—Central American Common Market
Capt.—Captain
CARE—Cooperative for American Remittances to Everywhere, Inc.
CARICOM—Caribbean Community and Common Market
CCC—Customs Cooperation Council
CDB—Caribbean Development Bank
CEAO—West African Economic Community (Communauté Économique de l'Afrique de l'Ouest; replaced UDEAO)
CEMA—see CMEA
CENTO—Central Treaty Organization
CERN—European Organization for Nuclear Research
CFA—Communauté Financière Africaine
CFP—Communauté Française du Pacifique
CGT—Confédération Générale du Travail
CIA—Central Intelligence Agency [of the US]
c.i.f.—cost, insurance, and freight
cm—centimeter(s)
CMEA—Council for Mutual Economic Assistance
Co.—company
Col.—colonel
COMECON—see CMEA
comp.—compiled, compiler
Cons.—Conservative
Corp.—corporation
cu—cubic
cu m—cubic meters
cwt—hundredweight

d—daily
d.—died
DDT—dichlorodiphenyltrichloroethane
Dem.—Democratic
DPT—diphtheria, pertussis, and tetanus
Dr.—doctor
DPRK—Democratic People's Republic of Korea (North Korea)
DRV—Democratic Republic of Vietnam (North Vietnam)
dwt—deadweight tons
e—evening
E—east
EAC—East African Community
EAEC—see EURATOM
EC—European Communities
ECA—Economic Commission for Africa [of the UN]
ECAFE—see ESCAP
ECE—Economic Commission for Europe [of the UN]
ECLAC—Economic Commission for Latin America and the Caribbean [of the UN]
ECOWAS—Economic Community of West African States
ECSC—European Coal and Steel Community
ed.—editor, edited, edition
EEC—European Economic Community (Common Market)
EFTA—European Free Trade Association
e.g.—exempli gratia (for example)
ESCAP—Economic and Social Commission for Asia and the Pacific [of the UN]
ESCWA—Economic and Social Commission for Western Asia [of the UN]
ESRO—European Space Research Organization
est.—estimate(d)
et al.—et alii (and others)
EURATOM—European Atomic Energy Community
f.—founded
F—Fahrenheit
FAO—Food and Agriculture Organization [of the UN]
ff.—following
fl.—flourished
FM—frequency modulation
f.o.b.—free on board
Fr.—France, French
FRG—Federal Republic of Germany (West Germany)
FSM—Federated States of Micronesia
ft—foot, feet
ft^3—cubic foot, feet
Ft.—Fort
G-77—Group of 77
GATT—General Agreement on Tariffs and Trade
GCC—Gulf Cooperation Council
GDP—gross domestic product
GDR—German Democratic Republic (East Germany)
Gen.—General
GHz—gigahertz
gm—gram(s)
GMT—Greenwich Mean Time
GNP—gross national product
GRT—gross registered tons (tonnage)

GSP—gross social product
HIV—human immunodeficiency virus
HMSO—Her Majesty's Stationery Office [of the UK]
ha—hectare(s)
I.—Island
IADB—*see* IDB
IAEA—International Atomic Energy Agency
IATA—International Air Transport Association
IBRD—International Bank for Reconstruction and Development (World Bank)
ICAO—International Civil Aviation Organization
ICC—International Control Commission
ICFTU—International Confederation of Free Trade Unions
ICSU—International Council of Scientific Unions
IDA—International Development Association
IDB/IADB—Inter-American Development Bank
i.e.—id est (that is)
IFAD—International Fund for Agricultural Development
IFC—International Finance Corporation
IGO—intergovernmental organization
IGY—International Geophysical Year
ILO—International Labor Organization
IMCO—*see* IMO
IMF—International Monetary Fund
IMO—International Maritime Organization (formerly IMCO)
in—inch(es)
Inc.—incorporated
Indep.—Independent
INSTRAW—International Research and Training Institute for the Advancement of Women [of the UN]
INTELSAT—International Telecommunications Satellite Consortium
INTERPOL—International Criminal Police Organization
IRU—International Relief Union
Is.—islands
ITU—International Telecommunication Union
IUCN—International Union for the Conservation of Nature and Natural Resources
IWC—International Whaling Commission; International Wheat Council
kg—kilogram(s)
kHz—kilohertz
km—kilometer(s)
km/hr—kilometer(s) per hour
kw—kilowatt(s)
kwh—kilowatt-hour(s)
L.—Lake
LAFTA—Latin American Free Trade Association
LAIA—Latin American Integration Association
lb—pound(s)
Lieut.—lieutenant
Ltd.—limited
m—meter(s); morning
m³—cubic meter(s)
mg—milligram(s)
MHz—megahertz
mi—mile(s)
mm—millimeter(s)
mph—mile(s) per hour
MPR—Mongolian People's Republic
Mt.—Mount
Mtn.—mountain(s)
Mw—Megawatt(s)
N—north
NA—not available
NATO—North Atlantic Treaty Organization
n.d.—no date

n.e.s.—not elsewhere specified
Neth.—Netherlands
NGO—nongovernmental organization
n.i.e.—not included elsewhere
NMP—net material product
NZ—New Zealand
OAPEC—Organization of Arab Petroleum Exporting Countries (subgroup of OPEC)
OAS—Organization of American States
OAU—Organization of African Unity
OCAM—African and Malagasy Common Organization
OECD—Organization for Economic Cooperation and Development
OIHP—International Office of Public Health (Office International d'Hygiène Publique)
O.M.—Order of Merit
OPEC—Organization of Petroleum Exporting Countries
orig.—original [edition]
oz—ounce(s)
p.—page
PAHO—Pan American Health Organization
PC of A—Permanent Court of Arbitration
PDRY—People's Democratic Republic of Yemen (South Yemen)
PL—Public Law
PLO—Palestine Liberation Organization
PM—after noon
pop.—population
Port.—Portugal, Portuguese
pp.—pages
PRC—People's Republic of China
r.—reigned
R.—river
Ra.—Range
Rep.—Republic
rev.—revised
ROC—Republic of China (Taiwan)
ROK—Republic of Korea (South Korea)
RVN—Republic of Vietnam (South Vietnam)
s—South
S.A.—Société Anonyme
SAARC—South Asian Association for Regional Cooperation
SDI—Strategic Defense Initiative
SDRs—Special Drawing Rights
SEATO—Southeast Asia Treaty Organization
SELA—Latin American Economic System (Sistema Económica Latinoamericano)
Sgt.—sergeant
SHAPE—Supreme Headquarters Allied Powers Europe
SPC—South Pacific Commission
sq—square
SRV—Socialist Republic of Vietnam
SSR—Soviet Socialist Republic
St.—Saint
tr.—translated
TB—tuberculosis
TV—television
UAE—United Arab Emirates
UAR—United Arab Republic
UCC—Universal Copyright Convention
UDEAC—Central African Customs and Economic Union (Union Douanière et Économique de l'Afrique Centrale)
UDEAO—*see* CEAO
UEAC—Central African Economic Union (Union des États de l'Afrique Centrale)
UHF—ultra high frequency
UK—United Kingdom of Great Britain and Northern Ireland
UMOA—West African Monetary Union (Union Monétaire Ouest

Africaine)
UN—United Nations
UNCHS—UN Center for Human Settlements (Habitat)
UNCTAD—UN Conference on Trade and Development
UNDOF—UN Disengagement Observer Force
UNDP—UN Development Program
UNDRO—UN Disaster Relief Coordinator, Office of
UNEF—UN Emergency Force
UNEP—UN Environment Program
UNESCO—UN Educational, Scientific and Cultural Organization
UNFICYP—UN Peacekeeping Force in Cyprus
UNFPA—UN Population Fund
UNHCR—UN High Commissioner for Refugees
UNICEF—UN Children's Fund
UNIDO—UN Industrial Development Organization
UNIFIL—UN Interim Force in Lebanon
UNITAR—UN Institute for Training and Research
UNMOGIP—UN Military Observer Group in India and Pakistan
UNRWA—UN Relief and Works Agency for Palestine Refugees
UNSO—UN Sahelian Office

UNTSO—UN Truce Supervision Organization
UNU—UN University
UNV—UN Volunteers
UPU—Universal Postal Union
US—United States of America
USIA—US Information Agency
USSR—Union of Soviet Socialist Republics
VHF—very high frequency
vol., vols., Vol., Vols.—volume(s)
w—west
WEU—Western European Union
WFC—World Food Council
WFP—World Food Program
WFTU—World Federation of Trade Unions
WHO—World Health Organization
WIPO—World Intellectual Property Organization
WMO—World Meteorological Organization
WTO—Warsaw Treaty Organization; World Tourism Organization
YAR—Yemen Arab Republic (North Yemen)

Glossary of Religious Holidays

BUDDHIST HOLIDAYS

Buddhist religious practice stems from the Hindu belief that every new moon or full moon day should be set apart for observance. In Buddhism, the half-moon days also have special status. In Sri Lanka, each Poya day—the day of the rise of the full moon of each month of the Buddhist calendar—is a public holiday. The following observances are common in Southeast Asia.

Songran. The Buddhist New Year is a three-day springtime water festival, in which images of the Buddha are bathed.

Vesak. This last full moon day of Visakha highlights a three-day celebration of the birth, enlightenment, and death of the Buddha. It falls in April or May.

Waso (Varsa; Vassa). This holiday begins the Buddhist equivalent of Lent, a period between July and October (the rainy season in Southeast Asia), during which Buddhist monks may not leave their cloisters. The season starts with the full moon of the month of Asalha and ends with a festival during the full moon of the month of Thadingyut.

CHRISTIAN HOLIDAYS

The chief Christian holiday is **Easter**, the annual celebration of the resurrection of Jesus Christ. Like Passover, the Jewish feast from which it is derived, the date of observation is linked to the phases of the moon. Since the Christian calendar is a solar one rather than a lunar one, the date of Easter changes from year to year. Easter is celebrated on the first Sunday after the first full moon following the spring equinox; in the Gregorian calendar, it can occur as early as 22 March or as late as 25 April. The Easter date determines the date of many other Roman Catholic holidays, such as Ash Wednesday, Ascension, and Pentecost.

Important Christian celebrations and feasts that invariably occur on Sunday are not listed as holidays in the country articles because Sunday itself is a holiday ("holy day") in predominantly Christian countries. In these lands, it is the day of rest and worship, occurring on the day after the Jewish Sabbath, from which it is derived, in commemoration of Christ's resurrection on Easter Sunday.

The names and dates of the Christian holidays listed below are almost all based on Roman Catholic observances. Some of these holidays are also observed by Protestant denominations. By contrast, all countries where Eastern Orthodox rites predominate are Communist-ruled except Greece and the Greek-held portion of Cyprus; in the Communist countries, Christian holidays are not national holidays. For religious celebrations, some Eastern Orthodox churches retain the Julian calendar, which is 13 days behind the Gregorian calendar. Eastern Orthodox holidays do not fully correspond to the list of church holidays given below.

Solemnity of Mary, Mother of God. Observed on 1 January, this celebration was, before a 1969 Vatican reform, the Feast of the Circumcision of Our Lord Jesus Christ.

Epiphany of Our Lord. Traditionally observed on 6 January but now observable on the Sunday falling between 2 January and 7 January, this feast commemorates the adoration of the Magi, who journeyed to the place of Jesus' birth. In the Orthodox churches, however, it is the feast celebrating Jesus' baptism.

St. Dévôte Day. Observed on 27 January in Monaco in honor of the principality's patron saint, this day celebrates her safe landing after a perilous voyage, thanks to a dove who directed her ship to the Monaco shore.

Candlemas. A national holiday on 2 February in Liechtenstein, this observation is now called the Presentation of the Lord, commemorating the presentation of the infant Jesus in the Temple at Jerusalem. Before a 1969 Vatican reform, it commemorated the Purification of Mary 40 days after giving birth to a male child in accordance with a Jewish practice of the time.

St. Agatha's Day. On 5 February is celebrated the feast day of the patron saint of San Marino. St. Agatha is also the patron saint of nurses, firefighters, and jewelers.

Shrove Monday and Shrove Tuesday. These two days occur just prior to the beginning of Lent (a term which derives from the Middle English *lente*, "spring"), the Christian season of penitence that ends with Easter Sunday. These are days of **Carnival**, public holidays of feasting and merriment in many lands. Shrove Tuesday is also known as **Mardi Gras**.

Ash Wednesday. The first day of Lent, observed 46 days before Easter, is so called from the practice of placing ashes on the forehead of the worshiper as a sign of penitence. In the Roman Catholic Church, these ashes are obtained from burning palm branches used in the previous year's **Palm Sunday** observation. (Palm Sunday commemorates the entry of Jesus into Jerusalem a week before Easter Sunday, and it begins **Holy Week**. On Ash Wednesday, the ashes are placed on the forehead of the communicant during Mass. The recipient is told, "Remember that you are dust, and unto dust you shall return" or "Turn away from sin and be faithful to the Gospel."

St. Patrick's Day. This holiday, observed on 17 March, is celebrated in Ireland to honor its patron saint.

St. Joseph's Day. The feast day in honor of Mary's husband is observed on 19 March as a public holiday in several countries.

Holy (Maundy) Thursday. The Thursday preceding Easter commemorates the Last Supper, the betrayal of Jesus by Judas Iscariot, and the arrest and arraignment of Jesus. In Rome, the pope customarily performs a ceremony in remembrance of Jesus' washing of his apostles' feet (John 13:5–20).

Good Friday. The day after Holy Thursday is devoted to remembrance of the crucifixion of Jesus and is given to penance and prayer.

Holy Saturday. This day commemorates the time during which Jesus was buried and, like Good Friday, is given to solemn prayer.

Easter Monday. The day after Easter is a public holiday in many countries.

Prayer Day. This Danish public holiday is observed on the fourth Friday after Easter.

Ascension. One of the most important Christian feasts, Ascension is observed 40 days after Easter in commemoration of Jesus' ascension to heaven.

Pentecost Monday (Whitmonday). This public holiday in many countries occurs the day after Pentecost (derived from the ancient Green *pentekostos*, "fiftieth"), or **Whitsunday**, which commemorates the descent of the Holy Spirit upon Jesus' apostles on the seventh Sunday after Easter and is derived from the Jewish feast of Shavuot. It was an important occasion for baptism in the early church, and the name "Whitsunday" originated from the white robes worn by the newly baptized.

Corpus Christi. This holiday in honor of the Eucharist is observed on the Thursday or Sunday after **Trinity Sunday**, which is the Sunday after Pentecost. In the Roman Catholic and Eastern Orthodox Churches, the Eucharist is a sacrament in which the consecrated bread and wine literally become the body and blood of Jesus Christ, a belief stemming from New Testament accounts of the Last Supper.

Sacred Heart. The Friday of the week after Corpus Christi is a holiday in Colombia. The object of devotion is the divine person of Jesus, whose heart is the symbol of his love for mankind.

Day of St. Peter and St. Paul. This observance, on 29 June, commemorates the martyrdom of the two apostles traditionally believed to have been executed in Rome on the same day (c. AD 67) during the persecution of Christians ordered by Emperor Nero.

St. James' Day. Observed on 25 July, this day commemorates St. James the Greater, one of Jesus' 12 apostles. St. James is the patron saint of Spain.

Feast of Our Lady of Angels. This feast, on 2 August, is celebrated as a national holiday in Costa Rica in honor of the Virgin Mary. Pilgrimage is made to the basilica in Cartago, which houses a black stone statue of the Virgin.

Assumption. This holiday, observed on 15 August in many countries, celebrates the Roman Catholic and Eastern Orthodox dogma that, following Mary's death, her body was taken into heaven and reunited with her soul.

Crowning of Our Lady of Altagracia. Another holiday in honor of Mary, this day is celebrated in the Dominican Republic on 15 August with a pilgrimage to her shrine. (**Altagracia Day,** 21 January, is also a holiday in the Dominican Republic.)

Day of Santa Rosa de Lima. The feast day in honor of the first native-born saint of the New World, declared patron saint of South America by Pope Clement X in 1671, is 23 August, but in Peru, she is commemorated by a national holiday on 30 August.

Day of Our Lady of Mercy (Las Mercedes). Another holiday in honor of Mary, this observance on 24 September is a holiday in the Dominican Republic.

All Saints' Day. On 1 November, a public holiday in many countries, saints and martyrs who have no special festival are commemorated. In the Middle Ages, it was known as **All Hallows' Day**; the evening of the previous day, October 31, was called **All Hallow Even,** from which the secular holiday **Halloween** is derived.

All Souls' Day. This day, 2 November, is dedicated to prayer for the repose of the souls of the dead.

Immaculate Conception. This day, 8 December, celebrates the Roman Catholic dogma asserting that Mary's conception, as the future mother of God, was uniquely free from original sin. In Paraguay, it is observed as the Day of Our Lady of Caacupé.

Our Lady of Guadalupe. This Mexican festival, on 12 December, celebrates a miracle that the Virgin Mary is believed to have performed on this day in 1531, when she appeared before an Amerindian peasant and told him to build a shrine in her honor. The shrine is now the site of a basilica in the Mexico City area.

Christmas. The annual commemoration of the nativity of Jesus is held on 25 December. A midnight Mass ushers in this joyous celebration in many Roman Catholic churches. The custom of distributing gifts to children on **Christmas Eve** derives from a Dutch custom originally observed on the evening before **St. Nicholas' Day (6 December).** The day after Christmas—often called **Boxing Day,** for the boxed gifts customarily given—is a public holiday in many countries.

St. Stephen's Day. The feast day in honor of the first martyred Christian saint is 26 December, the day after Christmas. St. Stephen is the patron saint of Hungary.

HINDU HOLIDAYS

Hindu holidays are based on various lunar calendars, with an extra month inserted at intervals that vary from year to year, in order to keep festivals from shifting in relation to the seasons. The bright half of the month is that in which the new moon advances to the full moon; the dark half lasts from full moon to new moon. It is said that no nation has more festivals than India. Most are of only local or regional importance, but the following are national holidays in India and other countries with large Hindu populations.

Raksha Bandhan. During this festival, which usually falls in August, bracelets of colored thread and tinsel are tied by women to the wrists of their menfolk, thus binding the men to guard and protect them during the year. It is celebrated on the full moon of Sravana.

Ganesh Chaturthi. The festival, honoring Ganesh (Ganesha), god of prosperity, is held on the fourth day of the bright fortnight of the month of Bhadrapada, corresponding to August or September.

Durga Puja. This holiday honors the Divine Mother, wife of Shiva and the principle of creation, in her victory over the demon Mashishasura. It is held during the first 10 days of the bright fortnight of Asvina (Navaratri), a period corresponding to September or October. The last day is Dussehra, an autumn festival that celebrates the victory of the god Rama over Ravana, king of demons.

Dewali (Deepavali; Divali). Dewali is the Hindu Festival of Lights, when Lakshmi, goddess of good fortune, is said to visit the homes of humans. The four- or five-day festival comes at the end of Asvina and the beginning of Karttika, a time corresponding to October or November.

Shivarati (Mahashivarati). Dedicated to the god Shiva, this holiday is observed on the 13th day of the dark half of Magha, corresponding to January or February.

Thaipusam. A holiday in Malaysia, Thaipusam honors Subrimaya, son of Shiva and an important deity in southern India. The three-day festival is held in the month of Magha according to when Pusam, a section of the lunar zodiac, is on the ascendant.

Holi. A festival lasting 3 to 10 days, Holi closes the old year with processions and merriment. It terminates on the full moon of Phalguna, the last month, corresponding to February or March.

JEWISH HOLIDAYS

The basic Jewish holy day is the **Sabbath,** the seventh day of each week, starting at sundown on Friday and ending at nightfall on Saturday. This is a day of rest and is devoted to worship, religious study, and the family.

Other Jewish holidays (all starting at sundown and ending at nightfall) occur on specific days of specific months of the Jewish calendar, which consists of 12 alternating months of 29 or 30 days (two months are variable), conforming to the lunar cycle of roughly 29½ days. In order to reconcile the lunar year of 353, 354, or 355 days with the solar year of 365¼ days, a 30-day month (Adar Sheni) is added 7 times within a 19-year cycle. In this way, Jewish festivals retain their seasonal origins. The following list, arranged in the order of the Jewish calendar, shows Jewish religious holidays observed in the State of Israel.

Rosh Hashanah. The Jewish New Year is celebrated on 1 Tishri, the first month. In synagogues, the sounding of the shofar (ram's horn) heralds the new year. Rosh Hashanah begins the observance of the Ten Penitential Days, which culminate in Yom Kippur. Orthodox and Conservative Jews outside Israel celebrate 2 Tishri, the next day, as well.

Yom Kippur. The Day of Atonement, spent in fasting, penitence, and prayer, is the most solemn day in Judaism. It takes place on 10 Tishri.

Sukkot. This ancient Jewish harvest festival, which begins on 15 Tishri, recalls the period in which harvesters left their homes to dwell in the fields in sukkot, or booths—small outdoor shelters of boards, leaves, and branches—in order to facilitate gathering the crops before the seasonal rains began. In religious terms, it commemorates the 40 years of wandering in the desert by the ancient Hebrews after their exodus from Egypt. The 8th day of Sukkot and the 22d day of Tishri is **Shmini Azeret/Simhat Torah**, a joyous holiday in which the annual cycle of reading the Torah (the Five Books of Moses) is completed and begun anew. Outside of Israel, Simhat Torah and the beginning of a new reading cycle are celebrated on the next day, 23 Tishri.

Hanukkah. The Festival of Lights, corresponding roughly to the winter solstice, is celebrated over an eight-day period beginning on 25 Kislev, the third month. Also known as the Feast of Dedication and Feast of the Maccabees, Hanukkah commemorates the rededication of the Temple at Jerusalem in 164 BC. According to tradition, the one ritually pure container of olive oil, sufficient to illuminate the Temple for one day, miraculously burned for eight days, until new oil could be prepared. A feature of the Hanukkah celebration is the lighting in each Jewish home of an eight-branched candelabrum, the menorah (hanukkiah). This festival, though not a public holiday in Israel, is widely observed with the lighting of giant hanukkiot in public places.

Purim. This holiday, celebrated on 14 Adar (Adar Sheni in a leap year), joyously commemorates the delivery of the Jews from potential annihilation at the hands of Haman, viceroy of Persia, as described in the Book of Esther, which is read from a scroll (megillah). The day, though not a public holiday in Israel, is widely marked by charity, exchange of edible gifts, and feasting.

Pesach (Passover). Pesach, lasting seven days in Israel and eight outside it, begins on 15 Nisan, at roughly the spring equinox, and recalls the exodus of the Hebrews from Egypt and their delivery from bondage. The chief festival of Judaism, Pesach begins with a ceremonial family meal, or seder, at which special foods (including unleavened bread, or matzoh) are eaten and the Passover story (Haggadah) is read.

Shavuot. This festival, on 6 Sivan, celebrates the presentation of the Ten Commandments to Moses on Mt. Sinai and the offering of the first harvest fruits at the temple in Jerusalem. The precursor of the Christian Pentecost, Shavuot takes place on the 50th day after the first day of Pesach.

Tishah b'Av. This holiday, which takes place on 9 Av, commemorates the destruction of the First Temple by the Babylonians (Chaldeans) in 586 BC and of the Second Temple by the Romans in AD 70. It is observed by fasting.

The Jewish calendar begins with the traditional date of Creation, equivalent to 3761 BC on the Christian calendar.

MUSLIM HOLIDAYS

Like the Jewish calendar, the Islamic calendar consists of 12 months alternating between 29 and 30 days. A normal year is 354 days; a leap day is added to the last month (Dhu'l-Hijja) 11 times during a 30-year cycle in order to keep the calendar in conformity with the phases of the moon. Like the Jewish day, the Islamic day runs from sundown to sundown. Unlike the Jewish calendar, however, the Islamic calendar makes no attempt to align itself with the solar year by the periodic addition of an extra month; therefore, over the course of time, Islamic festivals may occur at any season. Like the Christian and Jewish calendars, the Islamic calendar has a seven-day week. Friday is the principal day of worship; although work is not forbidden on that day, it is suspended during the midday prayer session. The following list gives Muslim holy days that are observed as public holidays in one or more of the predominantly Muslim countries. Except where noted, a transliteration style reflecting pronunciation practice in the Arab countries is given. Not given here are certain special Muslim holidays in Iran, the only Muslim country in which the Shi'i form of Islam predominates.

Muslim New Year. Although in some countries 1 Muharram, which is the first month of the Islamic year, is observed as a holiday, the new year is in other places observed on Sha'ban, the eighth month of the year. This practice apparently stems from pagan Arab times. Shab-i-Bharat, a national holiday in Bangladesh on this day, is held by many to be the occasion when God ordains all actions in the coming year.

'Ashura. This fast day was instituted by Muhammad as the equivalent of the Jewish Yom Kippur but later became voluntary when Ramadan replaced it as a penitential event. It also commemorates Noah's leaving the ark on Mt. Ararat after the waters of the Great Flood had subsided. In Iran, the martyrdom of Husayn, grandson of Muhammad, is commemorated with passion plays on this day.

Milad an-Nabi. The traditional birthday of Muhammad is celebrated on 12 Rabi al-Awwal, the third month of the Islamic year.

Laylat al-Miraj. This holiday, celebrated on 27 Rajab, the seventh month, commemorates the night of Muhammad's miraculous ascension to heaven, during which he received instructions from Allah on the requirements for daily prayer.

Ramadan. The first day of Ramadan (the ninth month) is a public holiday in many countries, although the religious festival does not officially begin until the new moon is sighted from the Naval Observatory in Cairo, Egypt. The entire month commemorates the period in which the Prophet received divine revelation and is observed by a strict fast from sunrise to sundown. This observance is one of Islam's five main duties for believers.

Laylat al-Qadr (Night of Power). This commemoration of the first revelation of the Koran (Qur'an) to Muhammad usually falls on 27 Ramadan.

'Id al-Fitr. The Little Festival, or Breaking-Fast-Festival, which begins just after Ramadan, on 1 Shawwal, the 10th month, is the occasion for three or four days of feasting. In Malaysia and Singapore, this festival is called Hari Raya Puasa; in Turkey, Şeker Bayrami.

'Id al-'Adha'. The Great Festival, or Sacrificial Feast, celebrates the end of the special pilgrimage season, or Hajj, to Mecca and Medina, an obligation for Muslims once in their lifetime if physically and economically feasible. The slaughter of animals pays tribute to Abraham's obedience to God in offering his son to the Lord for sacrifice; a portion of the meat is supposed to be donated to the poor. The feast begins on 10 Dhu'l-Hijja and continues to 13 Dhu'l-Hijja (14 Dhu'l-Hijja in a leap year). In Malaysia and Singapore, this festival is celebrated as Hari Raya Haji; in Indonesia, Lebaran Haji; in Turkey, Kurban Bayrami.

The Islamic calendar begins with the entry of Muhammad into Medina, equivalent to AD 622 on the Christian calendar.

Glossary of Special Terms

The following is a selected list, with brief definitions and explanations, of terms that appear frequently in these volumes. Not included below are UN organs and related agencies, which are discussed under their own headings elsewhere.

adult literacy: the capacity of adults to read and write, as defined by divergent national criteria of age and ability.

ad valorem tax: a levy based on a fixed percentage of an item's value; ad valorem taxes include sales taxes, property taxes, and the majority of import duties.

African Development Bank: IGO founded in 1963 and with its headquarters at Abidjan, Côte d'Ivoire; coordinates its members' development finances and provides loans.

animism: the belief that natural objects and phenomena have souls or innate spiritual powers.

Asian Development Bank: IGO founded in 1966 and with its headquarters at Manila, Philippines; seeks to encourage economic growth in Asia and the Far East and provides long-term, large-scale loans, with emphasis on the developing countries.

Association of South-East Asian Nations (ASEAN): IGO founded in 1967 and with its headquarters at Jakarta, Indonesia; promotes economic cooperation among its members.

balance of payments: a systematic record of all financial transactions between one country and the rest of the world.

bank of issue: a bank empowered to issue currency.

capital account: all additions to or subtractions from a stock of investment.

Caribbean Community and Common Market (CARICOM): IGO founded in 1973 and with its headquarters in Georgetown, Guyana; seeks the establishment of a common external tariff and common trade policy among its members and promotes increased cooperation in agricultural and industrial development in the Caribbean region.

cash economy: see **money economy.**

central bank: a financial institution that handles the transactions of the central government, coordinates and controls the nation's commercial banks, and regulates the nation's money supply and credit conditions.

Colombo Plan: formally known as the Colombo Plan for Cooperative Economic Development in Asia and the Pacific, a multinational mutual assistance program that took effect in 1951 and has its headquarters in Colombo, Sri Lanka.

commercial bank: a bank that offers to businesses and individuals a variety of banking services, including demand deposit and withdrawal by check.

Commonwealth of Nations: voluntary association of the UK and its present dependencies and associated states, as well as certain former dependencies and their dependent territories. The term was first used officially in 1926 and is embodied in the Statute of Westminster (1931). Within the Commonwealth, whose secretariat (established in 1965) is located in London, England, are numerous subgroups devoted to economic and technical cooperation.

constant prices: money values calculated so as to eliminate the effect of inflation on prices and income.

Council for Mutual Economic Assistance (CMEA): also known as COMECON, an IGO established to foster economic and technical cooperation within the Communist bloc, including the USSR, most Eastern European countries, and several other nations. Founded in 1949, CMEA has its headquarters in Moscow.

Council of Europe: IGO founded in 1949 and with its headquarters in Strasbourg, France; promotes consultation and cooperation among European countries.

crude birthrate: the number of births in a year per 1,000 estimated midyear population.

crude death rate: the number of deaths in a year per 1,000 estimated midyear population.

current account: the flow of goods and services, as measured by payments for and receipts from imports and exports, including interest and dividends.

currency in circulation: the tangible portion of a nation's money supply, composed of bank notes, government notes, and coins.

current prices: money values that reflect prevailing prices, without excluding the effects of inflation.

customs duty: a tax imposed on the importation or exportation of goods.

customs union: an arrangement between governments to establish a common tariff policy and remove customs barriers between them.

demand deposit: a bank deposit that can be withdrawn by the depositor without previous notice to the bank.

direct tax: a tax that cannot be shifted from the original payer to the ultimate consumer of a good or service; direct taxes include the income tax and the poll tax.

Economic Community of West African States (ECOWAS): IGO founded in 1975 and with its headquarters at Lagos, Nigeria; seeks to establish a common tariff policy and promote economic cooperation among its members.

economically active population: see **labor force.**

endangered species: a type of plant or animal threatened with extinction in all or part of its natural range. For the Seventh Edition, listings of endangered animal species are as compiled for each country by the International Union for Conservation of Nature and Natural Resources.

European Communities (EC): collective name for a supranational organization encompassing, among other entities, the European Coal and Steel Community, established in 1952; the European Economic Community (EEC, or European Common Market), founded in 1958; and the European Atomic Energy Community (EURATOM), also established in 1958. All EC members also participate in the European Parliament, which meets in Strasbourg and Luxembourg, and the Court of Justice, which sits in Luxembourg.

European Free Trade Association (EFTA): customs union established in 1960 and with its headquarters in Geneva, Switzerland.

factor cost: a concept used in determining the value of the national product in relation to the economic resources employed.

fertility rate: the average number of children that would be born to each woman in a population if she were to live through her childbearing lifetime bearing children at the same rate as women in that age range actually did in a given year.

fly: the part of a flag opposite and parallel to the one nearest the flagpole.

foreign exchange: all monetary assets that give residents of one country a financial claim on another.

gross domestic product (GDP): the total gross expenditure, in purchasers' values, on the domestic supply of goods and services (final use).

gross national product (GNP): the total monetary value of all final goods and services that a nation produces.

Group of 77 (G-77): IGO founded in 1967 to represent the interests of the developing countries and taking its name from the 77 developing nations that signed the Joint Declaration of the first UN Conference on Trade and Development (UNCTAD).

Gulf Cooperation Council (GCC): IGO founded in 1981 and with its headquarters in Riyadh, Sa'udi Arabia; aims at increasing cooperation among nations of the Persian (Arabian) Gulf region in matters of security and economic development.

hoist: the part of a flag nearest the flagpole.

indirect tax: a tax levied against goods and services; sales taxes, excise taxes, and import duties are generally regarded as indirect taxes.

infant mortality rate: the number of deaths of children less than one year old per 1,000 live births in a given year.

installed capacity: the maximum possible output of electric power at any given time.

Inter-American Development Bank (IDB): IGO established in 1959 and with its headquarters in Washington, D.C.; provides technical assistance and development financing to member nations in Latin America and the Caribbean.

intergovernmental organization (IGO): a body, such as the UN, to which only governments belong.

international reserves: cash and other international assets readily convertible into cash for the settlement of international accounts by a government.

invisibles: exports and imports of services (e.g., shipping charges, banking services, royalties, rents, and interest).

labor force: the number of people in a population available for work, whether actually employed or not.

Latin American Integration Association (LAIA): IGO founded in 1980 as the successor to the Latin American Free Trade Association and with its headquarters in Montevideo, Uruguay; seeks to foster economic cooperation among Latin American nations.

League of Arab States (Arab League): IGO founded in 1945 and with its headquarters in Tunis, Tunisia (formerly in Cairo, Egypt); attempts to coordinate national and international political activities of its members, to revive and diffuse the cultural legacy of Arabs, and to develop Arab social consciousness.

life expectancy: the expected life span of a newborn baby at any given date.

lingua franca: a language widely used as a means of communication among speakers of other languages.

Marshall Plan: formally known as the European Recovery Program, a joint project between the US and most Western European nations under which $12.5 billion in US loans and grants was expended to aid European recovery after World War II. Expenditures under the program, named for US Secretary of State George C. Marshall, were made from fiscal years 1949 through 1952.

money economy: a system or stage of economic development in which money replaces barter in the exchange of goods and services.

most-favored-nation clause: a provision in commercial treaties between two or more countries that guarantees that all partners to the agreement will automatically extend to each other any tariff reductions that they offer to nonmember countries.

Net material product: the total net value of goods and "productive" services, including turnover taxes, produced by the economy in the course of a given time period.

net natural increase: the difference between the crude birthrate and the crude death rate.

nongovernmental organization (NGO): a body, such as the International Chamber of Commerce or Amnesty International, in which organizations and individuals participate, often without government control or sponsorship.

Nordic Council: IGO founded in 1952 and with its headquarters in Stockholm, Sweden; a consultative body on matters of common interest to the Nordic (Scandinavian) countries.

North Atlantic Treaty Organization (NATO): IGO established in 1949 and with its headquarters in Brussels, Belgium; fosters cooperation in defense and other matters.

Organization of African Unity (OAU): IGO established in 1963 and with its headquarters in Addis Ababa, Ethiopia; attempts to promote African unity and development, eradicate colonialism, and coordinate members' economic, political, diplomatic, educational, cultural, health, scientific, and defense policies.

Organization of American States (OAS): IGO founded in 1948 and with its headquarters in Washington, D.C.; seeks to achieve peaceful settlement of members' disputes, promote solidarity in defense matters, and foster cooperation in the health, economic social and cultural fields.

Organization for Economic Cooperation and Development (OECD): IGO established in 1961 as the successor to the Organization for European Economic Cooperation and with its headquarters in Paris; attempts to promote economic growth, social welfare, higher living standards, and financial stability in member countries.

Organization of Petroleum Exporting Countries (OPEC): IGO founded in 1960 and with its headquarters in Vienna, Austria; seeks to coordinate its members' production and pricing of crude petroleum.

Pan American Health Organization (PAHO): IGO founded in 1902 as the International Sanitary Bureau; its headquarters are now in Washington, D.C. An OAS affiliate, PAHO seeks to improve health and environmental conditions in the Americas.

per capita: per person.

proved reserves: the quantity of a recoverable mineral resource (such as oil or natural gas) that is still in the ground.

public debt: the amount owed by a government.

retail trade: the sale of goods directly to the consumer.

smallholder: the owner or tenant of a small farm.

subsistence economy: the part of a national economy in which money plays little or no role, trade is by barter, and living standards are minimal.

supranational: transcending the limitations of the nation-state.

time deposit: money held in a bank account for which the bank may require advance notice of withdrawal.

turnkey project: a factory or other installation wholly built by a company of one country at a site in another country, which then assumes complete operational control over it, paying the builder in cash, credits, or a share of the proceeds.

turnover tax: a tax on transactions of goods and services at all levels of production and distribution.

value added by manufacture: the difference, measured in national currency units, between the value of finished goods and the cost of materials needed to produce them.

value-added tax (VAT): see **ad valorem tax.**

visibles: international transactions involving movement of tangible goods.

Warsaw Treaty Organization (WTO): IGO commonly known as the Warsaw Pact; attempts to promote the collective security of its members. Founded in 1955, the alliance has its headquarters in Moscow.

wholesale trade: the sale of goods, usually in bulk quantities, to intermediaries for ultimate resale to consumers.

work force: see **labor force.**

GENERAL BIBLIOGRAPHY

A

ABECOR. *Country Reports.* London: Barclays Bank PLC, 1997.

Ackerman, Robert H. "Economic and Medical Directions in the Czech Republic and Hungary." *The American Journal of Surgery* 167 (February 1994).

American Automobile Manufacturers Association. *World Motor Vehicle Data 1997 Edition.* Washington, D.C.: American Automobile Manufacturers Association, 1997.

Anderson, Ian E., ed. *Editor and Publisher Market Guide 2000.* 7th ed. New York: The Editor and Publisher Company, December 1999.

Argakas, Kullo, et. al. *The Baltic States, A Reference Book.* Tallinn, Estonia: Estonian Encyclopedia Publishers, 1991.

Argentina, Republic of. Secretariat of Science and Technology, National Bureau of International Affairs. *National System of Science and Technology.* Washington, D.C.: Embassy of Argentina, 1994.

Arthur Andersen & Co. *Asia and the Pacific, a Tax Tour.* New York: Arthur Andersen & Co., 1993.

———. *A Tax Guide to Europe.* New York: Arthur Andersen & Co., 1992.

———. *A Tax Guide to the Americas.* New York: Arthur Andersen & Co., 1991.

Asian Development Bank, ed. *Asian Development Outlook 2000.* Manila, Philippines: Asian Development Bank, June 2000.

———. *Key Indicators of Developing Asian and Pacific Countries 2000.* Manila, Philippines: Asian Development Bank, November 2000.

Asian Survey. *Survey of Asia 1993.* Berkeley: University of California Press, 1994.

Australian Bureau of Statistics. *Year Book Australia 2000.* Canberra, Australia: Australian Bureau of Statistics, 2000.

B

Bagby, Meredith E. *Annual Report of the United States of America: What Every Citizen Should Know about Where Each Tax Dollar Goes and Why.* New York: HarperBusinesss, 1996.

Bankers' Almanac. West Sussex: Reed Information Services, 1997.

Bellamy, Carol, ed. United Nations Children's Fund. *The State of the World's Children.* New York: Oxford University Press, 1997.

Best's Insurance Reports—International. Oldwick, N.J.: A. M. Best Co., 1997.

Bilello, Susan. "Mexico: The Rise of Civil Society." *Current History* 95, no. 598 (February 1996).

Rajewski, Brian, ed. *Countries of the World and Their Leaders Yearbook 2000.* Detroit: The Gale Group, 1999.

Brana-Shute, Gary. "Suriname: The Nation Against the State." *Current History* 94, no. 589 (February 1995).

Briggs, Asa, ed. *A Dictionary of 20th-Century World Biography.* New York: Oxford University Press, 1993.

British Petroleum Company. *BP Statistical Review of World Energy.* London: BP Education Service, 1996.

Brown, W. Norman. *The United States and India, Pakistan, Bangladesh.* Cambridge: Harvard University Press, 1972.

Bryan, Anthony T. "Haiti: Kick Starting the Economy." *Current History* 94, no. 589 (February 1995).

Bryden, Matthew. "Somalia: The Wages of Failure." *Current History* 94, no. 591 (April 1995).

Bungs, Dzintra. "Latvia: Transition to Independence Complicated." *RFE/RL Research Report* (7 January 1994): 96–98.

———. "Russia Agrees to Withdraw Troops from Latvia." *RFE/RL Research Report* (3 June 1994): 1–9.

Business International Limited. *Country Profiles.* London: Business International Limited, 1991–94.

C

Caribbean/Latin American Action. *Caribbean/Latin America Profile 2000.* Washington, D.C.: Caribbean Latin American Action, 1998.

Centers for Disease Control and Prevention. *Health Information for International Travel 1999/2000.* Washington, D.C.: U.S. Government Printing Office, July 1999.

Central Office of Information. *Britain 1993: An Official Handbook.* London: HMSO Publications Centre, 1993.

Central Intelligence Agency. *World Factbook 1999.* Washington, D.C.: U.S. Government Printing Office, 1999.

Chernick, Marc W. "Colombia's Fault Lines." *Current History* 95, no. 598 (February 1996).

Chew, Allen. *An Atlas of Russian History.* Rev. ed. New Haven: Yale University Press, 1970.

Chretien, Jean-Pierre. "Burundi: The Obsession with Genocide." *Current History* 95, no. 601 (May 1996).

CIA Directorate of Intelligence. *Chiefs of State and Cabinet Members of Foreign Governments: A Directory.* Washington, D.C.: U.S. Government Printing Office, June 1994.

———. *Handbook of International Economic Statistics, 1998.* Washington, D.C.: U.S. Government Printing Office, 1998.

Constable, Pamela. "A Fresh Start for Haiti?" *Current History* 95, no. 598 (February 1996).

Continuous Reporting System on Migration (SOPEMI). *Trends in International Migration.* Paris: Organization for Economic Co-operation and Development (OECD), 1992.

Coopers and Lybrand. *International Tax Summaries.* New York: John Wiley and Sons, 1992.

Corradi, Juan E. "Menem's Argentina, Act II." *Current History* 94, no. 589 (February 1995).

Cramer, Christopher. "Rebuilding South Africa." *Current History* 93, no. 583 (May 1994).

Crystal, David. *The Cambridge Encyclopedia of Language*. Cambridge: Cambridge University Press, 1994.

D

Daniels, Lorna. *Business Information Sources*. Berkeley, Calif.: University of California Press, 1993.

da Silva, Carlos Eduardo Lins. "Plato in the Tropics: The Brazilian Republic of Guardians." *Current History* 94, no. 589 (February 1995).

Department of Economic and Social Information and Policy Analysis. *World Urbanization Prospects. The 1996 Revision*. New York: United Nations, 1998.

Department for Economic and Social Information and Policy Analysis, Statistical Division. *Housing in the World: Graphical Presentation of Statistical Data*. New York: United Nations, 1993.

———. *Population and Vital Statistics Report*. Series A vol. XLVI, no. 1. New York: United Nations, 1994.

Des Forges, Alison. "Burundi: Failed Coup or Creeping Coup?" *Current History* 93, no. 583 (May 1994).

de Waal, Alex, and Rakiya Omaar. "The Genocide in Rwanda and the International Response." *Current History* 94, no. 591 (April 1995).

Directory of World Stock Exchanges. London: The Economist Publications, 1988.

Dresser, Denise. "Mexico: Uneasy, Uncertain, Unpredictable." *Current History* 96, no. 607 (February 1997).

E

Economic Commission for Latin America and the Caribbean. *Statistical Yearbook for Latin America and the Caribbean*, 1998 ed. New York: United Nations, 1999.

Economist Intelligence Unit. *Country Profile*. London: The Economist Intelligence Unit, 1988–.

———. *Country Report: An Analysis of Economic and Political Trends Every Quarter*. London: Economist Intelligence Unit, 1988–.

———. *Country Reports*. London: Economist Intelligence Unit, 1994.

———. *The Economist Book of Vital World Statistics*. New York: Random House, 1990.

Euromonitor. *International Marketing Data and Statistics*. London: Euromonitor, 1998.

———. The *World Healthcare Marketing Director*. London: Euromonitor, 1993.

Europa Publications Limited. *Africa South of the Sahara 2000*. 29th ed. London: Europa Publications Limited, 1999.

———. *The World of Learning*. 43rd edition. London: Europa Publications Limited, 1993.

Evandale's Directory of World Underwriters 2000. London: Evandale Publishing, 2000.

F

Fairbank, John K., Edwin O. Reischauer, and Albert M. Craig. *East Asia: Tradition and Transformation*. Boston: Houghton Mifflin Company, 1989.

Far Eastern Economic Review. *All-Asia Travel Guide*. 16th ed. Hong Kong: Review Publishing Co. Ltd., 1993.

Financial Times. *Financial Times World Insurance Yearbook*. London: Cartermill International, 1996.

Food and Agriculture Organization of the United Nations. *FAO Production Yearbook 1998*. vol. 52. New York: United Nations, 1999.

———. *FAO Trade Yearbook 1998*. vol. 52. New York: United Nations, 2000.

———. *FAO Yearbook: Fishery Statistics, Catches and Landings*. vol. 72. New York: United Nations, 1993.

———. *FAO Yearbook: Fishery Statistics: Commodities 1997*. vol. 85. New York: United Nations, 1999.

———. *FAO Yearbook of Forest Products, 1993–1997*. New York: United Nations, 1999.

Foreign and Commonwealth Office. *Commonwealth Yearbook 2000*. London: HMSO Publications Centre, 2000.

Foye, Stephen. "Russia Will Not Meet Deadline for Baltic Withdrawal." *RFE/RL Daily Report* (11 July 1994).

Fuller, Elizabeth. "Armenia's Constitutional Debate." *RFE/RL Research Report* (27 May 1994): 6–9.

———. "The Challenges to Armenia's Non-Communist Government." *RFE/RL Report on the USSR* (3 May 1991): 19–24.

———. "The Transcaucasus." *RFE/RL Research Report*. (22 April 1994): 38–41.

———. "Transcaucasia: Ethnic Strife Threatens Democratization." *RFE/RL Research Report* (1 January 1993): 17–24.

———. "The Transcaucasus: War, Turmoil, Economic Collapse." *RFE/RL Research Report* (7 January 1994): 51–58.

G

Girnius, Saulius. "The Baltic States." *RFE/RL Research Report* (22 April 1994): 5–8.

———. "Lithuania: Former Communists Fail to Solve Problems." *RFE/RL Research Report* (7 January 1994): 99–102.

———. "Lithuania: Former Communists Return to Power." *RFE/RL Research Report* (1 January 1993): 99–101.

Glickman, Harvey. "Tanzania: From Disillusionment to Guarded Optimism." *Current History* 96, no. 610 (May 1997).

Goldstein, Melvyn C., and Cynthia M. Beall. *The Changing World of Mongolia's Nomads*. Berkeley: University of California Press, 1994.

Grant, James P., ed. United Nations Children's Fund. *The State of the World's Children*. New York: Oxford University Press, 1994.

Grundy, Kenneth W. "South Africa: Putting Democracy to Work." *Current History* 94, no. 591 (April 1995).

Gunthorp, Dale, ed. *The Commonwealth Yearbook 1996*. London: Hanson Cooke Ltd. for the Commonwealth Secretariat, 1996.

H

1994 Handbook of World Stock and Commodity Exchanges. Oxford: Blackwell, 1994.

Handley, Antoinette, and Jeffrey Herbst. "South Africa: The Perils of Normalcy." *Current History* 96, no. 610 (May 1997).

Hane, Mikiso. *Modern Japan, A Historical Survey*. Boulder: Westview Press, 1986.

Hiatt, Fred. "Voters in Ukraine, Belarus Oust Their Leaders." *The Washington Post* (12 July 1994).

Holiday, David. "Guatemala's Long Road to Peace." *Current History* 96, no. 607 (February 1997).

Holm, John D. "Botswana: One African Success Story." *Current History* 93, no. 583 (May 1994).

Holmquist, Frank, and Michael Ford. "Stalling Political Change: Moi's Way in Kenya." *Current History* 94, no. 591 (April 1995).

Hongkong and Shanghai Banking Corporation. *Business Profile Series*. Hong Kong: Hongkong and Shanghai Banking Corporation Limited.

Hubbard, Monica M., and Beverly Baer, eds. *Cities of the World.* 4th ed. Detroit: The Gale Group, 1993.

I

Institute of the History of Natural Sciences, Chinese Academy of Sciences. *Ancient China's Technology and Science.* Beijing: Foreign Languages Press, 1983.

Inter-American Development Bank. *Annual Report 1998–1999.* Washington, D.C.: Inter-American Development Bank, 1999.

———. *Economic and Social Progress in Latin America: 1998–1999 Report.* Washington, D.C.: Inter-American Development Bank, November 1999.

———. *Latin America in Graphs: Demographic, Economic and Social Trends 1994–1995.* Washington, D.C.: Inter-American Development Bank, 1995; distributed by Johns Hopkins University Press.

International Civil Aviation Organization. *ICAO Statistical Yearbook, Civil Aviation Statistics of the World 1997–2000.* Montreal: International Civil Aviation Organization, 1997.

International Committee of the Red Cross. *Annual Report 1998.* Geneva: ICRC Publications, 1999.

International Finance Corporation. *Emerging Stock Markets Factbook 1999.* Washington, D.C.: International Finance Corporation, 1999.

International Institute for Environment and Development and World Resources Institute. *World Resources 1998–99.* New York: Basic Books, 1998.

International Institute for Strategic Studies. *The Military Balance 1999/2000.* London: Oxford University Press, 1999.

International Iron and Steel Institute. *World Steel in Figures.* Brussels: International Iron and Steel Institute, 1993.

International Labour Office. *1999 Year Book of Labour Statistics.* 58th issue. Geneva: International Labour Office, 1999.

———. *Sources and Methods: Labour Statistics 1996.* vol. 5, 55th ed. Geneva: International Labour Office, 1997.

———. *World Employment 1996–97.* Geneva: International Labour Office., 1996.

International Monetary Fund. *Balance of Payments Statistics Yearbook.* Parts 1, 2, and 3. Washington, D.C.: International Monetary Fund, 1999.

———. *Balance of Payments Textbook.* Washington, D.C.: International Monetary Fund, 1996.

———. *Direction of Trade Statistics Quarterly.* Washington, D.C.: International Monetary Fund, December 1996.

———. *Direction of Trade Statistics Yearbook 1999.* Washington, D.C.: International Monetary Fund, June 1999.

———. *Government Finance Statistics Yearbook.* Washington, D.C.: International Monetary Fund, 1999.

———. *International Financial Statistics.* Washington, D.C.: International Monetary Fund, 1999.

———. *International Financial Statistics Yearbook 1999.* Washington, D.C.: International Monetary Fund, 1999.

J

Jamison, Ellen, ed. *World Population Profile: 1991.* Washington, D.C.: U.S. Government Printing Office, 1991.

Joseph, Richard. "Nigeria: Inside the Dismal Tunnel." *Current History* 95, no. 601 (May 1996).

K

Kand, Villu "Estonia: A Year of Challenges." *RFE/RL Research Report,* 7 January 1994, 92–95.

Khader, Bichara, and Bashir el-Wifati, eds. *The Economic Development of Libya.* London: Croom Helm, 1987.

Knight, Virginia Curtin. "Zimbabwe's Reluctant Transformation." *Current History* 95, no. 601 (May 1996).

L

Leppingwell, John W. R. "Ukrainian Parliament Removes START-1 Conditions." *RFE/RL Research Report* (25 February 1994): 37–42.

Lloyd, Robert B. "Mozambique: The Terror of War, the Tensions of Peace." *Current History* 94, no. 591 (April 1995).

Lukashuk, Alexander, "Belarusian Draft Constitution: A Controversial Step Forward." *RFE/RL Research Report* (30 October 1992): 43–48.

M

MacFarquhar, Roderick, ed. *The Politics of China, 1949–1989.* Cambridge: Cambridge University Press, 1993.

Maddux, David, ed. *1999 International Year Book: the Encyclopedia of the Newspaper Industry.* 79th ed. New York: The Editor and Publisher Company, 1999.

Maingot, Anthony P. "Haiti: The Political Rot Within." *Current History* 94, no. 589 (February 1995).

Maren, Michael. "Somalia: Whose Failure?" *Current History* 95, no. 601 (May 1996).

Markus, Ustina. "Belarus: Slowly Awakening to New Realities." *RFE/RL Research Report* (7 January 1994): 42–46.

———. "Lukashenka Wins Election." *RFE/RL Daily Report* (11 July 1994).

McCleary, Rachel M. "Guatemala: Expectations for Peace." *Current History* 95, no. 598 (February 1996).

McCormick, Shawn H. "Zaire II: Mobutu, Master of the Game?" *Current History* 93, no. 583 (May 1994).

McCoy, Jennifer L., and Shelley A. McConnell. "Nicaragua: Beyond the Revolution." *Current History* 96, no. 607 (February 1997).

McDevitt, Thomas, ed. *World Population Profile 1996.* Washington, D.C.: U.S. Government Printing Office, 1996.

Meisner, Maurice. *Mao's China and After, A History of the People's Republic.* New York: The Free Press, 1989.

Montgomery, Tommie Sue. "Constructing Democracy in El Salvador." *Current History* 96, no. 607 (February 1997).

Morrison, Christian. *Adjustment and Equity in Morocco.* Paris: Development Centre Studies, 1991.

Mortimer, Robert. "Algeria: The Dialectec of Elections and Violence." *Current History* 96, no. 610 (May 1997).

N

Nahaylo, Bohdan, and Victor Swoboda. *Soviet Disunion: A History of the Nationalities Problem in the USSR.* New York: The Free Press, 1990.

Nahaylo, Bohdan. "More on Ukrainian Election Results." *RFE/RL Daily Report* (12 April 1994).

Nakanishi, Akira. *Writing Systems of the World.* Tokyo, Japan; Rutland, Vt.: Charles E. Tuttle Company, 1992.

National Science Board. *Science and Engineering Indicators 2000.* Washington, D.C.: U.S. Government Printing Office, 2000.

Nordic Statistical Secretariat, ed. *Yearbook of Nordic Statistics.* Stockholm: Nordic Council of Ministers, 1999.

Nzongola-Ntalaja, Georges. "Zaire I: Moving Beyond Mobutu." *Current History* 93, no. 583 (May 1994).

O

OECD. *Economies at a Glance: Structural Indicators*. Paris: Organization for Economic Co-operation and Development (OECD), 1996.

———. *Revenue Statistics of OECD Member Countries: 1965–1998*. Paris: Organization for Economic Co-operation and Development (OECD), 2000.

———. *Trends in International Migration. Annual Report 1999*. Organization for Economic Co-operation and Development (OECD), 1999.

OECD Tourism Committee. *Tourism Policy and International Tourism in OECD Member Countries*. Paris: Organization for Economic Co-operation and Development (OECD), 1992.

Office of Conference Services; Translation Division; Documentation, Reference and Terminology Section. *Terminology Bulletin No. 345: Country Names*. New York: United Nations, 1993.

Oloka-Onyango, J. "Uganda's 'Benevolent' Dictatorship." *Current History* 96, no. 610 (May 1997).

Omaar, Rakiya. "Somaliland: One Thorn Bush at a Time." *Current History* 93, no. 583 (May 1994).

OPEC. *OPEC Annual Report 1998*. Vienna: Organization of the Petroleum Exporting Countries, 1999.

Organization of American States. *OAS Annual Report of the Inter American Commission on Human Rights*. Washington, D.C.: Organization of American States, 1998–99.

P

Palmer, David Scott. "'Fujipopulism' and Peru's Progress." *Current History* 95, no. 598 (February 1996).

Pateman, Roy. "Eritrea Takes the World Stage." *Current History* 93, no. 583 (May 1994).

Population Council. *Family Planning and Population: A Compendium of International Statistics*. New York: The Population Council, 1993.

Price Waterhouse. *Corporate Taxes: A Worldwide Summary*. Information Guide Series. New York: Price Waterhouse, 1996.

———. *Doing Business in . . . .* Information Guide Series. New York: Price Waterhouse, 1994.

———. *Individual Taxes: A Worldwide Summary*. Information Guide Series. New York: Price Waterhouse, 1996.

Programme Evaluation and Communications Research Unit (PECRU). *World Media Handbook 1995*. New York: United Nations Department of Public Information (DPI), 1995.

R

Rahr, Alexander. "The First Year of Russian Independence." *RFE/RL Research Report* (1 January 1993): 50–57.

Reno, William. "The Business of War in Liberia." *Current History* 95, no. 601 (May 1996).

———. "Privatizing War in Sierra Leone." *Current History* 96, no. 610 (May 1997).

Ropp, Steve C. "Panama: Tailoring a New Image." *Current History* 95, no. 598 (February 1996).

Rosenblum, Peter. "Endgame in Zaire." *Current History* 96, no. 610 (May 1997).

Ruhl, J. Mark. "Doubting Democracy in Honduras." *Current History* 96, no. 607 (February 1997).

S

Salt, John. *Migration and Population Change in Europe*. Research Paper No. 19. New York: United Nations, 1993.

Sayeed, Khalid B. *The Political System of Pakistan*. Boston: Houghton Mifflin Co., 1967.

Schiff, Ben. "The Afrikaners after Apartheid." *Current History* 95, no. 601 (May 1996).

Schirokauer, Conrad. *A Brief History of Chinese Civilization*. San Diego: Harcourt, Brace, Jovanovich, 1991.

Seton-Watson, Hugh. *The Russian Empire, 1801–1917*. Oxford: Oxford University Press, 1967.

Sivard, Ruth Leger. *World Military and Social Expenditures 1996*. 16th ed. Washington. D.C.: World Priorities, 1996.

Shafir, Shlomo. *American Jews and Germany after 1945, Points of Connection and Points of Departure*. Cincinnati: American Jewish Archives, 1993.

Slater, Wendy. "Russia: The Return of Authoritarian Government?" *RFE/RL Research Report* (7 January 1994): 22–31.

———. "Russian Duma Sidelines Extremist Politicians," *RFE/RL Research Report* (18 February 1994): 5–9.

Smith, Gaddis. "Haiti: From Intervention to Intervasion." *Current History* 94, no. 589 (February 1995).

Smith, Wayne S. "Shackled to the Past: The United States and Cuba." *Current History* 95, no. 598 (February 1996).

Socor, Vladimir. "Moldova's Dniester Ulcer." *RFE/RL Research Report* (1 January 1993): 12–16.

———. "Moldova's Political Landscape: Profiles of the Parties." *RFE/RL Research Report* (11 March 1994): 6–14.

———. "Moldova: Democracy Advances, Independence at Risk." *RFE/RL Research Report* (7 January 1994): 47–50.

———. "Moldovan Election Results." *RFE/RL Daily Report* (15 March 1994).

———. "Ukraine: A Year of Crisis." *RFE/RL Research Report* (7 January 1994): 38–41.

———. "Political Parties in Ukraine's Elections." *RFE/RL Daily Report* (14 April 1994).

Solomon Brothers. *Economic and Market Analysis: International Bond Market Analysis*. New York: Solomon Brothers, Inc., September 1993.

Standard and Poor's and IFC. *Emerging Stock Markets Factbook 2000*. Washington, D.C.: The World Bank, 2000.

Statistical Directorate. *National Accounts 1979–1991*. Paris: Organization for Economic Co-operation and Development (OECD), 1993.

Statistics Canada. *Canada Year Book 1999*. Ottawa: Statistics Canada, 1999.

Statistics Sweden. *Sweden in Figures*. Stockholm: Statistics Sweden, 1992.

Stetler, Susan L., ed. *Almanac of Famous People*. 4th ed. Detroit: The Gale Group, 1989.

Stockholm International Peace Research Institute. *SIPRI Yearbook 1999: Armaments, Disarmament and International Security*. New York: Oxford University Press, 1999.

———. *SIPRI Yearbook 1993: World Armaments and Disarmament*. New York: Oxford University Press, 1993.

Suberu, Rotimi T. "The Democratic Recession in Nigeria." *Current History* 93, no. 583 (May 1994).

Svetova, Svetlana, and Roman Solchanyk. "Chronology of Events in Crimea." *RFE/RL Research Report* (13 May 1994): 27–33.

T

Taylor, Richard, and Kiki Thomas. "Mortality Patterns in the Modernized Pacific Island Nation of Nauru," *The American Journal of Public Health* (February, 1985) 75:2.

Teague, Elizabeth. "Russia's Local Elections Begin," *RFE/RL Research Report* (18 February 1994): 1–4.

Thomson Bank Directory. Skokie, Ill.: Thomson Financial Publications, 1991–.

Thorson, Carla. "Russia's Draft Constitution." *RFE/RL Research Report* (3 December 1993): 9–15.

Tolz, Vera. "Russia's New Parliament and Yeltsin: Cooperation Prospects," *RFE/RL Research Report* (4 February 1994): 1–6.

———. "Russia's Parliamentary Elections: What Happened and Why," *RFE/RL Research Report* (14 January 1994): 1–8.

Treadgold, Donald W. *Twentieth Century Russia.* 7th ed. Boulder: Westview Press, 1990.

U

U.S. Arms Control and Disarmament Agency. *World Military Expenditures and Arms Transfers 1996.* Washington, D.C.: U.S. Arms Control and Disarmament Agency, 1997.

U.S. Agency for International Development, Bureau for Management, Office of Budget. *U.S. Overseas Loans and Grants and Assistance from International Organizations.* Washington, D.C.: U.S. Government Printing Office, 1997.

U.S. Bureau of the Census. *Statistical Abstract of the United States 1999.* Washington, D.C.: U.S. Government Printing Office, January 2000.

U.S. Department of Agriculture, Foreign Agricultural Service. *Wood Products Trade and Foreign Markets: EC Market Profile Issue.* Washington, D.C.: U.S. Government Printing Office, 1993.

———. *Wood Products Trade and Foreign Markets: Annual Production, Consumption, and Trade Issue.* Washington, D.C.: U.S. Government Printing Office, 1993.

U.S. Department of Commerce. *International Business Practices.* Washington, D.C.: U.S. Government Printing Office, 1993.

U.S. Department of Commerce, Economics and Statistics Administration, Office of Business Analysis. *NTDB: The Export Connection CD-ROM.* Washington, D.C.: U.S. Government Printing Office, March–August 1994. This CD-ROM includes a wide variety of U.S. Government publications including the following which were used in the compilation of this encyclopedia:

> *Commercial Activities Reports;*
> *Country Marketing Plans;*
> *Foreign Economic Trends;*
> *Country Commercial Guides;*
> *Country Reports on Economic Policy and Trade Practices;*
> *Handbook of Economic Statistics;*
> *International Labor Statistics;*
> *U.S. Foreign Trade Highlights;*
> *Market Research Reports;*
> *International Business Practices;*
> *Foreign Labor Trends;*
> *Background Notes;*
> *BINIS Bulletin (Newly Independent States)*

U.S. Department of Defense. *Defense 99 Almanac.* Alexandria, Va.: American Forces Information Service, 1999. Text-fiche.

U.S. Department of Energy, Energy Information Administration. *Country Profiles: 1993; An Energy Overview of Important Countries in the World Oil Market.* Washington, D.C.: U.S. Government Printing Office, 1993.

———. *Energy Use and Carbon Emission: Some International Comparisons.* Washington, D.C.: U.S. Government Printing Office, March 1994.

———. *International Energy Outlook 1999.* Washington, D.C.: U.S. Government Printing Office, September 1999.

———. *International Energy Annual, 1998.* Washington, D.C.: U.S. Government Printing Office, March 2000.

———. *International Petroleum Statistics Report.* Washington, D.C.: U.S. Government Printing Office, September 1993.

U.S. Department of Health, Education, and Welfare. *Social Security Programs Throughout the World, 1999.* Washington, D.C.: U.S. Government Printing Office, October 1999.

U.S. Department of State. *Country Reports on Economic Policy and Trade Practices.* Joint Committee Print. Washington, D.C.: U.S. Government Printing Office, 2000.

———. *Country Reports on Human Rights Practices 1997.* Washington, D.C.: U.S. Government Printing Office, 1998.

———. *Diplomatic List. Fall 1996.* Washington, D.C.: U.S. Government Printing Office, 1996.

———. *Foreign Consular Offices in the United States: Fall/Winter 1999.* Washington, D.C.: U.S. Government Printing Office, March 2000.

U.S. Department of State, Bureau of Intelligence and Research. *Geographic and Global Issues Quarterly* (U.S. Government Printing Office) vol. 3, no. 1–4 (1994).

U.S. Department of the Interior. *Endangered and Threatened Wildlife and Plants.* Washington, D.C.: U.S. Government Printing Office, 1992.

U.S. Department of the Interior, Bureau of Mines. *Mineral Perspectives: The Mineral Economy of Mexico.* Washington, D.C.: U.S. Government Printing Office, 1992.

———. *Minerals Today* (U.S. Government Printing Office) June 1993.

———. *Minerals Yearbook: Minerals in the World Economy.* Washington, D.C.: U.S. Government Printing Office, 1991.

U.S. Department of the Interior, U.S. Geological Survey. *Minerals Yearbook Area Reports: International 1997 Asia and the Pacific.* Washington, D.C.: U.S. Government Printing Office, 1999.

———. *Minerals Yearbook Area Reports: International 1997 Latin America and Canada.* Washington, D.C.: U.S. Government Printing Office, 1999.

U.S. Department of Transportation, Maritime Administration. *Merchant Fleets of the World.* Washington, D.C.: U.S. Government Printing Office, October 1999.

U.S. Library of Congress. Congressional Research Service. *International Science and Technology: Issues for U.S. Policymakers* (a report for the Committee on Science, Space, and Technology of the U.S. House of Representatives). Coordinated by Glenn J. McLoughlin. June 1994.

———. *Country Studies/Federal Research Division, Library of Congress.* Washington, D.C.: Library of Congress, 1997.

U.S. Public Health Service. Health Information for International Travel 1996–97. Washington, D.C.: U.S. Government Printing Office, 1996.

U.S. Social Security Administration, Office of Research and Statistics. *Social Security Programs Throughout the World—1999.* Washington, D.C.: U.S. Government Printing Office, 1999.

UNESCO. *Statistical Yearbook.* Lanham, Md.: UNESCO Publishing and Bernan Press, 1999.

———. *World Education Report 1998.* Oxford: UNESCO Publishing, 1998.

United Nations. *The State of the World's Children 2000.* New York: UN Publications, 2000.

———. *National Accounts Statistics: Main Aggregates and Detailed Tables, 1995.* New York: United Nations, 1999.

———. *United Nations System of Organizations and Directory.* New York: United Nations, 1994.

United Nations Conference on Environment and Development. *Nations of the Earth Report.* New York: United Nations, 1993.

United Nations Conference on Trade and Development. *Handbook of International Trade and Development Statistics: 1996/1997.* New York: United Nations, 1999.

United Nations Department for Economic and Social Information and Policy Analysis. *1997 International Trade Statistics Yearbook.* vols. I and II. New York: United Nations, 1999.

———. *Monthly Bulletin of Statistics*. vol. LI, no. 1. New York: United Nations, January 1997.

———. *Statistical Yearbook, 1996*. 43rd ed. New York: United Nations, 2000.

———. *World Statistics Pocketbook*. New York: United Nations, 1999.

United Nations Department of International Economic and Social Affairs. *World Population Policies*. 3 vols. New York: United Nations, 1987–90.

United Nations Development Program. *Human Development Report 2000*. New York: Oxford University Press, 2000.

United Nations General Assembly. *Report of the Commissioner-General of the United Nations Relief and Works Agency for Palestine Refugees in the Near East*. 51st Sess., 1 July 1995–30 June 1996. New York: United Nations, 1996.

United Nations High Commissioner for Refugees. *The State of the World's Refugees: The Challenge of Protection*. New York: Penguin Books, 1993.

W

Wasylyk, Myron. "Ukraine on the Eve of Elections." *RFE/RL Research Report* (25 March 1994): 44–50.

Wenner, Manfred W. *The Yemen Arab Republic*. Boulder: Westview Press, 1991.

Wishnevsky, Julia. "Problems of Russian Regional Leadership." *RFE/RL Research Report* (13 May 1994): 6–13.

World Bank. *Russian Economic Reform: Crossing the Threshold of Structural Change* (A World Bank Country Study). Washington, D.C.: World Bank, 1992.

———. *Trends in Developing Economies 1996*. Washington, D.C.: World Bank, 1996.

———. *World Bank Annual Report 1999*. Washington, D.C.: World Bank, 1999.

———. *World Bank Atlas 2000*. Washington, D.C.: World Bank, 2000.

———. *World Development Indicators 2000*. Washington, D.C.: World Bank, 2000.

———. *World Development Report 1993: Investing in Health*. New York: Oxford University Press, 1993.

———. *World Development Report 1995: Workers in an Integrating World*. New York: Oxford University Press, 1995.

———. *World Development Report 1996: From Plan to Market*. New York: Oxford University Press, 1996.

———. *World Development Report 1999/2000: Entering the 21st Century*. New York: Oxford University Press, 1999.

———. *World Tables 1994*. Baltimore: Johns Hopkins University Press, 1994.

World Health Organization. *1995 World Health Statistics Annual*. Geneva: World Health Organization, 1997.

World Resources Institute; United Nations Environment Programme; United Nations Development Programme; World Bank. *World Resources 1998–99*. New York: Oxford University Press, 1998.

World Tourism Organization. *Compendium of Tourism Statistics 1993–1997*. 19th ed. Madrid: World Tourism Organization, 1999.

———. *Tourism Market Trends: Africa 1989–1998*. 1999 ed. Madrid: World Tourism Organization, 1999.

———. *Tourism Market Trends: Americas 1989–1998*. 1999 ed. Madrid: World Tourism Organization, 1999.

———. *Tourism Market Trends: East Asia & the Pacific 1989–1998*. 1999 ed. Madrid: World Tourism Organization, 1999.

———. *Tourism Market Trends: Europe 1989–1998*. 1999 ed. Madrid: World Tourism Organization, 1999.

———. *Tourism Market Trends: Middle East 1989–1998*. 1999 ed. Madrid: World Tourism Organization, 1999.

———. *Tourism Market Trends: South Asia 1989–1998*. 1999 ed. Madrid: World Tourism Organization, 1999.

———. *Yearbook of Tourism Statistics*. 51st ed. Madrid: World Tourism Organization, 1999.

Wright, John W., ed. *The Universal Almanac 1997*. Kansas City: Andrews and McMeel, 1997.

Z

Zunes, Stephen. "Western Sahara: Peace Derailed." *Current History 95*, no. 601 (May 1996)

INDEX TO COUNTRIES AND TERRITORIES

This alphabetical list includes countries and dependencies (colonies, protectorates, and other territories) described in the encyclopedia. Countries and territories described in their own articles are followed by the continental volume (printed in *italics*) in which each appears. Country articles are arranged alphabetically in each volume. For example, Argentina, which appears in *Americas*, is listed this way: Argentina—*Americas*. Dependencies are listed here with the title of the volume in which they are treated, followed by the name of the article in which they are dealt with. In a few cases, an alternative name for the same place is given in parentheses at the end of the entry. The name of the volume *Asia and Oceania* is abbreviated in this list to *Asia*.

Adélie Land—*Asia:* French Pacific Dependencies: French Southern and Antarctic Territories
Afars and the Issas, Territory of the—*Africa:* Djibouti
Afghanistan—*Asia*
Albania—*Europe*
Algeria—*Africa*
American Samoa—*Asia:* US Pacific Dependencies
Andaman Islands—*Asia:* India
Andorra—*Europe*
Angola—*Africa*
Anguilla—*Americas:* UK American Dependencies: Leeward Islands
Antarctica—*United Nations:* Polar Regions
Antigua and Barbuda—*Americas*
Arctic—*United Nations:* Polar Regions
Argentina—*Americas*
Armenia—*Europe*
Aruba—*Americas:* Netherlands American Dependencies: Aruba
Ashmore and Cartier Islands—*Asia:* Australia
Australia—*Asia*
Austria—*Europe*
Azerbaijan—*Asia*
Azores—*Europe:* Portugal

Bahamas—*Americas*
Bahrain—*Asia*
Bangladesh—*Asia*
Barbados—*Americas*
Basutoland—*Africa:* Lesotho
Bechuanaland—*Africa:* Botswana
Belarus—*Europe*
Belau—*Asia:* Palau
Belgium—*Europe*
Belize—*Americas*
Benin—*Africa*
Bermuda—*Americas:* UK American Dependencies
Bhutan—*Asia*
Bolivia—*Americas*
Bonin Islands—*Asia:* Japan (Ogasawara Islands)
Borneo, North—*Asia:* Malaysia
Bosnia and Herzegovina—*Europe*
Botswana—*Africa*
Bouvet Island—*Europe:* Norway
Brazil—*Americas*
British Antarctic Territory—*Americas:* UK American Dependencies

British Guiana—*Americas:* Guyana
British Honduras—*Americas:* Belize
British Indian Ocean Territory—*Africa:* UK African Dependencies
British Virgin Islands—*Americas:* UK American Dependencies
Brunei Darussalam—*Asia*
Bulgaria—*Europe*
Burkina Faso—*Africa*
Burma—*Asia:* Myanmar
Burundi—*Africa*

Caicos Islands—*Americas:* UK American Dependencies
Cambodia—*Asia*
Cameroon—*Africa*
Canada—*Americas*
Canary Islands—*Europe:* Spain
Cape Verde—*Africa*
Caroline Islands—*Asia:* Federated States of Micronesia; Palau
Carriacou—*Americas:* Grenada
Cayman Islands—*Americas:* UK American Dependencies
Central African Republic—*Africa*
Ceuta—*Europe:* Spain
Ceylon—*Asia:* Sri Lanka
Chad—*Africa*
Chile—*Americas*
Chilean Antarctic Territory—*Americas:* Chile
China—*Asia*
Christmas Island (Indian Ocean)—*Asia:* Australia
Christmas Island (Pacific Ocean)—*Asia:* Kiribati
Cocos Islands—*Americas:* Costa Rica
Cocos (Keeling) Islands—*Asia:* Australia
Colombia—*Americas*
Columbus, Archipelago of—*Americas:* Ecuador (Galapagos Islands)
Comoros—*Africa*
Congo—*Africa*
Congo, Democratic Republic of (former Zaire)—*Africa*
Cook Islands—*Asia:* New Zealand
Coral Sea Islands—*Asia:* Australia
Corn Islands—*Americas:* Nicaragua
Costa Rica—*Americas*
Côte d'Ivoire—*Africa*
Croatia—*Europe*
Cuba—*Americas*
Curaçao—*Americas:* Netherlands American Dependencies: Netherlands Antilles
Cyprus—*Asia*

Line Islands—*Asia:* Kiribati
Lithuania—*Europe*
Luxembourg—*Europe*

Macau—*Asia:* China
Macedonia, Former Yugoslav Republic of—*Europe*
Macquarie Island—*Asia:* Australia
Madeira—*Europe:* Portugal
Madagascar—*Africa*
Malagasy Republic—*Africa:* Madagascar
Malawi—*Africa*
Malaya—*Asia:* Malaysia
Malaysia—*Asia*
Malden and Starbuck Islands—*Asia:* Kiribati
Maldive Islands—*Asia:* Maldives
Maldives—*Asia*
Mali—*Africa*
Malta—*Europe*
Malvinas—*Americas:* UK American Dependencies
  (Falkland Islands)
Mariana Islands—*Asia:* US Pacific Dependencies
Marquesas Islands—*Asia:* French Pacific Dependencies:
  French Polynesia
Marshall Islands—*Asia*
Martinique—*Americas:* French American Dependencies
Matsu Islands—*Asia:* Taiwan
Mauritania—*Africa*
Mauritius—*Africa*
Mayotte—*Africa:* French African Dependencies
Melilla—*Europe:* Spain
Mexico—*Americas*
Micronesia, Federated States of—*Asia:* Federated States
  of Micronesia
Midway—*Asia:* US Pacific Dependencies
Moldova—*Europe*
Monaco—*Europe*
Mongolia—*Asia*
Montserrat—*Americas:* UK American Dependencies:
  Leeward Islands
Morocco—*Africa*
Mozambique—*Africa*
Muscat and Oman—*Asia:* Oman
Myanmar—*Asia*

Namibia—*Africa*
Nauru—*Asia*
Navassa—*Americas:* US
Nepal—*Asia*
Netherlands—*Europe*
Netherlands American Dependencies—*Americas*
Netherlands Antilles—*Americas:* Netherlands American
  Dependencies
Nevis—*Americas:* St. Kitts and Nevis
New Caledonia—*Asia:* French Pacific Dependencies
New Guinea—*Asia:* Papua New Guinea
New Hebrides—*Asia:* Vanuatu
New Zealand—*Asia*
Nicaragua—*Americas*
Nicobar Islands—*Asia:* India
Niger—*Africa*
Nigeria—*Africa*
Niue—*Asia:* New Zealand
Norfolk Island—*Asia:* Australia
North Borneo—*Asia:* Malaysia
Northern Ireland—*Europe:* United Kingdom
Northern Mariana Islands—*Asia:* US Pacific Dependencies
Northern Rhodesia—*Africa:* Zambia

North Korea—*Asia:* Korea, Democratic People's Republic of
North Vietnam—*Asia:* Vietnam
Northwest Territories—*Americas:* Canada
Norway—*Europe*
Nosy Boraha and Nosy Be—*Africa:* Madagascar
Nyasaland—*Africa:* Malawi

Ocean Island—*Asia:* Kiribati (Banaba)
Ogasawara Islands—*Asia:* Japan (Bonin Islands)
Okinawa—*Asia:* Japan
Oman—*Asia*
Outer Mongolia—*Asia:* Mongolia

Pacific Islands, Trust Territory of the—*Asia:* Federated States of
  Micronesia; Marshall Islands; Palau; US Pacific Dependencies
Pakistan—*Asia*
Pakistan, East—*Asia:* Bangladesh
Palau—*Asia*
Palmyra Atoll—*Asia:* US Pacific Dependencies
Panama—*Americas*
Papua New Guinea—*Asia*
Paracel Islands—*Asia:* China (Xisha Islands)
Paraguay—*Americas*
Peru—*Americas*
Peter I Island—*Europe:* Norway
Petit Martinique—*Americas:* Grenada
Philippines—*Asia*
Phoenix Islands—*Asia:* Kiribati
Pitcairn Island—*Europe:* United Kingdom
Poland—*Europe*
Polar Regions—*United Nations*
Portugal—*Europe*
Portuguese Timor—*Asia:* East Timor
Puerto Rico—*Americas:* United States

Qatar—*Asia*
Queen Maud Land—*Europe:* Norway
Quemoy Islands—*Asia:* Taiwan

Ras al-Khaimah—*Asia:* United Arab Emirates
Réunion—*Africa:* French African Dependencies
Rhodesia—*Africa:* Zimbabwe
Río Muni—*Africa:* Equatorial Guinea
Romania—*Europe*
Ross Dependency—*Asia:* New Zealand
Ruanda-Urundi—*Africa:* Burundi; Rwanda
Russia—*Europe*
Rwanda—*Africa*
Ryukyu Islands—*Asia:* Japan

Sabah—*Asia:* Malaysia
St. Christopher—*Americas:* St. Kitts and Nevis
St. Christopher and Nevis—*Americas:* St. Kitts and Nevis
St. Helena—*Africa:* UK African Dependencies
St. Kitts—*Americas:* St. Kitts and Nevis
St. Kitts and Nevis—*Americas*
St. Lucia—*Americas*
St. Pierre and Miquelon—*Americas:* French American
  Dependencies
St. Vincent and the Grenadines—*Americas*
Sala y Gómez Island—*Americas:* Chile
Samoa, American—*Asia:* US Pacific Dependencies
Samoa, Western—*Asia:* Samoa
San Ambrosio Island—*Americas:* Chile
San Andrés and Providentia—*Americas:* Colombia
San Felix Island—*Americas:* Chile
San Marino—*Europe*

INDEX TO THE UNITED NATIONS AND RELATED AGENCIES